T0398205

Monetary Economics in Globalised
Financial Markets

Ansgar Belke · Thorsten Polleit

Monetary Economics in Globalised Financial Markets

 Springer

Prof. Dr. Ansgar Belke
University Duisburg-Essen
Faculty of Economics
    and Business Administration
Chair for Macroeconomics
Universitätsstr. 12
45117 Essen
Germany
ansgar.belke@uni-due.de

Honorary Prof. Dr. Thorsten Polleit
Frankfurt School of Finance & Management
Sonnemannstr. 9-11
60314 Frankfurt am Main
Germany
info@frankfurt-school.de

ISBN 978-3-540-71002-8   e-ISBN 978-3-540-71003-5
DOI 10.1007/978-3-540-71003-5
Springer Dordrecht Heidelberg London New York

Library of Congress Control Number: 2009920050

Cover design: WMXDesign GmbH, Heidelberg

Printed on acid-free paper

Springer is part of Springer Science+Business Media (www.springer.com)

To our parents
Ursula and Winfried Belke
Anita and Horst Polleit

Preface

An old song has it that *money makes the world go round.* Indeed, money, the universally accepted means of exchange, plays a pivotal role in turning the wheels of an increasingly globalized world economy, characterised by increasing cross-border trade in goods and services and financial transactions. Given the undeniable importance of money for domestic and international economic dispositions, we therefore do not heed the old saying *The best advice about money is not to talk about it* in this book. On the contrary, we will talk about money quite extensively.

At the time of writing, the global monetary architecture experiences an unprecedented credit market turmoil, which started in the US subprime mortgage market in July/August 2007 and spread to virtually all major financial markets. The ultimate consequences of this financial earthquake are hard to predict in terms of their impact on the global economy and its monetary order in the years to come. Nevertheless, throughout our book the reader will find plenty of analyses of the factors and events which may have sown the seeds of the current crisis.

With this book we want to provide students with an integrated overview about the major building blocks of monetary economics – that are monetary theory, capital market theory and monetary policy theory. In doing so, we will draw heavily on the work of many leading scholars. On top of that, we will provide numerous graphs and econometric examples, which may help illustrating, and thereby improving the understanding of, the theoretical issues under review.

We also want to show that one can address nearly all the core issues in monetary economics with a systematic modern approach which does not neglect econometrics but that also pays attention to the nuances of micro foundations. The book is aimed at second- and third-year undergraduate and graduate courses in monetary economics and international finance.

We would like to thank Professor Dr. Dieter Gerdesmeier and the colleagues at the Frankfurt School of Finance & Management, Frankfurt, Daniel Gros, PhD, Director Centre for European Policy Studies, Brussels, Dr. Eduard Hochreiter, The Joint Vienna Institute, Vienna, Professor Dr. Wim Kösters, University of Bochum, and Professor Dr. Martin Leschke, University of Bayreuth for many fruitful discussions and invaluable support. We are also grateful for financial and intellectual support from the Oesterreichische Nationalbank (OeNB) where the first author stayed as a research professor when the first drafts of this book were written. The quality of the book profited most from the feedback by our students at the Universities of Vienna, Stuttgart, Bayreuth, Frankfurt, Stuttgart-Hohenheim, Duisburg-Essen Berlin and Saarbrücken. Technical assistance by students from the Universities of Duisburg-Essen and Hohenheim, especially from Kai Müller-Berner and Markus Ortel is gratefully acknowledged as well. Needless to say, we take full responsibility for any remaining shortcomings and errors.

Frankfurt and Berlin   *Ansgar Belke*
April 2009   *Thorsten Polleit*

Contents

Chapter 1
Money and Credit Supply

> *"(...) a world monetary system has emerged that has no historical precedent: a system in which every major currency in the world is, directly or indirectly, on an irredeemable paper money standard (...). The ultimate consequences of this development are shrouded in uncertainty."*
>
> – Milton Friedman (1994), Money Mischief, p. 249.

1.1 Money Definition, Functions, Kinds and Origin

1.1.1 Definition and Functions

"Money is a little like an airplane – marvellous when it works, frustrating when it is immobilised, and tragic when it crashes."[1] Money is one of man's great inventions, and it is a crucial part of the pervasive framework of a society organised along the lines of free markets – characterised by *private property, the division of labour* and *free trade*. It has become common practise to define money as the *universally accepted means of exchange*. In that sense, *money is anything that is generally accepted in exchange transactions.*

People use money because of *uncertainty*. Uncertainty is inherent in human life. The future course of events is unknown. If the future was known, there wouldn't be any need for people holding money. They could simply make all their dispositions today – as under certainty they would know, as of today, their future income, preferences and wants. In a world of certainty, there is actually no need for anyone to hold money.

As a universally accepted means of exchange, money is the *most liquid good* in the economy. The term *liquidity* is used to describe the ease with which an asset can be exchanged against other goods and services. Other (financial) assets vary widely as far as their degree of liquidity is concerned. For instance, stocks and bonds, representing rather homogenous types of assets traded on primary and secondary markets,

---

[1] Harriss (1961), p. 3.

A. Belke, T. Polleit, *Monetary Economics in Globalised Financial Markets*,
DOI 10.1007/978-3-540-71003-5_1, © Springer-Verlag Berlin Heidelberg 2009

tend to be even more liquid than assets such as, for instance, cattle, real estates and housing, but stocks and bonds are less liquid than money.

When deciding in what form to hold their wealth, market participants have to balance the issue of *liquidity* of each possible asset against the asset's capacity to serve as a *store of value*. Money is certainly the most liquid asset, but it is usually far from being a perfect *store of value*. This is because peoples' preferences change over time. As result, the value of goods and services, including money, changes over time.

Money is often defined by the functions it fulfils, thereby contributing in different ways to the workings of the economy:

– First and foremost, money is a *medium of exchange*; this is the most obvious function of money. Using money in buying and selling frees people from the need to *barter*, that is to make *direct* exchanges in the form of things for things. Making use of money leads to *indirect* exchange, and this avoids the problem of *double coincidence*, the necessary prerequisite for making possible barter trade.
– Second, money serves as a *unit of account* (*numéraire*). Exchanges in the market (purchases, loan and wage contracts, etc.) are usually made by using money units rather than a quantity of goods and services. This reduces *transaction costs*, thereby allowing for an overall *increase in productivity*. To show this, assume that there are n goods, so that in a barter economy the individual would have to know $(n^2 - n)/2$ independent exchange ratios between the n goods. Using money as a unit of account, however, an individual would need to know just $n - 1$ exchange ratios.

  To give an example of the productive effect of using money as a *numéraire*, assume there are 4 goods. Using the formula above, people would have to deal with 6 individual exchange ratios, namely:

  X1 : X2 = 1 : 2   X2 : X3 = 2 : 3
  X1 : X3 = 1 : 3   X2 : X4 = 2 : 4
  X1 : X4 = 1 : 4   X3 : X4 = 3 : 4

  Let us use X1 as the unit of account. Then we have:

  X2 = 2 X1
  X3 = 3/2 X2 = 3 X1
  X4 = 4/3 X3 = 4 X1.

  Using money as a *numéraire* reduces the number of exchange ratios to three. If we had 100 goods, people in a barter economy would need to know 4950 individual exchange ratios. However, this number declines to 99 if money is used as the unit of account.
– Third, money serves as a *store of value*. Exchanges for which money serves so well as a medium of exchange do not take place simultaneously. Quite often, people receive money one day and pay it out at a later point in time. If the price of a vendible good is fixed in terms of a unit of account, and if the unit of account

is the universally accepted means of exchange in the future, it can serve as a store of value. In that sense, money's function as a store of value gives its holder economic freedom through time: holding money is an option of what to buy. It gives its holder the power to delay the acquisition of goods and services to a convenient time.

- Fourth, and this actually follows from the other three functions, money can serve a *standard of deferred payment*. As there tend to be current transactions that extend into the future (such as, for instance, building factories, railroads, etc.), people need something to serve as a standard for payments to be made in the future. In developed economies, people save money and lend it, often through financial institutions, to businesses or governments, and people prefer to express the agreement in money terms.

In contrast to this *mainstream economic* characterisation of the functions of money, Ludwig von Mises (1881–1973) noted that the medium of exchange would be money's *only* function. All other functions which people ascribe to money – unit of account, store of value and standard of deferred payment – would be "merely particular aspects of its primary and sole function, that of a medium of exchange."[2] As he noted, the functions of money as a unit of account and transmitter of value through time and space can indeed be traced back to its function as medium of exchange.

It is often said that money would *measure value*. However, from the viewpoint of a *subjectivist value theory* such a conclusion would appear to be erroneous. In a free market, exchange is voluntary and mutually beneficial. People exchange those goods and services which they consider less valuable against those vendible items they value more highly. In that sense, human action is expressive of *preferences*. In fact, each person values what he acquires more highly than what he surrenders. Exchange is therefore not about *value identity* or *value equivalency*.

Take, for instance, the case in which Mr Miller willingly exchanges US$1 against an apple in a grocery shop. Obviously he values the apple more highly than one US dollar. The shopkeeper, in turn, exchanges an apple against US$1 because from his viewpoint one US dollar is *more* valuable than the apple. That said, for Mr Miller the apple is worth *more* than US$1, while for the seller the US$1 is *more* valuable than the apple surrendered. In that sense, the US dollar price of the apple does not measure the value of the apple from the viewpoint of the buyer and seller.

If the value of the US dollar were equal to the value of the apple from the viewpoint of the buyer and seller, what would be the point of engaging in a trade? In such a case neither the buyer of the apple nor its seller could improve their individual utility. In fact, if the US dollar and the apple were of identical value from the viewpoints of the market participants, there would be no economic incentive at all for them to enter into any transaction.

---

[2]Mises (1996), p. 401.

In this context it might be of interest to raise the following question: Can there be a constant value of money? From an economic viewpoint there is no doubt that money is a *good*, as it has economic value for market participants. In fact, money is the most liquid good. It can be easily and readily exchanged against other good and service. If money is a good, however, it must necessarily fall under the *law of diminishing marginal utility*. The latter holds that the marginal utility of a given unit of a vendible item decreases (increases) as the supply of such units increases (decreases). In other words: a change in the supply of a good, including the *good money*, leads to a change in the good's marginal utility.

A change in the stock of money M in the purse of Mrs Smith would lead her to revalue M: As the supply of M changes, Mrs Smith will assign a different *value-rank* to M. From the viewpoint of Mrs Smith, the first US dollar received commands a higher value than, say, an additional US dollar earned when Mrs Smith owns a million US dollar already. That said, the search for a once-and-for-all stable, that is constant-valued, good is, generally speaking, an illusionary undertaking. Even money, the most liquid good, cannot fulfil such a requirement.

Can There be "Stable Money"? No, Says the Law of Diminishing Marginal Utility

The *law of diminishing utility* is attributable to the work of Hermann Heinrich Gossen (1810–1858), Leon Walras (1834–1923), Carl Menger (1840–1921) and William Stanley Jevons (1835–1882). Because of its importance in economic theory for *determining the value of a good*, the *law of diminishing marginal utility* shall be outlined in some more detail. To start with, an individual's utility can be formalised as:

$$U = f(x_1, x_2, \ldots, x_n), \tag{1.1}$$

that is his/her utility is determined by consuming goods $x_1, x_2, \ldots, x_n$.

It is assumed that the marginal utility from consuming one unit more of, say, x_1 is positive:

$$\frac{\partial U}{\partial x_1} = f_1' > 0. \tag{1.2}$$

This condition reflects the assumption of non-satisfaction.

Further, it is assumed that with growing consumption of x_1 the marginal utility declines:

$$\frac{\partial^2 U}{\partial^2 x_1^2} = f_1'' < 0. \tag{1.3}$$

Equations (1.2) and (1.3) reflect the *First Law of Gossen.*

Furthermore, it is assumed that marginal utility from consuming one unit more of x_1 increases if one unit more of the other good x_2 is consumed:

$$\frac{\partial^2 U}{\partial^2 x_1 \partial x_2} = f''_{12} > 0. \qquad (1.4)$$

Figure 1.1 shows the utility function for varying levels of x_1 given two different level of x_2.

Fig. 1.1 Utility function

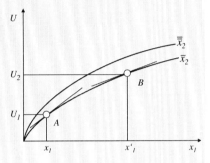

Now assume that, for simplicity, there is a given level of utility, $\bar{U}$, which depends on the levels of x_1 and x_2:

$$\bar{U} = f(x_1, x_2) \text{ or, when solving for } x_1 \qquad (1.5)$$

$$x_1 = \tilde{f}(x_2, \bar{U}) = \tilde{\tilde{f}} = (x_2). \qquad (1.6)$$

Equation (1.6) is the so-called indifference curve, that is the locus of all combinations of x_1 and x_2 which yield the same level of utility $\bar{U}$. This curve is graphically displayed in Fig. 1.2.

Fig. 1.2 Indifference curve
for a given level of utility, $\bar{U}$

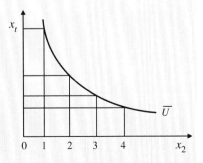

The slope at any point on an indifference curve equals the rate at which the consumer is willing to substitute one good for another. This rate is called the *marginal rate of substitution* (MRS). It shows how much of a good someone requires in order to be compensated for a one unit reduction in the consumption of another good. The MRS can be calculated by the total differential of the utility function:

$$dU = f_1' dx_1 + f_2' dx_2,$$

where d are small (but not infinitesimal small) changes.

Along the indifference curve we have:

$$0 = f_1' dx_1 + f_2' dx_2, \text{ or equally:}$$

$$\frac{f_2'}{f_1'} = -\frac{dx_1}{dx_2}.$$

That said, the MRS for substituting x_1 through one additional unit of x_2 equals the reciprocal of the marginal utilities for the goods under review (with a negative sign).

If money qualifies as a good, it should be subject to the law of diminishing marginal utility. This law contradicts the notion of a stable, that is constant-valued, good. An individual would rank the marginal utility of a larger sized unit of a good higher than that of a smaller sized unit of the same good; and any increment to the supply of a good by an additional unit will be ranked lower (valued less) than any same-sized unit of this good already in one's possession. So a change in the supply of a good must lead to a change in the good's marginal utility. From this viewpoint, the concept of stable, or constant-valued, money would be misleading (Hoppe, 1994).

1.1.2 Kinds of Money

There is a fascinating history of money – in terms of its evolution and in terms of the various kinds of goods which served as money. Unfortunately, this history is much too long and complicated to summarize here. We have to confine ourselves to a very brief overview on the different kinds of money that have emerged in the more recent history:

- *Commodity money* represents a physical commodity – a good produced and originally valued for its commercial use (such as, for instance, gold and silver) – that has come to be used as the generally accepted means of exchange.
- *Fiat money* is a coin or piece of paper of insignificant commodity value that a government has declared to be money and to which the government has given *legal tender* quality. Typically, fiat money neither represents nor is a claim for commodity money. It is issued without any intention to redeem it, and consequently the issuer does not set aside any *reserves* for that purpose.
- *Credit money* is created through a credit transaction such as, for instance, a bank extending a loan to a non-bank. As a rule, credit money is not physically backed by a commodity.
- *Tokens* are usually minor or subsidiary coins. Typically, the value of the metal content of a token is lower than its face value; a token's exchange value exceeds its commodity value.
- *Central bank money* is money issued by the central bank in the form of demand deposits (book entries) and paper notes.
- *Commercial bank money* is money issued by a commercial bank, nowadays usually in the form of demand deposits.
- *Money substitutes* are anything generally known to be freely and readily exchangeable into money, whether or not a legal requirement to do so exists.

Money that takes the form of a commodity is said to have *intrinsic value*. The term intrinsic value implies that the means of exchange would have value from the point of view of market agents even if it was not used as money. For instance, gold and silver, which served as money in the past, have intrinsic value – they are used for industrial and/or jewellery purposes. When gold is used as money (or paper money that is convertible into gold on demand), the economy is said to be operating under a *gold standard*.

Today's monies represent *non-redeemable paper*, or *fiat*, *money* over which the government holds the *supply monopoly*. It is money without any intrinsic value. It was established as money by government decree and not, as was the case with commodity based money, by the free choice of market agents. Part of the acceptability of fiat money is the result of government law. *Legal tender*, or forced tender, is payment that, by law, cannot be refused in the settlement of debts denominated in the same currency. Legal tender is a status which may be conferred on a certain type of money.

Currency School Versus Banking School

The debate about what qualifies as money is actually closely related to the dispute between the Currency School and the Banking School in the 19th century.

The *Currency School* originated from the writings of David Ricardo (1772–1823). It argued that excessive issuing of banknotes was a major cause of inflation. Currency School economists supported the British Bank Act of 1844 (or Peel's Bank Act, named after Robert Peel (1788–1850)), which prohibited the issuance of banknotes against anything except 100% gold reserves. However, the Act did permit the expansion of *demand deposits* subject to transfer or withdrawal by check against short term commercial paper of the type approved by the *Banking Principle*. This paved the way towards *fractional reserve banking* (that is allowing banks to expand their money supply beyond their gold reserves) and *elastic currency* (that is expanding money supply as trade increases and vice versa).

The Currency School was opposed by the *Banking School*. Drawing on the writings of Adam Smith (1723–1790), it espoused the *Banking Principle* or *Fullarton Principle* (named after John Fullarton (1780–1849)). The Banking School holds that as long as a bank maintains the convertibility of its banknotes into specie (gold), for which it should keep *adequate reserves*, (that is less than 100%), reserves it is impossible for the bank to over-issue its banknotes (when extending credit). The Banking School reasoned that the issuance of gold-backed banknotes would stimulate business activity, would not raise prices, and that the quantity of notes issued would be limited by the needs of trade rather than the desire of the issuing bank. It claimed that note-holders would promptly present for redemption all banknotes issued in excess of the needs of trade (business) under the so-called *law of reflux*. As a result, a trade-related rise in the money stock would not be inflationary.

1.1.3 Origin of Money

Where does money come from? According to the Austrian School of Economics, historical experience shows that money, the *universally accepted means of exchange*, emerged from free market forces. People learned that moving from direct (barter) trade to indirect trade – that is exchanging vendible goods against a good that might not necessarily be demanded for consumption or production in the first place – would lead to a higher standard of living.

Driven by peoples' self-interest and the insight that directly traded goods possess different degrees of marketability, some market agents started demanding specific goods not for their own sake (consumption or production) but for the sake of using them as a medium of exchange. Doing so entails a number of advantages. If money is used as a means of exchange, there does not have to be a "double coincidence of wants" to make trade possible. In a barter economy, it would take Mr. *A* to demand the good Mr. *B* has to offer, and Mr. *B* to demand the good that Mr. *A* wants to surrender. By accepting not only directly useful consumption and production goods, but also goods with a higher marketability than those surrendered, individuals can benefit more fully from the economic advantages of the division of labor and free trade.

Everyone recognizes the benefits of a universally accepted medium of exchange, but how does money come into existence? The *Austrian School of Economics* has offered a comprehensive explanation of the historical origin of money, actually based on the influential work of Carl Menger (1840–1921):

- In a barter economy, self-interested individuals would be reluctant to surrender real goods and services in exchange for intrinsically worthless pieces of paper or even relatively useless metal.
- It's true, however, that once *everyone else* accepts money in exchange, any individual is also willing to do so. But how could human beings reach such a position in the first place?
- According to Menger, money emerged spontaneously through the self-interested actions of individuals. No single person sat back and conceived of a universal medium of exchange, and no government action was necessary to effect the transition from a condition of barter to a money economy.
- Menger pointed out that even in a state of barter, goods would have different degrees of *marketability* or *saleability*. The more saleable a good, the more easily its owner could exchange it for other goods.
- Over time, Menger argued, the most saleable goods were desired by more and more traders because of this advantage. And as more people accepted these goods in exchange, the more saleable they became.
- Eventually, certain goods outstripped all others in this respect, and became *universally* accepted in exchange by the sellers of other goods. At this point, *money* had emerged on the market.

Market agents preferred holding the most marketable commodity over those of less marketability: "(...) there would be an inevitable tendency for the less marketable of the series of goods used as a media of exchange to be one by one rejected until at least only a single commodity remained, which was universally employed as a medium of exchange; in a word, money."[3]

In that sense, money emerged from a commodity. It is against the background of this reasoning that Mises put forward his *regression theorem*, which holds that "no good can be employed for the function of a medium of exchange which at the

---

[3]Mises (1981), p. 45.

very beginning of its use for this purpose did not have exchange value on account of other employments."[4] Experience shows that it was mostly gold (and, to a lesser extent, silver) that became the universally accepted means of exchange.

Today, however, the universally accepted means of exchange is government-controlled paper, or fiat, money. It is no longer backed by, or related to, a scarce commodity freely chosen by the market. Such a money regime was brought on its way by *going off the gold standard*: governments decided to end gold redemption of the outstanding money stock. To put it differently: by suspending peoples' *property right* to exchange their money holdings into specie, the fiat money system was established.[5]

Currency Competition Versus Money Supply Monopoly?

Today, the quality and quantity of national monies is determined by national states: the government holds the money supply monopoly. While being widely accepted by *mainstream economists*, government-controlled *irredeemable paper money standards* have not remained unchallenged. Friedrich August von Hayek (1899–1992) wrote in his *Choice in Currency: a Way to Stop Inflation* (1976): "[P]ractically all governments of history have used their exclusive power to issue money in order to defraud and plunder the people."

It was against this insight that Hayek proposed the abolition of the government's monopoly over the issue of fiat money. In his 1978 Hobart Special Paper No. 70, Hayek outlined his concept of free competition in monetary affairs: "The purpose of this scheme is to impose upon existing monetary and financial agencies a very much needed discipline by making it impossible for any of them, or for any length of time, to issue a kind of money substantially less reliable and useful than the money of any other. As soon as the public became familiar with the new possibilities, any deviations from the straight path of providing a honest money would at once lead to the rapid displacement of the offending currency by others. And the individual countries, being deprived of the various dodges by which they are now able temporarily to conceal the effects of their actions by 'protecting' their currency, would be constrained to keep the value of their currencies tolerably stable."

Hayek was of the opinion that his proposal would, if implemented, contribute to the overall stability of the economy. In his monograph, he wrote: "The past instability of the market economy is the consequence of the exclu-

---

[4]Mises (1996), p. 410.

[5]In this context see *What has Government Done to Our Money?* first published in 1963 by the historian, philosopher and economist Murray N. Rothbard (2005).

sion of the most important regulator of the market mechanism, money, from itself being regulated by the market process."[6]

Hayek's proposal kindled a lively and far-reaching debate on the role of government in the monetary system, a debate that addresses the choice between a free-market monetary regime and government management of the monetary system via a central bank (Issing, 1999). Hayek's proposal was considered profound and radical that even some leading advocates of a laissez-faire approach to most aspects of economic life (Milton Friedman, for example) were put on the defensive.

Long before Hayek, Ludwig von Mises (1881–1973) had already called for putting an end to the system of government monopolistically issued fiat money, paving the way for a system of *free banking*, with the market deciding about which kind of *sound money* they would like to hold. To Mises, this would be money backed by 100-percent in gold. Mises advocated the *sound money principle* because: "(...) it was devised as an instrument for the protection of civil liberties against despotic inroads on the part of governments. Ideologically it belongs to the same class with political constitutions and bills of rights."[7]

In his essay *The Return to Sound Money* (1953), Mises, in an attempt to show that the reestablishment and preservation of the gold standard would be economically and technically possible, made the following recommendation (in view of the US situation at that time): "The first step must be a radical and unconditional abandonment of any further inflation. The total amount of dollar bills, whatever the name or legal characteristic may be, must not be increased by further issuance."[8]

1.2 From the Gold to the Paper Money Standard

1.2.1 The Gold Standard

Originally, economists used to think in terms of *commodity price rules* for issuers of currency to follow. For them the most natural way was to implement a system of *property-rights-respecting rules*, which imposed on the issuers of currency the obligation to maintain a particular exchange rate between their currencies and one or more commodities.

---

[6]Hayek (1976), p. 192.

[7]Mises (1981), p. 454.

[8]Ibid, p. 491.

If a bank issues, say, US$1 bills, a commodity standard requires it to ensure that the US$1 bills always exchange for a given amount of a commodity. Because the issuer would maintain a fixed exchange rate between the US$1 bills and a particular quantity (or quantities) of one or more real goods, the nominal price of that good (or goods) would be fixed. Currency issued under these conditions is said to be *fully convertible*.

Commodity standards were the historical norm. The perhaps best remembered commodity standard is the *international gold standard*.[9] Britain adopted a de facto gold standard in 1717 after the master of the mint, Sir Isaac Newton (1643–1727), re-valued the silver guinea and formally adopted the gold standard in 1819, when the British Parliament abandoned long-standing restrictions on the export of gold coins and bullion from Britain. The US, though formally on a *bimetallic gold and silver standard*, switched to gold de facto in 1834 and de jure in 1900. In 1834, the US fixed the price of gold at US$20.67 per ounce. It remained at that level until 1933.

The period from 1870s to 1914 is known as the *classical gold standard*. The gold standard was a system of rules. It required the issuer of currency to maintain the exchange rate of currency against gold. If the demand for currency rose, individuals could go to the banks of issue and ask for gold to be converted into the currency they desired to hold. If the demand for currency fell, they could go to banks of issue and ask for currency to be converted into gold.

Perhaps most prominently, the Bank of England *played by the rules* over much of the period between 1870 and 1914. Whenever Great Britain faced a balance of payments deficit and, as a result, the bank saw the country's gold reserves declining, it raised its interest rate. Rising rates were supposed to dampen economic expansion and cause a fall in national goods prices. Higher interest rates and slower economic expansion would stem short-term capital outflow and attract short-term funds from abroad, thereby working towards balancing the balance of payment.

The classical gold standard was destroyed with the emergence World War I, when governments resorted to inflationary finance. It was briefly reinstated from 1925 to 1931 in the form of a *gold exchange standard*. Under the latter, countries could hold gold, US dollar or British pounds as reserves, except for the US and the UK, which held reserves only in gold. This monetary regime broke down in 1931 following Britain's departure from gold in the face of massive gold and capital outflows.[10] In 1933, US President Franklin D. Roosevelt (1882–1945) nationalized gold owned by private citizens and abrogated contracts in which payment was specified in gold.

Between 1946 and 1971 the world financial system operated under the *Bretton Woods System*. Most countries settled their international balances in US dollar, but

---

[9]For an excellent survey about the performance of the gold standard in different historical periods see Eichengreen and Flandreau (1997).

[10]On the error of Britain to return to the gold standard at a pre-war overvalued US$4.86 per pound sterling and its consequences in leading to the 1929 depression, see Robbins (1934). See also Bordo and Eichengreen (1993) and Eichengreen (1992), pp. 3–28.

the US government promised to redeem other central banks' holdings of US dollar for gold at a fixed rate of US$35 per ounce. However, persistent US balance of payments deficits steadily reduced US gold reserves. This, in turn, eroded confidence in the ability of the US to redeem its currency in gold. Finally, on 15 August, 1971, US President Richard Nixon (1913–1994) announced that the US would no longer redeem currency for gold (*closing the gold window*).

In today's government controlled fiat money system, gold has lost its monetary function. However, gold has remained a kind of *ultimate means of payment*, protecting investors against financial crises and inflation. Like any other good, the gold price depends on supply and demand. But unlike, say, corn and wheat, where most of the supply comes from the current year's crop, gold is storable and most of its supply comes from past production, built up over centuries. That said, the market price of gold behaves less like the price of a commodity than like the price of a long-lived asset. *Expectations* are therefore important for the market value of gold vis-à-vis paper money: The gold price (in, for instance, US dollar) is forward-looking, and today's price depends heavily on the expected demand for and supply of gold in the future. As a result, one would expect that *the price of gold is positively related to paper money inflation expected in the future* (Haubrich, 1998).

Figure 1.3 shows the development of the gold price in US dollar per troy ounce from 1820 to 2008 in nominal and real terms. After the US announced in August 1971 that it would no longer redeem foreign central banks' US dollar in gold, the US dollar gold price started rising. It rose to more than US$800 per ounce in the early 1980s, and declined thereafter. Following the bursting of the *New Economy-hype*, in 2001/02, the gold price in US dollar rose strongly, reaching more than US$1000 in March 2008 as investors became increasingly concerned about the consequences of

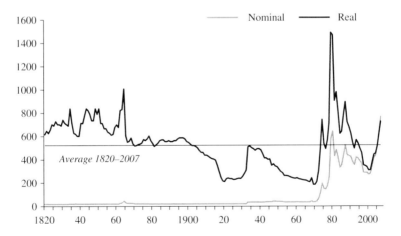

Fig. 1.3 History of the US dollar gold price per troy ounce
Source: Global Financial data; own calculations. The real gold price was calculated by deflating the nominal price with the US BLS consumer price index, from September 2007 backwards.

the *international credit market turmoil* which started in July/August 2007. However, in inflation adjusted terms, the rise in the gold price was much less pronounced than the one seen in the early 1980s.

1.2.2 Gold Standard and the Price Level

The economy's price level in terms of money prices of goods (in, say, US dollar) can be written as follows (Hallwood & MacDonald, 1994, p. 273):

$$\frac{\$}{goods} = \frac{\$}{one\ ounce\ gold} \times \frac{one\ ounce\ gold}{goods}.$$

Under the gold standard, the US dollar price of goods depended on the money price of gold *and* the amount of gold relative to goods. The money price for gold was set by law; it was the right of the gold holder to convert his money holdings into a specific weight of gold at any one time. The gold-goods relation, in turn, was a result of the free market.

A decline in the production of goods and/or a rise in gold supply for monetary purposes would increase the gold-to-goods ratio. If there was, for example, a strong increase in the supply of gold (gold discovery), there would be too much gold to clear the gold market at prevailing prices, and so the relative price of gold would have to fall.[11] Any factor that alters the gold-to-goods ratio would also alter the price level. Since the nominal price of gold would be fixed by the rules of the gold standard, the relative price of gold could only fall and clear the gold market if other prices adjusted upward. That said, the gold standard would *not necessarily guarantee an anchoring of the economy's price level* (Cooper, 1982) – but it actually did this over relatively long periods of time.

1.2.3 Trade, Gold Movements, Prices and Income

Under the gold standard, gold was the internationally accepted means of exchange. Exchange rates between international currencies were de facto fixed: each national currency was fixed vis-à-vis gold, and so the exchange rates between national currencies were also fixed. What is more, the gold standard led to an *automatic balancing* of countries' current account positions, an effect which had important consequences for domestic prices, incomes and employment levels.

Consider, for example, the case in which the US runs up a *trade surplus* vis-à-vis the UK. To settle the bill, gold is shipped from the latter to the former. The incoming

---

[11] The California gold rush in 1848 is a case in point. The newly produced gold increased the US money supply, which then raised domestic expenditures, nominal income, and ultimately, the price level.

stock of gold increases US banks' gold reserves. Money and credit become *easier* in the US, and bank lending increases. Business activity expands, with prices drifting upwards as the economy reaches full employment. The opposite is happening in the UK. Here the stock of money contracts as banks have to reduce outstanding currency. Business activity and employment decline, and goods prices fall.

Stronger economic activity in the US stimulates imports, thereby reducing the US trade surplus (*income effect*). At the same time, upward pressure on prices makes the US a more inviting place for sellers from the UK (*price effect*). In the US, domestically produced goods become less competitive. So whereas the US trade surplus declines, the trade balances of its trading partner countries improve, bringing the trade balances of the countries involved back towards zero.

Under the gold standard, the combined result of the *price* and *income* effect act to offset the conditions which originally caused the movement of gold between the countries. If the gold standard is allowed to work, it keeps the economies involved from getting too far from a position of a balanced trade balance. In fact, gold flows could be expected not to continue for long in one direction. Of course, the timing of the gold flows depends on the responsiveness (i) of the monetary system to gold movements among countries and (ii) of the economies to changes in monetary conditions.

Under the gold standard, periods of a prolonged decline in the countries' price levels were no exception. According to Bordo, Landon-Lane and Redish (2004), price declines in the late 19th century reflected both *positive aggregate supply shocks* and *negative money supply shocks*. However, the negative money supply shocks had little effect on output. The authors' findings contrast therefore greatly with the experience of following prices during the Great Depression in 1929–1933. In fact, following prices in the 19th century were primarily beneficial. They did not exert negative effects on output and employment growth.

In sum, the gold standard automatism secured *a very high degree of international free trade and capital market integration*. Disequilibria in international trade were adjusted by way of changing domestic prices and employment levels in the countries involved. A country under the gold standard could not decouple itself from the international competition and business cycle situation. It could not take recourse to autonomous national fiscal and/or monetary policies.

Gold Standard Model with Two Countries

In a *simple gold standard* model, M (M^*) is the home (foreign) country's money supply (Hallwood & MacDonald, 1994, p. 273). It is determined by the respective prices of gold (g and g^*) in terms of home and foreign country currencies, the physical amount of monetary gold (G and G^*) deposited with the banking system and the ratios of monetary gold to the money supply, that are r and r^* (gold-reserve ratios). That said, the money supply in the domestic and foreign country can be written as:

$$M = \frac{1}{r}gG \text{ and } M^* = \frac{1}{r^*}g^*G^*,$$

respectively. A rise in the gold stock, or the money price of gold or a decline
in the gold-reserve ratio increases the money supply.

If gold can be transported freely between countries without costs, gold
market arbitrage will ensure that:

$$S = \frac{g}{g^*},$$

where S is the domestic country's exchange rate (defined as the domestic currency price of the foreign currency). If transactions costs are, say, 1 percent of
the price of gold, the exchange rate may vary in a band of ± 1 on either side of
S. Under the gold standard, the money prices of gold (g and g^*) and the gold-
reserve ratios (r and r^*) are held constant. That said, only a rise in a country's
gold stock (G and G^*) increases the country's money supply: For instance,
any inflow of gold (as a result of a trade surplus and/or new gold discoveries)
increases the domestic gold stock. If the latter is held with the domestic banking sector, domestic money supply increases. As domestic prices increase,
gold will flow out of the country, reducing domestic money supply and thus
prices. A change in the world's gold stock would, sooner or later, affect prices
in all the countries adhering to the gold standard.

1.2.4 Pros and Cons of the Gold Standard

The international gold standard was a period of more or less *stable price levels*.[12]
It provided a mechanism to ensure an automatic retiring of excess currency from
circulation. Under a fiat system, there is no procedure to return excess currency to a
central bank that issues more currency than people are willing to hold at prevailing
prices. Here, prices have to rise in order to restore the market equilibrium – and that
is part of the explanation why fiat money systems have been producing so much
inflation in the past.

The rules of the gold standard worked successfully for the core countries of the
classical gold standard: the UK, France and the US. By and large, this was also
true for the smaller countries of Western Europe and the British Dominions, but
not for the peripheral nations of Southern and Eastern Europe and Latin America.
Their experience was characterized by frequent suspensions of convertibility and
devaluations (Bordo & Schwartz, 1999).

---

[12]On the theory of commodity money, see, for instance, Friedman (1953).

The gold standard provided the issuer of currency with rather *simple rules* to follow (Bordo & Kydland, 1995). It was merely required that an issuer stands ready to take back its currency on demand from the public against gold. There was no need for currency-issuing banks to try to estimate the public's demand for currency. All they had to do was to *honour their legal commitments* and convert the money issued into specie upon demand. The gold standard was thus very simple to operate.

The gold standard also had its (alleged) *drawbacks*. One obvious drawback was that the price level under the gold standard was only as stable as the relative price of gold. If the relative price of gold was unstable, then so too was the price level, and the historical record of the gold standard suggests that this concern about price level instability is not unfounded. The price level under the historical gold standard was rarely stable from one year to the next, but it remained stable over the long-run. However, price changes were seldom as economically and politically damaging as those that have characterized the world since the collapse of the Bretton Woods System (Bordo, 1993; Cooper, 1982).

Also, a gold standard involves certain *resource costs* – the costs of mining and handling gold that is used in the operation of the standard.[13] In the historical gold standard, people used gold coins, which were a more costly medium of exchange to produce and maintain than pieces of paper or bank deposits. Those resource costs gave rise to considerable concern, and their existence led many economists to argue that commodity standards were less efficient than fiat money systems because the latter involved no comparable costs and could (so it was claimed) deliver otherwise similar outcomes.

There are good reasons to believe these claims were exaggerated, however, but there is certainly no denying that the resource cost argument was a major reason why the majority of economists opposed the gold standard. Further drawbacks of the gold standard typically refer to (i) uncertainties about the possibility of keeping the growth of gold (and therefore money) supply in line with output expansion and (ii) the considerable macro-economic influence of countries with a potentially large gold production.[14]

---

[13]Milton Friedman estimated the cost of maintaining a full gold coin standard for the US in 1960 to be more than 2.5 percent of GNP. In 1990 this cost would have been US$137bn (Friedman, 1959). Initially, Friedman proposed to replace the gold standard by a "less costly" paper money standard bound by a strict money growth rule (Friedman, 1986, 1987). In the 1980s, he changed his mind, reconsidered the costs of inflation in the absence of a strict rule, and called for abolishing the Federal Reserve System (though not replacing it with a gold standard).

[14]For an excellent survey of the main drawbacks of the gold standard see, for instance, Krugman and Obstfeld (2006), p. 472.

1.2.5 The End of the Gold Standard

Four main monetary regimes can be identified in the recent monetary history of the western industrialised world: the classical gold standard (1821–1914); the interwar gold exchange standard (1925–1931); the Bretton Woods System (1946–1971); and the present system of irredeemable paper money systems (Bordo & Schwartz, 1997).

It was in the early 20th century that the gold standard became discredited by economists who believed that it must be possible to improve on it, and by governments and central banks that became increasingly impatient with the constraints the gold standard imposed on their ability to issue currency and manipulate interest rates as they pleased.

Clearly, the functioning of the gold standard rested on certain attitudes and beliefs which came to an end with the emergence of new economic paradigms after the end of World War II. National politics, increasingly inspired by policies of market interventionism, were no longer willing to accept unemployment and business cycle swings. The prevailing political and economic ideology of the day, the power of pressure groups and vested interests made it difficult and undesirable for democratically elected governments to uphold the gold standard.

With the emergence of *Keynesian economics* – which promised to provide the tools for smoothing the business cycle and lower unemployment – the gold standard was increasingly considered as being *rigid* and an *outdated regime*, representing a major hurdle to improvements in social welfare. In particular, hopes that monetary policy could become an instrument to stimulate growth and employment have played an important role for the demise of a commodity based monetary standard. The fact that the gold standard places constraints on the use of monetary policy was perceived as a drawback. Especially in the case of a worldwide recession, it was considered to be desirable for all countries to expand their money supplies jointly even if this led to inflation.

Robert Triffin (1960) drew attention to the *confidence problem* as the long-run fundamental problem of the Bretton Woods System. The inflationary US monetary policy as from the late 1960s caused an international inflation problem. Due to US inflation, the US dollar exchange rate depreciated vis-à-vis other currencies. To keep the exchange rate of the US dollar stable against their currencies (a requirement of the Bretton Woods system), foreign central banks had to buy US dollar against issuing domestic currency, which led to domestic inflation.

The US inflation policy caused a situation in which the US could no longer meet its obligations to convert all US dollars issued into gold. Knowing that their US dollar holdings would no longer be as good as gold, international central banks became unwilling to accumulate more US dollars. Some of them started converting their paper US dollars into gold, causing the US gold stock to dwindle (Fig. 1.4). To stop the outflow of gold, US president Richard Nixon, on 15 August 1971, closed the *gold window*: de facto, the US stopped converting Greenback into gold upon demand. Finally, one has to note that the functioning of the Bretton Woods System rested on the monetary discipline of the US. In that sense, the problems experi-

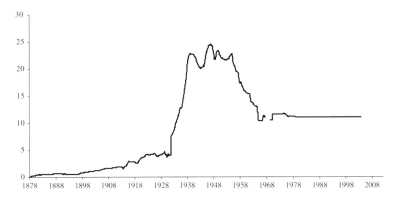

Fig. 1.4 US gold stock, US$bn
Source: NBER, Thomson Financial. Up to 1970, US monetary gold stock, thereafter US gold reserves.

enced under the Bretton Woods System do not qualify as a critique of the economic attractiveness of the gold standard per se.

1.3 Money and Credit Creation

Modern day's government controlled paper money standards, in which central banks hold the money supply monopoly, rest on two types of money: *base money* (or *high powered money*) is issued by the central bank, and *commercial bank money* is issued by commercial banks. The stock of base money includes banks' and non-banks' holdings of notes and coins (*cash*) and their respective demand deposits held with the central bank. The stock of commercial bank money consists of non-banks' deposits held with commercial banks.

1.3.1 Base Money Supply

A central bank *creates* base money whenever it buys an asset from or extends credit to banks and non-banks. It *destroys* base money whenever it sells an asset to banks and non-banks or demands repayments of credit extended. To give a simple example, let us assume that the central bank buys securities (say, a treasury bill) in the amount of US$100 from commercial banks. The central bank records the securities on its asset side and, uno actu, issues a liability vis-à-vis the banking sector in the form of a demand deposit (Fig. 1.5a). In the balance sheet of the banking sector, securities are exchanged against a base money deposit (Fig. 1.5b).

Open market operations represent the most important instrument for central banks to affect the liquidity situation in the banking sector. A central bank's purchase of securities increases the quantity of base money because the central bank

Assets	Balance sheet of the central bank	Liabilities
Securities	+100	Bank's demand deposits	+100
	100		*100*

Fig. 1.5a The central bank buys securities

Assets	Balance sheet of the commercial bank sector	Liabilities
Securities	100	Liabilities	100
	−100		
Base money demand deposit	+100		
	100		*100*

Fig. 1.5b Commercial banks sell securities

creates new money balances by crediting the account of the seller's bank held at the central bank. Conversely, sales of securities decrease the quantity of base money because the central bank extinguishes balances when it debits the account of the purchaser's depository institution at the central bank. In contrast, when financial institutions, business firms, or individuals conduct transactions among themselves, they simply redistribute existing balances held with the central bank without changing the aggregate level of those balances.

Foreign Reserve Holdings – Accumulation Trends and Implication for Central Bank Money Supply

In March 2006, a study published by the ECB (2006b) showed world foreign exchange reserves standing at around US$4.0trn, up from US$1.2trn seen in January 1995 (Fig. 1.6). Reserve accumulation in this period exhibited four features that seemed largely unprecedented; three of these features became particularly prominent in the period 2002–2004:

- *First*, world reserves grew by around 85% (or 91% if the first eight months of 2005 were included), a pace three times faster than in the period 1999–2001.
- *Second*, monetary authorities in Asia, including Japan until March 2004, accounted for the bulk of the accumulation; eight of them ranked among the ten largest reserve holders.
- *Third*, fewer official creditors held an increasingly larger share of the total accumulation. The top five reserve accumulating central banks, which accounted for almost 57% of the total reserve accumulation on average

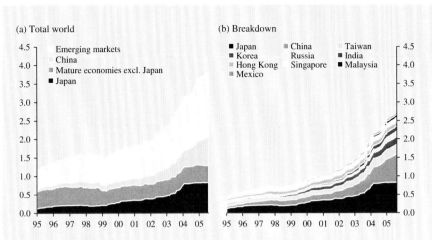

Fig. 1.6 International foreign reserves, US$trn
Source: IMF, International Financial Statistics and WEO, ECB. – Period February 1995 to September 2005.

in the period 1995–2001, increased their share to more than 68% of the total world accumulation in 2004. The top two, Japan and China, accounted for about half of the total world accumulation in 2002–2004, holding around 40% of the total world stock of reserves.
– *Fourth*, oil exporting countries, whose combined current account surpluses were estimated to have exceeded that of the Asian economies in 2005, emerged as a new major group of net capital exporters in the world economy.

The unprecedented accumulation of official foreign assets can be seen as the outcome of three main drivers (De Beaufort Wijnholds & Søndergaard, 2007):

– First, in the aftermath of the financial crises that occurred in the 1990s and early 2000s, many emerging market economies (EMEs) felt the need to self-insure against future crises, building up Foreign reserves.
– Second, at the beginning of their recoveries and following strong depreciation of their currencies, the crisis-hit Asian economies pursued export-led growth supported by exchange rate regimes pegging their currencies mostly to the US dollar. This is especially the case for several emerging Asian countries, whose reserve levels have grown far beyond what can reasonably considered economically reasonable.[15]

---

[15]Various opinions on Asian exchange rate and reserves policies are examined in ECB (2007), and the costs and benefits of currency undervaluation are also discussed.

– Third, certain features of the domestic financial systems of EMEs, especially in Asia, are likely to have played a role. Such characteristics relate
mainly to: (i) underdeveloped local financial systems, entailing difficulties in properly channelling domestic private savings to investment as well
as inefficient and/or costly hedging markets; (ii) the tendency towards
dollarisation of official and/or private cross-border assets on the part
of certain creditor EMEs; and (iii) an excess of domestic savings over
investment.

Now consider the case in which an Asian central bank tries to prevent the
country's exchange rate from *appreciating* against the US dollar. Whenever
the domestic currency rises vis-à-vis the Greenback, the Asian central bank
would have to buy US dollar against issuing domestic currency (Fig. 1.7). The
Asian central bank would report the purchased US dollar amount (translated
into domestic currency) on the asset side of its balance sheet (1a), while the
currency issued would be recorded on the liability side (1b).

Any such intervention would increase the Asian country's base money supply. If the central bank wants to *neutralise* the increase in base money supply,
it would have to sell securities (or any other asset) to the banking sector and/or
the private sector. As the buyer would have to pay with base money, the central
bank's security holdings (2a) and liabilities (2b) would be reduced in the same
amount. The commercial banking/non-banking sector would end up with less
base money and more securities in its portfolio.

Assets	Balance sheet of the central bank	Liabilities
1a) Foreign bank deposits	+100	1b) Banks' deposits	+100
2a) Securities	−100	2b)	−100

Fig. 1.7 Central bank buying and neutralising of foreign currency

1.3.2 Central Bank Balance Sheet

The interaction between the monetary authority and commercial banks are reflected
in the balance sheet of the central bank. In the following, a closer look shall be taken
at the structures of the balance sheets of the US Federal Reserve and the Eurosystem.

1.3.3 The US Federal Reserve

1.3.3.1 Asset Side of the Balance Sheet

Figure 1.8 shows the consolidated balance sheet of the US Federal Reserve Banks in US dollar as of the end of October 2007. The item S*ecurities, repurchase agreements, and loans* on the asset side is by far the largest category of assets. It basically represents the Fed's holdings of securities, which consist primarily of Treasury securities (in the past it has also included banker's acceptances). The total amount of securities is controlled by open market operations (the Fed's purchase and sale of these securities). *Loans* represent Fed lending to banks. The amount is affected by the Fed's setting the discount rate (the interest rate that the Fed charges banks for these loans). These two Fed assets earn interest. Because the liabilities of the Fed do not pay interest, the Fed makes a profit every year.

The items *Gold certificate account* and *Special drawing rights* (SDRs) *account* represent the Fed's gold holdings and SDRs issued to governments by the International Monetary Fund (IMF) to settle international debts. When the Treasury acquires gold or SDRs, it issues certificates to the Fed that are claims on the gold or SDRs; it is then credited with deposit balances at the Fed. The gold and SDR accounts are made up of these certificates issued by the Treasury.

The item *Coin* is actually the smallest item in the balance sheet, consisting of Treasury currency (mostly coins) held by the Fed.

Cash items in process of collection arise from the Fed's check-clearing process. When a check is given to the Fed for clearing, the Fed will present it to the bank

Assets		Liabilities	
1 Gold certificate account	11,037	20 Federal Reserve notes, net of F.R. Bank holdings	778,155
2 Special drawing rights certificate account	2,200	21 Reverse repurchase agreements	38,055
3 Coin	1,251	22 Deposits	25,915
4 Securities, repurchase agreements, and loans	828,178	23 Depository institutions	20,720
5 Securities held outright	779,586	24 US Treasury, general account	4,307
6 US Treasury	779,586	25 Foreign official	0,601
7 Bills	267,019	26 Other	0,287
8 Notes, bonds, nominal	470,984	27 Deferred availability cash item	2,955
9 Notes, bonds, inflation indexed	36,911	28 Other liabilities and accrued dividends	5,724
10 Inflation compensation	4,672	29 Total capital	36,126
11 Federal agency	0,000	30 Capital paid in	17,947
12 Repurchase agreements	48,500	31 Surplus	15,455
13 Loans	0,092	32 Other capital accounts	2,724
14 Items in the process of collection	2,210		
15 Bank premises	2,118		
16 Other assets	39,936		
17 Denominated in foreign currencies	22,417		
18 All other	17,519		
19 *Total assets*	*886,929*	33 *Total liabilities*	*886,929*

Fig. 1.8. Consolidated balance sheet of Federal Reserve Banks, US$mn, end of month October 2007
Source: Federal Reserve Bulletin, Statistical Supplement, January 2008, Table 1.18 Federal Reserve Banks, Condition and Federal Reserve Note Statements.

on which it is written and will collect funds by deducting the amount of the check from the bank's deposits (reserves) with the Fed. Before these funds are collected, the check is a cash item in process of collection, and it is recorded as a Fed asset.

Other Federal Reserve assets include deposits and bonds denominated in foreign currencies as well as physical goods such as computers, office equipment and buildings owned by the Fed.

1.3.3.2 Liability Side of the Balance Sheet

Turning to the liability side of the Fed's balance sheet, *Federal Reserve notes, net of F.R. Banks holdings* are banknotes outstanding issued by the Fed and held by the public. (Note that currency held by depository institutions is also a liability of the Fed, but it is counted as part of the reserves liability).[16]

The item *Reserves* shows banks' deposits at the Fed. Reserves consist of deposits at the Fed plus currency that is physically held by banks (*vault cash*). Reserves are assets for commercial banks but liabilities for the Fed: banks can demand payment on them at any time and the Fed is required to satisfy its obligation by paying Federal Reserve notes.

Total reserves can be divided into two categories: reserves that the Fed requires banks to hold (required reserves) and any additional reserves the banks choose to hold (excess reserves). For example, the Fed might require that for every dollar of deposits at a depository institution a certain fraction (say, 10 cents) must be held as reserves. This fraction (10%) is called the required reserve ratio.

Furthermore, there are *US Treasury deposits*, that are deposits held by the Treasury with the Fed.

Foreign and other deposits include the deposits with the Fed owned by foreign governments, foreign central banks, international agencies (such as the World Bank and the United Nations), and US government agencies (such as the Federal Deposit Insurance Corporation (FDIC) and Federal Home Loan banks).

Deferred-availability cash items arise from the Fed's check-clearing process. When a check is submitted for clearing, the Fed does not immediately credit the bank that submitted the check. Instead, it promises to credit the bank within a certain time limit, which never exceeds two days. These promises are the deferred-availability items and are a liability of the Fed.

The items *Other Federal Reserve liabilities* and *capital accounts* include all the remaining Federal Reserve liabilities not included elsewhere on the balance sheet. For example, stocks in the Federal Reserve System purchased by member banks are included in this item.

---

[16]Banknotes issued by the Fed are IOUs of the Fed to the bearer. IOU is an abbreviation of the phrase "I owe you". An IOU in the business community is a legally binding agreement between a borrower and a lender. Unlike most liabilities, however, Fed banknotes promise to pay back the bearer solely with Fed banknotes. For instance, if someone hands over a $100 bill to the Federal Reserve and demands payment, he will receive two $50s, five $20s, ten $10s, or one hundred $1 bills. That is the Fed pays off IOUs with other IOUs.

Fed Open Market and Credit Operations in the Course of the Credit Market Turmoil 2007/2008

In the last decades, the US Fed has been providing banks' *total reserves* via open market operations, so that total reserves basically equalled *non-borrowed reserves* (Fig. 1.9). This changed following the international credit market turmoil starting in July/August 2007. In June 2007, total reserves stood at US$41.8bn, total borrowing at US$0.2bn and non-borrowed reserves at US$41.6bn. In June 2008, total reserves amounted to US$43.4bn, while total borrowed had risen to US$171.3bn and non-borrowed reserves fallen to a negative US$127.9bn.

By definition, *non-borrowed reserves* equal *total reserves* minus *borrowed reserves*. Borrowed reserves are equal to credit extended through the Fed's regular discount window programs and credit extended through the Term Auction Facility (TAF). To maintain total reserves consistent with the Federal Open Market Committee (FOMC) target federal funds rate, an increase in borrowed reserves must generally be met by a commensurate decrease in non-borrowed reserves, which is accomplished through a reduction in the Fed's holdings of securities and other assets. The negative level of non-borrowed reserves is the result of the fact that TAF borrowings are larger than total reserves.

These changes were reflected in the Federal Reserve banks' asset structure (Fig. 1.10). Most important, *securities held outright* (that are US Treasury and Federal agency securities) fell from around US$790bn in July 2007 to

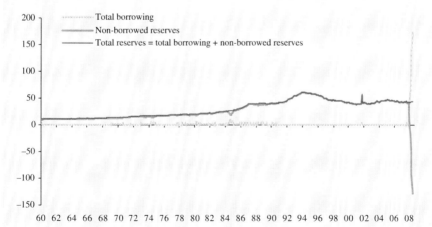

Fig. 1.9 US banks' base money reserves, US$bn
Source: Federal Reserve Bank of St. Louis.

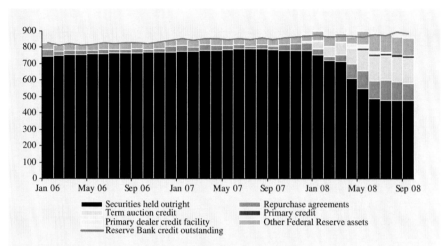

Fig. 1.10 Selected assets of Federal Reserve banks, US$bn
Source: Thomson Financial, Federal Reserve.

US$479bn in September 2008, basically compensated for by a rise in *repurchase agreements*, *TAF* and *primary credit*. In other words: the Fed returned low risk government paper to commercial banks, and lent base money to banks by accepting risky assets as collateral. By doing so, banks were (temporarily) relieved from risky assets (which, as a rule, need to be backed by (costly) equity capital).

1.3.3.3 Calculating the Monetary Base

Federal Reserve notes (currency) outstanding and reserves are referred to as the Fed's monetary liabilities. Adding to these liabilities the US Treasury's monetary liabilities (Treasury currency in circulation, primarily coins), one gets an aggregate which is called the *monetary base* (or *high powered money*). The monetary base is an important part of the money supply, because increases in it tend to lead to a multiple increase in commercial banks' money supply.

If Treasury currency and Federal Reserve currency are added together into currency in circulation, C, the monetary base equals the sum of C plus reserves, R. The monetary base MB is expressed as follows:

$$MB = Federal\ Reserve\ notes + Treasury\ currency - coin + reserves$$
$$= C + R.$$

The items on the right-hand side of this equation indicate how the base is actually *used*. They are called uses of the monetary base.

This equation does not tell us the factors that determine the monetary base. This issue can be solved by taking a look at the Fed's balance sheet. Because the Federal Reserve notes and reserves in the *uses of the monetary base* are Fed liabilities, the assets-equals-liabilities-property of the balance sheet one can solve for these items in terms of the Fed balance sheet items that are included in the sources of the base. Specifically, Federal Reserve notes and reserves equal the sum of all the Fed assets minus all the other Fed liabilities:

Federal Reserve notes + reserves = Securities + discount loans + gold and SDRs + coin + cash items in process of collection + other Federal Reserve assets – Treasury deposits – foreign and other deposits – deferred-availability cash items – other Federal Reserve liabilities and capital.

The two balance sheet items related to check clearing can be collected into one term called *float*, defined as *Cash items in process of collection* minus *Deferred-availability cash items*. Substituting all the right-hand-side items in the equation for Federal Reserve notes + reserves in the uses-of-the-base equation, we obtain the following expression describing the sources of the monetary base:

MB = Securities + discount loans + gold and SDRs + float + other Federal Reserve assets + treasury currency – Treasury deposits – foreign and other deposits – other Federal Reserve liabilities and capital.

Accounting logic provides an equation that identifies the nine factors influencing the monetary base. An increase of the first six factors enhances the monetary base, while increases in the last three items reduce the monetary base.

1.3.4 The Eurosystem

1.3.4.1 Asset Side of the Balance Sheet

Figure 1.11 shows a *stylised* balance sheet of the Eurosystem. There are three main liquidity-providing items recorded on the assets side of the balance sheet: *refinancing to credit institutions*, *marginal lending facility* and *net foreign assets*. Refinancing to credit institutions refers to the amount outstanding of base-money-providing open market operations. These operations include the main and long-term open market operations; liquidity providing fine-tuning operations and structural operations would also be included under this item. The marginal lending facility refers to overnight base money credit provided to those credit institutions that have recourse to this facility. Net foreign assets refer to assets in foreign currency owned by the central bank, net of any central bank liabilities denominated in foreign currency.

1.3.4.2 Liability Side of the Balance Sheet

On the liabilities side, there are five main items. These are *credit institutions' holdings on current accounts*, the *deposit facility*, *banknotes in circulation*, *government*

Standardised central bank balance sheet	
Assets	*Liabilities*
- Refinancing to credit institutions - Marginal lending facility - Net foreign assets	- Credit institutions' holdings on current accounts (reserves) - Deposit facility - Banknotes in circulation - Government deposits - Other factors (net)
Can be rearranged as follows:	
Liquidity supply through monetary policy operations	
"refinancing to credit institutions" plus "marginal lending facility" minus "deposit facility"	
equals	
Autonomous factors	
"banknotes in circulation" plus "government deposits" minus "net foreign assets" plus "other factors (net)"	
plus	
Reserves	
"credit institutions' holdings on current accounts"	

Fig. 1.11 Stylised balance sheet of the Eurosystem
Source: ECB (2005), p. 85.

deposits and *other net factors*. The item credit institutions' holdings on current accounts refers to balances owned by credit institutions and held with the central bank in order to meet settlement obligations from interbank transactions and to fulfil reserve requirements (also referred to as *reserves*). The deposit facility refers to banks' overnight balances held with the Eurosystem. Banknotes indicate the value of the banknotes put into circulation by the central bank at the request of credit institutions. This is usually the largest item on the liabilities side. Government deposits reflect the existence of current account balances held by national treasuries with national central banks. Finally, other net factors are a balancing item encompassing the remaining items on the balance sheet.

1.3.4.3 Illustration

A simple version of the Eurosystem's balance sheet as of 29 February 2008 is shown in Fig. 1.12. On the asset side, item (5.) *Lending to euro area credit institutions in euro* reflects open market operations with the euro area banking sector. This item represents the most important procedure for affecting the amount of base money in banks' portfolios.

Assets		Liabilities	
1. Gold and gold receivables	201.3	1. Banknotes in circulation	654.0
2. Claims on non-euro area residents in foreign currency	137.9	2. Liabilities to euro area credit institutions in euro	195.6
3. Claims on euro area residents in foreign currency	24.7	3. Other liabilities to euro area credit institutions in euro	0.2
4. Claims on non-euro area residents in euro	14.6	4. Debt certificates issued	0.0
5. Lending to euro area credit institutions in euro	451.5	5. Liabilities to other euro area residents in euro	80.7
6. Other claims on euro area credit institutions in euro	30.8	6. Liabilities to non-euro area residents in euro	34.4
7. Securities of euro area residents in euro	106.1	7. Liabilities to euro area residents in foreign currency	0.7
8. General government debt in euro	38.6	8. Liabilities to non-euro area residents in foreign currency	18.6
9. Other assets	333.3	9. Counterpart of special drawing rights allocated by the IMF	5.3
		10. Other liabilities	130.9
		11. Revaluation accounts	147.7
		12. Capital and reserves	70.6
Total	1338.8		1338.8

Fig. 1.12 Stylised balance sheet of the Eurosystem, in €bn, 29 February 2008
Source: ECB, Deutsche Bundesbank. Differences are due to rounding.

On the liability side, item (2.) *Liabilities to euro area credit institutions in euro* shows banks' deposits in base money held with central banks of the Eurosystem. This item largely represents of banks' minimum reserve requirement holdings (as banks tend to keep *excess reserves* close to zero). The total amount of base money outside the central bank would be commercial banks' deposits with the central bank plus the stock of cash (coins and notes) outstanding.

1.3.5 Credit and Money Creation

Commercial banks need base money for at least three reasons: (i) making inter-bank payments; (ii) meeting any *cash drain* as non-banks want to keep a portion of their deposits in cash (notes and coins); and (iii) holding a certain portion of their liabilities in the form of base money with the central bank (*minimum reserves*).

For a start, let us assume that there is *only one bank* in the economy. In addition, all payments are transacted cashlessly. Money is created whenever the bank buys an asset (security, stock, foreign exchange holdings etc.) from non-banks and issues its own liabilities in return (which are considered as money). For instance, in our example the bank buys bonds from non-banks in the amount of US$100 (Fig. 1.13a).

The bank's balance sheet volume increases in the amount of the asset purchased. The balance sheet of the non-banking sector records a change in the structure of the

Assets	Balance sheet of the bank		Liabilities
Securities		+100	Sight deposits	+100
Others		600	Equity capital	600
		700		*700*

Fig. 1.13a

Assets	Balance sheet of the non-bank sector	Liabilities
Securities	−100	
Sight deposits with the bank	+100	

Fig. 1.13b

Assets	Balance sheet of the bank		Liabilities
Loans to non-banks		1000	Sight deposits	1000
Others		600	Equity capital	600
		1600		*1600*

Fig. 1.14a

Assets	Balance sheet of the non-bank sector	Liabilities
Sight deposits bank	+1000	Liabilities	+1000

Fig. 1.14b

asset side: securities holdings decline and in the same amount sight deposits held with the bank increase (Fig. 1.13b).

Alternatively, the bank can create money if it extends loans to non-banks. Assume the bank extends loans in the amount of US$1000 to firms. In such a case, the bank's balance sheet volume increases in the amount of credit extended (Fig. 1.14a). At the same time, the non-banking sector's assets and liabilities rise in the amount of sight deposits, e.g. liabilities vis-à-vis the bank (Fig. 1.14b).

1.3.6 Multiple Credit and Money Creation

If there is just one bank in the economy, and all payments are being made with sight deposits, the bank's capacity for creating credit and money would be unlimited. This is, of course, not what can be observed in reality, and so we change our assumptions as follows. First, we assume that there are *many banks*. Second, we assume that some payments are made with cash, so we take into account that *banks need central bank money*. In such a world, the banking sector's capacity for creating money and credit is *limited* by:

- *non-banks' cash holdings*, that is banks are required to hold a certain fraction of their liabilities vis-à-vis non-banks in cash (*working balances* in the form of coins and notes); and
- *commercial banks' minimum reserve holdings*, as banks are required to keep a certain amount of balances with the central bank in the form of base money.

In a first step, we will consider the banking sectors' capacity to create money and credit if non-banks do not demand cash balances (in relation to their sight deposits held with banks). Let us assume that non-banks deposit cash and coins in the amount of US$100 with the banking sector and that the banking sector issues liabilities in the form of sight deposits in the same amount (Fig. 1.15a).

Assuming a minimum reserve rate of 2%, the banking sector is required to keep US$2 as minimum reserves. *Excess reserves* amount to US$98 (Fig. 1.15b). With the latter, the banking sector as a whole can extend loans to the private sector until the excess reserves are fully absorbed by minimum reserves. This is the case if excess reserves, *ER*, equal the minimum reserve rate, *r*, multiplied by the stock of additional loans, ΔL:

$$\Delta L \cdot r = ER, \text{ or}$$

$$\Delta L = \frac{1}{r} \cdot ER.$$

In view of the example above, the balance sheet would now look as follows (Fig. 1.15c): With an excess reserve of US$98, the banking sector can create additional loans and, at the same time, increase the stock of payments (that is M1) in the amount of US$4900.

In view of the transactions above, the banking sector's money creating capacity is given by the following relation:

Assets	Balance sheet of the banking sector		Liabilities
Cash and notes	100	Sight deposits	100
Others	600	Equity capital	600
	700		700

Fig. 1.15a

Excess reserves	98	Sight deposits	100
Minimum reserves	2		
Others	600	Equity capital	600
	700		700

Fig. 1.15b

Assets	Balance sheet of the banking sector	Liabilities
Minimum reserves	100	Sight deposits	5000
Loans (ΔL)	4900		
Others	600	Equity capital	600
	5600		5600

Fig. 1.15c

$$M \cdot r = B^{cbk}, \text{ or}$$

$$M = \frac{1}{r} \cdot B^{cbk},$$

where $1/r = m$ is the money multiplier.

The *maximum money creation potential of the banking sector*, M^{pot}, depends on the amount of central bank money available to banks, that is banks' central bank money holdings, B^{cbk}, plus non-banks' central bank money holdings, B^{nbk}, which could be attracted by commercial banks:

$$M^{pot} = m \cdot B, \text{ with } B = B^{nbk} + B^{cbk}.$$

The analysis shall now be extended by taking into account that non-banks prefer to keep a certain fraction of their sight deposits in the form of cash and coins – so that banks face a *cash drain*. Banks are required to keep minimum reserves *and* working balances in central bank money. Let us assume that the working balances ratio is $c = 5\%$. That said, for each unit of non-banks' sight deposit the banking sector is required to hold $c + r = 7\%$ in the form of base money. For maintaining its liquidity, banks' holdings of central bank money must satisfy the following restriction:

$$ER - c \cdot L \geq 0.$$

Note that $L \cdot (1 - c)$ represents the remaining potential for additional loan and money creation. Or, to put the above liquidity condition differently, we can write:

$$ER - \underbrace{c \cdot \Delta L}_{Cash\ holdings} = \underbrace{\Delta L}_{Sight\ deposits} \cdot r, \text{ or}$$

$$\underbrace{}_{\Delta MR}$$

$$ER = \Delta L \cdot (r + c), \text{ or}$$

$$\Delta L = \frac{1}{0.07} \cdot 93 \approx 1329.$$

Taking into account banks' holdings of working balances, the *modified money creation multiplier* is:

$$m = \frac{1}{r + c}.$$

Turning back to our example, let us assume that non-banks' deposit notes and coins in the amount of US\$100 with the commercial banking sector in period $t = 0$ (Fig. 1.16a). In period $t = 1$, excess reserves are used for multiple money and credit creation (Fig. 1.16b).

Using the modified money creation multiplier m, one can calculate the *banking sector's maximum lending* (as opposed to money creation) *potential*. In the multiple money and credit creation process, the stock of sight deposits, M, must equal the sum of minimum reserve holdings and working balances, B^{cbk}, plus the amount of loans created (L):

$$M = B^{cbk} + L, \text{ or with } M = m \cdot B^{cbk}:$$

$$L = m \cdot B^{cbk} - B^{cbk} = B^{cbk}(m - 1),$$

where $m - 1$ is the credit multiplier.

Assets	Balance sheet of the banking sector		Liabilities
Central bank money	+100	Sight deposits	+100
Thereof:			
(a) Minimum reserves	+2		
(b) Working balances	+5		
(c) Excess reserves	+93		
Others	600	Equity capital	600
	700		700

Fig. 1.16a Banks receive central bank money $(t = 0)$

Assets	Balance sheet of the banking sector		Liabilities
Central bank money	100	Sight deposits	1429
Thereof:			
(a) Minimum reserves	+28.6		
(b) Working balances	+71.4		
(c) Excess reserves	+0		
Loans (ΔL)	1329		
Others	600	Equity capital	600
	2029		2029

Fig. 1.16b Multiple money and credit creation $(t = 1)$

Under a given stock of central bank money, the banking sector's money and credit creation capacity varies with changes in c and r. If, for instance, non-banks' preferences for holding cash decreases, or the central bank lowers the reserve rate r, banks' potential for expanding money and credit supply increases (other things equal).

The traditional money and credit multiplier theory has been subject to various criticisms. Most importantly, it has been claimed that market agents do not only hold sight deposits but tend to shift from sight deposits into, for instance, time and savings deposits. Modern approaches to the money multiplier try to take into account these *shifting processes.*

1.3.7 The Tinbergen Approach to the Money Multiplier

To start with, the stock of M1 is defined as:

$$M1 = C^{nbk} + Si, \tag{1.7}$$

where $C^{nbk} =$ cash in the hands of non-banks and $Si =$ non-banks' sight deposits. The monetary base, B, is:

$$B = C^{cbk} + MR, \tag{1.8}$$

where $MR =$ minimum reserves.

The total amount of cash in the economy is:

$$C = C^{cbk} + C^{nbk}. \tag{1.9}$$

If there is just a single minimum reserve ratio, banks' minimum reserve holdings can be calculated as:

$$MR = r(Si + T + SAV), \tag{1.10}$$

where $T =$ time deposits and $SAV =$ savings deposits.

According to the *Tinbergen approach*, non-banks will hold sight deposits, time deposits and savings deposits in a certain proportion, namely:

$$C^{nbk} = c \cdot Si, \text{ with } c = \text{cash coefficient}, \tag{1.11a}$$

$$T = t \cdot Si, \text{ with } t = \text{time deposit ratio, and} \tag{1.11b}$$

$$SAV = sd \cdot Si, \text{ with } sd = \text{savings deposit ratio.} \tag{1.11c}$$

Substituting Eqs. (1.11b) and (1.11c) in (1.10) yields:

$$MR = r \cdot Si(1 + t + sd). \tag{1.12}$$

Substituting Eqs. (1.9) in (1.8) and taking into account the above leads to:

$$
\begin{aligned}
B &= C - C^{nbk} + MR \\
&= C - c \cdot Si + r \cdot Si(1 + t + sd) \\
&= C + Si\,[r(1 + t + sd) - c].
\end{aligned}
$$

(1.13a)

Solving for Si yields:

$$
Si = \frac{1}{r(1 + t + sd) - c} \cdot (B - C).
$$

(1.13b)

Using Eq. (1.11a), we can write the stock of payments as:

$$
M1 = c \cdot Si + Si = Si(1 + c) = \frac{1 + c}{r(1 + t + sd) - c} \cdot (B - C)
$$

(1.14)

Against the background of Eq. (1.14), the money multiplier for a broadly defined money aggregate ($M3 = M1 + T + SAV$) can be easily derived as:

$$
M3 = Si(1 + c) + t \cdot Si + sd \cdot Si = \frac{1 + c + t + sd}{r(1 + t + sd) - c} \cdot (B - C)
$$

(1.15)

Of course, the parameters of the money multipliers are *functions of other variables*. For instance, the holding of cash can be expected to depend on interest rates (opportunity costs of money holdings); the same applies to t and sd. This, in turn, suggests that banks, via changing deposit interest rates, are in a position to affect the money multipliers. Figures 1.17 (a) and (b) show the money multipliers for US M1, M2, M3 and M2 Minus from 1960 to December 2007. The multipliers were not

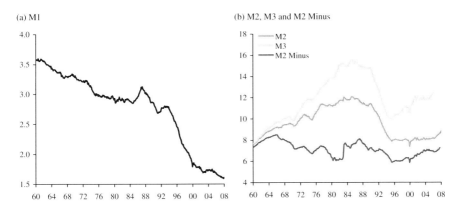

Fig. 1.17 Money multipliers in the US
Source: Federal Reserve Bank of St. Louis, Bloomberg; own calculations. – Period: January 1960 to December 2007 (for M3: February 2006). – The multiplier is defined as the stock of money divided by the Board of Governors Monetary Base (adjusted for changes in reserve requirements).

constant over time, indicating that changes in base money had time-varying effects on commercial bank money aggregates.

Bank Lending and Bank Equity Capital

The central bank's supply of base money is not the only restriction influencing commercial banks' scope of creating credit and money. This is because banks have *to employ equity capital* when taking risky positions on their balance sheets: Government regulations require banks to keep a certain ratio between risky assets (such as, for instance, loans and corporate bonds) and equity capital.

In the example below, it is assumed that the minimum reserve ratio on demand and time deposits is 2%, respectively. Given that the stock of demand plus time deposit amounts to US$3000, minimum reserves amount to U$60.[17] What is more, it is assumed that the required capital ratio is 8%.[18] Economically speaking, the capital requirement works as a multiplier: with a given US-dollar of equity capital, banks can create US$12.5 of credit (that is 1 divided by 0.08).

Assets	Consolidated balance sheet of the banking sector		Liabilities
Base money		60	Demand deposits	1500
of which:			Time deposits	1500
minimum reserves		60	Long-term liabilities	3040
Loans	3500		
Bond holdings	3000	Equity capital	520
Total assets	6560	*Total liabilities*	6560

Assets	Consolidated balance sheet of the central bank		Liabilities
Securities	60	Commercial banks' base money	60
Other assets	10	Equity capital	10
Total assets	70	*Total liabilities*	70

---

[17]With a base money supply of US$60 and a minimum reserve ratio of 2%, banks can, in a first step, increase credit and money supply by US$3000, respectively (that is US$60 divided by 0.02). If, in a second step, banks make their clients shifting, say, sight deposits of US$2000 into longer-term liabilities (which are not subject to minimum reserves), base money in the amount of US$40 can be freed up; this allows an additional credit and money creation of US$2000.

[18]The 1988 Basle Accord (Basle I) is the globally agreed standard by which supervisors calculate and set capital charges for internationally active banks. The Accord sets out rules which require firms to hold a minimum of 8% capital to mitigate against credit and market risk. Building on Basle I, the new Basle Framework for the International Convergence of Capital Measurement and Capital Standards (Basel II) came into force in Europe at the end of 2006. The key objective of the new capital adequacy framework is to bring in line banks' capital requirements more closely with the actually incurred risk than in the past and to take account of recent innovations in the financial markets as well as in institutions' risk management.

Now we assume that, after years of a credit and money fuelled boom, borrowers start defaulting. As a result, the values of banks' holdings of loans and bonds need to be written down by, say, US$65, respectively. As a result, loans are recorded at US$3435 and bonds at US$2935, with banks' equity capital declining to US$390.

Assets		Consolidated balance sheet of the banking sector	Liabilities
Base money	60	Demand deposits	1500
of which:		Time deposits	1500
minimum reserves	*60*	Long-term liabilities	3040
Loans	3435		
Bond holdings	2935	Equity capital	390
Total assets	*6430*	*Total liabilities*	*6430*

The write-offs make banks' equity capital ratio drop to 6.1%, which is lower than what banks are required to maintain. Banks would now basically have *two options to stay in business*: getting rid of risky assets and/or issuing new equity.[19] Raising new equity capital might be costly in times of financial market stress, while selling risky assets in times of crisis (*fire sale*) may suppress asset valuations, thereby increasing banks' capital losses further. In fact, it may trigger a downward spiral: falling asset prices, more capital losses, rising investor concern about the solidity of the banking sector, higher funding costs – potentially ending in bank failures on a grand scale.

For the sake of simplicity let us assume that banks succeed in selling bonds in the amount of US$1495 to non-banks (insurance companies, pension funds etc.). This would bring banks' equity capital ratio back to 8%. However, demand deposits decline to US$5, as non-banks exchange demand deposits for bonds, so that banks' liabilities in the form of demand deposits are *destroyed*. Banks' excess reserves increase to US$29.9. However, given their diminished equity capital base, banks could not expand credit and money supply any further.

Assets		Consolidated balance sheet of the banking sector	Liabilities
Base money	60	Demand deposits	5
of which:		Time deposits	1500
minimum reserves	*30,1*	Long-term liabilities	3040
excess reserves	*29,9*		
Loans	3435		
Bond holdings	1440	Equity capital	390
Total assets	*4935*	*Total liabilities*	*4935*

---

[19]Of course, authorities could relax the capital requirement. However, such a measure would, as a rule, be effective only if banks' write-offs do not exceed their equity capital. What is more, a lowering of the capital requirement might erode the public's confidence in the financial health of the banking sector.

1.3.8 Open Market Operations

Open market operations have become the primary tools of monetary policies for supplying base money to commercial banks. In what follows, we will take a brief look at the open market regimes in the US and the euro area. Operating procedures tend to be fairly similar to one another, though details may differ from currency area to currency area.

1.3.8.1 Open Market Operations in the US

In the US, open market operations are arranged by the Domestic Trading Desk (*Desk*) at the Federal Reserve Bank of New York under the authorization from the FOMC, which was created by statute to direct open market operations (Edwards, 1997; Akhtar, 1997). Each morning, the Desk decides whether an open market operation is necessary and, if so, whether it should be an outright or a temporary operation.

If the Fed's *staff projections* point to a large and persistent imbalance between the demand for and supply of reserves (for longer-terms, such as a month or more), the Desk may conduct an *outright* purchase or sale of securities. Such transactions raise or lower the size of the Fed's portfolio (and thus add or reduce reserve balances) permanently. If *staff projections* suggest only a short-lived need to add or drain reserve balances, the Desk usually conducts a *temporary* operation. Such operations are actually far more common than outright operations.

By trading government securities, the New York Fed affects the *federal funds rate*, which is the interest rate at which depository institutions lend balances to each other overnight. As a monopoly supplier of base money, the FOMC sets the target

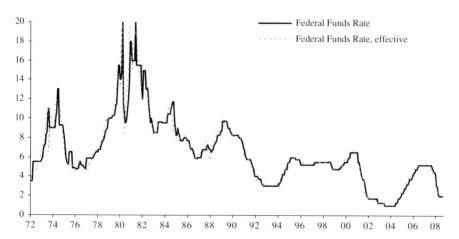

Fig. 1.18 Federal Funds Rate, actual and effective (%)
Source: Thomson Financial.

rate of the federal funds rate for trading in the federal funds market. As a rule, the federal funds rate tends to be closely aligned to the federal funds target rate (Fig. 1.18).

The Fed's Open Market Regime

The Feds open market operations involve the buying (increasing base money supply) and selling (reducing base money supply) of government securities in the *secondary market* (that is in the market in which previously issued securities are traded). Open market operations are the most prominent instrument for supplying base money.

− *Outright operations* are used when reserve shortages or excesses are expected to be persistent for a relatively long period. The Desk may take recourse to outright purchases or sales (and redemptions) of government securities, which permanently affect the amount of the base money supply.
− *Temporary operations* are transactions that will unwind after a specified number of days. As a rule, temporary open market operations help to offset short-lived imbalances between the demand for and supply of reserves. The Fed's Desk uses *repurchase agreements* to add reserves and *matched-sale purchase transactions* to drain reserves on a temporary.
− Under *repurchase agreements* for expanding base money supply, the central bank purchases securities from its counterparties and agrees to resell the securities on a specified date in the future.
− *Matched sale–purchase transactions* (which are akin to reverse repurchase agreements) are the method by which the Fed drains reserve balances temporarily. The Fed agrees to sell a short-dated Treasury bill at a specified price, and the buyer simultaneously enters into another agreement to sell the bill back to the Fed on a specific date.
− Finally, it should be noted that the Desk can reduce the size of the Fed's security holdings by *redeeming* some of its maturing securities rather than exchanging all of them for new securities. Such an approach makes it possible to reduce the portfolio gradually without formally entering the market. When replacement securities are not available, the Desk must redeem its maturing holdings.

Source: *Edwards* (1997), Open Market Operations in the 1990s, Federal Reserve Bulletin, pp. 859–874.

1.3.8.2 Open Market Operations in the Euro Area

For the Eurosystem, open market operations play an important role in the monetary policy of steering interest rates, managing the liquidity situation in the market and signalling the stance of monetary policy (ECB, 2006b). With regard to their aims, open market operations can be divided into the following *four categories*:

- *Main refinancing operations*, which are regular liquidity-providing reverse transactions with a weekly frequency and a maturity of normally one week. These operations provide the bulk of refinancing to the financial sector.
- *Longer-term refinancing operations*, which are liquidity-providing reverse transactions with a monthly frequency and a maturity of normally three months. These operations are aimed at providing counterparties with longer-term refinancing.
- *Fine-tuning operations*, which are executed on an ad hoc basis with the aim of managing the liquidity situation in the market and steering interest rates, in particular in order to smooth the effects on interest rates caused by unexpected liquidity fluctuations in the market.
- *Structural operations*, which are carried out through the issuance of debt certificates, reverse transactions and outright transactions. These operations are executed whenever the ECB wishes to adjust the structural position vis-à-vis the financial sector (on a regular or non-regular basis), i.e. to make the liquidity deficit large enough to make the banking system consistently dependent on liquidity-providing open market operations.[20]

Five types of *instruments* are available to the Eurosystem for the conduct of open market operations: *reverse transactions* (applicable on the basis of repurchase agreements or collateralised loans), *outright transactions*, the *issuance of debt certificates*, *foreign exchange swaps* and the *collection of fixed-term deposits*. Open market operations can be executed on the basis of standard tenders, quick tenders or bilateral procedures.

The ECB's *standing facilities* are aimed at providing and absorbing overnight liquidity, signal the general stance of monetary policy and bound overnight market interest rates. Two standing facilities are available to eligible counterparties on their own initiative, subject to their fulfilment of certain operational access conditions:

- Counterparties can use the *marginal lending facility* to obtain overnight liquidity from national central banks (NCBs) against eligible assets. Under normal circumstances there are no credit limits or other restrictions on counterparties' access to the facility apart from the requirement to present sufficient underlying assets. The interest rate on the marginal lending facility normally provides a ceiling for the overnight market interest rate.

---

[20]The main focus here is the structural liquidity deficit position of the euro area banking system (i.e. its position vis-à-vis the Eurosystem net of monetary policy operations). See ECB (1999), p. 41.

– Counterparties can use the *deposit facility* to make overnight deposits with NCBs. Under normal circumstances, there are no deposit limits or other restrictions on counterparties' access to the facility. The interest rate on the deposit facility normally provides a floor for the overnight market interest rate.

1.3.8.3 Example: The ECB's Variable and Fixed Tender Procedure

Open market operations can be directed at achieving a desired base money supply or a desired interest rate for base money, but it may not be possible to achieve both at once. The greater the emphasis on a quantity objective is, the more short-run changes in the demand for balances will influence the interest rate; and the greater the emphasis on an interest rate objective is, the more shifts in demand will influence base money supply. Technically speaking, there are two major open market procedures (Fig. 1.19):

– First, under a *variable rate tender* the counterparties bid *both* the amount of money they want to transact with the central bank and the interest rate at which they want to enter into the transaction. The amount of base money is then set by the central bank. The settlement of base money across bidding banks is conducted via either the Dutch (or single rate) auction or the American (multiple rate) auction.
– Second, under a *fixed rate tender* (or volume tender) procedure the interest rate is specified in advance by the central bank and participating counterparties bid the amount of money they want to borrow at the fixed interest rate.

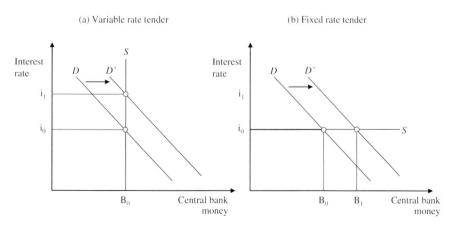

Fig. 1.19 Variable and fixed rate tender
Note: i = interest rate, B = base money, D = demand for base money, S = supply of base money.

To give an example, consider the case in which the central bank decides to provide liquidity to the market by means of a reverse transaction organised with a *fixed rate tender procedure*. Three counterparties submit the following bids:

Counterparty	Bid (€mn)
Bank 1	30
Bank 2	40
Bank 3	70
Total	*140*

The central bank decides to allot a total of €105 million. The percentage of allotment is: $105/(30 + 40 + 70) \cdot 100 = 75\%$. The specific allotments to the counterparties are:

Counterparty	Bid (€mn)	Allotment (€mn)
Bank 1	30	22.5
Bank 2	40	30.0
Bank 3	70	52.5
Total	*140*	*105.0*

The Eurosystem's Open Market Regime

The ECB actively influences the demand for base money, as it requires credit institutions to hold *minimum reserves*. The amount of required reserves to be held by each institution is determined by its *reserve base*. The reserve base is defined in relation to the elements of the credit institution's balance sheet. In order to determine the reserve requirement, the reserve base is multiplied by a reserve ratio (which was set at 2% at the start of EMU).

The first key function of the minimum reserve system is *to stabilise money market interest rates*. This function is performed by the averaging provision. The averaging provision allows credit institutions to smooth out daily liquidity fluctuations (e.g. those arising from fluctuations in the demand for banknotes), since transitory reserve imbalances can be offset by opposite reserve imbalances generated within the same maintenance period. A second important function assigned to the minimum reserve system is the *enlargement of the structural liquidity shortage of the banking system*. The need for credit institutions to hold reserves with the NCBs contributes to increasing the demand for central bank refinancing which, in turn, makes it easier for the ECB to steer money market rates through regular liquidity providing operations.

Turning to the supply of base money, the *main refinancing operations* are the most important open market operations and represent the key monetary policy instrument of the Eurosystem. Through the main refinancing operations the central bank lends funds to its counterparties. Lending is always against collateral, in order to protect the Eurosystem against financial risks. Lending through open market operations normally takes place in the form of *reverse transactions* (see Table 1.1). In reverse transactions of this kind the central bank buys assets under a repurchase agreement or grants a loan against assets given as collateral. Reverse transactions are therefore temporary open market operations which provide funds for a limited and pre-specified period only.

Table 1.1 Eurosystem reverse transactions

Reverse transactions are the main open market instrument of the Eurosystem and can be used for all kinds of liquidity-providing open market operations. The Eurosystem has *three other instruments* available to it for the conduct of fine-tuning operations: outright transactions, foreign exchange swaps and the collection of fixed-term deposits. Finally, for structural operations the ECB may issue debt certificates.

1. Reverse transactions. Reverse transactions refer to operations where the Eurosystem buys or sells eligible assets under repurchase agreements or conducts credit operations against eligible assets provided as collateral. Reverse transactions are used for the main refinancing operations and the longer-term refinancing operations. In addition, the Eurosystem can use reverse transactions for structural and fine-tuning operations. Where a reverse transaction takes the form of a repurchase agreement, the difference between the purchase price and the repurchase price corresponds to the interest due on the amount of money borrowed or lent over the maturity of the operation, i.e. the repurchase price includes the interest to be paid. The interest rate on a reverse transaction in the form of a collateralised loan is determined by applying the specified interest rate on the credit amount over the maturity of the operation.

2. Outright transactions. Outright open market transactions refer to operations where the Eurosystem buys or sells eligible assets outright on the market. Outright open market operations are only available for structural and fine-tuning purposes.

3. Foreign exchange swaps. Foreign exchange swaps executed for monetary policy purposes consist of simultaneous spot and forward transactions in euro against a foreign currency. They can be used for fine-tuning purposes, mainly in order to manage the liquidity situation in the market and to steer interest rates.

4. Collection of fixed-term deposits. The Eurosystem may invite counterparties to place remunerated fixed-term deposits with the NCB in the Member State in which the counterparty is established. The collection of fixed-term deposits is envisaged only for fine-tuning purposes in order to absorb liquidity in the market.

5. Issuance of ECB debt certificates. The ECB may issue debt certificates with the aim of adjusting the structural position of the Eurosystem vis-à-vis the financial sector so as to create or increase a liquidity shortage in the market.

Source: ECB (2006b), The Implementation of Monetary Policy in the Euro Area, General Document of Eurosystem Monetary Policy Instruments and Procedures, September.

For the purpose of controlling short-term interest rates in the money market
and, in particular, restricting their volatility, the Eurosystem also offers two
standing facilities to its counterparties, the *marginal lending facility* and the
deposit facility. Both facilities have an overnight maturity and are available to
counterparties on their own initiative. The interest rate on the marginal lending
facility is normally substantially higher than the corresponding market rate,
and the interest rate on the deposit facility is normally substantially lower than
the market rate. As a result, credit institutions use the standing facilities when
there are no other alternatives. Since – except for the collateral requirements
of the marginal lending facility – there are *no limits* on the access to these
facilities, their interest rates normally provide a ceiling and a floor for the
overnight rate in the money market.

By setting the rates on the standing facilities, the ECB Governing Council
determines the *corridor* within which the overnight money market rate can
fluctuate. The chart below shows the development of the key ECB interest
rates from January 1999 to August 2007 (weekly data). It shows how the
interest rates on the standing facilities have provided a ceiling and a floor
for the overnight market interest rate (EONIA). It represents the weighted
average of all uncollateralised overnight loans made by a panel of the banks
most active in the money market.

Figure 1.20 shows that EONIA had generally remained close to the
rate of the main refinancing operations, illustrating the importance of
these operations as the main monetary policy instrument. Also, EONIA
exhibited a pattern of occasional spikes, which were related to the minimum reserve system. Finally, the chart illustrates that the differences

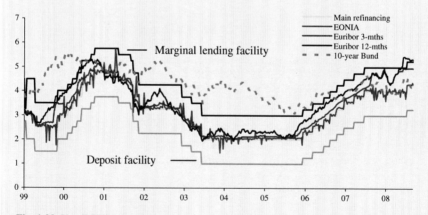

Fig. 1.20 Key ECB interest and money market rates (%)
Source: Thomson Financial.

between the standing facility rates and the rate on the main refinancing operations were kept unchanged between April 1999 and December 2005 (± 1 percentage point).

1.3.9 A Closer Look at the Demand for Base Money

The commercial banking sector's demand for base money is usually driven by three factors: (i) minimum reserve requirements, (ii) *cash drain* and (iii) *working balances*. In a more sophisticated approach, Heller and Lengwiler (2003) develop a model in which a bank's demand for central bank money depends on the joint distribution of the transaction volume, reserve requirements, and the interest rate. By *adding uncertainty* over the cash flows to a Baumol-Tobin framework, Miller and Orr (1966) show that the demand for money depends not only on the interest rate and transaction costs, but also on the variance of the cash flows; Poole (1968) explicitly incorporates both reserve requirements and stochastic payment flows into a demand function for reserves.

1.3.9.1 Re (i): Minimum Reserves

For influencing the (structural) demand for base money, most central banks require credit institutions to hold compulsory balances in the form of central bank money, or *minimum reserves*. The amount of required reserves to be held by each institution is typically defined in relation to an institute's liabilities vis-à-vis non-banks as reported in its balance sheet. This so-called *reserve base* is then multiplied by the (respective) reserve ratio.

As a rule, reserve requirements can only be satisfied by holding base money deposits with the central bank. However, minimum reserve requirements differ from country to country. In the US, for instance, depository institutions subject to minimum reserves must hold reserves in the form of vault cash or deposits with Federal Reserve Banks (Blenck, Hasko, Hilton, & Masaki, 2001, p. 25).[21] Banks within the Federal Reserve System may also establish a required clearing balance, which affects the demand for balances in a way that is virtually identical to reserve requirements.

---

[21]The Fed allows banks to satisfy its reserve requirements with currency held on the bank's premises (*vault cash*). Each depository institution's level of *applied vault cash* in a maintenance period is calculated as the average value of the vault cash it held during an earlier computation period, up to the level of its reserve requirements. Thus, the level of applied vault cash is lagged and known prior to the start of each maintenance period. Applied vault cash is included in official measures of reserves.

Most central banks allow banks to make use of *averaging provisions*. This means that compliance with reserve requirements is determined on the basis of the average of the daily balances on the counterparties' reserve accounts over a *reserve maintenance period* (say, one month). The ability of banks to *average* their balance holdings within a maintenance period so as to meet requirements helps moderate the impact that daily variations in the actual supply of balances outside the control of the central bank would have on inter-bank rates.

To ensure that the minimum reserve system neither puts a burden on the banking system nor hinders the efficient allocation of resources, some central banks remunerate banks' minimum reserves. For instance, in the euro area, remuneration corresponds to the average, over the maintenance period, of the *marginal rate of allotment* (weighted according to the number of calendar days) of the main refinancing operations. The marginal tender rates are normally close to the short-term money market interest rates.

As a rule, banks would keep base money holdings at a minimum. Figure 1.21 (a) shows euro area monetary financial institutions' excess reserve holdings – defined as current account holdings of base money above minimum reserve requirements – from February 1999 to January 2008 (monthly averages). Figure 1.21 (b) shows

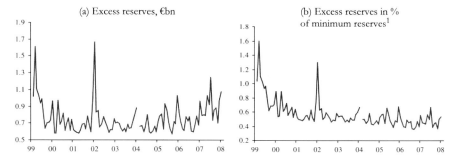

Fig. 1.21 Base money holdings in the euro area (monthly averages)
Source: ECB, own calculations. [1]Current account minus minimum reserves.

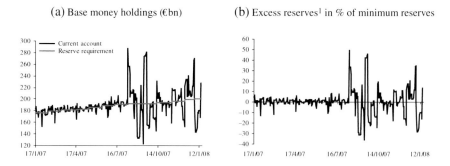

Fig. 1.22 Base money holdings in the euro area (daily basis)
Source: ECB, own calculations. [1]Current account minus minimum reserves.

excess reserves in percent of minimum reserves, amounting to no more than 0.5 percent, on average, for the period 2001–2008.

Figure 1.22 (a) and (b) show daily base money holding of euro area monetary financial institutions for the period January 2007 to January 2008. Up to the start of the international credit market turmoil (which unfolded around July/August 2007) current account holdings were closely aligned to minimum reserve requirements. In the period of financial market turmoil, however, current account holdings started fluctuating widely – driven by marked changes in the demand for and supply of base money.

1.3.9.2 Re (ii): Cash Drain

People tend to hold a portion of their sight deposits in cash. That said, part of banks' sight deposits is withdrawn in cash. Cash holding preferences may change over time, though, and they tend to differ from country to country. Table 1.2 provides some insight into various countries' cash holding coefficients, both in percent of GDP and in percent of the narrowly defined stock of money. For instance, cash holdings were substantially higher in Japan than say, in France and the UK in the periods under review.

In the US, the stock of M1 in relation to nominal GDP has been declining since the late 1950s – except for the period from the early 1980s to the early 1990s (Fig. 1.23). *Financial innovations* might have induced people to hold fewer means of payments relative to their incomes. What is more, currency in circulation in percent of GDP fell until the early 1980s, then rose until 2003 and declined thereafter.

Table 1.2 Banknotes and coins in circulation

	'97	'98	'99	'00	01	'97	'98	'99	00	'01
	I. In % of GDP					II. In % of narrow money				
Belgium	5.0	4.8	5.1	4.8	2.8	26.5	23.8	20.4	19.3	11.8
Canada	3.4	3.5	3.8	3.3	3.5	14.2	14.5	15.6	13.7	13.0
France	3.3	3.2	3.3	3.1	2.0	13.1	12.9	12.7	11.9	7.4
Germany	6.7	6.4	6.6	6.2	3.3	27.1	24.1	23.5	21.9	11.3
Hong Kong	6.1	6.4	8.1	7.2	7.9	42.8	45.5	48.5	45.0	44.2
Italy	5.4	5.5	5.9	6.0	4.7	16.1	16.1	14.4	14.3	11.3
Japan	10.1	10.5	11.7	12.1	13.1	25.8	25.3	24.8	25.0	23.7
Netherlands	5.3	4.8	4.6	4.2	2.1	15.7	14.1	12.8	11.4	5.7
Singapore	7.6	7.4	8.0	7.1	7.7	38.9	37.2	36.4	33.9	32.9
Sweden	4.1	4.1	4.3	4.3	4.5	...	...	...	...	...
Switzerland	7.8	7.9	8.2	7.9	8.7	15.6	15.5	15.3	15.8	16.7
UK	3.0	3.0	3.1	3.2	3.3	5.0	5.0	5.0	5.0	5.0
US	5.1	5.3	5.6	5.4	5.8	39.0	41.4	45.4	48.1	48.6
CPSS	5.9	6.4	6.8	6.5	6.2	23.3	23.1	23.6	23.7	21.9

Source: Bank for International Settlements (2003), Table 1. – Converted at end-of-year exchange rates. – CPSS represents average excluding those countries where data are not available.

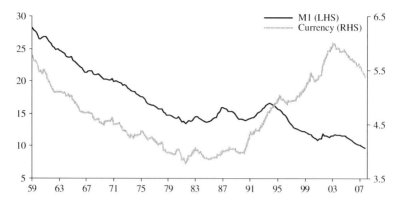

Fig. 1.23 US means of payment in percent of nominal GDP
Source: US Federal Reserve Bank of St. Louis, own calculations. Period: 1959-Q1 to 2007-Q4

This finding might reflect the decline in CPI inflation since the early 1980s (thereby lowering the opportunity costs of cash holdings) and changes in the demand for US currency held by abroad (Porter & Judson, 1996).

1.3.9.3 Re (iii): Working Balances

Commercial banks demand base money (*working balances*) for making inter-bank payments (Bank for International Settlements, 2003). Whereas non-banks usually settle accounts receivables and liabilities by transferring commercial bank money balances (sight deposits), inter-bank payments are made by transferring deposits held with the central bank among commercial banks (Fig. 1.24).

Assets	Balance sheet of the central bank		Liabilities
Assets	100	Sight deposits (bank 1)	100
			–100
		Sight deposit (bank 2)	*+100*
	100		*100*

Assets	Balance sheet of the bank 1		Liabilities
Deposit with central bank	100	Sight deposits (non-bank A)	100
	–100		*–100*
	0		*0*

Assets	Balance sheet of the bank 2		Liabilities
Deposit with central bank	*+100*	Sight deposits (non-bank B)	*+100*
	100		*100*

Fig. 1.24 Assume non-bank *A* transfers US$100 from his account held with bank 1 to non-bank *B*, who keeps his account with bank 2. If paying US$100 to bank 2, bank 1 simply transfers its base money holdings with the central bank to the account bank 2 holds with the central bank

1.3.10 Supply of and Demand for Base Money

The central bank is the *monopoly supplier* of base money. At the same time, the central bank can, via imposing minimum reserve requirements, exert a (pre-dominant) influence on the demand for central bank money. That said, the central bank is in a (comfortable) position to manage the conditions in the market for central bank money (usually referred to as *money market*), that is determining the quantity of base money or the interest rate on base money balances.

Figure 1.25 shows a simple model of the inter-bank money market (for, say, 1-month money), where the interest rate is determined by the demand for and supply of base money. The demand is determined by minimum reserves, the cash drain and working balances. Supply is determined by the central bank's regular operations and by autonomous factors (such as, for instance, deposits being shifted from central bank to commercial bank accounts and vice versa).

In their money market operations central banks aim to ensure an *orderly functioning* of the money market, helping credit institutions to meet their liquidity needs in a smooth manner. This is typically achieved by providing regular refinancing to banks and facilities that allow them to deal with end-of-day balances and to cushion transitory liquidity fluctuations. What is more, central banks tend to signal their monetary policy stance to the money market via changing the conditions under which the central bank is willing to enter into transactions with commercial banks.

Virtually all major central banks have chosen a short-term interest rate as their *operational target* of monetary policy. In many cases the operational target is represented by an overnight interest rate charged to banks that borrow overnight from

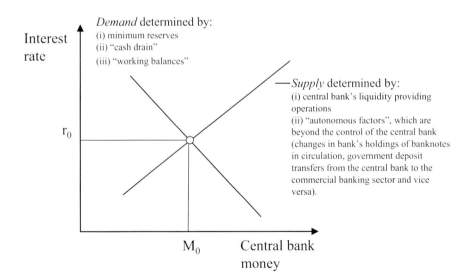

Fig. 1.25 Supply and demand for central bank money

the central bank. Via exerting a dominant influence over the overnight interest rate, the central bank is usually able to influence interest rates for credit transactions with a longer maturity, say 1- and 3-months or more. Table 1.3 gives an overview about the definition official central bank rates.

Why do most central banks *focus on shortterm (overnight) interest rates* rather than long-term interest rates when implementing monetary policy? The answer to that question is that targeting longer-term rates would lead to an *anomaly* for the time series properties of short-term rates and thus the yield curve (Bindseil, 2004, p. 78).

Consider the case in which a central bank targets the 90-day (approximately the 3-months) money market interest rate. Let us assume that the central bank is predictable in terms of forthcoming rate changes, thereby keeping the market rate at its target level with a relatively high degree of precision. Moreover, assume the central bank is, on day τ, expected to lower its 90-day interest rate from the current level of 5 to 4%. What would be the *consequence*, at least in theory, *for the overnight rate around day* τ if the expectation hypothesis of the term structure of interest rate holds?

The 90-day horizons on day $\tau - 1$ and on day τ obviously overlap by 89 days. The expectation hypothesis, in a simplified linear form, would hold that:

$$i_{90,t} = \sum_{j=0}^{89} i_{1,t+j}/90,$$

where $i_{90,t}$ is the 90-day interest rate and $i_{1,t}$ is the overnight rate, both on day t. The difference in the 90-day rate between $\tau - 1$ and τ would have to be translated in terms of overnight rates, in fact exclusively into the overnight rates on day $\tau - 1$ (which is not included in the calculation for τ) and on $\tau + 89$ (which is not included in the calculus for $\tau - 1$), such that:

$$i_{1,\tau-1} - i_{1,\tau+89} = (i_{90,\tau-1} - i_{90,\tau})90.$$

When $i_{1,\tau+89} = 4\%$, this would imply $i_{1,\tau-1} = 94\%$, which would really represent an *anomaly*: it would be an irritating outcome since it would suggest that there would be a *strong increase* in the overnight rate, although the level of rates is *lowered*.

Now consider the case in which the central bank *targets an overnight rate* of 5% until $\tau - 1$, and then, on day τ, lowers the rate to 4%. The 90-day rate would simply move on $\tau - 89$ from 5% to approximately 4.99%, and would become lower by approximately 1 basis point on each of the following days. As a result, the adaptation of long-term rates takes place *in the smoothest possible way* if the overnight rate is targeted and changed in a predictable way.

Table 1.3 Selected international official interest rates

Central bank	Official rates	Type
US Federal Reserve	Federal Funds Rate:	Rate charged to depository institution on an *overnight* sale of immediately available funds (balances at the Federal Reserve) to another depository institution.
	Federal Funds Target Rate:	Federal Funds Rate set by the US Federal Reserve.
	Discount rate:	Rate charged to commercial banks and other depository institutions on (*overnight*) loans they receive from their regional Fed's lending facility (*discount window*), of which there are three types: primary credit, secondary credit, and seasonal credit, each with its own interest rate. All discount window loans are fully secured.
Bank of Japan***	Uncollateralized overnight call rate:	In recent years, the Bank of Japan has targeted a specific level of the uncollateralized overnight call rate, with open market operations aimed at increasing the provision of funds when the overnight call rate is above target, and at decreasing the provision of funds when the overnight call rate is below target. The funds whose provision the Bank modifies in its day-to-day open market operations are the current account balances that private financial institutions hold at the central bank.
European Central Bank	Main refinancing rate:	Rate of regular open market operation with counterparties in the form of a reverse transaction using *weekly* standard tenders.
	Marginal lending facility rate:	Rate at which counterparties may receive *overnight credit* from a national central bank; usually 50bp higher than main refinancing rate.
	Deposit facility rate:	Rate at which counterparties may make *overnight deposits* at a national central bank; usually 50bp lower than main refinancing rate.

Table 1.3 (continued)

Central bank	Official rates	Type
Bank of England	Bank's official (repo) rate:	Rate charged to commercial banks borrowing funds (via repo transactions) from the Bank of England.
	Standing lending facility rate:	Rate at which counterparties can *borrow overnight funds* from the Bank of England. Usually the rate is set at a 100bp spread over the Bank's official rate. On the final day of the reserve maintenance period the rate is 25bp above the Bank's official rate.
	Standing deposit facility rate:	Rate at which counterparties can *make overnight deposits* with the Bank of England. The rate is set 100bp below the Bank's official rate. On the final day of the maintenance period, the rate on the standing deposit facility is 25bp below the Bank's official rate.
Bank of Canada**	Target for the Overnight Rate:	Rate at which major financial institutions borrow and lend one-day funds among themselves in the Large Value Transfer System (LVS). It has an *operating band*, which is 0.5 percentage point wide, with the Target for the Overnight Rate at its centre.
	Bank Rate:	The Bank Rate is always at the top end of the operating band. The upper and lower limits of the operating band are the rates at which the Bank of Canada will, respectively, loan one-day funds to financial institutions that operate in the LVTS, or pay interest on one-day funds deposited at the Bank by financial institutions.
Swedish Riksbank	Repo rate:	The rate that banks receive or pay when depositing or borrowing funds at the Riksbank for a period of *seven days*.
	Lending rate:	*Overnight* rate of interest paid by banks on money borrowed from the Riksbank.
	Deposit rate:	*Overnight* rate of interest paid by the Riksbank on money held in accounts with banks.
Swiss National Bank*	3-months Libor target rate:	Money market rate (with a bandwidth of ±100bp) that is steered/targeted by open market (repo) operations.
	Repo rate:	Rate of (weekly) repurchase operations with commercial banks, through which the Swiss National Bank seeks to affect the 3-months Libor target rate.

*As from March 2006; **Since October 2000; ***Since September 2000.
Source: Various central banks.

1.3.11 Impact of Short- on Long-Term Rates

According to the *expectations theory of the term structure*, the longer-term interest rate is a weighted average of the short-term interest rates expected to prevail over the life of the bond.[22] The investor should be indifferent between making *n* consecutive investments in one-period bonds and investing in an *n*-period bond. For example, let time be months. The expectations theory would then suggest that the two-month interest rate should be equal to the average of today's one-month interest rate and the expected one-month rate next month.

The central bank controls the short-term interest rate in the market for base money. How do long-term market yields react to short-term rate changes? To shed some light on the question, a simple bi-variate model shall be applied for the US Rudebusch Swanson & Wu, 2006. It will be tested as to whether changes in short-term interest rates, as determined by the central bank, *Granger-caused* changes in the 10-year interest rate. These tests will be run for the two periods: June 1975 to December 2005 and August 1987 to December 2005.[23] The Federal Funds Rate and the 10-year Treasury yield are shown in Fig. 1.26 and the statistics of the data under review are summarized in Table 1.4.

The Federal Funds Rate and the long-term interest rate are *highly persistent* in the periods under review as indicated by the autocorrelation coefficients. It is

Fig. 1.26 Federal funds rate and 10-year Treasury yield (%)
Source: Thomson Financial, Federal Reserve Bank of St. Louis.

---

[22]The expectation theory of the term structure is the oldest and most common theory of the term structure and is generally traced back to Fisher (1911). For understanding the term structure of interest rates see, for instance, Poole (2005).

[23]For an analysis of the period 1974 to 1979, see Cook and Hahn (1989) and Rudebusch (1995). For a more recent period, namely 1990 to 2001, see Kuttner (2001).

Table 1.4 Summary statistics

	Mean	Std. dev.	Auto-corr.	Correl.
I. June 1975 to December 2005 (No. of obs.: 371)				
Federal Funds Rate	6.46	3.52	.985	.882
10-year Treasury yield	7.81	2.64	.990	
II. August 1987 to December 2005 (No. of obs.: 371)				
Federal Funds Rate	4.79	2.25	.993	.812
10-year Treasury yield	6.31	1.58	.980	

Source: Thomson Financial; own calculations. – Monthly data.

also interesting to note that the Federal Funds Rate has a higher standard deviation (volatility) than the long-term interest rate. The standard test fails to reject the unit root hypothesis in the levels of the series. Granger-causality tests are therefore conducted on the basis of changes in interest rates, that is in their *first-order differences*.

Tables 1.5a, b below show the results of the Granger-causality tests for the two periods under review. For each sample period, lags of up to 8 months were included in the bi-variate VAR model. Δf_t denotes the monthly change in the Federal Funds Rate, while Δi_t is the monthly change in the 10-year Treasury yield. The numbers in parentheses are the respective *p*-values. Large χ^2-statistics, or small *p*-values, reject the null hypothesis of no Granger causality.

For the period June 1975 to December 2005, the null hypothesis that changes in long-bond yields do not cause changes in the policy rate can be rejected for time lags of 1-, 2- and 3-months. In other words, the bond market appeared to be able to predict changes in the monetary policy target rate or, to put it differently, *expectations about forthcoming monetary policy changes were reflected in the bond yields at an early stage*. The null hypothesis that changes in the Federal Funds Rate do not Granger-cause changes in the 10-year yield has to be rejected at the 5%-level for

Table 1.5a χ^2-statistics from Granger-causality tests, 1975–2005

Lag length	$H_0 : \Delta f_t$ does not cause Δi_t		$H_0 : \Delta i_t$ does not cause Δf_t	
1	0.8055	(.3701)	58.49	(.0000)
2	2.7903	(.0627)	32.97	(.0000)
3	2.5471	(.0558)	21.58	(.0000)
4	4.5929	(.0013)	15.34	(.0000)
5	3.0349	(.0107)	12.94	(.0000)
6	3.6108	(.0017)	10.92	(.0000)
7	4.6485	(.0000)	10.54	(.0000)
8	3.8043	(.0003)	8.863	(.0000)

No. of observations: 366. – *Legend*: Δf_t represents the monthly change in the Federal Funds Rate, Δi_t the monthly change in the 10-year Treasury yield. – Optimal lag length is 3 months according to *AIC* and *SC*. – Large χ^2-statistics, or small *p*-values, reject the null hypothesis of no Granger causality.

Table 1.5b χ^2-statistics from Granger-causality tests, 1987–2005

Lag length	$H_0 : \Delta f_t$ does not cause Δi_t	$H_0 : \Delta i_t$ does not cause Δf_t
1	1.110 (.2932)	7.6354 (.0062)
2	.1331 (.8754)	5.0498 (.0072)
3	.4294 (.7322)	5.7216 (.0001)
4	.3424 (.8491)	4.1104 (.0032)
5	.2975 (.9139)	3.3759 (.0059)
6	.3022 (.9353)	2.7284 (.0143)
7	.2951 (.9553)	2.5895 (.0140)
8	.3165 (.9592)	2.2880 (.0229)

No. of observations: 220. – *Legend:* Δf_t represents the monthly change in the Federal Funds Rate, Δi_t the monthly change in the 10-year Treasury yield. Optimal lag length is 7 months according to *AIC* and 2 months according to *SC*. – Large χ^2-statistics, or small *p*-values, reject the null hypothesis of no Granger causality.

all time lags under review. For the period August 1987 to December 2005, the null hypothesis $H_0 : \Delta f_t$ does not cause Δi_t cannot be rejected for all time lags, while the null hypothesis $H_0 : \Delta i_t$ does not cause Δf_t has to be rejected for all time lags under review.

The results suggest that Fed rate changes may have had different effects on the long-term interest rate over time. Presumably, long-term bond yields incorporate expectations about the forthcoming short-term interest rates, so it may not come as a surprise to find, statistically speaking, long-term bond yields Granger-cause short-term interest rates (Hamilton, 1994).

1.3.12 Exogenous Versus Endogenous Money Supply

1.3.12.1 The Statistical Issue

A variable is said to be *endogenous* in a model if it is at least partly a function of other parameters and variables in the model. In contrast, a variable is said to be *exogenous* if it is not determined by other parameters and variables in the model, but is set externally, and any changes to it come from external forces. In economics, the issue about exogenity and endogenity of a variable is typically decided either by theoretical or statistical procedures.

The Auto Regressive Distributed Lag (ARDL) procedure developed by Pesaran and Shin (1999) has become the standard approach for analysing the issue of exogeneity. Assume the following ARDL(p, q) model, where the underlying variables are identified as $I(1)$, and a long-run stable (cointegrating) relation exists between y_t and x_t:

$$y_t = \alpha_0 + \sum_{i=1}^{p} \phi_i y_{t-i} + \beta' x_t + \sum_{i=0}^{q-1} \beta_i^{*\prime} \Delta x_{t-i} + \eta_t, \qquad (1.16)$$

where η_t is the disturbance term.

Pesaran and Shin (1999) have shown that even when the x's are endogenous, valid asymptotic inferences on the short- and long-run parameters can be drawn once an appropriate choice of the order of the ARDL model is made. According to Pesaran (1997), the Akaike Information Criterion (AIC) and Schwarz Bayesian Criterion (SC) perform well in small samples, although the SC is slightly superior to the AIC (Pesaran & Shin, 1999). By utilising the residuals from equation above, consider the following error correction model:

$$\Delta y_t = \alpha_1 + \sum_{i=1}^{n} \beta_{y,i} \Delta y_{t-i} + \sum_{i=0}^{m} \beta_{xi} \Delta x_{t-i} + \alpha_3 \mu_{t-1} + \varepsilon_t, \qquad (1.17)$$

where μ_{t-1} is the lagged error correction term obtained from the residuals in Eq. (1.16) and ε_t is the short-run random disturbance term. From Eq. (1.17), the null hypothesis that x does not Granger cause y would be rejected if the lagged coefficients of the β_{xi}'s are jointly significant based on a standard F-test (or Wald-test). Accordingly, the null hypothesis that y does not cause x would be rejected if the lagged coefficients of the β_{yi}'s are jointly significant.

Equation (1.17) provides an interesting alternative to the Granger causality test. The standard Granger causality procedure is based on *past changes* in one variable explaining *current changes* in another. If, however, variables share a common trend, then *current* adjustments in y towards its long-run equilibrium value are partly the result of *current* changes in x. Such causality can be detected by investigating the error correction representation of Eq. (1.17) and checking whether the error correction term μ_{t-1} is statistically significant –, but this is not possible under the standard Granger causality test. If variables are cointegrated, then causality must exist in at least one direction, which is not always detectable if the results are only based on the standard Granger procedure (Granger, 1988).[24]

It should be noted that standard Granger causality tests are only indicative of whether one variable *precedes* another (Maddala, 1988; Urbain, 1992). In many empirical studies, causality through the error correction term is used as a test for *weak exogeneity*, since it shows how the short-run coefficients of the variables adjust towards their long-run equilibrium values (Engle & Granger, 1987; Harris, 1995).

Thus, in addition to first showing that a variable is *weakly exogenous* through the error correction term, the definitions developed by Engle, Hendry and Richard (1983) can be used to determine whether a variable is *strongly exogenous* (Charemza & Deadman, 1997). If a variable is *weakly exogenous* through the error correction term, and the lagged values are also jointly significant, then the variable is said to

---

[24]For recent econometric applications see Belke and Polleit (2006a, b; c).

be *strongly exogenous*. Since weak exogeneity is a necessary condition for efficient estimation, more weight will be attached to causality through the error correction term as opposed to causality through the standard Granger procedure which only detects short-run causality.

1.3.12.2 The Theoretical Issue

Mainstream macroeconomic models – based on the Keynesian IS-LM-AS set up for describing the economy in the short-run and using the classical/neoclassical model for the long-run – assume that the money stock is *exogenously determined* by the central bank. In contrast, (Post-)Keynesian and a more heterodox school of economists argue that money supply, including base money, would be *endogenous* (Kaldor & Trevithick, 1981; Kaldor, 1982; Lavoie, 1984; Moore, 1988, 1989; Palley, 1991; Arestis & Sawyer, 2002). These authors maintain that money is actually the consequence of economic activity, and not the cause of it.[25]

Indeed, at first glance this view appears to fit quite well with today's central banking practice in, for instance, the money market. Most central banks set a fixed interest rate and accommodate the demand for high-powered money; it follows that the money supply is a *result* and not a *cause* of changes in money income, and that money supply varies in relation to prices and output (Kaldor & Trevithick, 1981).

In principle, the *accommodation view* of an endogenous money supply is supported by the *structuralist view*. In contrast to the former, the latter argues that banks' loan supply schedule would be positively related to the interest rate (Pollin, 1991; Palley, 1994).[26] It is argued that, under a money supply monopoly, central banks are well in a position to constrain base money supply, so that full accommodation would be an unrealistic assumption, and that ultimately an increase in bank credit and money creation would be accompanied by higher interest rates (Palley, 1994).

At a normative level, (Post-)Keynesians challenge any monetarist claims that economic fluctuations are the product of misguided monetary policies. They also challenge the efficacy of monetarist policy – that is targeting of monetary aggregates. Instead, this school recommends interest rate targeting policies and regulatory controls – such as asset based reserve requirements – that would automatically restrict the ability of the financial sector to expand lending.[27]

---

[25]Heterodox economists believe that the profit motive, as well as profit-seeking financial innovations, plays a role in the creation of money by the banking system. In a survey paper on endogenous money - structuralists versus horizontalists, Wray (2007) concludes that the central bank's influence on the quantity of money is indirect and unpredictable, and therefore should be of little interest to economists.

[26]Davidson (1988) associates an exogenous money supply with a perfectly inelastic money supply function and an endogenous money supply with a less than perfectly inelastic money supply function. See in this context also Davidson (1989) and Goodhart (1989).

[27]What about the central bank's official interest rate, then? For most mainstream economists, the central bank reaction function – when modelled as a Taylor rule (Taylor, 1993) – is based on a

So is the stock of money supply endogenous or exogenous in nature? It is fair to answer this question against the backdrop of the prevailing monetary regime. Under today's government money supply monopoly the money stock should be considered *exogenous*: It is the central bank that has the power to determine the stock of money in the hands of the public (abstracting from any control problems). Under a free market money regime, in contrast, the money stock would qualify as being *endogenously* determined.

1.4 Money Aggregates

In principle, an economy's stock of money would include *all assets which can fulfil the function of money*. In practise, however, various (simple-sum) aggregations of the means of payments and selected liabilities of the banking sector (at times even other financial assets such as, for instance, money market funds, repos etc.) have been defined as *monetary aggregates*. Definitions of monetary aggregates tend to vary from country to country, though. In what follows, we will take a closer look at the definitions and developments of monetary aggregates in a number of countries.

1.4.1 International Definitions of Money Aggregates

1.4.1.1 United States

The Fed publishes weekly and monthly data on three money supply measures – M1, M2, and (until February 2006) M3 – as well as data on the total amount of debt of the nonfinancial sectors of the US economy (Table 1.6). The monetary aggregates reflect the different degrees of liquidity that different types of bank liabilities have. The narrowest measure, M1, is restricted to the most liquid forms of money. M2 includes M1, plus savings accounts, time deposits of under US$100,000, and balances in retail money market mutual funds. M3 included M2, large-denomination (US$100,000 or more) time deposits, balances in institutional money funds, repurchase liabilities issued by depository institutions, and Eurodollars held by US residents at foreign branches of US banks and at all banks in the UK and Canada.

   William Poole (1991) first coined the term MZM when he proposed a measure of money encompassing all of the monetary instruments with zero maturity (Carlson & Keen, 1996). The assets included in MZM are essentially redeemable at par on demand, comprising both instruments that are directly transferable to third parties

---

target rate of inflation and a target rate of output growth. But once these targets are fixed, realized inflation and growth are the dominant endogenous variables in the central bank reaction function. One could say that the only autonomy left to the central bank is to decide about the timing of the change in the interest rate.

Table 1.6 US monetary aggregates

Indicator	Definition
Adjusted Monetary Base:	The sum of currency in circulation outside Federal Reserve Banks and the U.S. Treasury, deposits of depository financial institutions at Federal Reserve Banks, and an adjustment for the effects of changes in statutory reserve requirements on the quantity of base money held by depositories.[1]
Adjusted Reserves:	The sum of vault cash and Federal Reserve Bank deposits held by depository institutions and an adjustment for the effects of changes in statutory reserve requirements on the quantity of base money held by depositories. This spliced chain index is numerically larger than the Board of Governors' measure, which excludes vault cash not used to satisfy statutory reserve requirements and Federal Reserve Bank deposits used to satisfy required clearing balance contracts.[2]
M1:	The sum of currency held outside the vaults of depository institutions, Federal Reserve Banks, and the U.S. Treasury; travelers checks; and demand and other checkable deposits issued by financial institutions (except demand deposits due to the Treasury and depository institutions), minus cash items in process of collection and Federal Reserve float.
MZM:	M2 minus small-denomination time deposits, plus institutional money market mutual funds (that is, those included in M3 but excluded from M2).1 The label MZM was coined by William Poole (1991); the aggregate itself was proposed earlier by Motley (1988).
M2:	M1 plus savings deposits (including money market deposit accounts) and small-denomination (under \$100,000) time deposits issued by financial institutions; and shares in retail money market mutual funds (funds with initial investments under \$50,000), net of retirement accounts.
M3:	M2 plus large-denomination (\$100,000 or more) time deposits; repurchase agreements issued by depository institutions; Eurodollar deposits, specifically, dollar-denominated deposits due to nonbank US addresses held at foreign offices of U.S. banks worldwide and all banking offices in Canada and the United Kingdom; and institutional money market mutual funds (funds with initial investments of \$50,000 or more).

Source: Federal Reserve Bank of St. Louis, *MonetaryTrends*. – [1]This series is a spliced chain index; see Anderson and Rasche (1996a, b, 2001, Anderson, Rasche, & Jeffrey, 2003). – [2]Anderson and Rasche (1996a, 2001, Anderson, Rasche, & Jeffrey, 2003).

and those that are not. This concept excludes all securities, which are subject to risk of capital loss, and time deposits, which carry penalties for early withdrawal; Motley (1988) had earlier proposed such a similar measure (non-term M3). In sum, MZM includes all types of financial instruments that are, or can be easily converted into, transaction balances without penalty or risk of capital loss.

A Little History of Monetary Aggregates in the US

The Fed began reporting monthly data on the level of currency in circulation, demand deposits, and time deposits in the 1940s, and it introduced M1, M2, and M3 in 1971. The Full Employment and Balanced Growth Act of 1978, known as the Humphrey-Hawkins Act, required the Fed to set one-year target ranges for money supply growth twice a year and to report the targets to Congress. During the heyday of the monetary aggregates, in the early 1980s, analysts paid a great deal of attention to the Fed's weekly money supply reports, and especially to the reports on M1. If, for example, the Fed published a higher-than-envisaged M1 number, the markets surmised that the Fed would soon raise interest rates to bring money supply growth back to target.

Following the introduction of NOW accounts in 1981, the relationship between M1 growth and measures of economic activity, such as nominal GDP, broke down. Depositors moved funds from savings accounts – which are included in M2 but not in M1 – into NOW accounts, which are part of M1. As a result, M1 growth exceeded the Fed's target range in 1982, even though the economy experienced its worst recession in decades. In late 1982 the Fed de-emphasized M1 as a guide for monetary policy, and it stopped announcing growth ranges for M1 in 1987.

By the early 1990s, the relationship between M2 growth and the performance of the economy also had weakened. Interest rates were at the lowest levels in more than three decades, prompting savers to move funds out of the savings and time deposits that are part of M2 into stock and bond mutual funds, which are not included in any of the money supply measures. Thus, in July 1993, when the economy had been growing for more than two years, Fed Chairman Alan Greenspan remarked in his Congressional testimony that: "if the historical relationships between M2 and nominal income had remained intact, the behavior of M2 in recent years would have been consistent with an economy in severe contraction. (. . .) The historical relationships between money and income, and between money and the price level have largely broken down, depriving the aggregates of much of their usefulness as guides to policy. At least for the time being, M2 has been downgraded as a reliable indicator of financial conditions in the economy, and no single variable has yet been identified to take its place."

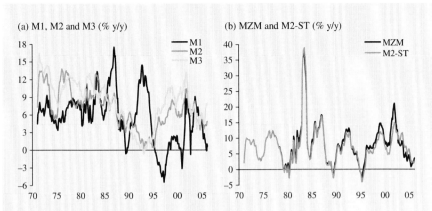

Fig. 1.27 Monetary aggregates in the US
Source: Bloomberg; own calculations. – M2-ST is the stock of M2 minus short-term deposits. – M3 up to February 2006. – Period: January 1971 to July 2008.

In 2000, when the Humphrey-Hawkins legislation requiring the Fed to set target ranges for money supply growth expired, the Fed announced that it was no longer setting such targets, because money supply growth does not provide a useful benchmark for the conduct of monetary policy. However, the Fed said, too, that "(. . .) the FOMC believes that the behavior of money and credit will continue to have value for gauging economic and financial conditions." Figure 1.27 shows the annual growth rates of US money stocks since the early 1970s.

Sources: US Federal Reserve, Monetary Policy Report forwarded to the Congress on July 20, 2000.

1.4.1.2 Euro Area

In the euro area, the ECB publishes a narrow aggregate, M1, an intermediate aggregate, M2, and a broad aggregate, M3. Table 1.7 shows the definitions of euro area M1, M2 and M3. All monetary aggregates include only positions of residents in the euro area which are held with a monetary financial institution (MFI) located in the euro area. As euro area residents' holdings of liquid assets denominated in foreign currency can be close substitutes for euro-denominated assets, the Eurosystem has decided to include such assets in the money definitions if they are held with MFIs located in the euro area.

Figure 1.28 shows the annual growth rates of the monetary aggregates in the euro area since the early 1980s. Right from the start, the monetary aggregate M3 was made to play an important part in the ECB monetary policy making. The Governing

Table 1.7 Euro area monetary aggregates

Liabilities*	M1	M2	M3
Currency in circulation	X	X	X
Overnight deposits	X	X	X
Deposits with an agreed maturity up to 2 years		X	X
Deposits redeemable at a period of notice up to 3 months		X	X
Repurchase agreements			X
Money market fund (MMF) shares/units			X
Debt securities up to 2 years			X

*Liabilities of the money-issuing sector and central government liabilities with a monetary character held by the money-holding sector. More specifically, the Eurosystem defines its money aggregates as follows:

—Narrow money (M1) includes currency, i.e. banknotes and coins, as well as balances which can immediately be converted into currency or used for cashless payments, i.e. overnight deposits.

—"Intermediate" money (M2) comprises narrow money (M1) and, in addition, deposits with a maturity of up to two years and deposits redeemable at a period of notice of up to three months. Depending on their degree of moneyness, such deposits can be converted into components of narrow money, but in some cases there may be restrictions involved, such as the need for advance notification, delays, penalties or fees. The definition of M2 reflects the particular interest in analysing and monitoring a monetary aggregate that, in addition to currency, consists of deposits which are liquid.

—Broad money (M3) comprises M2 and marketable instruments issued by the MFI sector. Certain money market instruments, in particular money market fund (MMF) shares/units and repurchase agreements are included in this aggregate. A high degree of liquidity and price certainty make these instruments close substitutes for deposits. As a result of their inclusion, M3 is less affected by substitution between various liquid asset categories than narrower definitions of money, and is therefore more stable.

Source: ECB (1999, p. 35).

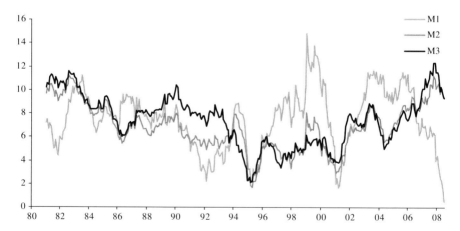

Fig. 1.28 Monetary aggregate growth in the euro area (% y/y)
Source: ECB data; own calculations. – Period: January 1981 to July 2008.

Council of the ECB decided to announce a reference value for the annual growth rate of M3, originally set at $4\frac{1}{2}\%$ p.a., for keeping inflation, in the medium- to long-term, at around 2% p.a. (ECB, 1999). However, the ECB's monetary policy led to an M3 growth much higher than that: in the period January 1999 to July 2008, average annual M3 growth amounted to 7.3%.[28]

Money and the Consolidated Banking Balance Sheet

The *consolidated balance sheet of the MFI sector* shows the assets and liabilities of those financial intermediaries that are considered to be money creating in the euro area. This statistic forms the basis for calculating monetary aggregates. Consolidation, in the context of monetary statistics, means netting out inter-MFI positions (transactions):

- deposits and loans from MFIs (liabilities) less claims against MFIs (assets); and
- liabilities arising from issued debt and equity securities less the amount of such instruments on the side of MFI owned assets.

The counterparts of the M3 monetary aggregate consist of those asset and liability items on the consolidated balance sheet of the MFI sector which are not included in the M3 monetary aggregate. The calculation of M3 and counterparts from the MFI consolidated balance sheet is shown in Fig. 1.29.

The items in the consolidated balance sheet of the euro area MFI are defined as follows:

- *Credit to residents* is defined as loans granted to non-MFI residents plus securities held by the MFI sector but issued by non-MFI residents.
- *Net external assets* are defined as *external assets* held by MFIs less *external liabilities* of MFIs. External assets include foreign-currency cash holdings

Assets	Liabilities
- Credit to euro area residents	M3
- External assets	- Long-term financial liabilities
- Other assets	- External liabilities
	- Other liabilities (including deposits held by central government)

Fig. 1.29 Consolidated balance sheet of the euro area MFI

[28]The prominent role of M3 in the ECB strategy de facto ended with the bank's strategy revision from May 2003 (ECB 2003, p. 79). The stock of M3 was downgraded from an information/intermediate (target) variable of monetary policy to a mere *cross-checking variable*.

of MFIs, holdings of securities issued by non-residents and held by MFIs, credit to non-residents (including banks), gold, and special drawing rights (SDRs). External liabilities include deposits and received loans from non-residents, and the counterpart of SDRs.

– *Longer-term financial liabilities* are deposits and received loans with an agreed maturity of over two years, deposits redeemable at a period of notice of over three months, securities with a maturity of over two years issued by the MFI sector, plus capital, reserves and provisions.
– *Other counterparts* comprise *remaining assets* (including fixed assets) minus *remaining liabilities* (including deposits that the central government holds with the MFI sector and the consolidated surplus).

Using the balance sheet identity, M3 is defined as:

M3 = credit to euro area residents + net external assets – longer-term financial liabilities + other counterparts.

Figure 1.30a shows the *counterparts of euro area M3* from September 1998 to March 2007 in €bn. The most important counterpart of M3 is credit to the private sector and the general government. Longer-term financial liabilities represent the most important item in terms of reducing the stock of M3. Figure 2.30b shows that the strongest contribution to the rise in M3 came from the growth in M1. In the period under review, the M1 contributed, on average, 3.8 percentage points to the annual M3 growth rate of 6.8%; M2-M1 contributed 2.1 percentage points while M3-M2 contributed 0.9 percentage points.

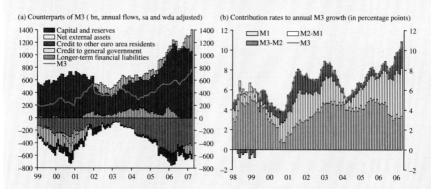

Fig. 1.30 Euro area M3, counterparts and contribution to growth
Source: ECB; own calculations. M3 can be calculated as: credit to the private sector + credit to general government + net external assets – longer-term financial liabilities (excluding capital and reserves) + other counterparts (including capital and reserves). Longer-term financial liabilities (excluding capital and reserves) are shown with an inverted sign, since they are liabilities of the MFI sector.

1.4.1.3 Japan

The Bank of Japan (BoJ) has been publishing the Money Stock Statistics (MSS) since 1955. The statistics characterise *money* as cash currency in circulation and deposit money, held by money holders such as non-financial corporations, individuals, and local governments (Bank of Japan, 2004). In Japan, four monetary aggregates – M1, M2+CDs, M3+CDs and broadly-defined liquidity – are compiled and published on a regular basis (Table 1.8). Figure 1.31 shows the annual growth rate of selected Japanese monetary aggregates since the early 1970s.

Table 1.8 Definition of monetary aggregates in Japan

M1	=	Cash currency in circulation + deposit money
M2+CDs	=	M1 + quasi-money + CDs
M3+CDs		M2+CDs + deposits of post offices + other savings and deposits with financial institutions + money trusts
Broadly-defined liquidity	=	M3+CDs + pecuniary trusts other than money trusts + investment trusts + bank debentures + commercial paper issued by financial institutions + repurchase agreements and securities lending with cash collateral + government bonds + foreign bonds
Whereas:		
Cash Currency in circulation	=	*Banknotes in circulation + coins in circulation*
Deposit money	=	*Demand deposits (current deposits, ordinary deposits, saving deposits, deposits at notice, special deposits and deposits for tax payments) – checks and notes held by the surveyed financial institutions*
Quasi-money	=	*Time deposits + deferred savings + instalment savings + nonresident yen deposits + foreign currency deposits*

Source: Bank of Japan (2004), p. 1.

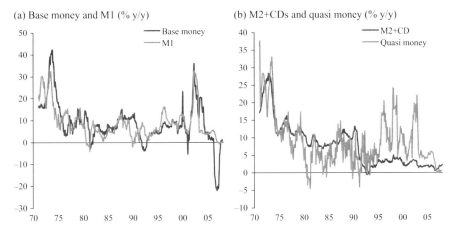

(a) Base money and M1 (% y/y)   (b) M2+CDs and quasi money (% y/y)

Fig. 1.31 Monetary aggregates in Japan
Source: Thomson Financial, IMF; own calculations. – Period: January 1971 to January 2008.

Table 1.9 Definition of Swiss monetary aggregates

Stock M1	Currency in circulation	Notes and coins in circulation + current accounts at the SNB + sight deposit accounts of trade and industry at the SNB – notes and coins at banks and post offices
	Sight deposits	Sight deposits at banks + postal account balances – postal account balances of the banks and the Federal government
	Tradnsaction accounts	Deposits in the form of savings accounts and investments for payment purposes
Money stock M2	Money stock M1	
	Savings deposits	Liabilities vis-à-vis clients in savings account and investment form
	(excl. vested pension benefits and pension fund accounts)	– transaction accounts – vested pension benefit and pension fund accounts
Moncy stock M3	Money stock M2 Time deposits	

Source: Swiss National Bank (2008).

1.4.1.4 Switzerland

Since 1975, the National Bank has distinguished between three monetary aggregates, namely M1, M2 and M3. In 1985, the statistics of monetary aggregates were compiled on a more comprehensive banking statistical basis. Since then Swiss statistics of monetary aggregates have also included the Principality of Liechtenstein, thus covering the entire Swiss currency area. The most liquid monetary aggregate M1 – money supply in a narrow sense – comprises currency in circulation and sight deposits at banks and at the post office (Table 1.9).

The aggregate M2 consists of M1 plus savings deposits, while the money stock M3 corresponds to the sum of M2 plus time deposits. M3 also contains transaction account balances since these were generally a part of the savings deposits. The pension fund monies invested in schemes with restricted terms and tax benefits, also referred to as *tied pension fund monies* (2nd and 3rd pillar of the old age pension scheme) were likewise included in the definition of M3. Figure 1.32 depicts the annual growth rates of the Swiss stock of money since the middle of the 1980s.

Digression: Divisia Monetary Aggregates

Money is typically defined according to the functions it performs (Osborne, 1992) – means of exchange, standard of account, store of value and standard of deferred payment –, with the medium-of-transaction function distinguishing money from any other asset. However, as shown earlier, it has become commonplace for monetary

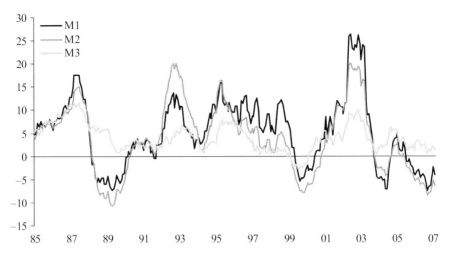

Fig. 1.32 Monetary aggregates in Switzerland (% y/y)
Source: SNB, Bloomberg; own calculations. – Period: December 1985 to January 2008.

aggregates to include financial assets that do not serve as money.[29] For example, *broadly defined* monetary aggregates include savings and time deposits, or holdings in mutual funds, despite the fact that they cannot be used to make transactions.

Such an approach has been criticised. For instance, *simple-sum aggregation* assumes that the different monetary components included in the aggregates are perfect substitutes from the viewpoint of the money holder, and the components that are excluded are assumed to have no substitutive relationship with money. What is more, the monetary components in simple-sum aggregates have the same weight. That said, the theoretical foundation of the simple-sum aggregation approach appears to be weak.

An alternative is the concept of the *Divisia index*[30], a measure of the money supply that gives greatest weight to those components most used in transactions. Divisia money uses a form of aggregation that weights the components of money according to their usefulness in transactions. For example, notes and coin are very useful for making transactions, and pay no interest, while time deposits pay interest, but are less useful for making transactions. Thus Divisia money might be expected to have stronger links to aggregate spending than a simple-sum money aggregate. One way to see how the Divisia index compares with simple-sum approach is to

---

[29]In accordance with aggregation theory, a monetary aggregate is defined over a weakly separable block in the utility function. This definition is rarely implemented because tests for blockwise weak separability are biased towards rejection; a single rejection in the data renders the formation of a separable group impossible. For a discussion of separability tests and applications to US monetary data, see Swofford and Whitney (1986, 1987, 1988, 1994).

[30]The term Divisia index is used refers to the Törnqvist-Theil discrete time approximation to the continuous time index suggested by Divisia (1925).

assume that individuals maximize a utility function composed of a number of real monetary assets and commodities that are directly consumed.[31]

Weak Separability of Utility Functions

An individual's utility function (u) is given as follows (Reimers, 2002):

$$u = u(c_1, c_2, l, m_1, m_2), \qquad (1.18)$$

where c_1 and c_2 are consumer goods, l represents leisure time, and m_1 and m_2 are financial assets which are actually money or money substitutes. *Weak separability* implies that some *arguments* of the utility function can be put together. This is possible if the marginal rate of substitution between any two goods of the same group is independent of the quantity of goods in another group. On the assumption of weak separability for the two financial assets, the utility function may be written as:

$$u = u(c_1, c_2, l, M(m_1, m_2)) \text{ with} \qquad (1.19)$$

$$\frac{\partial(\partial m_1/\partial m_2)}{\partial c_1} = 0 \text{ for } i = 1, 2. \qquad (1.20)$$

The former says that the marginal rate of substitution between the financial assets m_1 and m_2 is not influenced by changing quantities of c_1. Weak separability is the necessary condition for generating the structure of a utility-tree (Reischle, 2000, pp. 184–217).

The total utility function is a function of a sub-utility function:

$$u = f(u_c(C), u_l(l), u_m(M)). \qquad (1.21)$$

With utility levels u_c and u_l given, utility maximisation will be reduced to the maximization of u_m under this constraint:

$$\sum_{i=1}^{2} p_i m_i = y_m \qquad (1.22)$$

where p_i is the price and m_i is the quantity of the financial asset i, y_m is the expenditure on M. The demand for the particular components of M depends only on the relative prices (p_m) of the particular financial assets and on the amount of expenditure spent on financial assets:

---

[31] Aggregation of real monetary assets is equivalent to aggregating nominal assets and deflating the monetary services index afterwards (see Anderson, Jones, & Nesmith, 1997b). For calculating a Divisia index for the euro area see Wesche (1997).

$$m_i = \theta_i(p_m, y_m) \text{ for } i = 1, 2. \tag{1.23}$$

The total income $y = y_c + y_l + y_m$ and the prices p_c and p_l affect the demand for group m assets only via y_m (general substitution effect). When y_m is given, p_c and p_l can be disregarded. All prices p_c exert a proportionate influence on m_i.

Constructing a Divisia Monetary Aggregate

The considerations outlined above allow constructing Divisia monetary aggregates as proposed by Barnett (1978, 1980). Let us assume that there is a benchmark asset with yield R_t, which provides no monetary services and is held solely to transfer wealth intertemporally. Holding the liquid asset i with yield $r_{i,t}$ costs $R_t - r_{i,t}$ per unit of currency in period t. Total transaction costs in period t can be expressed as:

$$K_t = \sum_{i=1}^{L} (R_t - r_{i,t})m_{i,t}, \tag{1.24}$$

where $m_{i,t}$ is the value of monetary component i and L is the number of considered components. The expenditure share of the ith asset is:

$$s_{i,t} = \frac{(R_t - r_{i,t})m_{i,t}}{K_t} = \frac{(R_t - r_{i,t})m_{i,t}}{\sum_{i=1}^{L}(R_t - r_{i,t})m_{i,t}}. \tag{1.25}$$

Real user costs are:

$$\chi_{i,t} = \frac{R_t - r_{i,t}}{1 + R_t}. \tag{1.26}$$

Furthermore, let us assume that the transaction technology can be described by the general, twice differential, homogeneous function:

$$m_t = M(m_{i,t}, \ldots, m_{L,t}). \tag{1.27}$$

Minimizing the transaction costs (1.24), subject to (1.27), results in a Divisia monetary index:

$$d \ln DM_t = \sum_{i=1}^{L} s_{i,t} d \ln m_{i,t}, \tag{1.28}$$

where $d\ln$ denotes the ln-differential of a variable. In discrete time, usually the Törnquist-Theil approximation of the Divisia index is used:

$$\Delta \ln DM_t = \sum_{i=1}^{L} \tilde{s}_{i,t} \Delta \ln m_{i,t}, \tag{1.29}$$

with $\tilde{s}_{i,t} = (s_{i,t} - s_{i,t-1})0.5$.[32] The price dual of the Divisia quantity index is given by:

$$\Delta \ln Pd_t = \sum_{i=1}^{L} \tilde{s}_{i,t} \Delta \ln(R_t - r_{i,t}).\qquad(1.30)$$

Equivalently, it is calculated by

$$Pd_t = \frac{\sum_{i=1}^{L}(R_t - r_{i,t})m_{i,t}/(1 + R_t)}{DM_t}$$

since $Pd_t = DM_t \cdot K_t$.

The Divisia index refers to the growth rate of monetary services provided by the monetary components (Gaab & Mullineux, 1996), so that the levels of monetary services have to be recovered following normalisation. What is more, the user cost s_i is to be interpreted as the cost of purchasing an additional unit of monetary service of the i-th monetary component.

A disadvantage of the Divisia aggregate is that it measures money on the basis of the changes in the logarithm of its components. As a result, the Divisia aggregate can not handle the introduction of new assets: Because the logarithm of zero is minus infinity, the formula for the Divisia aggregate implies that the growth rate of the Divisia index equals infinity when a new asset is introduced. Thus, in a period when a new monetary asset is introduced, one has to set the growth rate of the new asset to zero.[33]

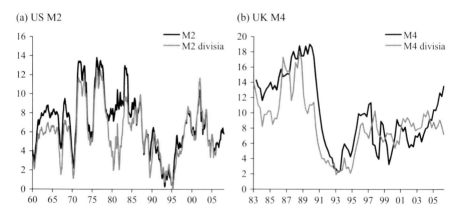

Fig. 1.33 Money and divisia money in the US and the UK
Source: Federal Reserve Bank of St. Louis, Ecowin, Bank of England; own calculations. – Period: January 1960 to February 2008 (M2-Divisia: February 2006). – UK: Q1 1983 to Q4 2007.

---

[32]See Barnett, Offenbacher and Spindt (1984), p. 1052.
[33]Gaab and Mullineux (1996) mention further problems posed by calculating Divisia indices.

Figures 1.33a, b show annual growth rates of simple-sum and Divisia money aggregates in the US and the UK. In both currency areas, Divisia monies grew, on average, relatively closely aligned with their simple-sum counterparts. While Divisia money aggregate has certainly a more sophisticated theoretical underpinning than a simple-sum monetary aggregate, it remains up to debate as to whether they would do a better job in term of providing information about (future) price and real output developments.

1.5 Impact of Portfolio Shifts on Money

Under today's government-controlled paper money systems, bank lending goes hand in hand with an increase in the money stock. In that sense, one would expect that a rise in economic activity, if financed by bank credit, will be reflected in bank credit and money aggregates. In practise, however, the relation between credit, money and economic activity might not be so straightforward, largely due to the existence of so-called *portfolio shifts* on the part of banks and non-banks. Taking a closer look at these developments might help improving the understanding of the information content of bank credit and money aggregates in terms of (forthcoming) inflation and economic growth.

1.5.1 Autonomous Bank Refinancing

To illustrate the process of *autonomous refinancing*, we assume that the banking sector's monetary base amounts to €80, held as minimum reserves (Fig. 1.34). The reserve ratio on sight deposits (Si), term deposits (Ti) and savings deposits (SAV) is 2%, respectively, while deposits with a maturity of more than 2 years (Li) are exempted from minimum reserves. Bank credit supply amounts to €6000, the stock of M1 amounts to €1000, M2 to €2500 and M3 to €4000.

Assume that credit demand increases, while excess reserves are zero. In an effort to use the given monetary base more efficiently, banks would offer their clients higher returns on deposits which are exempted from minimum reserves. If, for instance, non-banks shift €500 from Si (subject to minimum reserves) to Li (exempt

Assets	Balance sheet of the banking sector		Liabilities
Minimum reserves	80	Sight deposits (Si)	1000
Credit	6000	Term deposits (Ti)	1500
Securities	1000	Savings deposits (SAV)	1500
Others	550	Long-term deposits (Li)	3000
		Equity capital	630
	7630		*7630*

Fig. 1.34

Assets	Balance sheet of the banking sector		Liabilities
Minimum reserves	80	Sight deposits (Si)	1000
Credit	6500	Term deposits (Ti)	1500
Securities	1000	Savings deposits (SAV)	1500
Others	550	Long-term deposits (Li)	3500
		Equity capital	630
	8130		8130

Fig. 1.35

from minimum reserves), excess reserves rise to €10. Banks can expand credit and money supply by €500: 10 times 1/0.02 (Fig. 1.35).

The portfolio shift led to a decline in the stock of M1 by €500, while banks' credit expansion restored the money stock to its original level. That said, the portfolio shift leaves the money stocks M1, M2 and M3 unchanged; they do not show an expansionary impulse. As the rise in bank credit should be accompanied by a higher level of economic activity, the *velocity of M1* – defined as nominal income divided by M1 – *must have risen*.[34]

1.5.2 Bank Refinancing Via Selling Assets

Banks can refinance their lending business by selling assets (loans, bonds, asset backed securities (ABS), etc.) to non-banks. By doing so, sight deposits are destroyed, thereby lowering minimum reserves, that is creating excess reserves. Taking the example in Fig. 1.36, assume banks sell corporate bonds worth €500 to *hedge funds*. Here, bank assets and liabilities (the latter in the form of sight deposits) decline by €500, resulting in excess reserves of €10.

Assets	Balance sheet of the banking sector		Liabilities
Minimum reserves	80	Sight deposits (Si)	1000
Credit	6500	Term deposits (Ti)	1500
Securities	500	Savings deposits (SAV)	1500
Others	550	Long-term deposits (Li)	3000
		Equity capital	630
	7630		7630

Fig. 1.36

---

[34]In this context it should be noted that if banks' *working balances* exceed the required reserve holdings for deposits with longer maturities, banks have an incentive to induce non-banks to shift sight deposits to longer-term deposits. If, for instance, the reserve ratios for sight and time deposits are equal, and if the reserve ratio is smaller than the working balance ratio for sight deposits w, that is $r_T = r_S < w$, it is profitable for banks to induce non-banks to shift from sight into time deposits. By doing so, excess reserves rise.

If banks take advantage of excess reserves by expanding bank credit to non-banks, M1, M2 and M3 are restored to their original levels, while the economy's total credit supply (that is bank credit/security holdings plus credit held outside the banking sector) increases. Again, the stock of monies would not indicate the underlying expansionary impact of the transaction.

1.5.3 Disintermediation

Disintermediation represents a process in which bank loans are (increasingly) replaced by credit supplied by non-banks such as, for instance, insurance companies, mutual funds, hedge funds, etc. (Polleit, 1996): Non-banks such as corporates and public agencies would secure their debt funding by issuing money and capital market instruments. What is more, disintermediation implies that non-banks substitute bank deposits such as, for instance, term deposits, for notes issued either by corporates (CPs, short-term notes, etc.) and/or public agencies (Treasuries, short-term notes, etc.).

Taking Fig. 1.34 as a starting point, assume that non-banks substitute time deposits in the amount of €500 for short-term paper issued by state agencies (Fig. 1.37a). On the asset side of the balance sheet of non-banks time deposits are replaced by short-term paper (Fig. 1.37b). Sight deposits, which had been created by shifting time into sight deposits, are transferred to the issuer's account. The total credit supply has increased in the amount of short-term paper purchased by non-banks. The stock of M1 has increased, while the levels of M2 and M3 have remained unchanged.

Assets	Balance sheet of the banking sector		Liabilities
Minimum reserves	80	Sight deposits (Si)	1000
			+500
Credit	6000	Term deposits (Ti)	1500
			–500
Securities	1000	Savings deposits (SAV)	1500
Others	550	Long-term deposits (Li)	3000
		Equity capital	630
	7630		*7630*

Fig. 1.37a

Assets	Non-bank balance sheet		Liabilities
Term deposits	1500		
	–500		
Short-term notes	*+500*		
	1500		*1500*

Fig. 1.37b

1.5.4 Inversion of the Yield Curve

Irving Fisher's (1911) *expectation theory of the yield curve* and John R. Hicks' (1946) *liquidity premium theory* suggest that long-term yields should, in general, exceed short-term rates.[35] However, once in a while the yield curve inverts, that is long-term yields fall below short-term rates. In such periods, monetary aggregates can show a rather strong expansion, even though there is no accompanying increase in bank lending. Money supply growth may therefore *overstate* the underlying money creation dynamics.

The Shape of the Yield Curve

Figures 1.38a, b show long- and short-term interest rates in Germany and the US, respectively, for the period January 1978 to April 2007. The level of long-term yields was, on average, higher than the level of short-term interest rates. As a result, the yield curve – that is the difference between long- and short-term rates (*spread*) – was positive most of the time.

Bond yields tend to move higher as maturities lengthen, resulting in a *positive slope* of the yield curve. The longer the maturity of the bond is, the higher is the risk for the investor. And the higher the risk is, the higher must be

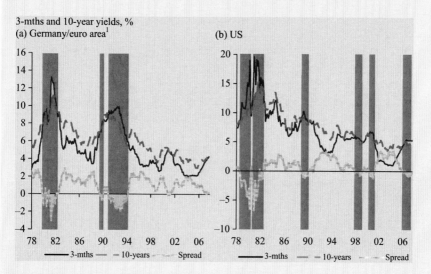

Fig. 1.38 3–months and 10-year yields in Germany and the US
Source: IMF; on calculations. [1] As from 1 January 1999 euro area data; Bund yields throughout the total period. The spread is 10-year yield minus 3-mths rate.

---

[35] See in this context Chapter 4 of this book.

the yield on the bond for making investors holding risky assets. If the spread between long- and short yields becomes large (small), the yield curve is said to become *steep* (or *flat*).

In that sense, an *inverted* yield curve – defined as long-term yields trading below short-term rates – would appear to be an *abnormal* situation: Investors would accept a lowering of the yield as the maturity of the bond (and therefore the risk) increases. However, there might be *economic reasons* for an inversion of the yield curve.

If, for instance, the central bank raises official short-term interest rates for bringing down inflation, investors might believe that the restrictive monetary policy does not last long, and will be followed by a lowering of rates. As long-term yields – as suggested by the term structure of interest rates – are based on the expected course of future short-term rates, forward looking investors might start buying bonds well in advance of the actual decline in official rates (in the hope to make capital gains and lock-in a favourable return).

Such buying activity raises (lowers), ceteris paribus, bond prices (yields). Long-term yields may fall below short-term rates. For instance, the Fed's fight against inflation in the late 1970s/early 1980s led to an inversion of the yield curve; the same happened when the Deutsche Bundesbank raised interest rates sharply in the course of the German reunification period at the beginning of the 1990s.

Financial market *shocks* can also lead to inversions of the yield curve. For instance, the Russian, Asian and LTCM crises in 1997–1998 increased the demand for asset with little perceived risk such as government bonds (*flight to quality*). If central banks are expected to cut interest rates in view of a major financial market shock, investors might well start buying in anticipation of forthcoming rate cuts (ECB, 2007, p. 28).

For instance, in Germany the yield curve inverted in 1993/1994 after the Deutsche Bundesbank had raised rates strongly and the market expected declining inflation and a slowdown in economic growth. Taking advantage of the inversion of the yield curve, non-banks increased their demand for short-term deposits relative to long-term deposits, resulting in a marked increase in the stock of M3.[36]

Assume that non-banks shift €500 of long-term bank liabilities to time deposits. As the former are not subject to minimum reserves, the banking sector's demand for monetary base increases by €10 (Fig. 1.39). If the central bank does not supply additional base money (as it pursues a restrictive monetary policy), banks would

---

[36]For instance, in the German reunification period, ongoing uncertainty about property rights led to a marked delay of investment activity. In such an environment, non-banks tended to park their money balances on short-term bank deposits. As the latter was included in the definition of the German stock of money, the stock of M3 was bloated up by a considerable margin, misleadingly indicating an expansionary monetary policy. See Westerheide (1995), p. 115.

Assets	Balance sheet of the banking sector		Liabilities
Minimum reserves	80	Sight deposits (Si)	1000
			−500
Credit	6000	Term deposits (Ti)	1500
	−500		*+500*
Securities	1000	Savings deposits (SAV)	1500
Others	550	Long-term deposits (Li)	3000
			−500
		Equity capital	630
	7130		*7130*

Fig. 1.39

have to reduce their supply of loans and money by €500, respectively, to bring minimum reserves in line with the stock of base money.

In our example, the portfolio shifts, induced by an inverted yield curve, have effectively reduced the stock of bank credit to €5500 and the stock of M1 to €500, leaving the levels of M2 and M3 unchanged at €4000. A rise in the money stocks (be it M1, M2 or M3) in a period of an inverted yield curve is possible if, and only if, the central bank increases the base money supply in view of banks' rising demand for minimum reserves.

1.6 A Look at "Global Liquidity"

Given the already *high* and still growing *level of integration of international financial markets*, it seems plausible to assume that *cross-country* capital flows have become an increasingly important factor for influencing *domestic* business cycles, determining domestic monetary developments and exerting a strong impact on the pricing of domestic financial assets. The interest in the sources of international business fluctuations and the impact of money on asset returns on the one hand and the role played by international spill-overs of monetary policy shocks on the other hand has motivated various analyses in this field (Baks & Kramer, 1999; Sousa & Zaghini, 2003; ECB, 2004, pp. 10–12; BIS, 2004, pp. 70– 73).

According to the *push channel*, high money growth in one currency area may lead to *capital flows* into foreign countries, provoking a rise in money growth and higher asset returns; according to the *pull channel*, high domestic money growth may lead to domestic asset price inflation and, as a result, attract foreign capital, thereby depressing asset prices in the countries where the capital flows originated. These effects may operate not only at times of stress in financial markets, but also in *normal times*.

In the absence of capital flows between regions, it may be the existence of *common international exogenous shocks* that leads to co-movements of money expansion in different countries. From a single country perspective, such co-movements can be indicative of the sources of the shocks hitting the domestic economy.

For instance, shocks associated to international *stock price volatility* may lead to increases in both *domestic and foreign money growth* due to a worldwide increased preference for holding liquid assets. In this case information on foreign developments may help to confirm that such a liquidity preference shock was the likely cause of the observed fluctuation in domestic monetary aggregates. In this context it may be of interest to form a view about a global money aggregate, that is *global liquidity*.

1.6.1 Calculating a Global Liquidity Aggregate

There are several ways to calculate measures of *global liquidity* (Baks & Kramer, 1999). For instance, one can calculate the growth rate of money for each country (in domestic currency) and weight the national growth rates by the respective country's GDP in global GDP (measured in, for instance, US dollar at constant purchasing power parities) and sum it up:

$$\sum_{i=1}^{n} w_{i,t} \left(\frac{m_{i,t} - m_{i,t-1}}{m_{i,t-1}} \right),$$

where $m_{i,t}$ denotes domestic currency money of country i (out of a total of n countries) in period t and $w_{i,t}$ denotes the share of country i in total GDP.

Alternatively, one may want to calculate a simple sum global money aggregate based on the sum of domestic money stocks, which are converted into a common currency (that is by dividing the domestic stock of money by the respective exchange rates), and then calculate the respective growth rate:

$$\frac{\sum_{i=1}^{n} m_{i,t}/e_{i,t} - \sum_{i=1}^{n} m_{i,t-1}/e_{i,t-1}}{\sum_{i=1}^{n} m_{i,t-1}/e_{i,t-1}},$$

where $e_{i,t}$ denotes the exchange rate of country i in period t (units of local currency per US dollar).[37]

Figure 1.40a shows global liquidity and global nominal GDP (which take the value of 100 in 1980-Q1, respectively). Global liquidity and global nominal GDP represent the simple sums of broad monetary aggregates and national nominal GDP in the euro area, the US, the UK, Japan and Canada converted into US dollar using purchasing power parity exchange rates (ECB, 2004, p. 10).[38] Until around the

---

[37]Using market exchange rates to convert local currency money may impart some volatility to the global monetary aggregate, so that using (say) a moving average would reduce this effect. Alternatively, one may use relative PPP at a given point in time.

[38]Among international central banks, the ECB explicitly addressed the issue of rising global liquidity in January 2004 for the first time (as far as we are informed).

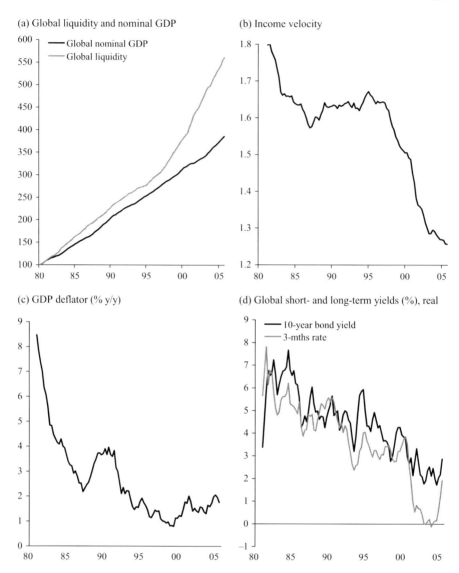

Fig. 1.40 Global money growth and key macro-economic variables
Source: Thomson Financial; own estimates. Period: 1980-Q1 to 2005-Q4. – The monetary aggregates are M2 for the US, M3 for the euro area, M2 plus certificates of deposits for Japan, M4 for the UK, and M2+ for Canada. – Global liquidity and global nominal GDP represent the simple sums of broad monetary aggregates and national nominal GDP in the euro area, the US, the UK, Japan and Canada converted into US dollar using purchasing power parity exchange rates. – The global GDP deflator, and short- and long-term yields represent GDP weighted sums of national annual rates (that is 3-months money market rates and 10-year government bond yields).

middle of the 1990s, global liquidity and global nominal output expanded more or less at a similar pace. In the period thereafter, however, the former clearly started outpacing the latter.

As a result, the income velocity of global liquidity declined sharply as from around 1995 (Fig. 1.40b). The income velocity fell from around 1.65 at the end of 1994 to 1.25 at the end of 2005. To put it differently: Real money holdings relative to real income increased substantially. Global inflation – as expressed by the annual rise in the GDP deflator –, however, remained relatively subdued in the period of strong global liquidity growth (Fig. 1.40c).

Short- and long-term real interest rates (that is nominal rates minus the annual change in the GDP deflator) kept declining throughout the period under review (Fig. 1.40d). In particular, starting in the second half of 2001 short-term real rates fell to unprecedented low levels as central banks throughout the world lowered borrowing costs in response to the stock market correction, the 9/11 terror attacks on the US and a weakening of growth in major industrial countries.

What will be the consequences of the strong rise in global liquidity starting around the middle of the 1990s? Although it is possible that a higher liquidity preference might become a structural phenomenon (that is manifesting itself in a stronger (trend) decline in the income velocity of broadly defined monetary aggregates), there is of course also the risk of the strong rise in global liquidity leading to higher *global inflation*, renewed *global asset price bubbles* and/or inflation-induced economic disequilibria/crises in the future.

1.6.2 The Effects of Cross-Border Selling of National Currency on National Monetary Aggregates

In a final step we want to analyse how international payments would affect the stock of domestic monetary aggregates. To start with, assume a US corporation is a *seller of the dollar*, exchanging US$100 against euro at an exchange rate of EURUSD of 1.25. The US corporation's holdings of US dollar decline by US$100, while its euro balances, held with a US bank, rises in the amount of €80 (Fig. 1.41). The US based bank, in turn, records an account receivable in the amount of €80 vis-à-vis a bank located in the euro area.

Accordingly, deposits of the *seller of the euro* decline by €80 (the equivalent of US$100), whereas his US$ account, held with the bank in the euro area, rises by US$100. The euro area based bank records a US$ liability in the amount of US$80 and records a deposit with the US bank in the amount of US$100 (see lower table of Fig. 1.41).

National monetary aggregates typically include residents' deposits denominated in both domestic and foreign currencies, while they exclude domestic deposits held by non-residents. That said, the transaction as outlined above should leave the stocks of money in both countries unaffected. However, for calculating the domestic money stock residents' holdings of foreign currency denominated deposits have

Assets	Balance sheet US banks		Liabilities
	US depositor		US$100
			−US$100
Deposit with euro area bank	+€80		+€80
	Euro area bank deposit		+US$100

Assets	Balance sheet euro area banks		Liabilities
	Euro area depositor		€100
			−€80
Deposit with US bank	+US$100		+US$100
	US bank deposit		+€80

Fig. 1.41

to be converted into domestic currency. Changes in exchange rates could – if not statistically corrected for – affect the domestic stock of money.

Digression: Key Facts About Major Central Banks

The US Federal Reserve System

Objectives

The goals of monetary policy are spelled out in the Federal Reserve Act, which specifies that the Board of Governors and the Federal Open Market Committee should seek "to promote effectively the goals of maximum employment, stable prices, and moderate long-term interest rates."

Federal Reserve Open Market Committee

The Federal Reserve Act of 1913 gave the Federal Reserve responsibility for setting monetary policy. The Federal Reserve controls the three tools of monetary policy – open market operations, the discount rate, and reserve requirements.[39] *The Board of Governors of the Federal Reserve System* is responsible for the discount rate and reserve requirements, and the F*ederal Open Market Committee* ("FOMC") is responsible for open market operations. Using the three tools, the Federal Reserve influences the demand for, and supply of, balances that depository institutions hold at Federal Reserve Banks and in this way alters the federal funds rate.

---

[39]These and the following explanations are taken from the web site of the US Federal Reserve Board, Washington DC, and The Federal Reserve System (2005), Purposes and Functions, Washington DC.

The FOMC consists of twelve members – the seven members of the Board of Governors of the Federal Reserve System; the president of the Federal Reserve Bank of New York; and four of the remaining eleven Reserve Bank presidents, who serve one-year terms on a rotating basis. The rotating seats are filled from the following four groups of Banks, one Bank president from each group: Boston, Philadelphia, and Richmond; Cleveland and Chicago; Atlanta, St. Louis, and Dallas; and Minneapolis, Kansas City, and San Francisco. Nonvoting Reserve Bank presidents attend the meetings of the Committee, participate in the discussions, and contribute to the Committee's assessment of the economy and policy options.

The seven Board members are appointed by the President of the United States and confirmed by the US Senate. The full term of a Board member is fourteen years, and the appointments are staggered so that one term expires on January 31 of each even-numbered year. After serving a full term, a Board member may not be reappointed. If a member leaves the Board before his or her term expires, however, the person appointed and confirmed to serve the remainder of the term may later be reappointed to a full term.

The Chairman and the Vice Chairman of the Board are also appointed by the President and confirmed by the Senate. The nominees to these posts must already be members of the Board or must be simultaneously appointed to the Board. The terms for these positions are four years.

The FOMC holds eight regularly scheduled meetings per year. At these meetings, the Committee reviews economic and financial conditions, determines the appropriate stance of monetary policy, and assesses the risks to its long-run goals of price stability and sustainable economic growth. Usually, the FOMC meeting is for one day. The meetings in January-February and June-July are two-day meetings.

Meetings and Proceedings of the FOMC

By law, the FOMC must meet at least four times each year in Washington, DC. Since 1981, eight regularly scheduled meetings have been held each year at intervals of five to eight weeks. If circumstances require consultation or consideration of an action between these regular meetings, members may be called on to participate in a special meeting or a telephone conference, or to vote on a proposed action by telegram or telephone. At each regularly scheduled meeting, the Committee votes on the policy to be carried out during the interval between meetings. Attendance at meetings is restricted because of the confidential nature of the information discussed and is limited to Committee members, nonmember Reserve Bank presidents, staff officers, the Manager of the System Open Market Account, and a small number of Board and Reserve Bank staff.

Press Releases: A statement is released at about 2:15 p.m. on the final day of each FOMC meeting. The disclosure policy has evolved over the years as the FOMC has sought to provide more information on its views on economic activity and risks to the outlook.

Minutes: The Committee unanimously decided to expedite the release of its minutes. The minutes of regularly scheduled meetings will be released three weeks after the date of the policy decision. The first set of expedited minutes were released at 2 p.m. EST on January 4, 2005. Since March 2002, the statement has included each member's vote on monetary policy decisions.

Transcripts: Procedures adopted by the FOMC provide for the public release of transcripts for an entire year of meetings with a five-year lag.

European Central Bank

Objectives

The primary objective of the Eurosystem monetary policy is specified by the Maastricht Treaty (article 105 (1)) as the maintenance of price stability. Moreover, and "without prejudice to the objective of price stability", the Eurosystem shall also "support the general economic policies in the Community with a view to contributing to the achievement of the objectives of the Community" which include a "high level of employment" and "sustainable and non-inflationary growth."

ECB, ESCB and Eurosystem

On 1 January 1999, the European Central Bank (ECB) assumed responsibility for monetary policy in the euro area. The European System of Central Banks (ESCB) comprises the ECB and the national central banks (NCBs) of all EU member states. The term "Eurosystem" denotes the ECB and the NCBs of those EU member states that have adopted the euro currency.

According to the Treaty, the basic tasks to be carried out through the Eurosystem are (i) the definition and implementation of the monetary policy of the euro area; (ii) the conduct of foreign exchange operations; (iii) the holding and management of the official foreign reserves of the Member States; and (iv) the promotion of the smooth operation of payment systems.

Decision Making Bodies

There are two decision-making bodies of the ECB which are responsible for the preparation, conduct and implementation of the single monetary policy: the ECB Governing Council and the ECB Executive Board. A third decision-making body is the ECB General Council.

The Governing Council of the ECB consists of the six members of the Executive Board and the governors of the euro area NCBs.[40] Both the Governing Council and the Executive Board are chaired by the President of the ECB or, in his absence, by the Vice-President. The responsibilities of the Governing Council are: (i) to adopt

---

[40]As of July 2005, there were 12 governors in the Governing Council. In 2008, this number has grown to a total of 15 governors. With the Slovakia NCB governor knocking on the area's door as the potential 16th member.

the guidelines and take the decisions necessary to ensure the performance of the tasks entrusted to the Eurosystem; and (ii) to formulate the monetary policy of the euro area. The Council usually meets two times per months.

In accordance with the Statute of the ESCB, the formulation of monetary policy for the euro area includes taking decisions on "intermediate monetary objectives, key interest rates and the supply of reserves" in the Eurosystem. Moreover, the Governing Council shall establish the necessary guidelines for the implementation of those decisions.

The Executive Board of the ECB consists of the President and the Vice-President and four other members, all appointed by common accord of the Heads of State or Government of the euro area countries for an eight year term. In accordance with the Statute of the ESCB, the Executive Board: (i) prepares the meetings of the Governing Council; (ii) implements monetary policy in accordance with the guidelines and decisions laid down by the Governing Council and, in so doing, gives the necessary instructions to the euro area NCBs; (iii) is responsible for the current business of the ECB; and (iv) assumes certain powers delegated to it by the Governing Council, which may include powers of a regulatory nature.

The General Council of the ECB is composed of the President and the Vice-President of the ECB and the governors of the NCBs of all EU Member States (15 in 2003; 25 following the enlargement of the EU as of 1 May 2004). It will remain in existence for as long as there are Member States that have not adopted the euro as their currency. The General Council has no responsibility for monetary policy decisions in the euro area, though.

Long terms of office for the members of the Governing Council, and a rule stipulating that members of the Executive Board cannot be re-appointed, shall contribute to minimising potential political influence on individual members of the ECB's decision-making bodies.

The Statute of the ESCB states that the Governing Council shall act by a simple majority when taking decisions on monetary policy and on the other tasks of the Eurosystem. Monetary policy decisions in the euro area must be based on a euro area perspective. Each member of the Governing Council has one vote. In the event of a tie, the President of the ECB has a casting vote. When taking decisions, the members of the Governing Council do not act as national representatives but in a fully independent, personal capacity.

Prior to the accession of ten additional countries to the EU on 1 May 2004, on 21 March 2003 the European Council approved an amendment to the Statute of the ESCB which provides for an adjustment of the voting modalities in the Governing Council. According to the new voting system, the six members of the Executive Board will maintain a permanent voting right, but the voting rights of NCB Governors will be subject to a rotation scheme once the number of euro area countries exceeds 15. However, all Governors will participate in all meetings of the Governing Council, irrespective of whether they hold a voting right at the time.

Meetings and Communication

The Governing Council usually meets twice a month at the Eurotower in Frankfurt am Main, Germany. At its first meeting each month, the Governing Council assesses monetary and economic developments and takes its monthly monetary policy decision. At its second meeting, the Council discusses mainly issues related to other tasks and responsibilities of the ECB and the Eurosystem.

Immediately after the first Governing Council meeting of the month, a monthly press conference is held by the ECB President and the Vice-President, in which the policy action of the bank is explained in detail. The press conference includes a question and answer session, which is attended by various media representatives from across the euro area and beyond. Transcripts of the press conference are made available on the ECB's website a few hours after the closing of the press conference. The ECB does not publish details as far as majority voting in the ECB Governing Council is concerned.

The President of the ECB appears four times a year before the European Parliament's Committee on Economic and Monetary Affairs. The President explains the ECB's policy decisions and then answers questions posed by Committee members. Other communication channels are public engagements (speeches etc.) by ECB Executive Board members and the Presidents of the NCBs.

Bank of Japan

Objectives

According to the Bank of Japan ("BoJ") Law ("Law"), the objective of the BoJ is to issue banknotes and to carry out currency and monetary control. In addition, the BoJ's objective is to ensure smooth settlement of funds among banks and other financial institutions, thereby contributing to the maintenance of an orderly financial system (article 1). The Law stipulates the BoJ's principle of currency and monetary control as follows: Currency and monetary control shall be aimed at, through the pursuit of price stability, contributing to the sound development of the national economy (article 2).

Decision Making Bodies

The *Policy Board* is established as the BoJ's highest decision-making body. The Law stipulates that monetary policy shall be decided by the Policy Board at Monetary Policy Meetings (MPMs), which are two day affair. At MPMs, the Board first discusses the economic and financial situation and then decides various matters relating to monetary policy, including the following: (1) the guideline for money market operations; (2) the official discount rate; (3) reserve requirement ratios; (4) the BoJ's view of economic and financial developments; and (5) the types and the terms and conditions of bills and bonds eligible for money market operations. The Board also oversees the fulfilment of the duties of Bank executives, excluding Executive Auditors and Counsellors.

Bank executives are members of the Policy Board (including the Governor and Deputy Governors), *Executive Auditors*, *Executive Directors*, and *Counsellors*. Of the above executives, the Governor, the two Deputy Governors, and six other members of the Policy Board make up the Policy Board. The Governor, the Deputy Governors, and other members of the Policy Board are appointed by the Cabinet, subject to the consent of the House of Representatives and the House of Councillors. Executive Auditors are appointed by the Cabinet. Executive Directors and Counsellors are appointed by the Minister of Finance on the recommendation of the Board.

The term of office is five years for the Governor, Deputy Governors, and other members of the Policy Board, four years for Executive Auditors and Executive Directors, and two years for Counsellors. Bank executives, excluding Executive Directors, are not dismissed against their will during their term of office except in the situations prescribed in the Law, such as where they receive a ruling of commencement of bankruptcy proceedings.

Meetings and Communication

Board decisions are announced, in principle, immediately after the meeting concerned. Discussions that take place during the course of the decision-making process are disclosed in the minutes. The latter include the majority voting results but do not show the individual votes of the voting members. The BoJ held 15 MPMs in the fiscal year 2004.

Also in 2004, the BoJ continued efforts to present its basic thinking on the conduct of monetary policy together with its evaluation of economic and price developments in a timely and lucid manner. Such efforts included releasing interim assessments of economic and price developments in July 2004 and January 2005, three months after the releases of the periodically *Outlook for Economic Activity and Prices* in April and October, as well as releasing "The Bank's View" of the *Monthly Report of Recent Economic and Financial Developments* on the same day as the first MPM of the month.

Bank of England

Objectives

In relation to monetary policy, the objectives of the Bank of England shall be (a) to maintain price stability, and (b) subject to that, to support the economic policy of Her Majesty's Government, including its objectives for growth and employment. The Treasury may by notice in writing to the Bank specify (a) what price stability is to be taken to consist of, or (b) what the economic policy of Her Majesty's Government is to be taken to be.

Committees

The *Court of Directors* ("Court") consists of the Governor, two Deputy Governors and 16 Directors. The Directors are all non-executive. The Governors are appointed by the Crown for five years and the Directors for three years. Under the Act, the responsibilities of Court are to manage the Bank's affairs, other than the formulation of monetary policy, which is the responsibility of the Monetary Policy Committee. This includes, inter alia, determining the Bank's objectives and strategy,

The *Committee of Court* ("NedCo") consists of all the non-executive Directors, with a chairman designated by the Chancellor of the Exchequer. The chairman of NedCo is also Deputy Chairman of Court. NedCo has responsibilities for reviewing the Bank's performance in relation to its objectives and strategy, and monitoring the extent to which the Bank's financial management objectives are met. NedCo is also responsible for reviewing the procedures of the MPC, and in particular whether the Committee has collected the regional, sectoral and other information necessary for formulating monetary policy.

The Bank of England Act establishes the *Monetary Policy Committee* ("MPC") as a Committee of the Bank, subject to the oversight of NedCo, and sets a framework for its operations. Under the Act, the Bank's objectives in relation to monetary policy are to maintain price stability and, subject to that, to support the Government's economic policies, including its objectives for growth and employment. At least once a year, the Government specifies the price stability target and its growth and employment objectives. The monthly MPC meeting itself is a two-day affair. On the first day, the meeting starts with an update on the most recent economic data. On the following day, a summary of the previous day's discussion is provided and the MPC members individually explain their views on what policy should be. The interest rate decision is announced at 12 noon on the second day.

Meetings and Communication

The MPC must meet at least monthly; its members comprise the Governor and Deputy Governors, two of the Bank's Executive Directors and four members appointed by the Chancellor. The MPC's decisions are announced after each monthly meeting and minutes of their meetings are released on the Wednesday of the second week after the meeting takes place. The minutes show the results of the majority voting without show the votes of the individual members.

The *Inflation Report* (which include the MPC's projections of inflation and output) and *MPC Minutes* are the Bank's major regular publications on the operation of the policy framework. In addition, the *Quarterly Bulletin* carries background articles describing pieces of analysis that underpin the MPC's thinking, as well as articles describing developments in the markets and analysis relevant to other aspects of the Bank's work.

Public appearances by MPC members represent an important part of the Bank's effort to build public understanding of monetary policy. The Governor and other MPC members usually give evidence to the Treasury Select Committee of the House of Commons, as well as to other Parliamentary Committees.

References

Akhtar, M. A. (1997). Understanding open market operations, Federal Reserve Bank of New York (http://research.stlouisfed.org/aggreg/meeks.pdf).

Anderson, R. G., & Rasche, R. H. (1996a, March/April). A revised measure of the St. Louis adjusted monetary base, *Federal Reserve Bank of St. Louis Review*, *78*(2), 3–13.

Anderson, R. G., & Rasche, R. H. (1996b, November/December). Measuring the adjusted monetary base in an era of financial change. *Federal Reserve Bank of St. Louis Review*, *78*(6), 3–37.

Anderson, R. G., & Rasche, R. H. (2001, January/February), Retail sweep programs and bank reserves, 1994–1999. *Federal Reserve Bank of St. Louis Review*, *83*(1), 51–72.

Anderson, R. G., Rasche, R. H., & Jeffrey L. (2003, September/October,). A reconstruction of the Federal Reserve Bank of St. Louis adjusted monetary base and reserves. *Federal Reserve Bank of St. Louis Review*, *85*(5), 39–70.

Arestis, P., & Sawyer, M. (2002, November 14–16). *Can monetary policy affect the real economy?, international conference on economic policies: perspectives from the Keynesian heterodoxy.* Dijon: Université de Bourgogne.

Baks, K., & Kramer, C. (1999). *Global liquidity and asset prices: measurement, implications and spillovers.* IMF Working Paper, 168, Washingon, DC.

Bank for International Settlements (2003). The role of central bank money in payment systems. Committee on Payment and Settlement Systems, August, Basle.

Bank of England (2002). *The Bank of England's operations in the sterling money market*, May (http://www.bankofengland.co.uk/markets/money/stermm3.pdf).

Bank of Japan (2004, June). Guide to Japan's money stock statistics Tokyo.

Barnett, W. A. (1978). The user cost of money. *Economics Letters*, *1*, 145–149.

Barnett, W. A. (1980). Economic monetary aggregates: an application of index number and aggregation theory. *Journal of Econometrics*, *14*, 11–48.

Barnett, W. A., Offenbacher, E. K., & Spindt, P. A. (1984). The new Divisia monetary aggregates. *Journal of Political Economy*, *92*, 687–710.

Beaufort Wijnholds, J. O. de, & Søndergaard, L. (2007). Reserve accumulation: objective or by-product?. Occasional Paper Series, 73, September, European Central Bank, Frankfurt/Main.

Belke, A., & Polleit, T. (2006a). (How) do stock market returns react to monetary policy? An ARDL cointegration analysis for Germany. *Kredit & Kapital*, *38*(3), 335–366.

Belke, A., & Polleit, T. (2006b). Monetary policy and dividend growth, in Germany: long-run structural modelling versus bounds testing approach. *Applied Economics*, *38*(12), 1409–1423.

Belke, A., & Polleit, T. (2006c). Dividend yields for forecasting stock market returns: an ARDL cointegration analysis for Germany. *Ekonomia*, *9*(1), 86–116.

Bank for International Settlements (2004), Annual Report, Basle.

Bindseil, U. (2004). *Monetary policy implementation: theory, past, and present.* New York: Oxford University Press.

Blenck, D., Hasko, H., Hilton, S., & Masaki, K. (2001, December). *The main features of the monetary policy frameworks of the Bank of Japan, the Federal Reserve and the Eurosystem.* BIS Papers, 9, Bank for International Settlements, Basle.

Bordo, M. D. (1993, April–May). The gold standard, Bretton Woods, and other monetary regimes: A historical appraisal, in: Dimensions of Monetary Policy, Essays in Honor of Anatole B. Balbach, special issue of the Federal Reserve Bank of St. Louis Review, pp. 123 – 91.

Bordo, M. D., & Eichengreen, B. (1993). Implications of the great depression for the development of the international monetary system. In M. D. Bordo, C. Goldin, & E. N. White (Eds.), *The defining moment: the great depression and the American economy in the 20th century* (pp. 403–454). Chicago: University of Chicago Press.

Bordo, M. D., & Kydland, F. E. (1995, October). The gold standard as a rule: an essay in exploration, *Explorations in Economic History, 32*, 423–64, and NBER Reprint, 2023, January 1996.

Bordo M. D., & Schwartz, A. J. (1997). *Monetary policy regimes and economic performance: the historical period.* NBER Working Paper, 6201, National Bureau of Economic Research, Cambridge/MA.

Bordo, M. D., & Schwartz, A. J. (1999). Monetary policy regimes and economic performance: the historical record. In J. Taylor, & M. Woodford (Eds.), *Handbook of macroeconomics*, Elsevier Vol. 1A, pp. 149–234.

Bordo, M. D., Landon-Lane, J., & Redish, A. (2004). *Good versus bad deflation: lessons from the gold standard era*. NBER Working Papers, 10329, National Bureau of Economic Research, Cambridge, MA.

Carlson, J. B., & Keen, B. D. (1996). MZM: a monetary aggregate for the 1990s? *Economic Review, Federal Reserve Bank of Cleveland, Q II*, 15–23.

Charemza, W. W., & Deadman, D. F. (1997), *New directions in econometric practice* (2nd ed.). Cheltenham, UK: Edward Elgar.

Cook, T., & Hahn, T. (1989). The effect of changes in the federal funds rate target on market interest rates in 1970s. *Journal of Monetary Economics*, *24*, 331–351.

Cooper, R. N. (1982). The gold standard: Historical facts and future prospects. *Brooking Papers on Economic Activity*, *1*, 1–45.

Davidson, P. (1988), Endogenous money, the production process, and inflation analysis. *Economie Appliquee*, *XLI*(1), 151–169.

Davidson, P. (1989). On the endogeneity of money once more. *Journal of Post Keynesian Economics*, *XI*(3), 488–490.

Divisia, F. (1925). L'indice Monétaire et la Théorie de la Monnaie. *Revue d'Economie Politique*, *39*, 980–1008.

ECB (1999, February). Euro area monetary aggregates and their role in the eurosystem's monetary policy strategy. *Monthly Bulletin*, Frankfurt/Main, 29–46.

ECB (2003, June). The outcome of the ECB's evaluation of its monetary policy strategy, Frankfurt/Main, 79–92.

ECB (2004, January). *Monthly Bulletin*, Frankfurt/Main (here: Box I).

ECB (2006a, September). The implementation of monetary policy in the euro area. General Documentation on Eurosystem Monetary Policy – Instruments and Procedures.

ECB (2006b). *The accumulation of foreign reserves*, Occasional Paper Series No. 43, March, European Central Bank, Frankfurt/Main.

ECB (2007, September). *Monthly Bulletin*, Frankfurt/Main.

Edwards, C. L. (1997). Open market operations in the 1990s. *Federal Reserve Bulletin*, 859–874.

Eichengreen, B. (1992). *Golden fetters: The gold standard and the great depression 1919–1939*. New York: Oxford University Press.

Eichengreen, B., & Flandreau, M. (1997). *The gold standard in theory and history* (2nd ed.). London: Routledge.

Engle, R. F., & Granger, W. J. (1987). Cointegration and error correction: representation, estimation, and testing. *Econometrica*, *55*, 251–276.

Engle, R. F., Hendry, D. F., & Richard, J.-F. (1983). Exogeneity. *Econometrica*, *51*, 277–304.

Fisher, I. (1911). *The purchasing power of money: its determination and relation to credit, interest, and crises publisher*. New York: The Macmillan Company Location.

Friedman, M. (1953). Commodity-reserve currency. *Milton Friedman, essays in positive economics*. Chicago, IL: University of Chicago Press.

Friedman, M. (1959). *A program for monetary stability*. New York: Fordham University Press.

Friedman, M. (1986, June). The resource cost of irredeemable paper money. *Journal of Political Economy*, *94*, 642–647.

Friedman, M. (1987). Monetary policy for the 1980s. In J. H. Moore (Ed.), *To promote prosperity: U.S. domestic policy in the mid-1980s*. Stanford, CA: Hoover Institution Press (1984), Reprinted in: K. Leube (Ed.), *The essence of Friedman*. Stanford, CA: Hoover Institution Press.

Friedman, M. (1994). *Money mischief*. Mariner Books San Diego, New York, London.

Gaab, W., & Mullineux, A. (1996). Monetary aggregates and monetary policy in the UK and Germany. In D. Duwendag (Ed.), *Finanzmärkte, Finanzinnovationen und Geldpolitik*. Berlin: Duncker & Humblot.

Goodhart, C. A. E. (1989). Has Moore become too horizontal?. *Journal of Post Keynesian Economics*, *12*(1), 29–34.

Granger, C. W. J. (1988), Some recent developments in a concept of causality. *Journal of Econometrics*, *39*, 199–211.

Hamilton, J. (1994). *Time series analysis*. Princeton, New Jersey: Princeton University Press.

Hallwood, C. P., & MacDonald, R. (1994). *International money and finance* (2nd ed.), Oxford UK & Cambridge USA: Blackwell.

Harriss, C. L. (1961). *Money and banking*. ALLYN and BACON, INC., Boston.

Harris, R. I. D. (1995). *Cointegration analysis in econometric modelling, London*. Prentice Hall.

Haubrich, J. G. (1998). *Gold prices, economic commentary*. Federal Reserve Bank of Cleveland, December.

Hayek, F. A. von (1976). *Choice in currency – a way to stop inflation*. Institute of Economic Affairs (IEA) Occasional Paper, 48, London.

Hayek, F. A. von (1978). *Denationalisation of money – the argument refined*. Hobart Special Paper, 70, 2nd (extended) ed., Institute of Economic Affairs (IEA), London.

Heller, D., & Lengwiler, Y. (2003). Payment obligations, reserve requirements, and the demand for central bank balances. *Journal of Monetary Economics*, *50*, 419–432.

Hicks, J. R. (1946). *Value and Capital*. London: Clarendon Press.

Hoppe, H.-H. (1994). How is fiat money possible? *Review of Austrian Economics*, *7*(2), 49–74.

Baks, K., Kramer, C. (1999), *Global Liquidity and Asset Prices. Measurement, implications, and Spillovers*, IMF Working Paper, 99/168.

Issing, O. (1999, May 27). *Hayek – currency competition and European Monetary Union*. London: Annual Hayek Memorial Lecture hosted by the Institute of Economics Affairs.

Kaldor, N. (1982). *The scourge of monetarism*. New York: Oxford University Press.

Kaldor, N., & Trevithick, J. A. (1981). A Keynesian perspective on money. *Lloyds Bank Review*, *139*, 1–19.

Krugman, P. R., & Obstfeld, M. (2006). International economics – theory & policy. Boston: Pearson/Addison-Wesley.

Kuttner, K. N. (2001). Monetary policy surprises and interest rates: evidence from the Fed funds future market. *Journal of Monetary Economics*, *47*, 523–544.

Lavoie, M. (1984). The endogenous flow of credit and the post Keynesian theory of money. *Journal of Economic Issues*, *XVIII*(3), 771–797.

Maddala, G. S. (1988). *Introduction to econometrics*. New York: Macmillan.

Miller, M., & Orr, D. (1966). A model of the demand for money by firms. *The Quarterly Journal of Economics*, *80*, 413–435.

Mises, L. von (1981). *The theory of money and credit*. Indianapolis: Liberty Fund.

Moore, B. J. (1988). *Horizontalists and verticalists*. Cambridge: Cambridge University Press.

Moore, B. J. (1989). A simple model of bank intermediation. *Journal of Post Keynesian Economics*, *12*(1), 10–28.

Motley, B. (1988). *Should M2 be redefined?*, in: Federal Reserve Bank of San Francisco, Review, Winter, pp. 33–51.

Osborne, D. K. (1992). Defining money, In P. Newman, M. Milgate, & J. Eatwell (Eds.), *The New Palgrave Dictionary of Money and Finance* (pp. 602–206). Toronto, ON, Macmillan.

Palley, T. I. (1991). The endogenous money supply: consensus and disagreement. *Journal of Post Keynesian Economics*, *13*(3), 397–403.

Palley, T. I. (1994). Competing views of the money supply process. *Metroeconomica*, *45*(1), 397–403.

Pesaran, M. H. (1997). The role of economic theory in modelling the long run. *The Economic Journal*, *107*(1), 178–191.

Pesaran, M. H., & Shin, Y. (1999). An autoregressive distributed lag modelling approach to cointegration analysis. In S. Strom, & P. Diamond (Eds.), *Econometrics and economic theory in the 20th century: The Ragnar Frisch centennial symposium*. Chapter 11, Cambridge: Cambridge University Press.

Polleit, T. (1996), Finanzierung, Disintermediation und Geldpolitik, LitVerlag, Minister.

Pollin, R. (1991). Two theories of money supply endogeneity: Some empirical evidence. *Journal of Post Keynesian Economics*, *13*(3), 366–396.

Poole, W. (1968). Commercial bank reserve management in a stochastic model: Implications for monetary policy. *The Journal of Finance, 23*, 769–791.

Poole, W. (1991). *Congressional testimony before the subcommittee on domestic monetary policy of the Committee on Banking.* Finance and Urban Affairs.

Poole, W. (2005). Understanding the term structure of interest rates, Speech, 14 June http://stlouisfed.org/news/speeches/2005/6_14_05.html.

Porter, R. D., & Judson, R. A. (1996, October). The location of U.S. currency: How much is abroad?. *Federal Reserve Bulletin,* 883–903.

Reimers, H.-E. (2002). *Analysing Divisia aggregates for the euro area.* Deutsche Bundesbank, Discussion Paper, 13, Frankfurt/Main, May.

Reischle, J. (2000). Der Divisia-Geldmengenindex: Eine Analyse seiner theoretischen Grundlagen, Europäische Hochschulschriften, Peter Lang Verlag: Frankfurt am Main.

Robbins, L. (1934). *The great depression.* New York: Macmillan.

Rothbard, M. N. (2005). What has government done to our money?. US Alabama: Ludwig von Mises Institute.

Rudebusch, G. (1995). Federal reserve interest rate targeting, rational expectations, and the term structure. *Journal of Monetary Economics, 35*, 245–274.

Rudebusch, G. D., Swanson, E. P. & Wu, T. (2006). The bond yield "conundrum" from a macro-finance perspective. Federal Reserve Bank of San Francisco Working Paper 2006–16, San Francisco.

Sousa, J., & Zaghini, A. (2003). *Monetary policy shocks in the Euro Area and global liquidity spillovers.* ECB Working Paper, 309, European Central Bank, Frankfurt/Main.

Swiss National Bank (2008), Statistical Bulletin, December.

Swofford, J. L., & Whitney, G. A. (1986). Flexible functional forms and the utility approach to the demand for money: A nonparametric analysis. *Journal of Money, Credit, and Banking,* 18(3) 383–389.

Swofford, J. L., & Whitney, G. A. (1987). Nonparametric tests of utility maximization and weak separability for consumption, leisure and money. *Review of Economics and Statistics, 69,* 458–464.

Swofford, J. L., & Whitney, G. A. (1988). A comparison of nonparametric tests of weak separability for annual and quarterly data on consumption, leisure, and money. *Journal of Business and Economic Statistics,* 6(2), 241–246.

Swofford, J. L., & Whitney, G. A. (1994, January/February). A revealed preference test for weakly separable utility maximization with incomplete adjustment. *Journal of Econometrics,* 235–249.

Taylor, J. B. (1993). Discretion versus policy rules in practice. Carnegie-Rochester Conference Series on Public Policy, Elsevier, 39, pp. 195–214.

Triffin, R. (1960). *Gold and the dollar crisis.* New Haven: Yale University Press.

Urbain, J. (1992). On the weak exogeneity in error correction models. *Oxford Bulletin of Economics and Statistics,* 54(2), 187–207.

Wesche, K. (1997, September/October). The demand for Divisia money in a core monetary union. Review, Federal Reserve Bank of St. Louis, 51–60.

Westerheide, P. (1995). Potentialorientierte Geldmengenpolitik, Die Zinsstruktur als geldpolitisches Problem, Wiesbaden.

Wray, R. (2007). *Endogenous money: Structuralist and horizontalist,* Levy Working Paper, 512, The Levy Economics Institute of Bard College, New York.

Chapter 2
Money and Credit Demand

> A medium of exchange is a good which people acquire neither
> for their own consumption nor for employment in their own
> production activities, but with the intention of exchanging it at a
> later date against those goods which they want to use either for
> consumption or for production.
>
> Mises, L. v. (1996), Human Action, p. 401.

2.1 Classical Demand for Money Theory

The quantity theory of money, dating back to contributions made in the mid-16th century by Spanish Scholastic writers of the *Salamanca School*, is one of the oldest theories in economics (de Soto, 2006, p. 603). In his book *The Purchasing Power of Money* (1911), Fisher gave the quantity theory, as inherited from his classical and pre-classical predecessors, its modern formulation. Fisher's version, typically termed *equation of exchange* or *transaction approach* can be stated as:

$$M \cdot V_T = T \cdot P_T, \tag{2.1}$$

where M = stock of money, V_T = velocity of the stock of money to finance the transaction volume, T, and P_T = price level.

According to the neo-classical assumptions – namely that the economy is running at full potential and V is constant – P would move in strict proportion to changes in M: A rise (decline) in the economy's stock of money would increase (reduce) the price level. In this theoretical framework, *money is neutral* as far as its effects on output are concerned. Changes in M affect P, but do not have any impact on Y or V.

A. Belke, T. Polleit, *Monetary Economics in Globalised Financial Markets*,
DOI 10.1007/978-3-540-71003-5_2, © Springer-Verlag Berlin Heidelberg 2009

2.1.1 The Cambridge Approach

The *Cambridge approach* or *cash balance approach* is associated with Arthur C. Pigou (1917) and Alfred Marshall (1923).[1] It differs from Fisher's approach in three aspects. *First*, the Cambridge approach is a microeconomic approach, describing *individual* choice rather than market equilibrium. It asks: what determines the amount of money an individual would wish to hold, given that the desire to conduct transactions makes money holding attractive. The Cambridge approach moved the analytical focus from a model where the velocity of money was determined by making payments to one where market agents have a *demand for money* (Cuthbertson & Barlow, 1991, p. 16). *Second*, money is held not only as a medium of exchange for making transactions as in Fisher's case, but also as a *store of value*, providing satisfaction to its holder by, for instance, adding convenience and security. And *third*, the concept of money demand comes across *more explicitly* as will be discussed in more detail below; Cambridge economists pointed out the role of *wealth* and the *interest rate* in determining the demand for money.

Formalizing the Cambridge approach, Pigou *assumed* that for an individual the level of wealth, the volume of transactions and the level of income – at least over short periods – would move in stable portions to one another. Other things being equal, the nominal demand for money, M_d, is then proportional to the nominal level of the transaction volume, PT:

$$M_d = kPT, \qquad (2.2)$$

where k represents the *cash holding coefficient*. The latter is simply the reciprocal of the velocity of money, that is: $V = 1/k$. If money supply, M_s, equals money demand M_d, we can write:

$$
\begin{aligned}
M_S &= M_D = kPT \\
M &= \tfrac{1}{V}PT \\
MV &= PT,
\end{aligned}
\qquad (2.3)
$$

with the latter expression representing the familiar equation of exchange.

The Cambridge formulation of the quantity theory provides a description of monetary equilibrium within the neo-classical model by focusing on peoples' demand for money, especially the demand for real money balances, as the important factor determining the equilibrium price level consistent with a given quantity of money. The emphasis which the Cambridge formulation placed on the demand for money and implicitly also on its determinants like, for instance, interest rates, strongly influenced both the Keynesian and the Monetarist theories.

---

[1] Humphrey (2004) notes that Marshall in his early manuscript Money (1871) as well as in his book Economics of Industry (coauthored with his wife in 1879) gave the quantity theory, as inherited from his classical predecessors, its distinctive Cambridge cash-balance formulation.

2.1.2 The Role of Wealth in the Transaction Approach

In most analyses, the velocity of money is calculated on the basis of current output, or gross domestic product (GDP). However, the latter does not take into account the economy's *stock of wealth*, or *stock of assets* (such as, for instance, equities, bonds, housing, etc.). To make explicit the role of the economy's stock of wealth for the velocity of money, the equation of exchange (2.1) can be written as follows:

$$M \cdot V_T = \left(Y^\alpha \cdot S^{1-\alpha}\right) \cdot \left(P_Y^\beta \cdot P_S^{1-\beta}\right), \tag{2.4}$$

where M = stock of money, V_T = velocity of the stock of money to finance the economy's total transaction volume, Y = real output, S = stock of (financial) wealth, while P_Y and P_S represent the price level of real output and (financial) assets, respectively. $\alpha(1-\alpha)$ is the share of real output (financial assets) in the economy's total transaction volume, and β is the share of output's (financial assets') price level in the total price level. Taking logarithms and solving for the *velocity of the transaction volume*, Eq. (2.4) can be stated as:

$$v_T = \alpha \cdot y + (1 - \alpha) \cdot s + \beta \cdot p_Y + (1 - \beta) \cdot p_S - m. \tag{2.5}$$

In most analyses, however, the transaction equation is based on current real output (that is GDP) rather than the economy's total transaction volume:

$$M \cdot V_Y = Y \cdot P_Y, \text{ or in log form and solving for the velocity} \tag{2.6}$$

$$v_Y = y + p_y - m. \tag{2.7}$$

According to this representation, the traditional *income velocity* of money in log form will be negative (positive) if nominal money supply exceeds (falls below) nominal income. The *difference* between the velocity of the transaction volume and the velocity of current income is:

$$v_T - v_y = (y - s) \cdot (\alpha - 1) + (p_Y - p_S) \cdot (\beta - 1). \tag{2.8}$$

Under the assumption that $0 < \alpha$, $\beta < 1$, which is equivalent to $\alpha - 1$, $\beta - 1 < 0$, Eq. (2.8) suggests that the transaction volume velocity of money will exceed the income velocity of money if financial wealth exceeds output ($y < s$) and/or the price level of financial wealth exceeds the price level of current output ($p_Y < p_S$).

For instance, the income velocity of the euro area money stock M3 – after having shown a more or less stable linear decline since the early 1980s – started falling more strongly as from 2001 (Fig. 2.1). This finding could be an indication that the increase in the stock of M3 increasingly affected nominal wealth (such as, for instance, stock and real estate prices) rather than nominal income.

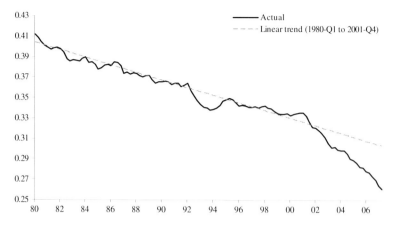

Fig. 2.1 Euro area income velocity of M3, actual and trend
Source: Thomson Financial, ECB; own calculations. – The income velocity of M3 was calculated by dividing nominal GDP by the stock of M3. Period: 1980-Q1 to 2008-Q1.

Time Series Properties of the Velocity Series

Figure 2.2(a) shows the Japanese income velocity of *broad money* – defined as the difference between nominal GDP and broad money (in natural logarithms) for the period 1980-Q1 to 2005-Q4. Two linear trend lines for income velocity

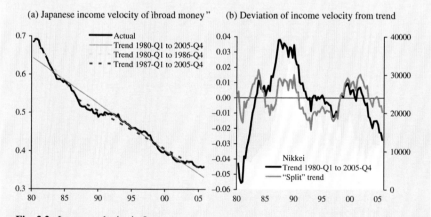

Fig. 2.2 Income velocity in Japan
Source: Thomson Financial; own estimation. - Income velocity is defined as nominal GDP minus stock of broad money (all variables in logarithms). - Period: 1980-Q1 to 2005-Q4.

are also shown: a trend line for the period 1980-Q1 to 2005-Q4 and a *split trend* line that runs from 1980-Q1 to 1986-Q4, thereafter adopting a flatter trend decline. Figure 2.2(b) shows the deviations of actual from trend income velocities of money, index, together with the Nikkei stock market.

A visual inspection suggests that the strong rise in the Nikkei around the second half of the 1980s was accompanied by the income velocity of money moving below its long-run trend, while the decline in stock prices in the period thereafter was accompanied by income velocity moving back up towards the long-run trend. That said, the *assumed* trend figure of the income velocity of money may have important analytical implications.

The time series properties of the income velocity of money affect the analyses related to its medium- to long-term trend. If the log level of income velocity of money, v_t, at time t is stationary around a linear trend t, i.e.:

$$v_t = a + \beta \cdot t + \varepsilon_t, \quad t = 1, \dots, T, \tag{2.9}$$

where ε is a mean-zero stationary process (a random process which has a constant and time independent variance), then the medium-term velocity developments can be described by estimates of β from Eq. (2.9).

If velocity is assumed to be stationary, its variance is constant over time and the covariance between two time instances depends only on the distance, or lag, between them and not on the actual time at which the covariance is calculated. In this case, the impact of shocks on velocity will vanish over time.

In contrast, the log level of velocity is non-stationary if it is a random walk, for instance with drift parameter μ:

$$v_t = v_{t-1} + \mu + \eta_t, \quad t = 1, \dots, T, \tag{2.10}$$

where η_t is some mean-zero stationary process, and the lagged coefficient on velocity is assumed to be one, which explains why the series is said to contain a unit root.

The impact of a random shock on the velocity of money would never disappear as velocity can equivalently be written as an accumulation of past historical shocks:

$$v_t = v_0 + \mu \cdot t + \sum_{j=0}^{t} \eta_j, \quad t = 1, \dots, T. \tag{2.11}$$

As a consequence, the variance of velocity would become a function of time t. In theory, then, under the unit root assumption, deviations of velocity from $\mu \cdot t$ would increase over time. However, the size of the random walk component will also determine how far actual velocity might deviate from the linear trend in a specific period of time.

Under the unit root assumption, velocity can be differenced to obtain a stationary series. Taking the time difference of velocity in Eq. (2.10) and using the specification $\Delta v_t \equiv v_t - v_{t-1}$, yields:

$$\Delta v_t = \mu + \eta_t \quad t = 1, \ldots, T. \tag{2.12}$$

This would permit the estimation of the drift term μ which could form the basis for the expectation of the money velocity trend over the medium-term.

In sum, the choice between models (2.9) and (2.10) may have important economic implications. In the context of model (2.10), under the unit root assumption, velocity would be treated as a non-stationary time series to which shocks accumulate over time. In model (2.9), velocity would be treated as a stationary time series; shocks would have no permanent impact on velocity. Regressing the level of velocity on a time trend in model (2.9) would be appropriate but not in model (2.10).

See, for instance, Harvey (1990), Greene (2003) and Brand, Gerdesmeier, Roffia (2002), p. 14.

2.2 Keynesian Money Demand Theory

The Keynesian theory of money demand (or: *liquidity preference theory*) focuses on the motives that lead people to hold money. More specifically, John Maynard Keynes (1936) distinguished between the demand for *transaction balances* (including the demand for *precaution balances*), L_T, and the demand for *speculative balances*, L_S:[2]

$$L_T = L_t(Y) = kY, \text{ with } \partial L_T / \partial Y > 0 \text{ and} \tag{2.13}$$

$$L_S = L_S(r) = R - dr, \text{ with } \partial L_S / \partial r < 0 \text{ and } \partial^2 L_S / \partial r^2 < 0, \tag{2.14}$$

where k = income balance coefficient, Y = nominal output, R = autonomous speculative balance, d = interest rate elasticity and r = representative interest rate.

Combining the demand for transaction balances (2.13) and speculative balances (2.14) yields the *Keynesian demand for money*:

---

[2]"Money held for each of the three purposes forms, nevertheless a single pool, which the holder is under no necessity to segregate into three water-tight compartments; for they need not be sharply divided even in his own mind, and the same sum can be held primarily for one purpose and secondarily for another". Keynes (1973), p. 195.

$$L = L_T + L_S = kY + L_S(r). \tag{2.15}$$

In equilibrium, money supply, M, equals money demand, that is, in real terms, $M/P = L$. Similar to the quantity theory, the transaction demand for money emphasises the role of money as a means of payment, suggesting that the transaction demand for money depends on the level of current income. The store-of-value function is reflected in the speculative motive of the demand for money.

In the Keynesian theory, market agents' portfolio decisions are driven by expectations regarding future bond prices, e.g. bond yields. Bonds are willingly held if the expected total return (defined as the sum of interest payable on the bond and expected capital gains) is greater than zero.[3]

The pricing formula for the bond market (for *consols*) is:

$$BP = \frac{n}{r} \cdot NV, \tag{2.16}$$

where BP = bond market price, n = nominal coupon of the bond (in percent of its nominal value), r = effective yield in the bond market (market rate), and NV = nominal value of the bond. For example, if $n = 5\%$ p.a., $NV = $ US\$100 and $r = 5\%$ p.a., then $BP = $ US\$100. If r rises to 10%, BP falls to US\$50.

Now assume that each investor has an estimate of the *normal* market yield, r^{normal}, which might deviate from the current market yield. Depending on the subjectively perceived normal yield, an individual investor is expecting a capital gain or loss from bond holdings:

$$expected\ loss\ on\ bond\ holdings = BP - BP^e, \tag{2.17}$$

with BP^e as the expected bond price in the future. We can rewrite Eq. (2.17) as follows:

$$expected\ loss\ on\ bond\ holdings = \frac{n}{r} \cdot NV - \frac{n}{r^{normal}} \cdot NV \tag{2.18}$$

The income from coupon payments on the bond is:

$$interest\ income = n \cdot NV. \tag{2.19}$$

That said, an investor will hold interest bearing bonds if interest income is higher than expected capital losses from holding bonds:

$$\underbrace{n \cdot NV}_{Interest\ income} > \underbrace{\frac{n}{r} \cdot NV - \frac{n}{r^{normal}} \cdot NV}_{expected\ capital\ losses} \tag{2.20}$$

---

[3]Note that if a bond's market price equals its par value, the bond's return equals its nominal coupon. If the bond's market price is higher (lower) than its par value, the bond's return is lower (higher) than its nominal coupon.

or, equivalently:

$$1 > \frac{1}{r} - \frac{1}{r^{normal}} \quad \text{or} \tag{2.20a}$$

$$r > \frac{r^{normal}}{1 + r^{normal}} \tag{2.20b}$$

The level of r, which fulfils Eq. (2.20b), is called the *critical market yield*. At the critical yield, the investor is *indifferent* as interest income from bond holdings equals expected capital losses of bond holdings. That said, one can draw the following conclusions:

– If the market rate is *above* the critical yield level, interest income is higher than the expected capital losses, so that the investor decides to keep his total wealth *in bonds*.
– If the market yield is *below* the critical market yield, the investor would decide to keep his total wealth *in money balances*, as he fears capital losses related to a forthcoming rise in market yields.

The Keynesian demand for speculative balances is therefore a decision to hold *either* money *or* interest bearing bonds (Fig. 2.3a). Assuming that different people have different estimates of the normal yield and, as a result the critical yield, one can finally construct an *aggregated* demand for speculative balances (Fig. 2.3b). The resulting aggregated money demand curve has a continuous shape with a negative slope, since with a decreasing market interest rate more and more investors will expect an increase of this rate and, therefore, prefer to hold money instead of bonds.

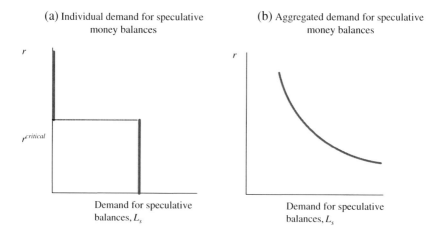

Fig. 2.3 Keynesian demand for speculative balances

In our example, assume that the normal yield is 10% p.a. According to Eq. (2.20b), the critical market yield is:

$$r^{critical} = \frac{0.1}{1 + 0.1} \approx 9\%. \tag{2.20c}$$

So if the market yield is less than 9%, the investor wouldn't want to hold any bonds as expected capital losses are higher than interest income.

It is important to note that in the Keynesian liquidity theory, *the speculative demand for money always equals the supply of bonds and vice versa*.[4] As it is important for the understanding of the portfolio approach underlying the Keynesian theory, this aspect shall be explained in some more detail.

In a *first step*, let us assume the economy's number of bonds outstanding, b_0, can be traded at any time. Moreover, the demand for bonds, B_D, which is assumed to be independent of the bond price, amounts to US$100. Given a bond supply of $b_0 = 1$ (for instance, 1 million bonds outstanding), the equilibrium price is US$100 (Fig. 2.4a). Alternatively, would the number of offered bonds increase to, say, $b_1 = 2$, the equilibrium price of bonds, P_B, would fall to US$50.

In a *second step*, we show the relation between bond prices (vertical axis) and the market capitalisation of bonds (horizontal axis), that is b times P_B (Fig. 2.4b). The economy's total bond demand, $B_D = US\$100$, is assumed to be given, represented by the vertical line. Bond supply, BS_0, is represented by a line with a 45° slope ($tg\alpha = 1$ if $b_1 = 1$); assuming $b_1 = 2$, the higher bond supply would be represented by BS_1 (with $tg\alpha = 0.5$), since the market volume would double in this case (when compared to BS_0).

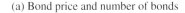
(a) Bond price and number of bonds

(b) Bond price and market volume

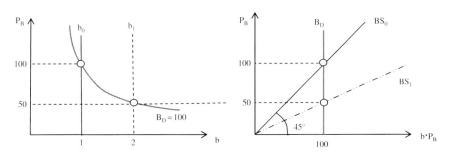

Fig. 2.4 Demand and supply for bonds in the Keynesian liquidity preference theory

---

[4]See Borchert (2001), pp. 120.

In a *third step*, we replace the bond price on the vertical axis of Fig. 2.4b by the bond yield r, where:

$$r = \frac{NV \cdot n}{P_B},$$

with NV = nominal value of the bond, n = coupon and P_B = bond market price.

In view of the pricing formula above, the *bond demand curve* stays the same as before, and the *bond supply curve* converges asymptotically towards the vertical and horizontal axis (Fig. 2.5).[5] The higher bond price $P_B = 100$ in Fig. 2.4(b) cor- responds with the lower bond yield r_0 in Fig. 2.5, and the lower bond price $P_B = 50$ with the higher bond yield r_1. In Fig. 2.5, *bond demand equals money supply* (and vice versa), that is $B_D = M_S$, which is representing the demand for speculative balances.

That said, a given liquidity preference function is actually defined on the basis of a given stock of bonds *and* a given stock of money, whereas bonds and money represent the economy's total stock of wealth, W:

$$L_s = L_s(r, W), \text{ mit } \partial L_s / \partial W > 0. \tag{2.21}$$

An increase in the supply of bonds would move the liquidity preference curve upwards: under a given stock of money, an increase in the supply of bonds would be associated with a higher interest rate. So any open market operation by the central bank, for instance, which brings about a change in money supply, would also affect the location of the liquidity preference function.

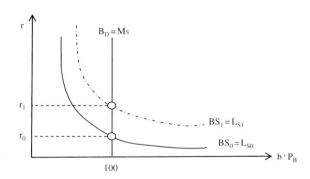

Fig. 2.5 Keynesian liquidity preference

---

[5] If the above bond pricing formula is valid and the price of the bonds P_B converges towards zero, the interest rate r tends to infinity and vice versa. Hence, the curve depicting the bond supply reveals the shape described above.

2.2.1 Explaining the Trend of Income Velocity of Money

The Keynesian demand for money theory can be integrated in the quantity theory framework for analysing the behaviour of the income velocity of money. The long-run demand for real money balances is:

$$m_t - p_t = \beta_0 + \beta_1 y_t - \beta_2 r_t + \varepsilon_t, \qquad (2.22)$$

where y_t is the log of real income in period t, β_0 is a constant term, β_1 and β_2 represent the income and interest rate elasticities of money demand, respectively, and r_t is the interest rate. If ε_t is a stationary stochastic process with zero mean, Eq. (2.22) describes a cointegrated long-run relationship (King & Watson, 1997).

Combining equation (2.22) with the log version of the transaction equation, that is $m - p = y - v_Y$, yields the following expression for the *income velocity* of money:

$$v_{y,t} = -\beta_0 + (1 - \beta_1) \cdot y_t + \beta_2 \cdot r_t - \varepsilon_t. \qquad (2.23a)$$

As far as r_t is concerned, it would be appropriate for a broadly defined monetary aggregate to use the difference between the opportunity cost of money holdings and the (weighted) yield paid on deposits included in the definition of money. If the yield spread is stationary, however, the interest component in (2.23a) could not be held responsible for the velocity of money's trend behaviour. Under this assumption, the functional specification of the demand for money would actually be *tied to current income* as the interest rate r drops out:

$$v_{y,t} = -\beta_0 + (1 - \beta_1) \cdot y_t - \varepsilon_t. \qquad (2.23b)$$

If the log velocity in time t fluctuates randomly around a constant term, it becomes $v_{y,t} = v_0 + \varepsilon_t$. With ε_t being a stationary zero mean process, the equilibrium level of log velocity would be $v^* = v_0$. Hence, calculating trend velocity finally yields:

$$v^* = v_0 + (1 - \beta_1) \cdot y^*, \qquad (2.24)$$

with y^* log of potential output. If, for instance, β_1 exceeds unity, the income velocity of money would predict a declining trend over time as long as potential output is growing (assuming throughout that the opportunity costs of money holdings is integrated of order zero ($I(0)$).

2.2.2 Some Empirically Testable Money Demand Hypotheses

In view of the findings above, there are some *testable relationships* which have become important in empirical analyses of money demandfunctions (Herwartz &

Reimers, 2006). To start with, one may be concerned with *cointegration* between money, prices and real output, based on the static representation of real money, which corresponds to:

$$m_t - p_t = \beta_0 + \beta_1 y_t + z_t, \tag{2.25}$$

excluding interest rates for reasons stated above, and with z_t being a stationary stochastic process with zero mean. To test for cointegration, the potential cointegrating relationship may be written to allow the interpretation of a price equation:

$$p_t = -\beta_0 - \beta_1 y_t + \beta_2 m_t - z_t. \tag{2.26}$$

The first hypothesis to consider is then:

$H_1 : p_t, m_t$ and y_t are cointegrated with cointegration rank $r = 1$.
  Second, deviations from the long-run relation should not affect the change in output:
$H_2 :$ Output is weakly exogenous.
  Third, the coefficients of prices and money should be equal in absolute terms:
$H_3 : \beta_2 = 1$ which suggests *price homogeneity*.
  Fourth, if the cointegration relation is normalised such that the coefficient of the price level is unity, the coefficient of real output is unity:
$H_4 : \beta_1 = 1,$
  implying that the velocity of money is constant in the long-run. If $\beta_1 > 1$, trend income velocity follows a downward trend over time.

The Keynesian money theory has had a profound impact. Most importantly, it has ended the dichotomy the (neo-) classical theory assumed between the economy's real and monetary sector. Under the assumption that investment spending and the demand for money depend on the interest rate, the central bank, by changing the stock of money and thereby affecting the interest rate, was supposed to exert an impact on aggregate demand. Over time, elements of the Keynesian money demand system have been developed further, particularly in portfolio-oriented money demand theories.

Overview of Functional Forms of Money Demand

Table 2.1 summarizes the salient features of various functional forms which are now widely used for estimating money demand functions.

The elasticity E of a variable M (such as, for instance, money) with respect to another variable X (say, the interest rate) is defined as:

Table 2.1 Functional forms of money demand

Model	Equation	Slope $\left(= \frac{dY}{dX}\right)$	Elasticity $\left(= \frac{dY}{dX}\frac{X}{Y}\right)$
Linear	$Y = \beta_1 + \beta_2 X$	β_2	$\beta_2 \left(\frac{X}{Y}\right)^*$
Log-linear or log-log	$\ln Y = \beta_1 + \beta_2 \ln X$	$\beta_2 \left(\frac{Y}{X}\right)$	β_2
Log-lin	$\ln Y = \beta_1 + \beta_2 X$	$\beta_2(Y)$	$\beta_2(X)^*$
Lin-log	$Y = \beta_1 + \beta_2 \ln X$	$\beta_2 \left(\frac{1}{X}\right)$	$\beta_2 \left(\frac{1}{Y}\right)^*$
Reciprocal	$Y = \beta_1 + \beta_2 \left(\frac{1}{X}\right)$	$-\beta_2 \left(\frac{1}{X^2}\right)$	$-\beta_2 \left(\frac{1}{XY}\right)^*$

Note: An asterisk indicates that the elasticity coefficient is variable, that is depending on the value taken by X or Y or both.

$$E = \frac{\%change\ in\ Y}{\%change\ in\ X}$$

$$E = \frac{(\Delta Y/Y) \cdot 100}{(\Delta X/X) \cdot 100}$$

$$E = \frac{\Delta Y}{\Delta X}\frac{X}{Y}$$

$$E = slope \cdot (X/Y),$$

where Δ denotes a (small) change. If Δ is sufficiently small, it can be replaced by the calculus derivate notation dY/dX.

Take, for instance, the following money demand function:

$$\ln M = \beta_1 + \beta_2 \ln Y + \beta_3 \ln r + e, \tag{2.27}$$

where M = (real) stock of money, Y = real output and r = interest rate and e = i.i.d. error term. This equation can also be estimated using the level instead of the logarithm of the interest rate:

$$\ln M = \beta_1 + \beta_2 \ln Y + \beta_3 r + e. \tag{2.28}$$

In Eq. (2.28), the coefficient of r represents the *semi-elasticity*. It shows by how much *percent* the real demand for money changes in response to a change in the interest rate of 1 percentage point (that is, for instance, the rate rising from 5% to 6%).

In contrast, Eq. (2.27) shows how the demand for money changes in response to a given percentage point change in the interest rate (say, a one percent change from 5.0% to 5.05%). That said, the semi-elasticity is defined as:

$$\beta_2 = \frac{d \ln M}{dr} = \frac{dM/M}{dr}. \tag{2.29}$$

Source: Gurajati (1995), pp. 167–178.

2.3 Portfolio Oriented Money Demand Theory

2.3.1 Monetarist Money Demand

Milton Friedman (1956) extended Keynes' speculative money demand within the framework of asset price theory, treating money as a good as any other durable consumption good. To Friedman, the demand for money is a function of a great number of factors. His analysis refers to nominal magnitudes in the first place. Taking this as a starting point, he derives the real money demand from nominal money demand under certain assumptions.

Perhaps most important, Friedman maintains that it is *permanent income* – and not *current income* as in the Keynesian theory – that determines the demand for money. If W^n represents market agents' total wealth, which comprises all sources of income – among them human capital and all consumable services –, and r is the representative market yield, nominal income per period is: [6]

$$Y^n = W^n \cdot r.$$

With W^n and r assumed to be relatively stable, market agents' permanent income can be also expected to be rather stable when compared with current income.

More specifically, Friedman's *monetarist demand function for money* can be summarized as follows (Felderer & Homburg, 2005, p. 244):

$$L^n = f \left(\underset{(+)}{P}, \underset{(-)}{r_B}, \underset{(-)}{r_E}, \underset{(-)}{\frac{\dot{P}}{P}}, \underset{(+)}{\frac{Y^n}{r}}, \upsilon \right). \tag{2.30}$$

---

[6]Such a specification can be interpreted as an income or wealth hypothesis. See Meltzer (1963), p. 220.

According to Eq. (2.30), the nominal demand for money:

- is positively related to the price level, P, as market agents are expected to hold a certain stock of real rather than nominal money balances. If the price level rises (falls), the demand for money increases (decreases);
- rises (falls) if the opportunity costs of money holdings – that are bonds and stock returns, r_B and r_E, respectively – decline (increase);
- is influenced by inflation, $\dot{P}/P$ (or: dP/dt). A positive (negative) inflation rate reduces (increases) the real value of money balances, thereby increasing (reducing) the opportunity costs of money holdings. Whereas a *one-off* increase in the price level would increase the demand for money, inflation – that is an ongoing increase in the economy's price level – will lead to a decline in money demand.
- is a function of total wealth, which is represented by permanent income divided by the discount rate r, defined as the average return on the five asset classes in the monetarist theory world, namely money, bonds, equity, physical capital and human capital, υ (which is, for the sake of clarification, explicitly shown in Eq. (2.30)).

Furthermore, Friedman assumes that r, which cannot be measured directly, would correspond more or less with r_B and r_S, so that r (and υ) can be dropped from the equation:

$$L^n = f\left(P, r_B, r_E, \frac{\dot{P}}{P}, Y^n \right). \tag{2.31}$$

If market agents do not suffer from *money illusion*, a change in P and a change in Y^n by the multiple λ will change the demand for money by the same amount (*homogeneity hypothesis of money demand*):

$$\lambda \cdot L^n = f\left(\lambda \cdot P, r_B, r_E, \frac{\dot{P}}{P}, \lambda \cdot Y^n \right). \tag{2.32}$$

If (2.32) holds true for any arbitrary realisation of the parameter λ, we can, for instance, define $\lambda = 1/Y^n$. Substituting this expression in (2.32) yields:

$$\frac{1}{Y^n} \cdot L^n = f\left(\frac{P}{Y^n}, r_B, r_E, \frac{\dot{P}}{P}, 1 \right) \text{ and, by rearranging,} \tag{2.33}$$

$$L^n = f\left(\frac{P}{Y^n}, r_B, r_E, \frac{\dot{P}}{P}, 1 \right) \cdot Y^n. \tag{2.34}$$

According to Eq. (2.34), Friedman's demand for money is a stable function (i.e., f(.) times Y_n) of several variables – rather than a numerically constant number as is assumed in the (neo-)classical theory. The velocity of money v ($= Y_n/L_n$) is the reciprocal of f(.), which, according to (2.34), is equal to L_n/Y_n. That said, we can write (dropping the "1"):

$$v \left(\frac{Y^n}{P}, r_B, r_E, \frac{\dot{P}}{P} \right) = 1/f \left(\frac{P}{Y^n}, r_B, r_E, \frac{\dot{P}}{P}, 1 \right). \qquad (2.35)$$

Imposing market equilibrium, $M = L^n$, we arrive at the new formulation of the equation of exchange:

$$M \cdot v \left(\frac{Y^n}{P}, r_B, r_E, \frac{\dot{P}}{P}, \right) = Y^n, \qquad (2.36)$$

which actually restates the *traditional specification of the quantity theory*.

In this context it seems interesting to highlight the effect a one-off money supply increase might exert on the real economy from the point of view of the Monetarists. With the economy running at full capacity, a one-off increase in money supply of, say, 5%, can be expected to increase (future) inflation. This, in turn, would reduce peoples' demand for money, thereby increasing the velocity of money $v = Y^N/M$ by, say, 2%.

As a result, Friedman's money demand function suggests that the percentage increase in *nominal income* should be higher than a given percentage increase in money supply, namely 7% in our example (that is 5% money growth plus a 2% increase in velocity). However, as soon as the additional money supply has fully translated into an increase of the price level, inflation returns back to its previous level, increasing the demand for money, thereby lowering the velocity of money by 2%. Finally, after all adjustments have run their course, nominal output is expected to have risen by 5%, corresponding to the increase in the stock of money. To sum up, Monetarists would expect that a one-off increase in the money supply would exert cyclical swings of the economy's nominal income.

2.3.2 Post-Keynesian Money Demand Theory

Two characteristics of money provide the starting point for *Post-Keynesian* theories of money demand. *First*, the analysis of the transaction function of money has brought forward *inventory models*. *Second*, the study of the store-of-value function of money has inspired *asset* or *portfolio model* approaches, in which money is held as part of market agents' overall asset portfolios. Our discussion begins with the inventory model approach to transaction balances.

2.3.2.1 Inventory Model Approach to Transaction Balances

Baumol (1952) and Tobin (1956) developed a deterministic theory of money demand in which money was essentially viewed as an *inventory* held for transaction purposes. Although relatively liquid financial assets other than money (such as, for instance, time and savings deposits) offer a positive return, the transaction costs of going between money and these assets justifies holding money. *Inventory models* actually assume two media for storing value: money and an interest bearing alternative asset. What is more, inventory models state that there is a fixed cost of making transfers between money and the alternative asset. Finally, it is assumed that all transactions involve money as the means of exchange, and that all relevant information is known with certainty.

Let us assume that a household receives a nominal income of PY in each period (say, a month), spending if at a constant rate over the period. Money which is not needed for purchasing will be put in an interest-bearing account. As goods are purchased with cash, the household needs to go to his bank at least once (for converting sight deposits into cash). Each visit to the bank has a nominal cost c attached to it, and c should be thought of as the opportunity cost (such as time spent queuing, shoe leather costs, fees for using online banking services, etc). If n is the number of visits to the bank during the month, the monthly cost will be: $n \cdot c$. To reduce costs, the household might wish to hold more cash. However, holding more cash comes at a cost in the form of foregone interest income. If i is the monthly interest rate on the savings account (the alternative to cash), holding an average nominal balance M over the month gives an opportunity cost of: $i M$. Figure 2.6 illustrates the average transaction balance holdings as a function of n. PY denotes the incoming payment per month. If, for instance, the household spends his money continuously over the period, his money account is zero at the end of the month.

For evenly-spaced visits to the bank, the average money balance is PY/n. These n trips occur every $1/n$th of a month. The area of eachtriangle represents the average

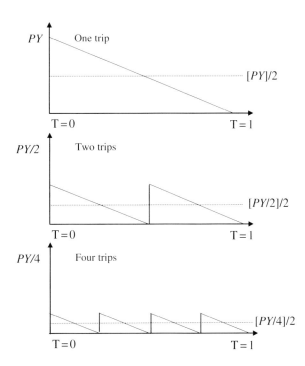

Fig. 2.6 Number of bank trips and average money holdings

money amount held between two trips. That said, the average money holdings as a function of the number of bank trips, n, are:

$$average\ money\ holdings\ between\ n\ bank\ trips,\ M = \frac{PY}{2n}. \quad (2.37)$$

The opportunity cost is the foregone interest on the average money holdings:

$$opportunity\ costs = M \cdot i. \quad (2.38)$$

Transaction costs are a function of the transaction costs per bank trip, c, and n:

$$transaction\ costs = c \cdot n. \quad (2.39)$$

Total costs, TC, taking into account the opportunity costs of money holdings and transaction costs, are therefore:

$$TC = M \cdot i + cn. \quad (2.40a)$$

As $n = \frac{PY}{2M}$ (remember that the average money holdings between n bank trips amount to $M = \frac{PY}{2n}$), one can write:

$$TC = M \cdot i + c \cdot \frac{PY}{2M}. \quad (2.40b)$$

The optimization of money holdings is equivalent to:

$$TC = M \cdot i + c \cdot \frac{PY}{2M} \rightarrow \min. \quad (2.40c)$$

The minimum costs of money holdings are obtained by taking the first derivative of equation (2.40c) with respect to M, setting the result to zero:

$$\frac{\partial TC}{\partial M} = i - \frac{cPY}{2M^2} = 0. \quad (2.41)$$

Since the sufficient condition of a cost minimum is fulfilled (note that the realization of the second derivation is positive), the optimal holding of transaction balances is the following *square root formula*:

$$M^* = \sqrt{\frac{cPY}{2i}}. \quad (2.42)$$

Expression (2.42) states that the optimal average money holding is:

– a positive function of real economic activity Y,
– a positive function of the price level P,

– a positive function of transactions costs c, and
– a negative function of the nominal interest rate i.

If we define the *real* cost of transactions, c^{real}, as $c^{real} = c/P$, the square root formula can be expressed in terms of real money demand:

$$\left(\frac{M}{P}\right)^* = \sqrt{\frac{c^{real} Y}{2i}}. \tag{2.43}$$

The real demand for transaction balances in natural logarithms, $m - p$, can be written as:

$$m - p = 0.5 \ln\left(\frac{c^{real}}{2}\right) + 0.5 \ln Y - 0.5 \ln i. \tag{2.44}$$

It is determined by the constant $c^{real}/2$, real income and the interest rate. Accordingly, the income elasticity of money is:

$$\varepsilon_{m-p,\, Y} = \frac{d(M/P)}{M/P} : \frac{dY}{Y} = \frac{d \ln(m - p)}{d \ln Y} = 0.5. \tag{2.45}$$

The interest rate elasticity of money demand can be written as:

$$\varepsilon_{i,Y} = \frac{d(M/P)}{M/P} : \frac{di}{i} = \frac{d \ln(m - p)}{d \ln i} = -0.5. \tag{2.46}$$

To conclude, in contrast to the Keynesian demand for transaction balances, the *transaction demand* of Baumol and Tobin is also a function of interest rates. What is more, the income elasticity suggests *economies of scale* of transaction money holdings. A rise in real income by, say, 1 percentage point would, according to Tobin and Baumol, be followed by a 0.5 percentage point increase in real balance holdings – rather than a proportional increase as suggested by the transaction equation.[7]

2.3.2.2 Tobin's Demand for Speculative Balances

Tobin's *mean-variance analysis* of the demand for speculative money holdings is in fact an application of the theory of portfolio choice. Tobin (1958) assumes that the utility which people derive from their asset holdings is *positively* related to the *expected return of the portfolio* and *negatively* related to the *risk of the asset portfolio*, with the latter being measured by the variance (or standard deviation) of asset returns.

An individual's preference for *return and risk* can be illustrated by means of *indifference curves* as shown in Fig. 2.7. In the *expected return-risk-space*, the indif-

---

[7]The approach to money demand derived in this section may, for instance, be also applied to professional cash managers in large firms and, in particular, to investment and commercial banks' management of base money holdings.

Fig. 2.7 Indifference curves in the mean-variance model

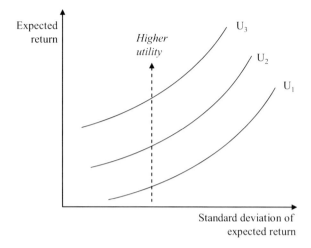

ference curves slope upward because an individual is willing to accept more risk if it is accompanied by a higher expected return. When we turn to higher indifference curves, utility is higher because for the same level of risk, the expected return is higher. Against this background, we now take a closer look at the mean-variance model for explaining the demand for speculative balances.

To start with, we assume that *total wealth*, W, consists of the stock of money, M, and the stock of bonds, B, that is:

$$\overline{W} = M + B, \tag{2.47}$$

where B represents the market value of bonds, that is the bond price, P_X, times the number of outstanding bonds, b. The expected return on a bond portfolio, R^e, is determined by the interest payment, r, and the expected capital gain, g:

$$R^e = r \cdot B + g \cdot B = (r + g) \cdot B. \tag{2.48}$$

In contrast to Keynes, expected capital gains are *no longer* assumed to be known *with certainty* but characterized by a measure of the distribution of possible returns around the mean value:

$$g \sim N(\bar{g}, \sigma_g^2),$$

where the expected capital gain is $E(g) = \bar{g}$ and the variance of the capital gain is $\text{var}(g) = \sigma_p^2$.

If all bonds are assumed to have the same risk, σ_g, the total portfolio risk is:

$$\sigma_P = \sigma_g \cdot B. \tag{2.49}$$

Solving (2.49) for B and inserting in (2.48) yields the *transformation curve*, showing the opportunity locus of all possible combinations of R^e and σ_p for alternative asset allocations:

$$R^e = \frac{r + \bar{g}}{\sigma_g} \cdot \sigma_P. \qquad (2.50)$$

The utility function of a *risk averter* can be written as follows:

$$U = U(R^e, \sigma_p), \quad \text{where} \quad \frac{\partial U}{\partial R^e} > 0, \quad \frac{\partial U}{\partial \sigma_P} < 0, \quad \frac{\partial^2 U}{\partial^2 \sigma_P} > 0. \qquad (2.51)$$

Note that the last inequality implies that the utility loss induced by risk becomes increasingly larger – for a given level of return.

The optimal portfolio can be calculated by applying the *Lagrange technique*:

$$L = U(R^e, \sigma_P) + \lambda \left(R^e - \frac{r + \bar{g}}{\sigma_g} \sigma_P \right) \overset{!}{\to} \max. \qquad (2.52)$$

Differentiating (2.52) for R^e and σ_P, setting the first derivations to zero and solving for λ yields:

$$\lambda = -\frac{\partial U}{\partial R^e} \quad \text{and} \qquad (2.53a)$$

$$\lambda = -\frac{\partial U}{\partial \sigma_P} \cdot \frac{\sigma_g}{r + \bar{g}}. \qquad (2.53b)$$

Equating (2.53a) and (2.53b) and rearranging yields the optimum condition:

$$-\frac{\partial U}{\partial R^e} = \frac{\partial U}{\partial \sigma_P} \cdot \frac{\sigma_g}{r + \bar{g}} \quad \text{or} \quad \frac{\partial U}{\partial R^e} \cdot (r + \bar{g}) = \frac{\partial U}{\partial \sigma_P} \cdot \sigma_g. \qquad (2.54)$$

Equation (2.54) shows that, in the optimum, the slope of the indifference curve is equal to the slope of the transformation curve: the increase in utility from holding an additional bond unit $[(r + \bar{g}) \cdot (\partial U / \partial R^e)]$ equals the decline in utility from taking additional risk $[\sigma_g \cdot \partial U / \partial \sigma_p]$.

To calculate the actual portfolio structure, we make use of the total wealth restriction (2.47): $\bar{W} = M + B$. Solving for M and substitution B by the term $\sigma_P / \sigma_g = B$, we can write:

$$M = \bar{W} - \frac{1}{\sigma_g} \sigma_P, \qquad (2.55)$$

which shows the *demand for money* as a function of total wealth, the individual risk of bonds and the total bond portfolio risk.

That said, in Tobin's theory of the demand for speculative balances individuals are capable of holding money as well as bonds (mixed portfolios). This is different

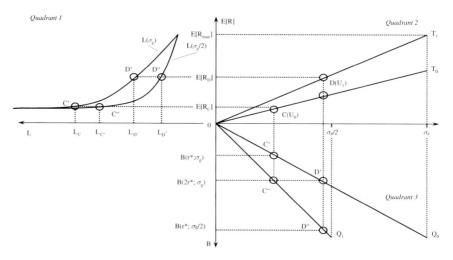

Fig. 2.8 Optimal portfolio and money demand

from Keynes and his liquidity preference theory, in which an individual holds *either* money or bonds; in the liquidity preference theory, the possibility of holding mixed portfolios is limited to the macroeconomic level.

The results are illustrated in Fig. 2.8. Quadrant 1 shows the demand for speculative balances as a negative function of expected return insert eq. (2.50) in (2.55). Quadrant 2 depicts the transformation curve (Eq. 2.50), represented by T_0. Quadrant 3 plots the relation between risk and bond holdings.

At point $C(U_0)$ the slope of the indifference curve equals the slope of the transformation curve, representing the investor's optimum portfolio choice. Here, the bond holding is $B(r^*, \sigma_g)$. The optimal money holding is L_C, corresponding to point C'. In the following, the implications of *three scenarios* for the demand for money and bond holdings shall be analyzed, namely a change in the investor's estimate of (i) return, (ii) risk and (iii) a change in taxes.

2.3.2.3 Re (i): Change in Expected Return

Let us assume that – starting from point $C(U_0)$ – the bond yield rises from r^* to $2r^*$. As a result, the transformation curve steepens (from $0T_0$ to $_20T_1$). The new optimum is in point $D(U_1)$. Bond holdings increase to $B(2r^*, \sigma_g)$ – with the risk-bond relation remaining unaffected –, giving the new risk-bond relation at point D'' in quadrant 3. Accordingly, with a growing share of bonds in the portfolio, the demand for money balances declines – *along* the liquidity preference curve in quadrant 1 $L(\sigma_g)$ – from L_C to $L_{D'}$. That said, a given liquidity preference curve reflects different levels of return expectations under a given risk perception.

2.3.2.4 Re (ii): Change in Risk

Starting with the optimum portfolio in $C(U_0)$, the assumption is that investors cut their risk estimate in half, from σ_g to $\sigma_g/2$. As a result, the transformation curve in quadrant 2 will double in slope, from $0T_0$ to $_20T_1$. Consequently, the new optimum point $D(U_1)$ corresponds to bond holdings of $B(r^*, \sigma_g/2)$, now expressed by point D'' in quadrant 3. With a higher share of bonds in the optimal portfolio, an unchanged expected return of r^* implies a corresponding decline in liquidity preference from L_C to $L_{D''}$. The *liquidity preference curve* becomes *steeper*, leading to this new equilibrium D'' in quadrant 1. That said, the change in risk perception entails a *change in the interest rate elasticity* of the liquidity preference curve (note that an unchanged demand for transaction balances is assumed). Generally speaking, the Tobin model would suggest that for a given expected return the interest rate elasticity of speculative money demand declines (rises) when the risk perception declines (increases).

Heightened Investor Uncertainty and Money Holdings

The period between 2000 and 2003 provides an illustration of how changes in investor risk and return perception can (temporarily) influence the demand for money – as suggested by Tobin's theory of the demand for speculative balances. The early years of the 21st century were characterised by *heightened financial market uncertainty*.

The key events include the bust marking the end of the IT-driven "New Economy" boom, the terrorist attacks in the US on 11 September 2001, a spate of accounting scandals on both sides of the Atlantic in the aftermath of the equity market correction, and the start of the wars in Afghanistan in late 2001 and in Iraq in early 2003. All these events contributed in one way or another to a significant and protracted fall and heightened volatility in global stock prices from mid-2000 onwards.

As a consequence of strongly increased investor risk perception, *extraordinary portfolio shifts* affecting monetary aggregates took place. These shifts strongly influenced money growth in many countries in a way that could not be easily explained by the conventional determinants of money demand, such as prices, income and interest rates.

At the global level, precautionary and speculative motives significantly influenced the overall demand for money during that period. The fact that common global shocks might have influenced the demand for money in several regions was illustrated by a rather *close co-movement* of the growth rates of broad monetary aggregates during the period of heightened financial market turmoil.

Figures 2.9(a to d) show annual money supply growth rates and measures of stock market volatility in the US, the euro area, Switzerland and the UK for

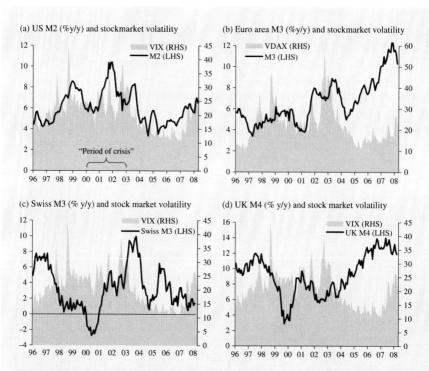

Fig. 2.9 Money demand in times of crisis
Source: Bloomberg; own calculations.

the period January 1996 to April 2008.[8] In the currency regions under review,
the (drastic) increases in stock market volatility indeed appear to have been
accompanied by a growing demand for money. The ECB (2005, p. 73) came
to the conclusion that the crisis period from 2000 to 2003 "triggered considerable flows into safe haven investments, especially monetary assets. Money
demand therefore increased significantly. Due to the increasing globalisation
of financial markets, shocks that increase global uncertainty are likely to have
a considerably stronger effect on euro area monetary holdings than in previous
decades."

2.3.2.5   Re (iii): Increase in Taxes

Suppose the initial position of the investor is $D(U_1)$ on the transformation line $0T_1$,
with bond holdings of $B(2r^*, \sigma_g)$ and money demand at $L_{D'}$. Now, investors cut in
half expected returns (from $2r^*$ to r^*) and perceived risk (from σ_g to $\sigma_g/2$). The

---

[8]In the case of the US, Switzerland and UK, stock market volatility is expressed by the market
traded volatility index of the S&P's 500; in the case of the euro area it is the V-DAX.

transformation curve will remain unchanged at $0T_1$, and investors will still wish to obtain the combination of risk and reward depicted by $D(U_1)$. This combination, however, requires investors to double their holdings of bonds, that is moving to $B(r^*, \sigma_g/2)$; the tax change moves the risk-consol relation from $0Q_0$ to $0Q_1$. Accordingly, the demand for cash declines from $L_{D'}$ to $L_{D''}$.

Digression: Income Velocities of US Monetary Aggregates

Figures 2.10 (a–d) show the income velocities of US monetary aggregates – that is M1, M2, M2-ST (the latter being M2 minus time deposits) – for the period 1960-Q1 to 2008-Q1 and the income velocity of M3 up to 2006-Q1. Two findings stand out. First, the income velocities for all aggregates are *not numerical constants*, as suggested by the (neo)classical quantity theory. Second, the income velocities tend to exhibit rather *pronounced swings* over time.

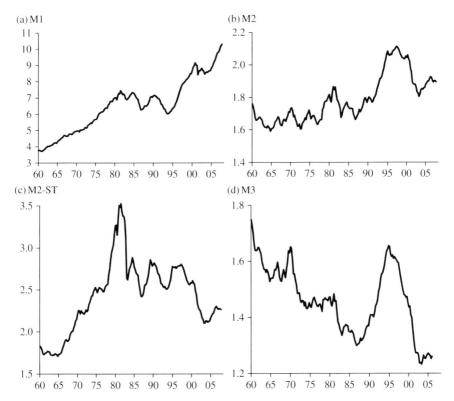

Fig. 2.10 Income velocities of US monetary aggregates
Source: Bloomberg, Federal Reserve Bank of St. Louis; own calculations. – The velocities were calculated by dividing nominal GDP by the stock of money. – M2-ST is M2 minus time deposits. – Period: 1960-Q1 to 2008-Q1 (M3: until 2006-Q1)

Take, for instance, the income velocity of the stock of M1. Its trend pointed upwards from the late 1960s until around 1981-Q1. From then on until the end of 1994, the trend of income velocity of M1 declined, and started rising thereafter. In the period under review, the income velocity of M2 exhibited an *upward trend*, accompanied with a rather strong rise in the early 1990s. By contrast, the income velocity M3 suggests a long-term *downward trend*.

Time-varying income velocities of money do not necessarily indicate *unstable* income velocities of the money. In fact, the crucial question is whether a monetary aggregate's income velocity – or, its reciprocal, the demand for money – is a reliable function of various observable variables such as, for instance, output, prices, risk perception, and interest rates. In that sense, changes in the income velocity would reflect changes in its determining factors.

From the mid-1980s to the early 1990s, the income velocity of M2 was perceived to be reasonably stable and the most reliable of the alternative money measures. M2 and nominal GDP had grown at approximately the same rate over the previous 30 years, suggesting a simple and robust relationship that provided monetary policy makers with an uncomplicated framework for setting monetary targets. This relationship was summarized by the trendless long-run average of M2 velocity up to the end of the 1980s.

Movements of actual income velocity of M2 away from this level were *positively correlated with the opportunity costs* of M2 holdings, measured as the spread between the 3-months Treasury Bills rate and the weighted average returns on deposits included in the stock of M2 (Fig. 2.11). When short-term interest rose, opportunity costs of M2 holdings increased because the rates on components of M2 did not climb as fast as market interest rates.

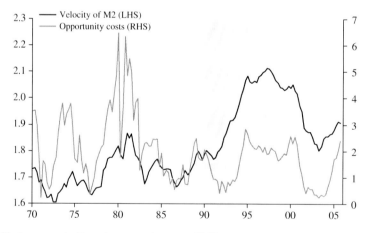

Fig. 2.11 Income velocity and opportunity costs of M2
Source: Federal Reserve Bank of St. Louis, Bloomberg; own calculations. – The income velocity of the monetary aggregate was calculated by dividing nominal GDP by the stock of M2. – Period: 1970-Q1 to 2005-Q4. – Opportunity costs of M2 holdings is calculated by the 3-months Treasury Bills rate minus the weighted average return of deposits included in M2.

In the first half of the 1990, however, income velocity of M2 rose substantially above its long-term trend level, despite a considerable decline in M2 opportunity costs (Hallman & Anderson, 1993). Conventional M2 demand function, which modelled the relationship between M2 and variables such as output and interest rates *began to go off track*. As the link between M2 and GDP deteriorated, the forecasting ability of M2 money demand equations suffered. Friedman and Kuttner (1992) argued that by the early 1990s the relationship between M2 and GDP had weakened,[9] and in July 1993 Federal Reserve Chairman Alan Greenspan reported that: "(...) *at least for the time being, M2 has been downgraded as a reliable indicator of financial conditions in the economy, and no single variable has yet been identified to take its place*."

The difficulties in forecasting M2 spurred a fair amount of research examining whether the deterioration in the M2 equation's forecasting ability was temporary, or whether more fundamental factors – such as flaws in the construction of the opportunity cost, the M2 aggregate, or both – were at work. Carlson and Parrott (1991), and Duca (1992) argued that the existence of troubled US thrift institutions and the length of time it took the Resolution Trust Corporation to resolve the thrifts' difficulties helped explain the weakness in M2.

Duca found that the change in the volume of cumulated deposits at resolved thrifts accounted for a large part of the decline in M2 growth. Orphanides, Reid and Small (1994) and Duca (1995) examined whether some of the weakness in M2 growth reflected a substitution by households away from M2-type deposits and into bond and equity mutual funds. They found that this substitution effect appeared to account for only a small part of the M2 weakness. Collins and Edwards (1994) tried to restore the hitherto stable demand function by redefining M2 (that is including additional instruments such as bond mutual funds in M2).

Carlson and Keen (1995) suggest that preliminary evidence indicates that the relationship between M2, inflation, and output may have stabilized. The prediction errors of the M2 demand model have essentially remained unchanged since 1992. This is consistent with *a permanent one-time shift in the level of M2 relative to income*. Such an outcome would be the case if the forces underlying the deceleration of M2 – such as, for instance, restructuring of credit markets and financial innovation – had worked themselves out.

Koenig (1996a, b) notes that attributing the slowdown in M2 growth to the thrift resolution process had largely been abandoned in dealing with the demand for M2 function. The focus instead has shifted to an examination of the competitiveness problems of financial intermediaries in the face of tighter regulations and stricter capital standards. Koenig proposes an alternative approach by altering the opportunity cost measure to include a long-term Treasury bond rate in the M2 demand function.

---

[9]The work of Estrella and Mishkin (1997) provided further support for this finding.

Lown, Peristiani and Robinson (1999) argue that the financial conditions of depository institutions were a major factor behind the unusual pattern of M2 growth in the early 1990s. By constructing alternative measures of M2 based on banks' and thrifts' capital positions, the authors show that the anomalous behavior of M2 in the early 1990s disappears. After accounting for the effect of capital constrained institutions on M2 growth the unusual behavior of M2 velocity during the early 1990s can be explained, and a more stable relationship between M2 and the ultimate goals of policy can be established. Lown and Peristiani conclude that M2 may contain useful information about economic growth during periods when there are no major disturbances to depository institutions.

Following Carlson and Keen (1995), the income velocity of M2 shall be estimated on the basis of a *level shift variable* which takes account of the *rise in income velocity starting in the early 1990s*. The shift parameter takes the value of 0 from 1970-Q1 to 1989-Q4, then rises linearly to 1 until 1994-Q4 and remains constant thereafter. The estimation result is shown in Fig. 2.12(a), which depicts the actual and estimated income velocity of M2 and the deviation from mean (residual).

Following the adjustment suggested by Carlson and Keen (1995), the historical relation between deviations of income velocity from its long-run trend and M2 opportunity costs can actually be restored (Fig. 2.12b). One implication of this result might be that M2 velocity has stabilized at a higher level, while the short-run relationship between swings in the income velocity of M2 and the opportunity cost of M2 holdings has remained basically unchanged.

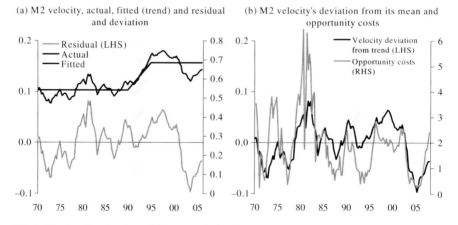

(a) M2 velocity, actual, fitted (trend) and residual and deviation   (b) M2 velocity's deviation from its mean and opportunity costs

Fig. 2.12 Actual and estimated income velocity of M2
Source: Bloomberg; own calculations. – With Carlson and Keen (1995), the trend income velocity is estimated to 0 from 1970-Q1 to 1989-Q4, thereafter rising linearly to 1 until 1992-Q4 and remaining constant at that level. – The regression is: $VM2_t = a + TL_t + \varepsilon_t$, where $VM2$ = income velocity of money, TL takes account of the level shift in the income velocity of M2, ε_t is i.i.d. "white noise" error term. – Period 1968-Q1 to 2005-Q4.

2.4 Money-in-the-Utility Function and Cash-In-Advance Models of Money Demand

An alternative theoretical explanation of why people wish to hold money can be found in money-in-the-utility-function (MUF) and cash-in-advance (CIA) theories of money demand. Both approaches do justice to the notion that people derive *utility* from holding money.

2.4.1 Money-in-the-Utility Function of Money Demand

The utility function of a representative market agent is:

$$U_t = \sum_{s=t}^{\infty} \beta^{s-t} u \left(C_S, \frac{M_S}{P_S} \right),$$ (2.56)

where β is the discount factor, C real consumption, M_t nominal stock of money (acquired at the beginning of period t and held to the end of t), and P is the price level. We assume further that the marginal utility of consumption and real money holdings is positive, and that the utility function is strictly concave.

What is more, it is assumed that in a one-good-only open economy the purchasing power parity (*PPP*) holds:

$$P_t = \varepsilon_t P_t^*,$$ (2.57)

where ε represents the price of foreign currency in domestic currency. Since P^* is assumed to be constant, the domestic price level P is expressed by the exchange rate ε.

Now assume that a market agent's utility depends on consumption and leisure so that:

$$\alpha \log C + (1 - \alpha) \log(\bar{L} - L_t),$$ (2.58)

where $\bar{L} - L_t$ denotes leisure, and α $(1 - \alpha)$ shows the portion of an individual's limited budget that is devoted to consumption (leisure), with $0 \leq \alpha \leq 1$.

Now let us assume that an individual's leisure is an increasing function of real money holdings relative to consumption:

$$\bar{L} - L_t = \bar{L} \left(\frac{M_t/P_t}{C_t} \right)^{\beta},$$ (2.59)

with $0 < \beta < \frac{\alpha}{1 - \alpha}$. When combining equations (2.58) and (2.59), one yields:

$$[\alpha - \beta(1 - \alpha)] \log C_t + \beta(1 - \alpha) \log \frac{M_t}{P_t}.$$ (2.60)

As Eq. (2.60) shows, real money holdings have now entered a market agent's utility function and, as a result, provide an explanation why people may wish to hold money balances.

2.4.2 Cash-in-Advance Models of Money Demand

An alternative way of formulating the demand for money is to assume a *cash-in-advance* (CIA) restriction (Clower, 1967). The CIA model represents a rather extreme micro-founded transaction approach to the demand for money: money demand is determined by the need to make purchases rather than economizing. In a popular variant of the CIA model (Lucas, 1982), agents must acquire currency in period $t - 1$ to cover the consumption purchases they make in period t (Obstfeld & Rogoff, 1999, p. 547). The market agent's challenge is to maximize the utility (U) of consumption (C) according to the following equation:

$$U_t = \sum_{s=t}^{\infty} \beta^{s-t} u(C_s), \qquad (2.61)$$

where β is the discount factor. Money does not enter the utility function. However, Eq. (2.61) is subject to the individual market agent's budget constraint, which is:

$$B_{t+1} + \frac{M_t}{P_t} = (1+r)B_t + \frac{M_{t-1}}{P_t} + Y_t - C_t - T_t, \qquad (2.62a)$$

where B represents holdings of bonds issued by non-residents (we assume, for simplicity, that residents don't issue debt), which are denominated in terms of real output, Y is real income and T are real taxes. The *timing convention* is that M_t is the nominal stock of money which is accumulated during period t and then carried over into $t + 1$.

What is more, the CIA constraint is:

$$M_{t-1} \geq P_t C_t, \qquad (2.62b)$$

that is nominal consumption spending in t must be lower or equal the stock of nominal money held in $t - 1$. What about the interest rate (that is the opportunity cost) of money holdings? If the interest rate is positive, people wouldn't want to hold money in excess of next period's consumption spending, as they could earn a return by investing the money. If the nominal interest rate is zero, the CIA constraint is:

$$M_{t-1} = P_t C_t. \qquad (2.62c)$$

Using (2.62c) to eliminate M_t and M_{t-1} from Eq. (2.62a) yields:

$$B_{t+1} = (1+r)B_t + Y_t - T_t - \frac{P_{t+1}}{P_t} + C_{t+1}; \qquad (2.63)$$

note that the last term on the right hand side of (2.63) is from substitution $M_t/P_t = (P_{t+1}/P_t)C_{t+1}$; its meaning will become clear shortly.

The intertemporal Euler condition can be calculated by maximizing the following function with respect to B_s:

$$U_t = \sum_{s=t}^{\infty} \beta^{s-t} u \left\{ \frac{P_{s-1}}{P_s}[(1+r)B_{s-1} - B_s + Y_{s-1} - T_{s-1}] \right\}. \tag{2.64}$$

Because we have $C_t = M_{t-1}/P_t$, with M_{t-1} given in t, C_t is predetermined – given by past history – in the individual's maximization problem, and therefore not subject to choice on date t.

Differentiating (2.64) with respect to B_s (for $s > t$) yields:

$$\frac{P_{s-1}}{P_s}u'(C_s) = (1+r)\frac{P_s}{P_{s+1}}\beta u'(C_{s+1}). \tag{2.65}$$

Now we take recourse to the *Fisher parity*, which expresses the nominal interest rate as the real interest rate plus inflation:

$$1 + i_{s+1} = (1+r)(P_{s+1}/P_s). \tag{2.66}$$

Dividing both sides of (2.65) by $1 + r$ and using (2.66) yields:

$$\frac{u'(C_s)}{1 + i_s} = (1+r)\beta\frac{u'(C_{s+1})}{1 + i_{s+1}}. \tag{2.67}$$

According to Eq. (2.67) the additional cost for money held between $s - 1$ and s is i_s. The cost is i_{s+1} for money balances held between s and $s + 1$. Note that consumption involves an additional cost, as the agent component must wait one full period between the date he converts bonds or output into cash and the date he can consume. In that sense the nominal interest rate acts as a consumption tax. In a stationary equilibrium (constant money growth), nominal interest rates and the implied consumption tax are constant, and Eq. (2.67) would equal the usual Euler equation (2.64).

It is important to note that the money demand equation for this kind of CIA model is determined by consumption, rather than by total income:

$$\frac{M_{t-1}}{P_t} = C_t. \tag{2.68}$$

In this simple CIA model, anticipated inflation does not affect money demand (as it would, for instance, in Friedman's theory). As this is theoretically unappealing, Lucas and Stokey (1987) developed a model which combines the features of the CIA and the MUF approach. Cash needs to be held to finance consumption purchases, but the agent has some flexibility in allocating consumption between goods subject to the CIA constraint (*cash goods*) and goods that can be purchased in exchange for securities (*credit goods*). This feature of the CIA constraint generates a non-zero interest rate elasticity of real money demand.

A simple variant of the CIA model as put forward by Helpman (1981) and Lucas (1982) gives consumers the opportunity to use cash acquired in period t for consumption later in period t. The producers of goods who receive the cash must hold it between periods. The CIA constraint (2.62b) is then:

$$M_t \geq P_t C_t. \tag{2.69}$$

Here, inflation does not affect consumption decisions. However, the model holds that inflation influences the budget constraints of *producers*. The latter would hold money between periods in proportion to current sales, so that inflation becomes a production tax rather than a consumption tax in this model.[10]

2.5 Estimating Money Demand Functions for the US and the Euro Area

2.5.1 Money Demand in the US

During the 1980s, M2 became the primary intermediate target of US monetary policy. Since the early 1990s, however, the reliability of money measures as targets or indicators of monetary policy has been called into question. In 1993 the FOMC "downgraded" the role of M2. Though the "traditional" M2 relation broke down somewhere around 1990, there is some evidence that the disturbance might be a *permanent upward shift in M2 velocity*, which began in the early 1990s and was largely over by 1994. In terms of the monetary aggregates MZM and M2M, Carlson, Hoffman, Keen, and Rasche (2000) found strong evidence of a stable money demand relationships through the 1990s.

To revisit the issue, the long-run demand function for US monetary aggregates can be formulated as:

$$m_t - p_t = \beta_0 + \beta_1 y_t - \beta_2 i_t^{opportunity} + \beta_3 dum_t + \varepsilon_t, \tag{2.70}$$

where m_t is the stock of money, p_t is the GDP deflator, y_t is real output (all variables in natural logarithms). The opportunity costs of money holdings is the difference between the 3-months money market rate and the yield of money included in M2:

$$i_t^{opportunity} = \ln(1 + i_t^{3-mths}/100) - \ln(1 + i_t^{M2\ own\ rate}/100). \tag{2.71}$$

Finally, *dum* is a dummy variable, taking the value of 0 from 1968-Q1 to 1989-Q4, then *dum* rises linearly to 1 until 1994-Q1 and remains at that level thereafter

---

[10]See in this context also the work of Aschauer and Greenwood (1983).

	Sample periods			
	1970-Q4 to 1989-Q4	1970-Q4 to 1995-Q4	1970-Q4 to 2000-Q4	1970-Q4 to 2005-Q4
	I. Long-run relation			
y_t	−8.862	−0.872	−0.877	−0.862
	(0.014)	(0.012)	(0.022)	(0.045)
$i_t^{opportunity}$	3.255	3.264	4.177	7.313
	(0.296)	(0.275)	(0.485)	(0.905)
Dum	–	0.139	0.115	0.089
		(0.011)	(0.014)	(0.030)
Constant	3.901	3.979	4.014	3.826
Unit root tests:				
Lag 2	−3.02 [0.03]	−3.42 [0.01]	−3.09 [0.02]	−2.89 [0.04]
Lag 4	−3.21 [0.02]	−3.63 [0.00]	−3.09 [0.02]	−2.95 [0.04]
Lag 6	−4.72 [0.00]	−5.25 [0.00]	−4.15 [0.00]	−3.79 [0.00]
	II. ECM			
Lags	2	2	2	2
EC_{t-1}	−0.334	−0.300	−0.158	−0.055
R^2	0.61	0.61	0.57	0.51

Fig. 2.13 Long-run demand for US real M2, *conventional*
Source: Federal Reserve Bank of St. Louis, Thomson Financial; own calculations. *Legend*: The price level is approximated by the GDP deflator, y_t is real output (in natural *ln*). The opportunity costs of money holdings is the difference between the 3-months money market rate and the yield of money included in M2: $i_t^{opportunity} = \ln(1 + i_t^{3-mths}/100) - \ln(1 + i_t^{M2\ own\ rate}/100)$; *dum* is a dummy variable, taking the value of 0 from 1970-Q4 to 1989-Q4, then *dum* rises linearly to 1 until 1994-Q4, and remains constant at that level thereafter. – *EC* represents the error correction term of the first difference equation. – Lags in quarters. – (.) are standard errors, [.] *p*-values. – Results of the *ADF*-tests.

(Carlson, Hoffman, Keen, & Rasche, 2000). Figure 2.13 shows the cointegration results following the Johansen methodology for four sample periods.

The Johansen Procedure – an Overview

The finding that many macroeconomic time series may contain a *unit root* has encouraged the development of the theory of non-stationary time series analysis. Engle and Granger (1987) pointed out that a linear combination of two or more non-stationary series may be stationary. If such a stationary linear combination exists, the non-stationary time series are *cointegrated*. The stationary linear combination is called the cointegrating equation and may be interpreted as a long-run equilibrium relationship which exists among the variables under review.

The purpose of the cointegration test is to determine whether a group of non-stationary series are cointegrated or not. The presence of a cointegrating relation forms the basis of the vector error correction model (VEM). To outline the Johansen (1988, 1991, 1995) und Johansen und Juselius (1990) cointegreation technique, we start with a vector autoregressive (VAR) model of order p:

$$y_t = A_1 y_{t-1} + \ldots + A_p y_{t-p} + Bx_t + \varepsilon_t \qquad (2.72)$$

where y_t is a vector of non-stationary $I(1)$ variables, x_t is a d-vector of deterministic variables, and ε_t is a vector of innovations. We can rewrite the VAR as:

$$\Delta y_t = \Pi y_{t-1} + \sum_{i=1}^{p-1} \Gamma_i \Delta y_{t-i} + Bx_t + \varepsilon_t, \qquad (2.73)$$

where

$$\Pi = \sum_{i=1}^{p} A_t - I \text{ and } \Gamma_i = - \sum_{j=i+1}^{p} A_j. \qquad (2.74)$$

Granger's representation theorem asserts that if the coefficient matrix Π has reduced rank (such that $r < k$), then there exist $k \times r$ matrices α and β each with rank r such that $\Pi = \alpha \beta'$ and $\beta' y_t$ is $I(0)$. r is the number of cointegrating relations (the rank) and each column of β is the cointegrating vector. The elements of α are the adjustment parameters in the VEC model. Johansen's method is to estimate the Π from an unrestricted VAR and to test whether we can reject the restrictions implied by the reduced rank of Π.

To determine the number of cointegrating relations conditional on the assumptions made about the trend, one can proceed sequentially from $r = 0$ to $r = k - 1$ until one fails to reject the null hypothesis. The trace statistic tests the null hypothesis of r cointegrating relations against the alternative of k cointegrating relations, where k is the number of endogenous variables, for $r = 0, 1, \ldots, k - 1$. The alternative of k cointegrating relations corresponds to the case where none of the series has a unit root and a stationary VAR may be specified in terms of the levels of all of the series. The trace statistic for the null hypothesis of r cointegrating relations is computed as:

$$LR_{tr}(r|k) = -T \sum_{i=r+1}^{k} \log(1 - \lambda_i) \qquad (2.75)$$

where λ_i is the i-th largest eigenvalue of the Π matrix. The maximum eigenvalue statistic shows the results of testing the null hypothesis of r cointegrating relations against the alternative of $r + 1$ cointegrating relations. This test statistic is computed as:

$$LR_{\max}(r|r+1) \qquad = \qquad -T\log(1+\lambda_{r+1})$$
$$= LR_{tr}(r|k) - LR_{tr}(r|r+1) \qquad (2.76)$$
$$\text{for } r = 0, 1, \ldots, k-1.$$

The estimated coefficients of the long-run demand for real M2 exhibit economically *plausible signs and magnitudes*. For all sample periods, the income elasticity
of money demand remains in a relatively narrow band of between 0.88 and 0.86. The
variability of the interest rate elasticity is much stronger, though, varying between
3.26 for the period 1970-Q4 to 1989-Q4 and 7.31 for the total period under review.
The results of the ADF-tests suggest that the null hypothesis of a unit root in the
residuals can be rejected at standard levels for all estimations. That said, the findings seem to indicate that there is a long-run relation between real money demand,
real output and the opportunity costs of money holdings in the US. Also, the error
correction terms (*EC*) are statistically significant and have a negative sign, suggesting that deviations of real money holdings from the level suggested by the long-run
equation are corrected over time.

Figure 2.14(a) displays the EC terms of the estimation results for the four sample
periods. As can be seen, the EC terms fluctuate around the zero line, reflecting the
fact that real M2 holdings tend to deviate temporarily from the long-run equilibrium
value. What is more, the longer the sample periods are for which the coefficients
were estimated, the higher is the volatility of the EC term. This could suggest that
in the 1990s, in addition to the long-run determinants of money demand, numerous
additional factors (*shocks*) might have affected money demand.

In a second step, the demand for real M2 balances is analysed using a different
definition of the price level. In fact, the price level was calculated as a weighted

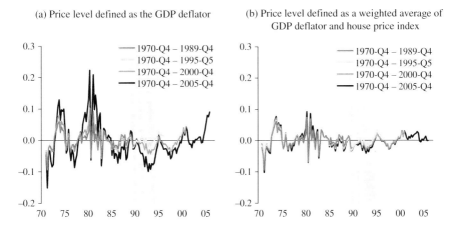

Fig. 2.14   Deviation of US real M2 holdings from equilibrium
Source: Federal Reserve Bank of St. Louis, Thomson Financial; own calculations.

	Sample periods			
	1970-Q4 to 1989-Q4	1970-Q4 to 1995-Q4	1970-Q4 to 2000-Q4	1970-Q4 to 2005-Q4
	I.Long-run relation			
y_t	−0.779	−0.799	−0.806	−0.797
	(0.024)	(0.019)	(0.019)	(0.021)
$i_t^{opportunity}$	3.522	3.458	3.767	4.292
	(0.452)	(0.370)	(0.392)	(0.388)
Dum	−	0.141	0.131	0.126
		(0.016)	(0.012)	(0.014)
Constant	4.505	4.676	4.732	4.646
Unit root tests:				
Lag 2	−3.96 [0.00]	−4.11 [0.00]	−3.98 [0.00]	−4.17 [0.00]
Lag 4	−3.43 [0.01]	−3.50 [0.01]	−3.41 [0.01]	−3.65 [0.00]
Lag 6	−4.59 [0.00]	−4.75 [0.00]	−4.63 [0.00]	−4.81 [0.00]
	II.ECM			
Lags	2		2	2
EC_{t-1}	−0.193	−0.168	−0.146	−0.116
R^2	0.52	0.54	0.54	0.49

Fig. 2.15 Long-run demand for US real M2, *amended*
Source: Federal Reserve Bank of St. Louis, Thomson Financial; own calculations. *Legend*: The price level is the weighted average of the GDP deflator (80%) and the US housing price index (20%), y_t is real output (in natural *ln*). The opportunity costs of money holdings is the difference between the 3-months money market rate and the yield of money included in M2: $i_t^{opportunity} = \ln(1 + i_t^{3-mths}/100) - \ln(1 + i_t^{M2\ own\ rate}/100)$; *dum* is a dummy variable, taking the value of 0 from 1970-Q4 to 1989-Q4, the *dum* rises linearly to 1 until 1994-Q4, and remains constant at that level thereafter. – *EC* represents the error correction term of the first difference equation. – Lags in quarters. – (.) are standard errors, [.] *p*-values. – Results of the *ADF*-tests.

average of the GDP deflator and a US wide *housing* price index. The underlying idea is that market agents might hold nominal M2 balances in relation to a price level much broader defined than the GDP deflator (or, for that matter, the consumer price index). The estimation results are shown in Fig. 2.15.

As in the conventional estimation, *income and interest elasticity* of money demand have *plausible signs and magnitudes*. Especially in the period 1970-Q4 to 2005-Q4 the interest elasticity rises only slightly compared to the sub-periods and the conventional estimation results. Again, the *EC* terms are statistically significant, suggesting that money holding disequilibria are reduced over time.

Figure 2.14(b) shows the EC terms for the estimates above. The *volatility of the EC terms is much smaller than in the conventional estimates*. With the parameters of the long-run demand function for real M2 being relatively stable for all sub-periods under consideration, it seems that using a weighted price level might be a promising approach to formulate and (re-)establish a stable demand for money function in the US.

Stock Prices in the Demand for Money Function

To highlight the long-run relation between stock prices, dividend yields and central bank short-term interest rates, the arbitrage model of Cassola and Morana (2002) will be outlined. It can form a theoretical framework for integrating the stock market into the demand for money theory.

Money Demand

The demand for real money, rm, is defined as a function of output, y, and a vector of relative asset returns:

$$rm_t = \phi_1 y_t - \phi' s_t, \tag{2.77}$$

where s_t is a vector of yields of alternative assets and ϕ is a vector of parameters. It is assumed that there is a stationary combination of the yield spreads:

$$\phi' s_t = \varepsilon_{rm,t} \sim I(0) \text{ where } \varepsilon_{rm,t} = \rho_1 \varepsilon_{rm,t-1} + \upsilon_{s,t} \text{ is an AR(1)}$$
with $\rho_1 < 1$ and $\upsilon_{s,t}$ white noise.

Term structure of interest rates

The first arbitrage relationship is between short- and long-term yields:

$$l_t = i_t + \phi_l + \varepsilon_{l,t}, \tag{2.78}$$

where $\varepsilon_{l,t} = \rho_2 \varepsilon_{l,t-1} + \upsilon_{l,t}$ with $\rho_2 < 1$ and $\upsilon_{l,t}$ white noise. The expectation theory of the term structure of interest rates can be written in logarithmic form as:

$$l_t = \frac{1}{n} \sum_{j=0}^{n-1} E_t \left[i_{t+j} \right] + \phi_l, \tag{2.79}$$

where l_t is expressed as an average of expected one period yields, $E_t \left[i_{t+j} \right]$, ϕ_l is a term premium and n is the maturity of the bond. Substracting i_t from both sides yields:

$$l_t - i_t = \frac{1}{n} \sum_{j=0}^{n-1} E_t \left[i_{t+j} - i_t \right] + \phi_l \text{ with } \frac{1}{n} \sum_{j=0}^{n-1} E_t \left[i_{t+j} - i_t \right] = \varepsilon_{l,t}. \tag{2.80}$$

Fisher Parity

The second arbitrage relationship is the Fisher parity. It links the long-term asset return, i, with the short-term interest rate:

$$i_t = \phi_{fp} + \phi_2 \pi_t + \varepsilon_{i,t}, \tag{2.81}$$

where ϕ_{fp} represents the real short-term interest rate plus the inflation risk premium and $\varepsilon_{i,t} = \rho_3 \varepsilon_{i,t-1} + \upsilon_{i,t}$ with $\rho_3 < 1$ and $\upsilon_{i,t}$ white noise.

The real asset return can be formulated as:

$$1 + \rho_t = (1 + \rho) \exp(\varepsilon_{\rho,t}). \tag{2.82}$$

The Fisher parity for the short-term interest rate can be written as:

$$1 + R_t = (1 + \rho_{t+1})(1 + \pi^*_{t+1}) \exp(\varepsilon_{rp,t+1}). \tag{2.83}$$

R_t is the gross nominal return on a short-term investment for the period t to $t+1$. $\varepsilon_{rp,t} = \rho_4 \varepsilon_{rp,t-1} + \upsilon_{rp,t}$ is the error term reflecting fluctuations in the real return and inflation with $\rho_4 < 1$ and $\upsilon_{rp,t}$ white noise.

The expected inflation is given by:

$$(1 + \pi^*_t) = (1 + \pi_t) \exp(\upsilon_{\pi^*,t}), \tag{2.84}$$

where $\upsilon_{\pi^*,t}$ is a stationary process.

Inserting (2.82) and (2.84) in (2.83) yields:

$$1 + R_t = (1 + \rho)(1 + \pi_{t+1}) \exp(\varepsilon_{rp,t+1} + \varepsilon_{\rho,t+1} + \upsilon_{\pi^*,t+1}). \tag{2.85}$$

For the long-term asset return, one yields the log-linear approximation:

$$i_t = \rho + \varepsilon_{rp,t} + \pi_{t+1} + \varepsilon_{\rho,t+1} + \upsilon_{\pi^*,t+1}, \tag{2.86}$$

which actually represents Eq. (2.81) if the unity coefficient on actual inflation is dropped. If (2.81) is inserted in (2.79) one yields:

$$l_t = \phi_{fp} + \phi_l + \phi_2 \pi_t + \varepsilon_{i,t} + \varepsilon_{i,t}, \tag{2.87}$$

which represents the long-run Fisher parity.

Stock Market and Output

The third arbitrage relation links the stock market to real output:

$$f_t = \phi_f + \phi_3 y_t + \varepsilon_{f,t}, \tag{2.88}$$

where f_t is the log real stock market capitalization and $\varepsilon_{f,t} = \rho_5 \varepsilon_{f,t-1} + \upsilon_{f,t}$ with $\rho_5 < 1$ and $\upsilon_{f,t}$ white noise. The present value model is:

$$F_t = E_t \left[\sum_{j=1}^{\infty} (1 + \upsilon)^{-j} D_{t+j} \right], \tag{2.89}$$

where F_t is the real stock market capitalization, υ is the real risk-adjusted discount rate and D_t is the real dividend paid at time t. Assuming a constant rate of growth for dividends (g), the Gordon (1962) growth model is:

$$F_t = \frac{1 + g}{\upsilon - g} D_t. \tag{2.90}$$

If dividends are constant over time, the formula can be reduced to:

$$\frac{D_t}{F_t} = \upsilon, \tag{2.91}$$

where the dividend yield D_t/F_t equals the real risk-adjusted rate of return on capital.

The relation between real dividends and output is:

$$D_t = kY_t^{\phi_3} \exp(\varepsilon_{d,t}), \tag{2.92}$$

with $\varepsilon_{d,t} = \rho_6 \varepsilon_{d,t-1} + \upsilon_{d,t}$ with $\rho_6 < 1$ and $\upsilon_{d,t}$ white noise, so that Eq. (2.88) can be written as:

$$f_t = \ln \left(\frac{1 + g}{\upsilon - g} \right) + \ln k + \phi_3 y_t + \varepsilon_{d,t}. \tag{2.93}$$

Equations (2.86) and (2.93) have important implications for the relation between the bond and stock markets. If dividends are assumed to be constant the equation above can be written as:

$$f_t - \phi_3 y_t = -\ln \upsilon + \ln k + \varepsilon_{d,t}. \tag{2.94}$$

The long-term real yield is:

$$l_t - \phi_2 \pi_t = \rho + \varepsilon_{rp,t} + \varepsilon_{\rho,t} + \phi_l + \upsilon_{\pi^*,t} + \varepsilon_{l,t}. \tag{2.95}$$

The relation between stock prices and the return on capital would be:

$$-\ln \upsilon + \ln k + \varepsilon_{d,t} \approx \rho + \varepsilon_{rp,t} + \upsilon_{\pi^*,t} + \varepsilon_{l,t}. \tag{2.96}$$

These relations suggest that there should be a stable linkage between the stock market, inflation, long- and short-term interest rates as set by the central bank.

Source: Cassola and Morana (2002).

2.5.2 Euro Area Money Demand 1980-Q1 to 2001-Q4

Empirical evidence supports the *existence of a stable long-run relationship* between money and output in the euro area (Bruggemann, Donati, & Warne, 2003). In fact, there is evidence that broad money demand has been more stable in the euro area than in other large economies (Calza & Sousa, 2003). First, some of the factors affecting money demand stability outside the euro area were country-specific. Second, the impact of financial innovation was relatively small in the euro area. Third, money demand in the euro area may have been more stable because it is an aggregation of money demand functions in individual countries. Figure 2.16 provides a selection of studies of the euro area demand function for broad money.

A first impression on the properties of the demand for money in the euro area can be derived from taking a look at the *income velocity of M3* (Fig. 2.17(a)). In the period 1980-Q1 to the end of 2001 a linear function approximated the trend decline of M3 income velocity quite well. Thereafter, velocity appears to fall much stronger, indicating that money supply growth was markedly higher than nominal income growth. Figure 2.17(b) shows the deviations of actual income velocity from two trend lines, one calculated for 1980-Q1 to 2001-Q4 and one calculated for 1980-Q4 to 2005-Q4.

Given possible interdependencies among the variables which are typically seen as representing the explanatory variables of the long-run demand function for money, the latter cannot be estimated as a single equation. In fact, the demand for money should be estimated with a cointegration approach (Johansen, 1995). The individual equations of the system are as follows:

$$m_t - p_t = \beta_{0,1} + \beta_{1,1} y_t + \beta_{2,1} i_t^l + \beta_{3,1} i_t^s + \beta_{4,1} i_t^0 + \beta_{5,1} \pi_t + \varepsilon_{t,1} \tag{2.97}$$

$$i_t^s = \beta_{0,2} + \beta_{2,2} i_t^l + \beta_{4,2} i_t^o + \beta_{5,2} \pi_t + \varepsilon_{t,2} \tag{2.98}$$

Authors	Sample	Money demand
Brand & Cassola (2000)	1980:1 – 1999:3	$m_t - p_t = 1.221 y_t - 1.61 i_t^l$
Coenen & Vega (2001)	1980:1 – 1998:4	$m_t - p_t = 1.125 \, y_t - 0.865 \, (i_t^l - i_t^s) - 1.512\pi_t$
Funke (2001)	1980:3 – 1988:4	$m_t - p_t = 1.21 \, y_t - 0.3 i_t^s + 0.06 \, D86$
Brand et al. (2002)	1980:1 – 2001:2	$m_t - p_t = 1.34 \, y_t - 0.45 i_t^l$
Golinelli & Pastorello (2002)	1980:3 – 1997:4	$m_t - p_t = 1.373 \, y_t - 0.68 i_t^l$
Kontolemis (2002)	1980:1 – 2001:3	$m_t - p_t = 1.373 \, y_t - 0.451 i_t^s$
Holtemöller (2004)	1984:1 – 2001:4	$m_t - p_t = 1.275 \, y_t - 0.751 i_t^l$
Müller (2003)	1984:1 – 2000:4	$m_t - p_t = 1.57 \, y_t - 2.22 i_t^l + 1.87 i_t^s$
Bruggemann et al. (2003)	1981:3 – 2001:4	$m_t - p_t = 1.38 \, y_t - 0.81 i_t^s + 1.31 i_t^o$
Dreger & Wolters (2006)	1983:1 – 2004:4	$m_t - p_t = 1.24 \, y_t + 5.16\pi_t$

Fig. 2.16 Examples of euro area money demand studies
Source: Nautz and Ruth (2005, p. 9) – Description of the Variables: m: (log) nominal money supply, p (log) price level, y (log) gross domestic product (GDP), i_t^l long-term nominal interest rate, i_t^s short-term nominal interest rate, i^o own rate of M3 (see Bruggemann et al., 2003, p. 37), π_t annualized quarterly inflation (derived from GDP deflator; see Coenen & Vega 2001, p. 731), $D86$ dummy variable (see Funke, 2001, p. 705; also Coenen & Vega, 2001, p. 733)

The first equation represents the demand function for real balances ($m_t - p_t$), depending on real income (y_t), the long- and short-rate (that is i_t^l and i_t^s, respectively), the M3 own rate (i_t^o), and inflation (π_t, that is the first difference of the logarithm of the quarterly GDP deflator, annualized). The second equation relates the short-term interest rate to the long-term interest rate, the M3 own rate and inflation; combined the second equation captures the *Fisher parity* and the *term structure of interest rates* (Belke and Polleit, 2006). The time series are shown in Fig. 2.18.

Combining the variables in a vector $X_t = (m_t - p_t, y_t, i_t^l, i_t^s, i_t^o, \pi_t)'$, the model can be formalized as $\hat{\beta}' X_t = \varepsilon_t$, or:

$$\hat{\beta}' X_t = \begin{bmatrix} -1 & \beta_{1,1} & 0 & \beta_{3,1} & \beta_{4,2} & 0 \\ 0 & 0 & \beta_{2,2} & -1 & \beta_{4,2} & \beta_{5,2} \end{bmatrix} \begin{bmatrix} m_t - p_t \\ y_t \\ i_t^l \\ i_t^s \\ i_t^o \\ \pi_t \end{bmatrix} = \begin{bmatrix} \varepsilon_{t,1} \\ \varepsilon_{t,2} \end{bmatrix}$$

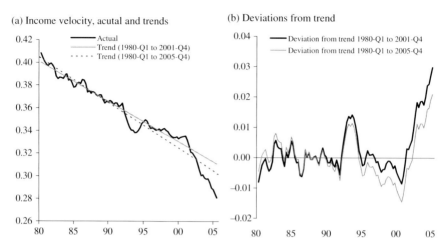

Fig. 2.17 Euro area M3 income, actual and trend, and deviations from trend
Source: ECB, Thomson Financial; own estimates. Income velocity was calculated by substracting the stock of M3 from nominal GDP (all variables in logarithms). Period: 1980-Q1 to 2005-Q4.

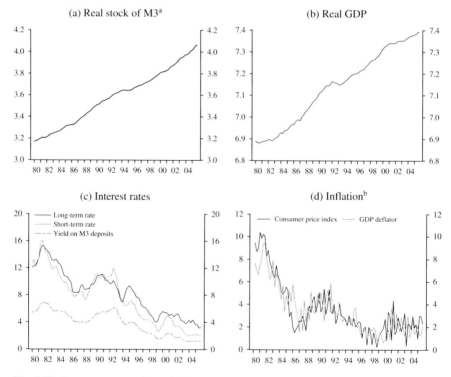

Fig. 2.18 Euro area money demand, data overview
Source: ECB, Thomson Financial. [a]Logarithm of the stock of M3 minus logarithm of GDP deflator. [b]First difference of the log of the quarterly consumer price index and GDP deflator, annualized. Period: 1980-Q1 to 2005-Q4.

For the period 1980-Q1 to 2001-Q4, the cointegration analysis between real stock of money, GDP, long- and short-term interest rates, the M3 own rate and inflation yields the following results:

$$
\hat{\beta}' X_t = \begin{bmatrix} 1 & \underset{(0.04)}{-1.35} & 0 & \underset{(0.0001)}{0.004} & 0 & 0 \\ 0 & 0 & \underset{0.10}{0.28} & 1 & \underset{(0.15)}{-1.71} & \underset{(0.10)}{-0.81} \end{bmatrix} \begin{bmatrix} m_t - p_t \\ y_t \\ i_t^l \\ i_t^s \\ i_t^o \\ \pi_t \end{bmatrix}
$$

Chi-squared $(4) = 0.68$ [0.88]; standard errors in brackets.

Examining the first cointegration relation (that is the first row), which resembles a long-run money demand relation, one finds that the estimated coefficient on output is 1.35. It is greater than unity and of a similar magnitude indicated by earlier studies on euro area money demand (Brand & Cassola, 2000; Golinelli & Pastorello, 2002; Calza, Gartner, and Sousa, 2001). The demand on real money holdings increases (declines) if the short-term interest rate declines (rises), as suggested by the coefficient 0.004. Turning to the second vector (that is the second row), the coefficient on the long-term interest rate (0.28) suggests that long-term interest rates rise when short-term rates decline and vice versa. What is more, the yield on M3 holdings and inflation move up (down) when short-term rates fall (rise).

Overall, real money, real income, long- and short-term rates, the M3 own yield and inflation are trending together and form two long-run, or steady state, relations, where the *first* vector can be interpreted as the *long-run money demand*. Figure 2.19(a) and (b) show the residuals of the cointegration relations. The *ADF*-tests suggest that the null hypothesis of a unit root in the residuals can be rejected.

Alternatively, a money demand system might be modelled taking into account stock markets. In this case, a three equations system might be formulated:

$$m_t - p_t = \beta_{0,1} + \beta_{1,1} y_t + \beta_{2,1} i_t^l + \beta_{3,1} i_t^s + \beta_{4,1} \pi_t + \beta_{5,1} s + \varepsilon_{t,1} \qquad (2.99)$$

$$i_t^l = \beta_{0,2} + \beta_{3,2} i_t^s + \beta_{4,2} \pi_t + \varepsilon_{t,2} \qquad (2.100)$$

$$s_t = \beta_{0,3} + \beta_{1,3} y_t + \varepsilon_{t,3}. \qquad (2.101)$$

The first equation represents the long-run demand function for real balances $(m_t - p_t)$, depending on real income (y_t), long- and short-rates (that is i_t^l and i_t^s, respectively), inflation π_t (first difference of quarterly changes in the GDP deflator, annualized) and real stock performance, s_t. The second equation shows the combined Fisher parity and the term structure of interest rates. The third equation relates real stock market performance with real GDP. The result of the cointegration analysis for the period 1980-Q1 to 2001-Q4 is shown below:

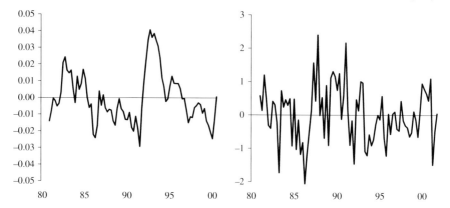

(a) Residual of the long-run demand function for real M3 holdings

(b) Residual of the combined test of the (i) term structure of interest rates and (ii) Fisher parity

Fig. 2.19 –Estimated cointegration relations for euro area M3 money demand over the period 1981-Q1 to 2001-Q4
Source: ECB; Thomson Financial; own calculations. – The *ADF*-tests reject the null hypothesis of a unit root in the residuals at the 5- and 1-percent level, respectively.

$$\begin{bmatrix} 1 & \underset{(0.02)}{-1.380} & \underset{(0.00)}{0.012} & 0 & 0 & 0 \\ 0 & 0 & 1 & \underset{(0.06)}{-0.197} & \underset{(0.09)}{-0.266} & 0 \\ 0 & 1 & 0 & 0 & 0 & \underset{(0.01)}{-0.166} \end{bmatrix} \begin{bmatrix} m_t - p_t \\ y_t \\ i_t^l \\ i_t^s \\ \pi_t \\ s_t \end{bmatrix}$$

Chi-squared $(5) = 6.04$ [0.19]; standard errors in brackets.

The first vector might be interpreted as the long-run demand for real balances. The income elasticity is 1.38, while money demand responds negatively to rises in long-term interest rates. A long-run relation can be established between long- and short-term rates and inflation, as represented by the second vector. The third vector relates real output positively to real stock prices. The results of the difference equations – which estimate changes in real M3 holdings as a function of lagged changes in the other variables of the cointegration system (VAR in first differences) – are

	$\Delta(m_t - p_t)$	$\Delta(y_t)$	$\Delta(i_t^l)$	$\Delta(i_t^s)$	$\Delta(\pi_t)$	$\Delta(s_t)$
Lags	2	2	2	2	2	2
$ECT1_{t-1}$	−0.164	0.104	−1.944	−21.15	19.93	0.710
	(−3.74)	(1.90)	(−0.39)	(−2.87)	(1.78)	(1.12)
$ECT2_{t-1}$	−0.000	0.001	−0.333	0.112	0.310	−0.040
	(−0.33)	(1.09)	(−2.75)	(0.62)	(1.12)	(−1.45)
$ECT3_{t-1}$	0.035	−0.076	5.626	5.918	−11.64	0.639
	(1.52)	(−2.61)	(2.15)	(1.50)	(−1.95)	(1.07)
R2	0.45	0.28	0.27	0.31	0.47	0.26

Fig. 2.20   Results of the first difference estimates, 1980-Q1 to 2001-Q4; *t*-values in brackets

shown in Fig. 2.20. The error term of the long-run demand function of real M3, $ECT1_{t-1}$, has a negative sign, implying that excess real money holdings are reduced over time.

2.5.3 Euro Area Money Demand 1980-Q1 to 2006-Q1

Since 2001, euro area M3 growth has been constantly above the ECB's $4\frac{1}{2}$ percent reference value. Hitherto stable standard money demand models fail to explain the observed monetary developments. One explanation for this phenomenon claims that an environment of increased macroeconomic uncertainty in conjunction with low asset yields has enhanced the preference for liquidity. Greiber and Lemke (2005) produced indicators (mainly based on financial market data) for measuring *investor uncertainty*. They show that uncertainty helps to explain the increase in euro area M3 over the period 2001 to 2004. In particular, a cointegrated money demand relationship can be established for samples that include these periods.

Euro Area Money Demand Stability Reconsidered

While a wide range of recent studies deals with the money demand relationship in the euro area, it has been analyzed almost exclusively on the basis of *aggregate* euro area data. Most of these studies exclusively use synthetic data for the pre-EMU period,[11] but the more recent papers add data on the first years of EMU.[12] Overviews are presented by Golinelli and Pastorello (2002) and Brand, Gerdesmeier & Roffia (2002).

Almost all papers find euro area money demand to be stable until the EMU started in 1999, even though they differ in many respects (sample, variables, estimation procedure, geographic area, aggregation method). A further outstanding result for studies with sample periods ending prior to 1999 is the higher stability of the area-wide compared to the country-specific money demand functions. It is, however, not clear how this can be explained properly; whether it is just a "statistical artefact" (Müller & Hahn, 2001), the positive influence of the traditionally stable German money demand (Calza & Sousa, 2003), or the neutralization of currency substitution movements across the union. On the other hand, as argued by Müller and Hahn (2001) and Hayo (1999), it is not clear whether the better stability properties of aggregate euro area money demand have persisted since the introduction of the euro.

---

[11] See, among others, Gottschalk (1999), Hayo (1999), Bruggemann (2000), Clausen and Kim (2000), Coenen and Vega (2001), Funke (2001), Müller and Hahn (2001), and Golinelli and Pastorello (2002).

[12] See, for instance, Brand and Cassola (2000), Calza, Gerdemeier and Levy (2001), Kontolemis (2002), Bruggemann et al. (2003), Greiber and Lemke (2005) and Carstensen (2006).

The stability issue has received particular attention since M3 growth started to accelerate in 2001. Due to the strong M3 growth, Kontolemis (2002) finds evidence for money demand instability in the third quarter of 2001, the last observation in his sample. In a comprehensive stability analysis Bruggemann, Donati & Warne (2003) apply the fluctuation and Nyblom–type stability tests proposed by Hansen and Johansen (1999) and obtain mixed results but finally conclude that there are some specifications of long-run money demand that seem to be stable.

This result is challenged by Carstensen (2006) and Greiber and Lemke (2005). They argue that conventional money demand functions become unstable during the recent period of strong M3 growth and should be augmented with measures of *macroeconomic or financial uncertainty*, which account for the observation reported by the ECB (2003) that, following the terrorist attacks of September 2001 and the burst of the new economy bubble, large funds were reallocated into safe and liquid assets that are part of M3. However, these augmented specifications seem to be unable to explain the increase in M3 growth since the middle of 2004 (ECB, 2005; Alves, Marques, & Sousa, 2006). In contrast, Dreger and Wolters (2006) are still able to find a stable money demand function using data until the end of 2004. Therefore, the question whether long-run money demand is stable in the euro area still remains unsettled.

The focus on aggregate euro area data and euro area wide money demand stability may not be surprising since the ECB should be exclusively concerned with economic developments in the euro area as a whole. However, a disaggregate analysis on the basis of individual country data can lead to additional important insights both for EMU member countries and for the euro area as a whole (Belke & Gros, 2007; Belke & Heine, 2006). As concerns the individual EMU member countries and their central banks, they should be interested in the timely detection of national imbalances. Assuming that monetary aggregates and, in particular, money overhangs which are defined as the deviation of actual M3 from the money demand equilibrium, carry important information with respect to the state of the monetary and financial system, they should closely track the evolution of these quantities at the country level. This is ever more important if one follows Milton Friedman's dictum that inflation is always and everywhere a monetary phenomenon because then money overhangs indicate future inflationary pressure for the respective country.

But a sensible measure of excess money is not necessarily invariant to the country of interest. This obviously holds for the 4.5% reference value that was derived by the ECB from aggregate developments in the euro area and, thus, disregards specific developments in the individual member countries. This may also hold true for more elaborate measures like the money overhang because the monetary and banking systems, the preferences of households and, hence, the money demand functions are probably not equal across countries. As concerns the euro area as a whole, there are at least three reasons why national developments should be of interest. First, for the optimal conduct of monetary policy it may prove beneficial to use national information if the national monetary transmission mechanisms are asymmetric (Belke & Heine, 2006; de Grauwe & Senegas, 2003). Second, and related to the first point, inflation forecasts constructed by aggregating country-specific models outperform inflation forecasts constructed by using aggregate euro area data only (Marcellino, Stock, & Watson, 2003). Similarly, country specific inflation helps to explain area wide inflation even after controlling for aggregate macroeconomic information (Beck, Hubrich, & Marcellino, 2006; Carstensen, Hagen, Hossfeld, & Salazar Neaves, 2008). This implies that if monetary developments have predictive content for inflation, it should pay off to augment the aggregate information set with national money overhang measures. Third, even if the national variables did not carry additional information over aggregated variables, the construction of the ECB Governing Council would nevertheless entail considerable importance for national developments because the majority of the council members represent national central banks and may experience political pressure if the national developments diverge from the aggregate ones (Carstensen et al., 2008; Heinemann & Huefner, 2004). In such a situation, it is possible that they will feel committed to the countries they represent rather than to the euro area as a whole.

In this context, Carstensen et al. (2008) analyze the money demand functions of the four largest EMU countries and a four-country (EMU-4) aggregate. They identify *reasonable and stable money demand relationships* for Germany, France and Spain as well as the EMU-4 aggregate *based on a M3 money aggregate*. In the case of Italy, results are less clear. From the estimated money demand functions, they derive both EMU-4 and country-specific measures of the money overhang. They find that the EMU-4 M3 overhang measure strongly correlates with the country-specific measures, particularly since the start of EMU, and that these measures are useful for predicting country-specific inflation. The analyses show, however, that the aggregate money overhang is an important, but not an exhaustive indicator at the disaggregate level.

Similar results have recently been provided by Hamori and Hamori (2008). They analyzed the stability of the money demand function using panel data from January 1999 through March 2006, covering eleven euro area countries (Austria, Belgium, Finland, France, Germany, Ireland, Italy, Luxembourg, Netherlands, Portugal, and Spain). The author, find that the money demand function was stable with respect to M3. This arguably supports the suitability of the ECB's focus on M3 money supply in its monetary policy.

A cointegration system for real M3 holdings for the period 1980-Q1 to 2006-Q1, including the stock market and a measure of volatility of stock prices, might look as follows:

$$m_t - p_t = \beta_{0,1} + \beta_{1,1} y_t + \beta_{2,1} i_t^l + \beta_{3,1} i_t^s + \beta_{4,1} s_t + \beta_{5,1} s v_t + \beta_{6,1} \pi_t + \varepsilon_{t,1} \quad (2.102)$$

$$i_t^s = \beta_{0,2} + \beta_{2,2} i_t^l + \beta_{6,2} \pi_t + \varepsilon_{t,2} \quad (2.103)$$

$$s_t = \beta_{0,3} + \beta_{1,3} y_t + \varepsilon_{t,3}. \quad (2.104)$$

The first equation represents the long-run demand function for real balances $(m_t - p_t)$, depending on real income (y_t), long- and short interest rates (that is i_t^l and i_t^s, respectively), real stock performance, s_t, stock market volatility, $s v_t$, and inflation π_t. The second equation shows the combined Fisher parity and the term structure of interest rates. The third equation relates real stock market performance to real GDP. The real stock market performance and the volatility measure are shown in Fig. 2.21a, b.

The results of the cointegration analysis for the period 1980-Q1 to 2006-Q1 are given below:

$$
\begin{bmatrix}
1 & -1.251 & 0.232 & 0 & 0 & 0 & 0.008 \\
 & {\scriptstyle(0.03)} & {\scriptstyle(0.02)} & & & & {\scriptstyle 0.00} \\
0 & 0 & 1 & -1.031 & -0.157 & -0.313 & 0 \\
 & & & {\scriptstyle(0.22)} & {\scriptstyle(0.07)} & {\scriptstyle(0.12)} & \\
0 & 1 & 0 & 0 & 0 & -0.154 & 0 \\
 & & & & & {\scriptstyle(0.01)} &
\end{bmatrix}
\begin{bmatrix}
m_t - p_t \\
y_t \\
i_t^l \\
i_t^s \\
\pi_t \\
s_t \\
s v_t
\end{bmatrix}
$$

Chi-squared (5) = 10.8 [0.05], standard errors in brackets.

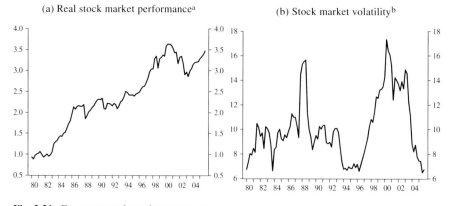

(a) Real stock market performance[a]   (b) Stock market volatility[b]

Fig. 2.21   Euro area stock market measures
Source: ECB, Thomson Financial. [a]Logarithm of the euro area stock market performance index minus the logarithm of GDP deflator. [b]Moving standard deviation of weekly first differences of logarithms of the stock market performance index over a gliding 52-week window.

	$\Delta(m_t-p_t)$	$\Delta(y_t)$	$\Delta(i_t^l)$	$\Delta(i_t^s)$	$\Delta(\pi_t)$	$\Delta(s_t)$	$\Delta(sv_t)$
Lags	3	3	3	3	3	3	3
ECT_1	−0.048	−0.021	**−1.557**	−0.098	12.34	**−1.701**	−17.63
	(−1.31)	(−0.66)	**(−4.03)**	(−0.16)	(1.59)	**(−2.49)**	(−1.79)
ECT_2	−0.001	0.003	−0.080	0.006	0.728	**0.067**	−0.347
	(−0.46)	(1.68)	(−3.39)	(−0.15)	(1.54)	(1.62)	(−0.58)
ECT_3	0.001	−0.023	0.501	0.050	−6.854	1.038	0.257
	(0.03)	(−1.14)	(2.05)	(1.35)	(−1.24)	(2.40)	(0.04)
R2	0.45	0.28	0.27	0.31	0.47	0.26	0.12

Fig. 2.22   Results of the first difference estimates, 1980-Q1 to 2006-Q1; t-values in brackets

Compared with the results for the period 1980-Q1 to 2001-Q1, income elasticity of the demand for real M3 has declined slightly (presumably due to the inclusion of a variable corresponding to wealth), whereas the interest rate elasticity of money holdings has increased quite markedly. Turning to the results of the difference equations (Fig. 2.22), it becomes evident that the error correction term of the long-run demand function for real M3 retains its negative sign, but is no longer statistically significant. At the same time, however, excess money holdings appear to have affected long-term yields and real stock prices.

These findings might indicate why strong money expansion, which actually set in around 2001, has not (yet) shown up in the economy's price level of current production. It might well be that excess money has been used to buy financial assets such as, for instance, bonds and stocks, thereby creating *asset price inflation* rather than consumer price inflation. Against this background it would be premature to argue that the demand function of M3 would have become unstable.

2.6   Credit Demand

When it comes to formulating models for credit demand, most studies include an economic activity variable (such as real GDP or industrial production) and financing costs (market interest rates or bank lending rates) as its main determinants.[13] However, there seems to be no consensus in the literature about *how* economic activity affects credit demand. Some empirical findings point to a positive relation between the two variables based on the notion that economic growth would have a positive effect on expected income and profits. According to this argument, firms' profit making enables private agents to support higher levels of indebtedness and, consequently, finance consumption and investments through credit (Kashyap, Stein, & Wilcox, 1993). An additional aspect would be that expectations of higher activity

---

[13]In the following, we focus on the US. For credit demand analyses in the euro area see, for instance, De Nederlandsche Bank (2000) which estimates national equations for bank loans to the private sector in several EU countries, Japan and the USA. Vega (1989) focuses on aggregate credit demand in Spain. Also, see Calza, Gartner, and Sousa (2001) for an analysis of the demand for bank loans to the private sector in the euro area.

and productivity can lead to a larger number of projects becoming profitable which, in turn, entails a higher demand for credit to fund them.

By contrast, studies focusing on the US economy question the existence of a stable relationship between credit and economic activity. Some go even further and argue that, if any such relationship existed, it might actually turn out to be *negative* (Bernanke & Gertler, 1995; Friedman & Kuttner, 1993). The main line of argument is that an increase in contemporary productivity (as opposed to expected productivity) leads to a rise in output and, ultimately, profits. During expansionary phases, companies might prefer to rely more on internal sources of finance and reduce external financing. Similarly, households may want to take advantage of higher incomes in expansion phases to reduce their debt. On the other hand, in recessions, when both disposable income of households and firms' profitability decline, households and corporations may increase their demand for bank credit in order to smooth out the impact of lower incomes and profits.

Most empirical Credit demand studies include a measure of the cost of loans as an explanatory variable, and in many cases come up with a negative sign of its estimated coefficient. The negative relationship between the demand for loans and their cost appears to be rather uncontroversial, though some studies have pointed out that the price of loans should be adjusted to reflect the opportunity cost of bank loans (i.e. the cost of alternative sources of finance should be netted out as in Friedman & Kuttner, 1993). The underlying argument is that the demand for loans will depend not only on the rate of borrowed funds, but also on their relative price (that is relative to the cost of funds obtained from other internal or external sources). However, this issue is more relevant for non-financial corporations than for households since the latter have limited access to financing from sources other than the banking sector.

In the following, the *demand function for bank loans* in the US shall be analysed. Figure 2.23(a) shows the nominal growth of US bank loans and US GDP for the period 1969-Q1 to 2005-Q3. Eyeballing the time series suggests a *positive relation*

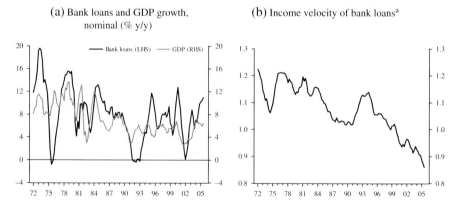

Fig. 2.23 US bank loans and economic activity
Source: Bloomberg, Federal Reserve Bank of St. Louis. Period: 1968-Q1 to 2005-Q3. – [a]Nominal GDP minus stock of bank loan, both in natural logarithms.

between economic expansion and loan supply. Figure 2.23(b) displays the *income velocity of bank loans* for the period 1968-Q1 to 2005-Q3, that is the difference between the logarithm of nominal GDP and the logarithm of the stock of bank loans. The series exhibits a *downward trend*, suggesting that, on average, the growth of nominal bank loans exceeded nominal output growth in the period under review.

The empirical model of the demand function for US bank loans shall be based on the following long-run relationship:

$$l_t - p_t = \alpha + \beta_1 y_t + \beta_2 def_t + \beta_3 \Delta cpi_t + \beta_4 s_t + \beta_5 i_t^{prime} + \beta_6 i_t^{5-year} + \beta_7 i_t^{fftr} + \varepsilon_t \tag{2.105}$$

where l, p and y stand for bank loans, GDP deflator and real GDP, respectively, in logarithms. Further, *def* stands for the default rate of US corporate bonds, and shall capture the degree of lenders' risk aversion. Δcpi is the first difference in the natural logarithm of the consumer price index. s stands for the real stock market performance index (deflated with the consumer price index). i_t^{prime}, i_t^{5-year} and i_t^{fftr} represent the prime loan rate, the 5-year bond rate and the Federal Funds Rate, respectively. Finally, ϵ is the i.i.d. error term. Figure 2.24(a–d) shows the time series under review.

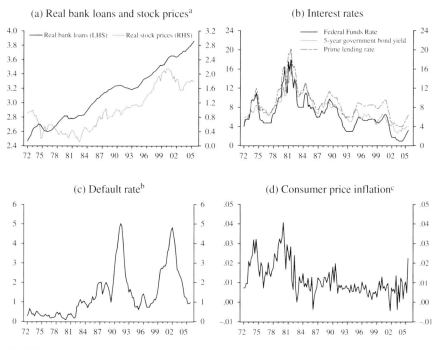

Fig. 2.24   Data overview
Source: Thomson Financial, Bloomberg, Federal Reserve Bank of St. Louis, Moody's; own calculations. [a]Bank loans deflated with the GDP deflator, stock prices with the consumer price index. [b]US default rate, all US corporate bonds, Moody's. [c]First differences of natural logarithms.

Fig. 2.25 VEC residual
serial correlation LM-tests
Notes: H_0: no serial
correlation at lag order
$h.$ – Included observations:
134. – Probs from
chi-squared with 36 df.

Lags	LM-Statistic	Probability
1	76.170	0.142
2	71.597	0.240
3	70.130	0.280
4	73.976	0.185
5	57.761	0.695
6	77.505	0.120

The results of ADF-tests suggest that for all variables under review the null hypothesis of a unit root cannot be rejected. As a result, all variables are treated as non-stationary ($I(1)$). The cointegration properties of the data were analysed by using the Johansen methodology. For determining the optimal lag lengths of the conintegration system, a vector auto regression (VAR) model for $l-p$, def, Δcpi, s, i_t^{prime}, i_t^{5-year} and i_t^{fftr} was estimated for the period 1974-Q2 to 2005-Q3.

The criterion for selecting the optimal lag length of the VAR consists of choosing exactly that number of lags that is needed to eliminate the vector autocorrelation in the residuals. The optimal lag length was determined by calculating and comparing the empirical realisations of the information criteria for the VARs. The Akaike information criterion reaches its maximum at a lag of 8 quarters, the Schwarz-criterion at a lag of 1 and the Hannan-Quinn criterion at a lag of 2 quarters. A lag of 4 quarters suggested no autocorrelation in the residuals (Fig. 2.25).

The cointegration model allows for an unrestricted constant with a linear deterministic trend in the variables but not in the cointegration relationship. The test results in Fig. 2.26 reveal that one cannot reject the existence of one cointegration vector driving the time series at lag 4. However, the use of a system with 3 lags would strongly speak in favour of using at least 2 cointegration vectors.

Assuming two cointegration vectors, the long-run relation between the real stock of bank loans, output, interest rates, inflation and the stock market can be stated as follows (asymptotic standard errors in brackets):

H_0: rank $= p$	Maximum eigenvalue test-statistic	95% critical value	Trace test-statistic	95% critical value
$p = 0$	65.896*	52.363 [.001]	190.529*	159.529 [.000]
$p \leq 1$	41.891	46.231 [.136]	124.655	125.615 [.057]
$p \leq 2$	30.852	40.078 [.369]	82.764	95.753 [.278]
$p \leq 3$	21.756	33.877 [.627]	51.911	69.819 [.553]

Fig. 2.26 Johnsen test for cointegration, lag two quarters (MacKinnon, Haug, & Michelis, 1999) *denotes the rejection of the null hypothesis at the .05 level. – Probabilities in brackets. The Trace-test and the Max-eigenvalue indicate 1 cointegrating eqn(s) at the .05 level.

$$
\hat{\beta}' X_t = \begin{bmatrix} 1 & \underset{(.09)}{-1.683} & 0 & \underset{(.01)}{.049} & 0 & \underset{(.02)}{.089} & \underset{(.02)}{-.106} & 0 \\ 0 & 0 & \underset{(.05)}{.181} & 0 & \underset{(.33)}{1.653} & \underset{(.14)}{-.987} & \underset{(.18)}{.149} & 1 \end{bmatrix} \begin{bmatrix} l_t - p_t \\ y_t \\ \Delta cpi_t \\ def_t \\ s_t \\ i_t^{prime} \\ i_t^{5-year} \\ i_t^{fftr} \end{bmatrix}
$$

Chi-squared $(4) = 8.36$ [.079].

The first vector might be interpreted as the *demand function for real bank loans*. The income coefficient of 1.68 reflects the downward trend of the income velocity of bank loans. A possible explanation is that GDP might not capture the impact of wealth, which might also relevant to explain credit demand. What is more, real bank loan demand declines when borrowing costs rise. Credit demand rises if there is a rise in the 5-year interest rate, though.

The second vector captures four long-run relations: (i) the Fisher parity, linking long-term interest rates and inflation, (ii) the term structure of interest, establishing a long-run relation between short- and long-term interest rates, (iii) the relation between the lending rate and the riskless 5-year rate (a proxy for the credit spread) and (iv) the relation between real stock prices and bond yields.

Figure 2.27(a) shows the residuals of the long-run demand function of real bank loans. The ADF-test rejects the null hypothesis of a unit root. The ECT is scaled so that deviations from the long-term equilibrium relationship average zero over the sample period. If the ECT is above (below) the zero line, the level of real loans is above (below) the equilibrium level. In that sense, a positive (negative) ECT can be interpreted as an "over-supply" (under-supply) of real loans.

Figure 2.27(b) shows the ECT of the combined long-run relation between interest rates, inflation and real stock prices. The ADF-test rejects the null hypothesis of a

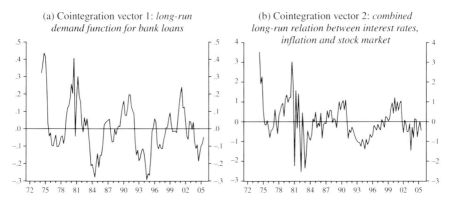

Fig. 2.27   Estimated cointegration relations for a model of the demand for real bank loans in the US

unit root. Finally, it should be noted that the volatility of the ECT of the second cointegration vectors is – measured on the basis of the standard deviation – around six and a half times the volatility of the ECT of the first vector.

The use of a VECM provides the opportunity to specify the long- and short-run dynamics of the variables under review, while also capturing potential endogeneity of the determinants of credit demand. In particular, while the cointegrating vector is generally interpreted as a long-run equilibrium relationship, the estimates of the short-term dynamics help to characterise the process of adjustment towards the long-run equilibrium.

The coefficient of the error correction term of the long-run demand function for real bank loans (ECT1) is statistically significant for explaining changes in real loan demand (Fig. 2.28). The sign of the ECT1 is negative, suggesting that an over-supply of bank loans is corrected by a decline in real bank loans in future periods. The magnitude of the coefficient is rather small, though, suggesting that in case of deviations of real loans from their equilibrium level the adjustment towards the long-run level takes quite some time.

The results of the misspecification tests for the single difference equations are presented in Fig. 2.29. The null hypothesis of autocorrelation in the single equation residuals can be rejected for all equations. ARCH effect can be detected only for real stock prices. Except for i_t^{5-year}, no ARCH effect (at lag 4) can be detected. A violation of the normality assumption can be detected for $l_t - p_t$, def_t, Δcpi and s_t. The multivariate test statistics for autocorrelation, normality and heteroscedasticity are satisfactory.

	$\Delta(l_t - p_t)$	$\Delta(y_t)$	$\Delta(\Delta cpi)$	$\Delta(def_t)$	$\Delta(s_t)$	$\Delta(i_t^{prime})$	$\Delta(i_t^{5-year})$	$\Delta(i_t^{ffir})$
ECT1	−0.053	−0.018	2.941	−0.028	−0.033	−3.518	1.550	−1.850
	−0.017	−0.013	−3.907	−0.422	−0.149	−1.243	−1.173	−1.211
	[−3.08]	[−1.37]	[0.75]	[−0.06]	[−0.22]	[−2.83]	[1.32]	[−1.52]
ECT2	0.003	0.001	−0.346	0.109	−0.025	0.497	−0.181	0.103
	−0.002	−0.002	−0.517	−0.056	−0.020	−0.164	−0.155	−0.160
	[1.30]	[0.69]	[−0.66]	[1.95]	[−1.27]	[3.02]	[−1.16]	[0.64]
R2	0.655	0.445	0.560	0.592	0.317	0.714	0.401	0.808
Adj. R2	0.526	0.237	0.395	0.440	0.062	0.607	0.177	0.736
Sum sq. resids	0.007	0.004	374.3	4.364	0.545	37.87	33.74	35.96
S.E. equation	0.009	0.007	2.028	0.219	0.077	0.645	0.609	0.629
F-statistic	5.073	2.142	3.401	3.884	1.244	6.681	1.788	11.24
Determinant resid covariance (dof adj.)	2.47E–14							
Determinant resid covariance	1.83E–15							
Log likelihood	707.6439							
Akaike information criterion	−6.53403							
Schwarz criterion	0.128981							

Fig. 2.28 Estimated error correction terms of the VECM
Legend: Standard errors in (.) and *t*-statistics in [.].

	Autocorrelation (4th order)[a]	ARCH effects (4th order)[b]	Hetero-scedasticity[c]	Normality test[d]
I. Single equation tests				
$l_t - p_t$	1.652 [.169]	.286 [.886]	1.092 [.368]	5.365 [.068]
y_t	.242 [.914]	.125 [.973]	.459 [.998]	277.6 [.000]
def_t	1.977 [.105]	2.177 [.076]	.722 [.900]	1.269 [.530]
Δcpi	1.346 [.259]	1.237 [.299]	1.009 [.489]	4.445 [.108]
s_t	.467 [.759]	2.465 [.005]	.880 [.694]	.195 [.907]
i_t^{prime}	1.094 [.368]	3.994 [.004]	.944 [.593]	39.11 [.000]
$i_t^{5\text{-}year}$	2.171 [.079]	2.234 [.069]	1.808 [.001]	12.85 [.002]
i_t^{fftr}	2.194 [.076]	1.005 [.408]	.749 [.873]	95.37 [.000]

II. Multivariate tests		
Autocorrelation (4th order)[a]	Vector normality test	Heteroscedasticity (joint test)[c]
79.439 [.092]	99.062 [.000]	2506.7 [.200]

Fig. 2.29 Diagnostic tests of selected models
Legend: *p*-values in brackets. [a]Lagrange multiplier (LM) test for autocorrelation by Godfrey (1978). – [b]Test for ARCH based on (Engle, 1982). [c]Heteroscedasticity test suggested by White (1980). [d]Jarque-Bera test.

Weak exogeneity tests can be performed on the equations for *def*, Δcpi, *s*, i_t^{prime}, $i_t^{5\text{-}year}$ and i_t^{fftr} in order to determine whether, in the spirit of a general-to-specific approach, it would be legitimate to specify the demand for loans as a single equation model instead of a system. The test is performed by assessing the statistical significance of the coefficient of the ECTs in each of the equations of the system other than the equation for loans. If the ECT is found not to be significant in a specific equation, this implies that there is no information loss from excluding that equation from the system.

The tests show that the null hypothesis of weak exogeneity cannot be rejected for all equations except for the prime lending rate. This implies that the VECM approach cannot be reduced to a single equation. Although on the basis of the weak exogeneity it would be possible to exclude this variable from the system and proceed with a smaller VECM (conditioned on these variables), one may decide to continue to retain the full system. One implication of the test result is that, in order to describe the dynamics of the adjustment of real loans to its equilibrium level, it cannot be assumed that in case real loans deviate from equilibrium the return to it will necessarily be prompted only by adjustments in real loans themselves. In fact, deviations from equilibrium may lead to movements also in the prime lending rate.

Figure 2.30 shows impulse-response functions of the VECM. It shows the reaction of real bank loans to a Cholesky one standard deviation of (i) real GDP, (ii) the prime lending rate, (iii) the default rate and (iv) the Federal Funds Rate. An increase in real GDP tends to raise the demand for real bank loans until 7 quarters following

Fig. 2.30 Impulse response functions of real bank loans from the VECM
Legend: The lines show the responses of real bank loans to Cholesky one standard innovations to the variables under review. The *x*-axis shows quarters, the *y*-axis shows the first differences of the natural logarithm of real bank loans (that is the quarter-on-quarter percentage change).

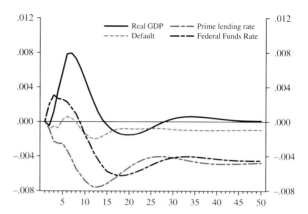

the impulse. An increase in the prime lending rate reduces the demand for real bank loans; the effect remains negative throughout the period under review. A hike of the Federal Funds Rate, however, increases the demand for real bank loans in the first 9 quarters. Thereafter, the negative impact kicks in. Finally, an increase in the default rate reduces the demand for bank loans.

References

Alves, N., Marques, C. R., & Sousa, J. (2006). Some issues concerning the use of M3 for monetary policy analysis in the euro area. *Banco de Portugal Economic Bulletin, 12*, 1–15.

Aschauer, D. A., & Greenwood, L. (1983). A further exploration in the theory of exchange rate regimes. *Journal of Political Economy, 91*, 868–875.

Baumol, W. J. (1952). The transactions demand for cash: An inventory theoretic approach. *Quarterly Journal of Economics, 66*, 545–556.

Beck, G. W., Hubrich, K., & Marcellino, M. (2006). *Regional inflation dynamics within and across Euro Area Countries and a comparison with the US. ECB Working Paper* No. 681, European Central Bank, Frankfurt/Main, October.

Belke, A., & Polleit, T. (2006). Money and Swedish inflation. *Journal of Policy Modeling, 28*, 931–942.

Belke, A., & Gros, D. (2007). Instability of the eurozone? In M. Heise, R. Tilly, P. J. J. Welfens (Eds.), *50 Years of EU dynamics – integration, financial markets and innovations* (pp. 75–108). New York: Springer.

Belke, A., & Heine, J. (2006). Specialisation patterns and the synchronicity of regional employment cycles in Europe. *Journal of International Economics and Economic Policy, 3*, 91–104.

Bernanke, B., & Gertler, M. (1995). *Inside the black box: The credit channel of monetary policy transmission. NBER Working Paper* No. 5146, National Bureau of Economics Research, Cambridge, MA.

Borchert, M. (2001). Geld und Kredit (7th ed.), Oldenbourg.

Brand, C., & Cassola, N. (2000, November). *A money demand system for euro area M3*, European Central Bank. *Working Paper* No. 39, Frankfurt/Main.

Brand, C., Gerdesmeier, D., & Roffia, B. (2002, May). *Estimating the trend of M3 income velocity underlying the reference value of monetary growth.* Occasional Paper No. 3, European Central Bank, Frankfurt (Main).

Bruggemann, A. (2000). The stability of EMU-wide money demand functions and the monetary policy strategy of the European Central Bank. *Manchester School, 68*, 184–202.

Bruggemann, A., Donati, P., & Warne, A. (2003, September). *Is the demand for Euro Area M3 stable?* European Central Bank, *Working Paper Series*, No. 255, Frankfurt/Main.

Calza, A., & Sousa, J. (2003, September). *Why has broad money demand been more stable in the euro area than in other economies? A Literature Overview*, European Central Bank, *Working Paper Series*, No. 261.

Calza, A., Gartner, C., & Sousa, J. (2001, April). *Modelling the demand for loans in the private sector in the Euro Area.* European Central Bank, *Working Paper*, No. 55 Frankfurt/Main.

Calza, A., Gerdesmeier, D., & Levy, J. (2001). *Euro area money demand: measuring the opportunity costs appropriately. IMF Working Paper* No. 01/179, International Monetary Fund, Washington/DC.

Carlson, J. B., & Keen, B. D. (1995), M2 growth in 1995: A return to normalcy, http://www.clevelandfed.org/Research/com96/1295.htm#8

Carlson, J. B., & Keen, B. D. (1995, December). *M2 growth in 1995: A return to normalcy?* Federal Reserve Bank of Cleveland.

Carlson, J. B., & Parrott, S. E. (1991). The demand for M2, opportunity cost, and financial change, Federal Reserve Bank of Cleveland Economic Review (Second Quarter), 2–11.

Carlson, J. B., Hoffman, D. L., Keen, B. D., & Rasche, R.H. (2000). Results of a study of the stability of cointegrating relations comprised of broad monetary aggregates. *Journal of Monetary Economics, 46*(2), 345–383.

Carstensen, K. (2006). Stock market downswing and the stability of european monetary union money demand. *Journal of Business and Economic Statistics, 24*, 395–402.

Carstensen, K., Hagen, J., Hossfeld, O., & Salazar Neaves, A. (2008). *Money demand stability and inflation prediction in the four largest EMU countries. Ifo Working Paper* No. 61, CESifo, Munich.

Cassola, N., & Morana, C. (2002, January). *Monetary policy and the stock market in the Euro Area. ECB Working Paper* No. 110.

Clausen, V., & Kim, J.-R. (2000). The long–run stability of European money demand. *Journal of Economic Integration, 15*, 486–505.

Clower, R. W. (1967, December). A reconsideration of the microfoundations of monetary theory. *Western Economic Journal, 6*, 1–8.

Coenen, G., & Vega, J.-L. (2001). The demand for M3 in the Euro Area. *Journal of Applied Econometrics, 16*, 727–748.

Collins, S. & Edwards, C. L. (1994, November/December). An alternative monetary aggregate: M2 plus household holdings of bond and equity mutual funds. *Federal Reserve Bank of St. Louis, Review*, 7–29.

Collins, S., & Edwards, C. L. (1994, November/December). Redefining M2 to include bond and equity mutual funds. *Federal Reserve Bank of St. Louis, 76*, 7–30.

Cuthbertson, K., & Barlow, D. (1991). Disequilibrium, buffer stocks and consumers expenditure on non-durables. *Review of Economics and Statistics, 73*(4), 643–653.

de Grauwe, P., & Senegas, M.-A. (2003). *Common monetary policy with transmission asymmetry and uncertainty: Is there a case for using national data in EMU?* manuscript, Leuven: Katholieke Universiteit Leuven.

De Nederlandsche Bank (2000), EUROMON – The Nederlandsche Bank's multi-country model for policy analysis in Europe, Amsterdam, pp. 83–85.

De Soto, J. H. (2006), *Money, bank credit, and economic cycles.* US Alabama: Ludwig von Mises Institute.

Dreger, C., & Wolters, J. (2006). *Investigating M3 money demand in the euro area – new evidence based on standard models.* DIW Discussion Papers No. 651, Dentselres Insti   draft Berlin March.

Duca, J. (1992). The case of the missing M2. *Federal Reserve Bank of Dallas Economic Review* (2nd Quarter), 1–24.

Duca, J. (1995). Should bond funds be added to M2? *Journal of Banking and Finance, 19*, 131–152.

Duca, J. V. (1992). The case of the missing M2. *Federal Reserve Bank of Dallas Economic Review* (2nd Quarter), 1–24.

ECB (2001, January). Monetary policy-making under Uncertainty, *Monthly Bulletin*, European Central Bank, Frankfurt/Main 43–55.

ECB (2003). *Background studies for the ECB's evaluation of its monetary policy strategy*. Frankfurt/Main: European Central Bank.

ECB (2005, October). Money demand and uncertainty. *Monthly Bulletin*, Frankfurt/Main: European Central Bank, 57–73.

Engle, R. F. (1982). Autoregressive Conditional Heteroskedasticity with Estimates of the Variance of UK Inflation, in: Econometrica, 50, pp. 987–1008.

Engle, R. F., & Granger, C. W. J. (1987). Co-integration and error correction: Representation, estimation, and testing. *Econometrica, 55*, 251–276.

Estrella, A., & Mishkin, F. S. (1997). Is there a role for monetary aggregates in the conduct of monetary policy? *Journal of Monetary Economics, 40*, 279–304.

Felderer, B., & Homburg, S. (2005). Makroökonomik und Neue Makroökonomik (9th ed.), Berlin et. al.

Fisher, I. (1911). *The purchasing power of money: Its determination and relation to credit, interest, and crises*. New York: Macmillan, reprinted, New York, Augustus M. Kelley, 1963.

Friedman, B. M., & Kuttner, K. N. (1992). Money, income, prices, and interest rates. *American Economic Review, 82*, 472–92.

Friedman, B., & Kuttner, K. N. (1993). Economic activity and the short-term credit markets: An analysis of prices and quantities. *Brookings Papers on Economic Activity, 2*, 193–283.

Friedman, M. (1956). The quantity theory of money – a restatement. In M. Friedman (Ed.), *Studies in the quantity theory of money*. Chicago.

Funke, M. (2001). Money demand in Euroland. *Journal of International Money and Finance, 20*, 701–713.

Godfrey, L. (1978). Testing against general autoregressive and moving average error models when the regressors include lagged dependent varibles, in: Econometrica, 46, pp. 1293–1302.

Gordon, M. (1962). *The Investment, Financing, and Valuation of the Corporation*. Irwin, Homewood, IL.

Golinelli, R., & Pastorello, S. (2002). Modelling the demand for M3 in the euro area. *The European Journal of Finance, 8*, 371–401.

Gottschalk, J. (1999). On the monetary transmission mechanism in Europe. *Journal of Economics and Statistics, 219*, 357–374.

Greene, W. H. (2003). *Econometric analysis* (5th ed.), Upper Saddle River, NJ: Prentice-Hall.

Greenspan, A. (1993, September). Statement to congress. *Federal Reserve Bulletin, 79*, 849–55.

Greiber, C., & Lemke, W. (2005). *Money demand and macroeconomic uncertainty*. Deutsche Bundesbank Discussion Paper, No. 26, Deutsche Bundesbank, Frankfurt/Main.

Gurajati, N. D. (1995). *Basic econometrics* (3rd ed., pp. 167–178), New York: MacGraw-Hill.

Hallman, J. J., & Anderson, R. G. (1993). Has the long-run velocity of M2 shifted? Evidence from the P*-model. *Federal Reserve Bank of Cleveland Economic Review* (first quarter), 14–26.

Hamori, S., & Hamori, N. (2008). Demand for money in the euro area. *Economic Systems, 32*(3), 274–284.

Hansen, H., & Johansen, S. (1999). Some tests for parameter constancy in cointegrated VAR-models. *Econometrics Journal, 2*, 306–333.

Harvey, A. (1990). *Forecasting, structural time series models and the Kalman filter*. Cambridge: Cambridge University Press.

Hayo, B. (1999). Estimating a European demand for money. *Scottish Journal of Political Economy, 46*, 221–244.

Heinemann, F., & Huefner, F. P. (2004). Is the view from the Eurotower purely European? National divergence and ECB interest rate policy. *Scottish Journal of Political Economy, 51*, 544–558.

Helpman, E. (1981, October). An exploration of the theory of exchange rate regimes. *Journal of Political Economy, 89*, 865–890.

Herwartz, H., & Reimers H.-E. (2006). Long-run links among money, prices and output: World-wide evidence. *German Economic Review, 7*, 65–86.

Holtemöller, O. (2004). A monetary vector error correction model of the euro area and implications for monetary policy. *Empirical Economics, 9*, 553–574.

Humphrey, T. M. (2004). *Alfred Marshall and the quantity theory. Federal Reserve Bank of Richmond Working Paper*, No. 04.

Johansen, S. (1988), Statistical analysis of cointegration vectors. *Journal of Economic Dynamics and Control, 12*(2–3), 231–254.

Johansen, S. (1991). Estimation and hypothesis testing of cointegration vectors in Gaussian vector autoregressive models. *Econometrica, 59*(6), 1551–1580.

Johansen, S. (1995). *Likelihood-based inference in cointegrated vector autoregressive models.* New York: Oxford University Press.

Johansen, S., & Juselius, K. (1990). Maximum likelihood estimation and inference on cointegration – with applications to the demand for money. *Oxford Bulletin of Economics and Statistics, 52*(2), 169–210.

Kashyap, A., Stein, J., & Wilcox, D. (1993). Monetary policy and credit conditions: evidence from the composition of external finance. *American Economic Review, 83*, 8–98.

Keynes, J.M. (1973, 1936), *The general theory of employment, interest, and money*, Macmillan, Cambridge University Press, London.

King, R. G., & Watson, M. W. (1997). Testing long-run neutrality, economic quarterly. *Federal Reserve Bank of Richmond, 83*, 69–101.

Koenig, E. (1996a), Long-term interest rates and the recent weakness in M2. *Journal of Economics and Business, 48*, 81–101.

Koenig, E. (1996b). Forecasting M2 growth: An exploration in real time. *Economic Review, Federal Reserve Bank of Dallas* (Second Quarter), 16–26.

Kontolemis, Z. G. (2002). *Money demand in the euro area: where do we stand (today)?* IMF *Working Paper* No. 02/185, International Monetary Fund, Washington.

Lown, C., Peristiani, S., & Robinson, K. J. (1999). *What was behind the M2 breakdown? Federal Reserve Bank of Dallas Financial Industry Studies Working Paper* No. 02/99.

Lucas, R. E. Jr. (1982, November). Interest rates and currency prices in a two-country world. *Monetary Economics, 10*, 335–360.

Lucas, R. E. Jr., & Stokey, N. (1987). Money and interest in a cash-in-advance economy. *Econometrica, 55*, 491–513.

MacKinnon, J. G., Haug, A., & Michelis, L. (1999). Numerical distribution functions of likelihood ratio tests for cointegration. *Journal of Applied Econometrics, 14*, 563–577.

Marcellino, M., Stock, J. H., & Watson, M. W. (2003). Macroeconomic forecasting in the euro area: Country-specific versus area-wide information. *European Economic Review, 47*, 1–18.

Marshall, A. (1923). *Money, credit and commerce.* London: Macmillan.

Marshall, A. (1871). Money. In J. Whitaker (Ed.), 1975, *The early economic writings of Alfred Marshall* (Vol. 2), London: Macmillan.

Marshall, A., & Marshall, M. P. (1879). The economics of industry. London: Macmillan.

Meltzer, A. H. (1963). The demand for money: The evidence from time series. *Journal of Political Economy, 71*, 219–246.

Müller, C. (2003). *Money demand in Europe: An empirical approach.* Heidelberg: Physica-Verlag.

Müller, C., & Hahn, E. (2001). Money demand in europe: evidence from the past. *Kredit und Kapital, 34*, 48–75.

Nautz, D., & Ruth, K. (2005). *Monetary disequilibria and the Euro/Dollar exchange rate.* Deutsche Bundesbank, Discussion Paper, Series 1, No. 18 Frankfurt/Main.

Obstfeld, M., & Rogoff, K. (1999). *Foundations of international macroeconomics.* Massachusetts: MIT Press, Cambridge.

Orphanides, A., Reid, B., & Small, D. H. (1994, November/December). The empirical properties of a monetary aggregate that adds bond and stock funds to M2. *Federal Reserve Bank of St. Louis, Review*, 31–51.

Pigou, A. C. (1917). The value of money. *Quarterly Journal of Economics, 32*, (1917–1918), Reprinted in: Readings in Monetary Theory, F. A. Lutz, & L. W. Mints (Eds.), Philadelphia, 1951, pp. 162–183.

Tobin, J. (1956). The interest-elasticity of transactions demand for cash. *Review of Economics and Statistics, 38*, 241–247.

Tobin, J. (1958). Liquidity preference as behavior towards risk. *Review of Economic Studies, 25*(2), 65–86.

Vega, J. L. (1989). Las variables de crédito en el mecanismo de transmission de la política monetaria: el caso español, Documento de Trabajo del Banco de España. 8902, Madrid.

White, H. (1980). A heteroskedasticity-consistent covariance matrix estimator and a direct test for heteroskedasticity, in: Econometrica, 48, pp. 817–838.

Chapter 3
Interest Rate Theories

The financial public, too, believes that the Fed can control interest rates, and that belief has spread to the Treasury and Congress. As a result, every recession brings calls from the Treasury, the White House, Congress, and Wall Street for the Fed to "to bring down interest rates." Counterbalancing pleas, at times of expansion, for the Fed to raise interest rates are notable by their absence.

Friedman, M. (1994), Money Mischief, p. 209.

3.1 Introductory Remarks

The interest rate plays an important role in economics, especially so in monetary theory. It may therefore come as a surprise that a consensus has not (yet) emerged as far as the nature and the determinants of the interest rate are concerned. In fact, the nature of the *interest rate phenomenon* has remained subject to, at times controversial, debate. In his book Man, Economy and State, first published in 1962, Murray N. Rothbard wrote (2001, p. 389): "Perhaps more fallacies have been committed in discussions concerning the interest rate than in the treatment of any other aspect of economics."

In a historic perspective, the dealing with and the examination of the interest rate phenomenon has actually always been strongly influenced by ideological and political considerations. For instance, the controversies of the Middle Ages over usury were by no means attempts to examine the nature of the interest rate. However, this changed with the work of the economists of the Austrian School of Economics and the (neo-)classical school. They interpreted the interest rate as a *real phenomenon*. As such, the interest rate phenomenon would not be related to the existence of money as such. They showed that even in a barter economy would there would be an interest rate.

In his book *Capital and Interest*, Eugen von Böhm-Bawerk wrote in 1890: Interest "(...) may be obtained from any capital, no matter what be the kind of goods of which the capital consists: from goods that are barren as well as from those that are naturally fruitful; from perishable as well as from durable goods; from goods

A. Belke, T. Polleit, *Monetary Economics in Globalised Financial Markets*,
DOI 10.1007/978-3-540-71003-5_3, © Springer-Verlag Berlin Heidelberg 2009

that can be replaced and from goods that cannot be replaced; from money as well as from commodities. (. . .) It is, if one may use such an expression about mundane things, capable of an everlasting life."[1]

The interpretation of the interest rate as a real phenomenon was challenged by the work of John Maynard Keynes (1883–1946). According to his *liquidity preference theory*, the interest rate is a *monetary phenomenon*, determined by the supply of and demand for money. To Keynesians, the rate of interest (i) determines investment and, at the same time, (ii) is being determined by the interplay of the demand for and supply of money, with real factors obviously not playing any role.[2]

The conclusion was that the interest rate – once the government holds the monopoly over the money supply – would qualify as a *policy variable*: by manipulating the interest rate, investment, output and employment can be affected by the government. The impact of the Keynesian interest rate theory was profound as far as economics and macro-economic policy making is concerned. To this day, central banks prefer a steering of (short-term) interest rates rather than limiting the supply of (base) money in an effort to preserve the exchange value of money and support growth and employment.

Such a viewpoint stands in a rather sharp contrast to the Austrian and (neo-)classical economists, both in terms of theoretical reasoning and practical and public policy implications. For instance, Ludwig von Mises (1881–1973), one of the leading Scholars of the Austrian School of Economics, stated that the interest rate "is neither the impetus to saving nor the reward or the compensation granted for abstaining from immediate consumption. It is the ratio in the mutual valuation of present goods against future goods."[3]

When looking at today's financial markets, there are actually many kinds of interest rates. For instance, there are interest rates for consumer, corporate and mortgage loans; interest rates for savings and time deposits, and those for government and corporate bonds; there are short- and long-term interest rates; and there are official interest rates, set by central banks, and interest rates set by supply and demand in the market place; there are interest rates in the form of spot and forward interest rates, and there are nominal and real interest rates.

Interest rates have been fluctuating considerably over time. Figure 3.1(a) and (b) show short- and long-term US interest rates for the period 1934–2008, respectively, together with annual CPI inflation. Perhaps most notably, real interest rates, while having been positive on average in the period under review, fell into negative territory on various occasions; this finding applies more to short- than to long-term interest rates, though.

These observations encourage a number of challenging questions: What determines the height of the interest rate? Why do interest rates vary over time? Why

---

[1] Eugen von Böhm-Bawerk (1890), p. 1.

[2] In practice, however, Keynesians treat the liquidity preference *not* as determining the rate of interest, but as *being determined* by it. See Rothbard (2001), p. 688.

[3] Mises, L. v. (1996) p. 527.

(a) Short-term interest rates   (b) US corporate yields

Fig. 3.1   Long-term history of US interest rates (%), 1934–2008
Source: Federal Reserve Bank of St. Louis; own calculations. – The real rate was calculated by subtracting the annual change in the CPI from the nominal rate. – Shaded areas: periods in which the real rate was negative. Corporate yield represents BAA rated bonds

tend real (or inflation-adjusted) interest rates to be positive on average? Is it possible to think that real interest rates might become negative at some stage? For answering these questions, we first of all need to understand the nature and determinants of the interest rate. To this end, a theoretical framework is required.

In what follows, we will focus on the most popular theories, namely (Sect. 3.2) the interest rate theory of the Austrian School of Economics, followed by (Sect. 3.3) the neo-classical theory and (Sect. 3.4) Knut Wicksell's *loanable funds theory*. While the former theories would characterise the interest rate as a real phenomenon, we will finally consider (Sect. 3.5) the *Keynesian liquidity preference theory*, which holds that the interest rate is a monetary phenomenon. Thereafter, we will briefly touch upon the issues of (Sect 3.6) nominal versus real interest rates and (Sect. 3.7) *credit spreads*.

3.2 The Austrian Theory of the Interest Rate

The interest rate theory of the Austrian School of Economics basically rests on the work of Eugen Böhm von Bawerk (1841–1914). In his book *History and Critique of Interest Theories*, published in 1884, he put forward the concept of *time preference*. According to this theory, the interest rate is an expression of people assigning greater value to goods and services available today than goods and services available at some future point in time.

It should be noted right from the start that to Austrian economists time preference is not a psychological or physiological concept, but it simply follows from the logical structure of action present in the mind of human beings: namely that every action requires time to attain its objective, and that time is always scarce for mortal man. Having said that, a present good is, and must invariably be, valued more highly than the same good available in the future.

Time preference must necessarily be positive, according to the Austrian theory. In fact, a negative time preference would be an absurdity for goal-pursing man. If a good is valued more highly in the future than at present, people would never consume, as postponing consumption from the present to the future will always add to utility. However, with a negative time preference this would hold true today as it does in the future. A negative time preference is therefore impossible as it implies that acting man can ever attain his goals.

The interest rate is a free market phenomenon. People exchange goods and services which they consider less valuable against those vendible items they value more highly. For instance, Mr Miller is willingly exchanging US$1 against an apple as he values the apple higher than one US dollar. Likewise, the shopkeeper exchanges the apple against US$1 because from his viewpoint the dollar is more valuable than the apple.

This principle does not only hold true for *exchanges of present-against-present-goods* (as in the example above) but also for *present-against-future-goods*. Present goods are goods that are readily available for consumption today, while future goods are those goods that will become – through the production process, which requires foregoing consumption today – present goods available at a future point in time.

Most exchanges in the market place involve indirect exchange, involving money as *the universally accepted means of exchange*. Money is a *present good*, and as such it is a perfectly marketable good. There are actually two kinds of transactions in which present goods are exchanged against future goods. Both take place in the so-called *present-future goods market* (or *time market*):

– *First*, there are transactions in which entrepreneurs buy present goods and use them as production input factors (*cash transaction*). In a time-consuming production process, present goods are transformed into future consumption goods. The entrepreneur hopes that the proceeds of future output will exceed input costs and compensate him for all his efforts.
– *Second*, there are *credit transactions*. For instance, *A* gives a certain amount of money to *B* in exchange for a claim to future money. *A* is *lender* (with a claim to future money) while *B* is *borrower* (required to repay borrowed money in the future). The transaction, starting in the current period, is to be completed in a future period (when *B* repays the loan by transferring the agreed amount of money to *A*).

For instance, firms demand present goods (such as, for instance, iron, coal, etc.) for transforming them into present goods available at some point in the future. In exchange for acquiring present goods, firms offer future goods in the form of promises to pay future money, that are dividend payments or, if present goods were acquired through a credit transaction, repaying the loan plus interest. In that sense, the interest rate is related to exchanging present goods against future goods: The interest rate is an exchange ratio. For instance, if 100 ounces of gold exchange for the prospect of obtaining 105 ounce of gold in one year, then the rate of interest is 5% p.a. That said, *the interest rate is the time-discount rate, or better: time preference rate, of future to present money.*

The free market interest rate reflects the aggregated individual time preference rates, or the *social rate of time preference*. It is the interest rate that equilibrates the supply of present goods (savings) with the demand for present good (investment). If peoples' time preference *falls* (*rises*), that is peoples' time preference for present goods over future goods *declines* (*increases*), people will consume less (*more*) out of current income and save and invest more (*less*).

In a society, individuals can be expected to differ as far as their time preference is concerned. Some individuals may have a *high* time preference, other may have a *low* time preference. The former are more willing to consume in the present and less willing to defer consumption to the future, while the latter tend to save more and consume less out of current income. In an economy populated by patient individuals (low time preference people) and less patient individuals (high time preference people) lending and borrowing of money will result.

Individuals with a low time preference value present goods less than a certain higher quantity of future goods. In contrast, individuals with a high time preference are willing to forego more future goods for the sake of enjoying an additional unit of present goods. As a result, individuals with a low time preference will, as a rule, be inclined to lend to individuals with a high time preference.

Austrian economists explain the market interest rate (or the *pure rate of interest*) through peoples' time preference. This can be illustrated in a more formal way. The *law of diminishing marginal utility* is typically applied in the context of an individual making a choice between *present goods*. However, the analysis can be easily applied to an individual making *choices between present and future goods*.

Assume an individual's utility is a function of consuming present goods (m_t) and future goods (m_{t+1}):

$$U = f(m_t,\ m_{t+1}). \tag{3.1}$$

The marginal utility from consuming one unit more of m_t increases total utility:

$$\frac{\partial U}{\partial m_t} = f'_{m_t} > 0. \tag{3.2}$$

Further, it is assumed that with growing consumption of m_t the marginal utility declines:

$$\frac{\partial^2 U}{\partial m_t^2} = f''_{m_t} < 0. \tag{3.3}$$

Equations (3.2) and (3.3) correspond to the *First Law of Gossen* (named after Hermann Heinrich Gossen, 1853).

Furthermore, it is assumed that the marginal utility from consuming one unit more of m_t increases if an additional unit of m_{t+1} is consumed.

$$\frac{\partial^2 U}{\partial m_t \partial m_{t+1}} = f''_{m_t,\ m_{t+1}} > 0. \tag{3.4}$$

Fig. 3.2 Utility function

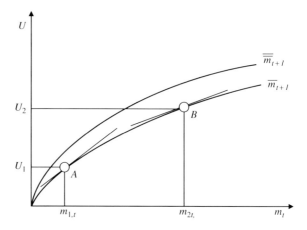

Figure 3.2 shows a utility curve with the properties as outlined in the equations above. In point A, the level of consumption is low ($m_{t,1}$), while its marginal utility is high, as expressed by the steepness of the utility curve. In contrast, the consumption level is higher in point B ($m_{t,2}$), whereas the marginal utility is lower than in point A.

Now assume that, for simplicity, there is a given level of utility, $\overline{U}$, which depends on m_t and m_{t+1}:

$$\overline{U} = f(m_t,\ m_{t+1}) \text{ or, when solving for } m_t \qquad (3.5)$$

$$m_t = \tilde{f}(m_{t+1},\ \overline{U}) = \overset{\approx}{f} = (m_{t+1}). \qquad (3.6)$$

Equation (3.6) is the so-called indifference curve. It shows all combinations of m_t and m_{t+1} which yield the same level of utility $\overline{U}$. It is shown in Fig. 3.3.

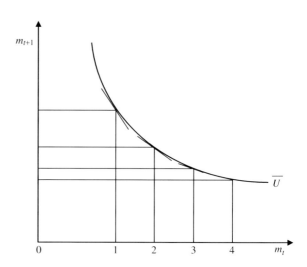

Fig. 3.3 Indifference curve
for a given level of utility $\overline{U}$

The slope at any point on the indifference curve equals the rate at which the consumer is willing to substitute present goods for future goods. This exchange rate reflects the time preference: It shows how much of a present good must be given up in order to get hold of an additional unit of the future good. The time preference can be calculated by the total differential of the utility function:

$$dU = f'_{m_t} dm_t + f'_{m_{t+1}} dm_{t+1}, \qquad (3.7)$$

where d represent small (but not infinitesimal small) changes.

Along the indifference curve we have:

$$0 = f'_{m_t} dm_t + f'_{m_{t+1}} dm_{t+1}, \text{ or equally } : \qquad (3.8)$$

$$\frac{f'_{m_{t+1}}}{f'_{m_t}} = -\frac{dm_t}{dm_{t+1}}. \qquad (3.9)$$

The time preference rate for substituting m_t through one additional unit of m_{t+1} equals the reciprocal of the marginal utilities for the goods under review (with a negative sign). Of course, the time preference rate depends on the amount of present goods already offered against future goods. The higher (smaller) the quantity of present goods that have already been exchanged against future goods, the higher (lower) will be the time preference rate.

Figure 3.4(a) shows an individual's indifference function for present goods (m_t) and future goods (m_{t+1}), both expressed in money terms. The time preference rate is the rate at which one unit of m_t exchanges for m_{t+1}. The more (less) m_t is exchanged against m_{t+1}, the higher (lower) becomes the time preference rate. This explains why the supply of present goods is positively related to the interest rate (Fig. 3.4(b)); as present goods are exchanged against future goods, the supply of present goods is simply the demand for future goods.

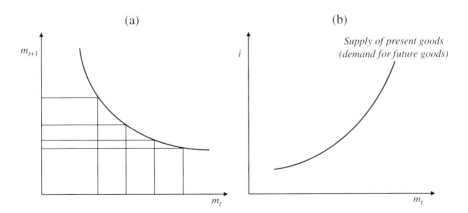

Fig. 3.4 Indifference curve, time preference and supply of present goods

What about the demand for present goods, then? Economic production means that necessary that currently available goods (present goods) are used as input factors of production; entrepreneurs transform present goods into future goods (that are present goods available at a future point in time). How does the demand for present goods relate to the interest rate? Again, this question can be answered by looking at an individual's time preference schedule.[4]

The right part of Fig. 3.5 shows the familiar supply schedule for present goods in relation to the interest rate. According to the law of diminishing marginal utility, an individual's time preference becomes infinite after a certain amount of present goods has been supplied in the time market. The reason is that man must consume in the present, so he cannot save all of his current income. And it is this fact that will drastically limit man's savings, regardless of the interest rate. Accordingly, the supply of money schedule becomes, at some point, a vertical line.

At the other end of the spectrum, time preference implies that at some (minimum) interest rate level – which varies from person to person – an individual does no longer save. For instance, an individual cannot – given the fact that he values present goods higher than future goods – prefer 3 ounces (or less) of future money over 3 ounces of present money. So what happens if an individual's present money supply curve hits the vertical axis?

For an individual, the marginal utility of present money may fall too fast, as compared with that of future money, for him to become *net demander of present goods* at a low interest rate; his time preference ratio is too low, and his time market curve drops to zero left of where the vertical axis meets the horizontal axis. Another individual, however, may have a high time preference, so that at a low

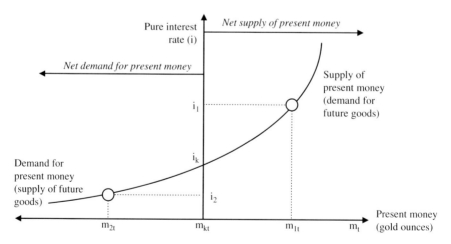

Fig. 3.5 An individual's time market curve

[4]For the following explanation, see Rothbard (2001), pp. 313 and 326.

interest rate he actually becomes a net demander of present goods (that is a *net supplier of future goods*).

Figure 3.5 shows a *continuous curve of an individual's activity in the time market*. The right part shows his supply of present goods: At higher interest rates, down to where it hits the vertical axis, he is a net supplier of present goods. The left part represents the individual's net demand for present goods, which rises (falls) with falling (rising interest rates). The borrower of present goods continues to borrow until the marginal utility of the next unit of money in the present will decline enough to be outstripped by the marginal utility of having a higher quantity of present goods in the future. As a result, the demand for present goods (that is the supply of future goods) must be negatively related to the interest rate.

Under the law of diminishing marginal utility, individuals have similar time-market schedules. The schedules of all individuals will be such that at higher rates of interest there will be a greater tendency towards net saving, while lower interest rates will be associated with less saving, until the individual becomes a net demander for present goods. Likewise, lower (higher) interest rates will be accompanied by rising (declining) demand for present goods.

If the individuals' time market schedules are aggregated, one obtains the familiar supply and demand curves as shown in Fig. 3.6. The intersection of the supply of and the demand for present goods determines the equilibrium rate of interest i_0. In equilibrium, $Om_{t,0}$ is the amount of present goods that will be saved and invested. At a higher interest rate than i_0, present goods supplied would exceed future goods supplied in exchange, and excess savings would compete with one another until the price of present goods in terms of future goods would decline toward equilibrium. If the rate of interest were below i_0, the demand for present goods by suppliers of future goods would exceed the supply of savings, and the competition of this demand would push interest rates up toward equilibrium.

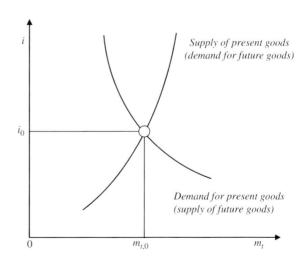

Fig. 3.6 Market equilibrium in the time market

The equilibrium market interest rate, which aligns the supply of present goods with the demand for present goods, is determined by peoples' time preference. Against this background it is understandable that Austrian economists would conclude that the interest rate – as Rothbard put it – "is determined by the time preferences of the individuals in the society, and by no other factor."[5] The equilibrium market interest rate reflects lenders' and borrowers' utility maximisation effort. Lenders (low time preference people) will continue to lend until the marginal utility from lending an additional unit of money falls enough to be outstripped by the marginal utility of the present use of that unit of money. Borrowers (high time preference people) will continue to borrow until the marginal utility of the additional unit of money in the present will fall enough to be outstripped by the marginal utility of having more money in the future.

3.3 The Neo-Classical Theory of the Interest Rate

Like the Austrians, the neo-classical interest rate theory explains the interest rate as a real economic phenomenon. However, it assumes that the market equilibrium interest rate is determined by the interaction of peoples' marginal utility of exchanging present against future goods *and* the *economy's marginal return on capital*. In what follows, we will review the elements of the neo-classical theory of the interest rate in some more detail.[6]

3.3.1 The Intertemporal Budget Constraint

Assume an individual has an income of $\bar{e}_t$ in period t and income zero in $t + 1$. For generating consumption in $t + 1$, the individual can consume less than $\bar{e}_t$ in t ($\bar{e}_t > c_t$) so that savings (s) amount to $\bar{e}_t - c_t = s_t$. Savings can be invested at an interest rate i, so that consumption in $t + 1$ is $c_{t+1} = s_t(1 + i)$. If the individual does not consume in t, that is save and invest $\bar{e}_t$, income in $t + 1$ would be $\bar{e}_{t+1} = \bar{e}_t(1+i)$. The possible combinations of c_t and c_{t+1} are shown in Fig. 3.7(a).

If, however, an individual receives an income of $\bar{e}_{t+1}$ in $t + 1$ and an income of zero in t, we assume that he can borrow at the interest rate i, consume in t, and then repay the loan with savings in $t + 1$: $s_{t+1} = \bar{e}_{t+1} - c_{t+1} = c_t(1+i)$. Consumption in t would amount to $c_t = \bar{e}_{t+1}/(1+i)$ if there is no consumption in $t + 1$. This finding is shown in Fig. 3.7(b).

Assume the individual receives income in period t, $\bar{e}_t$, and in $t + 1$, $\bar{e}_{t+1}$. Saving makes it possible let consumption exceed income in $t + 1$, so that $c_{t+1} > \bar{e}_{t+1}$; savings and investment makes it also possible that $c_t > \bar{e}_t$. The combinations

[5]Rothbard (2001), p. 389.
[6]In the following, we draw heavily on Schumann (1987), pp. 87.

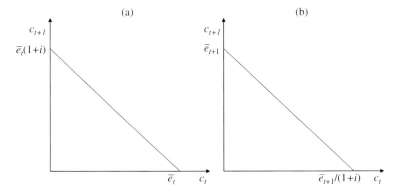

Fig. 3.7 Intertemporal budget constraint

of c_t and c_{t+1} are represented by the *intertemporal budget constraint*. It can be formulated as:

$$c_{t+1} = -(1+i)c_t + \bar{e}_{t+1} + \bar{e}_t(1+i) \text{ or}$$
$$c_t + \frac{c_{t+1}}{1+i} = \bar{e}_t + \frac{\bar{e}_{t+1}}{1+i}. \tag{3.10}$$

Figure 3.8 shows the intertemporal budget constraint, together with a utility function. The slope of the intertemporal budget constraint is $-(1+i)$. Point C^* represents the individual's optimal intertemporal consumption allocation. In the optimum, the (absolute) *marginal rate of substitution* (MRS) *of future against current consumption equals* $(1+i)$. Consumption amounts to c_t^* in t and c_{t+1}^* in $t+1$. Savings in t amount to $s_t^* = \bar{e}_t - c_t^*$, which are then invested at the interest rate i, so that $\bar{e}_{t+1}$ is raised by $s_t^*(1+i)$.

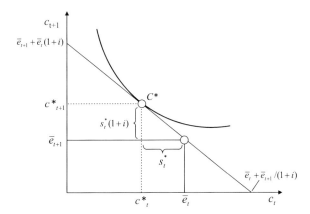

Fig. 3.8 Intertemporal budget constraint and the utility function

This result can also be presented in a more formal way. To determine the optimum of intertemporal consumption, we can make use of a *Lagrange function*:

$$L = f(c_t, \ c_{t+1}) + \lambda \left(c_t + \frac{c_{t+1}}{1+i} - \bar{e}_t - \frac{\bar{e}_{t+1}}{1+i} \right). \tag{3.11}$$

Deriving the first derivatives of (3.11) with respect to c_t, c_{t+1} and λ, and setting the result to zero, yields:

$$\frac{\partial L}{\partial c_t} = \frac{\partial f}{\partial c_t} + \lambda = 0$$

$$\frac{\partial L}{\partial c_{t+1}} = \frac{\partial f}{\partial c_{t+1}} + \lambda \frac{1}{1+i} = 0 \tag{3.12}$$

$$\frac{\partial L}{\partial \lambda} = c_t + \frac{c_{t+1}}{1+i} - \bar{e}_t - \frac{\bar{e}_{t+1}}{1+i} = 0.$$

The first two equations say that the MRS of future consumption against current consumption (that is the reciprocal of the marginal utilities in the period t and $t + 1$) equals the discount factor $1 + i$:

$$\left| \frac{dc_{t+1}}{dc_t} \right| = \frac{\partial f}{\partial c_t} : \frac{\partial f}{\partial c_{t+1}} = 1 + i, \ \text{which can also be stated as} \tag{3.13}$$

$$\frac{\partial f}{\partial c_t} = \frac{\partial f}{\partial c_{t+1}} \cdot (1 + i). \tag{3.14}$$

If a market agent wants to optimise his intertemporal consumption, the marginal utility of additional consumption in t must equal the marginal utility of consumption in $t + 1$ times $(1 + i)$. This result is intuitively plausible: a unit of income saved in t and invested at the rate of interest i will yield an income of $1 + i$ in $t + 1$.

3.3.2 The Intertemporal Production Frontier (IPPF)

So far it has been assumed that any amount of savings can be invested at a positive interest rate, providing an incentive to transform current consumption into future consumption. However, investment increases as savings rise. As a result, one would expect that the marginal return on investment declines. Indeed, this is what the *law of diminishing marginal returns* suggests. A neo-classical production function is $e = f(x_i, \ ..., \ x_n)$, with $i = 1, \ ..., n$. Assuming that there is just one variable input factor, the upper part of Fig. 3.9 relates the level of output e to the level of input x, while the lower part relates the marginal return on x, $\partial e / \partial x$, to the level of input x. The production function implies positive, but diminishing marginal returns. In point A input x is low and the marginal return on x is high. In point B, input x is high and the marginal return on x is low.

Fig. 3.9 Law of diminishing
marginal return

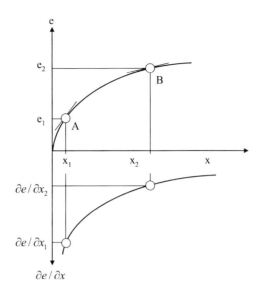

It is the law of diminishing marginal return that explains the shape of the *intertemporal production possibilities frontier* (IPPF) as illustrated in Fig. 3.10. The IPPF shows the possible combinations of current income, e_t, and future income, e_{t+1}, that can be achieved by investing savings at the prevailing production function.

Assume an individual has chosen $e_t = A$ and $e_{t+1} = D$. Now savings out of current income are increased by AB. Investing the proceeds yields an additional income of DE in $t + 1$. Saving an additional unit out of current income of, say, BC (with $BC = AB$) and investing it yields an additional income of EF in $t + 1$. However, given the law of diminishing marginal returns, we find that $EF < DE$.

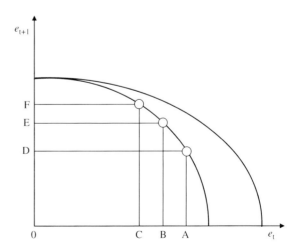

Fig. 3.10 Intertemporal
production possibility frontier
(IPPF)

Consuming a unit of current income in t comes at a cost, namely foregone consumption in $t + 1$ (*opportunity costs*). That said, the slope of the IPPF shows the *opportunity costs* of current consumption – which is simply the rate at which current consumption can be transformed into future consumption – as determined by the law of diminishing marginal returns.

It should be noted that combinations of e_t and e_{t+1} that lie below the IPPF would suggest that the individual would not make efficient use of scarce resources; and that combinations of e_t and e_{t+1} outside the IPPF would not be attainable. A shift of the IPPF to the right, as illustrated in Fig. 3.10, would signal, for instance, that production has become more efficient (as, for instance, new production technologies have been made available). As a result, the opportunity costs of current consumption decline.

3.3.3 Determining the Market Interest Rate

Figure 3.11(a) shows the intertemporal budget constrain KL, together with the IPPF, as represented by the line CG. Assume point G is realised. If savings are increased by JA, BI is the income received in $t + 1$ as a result of having invested savings in t (consumed less).

If it is the objective of individuals to maximise income in t and $t + 1$, that is $e_t + e_{t+1}$, the individual would want to realise point F, where the slopes of the intertemporal budget constrain equals the slope of the IPPF. However, one may expect that an individual wouldn't necessarily want to realise point F, but would try to maximise his individual utility function:

$$U_t = f(e_t, e_{t+1}), \tag{3.15}$$

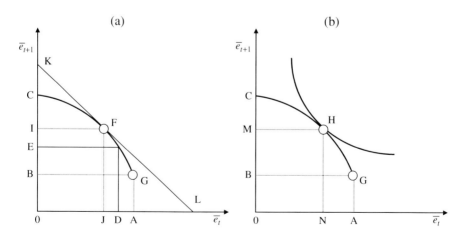

Fig. 3.11 Intertemporal budget constraint, IPPF and the utility function

which makes utility dependent on current and future consumption. In Fig. 3.11(b) the optimum of intertemporal consumption allocation is in point H. Here, the time preference rate equals the marginal return on investment – as expressed by the slope of the IPPF.

Marginal Utility, Expectations Under Risk and the Shape of Indifference Curves

The three co-discoverers of the marginal principle, which was applied to utility theory in the early 1870s, were the British Philosopher Jeremy Bentham (1748–1832), the Austrian Economist Carl Menger (1840–1921) and the French Economist Léon Walras (1834–1919). However, perhaps the most important contribution to the *marginal revolution* came from the German civil servant Herman Heinrich Gossen (1810–1858) with his book published in 1854.[7] Later theorists saw that the marginal principle could actually be applied to virtually any choice problem. Modern microeconomic theory and the micro-foundations of macroeconomics trace their origins to the *marginal revolution*.

Financial theory frequently sets up portfolios where the individual chooses a set of assets in order to maximize profits. For instance, a given level of wealth will imply a certain level of satisfaction for the individual as he contemplates the goods he could purchase with his wealth. If the level of wealth is doubled, the level of satisfaction rises, but it may not double. All information which affects the degree of satisfaction which the investor derives from available portfolios of goods is incorporated into the utility function.

The *utility function* is a mathematical expression of an individual's ranking of available portfolios. Such a function associates with each portfolio a real number. For instance, if a bundle of goods X yields a higher number than another bundle Y, the investor prefers X to Y. If both bundles yield the same number, the investor derives the same utility from both bundles and is said to be *indifferent* between them.

Modern economic theory assumes *ordinal utility* functions, a concept that is ascribed to Vilfredo Pareto (1848–1923). Ordinal utility functions rank; they do not register the amount of utility as *cardinal utility* measures do. A cardinal utility function would imply that increments to a person's utility can be measured and, as a result, compared to changes in another person's utility. An ordinal utility function simply indicates that utility is higher or lower, but does not say how much utility change has occurred.

---

[7]Gossen's rare and little known German book *Die Entwicklung der Gesetze des menschlichen Verkehrs und der daraus fließenden Regeln für menschliches Handeln* (1854) was rediscovered more than twenty years later by Robert Adamson (1852–1902), a Scottish Professor of Logic and Philosophy, and reported to the eminent English economist, William Stanley Jevons (1835–1882), who brought it to the attention of the economic profession.

The consequence is that in ordinal utility theory the absolute rate of change in utility is meaningless. What would make sense, however, is talking about positive, negative or zero marginal utility, for these obviously would be invariant with respect to any ordinal utility function that reflected the rankings of a consumer. In that sense, the theory of ordinal utility has humbler assumption than the theory of cardinal utility.

If the individual consumes one bottle of beer, the *additional* satisfaction from consuming an *extra* bottle may not be as great as from the first. For this assumption, the Austrian Economist Friedrich von Wieser (1851–1926) coined the term *diminishing marginal utility*. The combined findings that (i) an additional consumption of a good yields a positive marginal utility and that (ii) the additional satisfaction from consuming an extra unit may not be as great as the satisfaction from consuming the previous one is called *Gossen's First Law*. *Gossen's Second Law* denotes that in an optimum the exchange ratio of goods (that is their prices) is equal to the ratio of marginal utilities of the goods under review.

Utility theory can be applied to decisions involving uncertain outcomes. For instance, investors can be classified as *risk avers*, *risk loving* or *risk neutral* in terms of the shape of their utility function. Using utility theory, one can also examine how individuals might evaluate utility which arises at different points in time, that is the concept of discounted utility, in a multi-period or inter-temporal framework.

Expected Value and Expected Utility

A random variable X can take the discrete values $x_1, ..., x_2, ..., x_n$, with a discrete probability function (DPF):

$$f(x) = \text{Prob}(X = x) \text{ for } i = 1, \dots, n \text{ and } i = 0 \text{ for } x \neq x_i.$$

For example, in a throw of two dice X the outcome might take one of the 11 values shown below.

$x =$	2	3	4	5	6	7	8	9	10	11	12
$f(x) =$	1/36	2/36	3/36	4/36	5/36	6/36	5/36	4/36	3/36	2/36	1/36

The 11 numbers do not have an equal probability of coming up. The probability distribution can be easily verified. There are 36 combinations that produce the 11 outcomes. One outcome is favorable to number $x = 2$, two are favorable to $x = 3$ (that is the sum 3 can occur either as 1 on the first die and 2 on the second, or as a 2 on the first die and a 1 on the second), and so on.

If X is a continuous variable, the $f(x)$ is said to be a DPF of X if:

$$f(x) \geq 0$$

$$\int_{-\infty}^{\infty} f(x)dx = 1 \text{ and}$$

$$\int_{a}^{b} f(x)dx = P(a \leq x \leq b).$$

The expected value of a discrete X is defined as:

$$E(X) = \sum_{x} x f(x),$$

where Σ_x noted the sum over all x where $f(x)$ is the discrete DPF of X.
The outcome of the throw of two dice is therefore:

$$E(X) = 2 \cdot (1/36) + 3 \cdot (2/36) + \ldots + 12 \cdot (1/36) = 7.$$

If X is continuous random variable, the expected value is:

$$E(X) = \int_{-\infty}^{\infty} x f(x)dx.$$

If, from the individual investor point of view, an expected value of X is associated with a certain level of expected utility, U, we can write: $E(U) = U(E(X))$.

Risk

After von Neumann and Morgenstern (1944) had axiomatized expected utility, it quickly became the dominant paradigm for modeling decision making under uncertainty. Their utility functions have certain properties. One is that utility functions usually reflect the preference *more-is-better-than-less*. This implies that the first derivative of the utility function is positive:

$$U'(x) > 0,$$

where $U'(x) = \partial U(x)/\partial x$. To give an example, in a game the throw of a coin yields either US\$10 for a head or US\$0 for a tail. The expected utility (or, in this case, the expected value of the game) is:

$$0.5 \cdot US\$10 + 0.5 \cdot US\$0 = 5.$$

Suppose the gambler would have US$5 ready in cash; thus US$5 is the outcome from not playing the game. If the investor is *risk averse*, he won't go for a fair gamble. In our case, US$5 for certain is preferred to an equal chance of US$10 or US$0. This implies that the second derivative of the utility function is negative:

$$U''(x) < 0.$$

To see this, note that the utility from not investing $U(5)$ must exceed the expected utility from investing:

$$U(5) > 0.5 \cdot U(10) + 0.5 \cdot U(0).$$

Rearranging yields:

$$U(5) - U(0) > U(10) - U(5).$$

It says is that the utility of a riskless return is preferred over the same utility of a risky return. The utility function of a risk averter has a concave shape in the utility-return space as shown in Fig. 3.12.

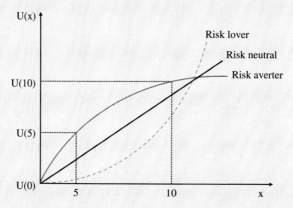

Fig. 3.12 Utility functions

It is easy now to understand that for a *risk lover* the utility function is convex, while for a risk neutral investor, who is indifferent to the gamble or the certain outcome, the utility function is linear. As a result, we can write:

$U''(x) < 0$ risk averse,
$U''(x) = 0$ risk neutral, and
$U''(x) > 0$ risk loving.

A risk averse investor is also said to experience diminishing marginal utility of wealth: each additional unit of x adds less to utility the higher the initial level of x, so that: $U''(x) < 0$. The degree of risk aversion is reflected in the concavity of the utility function in Fig. 3.12; it corresponds to the absolute size of $U''(x)$.

3.3.4 Sum of the Parts: the Neo-Classical Interest Rate

The neo-classical interest rate theory is often illustrated by the savings-investment cross as shown in Fig. 3.13. Savings (S) are assumed to be positively related to the interest rate (i): the higher (lower) the interest rate, the higher (lower) is the supply of savings. Investment (I), in contrast, is a function negatively related to the interest rate: the higher (lower) the interest rate is, the lower (higher) is the demand for investment. The intersection of the savings and the investment schedule determines the market clearing interest, i_0, where savings amount to S_0 and investment to I_0.

The *investment schedule* is based on the neo-classical production function, which relates output e to input x (Fig. 3.14(a)). The lower (higher) x is, the higher (lower) is the marginal return on x (other things being equal). As a result, a low level of investment would be associated with a high marginal return on investment and vice versa – which explains the negative slope of the demand for investment as depicted in Fig. 3.14 (b).

What about the shape of the *savings schedule*? According to *the theory of time preference,* people prefer current consumption over future consumption. Against this backdrop, people would be willing to transfer current consumption into future consumption only (that is save part of current income) if they are compensated for by a higher future income. The higher (lower) the amount of savings out of current income is, the higher (lower) is the marginal rate of substitution of current consumption against future consumption (Fig. 3.15(a)). As a result, a growing supply of savings would be positively related to the interest rate (Fig. 3.15(b)).

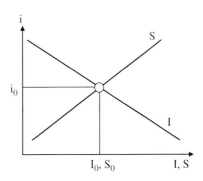

Fig. 3.13 Investment and savings

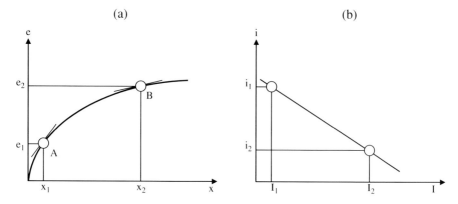

Fig. 3.14 Neo-classical production function and investment demand

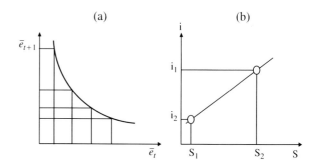

Fig. 3.15 Time preference
and the savings supply

The Neo-Classics: The Marginal Efficiency of Capital

The production function of a representative firm in the neo-classical theory
framework can be formulated as:

$$Y = F(N, C),$$

where Y is ouput, N is labor and C is capital. The firm's nominal profit function
is:

$$\underbrace{\psi}_{Profit} = \underbrace{P \cdot Y}_{Revenue} - \underbrace{w \cdot N^d}_{Wage\ costs} - \underbrace{i \cdot B^*}_{Capital\ costs} \ ,$$

where ψ = profit, P = price level, w = wage, N^d = planned demand for labor,
i = interest rate and B^* = planned level of debt, with $i \cdot B^*$ representing the
amount of money to be paid on borrowed funds.

Investment (I) is the change in the stock of capital from the beginning to the end of the period:

$$I = C - C_0,$$

and leads to the optimal stock of capital.

It is assumed that the firm finances its investment solely by debt:

$$P \cdot I = \Delta B^*.$$

The latter actually says that the amount invested equals real investment times the price level. To put it differently, the investment equals the increase in the firm's real level of debt: $I = \Delta B^*/P$.

Inserting the production function, the investment function and the function for the increase in debt into the firm's profit function, we yield:

$$\psi = P \cdot F(N, C) - w \cdot N^d - i(B_0 + P(C - C_0)).$$

If it acts as a price taker (that is accepting P, w and i as given), the firm's profit is a function of N and C. Maximizing the firm's profit function yields:

$$\frac{\partial \psi}{\partial N} = P \cdot \frac{\partial F}{\partial N} - w \overset{!}{=} 0,$$

$$\frac{\partial \psi}{\partial C} = P \cdot \frac{\partial F}{\partial C} - i \cdot P \overset{!}{=} .0.$$

Solving these two equations yields the optimal labor and capital input, which are:

$$w = P \cdot \frac{\partial F}{\partial N} \text{ and } i = \frac{\partial F}{\partial C},$$

respectively.

In the market optimum, the interest rate would equal the marginal efficiency of capital (while the real wage would equal the marginal product of labor). This finding makes clear how the neo-classical theory differs from the Austrian School in explaining the interest rate: To Austrians, the interest rate is simply expressive of peoples' time preferences, while neo-classic take recourse to the concept of time preference *and* the productivity theory of capital.

3.4 Knut Wicksell's Theory of the Interest Rate

3.4.1 Wicksell's Loanable Funds Theory

The Swedish economist Knut Wicksell (1851–1926), in an effort to explain the effect of the interest rate on commodity prices, made a distinction between the *neutral interest rate* and the *market interest rate*.[8] According to Wicksell, the neutral interest would be the rate of interest where the economy would be in equilibrium, that is where current output would be at its potential, and overall money prices would remain unchanged. As such, the neutral real interest rate is an *equilibrium* interest rate.

As Wicksell put it (1965, p. 102): "There is a certain rate of interest on loans which is neutral in respect to commodity prices, and tend neither to raise nor to lower them. This is necessarily the same as the rate of interest which would be determined by supply and demand if no use were made of money and all lending were effected in the form of real capital goods. It comes to much the same thing to describe it as the current value of the natural rate of interest on capital."

In Wicksell's theory, the market interest is the rate of interest in the loan market, as determined by the supply of and demand for money. By increasing (restricting) their loan supply, banks would be in a position to lower (raise) the market interest rate. If, for instance, the market rate falls below the natural rate (due to banks increasing their supply of loans), the economy would expand and, if output exceeds its potential level, prices would rise. If, however, the market rate of interest exceeds the economy's neutral interest rate, output would contract and prices would decline.

According to Wicksell, the neutral market interest rate is a *real phenomenon*. He wrote: "There is a certain rate of interest on loans which is neutral in respect to commodity prices, and tend neither to raise nor to lower them. This is necessarily the same as the rate of interest which would be determined by supply and demand if no use were made of money and all lending were effected in the form of real capital goods. It comes to much the same thing to describe it as the current value of the natural rate of interest on capital."

While the interest rate in financial markets is determined by demand for and supply of money, the neutral interest rate is set by real factors, and money as such has nothing to do with it. Wicksell wrote: "Now if money is loaned at this same rate of interest [that is, the neutral interest rate], it serves as nothing more than a cloak to cover a procedure which, from the purely formal point of view, could have been carried on equally well without it. The conditions of economic equilibrium are fulfilled in precisely the same manner."

---

[8]Wicksell introduced the natural rate in the 1898 paper *The Influence of the Rate of Interest on Commodity Prices* (reprinted in E. Lindahl, ed., Selected Papers on Economic Theory). He expanded the idea in *Geldzins und Güterpreise* (1898), translated by Kahn as *Interest and Price* in 1936.

Fig. 3.16 Increasing the
supply of money

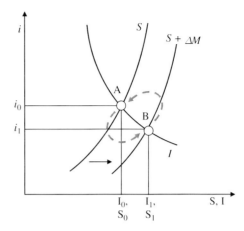

Against the background of Wicksell's distinction between the neutral interest rate
and the market interest rate, the *theory of loanable funds* was established. It explains
why the market interest rate can deviate from the neutral interest rate – which is the
case when banks increase the stock of money. Assume, for instance, the supply
of savings (S) equals the demand for investment (I), which is represented in point
A in Fig. 3.16. The neutral market rate and market interest rates are represented
by i_0, and savings and investment amount to S_0 and I_0, respectively. Now banks
increase the stock of money by ΔM (through lending money). As a result, the total
supply of *loanable funds* – that is $S + \Delta M$ – moves S to the right, lowering the
market interest rate to i_1. In the new market equilibrium, which is reached in point
B, savings amount to S_1 and investment to I_1.

However, the increase in savings and investment has been brought about by an
artificial lowering of the market interest rate (through increasing the supply of
money via credit expansion), while the neutral market interest rate remains unaffected. As a result, point B would represent a *temporary equilibrium*. Savings and
investment are now higher than people prefer according to their *time preference*.
People will, sooner or later, reduce their savings and investment and increase consumption, and the economy would move back to point A.

Alternatively, the demand for present goods may rise as people prefer to hold
more real balances (ΔH). Starting from the equilibrium point A, the demand schedule for present goods would move to the right by ΔH (Fig. 3.17). The shift reflects
an increase in peoples' time preference, as less present goods are now offered for
future goods. As a result, the market interest rate *and* the neutral interest rate rise
from to i_0 to i_1, with savings and investment rising to S_1 and I_1. Compared with an
increase in the stock of money (created via credit expansion), point B represents a
long-run equilibrium.

In market equilibrium, the market interest rate (as determined in the loan market) equals the neutral interest rate. Wicksell's distinction between the neutral interest rate (as determined by peoples' time preference) and the market interest rate

Fig. 3.17 Increasing the demand for money

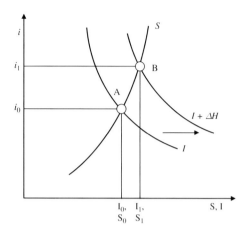

provides a theoretical framework for analysing, for instance, the impact changes in bank lending have on the business cycle. In the *Austrian monetary business cycle theory,* for instance, an economic boom emerges whenever government manipulations of the money supply push the market interest rate below the neutral interest rate – it causes a that will be followed by bust sooner or later.

Wicksell's Cumulative Process: a Monetary Process

In what follows, it will be shown that the Wicksell process – in which the market interest rate diverges from the natural interest rate – is caused by banks' loaning to non-banks through which the stock of money is increased. In fact, the Wicksell process is set into motion by an expansion of the economy's money supply.

Using the formal representation of *Wicksell's cumulative process* put forward by Humphrey (1997), it is assumed that savings (S) are deposited with banks, and that investment demand (I) determines the demand for loans (LD) which, in turn, are supplied by banks (LS). The interest rate on loans is i, while the natural rate is r, that is the rate that equilibrates saving and investment ($I = S$).

Furthermore, *excess demand* (that is actual demand over potential output) is E. As banks create additional deposits (D) when extending loans to non-banks, the change in deposit supply is dD/dt. The change in the price level (P) is dP/dt, and the change in the market interest rate is di/dt.

According to the first equation, planned investment will exceed planned savings if i falls below r:

$$I - S = a(r - i);$$ (3.16)

here a relates the investment-saving gap to the difference between the natural rate and the market rate.

The second equation says that the excess of investment over saving equals the additional demand deposits created by bank loan extension:

$$dD/dt = I - S.$$ (3.17)

Assuming that investment is financed by loans, we can write: $LD = I(i)$, where $I(i)$ is the function linking desired investment to the loan rate of interest. That said, banks loan supply is: $LS = S(i) + dD/dt$, that is banks loan supply equals savings deposited plus newly created deposits.

The third equation says that new deposits are used for demanding goods and services, therefore inducing excess demand. [Note that it is assumed that the economy is at full employment.] That said, we can write:

$$dD/dt = E.$$ (3.18)

Assuming that additional deposits create excess demand, one can assume that this causes prices to go up:

$$dP/dt = bE,$$ (3.19)

where the coefficient b is the factor of proportionality between price level changes and excess demand.

Substituting Eqs. (3.16), (3.17), and (3.18) into (3.19), one yields:

$$dP/dt = ab(r - i).$$ (3.20)

It says that the discrepancy between the natural rate and the market rate is to be held responsible for changes in the price level.

Substituting (3.16) into (3.17) yields:

$$dD/dt = a(r - i),$$ (3.21)

which shows that the change in deposits is also a function of the discrepancy between the natural rate and the market rate.

The final equation relates the change in the market interest rate to changes in the price level:

$$di/dt = gdP/dt;$$ (3.22)

here, g is the factor of proportionality. Equation (3.22) takes account of the fact that banks must, sooner or later, increase the loan rate to protect their gold holdings from inflation-induced demands for cash. The equation assumes that banks raise rates in response to price changes. The equation ensures that the loan rate eventually converges to its natural equilibrium level. This can be seen by substituting Eq. (3.20) into the above formula to obtain:

$$di/dt = gab(r - i). \tag{3.23}$$

Solving this equation for the time path of i yields:

$$i(t) = (i0 - r)e^{-gabt} + r, \tag{3.24}$$

where t is time, e is the base of the natural logarithm system, i_0 is the initial disequilibrium level of the loan rate, and r is the given natural rate. With the passage of time, the first term on the right-hand side vanishes and the loan rate converges to the natural rate. At this point, monetary equilibrium is restored. Saving equals investment, excess demand disappears, deposit expansion ceases, and prices stabilize at their new, higher level.

Source: Humphrey (1997).

3.4.2 The Concept of the Real Neutral Interest Rate

Wicksell's natural rate of interest is the rate at which the demand for loans equals the supply of savings. A high or low level of the natural real rate of interest cannot necessarily be said to be "positive" or "negative", though. For instance, with unchanged savings a rise in investment demand would bring up the interest rate and a rise in output. In contrast, with unchanged investment a decline in savings would result in higher interest rates, this time accompanied by a decline in investment and output.

The natural real interest rate concept is important for monetary policies, which nowadays try to deliver high output and employment growth accompanied by low consumer price inflation. Unfortunately, the natural real interest rate level cannot be directly observed. If anything, one can only try to estimate the rate on the basis of specific assumptions, while the reliability of the resulting estimations depends crucially on the assumptions made.

In recent years, the concept of the neutral interest rate has gained prominence in academia (Woodford, 2000, 2003; Bomfin, 2001; Neiss & Nelson, 2003). Economic theory identifies a number of determinants of the natural real interest rate. Perhaps the most important are: (i) peoples' time preference, (ii) productivity and population growth, (iii) fiscal policy and risk premia, and (iv) the institutional structure of financial markets. We will now take a brief look at these determinants.

3.4.2.1 Time Preferences

The most intuitive, and theoretically well founded, determinant of the natural
real rate of interest is *time preference*. As noted earlier, time preference means
that present goods command a premium over future goods. A rising (declining)
time preference means that, other things being equal, people prefer to consume
more (less) out of current income, thereby reducing (increasing) savings. With an
unchanged investment schedule (which can also be explained by peoples' time preference), a decline (rise) in savings argues for a rise (fall) in the natural real rate of
interest. That said, it is peoples' time preference that determines the natural real rate
of interest.

3.4.2.2 Productivity and Population Growth

For firms, an increase in productivity growth implies higher returns on physical
investment. To meet an increase in investment demand, the natural real rate of interest must rise to increase the supply of savings. In addition, productivity growth may
affect consumers' borrowing and lending to the extent that productivity growth may
have repercussions on peoples' expected rate of income growth. For instance, a situation in which households anticipate higher real incomes in the future may induce
them to increase their consumption relative to their current income. This, again,
would tend to work towards a rise in the natural real rate of interest.

An increase in an economy's working age population normally leads to an expansion of the workforce. Because the additional workers have to be equipped with
capital, a rise in firms' investment may be required. If, for instance, a rise in investment demand is not matched by increased savings, the natural real interest rate will
have to increase to balance investment and available savings. For an illustrate of
productivity and population growth in the US and Japan see Fig. 3.18.

3.4.2.3 Fiscal Policy and Risk Premia

In most countries, governments have become large (chronic) borrowers and thereby
exert a significant impact on the real rate of interest. Public sector borrowing represents a demand for peoples' savings. If the private sector does not fully adjust
its savings in response to, say, a rise in government borrowing – that is reducing
its consumption –, the natural real rate of interest rises in order to equilibrate the
demand for and supply of savings.

A prominent example of this *non-neutrality of budget decisions* can be found
in the field of social security. Typically, increases in social security transfers have
been found to reduce private savings: Households are economically encouraged to
cut back on their savings (which would be put aside if no government sponsored
social security system were in place). As a result, a higher real interest rate would
be required to finance social security benefits compared with a situation of privately
funded social security.

US

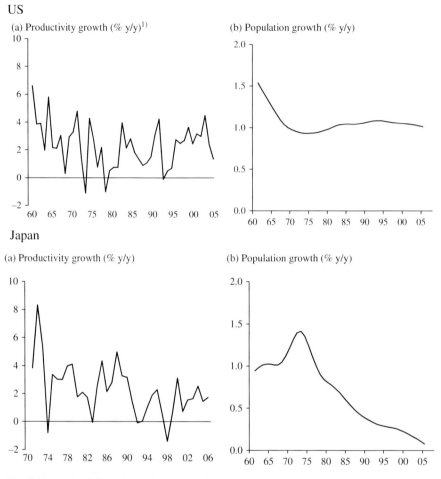

Fig. 3.18 Productivity and population growth
Source: Bloomberg, IMF; own calculations. [1]Business sector. Productivity is defined as real output per total employment

Alternatively, if the government runs up a deficit, and private agents decide to save more and consume less out of current income in order to offset a likely increase in taxes in the future, this would have no impact on the real interest rate, as saving would then increase one-to-one with the government's borrowing requirements, with no implications for the real rate that clears the market for funds.

In addition, risk premia may also play a role. For example, *exchange rate risk premia* as well as *inflation risk premia* may affect the level of the natural real rate of interest. Exchange rate risk premia could be significant in countries where inflation is high and volatile and where the credibility of monetary policy is low. Uncertainties related to future exchange rate development and inflation can make people demand a higher compensation for exchanging current consumption for future consumption – and thus increase the natural real rate of interest.

3.4.2.4 Institutional Structure of Financial Markets

The *institutional structure of financial markets* represents another relevant factor determining the natural real interest rate. For instance, the efficiency of financial markets can make an important contribution to an optimal allocation of savings across time and across investment projects. For example, an improving financial market structure (in terms of, for instance, the degree of competition among banks and other financial intermediaries) can enlarge the range of assets available to savers in terms of return, risk and liquidity. This, in turn, may have the overall effect of encouraging households to save more, thereby leading to a lower level of the equilibrium real interest rate.

A Simple Model of the Neutral Interest Rate

In view of the above, one might be inclined to model the neutral real interest rate as a function of a number of factors: time preference, the economy's long-term potential growth rate (including demographic developments), fiscal policy and institutional factors. The relationship between these variables and the equilibrium rate can be described by a simple neo-classical, or *golden rule growth*, model (Laubach & Williams, 2001):

$$ r* = \left(\frac{1}{\sigma}\right) q + \theta + n, $$

where r^* is the equilibrium real interest rate, q is the rate of technological change, σ denotes the coefficient of relative risk aversion, θ is the time preference, and n represents the rate of population growth. The formula can be interpreted as follows:

- An increase (decrease) in q increases (decreases) the return on investment. Given an unchanged level of savings, the ensuing rise (fall) in demand for investment funds drives up (lowers) the equilibrium real interest rate.
- The equilibrium real interest rate is inversely related to σ. An increase (decrease) in relative risk aversion causes savers to save more (less) which, assuming an unchanged investment schedule, leads to a decrease (increase) in the equilibrium real interest rate.
- An increase in θ would reduce savings: people decide to consume more (save less) out of current income. Given an unchanged demand for investment, such an increase leads to a rise in the equilibrium real interest rate.
- An increase in n enhances the economy's labour supply and tends to raise its potential growth rate. With unchanged savings, the ensuing higher investment demand drives up the equilibrium real interest rate.

3.4.3 Estimating the Natural Real Interest Rate

As noted earlier, the natural real rate of interest cannot be observed directly. However, there are basically four methods for finding out what the natural real interest rate could be, namely: (i) calculating averages of ex-post real interest rates, (ii) using real yields of inflation-index bonds and making use of (iii) time series and (iv) structural models.

3.4.3.1 Long-Term Averages of Actual Real Interest Rates

The underlying idea of calculating averages of actual real interest rates over a long time span is that (short-term) deviations between the actual and natural real interest rate should wash out. In a long-enough sample period resource slack probably averages zero, which could suggest that the long sample average of the real interest equals the natural real interest rate.

Deciding about the sample period has, of course, a material bearing on the outcome. For instance, including periods of generally low rates – such as 1950s – or high real rate periods, such as the early 1980s – make a big difference on the calculation results. What is more, the results depend on the interest rate maturity under review: natural real interest rates (Fig. 3.19–3.21) calculated on the basis of long-term yields should be higher than those calculated on the basis of short-term interest rates.

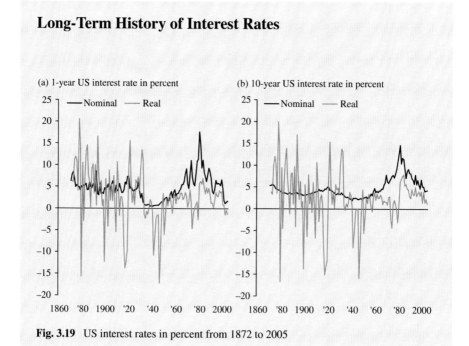

Fig. 3.19 US interest rates in percent from 1872 to 2005

	1-year rate			10-year rate			Inflation
	Av.	Min.	Max.	Av.	Min.	Max.	Av.
1872 – 2005	2.5	–17.1	20.6	2.4	–16.7	20.0	2.2
1871 – 1913	5.4	–15.6	20.6	4.1	–16.7	20.0	–0.3
1946 – 2005	1.4	–4.6	6.9	1.9	–15.9	7.8	4.1
1946 – 1970	0.3	–4.6	3.7	0.5	–15.9	4.4	3.1
1971 – 2005	2.1	–2.6	6.9	2.8	–4.3	7.8	4.8

Fig. 3.20   Short- and long-term real yields in the US in percent, 1872–2005
Source: Global Financial Data, R. Shiller; own calculations

	Real short-term interest rate				Average inflation			
	1981-Q1–2005-Q1	1981–1989	1990–1998	1999–2005-Q1	1981-Q1–2005-Q1	1981–1989	1990–1998	1999–2005-Q1
Euro area	3.9	4.8	4.7	1.2	3.7	5.8	2.9	2.0
US	2.2	3.9	1.8	0.4	3.5	4.7	3.1	2.5
UK	3.9	4.9	4.1	2.3	4.4	6.3	4.0	2.3
Japan	2.1	3.6	1.6	0.5	1.1	2.0	1.4	–0.5
Australia	4.2	4.9	4.8	2.0	4.8	8.2	2.6	3.1
Canada	3.8	5.1	4.1	1.3	3.7	6.1	2.3	2.3

Fig. 3.21   International overview: simple averages of the real short-term interest rate in percent, 1981-Q1 to 2005-Q1
Source: Browne and Everett (2005), p. 128

The estimation technique based on simple averages of actual real interest rates can be refined in order to take into account the specific events (shocks) that may well have distorted the *true* picture. In economic literature, the refined computation is often conducted by deriving the natural real interest rate from estimations of the Taylor rule (1993) such as:

$$r_t = r^* + a(\pi_t - \pi^*) + bx_t,$$

where r_t corresponds to the real short-term interest rate, r^* represents the natural real interest rate, π_t denotes the percentage change in the price level from time $t - 1$ to t, π^* symbolises the inflation objective of the central bank, and x_t stands for the output gap at time t.

The rule implies that the central bank allows deviations of the actual real interest rate from the natural real interest rate if inflation is not consistent with the central bank's objective, or if the output gap is non-zero. In order to estimate the natural real interest rate r^*, the average of the real interest rates observed is then corrected for those fluctuations in actual real interest rates which are due to inflation being different from its target or the output gap being positive or negative.

By proceeding in this way, Gerdesmeier and Roffia (2003) calculate that the (short-term) natural real interest rates were between 2.1% and 3.2% in the euro area for the period 1985 to 2002. However, in the sample period starting from 1993, lower levels of the equilibrium rate, between 1.8% and 2.9%, were estimated. Using this approach for the US economy, when π^* is taken to be 2%, Reifschneider and Williams (2000) report a value of 2.5% for the equilibrium real rate of interest. The authors also state that lower inflation targets yield higher equilibrium real interest rates. They report an equilibrium real rate of 3.5% for an inflation target in the region of 0 to 1%.

How do Real Yields Relate to Growth?

According to the neo-classical theory, the market equilibrium real interest rate should equal to the economy's marginal efficiency of capital. In that sense, it might be of interest to take a brief look at the relation between market yields and the economy's GDP growth rate.

Figure 3.22(a) shows US annual nominal GDP growth and yields for AAA and BAA rated corporate bonds in percent for the period 1962 to early 2008. Two facts stand out. First, nominal GDP growth and nominal yields were positively correlated. Second, nominal GDP growth tended to exceed nominal yields from the early 1960s to the early 1980s, while the reverse held true in the period thereafter.

Figure 3.22(b) shows real GDP growth and real AAA and BAA corporate yields in percent. The latter were calculated by subtracting the annual change in the GDP deflator from the nominal yield level. To eliminate the *noise* from the data, Fig. 3.22(c) shows *smoothed series* of real GDP growth and real corporate yields, calculated by applying the Hodrick-Prescott (HP) Filter.

The data suggest that the relation between (real) growth and (real) bond yields has not been straightforward in the past. The observed discrepancy might be explained by a number of factors. First, bond yields are formed on the basis of the expected average development of real output and inflation *over the remaining maturity of the bond* – a view which might *ex post* differ (markedly) from the actual turnout of GDP and inflation.

Second, the inflation period in the early 1970s and 1980s (and the associated fluctuations in real economic activity) should have increased the (inflation) risk premium demanded by investors for holding bonds, thereby driving a wedge between real yields and real growth. With the decline in CPI inflation in the last decades, however, real yields have converged back towards real GDP growth.

(a) Nominal GDP (% y/y) and corporate yields (%)

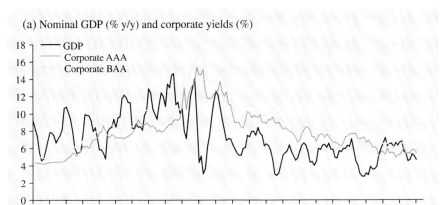

(b) Real GDP (% y/y) and corporate yields (%)

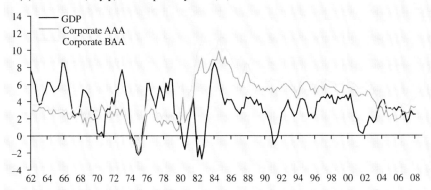

(c) Trend real GDP (% y/y) and corporate yields (%)

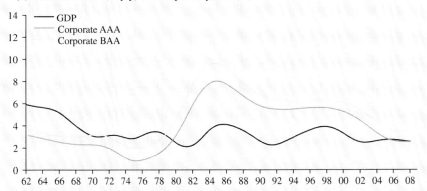

Fig. 3.22 US GDP growth and corporate bond yields (%)
Source: Thomson Financial, Bloomberg, own calculations. Real yields were calculated by subtracting the annual change in the GDP deflator from nominal yields. The series were calculated by applying the Hodrick-Prescott (HP) Filter to real series

3.4.3.2 Real Yields of Inflation Index Bonds

One may equate the *natural real interest rate* to the real yield of market traded *inflation indexed bonds*. Such an approach builds on the view that the market expectation is the best measure available for the natural real interest rate. At a sufficiently long horizon, it is reasonable to assume that a real long-term bond yield should be a valid indication of the natural real interest rate. Figure 3.23(a) and (b) show the real yields taken from US and euro area government inflation linked bonds from 1999 to May 2008. While this approach has advantages over calculating ex-post historical averages – namely its forward-looking character, its simplicity and its availability on a high frequency basis –, it also has several shortcomings.

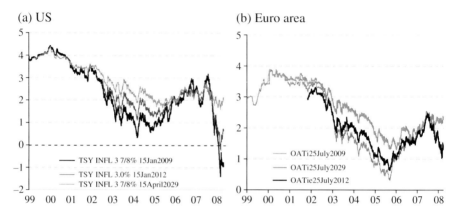

Fig. 3.23 Real yields of inflation-linked government bonds in percent
Source: Bloomberg; own calculations. – Daily data. – Negative real yields on short-dated US inflation linked bonds can be ascribed to dislocations in financial markets. With the emergence of the US subprime crisis in summer 2007, the US Fed cut interest rates from 5.25% in September 2007 to 2.0% in April 2008, thereby having brought short-term yields below annual CPI inflation

To start with, inflation linked bond yields and therefore the measures for the normal interest rate, may be distorted by premia, e.g. due to liquidity or tax factors, which may vary over time. What is more, inflation linked bond yields cannot measure the natural real interest rate per se, but only the market perception thereof, which might – at times of exceptional optimism or pessimism – be distorted. A further limitation is that for many currencies there are no long time series for inflation linked bonds available. For instance, in the US, the US Treasury started issuing Treasury inflation protected securities (TIPS) in January 1997 (Sack & Elsasser, 2004; Dupont & Sack, 1999). In the euro area, bonds indexed to the euro area HICP (excluding tobacco) have only existed since November 2001. So the time span of available data might be too short to form a final view on whether real bonds yields correspond with the natural real rate of interest.

3.4.3.3 Time Series Models

To take the possibility of persistent time variations in the natural real interest rate into account, a small but growing body of literature, especially building on US data, has put forward simple time series models which explicitly allow for a time-varying natural real interest rate. These approaches are based on the so-called *unobservable-component technique*, which help to disentangle the trend movements in the natural real interest rate from transitory, or higher-frequency, fluctuations in real (short-term) interest rates.

For instance, Cuaresma, Gnan, and Ritzberger-Grünwald (2005) used such a technique to calculate the equilibrium real interest rate in the euro area, using a multivariate econometric model on monthly data for industrial production, the real interest rate and inflation from 1991 to 2002, applying the Kalman filter. The natural real interest rate, corresponding to the non-stationary component of the real rate series, is found to have declined to levels around, or slightly above, 2 percent in most recent years.

An advantage of the statistical filtering approach is that it provides for time variation in the natural real interest rate. In addition, the estimates show relatively little dependence on the precise specification of the model used. However, the methodology does not allow for making a structural interpretation of the changes in the equilibrium real rate, i.e. the approach does not tell us anything about possible structural reasons for the time variations in the (natural) real interest rate.

3.4.3.4 Structural Models

The problem just described can be addressed by using fully specified *structural models* of the economy. One class these structural models are general equilibrium models constructed on the basis of explicit *optimising behaviour* on the part of households and firms; typically, prices are assumed to be sticky, that is prices do not adjust instantaneously to economic changes. Such an approach can deal with the problem of calculating a time-varying natural real interest rate and, at the same time, provide an explanation for the identified changes in the natural real interest rate.

In particular, the general equilibrium models can be used to generate a time path for the natural real interest rate over a certain period by constructing a *flexible-price scenario*, characterised by the absence of nominal rigidities in the economy. The path of the natural real interest rate is then identified with the path of the actual real interest rate that the model generates in response to the estimated shocks under the counterfactual scenario (Smets & Wouters, 2002). However, the results of such exercises depend heavily on the analyst's specific model assumptions and give therefore a subjective rather than an objective picture. Figure 3.24 shows selected studies on the neutral interest rates in the US and the euro area.

3.5 The Keynesian Liquidity Preference Theory

According to John Maynard Keynes (1883–1946), the interest rate is determined by the interaction of two factors: the demand for money – termed *liquidity preference* – and the *supply of money*. In the Keynesian view, the interest rate is therefore a purely *monetary phenomenon*.

Authors	Model	Area and period	Results
Mésonnier and Renne (2004)	Kalman filter with Philips curve and output gap equations	Euro area Q1 79-Q4 02	Year 2001: real neutral interest rate close to 1%
Giammarioli and Valla (2003)	Stochastic Dynamic General Equilibrium	Euro area Q4 73-Q2 00	Positive interest rate gap over 1999-2000
Amato (2005)	HP and Kalman filter with a consumption equation	Euro area (Germany prior to 1999) and US 1970–2001	Neutral at 2.5/2.75% for both the euro area and the US
Cuaresma et al. (2005)	Kalman filter with statistical equation	Euro area Jan 1991 to March 2002	Year 2001: neutral real interest rate slightly below 1%
Manrique and Marques (2004)	Kalman filter with Philips curve and output gap equations	US and Germany/euro Q2 62-Q4 01	US: neutral at 2.5% in 2002; euro area: neutral at 1.5% in 2002
Laubach and Williams (2003)	Kalman filter with Philips curve and output gap equations	US Q1 61-Q2 02	2001: natural rate of interest at around 3%

Fig. 3.24 Selected studies on the neutral interest rate

In the Keynesian theory, market agents can *either* hold money *or* keep their wealth in interest bearing bonds (*consols*); it is not possible to hold both. As there are just two assets – money and bonds –, the supply of (demand) bonds is equal to the demand for (supply of) money; that is bonds are traded against money and vice versa.

Money is demanded for three reasons: the transaction and precaution motive (depending on income) and the speculative motive (depending on the interest rate). What is more, people are said to hold bonds (money) when the interest rate is high (low), as then the opportunity costs of holding money is high (low). This actually explains the negative relation of the demand for money to the interest rate in Fig. 3.25. The economy's stock of money is assumed to be given, represented as a vertical line.

The equilibrium in the money market is in point *A*, where the money demand schedule intersects with the money supply curve. Here, the equilibrium interest rate is i_0. In point *B*, the demand for money would be lower than the amount supplied. Market agents would keep demanding bonds, pushing up bond prices (that is lowering the bond yield), thereby moving the money market towards point *A*. In point *C*, the demand for money outstrips the amount supplied. In an effort to increase money holdings, market agents keep selling bonds, thereby lowering bond prices (that is increasing bond yields), restoring the money market equilibrium in point *A*.

Fig. 3.25 Keynesian
liquidity preference and the
money stock

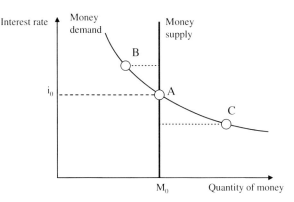

Viewed in this sense, the interest rate in the Keynesian liquidity preference theory is characterised as a purely *monetary phenomenon*, actually decoupled from
real economic developments. In the Keynesian system, neither time preference nor
the marginal efficiency of capital play a role in determining the equilibrium market
interest rate. The Keynesian explanation was actually intended to turn a back on the
neo-classical theory and the insights put forward by the Austrian School of Economics. In *The General Theory of Employment, Interest, and Money*, published in
1936, Keynes wrote (p. 21): "(...) classical economists are fallaciously supposing
that there is a nexus which unites decisions to abstain from current consumption
with decisions to provide for future consumption."

With the interest rate theoretically deprived of its essential function as outlined
by the neo-classical school – let alone the Austrians School of Economics –, the
Keynesian theory provided a prima facie argument for government interventionism
in terms of interest rate management. As Garrison (2002) wrote: "(...) Keynes's
verdict of "no nexus" left interest rates up for grabs. And if they weren't doing their
job, maybe they could be used for macro-management."

3.6 Nominal Versus Real Interest Rates

In the last few years a number of governments have issued bonds whose coupon
and principal at redemption are indexed to a consumer price index. The yield spread
between comparable conventional bonds and index linked bonds should therefore
reflect, among other things, market agents' inflation expectations over the residual
maturity of the bond. This yield spread is often referred to as *break even inflation*
(BEI), indicating the level of expected inflation at which an investor would be indifferent as to which of the two types of bond to hold.

In line with the *Fisher parity* (1907), the nominal yield of a bond, i_{nom}, can be
stated as follows:

$$(1 + i_{nom}) = (1 + i_{real})(1 + \pi^e)(1 + \phi), \tag{3.25}$$

whereas i_{real} = real rate component, π^e = inflation expectation and ϕ = risk premium. The BEI can be calculated as:

$$(1 + i_{nom})/(1 + i_{real}) = (1 + \pi^e)(1 + \phi). \qquad (3.26)$$

The BEI provides interesting insights into the private sector's *true* inflation expectations, as it is calculated on the basis of *market prices*. What is more, conventional and index linked bonds are issued over a variety of original maturities, so that the BEI is available for a larger number of horizons than usually reported in inflation expectation surveys. However, the BEI is, as a rule, an imperfect indicator of market agents' long-term inflation expectations (Sack, 2000):

– The BEI incorporates an *inflation risk premium* required by investors to be compensated for *inflation uncertainty* when holding nominal coupon bearing bonds. Future inflation erodes the payments on a nominal security in real terms but not those on an index-linked bond. Investors are therefore likely to demand a premium as compensation for holding long-term nominal securities, and, as they are typically risk-averse, such a premium is likely to vary over time. Moreover, the inflation risk premium can be expected to increase with the maturity of the bond. This premium tends to *bias the BEI upwards*.
– As market liquidity for inflation indexed bonds is typically lower than that for comparable nominal bonds, this may lead to a *higher liquidity premium* embedded in the yields on index linked bonds. This liquidity premium would therefore tend to *bias the BEI rate downwards*.
– The BEI may sometimes be biased as a result of technical and institutional market factors (related to, for instance, taxation and regulation), which may have little to do with changes in inflation expectations. Unfortunately, the *distortion effect* of changes in legislation and market practices on the BEI is difficult to isolate and quantify.

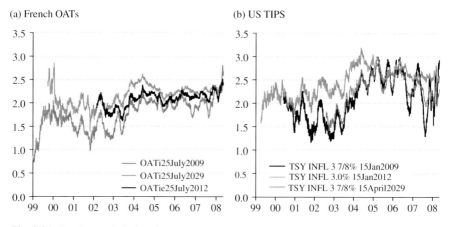

Fig. 3.26 Break-even-inflation the euro area and the US (%)
Source: Bloomberg, own calculations. – Daily data

Figures 3.26(a) and (b) show the BEI for various maturities for the euro area and the US from 1999 to May 2008. Throughout the period under review, the euro area BEI have been oscillating around 2.0%, the level of consumer price inflation the European Central Bank considers compatible with its price stability mandate. In the US, the BEIs were around 2.5% on average, a level which is typically interpreted as being in line with the US Fed's mandate of keeping inflation low.

3.7 Credit Spreads

One key economic principle is that the higher the risk of investment is, the higher is the risk compensation demanded by investors (*high risk, high return*). For instance, investors tend to demand a higher risk compensation for investing in emerging market economies when compared with investing in western developed markets; for instance, economic and/or political risks tend to be higher in the former than in the latter. When it comes to credit market transactions, lenders demand a compensation for risk, which tends to rise with the (perceived) level of risk involved.

A measure of investment risk is the so-called *credit spread*. Generally speaking, the credit spread is the yield differential between risky and low-risk bonds (such as government securities).[9] To give an illustration, Fig. 3.27 depicts the credit spread between US Baa- and Aaa-rated corporate bond yields from January 1922 to October 2007. Two facts stand out. *First*, the credit spread was always positive in the

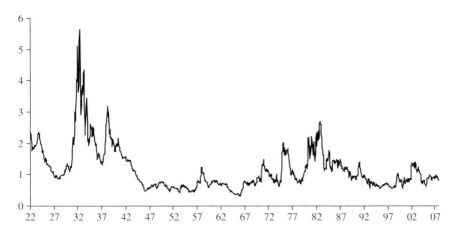

Fig. 3.27   Credit spread between US Baa- and Aaa-rated corporate bonds (%)
Source: Federal Reserve Bank of St. Louis, own calculations. – Period: January 1948 to October 2007

---

[9]Of course, government bonds are not, as a rule, riskless, as is often stated. Like any other debt security, government bonds are subject to price risks and, most importantly, repayment risks.

period under review. *Second*, it fluctuated substantially, reaching close to 6% in the early 1930s and a low point of 0.3% in early 1966.

Growing (declining) investor confidence in a borrower's credit quality should argue for a tightening (widening) of credit spreads. For instance, a more optimistic assessment of a firm's credit quality should translate into higher demand for its outstanding bonds. As a result, the price of the bond rises, and its yield declines relative to risk-free bonds, suppressing the credit spread. Likewise, investor concern about firms' deteriorating credit quality should make investors shying away from risky bonds. The selling of bonds should depress their prices, thereby widening the credit spread vis-à-vis less risky bonds.

One would expect that in a market environment of high (low) market interest rates credit spreads should be high (low). For instance, if the interest rate level is high due to high inflation, investment becomes more risky, as inflation creates distortions in the economy's relative price mechanism, increasing the risk of firms making bad investments. As investors seek higher compensation for holding risky assets, credit spreads widen. Figure 3.28 would actually support the notion that the higher the yield level is, the higher is the credit spread level.

However, there are reasons why the credit spread could reflect more than just the (perceived) credit quality of the respective borrower for at least two reasons:

– *First*, there tend to be *liquidity premia*. Even in large capital markets (such as the US and the euro area), most risky corporate bonds trade in relatively *thin* markets. This means that it is typically more costly to undertake transactions in these instruments than in equities and Treasuries. Investors must be compensated for this.

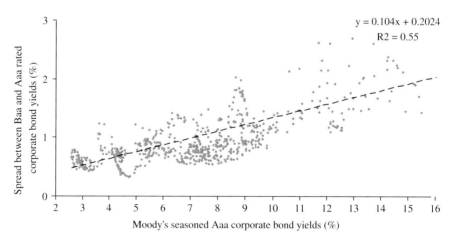

Fig. 3.28 US corporate spreads and interest rate level (%)
Source: Federal Reserve Bank of St. Louis, own calculations. – Period: January 1948 to October 2007

(a) Spreads over US Treasury yields (in basis points)

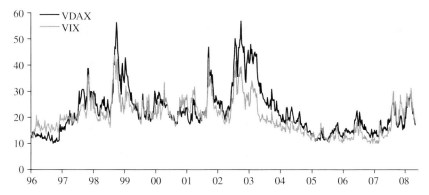

(b) Yield levels (%)

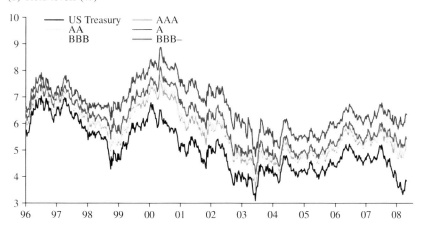

(c) Corporate yields over US Treasury yields in basis points (10-years)

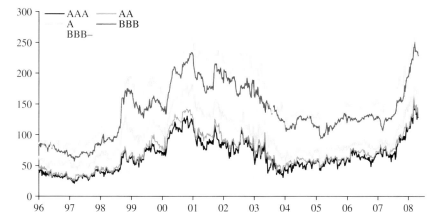

Fig. 3.29 US Treasury and corporate US yields (10-years)
Source: Thomson Financial, own calculations. – Period: January 1996 to May 2008

– *Second*, there is *taxation*. For instance, in many countries corporate bonds are subject to taxes, whereas government bonds are not. Since investors compare returns across instruments on an *after-tax basis*, arbitrage arguments imply that the yield on corporate debt will be higher to compensate for the payment of taxes.

To give a final illustration of the relation between corporate and government yields in times of financial market strain, Fig. 3.29(a) shows stock market volatility measures for the US (VIX index) and Germany (VDAX) for the period January 1996 to May 2008.[10] The shaded areas represent periods of elevated stock market volatility. Stock market volatility rose strongly towards the end of 1998/early 1999, as a response to the market turmoil associated with the LTCM debacle. Volatility also rose markedly after the 9/11 terror attacks in the US and in the aftermath of the bursting of the New Economy boom around 2001.

Figure 3.29(b) shows the yields of the 10-year US Treasury and various US corporate credits (with ratings categories ranging from AAA to BBB-). In the period under review, corporate yields, on averages, followed those on the US Treasury quite closely. However, in periods of elevated volatility (as measured by the stock market volatility indices), spread levels tended to widen, basically because government bond yields declined more strongly than corporate bond yields (Fig. 3.29(a)).

Periods of heightened investor risk aversion tend to be associated with a *flight to quality*, that is investors are increasingly willing to hold relatively riskless government bonds compared to risky corporate bonds. It should be noted here, however, that corporate spreads actually declined in 2002/2003, a situation of elevated stock market volatility. This finding might be explained by the fact that the fall in stock market valuations had bottomed out towards the end of 2002, and investors were increasingly stepping up their demand for risky assets, including corporate bonds.

References

Amato, J. D. (2005). *The role of the natural rate of interest in monetary policy*, Bank for International Settlements, *Working Paper* 171, Basle March.

Bomfin, A. N. (1997). Measuring equilibrium real interest rates: what can we learn from yields on indexed bonds? *Federal Reserve Board*, Finance and Economics Discussion Series, No. 53.

Böhm-Bawerk, E. v. (1890). *Capital and interest: A critical history of economical theory*. London: MacMillan.

Browne, F., & Everett, M. (2005). Assessing interest-rate risk from the constituent components. Central Bank and Financial Services Authority of Ireland, Financial Stability Report, pp. 123–137.

---

[10]The VDAX is a measure for the implied volatility of the German stock market index (DAX) over the coming 45 days, calculated on the basis of prices of options on stocks listed in the DAX. A high (low) VDAX means that the expected volatility of the DAX is high (low). The level of the VDAX does not say anything about the direction of expected price changes, though. VIX stands for the Chicago Board Options Exchange Volatility Index, a measure of the implied volatility of S&P 500 index options, representing the market's expectation of volatility over the next 30 day period.

Cuaresman, J. C., Gnan, E., & Ritzberger-Grünwald, D. (2003). The natural rate of interest – concepts and appraisal fort the euro area. *Monetary Policy & The Economy, Q5*, 29–47.

Dupont, D., & Sack, B. (1999, December). The treasury securities market: overview and recent developments. *Federal Reserve Bulletin* 785–806.

Fisher, I. (1907). *The rate of interest.* New York: Macmillan, reprinted in Fisher (1997). The Works of Irving Fisher, 3., William J. Barber (Ed.), London: Pickering and Chatto.

Friedman, M. (1994). *Money mischief, episodes in monetary history.* San Diego: Hartcourt Brace & Company.

Garrison, R. W. (2002, September). Ditch the Keynesians, Why policy-infected interest rates must go. *Barron's, 82*(35), 2.

Gerdesmeier, D., & Roffia, B. (2003, January). *Empirical estimates of reaction functions for the euro area. ECB Working Paper* No. 206 Frankfurt/Main.

Gossen, H. H. (1854). Entwicklung der Gesetze des menschlichen Verkehrs und der daraus fließenden Regeln für menschliches Handeln, Braunschweig, Viehweg.

Giammarioli, N., & Valla, N. (2003, May). *The natural real rate of interest in the euro area. ECB Working Paper* No. 233 European Central Bank.

Humphrey, T. M. (1997). Fisher and Wicksell on the quantity theory. Federal Reserve Bank of Richmond, *Economics Frankfurt/Main Quarterly, 83/4*, Fall, 71–90.

Keynes, J. M. (1973, 1936), *The general theory of employment, interest, and money.* Cambridge: Cambridge University Press.

Laubach, T., & Williams, J. (2001). Measuring the natural rate of interest. Federal Reserve Board Finance and Economic Discussion Series, No. 56.

Laubach, T., & Williams, J. C. (2003). Measuring the natural rate of interest. *Review of Economics and Statistics*, 85(4), 1063–1070.

Manrique, M., & Marques, J. M. (2004). *An empirical approximation of the natural rate of interest and potential growth. Working Paper* 0416, Banco de España Madrid.

Mésonnier, J. S., & Renne, J. P. (2004). *A time-varying natural rate of interest for the euro area. Working Paper* 115, Banque de France Paris.

Mises, L. v. (1996). *Human action* (4th ed., p. 527), San Francisco: Fox & Wilkes.

Neiss, K. S., & Nelson, E. (2003). The real interest rate gap as an inflation indicator. *Macroeconomic Dynamics*, 7(2), 239–262.

Neumann, J. v., & Morgenstern, O. (1944). *Theory of games and economic behavior.* Princeton: Princeton University Press.

Reifschneider, D., & Williams, J. C. (2000). Three lessons for monetary policy in a low-inflation era. *Journal of Money, Credit and Banking*, 32(4), 936–966.

Rothbard, M. N. (2001, 1962). *Man, economy, and state, power and market, a treatise on economic principles* (p. 389). Auburn, AL: Ludwig von Mises Institute.

Sack, B. (2002). A *monetary policy rule based on nominal and inflation-indexed treasury yield,* Board of Governors of the Federal Reserve System. Washington, DC: Division of Monetary Affairs.

Sack, B., & Elsasser, R. (2004, May). Treasury inflation-indexed debt: A review of the U.S. experience. Federal Reserve Bank of New York, *Economic Policy Review, 10*(1), 47–63.

Schumann, J. (1987). *Grundzüge der mikroökonomischen Theorie* (5th ed.), Berlin: Springer Verlag.

Smets, F., & Wouters, R. (2002, August). An *estimated stochastic dynamic general equilibrium model of the euro area. ECB Working Paper*, 171 European Central Bank Frankfurt/Main.

Woodford, M. (2000). *A Neo-Wicksellian framework for analyzing monetary policy. Working Paper*, Princeton University Press.

Woodford, M. (2003). *Interest and prices.* Princeton, New York: Princeton University Press.

Wicksell, K. (1898, 1965). *Interest and Prices*, translated by R. F. Kahn, London, Macmillan; reprinted New York, Augustus M. Kelley.

Wicksell, K. (1969). *The influence of the rate of interest on commodity prices.* Reprinted in Knut Wicksell, Selected Papers on Economic Theory, E. Lindahl (Ed.), New York, pp. 67–89.

Chapter 4
Financial Market Asset Pricing

> *When someone with experience proposes a deal to someone with money, too often the fellow with money ends up with the experience, and the fellow with experience ends up with the money.*
>
> Warren Buffet (2007, p. 22).

4.1 Prices, Returns and Distributions

4.1.1 Prices and Returns

Financial asset prices and their returns are closely linked, simply because returns are calculated on the basis of prices from different points in time. In theoretical and empirical work, however, returns tend to play a more prominent role than prices, given their relatively attractive statistical properties (Lucas, 1978). In what follows, we will take a brief look at various financial asset return measures.

4.1.1.1 Holding Period Returns

The one-period holding period return of an asset (in this case a stock), H_{t+1}, can be formulated as (Campbell, Lo, & MacKinlay, 1997, p. 9):

$$H_{t+1} = \left[\frac{P_{t+1} - P_t}{P_t} \right] + \frac{D_{t+1}}{P_t}. \tag{4.1}$$

The first term on the right hand side is the capital gain/loss of P from period t to $t + 1$. The second term is the dividend yield, with D being the dividend payment. H_{t+1} can be easily calculated *ex post*. Calculating ex ante requires forecasts for P_{t+1} and D_{t+1}. It also follows that the future one-period holding H_{t+1} between $t + i$ and $t + i + 1$ is:

A. Belke, T. Polleit, *Monetary Economics in Globalised Financial Markets*, DOI 10.1007/978-3-540-71003-5_4, © Springer-Verlag Berlin Heidelberg 2009

$$1 + H_{t+i+1} = \left[\frac{P_{t+i+1} + D_{t+i+1}}{P_{t+i}} \right]. \tag{4.2}$$

Hence, if one money unit is invested in the stock (and all dividend payments are reinvested in the stock), then *ex post* the payout over n periods is:

$$Z = A[1 + H_{t+1}][1 + H_{t+2}] \ldots [1 + H_{t+n}]. \tag{4.3}$$

The one-period holding period return formula can be applied to any kind of financial asset. For instance, for a coupon paying bond with an initial maturity of n periods and periodical coupon payments C, the one-period holding return for n periods is:

$$H_{t+1}^{(n)} = \frac{P_{t+1}^{(n-1)} - P_t^{(n)}}{P_t^{(n)}} + \frac{C}{P_t^{(n)}}. \tag{4.4}$$

4.1.1.2 Compounding Returns

The concept of compounding returns is an important one, as they give us multi-period returns. The *simple net return*, R_t on the asset between period $t - 1$ and t, is:

$$R_t = \frac{P_t}{P_{t-1}} - 1. \tag{4.5}$$

For the *simple gross return* on the asset we can write: $1 + R_t$. From this definition it follows that the asset's gross return over the most recent k periods from date $t - k$ to date t (that is: $1 + R_t(k)$) is equal to the product of the k single-period returns from $t - k + 1$ to t:

$$\begin{aligned} 1 + R_t(k) &\equiv (1 + R_t) \cdot (1 + R_{t-1}) \ldots (1 + R_{t-k+1}) \\ &= \frac{P_t}{P_{t-1}} \cdot \frac{P_{t-1}}{P_{t-2}} \cdot \frac{P_{t-2}}{P_{t-3}} \ldots \frac{P_{t-k+1}}{P_{t-k}} = \frac{P_t}{P_{t-k}}. \end{aligned} \tag{4.6}$$

The net return over the most recent k periods, written $R_t(k)$, equals its k-period gross return minus one.

In practise, investors quite often focus on a one-year investment horizon. Multi-year returns are often *annualized* to allow comparisons between different investment horizons:

$$Annualized\,[R_t(k)] = \left[\prod_{j=0}^{k-1}(1 + R_{t-j}) \right]^{1/k} - 1. \tag{4.7}$$

To annualize multi-year returns, investors often use a first-order Taylor expansion formula:

$$Annualized\,[R_t(k)] \approx \frac{1}{k} \sum_{j=0}^{k-1} R_{t-j}. \tag{4.8}$$

If, however, the volatility of returns plays an important role – that is if the higher-order terms in the Taylor expansion are not negligible – the results of Eq. (4.8) may become questionable. That said, the only advantage of such an approximation is convenience – it is easier to calculate arithmetic rather than a geometric averages.

4.1.1.3 Continuous Compounding

The continuously compounded return, or log return r_t, of an asset can be defined as the logarithm of its gross return $(1 + R_t)$:

$$r_t \equiv \log(1 + R_t) = \log \frac{P_t}{P_{t-1}} = p_t - p_{t-1}, \tag{4.9}$$

where $p_t \equiv \log P_t$. Here, R_t is a *simple* return, while r_t is the continuously compounding return. The advantages of the latter become clear if one considers multi-period returns:

$$\begin{aligned} r_t(k) = \log(1 + R_t(k)) &= \log((1 + R_t) \cdot (1 + R_{t-1}) \cdots (1 + R_{t-k+1})) \\ &= \log(1 + R_t) + \log(1 + R_{t-1}) + \cdots + \log(1 + R_{t-k+1}) \\ &= r_t + r_{t-1} + \cdots + r_{t-k+1}. \end{aligned} \tag{4.10}$$

The continuously compounded multi-period return is the sum of continuously compounded single-period returns. Continuous compounding is of great help in statistical analyses: it is much easier to derive the time-series properties of additive processes than of multiplicative processes.

However, continuously compounded returns have a serious disadvantage. The simple return on an asset portfolio is a weighted average of its simple returns, with the weight of each asset representing the share of the portfolio's total value invested in that particular asset. If asset i has a share of w_{ip} in portfolio p, then the return on the portfolio at time t, R_{pt}, is related to the returns on individual assets, $R_{it}, i = 1 \ldots N$, by $R_{pt} = \sum_{i=1}^{N} w_{ip} R_{it}$.

Continuously compounded returns, however, do not share this property: the log of a sum is not the same as the sum of logs; r_{pt} does not equal $\sum_{i=1}^{N} w_{ip} r_{it}$. In practise, however, this aspect is typically of minor importance. When measured over short periods (say, a day or week), returns tend to be relatively small, and the continuously compounded return on a portfolio tends to be actually fairly close to the weighted average of the continuously compounded returns on the individual assets: $R_{pt} \approx \sum_{i=1}^{N} w_{ip} r_{it}$.

4.1.2 *Joint, Marginal, Conditional and Unconditional*
   Distributions

Investors cannot predict with certainty future financial asset prices; in fact, future prices are uncertain. That said, uncertainty is the crucial ingredient in the theoretical and empirical work on financial asset pricing in capital markets. It is therefore important to give a brief overview about the types of uncertainty that asset prices might exhibit over time.

Statistically speaking, asset prices are an outcome of a random experiment. The outcome variable, X, is called a *random variable*: until X is realized, it is uncertain. One has to assign probabilities to potential outcomes (realizations of X) to quantify the degree of uncertainty. In terms of financial asset pricing, extrapolating of past observations has ever since been a favored method for arriving at an opinion of what the future will bring.[1]

A random variable might be discrete or continuous. A *discrete variable* is either finite in number or countably infinite. For a *continuous variable*, the set of outcomes is infinitely divisible and, as a result, uncountable. In statistical analyses, capital letters are often used for the name of the random variable, and lowercase letters for the value it takes. Thus, the probability (P) that X takes the value of x can be denoted as $P(X = x)$. A *probability distribution* is actually a listing of all possible outcomes, or events, with a probability assigned to each outcome.

For a discrete variable, the probability distribution is:

$$f(x) = P(X = x).$$

The axiom of probability requires that:

$$0 \leq P(X = x) \leq 1 \text{ and}$$

$$\sum_{i=1}^{n} f(x_i) = 1.$$

If the random variable is continuous, the probability associated with any particular point is zero, and positive probabilities can only be assigned to intervals in the range of x. The *probability density function* (PDF) is defined as $f(x) \geq 0$, so that:

$$P(a \leq x \leq b) = \int_a^b f(x)dx \geq 0,$$

---

[1]Of course, one may well say that the reliance on the frequency of past occurrences might be extremely hazardous. Frank H. Knight (1964, p. 226) noted that a past occurrence "(...) is so entirely unique that there are no others or not a sufficient number to make it possible to tabulate enough like it to form a basis for any inference of value about any real probability in the case we are interested."

Fig. 4.1 Example: joint PDF
of X and Y

		\multicolumn{4}{c}{X}
		-2	0	2	4
Y	3	0.30	0.10	0.22	0.00
	5	0.00	0.15	0.05	0.18

which describes the area under $f(x)$ in the range from a to b. For a continuous variable, we have:

$$\int_{-\infty}^{\infty} f(x)dx \geq 1.$$

4.1.2.1 Joint Probability Density Function (PDF)

The joint PDF gives the probability that X takes a value of x and, simultaneously, Y takes a value of y. More formally, assume X and Y are two discrete random variables. For the discrete joint PDF we can write:

$$f(x, y) = P(X = x \text{ and } Y = y)$$
$$= 0 \text{ when } X \neq x \text{ and } Y \neq y.$$

In view of the example given in Fig. 4.1, for instance, the joint probability that $X = -2$ while $Y = 5$ is zero. Likewise, the probability that X is zero while Y simultaneously takes the value of 3 is 0.10; and so on.

4.1.2.2 Marginal PDF

The marginal PDF gives the probability of a random variable X obtained by summing (or, in the case of continuous variables: integrating) the joint distributions over all values of the other random variable Y. $f(x)$ and $f(y)$ are called marginal PDFs:

$$f(x) = \sum_{y} f(x, y) \text{ and } f(y) = \sum_{x} f(x, y), \text{ respectively,}$$

where the Σ_y means the sum over all values of Y and Σ_x means the sum over all values of X.

Using the example above, the marginal PDF of X is:

$$f(x = -2) = 0.30 + 0.00 = 0.30$$
$$f(x = 0) = 0.10 + 0.15 = 0.25$$
$$f(x = 2) = 0.22 + 0.05 = 0.27$$
$$f(x = 4) = 0.00 + 0.18 = 0.18.$$

Likewise, the marginal PDF of Y is :

$$f(y = 3) = 0.30 + 0.10 + 0.22 + 0.00 = 0.62$$
$$f(y = 5) = 0.00 + 0.15 + 0.05 + 0.18 = 0.38.$$

4.1.2.3 Conditional and Unconditional PDF

The conditional PDF gives the probability that X takes on the value of x given that Y has taken a value of y. For instance, simple regression analysis estimates the behavior of the dependent variable (say, for instance, money supply) conditional upon the values of other variables (say, for instance, real output and interest rates). The conditional PDF for X can be formalized as:

$$f(x|y) = P(X = x|Y = y).$$

Similarly, the conditional PDF of Y is:

$$f(y|x) = P(Y = y|X = x).$$

The conditional PDF of one variable is simply the ratio between the *joint PDF* to the *marginal PDF* of another variable. The conditional PDFs for X and Y are, respectively:

$$f(x|y) = f(x, y)/f(y) \text{ and } f(y|x) = f(x, y)/f(x).$$

In view of the example above, the conditional probabilities can be calculated as:

$$f(X = -2|Y = 3) = f(X = -2, Y = 3)/f(Y = 3)$$
$$= 0.30/0.62 = 0.48$$
$$f(Y = 5|X = 0) = f(Y = 5, X = 0)/f(X = 0)$$
$$= 0.15/0.25 = 0.60.$$

Actually, every probability of an outcome is conditional – as it depends on many factors. For instance, the probability that the US dollar appreciates from US$1.50 per euro to US$1.00 per euro might depend on the yield differential between the US and the euro area, growth perspectives, fiscal policies, and many other variables. However, if all these unspecified conditions are taken for granted, the probability of the Greenback gaining in value against the euro can be interpreted as an *unconditional*, or *a priori*, *probability*.

For instance, assume that the investor determines the unconditional probability on the basis of past data, where the US-dollar exchange rate vis-à-vis the euro in the last 200 trading days appreciated 0.5% per day in 100 days and depreciated 0.3% per day in 100 days. The unconditional probability that the US-dollar will appreciate against the euro would be 10% (that is the expected return of 0.2% per day divided by 200 trading days).

4.1.2.4 Statistical Independence

If two random variables X and Y are statistically independent, we can write:

$$f(x, y) = f(x)f(y).$$

Statistical independence implies that the joint PDF can be expressed as the product of the two variables' marginal PDFs. It can be easily shown that X and Y in the example above are not statistically independent: the product of the two marginal PDFs is not equal to the joint PDF.

4.1.2.5 Continuous Joint PDF

When turning to continuous joint PDF, just assume that X and Y are continuous rather than discrete variables. Their PDF $f(x, y)$ is:

$$f(x, y) \geq 0$$

$$\int_{-\infty}^{\infty} \int_{-\infty}^{\infty} f(x, y) dx dy = 1 \text{ or}$$

$$\int_{c}^{d} \int_{a}^{b} f(x, y) dx dy = P(a \leq x \leq b, c \leq y \leq d).$$

The marginal PDF of X and Y is:

$$f(x) = \int_{-\infty}^{\infty} f(x, y) dy \text{ and}$$

$$f(y) = \int_{-\infty}^{\infty} f(x, y) dx, \text{ respectively.}$$

4.1.2.6 Random Variables and the Normal PDF

A random variable can be characterized by its *expected value* (calculated as the sample mean) and its *variance*. The most commonly used PDF is the *normal distribution*. A continuous random variable X, for instance, is said to be normally distributed if its PDF follows:

$$f(x) = \frac{1}{\sigma \sqrt{2\pi}} \exp\left(-\frac{1}{2}\frac{(x - \mu)^2}{\sigma^2}\right) \quad -\infty < x < \infty,$$

where the parameters of the distributions are μ and σ^2, the mean and the variance of the distribution, respectively. The PDF is symmetrical around its mean value, μ, and approximately 68% of the area under the normal curve lies between the values of $\mu \pm \sigma$, about 95% of the area lies between $\mu \pm 2\sigma$, and about 97% of the area lies between $\mu \pm 3\sigma$.

When dealing with asset returns, one may want to consider *higher moments* of the PDF. The third and fourth moment, which are defined as $E(X - \mu)^3$ and $E(X - \mu)^4$, respectively, allow analyzing the shape of the probability function, that is its *skewness* (or lack of symmetry) and *kurtosis* (or tallness or flatness) as depicted in Fig. 4.2 .[2]

The third moment, the measure of *skewness*, is defined as:

---

[2]Note that the second moment about the mean is the variance.

Fig. 4.2 Skewness and
kurtosis of a random variable

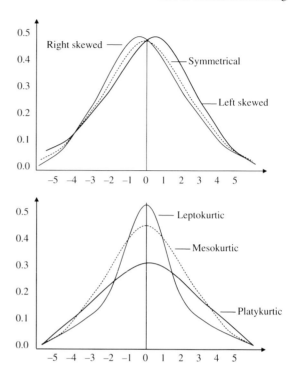

$$S(X) = \frac{\left[E(X - \mu)^3\right]^2}{\left[E(X - \mu)^2\right]^3}.$$

The fourth momentum, the measure of *kurtosis*, is:

$$K(X) = \frac{E(X - \mu)^4}{\left[E(X - \mu)^2\right]^2}.$$

A PDF with $K < 3$ is called *platykurtic* (fat or short-tailed), those with $K > 3$ are
called *leptokurtic* (slim or long tailed). If $K = 3$, the kurtosis is said to be *mesokurtic*,
of which the normal distribution is the prime example. The measures of skewness
and kurtosis can be used to determine whether a random variable follows a normal
PDF – which represents one of the crucial assumptions of the Gaussian classical
linear regression model.

The asymptotic, or large sample, Jarque-Bera (JB) test of normality (Jarque &
Bera, 1987) computes the skewness (S) and kurtosis (K) measures of the OLS residuals and uses the following test statistic:

$$JB = n\left[\frac{S^2}{6} + \frac{(K - 3)^2}{24}\right],$$

where $(K - 3)$ represents excess kurtosis, as for a normal distribution $S = 0$ and $K = 3$. If the p-value of the chi-square statistic is sufficiently low, one can reject the hypothesis that the residuals are normally distributed.

4.1.2.7 From the Unconditional to the Log-Normal Distribution

What if the conditional distribution of an asset return differs from its marginal or unconditional distribution? Well, the conditional distribution would be relevant for the investor if he wants to predict an asset's return. However, the unconditional distribution of returns would remain important to the investor, especially so if he expects the predictability of asset returns to be rather small.

The most common model for asset returns is the independently and identically distributed (i.i.d.) normal model. It holds that returns are independent over time and identically and normally distributed. For instance, the original formulation of the Capital Asset Pricing Model (CAPM) is based on the assumption of normality of asset returns. However, it should be noted that the i.i.d. normal model suffers from at least two important shortcomings.

First, most financial assets have a maximum loss potential. For example, a stock or bond investor cannot lose more than his investment in the stock or bond. That said, the maximum loss for the investor would be 100% of the capital invested. The normal distribution, however, does not allow for such a limit to losses; it actually allows for losses of more than 100%. *Second*, if one assumes that one-period returns are normally distributed, the multi-period returns cannot also be normally distributed: this is because multi-period returns are the *products* of one-period returns. Of course, the *sum* of normally distributed one-period returns would be normally distributed. However, it would not be economically meaningful. (Note that only the sum of single-period continuously compounded returns does have a meaningful interpretation as a multi-period continuously compounded return.)

4.1.2.8 The Lognormal Distribution

A continuous random variable X follows a lognormal distribution if its natural logarithm, $\ln(X)$, follows a normal distribution. Assume that the continuously compounded one-period return, $r_{it} \equiv \log(1 + R_{it})$, is i.i.d. normal.[3] The lognormal model can be stated as:

$$r_{it} \sim N(\mu_i, \sigma_i^2). \tag{4.11}$$

According to the lognormal model – assuming that the mean and variance of r_{it} are μ_i and σ_i^2, respectively –, the mean and variance can be calculated as:

---

[3]The lognormal model has a rather prominent history. The dissertation of the French mathematician Louis Bachelier (1900) contained the mathematics of Brownian motion and heat conduction, five years prior to Albert Einstein's (1879 – 1955) array of four distinguished "Annus Mirabilis Papers" published in "Annalen der Physik" in the year 1905. Over time, the lognormal model has become the basic model of in the field of financial asset pricing.

$$E[R_{it}] = e^{\mu_i + \frac{\sigma_i^2}{2}} - 1 \tag{4.12}$$

$$Var[R_{it}] = e^{2\mu_i + \sigma_i^2}[e^{\sigma_i^2} - 1]. \tag{4.13}$$

However, if the mean and variance of the lognormal (i.i.d.) one-period returns R_{it} are m_i and s_i^2, respectively, the mean and variance of r_{it} would be:

$$E[r_{it}] = \log \frac{m_i + 1}{\sqrt{1 + \left(\frac{s_i}{m_i+1}\right)^2}}, \tag{4.14}$$

$$Var[r_{it}] = \log\left[1 + \left(\frac{s_i}{m_i + 1}\right)^2\right]. \tag{4.15}$$

As can be seen, the lognormal model does not violate the limited liability restriction. There is a lower bound of zero for $(1 + R_{it})$, which is – provided r_{it} is i.i.d. – satisfied by $(1 + R_{it}) = e^{r_{it}}$.

Skewness and kurtosis can be estimated in a sample of data by constructing the obvious sample averages:
the sample mean

$$\hat{\mu} \equiv \frac{1}{T} \sum_{t=1}^{T} \varepsilon_t, \tag{4.16}$$

the sample variance

$$\hat{\sigma}^2 \equiv \frac{1}{T} \sum_{t=1}^{T} (\varepsilon_t - \hat{\mu})^2, \tag{4.17}$$

the sample skewness

$$\hat{S} \equiv \frac{1}{T\hat{\sigma}^3} \sum_{t=1}^{T} (\varepsilon_t - \hat{\mu})^3, \tag{4.18}$$

and the sample kurtosis

$$\hat{K} \equiv \frac{1}{T\hat{\sigma}^4} \sum_{t=1}^{T} (\varepsilon_t - \hat{\mu})^4. \tag{4.19}$$

Figure 4.3(a) and (b) show the frequency distribution of daily returns of the US and Japanese stock market performance indices from the beginning of 1995 to August 2006. In the US, Japan and Germany, there is negative skewness, implying that the distributions have a long left tail. In all cases, kurtosis exceeds 3; the distributions are peaked (leptokurtic) relative to the normal distribution. The Jarque-Bera

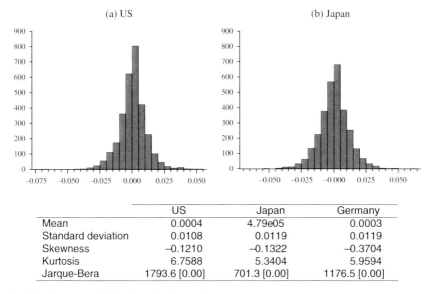

Fig. 4.3 Frequency distribution of daily stock returns

Source: Thomson Financial, own calculations. – Returns represent first differences of log levels; continuously compounded stock returns. – The stock market indices represent the performance indices (including capital gains and dividends). – Period: January 1995 to 18 August 2006.

tests suggest that the null hypothesis of a normal distribution can be rejected for both stock returns under review.

4.2 Stylised Facts for International Asset Price Linkages

4.2.1 Latest Developments

Examining financial newspapers suggests that (sharp) asset price changes are *event-based*, that is they appear to respond to economic and political *news*. This, in turn, suggests that different assets classes (bonds, stocks, etc.) in different markets (US, euro area, Japan, etc.) may be influenced by the same news or *information*. Indeed, time series analysis seems to indicate that random variations of financial asset prices do share some non-trivial statistical properties. Such properties, common across a wide range of instruments, markets and time periods are called *stylized facts*.

There are a number of reasons why financial market participants show great interest in understanding the statistical properties of asset prices. Private investors may hope that *additional knowledge* of the behaviour of asset prices could help detecting profitable trading opportunities and optimising portfolio diversification. Central banks, in turn, may want to form a view about how monetary policy actions (changes in interest rates and money supply) affect asset prices, which, in turn, have an effect on growth, employment and inflation.

In increasingly globalised financial markets, forming a view of asset price behaviour and its impact on real economic and monetary variables has become an ever greater intellectual challenge: Market trading volumes are growing rapidly; financial products turn out to be increasingly complex and interrelated across international market segments; cross-border capital flows are on the rise; the number of market participants from different currency areas is growing; and regulatory backgrounds are becoming increasingly important for buying and selling decisions on the part of private and institutional investors.

Do different financial markets crash jointly or is the fall of one the gain to another market? The answer to this question is crucial for the *stability* of international financial system (Hartmann, Straetmans, & Vries, 2005). The more markets crash simultaneously, the higher is the danger that even large market players (leading banks, insurance companies, mutual funds, hedge funds, etc.), holding wisely diversified

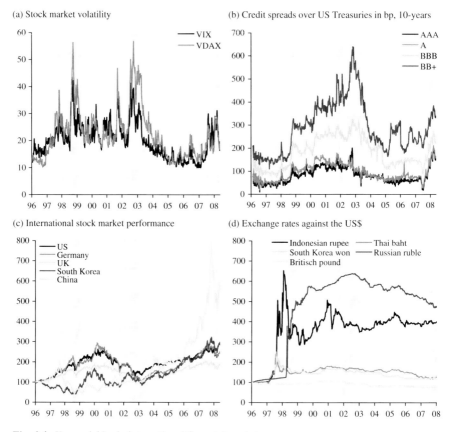

Fig. 4.4 Key variables in international financial markets
Source: Bloomberg, Thomson Financial, own calculations. – VIX and VDAX = market traded volatility of the US S&P 500 and German DAX, respectively. – The stock market performance indices reflect dividends and capital gains. – Stock markets and exchange rates were set to 100 in January 1996. – Period: January 1996 to May 2008. – The shaded areas represent periods of elevated stock market volatility.

and managed trading portfolios, could run into trouble, potentially causing serious frictions in financial markets and the real economy.

The latest series of international financial market crises – such as, for instance, the *East Asian financial crisis*, which started in July 1997, the *Russian debt default crisis* in August 1998, the crisis triggered by the collapse of *Long Term Capital Management* (LTCM) in autumn of 1998, the *international stock market collapse* starting towards the end of 2000 and, most recently, the *international credit market turmoil* starting in July/August 2007 – has left little doubt about how closely connected and integrated international financial markets have become.[4]

The financial market turbulence seen in recent years produced strong price (co-)movements in various securities markets worldwide (Domanski & Kremer, 2000). In most cases, it triggered a general reassessment of credit risk, leading to a drying-up of market liquidity, even in some of the largest securities markets (International Monetary Fund, 1998, p. 38). As a result, the co-movement of returns cross-markets underwent dramatic changes, challenging portfolio allocation and risk management strategies which rely on constant historical co-movements of asset prices. Figure 4.4(a–d) provide an illustration of market developments in *normal times* and periods of crisis (in terms of elevated stock market volatility) as far as credit spreads, stock market performances and FX developments are concerned.

The Long-Term Capital Management (LTCM) Crisis

In September 1998, the near-default of the hedge fund Long Term Capital Management (LTCM) caused a kind of earthquake in world financial markets.[5] LTCM was founded in early 1994 by John Meriwether, former Vice Chairman of the Salomon Brothers investment bank, and former US Fed Vice Chairman David Mullins. Among its principals and investors were many from Wall Street and academia, including Nobel Prize laureate Myron Scholes.

At the beginning of 1998, LTCM managed approximately US$4.8 billion of assets. The fund used sophisticated "relative value" arbitrage strategies: it tried to identify exploitable price discrepancies in global fixed income and

---

[4]For thorough and insightful reviews of the financial crises, see, for instance, the Quarterly Reviews published by the Bank for International Settlements.

[5]The US President's Working Group on Financial Markets (1999) characterized hedge funds as "any pooled investment vehicle that is privately organized, administered by professional investment managers, and not widely available to the public". The ECB (2005, p. 69) defines hedge funds as "a fund, whose managers generally have no or very limited restrictions on the use of various active investment strategies to achieve positive absolute returns, and receive performance-related fees. Such strategies often involve leverage, derivatives, long and short positions in securities or any other assets in a wide range of markets".

equity markets, betting on discrepancies to converge towards levels observed in the past. Right from the start, LTCM was extremely successful, generating an attractive "outperformance" for its shareholders. The market environment was quite favourable for the fund's investment philosophy: there was a trend decline in consumer price inflation, risk spreads and interest rate levels, and a trend rise in stock prices.

LTCM investments were financed by a high leverage, with balance sheet assets being more than 25 times higher than equity capital. The fund's impressive track record the and reputation of its principals resulted in favourable credit funding terms. What is more, the large trading volume made the fund a very desirable counterparty for investment and commercial banks.

In September 1998, however, the Russian debt crisis hit. It caused a far-reaching re-pricing in global fixed income markets. Investors, losing their risk appetite, rushed from risky into less risky assets (*flight-to-quality*). Spreads on riskier debt widened dramatically vis-à-vis government bonds, and *market liquidity* dried up in many market segments. What is more, correlations between financial markets calculated on price behaviour observed in the past broke down. The investments made by LTCM began to lose value. In early September, LTCM notified its investors that it had lost US$1.8bn of its equity capital, and the fund was forced to unwind its positions at unfavourable terms in order to meet *margin calls* and satisfy its overall liquidity demands.

The problems were compounded by the size of the LTCM investments in certain markets. At the end of August 1998, LTCM had already lost over 50% of its equity. What started as a liquidity crisis could have led to default. A *meltdown* was avoided when the US Federal Reserve, under the New York Fed President Bill McDonough, coordinated a bailout by the consortium of the fund's 16 main bankers. LTCM insolvency, it was feared, would have led to even larger losses to creditors and further disruptions in already very fragile markets.

The LTCM case highlighted the fact that market participants had failed to account for potential future credit exposures arising from the interaction of different markets, market liquidity and credit risks. None of the prime brokers was aware of the full size and the riskiness of the LTCM portfolio. Advantageous credit terms evaporated quickly under stressed conditions, as creditors changed their stance dramatically, which further magnified the severity of the liquidity shortage.

Sources: Vaughan, D. A. (2003), Selected Definitions of Hedge Fund, comments for the US SEC Roundtable on Hedge Funds, 14–15 May. Also, The President's Working Group on Financial Markets (1999), Hedge Funds, Leverage, and the Lessons of Long-term Capital Management, April; ECB (2005), Hedge Funds and their implications for financial stability, ECB Occasional Papers, No. 34, August.

4.2.2 Descriptive Statistics and Some Tests

There are a number of univariate descriptive statistics that allow characterizing asset returns. To start with, the *mean* is the average value a series. It can be obtained by simply adding up the realisations of the series and dividing it by the number of observations.

The *maximum* and *minimum* values of the returns might help to compare the "spikes" in the series, giving a view about the magnitude of *outliers* (relative to the mean).

The volatility of asset returns is usually measured by the *variance*, or its root, the *standard deviation*. It gives an indication of how closely or widely the individual asset returns are spread around their mean value of the sample period. It is measured as:

$$\sigma_x^2 = \frac{1}{n} \sum_{i=1}^{n} (x_i - \mu)^2, \tag{4.20}$$

where μ is the mean value of the variable x in the sample period. The higher (lower) the variance is, the higher (lower) an asset's volatility is.

As outlined earlier, *skewness* measures the asymmetry of a series' distribution around its mean, *kurtosis* its peakedness/flatness. As outlined earlier, both are inputs for the *Jarque-Bera* test statistics that allows testing whether a series is normally distributed.

The term *autocorrelation* might need some explanation. Assume the variable y can be estimated by the linear equation: $y_t = \beta_0 + \beta_1 x_t + u_t$. If the error terms u_t and u_{t-1} are correlated, y_t does not only depend on x_t but also on u_{t-1}, as the latter determines (to some extent) u_t. So if there is autocorrelation, past estimation errors would help predicting future values of y. In a simple OLS estimate, however, one crucial assumption is that there is no autocorrelation between the disturbances:

$$\text{cov}(u_i, u_j | x_i, y_j) = E[u_i - E(u_i)|x_i][u_j - E(u_j)|x_j] = 0, \tag{4.21}$$

where *cov* means covariance, with i and j denoting points in time ($i \neq j$).

The autocorrelation function (ACF) allows analyzing the stochastic process of a single time series. The ACF at a lag k is defined as:

$$\rho_k = \gamma_k / \gamma_0 = (\text{covariance at lag } k)/(\text{variance}). \tag{4.22a}$$

The sample covariance at lag k, $\hat{\gamma}_k$, and the sample variance, $\hat{\gamma}_0$, are:

$$\hat{\gamma}_k = \sum_{t=k+1}^{T} (x_t - \bar{x})(x_{t-k} - \bar{x}) \text{ and} \tag{4.22b}$$

$$\hat{\gamma}_0 = \sum_{t=1}^{T} (x_t - \bar{x})^2, \tag{4.22c}$$

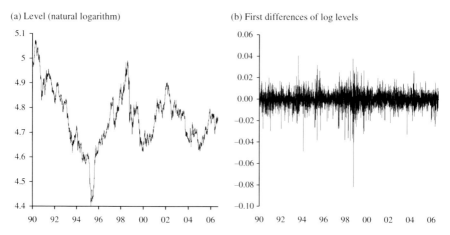

Fig. 4.5 US-dollar exchange rate versus the Japanese yen
Source: Bloomberg; own calcuations.

respectively, where T is the sample size and $\bar{x}$ the sample mean.[6] That said, the sample ACF is:

$$\hat{\rho}_k = \hat{\gamma}_k / \hat{\gamma}_0. \tag{4.23}$$

Like the ACF, the partial autocorrelation function (PACF) measures the correlation between observations that are k periods apart. However, it measures the correlation between a variable x and its lagged values x_{t-k} after removing the effect of the intermediate x's.

The Ljung-Box (LB) statistic (Ljung & Box, 1978) is a test for the *joint* hypothesis that there is no autocorrelation up to order k:

$$LB = T(T+2) \sum_{k=1}^{m} (\hat{\rho}_k^2)/(T-k) \sim \chi_m^2, \tag{4.24}$$

where T = sample size and m = lag length; in large samples, Q- and LB-statistics follow the chi-square statistics with m df.

To illustrate, Fig. 4.6 shows the autocorrelation and partial autocorrelation coefficients and the Q-statistics (including their p-values) for daily levels and daily changes in the exchange rate of the US-dollar versus the Japanese yen (as shown in Fig. 4.5) for the period January 1990 to August 2006. For levels, the ACs are fairly high, suggesting that the series is first-order serially correlated. They decline only very gradually with an increase in k and remain statistically significant from

---

[6]To be precise, the degree of freedom (df) for estimating the true but unknown variance would be $n - k$, not n independent observations, with k = number of restrictions put on them. In large samples, however, one often uses n.

Fig. 4.6 Autocorrelation, partial autocorrelations and Q-statistics for the exchange rate of the US-dollar versus the Japanese yen, period: January 1990 to August 2006 Source: Bloomberg; own calculations. – AC is autocorrelation, PAC is the partial autocorrelation coefficient, Q-statistics is the Ljung-Box Q-statistics, p is the probability for the null hypothesis that there is no autocorrelation up to the order k (number of days). – Daily changes represent first differences of log values

Lags (k)	Log levels				First differences in log levels			
	AC	PAC	Q-stat	p-value	AC	PAC	Q-stat	p-value
1	0.998	0.998	4328.1	0.000	−0.006	−0.006	0.1671	0.683
2	0.995	−0.010	8636.9	0.000	−0.012	−0.012	0.7636	0.683
3	0.993	0.012	12927	0.000	−0.043	−0.043	8.8119	0.032
4	0.991	0.047	17201	0.000	0.003	0.002	8.8510	0.065
5	0.989	−0.007	21457	0.000	0.011	0.010	9.3532	0.096
6	0.987	−0.010	25696	0.000	0.002	0.001	9.3753	0.154
7	0.985	−0.007	29918	0.000	0.005	0.005	9.4785	0.220
8	0.983	−0.006	34122	0.000	0.010	0.011	9.9195	0.271
9	0.980	−0.011	38308	0.000	0.012	0.013	10.572	0.306
10	0.978	−0.012	42476	0.000	0.024	0.025	13.169	0.214
11	0.976	−0.022	46624	0.000	−0.010	−0.008	13.571	0.258
12	0.973	0.006	50754	0.000	−0.005	−0.004	13.703	0.320
13	0.971	0.002	54865	0.000	0.019	0.021	15.360	0.285
14	0.969	−0.022	58957	0.000	0.005	0.004	15.466	0.347
15	0.966	−0.001	63029	0.000	0.001	0.001	15.472	0.418
16	0.964	−0.006	67082	0.000	−0.005	−0.004	15.592	0.482
17	0.961	0.003	71116	0.000	−0.006	−0.006	15.752	0.541
18	0.959	0.008	75131	0.000	0.009	0.008	16.091	0.586
19	0.957	−0.003	79127	0.000	0.029	0.028	19.656	0.416
20	0.954	−0.018	83103	0.000	−0.015	−0.015	20.624	0.420
21	0.952	0.014	87061	0.000	−0.014	−0.012	21.431	0.433
22	0.949	0.004	90999	0.000	0.007	0.008	21.632	0.482
23	0.947	−0.011	94919	0.000	0.033	0.030	26.437	0.281
24	0.945	−0.028	98819	0.000	−0.020	−0.021	28.208	0.251
25	0.942	0.013	102699	0.000	0.025	0.027	30.982	0.190
26	0.940	−0.024	106559	0.000	0.008	0.010	31.253	0.219
27	0.937	−0.009	110399	0.000	−0.003	−0.005	31.293	0.259
28	0.934	0.017	114219	0.000	0.001	0.002	31.295	0.304
29	0.932	−0.003	118018	0.000	0.002	0.002	31.309	0.351
30	0.929	−0.002	121797	0.000	−0.006	−0.005	31.442	0.394

zero. The PAC drops dramatically, and all PACs after $k = 1$ are statistically insignificant from zero. The Q-statistics for the null hypothesis that all autocorrelation are simultaneously zero are high and p-values zero. That said, the log of the exchange rate level series reveals autocorrelation. Turning to daily changes in the exchange rate, the ACs and PACs are very low, suggesting little autocorrelation among the daily changes of the exchange rate. Except for $k = 3$, the joint null that there is no autocorrelation cannot be rejected as indicated by the Q-statistics.

Finally, financial asset prices are volatile, given that they are sensitive to *news* concerning expected economic and political developments (such as, for instance, business cycle swings and changes in government monetary and fiscal policies). This suggests that the variance of forecasts errors is not a constant but varies from period to period. If this is the case, there would be autocorrelation in the variance of the forecast error, or *autoregressive conditional heteroskedasticity* (ARCH) in the residuals.

To show this, assume the following autoregressive model with p lags:

$$x_t = \beta_0 + \beta_1 x_{t-1} + \beta_2 x_{t-2} + \ldots \beta_p x_{t-p} + u_t. \tag{4.25}$$

Furthermore, assume that the error term is conditional on information available at $t-1$:

$$u_t \sim N[0, (\alpha_0 + \alpha_1 u_{t-1}^2)], \tag{4.26}$$

actually saying that the error term u is normally distributed with zero mean and a variance of $(\alpha_0 + \alpha_1 u_{t-1}^2)$. The variance of u thus depends on the lagged squared error term, suggesting serial correlation, which is called an ARCH(1) process. To generalize, an ARCH process is:

$$\text{var}(u_t) = \sigma_t^2 = \alpha_0 + \alpha_1 u_{t-1}^2 + u_{t-2}^2 + \ldots + \alpha_p u_{t-p}^2. \tag{4.27}$$

If there is no autocorrelation in the variance of u (or a homoscedastic error variance), the result is $H_0 : \alpha_1, \alpha_2, \ldots, \alpha_p = 0$ and $\text{var}(u_t) = \alpha_0$. According to Engle (1982), the test for the null hypothesis of no heteroscedasticity can be made by the following (auxiliary) regression:

$$\hat{u}_t^2 = \hat{\alpha}_0 + \hat{\alpha}_1 \hat{u}_t^2 + \hat{\alpha}_2 \hat{u}_{t-1}^2 + \ldots + \hat{\alpha}_p \hat{u}_{t-p}^2, \tag{4.28}$$

with $\hat{u}$ estimated in the model $x_t = \beta_0 + \beta_1 x_{t-1} + \beta_2 x_{t-2} + \ldots \beta_p x_{t-p} + u_t$. The null hypothesis can be tested using the F-test or by computing nR^2, where R^2 is the coefficient of determination of the auxiliary regression, given that nR^2 follows the chi-square distribution with df equal to the number of autoregressive terms in the auxiliary regression ($nR^2 \sim \chi_p^2$). The Lagrange multiplier (LM) ARCH(q) model (which follows a chi-square distribution) allows testing the null hypothesis that there is no ARCH up to order q in the residuals. If the p-value is low, one can reject the null of no ARCH in the residuals.

4.2.2.1 Empirical Findings for International Asset Returns

Figure 4.7 shows univariate summary statistics for weekly returns of selected bond and stock price indices from the US, Japan, Germany and the UK for the period 1980 to 2005.[7] Over the entire sample period, stock markets generated higher and more volatile returns than bond markets, as suggested by the series' mean values. However, a comparison of the minimum and maximum values suggests that the largest jumps relative to the mean return were much higher in bond than in stock markets.

---

[7]The calculations ignore exchange rate changes as they are computed on the basis of local currencies. This is, de facto, equivalent to the assumption that international investments are fully hedged against currency risk, but without cost.

Market	Mean	Min	Max	SD	S	K	JB	AC(1)	LB(4)	ARCH(4)
1. Bond market										
US 10yrs	0.02	−6.23	8.53	1.26	0.29	6.19	571.6	−0.05	3.06	4.43 [.35]
US 2yrs	0.01	−2.57	2.57	0.41	0.58	9.97	2715.9	0.05	3.11	150.9 [.00]
Japan 10yrs	0.04	−7.07	5.34	0.89	−0.69	12.17	3928.8	0.01	0.14	2.93 [.57]
Japan 2yrs	−0.03	−1.52	1.22	0.19	−0.52	10.98	3237.2	0.21	55.15	50.7 [.00]
Germany 10yrs	0.02	−5.18	5.55	0.82	−0.18	6.75	771.8	0.03	1.37	49.3 [.00]
Germany 2yrs	0.01	−1.32	1.15	0.24	−0.27	7.15	951.6	0.10	12.49	43.2 [.00]
UK 10yrs	0.05	−10.38	7.36	1.27	−0.62	10.55	3180.1	−0.04	2.21	3.86 [.43]
UK 2yrs	0.00	2.03	3.03	0.42	0.41	8.87	1909.2	−0.04	1.83	84.1 [.00]
2. Stock markets										
US	0.24	−29.59	11.12	2.43	−1.42	21.17	19793.1	−0.09	10.45	18.5 [.00]
Japan	0.14	−15.08	13.33	2.73	−0.28	5.79	457.8	−0.07	7.29	52.4 [.00]
Germany	0.19	−14.69	10.75	2.59	−0.52	5.75	491.3	−0.03	1.02	127.9 [.00]
UK	0.27	−20.81	10.65	2.34	−0.89	10.16	3073.8	0.00	0.00	94.5 [.00]

Fig. 4.7 Univariate summary statistics on weekly returns
Source: Thomson Financial; own calculations. – Bond market prices are represented by bond indices for 2- and 10-year benchmark government bonds. The stock market indices are broad-market value-weighted indices, covering around 80% of the countries' total market capitalisation. – Weekly returns are expressed as first differences of log prices, multiplied by 100; *Legend: SD* = standard deviation. – S = skewness. – K = excess kurtosis. – JB = Jarque-Bera statistic for normality. – AR(1) first order autorcorrelation coefficient. – LB(4) = Ljung-Box statistic for autocorrelation up to order 4. – ARCH(4) = ARCH-LM test with 4 lags (for squared returns), p-values in brackets. – Total sample: January 1980 to January 2005. – Japanese 2-year bond returns start on 1/1/1982, 10-year returns on 1/9/1984

Despite these marked differences, both asset classes share many other features, typical of higher-frequency asset price behavior. *First*, returns exhibit substantial non-normality (as can be seen from Jarque-Bera statistics) which mainly stems from excess kurtosis. That is, the distributions of short-term returns are characterised more by fat tails than by asymmetry (skewness). *Second*, autocorrelation (AC(1)) is generally low and tends to be insignificant. And *third*, ARCH tests reveal strong volatility clustering in all stock and in more than half of the bond returns. These properties suggest using a time-series framework for modelling short-term asset returns which captures serial correlation in the conditional means and variances, and which generates unconditionally leptokurtic, but not necessarily skewed returns.

4.2.3 *Measuring International Asset Return Linkages*

The linkages between returns on assets traded in financial markets can be measured along the lines of three dimensions (Kremer, 1999):

(i) *Causality* of asset price changes, which provides an answer to the question about the cause-and-effect relationship between variables. The issue of causality can be addressed by, for instance, Granger causality tests (Granger, 1969)

(ii) *Co-movement*, which can be operationalised by simple correlation coefficients. The higher (smaller) the correlation coefficient is, the higher is the co-movement of asset prices under review.

(iii) *Convergence*, which can be measured by applying *cointegration techniques*. Cointegration between two or more time series means that the time series under review show a tendency to converge over time.

For analysing asset prices linkages, a brief look shall be taken at stock and bond markets in the US, Germany, the UK and Japan from the early 1980 until the beginning of 2006.

4.2.3.1 Re (i): Causality

One test of causality is to check whether the lags of one variable enter into the explanatory equation of another variable. The Granger (1969) approach to the question of whether X causes Y is to see how much of the current Y can be explained by past values of Y and then to see whether adding lagged values of X can improve the explanation. Y is said to be Granger-caused by X if X helps in the prediction of Y, or equivalently, if the coefficients on the lagged X's are statistically significant. Note that two-way causation is frequently the case; X Granger may cause Y and Y Granger may cause X.

It is important to note that the statement "X Granger causes Y" does not imply that Y is the effect or the result of X. Granger causality measures precedence and information content but does not by itself indicate causality in the more common use of the term. The Granger causality approach runs bi-variate regressions in the following form:

$$Y_t = a_0 + a_1 Y_{t-1} + \ldots a_n Y_{t-n} + \beta_1 X_{t-1} + \ldots \beta_n X_{t-n} + \varepsilon_t \text{ and} \qquad (4.29)$$

$$X_t = a_0 + a_1 X_{t-1} + \ldots a_n X_{t-n} + \beta_1 Y_{t-1} + \ldots \beta_n Y_{t-n} + \varepsilon_t, \qquad (4.30)$$

for all possible pairs of (X,Y) series in the group. The reported F-statistics are the Wald statistics for the joint hypothesis:

$$\beta_1 = \beta_2 = \ldots = \beta_n = 0$$

for each equation. The null hypothesis is that X does *not* Granger-cause Y in the first regression and that Y does not Granger-cause X in the second regression.

Stationarity, Non-Stationarity and Covariance

Any time series can be thought of as being generated by a *stochastic* or *random process*; a concrete data set (stock market prices, yields, exchange rate, etc.) can be interpreted as a (particular) realisation of the underlying stochastic, that is data, generating process. A type of stochastic process that has received a great deal of attention by time series analysts is the so-called *stationary stochastic process*.

A stochastic process is said to be stationary if its mean and variance are constant over time, and the value of covariance between two (sub-)time periods depends solely on the distance, or lag, between the two time periods and not on the actual time at which the covariance is calculated. To explain this in some more detail, let Y_t be a stochastic time series with the following properties:

– mean: $E(Y_t) = \mu$,
– variance: $\text{var}(Y_t) = E(Y_t - \mu)(Y_{t+k} - \mu)$, and
– covariance: $\gamma_k = E\left[(Y_t - \mu)(Y_{t+k} - \mu)\right]$,

where γ_k is the covariance between Y realisations k periods apart. So if $k = 0$, γ_0 represents simply the variance ($= \sigma^2$); if $k = 1$, γ_1 shows the covariance between two adjacent realisation of Y.

If Y is a stationary process, a shift of Y from Y_t to Y_{t+m} would imply that the mean, variance and covariance of Y_{t+m} must be the same as of Y_t. That said, a time series is stationary if its mean, variance and covariance (at various lags) remain the same no matter at what time we measure them. If a time series is not stationary in the sense just defined, it is called *non-stationary* (or, to be more precise, *weak stationary*). An often cited example of a non-stationary process is the stock market, which tends to show (at least in the past decades) a steady upward trend over time.

Variables are said to be stationary if they are integrated of the order 0, that is $I(0)$. Conversely, a non-stationary variable can be made stationary by differencing. A variable is said to be integrated of the order n – or: $I(n)$ – if differencing the variable n times yields an $I(0)$ process. If the series is differenced once and the differenced series is stationary, we say the original (random walk) series is integrated of order 1. Similarly, if the original series has to be differenced twice (that is taking the first difference of the first difference) to make it stationary, the original series is said to be $I(2)$.

The Dickey-Fuller test (DF-test), Augmented-Dickey-Fuller test (ADF-test), the Perron test and the Kwiatowski-test, among others, are examples for well-established procedures to test time series' stationarity, e.g. non-stationarity.

Note that standard Ordinary Least Squares (OLS) regressions rest on using stationary variables, otherwise regression results include the possibility of obtaining *spurious*, or dubious, results in the sense that superficially the results look good but on further scrutiny are suspect. In principle, regressing one $I(1)$ variable on another $I(1)$ variable the standard t– and F–tests are not valid.

For further reading: Enders (2004).

No. of lags	Null hypothesis	No. of observations	F-statistic	Probability
I. Nominal stock market levels				
Lag = 1	−ΔGER does not Granger cause ΔUS	322	0.34	0.559
	−ΔUS does not Granger cause ΔGER		4.61	0.032
Lag = 3	−ΔGER does not Granger cause ΔUS	320	0.75	0.519
	−ΔUS does not Granger cause ΔGER		2.61	0.051
Lag = 1	−ΔUK does not Granger cause ΔUS	322	0.71	0.400
	−ΔUS does not Granger cause ΔUK		2.56	0.111
Lag = 1	−ΔJAP does not Granger cause ΔUS	322	0.61	0.436
	−ΔUS does not Granger cause ΔJAP		3.57	0.059
II. Real stock market levels				
Lag = 1	−Δ GER does not Granger cause ΔUS	322	0.46	0.497
	−Δ US does not Granger cause ΔGER		5.88	0.016
Lag = 3	−ΔGER does not Granger cause ΔUS	320	0.78	0.505
	−ΔUS does not Granger cause ΔGER		3.16	0.025
Lag = 3	−ΔUK does not Granger cause ΔUK	320	0.96	0.327
	−ΔUS does not Granger cause ΔUK		3.47	0.063
Lag = 1	−ΔJAP not Granger cause ΔUS	322	0.86	0.353
	−ΔUS does not Granger cause ΔJAP		4.08	0.044

Fig. 4.8   Granger causality test results for US, German, UK and Japanese stock markets
Legend: *Lags* note the number of months. − Lag order selected by the Akaike and Schwarz information criteria. − *US* stands for the US stock market, *GER* for Germany, *UK* for the United Kingdom and *JAP* for Japan. − Δ stands for the first difference of log values. − Period: January 1980 to January 2006.
Source: Thomsonal Financial, own calculation.

Figure 4.8 shows the bi-variate Granger causality test results for nominal and real stock market performance indices for the period January 1980 to January 2006. All variables represent first differences of logarithms, which were found to be stationary ($I(0)$ variables). The number of time lags was determined by the Akaike and Schwarz criteria. Only the null hypothesis that changes in the nominal US stock market do not Granger cause those in Germany can be rejected at the 5-percent level (*p*-value of 0.032).

Turning to real stock returns, that are nominal stock returns adjusted for consumer price inflation (as shown in the lower part of Fig. 4.8), the null hypothesis that changes in the US stock market performance do not Granger cause changes in the German and Japan stock market performance can be rejected, but not for the UK.

Turning to nominal bond yields (Fig. 4.9), there seems to be a two-way causation between monthly changes in nominal US and German 10-years yields at the lag 1. At lag 2, however, the null hypothesis that changes in US yields do not Granger

No. of lags	Null hypothesis	No. of observations	F-statistic	Probability
I. Nominal 10-year yields				
Lag = 1	−ΔGER does not Granger cause ΔUS	322	5.49	0.019
	−ΔUS does not Granger cause ΔGER		31.9	0.000
Lag = 2	−ΔGER does not Granger cause ΔUS	321	2.09	0.124
	−ΔUS does not Granger cause ΔGER		15.0	0.000
Lag = 1	−ΔUK does not Granger cause ΔUS	322	6.77	0.009
	−ΔUS does not Granger cause ΔUK		5.61	0.018
Lag = 4	−ΔJAP does not Granger cause ΔUS	261	2.31	0.058
	−ΔUS does not Granger cause ΔJAP		3.51	0.008
II. Real 10-year yields				
Lag = 1	−ΔGER does not Granger cause ΔUS	322	1.02	0.312
	−ΔUS does not Granger cause ΔGER		2.54	0.112
Lag = 3	−ΔUK does not Granger cause ΔUS	320	10.9	0.000
	−ΔUS does not Granger cause ΔUK		1.97	0.117
Lag = 4	−ΔJAP does not Granger cause ΔUS	261	1.38	0.243
	−ΔUS does not Granger cause ΔJAP		1.92	0.107

Fig. 4.9 Granger causality test results for US, German, UK and Japanese nominal bond yields; Legend: *Lags* note the number of months. – Lag order selected by the Akaike and Schwarz information criteria. – *US* stands for the US 10-year government bond yields, *GER* for German, *UK* for the United Kingdom and *JAP* for Japanese 10-year government bond yields. – Δ stands for the changes in monthly yields. – Period: January 1980 to January 2006; Japan from January 1984. Source: Thomson Financial, own calculations.

cause German yields can be rejected (*p*-value 0.000), but not the other way round. At a lag of 1, there seems to be a two-way Granger causation between nominal yield changes in the US and the UK. Changes in US yields seem to Granger cause those in Japan (at lag 4).

In respect to real bond yields (that are nominal yields minus annual changes in consumer price inflation), there seems to be a two-way Granger causality between changes in US and German yields. At lag 3, the null that changes in UK yields do not Granger cause changes in US yields can be rejected. Finally, at lag 4, there seems to be no clear cut Granger causation between changes in US and Japanese yields.

4.2.3.2 Re (ii): Co-Movement of Various Asset Prices

Simple Gliding Correlation Coefficients

The *correlation coefficient* measures the linear association between two variables *x* and *y*. It lies between the limits of −1 and +1, with the sign depending on the

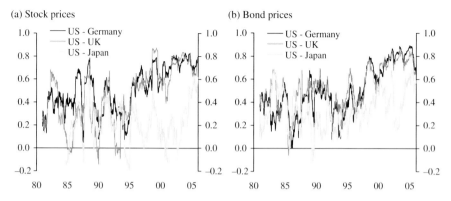

Fig. 4.10 Moving cross-country return correlations, 1980–2006
Source: Thomson Financial; own calculations. – Moving 52 week window. – The correlation of
stock price changes between the US and Germany over the period January 1980 to January 2006
was 0.49 on average; for the US and Japan 0.33 and for the US and the UK 0.53. – The correlation
between changes in bond prices of the US and Germany over the period January 1980 to January
2006 was 0.51 on average; for the US and the UK 0.45; for the period June 1984 to February 2005,
the coefficient for the US and Japan was 0.22.

numerator, the co-variation of the two variables. The closer the coefficient is to $+1$
(-1), the stronger is the positive (negative) co-movement between the two variables.[8]

Longer-term co-movements of cross-market asset prices can be measured by
gliding correlation coefficients of asset returns over a given (sub-)sample period.
For instance, Fig. 4.10(a) displays cross-correlation coefficients over a gliding 52
week window between changes in US stock prices and those in Germany, Japan and
the UK, respectively, from the early 1980s to the beginning of 2005.

The co-movement between stock market returns in the US and Germany and
the UK were positive and relatively high in the period under review. What is more,
since the second half of the 1990s the co-movement of stock market has increased
markedly. The correlation between changes in US and Japanese stock prices, however, was considerably lower. And only since the beginning of 2002 has it started
rising towards the correlation levels exhibited by Japan's peer markets vis-à-vis the
US.

Figure 4.10(b) shows the cross-country correlations over a gliding 52 week window between changes in US bond prices vis-à-vis those in Germany, Japan and the
UK from the early 1980s to the beginning of 2006. Whereas a relatively pronounced
co-movement of bond market returns can be observed between the US, Germany
and the UK, the correlation coefficients of the US market with Japan have become
noticeably weaker, especially so since around the middle of the 1990s. Only since

---

[8]Note that if x and y are statistically independent, the correlation coefficient is zero. However, if
the correlation coefficient is zero it does not necessarily mean independence of the two variables.

around 2002 has the co-movement between the Japanese and the other bond markets under review increased.

An increasing co-movement of stock and bond market returns might be explained by numerous factors. First and foremost, the growing internationalisation of investment portfolios might have contributed to a growing co-movement of international asset prices, as changes in one market could easily spill over into other market segments. What is more, a homogenisation of institutional investor risk management techniques might increasingly transmit "shocks" from one market to the other in periods of market stress, thereby increasing the degree of co-movement among international asset markets.

Modeling Volatility as a Measure of Risk

In conventional regression models, the variance of the error term is assumed to be constant. If a process is stable, the conditional variance will eventually decay to the long-run (unconditional variance.) However, many time series exhibit periods of unusually large volatility, followed by periods of relatively tranquility; and a large realization of the current period's disturbance increases the conditional variance in subsequent periods.

In this case, the assumption of a constant variance (homoscedasticity) would not be appropriate. For instance, an investor may wish to forecast the rate of return and the variance of the stock market over a given holding period. The unconditional variance (the long-run forecast of the variance) would be of little interest (and help) if the investor wants to buy and sell the asset within the period under review.

According to Engle (1982) it is possible to simultaneously model the mean and the variance of a time series. To show that Engle's conditional forecasts are superior to unconditional forecasts, suppose you estimate the stationary autoregressive moving average (ARMA) model $y_t = a_0 + a_1 y_{t-1} + \varepsilon_t$ and want to forecast y_{t+1} (Enders, 2004, p. 113). The conditional mean of y_{t+1} is $E_t y_{t+1} = a_0 + a_1 y_t$. Using this conditional mean to forecast y_{t+1}, the forecast error variance is:

$$E_t[(y_{t+1} - a_0 - a_1 y_t)^2] = E_t \varepsilon_{t+1}^2 = \sigma^2. \qquad (4.31)$$

In the case the unconditional forecasts are used, however, the unconditional forecast is the long-run mean $\{y_t\}$ sequence that is equal to $a_0/(1 - a_1)$. The unconditional forecast error variance is therefore:

$$E_t\{[y_{t+1} - a_0(1 - a_1)]^2\} = \sigma^2/(1 - a_1^2). \qquad (4.32)$$

Since $1/(1 - a_1^2) > 1$, the unconditional forecast has a greater variance than the conditional forecast. As a result, conditional forecasts are preferable.

Similarly, assume the variance of $\{\varepsilon_t\}$ is not constant and that sustained changes in the variance can be captured by an ARMA model. For instance, let $\{\varepsilon_t\}$ be the estimated residuals from the model: $y_t = a_0 + a_1 y_{t-1} + \varepsilon_t$. The conditional variance is:

$$\text{Var}\,(y_{t+1}|y_t) = E_t[(y_{t+1} - a_0 - a_1 y_t)^2] = E_t(\varepsilon_{t+1})^2. \tag{4.33}$$

Now assume that the time series' conditional variance is not constant over time. One strategy to forecast the conditional variance as an AR(q) process using squares of the estimated residuals:

$$\hat{\varepsilon}_t^2 = \alpha_0 + \alpha_1 \hat{\varepsilon}_{t-1}^2 + \alpha_2 \hat{\varepsilon}_{t-2}^2 + \dots \alpha_q \hat{\varepsilon}_{t+1-q}^2 + v_t, \tag{4.34}$$

where v is a white noise process. If all values of $\alpha_1, \alpha_2, \dots \alpha_n$ are zero, the estimated variance would be constant, that is α_0. The forecast of the conditional variance in $t + 1$ would be:

$$E_t \hat{\varepsilon}_{t+1}^2 = \alpha_0 + \alpha_1 \hat{\varepsilon}_t^2 + \alpha_2 \hat{\varepsilon}_{t-1}^2 + \dots \alpha_q \hat{\varepsilon}_{t+1-q}^2. \tag{4.35}$$

Equation (4.34) is called an autoregressive conditional heteroskedastic (ARCH) model.

Bollerslev (1986) extended Engle's original work, developing a method that models the conditional variance as an ARMA process. The error process is:

$$\varepsilon_t = v_t \sqrt{h_t}, \tag{4.36}$$

where $\sigma_v^2 = 1$ and

$$h_t = a_0 + \sum_{i=1}^{q} \alpha_i \varepsilon_{t-i}^2 + \sum_{i=1}^{p} \beta_i h_{t-i}. \tag{4.37}$$

As $\{v_t\}$ is a white noise process, the conditional and unconditional means of ε_t are equal to zero. The important point here is that the conditional variance of ε_t is the ARMA process given the expression h_t in equation (4.37).

The generalized ARCH(p, q) model – called GARCH(p, q) – allows for both autoregressive and moving average components in the heteroscedastic variance. If, for instance, $p = 0$ and $q = 1$, the first order ARCH model is simply a GARCH(0, 1) model. That said, if all β_i values are zero, the GARCH(p, q) model is equivalent to an ARCH(q) model.

The benefits of the GARCH model are that a high-order ARCH model may have a more parsimonious GARCH representation that is much easier to identify and estimate. (The more parsimonious the model is, the fewer are the model restrictions). This is particularly true as all coefficients in Eq. (4.37) must be positive. What is more, to make the variance finite, all characteristic roots of (4.37) must lie inside the unit circle.

To give an example, let us consider a GARCH(1,1) model for monthly changes in the logs of the US S&P 500 for the period January 1950 to February 2006. The mean and variance equations are:

$$r_t = c + \varepsilon_t \text{ and} \tag{4.38}$$

$$\sigma_t^2 = \omega + \alpha\varepsilon_{t-1}^2 + \beta\sigma_{t-1}^2, \tag{4.39}$$

respectively, where r represents the month-on-month change in the log of the S&P's 500 stock market index, c is a constant and ε is the i.i.d. error term. The model yields the following variance specification:

$$\sigma_t^2 = 9.42E - 05 + .087\varepsilon_{t-1}^2 + .861\sigma_{t-1}^2, \tag{4.40}$$
$$\underset{(.002)}{} \quad \underset{(.028)}{} \quad \underset{(.036)}{}$$

with standard errors in brackets. All coefficients are statistically significant at standard levels, and the null hypothesis of no ARCH in the residuals (LM-test) up to order 12 cannot be rejected. What is more, testing the standardized squared residuals indicates that there are no remaining GARCH effects. As the coefficient for α (.087) is lower than the coefficient β (.861), volatility reacts stronger to past volatility than to new information; that is volatility shocks seem to be quite persistent.

Figure 4.11 displays the US S&P's 500 return volatility according to the GARCH(1,1) model and, as from January 1990 onwards, the market traded volatility index VIX. As can be seen, the GARCH(1,1) modeled volatility and the VIX appear to be closely related. A simple cross-correlation suggests that the highest correlation coefficient (.76) is achieved when the lag between the two series is zero. So actual market expected volatility appears to be captured by past volatility realizations. (Note that the GARCH(1,1) model estimates current volatility on the basis past realizations.) In other words, market volatility expectations appear to be driven by some kind of an *adaptive expectation model*.

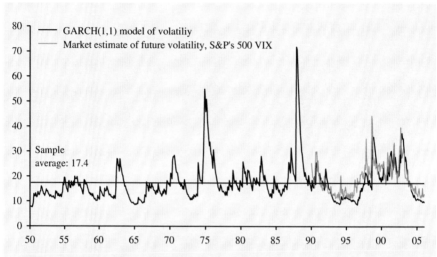

Fig. 4.11 US S&P's 500 volatility
Source: Bloomberg; own calculations. – First differences of log values. – Period: January
1950 to February 2006. See Bera and Higgins (1993)

Using ARCH Models for Measuring Return Linkages

A structural interpretation of the simple correlation coefficient as a measure of international asset price linkages is difficult (Domanski & Kremer, 2000): Simple gliding
correlation coefficients may only reflect the impact of a single price shock on such
short memory correlations. What is more, strong volatility clustering in short-term
returns (on a daily or weekly basis) and their unconditional non-normality have to
be taken into account. As a result, bivariate AR(1)-GARCH(1,1) specifications have
become a widely applied tool for analysing return linkages (Bollerslev et al. 1988).

To start with, the (near) unpredictability of short-term returns restricts the forecast for the conditional means to a simple AR(1) process such as:

$$r_{j,t} = \mu_{j,t} + \varepsilon_{j,t} \text{ with } \mu_{j,t} = E(r_{j,t}|\Omega_{t-1}) = a_j + \beta_j r_{j,t-1}, \qquad (4.41)$$

for $j =$ asset x, asset y. Here, $r_{j,t}$ is the return of asset j, $\mu_{j,t}$ stands for the expected
return conditional on information Ω_{t-1} and $\varepsilon_{j,t}$ is the error term. The error vector
ε_t is assumed to follow a bivariate normal distribution, with zero mean and a time-
varying covariance matrix H_t:

$$\varepsilon_t|\Omega_{t-1} \sim N(0, H_t). \qquad (4.42)$$

The system consists of three equations describing the dynamics of the elements of H_t. It can be summarised by a *vech representation*[9] of the bivariate GARCH(1,1) model:

$$
\begin{bmatrix} h_{x,t} \\ h_{xy,t} \\ h_{y,t} \end{bmatrix} = \begin{bmatrix} c_{11} \\ c_{12} \\ c_{13} \end{bmatrix} + \begin{bmatrix} a_{11} \ a_{12} \ a_{13} \\ a_{21} \ a_{22} \ a_{23} \\ a_{31} \ a_{32} \ a_{33} \end{bmatrix} \begin{bmatrix} \varepsilon_{x,t-1}^2 \\ \varepsilon_{x,t-1}\varepsilon_{y,t-1} \\ \varepsilon_{y,t-1}^2 \end{bmatrix} + \begin{bmatrix} b_{11} \ b_{12} \ b_{13} \\ b_{21} \ b_{22} \ b_{23} \\ b_{31} \ b_{32} \ b_{33} \end{bmatrix} \begin{bmatrix} h_{x,t-1} \\ h_{xy,t-1} \\ h_{y,t-1} \end{bmatrix}.
$$

$h_{j,t}$ is the conditional error variance of the return of asset j, $h_{xy,t}$ is the conditional covariance. For instance, $h_{x,t}$ is affected by lagged residuals and the lagged variance of asset y (namely via a_{12}, a_{13}, b_{12} and b_{13}). In addition, $h_{x,t}$ is influenced by the contemporaneous dependency represented by the covariance function $h_{xy,t}$. The correlation coefficient is:

$$
\rho_t = h_{xy,t}/(h_{x,t}h_{y,t})^{0.5}. \tag{4.43}
$$

This measure should be superior to the simple correlations since it is estimated within a consistent econometric framework.

However, estimating the vech representation raises two problems. First, positive definiteness of the variance covariance matrix is not guaranteed. Second, the system is overparameterised.[10] To tackle these problems, two restrictions are imposed on the system. First, a zero-restriction is imposed on all elements below and above the main diagonal of the coefficient matrices A and B. This *diagonal representation* suggested by Bollerslev et al. (1988) reduces the estimation burden to nine parameters. The conditional variance processes equal those of univariate GARCH models since neither squared lagged residuals nor the lagged variance of one variable appear in the variance equation of the other. That said, the transmission of international volatility can now occur only through the conditional covariance process. The diagonal representation of the bivariate base model (with some convenient changes in notation) looks as follows:

$$
\begin{bmatrix} h_{x,t} \\ h_{xy,t} \\ h_{y,t} \end{bmatrix} = \begin{bmatrix} c_{11} \\ c_{12} \\ c_{13} \end{bmatrix} + \begin{bmatrix} \alpha_x \ 0 \ 0 \\ 0 \ a_{xy} \ 0 \\ 0 \ 0 \ \alpha_y \end{bmatrix} \begin{bmatrix} \varepsilon_{x,t-1}^2 \\ \varepsilon_{x,t-1}\varepsilon_{y,t-1} \\ \varepsilon_{y,t-1}^2 \end{bmatrix} + \begin{bmatrix} b_x \ 0 \ 0 \\ 0 \ b_{xy} \ 0 \\ 0 \ 0 \ b_y \end{bmatrix} \begin{bmatrix} h_{x,t-1} \\ h_{xy,t-1} \\ h_{y,t-1} \end{bmatrix}.
$$

---

[9] The general form of a vech representation is (Domanski & Kremer, 2000, p. 137):

$$
vech(H_t) = vech(C) + \sum_{i=1}^{q} A_i vech(\varepsilon_{t-i}, \varepsilon'_{t-i}) + \sum_{j=1}^{p} B_j vech(H_{t-j}).
$$

The *vech* operator stacks all elements on and below the main diagonal of an $n \times n$ symmetric matrix column by column into an $n(n+1)/2$-dimensional vector. The coefficient matrices A and B are accordingly of dimension $n(n+1)/2 \times n(n+1)/2$) (Campbell et al., 1997, p. 490).

[10] A bivariate GARCH(1,1) models require 21 coefficients to be estimated for the variance covariance process alone.

Second, the model can be further simplified by assuming a constant correlation coefficient $\rho_t = \rho$ (Bollerslev, 1990). In this case, the conditional covariance function degenerates to the identity:

$$h_{xy,t} = \rho(h_{x,t}h_{y,t})^{0.5}. \tag{4.44}$$

Together with the two unchanged conditional variance processes, it forms the constant correlation representation which leaves seven parameters to be estimated. Positive definiteness of the variance covariance matrix is now guaranteed. Despite its restrictive nature (it does not permit any lagged international volatility spillovers), the constant correlation representation renders it quite useful. It provides a simple summary measure of international asset price linkages, immediately challenging the simple return correlation. What is more, it offers an easy way of directly testing specific hypotheses about possible determinants and the structural stability of the correlation coefficient. The upper part of Fig. 4.12 shows the results for

Bivariate AR(1)-GARCH(1,1) model for US and German weekly stock returns, diagonal representation
(a) Conditional variances   (b) Correlation

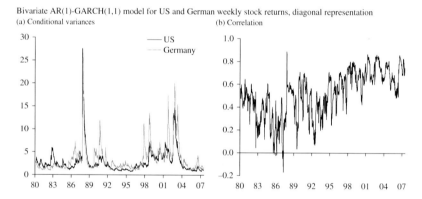

Bivariate AR(1)-GARCH(1,1) model for US weekly stock and 10-year bond returns, diagonal representation
(a) Conditional variances   (b) Correlation

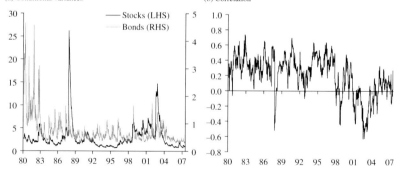

Fig. 4.12 International stock market volatility measures
Source: Thomson Financial; own calculations. – Period: January 1980 to June 2007. – Weekly returns are measured as first differences of log levels, annualised

weekly returns of US and German stock market indices on the basis of a bivariate AR(1)-GARCH(1,1) model for the period 1980 to June 2007. The lower part of Fig. 4.12 shows the same measures for weekly returns of US stocks and US bond prices.

4.2.3.3 Re (iii): Convergence of Asset Prices and Valuations

The co-movement of asset prices can be measured by taking recourse to cointegration analysis. Many economic theories suggest that a linear combination of non-stationary (that is $I(n)$ variables, or random walk stochastic processes) exists that must be stationary ($I(0)$). For instance, purchasing power parity and money demand analyses are fields of research in which cointegration techniques are typically applied.

Assume that the time series x_{1t}, x_{2t} and x_{3t} are $I(1)$, respectively. However, a linear combination in the form $\varepsilon_t = \beta_0 + \beta_1 x_{1t} + \beta_2 x_{2t} + \beta_t x_{3t}$ might be stationary, that is ε_t is $I(0)$ or, to put it differently, the residual does not have a "unit root". In such a case, the trends in the time series x_{1t}, x_{2t} and x_{3t} "cancel out" each other and the $I(1)$ variables are said to be cointegrated of order $(1,1)$. The vector $(\beta_0, \beta_1, \beta_2, \beta_3)$ is called the *cointegration vector*.

Simply speaking, cointegrated variables share the same stochastic trends and, as a result, cannot drift too far apart. Cointegrated variables have an "error correction" representation such that each responds to the deviation from the "long-run equilibrium": deviations from the equilibrium in the period under review will be reversed in later periods. In the case that the variables are cointegrated, and thus on the same "wavelength", the regression on the levels of the two variables is meaningful, and the traditional regression methodology, including standard $t-$ and F–tests, are applicable. Moreover, avoiding differencing the variables might well prevent any loss of valuable information provided by the variables under review.

ADF-Test as a Unit Root Test

A popular test for stationarity is known as the *unit root test*. To give an example, consider the following model:

$$y_t = y_{t-1} + u_t, \tag{4.45}$$

where u_t is the stochastic error i.i.d. white noise term, which is non-autocorrelated. The equation represents a first-order autoregression ($AR(1)$). If the coefficient of y_{t-1} would be 1, we would face the *unit root problem*: a non-stationary situation.

If the following regression is run:

$$y_t = \rho y_{t-1} + u_t, \tag{4.46}$$

and if it is found that $\rho = 1$, the stochastic variable y_t is said to have a unit root. A time series that has a unit root is known as a *random walk*. Substracting y_{t-1} from both sides of Eq. (4.46) yields:

$$\Delta y_t = (\rho - 1)y_{t-1} + u_t \text{ or } = \delta y_{t-1} + u_t, \tag{4.47}$$

where $\delta = (\rho - 1)$, which is known as the first difference operator. Testing the hypothesis $\rho = 1$ is equivalent to testing the hypothesis $\delta = 0$. Dickey and Fuller (1979) consider three different regression equations that can be used to test for the presence of a unit root:

$$\Delta y_t = \delta y_{t-1} + u_t, \tag{4.48a}$$

$$\Delta y_t = \beta_0 + \delta y_{t-1} + u_t \text{ and} \tag{4.48b}$$

$$\Delta y_t = \beta_0 + \beta_1 t + \delta y_{t-1} + u_t. \tag{4.48c}$$

The difference between the three regression equations concerns the presence of the deterministic elements β_0 and $\beta_1 t$. The first is a pure random walk model, the second adds an intercept (or drift term), and the third includes both a drift and a linear time trend.

The parameter of interest is δ. If $\delta = 1$, the $\{y_t\}$ sequence contains a unit root. The ADF-test involves estimating one (or more) of the equations above using OLS in order to obtain the estimated value of δ and the associate standard error. Comparing the resulting t-statistics with the appropriate value reported in the Dickey-Fuller tables allows to determine whether to accept or reject the null hypothesis of $\delta = 0$ (that is the time series under review has a unit root)[11].

4.2.3.4 Some Empirical Estimation

Long-Run Relation Between Stock Market Indices

Figure 4.13(a) shows nominal stock market performance indices for the US, Germany, the UK and Japan for the period January 1980 to April 2008. Figure 4.13(b) depicts the stock market performance in real, that is consumer price inflation-adjusted, terms. To find out as to whether there is a long-run relation between the stock market performances measures (in nominal and real terms) under review, one

---

[11] In their Monte Carlo study, Dickey and Fuller (1979) found that the critical values for $\delta = 0$ depend on the form of the regression and the sample size. Usually, the statistics are labelled τ, τ_μ and τ_τ, representing the statistics for the regression without constant and trend, the regression with a constant, and the regression with constant and linear trend, respectively.

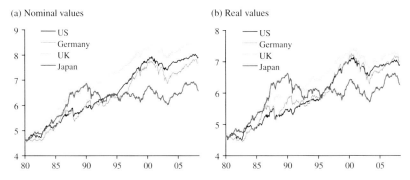

Fig. 4.13 International stock market performance indices
Source: Thomson Financial; own calculations. – Real values were calculated by deflating nominal values by consumer price indices. – All time series as natural logarithms (January 1980 = 100). – Period: January 1980 to April 2008

may regress the German, UK and Japanese stock market performance indices on the US stock market performance index. The test results are shown in Fig. 4.14.

The German and the UK stock markets react positively to changes in US stock market performance as evidenced by β_1's of 0.74 and 0.90, respectively. Changes in the Japanese stock market performance to changes in the performance of the

Estimation: $Y_{i,t} = \beta_0 + \beta_1 X_t + u_t$			ADF-tests of the residuals		
Y_i	β_0	β_1	AIC	Schwarz	Lag 12 mths
I. Nominal values with X = US stock market perfomance index					
Germany	1.084 (0.055)	0.736 (0.009)	–3.123**	–2.734*	–3.591***
UK	0.855 (0.064)	0.901 (0.010)	–1.796	–2.575*	–2.349
Japan	3.767 (0.151)	0.311 (0.026)	–1.635	–1.596	–1.888
II. Real values with X = US stock market performance index					
Germany	1.042 (0.072)	0.760 (0.013)	–2.959**	2.575*	–3.362***
UK	1.423 (0.066)	0.748 (0.012)	–1.778	–2.650*	–2.313
Japan	3.899 (0.185)	0.269 (0.034)	–1.623	–1.576	–1.950

Fig. 4.14 Long-run regression results between stock market performance indices
Source: Thomson Financial; own calculations. – All variables in natural logarithms. – *Legend*: */**/*** significant at the 10%/5%/1% level. – Standard errors in brackets. – Real values were calculated by deflating nominal indices with consumer prices indices. – *AIC* is the Akaike information criterion, *Schwarz* is the Schwarz information criterion. – Period: January 1980 to January 2006; monthly data

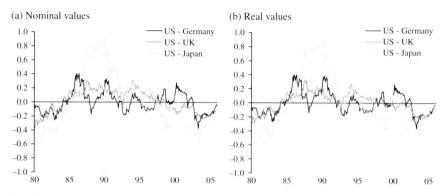

Fig. 4.15 Residuals of the long-run regressions
Source: Thomson Financial; own calculations

US stock market were also positive, but considerably lower (0.31). The results do not change much when the regressions are run for real stock market performance measures. The residuals of the regressions are depicted in Fig. 4.15.

The ADF-tests of the residuals suggest that there is a (statistically valid) long-run relation between the performance of the US and the German stock market (in nominal and real terms), but not between the US and the UK and the US and Japan. In other words, the residuals from regressing the German stock market performance on the performance of the US stock market appear to be stationary. In all other cases, however, the null hypothesis of a unit root of the residuals cannot be rejected at standard statistical levels.

The Long-Run Relations Between International Price-Earnings Ratios

The development of *price-earnings* (PE) *ratios* – defined as the relation between stock prices and corporate earnings per share – over time might help to form a view about the degree of convergence of international stock market valuations. Figure 4.16 shows the PE ratios for the stock markets in the US, Germany, Japan and the UK, respectively, for the period January 1980 to May 2008. Note that the

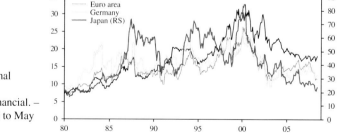

Fig. 4.16 International
PE-ratios
Source: Thomson Financial. –
Period: January 1980 to May
2008

PE ratios in all markets under review peaked around 2000/2001, when the "New Economy" boom reached its climax.

The Price-Earnings (PE) Ratio

The price earnings (PE) ratio of a stock is the share price of the firm divided by the firm's (annual) earnings per share. The PE ratio of a stock market index can be calculated accordingly: it is the average share price of the firms in the index (P) divided by the average (annual) earnings per share of the firms included in the index (EPS):

$$PE = P/EPS. \tag{4.49}$$

If, for instance, P is 100, while EPS are 10, the market's PE ratio would be 10 (that is: 100/10). In other words, if an investor buys the stock market at its current price, it would take him 10 years to recover his investment.

Basically two types of measurement issues arise in calculating PE ratios (Shen, 2000). One of them concerns the time period over which share prices and earnings are measured. The price in a PE ratio is usually the current market price of the stock or market index (such as the weekly or monthly average of daily closing prices). The timing of the earnings in such a calculation, however, may vary. There are two main conventions. The first is to use realized earnings (or *trailing earnings*), such as realized earnings in the past year, or averages of annual earnings for the past few years. The second convention is to use a forecast of earnings for the future such as, most prominently, predicted earnings for the current year or next year. That said, the PE ratio may depends substantially on the decisions made by the researcher.

PE Ratios and the Fed Model

PE ratios have become an important valuation measure for stock prices and stock markets alike. For instance, the Fed model postulates that the earnings yield E/P of a stock index (that is the reciprocal of the PE ratio) tends to move in the same direction as the bond yield r. If, for instance, the E/P is much less than r, one might expect a decrease in the equity prices P relative to E (or a rise in E relative to P) going forward. The idea is that bonds and stocks compete for investment funds, and funds tend to move towards the more attractive investment. This effect was studied in Ziemba and Schwartz (1991), and it became widely known with the Humphrey–Hawkins Report Board of the Governors of the Federal Reserve System (1997).

Empirical tests of the Fed model as made by, for instance, Koivu, Pennanen and Ziemba (2005) were based on a cointegration analysis of US, UK and German data. The results indicated that the Fed model has predictive power in forecasting changes in the equity prices, earnings and bond yields. The predictions were better in the US than in the other countries, though. Despite the empirical success in describing the behavior of stock prices and its enormous popularity among practitioners, the Fed model has also been criticized for being theoretically invalid; see, for instance, Asness (2003) and Campbell and Vuolteenaho (2003).

The main criticism is that the Fed model compares a nominal quantity r to the real quantity E/P. Rising (declining) nominal yields may not necessarily be negative (positive) for stock prices and earnings. The effect of rising yields (due to, for instance, higher expected inflation) on the PE ratio might be difficult to quantify as it affects both the numerator and the denominator (Modigliani & Cohn, 1979; Asness, 2000, 2003; Ritter & Warr, 2002; Campbell & Vuelteenaho, 2003). What is more, the Fed model does not take into consideration (potentially time-varying) risk premia. Using a (time-invariant) risk premium, Lander, Orphanides and Douvogiannis (1997) represent the Fed model as:

$$\frac{EPS_t}{P_t} = a + r_t, \qquad (4.50)$$

where a is an intercept (reflecting a constant risk premium) and r_t is the nominal long-term yield.

PE Ratios and the Net Present Value of Growth Opportunities (NPVGO)

The PE ratio should equal the reciprocal of the bond (or discount) yield, r (which includes a risk premium):

$$PE = 1/r. \qquad (4.51)$$

If firms pay out their earnings per share as dividends, that is $EPS = Div$, the stock price P can be represented as:

$$P = \frac{EPS}{r} = \frac{Div}{r}. \tag{4.52}$$

Now assume that firms retain part of their earnings, which is then invested in new (and risky) investments opportunities. The share price could then be written as follows:

$$P = \frac{EPS}{r} + NPVGO, \tag{4.53}$$

where NPVGO represents the net present value of the firm's growth opportunities. Dividing Eq. (4.53) by the earnings per share (*EPS*) yields:

$$\frac{P}{EPS} = \frac{1}{r} + \frac{NPVGO}{EPS}. \tag{4.54}$$

The left hand side of Eq. (4.54) represents the familiar PE ratio. The right hand side consists of two components. The term $1/r$ represents the value of the stock market if firms rest on their laurels, that is, if they simply distribute all earnings to the stockholder. The second term represents the additional value in relation to current EPS if the firm retains earnings in order to fund new (and risky) projects.

A high PE ratio could therefore suggest (i) a low discount rate (potentially implying a low risk premium) and/or (ii) strong expected future growth opportunities as represented by a high NPVGO. A good example of a period of PE ratios reaching exceptionally high levels was the "New Economy" hype in the second half of the 1990s, when investor growth and profit expectations became very (and, as was revealed later on: overly) optimistic (Shiller, 2000).

Figure 4.17 shows the reciprocal of the 10-year government bond yield, the NPVGO/EPS and the PE ratios in the US, Japan, Germany and the UK from the early 1980s to May 2008. In all markets under reviews, the NPVGO/EPS, after having been positive on average since the early 1980s, went into negative territory since around the beginning of the new millennium. For instance, with the US PE ratio being 18 in May 2008, the 10-year Treasury bond yield of 3.75% implied a NPVGO/EPS of −8.67%, that is a negative expected return on firms' new investment opportunities.

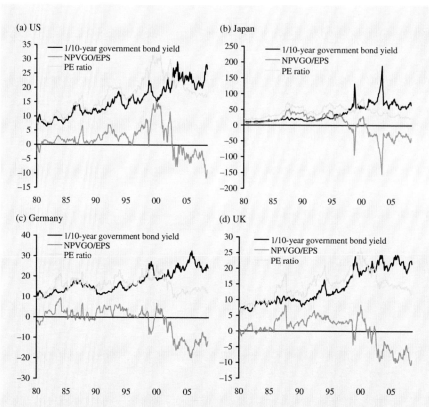

Fig. 4.17 Price earnings ratios, bond yields and the net present value of growth opportunities (NPVGO) in % of earnings per share
Source: Thomson Financial; own calculations. – *NPVGO/EPS* is the net present value of growth opportunities relative to earnings per share. It was calculated as *P/EPS – 1/r*. – Period: March 1973 to May 2008

Figure 4.18 shows long-run regression results of German, UK and Japanese stock market PE ratios on US stock market PE ratios for the period January 1980 to January 2006. According to the ADF-tests of the residuals (which are shown in Fig. 4.19), the null hypothesis of a unit root in the residuals for the US-German and US-UK case can be rejected. However it cannot be rejected in the US-Japanese case. That said, the PE ratios of the US, Germany and the UK appear to be on the same *wavelengths*, that is deviations between PE ratios in these currency relative to the US stock market tend to be corrected out over time.

Estimation: $Y_{i,t}^{*} = \beta_0 + \beta_1 X_t + u_t$			ADF-tests of the residuals		
Y_i^{*}	β_0	β_1	AIC	Schwarz	Lag 12 mths
I. PE-ratios with X = US PE ratio					
Germany	10.66 (0.495)	0.312 (0.027)	–3.159**	–3159**	–2.743*
UK	2.895 (0.216)	0.655 (0.012)	–3.598***	–4.056***	–2.397
Japan	19.94 (2.146)	1.375 (0.117)	–2.202	–2.202	–2.291
II. Dividend yields with X = US dividend yield					
Germany	1.075 (0.055)	0.407 (0.016)	–2.729*	–2.541	–2.821*
UK	2.220 (0.056)	0.629 (0.016)	–3.344**	–3.859***	–3.015**
Japan	0.424 (0.038)	0.183 (0.011)	–1.831	–1.706	–1.919

Fig. 4.18 Long-run regression results for PE ratios and dividend yields
Source: Thomson Financial; own calculations. – All variables in natural logarithms. – Legend: */**/*** significant at the 10%/5%/1% level. – Standard errors in brackets. – *AIC* is the Akaike information criterion, *Schwarz* is the Schwarz information criterion. – Period: January 1980 to January 2006; monthly data.

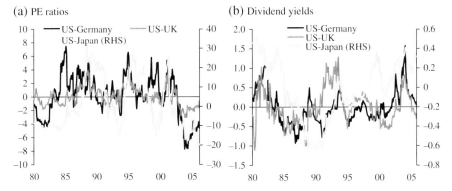

Fig. 4.19 Residuals of the long-run regressions
Source: Thomson Financial; own calculations

Digression: Price Earnings Ratios and Future Stock Market Performance

What do current price earnings (PE) ratios tell us about the stock market performance in the future? Fig. 4.20 plots the PE ratios of the US S&P's 500 stock market index (horizontal axis) against the average monthly changes in nominal stock prices

PE ratio and average nominal stock market performance ...
(a) ... in the coming 5-years   (b) ... in the coming 10-years

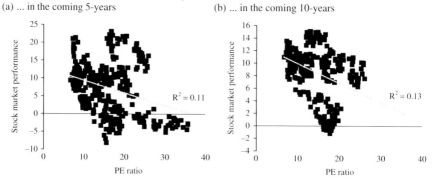

PE ratio and average real stock market performance ...
(c) ... in the coming 5-years   (d) ... in the coming 10-years

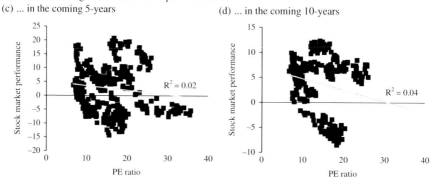

Fig. 4.20   S&P's 500 PE ratio and future stock price growth (1965–2006)
Source: Thomson Financial; own calculations. – Period January 1965 to March 2006. – Stock market performance is the average of first differences of log values in the coming 5- and 10-year period (annualised), respectively.

in (a) the coming 5-years and (b) 10-years (vertical axis) for the period 1965 to March 2006. Figure 4.20(c) and (d) show the same relations for real (that is inflation adjusted) stock returns. As can be seen, the relation between PE ratios and future (nominal and real) returns was negative, on average: High (low) PE ratios were followed by a declining (rising) stock market performance in the future.

Campbell and Shiller (1998) calculated the correlation between US PE ratios and subsequent growth in stock prices and earnings over the period 1872 to 1998. They found that the PE ratio was negatively (and statistically significantly) correlated with subsequent stock price growth but uncorrelated with subsequent earnings growth. These results suggest that changes in the PE ratio back toward the long-term average occurred mainly through changes in stock prices rather than changes in earnings growth. For the period 1965 to early 2006, a high (low) PE ratio of the US S&P's 500 stock market index was, if anything, followed by high (low) earnings growth (Fig. 4.21(a) and (b)).

PE ratio and average nominal earnings growth ...
(a)... in the coming 5 - years   (b) ... in the coming 10-years

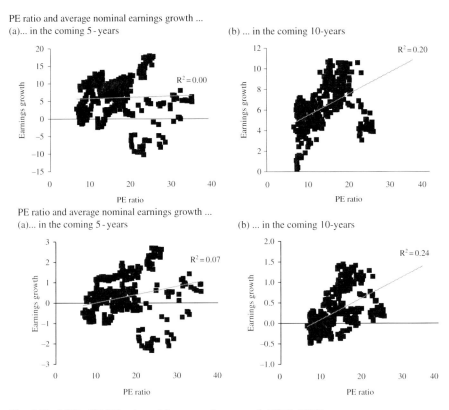

PE ratio and average nominal earnings growth ...
(a)... in the coming 5 - years   (b) ... in the coming 10-years

Fig. 4.21   S&P's 500 PE ratio and future earnings growth (1965–2006)
Source: Thomson Financial; own calculations. – For further explanations, see previous graphs.

In 1998, well before the global bull market (and the accompanying extraordinarily high PE ratios) came crashing down, Campbell and Shiller, who had worked extensively on the relation between actual PE ratios and future stock market performance, noted that (2001, p. 17): "Linear regressions of price changes and total returns on the log valuation ratios suggest substantial declines in real stock prices, and real stock returns below zero, over the next ten years." From August 2000, the US S&P stock market index fell from 1517.8 points to 841.2 points in February 2003 (and moved back to 1549.4 until October 2007).

Of course, one could think of economic reasons why PE ratios could potentially stay above their historical averages. *First*, one may argue that the economies worldwide might have entered a "New Era," in which globalization and accelerated technological progress allow economies to grow faster than in the past, justifying higher PE ratios. *Second*, stocks might appear less risky from the point of view of investors compared to previous periods, thereby justifying higher PE ratios. And *third*, the reduction of transaction costs (related to information and trading technologies) may contribute to higher PE ratios than in the past.

Long-Run Relation Between International Bond Yields

Figure 4.22(a) shows nominal 10-year government bond yields in the US, Japan, Germany and the UK. As can be seen, bond yields have been trending downwards in all currency areas under review. This finding might be explained by, for instance, a decline in expected inflation and, generally speaking, less volatile business cycles. Figure 4.22(b) plots the yield difference between US yields and Germany, UK and Japanese yields. Figure 4.22(c) and (d) show the same relations for real (that is inflation-adjusted) bond yields. It should be noted that in real terms the yield differentials between the US and the other currency areas under review were (much) lower when compared with nominal yield differentials.

The long-run regression results of German, UK and Japanese bond yields on US bond yields (in nominal and real terms) are shown in Fig. 4.23. The ADF-tests indicate that there is cointegration between long-term nominal yields in the US and the UK, the US and Japan, but not between the US and Germany. Turning to real yields,

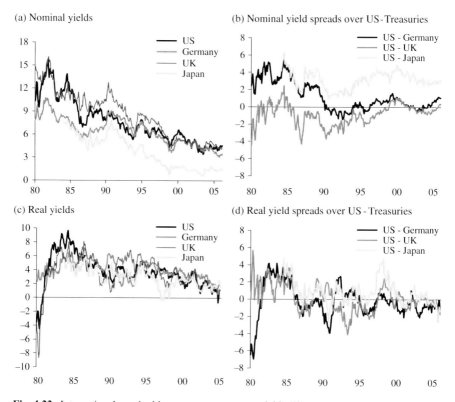

Fig. 4.22 International nominal long-term government yields (%)
Source: Thomson Financial; own calculations. Real yields were calculated by substracting current consumer price inflation from naominal yields. All yields represent 10-years government bond yields. - Period: January 1980 to Januare 2006; Japan starting January 1984.

Estimation: $Y_{i,t} = \beta_0 + \beta_1 X_t + u_t$			ADF-tests of the residuals		
Y_i	β_0	β_1	AIC	Schwarz	Lag 12 mths
I. Nominal yields with $X = $ US nominal yield					
Germany	2.416 (0.147)	0.525 (0.002)	−1.846	−1.978	−1.721
UK	0.997 (0.193)	0.981 (0.023)	−4.268***	−4.26***	−2.349
Japan	−2.236 (0.201)	0.865 (0.028)	−2.622*	−2.622*	−2.663*
II. Real yields with $X = $ US real yield					
Germany	2.798 (0.027)	0.314 (0.026)	−2.855*	−2.832*	−2.856*
UK	0.488 (0.168)	0.846 (0.038)	−3.273**	−3.761***	−2.539
Japan	1.207 (0.149)	0.455 (0.035)	−3.043**	−4.128***	−3.043**

Fig. 4.23 Long-run regression results between 10-year bond yields
Source: Thomson Financial; own calculations. – All variables in natural logarithms. –
Legend: */**/*** significant at the 10%/5%/1% level. – Standard errors in brackets. – Real values were calculated by substracting annual consumer price inflation from nominal yields. – *AIC* is
the Akaike information criterion, *Schwarz* is the Schwarz information criterion. – Period: January
1980 to January 2006; for Japan starting January 1984. – Monthly data.

the ADF-tests suggest cointegration between long-term US bond yields and those
of Germany, the UK and Japan. That said, the findings indicate that international
real long-term yields are (much) closer related than what nominal yields (which are
subject to currency areas' specific inflation targets) might suggest.

4.3 Rational Expectations and the Efficient Market Hypothesis

The Efficient Market Hypothesis (EMH) is a prominent concept in theoretical and
empirical analyses of financial markets.[12] It has evolved in the 1960s from the influential work of Eugene F. Fama 1965, 1970, 1976. The EMH holds that (financial)
asset prices (or asset returns) are determined by supply and demand in perfectly
competitive markets. Rational investors rapidly adjust asset prices to all relevant
information (Fama, Fisher, Jensen, & Roll, 1969). That said, at any point in time,
asset prices in an efficient market reflect all available relevant information (Fama,
1991, 1998). Individuals are not having any competitive advantages over their competitors as far as the acquisition and interpretation of information is concerned.

---

[12]The origins of the EMH can be tracked back at least as far as to the theoretical contributions of
Bachelier (1900) and Cowles (1933). The more modern literature begins with Samuelson (1965).

Perfect Capital Markets – or: Do we Need Realistic Assumptions?

The characteristic features of the neo-classical model are: perfect information, perfect capital markets and perfect competition. More specifically, a perfect market is typically characterised by the following factors:

- *No entry and exit barriers*. Investors can enter and exit the market at any point in time (without incurring any costs).
- *No tax asymmetries*. There is no different treatment of dividends and interest income, which could create asymmetric tax effects.
- *Financial assets are infinitely divisible*. Any financial asset can be bought and sold in any incremental of its face value.
- *No transaction costs*. Market agents' buying and selling is costless; there are no transactions costs (brokerage fees, taxes, etc.).
- *No restrictions on trading*. Taking long- and short-positions in the market is possible at any point in time.
- *Perfect competition*. All market agents act as price takers; no individual players can influence the market price.
- *All existing information is available to every participant without cost*: Acquiring and using information doesn't cost anything; there is no asymmetric information among market agents.

Of course, reality is quite different from the assumption made by the perfect capital market model. But this does not argue against its usefulness per se. Scientific models make certain assumptions, for exploring the subject matter in gradual steps. Accordingly, economic models are simplified replicas of reality. In that sense, one could hold the view that a *good model* includes just the most relevant features of the phenomenon the researcher is interested in analysing.

In fact, some researchers have argued that it would not matter at all whether a model's assumptions are realistic or not. What matters is the *quality of predictions* that can be derived from model's assumptions. To Milton Friedman, for instance, unrealistic assumptions would actually be an advantage (1953, p. 13): "(...) to be important (...) a hypothesis must be descriptively false in its assumptions." Friedman actually supported an *irrelevance-of-assumption* thesis.

The EMH assumes further that market agents have an understanding of how the economy works, and that they do not commit forecast errors systematically (LeRoy, 1989, p. 1583). What is more, the EMH is closely associated with the *random walk* of asset prices. The random walk theory holds that market relevant information in the future – *news* – is not foreseeable in the current period. As a result, an asset's current market price is the best predictor for its future price. No information available at time *t* or earlier can help improving the forecast of returns. The independence of forecast errors from the given set of information is known as the *orthogonality property* (and it is a widely used concept for empirical tests of the EMH).

In a world of the EMH, investors do not have the opportunity to *outperform* the market, that is generating a return on their investments that is in excess of a fair payment for the riskiness of the assets under review. That said, *abnormal profits* – that are profits in excess of the risk-free return – are assumed to be zero on average.

As the EMH allows a number of interesting and testable predictions about the behaviour of financial asset prices and returns, a vast amount of empirical research has been devoted to testing whether financial markets are efficient. Noting the *bad model problem* that plagues some of this research, Beechey, Gruen, and Vickery (2000), for instance, conclude that the EMH would be the right place to start thinking about price action in financial markets. However, the authors also note that the literature suggests that the EMH cannot explain all important features of financial asset price behaviour.

EMH and Anomalies

Many "anomalies" and statistically significant predictable patterns in stock returns have been uncovered in the literature, which obviously stand in contrast to the EMH (for an overview, see Fig. 4.24). If anomalies help outperforming the market on a systematic basis, the empirical evidence would argue against the EMH. Among the anomalies discussed in the literature are the following:

– *January effect*. A number of researchers have found that the month of January has been a very unusual month for stock market returns (Keim, 1983; Haugen & Lakonishok, 1988).
– *Size effect*. Over long periods, smaller company stocks generate larger returns than the stocks of large companies (Keim, 1983; Fama & French, 1992).
– *Value stock effect*. Stocks with low price earnings ratios (often called *value* stocks) appear to provide higher returns than stocks with high price to-earnings ratios (Nicholson, 1960; Ball, 1978).
– *Long-run return reversals*. When returns are measured over periods of days or weeks, the argument against the EMH is that some positive serial correlation exists. But studies have also shown evidence of negative serial correlation – that is, return reversals – over longer holding periods (Fama & French, 1988; Poterba & Summers, 1988; Fama, 1998).
– *No random walk*. More recent work by Lo and MacKinlay (1999) finds that short-run stock returns' serial correlations are not zero. The existence of *too*

many successive moves in the same direction make the authors rejecting the hypothesis that stock prices behave as random walks.

- *Overreaction*. Some studies have attributed return forecastability to the tendency of stock market prices to "overreact" to news (DeBondt & Thaler, 1995; DeBondt, 1995).
- *Return predictability*. Some stock performance measures such as, for instance, dividend yields, contain information to predict future returns (Fama & French, 1988; Campbell & Shiller, 1988).

Prediction	Empirical evidence
Asset prices move as random walks over time.	Approximately true. However: Small positive autocorrelation for short-horizon (daily, weekly and monthly) stock returns. Fragile evidence of mean reversion in stock prices at long horizons (3–5 years).
New information is rapidly incorporated into asset prices, and currently available information cannot be used to predict future excess returns.	New information is usually incorporated rapidly into asset prices, although there are some exceptions. On current information: In the stock market, shares with high returns continue to produce high returns in the short run (*momentum effect*). In the long run, shares with low price earnings ratios, high book-to-market-value ratios, and other measures of 'value' outperform the market (*value effect*). In the foreign exchange market, the current forward rate helps to predict excess returns; it is a biased predictor of the future exchange rate.
Technical analysis should provide no useful information.	Technical analysis is in widespread use in financial markets research. Mixed evidence about whether it generates excess returns.
Fund managers cannot systematically outperform the market.	Approximately true. Some evidence that fund managers systematically underperform the market.
Asset prices remain at levels consistent with economic fundamentals; they are not misaligned.	At times, asset prices appear to be significantly misaligned, for extended periods.

Fig. 4.24 Predictions and empirical evidence of the EMH
Source: Beechey et al. (2000, p. 5).

So does the EMH live up to empirical observation? Even though some anomalies have been shown to be quite robust, supporters of the EMH may argue that identification of anomalies tends to be (highly) dependent on the choice of the sample period. They may also argue that predictable excess returns are actually a compensation for risk, which might be incorrectly measured by the asset pricing models used. In addition, one could question whether the surveys have made use of the correct data: ex-post returns and ex-post risk premiums might not correspond to ex-ante investor expectations, which actually drive investment decisions. In sum, the EMH appears to be a rewarding approach for thinking about price formation in financial asset markets. However, both academic research and asset market experience suggest that the EMH might not explain all important features of asset price behaviour.

4.3.1 Formalising the EMH

The EMH assumes that the price P_t at time t incorporates all relevant information. Price changes between t and $t + 1$ are therefore solely a result of emerging *news*, which are, given the random walk assumption, unpredictable in t. The forecast error $\varepsilon_{t+1} = P_{t+1} - E_t P_{t+1}$ will therefore be zero on average and, in addition, uncorrelated with the information set Ω_t, which was available at the time the forecast was made. The latter is referred to as the rational expectation (RE) element of the EMH. The EMH-RE can be stated as:

$$P_{t+1} = E_t P_{t+1} + \varepsilon_{t+1}. \tag{4.55}$$

4.3.2 Orthogonality Property

The orthogonality property states that the forecast error must be independent of the information set Ω_t available at t or earlier:

$$E_t \varepsilon_{t+1} \equiv E_t (P_{t+1} - E_t P_{t+1}) \equiv E_t P_{t+1} - E_t P_{t+1} \equiv 0. \tag{4.56}$$

Generally speaking, the orthogonality property is violated if the error term ε_t is serially correlated. An example of a serially correlated error term is the first-order autoregressive process, AR(1):

$$\varepsilon_{t+1} = \rho \varepsilon_t + v_t, \tag{4.57}$$

where v_t is a (white noise) random element which is independent of the information set at time t. The forecast error, $\varepsilon_t = P_t - E_{t-1} P_t$, is known at time t and hence part of Ω_t. To see why serial correlation in ε_t violates the EMH, lag Eq. (4.55) by one period and multiply it by ρ, which gives:

$$\rho P_t = \rho(E_{t-1} P_t) + \rho \varepsilon_t. \tag{4.58}$$

Subtracting (4.55) from (4.58), rearranging and using $v_t = \varepsilon_{t+1} - \rho \varepsilon_t$ from (4.57), we have:

$$P_{t+1} = \rho P_t + (E_t P_{t+1} - \rho E_{t-1} P_t) + v_t. \tag{4.59}$$

The above equation shows that when ε is serially correlated, the price in $t + 1$ depends on the price in t and is therefore (partly) predictable from the information available today.[13] That said, the EMH implies no serial correlation in the error term.

4.3.3 Random Walk

Asset prices are typically said to follow a *random walk*. A time path of a random walk is often compared to a drunkard's walk. In the field of financial markets, the price of an asset, s, in $t + 1$ is:

$$s_{t+1} = s_t + \varepsilon_{t+1}. \tag{4.60}$$

If s_0 is the initial condition (the price in $t = 0$), it can be shown that the general solution to the first-order difference equation is:

$$s_t = s_0 + \sum_{i=1}^{t} \varepsilon_i. \tag{4.61}$$

The sequence ε_i imparts a persistent and random change in the conditional mean of the series. To see this, take expected values: $E s_t = E s_{t-m} = s_0$. It shows that the mean of the random walk is a constant. However, stochastic shocks have a persistent effect on the $\{s\}$ sequence. This becomes clear if we note that the conditional mean of s_{t+1} is:

$$E_t s_{t+1} = E_t(s_t + \varepsilon_{t+1}) = s_t. \tag{4.62}$$

The conditional mean of s_{t+s} is:

$$s_{t+s} = s_t + \sum_{i=1}^{s} \varepsilon_{t+i}. \tag{4.63}$$

When taking expectations, we can write:

$$E_t s_{t+s} = s_t + E_t \sum_{i=1}^{s} \varepsilon_{t+i} = s_t. \tag{4.64}$$

---

[13]The EMH places no restriction on the form of the second and third higher moments of the distribution of the error term. The RE places restrictions only on the behaviour of the first moment of the error term. See Cuthbertson (1996, p. 95).

If s takes a positive value, the conditional means for all s_{t+s} are equivalent. As a result, s_t is an unbiased predicator for s_{t+s}. Note, however, shocks (that are positive or negative values of ε_t) have a permanent effect on s_t. This is reflected in the forecast for s_{t+1}.[14]

The change in stock prices can also be partially deterministic (driven, for instance, by the prevailing monetary regime) and partially stochastic. Such a *random walk model plus drift model* can be written as:

$$s_t = s_{t-1} + a_0 + \varepsilon_t, \tag{4.65a}$$

where a_0 is a constant term. The general solution is:

$$s_t = s_0 + a_0 t + \sum_{i=1}^{t} \varepsilon_i. \tag{4.65b}$$

The behaviour of s_t is driven by two non-stationary factors: a linear deterministic trend and the stochastic trend $\Sigma \varepsilon_i$.

The n-step ahead forecast for the random walk model with drift yields:

$$\begin{aligned} s_{t+s} &= s_0 + a_0(t+n) \sum_{i=1}^{t+n} \varepsilon_t, \text{ or} \\ &= s_t + a_0 n + \sum_{i=1}^{n} \varepsilon_{t+i}. \end{aligned} \tag{4.66}$$

Taking conditional expectations of s_{t+s}, it follows that:

$$E_t s_{t+n} = s_t + a_0 n. \tag{4.67}$$

When compared with the pure random walk model, the forecast function of the random walk model with drift is not flat. In addition to s_t, one can extrapolate the deterministic change n times into future periods.

4.3.4 No Abnormal Returns

As noted earlier, the EMH assumes that investors cannot produce *abnormal* returns, that are returns which exceed the market risk-adjusted rate of return. While realised returns, R_{t+1}, will sometimes be above and sometimes below expected returns, $E_t R_{t+1}$, average unexpected returns, ε_{t+1}, will be zero:

$$\varepsilon_{t+1} = R_{t+1} - E_t R_{t+1}, \text{ or, when we include the expectation operator,} \tag{4.68}$$

$$E_t \varepsilon_{t+1} = E_t R_{t+1} - E_t R_{t+1} = 0. \tag{4.69}$$

---

[14] It can also be shown that the variance of a random walk is time-dependent.

If we want to draw any conclusion from (4.69), we need a model of how investors form a view about expected returns.

Let us consider a simple model in which (i) assets pay no dividends (so the expected return is the expected capital gain) and (ii) investors are willing to hold assets as long as expected, or required, returns are constant. In this case, the expected equilibrium return is:

$$E_t R_{t+1} = k. \tag{4.70}$$

Substituting (4.68) in (4.58) and rearranging yields:

$$R_{t+1} = k + \varepsilon_{t+1}, \tag{4.71}$$

where ε_{t+1} is white noise and independent of Ω_t. Assume further that the required return k on the risky asset consists of a risk-free return, r, and a risk premium, p (so that $k = r + p$), and that k is constant over time. For instance, a non-dividend paying stock yields:

$$R_{t+1} = (P_{t+1} - P_t)/P_t \approx \ln(P_{t+1}/P_t), \tag{4.72}$$

so that Eq. (4.71) implies that ex-post the *proportionate change* in the stock price will equal the constant plus a random error (which is expected to be zero on average). For the log of the future stock price we can write:

$$\ln P_{t+1} = k + \ln P_t + \varepsilon_{t+1}. \tag{4.73}$$

4.3.5 Market Relevant Information

For empirical tests of the EMH, one would need a definition of what constitutes "relevant information". In the literature, three types of the efficiency of financial markets have been put forward:

- *Weak form.* Current prices are assumed to incorporate all the information reflected in prices of the past. Under the weak form of the EMH one should not be able to profit from using information that is already known. That said, *technical*, or *chart analyses*, of historical price patterns (or trading data in general) would not permit outperforming the market.
- *Semi-strong form.* Current prices incorporate all publicly available information, that is past and current information. The semi-strong version of the EMH would still suggest that the investor should not be able to profit from using information that *everybody else* knows.
- *Strong form.* Current prices reflect all information that can possibly be known, including *insider information*. However, even here the investor should not be able to *systematically* outperform the market. Of course, an individual investor might gain profitable insider information. At the same time, however, the market

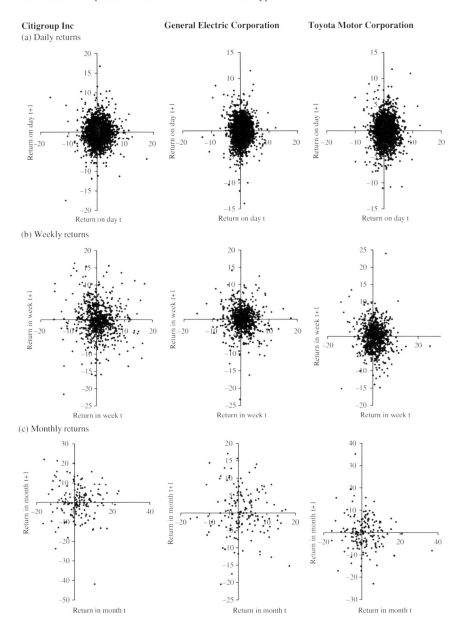

Fig. 4.25 Testing the weak form of the EMH
Source: Bloomberg; own calculations. – The returns are defined as first differences of log stock prices, multiplied by 100. – Period: January 1995 to May 2008.

anticipates, in an unbiased manner, future valuation relevant information (*news*), which cannot be anticipated even by the insider.

As noted above, under the weak form of the EMH, past information does not help identifying profitable trading opportunities. To give a simple illustration, Fig. 4.25 shows (a) daily, (b) weekly and (c) monthly stock price returns (in period t against period $t + 1$) of three publicly listed companies (Citigroup Inc., General Electric Corporation and Toyota Motor Corporation) for the period January 1995 to May 2008. In general, the correlation coefficients are very small. For instance, the correlation coefficient between daily returns in t and $t + 1$ is just 0.03 for Toyota, 0.03 for Citigroup and –0.01 for General Electric. That said, in these examples past returns appear to have been a poor guide when it comes to predicting future returns.

4.4 Bond Valuation – Basic Valuation Concepts

4.4.1 Prices, Yields and the RVF

4.4.1.1 Terminal Value of Investment

To many investors (such as, for instance, pensioners) it is of interest to know the terminal value of an investment. Consider an amount x invested for n years at a rate of R p.a., where R is a decimal such as, for instance, 0.1. Assume further the interest is paid at the end of each year. The terminal value of the investment after n years, TV_n, is then:

$$TV_n = x(1 + R)^n. \tag{4.74}$$

Of course, the frequency with which interest is paid matters for TV. If interest is paid m times per year, the terminal value at the end of the n years is:

$$TV_n^m = x \left(1 + \frac{R}{m} \right)^{mn}, \tag{4.75}$$

where m is the number of compounding periods per year.

To give an example, let $x = €100$, $R = 0.10$ (that is 10%) and $n = 5$. At various compounding periods per year, one obtains the following values of the investment at the end of 5 years:

Annual: TV_5^1 € $= 100 \left(1 + \dfrac{0.10}{1}\right)^{1(5)} = 100(1.10)^5 = $ €161.05

Semi-annual: TV_5^2 € $= 100 \left(1 + \dfrac{0.10}{2}\right)^{2(5)} = 100(1.05)^{10} = $ €162.89

Monthly: TV_5^{12} € $= 100 \left(1 + \dfrac{0.10}{12}\right)^{12(5)} = 100(1.0083)^{60} = $ €164.53

Daily: TV_5^{365} € $= 100 \left(1 + \dfrac{0.10}{365}\right)^{365(5)} = $ €164.86

Hourly: $TV_5^{365 \times 24}$ € $= 100 \left(1 + \dfrac{0.10}{8760}\right)^{365(24)(5)} = $ €164.87

As m increases, the interest rate actually becomes continuously compounded, so that the terminal value of the investment can be calculated as:

$$TV_n^c = \lim_{m \to \infty} x \left(1 + \frac{R}{m}\right)^{mn} = [e^{Rn}], \qquad (4.76a)$$

where $\exp = 2.71828\ldots$ So if €100 is invested for 5 years at 10% compounded continuously, the terminal value is:

$$TV_5^c = 100[e^{0.10(5)}] = 164.872. \qquad (4.76b)$$

In this context it is of interest to show what happens if the calculation switches between simple interest rates, periodic rates, effective annual rates and continuously compounded interest rates.

To start with, assume an investment of $x = $ €100 yields an interest rate of 2% each quarter. The effective annual rate, R^{eff}, can be calculated as:

$$x \left[1 + \frac{R}{m}\right]^m = 100 \left[1 + \frac{0.08}{4}\right]^4 = 108.24, \qquad (4.77)$$

so that the effective annual rate R^{eff} is 8.24%.

The relationship between the quoted rate R with payments m times per year and the *effective annual rate*, R^{eff}, is:

$$[1 + R^{eff}] = \left[1 + \frac{R}{m}\right]^m. \qquad (4.78a)$$

If, for example, the effective annual interest rate is 12%, and if we have quarterly interest payments, the compounded quarterly interest rate can be calculated by solving:

$$1.12 = \left[1 + \frac{R}{4}\right]^4 \qquad (4.78b)$$

for R, which then yields:

$$R = [(1.12)^{1/4} - 1]4 = 0.0287 \times 4 = 11.48. \tag{4.78c}$$

That said, the compounded quarterly interest rate is 2.87%, the simple interest rate would be 11.48% p.a. which, in turn, corresponds to an annual effective interest rate of 12% p.a.

Along the same line, one can switch between a rate R p.a., which applies to compounding over m periods, and an equivalent continuously compounded rate, R^c. To show this, assume an investor knows the m-period rate R and wishes to calculate R^c. The terminal investment values of x after n years must be equal when using either interest rate:

$$x \exp(R^c \cdot n) = x \left[1 + \frac{R}{m} \right]^{mn}, \text{ so that} \tag{4.79}$$

$$R^c = m \ln \left[1 + \frac{R}{m} \right]. \tag{4.80}$$

Accordingly, if R^c is known, we can calculate R as:

$$R = m \left[\exp(R^c/m) - 1 \right]. \tag{4.81}$$

4.4.1.2 Discounted Present Value (DPV)

What is today's value of a money unit to be received in the future? Let us assume the annual interest rate on a riskless investment over n years is $rs^{(n)}$.[15] We know that the future value of US$$x$ in n years (assuming annual interest payments) is:

$$TV_n = x(1 + rs^{(n)})^n. \tag{4.82}$$

That said, today's value of a payment of TV_n in n years time is simply x, so that the *discounted present value* (DPV) of TV_n is:

$$DPV = \frac{TV_n}{(1 + rs^{(n)})^n}. \tag{4.83}$$

The DPV concept is a reflection of the notion of the *time value of money*: a money unit today is worth more than the same amount of money to be received in the future.

---

[15] Note that the n-period bond will be a $(n-1)$ period bond after one period. For example, a bond which *when issued* had an original maturity of $n = 20$ years will after six years have a term to maturity of $n = 14$.

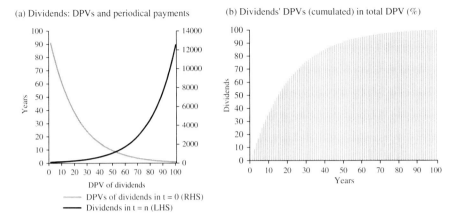

Fig. 4.26   Time value of money

4.4.1.3 Time Value of Money

A simple example might illustrate the concept of the time value of money. Let's assume a firm pays an annual dividend in the amount of ¥100 at the end of each period, and that the firm's dividend payment is expected to grow by 5% p.a. for the foreseeable future. Moreover, let the individual investor discount rate be 10% p.a. After 100 years, the DPV of dividend payments, and thus the value of the firm (that is the sum of all discounted cash flows), is ¥1980.9.

Figure 4.26(a) shows dividend payments from $t = 0$ to $t = 100$ (note that the series rises exponentially over time due to the interest-on-interest effect) and the DPV of periodical dividends, discounted to $t = 0$. The DPV series decays as the number of years increases – reflecting the time value of money. (Note that the rate of decline in the periodical DPVs of dividends slows down as the number of years increases.) Figure 4.26(b) shows the cumulated DPVs of dividends in percent of the firm's total DPV. More than 50% of the firm's DPV in $t = 0$ can be explained by the dividend DPVs in the first 15 years. The DPVs of dividends in the first 50 years account for 91% of the firm's DPV.

4.4.1.4 Pure Discount Bonds and Spot Yields

A zero bond (in short: *zero*) has a fixed redemption price M_n, an ex-post known maturity period, n, and pays no coupons in between. As a result, the return on a zero held to maturity is determined by the market price, P_t, and M_n (with $P_t < M_n$). If we assume a *one-year* $(n = 1)$ zero, the return is:

$$r s_t^{(1)} = \frac{M_1 - P_{1t}}{P_{1t}}, \tag{4.84}$$

where $r s_t^{(1)}$ is measured as a decimal (say, 0.05).

If one has to invest P_{1t} today for receiving M_1 in one year's time, the internal rate of return (IRR) concept can be applied:

$$P_{1t} = \frac{M_1}{(1 + y_{1t})}, \text{ so that the IRR, } y_{1t}, \text{ is} \qquad (4.85a)$$

$$y_{1t} = \frac{M_1 - P_{1t}}{P_{1t}}. \qquad (4.85b)$$

In other words: the one-year spot yield $rs_t^{(1)}$ is the IRR of the one-period zero.

Of course, the formula can be applied to a two year zero with a redemption price M_2. The annual (compound) interest rate $rs_t^{(2)}$ on the zero is:

$$P_{2t} = \frac{M_2}{(1 + rs_t^{(2)})^2}, \text{ which implies that} \qquad (4.86a)$$

$$rs_t^{(2)} = [M_2/P_{2t}]^{1/2} - 1. \qquad (4.86b)$$

In principle, it is possible to calculate (compound) spot rates for different maturities from the market prices of zeros.

Various Bond Return Measures

– The *internal rate of return* (IRR) is the interest rate that leads to a zero present value of the investment's cash flow stream. It implicitly assumes a *flat yield curve*.
– In terms of quoting bond returns, the IRR corresponds to the *yield to maturity* (YTM). The YTM can be used as a discrete or continuously compounded rate.
– The *holding period yield* (HPY), or the *redemption yield*, is the return on holding a bond from t to $t + 1$, including capital gains plus any coupon payment.
– The *spot rate* is the rate of return which applies to funds which are borrowed or lent today *over a given horizon*.
– The *forward rate* is the rate at which a contract is entered today, t, starting at future period $t + 1$, to be paid back in $t + 2$. Forward rates are typically synthesized from zero coupon bond prices. (Note that forward rates lie above (below) spot rates if the yield curve has a positive (negative) slope).

4.4.1.5 Coupon Paying Bonds

In most cases, bonds pay fixed coupons, C, which are ex ante known, at fixed intervals (annually or semi-annually) and have fixed redemption prices, M_n, payable at the end of the maturity. For instance, if the current market price of a coupon paying bond with n years left to maturity is $P_t^{(n)}$, the *yield to maturity* (YTM), R_t^y, which equals the IRR, is:

$$P_t^{(n)} = \frac{C}{(1 + R_t^y)} + \frac{C}{(1 + R_t^y)^2} + \cdots \frac{C + M_n}{(1 + R_t^y)^n}. \qquad (4.87)$$

The YTM is the *constant* rate of interest, bringing the DPV of future payments in line with the current market price. Equation (4.87) can be solved for R_t^y, as $P_t^{(n)}$, M_n and C are known. Note the subscript t on R^y. It denotes the fact that the yield to maturity changes as the bond's market price changes in t.

The YTM is a somewhat ambiguous measure. It implicitly assumes that coupon payments are reinvested at the *constant rate* R_t^y until the bond matures. To show this, consider the YTM for a two-period bond ($n = 2$) given by (4.87). After rearranging one yields:

$$(1 + R_t^y)^2 P_t = C(1 + R_t^y) + (C + M). \qquad (4.88)$$

The term on the left hand side is the terminal value (in two years) of the money amount invested at the constant annualised rate R_t^y. The right hand side of Eq. (4.88) is the amount $(C + M)$ paid at $t + 2$ and an amount $C(1 + R_t^y)$ which accrues at $t + 2$ after the first year's coupon payments have been reinvested at R_t^y. Since (4.88) and (4.87) are equivalent, the DPV formula assumes that the first coupon payment is reinvested at the start of year 2 at R_t^y. However, it is up to debate as to whether investors always believe that they will be able to reinvest *all* future coupon payments at the constant rate R_t^y.

There is another inconsistency in using the yield to maturity as a measure of the return on a coupon paying bond. Consider two bonds with different coupon payment streams $C_{t+i}^{(1)}$, $C_{t+i}^{(2)}$ but the same price, maturity date and maturity value. Using (4.87) this will imply two different yields to maturity R_{1t}^y and R_{2t}^y. If an investor holds both of these bonds in his portfolio and believes in Eq. (4.88) then he must be implicitly assuming that he can reinvest coupon payments for bond 1 between time $t + j$ and $t + j + 1$ at the rate R_{1t}^y and at a *different* rate R_{2t}^y for bond 2. But in reality the reinvestment rate between $t + j$ and $t + j + 1$ will be the same for both bonds and will equal the one period spot rate applicable between these years.

A *perpetuity* (or consol) is a coupon paying bond that is never redeemed by the issuer, so that $n \to \infty$. If the coupon is C p.a., and the bond's current market price is $P_t^{(\infty)}$, the return, $R_t^{(\infty)}$, is:

$$R_t^{(\infty)} = C/P_t^{(\infty)}. \qquad (4.89)$$

In fact, this measure corresponds to the YTM for perpetuity: if $n \to \infty$ in (4.87), it reduces to (4.89).

4.4.1.6 Spot Rates

Suppose an investor can lend money at the one year bond rate $rs^{(1)}$. For an investment of USx, the terminal value will be:

$$TV_1 = x(1 + rs^{(1)}).$$ (4.90a)

Suppose the interest on a two-year bond is $rs^{(2)}$ expressed at an annual compound rate. Then x invested will yield:

$$TV_2 = x(1 + rs^{(2)})^2.$$ (4.90b)

The *spot rate* assumes that the initial investment is *locked in* for the term of the contract. Spot yields can be used to discount payments accruing at *specific* dates in the future. The DPV of TV_2 is:

$$TV_2/(1 + rs^{(2)})^2,$$ (4.90c)

where $rs^{(2)}$ is the two-year spot rate.

Spot rates are calculated from market prices of zero bonds of different maturities. Since zeros offer a fixed one-off payment (namely the maturity value) in n years, their yields (expressed at an annual compound rate) can be expressed as a sequence of spot rates (that is $rs_t^{(1)}$, $rs_t^{(2)}$, ..., etc).

For example, if the redemption price of all zeros is TV, and the observed market prices of bonds with a maturity of $n = 1, 2, \ldots$ are $P_t^{(1)}$, $P_t^{(2)} \ldots$, and so on, each spot yield can be calculated as: $P_t^{(1)} = TV/(1 + rs_t^{(1)})$, $P_t^{(2)} = TV/(1 + rs_t^{(2)})^2$ and so on. For an n-period pure discount bond $P_t = TV/(1 + rs_t)^n$, where rs is the n-period spot rate, the formula is:

$$\ln P_t = \ln TV - n \ln(1 + rs_t).$$ (4.91a)

The price can also be expressed in terms of a continuously compounded rate, which is defined as $rc_t = \ln(1 + rs_t)$, and hence:

$$\ln P_t = \ln TV - n[rc_t], \text{ or}$$
$$P_t = TV \exp(-rc_t \cdot n).$$ (4.91b)

4.4.1.7 Approximating Spot Rates from Coupon Paying Bonds

If spot rates are available for all maturities,[16] the market price of an n-period coupon paying bond is determined as follows:

---

[16] If zero bonds are not available for all maturities, spot rates can be approximated using data on coupon paying bonds. For further details see McCulloch (1971, 1990).

$$P_t^{(n)} = \frac{C_{t+1}}{(1 + rs_t^{(1)})} + \frac{C_{t+2}}{(1 + rs_t^{(2)})^2} + \cdots + \frac{C_{t+n} + M_{t+n}}{(1 + rs_t^{(n)})^n} = \sum_{i=1}^n V_i, \qquad (4.92)$$

where M = redemption value, $V_i = C_{t+i}/(1 + rs_t^{(i)})^i$ for $i = 1, 2, \ldots n - 1$ and $V_n = (C_{t+n} + M_n)/(1 + rs_{t+n}^{(n)})^n$ for $i = n$. The market price is the DPV of future payments, where the discount rates are spot rates. In an information efficient market, Eq. (4.92) should hold. If it doesn't, investors can make *riskless arbitrage profits* by *coupon stripping*.

Governments typically do not issue zero notes or zero bonds. However, zeros can be created through coupon stripping, that is by separating coupon and principal payments of a security. After stripping, each cash flow of the security can be traded by itself, entitling its holder to a particular payment on a particular date. For instance, a 30-year US Treasury bond can be split into its 60 semi-annual coupon payments (*coupon strips*) and its principal payment (*principal strip*), thereby resulting in 61 individual zero securities.

To give an example for a riskless arbitrage opportunity through stripping, assume the market price of a coupon strip with the payment C_{t+1} in $t + 1$ is V_1, and that the market price of a coupon-plus-principal strip with the payment $C_{t+2} + M_{t+2}$ in $t + 2$ is V_2. The market price of a coupon bearing bond with a maturity of two years is $P_t^{(2)}$. Clearly, the bond can be viewed as a set of zero coupon bonds.

If, for instance, $P_t^{(2)} < V_1 + V_2$, the investor could purchase the two-year coupon bond and, at the same time, sell claims on the coupon payments in $t + 1$ and $t + 2$. By doing so, he can pocket a riskless profit in the amount of $V_1 + V_2 - P_t^{(2)}$. In an efficient market, the rise in the demand for the two-year coupon bearing bond would raise its price, while the selling of coupons would reduce prices of one- and two-year zero coupon bonds. As a result, riskless arbitrage would restore the equality in (4.92).

4.4.1.8 Forward Rates

The *forward rate* is the rate at which a contract is entered today, t, starting at future period N, and to be paid back at period $N + 1$. Forward rates are usually calculated from zero coupon bonds. Assume an investor buys a zero bond in t and simultaneously sells a number of X zeros with a maturity of N to be repaid in $N + 1$. The cash flows are shown in Fig. 4.27, (Cochrane, 2001, p. 350).

	1.	2.	3. = 1. + 2
	Buying N-period zero bond	Selling X ($N + 1$)-period zero bonds	Net cash flow
Period t:	$- P^{(N)}$	$+ X P^{(N+1)}$	$X P^{(N+1)} - P^{(N)}$
Period N:	1		1
Period $N + 1$:		$-X$	$-X$

Fig. 4.27 Calculating forwards rates from zero bonds

The number of bonds sold, X, that make today's cash flow zero, equals $P^{(N)}/P^{(N+1)}$. In fact, the investor has entered a synthesized loan contract from N to $N+1$. The forward rate at t for N to $N+1$ is:

$F_t^{(N,N+1)} = P_t^{(N)}/P_t^{(N+1)}$, or, when expressed in logarithms

$$f_t^{(N,N+1)} = p_t^{(N)} - p_t^{(N+1)}. \tag{4.93}$$

Of course, a bond price can be expressed as its DPV using forward rates:

$$
\begin{aligned}
p_t^{(N)} &= (p_t^{(N)} - p_t^{(N-1)}) + (p_t^{(N-1)} - p_t^{(N-2)}) + \dots (p_t^{(2)} - p_t^{(1)}) + p_t^{(1)} \\
&= -f_t^{(N-1,N)} - f_t^{(N-2,N-1)} - \dots - f_t^{(1,2)} - y_t^{(1)},
\end{aligned}
\tag{4.94}
$$

where $y_t^{(1)} = f_t^{(0,1)}$, so that one can write:

$$P_t^{(N)} = -\sum_{j=0}^{N-1} f_t^{(j,j+1)}. \tag{4.95}$$

In sum, the bond price today must be equal to the DPV of future payoffs valued at interest rates the investor can lock in today.

Changes in Bond Yields and Stock Prices and US Official Interest Rates

Figure 4.28 shows the Federal Funds Target Rate, the 10-year US Treasury yield and the US S&P's 500 for the period January to October 2006. On 29 June 2006 the US Federal Open Market Committee (FOMC) raised the Federal Funds Target Rate by 25 bp to 5.25% for the 17th consecutive time in the "rate hiking cycle". Subsequently, long-term bond yields declined, whereas stock prices increased. What kind of explanation provides financial market theory for such a market reaction?

As far as the bond market is concerned, the expectations hypothesis states that the yield offered on a long-term bond corresponds to the average of current and expected future short-term interest rates. So after the end of June 2006, investors seemed to have taken the view that the likelihood of further short-term rate hikes had decreased and that the official rate would decline sooner or later, translating into a decline of the long-term yield.

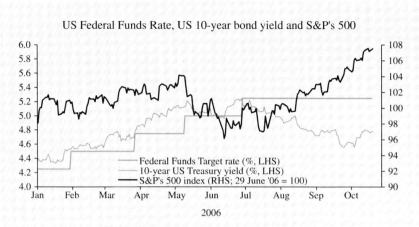

Fig. 4.28 US Federal Funds Rate, US 10-year bond yield and S&P's 500
Source: Thomson Financial, Bloomberg; daily data.

Likewise, the dividend discount model would suggest that the price of a stock corresponds to the sum of expected future dividends, discounted by a rate incorporating the risk-free interest rate and the risk premium investors require for holding the stock. All other things being equal (in particular earnings expectations), downward revisions in future expected (risk-free) short-term interest rates would exert downward pressure on long-term bond yields. A lowering of the discount rate, in turn, would argue for higher stock prices.

However, changes of other factors which influence bond and stock prices (such as, for instance, risk and/or liquidity premia) might, in certain circumstances, overshadow the impact of changes in expected monetary policy actions. That said, market agents shouldn't expect that there is at all times a "mechanical" reaction of bond yields and stock prices to changes in (expected) short-term interest rates.

See: ECB (2006b, Box 1, pp. 23–25).

4.4.1.9 Holding Period Yield (HPY) and the Rational Valuation Formula (RVF)

If an investor holds a coupon paying bond between t and $t + 1$, his return is the capital gain plus coupon payments. This measure of return is known as the one-period *holding period yield* (HPY):

$$H_{t+1}^{(n)} = \frac{P_{t+1}^{(n-1)} - P_t^{(n)} + C_t}{P_t^{(n)}}. \tag{4.96}$$

Investors do not know P_{t+1} at time t, though (while coupon payments are known at time t for all future time periods). They will have to form *expectations* of P_{t+1}.

The rational valuation formula (RVF) for bonds suggests that the *required one-period* return, or the HPY, on an n-period bond, k_t, is:

$$E_t \left[\frac{P_{t+1}^{(n-1)} - P_t^{(n)} + C_{t+1}}{P_t^{(n)}} \right] = k_t. \tag{4.97}$$

Solving Eq. (4.97) forward gives the *current bond price*: it is the DPV of future (known) coupon payments, discounted at the expected *one-period* spot returns k_{t+i}. For an n-period bond one yields:

$$P_t^{(n)} = E_t \left[\sum_{j=1}^{n} \frac{C_{t+j}}{\prod_{i=0}^{j-1} (1 + k_{t+i})} + \frac{M}{\prod_{i=0}^{n-1} (1 + k_{t+i})} \right], \tag{4.98}$$

where $M =$ the redemption payment. Here, the only variable the investor has to form expectations about is the one-period return k_{t+i} in future periods. As a rule, k_t can be broken down into a one-period risk-free interest rate, r_t, and a risk premium. However, when talking about the government bond market the risk premium on an n-period bond is frequently referred to as the *term premium*, $T_t^{(n)}$, so we can write:

$$k_{t+i} \equiv r_{t+i} + T_{t+i}^{(n)} \quad (i > 1) \tag{4.99}$$

where r_{t+i} is the *one-period* rate applicable between $t + 1$ and $t + i + 1$.

Note that government bonds are typically said to carry little or no risk of default.[17] In any case, risk arises either if bond investors wish to liquidate their holdings before the maturity date of the bond (*price uncertainty*); or if they hold the coupon paying bond to maturity, there is uncertainty as far as the reinvestment rate for coupon payments is concerned (*reinvestment risk*).

4.4.1.10 Duration

The value of a bond is inversely related to market interest rates. As a result, a long (short) bond position will gain (lose) in value if market yields decline. The *duration* has become a popular concept for measuring the *interest rate*, or *market risk* of a bond (portfolio). The duration can be defined in two ways: (i) as a measure of the average time (years) the investor has to wait to receive coupon payments and (ii) as a measure of the approximate sensitivity of a bond's value to a change in market interest rates. Both representations shall be briefly reviewed.

---

[17] However, this is actually a rather naïve assessment.

Risks for Fixed Income Investors

The investor in a fixed income security is exposed to various risks (Dattatreya & Fabozzi, 2001, p. 21).

- The *interest rate risk*, or *market risk*, denotes an unforeseen change in the bond's market price before it matures.
- Coupon payments are usually reinvested. The variability of the return on reinvestments is called *reinvestment risk*.
- *Liquidity risk* is the risk from a sudden, unexpected lack of marketability of a bond in the secondary market:[18] Buying and selling a given volume of bonds may be accompanied by large changes in prices.
- *Credit risk*, or *default risk*, refers to the risk that the issuer of the bond will be unable (or unwilling) to make timely principal and interest payments.
- *Inflation risk* implies that the loss in purchasing power of money turns out to be higher an expected by the investor.
- Cash flows, which are dominated in foreign currency, bear an *exchange rate risk*: the investor makes a loss (gain) if the domestic currency appreciates (depreciates) against the foreign currency.
- The possibility of any political or legal action that adversely affects the bond value is called *political risk,* or *legal risk*.

To start with, MacCaulay (1938) formulated the duration, D, of a bond with an a-priori known stream of payments, C, as:

$$D = \sum_{t=1}^{n} t C_t (1 + r)^{-t} / \sum_{t=1}^{n} C_t (1 + r)^t, \qquad (4.100)$$

where r is the market yield. Here, the duration is the *time weighted* average of the present value of a bond's payments in relation to the present value of the payments of the bond. For a zero bond which matures in n years, for instance, the duration is n years. For a coupon paying bond maturing in n years, in contrast, the duration will be less than n since some of the cash payments are received prior to n. In that sense, a coupon paying bond with a duration of, say, 4 years has a price sensitivity to market interest rate changes like a 4-year zero. That said, the higher (lower) the duration, the higher (lower) is the market risk of the bond related to changes in market interest rates.

---

[18] A prominent measure of liquidity is the *bid-ask spread* (that is the difference between the price for selling and buying a bond): the greater the bid-ask spread (for large transactions) is, the lower is the liquidity of the bond.

According to Hicks (1939), the duration can be expressed as the elasticity of the present value of a bond, PV, with respect to a change in the market interest rate, r:

$$\varepsilon = -\frac{\Delta PV/PV}{\Delta r/r}, \tag{4.101}$$

where $PV = \sum_{t=1}^{n} C_t(1+r)^{-t}$ and C are the cash flows. In this sense, an elasticity of, say, -0.2 means that the approximate decline in the bond price is 0.2% for a 100 basis point rise in the market yield.

In the case of a marginal change in r, the elasticity is:

$$\varepsilon = -\frac{dPV/PV}{dr/r} = -\frac{dPV}{dr} \cdot \frac{r}{PV}. \tag{4.102}$$

Differencing PV with respect to r yields:

$$dPV/dr = -\sum_{t=1}^{n} t C_t(1+r)^{-t} \cdot 1/(1+r). \tag{4.103}$$

Inserting the latter in the elasticity function yields:

$$\varepsilon = \frac{\sum_{t=1}^{n} t C_t(1+r)^{-t} \cdot}{1+r} \cdot \frac{r}{\sum_{t=1}^{n} C_t(1+r)^{-t}} \tag{4.104}$$

$$= D \cdot \frac{r}{1+r}.$$

Duration and Convexity

The duration is an approximation of a change in the bond price in response to a *small change* in the yield. For *large changes* in yields, however, the duration does not make a good job. This is because duration is a *linear* concept, whereas the *true* price-yield relation of a bond is *convex*. The duration is therefore a *conservative* concept: it underestimates the increase in bond prices as a result of declines in market yields, and it overestimates the decline in bond prices when yields rise.

Figure 4.29 shows the bond price-yield relationship, represented by the convex curve. The tangent line touches the latter where the bond price is P^* and the yield is y^*. For small changes in yields, the tangent line does not depart much from the bond's convex price-yield relationship; here, duration is a fairly good measure. The *estimation error*, however, gets larger the larger the change in the initial yield is.

To approximate the change in price that is not explained by duration, one may use the *convexity measure* (Fabozzi, Buetow, & Johnson, 2001, p. 112). It is approximated by the following formula:

$$convexity\ measure = \frac{PV_+ + PV_- - 2PV_0}{2PV_0(\Delta y)^2},$$

where +/– denote an increase/decline in y (in the amount of Δy).

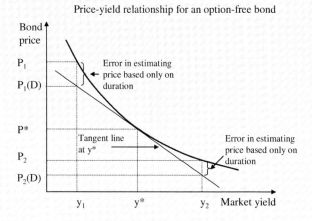

Fig. 4.29 – The convexity of a bond

To give an example, assume a bond with an issuing amount of US$100 with a 5.0% coupon p.a. and a maturity of 20 years. Given the market yield at 5.0%, the bond's PV_0 would be US$100, and its duration would be 13.09. The bond's price change in percent following a change in y is:

$$approximate\ percent\ price\ change = -duration \times \Delta y \times 100.$$

If, for instance, y rises from 5.0% to, say 5.2% (that is +20 bp, or 0.002 percentage points), we yield:

$$approximate\ percent\ price\ change = -13.09 \times 0.002 \times 100 = -2.618\%.$$

A 20 bp rise in the market yield to 5.20% implies $PV_+ = US\$97.55$, a 20 bp rate drop to 4.8% $PV_- = US\$102.54$. The convexity measure is therefore:

$$convexity\ measure = \frac{97.55 + 102.54 - 2 \cdot 100}{2 \cdot 100(0.002)^2} = 112.50.$$

The approximate percentage price change taking into account the bond's convexity is:

$$convexity\ adjustment = convexity\ measure\ x(\Delta y)^2 x\,100.$$
$$= 112.50 \times (0.002)^2 \times 100 = 0.045\%.$$

If the market yield rises from 5.0% to 5.2%, we saw earlier that the actual decline in the bond price was, according to the duration measure, 2.618%. The approximate change based on duration and the convexity adjustment is found by adding the two estimates:

$$estimated\ change\ using\ duration = -2.618\%$$
$$convexity\ adjustment\qquad\quad = +0.045\%$$
$$total\ estimated\ \%\ change\qquad = \overline{-2.573\%}.$$

If the market yield falls from 5.0% to, say, 4.8%, the actual rise in the bond price is 2.535%. The approximate price change based on duration and the convexity adjustment is:

$$estimated\ change\ using\ duration = +2.618\%$$
$$convexity\ adjustment\qquad\quad = +0.045\%$$
$$total\ estimated\ \%\ change\qquad = \overline{\ \ 2.663\%}$$

As a result, the duration combined with the convexity adjustment does a better job of estimating the sensitivity of a bond's change in price in response to a change in the market yield.

If the duration of a bond is known, it is possible to calculate the capital gain or loss following small changes in market rates. This, in turn, allows *hedging* the bond (portfolio) against market interest rate induced changes in its value. Assume a bond has duration D_L. The investor can *immunise* his long position vis-à-vis a rise in market interest rates by selling short a bond of the same duration.

Alternatively, the investor can immunise his portfolio by selling two bonds with maturity D_1 and D_2 such that:

$$\sum_{i=1}^{2} x_i D_i = D_L \text{ with } \sum_{i=1}^{2} x_i = 1, \tag{4.105}$$

and x_i the proportions of total assets held in the two bonds. In fact, this principle can be generalised to bond portfolios of all possible sizes.

Finally, it should be noted that such calculations only hold for small changes in yields and for parallel shifts in the (spot) yield curve. What is more, the duration changes as the remaining life of the bonds changes. As a result, the immunised portfolio must be continually rebalanced, so that the duration of assets and liabilities remains equal.

4.4.1.11 Nominal Versus Real Values

By deflating a bond's price P_t and its nominal coupon payments with a price index, the RVF can be formulated in real term (Modigliani & Cohn, 1979). The required *real* rate of return, k_t^*, is then the real interest rate (that is the nominal one-period rate, r, minus the expected one-period inflation, $E_t\pi_{t+1}$) plus a term premium:

$$k_t^* = (r_t - E_t\pi_{t+1}) + T_t = E_t(rr_t) + T_t, \tag{4.106}$$

whereas the real rate, rr_t, is assumed to be independent of inflation.

Inflation has a big impact on the value of a nominal coupon bearing bond: it reduces its real value. In terms of pricing, an increase in expected inflation will, other things being equal, increase nominal discount rates which causes the nominal bond price to decline. To show this, take the term at $t + 2$, for which we write: $(1 + k_{t+i}) = (1 + k_{t+i}^*)(1 + \pi_{t+i})$, so that:

$$P_t = \cdots + E_t[\frac{C_{t+2}}{(1 + k_t^*)(1 + k_{t+1}^*)(1 + \pi_{t+1})(1 + \pi_{t+2})}] + \cdots \tag{4.107}$$

Equation (4.107) can be rearranged into:

$$P_t = \cdots + E_t\left[\frac{C/(1 + \pi_{t+1})(1 + \pi_{t+2})}{(1 + k_t^*)(1 + k_{t+1}^*)}\right] + \cdots \tag{4.108}$$

That said, for constant real discount factors k_{t+i}^* the nominal bond price depends negatively on the expected future one-period rates of inflation.

Measuring the US Bond Markets' Inflation Expectation

Economic theory suggests that average *real* (inflation-adjusted) interest rates tend to rise with an increase in trend real GDP growth. Given real interest rates, average *nominal* interest rates tend to rise with an increase in investor inflation expectation. In the US, for instance, 10-year average real GDP growth drifted down from about 4% in the early 1960s to about 2% in the late 1970s and early 1980s, then returned to around 4.0% in the second half of the 1990s (Fig. 4.30).

The 5-year average of consumer price inflation (CPI) drifted up from less than 2% in the early 1960s to nearly 10% in 1980, then declined to around

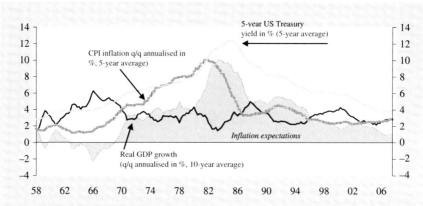

Fig. 4.30 US long-term yields, CPI inflation, real GDP growth and inflation expectations
Source: Thomson Financial, own calculations.

2.5% seen in the last decade. The 5-year average of the 5-year US Treasury yield rose from around 4% in the 1960s to 12% in the early 1980s. It fell back to less than 4% until the start of 2007.

These observations suggest that inflation expectations had a very important impact on long-term bond yields. On the one hand, bond yields rose when inflation accelerated, even though growth slowed, so inflation influenced bond yields more than real GDP growth did. On the other hand, bond yields fell when inflation decelerated, even though real GDP growth remained broadly stable.

Assuming an *adaptive expectation model*, the difference between the 5-year average of the 5-year US Treasury yield and the 10-year average of real GDP growth might be seen as an estimate of the bond market's 5-year *inflation expectation*. It is represented by the shaded area in the chart above. Inflation expectation oscillated around zero in the late 1950s and early 1960s, an environment of relatively subdued actual inflation.

Starting in the second half of the 1960s, however, actual inflation rose sharply to about 10% in the early 1980s. Thereafter, it started declining, reaching less than 1% in the first quarter of 2007. Inflation expectations fell below the 5-year average of annual consumer price inflation. The bond market's inflation expectation has thus receded considerably since the early 1980s, having returned to the levels seen in the late 1950s and 1960s. Clearly, with inflation fears approaching zero, bond yields could fall to match trend real growth, as was the pattern in the 1950s and early 1960s.

Source: Dewald, W. G. (1998), Bond Market Inflation Credibility, in: MonetaryTrends, Federal Reserve Bank of St. Louis, February.

4.4.2 Theories of the Term Structure of Interest Rates

4.4.2.1 Theories of the Term Structure of Interest Rates Using the HPY

The term structure of interest describes the relation between bond market yields and the maturities of the bonds under review at a given point in time. Figure 4.31 shows the yield levels of German government bonds for 1- to 10-year maturities from January 1970 to May 2008 in percent. Figure 4.32 shows term structures of interest rates at various points in time. For instance, the yield curve was positively sloped in May 2008 (that is long yields exceeded short yields), while it was negatively sloped in January 1992 (with short yields exceeding long yields) and actually flat in January 2003 (that is long rates were more or less at the same level as short rates).

How can we explain the slope of the term structure of interest rates? The box below provides an overview on the widely used theories of the term structure of interest rates (Cuthbertson, 1996, 1957). They actually differ in the assumptions regarding the term premium. In the following, the (pure) expectations hypothesis, the liquidity preference hypothesis, market segmentation and the preferred habitat hypothesis will be reviewed using the one-period holding period yield (HPY).

Pure Expectations Hypothesis (PEH)

If investors are risk neutral, the expected one-period HPY on bonds would be equal to the riskless return on a one-period investment, r_t:

$$E_t H_{t+1}^{(n)} = r_t \qquad (4.109)$$

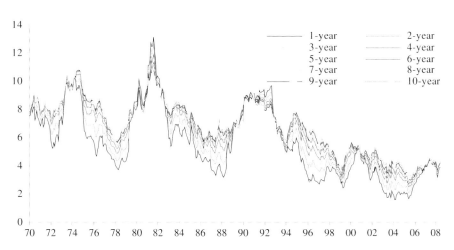

Fig. 4.31 German government bond yields (%)
Source: Thomson Financial.

Fig. 4.32 Selected term
structures of the German
bond yields (%)
Source: Thomson Financial.

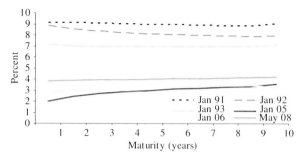

The *pure expectations hypothesis* (PEH) states that there is no term premium,
and that the discount factor in the RVF is simply $k_{t+i} = r_{t+i}$.

Assuming *rational expectations* (RE), one yields the PEH under RE:

$$H_{t+1}^{(n)} = E_t H_{t+1}^{(n)} + \eta_{t+1}^{(n)},$$

where $E_t(\eta_{t+1}^{(n)} \mid \Omega_t) = 0$, and $\eta_{t+1}^{(n)}$ is the one-period rational expectations forecast
error:

$$H_{t+1}^{(n)} - r_t = \eta_{t+1}^{(n)}. \tag{4.110}$$

Testing the PEH under RE requires that the *ex-post excess* HPY should have a
zero mean, that it is independent of all information at time t (Ω_t) and is serially
uncorrelated.

Expectations Hypothesis (EH), or Constant Term Premium

As the future is uncertain, investors would demand a compensation for risks. In this
case, the excess HPY includes a term for risk, that is a *term premium*, $T_t^{(n)}$:

$$E_t H_{t+1}^{(n)} = r_t + T_t^{(n)}. \tag{4.111}$$

How can we explain the term premium? One could assume that T is (i) constant
over time and/or (ii) independent of the term to maturity of the bond (so that $T_t^n =
T$). If the term premium is assumed to be constant, we would have the *expectations
hypothesis* (EH). When it comes to empirical testing, the EH-RE makes similar
predictions as the PEH-RE: namely no serial correlation in excess yields (that is the
constant term premium T and the discount factor, $k_t = r_t + T$), and that excess
yields should be independent of Ω_t.

Liquidity Preference Hypothesis (LPH)

The *liquidity preference hypothesis* (LPH) holds that the term premium depends (positively) on the maturity of the bond: $T_t^{(n)} = T^{(n)}$. The longer the maturity is the higher is the term premium and vice versa. Why? Compare, for example, the one-period HPY yield of a 30- and 5-year bond. The price volatility of the former would be higher than the price volatility of the latter. If this difference in volatility depends on the difference in the term to maturity, it should induce investors to demand a liquidity premium which depends on n.

What is more, the LPH states that the excess yield is a constant for bonds with the same maturity. At the same time, the LPH holds that the term premium increases with the maturity of the bond. In that sense, the expected excess HPY on a 10-year bond would exceed the expected excess HPY on a 2-year bond, but this difference would be constant over time.

That said, under the LPH we have $k_t = r_t + T^{(n)}$ as the discount factor in the RVF, and expected excess HPYs are given by:

$$E_t H_{t+1}^{(n)} - r_t + T^{(n)} \quad T^{(n)} > T^{(n-1)} > \ldots, \qquad (4.112)$$

so that we have a different constant for each bond of maturity n. The testable implications using regressions analysis for testing the LPH are identical to those of the PEH-EH.

Time Varying Risk

Of course, one could think of a time-varying term premium in the required return such as:

$$k_t = r_t + T(n, z_t), \qquad (4.113)$$

where n is the maturity of the bond and z_t is a set of variables that influences investors' perceptions of risk. While this seems to be a promising theoretical approach, the researcher has to specify the function T to make the expected excess HPYs operational.[19]

Market Segmentation Hypothesis (SMH)

The central idea of the SMH is that the slope of the yield curve depends on the relative supply and demand conditions in the market for longer-term funds relative to shorter-term funds. The shape of the yield curve at any point in time can thus be

---

[19]For instance, the Capital Asset Pricing Model (CAPM), which will be explained later in this chapter, could provide an analytical framework for explaining the term premium.

explained by (institutional) investors' asset/liability management constraints (regulatory or self-imposed) and/or creditors and debtors restricting their lending and borrowing activities to certain maturities (Cuthbertson, 1957).

In general, under the SMH the yield curve can be either upward sloping or downward sloping. For instance, if there is a large supply of money in the short-term market relative to demand, but a relative shortage of money supply in the long-term market relative to demand, the yield curve would be upward-sloping (that is long-term yields would exceed short-term yields). Similarly, a downward-sloping curve would be the result of relatively high money demand in the short-term market compared to the situation in the long-term market.

Preferred Habitat Theory (PHT)

Theoretically speaking, the PHT lies between the LPH and SMH. It holds that the shape of the yield curve is determined by investor expectations of future (short-term) interest rates and a risk premium (Modigliani & Sutch, 1966). It assumes that the risk premium does not necessarily rise with the maturity of the bond, as does the LPH. To the extent that supply of and demand for money in a particular maturity band does not match, some lenders and borrowers will have to shift to maturities showing opposite balances – as is the case under the SMH. For making creditors and debtors moving away from their preferred lending and borrowing maturities, however, an appropriate compensation for risk will be required, and so the PHT says that the term premium can be positive or negative.

Theories of the Term Structure of Interest Rates – An Overview

1. **Pure Expectations Hypothesis (PEH)**

   (i) Expected excess return is zero *or*
   (ii) the term premium is zero for all maturities:

   $$E_t H_{t+1}^{(n)} - r_t = 0 \quad R_t^{(n)} - E_t(r_{t+j}, s) = 0.$$

2. **Expectations Hypothesis, or constant term premium (EH)**

   (i) Expected excess return equals a constant which is the same for all maturities *or*
   (ii) the term premium T is a constant and the same for all maturities:

   $$E_t H_{t+1}^{(n)} - r_t = T \quad R_t^{(n)} - E_t(r_{t+j}, s) = T$$

3. **Liquidity Preference Hypothesis (LPH)**

   (i) Expected excess return on a bond of maturity n is a constant but the value of the constant is larger the longer the period to maturity *or*

   (ii) the term premium increases with n, the time period to maturity

$$E_t H_{t+1}^{(n)} - r_t = T^{(n)} \quad R_t^{(n)} - E_t(r_{t+j'} s) = T^{(n)} \text{ where } T^{(n)} > T^{(n-1)} \dots, \text{ etc.}$$

4. **Time varying risk**

   (i) Expected excess return on a bond of maturity n varies both with n and over time, and

   (ii) the term premium depends on the maturity n and varies over time

$$E_t H_{t+1}^{(n)} - r_t = T(n, z_t) \quad R_t^{(n)} - E_t(r_{t+j}, s) = T(n, z_t)$$

   where $T(\cdot)$ is some function of n and a set of variables z_t.

5. **Market Segmentation Hypothesis (SMH)**

   (i) Excess returns are influenced at least in part by the outstanding stock of assets of different maturities, and

   (ii) the term premium depends in part on the outstanding stock of assets of different maturities:

$$E_t H_{t+1}^{(n)} - r_t = T(z_t^{(n)}) \quad R_t^{(n)} - E_t(r_{i+j}, s) = T(z_t^{(n)})$$

   where $z_t^{(n)}$ stands for the *relative* holdings of assets of maturity n as a proportion of total assets held.

6. **Preferred Habitat Theory (PHT)**

   (i) Bonds which mature at dates which are close together should be reasonably close substitutes and hence have similar term premia.

Source: Cuthbertson (1996, p. 219).

Digression: **The Information Content of the US Term Spread for Future Economic Activity**

In the period June 2004 to June 2006, the US Federal Reserve raised the target for the Federal Funds Rate from 1.0% to 5.25%. In contrast to what happened in previous tightening cycles, long-term interest rates declined slightly over the same period, which caused a *flat yield curve*. In June 2007, the differential between the

(a) Term spread, real GDP growth and recessions in the US

(b) Probability of a US recession according to the term spread

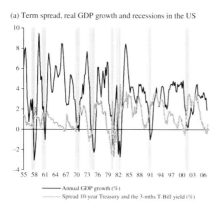

Annual GDP growth (%)
Spread 10-year Treasury and the 3-mths T-Bill yield (%)

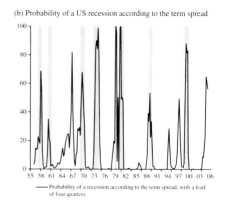

Probability of a recession according to the term spread, with a lead of four quarters

Fig. 4.33   A probit model for the US business cycle

yield on US 10-year government bonds and the 3-month US Treasury bill rate (that is the *term spread*) reached 49 basis points, a huge drop from 350 basis points seen in June 2004. On a monthly basis, the 10-year government bond yield even fell below the three-month interest rate at the end of 2005. Such a development in the term spread has typically been a forerunner of a slowdown in the US (Estrella, Rodrigues, & Schich 2003; Estrella, 2005).[20]

Figure 4.33(a) plots quarterly data for the term spread, together with the annual growth rate of real US GDP. The shaded areas indicate recessionary periods as defined by the NBER.[21] The chart illustrates that a sizeable drop in the steepness of the yield curve, making it flat or even inverted, has been on occasions followed – after periods of between two to four quarters – by a recession.

The Probit Model

What is the likelihood that a certain level of the term spreads indicates a forthcoming recession in the US? To address this issue, a simple probit regression analysis can be used. To start with, we assume that the indicator I_i is determined by an explanatory variable, in our case the yield spread, X, in such a

---

[20]The idea that an inverted yield curve signals a forthcoming recession was formalized empirically by a number of researchers in the late 1980s, including Laurent (1988, 1989), Harvey (1988, 1989), Stock and Watson (1989), Chen (1991), and Estrella and Hardouvelis (1991), primarily using US data. See also ECB (2006a).

[21]The NBER does not define a recession in terms of two consecutive quarters of decline in real GDP. Rather, a recession is a significant decline in economic activity spread across the economy, lasting more than a few months, normally visible in real GDP, real income, employment, industrial production, and wholesale-retail sales.

way that the greater I_i is, the greater is the probability of the economy falling into recession:

$$I_i = \beta_1 + \beta_2 X_i + u_i, \tag{4.114}$$

where u is the i.i.d. error term.

How is the (unobservable) I_i related to the actual event of the economy falling into recession? Let $Y = 1$ if the economy is in recession and $Y = 0$ if it is not. Now it is reasonable to assume that for each spread there is a critical threshold level of the index, call it I_i^*, such that if I_i exceeds I_i^*, the economy is in recession, otherwise it is not. The threshold I_i^* is not observable, but if one assumes that it is normally distributed with the same mean and variance, it is possible not only to estimate the parameters of the index in the equation above but also to get some information about the unobservable index itself.

Given the assumption of normality, the probability that I_i^* is less than or equal to I_i can be computed from the standardized normal CDF as:

$$
\begin{aligned}
P_i &= \Pr(Y = 1) = \Pr(I_i^* \le I_i) = F(I_i) = \frac{1}{\sqrt{2\pi}} \int_{-\infty}^{T_i} e^{-v^2} dv \\
&= \frac{1}{\sqrt{2\pi}} \int_{-\infty}^{\beta_1 + \beta_2 X_i} e^{-v^2/2} dv,
\end{aligned}
\tag{4.115}
$$

where v is a standardised normal variable, i.e. $v \sim N(0, 1)$. Since P_i represents the probability that an event will occur – here it is the probability of a recession –, it is measured by the area of the standard normal curve from $-\infty$ to I_i (Fig. 4.34).

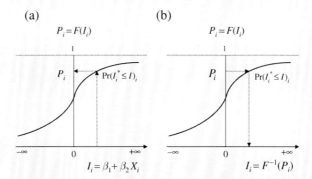

Fig. 4.34 Probit model; *Legend*: (**a**) Given I_i, read P_i from the ordinate, (**b**) given P_i, read I_i from the abscissa

To obtain information on I_i as well as β_1 and β_2 one can take the inverse of (2) and yields:

$$I_i = F^{-1}(I_i) = F^{-1}(P_i)$$

$$= \beta_1 + \beta_2 X_i,$$

(4.116)

where F^{-1} is the inverse of the normal CDF. What this means can be made clear from the graphs below. In graph (a) one obtains the cumulative probability of a recession given $I_i^* \leq I_i$, whereas in graph (b) one obtains (from the abscissa) the value of I_i given the value of P_i.

Applying a probit regression analysis on quarterly data, whereby the likelihood that the current quarter belongs to a recessionary phase is explained by the preceding four values of the term spread, it is found that, given the term spread at the end of September 2007, the probability of an imminent US recession was around 56% (Fig. 4.33(b)). The results reported by Estrella (2005), based on monthly data, indicate that, when the term spread is nil, there is a one-third probability of experiencing a recession after 12 months.

However, interpreting such empirical results requires quite some caution. The first reason why things could differ from the past is that a nearly inverted US yield curve could reflect a regime of particularly low long-term interest rates. The historically low level of long-term interest rate may reflect exceptionally low risk premia that are driven by an unusually high demand for long-term bonds rather than by fundamental macroeconomic factors. In particular, the US witnessed a surge in foreign investment in US government bonds since the last recession in 2001.

Second, when looking at survey evidence available up to Q3 2007, the perceived likelihood of a US recession over the next four quarters was significantly lower than that derived from the probit model, which features the term spread as the single explanatory variable. For example, according to the so-called *anxious index* published in the Federal Reserve Bank of Philadelphia's Survey of Professional Forecasters in June 2006, 17% of all the panellists covered foresaw negative quarter-on-quarter real GDP growth at the middle of 2007.[22]

In sum, the term spread in the US appears to contain valuable information as far as future economic expansion is concerned. However, it is important to bear in mind that it could be distorted by special factors such as, for instance, strong demand for long-term government bonds (from domestic and/or foreign investors), the precise impact of which is rather difficult to quantify.

---

[22]The "anxious index" can be found on the web site of the Federal Reserve Bank of Philadelphia.

Explaining the Term Structure of Interest Rates Using Spot Yields

The (continuously compounded) yield for a bond with a maturity n is $R_t^{(n)}$, and the one-period (continuously compounded) spot yield is r_{t+i}. The relationship between $R_t^{(n)}$ and a series of r_{t+i} can be established by assuming that the (continuously compounded) expected HPY equals the risk-free one-period spot yield plus a risk premium:

$$E_t h_{t+1}^{(n)} \equiv E_t[\ln P_{t+1}^{(n-1)} - \ln P_t^{(n)}] = r_t + T_t^{(n)}. \tag{4.117}$$

Equation (4.117) gives us the term structure relationship in terms of spot yields. With the redemption value of the bond, M, the continuously compounded rates are: $\ln P_t^{(n)} = \ln M - nR_t^{(n)}$. Substituting the latter expression in (4.117), one yields a forward difference equation:

$$nR_t^{(n)} = (n - 1)E_t R_{t+1}^{(n-1)} + r_t + T_t^{(n)}. \tag{4.118a}$$

Leading (4.118a) one period yields:

$$(n - 1)R_{t+1}^{(n-1)} = (n - 2)E_{t+1} R_{t+2}^{(n-2)} + r_{t+1} + T_{t+1}^{(n-1)}. \tag{4.118b}$$

When we take expectations of (4.118b) by writing $E_t E_{t+1} = E_t$ and substituting in (4.118a) yields:

$$nR_t^{(n)} = (n - 2)E_t R_{t+2}^{(n-2)} + E_t(r_{t+1} + r_t) + E_t(T_{t+1}^{(n-1)} + T_t^{(n)}). \tag{4.118c}$$

If we go on substituting for the first term on the RHS of (4.118c) and formulating that $(n - j)E_t R_{t+j}^{(n-j)} = 0$ for $j = n$, we obtain:

$$R_t^{(n)} = E_t R_t^{*(n)} + \Phi_t^{(n)}, \text{ with} \tag{4.119a}$$

$$R_t^{*(n)} = (1/n) \sum_{i=0}^{n-1} r_{t+i} \text{ and} \tag{4.119b}$$

$$\Phi_t^{(n)} = (1/n) \sum_{i=1}^{n-1} T_{t+i}^{(n-1)}. \tag{4.119c}$$

The result is that the n-period long-term interest rate equals a weighted average of expected future short rates r_{t+i} plus the average risk premium on the n-period bond until maturity, $\Phi_t^{(n)}$. The variable $R_t^{*(n)}$ is the *perfect foresight rate*. Subtracting r_t from both sides of (4.119b) and (4.119c), we yield:

$$S_t^{(n,1)} = E_t S_t^{*(n,1)} + E_t \Phi_t^{(n)}, \tag{4.120a}$$

where

$$S_t^{(n,1)} = R_t^{(n)} - r_t \tag{4.120b}$$

$$E_t S_t^{*(n,1)} = \sum_{i=1}^{n-1} (1 - i/n) E_t \Delta r_{t+i} \tag{4.120c}$$

Equation (4.120a) simply says that the actual spread $S_t^{(n,1)}$ between the n-period and the one-period rate is a weighted average of expected *changes* in short-term interest rates plus a term premium. The variable $S_t^{*(n,1)}$ is the *perfect foresight spread*.

The PEH and Spot Yields

As noted earlier, the PEH assumes that investors are risk neutral, that is they are indifferent to risk and base their investment decision only on *expected* returns. In this case, there is a straightforward arbitrage relation between long-term investments and a sequence of short-term investments. To show this, consider investment strategy I: investing US\$$A$ in a zero coupon bond with n years to maturity. The terminal value (TV) of the investment is:

$$TV_n = \$A(1 + R_t^{(n)})^n, \tag{4.121}$$

where $R_t^{(n)}$ is the (compound) rate on the n-period long bond.

Now consider investment strategy II: investing US\$$A$, and any interest earned, in a series of 'rolled-over' *one-period* investments, for n years. The *expected* terminal value $E_t(TV)$ of this series of one-period investments is:

$$E_t(TV) = \$A(1 + r_t)(1 + E_t r_{t+1})(1 + E_t r_{t+2})\ldots(1 + E_t r_{t+n-1}), \tag{4.122}$$

where r_{t+i} is the rate applicable between periods $t + i$ and $t + i + 1$.

The investment in the long bond (strategy I) gives a known terminal value, as the bond is held to maturity. Investing in a series of one-year investments (strategy II) gives a terminal value which is uncertain, as investors do not know the future one-period spot yields, r_{t+j}. However, under the PEH risk is ignored and hence the terminal values of the above two alternative investment strategies will be the same:

$$(1 + R_t^{(n)})^n = (1 + r_t)(1 + E_t r_{t+1})(1 + E_t r_{t+2})\ldots(1 + E_t r_{t+n-1}). \tag{4.123}$$

The equality holds because if the terminal value of investing in the long bond exceeds the *expected* terminal value of putting the money in a sequence of one-year investments, investors would at time t buy long bonds and sell short bonds. This would result in a rise in the current market price of the long bond and a fall in the long (spot) yield R_t. Simultaneously, selling of the short bond would cause a fall in its current price and a rise in r_t. Hence the equality in (4.123) would be quickly restored.

PEH: Tests Using Different Maturities

The PEH can be expressed in terms of the relationship between $R_t^{(n)}$ and *any m-period rate* $R_t^{(m)}$ for which $s = n/m$ is an integer:

$$R_t^{(n)} = (1/s) \sum_{i=0}^{s-1} E_t R_{t+im}^{(m)}. \tag{4.124}$$

It can be shown that the spread $S_t^{(n, m)} = (R_t^{(n)} - R_t^{(m)})$ is (i) an optimal predictor of future *changes in long-term rates* and (ii) an optimal predictor of (a weighted average of) future *changes in short rates*.

To show, in a *first step*, how the spread predicts changes in long-term rates, we make use of a simple example, writing (4.124) for $n = 6$, $m = 2$:

$$R_t^{(6)} = (1/3)[E_t(R_t^{(2)} + R_{t+2}^{(2)} + R_{t+4}^{(2)})]. \tag{4.125}$$

This equation is actually equivalent to writing:

$$E_t R_{t+2}^{(4)} - R_t^{(6)} = (1/2)S_t^{(6, 2)}. \tag{4.126}$$

If $R_t^{(6)} > R_t^{(2)}$, the PEH predicts that, on average, this should be followed by a rise in the long rate between t and $t + 2$. Assuming RE, Eq. (4.126) suggests a regression test of the EH such as:

$$R_{t+2}^{(4)} - R_t^{(6)} = \alpha + \beta[S_t^{(6, 2)}/2] + \eta_{t+2}, \tag{4.127}$$

where one would expect $\beta = 1$. Under RE, $S_t^{(6, 2)}$ is independent of η_{t+1} and therefore OLS yields consistent estimates; GMM correction to the standard errors might be required if there is heteroscedasticity in the error term, or if η_{t+2} is serially correlated due to the use of overlapping observations). For any (n, m), Eq. (4.127) is:

$$E_t R_{t+m}^{(n-m)} - R_t^{(n)} = [m/(n - m)]S_t^{(n,m)}. \tag{4.128}$$

In a *second step*, we now want to show how the spread predicts future changes in short-term rates. To this end, let us restate Eq. (4.125): $R_t^{(6)} = (1/3)[E_t(R_t^{(2)} + R_{t+2}^{(2)} + R_{t+4}^{(2)})]$. If we subtract $R_t^{(2)}$ from both sides of (4.125), we yield:

$$R_t^{(6)} - R_t^{(2)} = (1/3)[E_t(R_t^{(2)} + R_{t+2}^{(2)} + R_{t+4}^{(2)})] - R_t^{(2)}, \tag{4.129a}$$

that is we arrive at the perfect foresight spread $S_t^{(6,2)*}$. Rearranging (4.129a) yields:

$$S_t^{(6,2)*} = (-2/3)R_t^{(2)} + (1/3)[E_t R_{t+2}^{(2)} + E_t R_{t+4}^{(2)}] \quad \text{or} \tag{4.129b}$$

$$= (2/3)[E_t R_{t+2}^{(2)} - R_t^{(2)}] + (1/3)[E_t R_{t+4}^{(2)} - E_t R_{t+2}^{(2)}]. \tag{4.129c}$$

Equation (4.129c) says that the actual spread $S_t^{(6,\,2)*}$ is an optimal predictor of a weighted average of future *two-period* changes in the short-term rate $R_t^{(2)}$. If $S_t^{(6,\,2)} > 0$, agents expect on average that future (two-period) short rates should rise.

While $S_t^{(6,\,2)*}$ is an optimal predictor, this does not necessarily mean that it will forecasts the RHS of (4.129b) accurately. If there is substantial "news" between periods t and $t + 4$, $S_t^{(6,\,2)}$ may actually be a poor predictor. However, the spread is optimal in the sense that, under the EH, no variable other than S_t can improve one's forecast of future changes in short rates.

The generalization of (4.129a) is:

$$E_t S_t^{(n,m)*} = S_t^{(n,m)}, \tag{4.129d}$$

where

$$S_t^{(n,m)*} = \sum_{i=1}^{s-1} (1 - i/s)\Delta^{(m)} R_{t+im}^{(m)}. \tag{4.129e}$$

Equation (4.129e) suggests a straightforward regression-based test of the expectations hypothesis under RE:

$$S_t^{(n,m)*} = \alpha + \beta S_t^{(n,m)} + \omega_t. \tag{4.129f}$$

Under the EH, one would expect $\beta = 1$, and if the term premium is zero $\alpha = 0$. Since $S_t^{(n,\,m)}$ is, under RE, independent of information at time t, OLS yields unbiased estimates of the parameters; GMM estimates of the covariance matrix may be required. Note, however, that if the term premium is time varying and correlated with the spread then the parameter estimates in (4.129f) will be biased.

4.4.3 The Term Structure Spread and Future Short-Term Rate Changes

The theory of the term structure of interest rates under EMH-RE holds that the current spread between long- and short-term yields is an optimal predictor for future changes in short-term interest rates: The spread equals a weighted average of expected short-term interest rate *changes* over the life of the long bond *plus* a term premium. Making use of a simple OLS analysis, one can test the forecast accuracy by constructing the perfect foresight spread, $S_t^{n^{(*)}}$, for each bond maturity n from ex-post values of short-rate changes as:

$$S_t^{n^{(*)}} = \sum_{i=1}^{n-1} (1 - i/n) E_t \Delta r_{t+1} + \phi^{(n)}, \tag{4.130}$$

where $E(\,.\,)$ is the expectation operator, Δr is the change in short term interest rates and ϕ is the term premium. $S_t^{n^{(*)}}$ can then be regressed on the actual spread and a constant.

In the following, this shall be done for spreads between government bond yields and the one-month short-term interest rate in German and the US for the period January 1975 to August 2006, respectively. The bond maturities range from 1 year ($n = 12$) to 10 years ($n = 120$). The term premium is approximated by the difference in the sample means of the respective long-term yields and the one-month interest rate.[23]

The framework allows testing the EMH using a strict definition of RE: It is assumed that investors can predict future short-term rates perfectly save an i.i.d. error, which is orthogonal to all information at the time t (that is the point in time when the forecast is made):

$$\Delta r_{t+i} = E_t \Delta r_{t+i} + \eta_{t+i}. \tag{4.131}$$

Substituting Eq. (4.131) into Eq. (4.130) yields a testable hypothesis that the perfect foresight spread should equal the actual spread (which is the optimal predicator). Any differences between the two are purely random and uncorrelated with all information available in t or earlier:

$$S_t^{n^{(*)}} = S_t^n + \varepsilon_t^n. \tag{4.132}$$

Under the hypothesis (4.131), the regression error is a moving average process of the order $(n - 1)$ for monthly data:

$$\varepsilon_t^n = \sum_{i=1}^{n-1} (1 - i/n) \eta_{t+i}. \tag{4.133}$$

That said, the expected value of the compound forecast error is still zero, but successive error terms are autocorrelated and possibly heteroscedastic. As a result, the Newey and West (1987) methodology is applied, which shall correct for serial correlation and heteroscedasticity. The EMH-RE implies the two restrictions $\beta(n) = 1$ and $\alpha(n) = 0$. Figure 4.35 shows the p-values for the Wald tests of the first restriction (fourth line) and of both restrictions together (fifth line).

Except for the 1- and 2-year time horizon, the R2 statistics in Fig. 4.35 are relatively high for all maturities. They peak at the medium-term maturities of 6- and 7-years. The slope coefficients show a more pronounced hump-shaped pattern with

---

[23]So, in fact the liquidity preference hypothesis is tested, given the EH assumes constant and equal term premiums for all maturities.

Regression: $S_t^{n(pf)} = \alpha(n) + \beta(n)S_t^n + \varepsilon_t^n$. Estimation period: January 1975 to August 2006

		Long bond maturity in years $(n/12)$								
	1	2	3	4	5	6	7	8	9	10
Term premium $\phi(n)$	0.18	0.59	0.84	0.99	1.12	1.21	1.29	1.36	1.41	1.46
R2	0.13	0.19	0.30	0.45	0.62	0.72	0.63	0.58	0.53	0.51
$\alpha(n)$	−0.03	−0.29	−0.71	−1.19	−1.67	−2.07	−1.85	−1.64	−1.38	−1.30
	(0.18)	(0.31)	(0.33)	(0.32)	(0.31)	(0.12)	(0.33)	(0.29)	(0.25)	(0.33)
$\beta(n)$	0.86	1.24	1.61	1.94	2.17	2.18	1.72	1.33	1.05	0.92
	(0.21)	(0.33)	(0.32)	(0.21)	(0.18)	(0.13)	(0.15)	(0.12)	(0.09)	(0.12)
H0: $\beta(n) = 1$	0.52	0.47	0.06	0.00	0.00	0.00	0.00	0.00	0.59	0.51
H0: $\alpha(n) = 0$, $\beta(n) = 1$	0.80	0.59	0.05	0.00	0.00	0.00	0.00	0.00	0.00	0.00
Variance ratio (VR)	0.42	0.35	0.33	0.32	0.34	0.36	0.42	0.51	0.60	0.66

Fig. 4.35 Predicting future short-term rate changes with the current yield spread in Germany
Source: Thomson Financial, own calculations. – $S_t^{n(*)}$ is the "perfect foresight spread", where the risk premium is show in the first line of the table above. – S_t^n is the actual spread between the n-period bond yield and the one-month interest rate. – R2 is the coefficient of determination. $\alpha(n)$ and $\beta(n)$ are the coefficients (in brackets standard errors) for the constant and the actual spread, respectively, as estimated by the OLS method. – ε_t^n is the estimation error, which is autocorrelated of the order $n-1$ due to data overlap. – Standard errors in brackets, corrected for serial correlation and heteroscedasticity following Newey and West (1987). – The values shown for the hypothesis testing are p-values; the test statistics for the Wald test is distributed χ^2 (df) with $df = 1$ and 2 degrees of freedom. – The variance ratio (VR) is defined as the sample standard deviation of the actual spread, divided by the standard deviation of the perfect foresight spread. Number of observations: $379 - (n-1)$.

the highest value of 2.18 for the 6-year maturity. High (low) R2 statistics tend to be accompanied with large (small) slope coefficients. This suggests that, on average, investors could reliably predict medium-term, but not very near-term, developments of future changes in short-term rates. Whereas the direction of change has been anticipated quite well, the magnitudes of the medium-term short-term rate changes have been underestimated, causing the slope coefficients to exceed one to improve the regression fit.

These findings might be attributable to periods of high volatility in the sample, such as, for instance, the second oil price crisis in the early 1980s and the German reunification around the beginning of the 1990s. However, as these periods were temporary in nature, the effects of such interest rate shocks washed out over the medium-term. As a result, the slope coefficients for longer maturities (8- to 10-years) suggest that accumulated short-term rate changes are smaller compared with short-term maturities, and the slope coefficients are close to one.

The hypothesis that the slope coefficient is 1 cannot be rejected for 1-, 2-, 3-, 9- and 10-years. For medium-term maturities the actual spreads seem to be biased (with the slope coefficients much above one, the value implied by the EMH), although it is a relatively good predictor for future short-term rate changes. The best results from the EMH-RE are for the 1, 2- and 3-year maturities, with sufficiently high p-values for both restrictions.

The favourable model performance is also reflected in the *variance ratios* – the relation between the standard deviation of the actual spread divided by the standard deviation of the perfect foresight spread. In view of the null hypothesis of the RE, the variance of the perfect foresight spread must be higher than the variance of the actual spread. A high (low) variance ratio means therefore a low (high) forecast error variance. In the sample above, the variance ratios rise with the length of maturity, but do not reach one. Accumulated long-run forecast errors tend to be smaller than errors accumulated over shorter periods of time, reflecting a washing out of temporary volatile interest rate movements over longer periods. They reduce the bias in the slope coefficient and, as a result, weaken the evidence against the EMH.

Figure 4.36 shows the results for the US market. The R2 statistics are considerably lower compared with the findings for the German market, while the slope coefficients also follow a hump-shaped pattern. The slope coefficients are lower than those for Germany, though, indicating that for 3- to 8-years they also underestimated the magnitude of future changes in short-term rates, but to a somewhat smaller degree than in Germany. At the same time, the standard errors are much higher, reflecting considerable uncertainty of the predictions.

The hypothesis that the slope coefficient is 1 cannot be reject for maturities of 1-, 2-, 3-, 8-, 9- and 10-years. The strict EMH-RE, however, has to be rejected for all maturities except for 1- and 2-years. The variance ratios rise with the length of maturity, but remain, as is the case in Germany, below one. That said, with the length of maturity the forecast errors decline relative to the standard deviation of the actual spread.

Regression: $S_t^{n(pf)} = \alpha(n) + \beta(n)S_t^n + \varepsilon_t^n$. Estimation period: January 1975 to August 2006

	Long bond maturity in years ($n/12$)									
	1	2	3	4	5	6	7	8	9	10
Term premium $\phi(n)$	−0.07	0.28	0.45	0.59	0.72	0.82	0.92	0.95	0.99	1.03
R2	0.09	0.10	0.20	0.32	0.34	0.39	0.41	0.36	0.28	0.28
$\alpha(n)$	−0.06	−0.14	−0.46	−0.94	−1.25	−1.69	−2.04	−2.25	−2.38	−2.68
	(0.12)	(0.18)	(0.21)	(0.23)	(0.23)	(0.12)	(0.19)	(0.18)	(0.19)	(0.20)
$\beta(n)$	0.87	0.98	1.42	1.79	1.72	1.69	1.43	1.15	0.95	0.92
	(0.15)	(0.16)	(0.15)	(0.15)	(0.14)	(0.12)	(0.09)	(0.09)	(0.09)	(0.09)
H0: $\beta(n) = 1$	0.36	0.90	0.01	0.00	0.00	0.00	0.00	0.11	0.57	0.38
H0: $\alpha(n) = 0$, $\beta(n) = 1$	0.59	0.70	0.01	0.00	0.00	0.00	0.00	0.00	0.00	0.00
Variance ratio (VR)	0.34	0.32	0.31	0.29	0.33	0.36	0.43	0.49	0.52	0.53

Fig. 4.36 Predicting future short-term rate changes with the current yield spread in the US Source: Thomson Financial, own calculations. – $S_t^{n(*)}$ is the "perfect foresight spread", where the risk premium is show in the first line of the table above. – S_t^n is the actual spread between the n-period bond yield and the one-month interest rate. – R2 is the coefficient of determination. $\alpha(n)$ and $\beta(n)$ are the coefficients (in brackets standard errors) for the constant and the actual spread, respectively, as estimated by the OLS method. – ε_t^n is the estimation error, which is autocorrelated of the order $n-1$ due to data overlap. – Standard errors in brackets, corrected for serial correlation and heteroscedasticity following Newey and West (1987). – The values shown for the hypothesis testing are p-values; the test statistics for the Wald test is distributed χ^2 (df) with $df = 1$ and 2 degrees of freedom. – The variance ratio (VR) is defined as the sample standard deviation of the actual spread, divided by the standard deviation of the perfect foresight spread. Number of observations: $379 - (n-1)$.

4.5 Stock Valuation

4.5.1 Discounted Cash Flow Under EMH-RE

4.5.1.1 Stock Valuation

The discounted cash flow model is the most prominent concept for determining the *fundamental value* of stocks. If the expected *one-period* holding period return, $E_t H_{t+1}$, is q_t, the fundamental value of a stock, V_t, is the DPV of *expected* future dividends, $E_t D_{t+j}$:

$$V_t = E_t[\frac{D_{t+1}}{(1+q_1)} + \frac{D_{t+2}}{(1+q_1)(1+q_2)} + \cdots], \qquad (4.134)$$

where q_i is risk-adjusted return between time period $t+i-1$ and $t+i$.

For example, if $P_t < V_t$, the stock would be undervalued, and investors could purchase the undervalued stock and make a capital gain, as an increase in demand for the stock would increase its price, moving it towards V_t. In an efficient capital market, any such profitable trading opportunities should actually be immediately eliminated. Unfortunately, the investor cannot directly calculate V_t and compare it with P_t (which is observable), as D and q are not known in t and need to be estimated by the investor.

4.5.1.2 RVF for Stocks with Constant Expected Returns

If the expected return of a stock is assumed to be constant, the rational valuation formula (RVF) is:

$$E_t R_{t+1} = \frac{E_t V_{t+1} - V_t + E_t D_{t+1}}{V_t}, \qquad (4.135)$$

where V_t is the fundamental value of the stock at the end of period t and D_{t+1} are dividends paid between t and $t+1$; $E_t(.)$ is the expectation operator based the information set in t, Ω_t.

Assume investors are willing to hold the stock as long as it is expected to yield a constant return:

$$E_t R_{t+1} = k, \text{ with } k > 0. \qquad (4.136)$$

Using (4.135) and (4.136), we obtain a differential (Euler) equation which determines the movement in value over time:

$$V_t = \delta E_t(V_{t+1} + D_{t+1}), \qquad (4.137)$$

where the discount factor $\delta = 1/(1+k)$ with $0 < \delta < 1$.

Leading (4.137) one period yields:

$$V_{t+1} = \delta E_{t+1}(V_{t+2} + D_{t+2}).\tag{4.138}$$

Now we take expectations of (4.138), assuming information is only available up to time t:

$$E_t V_{t+1} = \delta E_t(V_{t+2} + D_{t+2}).\tag{4.139}$$

In deriving (4.139) we have made use of the *law of iterative expectations*:

$$E_t(E_{t+1}V_{t+2}) = E_t V_{t+2}.\tag{4.140}$$

Equation (4.140) says that the expectation formed in t of what one's expectation will be in $t + 1$ of the stock price in $t + 2$, which the expectation in t of V_{t+2} (as implied by the RE). Of course, (4.140) can be applied to all periods under review so that, for instance:

$$E_t V_{t+2} = \delta E_t(V_{t+3} + D_{t+3}), \text{ etc.}\tag{4.141}$$

Substituting (4.141) in (4.138), one yields:

$$V_t = \delta \left[\delta E_t(V_{t+2} + D_{t+2})\right] + \delta(E_t D_{t+1}).\tag{4.142}$$

If we continue to substitute up to N periods, the result is:

$$V_t = E_t \left[\delta D_{t+1} + \delta^2 D_{t+2} + \delta^3 D_{t+3} + \ldots + \delta^N (D_{t+N} + V_{t+N})\right].\tag{4.143}$$

Now let us assume that $N \to \infty$, so that $\delta^N \to 0$. If expected dividend growth is not explosive so that $E_t D_{t+N}$ remains finite and if $E_t V_{t+N}$ is also finite, we have:

$$\lim_{n\to\infty} E_t(\delta^N D_{t+N} + V_{t+N}) \to 0.\tag{4.144}$$

Equation (4.144) is known as a terminal condition (*transversality condition*), and it rules out rational speculative bubbles. Taking into account Eq. (4.144), Eq. (4.143) becomes:

$$V_t = E_t \sum_{i=1}^{\infty} \delta^i D_{t+i}.\tag{4.145}$$

If we add the assumption that investors simultaneously set the actual market price, P_t, equal to the fundamental value of the stock, V_t, the stock price is the discounted present value of expected future dividends:

$$V_t = P_t = E_t \sum_{i=1}^{\infty} \delta^i D_{t+i}.\tag{4.146}$$

If it is assumed that discount factors are time-varying rather than constant, Eq. (4.146) can be easily restated as:

$$V_t = P_t = E_t \left[\sum_{j=1}^{\infty} \left[\prod_{i=1}^{\infty} \delta_{t+i} \right] D_{t+j} \right]. \tag{4.147}$$

4.5.1.3 Gordon's Constant Dividend Growth Model

If we assume that dividends grow at a constant rate, g, the expected future dividends of a firm are:

$$E_t D_{t+k} = (1+g)^k D_t, \tag{4.148}$$

where r is the discount rate. The dividend discount model suggests that stock prices should be determined as follows:

$$P_t = \frac{D_t}{1+r} \sum_{k=0}^{\infty} \left(\frac{1+g}{1+r} \right)^k. \tag{4.149}$$

The well-known multiplier formula states that as long as $0 < c < 1$, we can write:

$$1 + c + c^2 + c^3 + \ldots = \sum_{k=0}^{\infty} c^k = \frac{1}{1-c}. \tag{4.150}$$

Such a geometric formula can be used as long as $\left(\frac{1+g}{1+r} \right) < 1$, that is as $r > g$. If this holds true, one can write:

$$P_t = \frac{D_t}{1+r} \cdot \frac{1}{1 - \left(\frac{1+g}{1+r} \right)} \quad \text{or} \tag{4.151a}$$

$$= \frac{D_t}{r-g}. \tag{4.151b}$$

That said, if dividend growth is constant, stock prices are a multiple of current dividends, and the multiple depends positively on the expected future growth rate of dividends and negatively on the discount yield. This formula is called the *Gordon growth model*.[24]

---

[24]The formula appeared in Gordon's 1962 book "The Investment, Financing and Valuation of the Corporation".

4.5.1.4 Gordon's Dividend Growth Model with Variations in Dividend Growth

Of course, expectations about future dividend growth might not be constant (Whelan, 2005). In fact, they may fluctuate around a steady growth trend. For instance, the dividends D in period t are:

$$D_t = d(1 + g)^t + u_t, \text{ where} \tag{4.152}$$

$$u_t = \rho u_{t-1} + \varepsilon_t; \tag{4.153}$$

here d is the current dividend and u is the error term.

According to Eq. (4.152), dividends grow at a constant rate g each period, while Eq. (4.153) says that dividends are affected by a cyclical component, u_t, modelled as a first-order autoregressive process (AR(1)). Here, ε_t is a zero-mean i.i.d. random shock term. Over large samples, u_t is expected to be zero, but deviations from zero will be more persistent the higher the value of the parameter ρ is.

Whelan, K. (2005), The Dividend-Discount Model of Stock Prices, Topic 4, EC4010, Note

The dividend discount model for stock prices when dividends follow the process as outlined above becomes:

$$P_t = \sum_{k=0}^{\infty} \left(\frac{1}{1+r}\right)^{k+1} E_t \left(d(1+g)^{t+k} + u_{t+k}\right). \tag{4.154}$$

The trend component can be written as:

$$\sum_{k=0}^{\infty} \left(\frac{1}{1+r}\right)^{k+1} E_t \left(d(1+g)^{t+k}\right) = \frac{d(1+g)^t}{1+r} \sum_{k=0}^{\infty} \left(\frac{1+g}{1+r}\right)^k$$
$$= \frac{d(1+g)^t}{r-g}. \tag{4.155}$$

Turning to the cyclical component, because $E(\varepsilon_{t+k}) = 0$ we have:

$$E_t u_{t+1} = E_t(\rho u_t + \varepsilon_{t+1}) = \rho u_t; \tag{4.156a}$$

$$E_t u_{t+2} = E_t(\rho u_{t+1} + \varepsilon_{t+2}) = \rho^2 u_t; \tag{4.156b}$$

$$E_t u_{t+3} = E_t(\rho u_{t+k-1} + \varepsilon_{t+k}) = \rho^3 u_t \tag{4.156c}$$

and so on. That said, the cyclical component can be written as:

$$\sum_{k=0}^{\infty} \left(\tfrac{1}{1+r}\right)^{k+1} E_t u_{t+k} = \frac{u_t}{1+r} \sum_{k=0}^{\infty} \left(\frac{\rho}{1+r}\right)^k$$
$$= \frac{u_t}{1+r-\rho}. \tag{4.157}$$

Putting the trend and cyclical components together, we yield:

$$P_t = \frac{d(1+g)^t}{r-g} + \frac{u_t}{1+r-\rho}.$$ (4.158)

According to this equation, stock prices do not grow at a constant rate. They depend positively on the cyclical component of dividends, u_t, and the more persistent the cyclical deviation is (that is the higher ρ is), the larger is the impact on the PV of discounted dividend payments and thus the stock price.

When taking averages over long periods, the u components of dividends and prices will average to zero. That said, over long time horizons averages the Gordon growth model should be correct. However, stock prices would tend to be temporarily high relative to dividends when dividends are expected to grow at above-average rates, and would be temporarily low when dividend growth is expected to be below average. That said, the Gordon growth model establishes long-run average valuations; it does not necessarily allow forecasting stock prices in the short-term.

4.5.1.5 *Excess* Volatility of Stock Prices ("Variance Bounds")

Are stock prices "excessively" volatile? If stock prices represent the discounted sum of expected future dividends, Shiller (1981) and LeRoy and Porter (1981) showed that the following relationship must hold: $Var(P_t^*) > Var(P_t)$. The variance (Var) of the *ex post* realized discounted sum of current and future dividends, P_t^* (or the *perfect foresight price*), must be greater than the variance of the actual stock price, P_t.

To show this, let us assume that the DPV of a stock can be written as follows:

$$P_t = \sum_{i=1}^{n-1} \delta^i E_t D_{t+i} + \delta^n E_t P_{t+n}.$$ (4.159)

In Eq. (4.159), P_t depends on the PV of expected future dividends plus the present value of the expected terminal price at the end of the investment period P_{t+n}; δ is the discount factor ($1/(1+k)$), whereas k is required return ($0 < \delta < 1$). The expectation operator is $E(\cdot)$.

The *perfect foresight price* of the stock, P_t^*, can be computed as:

$$P_t^* = \sum_{i=1}^{n-1} \delta^i D_{t+i} + \delta^n P_{t+n}.$$ (4.160)

The difference between P_t^* and P_t is the sum of the forecast errors of dividends, ω_{t+i}, weighted by the discount factors δ^i, where:

$$\omega_{t+i} = D_{t+i} - E_t D_{t+i}.$$ (4.161)

If investors make forecast errors, the relation between P_t^* and P_t is $P_t^* - P_t = \varepsilon_t$, so that $P_t^* = P_t + \varepsilon_t$, where ε_t represents the (discount factor) weighted error term for dividends in future periods. That said, the variance of P_t^* is:

$$Var(P_t^*) = Var(P_t) + Var(\varepsilon_t) + 2Cov(\varepsilon_t, P_t).^{25} \qquad (4.162)$$

Assuming that $Cov(\varepsilon_t, P_t) = 0$, as suggested by the EMH, we can write:

$$Var(P_t^*) = Var(P_t) + Var(\varepsilon_t). \qquad (4.163)$$

As the variance of the forecast error is positive, one can write:

$$Var(P_t^*) > Var(P_t). \qquad (4.164)$$

So if (i) investors are rational as far as processing information is concerned and (ii) the required return is constant, and (iii) stocks are priced according to the RVF, the variance of the perfect foresight price should exceed the variance of the actual price. That said, the variance ratio should exceed unity:

$$Variance\ ratio\ (VR) = \sigma(P_t^*)/\sigma(P_t) > 1.$$

If the inequality is violated, it is said that – on the basis of the underlying model – stock prices are "excessively" volatile.

Shiller (1981) showed that actual stock prices would be much too volatile to be in line with the RVF. Figure 4.37 depicts the real US S&P's 500 stock price index and three measures of PVs of future real dividend payments. The latter were calculated on the basis of (i) a constant discount rate, (ii) the market rate and (iii) the consumption per head growth rate. As can be seen, actual stock prices exhibited a higher volatility than the measures for perfect foresight prices. However, should such a finding make us rejecting the RVF under the EMH-RE?

If the model is not supported by empirical findings, is it the fault of the theory, the fault of the data, or the fault of both? In fact, the finding of excess volatility on the basis of variance bounds tests should be interpreted with great caution. Market agents' ex-ante dividend expectations cannot be directly observed, and they might differ from realized dividend payments. That said, using actual dividends as a proxy for dividend expectation in empirical testing might yield questionable results.

What is more, Flaving (1983) and Kleindon (1986) argued that small samples might lead to a *downward bias*, depending on the correlation of P_t^* and P_t. As the former has a higher autocorrelation than the latter, the variance of P_t^* would be estimated with a greater downward bias than the variance of P_t. What is more,

---

[25] Note that the variance of a variable x is: $Var(x) = \sum_{i=1}^{n} (x_t - \bar{x})^2/(n-1)$, where $\bar{x}$ is the sample mean an n is the number of observations.

Fig. 4.37 Actual US real
stock price and DPV of future
real dividends
Source: Global Financial
Data, Robert Shiller (update
of data shown in Chap. 26 of
market volatility, R. Shiller,
MIT Press, 1989, and
Irrational Exuberance,
Princeton 2005). – The stock
index and dividends were
deflated by using the CPI. –
Logarithmic scale.

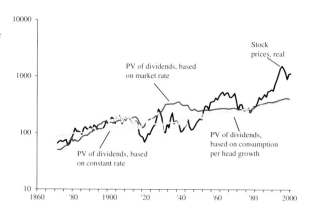

Hansen and Jagannathan (1991) refuted the constant discount rate assumption used
in variance bounds tests. Shoven (1987) has questioned the adequacy of dividends
as a proxy for the total payoffs expected by shareholders. Marsh and Merton (1986)
have discussed problems that can arise in variance bounds tests if corporate managers decide to smooth dividends over time.

Time Varying Expected Returns as a Cause for Stock Price Volatility?

To explain stock price volatility, one may want to allow for variations in expected
returns in the standard discounted cash flow model. Let us define the discount factor
as $R_t = 1 + r_t$, so that the PV of the discounted future dividends is:

$$P_t = \frac{D_t}{R_{t+1}} + \frac{P_{t+1}}{R_{t+1}}. \tag{4.165}$$

Leading Eq. (4.165) by one period gives the PV in period $t + 1$:

$$P_{t+1} = \frac{D_{t+1}}{R_{t+2}} \frac{P_{t+2}}{R_{t+2}}. \tag{4.166}$$

Substituting in Eq. (4.166) in Eq. (4.165) yields:

$$P_t = \frac{D_t}{R_{t+1}} + \frac{D_{t+1}}{R_{t+1}R_{t+2}} + \frac{P_{t+2}}{R_{t+1}R_{t+2}R_{t+3}}. \tag{4.167}$$

The general formula we would arrive at is:

$$P_t = \sum_{k=0}^{N-1} \frac{D_{t+k}}{\prod_{m=1}^{k+1} R_{t+m}} + \frac{P_{t+N}}{\prod_{m=1}^{N} R_{t+m}}. \tag{4.168}$$

Setting the limit of $t + N$ equal to zero and taking expectations, the dividend
discount model assuming variations in expected returns is:

$$P_t = \sum_{k=0}^{\infty} E_t \left(\frac{D_{t+k}}{\Pi_{m=1}^{k+1} R_{t+m}} \right). \tag{4.169}$$

According to Eq. (4.169), it may be new information about future stock returns rather than dividend payments that is to be held responsible for (excessive) stock price volatility.

Changes Interest Rates as a Cause for Stock Price Volatility?

In the RVF, (expected) changes in market interest rates (opportunity costs) affect current stock prices and their returns. In many models it is assumed that that there is an arbitrage equation linking stock and bond returns:

$$E_t R_{t+1} = E_t r_{t+1} + \phi. \tag{4.170}$$

Here, the expected return in the next period, $E_t R_{t+1}$, would equal next period's expected return on bonds, $E_t r_{t+1}$, plus a risk premium, ϕ (which is assumed to be constant).

Do interest rates qualify as drivers for stock price volatility? According to Campbell and Shiller (1988), the equation above is of little use for explaining stock market fluctuations. In their analysis, the authors put in forecasts for future interest rates and dividend growth into the right-hand-side of the equation and checked how close the resulting series is to the actual dividend price ratio. The conclusion is that expected fluctuations in interest rates contribute little to explaining the volatility in stock prices. A recent Federal Reserve Board study examining the link between monetary policy and the stock market comes to the same conclusions.[26]

Stock Market Returns and Interest Rates

What is the relationship between current market interest rates and future stock returns? In theory, one could think of rising (declining) stock returns as a response to a decline (rise) in market interest rates: for instance, lower market rates increase the PV of future cash flows and vice versa. Lower (higher) rates should also reduce (increase) firms' interest payments on debt, leading to higher (lower) cash flows and, as a result, a higher (lower) PV.

---

[26]See Bernanke and Kuttner (2004). They find that, on average, a hypothetical unanticipated 25 basis points cut in the federal funds rate target is associated with about a one percent increase in broad stock indexes. Using a methodology due to Campbell (1991) and Campbell and Ammer (2003), the authors find that the effects of unanticipated monetary policy actions on expected excess returns account for the largest part of the response of stock prices.

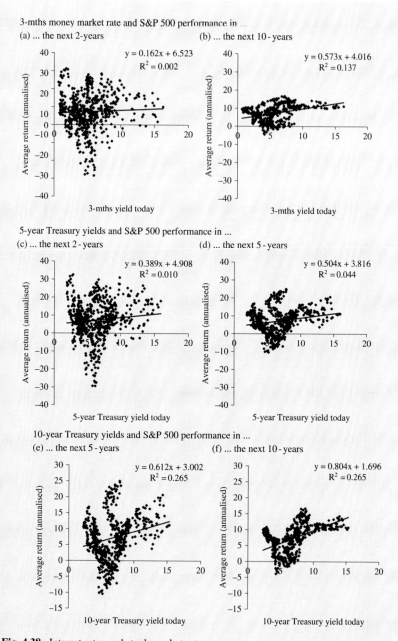

Fig. 4.38 Interest rates and stock market returns
Source: Federal Reserve Bank of St. Louis, Thomson Financial; own calculations. – Stock returns represent the first differences of log levels of the US S&P's 500 stock market index (annualized). – Period: April 1953 to July 2006.

In contrast, one could also think of a negative relation between current yields and future stock returns. If, for instance, interest rates reflect the economy's growth rate (that is its marginal efficiency of capital), a decline in market interest rates would correspond to lower future production and, as a result, firms' reduced ability to generate attractive returns on capital invested. In that sense, low interest rates would bode badly for future stock returns.

To form a view about the general relation between current market interest rates and future stock returns, Fig. 4.38 shows 3-months, 5-year and 10-year yields in the US (x-axis) plotted against the average performance of the US S&P's 500 stock market index over various future time spans (y-axis). The period under review is January 1953 to May 2008.

Generally speaking, the relation between today's level of interest rates and future average stock returns is positive (as indicated by the slope coefficients). What is more, for longer yield maturities and longer averaging stock return periods, the fit improves (as indicated by the coefficients of determination). These findings, however, may not come as a surprise.

Economically speaking, long-term rates should – if expectations are *not systematically false* – contain information about the economy's long-run growth (potential) and therefore be less affected by changes in cyclical growth and swings in short-term rates as determined by the central bank. In addition, the longer the average period under review is, the better should stock price changes correspond to the overall performance of the economy. As a result, long- rather than short-term rates should be more closely related to longer-term stock price changes.

In addition, CPI inflation is typically causing nominal long-term interest rates to go up (*Fisher effect*). If inflation also drives up nominal stock prices (as investors anticipate higher nominal firm cash flows in the future), nominal stock returns should increase in periods of (expected) rising inflation. This, in turn, would also suggest a positive relation between nominal long-term yields and nominal stock returns in the long-run.

Time-Varying Risk Premia as a Cause for Stock Price Volatility?

Finally, one could think of time-varying risk premia as a source of stock market volatility. From this viewpoint, the risk premium ϕ in Eq. (4.170) would be changing over time rather than being a constant. For instance, expected future stock returns over (riskless) short-term investments might vary, as investor sentiment concerning future stock returns might become "bullish" at some point, and it might turn into a "bearish" sentiment at another point in time. According to Campbell (1991), changing expectations about future equity premia lie behind most of the variations in stock returns.

Figure 4.39(a) shows the US S&P stock price index from January 1960 to May 2008, while Fig. 4.39(b) shows the US 3-month T-Bill rate. "Excess returns" on US stock investments – that is the risk premium for holding stocks rather than low-risk T-Bills – were calculated as the average stock price gains (on an annual basis)

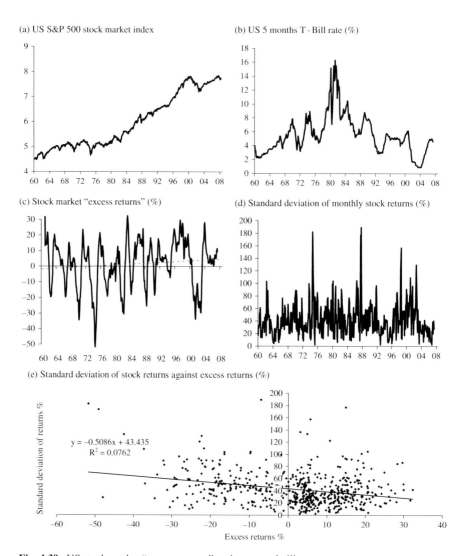

Fig. 4.39 US stock market "excess returns" and return volatility
Source: Bloomberg, own calculations. – Stock returns: twelve differences of monthly stock indices in logs. – Excess returns: average stock returns (on an annual basis) over the coming three month minus current 3-months money market rate. – Standard deviations are based on monthly stock returns (annualised) over the coming three months. – Period January 1960 to May 2008, monthly data.

over the coming three months minus the 3-months T-Bill rate (Fig. 4.39(c)). The standard deviations (volatility) of stock returns (on an annual basis) over the coming 3-months are depicted in Fig. 4.39(d), while Fig. 4.39(e) plots excess returns in the stock market against the volatility of stock returns.

On average, a negative relation between excess returns and stock return volatility can be observed in the period under review: The higher (lower) the risk premium from holding stocks is, the lower (higher) is the stock market volatility. Such a finding corresponds to the general finding that (sharply) declining stock returns (relative to short-term interest rates) tend to be accompanied by high stock return volatility and vice versa. However, as the coefficients of determination shows, the relation is rather weak, suggesting that there is more than changes in stock excess returns when it comes to explaining stock return volatility.

4.5.2 Dividend Yields, Expected Returns and the Campbell-Shiller Model

4.5.2.1 Dividends Yields and Expected Returns

To show how the dividend-price ratio is related to the discount rate and dividend growth in the RVF, let us take a look at its reciprocal, the price-dividend ratio (Cuthbertson, 1996, pp. 346):

$$\frac{P_t}{D_t} = E_t \left[\frac{(D_{t+1}/D_t)}{(1 + r_t)} + \frac{(D_{t+2}/D_t)}{(1 + r_t)(1 + r_{t+1})} + \frac{(D_{t+3}/D_t)}{(1 + r_t)(1 + r_{t+1})(1 + r_{t+3})} + \ldots \right],$$
(4.171)

where the stock price P_t has been divided by the dividend, D_t. The logarithmic approximation for dividend growth rates gives:

$$\frac{D_{t+2}}{D_t} = \frac{D_{t+2}}{D_{t+1}} \cdot \frac{D_{t+1}}{D_t} \approx \Delta d_{t+2} \cdot \Delta d_{t+1},$$
(4.172)

where Δd_{t+j} is the dividend growth rate. From (4.171) and (4.172) it can be seen that the RVF is consistent with the following conclusions (ceteris paribus):

(i) the current price-dividend ratio is positively related to future dividends growth rates Δd_{t+j};
(ii) the current price-dividend ratio is negatively related to future discount rates, r_{t+j}.

Inverting Eq. (4.172) gives the current dividend-price ratio, which can, by explicitly including expectations, written as:

$$(D_t/P_t) = f(\Delta d_{t+j}^e, \Delta r_{t+j}^e).$$
(4.173)

Equation (4.173) is a mere rearrangement of (4.171), so that we can draw the following conclusions (ceteris paribus):

(i) When investors expect dividends to grow in the future, the current stock price will be high and hence the dividend-price ratio will be low; and

(ii) when future discount rates are expected to be high, the current stock price will be low and hence the current dividend-price ratio will be high.

The considerations above suggest that dividend yields should contain relevant information for (expected) future stock returns. When allowing for time-varying stock returns, however, the relation between prices and returns becomes non-linear (Campbell et al., 1997, p. 260) and thus difficult to work with.

4.5.2.2 The Campbell-Shiller Model

Campbell and Shiller (1988) proposed a loglinear approximation of the present value concept for stock prices. Their log-linear relation between prices, dividends and returns provides an accounting framework: high prices must, sooner or later, be followed by high future dividends, low future returns, or some combination of the two. If investor expectations are consistent with this, high prices must be associated with high expected future dividends, low expected future returns, or some combination of the two. Similarly, high returns must be associated with upward revisions in expected future dividends, downward revisions in expected future returns, or some combination of the two (Campbell, 1991).

The log-linear model enables to calculate asset price behaviour under any model of time-varying expected returns. The log-linear model has the additional advantage that it is tractable under the empirically plausible assumption that dividends and returns follow log-linear processes. In the following, we derive a dividend discount model, which is based on the EMH and RE, to the stock market pricing. In line with Campbell and Shiller (1997, p. 260) the approximation formula for the continuously compounded one-period return on stocks is:[27]

$$h_{t+1} = k + \rho p_{t+1} + (1 - \rho)d_{t+1} - p_t, \qquad (4.174)$$

where h_{t+1} = approximate continuously compounded one-period return on stocks over the holding period $t + 1$. p_t = log of stock price at the end of t; d_{t+1} = log of dividend paid out before the end of period t + 1; $\rho \equiv 1/(\exp(\overline{d - p}))$, where $\overline{d - p}$ = average of log of dividend yield; and $k = -\log(\rho) - (1 - \rho)\log(1/\rho - 1)$.

Equation (4.174) shows a log-linear relation between stock prices, returns and dividends. It is a first-order linear difference equation in the stock price. Solving forward and imposing the terminal condition $\lim_{j \to \infty} \rho^j p_{t+j} = 0$ yields:

---

[27]The box below explains how the equation is formed.

$$p_t = \frac{k}{1-p} + \sum_{j=0}^{\infty} \rho^j [(1-\rho)d_{t+1+j} - h_{t+1+j}]. \qquad (4.175)$$

Equation (4.175) is an *ex post*-identity, which says that today's stock price is high if future dividends are high and/or future returns are low. Applying the conditional expectation operator $E_t x_{t+1} = E[x_{t+1}|\Omega_t]$, where Ω_t = market-wide information set available at the end of period t, and the law of iterative expectations, Eq. (4.175) be changed to an ex ante relation:

$$p_t = \frac{k}{1-\rho} + \sum_{j=0}^{\infty} \rho^j [(1-\rho)E_t d_{t+1+j} - E_t h_{t+1+j}]. \qquad (4.176)$$

Assuming homogenous expectations and instantaneous market clearing, the log stock price always equals its fundamental value, which is the specifically weighted, infinite sum of expected log dividends discounted by time-varying expected equilibrium returns. Combined with RE, Eq. (4.175) represents the rational valuation formula (RVF). The log-linear approximation framework has two advantages. First, it allows a linear, and thus simple, analysis of stock price behaviour. Second, it conforms to the empirically plausible assumption that dividends and stock return follow log-linear stochastic processes. For empirical analyses, Eq. (4.176) can be rearranged such that the log dividend yield (or log dividend–price ratio) is singled out as the left-hand variable:

$$d_t - p_t = -\frac{k}{1-\rho} + \sum_{j=0}^{\infty} \rho^j (-E_t \Delta d_{t+1+j} + E_t h_{t+1+j}). \qquad (4.177)$$

The current dividend yield should predict future returns if the discount rates used by forward-looking investors depend on expected holding period returns for subsequent periods, and if these expectations do not deviate systematically, and too much, from realised returns.[28]

Deriving at the Campbell-Shiller Model

The Campbell-Shiller Log-Linearisation

The one period holding return of a stock is (Cuthbertson et al., 1997):

$$H_{t+1} = \frac{P_{t+1} + D_{t+1} - P_t}{P_t}, \qquad (4.178)$$

---

[28]See Domanski and Kremer (1998, p. 26), who note that the term $E_t h_{t+1+j}$ is the equivalent to the expected future discount rate of the RVF.

where P_t is the stock price at the end of period t, D_{t+1} is the dividend payment in period $t+1$. Taking natural logarithms of the one period holding return (plus one), Eq. (1) can be written as:

$$h_{t+1} = \ln(1 + H_{t+1}) = \ln(P_{t+1} - D_{t+1}) - \ln(P_t). \quad (4.179)$$

If lower case letter represent logarithms, Eq. (2) becomes:

$$h_{t+1} = \ln\left[\exp(p_{t+1}) + \exp(d_{t+1})\right] - p_t. \quad (4.180)$$

The first term on the right hand side of Eq. (4.180) is a non-linear function in p_{t+1} and d_{t+1}. One can linearize it by taking first-order Taylor series expansion around the geometric mean of P and D:

$$\ln\left[\exp(p_{t+1}) + \exp(d_{t+1})\right] = k + \rho p_{t+1} + (1 - \rho)d_{t+1}, \quad (4.181)$$

where $\rho = P/(P + D)_t$, with ρ is a number of slightly less than unity and k is a constant.

Taylor Series Expansion

The term $(P_{t+1} + D_{t+1})$ can be approximated as (Cuthbertson, Hayes, & Nitzsche, 1997, p. 1005):

(i) $\ln(P_{t+1} + D_{t+1}) = \ln(e^{p_{t+1}} + e^{d_{t+1}}) \equiv f(p, d)$.

Since $\frac{\partial f}{\partial p} = \dfrac{e^{p_{t+1}}}{e^{p_{t+1}} + e^{d_{t+1}}}$ and $\frac{\partial f}{\partial d} = \dfrac{e^{d_{t+1}}}{e^{p_{t+1}} + e^{d_{t+1}}}$, a first order Taylor expansion of $f(p, d)$ around $\bar{p}$ and $\bar{d}$ gives:[29]

(ii) $f(p, d) \approx \ln(e^{\bar{p}} + e^{\bar{d}}) + (p_{t+1} - \bar{p})\dfrac{e^{\bar{p}}}{e^{\bar{p}} + e^{\bar{d}}} + (d_{t+1} - \bar{d})\dfrac{e^{\bar{d}}}{e^{\bar{p}} + e^{\bar{d}}}.$

Defining $\rho \equiv \frac{\bar{P}}{\bar{P}+\bar{D}} = \frac{e^{\bar{p}}}{e^{\bar{p}}+e^{\bar{d}}}$, one can write:

(iii) $f(p, d) \approx \ln(e^{\bar{p}} + e^{\bar{d}}) + (p_{t+1} - \bar{p})\rho + (d_{t+1} - \bar{d})(1 - \rho)$ or

(iv) $f(p, d) \approx \ln(\bar{P} + \bar{D}) + p_{t+1}\rho + (1 - \rho)d_{t+1} - \ln \bar{P} - (1 - \rho)\ln \bar{D}.$

Using (ii) and (iv) one yields:

---

[29] $\bar{p}$ and $\bar{d}$ are the arithmetic means of the log real stock price and dividends. Consequently, $\bar{P}$ and $\bar{D}$ are the geometric means of the real stock price and real dividends.

$$(v) f(p, d) \approx \ln(e^{\bar{p}} + e^{\bar{d}}) + (p_{t+1} - \bar{p})\rho + (d_{t+1} - \bar{d})(1 - \rho),$$

where $k \equiv \ln(\bar{P} + \bar{D}) - \rho \ln \bar{P} - (1 - \rho) \ln \bar{D}$.

Using equations (110) and (111), one yields:

$$h_{t+1} = k + \rho p_{t+1} + (1 - \rho)d_{t+1} - p_t. \tag{4.182}$$

If we add and subtract d_t in Eq. (4.182) and defining $\delta_t = d_t - p_t$ as the logarithm dividend price ratio, we yield:

$$h_{t+1} = k + \delta_t - \rho \delta_{t+1} + \Delta d_{t+1}. \tag{4.183}$$

Equation (4.183) can be interpreted as a linear forward difference equation in δ:

$$\delta_t = -k + \rho \delta_{t+1} + h_{t+1} - \Delta d_{t+1}. \tag{4.184}$$

Solving Eq. (4.184) by the forward recursive substitution method and assuming the transversality condition to hold, we yield:

$$\delta_t = \sum_{j=0}^{\infty} \rho^j \left[h_{t+j+1} - \Delta d_{t+j+1} \right] - k/(1 - \rho) \tag{4.185}$$

According to Eq. (4.185), the logarithm dividend price ratio can be expressed as the discounted sum of all future one period holding returns minus the discounted sum of all future dividend growth rates less a constant term. So if the current dividend price ratio is high because the current price is low then it means that in the future either required h_{t+j+1} are high or dividend growth rates Δd_{t+j+1} are low, or a combination of both.

Equation (4.185) represents an identity and holds almost exactly for actual data. However, it can be treated as an ex ante relationship by taking expectations of both sides of the equation conditional on the information available at the end of period t:

$$\delta_t = \sum_{j=0}^{\infty} \rho^j \left[E_t(h_{t+j+1}) - E_t(\Delta d_{t+j+1}) \right] - k/(1 - \rho). \tag{4.186}$$

It should be noted that δ_t is known at the end of period t and hence its expectation is equal to itself.

Testing the predictability of stock prices has become a central research topic in financial economics. Predictability is typically assessed in the context of a regression model in which real stock price growth or real stock returns over various time horizons are regressed on a variable thought to potentially explain future movements in stock prices. Popular forecasting variables include price-earnings and dividend-price ratios (Campbell & Shiller, 1988a, b; Fama & French, 1988; Hodrick, 1992; Shiller, 1984). Also, various interest rate measures such as the yield spread between long- and short-term rates, the quality yield spread between low- and high-grade corporate bonds or commercial paper and measures of changes in the level of short-term rates have been used to testing the predictability of stock returns (see Campbell, 1987; Fama & French, 1989; Hodrick, 1992; Keim & Stambaugh, 1986).

4.5.2.3 An Empirical Application of the Campbell-Shiller Model

Figure 4.40(a) shows the price-earnings ratios in the US, the euro area, Germany and Japan for the period January 1975 to May 2008, while Fig. 4.40(b) shows the respective dividend yields. In all the currency areas under review, dividend yields have trended downward from the early 1980s to around 2000. This trend was corrected around the end of 2000, and it can largely be explained by a sharp fall in stock prices relative to dividends which set in at that time.

As stock prices are assumed to depend on expected dividends and capital gains, the (log) dividend yield provides a noisy measure of variations in expected returns.[30] What is more, the regressions for dividend growth and profit growth are subject to the same omitted variables problem because, in that case, expected stock returns introduce noise. To circumvent these problems, the following stock market performance measures will be analyzed:

(i) holding period returns, h_t,
(ii) dividend growth rates, Δd_t,

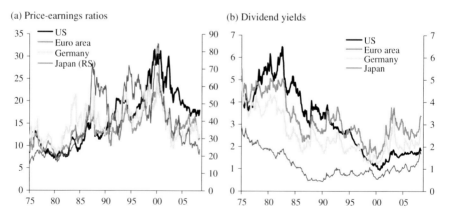

(a) Price-earnings ratios   (b) Dividend yields

Fig. 4.40 International PE ratios and dividend yields (%)
Source: Thomson Financial. – Period: January 1975 to May 2008.

---

[30]See Keim and Stambough (1986, p. 360).

(iii) the differences between holding period returns and dividend growth rates, $h_t - \Delta d_t$,

(iv) profit growth rates, Δp_t, and

(v) the differences between holding period returns and profit growth rates, $h_t - \Delta p_t$.

The sample period under review is January 1975 to April 2005. The return measures represent annualized first differences of the respective variables. Dividend yields are measured as the averages of dividends paid on the stock market index over the previous year, divided by the current level of the index.[31]

While a number of econometric difficulties are inherent in predictive regressions (see, for example, Stambaugh, 1986; Nelson & Kim, 1993), the consensus appears to be that some variables can, in fact, predict future movements in stock prices. The often-cited analyses of Fama and French (1988) and Campbell and Shiller (1988) find that price-dividends and price-earnings ratios predict future real stock returns using data spanning the late nineteenth to the late twentieth countries. The authors find that the price-dividends and price-earnings ratios have a limited ability of predict real stock price growth over the next year, but a strong and significant ability to predict real stock price growth over the next ten years. As indicated above, a number of subtle econometric issues arise that warrant caution in interpreting long-horizon predictive regressions.[32]

Figure 4.41 shows the results of long-horizon regressions of various stock performance measures on the dividend yield for holding periods of 1, 3, 12, 24, 36 and 48 months, respectively. An estimation horizon of more than one month ($H > 1$) induces serial correlation of the error terms even under the null hypothesis of no return predictability (zero coefficient on the dividend yield). In this case, the errors are correlated with the $H-1$ previous error terms. The alternative t-statistics shown in the table for the null hypothesis of a zero coefficient are corrected for serial correlation and possible heteroskedasticity as suggested by Newey and West (1987) using a lag length of $H-1$.[33]

The upper part of Figure 4.41 shows the main results for holding period returns. Here, the coefficients of determination ($R^2(H)$ statistic) increase with the forecast horizon. However, statistical significance can only be attached to the 12- to 48-month horizon.

The R^2 statistics for dividend growth follow a hump-shaped pattern with a peak at 12-month, with around 27% of explanatory power. Moreover, the coefficients of determination are much higher than for the holding period returns with the exception

---

[31] Summing dividends and profits over a full year removes any seasonal patterns in the performance variables, whereas the current stock index is used to incorporate the most recent information in stock prices.

[32] Nevertheless Campbell and Shiller (1998, p. 24) note that "it is striking how well the evidence for (long-horizon) stock market predictability survives the various corrections that have been proposed."

[33] See Campbell et al. (1997, pp. 534–536).

Regression equation: $1/H(x_{t+1}+...x_{t+H}) = \alpha(H)(d_t - p_t) + \varepsilon_{t+H,H}$

	\multicolumn{6}{c}{Forecast horizon (H)}
	1	3	12	24	36	48
\multicolumn{7}{c}{$x_t = h_t$}
$R^2(H)$	0.002	0.006	0.019	0.048	0.089	0.136
$\beta(H)$	8.507	7.967	7.546	8.639	9.209	9.246
t-Wert Newey and West	0.935	1.443	2.573	4.144	5.635	7.036
\multicolumn{7}{c}{$x_t = \Delta d_t$}
$R^2(H)$	0.042	0.109	0.269	0.203	0.134	0.108
$\beta(H)$	−18.28	−17.37	−15.52	−11.11	−7.809	−5.928
t-Wert Newey and West	−3.591	−3.893	−5.723	−4.498	−3.042	−2.353
\multicolumn{7}{c}{$x_t = h_t - \Delta d_t$}
$R^2(H)$	0.018	0.048	0.174	0.336	0.466	0.568
$\beta(H)$	26.79	25.35	23.07	19.75	17.02	15.17
t-Wert Newey and West	2.597	4.257	8.572	13.089	16.87	20.32
\multicolumn{7}{c}{$x_t = \Delta p_t$}
$R^2(H)$	0.010	0.024	0.037	0.033	0.043	0.046
$\beta(H)$	−16.84	−15.17	−9.839	−6.878	−6.142	−5.157
t-Wert Newey and West	−1.944	−2.989	−3.668	−3.404	−3.821	−3.878
\multicolumn{7}{c}{$x_t = h_t - \Delta p_t$}
$R^2(H)$	0.011	0.028	0.091	0.179	0.298	0.401
$\beta(H)$	25.35	23.13	17.39	15.52	15.35	14.40
t-Wert Newey and West	2.335	2.374	2.721	3.317	4.273	5.683

Fig. 4.41 Long horizon regression of German stock return measures on the log dividend yield ratio
Source: Thomson Financial, own calculation. Estimation period: January 1975 to April 2005, monthly data. h is the annualised one-month continuously compounded stock return in percent. Δd and Δp represent the annualised one-month continuously compounded dividend and profit growth rate, respectively. $\alpha(H)$ is the constant of the regression (not shown). $\beta(H)$ is the slope coefficient of the regression. Regression is estimated on the basis of OLS. $\varepsilon_{t+H,H}$ is the error term which is autocorrelated owing to data overlap for $H > 1$ under the null hypothesis of no predictability. Standard errors and t-values are corrected for serial correlation and heteroskedasticity in the equation using the method of Newey and West (1987). Number of observations: $364 - (H - 1)$.

of the 4-year horizon. They decline with the length of the forecast period, and the t-values retain a relatively high statistical significance.

The results for the holding period return less dividend growth are even more impressive. The R^2 stands at nearly 57% for the 4-year horizon. This suggests that the noise introduced by dividend growth is not negligible. Again, the coefficients decline with the length of the forecast period and all t-values indicate a relatively high statistical significance.

The explanatory power for profit growth is quite low; statistical significance can be attached to forecast horizons from 3-months to 4-years. The results for holding period returns less profit growth show a relatively high R^2 for the 4-year hori-

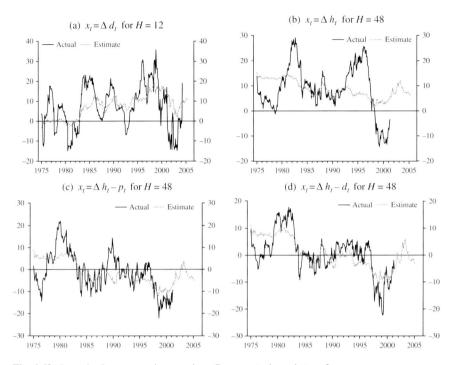

Fig. 4.42   Long-horizon regressions, various German stock market performance measures

zon. Again, the coefficients decline with the length of maturity, while the *t*-values are statistically significant. Figure 4.42 provides some graphical illustrations of the regression results.

Figure 4.43 shows the long-horizon regressions of US stock return measures on the log dividend yield. The results for the US show, in general, that the explanatory fit improves with the length of the forecasting horizon. However, the results for the various measures of stock market performance tend to be less impressive when compared with the results for the German stock market. The exceptions are, however, US holding period returns, which for the 12-month to 4-year horizon seem to "outperform" those in Germany. Also, the R^2 for dividend growth seems to continuously rise with the length of the forecasting period.

From the point of view of EMH-RE, the results for the German, US and Japanese stock market (see Fig. 4.44) suggest that dividend yields signal persistent time-variation in expected equilibrium returns. This, in turn, argues for rejecting the hypothesis that equilibrium returns are constant. It should be noted, however that the EMH postulates that *abnormal returns* are unpredictable, not that *actual returns* are predictable. Furthermore, high stock price volatility would be compatible with persistent movements in rationally expected returns and need not indicate irrational investor behaviour. Of course, as return predictability might result from *irrational bubbles* in stock prices, the question of whether the forecastability of stock returns

Regression equation: $1/H(x_{t+1} + ... x_{t+H}) = \alpha(H)(d_t - p_t) + \varepsilon_{t+H,H}$

	Forecast horizon (H)					
	1	3	12	24	36	48
	$x_t = h_t$					
$R^2(H)$	0.011	0.028	0.099	0.178	0.266	0.326
$\beta(H)$	10.53	9.747	9.385	9.224	9.736	9.552
t-Wert Newey and West	1.823	1.859	2.296	2.795	3.863	4.793
	$x_t = \Delta d_t$					
$R^2(H)$	0.006	0.015	0.061	0.113	0.119	0.124
$\beta(H)$	1.621	1.631	1.977	2.235	2.031	1.894
t-Wert Newey and West	1.071	1.147	1.781	2.703	2.874	3.099
	$x_t = h_t - \Delta d_t$					
$R^2(H)$	0.008	0.019	0.061	0.106	0.171	0.213
$\beta(H)$	8.908	8.115	7.408	6.989	7.705	7.658
t-Wert Newey and West	1.524	1.526	1.859	2.239	3.208	3.849
	$x_t = \Delta p_t$					
$R^2(H)$	0.001	0.003	0.001	0.001	0.003	0.001
$\beta(H)$	−1.149	−1.430	−0.689	0.389	0.630	0.338
t-Wert Newey and West	−0.323	−0.403	−0.213	0.154	0.368	0.267
	$x_t = h_t - \Delta p_t$					
$R^2(H)$	0.012	0.030	0.089	0.152	0.238	0.332
$\beta(H)$	11.68	11.18	10.073	8.837	9.106	9.213
t-Wert Newey and West	1.864	1.959	2.608	4.077	5.554	6.987

Fig. 4.43 Long-horizon regression of US stock return measures on the log dividend yield
Source: Thomson Financial, own calculations. Estimation period: January 1975 to April 2005, monthly data. h is the annualised one-month continuously compounded stock return in percent. Δd and Δp represent the annualised one-month continuously compounded dividend and profit growth rate, respectively. $\alpha(H)$ is the constant of the regression (not shown). $\beta(H)$ is the slope coefficient of the regression. Regression is estimated on the basis of OLS. $\varepsilon_{t+H,H}$ is the error term which is autocorrelated owing to data overlap for $H > 1$ under the null hypothesis of no predictability. Standard errors and t-values are corrected for serial correlation and heteroskedasticity in the equation using the method of Newey and West (1987). Number of observations: $364 - (H - 1)$.

would be driven by rational or irrational economic behaviour remains unanswered (Fama & French, 1989, p. 26).

In sum, the results presented above might provide some evidence that future stock returns contain predictable components, which are reflected in the current dividend yield. The finding that return predictability increases with the length of the holding period under review may well result from better predictability of the medium- to long-term developments when compared with short-term prospects of the economy. Of course, there should be some caution when it comes to the statistical reliability of long-horizon regressions.

Regression equation: $1/H(x_{t+1} + \ldots x_{t+H}) = \alpha(H)(d_t - p_t) + \varepsilon_{t+H,H}$

	Forecast horizon (H)					
	1	3	12	24	36	48
	$x_t = h_t$					
$R^2(H)$	0.018	0.048	0.174	0.318	0.438	0.534
$\beta(H)$	17.24	17.20	17.95	17.52	17.47	17.23
t-Wert Newey and West	2.667	2.991	4.553	6.188	7.595	9.427
	$x_t = \Delta d_t$					
$R^2(H)$	0.000	0.000	0.001	0.019	0.053	0.097
$\beta(H)$	−0.347	−0.411	0.272	1.261	1.682	2.048
t-Wert Newey and West	−0.211	−0.270	0.226	1.242	1.932	2.869
	$x_t = h_t - \Delta d_t$					
$R^2(H)$	0.017	0.048	0.172	0.301	0.423	0.517
$\beta(H)$	17.59	17.61	17.67	16.26	15.79	15.21
t-Wert Newey and West	2.793	3.150	4.800	6.106	6.991	8.178
	$x_t = \Delta p_t$					
$R^2(H)$	0.002	0.005	0.000	0.036	0.108	0.199
$\beta(H)$	−3.780	−3.542	0.163	4.390	6.014	7.059
t-Wert Newey and West	−0.947	−0.933	0.054	1.819	2.970	3.934
	$x_t = h_t - \Delta p_t$					
$R^2(H)$	0.019	0.051	0.133	0.158	0.200	0.230
$\beta(H)$	21.02	20.74	17.78	13.132	11.45	10.198
t-Wert Newey and West	2.901	3.219	4.288	4.373	4.279	4.169

Fig. 4.44 Long-horizon regression of Japanese stock return measures on the log dividend yield
Source: Thomson Financial, own calculations. Estimation period: January 1975 to April 2005, monthly data. h is the annualised one-month continuously compounded stock return in percent. Δd and Δp represent the annualised one-month continuously compounded dividend and profit growth rate, respectively. $\alpha(H)$ is the constant of the regression (not shown). $\beta(H)$ is the slope coefficient of the regression. Regression is estimated on the basis of OLS. $\varepsilon_{t+H,H}$ is the error term which is autocorrelated owing to data overlap for $H > 1$ under the null hypothesis of no predictability. Standard errors and t-values are corrected for serial correlation and heteroskedasticity in the equation using the method of Newey and West (1987). Number of observations: $364 - (H - 1)$.

4.5.2.4 Some Words of Caution: Data Persistence and the Quality of Long-Horizon Forecasts

As was shown above, the power to forecast the performance of the stock market using dividend yields as explanatory variables increases with the return horizon. Cochrane (2001, p. 391) notes that the results at different horizons are not separate facts, though. They reflect a single phenomenon: A slow-moving variable, such as the dividend yield, has little predictive power for short-term stock returns. However, the predictive power would add up with an increasing time horizon.

Assume the stationary return, r, is forecast using a stationary variable x:

$$r_{t+1} = ax_t + \varepsilon_{t+1}.$$

The variable x, in turn, is assumed to follow a AR(1) process:

$$x_{t+1} = bx_t + u_{t+1}.$$

From a statistically viewpoint, small values of a and a small R^2 in the first equation and a high persistence of x, as evidenced by a high b in the second equation, imply that an increase in the time horizon leads to an increase in a and R^2 (Cochrane, 2001, p. 392).

To show this, the average return over period $t + 1$ to $t + 2$ is:

$$r_{t+1} + r_{t+2} = a(1 + b)x_t + au_{t+1} + \varepsilon_{t+1} + \varepsilon_{t+2}.$$

The average return over period $t + 1$ to $t + 3$ is:

$$r_{t+1} + r_{t+2} + r_{t+3} = a(1 + b + b^2)x_t + abu_{t+1} + au_{t+2} + \varepsilon_{t+1} + \varepsilon_{t+2} + \varepsilon_{t+3}.$$

If b is close to 1, the coefficient for x increases with the length of the time horizon (almost linearly at first, then at a declining rate).

Turning to the finding that the regression fit improves as the forecast horizon increases, we need to take a look at the coefficient of determination:

$$R^2 = \sum_{i=1}^{n} (\hat{r}_i - \bar{r})^2 / \sum_{i=1}^{n} (r_i - \bar{r})^2,$$

where $\hat{r}$ is the estimated return, $\bar{r}$ is the sample mean of returns, and r is the actual return. The nominator shows the total variation of the estimated returns about their sample mean (that is the explained sum of squares), while the denominator gives the total variation of actual returns over their sample mean (that is the total sum of squares).

Forecasts of *expected returns* in the next several periods (on the basis of x) are only slightly less variable than next period's expected return forecast, and the two are highly positively correlated. Successive *actual returns*, however, are slightly negatively correlated with one another. As a result, in a multi-period regression, the variance of fitted values increases more rapidly than the variance of realized returns if expected returns are very persistent, thereby increasing R^2 as the time horizon increases (Fama & French, 1988, p. 18; Campbell et al., 1997, p. 271).

A Critical Voice: Ludwig von Mises on Empiricism

Today's mainstream economics has actually embraced *positivism*: in an attempt to investigate the truth of hypotheses in the field of social sciences, the positivists declare that measuring peoples' actions and their continual empirical testing (according to *if-then* statements) would be required, thereby allowing for scientific progress. However, such a view has not remained unchallenged. Perhaps most prominently, Ludwig von Mises questioned this viewpoint in the field of economics as a social science. Mises wrote (1960, p. 30):

"Human action always confronts experience as a complex phenomenon that first must be analyzed and interpreted by a theory before it can even be set in the context of an hypothesis that could be proved or disproved; hence the vexatious impasse created when supporters of conflicting doctrines point to the same historical data as evidence of their correctness. The statement that statistics can prove anything is a popular recognition of this truth. No political or economic program, no matter how absurd, can, in the eyes of its supporters, be contradicted by experience. Whoever is convinced a priori of the correctness of his doctrine can always point out that some condition essential for success according to his theory has not been met. Each of the German political parties seeks in the experience of the second Reich confirmation of the soundness of its program. Supporters and opponents of socialism draw opposite conclusions from the experience of Russian bolshevism. Disagreements concerning the probative power of concrete historical experience can be resolved only by reverting to the doctrines of the universally valid theory, which are independent of all experience. Every theoretical argument that is supposedly drawn from history necessarily becomes a logical argument about pure theory apart from all history. When arguments based on principle concern questions of action, one should always be ready to admit that nothing can "be found more dangerous and more unworthy of a philosopher than the vulgar pretension to appeal to an experience to the contrary," (. . .) and not, like Kant and the socialists of all schools who follow him, only when such an appeal shows socialism in an unfavorable light.

Precisely because the phenomena of historical experience are complex, the inadequacies of an erroneous theory are less effectively revealed when experience contradicts it than when it is assessed in the light of the correct theory."

4.6 Capital Asset Pricing Model (CAPM)

In the 1960s, William Sharpe (1964), John Lintner (1965) and Jack Treynor[34] and
Mossin (1966) came up with extending of James Tobin's portfolio approach inas-
much as the risky asset itself can be represented as an outcome of a portfolio
decision between risky assets and a risk free asset. It paved the way to the Capital
Asset Market Model (CAPM). The CAPM's theoretical message is pretty straightforward: the higher the (systematic) risk of an asset is, the higher is the asset's
return.

In what follows we will, in a first step, take a look at Harry M. Markowitz's
portfolio theory. In a second step, we will address the model of the capital market
line (CML). In a third step, some theoretical assumptions of the perfect market
model will be outlined followed by deriving the CAPM.

4.6.1 Portfolio Selection Theory

Harry M. Markowitz (1952) developed the portfolio selection theory. In his seminal research he cast the investor's portfolio selection problem in terms of expected
return and variance of return. He argued investors would optimally hold a mean-
variance efficient portfolio (mean variance criterion). A portfolio is said to be mean
variance efficient if there is no alternative which provides the investor (i) at a given
return with a lower variance, (ii) at a given variance with a higher return or (iii) a
higher return accompanied by a lower variance.

Let us define the variables as follows:

expected return of asset $i = \mu_i = E R_i$,
variance of returns of asset $i = \sigma_i^2 = \text{var}(R_i)$ and
covariance of returns between asset i *and* $j = \sigma_{ij} = \text{cov}(R_i, R_j)$.

For an investor facing a known set of n expected returns μ_i and variances σ_i^2
and $n(n-1)/2$ covariances σ_{ij} (or correlation coefficients ρ_{ij}), the formulas for the
expected return, return variance and variance of the portfolio are as follows. The
expected return of a portfolio p is the weighted average of the expected returns of
the assets $(i = 1, \ldots, n)$:

$$\mu_p = \sum_{i=1}^{n} x_i \mu_i, \tag{4.187}$$

where x_i = proportion of asset i in the portfolio and $\sum_{i=1}^{n} x_i = 1$.

The variance of the returns of a security i is defined as the simple variance:

$$\sigma_i^2 = E(R_i - \mu_i)^2. \tag{4.188a}$$

---

[34]Treynor's article was not published.

The variance of the portfolio p can be written as:

$$\sigma_p^2 = \sum_{i=1}^{n} x_i^2 \sigma_i^2 + \sum_{i=1}^{n}\sum_{\substack{j=1 \\ i \neq j}}^{n} x_i x_j \sigma_{ij} \text{ or} \qquad (4.188b)$$

$$\sigma_p^2 = \sum_{i=1}^{n} x_i^2 \sigma_i^2 + \sum_{i=1}^{n}\sum_{\substack{j=1 \\ i \neq j}}^{n} x_i x_j \rho_{ij} \sigma_i \sigma_j \qquad (4.188c)$$

where $\sigma_{ij} = \rho_{ij}\sigma_i\sigma_j$ with ρ_{ij} = correlation coefficient between the returns of asset i and j.

If $\rho = +1$, the two asset returns are perfectly positively (linearly) related, that is asset returns move in the same direction. For $\rho = -1$ the opposite holds, and for $\rho = 0$, asset returns are not (linearly) related. Thus, the riskiness of a portfolio consisting of two risky assets depends crucially on the sign and size of ρ. If $\rho = -1$, the portfolio risk can be eliminated by holding risky assets in a certain proportion. As long as ρ is positive (but less than +1), the riskiness of the portfolio can be reduced (although not to zero) by diversification. The *efficient frontier* shows all the combinations (μ_p, σ_p) which minimise the risk σ_p for a given level of μ_p (see Fig. 4.45).

In the portfolio theory, the determination of on optimal portfolio requires the knowledge of the (individual) utility function. The utility, or risk preference, function relates the investor utility, Φ, to the expected return, μ, and the standard deviation of expected returns, σ.

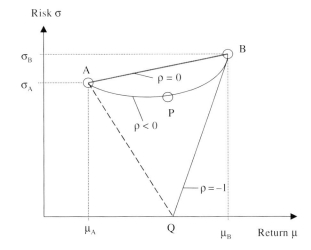

Fig. 4.45 Relation between risk and return (two risky assets)

Risk-Return Profiles of International Stock Markets – An Ex-Post View

Figure 4.46 shows various monthly averages of international stock market returns and their respective standard deviations for two time periods: February 1973 to March 2006 and January 1991 to March 2006. The risk-return combinations are shown in nominal as well as in real terms. On an ex-post basis,

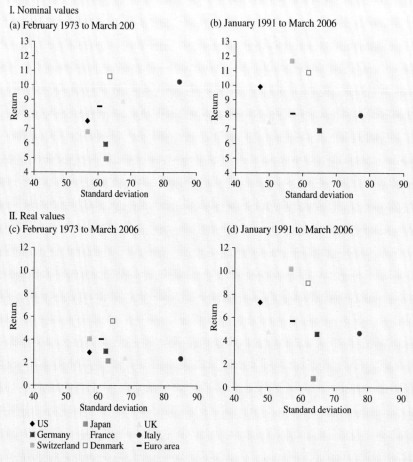

Fig. 4.46 Risk-return constellation of selected international stock markets
Source: Thomson Financial, IMF; own calculations. – The stock market returns are expressed in first differences of log values, annualised; the indices represent total return indices. – Real values were calculated by deflating nominal values with the national consumer price index.

a number of stock markets do not lie on the efficient frontier, that is on an ex-post basis they would not have qualified for being included in the efficient market portfolio. In reality, however, they were willingly held by investors.

How can this finding (which, at first glance, might suggest *irrational* investor behaviour) be explained? Well, the risk-return profiles were calculated on the basis of ex-post data. However, investors might have held different views about forthcoming risk-return profiles of the stock markets under review when the investment decisions were actually made. That said, all one could say is that – on an ex-post basis – investors may have made forecasting errors, but one could not say that they have behaved in an irrational way at the point in time when they made their investment decisions.

4.6.2 *Model of the Capital Market Line (CML)*

In the model of the CML it is assumed that investors can borrow or lend any amount at any time at a risk-free rate. This provides investors with the opportunity to choose between investing in risky and/or risk-free assets. The so-called "transformation line" is the risk-return relationship for any portfolio consisting of a combination of investments in the risk-free asset and a bundle of risky assets. There is no behavioural or optimisation by agents behind the derivation of the transformation line. In Fig. 4.47, the transformation line is a tangent to the efficient frontier. At each point on a given transformation line market agents hold the same bundle of risky assets. Along the transformation line the proportion held in risky and risk-free assets varies.

The amounts of the riskless asset and the bundle of risky assets held by individual investors depend on their preferences. A relatively risk averse investor will put some of his wealth in the risk-free asset and some in the market portfolio (point A'). A less risk averse investor might end up borrowing in order to invest more in the risky asset

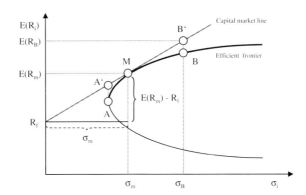

Fig. 4.47 Capital market line model (CML), transformation line

(point B'). Investment portfolios such as A and B would not be realised, as they are dominated by A' and B' in term of their risk-return profile. The individual portfolio is determined by the tangent of the investor's indifference curve to the CML. The slope of the indifference curve equals the marginal rate of substitution since it is the rate at which the individual will trade off more return for risk. The slope of the CML represents the market price of risk:

$$slope\ of\ the\ CML = (ER_m - R_f)/\sigma_m.$$

The market price of risk equals the difference between the expected return of the market portfolio, ER_m, and the risk-free rate, R_f, relative to the risk of the market portfolio, σ_m. Besides differences in risk preferences, the optimal portfolio of risky assets for all investors lies always on the CML. The return on the investor portfolio is thus:

$$ER_i = R_f + \frac{(ER_m - R_f)}{\sigma_m} \cdot \sigma_i, \tag{4.189}$$

that is the risk-free rate plus the market price of risk times the individual risk of the portfolio chosen.

4.6.3 Two-Fund Separation Theorem

The investment decision can be broken down into two separate decisions ("two-fund separation theorem"). In a *first step*, the choice of the optimal proportions of risky assets is made, which is independent of investor preferences. This decision depends only on the individual's view about expected returns, variances and covariances of the assets under review. Expectations about these variables are assumed to the homogeneous across investors. All investors therefore hold the same proportions of the risky assets in their portfolios, irrespective of their preferences.

Once investors have mimicked the market portfolio, we come to the *second step*: namely individual preferences enter the calculation. Individual investors decide how much to borrow (lend) in order to increase (reduce) the amount of funds invested in the market portfolio of risky assets. Most notably, this second decision does not affect the relative demand for risky assets (and their prices). As a result, the equilibrium returns on the set of risky assets are independent of individual investor preference, they depend only on market variables such as variances and covariances in the market.

4.6.4 The Capital Asset Pricing Model

The Capital Asset Pricing Model (CAPM) gives the equilibrium return on *individual* securities in the market portfolio. The CAPM actually says that only the systematic (or market) risk affects the equilibrium return on a risky asset, while the unsystematic (or idiosyncratic) risk can be diversified away and is therefore not compensated. In other words: The only thing an investor should worry about is how much an individual asset contributes to the risk of his portfolio as a whole. To show this, the expected return and standard deviation for any portfolio, p, consisting of n risky assets and a risk-free asset, r, can be written as (Cuthbertson, 1996, p. 45):

$$ER_p = \sum_{i=1}^{n} x_i ER_i + \left[1 - \sum_{i=1}^{n} x_i \right] \cdot r, \text{ and} \tag{4.190}$$

$$\sigma_p = \sqrt{\sum_{i=1}^{n} x_i^2 \sigma_i^2 + 2 \sum_{i=1}^{n} \sum_{j=1}^{n} x_i x_j \, \text{cov}\,(x_i, x_j)}_{\;\;i \neq j} \tag{4.191}$$

Here x_i represents the share of wealth held in asset i. In fact, the CAPM is the solution to minimising the variance of the portfolio subject to a given level of expected return, ER_p. The Langrangian is:

$$C = \sigma_p + \psi \left[ER_p - \sum x_i ER_i + \left(1 - \sum x_i \right) \cdot r \right]. \tag{4.192}$$

Choosing x_i $(i = 1, \ldots, n)$ to minimise Eq. (4.192) gives a set of first-order conditions:

$$\delta C / \delta x_1 = \frac{1}{2} (\sigma_p^2)^{-1/2} \left[2x_1 \sigma_1^2 + 2 \sum_{j=2}^{n} x_j \, \text{cov}\,(R_1, R_j) \right] - \psi(ER_1 - r) = 0 \tag{4.193a}$$

$$\delta C / \delta x_2 = \frac{1}{2} (\sigma_p^2)^{-1/2} \left[2x_2 \sigma_1^2 + 2 \sum_{j=1, j \neq 2}^{n} x_j \, \text{cov}\,(R_2, R_j) \right] - \psi(ER_2 - r) = 0 \tag{4.193b}$$

$$\delta C / \delta x_n = \frac{1}{2} (\sigma_p^2)^{-1/2} \left[2x_n \sigma_n^2 + 2 \sum_{j=1, j \neq n}^{n} x_j \, \text{cov}\,(R_n, R_j) \right] - \psi(ER_n - r) = 0. \tag{4.193c}$$

Differencing Eq. (4.192) with respect to ψ yields:

$$\delta C / \delta \psi = ER_P - \sum_{i=1}^{n} x_i ER_i - \left(1 - \sum_{i=1}^{n} x_i \right) \cdot r = 0. \tag{4.194}$$

Multiplying the (4.193a) with x_1, (4.193b) by x_2 etc., and summing over all equations yields:

$$\sigma_p = \psi \left[\sum_{i=1}^{n} x_i E R_i - \sum_{i=1}^{n} x_i r \right] = \psi \left[\sum_{i=1}^{n} x_i E R_i + \left(1 - \sum_{t=1}^{n} x_i \right) \cdot r - r \right].$$

$$(4.195)$$

At the point where $\sum_{i=1}^{n} x_i = 1$, we yield:

$$\sigma_m = \psi (E R_m - r) \text{ and} \tag{4.196}$$

$$1/\psi = (E R_m - r)/\sigma_m, \tag{4.197}$$

where $E R_m = \sum_{i=1}^{n} x_i E R_i$ is the expected return of the market portfolio. The term $1/\psi$ in (4.197) is the price of a unit risk, which is the same for all investors. Since Eqs. (4.193a), (4.193b) and (4.193c) hold for all investors irrespective of individual preferences, they can be used to derive the CAPM expressing for equilibrium returns on each individual share in the portfolio. The ith Eq. in (4.193c) at point $\sum_{i=1}^{n} x_i = 1$ is:

$$E R_i = r + \frac{1}{\psi \sigma_m} \left[x_i \sigma_i^2 + \sum_{j=1, i \neq j}^{n} x_j \operatorname{cov}(R_i, R_j) \right]. \tag{4.198}$$

If we substitute $1/\psi$ from Eq. (4.197) in Eq. (4.198) gives:

$$E R_i = r + \frac{E R_m - r}{\sigma_m^2} \left[x_i \sigma_i^2 + \sum_{j=1, i \neq j}^{n} x_j \operatorname{cov}(R_i, R_j) \right]. \tag{4.199}$$

We should note that:

$$\operatorname{cov}(R_i, R_m) = \operatorname{cov}\left[(R_i, (x_1 R_1, +x_2 R_2 + \ldots + x_n R_n)] \right]$$
$$= x_i \sigma_i^2 + \sum_{j=1, i \neq j}^{n} x_j \operatorname{cov}(R_i, R_j) \tag{4.200}$$

and substituting (4.200) in (4.199), one yields the CAPM expression for the equilibrium expected return on asset i:

$$E R_i = r + (E R_m - r)\beta_i \quad \text{with} \quad \beta_i = \operatorname{cov}(R_i, R_m)/\sigma_m^2.^{35} \tag{4.201}$$

---

[35] Adrian and Franzoni (2008) complement the conditional capital asset pricing model (CAPM) by introducing unobservable long-run changes in risk factor loadings. In this environment, investors rationally "learn" the long-run level of factor loading by observing realized returns. As a direct consequence of this assumption, conditional betas are modeled using the Kalman filter. Because of its focus on low-frequency variation in betas, the authors' approach circumvents recent criticisms

4.6.5 Estimating the Beta-Factor

The relationship between return and risk is commonly tested in the form of the market model (Blume, 1971, 1975, 1979; Clarkson, 1990; Fabozzi et al., 1978):

$$R_t = \alpha + \beta R_{m,t} + \varepsilon_t. \tag{4.202}$$

According to the capital asset pricing theory, the specification would be:

$$R_t - r_t = \beta(R_{m,t} - r_t) + \varepsilon_t. \tag{4.203}$$

The empirical formulation of the CAPM is:

$$R_t - r_t = \alpha + \beta(R_{m,t} - r_t) + \varepsilon_t. \tag{4.204}$$

Of course, these models tend to be subject to OLS estimation problems (such as, for instance, autocorrelation of residuals, non-normal distributions ("fat tails"), etc.). In particular, Eq. (4.203) – which represents a *regression through the origin*, as the model does not contain an explicit intercept term – should be used with caution. In such models the sum of residuals is non-zero; also, the coefficient of determination might not be meaningful.

To give a simple illustration of calculating the ex post beta-factor for individual stocks, Fig. 4.48 shows the regression results of the CAPM in its risk-premium form, that is regressing a stock's risk-adjusted return $(R_t - r_t)$ on the market's risk premium $(R_{m,t} - r_t)$ and a constant, α. Daily returns for two stocks and the market index (that SAP AG and Lufthansa AG vis-à-vis the German stock market index DAX) were calculated as first differences of log daily prices, multiplied by 100, the risk free rate was approximated by the 1-months Euribor interest rate. The estimates were made for two periods, namely 1 January 2000 to 27 July 2006 and 1 January to 30 December 2002.

The intercept α is positive for SAP, whereas it is negative for Lufthansa. This suggests that the technology stock generates a positive risk-adjusted return even if the stock market as a whole doesn't go up. In the case of the airline, α is negative: without the total market showing positive gains, the Lufthansa stock would yield a negative risk-adjusted return. What is more, the β-factor of SAP exceeds 1 in both samples, whereas Lufthansa's β-factor is smaller than 1. That said, in the periods under review, returns of the technology stock reacted more strongly to a given change in the market's return when compared with the returns of the airline stock.

---

of the conditional CAPM. When tested on portfolios sorted by size and book-to-market ratio, their learning-augmented conditional CAPM fails to be rejected.

Daily risk-adjusted returns in percent of SAP and DAX

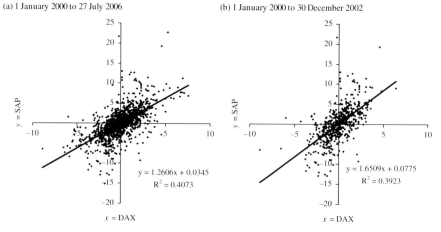

(a) 1 January 2000 to 27 July 2006

(b) 1 January 2000 to 30 December 2002

Daily risk-adjusted returns in percent of Lufthansa and DAX

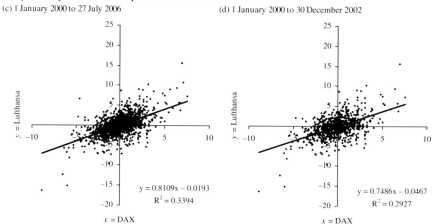

(c) 1 January 2000 to 27 July 2006

(d) 1 January 2000 to 30 December 2002

Fig. 4.48 Estimating the beta-factors for individual stocks;
Source: Bloomberg; own calculations. – The daily returns are expressed in first differences of the logs of price levels, multiplied by 100. – The risk free rate was approximated by the 1-months Euribor interest rate.

Credit Derivatives

In recent years, the international market for *credit derivatives* has been showing spectacular growth. In September 2008, the British Banker Association (BBA) estimated that the global market for credit derivatives would expand to US$33trn, compared with a market volume of around US$7trn seen at the end of 2006.

In general, credit derivatives are contracts that transfer the risk (and sometimes the return) of an asset from one counterparty to another without transferring ownership of the underlying asset (Kiff & Morrow, 2000) (See Fig. 4.49). *Credit default swaps* (CDS) transfer the potential loss on the underlying asset that can result from specific *credit events* (bankruptcy, failure to pay and restructuring). A *protection buyer* pays a periodic (or upfront) fee to a *protection seller* in exchange for a contingent payment if there is a credit event (chart a).

Total-rate-of-return swaps (TRORS) transfer the returns and risks on an underlying reference asset from one party to another. TRORS involve a *total return buyer*, who pays a periodic fee to a *total return seller* and receives the total economic performance of the underlying reference asset (such as, for instance, interest income) in return (chart b).

There are also *credit spread put contracts* and *credit spread call option contracts*. For instance, the former isolate and capture devaluations in a reference asset that are independent of shifts in the general market environment (such as, for instance, the yield curve). Essentially, they are default swaps that stipulate spread widening as a *credit event* (chart c).

Credit-linked notes are securities that effectively embed default swaps within a traditional fixed income structure. In return for a principal payment when the contract is made, they typically pay periodic interest plus, at maturity, the principal minus a contingent payment on the embedded default swap (chart d).

CDS can be combined to create new portfolio instruments. This use of CDS led to the evolution of the market in *collateralised debt obligations* (CDOs). In its simplest form, a CDO is a debt security issued by a special purpose vehicle (SPV) and backed by a diversified loan, bond or CDS portfolio.

Markets for credit derivatives allow a more efficient allocation of credit risk among market participants (Rule, 2001, p. 117). Credit derivatives enable banks to reduce concentrations of exposure and diversify risk beyond their customer base. Liquid markets for credit derivatives provide valuable price information. They allow financial institutions to lower their regulatory capital burden, take on more credit risk, thereby stimulating investment, growth and employment.

However, not everyone takes kindly to the evolution of credit derivatives. For instance, famous investor Warren Buffet wrote in his Letter to Berkshire Hathaway Shareholders on 21 February (2003, p. 15): "We try to be alert to any sort of megacatastrophe risk, and that posture may make us unduly apprehensive about the burgeoning quantities of long-term derivatives contracts and the massive amount of uncollateralized receivables that are growing alongside. In our view, however, derivatives are financial weapons of mass destruction, carrying dangers that, while now latent, are potentially lethal."

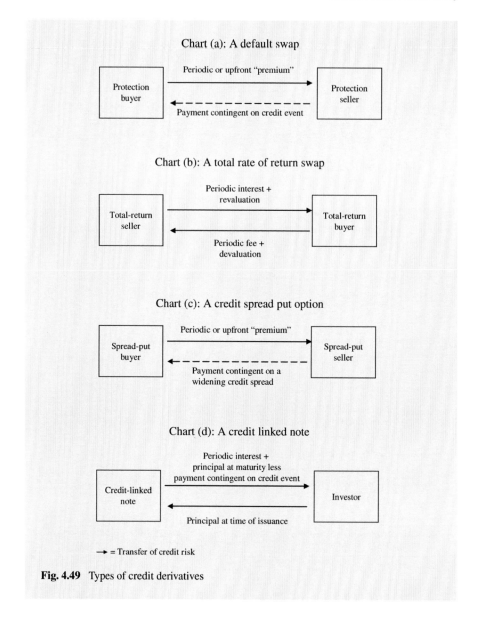

Fig. 4.49 Types of credit derivatives

4.7 Liquidity Provision – A Theoretical Framework

Clearly, liquidity seems to have played a central role within the financial crisis of 2007–2008. Hence, it is important to have a theoretical framework for reasoning about liquidity provisioning by the commercial banking system and its effect for crises. In the following, we briefly describe the relevant concepts using a couple of papers as considered, for instance, by Allen and Carletti (2008). We will come back to these concepts later in Sect 7.1 where we will discuss the genesis of and the policy lessons from the financial crisis of 2007/2008.

4.7.1 The Financial System as a Private Provider of Liquidity

Asset pricing theory in financial economics that delivers the tools for the valuation of assets and risk management heavily relies on the assumptions of perfect and complete markets and fully rational agents. Agents understand the risks involved in the investments made and price them in a correct fashion. In Sect 8.7 of this book we demonstrate that much of the theory that underlies central bank inflation-targeting (IT) policy in recent years relies on similar assumptions. In this frictionless world, financial institutions do not have any role to play. Hence, financial crises should never occur. However, they take place in reality, and as the financial crisis of 2007–2008 demonstrates, badly functioning money markets, financial institutions and their role as liquidity creators play an important role. Understanding the events of 2007–2008 in terms of models *without financial intermediaries* is extremely *difficult* if not impossible (Allen & Carletti, 2008a; Allen, Carletti, & Gale, 2008).

The first step in any investigation of the role of liquidity in financial crises is to develop a model of liquidity provision in the context of financial institutions and markets. The purpose is to get a grip on how a financial system is able to provide liquidity efficiently and what can go wrong with it. We also have to check *the potential role of central banks* in improving the allocation of resources and safeguarding financial stability when there appears to be a problem.

The standard model of banking which enables an assessment of the role of banks as providers of liquidity was introduced by the well-known contributions of Bryant (1980) and Diamond and Dybvig (1983). Assume that there is a short-term asset which provides liquidity in the next period and a long-term asset which bears a higher return which, however, comes at a later date. At the beginning, consumers are not quite sure when exactly they will be in need of liquidity and cannot directly insure themselves against this kind of risk. In this world the role of banks boils down to providing liquidity insurance to the depositors.

However, one drawback of the *original* banking models is that they *do not include financial markets*. To get a deeper understanding of the financial crisis of 2007–2008, it is essential to dispose of a theoretical framework including *both* financial intermediaries and markets. Allen and Gale (2004, 2007) among others develop such a model which has these properties. They claim that in modern financial systems financial institutions are essential for financial markets. Consumers first invest in financial intermediaries such as commercial banks and mutual funds and these institutions then invest in financial markets. The emergence of information and transaction costs renders it too costly for individual investors to trade directly within the full range of financial markets. Both financial intermediaries and markets play an important role in this environment. Financial intermediaries provide liquidity insurance to consumers against their individual risk of liquidity shocks. Markets allow financial intermediaries (and hence their depositors) to share aggregate risks. This general equilibrium framework allows the conduct of a normative analysis of liquidity provision by the financial system. It behaves like the Arrow-Debreu model of resource allocation except that it includes financial institutions. It serves as a benchmark for the efficient provision of liquidity by intermediaries and markets (and indirectly also by central banks).

Commercial banks grant consumers to deposit funds which they are able to withdraw when they are in need of liquidity. This liquidity provision allows banks to accumulate funds they can make use of in order to lend to firms to fund their long-run investments. Banks have to manage their liquidity so that they are able to exactly match the liquidity needs of their depositors. We have to differentiate *two types of uncertainty* with respect to liquidity needs. The first variant of uncertainty is represented by the fact that each individual bank is faced with *idiosyncratic* liquidity risk. At any given date its customers may have a certain degree of liquidity needs. The second type of uncertainty faced by banks is represented by an *aggregate* liquidity risk. In some periods aggregate liquidity demand turns out to be large whereas it is low in other periods. Hence, all banks are exposed to the same shock by means of aggregate risk. This type of shock increases or decreases the demand for liquidity which all banks face at the same time. The capability of banks to hedge themselves against these liquidity risks crucially depends on the functioning, or, more concretely, the completeness of financial markets (Allen & Carletti, 2008, p. 8ff.).

If financial markets prove to be really *complete*, the financial system provides liquidity efficiently. In other words, it ensures that the banks' liquidity shocks are hedged. One method to implement complete markets that allow every bank to hedge itself against idiosyncratic liquidity risk is the following. Each bank issues a small amount of a security, contingent on the idiosyncratic liquidity shock experienced by each *other* bank. With the funds generated by these securities, each bank buys all of the securities issued by the other banks that are contingent on its *own* idiosyncratic shock. Thus when a bank is hit by a high liquidity shock, it obtains the funds it needs to cover its liquidity requirements.[36]

The equilibrium prices of all these bank-specific securities together with securities that allow aggregate risk to be hedged lead to the efficient provision of liquidity by the financial system. The invisible hand of the market ensures that the pricing of the complete set of securities provides the correct incentives for the provision of liquidity by the banking system in every state of the world.

The key point here is *that the implementation of complete markets requires a large number of bank-specific securities*, but in practice we do not see anything that resembles this kind of situation or provides an equivalent allocation. One potential reason is that the infrastructure needed to make sure that all the securities required for markets to be overall complete can be very costly in practice and, hence, not

---

[36]See Allen et al. (2008) for a full description of how complete markets can be implemented.

convenient. Although, for instance, the current US financial system disposes of a wide array of securities and many of them are specifically contingent on the particular experiences of specific firms such as credit default swaps (CDS), it is still far away from really enabling the type of hedging transactions which is equivalent to the theoretical benchmark of complete markets.

However, if markets are *incomplete*, commercial banks can trade only a limited number of assets and *their ability to hedge liquidity risk changes significantly*. This incompleteness of markets causes an inefficient provision of liquidity by the financial system. This in turn can generate *cash-in-the-market pricing*, where even the prices of safe assets can fall below their fundamental value, and cause *financial fragility*, meaning that even small shocks can have large impacts on asset prices. In addition, *contagion* cannot be excluded. Shocks may then spread from one institution to another leading to a chain of bankruptcies. Allen and Carletti (2008), for instance, emphasize that these effects may provide one explanation of what can go wrong in imperfect financial markets.

4.7.2 Financial Fragility and Cash-in-the-Market Pricing

The main problem with incomplete markets consists of the fact that liquidity provision by the financial system turns out to be not efficient. The specific kind of risk management which ensures that the commercial bank or the intermediary disposes of the adequate amount of liquidity changes significantly as compared to the case of complete markets. In case of the latter it is possible, as described above, to employ securities in order to ensure that liquidity is received when it is needed. The price system makes sure that adequate liquidity is provided in every state and is priced properly state by state. In the case of complete markets, thus, banks and other intermediaries buy liquidity in states where it is scarce by selling liquidity in states where it is plentiful from their point of view. Hence, in this state of the world the financial system allows risk sharing and insurance (Allen & Carletti, 2008, p. 11ff.).

However, when markets are incomplete, liquidity provision is in contrast achieved by selling assets when liquidity is required. When liquidity is scarce asset prices are determined by the available liquidity or in other words by the cash in the market. It is necessary that a proportion of financial institutions hold extra liquidity that allows them to buy up assets when liquidity is scarce. These suppliers of liquidity are no longer compensated for the cost of providing liquidity state by state. Instead, the cost must be made up on average across all states and this is exactly where the main problem is located.

The providers of liquidity are endowed with the alternative of investing in a productive long asset. There is an opportunity cost of holding liquidity since the latter displays a lower return than the productive long asset. Agents must be able to make a profit in some states in order to be willing to supply liquidity. If no one held liquidity, the price of the long asset would collapse to a value of zero. This would create an incentive for some agents to hold liquidity because they can acquire assets cheaply. But if the price increased too much, then nobody would hold liquidity as this would not be profitable. Hence, in equilibrium the prices are bid to the level where the profit in the states where banks face high liquidity demand is sufficiently high to compensate the providers of liquidity for all the other states where they do not make any profit and simply bear the opportunity cost of holding liquidity. In other words, prices are low in the states where banks are in need of more liquidity. But this proves to be exactly the wrong point in time from an efficiency point of view for there to be a transfer from the banks who need liquidity to the providers of liquidity. In effect, there is negative insurance and a suboptimal degree of risk sharing. Volatility of asset prices is costly because depositors are risk averse and their consumption varies across banks with high and low idiosyncratic liquidity risk.[37] This leaves ample room for central bank intervention. By conducting open market operations to fix the price of the long asset (or equivalently fix the short term interest rate), central banks can remove the inefficiency stemming from the volatility of asset prices and achieve the same allocation as in case of complete markets (Allen et al., 2008).

Seen on the whole, when markets are incomplete, asset prices must be volatile to provide incentives for liquidity provision. This kind of asset price volatility can cause costly and inefficient crises. This establishes a market failure which provides the justification for central bank and other types of intervention to improve the resource allocation. Liquidity provision in the complete markets allocation might serve as a proper benchmark for assessing the effectiveness of such an intervention.

4.7.3 Contagion

A second important concept to be considered when markets are incomplete is *contagion*. The linkages between commercial banks which interbank markets provide imply that problems of one bank has the potential to spread over to other banks and can potentially disrupt the whole financial system. Allen and Gale (2000) analyze a variant of the basic model of liquidity provision described above to investigate how this process works and to check the inefficiencies involved.[38] As with financial fragility, the problem here is also related to liquidity provision but in a somewhat different way. The possibility of contagion arises from the overlapping claims which different banks have on one another rather than from asset price volatility. When one specific bank suffers from a shock and defaults as a consequence, the other banks are also hit by a loss because their claims on the troubled bank decrease in value. If this spillover effect is significant enough, it may cause *a crisis throughout the system*. In extreme cases, the crisis moves on from bank to bank, eventually having

---

[37] Allen and Carletti (2006, 2008a) analyze in detail how this pricing mechanism works.

[38] For a survey of the literature on contagion see Allen and Babus (2008).

an impact on a much larger set of banks than the one in which the original shock occurred (Allen & Carletti, 2008, p. 13ff.).

If there is a large degree of interdependence between banks in the sense that many banks hold the assets of others, there will be no de-coupling and there are many links through which a crisis can spread. On the other hand, however, the importance of each link will be smaller. This implies that a shock can be more easily absorbed by the capital buffer of each institution. If there are a few links but each of them involves a larger amount of funds, crises are more likely to spread because each bank's capital buffer will be overwhelmed if another bank fails. Thus the case of some interrelation but not too much represents the most likely situation for contagion to occur (Allen & Carletti, 2008, p. 13f.).

In general, contagion represents an extremely worrying phenomenon for policy makers. The *costs of bankruptcy* of financial institutions can be *large*. A whole string of bankruptcies across banks can impose tremendous damage on the financial system, and this in turn has the potential to have large spillovers to the real economy. If firms no longer have access to funding from commercial banks or other financial institutions then they may feel forced to cut investment and their intended level of output significantly.

Many factors affect the probability and the extent of contagion. One important factor which appears to have played a role in the current crisis relates to the use of *mark-to-market accounting*. This specific accounting method has the benefit of reflecting the *market value* of the balance sheets of financial institutions and thus of allowing regulators, investors and other users of accounting information to better assess the risk profile of financial institutions. This is true provided financial markets operate perfectly and prices correctly reflect the future earning power of assets. However, when markets do not work perfectly and prices do not throughout reflect the fundamental value as, for instance, in the case where there is *cash-in-the-market pricing*, mark-to-market accounting exposes the value of the balance sheets of financial institutions to short-term and excessive fluctuations, and it can ultimately generate contagion. If there emerges cash-in-the-market pricing in one sector of the financial system, other sectors are potentially affected by the price changes and may be forced to write down the value of their assets. [39]

4.7.4 Asymmetric Information

In our above discussion of liquidity provision, *asymmetric information* has played a relatively small role. In particular, the assets that are traded are not plagued by asymmetric information. In the financial crisis of 2007/2008, many people believe that asymmetric information has played a quite important role (see, for instance,

---

[39]See Allen and Carletti (2008a) for an extensive analysis of mark-to-market accounting when there is cash-in-the-market pricing.

Gorton, 2008). Bolton, Santos and Scheinkman (2008) have provided an interesting theory of liquidity provision with asymmetric information.

In their model they have three sets of agents. There are investors with a short horizon, intermediaries and investors with a long horizon. The basic source of inefficiency is asymmetric information about asset values between long-horizon investors and financial intermediaries. Long-horizon investors are not able to distinguish between an asset sale that is due to a liquidity need and an asset sale motivated by an offload of low quality securities. This asymmetric information creates an *adverse selection problem* and as a consequence also a price discount. Bolton, Santos and Scheinkman assume that over time, the intermediaries learn more about the assets in their portefeuille. This ensures that over time the adverse selection problem gets worse, and the price discount in case of a selling intermediary becomes greater.

The basic problem faced by an intermediary if it is confronted with a liquidity shock is whether to sell its assets now at a discount or to try and ride out the crisis. The danger of choosing the latter strategy is that the intermediary runs the risk of having to sell at a greater discount if the crisis lasts longer than expected. It is shown in this case that two types of rational expectations equilibrium exist. In what the so-called *immediate trading equilibrium*, intermediaries sell assets immediately to make sure they are endowed with enough liquidity. In the *delayed trading equilibrium* intermediaries try to ride out the crisis and only sell if they are forced to.

For some parameter values only the immediate trading equilibrium exists while for others both do. Surprisingly, Bolton, Santos and Scheinkman are able to show that the delayed trading equilibrium is Pareto superior when both equilibria exist. The reason is that short-horizon investors tend to undervalue long assets while long-horizon investors tend to undervalue cash. They derive a gain from inducing short horizon investors to hold more long assets and long-horizon investors more cash. This is exactly what the delayed trading equilibrium does. The asymmetric information problem is the worse the less is the gain since it impedes the operation of the market for the long assets.

References

Adrian, T., & Franzoni, F. (2008, October). *Learning about beta: Time-varying factor loadings, expected returns, and the conditional CAPM*, Federal Reserve Bank of New York Staff Report, 193 New York.

Allen, F., & Gale, D. (2000). Financial Contagion, Journal of Political Economy 108, 1–33.

Allen, F., & Babus, A. (2008). *Networks in finance*. Working Paper 08–07, Wharton Financial Institutions Center, University of Pennsylvania.

Allen, F. D., & Carletti, E. (2008). *The role of liquidity in financial crises*. Working Paper 08–33, Wharton Financial Institutions Center, University of Pennsylvania.

Allen, F., & E. Carletti (2008a). Mark-to-market accounting and liquidity pricing. *Journal of Accounting and Economics, 45*, 358–378.

Allen, F., & Gale, D. (2004). Financial intermediaries and markets. *Econometrica, 72*, 1023–1061.

Allen, F., & Gale, D. (2007). *Understanding financial crises, Clarendon lecture series in finance*. Oxford: Oxford University Press.

Allen, F., Carletti, E., & Gale, D. (2008). *Interbank market liquidity and central bank intervention*. Working paper, University of Pennsylvania Mimeo.

Arrow, K. J. (1971). Essays in theories of risk-bearing, Chicago: Markham Publishing Co.

Asness, C. (2000). Stocks vs. bonds: Explaining the equity risk premium. *Financial Analysts Journal, 56,* 96–113.

Asness, C. (2003). Fight the Fed model: The relationship between future returns and stock and bond market yields. *Journal of Portfolio Management, 30,* 11–24.

Bachelier, L. (1900). *Theory of speculation*, Paris: Gauthier-Villars, translated by A. James Boness and reprinted in Cootner, loc. cit.

Ball, R. (1978). Anomalies in relationships between securities' yields and yield-surrogates. *Journal of Financial Economics, 6,* 103–126.

Beechey, M., Gruen, D., & Vickery, J. (2000, January 01). *The efficient market hypothesis: A survey*, Research Discussion Paper, Economic Research Department Reserve Bank of Australia.

Bera, A. K., & Higgins, M. L. (1993). ARCH models: Properties, estimation and testing. *Journal of Economic Surveys, 7,* 305–362.

Bernanke B. S., & Kuttner, K. N. (2004). What explains the stock market's reaction to Federal Reserve policy?, by Ben Federal Reserve Board Finance and Economics Discussion Series, No. 2004–16, http://www.federalreserve.gov/pubs/feds/ 2004/200416/200416abs.html

Bernstein, P. L. (2005). *Capital ideas*. Hoboken, NJ: John Wiley & Sons, Inc.

Blume, M. E. (1971). On the assessment of risk. *Journal of Finance, 24,* 1–9.

Blume, M. E. (1975). Betas and their regression tendencies. *Journal of Finance, 30,* 785–795.

Blume, M. E. (1979). Betas and their regression tendencies: Some further evidence. *Journal of Finance, 34,* 265–267.

Bollerslev, T. (1986). Generalised autoregressive conditional heteroskedasticity. *Journal of Econometrics, 31,* 307–327.

Bollerslev, T. (1990). Modelling the coherence in short-run nominal exchange rates: A multivariate generalised ARCH approach. *Review of Economics and Statistics, 72,* 498–505.

Bollerslev, T., et al. (1988). On the correlation structure of the generalised conditional heteroscedastic process. *Journal of Time Series Analysis, 9,* 121–131.

Bolton, P., Santos, T., & Scheinkman, J. (2008). *Inside and outside liquidity*, Working paper, Columbia University Mimeo.

Bryant, J. (1980). A model of reserves, bank runs, and deposit insurance. *Journal of Banking and Finance, 4,* 335–344.

Buffet, W. (2007, February 28). Letter to Berkshire Hathaway Shareholders, p. 22.

Campbell, J. Y. (1987). Stock returns and the term structure. *Journal of Financial Economics, 18,* 373–399.

Campbell, J. Y. (1991). A variance decomposition for stock returns. *The Economic Journal, 101,* 157–179.

Campbell, J. Y., & Ammer, J. (2003). What moves the stock and bond markets? A variance decomposition for long-term asset returns. *Journal of Finance, 48*(1), 3–37.

Campbell, J. Y., Lo, A. W., & MacKinlay, A. C. (1997). *The econometrics of financial markets*. Princeton, NJ: Princeton University Press.

Campbell, J. Y., & Shiller, R. J. (1988). Stock prices, earnings, and expected dividends. *Journal of Finance, 43,* 661–676.

Campbell, J. Y., & Shiller, R. J. (1988a). The dividend-price ration and expectations of future dividends and discount factors. *Review of Financial Studies, 1,* 195–228.

Campbell, J. Y., & Shiller, R. J. (1997). Cointegration and tests of present value models. *Journal of Political Economy, 95,* 1062–1088.

Campbell, J. Y., & Shiller, R. J. (1998). Valuation ratios and the long-run stock market outlook. *Journal of Portfolio Management, 24*(2), 11–26.

Campbell, J. Y., & Vuolteenaho, T. (2003). *Inflation illusion and stock prices*. Mimeo: Harvard University.

Chen, N.-F. (1991). Financial investment opportunities and the macroeconomy. *Journal of Finance, 46,* 529–554.

Chiodo, A. J., & Owyang, M. T. (2002, November/December). *A case study of a currency crisis: The Russian default of 1998*. Review of the Federal Reserve Bank of St. Louis, pp. 7–18.

Clarkson, P. M., & Thompson, R. (1990). Empirical estimates of beta when investors face estimation risk. *Journal of Finance, 45*(2), 431–453.

Cochrane, J. H. (2001). *Asset Pricing*. Princeton, New Jersey: Princeton University Press.

Cowles A. (1933). Can stock market forecasters forecast? *Econometrica, 1,* 309–324.

Cuthbertson, J. M. (1957, November). The term structure of interest rates. *Quarterly Journal of Economics, 71,* 489–504.

Cuthbertson, K. (1996). *Quantitative financial economics, stocks, bonds and foreign exchange*. Chichester: John Wiley & Sons, Ltd..

Cuthbertson, K. et al. (1997, July). The behaviour of UK stock prices and returns. *The Economic Journal, 107*(443), 986–1008.

Cuthbertson, K., Hayes, S., & Nitzsche, D. (1997). The behaviour of UK stock prices and returns: Is the market efficient? *Economic Journal, 107*(443), 986–1008.

Dattatreya, R. F., & Fabozzi, F. J. (2001). Risks associated with investing in fixed income securities. In F. J. Fabozzi (Ed.), *The Handbook of Fixed Income Securities* (6th ed., pp. 21–29). New York: McGraw-Hill.

DeBondt, W. F. M. (1995). Financial decision-making in markets and firms: A behavioral perspective. In R. Jarrow et al (Eds.), *Handbook in OR&MS* (Vol. 9). Amsterdam: Elsevier Science B.V.

DeBondt, W. F. M., & Thaler, R. (1995). Does the stock market overreact? *Journal of Finance, 40,* 793–805.

Diamond, D., & Dybvig, P. (1983). Bank runs, deposit insurance, and liquidity. *Journal of Political Economy, 91,* 401–419.

Dickey, D. A., & Fuller, W. A. (1979). Distributions of the estimators for autoregressive time series with a unit root. *Journal of the American Statistical Association, 74*(366), 427–431.

Domanski, D., & Kremer, M. (1998). What *do asset price movements in germany tell monetary policy makers*? The Role of Asset Prices in the Formulation of Monetary Policy, BIS Conference Papers, 5, pp. 24–44.

Domanski, D., & Kremer, M. (2000). *The dynamics of international asset price linkages and their effects on german stock and bond markets*. International Financial Markets and the Implications for Monetary and Financial Stability, BIS Conference Papers, Bank for International Settlements, 8, pp. 134–158, Basle.

Enders, W. (2004). *Applied econometric time series* (2nd ed.). Alabama: Wiley.

Engle, R. (1982). Autoregressive conditional heteroskedasticity with estimates of the variance of United Kingdom inflation. *Econometrica, 50*(1), 987–1007.

Estrella, A. (2005). The yield curve as a leading indicator: Frequently asked questions. www.newyorkfed.org.

Estrella, A., & Hardouvelis, G. (1991). The term structure as a predictor of real economic activity. *Journal of Finance, 46*(2), 555–576.

Estrella, A., Rodrigues, A. P., & Schich, S. (2003). How stable is the predictive power of the yield curve? Evidence from Germany and the United States. *Review of Economics and Statistics 85*(3), 629–644.

European Central Bank (2005, August). *Hedge funds and their implications for financial stability*. Occasional Papers, No. 34.

European Central Bank (2006a, February), Monthly Bulletin, Frankfurt.

European Central Bank (2006b, October), Monthly Bulletin, Frankfurt.

Fabozzi F. J., & Francis, J. C. (1978). Industry effects and the determinants of beta. *Quarterly Review of Economics and Business, 19*(3), 61–74.

Fabozzi, F. J., Buetow, G. W., & Johnson, R. R. (2001). Measuring interest rate risk. In Fabozzi, F. J. (Ed.), *The Handbook of Fixed Income Securities* (6th ed., pp. 85–129). New York: McGraw-Hill.

Fama, E. F. (1965). The behavior of stock market prices. *Journal of Business, 38,* 34–105.

Fama, E. F. (1970). Efficient capital markets: A review of theory and empirical work. *Journal of Finance, 25*(1), 383–417.

Fama, E. F. (1976). *Foundations of finance*. New York: Basic Books.

Fama, E. F. (1991). Efficient capital markets: II. *Journal of Finance, 46*(5), 1575–1617.

Fama, E. F. (1998). Market efficiency, long-term returns, and behavioral finance. *Journal of Financial Economics, 49*, 283–306.

Fama, E. F., & French, K. R. (1988). Permanent and temporary components of stock prices. *Journal of Political Economy, 96*, 246–273.

Fama, E. F., & French, K. R. (1989). Business conditions and expected returns on stocks and bonds. *Journal of Financial Economics, 25*, 23–49.

Fama, E. F., & French, K. R. (1992). The cross-section of expected stock returns. *Journal of Finance, 47*, 427–465.

Fama, E. F., Fisher, L., Jensen, M., & Roll, R. (1969). The adjustment of stock prices to new information. *International Economic Review, 10*, 1–21.

Flaving, M. A. (1983). Excess volatility in the financial markets–A reassessment of the empirical evidence. *Journal of Political Economy, 91*, 246–273.

Friedman, M. (1953). *Essays in positive economics*. Chicago, IL: University of Chicago Press.

Gordon, M. J., (1962). *The investment, financing and valuation of the corporation*. Homewood, IL: Irwin.

Gorton, G. (2008). *The panic of 2007*, Presentation delivered at the 2008 Jackson Hole Symposium.

Granger C. W. J. (1969). Investigating causal relations by econometric models and cross-spectral methods. *Econometrica, 37*, 424–438.

Hansen, L. P., & Jagannathan, R. (1991). Implications of security market data for models of dynamic economies. *Journal of Political Economy, 99*, 225–262.

Hartmann P., Straetmans S., & Vries C. G. (2005, September). *Banking system stability: A cross-Atlantic perspective*. ECB Working Paper, No. 527.

Harvey, C. R. (1988). The real term structure and consumption growth. *Journal of Financial Economics, 22*, 305–333.

Harvey, C. R. (1989). Forecasts of economic growth from the bond and stock markets. *Financial Analysts Journal 45*(5), 38–45.

Haugen, R. A., & Lakonishok, J. (1988). *The incredible January effect*. Homewood: Dow Jones-Irwin.

Hicks, J. R. (1939). *Value and capital – An inquiry into some fundamental principles of economic theory* (1st ed.). Oxford (2nd ed., 1946). Oxford.

Hodrick, R. J. (1992). Dividend yields and expected stock returns: alternative procedures for inference and measurement. *Review of Financial Studies, 5*, 357–386.

Humphrey-Hawkins Report (1997, February 22). The Federal Reserve Board, Washington/DC.

International Monetary Fund (1998, September). International Capital Markets, Developments, Prospects, and Key Policy Issues, Washington/DC.

Jarque, C. M., & Bera, A. K. (1987). A test for normality of observations and regression residuals. *International Statistical Review, 55*, 163–172.

Keim, D. B. (1983). Size-related anomalies and stock return seasonality: further empirical evidence. *Journal of Financial Economics, 12*, 13–32.

Keim, D. B., & Stambaugh, R. (1986). Predicting returns in the stock and bond markets, Journal of Financial Economics, 357–390.

Kiff, J., & Morrow, R. (2000, Autumn). Credit derivatives. *Bank of Canada Review*, 3–11.

Kleindon, A. W. (1986). Variance bounds test and stock price valuation models. *Journal of Political Economy, 94*, 953–1001.

Knight, F. H. (1964). *Risk, uncertainty & profit*. New York: Century Press, originally published in 1921.

Koivu, M., Pennanen, T., & Ziemba, W. T. (2005). Cointegration analysis of the FED model. *Finance Research Letters, 2*, 248–259.

Kremer, M. (1999). Die Kapitalmarktzinsen in Deutschland und den USA: Wie eng ist der Zinsverbund? Eine Anwendung der multivariaten Kointegrationsanalyse, Economic Research Group of the Deutsche Bundesbank, Discussion Paper 2/99 Frankfurt/Main February.

Kumar, S., & Hyodo, K. (2001). Price-earnings ratios in Japan: Recent evidence and further results. *Journal of International Financial Management and Accounting, 12*(1), 24–49.

Lander J., Orphanides A., & Douvogiannis M. (1997, Summer). Earnings, forecasts and the predictability of stock returns: Evidence from trading the S&P. *Journal of Portfolio Management, 23*(4), 24–35.

Laurent, R. (1988). An interest rate-based indicator of monetary policy. *Federal Reserve Bank of Chicago Economic Perspectives, 12*(1), 3–14.

Laurent, R. (1989, July/August). Testing the spread. *Federal Reserve Bank of Chicago Economic Perspectives, 13*, 22–34.

LeRoy, S. F. (1989, December). Efficient capital markets and martingales. *Journal of Economic Literature, 27*, 1583–1621.

LeRoy, S. F., & Porter, R. D. (1981). The present-value relation: Tests based on implied variance bounds. *Econometrica, 49*(3), 555–574.

Lintner, J. (1965, February). The valuation of risk assets and the selection of risky investment in stock portfolios and capital budgets. *Review of Economics and Statistics, 47*, 13–37.

Ljung, G. M., & Box, G. P. E. (1978). On a measure of lack of fit in time series models. *Biometrica, 66*, 66–72.

Lo, A. W., & Craig MacKinlay, A. C., (1999). *A non-random walk down wall street*. Princeton: Princeton University Press.

Lucas, R. E. (1978). Asset prices in an exchange economy. *Econometrica, 46*, 1424–1446.

MacCaulay, F. R. (1938). Some theoretical problems suggested by the movement of interest rates, bond yields and stock prices in the United States since 1856. New York: National Bureau of Economic Research.

Markowitz, H. M. (1952). Portfolio selection. *Journal of Finance, 7*, 77–99.

Marsh, T. A., & Merton, R. C. (1986). Dividend variability and variance bounds tests for the rationality of stock market prices. *American Economic Review, 76*, 483–498.

McCulloch, J. (1971). Measuring the term structure of interest rates. *Journal of Business, 44*, 19–31.

McCulloch, J. (1990). U.S. government term structure data. In B. Friedman, & F. Hahn (Eds.), *The handbook of monetary economics*. Amsterdam: North Holland.

Mises, L. V. (1960). *Epistemological problems of economics*, US Alabama: Ludwig von Mises Institute.

Modigliani, F., & Cohn, R. (1979). Inflation, rational valuation and the market. *Financial Analysts Journal*, 24–44.

Modigliani, F., & Sutch, R. (1966). Innovation in interest rate policy. *American Economic Review, 56*, 178–197.

Mossin, J. (1966). Equilibrium in a capital asset market. *Econometrica, 34*(4), 768–783.

Nelson C. R., & Kim M. J. (1993). Predictable stock returns: The role of small sample bias. *Journal of Finance, 48*, 641–661.

Neumann, J. von, & Morgenstern, O. (1944). *Theory of games and economic behavior*. Princeton: Princeton University Press, (2nd ed., 1947, 3rd ed., 1953).

Newey, W., & West, K. (1987). A simple, positive semi-definite, heterscedasticity and autocorrelation consistent covariance matrix. *Econometrica, 55*, 703–708.

Nicholson, S. F. (1960, July/August). Price-earnings ratios. *Financial Analysts Journal*, 43–50.

Poterba, J., & Summers, L. (1988). Mean reversion in stock returns: Evidence and implications. *Journal of Financial Economics, 22*, 27–59.

Ritter, J. R., & Warr, R. S. (2002). The decline of inflation and the bull market of 1982–1999. *Journal of Financial and Quantitative Analysis 37*, 29–61.

Rule, D. (2001, June). The credit derivatives market: its development and possible implications for financial stability. *Bank of England Financial Stability Review*, 117–140.

Samuelson, P. A. (1965). Proof that properly anticipated prices fluctuate randomly. *Industrial Management Review, 6*, 41–49.

Sharpe, W. F. (1964, September). Capital asset pricing: A theory of market equilibrium under conditions of risk. *Journal of Finance, 19*, 425–442.

Shen, P. (2000). The PE ratio and stock market performance. *Federal Reserve Bank of Kansas City, Economic Review*, Fourth Quarter, 23–36.

Shiller, R. J. (1981). Do stock prices move by too much to be justified by subsequent changes in dividends? *American Economic Review, 71*, 421–436.

Shiller, R. J. (1984). Stock prices and social dynamics. *Brookings Papers on Economic Activity, 2*, 457–498.

Shiller, R. J. (1988). The probability of gross violations of a present value variance inequality. *Journal of Political Economy, 96*, 1089–1092.

Shiller, R. J. (2000). *Irrational exuberance*. Princeton, NJ: Princeton University Press.

Shoven, J. B. (1987). Tax consequences of share repurchases and other non-dividend cash payments to equity owners. In L. H. Summers (Ed.), *Tax policy and the economy*. (Vol 1). Cambridge, MA: NBER and MIT Press.

Stambaugh, R. F. (1986). *Bias in regressions with lagged stochastic regressors*. CRSP Working Paper 156, University of Chicago.

Stock, J. H., & Watson, M. W. (1989). *New indexes of coincident and leading economic indicators*. In O. J. Blanchard, S. Fischer,(Eds.), NBER Macroeconomics Annual 1989, pp. 352–394.

The President's Working Group on Financial Markets (1999, April 28). *Hedge funds, leverage, and the lessons of long-term capital management*, Washington D. C.

Vaughan, D. A. (2003). Selected definitions of hedge funds, Comments for the US SEC Roundtable on Hedge Funds, pp. 14–15.

Whelan, K. (2005). The Dividend-Discount Model of Flock Prices, Topic 4, EC4010, Note.

Ziemba, W. T., & Schwartz, S. L. (1991). *Invest Japan: The structure, performance and opportunities of Japan's stock, bond and fund markets*. Chicago, IL: Probus Publishing.

Chapter 5
Causes, Costs and Benefits of Sound Money

> Inflation is always and everywhere a monetary phenomenon.
> — Milton Friedman, Wincott Memorial Lecture, London,
> September 16, 1970

5.1 The Objective of Price Stability

In most countries, price stability has become the primary objective of monetary policy. In 2006, US Fed chairman Ben S. Bernanke said: "Price stability plays a dual role in modern central banking: It is both an *end* and a *means* of monetary policy." (...) "Central bankers, economists, and other knowledgeable observers around the world agree that price stability both contributes importantly to the economy's growth and employment prospects in the longer term and moderates the variability of output and employment in the short to medium term."

Price stability is considered as a situation in which the economy's price level does neither increase nor decrease over time; that said, price stability is a situation in which inflation (that is an ongoing increase in the economy's price level) and deflation (that is a ongoing decline in the economy's price level) are actually absent, or, to put it differently: price stability is a situation in which the purchasing power of money remains unchanged over time.

The idea of preserving the value of money by stabilising the economy's price level – which is actually typically represented by a consumer price index – is based on the work of Irving Fisher (1867–1947) between 1895 and 1922, in particular on Fisher's *The Making of Index Numbers* from 1922. Fisher was one of the first experts on the calculation of price index numbers, and he began the first weekly newspaper publication of a wholesale price index in 1923. Before that, the value of the currency was fixed against a certain amount of gold. In fact, Fisher's "index regime" has become the "state-of-the-art" concept in monetary policy.

A. Belke, T. Polleit, *Monetary Economics in Globalised Financial Markets*,
DOI 10.1007/978-3-540-71003-5_5, © Springer-Verlag Berlin Heidelberg 2009

5.1.1 The Index Regime – Measuring Price Stability

Measuring price stability requires the solving of the *index number problem*. The two most prominent types of indices for measuring changes in the purchasing power of money are named after two people who were involved in developing them: Ernst Louis Étienne Laspeyres (1834–1913) and Hermann Paasche (1851–1925).

The most commonly used index formula is the Laspeyres index. It measures the change in the cost of purchasing a certain basket of goods and services in the current period compared with a specified base period. The prices are weighted by quantities in the base period:

$$Laspeyres\ index = \frac{\sum (P_{i,t} Q_{i,0})}{\sum (P_{i,0} Q_{i,0})},$$

where

$P_{i,t}$ = price of item i ($i = 1, \ldots, m$) in period t
$P_{i,0}$ = price of item i ($i = 1, \ldots, m$) in the base period
$Q_{i,0}$ = quantity of item i ($i = 1, \ldots, m$) purchased in the base period.

The Paasche index compares the cost of purchasing a given basket of goods and services with the cost of purchasing the same basket in an earlier period. The prices are weighted by the quantities of the current period. This means that each time the index is calculated, the weights are different. The formula for the Paasche index is:

$$Paasche\ index = \frac{\sum (P_{i,t} Q_{i,t})}{\sum (P_{i,0} Q_{i,t})},$$

where

$P_{i,t}$ = price of item i ($i = 1, \ldots, m$) in period t
$P_{i,0}$ = price of item i ($i = 1, \ldots, m$) in the base period
$Q_{i,t}$ = quantity of item i ($i = 1, \ldots, m$) purchased in period t.

The Paasche index, which represents a formula with changing weights, involves the collection of substantial (additional) data, since information on peoples' expenditure patterns, as well as prices, must be obtained continuously. Usually, the time taken to process current expenditure data and to derive revised weights precludes the preparation of a timely Paasche index.

Because of the difference in the weightings in the Laspeyres index and the Paasche index, the two indices will produce different results for the same sample period. This is because, in real life, expenditure patterns change from period to period as new commodities become available and consumer tastes change. Such changes also occur in response to price changes. Buyers attempt to minimise total outlays, while attempting to maintain the same standard of living. They can be expected to increasingly purchase goods and services that are now less expensive than those purchased in the base period.

If this is the case, vendible items whose prices have risen more than the average price rise of all goods will tend to have weights in the current period that are relatively smaller than in the base period, and therefore will have a relatively smaller weight in a Paasche index than in a Laspeyres index. This means that a Paasche index will tend to give a lower estimate of the overall price level change than a Laspeyres index when prices are increasing (and, of course, a higher estimate when prices are decreasing).

In practice, the Laspeyres index and the Paasche index should give fairly similar results, though, provided the periods under considerations are not too far apart (say, a month). The greater the length of time between the two periods being compared, however, the more opportunity there is for differential price and quantity movements and hence differences as far as the changes in the Laspeyres and Paasche indices are concerned.

5.1.2 Headline Versus Core Indices

In recent years, the decision to use a consumer price index (CPI) for measuring inflation has become the subject of controversy (Motely, 1997; Bundesbank 2000). It has been argued that *headline* changes in the CPI might overstate actual inflation. For instance, seasonal food and energy prices can be volatile (from month to month), often due to temporary supply and demand constellations. In those instances, headline inflation, which includes volatile food and energy price components, tends to be less representative of underlying, or true, inflation. That said, it is argued that underlying inflation is much better captured by a measure of *core inflation* (Bryan & Cecchetti, 1994).

The discussion about focussing on *headline inflation* versus *core inflation* bears particular importance for monetary policy if and when the central bank follows a policy in which it changes interest rates in response to actual changes in the inflation measure relative to the inflation target (Mishkin, 2007). For instance, a common argument for ignoring changes in food and energy prices in inflation measures is that although these prices have substantial effects on the overall index, they often are quickly reversed (*one-off effects*) and therefore do not require a monetary policy response.

Negative (positive) supply side shocks are sudden increases (declines) in average goods prices. For instance, a negative supply side shock – such as, For instance, unusual harsh weather or cutbacks in oil exports by OPEC – can be expected to bring up the economy's level of prices, but not necessarily result in an ongoing rise in the economy's price level. That said, if the goal is to control inflation, monetary policy might "forgive" these one-off changes in the price level (and thus the purchasing power of money) – and refrain from taking any (corrective) monetary policy action.

From this point of view, policymakers' interest in core inflation is driven by the notion that core inflation is a (much) more appropriate target for monetary policy, as core inflation measures (much) better the *underlying trend loss of the purchasing power of money* – which is actually driven by monetary developments – when compared with a measure of headline inflation (Bryan, Cecchetti, & Wiggins, 1997; Cecchetti, 1997).

In addition, economists and policymakers have an interest in the concept of core inflation as such a measure might track the component of overall price level changes that are expected to persist for a longer-term time horizon (compared with changes in the headline price level). Against this backdrop, it is hoped that measures of core inflation might help in forecasting near- and medium-term inflation developments (Blinder, 1997; Bryan & Cecchetti, 1993, 1994).

The point of departure for virtually all attempts to measure core inflation is the observation that *headline changes* in a price index between two periods contain a *trend component*, constituting core inflation, and a *temporary component*, reflecting transitory (non-persistent) effects:[1]

$$\Delta P_t^{headline} = \Delta P_t^{trend} + \varepsilon_t, \qquad (5.1)$$

where Δ denotes a change against the previous period (say, on a monthly or annual basis), P represents the price index, and ε is the i.i.d. error term. Temporary disturbances in headline inflation can be caused by, say, the effects of weather conditions (droughts or floods) on goods prices, while the trend component reflects persistent changes in headline inflation. Of course, the analytical challenge for calculating measures of core inflation is to isolate the trend from temporary factors (that is: *stripping away the noise in the data*).

Table 5.1 provides an overview about the most commonly used concepts in practise. For instance, *excluding selected items* (such as, for instance, food, energy and taxes) from the overall consumer price index is perhaps the most simple and common procedure for calculating a measure of core inflation, while measures such as a *trimmed mean CPI* and a *median CPI* are somewhat more sophisticated methods for measuring the underlying trend in inflation.

Figure 5.1 shows various measures of (core) inflation in the US from the late 1950s to May 2008. As can be seen, the inflation measures under review diverged in the short- to medium term, but tended to move on the "same wavelength" over the longer-term. Not surprisingly, measures of core inflation – that are (i) changes in the CPI excluding food and energy, (ii) changes in the CPI trimmed mean and (iii) changes in the median CPI – were (much) less volatile than changes in headline CPI.

---

[1] Roger (1998) contains a discussion of the different views on core inflation. Wynne (1999) also deals with this problem at length.

Table 5. 1   Some measures of core inflation

Method	Procedure
CPI *ex energy*	Excludes just energy from the overall CPI.
CPI *excluding food and energy*	Excludes food and energy from the CPI because, historically, the price changes of these items have been highly volatile and temporary phenomena.
CPI *ex 8 components*	Excludes just some, and not all, food and energy items from the index. That is, the less volatile food and energy items remain in the index.
Trimmed mean (Bryan & Cecchetti, 1994)	Removes from CPI inflation all large relative price changes in each month, with the set of excluded components changing from month to month. The trimmed mean excludes the percent changes in prices that rank among the smallest or largest (in numerical terms) changes for the month. Both small and large percent changes represent large price movements relative to the average for the month.
Median CPI (Bryan & Cecchetti, 1994)	Trims all but the midpoint of the distribution of price changes. If, for example, the overall price index included 100 components with equal relative importance, the median CPI would simply be the 50th largest percent change in price.

Source: Clark (2001, p. 7).

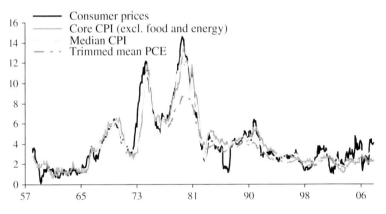

Fig. 5.1   Headline and core inflation measures in the US (%)
Source: Thomson Financial; US Bureau of Economic Analysis (BEA), Federal Reserve Bank of Dallas. – Monthly data. – Median CPI starts February 1964, trimmed mean CPI in January 1978.

5.1.3 Predictive Power of Core Inflation

One could argue that if core inflation reflects the underlying trend of headline infla-tion, today's core inflation may contain more information about the forthcoming

trend of headline inflation than total inflation itself (Laflèche & Armour, 2006). On
top of that, one could hold the view that any divergences between headline inflation
and core inflation will be temporary (and therefore corrected sooner or later): total
inflation may diverge from core inflation in the short-run, but not in the long-run.

A common way to test the hypothesis that divergences between headline inflation
and core inflation are temporary rather than persistent in nature is to estimate the
following equations (Hogan, 2001):

$$(\pi_{t+h} - \pi_t) = \alpha + \beta(\pi_t^{core} - \pi_t) + u_t, \tag{5.2}$$

and

$$(\pi_{t+h}^{core} - \pi_t^{core}) = a + B(\pi_t - \pi_t^{core}) + v_t, \tag{5.3}$$

where $\pi_{t+h} - \pi_t$ is the change in headline inflation from period t to $t + h$, $\pi_{t+h}^{core} - \pi_t^{core}$ is the change in core inflation, u and v are random i.i.d. error terms. If, for
instance, core inflation is above headline inflation, headline inflation must have been
affected by a specific shock that will be reversed later on. Headline inflation should
therefore be expected to increase in the future ($\beta > 0$), but core inflation should
remain unaffected ($B = 0$).

If the restrictions $\alpha = 0$ and $\beta = 1$ hold, Eq. (5.2) would become:

$$\pi_{t+h} = \pi_t^{core} + u_t. \tag{5.4}$$

Here, current core inflation would be an unbiased predictor of future headline
inflation. If this is the case, a rise in current core inflation (above the level that
is considered acceptable from the viewpoint of monetary policy) would actually
recommend a restrictive monetary policy, even if current headline inflation is still
low in the current period in order to prevent the latter from rising (too fast).

5.1.4 Role of Core Inflation in Monetary Policy

A number of central banks use core inflation for gauging the appropriate stance of
monetary policy (Table 5.2). However, measures of core inflation have their limitations. Core inflation can be misleading about what is really happening to the underlying inflation trend, as such a measure might not account for all types of shocks.
In fact, identifying the factors which drive changes in the overall CPI (in the future)
might be a rather difficult task.

For instance, a strong rise in oil prices might drive up headline inflation but may
leave measures of core inflation more or less unchanged. However, if employers
and employees agree on raising wages as a direct response to higher energy prices,
and firms can pass-through higher input costs onto goods prices, a measure of current core inflation might give a (highly) questionable indication of what is going to
happen with overall inflation in the future.

Table 5.2 Central banks' core inflation measures (examples)

Central bank	Core inflation measure	Use
Bank of Canada	CPI excluding food, energy and indirect taxes	Indicator*
Bank of England	Retail prices excluding mortgage interest rates	Target
US Federal Reserve Board	CPI excluding food and energy	Indicator
European Central Bank	HICP excluding food, energy and duties	Indicator
Reserve Bank of New Zealand	CPI excluding credit services	Indicator
Reserve Bank of Australia	Range of measures	Indicator
Swedish Riksbank	CPI excluding mortgage interest expenditure, indirect taxes, subsidies	Indicator
Bank of Thailand	CPI excluding raw food and energy	Target

*Published alongside headline measure and target range in Monetary Policy Report.
Source: Cutler (2001, p. 4).

In this context it should be noted that so far there is no unanimously agreed upon measure of core inflation. In fact, defining core inflation is actually an arbitrary undertaking. What is more, any divergence between headline inflation and core inflation should be, conceptually speaking, short-lived, given the idea that core inflation should strip away volatile relative price movements relative to headline inflation. That said, the choice for calculating a measure of core inflation has to be made on conceptual rather than empirical grounds.

Finally, the question about the *appropriate* measure of core inflation becomes (much) less pressing when inflation is not considered to be a variable which should determine changes in the stance of monetary policy. If, for instance, the central bank makes its interest rate setting policy dependent on so-called *intermediate variables* rather than on the final objective of policy – namely keeping inflation low –, the rationale for a distinction between headline and core inflation would be greatly diminished.

Headline and Core Inflation

Blinder (1997) identifies core CPI inflation as the durable or persistent component of the inflation of the economy's overall CPI. The persistent part of inflation should capture the on going element of price changes and therefore be correlated with future inflation, which is ultimately what policy makers care about (in a forward-looking policy framework). So how is headline and core inflation related?

Figure 5.2(a) shows annual changes in the US headline CPI and the core CPI (that is CPI excluding food and energy) for the period January 1980–September 2005, while Fig. 5.2(b) depicts the monthly changes in the price indices under review. Core inflation (on an annual as well as monthly basis) is – as one would expect – much less volatile than headline inflation.

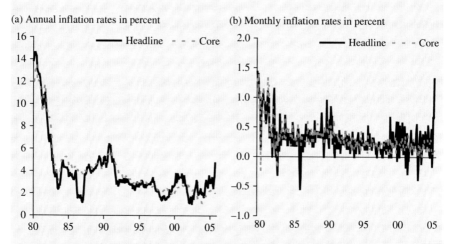

Fig. 5.2 US consumer price inflation, 1980–2005
Source: Bloomberg, own calculations.

The crucial question in this context is: Does core inflation "cause" headline inflation or is it the other way round? To shed some light on this question, one may take recourse to the concept of *Granger causality* (Table 5.3). Applying the Granger causality test (Granger, 1969), we make use of monthly changes

Table 5.3 Granger causality for US headline and core inflation

Null hypothesis	No. of observations	F-statistic	Probability
I. January 1980–September 2005[1]			
Lag = 12			
- Core does not Granger-cause headline	308	3.087	0.00040
- Headline does not Granger-cause core		1.119	0.34393
Lag = 2			
- Core does not Granger-cause headline	308	18.724	0.00000
- Headline does not Granger-cause core		0.9339	0.39412
II. January 1995–September 2005[2]			
Lag = 12			
- Core does not Granger-cause headline	129	1.286	0.23763
- Headline does not Granger-cause core		0.912	0.53723
Lag = 5			
- Core does not Granger-cause headline	129	1.302	0.26787
- Headline does not Granger-cause core		0.769	0.57390

Lag order of selection: [1] Sequential modified LR test statistic (LR) = 12, Final prediction error (FPE) = 12, Akaike information criterion (AIC) = 12, Schwarz information criterion (SC) = 2, Hannan-Quinn information criterion (HQ) = 2.
[2] LR = 12, FPE = 5, AIC = 5, SC = 1, HQ = 1; optimal lags not shown.
Source: Thomson Financial; own calculations.

in the price indices under review (which yield series that are stationary ($I(0)$) variables according to the ADF-tests).

For the period January 1980 to September 2005, one cannot reject the null hypothesis that headline inflation does not Granger cause core inflation, but the hypothesis is rejected that core does not Granger cause headline inflation. Therefore it appears that Granger causality runs from core to headline and not the other way round.

For the (much shorter) sub-sample January 1995 to September 2005, however, one has to reject both null hypotheses. In this sample period, a statistically clear-cut Granger causality between the variables cannot be identified; there is evidence that headline inflation Granger-causes core inflation and that core inflation Granger-causes headline inflation.

5.1.5 International Definitions of Price Stability

In recent years, many central banks have explicitly announced *numerical targets* for their objective of maintaining price stability. Generally speaking, the announcement of a numerical, or quantitative, target variable of monetary policy is believed to be a powerful instrument for anchoring market agents' inflation expectations and therefore providing a reliable point-of-departure for co-ordinating price and wage settings in the economy.

For instance, Orphanides and Williams (2003) analyse the effect of the announcement of a numerical inflation target in a model in which agents have imperfect knowledge about the structure of the economy, where market agents rely on adaptive learning. In such a framework, effective communication of an explicit inflation target (and strong emphasis on the primacy of price stability objective) by the central bank can indeed help anchoring inflation expectations and thereby reduce the costs associated with imperfect knowledge.

Table 5.4 gives an overview about the definitions of price stability as announced by central banks in major developed countries (Castelnuovo, Nicoletti-Altimari, & Rodriguez-Palenzuela, 2003, p. 10). While in all countries under review price stability is seen as the primary goal for monetary policy, actual practices of defining and announcing price stability targets vary across countries. In terms of the announced definitions of price stability, one can distinguish between the following arrangements:

- Central banks that have not announced a quantitative target;
- central banks that have provided a quantitative definition of price stability; and
- central banks that specified inflation targets.

The US Federal Reserve, for example, has refrained from explicitly announcing its definition of price stability. The former US Fed Chairman Alan Greenspan

Table 5.4 Inflation targets or definitions of price stability in selected industrial countries

Country	Indicator	Numercial value/definition/target	Ex ante horizon*	Accountability (ex post)*
1. Europe				
Euro area	HICP	– Below 2% (since 1999) – Definition of price stability	Medium term (not sole focus on inflation forecasts; prominent role for monetary developments, which exhibit a medium-term relation with prices)	Medium term
Memo item: Euro area countries prior to 1999¹				
Finland	CPI	– (about) 2% – Objective for 1998	Focus on two years ahead inflation forecast	
France	CPI	– Not exceeding 2% – Objective for 1998		Inflation in the year concerned
Germany	Not specified	– 2% before 1997 – 1.5–2% for 1998 "inflation norm"	Annual monetary target	Monetary developments in the year concerned
Italy	CPI	– Not exceeding 2% – Objective for 1998		
Spain	CPI	– 3.5–4% (January 1995 to 1996-Q1) – 3–3.25% (1996-Q1 to 1997-Q1) – below 3% during 1997 – below 2.5–2.75% for late 1997 – 2% for 1998		Inflation in the year concerned
European countries not in the euro area				
Norway	CPI Focus on core inflation	– 2½% with a fluctuation margin of ±1% – Target	Main focus on 2 years ahead inflation forecast	Timeless with escape clauses²

Table 5.4 (continued)

Country	Indicator	Numercial value/definition/target	Ex ante horizon*	Accountability (ex post)*
Sweden	CPI	– 2% with a fluctuation margin of ±1% (January 95–now) – Target	Main focus on 1–2 years ahead inflation forecast with possibility of extending horizon	Escape clauses[2]
Switzerland	CPI	– Below 2% – Definition of price stability	Medium term with a focus on three years ahead inflation forecast	Medium term
United Kingdom	RPIX (Retail Price Index excluding mortgage interest payments)	– 1–4% (October 92–June 97) – 2.5%[3] (June 97–now) – Target	Medium term (with a focus on two years ahead inflation forecasts)	Timeless with escape clauses[2]
2. Other OECD countries				
Australia	CPI	– 2–3%, (January 1993–now) – Target	Medium term	On average over the business cycle
Canada	CPI Focus on CPI excluding food energy, and the effect of indirect taxes	– Midpoint 2–4% (February 91–end-1992) – Midpoint 1.5–3.5% (end-92–mid 1994) – Midpoint 1–3% (December 1993 (revised)–February 2001; then renewed, and valid up to end-2006) – Target	Medium term with focus on to eight quarters ahead	
Japan	CPI	– No numerical value[4] – Qualitative definition of price stability	[5]	

(continued)

Table 5.4 (continued)

Country	Indicator	Numercial value/definition/target	Ex ante horizon*	Accountability (ex post)*
New Zealand	CPI (excluding credit services)	– 3–5%, range target (March 90–December 90) – 2.5–4.5%, range target (December 90–December 91) – 1.5–3.5% (December 91–December 92) – 0–2% (December 92–December 96) – 0–3% (December 96–November 2002) – 1–3% (November 2002–now) – Target	Medium term (prior to November 2002: main focus on 6–8 quarters ahead inflation forecast)	Medium term (future CPI between 1 and 3% on average over the medium term)
United States	Not specified Focus on several inflation measures	– No numerical value[6] – Qualitative definition of price stability		

[1] When adopting the broad economic policy guidelines in July 1995 the Ecofin indicated that a value of 2% would be the maximum rate of inflation compatible with price stability. This was reconfirmed in the 1998 guidelines.

[2] Timeless horizon implies that, in principle, the inflation target has to be maintained at all times. Escape clauses: when explicit contingencies under which a temporary deviation from price stability can be allowed are provided.

[3] If inflation as measured by the RPIX is more than one percentage point above or below the target of 2.5%, the Governor of the Bank of England needs to write an Open Letter of explanation to the Chancellor.

[4] The BoJ has defined price stability "as an environment where economic agents including households and firms can make decisions regarding such economic activity as consumption and investment without being concerned about the fluctuation of the general price level".

[5] On 19 March 2001 the BoJ announced that it will continue its policy of quantitative easing "until the CPI registers stably a zero percent or an increase year on year".

[6] The Chairman of the US Fed, Alan Greenspan, stated that "price stability obtains when people do not consider inflation a factor in their decisions".

Notes: * Ex ante horizon: the horizon over which the central bank will seek to pursue its objective or re-establish it after a shock has occurred. Accountability ex post: the time period over which the central bank is to be held accountable.

Source: Castelnuovo et al. (2003).

noted (2001): *"By price stability, however, I do not refer to a single number as measured by a particular price index. In fact, it has become increasingly difficult to pin down the notion of what constitutes a stable general price level".* [. . .]. *"For all these conceptual uncertainties and measurement problems, a specific numerical inflation target would represent an unhelpful and false precision. Rather price stability is best thought as an environment in which inflation is so low and stable over time that it does not materially enter into the decisions of households and firms."*

In contrast, the European Central Bank (ECB) has taken great efforts to give a precise definition of what is meant by price stability, the bank's primary objective as set out in the Maastricht Treaty. Right at the start of the monetary union, the ECB's Governing Council announced a quantitative definition of price stability: "Price stability is defined as a year-on-year increase in the Harmonised Index of Consumer Prices (HICP) for the euro area of below 2%." In May 2003, the ECB Governing Council clarified that, in the pursuit of price stability, it would aim to keep inflation below, but close to, 2% over the medium term, making deflation inconsistent with price stability. The explicit announcement of price stability shall make ECB monetary policy transparent, providing a clear and measurable yardstick against which the ECB can be held accountable, and provide guidance to the public for forming expectations of future price developments.

Table 5.4 shows that many central banks allow inflation to move within a predetermined band, or range. The announcement of a range – rather than a point – for acceptable inflation signals uncertainty surrounding future price developments and, most important, highlights the imperfect controllability of inflation at short-term horizons through monetary policy. In fact, a range for target inflation gives more flexibility to monetary policy to accommodate possible moderate and gradual variations (one-off shocks) in inflation over time (*escape clause*).

A possible drawback of an inflation range objective is that the bounds of the range may be seen as implying *hard edges*: it could lead market agents to believe that there are thresholds values which, if violated, trigger policy actions in a quasi-automatic fashion. A point objective may be preferable in this respect. Moreover, a point objective probably provides a more precise focal point for the formation of market agents' expectation as far as future (average) inflation is concerned when compared with an inflation range target.

Over short periods of time, deviations from a point inflation objective may be substantial, with potential negative effects on the credibility of the central bank, while a range enhances the likelihood that inflation will remain within the pre-announced objective. This latter view is not, however, uncontroversial. Bernanke (1999) argues that missing a range target (which may inevitably happen from time to time) may be perceived by the public at large as a more serious policy failure than missing a point target (which happens continuously and inevitably).

Moreover, under an inflation target range the public may focus excessively on whether current inflation is inside or outside of the pre-announced range, rather than on the magnitude of the deviations from the mid-point. This, in turn, may increase pressure on the central bank to act vigorously to keep inflation (at all times) within the pre-announced range. What may result is a monetary policy that induces excessive volatility in the real economy.

A reason that is often seen as supportive for an inflation range is the need to preserve *flexibility* in monetary policy. A range reflects a concern by central bank for macroeconomic stabilisation, in particular for avoiding excessive output and employment fluctuations when responding to threats to price stability.[2] Finally, it can be argued that a range might be preferable if there is the possibility that *optimal inflation* for the economy is unknown and, in addition, varies (gradually and moderately) over time.

5.1.6 Inflation Versus Price Level Objective

In mainstream economics there is a consensus that central banks should specify the objective of price stability by way of achieving low and stable inflation (*inflation targeting*). An alternative concept would be keeping the price level stable over time (*price level targeting*); for instance, Knut Wicksell (1898) was in a way, an early proponent of price level targeting. The objective of keeping inflation low and stable over time differs markedly from and keeping the price level stable over time (Carlstrom & Fuerst, 2002): Most importantly, while the former would ignore policy mistakes made in the past, the latter would not.[3] In fact, price level targeting policy would be even more ambitious than (a zero) inflation targeting.

Targeting zero inflation means that the central bank brings inflation to a halt, but it would leave the price level where it is at the end of any inflation period. In contrast, keeping the price level stable not only means that the central bank puts an end to inflation. It would *also* roll back any inflation of prices to some fixed target level. Price level targeting eradicates any upward drift of prices. As a result, a stable-price policy is (much) more stringent than a zero inflation policy.

Under an *inflation targeting* policy (with $\pi > 0$), the central bank allows the price level to rise over time. As can be seen from the left graph in Fig. 5.3, the price level would be allowed to increase from P_0 to P_1 and then further to P_2 at the pre-determined rate of π. If inflation in one year would rise by more than π, the price level would rise higher than desired. However, the central bank would not correct any policy error (*bygones are bygones*), but would increase the price level from an elevated level at the rate of π. Under a *price level targeting*, however, the central bank would keep the price level stable over time. That said, an increase in the price level from, say, P_0 to P_1 would have to be reversed (right hand side graph in Fig. 5.3).

---

[2]In this respect, there is clearly a link between the choice of a range and the horizon for the conduct of monetary policy.

[3]Regarding the problems related to a forward-looking inflation targeting, see Carlstrom and Fuerst (2001). According to the authors, some recent research indicates an inflation targeting can potentially leave money growth vulnerable to what is called "sunspot events" – extraneous and unpredictable events that set into motion self-fulfilling cycles of inflation expectations and realized inflation.

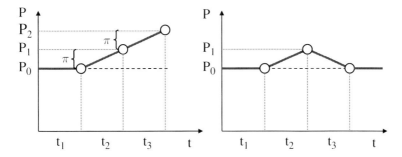

Fig. 5.3 Inflation targeting versus price level targeting

Why Not Go for a Declining Price Level?

One strong argument in favour of a falling rather than rising price level (that is a rising rather than falling value of money over time) is that such a regime would reflect the benefits of an advancing and growing economy: namely rising productivity. In fact, there are both *equality* and *efficiency* arguments for a declining price level.

The *equity* argument is that a drop in prices will make the gains in productivity available to everyone in the economy. If, however, the price level is kept stable, some members of society will not be able to share in the benefits of rising productivity because in practise not all people will be able to negotiate changes in money wages. To some extent, wage earners probably contribute to the increase in overall productivity; after all, at least some of an economy's efficiency gains can be expected to be a result of broader societal developments such as, for instance, education infrastructure and an enforced rule of law. Is it really plausible to assume that the downward drift in real costs is solely the fruit of those directly engaged in production? Yet it is only they who would benefit if the price level is not allowed to reflect productivity gains, that is working towards a rise in the purchasing power of money.

The *efficiency* argument is a bit more complex. The process of resource allocation operates most effectively if money costs and prices reflect (changes in) technological conditions. Here, relative prices change in response to changes in real costs. A stable price level in an environment of falling real costs would mean that relative prices might not reflect cost changes accurately.

Furthermore, price level stability tends to bring windfall profits where individual prices do not drop as productivity rises. This, in turn, could induce somewhat erroneous and wasteful decisions – as they typically occur when there is inflation. Finally, downward pressure on prices would force producers to step up efforts for improving efficiency.

However, a regime of a declining price level has attracted few, if any, supporters. The preference for a stable or slightly rising price level is actually based on three considerations:

- *First*, there is the view that, as a matter of economic justice, the gains in productivity ought to go to those actively and directly engaged in bringing them about.
- *Second*, the prospect of enjoying the fruits of cost reductions provides a powerful incentive to produce them. If the general price level is kept stable (rather trending downward in line with productivity gains), those producers who succeed in lowering costs benefit more than less efficient producers. The competitive pressure, of course, will operate to force individual prices down as costs fall. Nevertheless, in a regime of general price stability producers which contribute to progress by reducing input needed for a unit of output will not face the pressure of monetary forces that reduce the price level.
- And *third*, a declining price level, it is said, is bad for business psychology: Optimism may suffer when prices keep falling. For instance, those who hold inventory suffer losses; firms may delay expansion, modernisation, and the purchase of more advanced equipment if they expect the price to be lower in the future.[4]

Whatever the *balance of the pros and cons*, there is an institutional objection to pursuing a declining price level as an objective of monetary policy. Strongly organized groups do not wish for it, certainly not for the good and services they sell. Instead, they show a propensity for wage and price increases which exceed the gains in productivity. Usually, these lobby groups exert enough political influence to overweigh any politically feasible monetary pressures designed to translate falling real costs into declining prices for their output.

Consequently, if the price level were to fall, the less well organized groups would have to bear the great bulk of these effects. There is little reason to expect that these are the groups whose productivity increase is the highest. Nor is there a presumption that the relative position of those with weak bargaining strength would become any better than it is today. And how could the public ever reach agreement on the amount of the decline in prices to seek? In conclusion, there seems to be little chances that public opinion will support the policy objective of a declining price level.

---

[4]Of course, such a line of argument assumes "money illusion". In fact, if prices keep declining – and the downward trend can to some degree be anticipated – future nominal incomes would decline as well. Under perfect foresight, therefore, future real income and prices should not change.

5.1.7 Price Level Stability and Positive Supply-Side Shocks

In the following, the effects of *supply-side shocks* shall be analysed for a monetary policy regime under which the central bank (i) abstains from any market intervention and (ii) actively tries to keep the economy's price level stable (at all times).[5] The long-run equilibrium output is represented by a vertical neo-classical supply function. The short-term supply function is represented by a positively sloped *AS*-schedule in the price-level-income space, while the demand schedule is represented by a negatively sloped *AD*-curve.

5.1.7.1 Re (i): Supply Shock Without Policy Intervention

In equilibrium, output is Y^*, the price level P_0 and the interest rate i_0 (point A in Fig. 5.4). A *positive* supply side shock (triggered by, for instance, an increase in labour supply in the wake of an increasingly globalised economy) moves the *AS*-curve to AS'. As a result, output rises to $Y' (> Y)^*$, with the interest rate falling to $i_1 (< i_0)$ and the price level falling to $P_1 (< P_0)$ (point B); the decline in the price level moves the *LM*-curve to the right, from $\mathrm{LM}(M_0/P_0)$ to $\mathrm{LM}(M_0/P_1)$.

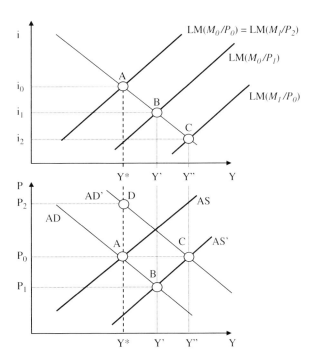

Fig. 5.4 Positive supply shock in the *IS-LM-* and *AD-AS*-system

---

[5]Of course, "negative supply shocks" could be analysed in the same framework.

With demand now exceeding supply ($Y^* < Y'$) and the central bank refraining from any intervention, the price level must rise from P_1 back to P_0 for bringing the economy back to its equilibrium output level. With the AS-curve returning to its vertical position, the rising price level forces the LM-curves back towards its initial location (point A).

5.1.7.2 Re (ii): Supply Shock with Policy Intervention

If the central bank wants to keep the price level at P_0, it would have to increase money supply from M_0 to M_1. As a result, the LM-curve moves to $LM(M_1/P_0)$ and the AD-curve to AD'.[6] The economy reaches point C, where the price level is back at P_0, the interest rate is i_2 ($< i_1 < i_0$) and output is Y'' ($> Y' > Y^*$).

With the AS-curve returning to its vertical position, however, the new equilibrium would now be point D, implying a price level of P_2 ($> P_1 > P_0$). To avoid the price level from rising above P_0, the central bank would have to reverse its initial increase in the money supply, that is reducing M_1 to M_0. The LM-curve would move back to the left, with the economy returning to point A.

5.1.7.3 Conclusion

A monetary policy that tries to keep the economy's price level stable when confronted with a (positive) supply-side shock leads to higher output volatility compared to a monetary policy of keeping the money supply constant. In contrast, if the central bank keeps the money supply unchanged in an environment of price shocks, output volatility would be lower and price level volatility would be higher when compared to the interventionist monetary policy approach.

A challenge for an interventionist monetary policy is, of course, the *problem of limited knowledge*: How do policy makers know if and when a (negative or positive) supply shock has a lasting or a temporary impact on the price level? In the first case, a policy response would be necessary, while in the second case the central bank could refrain from taking action. In addition, there is the question of the *time horizon* associated with the central bank's price level stability objective. If monetary policy tries to keep the price level stable at all times – that is trying to avoid even short-term fluctuations –, it would have to pursue an activist intervention policy, which might run the risk of increasing output and price level volatility.

5.1.8 Inflation Versus Price Level Targeting in a Simple Phillips Curve Model

The choice between price level and inflation targeting is often seen as involving a *trade-off* between low frequency price level uncertainty on the one side and high frequency inflation and output uncertainty on the other side (Svensson 2002). Price

---

[6]Note that the AD-schedule is defined as the equilibrium locus as implied by the LM-curve given a constant money supply.

level targeting thus offers the advantage of reduced long-term variability of the price level, but comes at the cost of increased short-term variability of inflation and output. Svensson (1997a) explains why a price level target can be used as a commitment mechanism to eliminate an *inflation bias* that results when a central bank tries to target an unrealistically high level of output.[7]

The model of Dittmar, Gavin, and Kydland (1999) builds on the model used by Svensson (1997b), representing an economy with sticky prices in which monetary policy can have real effects. The model has three elements: (i) a multi-period objective function for the central bank, (ii) an aggregate supply equation, and (iii) and rational expectations. The central bank's objective function is:

$$L = \sum_{t=0}^{\infty} \beta^t \left(\lambda y_t^2 + (\pi_t - \pi^*)^2 \right), \tag{5.5}$$

where y_t is the deviation of actual from target output (*output gap*) and $(\pi_t - \pi^*)$ is the deviation of inflation from its target. The central bank discounts future variability in the output and inflation gap by the factor β. λ relates the central bank's preference for output stability to its preference for inflation stability.

The economy is modelled as a short-run aggregate supply curve with persistence in the output gap:

$$y_t = \rho y_{t-1} + \alpha(\pi_t - \pi_t^e) + \varepsilon_t. \tag{5.6}$$

The introduction of a lagged output gap in this equation is important for comparing inflation and price level targeting. The time lag takes into account any frictions (rigid wages, taxes, etc.) that prevent instantaneous adjustment of output to unexpected changes in the price level. The slope of the short-run Phillips curve is given by α, which determines the response of the output gap to an unexpected inflation target deviation $(\pi_t - \pi_t^e)$.

Now assume the central bank follows *inflation targeting*. Under rational expectations we have: $\pi_t^e = E_{t-1}\pi_t$. The central bank's optimization problem is to find a trade-off between output and inflation variability. Minimizing this loss function – subject to the aggregate supply curve – leads to a rule for inflation that is contingent on the size of the output gap:

$$\pi_t^I = p_t^I - p_{t-1} = \pi^* - \frac{\alpha\lambda\rho}{1 - \beta\rho^2} y_{t-1} - \frac{\alpha\lambda}{1 - \beta\rho^2 + \alpha^2\lambda} \varepsilon_t \tag{5.7}$$

The subscript *I* indicates that the variable is determined by the inflation targeting rule, and p is the logarithms of the price level. Inflation is set in each period, and

---

[7]Gavin and Stockman (1991) explain why a society that cares about inflation (not price level) stability may still prefer a price level target if the source of inflation shocks is unobservable to the public.

is equal to the inflation target with countercyclical adjustments proportional to the lagged output gap and the error term.

If the central bank pursues *price level targeting*, the objective function is:

$$L = \sum_{t=0}^{\infty} \beta^t \left(\lambda y_t^2 + (p_t - p_t^*)^2 \right). \tag{5.8}$$

The central bank's price level targeting is therefore:

$$p_t^P = p_t^* - \frac{\alpha \lambda \rho}{1 - \beta \rho^2} y_{t-1} - \frac{\alpha \lambda}{1 - \beta \rho^2 + \alpha^2 \lambda} \varepsilon_t, \tag{5.9}$$

which gives the inflation rule as:

$$\pi_t^P = p_t^P - p_{t-1} = \pi^* - \frac{\alpha \lambda \rho}{1 - \beta \rho^2}(y_{t-1} - y_{t-2}) - \frac{\alpha \lambda}{1 - \beta \rho^2 + \alpha^2 \lambda}(\varepsilon_t - \varepsilon_{t-1}). \tag{5.10}$$

In Eq. (5.10) it is assumed that $p_t^* = \pi^* + p_{t-1}^*$. The superscript P indicates that the variable is determined by the price level targeting rule. According to (5.10), the central bank's reaction function rests on three elements. The first element is target inflation. The second and third elements are proportional, countercyclical adjustments to the change in the output gap from period $t-2$ to period $t-1$ and unexpected shocks from period $t-1$ to period t, respectively.

Now, what about the trade-offs between inflation and output under inflation targeting and price level targeting? Under inflation targeting, the bank sets inflation, π_t^I, as shown in Eq. (5.7). With rational expectations, the Phillips curve implies that the output gap can be expressed as:

$$y_t = \rho y_{t-1} + \frac{1 - \beta \rho^2}{1 - \beta \rho^2 + \alpha^2 \lambda} \varepsilon_t. \tag{5.11}$$

If the relative weight on output variability, λ, gets large, the coefficient on the error term converges to zero. If the variance of the output gap ε_t is σ_ε^2, Eq. (5.11) implies that the unconditional variance of the output gap is:

$$\sigma_y^2 = \frac{(1 - \beta \rho^2)^2}{(1 - \rho^2)(1 - \beta \rho^2 + \alpha^2 \lambda)^2} \sigma_\varepsilon^2. \tag{5.12}$$

If ε_t is uncorrelated with y_{t-1}, using the decision rule for π_t (namely Eq. (5.10)) to calculate the unconditional variance of inflation as:

$$\sigma_\pi^2 = \left(\frac{\alpha \lambda \rho}{1 - \beta \rho^2} \right)^2 \sigma_y^2 + \left(\frac{\alpha \lambda}{(1 - \beta \rho^2 + \alpha^2 \lambda)} \right)^2 \sigma_\varepsilon^2. \tag{5.13}$$

Simplifying yields a function only involving σ_ε^2:

$$\sigma_\pi^2 = \frac{\alpha^2 \lambda^2}{(1 - \rho^2)(1 - \beta\rho^2 + \alpha^2\lambda)^2} \sigma_\varepsilon^2. \tag{5.14}$$

Under price level targeting, the central bank sets inflation, π_t^P, as in Eq. (5.9). Under rational expectations (which implies: $p_t^e = E_{t-1}p_t$), we can write the output gap as:

$$y_t = \rho y_{t-1} + \frac{1 - \beta\rho^2}{1 - \beta\rho^2 + \alpha^2\lambda}\varepsilon_t. \tag{5.15}$$

The unconditional variance of the output gap as a function of λ is shown in Eq. (5.12). The unconditional variance of inflation, however, is given by:

$$\sigma_\pi^2 = \frac{2\alpha^2\lambda^2}{(1 + \rho)(1 - \beta\rho^2 + \alpha^2\lambda)^2} \sigma_\varepsilon^2. \tag{5.16}$$

A small λ makes the central bank to strive for keeping inflation and the price level close to its target. If the central bank places no weight on deviations of the output gap ($\lambda = 0$), the variance of the output gap is determined by persistence in the output gap, ρ, and the variance of technology shocks. Here, the bank optimizes by fixing inflation, or the price level, at its target in every period. There is no inflation variability, no inflation uncertainty, and a simple autoregressive process for the output gap. In contrast, if λ is high, the central bank would play the Phillips curve to control the output gap by letting inflation vary to a larger extent.

5.1.8.1 Some Simulations

To highlight the differences between the inflation/output variability trade-offs under inflation targeting and price level targeting one may take recourse to some simulations. The output gap variance and the inflation variance can be expressed as functions of the preference parameter λ while keeping the Phillips curve parameters unchanged. For a given λ, the bank's decision rules can be used to calculate an unconditional variance for both inflation and the output gap (a single point in Fig. 5.5). Varying λ will determine the location of the curve representing the trade off between σ_π^2 and σ_ε^2. In our example, the variance trade-off under the price level targeting regime lies everywhere below that for the inflation-targeting regime. In this case, society would prefer the price level targeting regime.

However, if the expressions for the unconditional variances of the output gap and inflation are examined, we can describe the position of these curves in terms of the autoregressive parameter, ρ, in the Phillips curve equation. Note that in either regime, if the bank places no weight on deviations of the output gap from its target, then the bank simply sets inflation, or the price level, equal to its target in every period. As the parameter λ approaches 0, therefore, the unconditional variance of

Output-inflation volatility trade-off

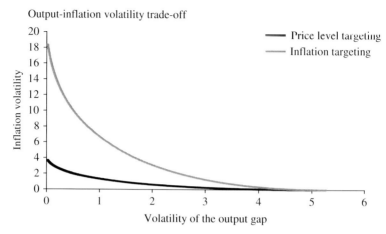

Fig. 5.5 Results of a simple simulation
Source: Dittmar et al. (1999), own calculations. – Parameters: $\alpha = 0.99$, $\beta = 0.50$ and $\rho = 0.90$.

inflation approaches 0, while the unconditional variance of output approaches that of the simple first-order autoregressive process $y_t = \rho y_{t-1} + \varepsilon_t$. Thus, the two trade-off curves intersect the σ_y^2-axis at the same point.

If the central bank's weight on deviations of the output gap from target becomes large, then the central bank sets the output gap equal to its target and manipulates the inflation rate to reach this goal. Thus, as the parameter λ approaches infinity, the variance of output approaches 0. The expressions for the unconditional variance of inflation show that as λ approaches infinity, the variance of inflation under an inflation targeting regime approaches $(\alpha^2(1 - \rho))^{-1}$, and the variance of inflation under a price level targeting regime approaches $2(\alpha^2(1 + \rho))^{-1}$. Therefore, assuming that the trade-off curves are convex for all parameter values, the trade-off curves under price level targeting regimes will lie below those for inflation-targeting regimes as long as:

$$2(\alpha^2(1 + \rho))^{-1} < (\alpha^2(1 - \rho))^{-1}, \tag{5.17}$$

or equivalently, $\rho > 0.5$. Note that the relative position of the trade-off curves does not depend on α, the slope of the short-run Phillips Curve, or on β, the central bank's discount factor.

We can gain some insight for the relative placement of the curves under the above condition by considering what happens as the auto-regressive parameter, ρ, approaches 1. As this happens, the output gap starts to behave more and more like a random walk. Under the inflation-targeting regime, the bank sets the inflation rate proportional to the output gap. Consequently, if the output gap behaves like a random walk, so will the inflation rate. Under the price level targeting regime, however, the bank sets the inflation rate proportional to the change in the output gap. Thus, even if the output gap becomes non-stationary as ρ approaches 1, the time path of the inflation rate remains stationary under such a regime.

5.1.8.2 Conclusion

If the output gap is relatively persistent, then targeting the *price level* rather than inflation results in a *better* monetary policy. Dittmar et al. (1999) present evidence from the G-10 countries showing that conventionally measured output gaps are highly persistent. The policy implication of assuming rational expectations and this Phillips curve model is therefore that central banks should set objectives for a price level, not inflation.

5.1.9 A Brief Look at Inflation History

Figure 5.6(a) and (b) show the price levels in the US and the UK for the period 1820–2007. In the total period under review, the US price level in the US rose 3,258%,

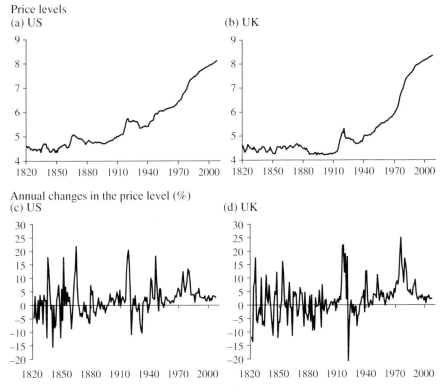

Fig. 5.6 Price levels and inflation in the US and UK, 1820–2007
Source: Global Financial Data; own calculations. US: BLS consumer price index; UK: retail price index. Price levels in natural logarithms $(1820 = \ln(100))$.

Table 5.5 Price level and inflation in the US and UK

| | 1821–2007 | | 1821–1913 | | 1974–2007 | |
	US	UK	US	UK	US	UK
Mean	2.0	2.2	0.7	−0.1	4.6	6.5
Median	1.9	2.1	0.0	−0.1	3.4	3.7
Maximum	21.8	25.0	21.8	17.4	13.3	25.0
Minimum	−15.5	−27.5	−15.5	−13.5	1.1	0.7
Standard deviation	5.7	6.9	5.9	6.0	3.2	5.8
No. of observations	*187*	*187*	*93*	*93*	*34*	*34*

Source: Global Financial Data; own calculations.

while in the UK the price level increase amounted to 4,072%. Figure 5.6(c) and (d) show annual changes in the price levels – typically interpreted as annual inflation in the currency areas under review.

Eyeballing the data suggests that under the gold standard era (which prevailed in much of the 19th century up to the start of World War II) price levels in the US and UK remained broadly stable (Table 5.5). Indeed, from 1821 to 1913 inflation was, on average, 0.7% p.a. in the US and slightly negative in the UK. In the period 1974–2007, the fiat paper money era, average inflation amounted to 4.6% p.a. in the US and 6.5% p.a. in the UK. What is more, inflation volatility (measured as the standard deviation of annual changes in the price levels) was somewhat higher under the gold standard compared with the period of fiat money. Most notably, the data review suggests that high inflation actually came when the (free market) gold standard was replaced by government run paper money standards.

5.2 Causes of Inflation

Generally speaking, inflation can be defined as *a continuous increase in the economy's overall price level*. Such a definition carries three important features. *First,* inflation is basically defined as a *process*. As such, inflation does not refer to a one-off increase in prices. It refers to an *ongoing* increase in prices over time.

Second, inflation is not just an ongoing increase in the price of a particular good but an ongoing rise in *all prices*. Of course, even if the economy's total level of prices is constant over time, some goods prices typically increase while other good prices decrease, in response to changes in supply and demand. There is inflation only when the prices of most, or all, goods and services are increasing over time.

Third, the above definition of inflation is *neutral* in the sense that it does not give a cause for ongoing increases in the economy's price level. For instance, an *excessive increase in the money supply* or *demand outstripping supply* may be held responsible for inflation. These so-called *causal definitions of inflation* usually result in the formulation of policies for fighting inflation.

In what follows, the causes of inflation as discussed in the field of monetary economics shall be reviewed in some more detail. To this end, the monetary inflation theory (Sect. 5.2.1), the non-monetary inflation theory (Sect. 5.2.2) and, as a special case, the fiscal theory of the price level (Sect. 5.2.3) will be considered.

5.2.1 Monetary Inflation Theory

The association between money growth and inflation is evidence for one of the principal monetarist propositions, as expressed by Milton Friedman's famous dictum: *inflation is always and everywhere a monetary phenomenon*. Sustained money growth in excess of the growth of output, adjusted for the trend change in income velocity of money, produces inflation. For ending inflation, money growth must be brought in line with the growth rate of real output, adjusted for the trend change in velocity. This line of thinking can be formalised by the *equation of exchange*.

5.2.1.1 The Equation of Exchange

The equation of exchange can be formalised as follows:

$$M \cdot V = Y \cdot P, \tag{5.18}$$

where M denotes the stock of money, V represents the income velocity of money, whereas Y and P stand for real output and the price level, respectively. Using logs (smaller case letters) and differences (Δ), the change in the price level can be rearranged to bring Δp to the left hand side:

$$\Delta p = \Delta m + \Delta v - \Delta y. \tag{5.19}$$

According to Eq. (5.19), inflation – defined as a persistent rise in the price level – would be a function of money growth, adjusted for the trend change in the income velocity of money, minus real output growth. If the income velocity of money is constant over time, Δv is zero, and inflation would emerge only if the stock of money grows in excess of output expansion.

(Neo-)Classical macroeconomis theory emphasizes a number of key long-run properties of the economy, including the *neutrality* (and even *superneutrality*) *of money* and the *quantity theory of money*. *Neutrality* holds if the equilibrium values of real variables are independent of the level of the money supply in the long-run. *Superneutrality* holds when the output growth rate is independent of the rate of growth in the money supply in the long-run.

The *quantity theory* of money holds that prices move proportionately to changes in the money supply, so that inflation is linked to money growth. It is assumed that the income velocity of money is constant and real output is always at its equilibrium level. Together, these propositions identify what monetary policy can achieve and what it cannot, delineating the responsibilities of central banks: Central banks have no effect on the level or growth rate of output in the long-run, but they do determine inflation.

Neutrality and Superneutrality of Money

Nowadays only few economists would dispute the *long-run neutrality of money*: namely that, in the long-run, an injection of additional money into the economy does not affect real magnitudes. A one-off permanent increase in the stock of money will (according to the quantity theory) increase prices eventually in proportion to the increase in the money stock, and all real variables will return to their original values. This is the *long-run neutrality of money hypothesis*.

According to the *long-run superneutrality of money hypothesis*, a permanent increase in the *growth rate* of the stock of money (from, say, 5–7% p.a.) does not affect real output in the long-run. Of course, there might be some effect on real magnitudes in the short-run, as market agents adjust their dispositions to the higher growth rate of money. But in the long-run the increased money supply growth rate does not have an impact on real magnitudes.

The discussion about neutrality of money refers to changes in the level of real output as a result of a one-off permanent rise in the money stock. However, real output in industrialized economies generally grows over time. A one-off shift in the level of real output would be a change from, say, US$100 to US$105, thereafter real output continues to grow at its previous rate. A permanent effect on the level of real output does not necessarily lead to a permanent effect on its growth rate. The key question to ask is: do permanent changes in the money growth affect the economic growth rate? Is money superneutral with respect to economic growth?

Figure 5.7 provides a very simple illustration of the hypotheses of neutrality and superneutrality of money in the US. It shows the relations between the stock of money (M1, MZM and M2) and real GDP, expressed in terms of annual growth rates and changes in annual growth rates, respectively. The period under review is 1959-Q1 to 2007-Q4.

The linear regression lines for M1 and MZM are basically horizontal, suggesting that there is little evidence for the money growth rate (changes in the money growth rate) to have a bearing on the growth rates of real GDP (changes in the GDP growth rate). For all relations under review the coefficients of determination are basically zero. In the case of M2, the relation to real GDP appears to be somewhat closer (a finding that might be attributable to the fact that M2 includes, in addition to the means of payments, wealth components which, in turn, could be related to real GDP).

In the short-run, changes in (the growth rate of) the stock of money might well affect (the growth rates of) real output. For instance, an increase in the money supply could induce (via the distortion of relative prices) a cyclical upswing. However, any such effects would be compensated for by the long-run effects such as a decline in real output as a consequence of the collapse of a monetary induced boom.

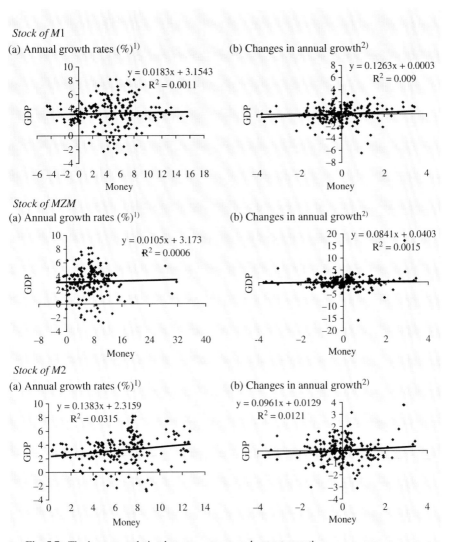

Fig. 5.7 The long-run relation between money and output growth
Source: Federal Reserve Bank of St. Louis, Thomson Financial, own calculations. – Period: 1959-Q1 to 2007-Q4. – 4th differences of log variables, multiplied with 100.

Finally, it should be noted that if money growth causes inflation, and if inflation exerts a negative impact on investment and total production, then (ongoing) shocks to the money stock, or to the money growth rate, can be expected to be detrimental for the investment, employment and the real economy. In such a case, the long-run superneutrality of money should not hold.

Source: In this context see, for instance Bullard (1999), Dwyer and Hafer (1999), King and Watson (1997), Lucas (1996), McCandless and Weber (1995), Weber (1994).

Milton Friedman's famous dictum, namely that inflation is always and everywhere a monetary phenomenon, rests on a number of assumptions imposed on Eq. (5.18). *First*, and in line with the (neo-)classical school of economics, real output is independent from the money supply. It is solely determined by the economy's endowment (that is labour, capital and technological progress). And if left on its own, output and employment will always be in equilibrium.[8]

Second, given the time needed for an economy to adjust to new data/developments, the income velocity of money may not be numerically constant, but may, in the short- to medium-term, oscillate around a certain trend value. As a result, an increase in the stock of money may not push up the price level immediately but will cause inflation in the long-run – reflecting the proposition of long-run neutrality of money, one of the central tenets of Friedman's interpretation of the quantity theory.

Third, money supply M is assumed to be exogenous and thus subject to the full control of the central bank: in a world in which only government controlled money circulates, it is indeed the government, or its agent, the central bank, that determines the outstanding stock of payment.

And *fourth*, Friedman's monetarism implies that changes in the stock of money are responsible for changes in nominal income: the *causality* runs from MV to PY. However, Friedman did not specify to which extent, in the short- to medium-run, real output and/or prices would be affected by an increase in money supply. As output is assumed to expand around potential, and the income velocity is a constant function of a number of variables, a persistent rise of the stock of money in excess of output should lead to inflation, though.

Friedman's Constant Money Growth Plan *Versus* Hayek's Competition of Currency Concept

To Milton Friedman, the power assigned to central bank decision makers – namely the ability to change the stock of money at will at any one time – is simply unacceptable. He does not dispute that a system in which the central bank has full autonomy over the money supply might be beneficial on some occasions. However, to Friedman it is irresponsible for a monetary system to be exposed to policymakers' mistakes (excusable or not) and their

---

[8]Note that Friedman's refusal to assume that output is constant or growing at a constant rate is one of the major pieces of evidence that his 1956 theory is not a restatement of the quantity theory.

(potentially) disastrous consequences. The examples of policy mistakes cited by Friedman include: the triggering of the Great Depression in the late-1920s and, more recently, the accelerating inflation in the 1970s (*Great Inflation*), both of which Friedman ascribes to policy mistakes made on the part of the US Federal Reserve Board.

Friedman recognises that, in practice, actual monetary policy decisions depend on numerous factors, such as bureaucratic needs, personal beliefs and values of the persons in charge, current and expected developments in the economy, and the political pressures to which the decision makers are exposed. In order to avoid policy mistakes and/or the misuse of power, Friedman recommends making the central bank politically independent and, in addition, subject monetary policy makers to a strict rule (*Chicago rule*): central banks action should, by a legal act, be confined to expanding the money supply at a constant rate over time (by, say, 3–5% p.a.) – a mandate that he believes should be enshrined in the country's constitution.[9] Friedman's famous *k-percent rule*, if implemented, would reduce the central bank's discretionary scope to zero;[10] and as central banks could no longer influence the money supply at will, there would be less risk for the economy falling victim to the consequences of a great monetary catastrophe.

Friedman does not oppose a commodity-based standard per se.[11] He believes that even a monetary commodity standard entails risks to a free market society and, as such, would not provide a solution to the problem of establishing a reliable money framework. According to Friedman, historically the gold standard has seldom existed as a pure system and, when it has, only for relatively short periods of time. Quite often, fiduciary money elements (such as notes issued in excess of a banks' gold holdings) entered the system. And once this had happened, it was difficult to avoid government meddling in monetary matters, with negative consequences for the value of the currency. For instance, the acceptance of fiduciary money as the means of payment makes the issuance of its own money virtually irresistible for the government.

Friedrich August von Hayek shared Friedman's deep scepticism regarding the threats that an ill-designed monetary system pose to a free society Hayek (1976): "(. . .) practically all governments of history have used their exclusive power to issue money in order to defraud and plunder the people."

---

[9]See Friedman (1960, pp. 77–99).

[10]In fact, such constant money growth rule had been advocated by Angell (1933) and Warburton (1952). See also Lee and Wellington (1984).

[11]Referring to the costs of using the gold standard, Friedman (1994, p. 41), Money Mischief, wrote: "While the welfare effects of the gold discoveries were almost surely negative, *it does not follow that the existence of a gold standard – or, more generally, a commodity standard – is a mistake and harmful to society.*"

He feared that the destruction of money "(...) is the inevitable result of a policy which regards all the other decisions as data to which the supply of money must be adapted so that the damage done by other measures will be as little noticed as possible. In the long run, however, such a policy makes governments the captives of their own earlier decisions, which often force them to adopt measures that they know to be harmful" (Hayek, 1960, p. 333).

Echoing the warnings Ludwig von Mises made back in 1912 in *The Theory of Money and Credit*, Hayek concluded that (Hayek, 1960, p. 333): "(...) the inflationary bias of our day is largely the result of the prevalence of the short-term view, which in turns stems from the great difficulty of recognising the more remote consequences of current measures, and from the inevitable pre-occupation of practical men, and particularly politicians, with the immediate problems and the achievements of near goals."

In his Hobart Paper Special No. 70, Hayek outlines his reasoning for having a competition of currencies, issued by private agents, rather than a state monopoly of money: "The purpose of this scheme is to impose upon existing monetary and financial agencies a very much needed discipline by making it impossible for any of them, or for any length of time, to issue a kind of money substantially less reliable and useful than the money of any other. As soon as the public became familiar with the new possibilities, any deviation from the straight path of providing an honest money would at once lead to the rapid displacement of the offending currency by others. And the individual countries, being deprived of the various dodges by which they are now able temporarily to conceal the effects of the actions by 'protecting' their currency, would be constrained to keep the value of their currencies tolerably stable."[12]

In sum, when it comes to establishing a monetary framework compatible with his vision of a free society, Friedman thinks it would be best to assign the money supply monopoly to the government. At the same time, he calls for a politically independent central bank to do the job, and he believes that the central bank should be stripped of all discretionary power. Hayek, in contrast, recommends a diametrically opposed and what many regard as a rather radical solution, namely the complete abolition of the government's monopoly over the issue of money, paving the way towards full competition in its supply by the private sector. So one may say that even though Friedman's plan does not seek to expel the government out of monetary affairs altogether, it actually indicates a much greater scepticism vis-à-vis government interference in the market compared to Hayek's proposal.

5.2.1.2 Money Growth and Inflation

The idea that persistent changes in the price level are associated with changes in the supply of money is one of the oldest and most established propositions in

---

[12]Quoted from Issing (1999)

economics. An early and influential analysis appeared almost 250 years ago: David Hume's 1752 essay *Of Money* analyzes the link between increases in money and the subsequent increase in prices. Economists since Hume repeatedly have observed that prolonged increases in prices are associated with increases in the nominal quantity of money.

In more recent analyses, Lucas (1980), Dwyer and Hafer (1988), McCandless and Weber (1995), Dewald (1998), Rolnick and Weber (1995, 1997), Dwyer & Hafer (1998) and others have found that changes in the nominal quantity of money and the price level are closely related. In fact, some economists have concluded from this evidence that the problem of controlling inflation has been successfully solved (Lucas, 1986): In view of the strong link between money growth and inflation a straightforward strategy for maintaining low inflation would be choosing the growth rate of money that corresponds to the desired long-run rate of inflation.

More recently, Dwyer and Hafer (1999) use data including observations on money growth relative to income and inflation for all countries for which data are available. The study examines data for two five-year periods, namely 1987–1992 and 1992–1997. The authors identify a positive proportional relationship between the price level and money relative to real income. The relation between inflation and money growth is evident in the data over long periods of time and over shorter periods for many countries.

In his essay *No money no inflation*, Mervin King (2002) concludes: "Evidence of the differences in inflation across countries, and changes in inflation over time, reveal the intimate link between money and prices. Economists and central bankers understand this link, but conduct their conversations in terms of interest rates and not the quantity of money. In large part, this is because unpredictable shifts in the demand for money mean that central banks choose to set interest rates and allow the public to determine the quantity of money which is supplied elastically at the given interest rate."

Despite its long history and substantial evidence, the predicted association between money growth and inflation remains disputed. Some economist may even say that money growth is largely, if not entirely, irrelevant for inflation. One possible explanation for this viewpoint is that the empirical relationship between money growth and inflation tends to hold only over time periods that are so long that the relationship is said to be uninformative for practitioners and policymakers, who are more concerned about inflation next month or next year.

Indeed, one should not expect that changes in money supply have an immediate effect on inflation. Taking into account adjustment processes, it may well take quite some time for the change in the money supply to make itself felt in price changes. However, *how long is the time horizon over which the link between money growth and CPI inflation emerges*? To answer this question, the relationship between money growth and inflation shall be examined across different time horizons (Fitzgerald, 1999).

To start with the US, the relations between annual M2 growth and CPI inflation from January 1970 to August 2007 are shown in Fig. 5.8(a)–(d). From eye-balling the series, it becomes obvious that movements in money growth have no

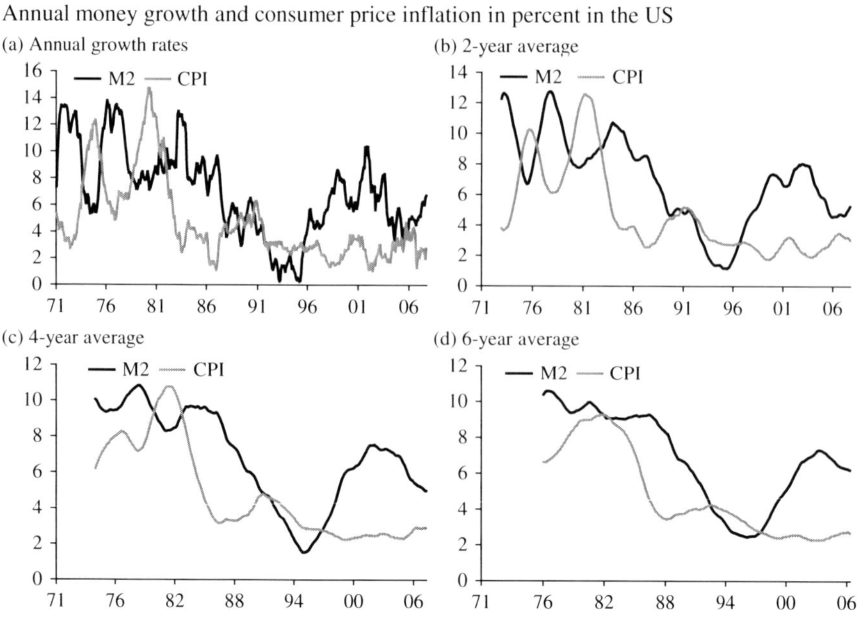

Annual money growth and consumer price inflation in percent in the US

(a) Annual growth rates

(b) 2-year average

(c) 4-year average

(d) 6-year average

Fig. 5.8 Money growth and inflation in the US
Source: ECB, Thomson Financial, Bloomberg; own calculations. – Period: January 1971–August 2007. – The simple correlation coefficient for contemporaneous relation is 0.27, for 2-year averages 0.38, for 4-year averages 0.61 and for 6-year averages 0.70.

clear relationship with CPI inflation over short periods. However, the relations, measured by simple correlation coefficients, are positive in all periods under review, and increase with a lengthening of the averaging periods under review. While money growth tended to correspond with the direction of CPI inflation, it did not always correspond to the level of forthcoming CPI inflation, though.

Turning to the *euro area*, Fig. 5.9 shows the relationships between annual money growth, measured as annual change in the stock of M3, and annual CPI inflation for the period January 1971 to August 2007. As is the case in the US, both series exhibit a positive relation in the periods under review, that is higher money supply growth was accompanied by higher CPI inflation and vice versa. The relation seems to be most pronounced when using gliding 6-year averages of growth rates, with the correlation coefficient reaching 0.93. Again, at a short-term horizon, changes in M3 did not show a close relation to CPI changes.

Like in the US and the euro area, the relationship between money and CPI inflation *in Japan* was positive (Fig. 5.10): A rise (decline) in money growth was accompanied by an increase (fall) in CPI inflation. What is more, the relationship between money growth and CPI inflation increased with the length of the averaging period under review. The strongest co-movement was for a 6-year average, with the correlation coefficient reaching 0.90.

Annual money growth and consumer price inflation in percent in the euro area

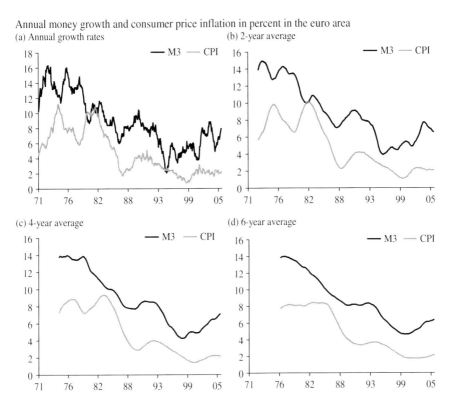

Fig. 5.9 Money growth and inflation in the euro area
Source: ECB, Thomson Financial, Bloomberg. Period: January 1971–July 2005, monthly data; own calculations. – The simple correlation coefficient for contemporaneous relation is 0.78, for 2-year averages 0.83, 4-year averages 0.90 and 6-year averages 0.93.

The analyses suggest that a relatively close relationship between money growth and CPI inflation existed over longer-term horizons in the countries under review. These findings should serve as a reminder that ignoring money growth for too long a period may be politically unwise. While money growth may not provide a particularly useful guide for short-run policymaking, empirical evidence suggests that the long-run trend of CPI inflation appears to be determined by the long-run growth rate of the money supply. That said, it would be quite hard to challenge conventional wisdom, namely that inflation is a monetary phenomenon, and that central banks should always keep an eye on the long run (see, for instance, Pill & Rautanen, 2006).

Of course, a reliable relation between money supply growth and CPI inflation hinges on a (trend) stable velocity of money. The US Fed has found the short-run relationship between money growth and inflation too unreliable for money growth

Annual money growth and consumer price inflation in percent in Japan

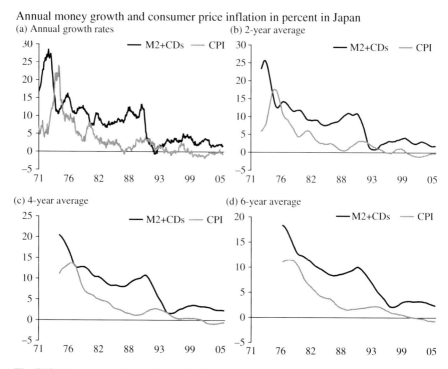

Fig. 5.10 Money growth and inflation in Japan
Source: ECB, Thomson Financial, Bloomberg. – Period: January 1971–July 2005; own calculations. – The simple correlation coefficient for contemporaneous relation is 0.59, for 2-year averages
0.72, 4-year averages 0.87 and 6-year averages 0.90.

to merit much attention. In the Humphrey–Hawkins Report presented 23 February 1999, the Fed stated: "Given continued uncertainty (...), the [Federal Reserve
Open Market] Committee would have little confidence that money growth within
any particular range selected for the year would be associated with the economic
performance it expected or desired."

There are two aspects which may reconcile the findings of a close long-run
relationship between money growth and CPI inflation and policymakers' (frequent) lack of interest in money growth rates. *First*, most studies that report a
close connection in the long-run use data for many countries, and it is sometimes noted that the finding appears to rely heavily on the presence of countries
with high rates of money growth and CPI inflation. It is much less clear that a
close relationship exists within countries with relatively small changes in money
growth.

Second, even if a close relationship between money growth and inflation exists in
the long-run, that relationship largely disappears when one considers relatively short
time horizons such as a year or a quarter. In conducting monetary policy, central
banks monitor and seek to influence CPI inflation and other economic variables

over annual and quarterly intervals. A close relationship between money growth and inflation that exists only over long time horizons appears therefore to be of little use to policymakers trying to control inflation over the next quarter or next year or so.

5.2.1.3 The Information Content of Money in a Low Inflation Environment

de Grauwe and Polan (2005) are among the critics of Friedman's dictum and the empirical results mentioned above. Using data for 165 countries and 30 years, they show that the strength of the correlation depends critically on the *level* of inflation. They report that regressions of inflation on money growth are significant only for inflation above 17.4% p.a., and so de Grauwe and Polan conclude that central banks should pay no attention to monetary developments as long as inflation is low or moderate.

However, such a conclusion would be premature, as shown by von Hagen and Hofmann (2003). Let us assume that the long-term price level, p^*, is a function of the trend level of money, m^* (small letter represent logarithmic values):

$$p_t^* = m_t^*. \tag{5.20}$$

What is more, actual price and money levels are assumed to fluctuate randomly around their trend values:

$$p_t = p_t^* + \mu_t \text{ and} \tag{5.21}$$

$$m_t = m_t^* + \xi_t, \tag{5.22}$$

where μ and ξ represent random shock terms.

Moreover, money supply grows with the drift term π^* and a random shock term ε:

$$\Delta m_t = \pi_t^* + \varepsilon_t. \tag{5.23}$$

Now assume that the two temporary level shocks μ and ε are uncorrelated. In this case the correlation between average inflation and average money supply growth over T periods is:

$$\rho_T = \frac{var(\varepsilon)}{\sqrt{var(\varepsilon) + 2T^{-1}var(\xi)}\sqrt{var(\varepsilon) + 2T^{-1}var(\mu)}}. \tag{5.24}$$

This representation yields two major conclusions. *First*, the correlation coefficient increases with T, over which the averages are computed: temporary level shocks wash out as the period under review increases. *Second*, periods characterized by a series of large money growth shocks, ε, will be accompanied by high correlation between money growth and inflation; when money growth shocks are small, the correlation becomes weaker. Thus, if declining and low money growth rates are accompanied with a decline in money growth volatility, the correlation coefficient for money growth and inflation becomes weaker.

Now suppose that the central bank follows a constant money supply rule in the sense that there are no longer any shocks to money growth. Under such a regime, the correlation between money growth and inflation would disappear altogether. However, trend inflation is determined by π^*, the trend money growth rate set by the central bank. Obviously, to conclude that money growth has no information about inflation would be completely unwarranted in this situation – and the finding of a low correlation coefficient would be misleading when it comes to analysing the role of money for inflation.

5.2.1.4 The Concept of "Core Money" and "Core Inflation"

Neumann and Greiber (2004) stress the role of *core money* for inflation. Core money is defined as the *excess of permanent nominal money over permanent real money demand*; the latter is equal to permanent output growth adjusted for the long-run income elasticity of money demand. A key characteristic of the core money concept is that short-run fluctuations of money growth, generated by the accommodation of money demand shocks, are eliminated as they do not invoke inflation.

In their approach, Neumann and Greiber use a standard Phillips curve which is combined with adaptive inflation expectation formation. Also, a link between inflation expectations and the growth of the money stock is established. The approach is in line with the quantity theory of money in the sense that a one-to-one long-run relation between core money growth and inflation exists.

To outline the concept, let us start with an expectation augmented Phillips curve (Neumann, 2003):

$$\pi_{t+1} = \pi_{t+1,t}^e + \beta(y_t - \bar{y}_t) + \varepsilon_{t+1}, \tag{5.25}$$

where π_{t+1} represents actual inflation in $t+1$, $\pi_{t+1,t}^e$ is expected inflation in period t for period $t+1$, y_t is the log of real output and $y_t - \bar{y}_t$ is the output gap; ε_{t+1} is the i.i.d. white noise term.

According to the Phillips curve, there are two channels for money to affect inflation. The first channel links actual inflation with expected inflation, driven by money growth. The second channel allows nominal money shocks as well as real demand shocks to affect future inflation. However, the latter channel cannot affect the inflation trend, as the output gap is zero on average.

Assume that inflation expectations for period $t+1$ follow an adaptive model:

$$\pi_{t+1}^e = \bar{\pi}_t + (1 - \alpha)(\pi_t - \bar{\pi}_t) \text{ or, equivalently,} \tag{5.26a}$$

$$\pi_{t+1}^e = \alpha \bar{\pi}_t + (1 - \alpha)\pi_t, \tag{5.26b}$$

where $0 \leq \alpha < 1$. Expected inflation in $t+1$ equals the expected core rate observed in t, $\bar{\pi}_t$, plus a fraction of transitional inflation in t.

Core inflation is modelled as a function of the equilibrium in the money market. The stock of money can be decomposed in a long- and a short-run component:

$$m_{r,t} = m_{r,t}^l + m_{r,t}^s, \text{ with} \tag{5.27a}$$

$$m_{r,t}^l = \lambda_l \bar{y}_t - \gamma_l (\bar{r}^l - \bar{r}^s) \text{ and} \tag{5.27b}$$

$$m_{r,t}^s = \lambda_s (y_t - \bar{y}_t) - \gamma_s (i_t^l - i_t^s) + v_t. \tag{5.27c}$$

Equation (5.27b) shows the long-run component of money demand. Here, the opportunity cost of money holdings are captured by the spread between long- and short-term real interest rates $\bar{r}^l$ and $\bar{r}^s$, respectively. Equation (5.27c) states the short-term demand for real money. It is assumed to be more volatile than the long-run demand function, due to stochastic demand shocks, v_t, cyclical deviations of actual from potential output ($y_t - \bar{y}_t$), and the nominal interest rate differential ($i_t^l - i_t^s$).

Similarly, the log of the nominal stock of money can decomposed into a permanent, or trend, component, $\bar{m}$, and a transitory component, $\bar{s}$:

$$m_t = \bar{m}_{t-1} + \Delta \bar{m}_t + s_t. \tag{5.28}$$

The permanent component of money growth, $\Delta \bar{m}$, represents the central bank's envisaged trend money growth rate. The transitory component reflects the central bank's response to temporary short-run events – for example, the partial or full accommodation of money demand shocks, v_t, – as well as discretionary innovations.

Combining money demand (5.27a) and money supply (5.27c), the core price level is the price level that equilibrates the permanent components of the supply of and demand for money:

$$\bar{p}_t = \bar{m}_t - \lambda_l \bar{y}_t + \gamma_l (\bar{r}^l - \bar{r}^s). \tag{5.29}$$

Assuming that ($\bar{r}^l - \bar{r}^s$) is stationary, the change in the core price level is:

$$\bar{\pi}_t = \Delta \bar{m}_t - \lambda_l \Delta \bar{y}_t. \tag{5.30}$$

The core rate of inflation responds to the difference between permanent nominal money growth and the permanent component of real money demand growth.

To derive the solution for inflation, it remains to combine (5.25), (5.26b), and (5.30), which yields:

$$\pi_{t+1} = \alpha (\Delta \bar{m}_t - \lambda_l \bar{y}_t) + (1 - \alpha)\pi_t + \beta(y_t - \bar{y}_t) + \varepsilon_{t+1}. \tag{5.31}$$

The first expression on the right hand side is core money growth – the excess of permanent nominal money growth over permanent real money demand growth. The long-run equilibrium the impact of core money on inflation should be unity. However, due to adaptive expectations in the short-run core money growth affects next period's inflation with a coefficient of less than unity. Thus it takes time until a change in the core rate of money growth is fully transformed into inflation, and the smaller α is, the longer it takes. The output gap provides a potential source for transitional inflation.

(Core) Money Growth and CPI Inflation

To analyse the impact of core money on CPI inflation, the well-known trans-action equation can be transformed as follows:

$$\Delta m + \Delta v = \Delta y + \Delta p \tag{5.32}$$

where $m =$ stock of money, $v =$ income velocity, $y =$ real output and $p =$ price level; small case letters represent logarithms and Δ represents first differences. Solving Eq. (5.32) for p yields:

$$\Delta p = \Delta m + \Delta v - \Delta y. \tag{5.33}$$

Assuming that the trend change of v is zero or constant, and that, in the long-run, y is a positive constant, one can write:

$$\Delta p = \Delta m, \tag{5.34}$$

that is the change in the stock of money determines the change in the price level. That said, an empirically testable equation would be:

$$\Delta p_t = \beta_0 + \beta_1 \Delta m_t + \varepsilon_t, \tag{5.35}$$

where ε is the i.i.d. error term. Note that under the assumptions made above, the constant β_0 would reflect changes in income velocity and output.

Figure 5.11 shows quarterly changes in the euro area consumer price index, the stock of M3, and a measure of M3 core for the period 1970-Q2 to 2007-Q2. The latter was determined by applying the Hodrick-Prescott-Filter to quarterly changes in the stock of M3.

Table 5.6 shows the results of analysing the long-run relation between changes in CPI inflation and changes in the stock of M3. They suggest that there is a stable, long-run relation between changes in the CPI and changes in M3 and M3 core; that is, the variables under review are on the same *wavelength*, or: they are *cointegrated*.

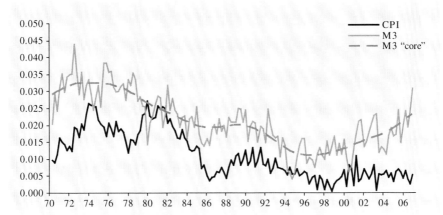

Fig. 5.11 Euro area CPI, M3 and M3 "core"; *Source:* Thomson Financials, ECB; own calculations. – The changes represent first differences of log levels

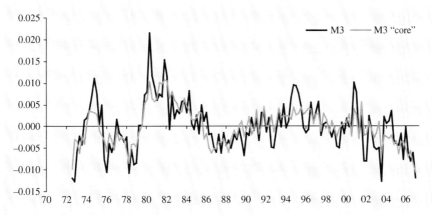

Fig. 5.12 Residuals of the long-run equation; *Source:* Thomson Financial, ECB; own calculations.

A 1% rise in M3 was associated with a 0.89% rise in CPI inflation, on average, while a 1% rise in M3 core led to a 0.96% rise in the CPI. Figure 5.12 shows the deviations of actual quarterly CPI inflation from the long-term path determined by M3 and M3 core growth, respectively. If the residual moves above (below) the zero line, CPI inflation can be expected to decline (rise) in the periods ahead. As from around 2001, money supply growth had signalled rising CPI inflation in future periods.

In Table 5.6, the first difference equations show that the error correction terms (*ect*) of the long-run relations prove to be statistically significant at standard levels for explaining changes in CPI inflation. This suggests that it is the change in money that drives CPI inflation (rather than the other way round). In fact, the results correspond quite nicely to one of Friedman's central hypothesis, namely that the growth of the stock of money determines the loss of purchasing power of money.

Table 5.6 The relation between CPI inflation and money growth

	I. Using M3	II. Using M3 core
I. Lag lengths (quarters)		
AIC	8	8
SIC	4	4
HQ	8	8
Chosen lag	8	8
II. Johansen test		
Trace statistic $r = 0$	16.787*	19.973*
Critical value 0.05	15.595	15.495
Prob.	(0.032)	(0.001)
Max-Eigen statistic $r = 0$	21.539*	16.006*
Critical value 0.05	15.495	14.26
Prob.	(0.005)	(0.026)
III. Long-run relations		
$\Delta \ln CPI_t$	1.000	1.000
$\Delta \ln M3_t$	−0.897	...
	(0.12)	
$\Delta \ln M3\,core_t$	...	−0.963
		(0.12)
Constant	0.007	0.009
IV. Error correction equations		
	$ect_{t-1,1}$	$ect_{t-1,2}$
$\Delta\,(\Delta \ln M3_t)$	−0.007	...
	[−0.08]	
$\Delta\,(\Delta \ln M3\,core_t)$	...	0.000
		[1.56]
$\Delta\,(\Delta \ln CPI_t)$	−0.200	−0.256
	[−4.04]	[−3.55]
R2	0.547	0.531

Legend: Period under review: 1970-Q1 to 2007-Q2. – *AIC* = Akaike information criterion, *SC* = Schwarz information criterion, *HQ* = Hannan-Quinn information criterion. – (.) standard errors, [.] *t*-values. – ln = natural logarithm, Δ = first difference, M3 = stock of M3, M3 core = filtered M3, CPI = consumer price index.
Source: Thomson Financial, ECB; own calculations.

5.2.1.5 Cagan's Model of Prices, Money and Hyperinflation

In his paper, Cagan (1956) studied hyperinflation in various countries (Austria, Germany, Hungary, Poland and Russia after World War I, and Greece and Hungary after World War II). As a stochastic discrete-time version of Cagan's model, the demand for real money balances M/P can be defined as a function of expected future inflation (Obstfeld and Rogoff, 1999, p. 515):

$$m_t^d - p_t = -\eta E_t(p_{t+1} - p_t), \tag{5.36}$$

where $m = \log M$, $p = \log P$, and η is the semi-elasticity demand for real balances with respect to expected future inflation. The model assumes rational expectations in the sense of Muth (1961). Cagan argues that in a hyperinflation, expected future inflation becomes the sole factor determining real money demand; the Cagan model is thus a special case of the *LM*-function.

According to the Fisher parity under perfect foresight, the nominal interest rate is the real interest rate plus inflation:

$$1 + i_{t+1} = (1 + r_{t+1})P_{t+1}/P_t. \tag{5.37}$$

The nominal interest and expected inflation will move in lockstep if the real interest rate is constant. This explains Cagan's simplification of making money demand a function of expected inflation.

Let us now assume that actual money demand meets supply ($m_t = m_t^d$). That said, the equilibrium is:

$$m_t - p_t = -\eta E_t(p_{t+1} - p_t). \tag{5.38}$$

Equation (5.38) is a first order stochastic difference equation, explaining the price level dynamics in terms of the money supply (which is the *forcing variable*). Assuming *non-stochastic perfect foresight*, one can solve Eq. 5.38 as:

$$m_t - p_t = -\eta(p_{t+1} - p_t). \tag{5.39}$$

Solving (5.39) for today's price level yields:

$$p_t = \frac{1}{1+\eta}m_t + \frac{\eta}{1+\eta}p_{t+1}. \tag{5.40}$$

Leading (5.40) by one period yields:

$$p_{t+1} = \frac{1}{1+\eta}m_{t+1} + \frac{\eta}{1+\eta}p_{t+2}. \tag{5.41}$$

Using (5.41) to eliminate p_{t+1} in (5.40) yields:

$$p_t = \frac{1}{1+\eta}\left(m_t + \frac{\eta}{1+\eta}m_{t+1}\right) + \left(\frac{\eta}{1+\eta}\right)^2 p_{t+2}. \tag{5.42}$$

Repeating this procedure to eliminate p_{t+2}, p_{t+3}, ..., the result is:

$$p_t = \frac{1}{1+\eta}\sum_{s=t}^{\infty}\left(\frac{\eta}{1+\eta}\right)^{s-t} m_s + \lim_{T\to\infty}\left(\frac{\eta}{1+\eta}\right)^T p_{t+T}. \tag{5.43}$$

Assuming that $\lim_{T\to\infty}\left(\frac{\eta}{1+\eta}\right)^T p_{t+T} = 0$, the condition for the equilibrium price level is:

$$p_t = \frac{1}{1+\eta}\sum_{s=t}^{\infty}\left(\frac{\eta}{1+\eta}\right)^{s-t} m_s.^{13} \tag{5.44}$$

It can easily be shown that the sum of the coefficients of the money supply term in (5.44) is actually 1:

$$\frac{1}{1+\eta}\left[1 + \frac{\eta}{1+\eta} + \left(\frac{\eta}{1+\eta}\right)^2 + \dots\right] = \frac{1}{1+\eta}\left(\frac{1}{1-\frac{\eta}{1+\eta}}\right) = 1. \tag{5.45}$$

As a result, the price level depends on a weighted average of future expected money supplies, with weights that decline geometrically as the future unfolds. The finding that the money weights sum up to one suggests that *money is fully neutral*: a change the level of money equates to a proportional change in the price level.

To explore the intuition of this finding a bit more, consider the case in which money supply is expected to remain unchanged at $\bar{m}$. In such an environment, inflation is zero: $p_{t+1} - p_t = 0$. Equation (5.39) implies then that the price level is constant at: $\bar{p} = \bar{m}$, which is also implied by (5.44).

Now consider the case in which money supply grows at a constant rate, μ, each period, that is: $m_t = \bar{m} + \mu t$. Here, one would at first glance think that the price level would also grow at: $p_{t+1} - p_t = \mu$. Substituting the latter in Eq. (5.40) yields:

$$p_t = m_t + \eta\mu. \tag{5.46}$$

The same solution is also implied by (5.44). Using the constant money supply rate, Eq. (5.44) can be written as:

---

[13] To ensure convergence of the first term of Eq. (5.43), the restriction which must be imposed is that money supply does not grow indefinitely at an exponential rate of $(1+\eta)/\eta$ or above.

$$p_t = \frac{1}{1+\eta} \sum_{s=t}^{\infty} \left(\frac{\eta}{1+\eta}\right)^{s-t} [m_t + \mu(s-t)].$$

$$= m_t + \frac{\mu}{1+\eta} \left[1 + \frac{\eta}{1+\eta} + \left(\frac{\eta}{1+\eta}\right)^2 + \dots\right] \sum_{s=t}^{\infty} \left(\frac{\eta}{1+\eta}\right)^{s-t} \qquad (5.47)$$

$$= m_t + \left(\frac{\mu}{1+\eta}\right) \eta(1+\eta) = m_t + \eta\mu.$$

The solution in (5.47), however, covers a more general money supply process. Assume an unanticipated announcement in $t = 0$ that money supply is going to rise sharply and permanently on a future date T. More specifically, assume the following:

$$m_t = \begin{cases} \bar{m}, & t < T \\ \bar{m}', & t \geq T \end{cases}$$

In view of such a money supply growth path, Eq. (5.44) gives the path of the corresponding price level, that is:

$$m_t = \begin{cases} \bar{m} + \left(\frac{\eta}{1+\eta}\right)^{T-t} (\bar{m}' - \bar{m}), & t < T \\ p_t = \bar{m}', & t \geq T \end{cases}$$

The corresponding graph is shown in Fig. 5.13. Notice how the price level increases at time 0 until it reaches its new steady state value on date T.

Generalisation of Cagan's Model

The price level path was determined by ruling out self-generating speculative bubbles (*assumption of no speculative bubbles*). Dropping this assumption, Eq. (5.43) would look as follows:

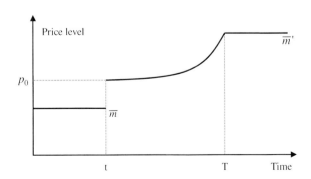

Fig. 5.13 Perfectly anticipated money supply increase

$$p_t = \frac{1}{1+\eta} \sum_{s=t}^{\infty} \left(\frac{\eta}{1+\eta}\right)^{s-t} m_s + b_0 \left(\frac{1+\eta}{\eta}\right)^t, \tag{5.48}$$

where b_0 is the initial deviation of p_0 from its fundamental value:

$$b_0 = p_0 - \frac{1}{1+\eta} \sum_{s=t}^{\infty} \left(\frac{\eta}{1+\eta}\right)^{s} m_s \tag{5.49}$$

The Cagan model is linear, and as a result, extending it to a stochastic version is rather simple (*the stochastic version*). Assuming that future money supply growth is uncertain, the no-bubble solution to (5.43) is:

$$p_t = \frac{1}{1+\eta} \sum_{s=t}^{\infty} \left(\frac{\eta}{1+\eta}\right)^{s-t} E_t\{m_s\}. \tag{5.50}$$

This solution differs from the perfect foresight solution (5.44) by replacing foreseen future money supplies by their expected values. Let, for instance, the money supply process be:

$$m_t = \rho m_{t-1} + \varepsilon_t, \quad 0 \le \rho \le 1, \tag{5.51}$$

where is ε_t is white noise (i.i.d.). Substituting Eq. (5.51) in (5.50), and noting that $E_t\{\varepsilon_{t+s} = 0\}$ for $s > t$, yields:

$$p_t = \frac{m_t}{1+\eta} \sum_{s=t}^{\infty} \left(\frac{\rho\eta}{1+\eta}\right)^{s-t} = \left(\frac{m_t}{1+\eta}\right) \frac{1}{1 - \frac{\rho\eta}{1+\eta}} = \frac{m_t}{1+\eta-\rho\eta}. \tag{5.52}$$

In the case $\rho = 1$, i.e. when money shocks are expected to be permanent, the solution reduces to the expression $p_t = m_t$, in analogy with the non-stochastic case.

5.2.2 Non-Monetary Inflation Theory

The non-monetary inflation theory rests on the *demand pull* and *cost push* explanation of inflation. *Demand pull inflation* is said to occur when total demand for goods and services outstrips total supply, resulting in higher equilibrium prices. Demand pull inflation can be triggered by various factors such as, for instance:

− A depreciation of the exchange rate increases the price competitiveness of domestically produced goods and services. If the economy is already at full employment, the increase in foreign demand for domestic products increases prices.

– A natural catastrophe reduces the economy's production capacity. With demand exceeding supply, the economy's price level is pushed upwards.

Cost push inflation is a type of upward pressure on the economy's price level caused by increases in the cost of goods and services where no suitable alternative is available. A situation that has been often cited in this context were the oil crises of the early 1970s and early 1980s, which some economists see as a major cause of the inflation experienced in the Western world at that time. Other developments that might result in cost push inflation are:

– Firms pass-through higher production costs such as, for instance, higher wages onto product prices;
– the government increases taxes for environmental purposes, which increase the cost of production and thus output prices;
– the domestic currency devalues vis-à-vis major trading partner countries, leading to higher import prices for commodities and intermediate products.

Figure 5.14(a) and (b) illustrate cost push and demand pull effects, respectively, on the price level. The aggregated demand function (*AD*) is assumed to have a negative slope in the price level-output-space, while the aggregated supply function (*AS*) shows a positive slope.

Providing some illustration to the above, Fig. 5.15(a) shows US CPI inflation and changes in unit labour for the period 1969-Q1 to 2005-Q4. Changes in unit labour costs and inflation show a relatively strong positive fit. Figure 5.15(b) plots inflation

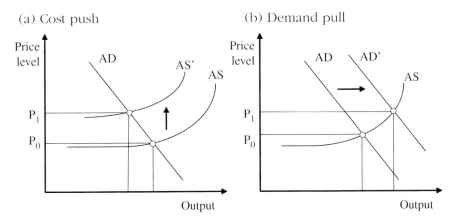

Fig. 5.14 Cost push and demand pull. Graph (**a**): Starting with P_0, a (negative) cost push shock moves the aggregated supply curve (*AS*) upwards to *AS'*. Given unchanged demand, the equilibrium price level rises to P_1, accompanied by a decline in output. – Graph (**b**): A (positive) demand pull effect moves the aggregated demand (*AD*) curve to the right (*AD'*). Given a positively sloped *AS* curve, the equilibrium price level rises to P_1 accompanied by an increase in equilibrium output

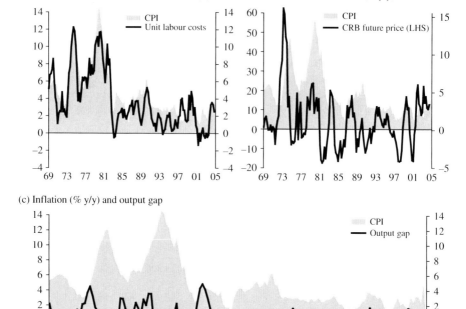

Fig. 5.15 US inflation and cost push and demand pull variables
Source: Bloomberg, Thomson Financial; own calculations. – Period under review: 1969-Q1 to 2005-Q4. – The correlation coefficient between consumer price inflation and unit labour cost growth is 0.88. – For consumer price inflation and CRB price changes (leading by 4 quarters) is 0.53. – The correlation coefficient between inflation and the output gap reaches its maximum of 0.38 when the latter leads inflation by 3 quarters; the output gap is potential GDP growth (calculated using a HP-Filter) minus actual GDP growth.

and changes in CRB future prices.[14] Again, the two series exhibit a positive relation. Finally, Fig. 5.15(c) shows inflation and the US output gap: The two series are also positively correlated, but the correlation coefficient is relatively small.

5.2.2.1 One-Off Price Level Effect Versus Inflation

What is of particular interest in this context is: Do cost push and demand pull effects lead to a *persistent* rise in the economy's price level, or do they just exert a transi-

---

[14]The CRB index used above is the Commodity Research Bureau Futures Price Index. It represents averages of commodity futures prices (through 6 months forward) of 17 major commodity futures markets.

tory/temporary effect? In the former case, cost push and demand pull effects would qualify as a source of inflation, in the latter case they would merely exert a one-off effect on the price level without affecting its rate of change over time.

Monetarists would argue that cost push and demand pull effect cannot lead to an ongoing rise in the economy's price level. From their viewpoint, cost push and demand pull effects just entail one-off effects on the economy's price level – provided these effects are not accommodated with an increase in the money stock. Keynesian oriented economists, in contrast, tend to argue that cost push and demand pull developments tend to be inflation-enhancing in character.

In this context it might be helpful to compare a *one-off* increase with an *ongoing* increase in the price level and their resulting effect on inflation. Assume the economy's price level (after having remained constant at, say, 100) rises, due to a cost push and/or a demand pull effect, to 160 in period 13, and remains at that level thereafter (Fig. 5.16(a)). Accordingly, the annual change in the price level, after having been zero so far, jumps to 60% from period 13 to 24, only to fall back to zero thereafter (Fig. 5.16(b)). Technically speaking, a *one-off (positive) demand pull and/or cost push effects would not lead to an ongoing rise in the annual change in the economy's price level, that is inflation.*

In contrast, an *ongoing rise* in the economy's price level is depicted in Fig. 5.17(a). Such a development would be consistent with persistent positive inflation; in this case the annual change in the economy's price level is positive throughout the periods under review (Fig. 5.17(b)). This conclusion holds true if the economy's price level rises at a constant rate per period or at an accelerating pace over time (as represented by the dotted lines).

Many phenomena – such as, for instance, a decline in productivity, rising oil prices, union power and related wage increases and rising import prices – can, in the short-run, exert upward pressures on the price level. However, in most cases it is far from clear as to whether such developments can exert a lasting effect on the price level. From a theoretical viewpoint, it hard to imagine an ongoing rise in the price level following cost push and/or demand pull effects if the latter are not

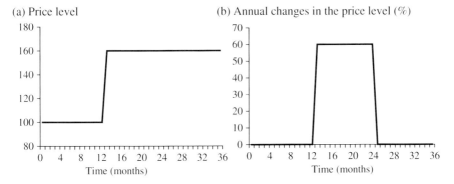

Fig. 5.16 One-off rise in the price level and inflation

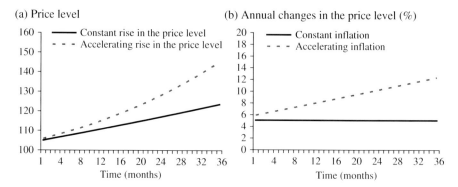

Fig. 5.17 Ongoing rise in the price level and inflation

accompanied by an increase in the money stock – which would then suggest that inflation is actually a monetary phenomenon.

5.2.2.2 Do "Models Without Money" Explain Inflation as a Non-Monetary Phenomenon?

It has become mainstream practice-for monetary policy analysis to use models that make no reference to money. McCallum (2001) has shown, however, that models without monetary aggregates do not imply that inflation is a non-monetary phenomenon. He specifies a model that reflects today's standard approach of modeling inflation without money and asks whether its adoption implies that inflation has little or nothing to do with money. McCallum's answer is "no."

The well-known forward-looking expectational IS function that can be justified by dynamic optimization (as explained by Kerr & King, 1996; McCallum & Nelson, 1999b; Woodford, 1995, 1999a and others) is:

$$y_t = b_0 + b_1(R_t - E_t \Delta p_{t+1}) + E y_{t+1} + v_t, \qquad (5.53)$$

with $b_1 > 0$, whereas y_t is the log of actual real output, R_t is the nominal short-term interest, $E(.)$ is the expectation operator, Δ is the first difference in the log of price level p_t; v_t is the stochastic disturbance term, representing shocks.

The first difference in the price level is:

$$\Delta p_t = \beta E_t \Delta p_t + \alpha(y_t - \bar{y}_t) + u_t, \qquad (5.54)$$

with $0 < \beta < 1, \alpha > 1$, where $\bar{y}_t$ is potential output (which is exogenous), and $(y_t - \bar{y}_t)$ is the output gap; u_t represents the stochastic error term of "cost push" shocks. Equation (5.54) is a price adjustment specification of the Calvo-Rotemberg type, basically the standard model of those in use.[15]

The policy rule of the Taylor (1993) type is:

$$R_t = \mu_0 + E_t \Delta p_{t+1} + \mu_1(E_t \Delta p_{t+j} - \pi^*) + \mu_2(y_t - \bar{y}_t) + e_t. \qquad (5.55)$$

According to (5.55), the central bank raises the real interest rate $R_t - E_t \Delta p_{t+1}$ if and when current or expected inflation exceeds target inflation π^* and/or the output gap is positive. Generally speaking, the central bank will make the parameter μ_0 to equal $\bar{r}$, the long-run average real rate of interest, which, in turn, equals $-b_0/b_1$.[16]

The system (5.53), (5.54), and (5.55) includes no money. Yet it is complete, in the sense that the three relations govern time paths for the three endogenous variables, y_t, Δp_t, and R_t. Of course, it would be possible to add to the system a money demand function such as:

$$m_t - p_t = c_0 + c_1 y_t + c_2 R_t + \eta_t, \qquad (5.56)$$

with $c_1 > 0, c_2 < 0$, where m_t is the nominal stock of money. However, is the latter not superfluous, in the sense that it does not affect the behavior of y_t, Δp_t, and R_t? Its only function would be to specify the amount of base money that is needed to implement the policy rule (5.55). Thus policy analysis involving y_t, $\bar{y}_t$, Δp_t, and R_t can be run without even specifying a money demand function such as (5.56).

Nevertheless, it would be wrong to view this model without any money, or to come to the conclusion that Eqs. (5.53), (5.54), and (5.55) imply a non-monetary model. For the central bank's control over the one-period nominal interest rate rests on its ability to control the quantity of (base) money. If some entity other than the central bank could exogenously manipulate the path of m_t, then (5.56), (5.53), and (5.54) would determine paths for y_t, Δp_t, and R_t with (5.55) being overruled.

According to the model above, inflation can be interpreted as a non-monetary phenomenon, governed by the Phillips curve equation (5.54). McCallum says that such a suggestion would be unjustified, as *the true issue in this regard is what controls long-run average inflation*. And in the model (5.53), (5.54), and (5.55), it can be shown that inflation is controlled entirely by the central bank.

For this argument let us assume that the long-run average value of the output gap is zero, that is $E(y_t - \bar{y}_t) = 0$ as is implied by the strict version of the natural rate hypothesis (Lucas, 1972; McCallum & Nelson, 1999). Then from (5.53) we have that, in the absence of growth, $E(R_t - \Delta p_{t+1}) = -b_0/b_1$, so that Eq. (5.55) implies that:

$$-b_0/b_1 = \mu_0 + \mu_1(E \Delta p_{t+j} - \pi^*) + \alpha E(y_t - \bar{y}_t). \qquad (5.57)$$

---

[15]There has recently been much controversy over the adequacy of the Calvo-Rotemberg specification since it itself supplies no persistence to the inflation rate; see Estrella and Fuhrer (2000) and Gali and Gertler (1999) for an introduction to the controversy.

[16]One may include the term R_{t-1} in the policy rule to represent interest rate smoothing.

It follows:

$$E \Delta p_t = \pi^* - ((b_0/b_1) + \mu_0)(1/\mu_1). \tag{5.58}$$

Consequently, if the central bank sets μ_0 equal to the average real interest rate, $-b_0/b_1$, then average inflation will equal the central bank's chosen target value π^*. And if it errs by (say) e in setting μ_0, average inflation will differ from π^* by e/μ_0. Basically, then, average inflation is determined by the central bank. Parameters α and β from the Phillips relationship (5.54) play no role.

5.2.3 Fiscal Theory of the Price Level

As was emphasized several times in this book, the traditional function of the central bank is to control the price level. This function is a natural implication of economic theory: The celebrated quantity theory of money can be summarized in Milton Friedman's dictum that "inflation is always and everywhere a monetary phenomenon." As reviewed, among others, in Robert Lucas' Nobel lecture (1996), there is a wealth of empirical evidence linking *price* movements to movements in the *money stock*. Standard monetarist doctrine derives a simple conclusion from this: simply make sure the central bank has an unwavering and credible *commitment to price stability*.

Recently, though, some economists have begun to reassess the foundations of this doctrine, generating an *alternative view* according to which a hard-nosed and independent central bank is not sufficient to guarantee price stability. According to this view, price stability requires not only an appropriate stance of monetary policy, but at the same time also an *appropriate fiscal policy*.[17] Since fiscal policy receives so much attention in this rather new view of price-level determination, Michael Woodford has called it the *fiscal theory of the price level*.[18] Throughout this chapter, we will refer to it as the FTPL. The latter maintains that the price level is (at least partly) determined by the budgetary policies of the fiscal authority.

Monetarist doctrine also incorporates that *both* fiscal and monetary policy must be selected appropriately if price stability is to be achieved. However, monetarism holds that if the central bank is tough, the fiscal authority will be nearly

---

[17]Cochrane (2000) goes so far as to say that monetary policy may be irrelevant to price determination. In his view, government-provided transactions assets are a vanishing component of all financial assets traded.

[18]Benhabib, Schmitt-Grohe, and Uribe (2002), Cochrane (1998a, 2000), Dupor (2000), Leeper (1991), Sims (1994, 2001), and Woodford (1994, 1995, 1996, 1998a, 1998b, 1998c, 2003) all advocate the FTPL, while Buiter (1999), Carlstrom and Fuerst (1999), Kocherlakota and Phelan (1999), and McCallum (1998) provide critical reviews. Other contributions supporting the theoretical foundations of the FTPL are contained in Bassetto (2002), Cochrane (1998a, 2003a, 2003b), Daniel (2003, 2004), Davig, Leeper, and Chung (2004), Gordon and Leeper (2002) and Woodford (2001).

automatically *compelled* to adopt an appropriate fiscal policy.[19] The FTPL denies this kind of automatism. Instead, it claims that unless steps are taken to credibly implement appropriate fiscal policies, the goal of price stability may remain elusive no matter how tough and independent the central bank is. The attack on the conventional position has come in two parts, *weak-form* FTPL and *strong-form* FTPL (Carlstrom & Fuerst, 1999).

5.2.3.1   Weak Form Fiscal Theory of the Price Level

I nearly all cases, weak-form FTPL takes an obvious link between monetary and fiscal policy as a starting point. Because seigniorage, i.e. the revenue from money creation, is a potential source of revenue, long-run both monetary and fiscal policy are determined jointly by fiscal budget constraints. Whether monetary or fiscal policy determines prices necessitates an assumption about which policymaker will be the first mover, the central bank or the fiscal authority (Belke, 2002). The weak form of the FTPL takes for granted that the fiscal authority moves first by committing to a path for primary budget surpluses/deficits, thereby forcing the monetary authority to generate the seigniorage needed to maintain solvency. Sargent (1986b) calls this a "game of chicken."

If both the monetary and the fiscal authority refuse to come up with and generate the seigniorage in need, the nation's debt-to-GDP ratio will grow at an unsustainable rate. This implies ever-increasing real rates of interest on government debt since the market requests larger and larger default premiums. This process cannot continue forever. Hence, one of the two players, the government or the central bank, must alter its behavior. Defenders of the weak-form FTPL assume the central bank will respond and generate the seigniorage needed to avoid default. Applying the above mentioned game-of-chicken analogy again, the weak-form FTPL claims that the monetary authority loses and is forced to "blink."

This version of the fiscal theory predicts that fiscal policy determines future inflation as well. Although this is true, it does so merely by determining future money growth. The traditional version of the FTPL, thus, is not at odds with the heart of the quantity theory because prices are still driven by current or future money growth. Sargent and Wallace's (1981) frequently celebrated example in which tight money today increases the price level occurs as future money growth and, by this, also future inflation increase.[20]

---

[19] See, above all, the last section of Sargent and Wallace (1981).

[20] This argument heavily relies on the theoretical assumption money demand is sufficiently elastic (greater than one). Note, however, that empirical estimates of the interest rate elasticity of money demand are uniformly less than one. Thus, Sargent and Wallace's unpleasant possibility that tight money leads to higher current prices is probably *only a theoretical curiosity*. The same is valid with respect to the strong-form FT, in which both the fiscal and monetary authorities move first (neither blinks), relies on large elasticities and thus is little more than an intellectual curiosity. Hence, it appears to us rather difficult to take these examples too seriously. See, for instance, Carlstrom and Fuerst (1999, pp. 25 and 31).

Fiscal dominance is exactly the assumption made by Sargent and Wallace (1981) in their classic paper, "*Some Unpleasant Monetarist Arithmetic*". They posit that "the path of [primary surpluses] is given and does not depend on current or future monetary policies. This assumption is ... about the behavior of the monetary and fiscal authorities and the 'game' that they are playing. Since the monetary authorities affect the extent to which seigniorage is exploited as a source of revenue, monetary and fiscal policies have to be coordinated. The question is which authority 'moves first' ... who imposes discipline on whom?" (Sargent, 1986b, pp. 170f.). Hence, the theory simply posits that the ultimate driver of the money supply is the fiscal authority. In other words, fiscal policy is assumed to be exogenous, while *money supply* movements are *endogenous*.

Expressed differently, Sargent and Wallace (1981) showed a natural way in which fiscal and monetary policies are related to each other by highlighting the role played by the government's *inter-temporal budget constraint*. One of the most important messages from the above mentioned "Unpleasant Monetarist Arithmetic" is that, regardless of the policy regime at work, a certain degree of coordination between fiscal and monetary decisions is always needed, conditional on the government's will to really honor its policy announcements (Mundschenk and von Hagen, 2002). Another critical observation drawn from the Sargent and Wallace story is that fiscal variables, like taxes or public debt, are only able to affect nominal variables, such as prices, money supply or nominal interest rates, as long as the central bank accommodates its policy in order to satisfy some fiscal requirements, printing as much money (i.e. collecting seigniorage) as required to cover a portion of the government's expenditures – in other words: when the fiscal-monetary plan is conducted under a fiscal-dominance regime. Overall, in their model economy the monetarist dictum still goes on: the price level is always a monetary phenomenon in spite of the eventual fiscal motivation of the observed monetary stance.

5.2.3.2 Strong Form Fiscal Theory of the Price Level

More recently, a *stronger* version of the fiscal theory has been posited. Strong-form FTPL maintains that fiscal policy determines future inflation, but *independent of* future money growth. Unlike the weak theory, according to which inflation still and ultimately represents a monetary phenomenon, the strong-form FTPL maintains that fiscal policy affects the price level and the path of inflation *independent of monetary policy* changes.

This newer version of the fiscal theory is possible since, in a wide variety of monetary models, the initial price level is not exactly pinned down. Accordingly, different initial price levels are consistent with different paths for future inflation. In contrast, prices are uniquely determined in the weak form of the FTPL analyzed by Sargent and Wallace. The strong-form FTPL assumes that the fiscal budget constraint, and thus fiscal policy, pins down the initial price level. Without this constraint, the initial price level may be indeterminate, even if the money supply is given exogenously – that is, even if the monetary authority moves first by committing to a path for the money stock. This scenario stands in sharp contrast with the weak-form FTPL according to which the money supply is endogenous in order to satisfy the government's budget constraint. The strong-form FTPL assumes that both fiscal and monetary policy are given exogenously and that prices adjust to ensure solvency. In this game of chicken, neither player blinks (see, for instance, McCallum, 1998).

Seen on the whole, thus, the FTPL has significant implications for the way central banks conduct business. The conventional view prescribes that central bankers should stay away from fiscal authorities to reduce the likelihood of being pressured into making poor monetary policy decisions. The FTPL implies that central bankers with a mandate to foster price stability must do more than simply make sure that their own house is in order; they also have to convince the fiscal authority to adopt a kind of fiscal policy which proves to be appropriate for price stability.

5.2.3.3   How Much Price Stability Is Desirable?

Price stability is an important goal of public policy. But to reach this goal, two key questions must be addressed. Not only: how can price stability be achieved? But also: how much price stability is desirable? The FTPL literature also draws attention to the second question – *how much price stability is desirable?* – which is both important and difficult. Sims (2001) and Woodford (1998a) were one of the first to point out that allowing the price level to fluctuate with unexpected shocks to the government budget constraint produces public finance benefits. For example, a negative fiscal shock such as a war or natural disaster drives up the price level. The latter can be regarded as being equivalent to taxing the holders of the government's nominal liabilities and promotes efficiency to the extent that it allows the authorities to keep labor tax rates smooth. In practice, this benefit is likely to be mitigated by all kinds of distortionary costs associated with price instability (Woodford, 1998a, pp. 59f.). Cochrane (1998b) is mindful of these costs when, in his analysis, he simply takes for granted that complete price stability is a fundamental social objective. In this vein, he emphasizes the need for some type of government security whose payoff fluctuates with shocks to the government budget constraint but does not generate the sort of distortionary costs usually associated with a fluctuating price level. Sims (2001) posits that public finance benefits overwhelm the distortionary costs associated with volatile prices. Accordingly, he conjectures that complete price stability is non-optimal. However, seen on the whole, a really convincing answer to the question of how much price stability is desirable still awaits a quantitative study that carefully balances benefits and costs.

Note that it is quite important to understand that the conventional view and the FTPL view differ in their views of the government's *inter-temporal budget equation*. That equation says that the value of government debt is equal to the present discounted value of future government tax revenues net of expenditures (that is, surpluses). The FTPL advocates, however, argue that there is no inherent requirement that governments treat this equation as a constraint on policy. In their view, the inter-temporal budget equation is instead an equilibrium condition: When something threatens to disturb the equation, the market-clearing mechanism finally moves the price level to restore equality. Michael Woodford has called this assumption – that government policy is not calibrated to satisfy the inter-temporal budget equation for all values of the price level – the *non-Ricardian assumption*. Another way of stating this assumption is that if the real value of government debt were to grow explosively, no adjustments to fiscal and monetary policy would be made to keep it in line.

5.2.3.4 Does the FTPL Provide Useful Input into the Design of Socially Efficient Policies?

Clearly, the non-Ricardian assumption is not a good characterization of policy in all times and places. Often governments do seem ready to adjust fiscal policy when the debt gets too large. For instance, when the U.S. government debt started to grow in the 1980s and 1990s, there was considerable pressure for some combination of a tax increase and expenditure decrease to bring the debt back in line. Woodford (1998b) himself acknowledges that the political reaction to growing debt in the 1980s and 1990s (as well as other considerations) indicates U.S. policy during the past two decades is probably not well characterized as non-Ricardian (see also the section "The FTPL and the Control of Average Inflation" in Christiano & Fitzgerald, 2000, p. 18). He argues that earlier episodes in U.S. postwar history – for example, the period from 1965 to 1979 – might be better characterized in this way.

Likewise, according to the Maastricht Treaty, members of the European Union formally record their intention to adjust fiscal policy in the event their debts grow too large. Another example is provided by the International Monetary Fund. The latter uses an array of sanctions and rewards to encourage member countries to keep their debts in line by suitably adjusting fiscal policy.

We would like to argue that for the FTPL to be an interesting positive theory, *it does not need to hold in all situations*. As Woodford (1998b) emphasizes, it may provide a useful characterization of actual policies in some contexts, even if it does not do so at all in others. For instance, the government budget constraint was essentially absent from the standard macroeconomic models of the 1960s and 1970s, and it played only a little role in Keynesian policy analysis (Sargent, 1987, p. 112). As a result, it is perhaps reasonable to suppose that the non-Ricardian assumption held for that period. This view is supported by Woodford (1998b) who elaborates the argument that U.S. policy may have been non-Ricardian in the 1960s and 1970s. Loyo (1999) argues that Brazilian policy in the late 1970s and early 1980s was non-Ricardian and that the FTPL provides a compelling explanation for Brazil's high inflation during that time (However, we feel legitimized to wonder whether it makes sense to assume that a theory like the FTPL, which focuses on the long-run properties of fiscal policy, holds for some periods and not others!).[21]

---

[21]The paper by Eduardo Loyo is an unpublished classic. Hyperinflation is usually interpreted as a result of the monetary financing o serious fiscal imbalances. Here, a fiscalist alternative is explored, in which inflation explodes because of the fiscal effects of monetary policy. Higher interest rates cause the outside financial wealth of private agents to grow faster in nominal terms, which in fiscalist models calls for higher inflation. If the monetary authority responds to higher inflation

Even if, in practice, policy has never been non-Ricardian, the FTPL might still hold interest as a normative theory, for two reasons. First, optimal policies might themselves be non-Ricardian (Sims, 2001; Woodford, 1998a). Second, the FTPL could serve as useful input into policy design, even if non-Ricardian policies are, in practice, bad. To see why they might be bad, consider legislators living in a non-Ricardian regime. Understanding that tax cuts or increases in government spending do not necessarily have to be paid for with higher taxes later, they might be tempted to embrace policies that imply too much spending and too much debt. Restricting fiscal policy by limiting government debt may be an effective way to deal with this problem.

Chari and Kehoe (2002) describe a model in which countries form a monetary union, and, absent debt constraints, the result is excessive debt. Bergin (2000) and McCallum (1999b) also discuss the fiscal monetary coordination problem in a monetary union in light of the FTPL's arguments. Woodford (1996) argues that a union without debt constraints is likely to end up with excessive price volatility. His reasoning uses the kind of logic surveyed in this section. He notes that if policy is non-Ricardian, then fiscal shocks must show up as shocks to the price level, regardless of monetary policy (this has become known as the "Woodford's really unpleasant arithmetic") He argues that price-level instability arising from this source is likely to be excessive in a monetary union that adopts a non-Ricardian policy. It is precisely because he believes non-Ricardian policy is a realistic possibility – a possibility which, in this case, he thinks is bad – that he approves of the explicit debt restrictions incorporated into the Maastricht Treaty.[22]

By establishing the logical possibility of non-Ricardian policy, the FTPL implies that such policies could occur, in the absence of specific measures to rule them out. As a result, the FTPL can be used to articulate a rationale for the type of debt limitations imposed by the IMF and by the Maastricht Treaty.

5.2.3.5 What Insights Does the FTPL Provide in the End? A Critical Assessment

What insights does the FTPL provide into the two questions about price stability we posed at the beginning of this review? That is, how can price stability be achieved? And, how much price stability is desirable? Conventional wisdom holds that if there is no doubt about the central bank's commitment to low and stable inflation, then low and stable inflation is exactly what will happen (Sargent and Wallace, 1981, last paragraph). According to the FTPL, however, this overstates the central bank's power. Still, it remains an open question just how severe the limitations on central

---

with sufficiently higher nominal interest rates, a vicious circle is formed. The model is particularly advantageous for hyperinflations in which most of the fiscal action concentrates in the interest bill on public debt and debt rollover, rather than seigniorage or primary budget deficits. Brazil in the late 1970s and early 1980s serves as a motivating case.

[22]For another similar discussion of the potential dangers of non-Ricardian policy, see Woodford (1998a, p. 60).

banks' powers are. These limitations may not be very great for modern, developed economies. Moreover, many approaches to the FTPL rely on large elasticities and thus are little more than an intellectual curiosities.

In the FTPL models that we have studied, the central bank can determine the average rate of inflation. However, it cannot perfectly control the variance of inflation because it cannot eliminate the impact of shocks to fiscal policy on the price level. But in a modern Western economy, the stock of outstanding nominal government liabilities is quite large – Judd's (1989) estimate for the United States puts it at one year's GDP. Therefore, a relatively small change in the price level can absorb a fairly large fiscal policy shock (Sims, 2001). In practice, then, the conventional answer to the first question may be roughly the right one, even under the FTPL. Regarding the second question, Sims (2001) has stressed the potential benefits of price volatility. Woodford (1998a) has made a similar suggestion. The result has also been obtained in Chari, Christiano, and Kehoe (1991). Variations in the price level in response to fiscal shocks have the effect of taxing and subsidizing holders of nominal government liabilities. Under certain circumstances, this can enhance the overall efficiency of government fiscal and monetary policy. But this result also raises questions, because it is obtained in an environment with few of the frictions observed in actual economies that make price volatility costly. Whether the result would survive the introduction of a realistic set of frictions – and a realistic set of alternative methods for dealing with fiscal shocks – is unclear at this time.

Given the long-reaching implications of the FTPL, the *validity of its basic postulates* has attracted much attention. Among the advocates of the FTPL, it is usually argued that the government is not limited in its actions by any inter-temporal budget constraint, that the real value of fiat government-issued money can be determined in a fiscalist world as the price of a private firm's equity (this is the so-called stock-analogy, defended by Cochrane, 2003a, 2003b and Sims, 1999) and, in general, that a non-Ricardian policy is theoretically as valid as it is a Ricardian one, with the assumptions underlying the former being neither unfeasible nor unrealistic (e.g. Daniel, 2003, 2004; Woodford, 1998a, 2001). Some critiques of the FTPL point towards the implausibility of non-Ricardian policies, since these policies imply that the government is allowed to violate its inter-temporal budget constraint at off-equilibrium prices (Buiter, 2000, 2002), the incompatibility of non-Ricardian policies with the requirements imposed by the Walrasian competitive equilibrium concept (Marimón, 2001), the possibility of government default under a non-Ricardian fiscal policy (Cushing, 1999) or the unrealistic assumption on the existence of a non-zero stock of nominal government-issued assets at the "beginning of the world" (Niepelt, 2004).

We take a more formal view on a similar topic in part VI.5 of this textbook where we investigate the relation between fiscal and monetary policy more deeply. Very readable introductory formal papers on the topic are also delivered, for instance, by Christiano and Fitzgerald (2000) and Carlstrom and Fuerst (1999).[23] Christiano and Fitzgerald (2000) explain the FTPL and elaborate on its implications for the

---

[23]For other useful introductions into the topic see Arce (2005).

two questions posed above, as well as for other issues. They first discuss the crucial assumption that differentiates the FTPL from the conventional view. Next, they summarize some of the key issues that any assessment of the FTPL must confront, then they briefly describe other issues addressed in the FTPL literature. Finally, they emphasize the connection between the FTPL and the traditional Ramsey literature on optimal monetary and fiscal policy. Carlstrom and Fuerst (1999), as a first step, analyze a partial-equilibrium model where real cash balances immediately jump to their steady state – that is, equilibria in which the level of real cash balances remains constant. As a second step, they broaden the analysis to a more fully specified general-equilibrium model, allowing for consideration of equilibria where the level of real balances varies with time and for consideration of strong-form FT. Third, they extend the discussion to models in which the central bank targets the interest rate and in which the money supply is endogenous, asking whether this case is an example of weak- or strong-form FT.

5.3 Costs and Benefits of Inflation

CPI inflation declined substantially in most western industrialised countries in the last decades (Dowd, 1994). This might explain why economic analyses of inflation have shifted from focusing on the problem associated with high inflation to exploring the costs and benefits of reducing inflation further from current levels (toward zero). It is often argued that the benefits from squeezing out the last few percentage points of inflation might well be less than the costs of doing so, in terms of foregone output and/or employment.

This literature has attempted to specify the nature of those costs and benefits, as well as provide some indication of the empirical magnitudes involved (Akerlof, Dickens, & Perry, 1996; Hess & Morris, 1996; Feldstein, 1997; Pakko, 1998; Chadha, Haldane, & Janssen, 1998). The studies have come up with a variety of results, both theoretically and empirically. However, a clear consensus on whether further attempts to reduce a relatively low level of inflation (towards zero) are justified on welfare grounds has not yet emerged.

A major difficulty faced by many of these studies is that they see the costs of inflation by focusing on the way inflation taxes money balances (Bailey, 1956). This perspective might be overly narrow, though, and changes in the theoretical landscape of economics in the last couple of decades make a re-examination of the costs of inflation a worthwhile undertaking (Horwitz, 2003). In particular, the maturation of public choice (Belke, 2000), the growth of New Institutionalism, and the revival of the Austrian school of economics have prompted more careful consideration of the workings of markets and institutions and the interaction between them when dealing with the costs of inflation.

5.3.1 Costs of Inflation

When dealing with the costs of inflation, the *costs of non-anticipated inflation* shall be addressed first, followed by the *costs of anticipated inflation*. Thereafter, the

382 5 Causes, Costs and Benefits of Sound Money

political-economic costs of inflation shall be discussed in some more detail. The paragraph concludes with outlining arguments why inflation is to be considered a *societal evil*.

5.3.1.1 Costs of Non-Anticipated Inflation

The *first*, and perhaps most obvious, problem is that inflation amounts to a *tax on money balances*, destroying the exchange value of money. As a result, actors are made to hold lower real money balances than they would in the absence of inflation, thereby creating a sub-optimal outcome. Various studies have attempted to quantify this inflation generated welfare loss by computing the money demand function and measuring the area underneath the curve that is eaten away by inflation.

A fairly rapid and strong fall in the value of money will impose further costs on money users. In struggling to keep up with rising prices, people economist on this money holdings have to make additional trips to the bank to replenish their desired nominal money balances. These costs may be called *shoe-leather costs*. In the age of the *internet* one might term these costs as *banking transaction costs*.

A *second* cost of inflation, in the standard view, is the *redistribution of wealth from creditors to debtors* (Alchian & Kessel, 1959). If the increase in the price level is unanticipated, debtors will be paying back their nominally denominated debts in real money that is worth progressively less. Unanticipated inflation reduces the burden on debtors and harms creditors. One might object that this is not really a cost, because it amounts to a contractual transfer, and that it is therefore not a net loss to society. However, inflation, particularly if rates are variable and unpredictable, may well cause lenders to reduce the overall amount of credit they supply, which would represent a real loss in comparison to an economy with non-inflationary money.

Third, inflation forces sellers to expend additional resources in order to change prices more frequently. These so-called *menu costs* will vary directly with changes in inflation. The more quickly prices are rising, the more often sellers will have to adjust prices. The time spent in remarking inventory, or reprogramming computers, reflects a cost imposed by inflation. Note, however, that these costs exist even if inflation is perfectly anticipated: Adjusting prices from their pre-inflation equilibrium values to their post-inflation equilibrium values still involves resource costs.

The first three problems were all related to changes in the *level* of prices. The *fourth* problem is that *changes* in the price level affect the distribution of relative prices across the economy. If inflation affects all nominal prices at the same time, and leaves relative prices unchanged, it would create all of the above costs. However, if inflation affects *relative prices*, then resources will be misallocated because some relative prices will no longer correspond to their equilibrium. So whereas the first three inflation related costs would put the economy at a new price level equilibrium with lower overall welfare, the fourth problem can cause the economy *to be out of equilibrium*, which would come in addition to any overall losses of welfare.

The literature offers a variety of explanations for how relative prices might be affected by inflation.[24] The *first effect* emerges from *menu costs*. If prices cannot be instantaneously changed as the money supply rises – due to, for instance, the costs involved in making changes – prices will be changed at discrete intervals. The nature of menu costs, plus other institutional factors in the marketplace, will lead to relative price distortions when firms make price changes. At any given time during inflation, some prices will be adjusted upward while others will not (Caplin & Spulber, 1987). As a result, at any given point in time, the vector of relative prices might not be the equilibrium one. The consequence is resource misallocation.

The *second effect* of inflation on relative prices is a version of the *signal extraction problem*. Prices provide information to market agents. This discovery of this insight is usually ascribed to Hayek (1945) and it has spawned a whole literature on the informational efficiency of prices. Inflation makes price signals informationally inefficient by injecting *noise* into the otherwise fully informative equilibrium price. This noise is what creates the signal extraction problem and the resulting relative price effects and resource misallocation. In his essay *Can We Still Avoid Inflation* Published 1970, Hayek wrote:

> There is of course, no doubt that temporarily the production of capital goods (*as a result of inflation, insertion by the authors*) can be increased by what is called "forced saving" – that is, credit expansion can be used to direct a greater part of the current services of resources to the production of capital goods. At the end of such a period the physical quantity of capital goods existing will be greater than it would otherwise have been. Some of this may be a lasting gain – people may get houses in return for what they were not allowed to consume. But I am not so sure that such a forced growth of the stock of industrial equipment always makes a country richer, that is, that the value of its capital stock will afterwards be greater – or by its assistance of all-round productivity be increased more than would otherwise have been the case. If investment was guided by the expectation of a higher rate of continued investment (or a lower rate of interest, or a higher rate of real wages, which all come to the same thing) in the future than in fact will exist, this higher rate of investment may have done less to enhance overall productivity than a lower rate of investment would have done if it had taken more appropriate forms.

During unanticipated inflations, agents have difficulty in distinguishing changes in the average level of prices from changes in the relative prices. For car producers, for instance, an increase in the price of cars might reflect an inflationary increase in aggregate demand, or a substitution away from other goods into cars, or both. To the extent that agents *misinterpret* a rise in the general price level as an increase in relative prices, and expand production capacity as a result of it, they move, supply away from the *true* economic equilibrium. In addition, agents will have to sort out how much of the price change is permanent and how much of it is temporary. Again, any error will lead to relative price effects, and with the structure of relative prices deviating from equilibrium, resource misallocation and economic waste will result.

---

[24]See the survey delivered by Dowd (1996).

5.3.1.2 Costs of Anticipated Inflation

When inflation is anticipated, its costs are substantially less, according to the standard view, when compared with those of unanticipated inflation. What remains are *shoe leather costs* and *menu costs*, it is said. However, even in case of perfectly anticipated inflation *additional* costs have to be taken into account.

To start with, inflation increases the opportunity costs of money holdings – as money holdings (coins, notes and demand deposits) typically do not yield an interest rate. Market agents can be expected to reduce their holdings of money. By doing so, they might be less flexible in responding to changing market conditions which, in turn, entail the *costs of suboptimal cash holdings* (Friedman, 1969; McCallum and Goodfriend, 1987).

If inflation rises strongly, or approaches a state of *hyperinflation*, market agents might want to stop using money altogether, *switching to other media* that may serve as money (such as, for instance, cigarettes). The (transaction) costs related to such a substitution process can be expected to be (quite) substantial.

If nominal income and capital gains are subject to taxation, inflation increases the *tax burden*; this holds true under both a *progressive* tax rate (*bracket creep*) and a constant tax rate.[25] Assume, for instance, a constant tax rate t, while i_r is the real return on investment, i_n is the nominal return, i_{eff} is the effective real return (after tax), π is inflation and Q is the nominal value of the investment. The nominal yield can be expressed as: $i_n = i_r + \pi + \pi i_r$. Assuming a one-period investment horizon, the real value of the investment is:

$$Q_r = \frac{Q(1+i_n) - Q \cdot i_n \cdot t}{1+\pi} \Leftrightarrow Q_r = \frac{Q(1+(1-t)(i_r + \pi + \pi \cdot i_r))}{1+\pi}. \quad (5.59)$$

The real effective return after tax is:

$$i_{eff} = \frac{(Q_r - Q)}{Q} = \frac{Q_r}{Q} - 1 = \frac{(1-t) \cdot i_r - \pi(t - (1-t) \cdot i_r)}{1 - \pi}. \quad (5.60)$$

The first derivate of i_{eff} with respect to π is:

$$\frac{\partial i_{eff}}{\partial \pi} = \frac{-t}{(1+\pi)^2} < 0. \quad (5.61)$$

That said, the higher inflation is, the lower is (given a constant tax rate) the effective real return on investment.

What is more, *inflation is an excellent example of the dynamics of interventionism*, as identified by Ludwig von Mises (1966, p. 716). Once inflation occurs, it

---

[25]The "bracket creep" is a situation where inflation pushes nominal income into higher tax brackets. The result is an increase in real taxes. This is a problem during periods of high inflation as income tax codes typically take a longer time to change.

sets off a sequence of events that leads to progressively more government involvement in the market process. The dissatisfaction caused by inflation (following, for instance, complains about rising prices from households and firms), resulting from the public's inability to connect the effects with the cause, creates opportunities for political actors to expand their influence. If the political demands are specific, as it is the case with unemployment, the scope for discriminating among possible programs and beneficiaries is very narrow. Politicians must respond to the specific demand.

The political benefits of inflation occur not just due to its discriminatory impact at its onset, but also from the induced increase in the quantity of future discriminatory programs being demanded. The process does not stop here, however. Once these programs are created in response to the diverse effects of inflation, further consequences follow. As with the creation of any government program, there is a class of beneficiaries who will be unwilling to give up those benefits. Programs created in response to inflation will create further opportunities for *rent-seeking* and rent-protecting behavior as those programs come up for periodic renewal or review.

By satisfying the political demands of one group, two other problems arise. First, other groups will have a greater expectation of their demands being satisfied and, as a result, will likely increase their rent-seeking expenditures (Tullock, 1967, p. 48). This will be particularly true the more inflation undermines market price signals, preventing the market process from improving economic welfare. Second, the existence of one set of government programs may well cause further undesirable unintended consequences in the market process, leading to not only intensified demands on the part of pre-existing rent-seekers, but new sets of demands on the political process by the victims of the new programs.

5.3.1.3 Inflation – A Collective Societal Evil

A large number of economic arguments point to the *benefits of sound money* as far as output and employment are concerned. Among the main arguments are:

- Price stability improves the transparency of the *relative price mechanism*, thereby *avoiding distortions* and helping to ensure that the market will *allocate real resources efficiently* both across uses and across time. An efficient allocation will raise the productive potential of the economy. Price stability creates an environment in which structural reforms implemented by national governments to increase the flexibility and efficiency of markets can be most effective.
- Stable prices *minimise the inflation risk premium* in long-term interest rates, thereby lowering long-term rates, supporting investment and growth.
- If the *future price level is uncertain, real resources are diverted to hedging* against inflation or deflation, rather than being put to productive use. Price stability avoids these costs and provides the environment for efficient real investment decisions. It also eliminates the real costs entailed when *inflation or deflation*

exacerbates the distortionary effects of the tax and welfare system on economic behaviour.

– Maintaining price stability *avoids the large and arbitrary redistribution of wealth and incomes* that arises in an inflationary environment, and therefore helps to maintain social cohesion and stability.

Several studies have shown that, across a large number of countries, nations with lower inflation appear, on average, to grow more rapidly (Barro, 1995, 1997). A number of empirical studies have shown that the costs incurred when inflation exacerbates the distortions inherent in tax and benefit systems are considerable (Feldstein, 1999). Extension of this analysis to several euro area countries suggests that the benefits of maintaining price stability in these contexts may be even higher than in the United States.

Some Theories About the "Great Inflation" in the US

During the 1970s US inflation reached its 20-th century peak, with levels exceeding 10% (Fig. 5.18). The causes of this *Great Inflation* have remained subject to debate (Lansing, 2000). In the literature, the great inflation has been explained on the one hand, by the so-called the *bad luck theory* (emphasizing events allegedly outside the Fed's control) and, on the other hand, by the *policy mistake theory* (stressing wrong decisions made by policymakers).[26]

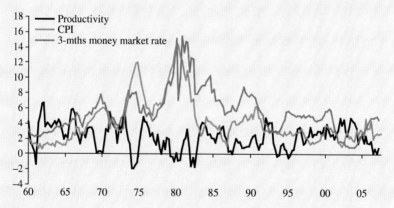

Fig. 5.18 US Effective Federal Funds Rate (%) and CPI and productivity (% y/y)
Source: Bloomberg, Federal Reserve Bank of St. Louis; own calculations.

---

[26] A number of authors have put forward formal models for explaining the Great Inflation in the US. See, for instance, Clarida, Gali, and Gertler (1999), Christiano and Gust (1999) and Albanesi, Chari, and Christiano (2003), Sargent (1986).

The "Bad Luck Theory"

Orphanides (1999) hypothesised that Fed policymakers of the 1970s acted in best faith but did not know that trend productivity growth and thus the US economy's potential growth rate had slowed drastically around the early 1970s (Lansing, 2002). As the Fed assumed too high a level of potential growth, it lowered interest when actual GDP growth rates declined, thinking a widening of the output gap would require easier monetary policy.

The Fed's policy turned out to be overly expansionary. The result was higher inflation. Inflation rose to a point where the Fed started raising interest rates. However, the upward momentum in inflation was so strong that the Fed could not turn things around until the early 1980s.

One problem with the bad luck theory is the timing of the emergence of inflation. It links the rise in inflation with the slowdown in potential growth. The slowdown in productivity growth started in the early 1970s, while inflation began to rise as from the middle of the 1960s.

Blinder (1982) put forward a theory that makes use of the bad luck argument. Oil and food price shocks, he argued, coupled with pent-up inflation from the release of the Nixon wage-price controls in 1974, account for most of the rise in inflation during the 1970s. Fed policymakers can be held responsible for the rise in inflation because they tried to offset the contractionary effects of the rise in oil prices with an overly expansionary monetary policy.

De Long (1997) criticises Blinder's explanation for two reasons. First, he notes that inflation began to rise in the mid-1960s, well before the first oil price shock. Second, he sees no evidence that the temporary bursts of inflation from the oil shocks affected the time path of wage inflation – which he sees as a prerequisite for the consumer price inflation trend.

The "Policy Mistake Theory"

Hetzel (1998) and Mayer (1999) analyse the views held by Fed policymakers during the 1960s and 1970s. The authors write that Fed officials believed incorrectly that inflation was largely determined by factors beyond the reach of monetary policy. What is more, wage-price controls in 1971 encouraged an expansionary monetary policy because it was thought that wage-price controls would restrain inflation.

De Long (1997) argues that policymakers' mistaken belief in an exploitable Phillips curve trade-off, coupled with a strong aversion to unemployment, led Fed policymakers to pursue an ill-fated policy to drive the unemployment rate down through an overly lax monetary policy. After having experienced the high costs of high inflation, the Fed moved eventually towards a monetary policy of disinflation.

Sargent (1999) develops a theory that builds on the *time-inconsistency problem* as put forward by Kydland and Prescott (1977). Discretionary policymakers are tempted to create *surprise inflation* in order to temporarily push unemployment below its natural rate. Private sector agents recognize this temptation and increase their inflation expectations above what is promised in terms of future inflation by the central bank. In equilibrium, no surprises occur but the economy ends up with higher than optimal inflation. According to Sargent, policymakers caused inflation because of their mistaken belief in an exploitable Phillips curve trade-off.

Parkin (1993) develops a theory assuming that an increase in the natural rate of unemployment leads to an increase in equilibrium inflation. This occurs because changes in the natural rate influence policymakers' temptation to engage in surprise inflation policy. Parkin argues that the Kydland-Prescott model predicts rising inflation during the 1960s and 1970s and declining inflation during the 1980s because demographic shifts have created a similar hump-shaped pattern in the natural rate of unemployment. During the 1960s and 1970s, the peak of the baby boom generation was passing through a period of high life-cycle unemployment.

Friedman's Dictum on the Cause of Inflation

The theories outlined above highlight the role of *monetary policy mistakes* (and/or *misuses of monetary policy*) for the Great Inflation in the US (Delong, 1995). However, they are not really insightful as far as the *ultimate cause of inflation* is concerned. That said, it might be worthwhile to remind us of Friedman's explanation why the ultimate cause of inflation often remains disputed (Friedman, 1994, p. 192): "No government willingly accepts the responsibility for producing inflation even in moderate degree, let alone at hyperinflation rates. Government officials always find some excuse – greedy businessmen, grasping trade unions, spendthrift consumers, Arab sheiks, bad weather, or anything else that seems remotely plausible. (N)ot one of the alleged culprits possesses a printing press on which it can legally turn out those pieces of paper we carry in our pockets and call money. (. . .) The recognition that *substantial inflation is always and everywhere a monetary phenomenon* is only the beginning of an understanding of the cause and cure of inflation."

5.3.2 Benefits of Inflation – The Phillips Curve

In the late 1950s, the British economist Arthur W. Phillips (1958) came up with an *inverse statistical relationship between annual changes in average wage rates and the rate of unemployment*: When the annual nominal wage growth rates were plotted against the unemployment rates for Great Britain in the period 1861–1957, they approximated a curve convex to the origin (Fig. 5.19). In years when unemployment rates were low, average nominal wage growth tended to grow strongly, while in years of high unemployment rates, nominal wages tended to grow little (or even declined).

Keynesian economists reasoned from this finding that *because* unemployment rates and growth rates of nominal wages are inversely related, the policy objectives of maintaining both low inflation and low unemployment would be in conflict. As wages represent a large share of the costs of production, rapid increases in nominal wages are bound to push up the economy's price level. Even more important, it was concluded that there is a *trade-off between inflation and unemployment*, and economic policy makers can choose the mix of inflation and unemployment that they find most acceptable according to political and ideological goals.

More specifically, one may argue that *conservative policy makers* are willing to prefer low inflation even at the cost of high unemployment, whereas *socialist policy makers* can be expected to pursue more inflationary policies because of their deeper commitments to the goal of full employment. The Phillips curve, assuming that it remains fixed and stable over time, seems therefore to provide a *kind of menu* of numerical combinations of inflation and unemployment that policy makers can choose from.

One result of the *Phillips curve trade-off theory* was to make inflation politically respectable. Low inflation was no longer seen as a failure of economic policy but more as a price to pay for keeping unemployment low. Political critics of inflation could now be denounced as advocates of increasing unemployment, thereby bringing misery to employees. Under the spell of the Phillips curve, the low inflation environment in most western industrialised gave way to high inflation in the 1960s and especially in the 1970s of the last century.

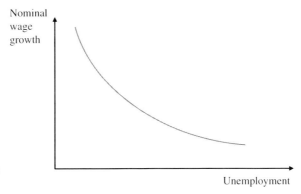

Fig. 5.19 Traditional Phillips curve

High inflation started coexisting with high unemployment. What is more, higher and higher doses of inflation seemed necessary to bring unemployment down to politically desired levels. Over time, however, it became obvious that high inflation was accompanied with high unemployment and lower output growth – the opposite of what was promised by the Phillips curve theory. What went wrong? To answer this question, we start with taking a closer look at the *traditional Phillips curve*.

5.3.2.1 The Traditional Phillips Curve

According to the traditional Phillips curve, the relation between nominal wage growth and unemployment can be formalised as:

$$\Delta \ln W_t = f(U_{t-1}) \text{ with } \frac{\partial f}{\partial U_{t-1}} < 0. \tag{5.62}$$

According to Eq. (5.62), a change of nominal wage growth ($\Delta \ln W_t$) between period t and $t-1$ is a negative function of unemployment in the previous period (U_{t-1}).

5.3.2.2 The Modified Phillips Curve

The modified Phillips curve, which was put forward by Samuelson and Solow (1960), shows the relation between *unemployment and inflation* (rather than nominal wage growth). It assumes that firms calculate prices according to a *mark-up formula*, so that the economy's price level is:

$$P_t = (1 + \phi)\frac{L_t}{Y_t} W_t. \tag{5.63}$$

The price level is determined by the profit mark-up, ϕ, and the total wages costs, $(L_t/Y_t) \cdot W_t$, where L represents labour, Y output and W the nominal (average) wage. (Note that L_t/Y_t is the reciprocal of labour productivity.)

Rearranging Eq. (5.63), the relation between labour productivity and the real wage is:

$$\frac{1}{(1 + \phi)} \frac{Y_t}{L_t} = \frac{W_t}{P_t}. \tag{5.64}$$

Under the assumption of firms' mark-up pricing, a change in labour productivity corresponds to a proportional change in real wages:

$$\Delta \ln \left(\frac{Y_t}{L_t}\right) = \Delta \ln \left(\frac{W_t}{P_t}\right) \text{ or} \tag{5.65a}$$

$$= \ln W_t - \ln P_t - \ln W_{t-1} + \ln P_{t-1} \tag{5.65b}$$

$$= \Delta \ln W_t - \Delta \ln P_t \tag{5.65c}$$

$$= \Delta \ln W_t - \pi_t. \tag{5.65d}$$

The left hand side of Eq. (5.65d) shows productivity growth of labour and is represented by λ. The right hand side shows the change in real wages, that is the difference between nominal wage growth and inflation (π). Assuming λ to be constant, there would be a stable relationship between the growth in nominal wages and inflation such as:

$$\Delta \ln W_t = \lambda + \pi_t. \tag{5.66}$$

Inserting Eq. (5.66) in (5.62) yields:

$$\pi_t = f(U_{t-1}) - \lambda. \tag{5.67}$$

That said, productivity growth (which is assumed to be constant) affects the magnitude of inflation. However, productivity growth does not have any impact on the *slope of the Phillips curve*. A permanent rise in productivity growth would move the modified Phillips curve to the right.

The Phillips Curve in the US

Figure 5.20 I.(a) shows a scatter diagram of the unemployment rate relative to consumer price inflation in the US for the period 1951:10 to 2005:1 (monthly data). The simple correlation coefficient for the contemporaneous time series is rather low (0.32). It is interesting to note that, if anything, the underlying relation seems to be *positive rather than negative* as suggested by the Phillips curve: higher (lower) inflation has been, on average, accompanied by rising (declining) unemployment in the US.

Figure 5.20 I.(b) shows the Phillips curve with inflation lagged by 33 months. The fit between the two series is much better, with the correlation coefficient standing at 0.69. However, there is still a positive relation between the unemployment rate and inflation in the period under review.

In the period 1951:10 to 1974:12, the relation between the unemployment rate and inflation was rather weak, both for the cotemporaneous and lagged specification (see Fig. 5.20 II.(c) and (d)). In fact the Phillips curve is actually a horizontal line.

The Phillips curve shows a positive slope for the period 1975:1 to 2005:1 (Fig. 5.20 III.(e) and (f)), with the correlation coefficients for both the contemporaneous and lagged relationships being relatively high (that is 0.59 and 0.72, respectively).

The findings suggest that the modified Phillips curve trade-off theory did not hold in the US for the sample periods under review. In fact, the findings suggest that inflation might have exerted a negative effect on investment, output and employment: unemployment did rise rather than fall in an inflationary environment.

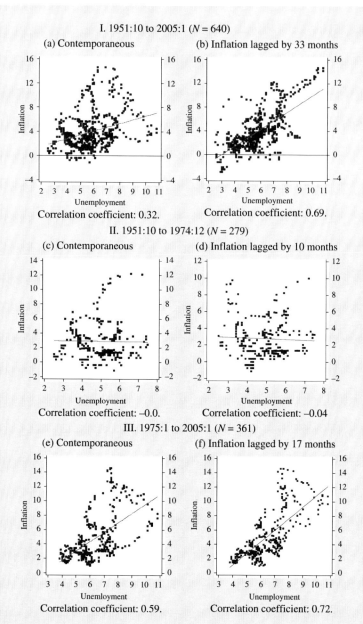

Fig. 5.20 Phillips curves in the US for alternative periods
Source: Bloomberg; own calculations. – Total sample period: January 1949–January 2005.
– Inflation defined as annual change in the consumer price index. – All variables are seasonally adjusted. – The time lags were determined by the maximum value of a cross correlation
analysis. – N = number of data points.

5.3.2.3 Expectation Based Phillips Curve

According to a hypothesis put forward by Milton Friedman (1968a, 1968b) and Edmund Phelps (1967), the economically relevant relation between unemployment and wages is determined by *real rather than nominal wages*. As a result, the authors substitute the nominal wage growth in Eq. (5.62) for real wage growth so that we yield:

$$\Delta \ln \left(\frac{W_t}{P_t} \right) = g(U_{t-1}) \text{ with } \frac{\partial g}{\partial U_{t-1}} < 0. \tag{5.68}$$

The change in the real wage is the difference between nominal wage growth and inflation:

$$\Delta \ln W_t - \pi_t = g(U_{t-1}). \tag{5.69}$$

What is important, Friedman (1968a, 1968b) and Phelps (1967, 1968) assume that future inflation is not known with certainty at the point in time when wages are determined. As a result, Friedman and Phelps insert expected inflation (π_t^e) in Eq. (5.69), which can be rearranged as:

$$\Delta \ln W_t = g(U_{t-1}) + \pi_t^e. \tag{5.70}$$

According to Eq. (5.70), nominal wage growth depends on the employment situation as well as market agents' inflation expectations.

Assuming constant productivity growth, Eq. (5.62) can be reformulated as follows:

$$\pi_t = g(U_{t-1}) - \lambda + \pi_t^e. \tag{5.71}$$

According to Eq. (5.71), productivity growth and expected inflation affect the location of the expectation based Phillips curve, but do not have an impact on its sloop.

Figure 5.21 shows negatively sloped Phillips curves for alternative inflation expectations. The Phillips curves move further to the right with rising inflation expectations. That said, the assumed long-run trade-off between unemployment and inflation, as suggested by the traditional and modified Phillips curves, does no longer exist. It just holds in the short-run if, and only if, actual inflation turns out to be higher than expected inflation.

Assume the economy is in equilibrium, unemployment stands at U^*, and inflation expectations are zero. Assume further that the government attempts to decrease unemployment below U^* (say, to U_1). The central bank increases the stock of money so that, with a time lag, inflation rises above expectations (in this case it exceeds zero). The decline in real wages induces firms to increase their demand for labour. Unemployment falls to U_1 as inflation rises to π_1. However, employees will seek compensation and demand higher nominal wages. As a result, real wages rise, the

Fig. 5.21 Long- and
short-run expectation based
Phillips curve

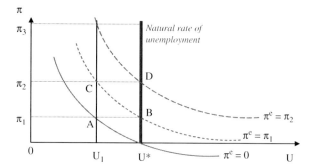

demand for labour declines, and unemployment moves back to U^*. The new equilibrium is B, where unemployment is unchanged, accompanied by higher inflation.

Under variable inflation expectations (as well as changes in productivity), there is no longer a stable long-run relation between unemployment and inflation. Assuming adaptive expectations and constant productivity growth, a long-run trade-off between unemployment and inflation is only possible under *accelerating inflation* over time – which leads to hyper inflation.

To show this, assume that actual and ex ante expected inflation are equal, that is $\pi = \pi^e$. In this case, the conclusion from using Eq. (5.71) is:

$$\lambda = g(U). \qquad (5.72a)$$

The reversal function of Eq. (5.72a) shows that unemployment (U) is determined by the real economy only (assuming constant productivity):

$$U = g^{-1}(\lambda). \qquad (5.72b)$$

According to Eq. (5.72b), the long-run Phillips curve is a vertical line. Here, the unemployment rate does no longer depend on monetary variables. It represents the *natural unemployment rate* (Friedman, 1968a, 1968b), which cannot be lowered on a persistent basis by monetary policy. The natural unemployment rate became known as the *non accelerating inflation rate of unemployment* or *NAIRU*, reflecting *structural* unemployment.

5.3.2.4 The Hysteresis-Based Phillips Curve

Up to now we assumed that the natural rate of unemployment is a kind of "natural constant", is driven only by structural characteristics of the economy, but is not path-dependent. But what happens to our above Phillips curve analysis if the natural rate of (un-employment becomes path-dependent, i.e. hysteretic? Some "new Keynesian" economists argue that there is no natural rate of unemployment in the sense of a rate to which the actual rate tends converge. Instead, when actual unemployment rises and remains high for some time, the NAIRU rises as well. The dependence of the NAIRU on actual unemployment is known as the hysteresis hypothesis (Cross, 1988). Hysteresis is a notion from ferromagnetics and refers to the influence of current market shocks on future market equilibrium conditions (expressed in Latin: "Semper aliquid haeret!"). As introduced by Phelps (1972), unemployment hysteresis describes *a sustained unemployment after a transitory shock*. In essence, the effect of the shock gets built into the natural rate of unemployment resulting in *changing the long run equilibrium*.

In general, there are two theoretical justifications for the existence of hysteresis. The first main justification is based on market rigidities. It is the view used in the insider-outsider model of Lindbeck and Snower (1988). This view stipulates that the existence of hysteresis is due to the power of labor unions that keep the equilibrium wage high, and therefore increases unemployment. Hence, one explanation for hysteresis in a heavily unionized economy is that unions directly represent the interests only of those who are currently employed (*insider-outsider approach*). Unionization undermines the ability of those outside the union to compete for employment. After prolonged layoffs employed workers inside the union may seek the benefits of higher wages for themselves, rather than moderating wage demands to promote the rehiring of unemployed workers. Market rigidity is also the basis for *the human capital approach* (Layard, Nickell, & Jackman, 1991). This kind of hysteresis effect deals with human capital depreciation during spells of unemployment which lowers the real wage necessary for re-entering the labor market. Complementary approaches stress the fact that during recessions physical capital is downsized more quickly than it is rebuilt in the next boom (*capital shortage approach*, Burda, 1988).

The second main justification for hysteresis is based on the anticipation of inflation in a Phillips Curve approach, whereby downward pressures on inflation lead to sustained high unemployment (Hall, 1979). In a more general sense, a change in the natural rate of unemployment can occur due to: (i) fluctuations in macroeconomic variables (Blanchard & Wolfers, 2000; Phelps, 1999), or (ii) institutional changes that affect employment conditions, such as labor market regulations. Hysteresis causes unemployment dynamics to be a non-stationary process that does not revert to its long run equilibrium. On the contrary, rejecting hysteresis implies that the unemployment dynamic is a stationary process that is flexible enough to easily revert to its long run equilibrium. Nevertheless, in the case of near hysteresis (*persistence*), market rigidities cause unemployment to remain in the economy because the speed of adjustment to the long run equilibrium level is slower.

On a more theoretical level testing for (un-) employment hysteresis has become synonymous in the mainstream literature with testing for stationarity in the (un-)employment data although maintaining "true" hysteresis according to the hysteresis concept in natural sciences involves much more than establishing a mere unit root in the time series (Sect. 5.3.3). However, it has proven rather difficult to disentangle persistence from pure hysteresis based on a limited data set due to near observational equivalence of both phenomena (Perron, 1989).

Taking the hysteresis approach for granted and accepting its main implications, one might argue in the framework of Fig. 5.21 that a temporarily expansionary monetary policy might be successful in the long run because U_1 will become the new natural rate of unemployment U^*; in the future after the three mechanisms described above have been effective. By this, lower short-term unemployment has been transformed to lower structural unemployment over time by counter-cyclical monetary policy. However, the downside to the hysteresis hypothesis is that once unemployment becomes high – as it did in Europe in the recessions of the seventies – it is relatively impervious to a monetary and fiscal stimulus, even in the short run. The hysteresis hypothesis appears to be more relevant to Europe, where unionization is higher and where labor laws create numerous barriers to hiring and firing, than it is to the United States, with its considerably more flexible labor markets.

Many macroeconomists have been interested and to a certain extend involved in the hysteresis debate since the mid-eighties, mainly from a labor market and Phillips curve perspective. European unemployment has been steadily increasing for the last fifteen years at the time of writing of the now-famous paper by Blanchard and Summers (1986, 1988) on hysteresis as a description and explanation of the roots of the European unemployment problem. At the time of writing, structural unemployment in continental Europe was expected to remain very high for many years to come. And these pessimistic expectations proved right in the end. In their paper, Blanchard and Summers argue that this fact implies that shocks have much more persistent effects on unemployment than standard theories can possibly explain. They develop a theory which can explain such persistence, and which is based on the distinction between insiders and outsiders in wage bargaining. They argue that if wages are largely set by bargaining between insiders and firms, shocks which affect actual unemployment tend also to affect equilibrium unemployment. They then confront the theory to both the detailed facts of the European situation as well as to earlier periods of high persistent unemployment such as the Great Depression in the US.

What we learned from the early debate about hysteresis in (un-) employment was mainly that the "true" (in the sense of accordance with ferromagnetics science) concept of hysteretic dependence as developed and conveyed by Cross (1994) and colleagues *clearly reaches beyond the pure random walk* ("unit root") *notion of the unemployment rate*, the latter implying not more than the degeneration of the adjustment process. Although one should be careful in science with claiming that a model is "true", the concept convinced me in view of its nice and elaborated Preisach-style micro foundations. Please note, that up to now empirical support in favour of the a latter is still rather difficult to gain in view of the special distributions of critical values, which have to be generated by certain Monte Carlo exercises. Hence, some additional will still be necessary to render policy consulting fully founded and more convincing. In this sense, empirics is a conditio sine qua non for sound (monetary) policy advice giving.

As already stated above, standard neoclassical economic analysis has microeconomic foundations in which some representative agent continuously responds to economic shocks. This yields economic equilibria their do not contain a memory of the past shocks. Since the seventies it has become reasonable clear that some important economic phenomena are not well described by such models. For example, expansionary shocks have reduced unemployment rates without leading to rising inflation rates predicted by standard models.

In this respect, one might think of the UK and Italy departure from the ERM in 1992 or the buoyant stock market of the nineties. The recent debate on inflation forecasts for the year 2003 clearly demonstrate that this view has not lost anything of its topicality up to now. In most years, it was rather obvious that high unemployment rates were compatible with increasing inflation in Euroland. As for as in the same way as relatively low unemployment rates have gone along with rather low inflation only recently when the credit crisis started policy consulting, is concerned we argued along these lines for instance in our regular ECB observer report and forecasted inflation rates for Euroland well above 2% although it was quite clear that unemployment would stay as high as before (Belke, Koesters, Leschke, & Polleit, 2002). However, we found ourselves in a minority position among the wide array called "EZB-Schattenrat" of ECB workers, among them the the ECB Shadow Committee which was founded some years ago by one of the leading German financial newspapers, the "Handelsblatt". ("EZB-Schattenrat"). In this respect, it should be noted that only three of eighteen members of the so-called shadow committee of the ECB, all of them Germans (!), at that time argued against a further lowering of interest rates in the euro area in view of inflation forecasts well above the targeted 2%.

The mathematical theory of hysteresis contributes to the analysis of situations including habit formation and the excess smoothness of consumption decisions, sunk costs and irreversibilities in investment and market entry decisions, and along the lines of 2008 Nobel prize win new Paul Krugman long-lasting effects of temporary exchange rate changes on international trade flows. This theory provides a toolbox of simple and complex models for hysteretic dependence. Combined with dynamical system theory, it yields qualitative insights into the short-term and long-term behaviour of such processes, and it forms – as mathematicians often put it – the basis for their reliable numerical simulation. However, it can be asked whether the use of hysteresis models goes significantly beyond a pure description of, e.g., economic processes. In other words: do hysteresis models have an inherent strategic value, which makes them indispensable in giving policy advice?

We would like to strengthen the case for hysteresis models when giving policy advice in areas in which path-dependent variables are relevant. For this purpose, we will focus on the debate about European Monetary Union from a public choice perspective and will emphasize the "two-handed approach" to economic policy. This approach can be traced back to the hysteresis approach and alludes to the fact that a combination of supply-side and demand-side measures is the most efficient way to tackle the bad performance of economic variables which exhibit path-dependence.[27] The main argument behind it is as follows. According to this view, the application of supply-side oriented measures lowers the magnitude of the demand shock necessary to reverse the effect of an adverse shock in the past. Demand-side measures enhance the probability of supply-side reforms. Since supply-side measures are often proposed by politicians adhering to neoclassical theory and demand-side measures are favoured by those who are advised by Keynesian economists or are heavily

---

[27] Again: for an excellent survey in this respect see the comprehensive volume on hysteresis in unemployment edited by Rod Cross (1988).

influenced by unions, policy advice derived from a hysteresis model typically has a high chance to lead to a political consensus. Moreover, politicians are rewarded for reform efforts with long-lasting benefits. Taken the significant reduction in polarisation of the political parties' programs in Western Europe as given, the mathematical theory of hysteresis might contribute to progress in a non-mathematical area, i.e. to a more efficient policy advice giving.

5.3.2.5 Why Is the Use of Full-Fledged Hysteresis Models So Attractive for Monetary Policy Consulting?

It is rather obvious that one should differentiate between different levels of the argument when judging on the usefulness of hysteresis models. First, hysteresis models might be seen as a medium to make economic relations more understandable to the public. In other words: they might be preferred by policy advisors because they are *intuitively understandable* rather quickly (for example because their components are well-known from every day-life respectively from school). However, the question arises how to judge a fully-fledged hysteresis model in this respect compared to the popular random walk hysteresis representation. Our personal guess would be that the former – though highly interesting in itself – has been presented up to now in a fashion much too complicated and too difficult to be understood by the recipients of policy advice.

Second, these models might be accepted by politicians and other recipients of policy advice more easily than those purely based on either Keynesian or supply-side "ideology" because their *economic policy implications are acceptable* in a political sense by a vast majority among them. Remember that the main message of policy advice arising from the "true" hysteresis models is to follow the "two-handed approach". I would like to call this kind of strategic considerations the search for a *politico-economic motivation of model choice*. In my view, the determinants of the choice of macro models to be used for policy consulting have not been investigated sufficiently up to now. Unfortunately, this is neither the case with respect to the choice of Economic Research Institutes by political parties seeking policy advice, nor with the problems arising from this "ideology bias" with respect to the credibility of the published policy advice resulting from this kind of procedure. Note that a lack of credibility of policy advice significantly hampers the implementation of the highly awaited structural reforms. According to the New Political Economy, in reality incentives should determine the model choice although time series econometrics has recently developed some criteria to choose between a more supply-side or a more Keynesian model by scientific criteria (see, for instance, Pesaran and Pesaran, 1997).

Third, models with hysteretic features are potentially attractive, because they up to now come together with *convincing empirical corroboration*. However, in this field there admittedly remains still a lot to be done. Much further empirical work will have to be invested in order to investigate the important question whether there is really convincing empirical evidence that hysteresis models do a better task in forecasting economic activity than non-hysteretic models and what do the usual model selection criteria tell us about this.

Fourth, a further caveat with respect to too much laxity in the application of hysteresis models might be the fact that persuading political leaders of the validity of hysteresis models might induce these leaders to act as if the latter are valid descriptions of reality (*Lucas critique,* see Lucas, 1976). The resulting economic policy actions might then be welcomed by policy advisors.

One potential *danger* of using hysteresis models in giving policy advice is connected with the fact that the former tend to favour the so-called "two-handed" approach and, thus, do not lead to the derivation of a clear-cut advice in the sense of policy measures which are either purely supply-side or purely demand-side oriented. In other words, the resulting piece of policy advice is *not unambiguous enough* to give clear-cut guidelines according to the principles of a sound "Ordnungpolitik" of the German style.[28] From another perspective, however, this might at the same time be the largest advantage because they lead to a political consensus with a higher probability and policy advice would be accepted more easier by the policy makers (see point 2 above).

The main focus behind this view is on the "*two-handed approach*" to economic policy originally brought forward by the Centre for European Policy Studies' Macroeconomic Policy Group, Brussels, in the midst of the eighties (see, for instance, Belke 2002). This landmark approach can be traced back to the hysteresis approach and alludes to the fact that a combination of supply-side and demand-side measures is the most efficient way to tackle the bad performance of economic variables, which exhibit path-dependence. The application of supply-side measures lowers the magnitude of the demand shock necessary to reverse the effect of an adverse shock in the past. At the same time, demand-side measures enhance the probability of supply-side reforms (a point stressed in the next paragraphs).

Since supply-side measures are often proposed by politicians adhering to neoclassical theory and demand-side measures are favoured by those who are advised by Keynesian type economists, policy advice derived from a hysteresis model typically has a high chance to lead to a political consensus. Moreover, and this strengthens the argument in favour of the "two-handed approach", politicians anticipate to be *rewarded for reform efforts with long-lasting benefits.* Given the reduction in polarisation of the political parties' programs in Western Europe (see, e.g., Chancellor Schroeder's policies based on the so-called Schroeder-Blair paper at the beginning of his first term, and his policy announcements which are shared by his "Superminister" Clement at the start of his second term), the mathematical theory of hysteresis might thus contribute to progress in a non-mathematical area, i.e. to a more efficient policy advice giving.

However, if politicians understand the special kind of dependence expressed by hysteresis models and legislation periods are limited to, let's say, four years, there might as well be an additional incentive for them to punish future governments with a bad economic performance today (which has an impact on the performance

---

[28]Instead, as expressed from a German point of view, the policy recommendations can best be characterized by a mixture of "Prozesspolitik" and "Ordnungspolitik".

tomorrow and so on). In this case, the chance of sound policies due to policy advice giving based on hysteresis models is admittedly rather limited. Hence, policy advice giving based on hysteresis models should be concentrated on the beginning of the legislation period.

Finally, the very influential *political economy of labour market reform* models of the Saint-Paul type are worth to be mentioned here with respect to strategic aspects of policy implementation (see, for instance, Saint-Paul 1996a). According to this strain of literature, the probability of supply-side reforms rises, e.g., if they are backed by demand-side measures. Thus, the complementarity of different labour market policies as one important policy implication inherent in hysteretic models is supported from another angle as well. Moreover, as shown above, politicians who believe in hysteresis have a reform bias quite different from those believing in, e.g., a natural rate of unemployment as a natural constant.

Let us now turn to the formal derivation of a full-fledged hysteresis model of a natural rate of employment in an open-economy context. The reader will see in a minute that the latter moves variably over time in a path-dependent fashion. Expressed in terms of the notion of the Phillips curve, the connection of inflation with unemployment becomes significantly less tight. Speaking differently, one specific realization of (un-) employment can be observed with different empirical realizations of the inflation rate. This property is emphasized if there is return uncertainty for firms.

5.3.3 A Path-Dependent Long-Run Phillips Curve – The Case of Hysteresis

This section deals with a generalisation of the hysteresis notion and, for this purpose, derives a micro-based macro model of employment hysteresis under uncertainty (Belke & Goecke, 2005). It can be shown that *one does not need any Neo-Keynesian type ingredients* like wage rigidities in order to derive hysteretic properties of (un-) employment. In a baseline micro model a band of inaction due to hiring- and firing-costs is widened by option value effects of exchange rate uncertainty. Based on this micro foundation an aggregation approach is presented. Under uncertainty, intervals of weak response to exchange rate reversals are introduced on the macro-level. "Spurts" in new employment or firing may occur after an initially weak response. Since these mechanisms may apply to other "investment" cases where the aggregation of microeconomic real options effects under uncertainty are relevant, they may even be of a more general interest in the broad range of topics included in our textbook.

5.3.3.1 Introduction

The usual presumption of EMU proponents has been that lowering exchange rate volatility promotes foreign trade. However, macroeconomic empirical evidence is far from conclusive in that respect (e.g. Côté, 1994). The possibility that exchange rate uncertainty could have an impact on labour market performance or at least on the relation between employment and its determinants has not been considered so far (Belke & Gros, 2001). The lack of a theoretical and empirical literature on the effect of exchange rate variability on employment is striking in view of the high policy relevance of the question (Dornbusch, 1987) and in view of the fact that there is considerable literature on the link between investment and uncertainty (Cushman, 1985; Darby, Hughes Hallet, Ireland, & Piscitelli, 1998). Given the high hiring and firing costs affecting European labour markets (Bentolila & Bertola, 1990; Saint-Paul, 1996) one would assume that the same arguments that underpin the presumed effect of volatility on investment should also apply to exchange rate volatility and employment. But given the weak results concerning the link between exchange rate volatility and trade, the prior of many economists seemed to be that exchange rate variability is not important and that there should be no link between exchange rate variability and (un)employment.

Côté (1994) and de Grauwe and Skudelny (1997) show that the empirical puzzle concerning the impact of exchange rate uncertainty and foreign trade might have been due to the *methods* chosen so far. In the light of their arguments (but relying on a totally different theoretical approach) this paper argues that – *on a micro level* – the absence of evidence of a strong impact of exchange rate variability on the volume of trade is due to neglecting a "band of inaction" of export activity based on sunk costs. Its impacts are amplified by volatility-induced uncertainty. This export inactivity band spills over to labour markets leading to stronger persistence in (un)employment.[29] In order to solve the empirical puzzle, the micro approach has to be transferred to the *macro-level*.

A macro interpretation of micro hysteresis and of uncertainty impacts on "investment" decisions cannot be performed in a straightforward way, since different firms have different "investment" thresholds. For this reason, we pay special attention to the *problem of aggregation*.[30] The examination of the persistent effects of only temporary exchange rate shocks on employment behaviour of single firms and on overall employment is conducted based on an aggregation approach, developed by Krasnosel'skii and Pokrovskii (1989) and Mayergoyz (1986) and introduced to economics by Amable, Henry, Lordon, and Topol (1991, 1995) and Cross (1994). This approach stresses the differences between hysteretic effects on the micro and on the macro level and the consequences of aggregation (*under certainty*): while at the micro level certain threshold values of the input variable have to be passed in order to produce branch-to-branch-transitions (i.e. shifts in the input-output relation), at the macro level small changes in the input variable can yield long-lasting

---

[29]For a more theoretical treatment see Belke and Goecke (1999).

[30]For aggregation problems in the presence of underlying non-linear micro relations see van Garderen, Lee, and Pesaran (1997). Generally, the aggregation is regarded as especially complicated in this case. Since we impose very stringent restrictions on the shape of the non-linearity, we are able to derive an exactly identified macro behaviour.

effects.[31] What is up to now not well-known in the literature is how the introduction of *un*certainty influences the transition from micro to macro behaviour. In this contribution we show that, under uncertainty, areas of non-reaction – corresponding to mechanical play the so-called "play"-area – have to be considered even at the macro level. Thus, similarities of macro relations ["play"] to micro behaviour [band of inaction] are enhanced by uncertainty.[32] The first result of the paper is that persistent aggregate (employment) effects do *not* necessarily result from small changes in the forcing (labour market) variables, as far as the changes occur inside the play-area. However, as far as changes go beyond the play-area, suddenly strong reactions (and persistence effects) will occur. With this, we theoretically capture the "spurts" commonly observed in aggregate hiring/firing or investment decisions explicitly based on an aggregation approach for heterogeneous firms.[33]

The further outline of this section is as follows. As a first step, the baseline micro model of employment hysteresis under certainty is described. As a second step, we deal with the aggregation approach under certainty. Third, we focus on modifications to our micro level analysis which become necessary by the consideration of uncertainty. As a fourth step, we present a method to solve the problem of aggregation of hysteresis from micro to total economy employment under uncertainty.

5.3.3.2 The Micro Model Under Certainty

We consider an extremely simple model of an exporting firm which has been active or passive in a foreign market in the past. Depending on its past state of activity this firm might either retain activity or exit (if it has been active in the past) respectively remain passive or enter the foreign market (if it has been passive). If a previously inactive firm enters the market, it has to bear entry costs, i.e. costs of hiring new labour. These expenditures cannot be regained and are therefore ex-post treated as sunk costs. Thus entering (leaving) can be compared with an investment (disinvestment) project.

---

[31] In this context, the terms "input" and "output" are used in a mathematical or physical sense ("input-output transducer"). The macro form is called "strong" hysteresis (Amable et al., 1991, 1994; Cross, 1994). Another recent strand of literature deals with models which are more general with respect to the non-linearities at the micro level than the one presented here. See e.g. Caballero, Engel, and Haltiwanger (1997). These models explain aggregate employment dynamics, but dispense with an explicit derivation of an aggregation mechanism over heterogeneous firms.

[32] For an overview of the variety of uses of the term "hysteresis" in economics for different path-dependent phenomena ranging from "band of inaction", "play" to "strong hysteresis" especially compared to the approximation of hysteresis via unit (zero) roots in difference (differential) equations see Amable et al. (1994) and Goecke (2002).

[33] For an (empirical) macro analysis of "spurts" in investment implicitly based on micro (i.e. threshold) models see Darby et al. (1998, pp. 24ff).

The firm j is assumed to be a price taker in the foreign and in the currency market. It produces one unit[34] of a final product using a_j units of labour, with the wage w being the price of labour, i.e. variable costs are $w \cdot aj$. Selling on the foreign market, the firm receives the price p^*. The gross profit (in domestic currency) on sales in the foreign market, without consideration of hiring and firing costs, is:[35]

$$R_{j,a,t} = p^* \cdot e_t - w_t \cdot a_j. \tag{5.73}$$

with:

t: time index
j: index for potential domestic exporters
$R_{j,a,t}$: gross profit of firm j in period t (if active)
e_t: exchange rate (home currency price of foreign exchange)
w_t: wage rate
a_j: input coefficient of labour of firm j
p^*: price of the domestic export good (in foreign currency).

We feel justified to ascribe the revenue volatility solely to exchange rate volatility, since it is well-known that short-term volatility of exchange rates exceeds the variability of prices, wages and productivity by far.[36] We assume $w_t = w$ and a_j to be constant and normalise p^* to unity. As a consequence, the exporters are forced to bear unit revenue changes (in their own currency) proportionally to the exchange rate changes. A weaker form of the results of our model stays valid, if p^* changes less than proportionally compared with the exchange rate. The same logic can be applied to import-competing firms, whose revenues are influenced by the exchange rate as well. Using this simplification, the gross profit of firm j follows as:

$$R_{j,a,t} = e_t - w \cdot a_j \text{ (if active), otherwise } R_{j,p,t} = 0 \text{ (if passive).} \tag{5.74}$$

It is assumed that the hiring costs H_j (including training costs) must be spent at the moment the entry is executed, and the firm has to pay firing costs F_j at the time it leaves the market (e.g. severance pay). If the firm later on decides to re-enter the market, the entire hiring costs must be repaid. If the firm is inactive for only one period, however, the staff must be completely re-set up and the hiring costs must be paid anew. Since switching the state of activity leads to a complete depreciation of hiring respectively firing costs, H_j and F_j have to be regarded as sunk costs ex post. The decision whether the firm should sell abroad or not, is reached by a comparison

---

[34] If an institutional firm is imagined to be divided into single production units, every unit is represented here individually. By this form of (fictitious) dis-aggregation a totally new erection as well as an enlargement of employment by an institutional firm can be included.

[35] For a related model see Baldwin and Krugman (1989, p. 638) and Goecke (1994). The index j used here indicates heterogeneity between firms.

[36] See for instance, Darby et al. (1998, pp. 1f.), Krugman (1989, p. 64).

of the expected present values of the returns with or without being active in the decision period t.

A firm j which has been active in the preceding period and will continue its activity will gain the period t revenue $R_{j,a,t}$. The discount factor is defined as $\delta = 1/(1 + i)$ with interest rate i. Since it expects the same revenue for the whole infinite future the present value of annuity due of continuing activity is $(e - w \cdot a_j)/(1 - \delta)$, which has to be compared to the present value of an instantaneous exit, i.e. firing costs $(-F_j)$. Equating both expressions leads to an exit trigger exchange rate value β_j for switching from employment to inactivity:

$$\beta_j = e^c_{j,exit} = w \cdot a_j - (1 - \delta) \cdot F_j \quad \text{with: exit if } e_t < \beta_j. \tag{5.75}$$

Therefore, the unit revenue e has to cover at least the wage costs $w \cdot a_j$ less the interest costs of exit. Hence, due to the sunk firing costs the price floor is below variable costs.

A previously non-active firm earns neither current nor future profits if it remains passive. If it enters the market and hires new employees it has to pay extra hiring costs H_j to be able to earn current and future profits: $-H_j + (e - w \cdot a_j)/(1 - \delta)$. With this, the entry trigger α_j is:

$$\alpha_j = e^c_{j,entry} = w \cdot a_j + (1 - \delta) \cdot H_j \quad \text{with: entry if } e_t > \alpha_j \text{ and } \alpha_j > \beta_j. \tag{5.76}$$

Due to the sunk hiring costs, the necessary unit revenue is larger than the variable costs. Combining both trigger values, a "band of inaction" results (Fig. 5.22). The latter implies that the current realisation of the exchange rate is not sufficient to determine the current state of the firm's activity. Depending on the past, the relationship between *input variable (exchange rate)* and *output variable (employment)*

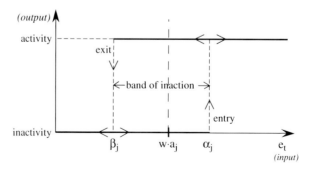

Fig. 5.22 Micro hysteresis for a single-unit firm j under certainty

is represented by different curves.[37] In order to select one of the multiple equilibria, the history of activity has to be regarded. In the case of micro hysteresis nonlinearity has a very simple form: there exist only two "branches" with a discontinuous branch-to-branch-transition when certain threshold-values are passed.

5.3.3.3 Macro Level: An Aggregation Approach

In this section we describe a procedure which allows an aggregation of heterogeneous single firms with an employment behaviour characterised by a micro hysteresis loop, resulting in a continuous macro loop of overall employment (see Amable et al., 1991, 1995; Cross, 1994; Goecke, 1994). Every potentially active firm is characterised by its α_j/β_j-set. Since $\alpha_j \geq \beta_j$, all α/β-points are located in the triangle area T above the 45°-line. The aggregation is done without any serious restriction of heterogeneity in the cost structure (concerning H_j, F_j and a_j) between the firms. Points on the 45°-line describe non-hysteretic employers (H_j, $F_j = 0 \Rightarrow \alpha = \beta$), the distance from the origin given by $w \cdot a_j$. For points above the line there is micro hysteresis in employment, the distance from the ($\alpha = \beta$)-line measured in north west direction determined by H_j and F_j.

In order to prevent extensive assumptions concerning the past exchange rate development, the exchange rate $e = 0$ is assumed as an initial level. Therefore, no firm is active initially. Starting from $e = 0$ the exchange rate rises, resulting in hiring by firms with the lowest costs (and the lowest entry rate α_j).[38] Hence, overall employment increases, as traced in Fig. 5.23(a).[39] The triangle T is divided into two shares: S_t^+ (including all active firms) and S_t^- (including all inactive firms). For increasing exchange rates, the share S_t^+ expands while S_t^- diminishes. The firms with a changing state of activity are described by the α/β-points in the hatched area. For rising rates, the S_t^+-expansion is indicated by an upward shift of the horizontal borderline.

In Fig. 5.23(b) a subsequent decrease in the exchange rate is traced: e_t falls from the highest value, the (local) maximum e_1^M. Therefore, S_t^+ decreases, since firms, which recently hired new employees, now leave the market when the exchange rate falls below their exit rate β_j. For decreasing exchange rates, the activity changes (hatched area) are illustrated by a left vertical shift of the $S_t^- - S_t^+$-borderline. (The corresponding macro reaction is path BC in Fig. 5.25.)

If the exchange rate rises again, after reaching the local minimum e_1^m (the lowest input level apart from the initial rate $e_0^m = 0$), $S_t;^+$ expands again. This is depicted in Fig. 5.23(c) once again by an upward shift of the right-horizontal part of the

---

[37] The reader should be aware that the terms "input" and "output" are used in a mathematical or physical sense.

[38] The exchange rate $e = 0$ has not to be understood in a strict way: The exchange rates could also be stated in a standardised form with $e = 0$ as the rate that induces an exit of all firms. See Amable et al. (1991, p. 10).

[39] The increase in overall employment takes place on the lowest branch (path OAB in Fig. 4).

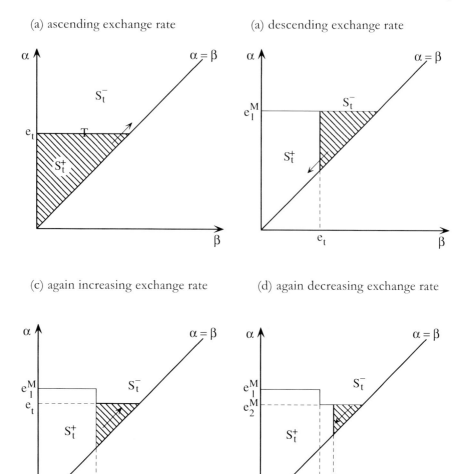

Fig. 5.23 Active firms under a volatile exchange rate
Source: Following Amable et al. (1991), Figs. 3 and 4.

borderline.[40] The result of the subsequent shifts is a "staircase-shape" of the border between the two parts of T. If the recently reached (local) maximum is lower than the highest maximum e_1^M, a staircase step in the borderline remains characterised by the coordinates ($\alpha = e_1^M / \beta = e_1^m$). If the exchange rate would have continued to increase and would have passed the original maximum, the α-coordinate of the "e_1^M-step" would have been "erased" and would have been replaced by the "new"

---

[40]The resulting macro reaction is depicted as path CD in Fig. 4.

e_1^M.[41] However, if (as traced in Fig. 5.23(c)) the new local maximum is lower than the "old" e_1^M, the maximum e_1^M remains and the new local maximum becomes the second highest, and is consequently labelled e_2^M.

Figure 5.23(d) illustrates a later decreasing exchange rate. The borderline is changed by a shift to the left of the lower vertical part (corresponding to DE in Fig. 5.25). If e_t does not fall below e_1^m with the new local minimum (disregarding the initial level) the second lowest minimum is given, labelled e_2^m. If the input were to fall under the "old" e_1^m, the β-coordinate of the corresponding staircase-step would be eliminated and the new local minimum would be (the "new") e_1^m.[42] If subsequent local maxima and minima are not as "extreme" as the preceding extrema, a new corner in the staircase border is created. On the other hand, local maxima which are higher than preceding maxima will erase the α-coordinate of the corresponding corners; subsequent local minima erase the β-coordinate of corners corresponding to higher preceding minima (Amable et al., 1991, pp. 11ff.). For a given exchange rate path, the remaining maxima are ordered by descending size and the remaining minima by ascending size; a sequence of local maxima e_i^M and local minima e_i^m results ($i=1,\ldots, p$). The α/β-coordinates of the outward corners of the staircase $S_t^+ - S_t^-$-borderline are given by the pairs ($\alpha = e_i^M$ and $\beta = e_i^m$). An illustration of the staircase borderline is drawn in Fig. 5.24(a) for rising and in (b) for falling exchange rates.

For ascending exchange rates the area S_t^+ (including all active firms) can be divided into two partial areas $\left(\sum_i^p S_i^+ \text{ and } \sigma_t^+ \right)$. Path-dependence is captured by the influence of the past input extrema on the area of the active (i.e. employing) firms.

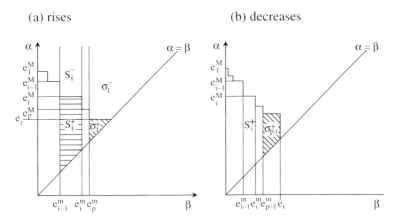

Fig. 5.24 Active firms when the exchange rate
Source: Following Amable et al. (1991), Figs. 5 and 8.

---

[41] For the erasing property see Mayergoyz (1986, p. 605).
[42] Consequently, starting with $e = 0$ erases all steps and so the whole influence of the past.

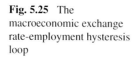

Fig. 5.25 The
macroeconomic exchange
rate-employment hysteresis
loop

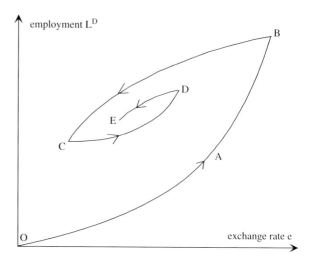

When the exchange rate decreases, the area S_t^+ is changed by shifts to the left of the lower right vertical part of the border. Only $\sigma_{p,t}^+$ is directly influenced by e_t, while $\sum_i^{p-1} S_i^+$ depends on past extrema. $\sigma_{p,t}^+$ diminishes with decreasing e_t, until the stage corresponding to the (highest not yet not-erased) minimum e_{p-1}^m is erased and the order $(p-1)$ of $\sum_i^{p-1} S_i^+$ is reduced by one.

Thus, the basic formal structure of the results for employment in the cases of rising and falling exchange rates is similar: an important constant term that is determined by the past extrema stands aside a term that is influenced by the current exchange rate e_t. The relations that are valid for the current exchange rate have been shifted by past input extrema. Consequently, every reversal in the *direction* of the exchange rate input path leads to a structural break in the exchange rate-employment (i.e. "input-output") relation.

In the case of micro hysteresis only two branches are possible. A jump between these two (not continuously linked) "branches" only occurs with the passing of certain threshold values. The continuous macro loop (Fig. 5.25) results from aggregation over a bulk of heterogeneous micro elements. Due to the lack of thresholds and to the fact that the path-dependence is captured by the local input variable extrema even small changes in the exchange rate can have durable effects on employment.[43]

The *distribution* of the heterogeneous firms in the α,β-space is important for the result of the analysis. A continuous distribution of the firms in the α,β-space

---

[43]See Mayergoyz (1986) and Amable et al. (1991, p. 2, 9, and 15). For a detailed mathematical analysis of various forms of hysteresis see Krasnosel'skii and Pokrovskii (1989) and Brokate and Sprekels (1996).

results in *continuous* macroeconomic loops in Fig. 5.25. The exact density of the $\alpha j, \beta j$-distribution will solely determine the curvature of the branches. The more all firms are clustered in a specific area (i.e. the more homogenous the firms are) the more curved are the branches. In the borderline case of a multiplicity of similar homogenous firms the macro-loop will degenerate to a loop of the form as depicted for a single firm in Fig. 5.22.

5.3.3.4 The Micro Model Under One-Off Uncertainty and the Possibility of Waiting

Uncertainty generates an option value of waiting, and therefore introduces a bias in favour of a "wait-and-see"-strategy. Since the firm's employment decision can be understood as an irreversible investment, we follow a real option approach. The firm's employment opportunity corresponds to a call option that gives the firm the right to employ (invest), hiring costs being the exercise price of the option, and to obtain a "project". The option itself is valuable, and exercising the employment investment "kills" the option. Analogously, disinvestment (firing) can be interpreted as a put option.

We analyse the effects of an expected future stochastic one-time shock on the band of inaction. However, assuming a risk-neutral firm, we abstract from risk-aversion. Focusing on employment impacts of uncertainty, we take up an idea originally proposed by Dornbusch (1987, pp. 8f.), Dixit (1989, p. 624, fn. 3), Bentolila and Bertola (1990), and Pindyck (1991, p. 1111). Option price effects are modelled in a technically sophisticated way in these references. Since we focus on the aggregation problem, we model micro uncertainty effects as simple as possible (based on the model by Belke & Goecke, 1999). However, the basic structure and the main micro effects of uncertainty are left unchanged compared to the cited references.

We suppose a non-recurring single stochastic change in the exchange rate, which can be either positive ($+\varepsilon$) or negative ($-\varepsilon$) (with $\varepsilon \geq 0$, mean preserving spread). For simplicity reasons, both realisations of the change ε are presumed to have a probability of $\frac{1}{2}$: $e_{t+1} = e_t \pm \varepsilon$ and $E_t(e_{t+1}) = e_t$. From period $t+1$ on, the firm will decide under certainty again. Thus, the trigger exchange rate value under certainty ("c-trigger") as derived above will become valid again. The stochastic change between t and $t+1$ leads to a widening of the band of inaction due to the possibility of a "wait-and-see"-strategy. Under certainty, the relevant alternative strategies are to enter or not for a previously inactive firm respectively to exit or not for a formerly active firm. Under uncertainty and the feasibility to delay an investment, a third alternative has to be taken into account: the option to wait and to meet the respective decision (i.e. entry or exit) in the future. The option to employ in the future is valuable because the future value of the "asset" obtained by employment is uncertain. If its value will decrease, the firm will not need to employ and will only lose what it will have spent to keep the employment opportunity. This limits the risk downwards and with this generates the inherent value of the option.

Under uncertainty a previously active (i.e. employing) firm has to decide whether to leave the market now or to stay active, including the option to leave later. It may appear advantageous for the firm to bear temporary period t losses, if there is a possibility of future gains. In this case the firm can avoid additional exit costs.[44] On the one hand, the firm anticipates the possibility of future gains if the future exchange rate turns out to be favourable $(+\varepsilon)$. On the other hand, the firm foresees that it can avoid future losses if the exchange rate change will be negative $(-\varepsilon)$ with a later exit in t+1.

The expected present value of the wait-and-see strategy in period t is defined as the probability-weighted average of the present values of both ε-realisations. Waiting implies a period t profit of $e - w \cdot a_j$. Conditional on the $(-\varepsilon)$-realisation, the firm will use its option to leave in t+1 causing discounted firing costs $\delta \cdot F_j$. In the case of the favourable $(+\varepsilon)$-realisation the firm will stay and earn annuity value $\delta \cdot (e + \varepsilon - w \cdot a_j)/(1 - \delta)$. Combining both, the expected present value of the wait-and-see strategy is:

$$E_t(V_{j,t}^{wait}) = e - w \cdot a_j - \frac{1}{2} \cdot \delta \cdot F_j + \frac{1}{2} \cdot \delta \cdot \frac{e + \varepsilon - w \cdot a_j}{1 - \delta}. \qquad (5.77)$$

The present value of an immediate exit is simply determined by firing costs: $E_t(V_{j,t}^{exit}) = -F_j$. Hence, the firm is indifferent between exit in t and "wait-and-see" if $E_t(V_{j,t}^{exit}) = E_t(V_{j,t}^{wait})$. As a consequence, the u-exit-trigger follows (with exit for $e_t < e_{j,exit}^u$):

$$e_{j,exit}^u = w \cdot a_j - (1 - \delta) \cdot F_j - \frac{\delta \cdot \varepsilon}{2 - \delta} = e_{j,exit}^c - \frac{\delta \cdot \varepsilon}{2 - \delta} = e_{j,exit}^c - \frac{\varepsilon}{1 + 2i}. \qquad (5.78)$$

A *previously inactive firm* has to decide whether to enter the market now or to stay passive, including the option to enter later. The firm anticipates the possibility of internalising future gains by an entry in t+1 if the future exchange rate turns out to be favourable $(+\varepsilon)$. Besides, the firm foresees that it can avoid future losses if the exchange rate change will be negative $(-\varepsilon)$ by staying passive. Waiting and staying inactive implies zero profits in t. Conditional on a $(+\varepsilon)$-realisation, the firm will use its option to enter in t+1 causing discounted hiring costs $\delta \cdot H_j$, gaining an annuity value of $\delta \cdot (e + \varepsilon - w \cdot a_j)/(1 - \delta)$. For a $(-\varepsilon)$-realisation the firm will remain passive. Consequently, the expected present value of the wait-and-see strategy for a previously inactive firm is given by $E_t(V_{j,t}^{wait})$ in Eq. (5.79). The expected present value of an immediate entry (without a re-exit) is $E_t(V_{j,t}^{entry})$:

$$E_t(V_{j,t}^{wait}) = -\frac{1}{2} \cdot \delta \cdot H_j + \frac{1}{2} \cdot \delta \cdot \frac{e + \varepsilon - w \cdot a_j}{1 - \delta};$$
$$E_t(V_{j,t}^{entry}) = -H_j + \frac{e - w \cdot a_j}{1 - \delta}. \qquad (5.79)$$

---

[44]Belke and Goecke (2005) abstract from a later re-entry (and analogously from a later re-exit by a previously inactive firm), and therefore neglect re-entry (re-exit) costs. For a more detailed presentation of the micro framework under uncertainty and for a simultaneous consideration of exit and re-entry (entry and re-exit) options see Belke and Goecke (1999).

The option value of having the flexibility to make the employment decision in the next period rather than to employ either now or never, can easily be calculated as the difference between the two expected net present values: $OV(e, \varepsilon) = E_t(V^{wait}_{j,t}) - E_t(V^{entry}_{j,t})$, with: $\partial OV/\partial e < 0$, $\partial OV/\partial \varepsilon > 0$. (An analogous logic can be applied to the disinvestment/firing put option case.) An increase in uncertainty enlarges the value of the option to employ later. The reason is that it enlarges the potential payoff of the option, leaving the downside payoff unchanged, since the firm will not exercise the option if the exchange rate falls. The firm is indifferent between entry in t and wait-and-see if $E_t(V^{entry}_{j,t}) = E_t(V^{wait}_{j,t})$, i.e. if $OV = 0$. The entry-trigger under uncertainty follows as (entry for $e_t > e^u_{j,entry}$):

$$e^u_{j,entry} = w \cdot a_j + (1 - \delta) \cdot H_j + \frac{\delta \cdot \varepsilon}{2 - \delta} = e^c_{j,entry} + \frac{\delta \cdot \varepsilon}{2 - \delta} = e^c_{j,entry} + \frac{\varepsilon}{1 - 2i}. \quad (5.80)$$

The entry (and exit) exchange rate trigger value under uncertainty is additively (subtractively) augmented by the term $\varepsilon/(1 + 2\,i)$. Thus *uncertainty leads to an expansion of the band of inaction*. Uncertainty increases the probability that a firm stays active (passive) if the current level of the revenue e has descended (ascended) from a formerly high (low) level that had earlier induced entry (exit). In our specific simple model the expansion of the band of inaction is even linear with respect to ε. Furthermore, in this simple set up the expansion is even independent of any aspects of heterogeneity.

5.3.3.5 Aggregation to the Macro Level Under Uncertainty

The qualitative property of micro hysteresis, i.e. the entry trigger being larger than the exit trigger, has not changed, when switching to uncertainty. However, the distance between the trigger values has been enlarged *for every firm*. With this, the aggregation approach described in detail further above can principally be applied to the case of uncertainty as well. We now focus on the implications of a switch from certainty to a situation with uncertainty for the shape and the location of the macro hysteresis loop.

Uncertainty leads to an outward shift of the entry and the exit trigger by $\varepsilon/(1 + 2i)$. Taking the situation under certainty described by Fig. 5.24 as a starting point, α_j moves to the north, and β_j slips westward by this amount. Thus, every (α_j, β_j)-combination characterising firm j is projected to the north-west. Hence the orthogonal distance of each point to the $(\alpha=\beta)$-45°-line is increased by $\sqrt{2(\varepsilon/(1 + 2i))^2}$. However, the non-hysteretic firms with H_j, $F_j = 0$ (located on the $\alpha=\beta$-line) retain their position even under uncertainty. Expressed graphically, the whole S^+_t-block comprising the active firms (and analogously the S^-_t-block describing the inactive firms) is shifted. A $\sqrt{2(\varepsilon/(1 + 2i))^2}$ –wide zone above and parallel

(a) has risen before   (b) has decreased before

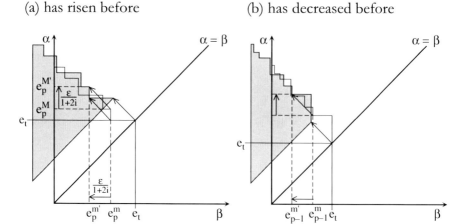

Fig. 5.26 Active firms after the introduction of uncertainty when exchange rate

to the $\alpha=\beta$-line free of firms emerges.[45] In Fig 5.26 the impacts of an introduction of uncertainty to a situation described by Fig. 5.26(a) and (b) are illustrated. Obviously, some firms with formerly positive exit rates may be shifted into the negative range. These firms would even bear negative revenues in order not to lose the sunk costs and the option value of waiting. Since in our simple model the unit revenue is expressed by the exchange rate which is expected to be positive, we will neglect the area on the LHS of the ordinate in our further analysis.

For simplicity reasons, with respect to the certainty situation we assume a preceding time path of the exchange rate which has produced a "staircase-borderline" with an infinite number of non-erased extrema resulting in infinitesimally small steps, resulting in a $(-45°)$-borderline with a negative slope equal to one. This procedure has the advantage to abstract from the differentiation concerning the actual direction of e underlying the parts (a) and (b) of Fig. 5.26 leaving the main effects of uncertainty on the aggregation procedure unaffected. All initially active firms are included in the triangle area S^+ depicted in Fig. 5.27(a). The initial exchange rate is given as e_0. The introduction of uncertainty thus results in a north-western shift of S^+ to the triangle $S^{+'}$ as illustrated in Fig. 5.27(b).

Taking e_0 as an initial value, an increase in the exchange rate up to e_1 does not affect any "hysteretic" firm (with H_j, $F_j > 0$) in the shifted triangle S'. Only "non-hysteretic" firms (with H_j, $F_j = 0$) on the $\alpha = \beta$-line change from inactivity to

---

[45]For reasons of simplicity, in this paper we have neglected the non-trivial problems which may arise when the possibility of a re-entry after an exit in t (respectively a re-exit after an entry in t) is given. A re-entry or a re-exit-behaviour might become optimal if the sunk costs (H_j and F_j) are "small" compared to the revenue change due to ε. As a consequence, these firms are not shifted by the full amount. This would result in a zone parallel to the $\alpha=\beta$-line which is not completely "de-populated" as derived above.

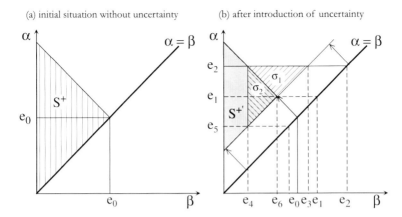

Fig. 5.27 Active firms dependent on the exchange rate

activity. Thus, in this "play" interval an increase in the exchange rate leads only to a weak reaction of employment, as it is depicted in Fig. 5.28 (as the movement from point A to B).[46] A further increase e.g. to the local maximum e_2 induces additional employment corresponding to the area σ_1 in Fig. 5.27(b) (point B to C in Fig. 5.28). While the initial weak reaction AB shows similarities to mechanical "play",[47] the

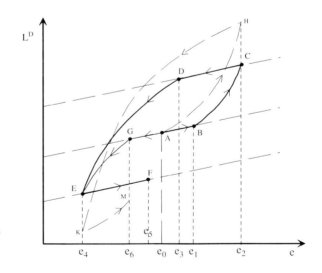

Fig. 5.28 Macro hysteresis loop under uncertainty (including "play")

---

[46]For reasons of simplicity, this reaction is depicted in a linear way. Expressed differently, non-hysteretic firms are assumed to be equally distributed on the $\alpha = \beta$-line.

[47]For a description of original play hysteresis, see Krasnosel'skii and Pokrovskii (1989, pp. 6ff.) and Brokate and Sprekels (1996, pp. 24f. and 42ff.).

subsequent additional increase BC leads to a strong reaction which can be titled "spurt" in employment. More concretely, after a reversal of the exchange rate the initially weak response of employment will evolve into a very strong response, once the thresholds of many firms are passed.[48] A reversal of the exchange rate towards e_3 will again cause a weak ("play") reaction (CD). A further decrease in the exchange rate to e_4 leads to an erasure of the formerly gained employment σ_1 as well as to new unemployment described by the area σ_2. Again a weak "play"-reaction follows for a subsequent increase to e_5 (EF). An exchange rate movement $e_0 \rightarrow e_1 \rightarrow e_2 \rightarrow e_3 \rightarrow e_4 \rightarrow e_5$ will result in a hysteresis loop determined by ABCDEF. In contrast, the corresponding hysteresis loop under certainty (as already described in Fig. 5.25) is depicted by the dotted path AHKM in Fig. 5.28.

Starting from the initial situation (e_0 respectively point A) again, now assume a decrease in the exchange rate from e_0 to e_6. As before, a "play"-reaction results (AG). A further decrease towards e_4 analogously leads to a "spurt" in unemployment described by σ_2 (GE).

As a main result, the introduction of uncertainty implies additional "play"-intervals in the macro loop with every reversal of the input direction. The width of the "play"-interval, i.e. ($e_2 - e_3$), ($e_5 - e_4$) or ($e_1 - e_6$) is given by the same amount: ($2\ \varepsilon)/(1 + 2\ i)$). This expression exactly equals the widening effect of uncertainty on the width of the microeconomic "band of inaction" for the single firm ($e^u_{j,entry} - e^u_{j,exit}$) as implied by Eqs. (5.78) and (5.80).[49] Due to our special initial situation, e_0 not being an extremum, the initial play intervals (AB or AG) amount to the half (i.e.: $\varepsilon/(1 + 2i)$).

The occurrence of "play"-intervals – implying a weak reaction with every reversal of the input (exchange rate) – results in a weaker reaction of the dependent variable (employment) compared to the situation without uncertainty. This weaker reaction corresponds to the fact that (a) the "play"-interval has to be passed in order to lead to permanent employment impacts and (b) a smaller number of firms is affected by exchange rate changes, since all "hysteretic" firms are shifted to the north-west by uncertainty. These mechanisms finally result in a "flatter" shape of the hysteresis loop under exchange rate uncertainty.

Our micro model is based on a risk-neutral single-unit (dis)employment decision under revenue uncertainty caused by exchange rate (step) volatility and fixed sunk (i.e. irreversible) hiring and firing costs. It is comparable to models incorporating irreversible investment decisions. However, we do not rely on the asymmetry of

---

[48]For a non-formal description of "spurts" in investment or in employment based on a microeconomic sunk cost mechanism under uncertainty see Pindyck (1988, pp. 980f.), and Belke and Goecke (2001b). Dixit and Pindyck (1994, pp. 15f.), vividly illustrate the non-linear reaction of US-employment after recovery in the mid 1993. However, in these contributions no explicit aggregation approach to derive macroeconomic behaviour is applied.

[49]However, this simple and clear result is due to our extremely simple micro model, where the expansion of the band of inaction is linear with respect to uncertainty ε and even independent of the heterogeneity between firms. But even in a more general formulation the widening of band of inaction will occur due to uncertainty and, thus a kind of a "depopulated" area parallel to the $\alpha = \beta$-line and play-hysteresis will result.

adjustment costs (Caballero, 1991) and on scrapping values (Darby et al., 1998), since we analyse "investments" in employment and not in real capital. In addition, the degree of competition in the output market and economies of scale (Caballero, 1991) do not play a predominant role since we analyze a single-unit decision.

However, at the price of the advantage of being very simple, our model shows limitations due to its partial equilibrium nature. In our model a firm only has the choice between export activity or to stop production at all. In this paper we do not consider the variety of further options a real world firm would have in a situation with an unfavourable and uncertain exchange rate. For example, the firm may have the option to reallocate its labour force from the production of exports to the production for the domestic market. Furthermore, a firm may have the option to internationally reallocate production via direct foreign investments in response to an appreciation of the domestic currency. The consideration of all these options lowers the importance of the non-linear persistent exchange rate effects in foreign trade on aggregate employment. Consequently, our approach may exaggerate the importance of exchange rate variability on aggregate employment.

In an extreme case with a perfect mobility of factors between the production of exports and the production for the domestic market – i.e. if the reallocation of factors is possible without generating any frictional costs – the loop in Fig. 5.28 would merely describe the distribution of a given supply of labour between both, the production of exports and the production for the domestic market. In such a situation we would have no effects of exchange rate changes on aggregate employment at all.

However, in reality we do have costs of reallocation. For example, selling an increased production on the domestic market may only be possible via cutting prices, and thus is not a profitable option for many firms. Furthermore, producing more goods specific for the domestic market may require specific skills and specific equipment. Training of new skill and establishing specific equipment may again result in sunk costs (of reallocation factors in an uncertain environment). Consequently, if we consider realistic imperfections concerning the reallocation of labor, e.g. due to limited intersectoral labour mobility and due to factor specifity, our intuition of exchange rate uncertainty effects on aggregate labor demand qualitatively may even hold in a more general context, however in a quantitatively reduced manner.

Of course, our theoretical results concerning macroeconomic play-areas as a consequence of sunk cost and uncertainty on a microeconomic level deserve an empirical evaluation with tight testable propositions concerning the relation between the exchange rate and *aggregate* employment. According to the theory developed in this paper, under uncertainty "play"-areas of weak reactions of aggregate employment on exchange rate changes have to be considered at the macro level. When changes go beyond the play-area a sudden switch to a strong reaction ("spurt") occurs. Moreover, the width of the play-area is a positive function of the degree of uncertainty. Thus we have three testable implications: (1) we expect to observe play-areas with a weak or even no effect of exchange rate changes and (2) a switch to a strong reaction of aggregate employment, i.e. structural breaks, if large exchange rate changes occur, and (3) a positive effect of the exchange rate variability on the width of the play-area.

In order to check how well the model is validated by the data, Belke and Goecke (2001a) apply a linear approximation of the loop depicted in Fig. 5.28 in order to approximate the play-shape of the relationship between exchange rate and employment. They develop an estimation algorithm based on a switching-regression approach and find empirical support for play-effects on West-German employment caused by real exchange rate variability. Based on an estimation of their switching-regression model (with quarterly observations from 1973:3 to 1996:1) they show that the non-linear model including play displays a significantly better performance than a standard linear regression model. They estimate play areas without any employment effects in response to exchange rate changes, if these changes are lower than about 10% (in case of an average degree of exchange rate uncertainty). Moreover, they find strong support for strong reactions ("spurts") if the magnitude of changes go beyond these play-areas. Furthermore, the estimation reveals a strong impact of exchange rate variation (measured as the standard deviation over preceding twelve months) on the size of the play areas. Thus, all three theoretical implications concerning the dynamics of aggregate labor demand are corroborated by this first attempt of an empirical validation.

5.3.3.6 Conclusions and Implications for Monetary Policy

In this section, non-linearities in the relation between total economy employment and the exchange rate are emphasized. A potential mechanism based on a band of inaction that is induced by sunk costs and could account for a "weaker" relationship between employment and its determinants has been augmented by exchange rate uncertainty. As a result of option value effects the band of inaction is widened and, thus, hysteresis effects are strongly amplified by uncertainty. Special attention has been paid to the problem of aggregation under uncertainty. It has been shown that under uncertainty "play"-areas have to be considered at the macro level. Thus, similarities of macro relations ["play"] to micro behavior [band of inaction] are enhanced by uncertainty.[50]

We ascribe the revenue volatility to exchange rate volatility. However, since uncertainty effects on the revenue ε is additively included in the revenue function, an interpretation of ε as an all comprising expression of uncertainty in exchange rates, foreign prices, wages and productivity is straightforward. Moreover, the relation between employment and all its driving forces (e.g. the wages) is affected by uncertainty. We focus on the calculation of exchange rate triggers, holding other determinants of employment constant. Similarly, one could calculate trigger values for e.g. wages resulting in a hysteresis-band concerning wages. An application of our aggregation approach based on wages is straightforward. According to our results, due to uncertainty, total economy employment is expected to be less sensitive than previously expected to movements in the exchange rate, foreign prices, wages and productivity.

---

[50]Thus, additional empirical studies in the manner of Parsley and Wei (1993) introducing uncertainty related zones of inaction may be adequate even on the macro level.

Moreover, the findings presented above may be of a more general interest, since the aggregation mechanisms detected here may apply to other cases where the aggregation of microeconomic real option effects under uncertainty becomes necessary. A prominent example in this context is of course monetary policy.

5.3.3.7 Monetary Policy and Investment Decisions – A Stylized Treatment of the Uncertainty Trap

The aim of this brief section is to investigate the effectiveness of monetary policy under cash flow uncertainty and investment irreversibility. If future net revenues are uncertain and investment expenditure cannot be recovered, there is an option value of waiting. The value of waiting derives from the possibility of deferring investment and see if tomorrow net revenue has gone up or down, minus the cost of delaying the income stream from investing today. The option value of waiting increases in the cost of immediate investment, and therefore the threshold revenue above which the firm finds investing today profitable. Alternatively, it lowers the interest rate which triggers immediate investment. A full-fledged model along these lines is presented by Belke and Goecke (2008). See also the chapter on monetary policy and uncertainty in this textbook.

Half a decade ago, in summer 2003, pressure on the European Central Bank to cut interest rates has been growing as short-term growth prospects for the euro area deteriorated. The arguments for even lower rates seemed to be compelling. Inflation was at that time wandering around the ECB's upper ceiling. Low growth was expected to cause downward pressure on the price level and ongoing uncertainty was assumed to dampen economic activity even further. However, a closer look at the economic implication of uncertainty suggests that monetary policy easing might have been in fact a poor strategy under this scenario. This is because in times of uncertainty, as we will show, the effectiveness of monetary policy generally decreases greatly (Greenspan, 2004; Jenkins & Longworth, 2002).

Where does uncertainty typically come from? One conjecture would be to trace uncertainty of revenues back to the events of September 11th, 2001, and ensuing war against terrorism which have shaken the hitherto prevailing geopolitical order. In addition, high uncertainty could also stem from certain macro-economic disequilibria such a, for instance, the US current account situation, the strong increase in corporate debt, corporate malfeasance etc. Finally, piecemeal reforms are made responsible for an environment uncertain for investors.

To deal with the influence of uncertainty on economic decisions, economists have developed the concept of the "option value of waiting". This formalises a common-sense rule: if a decision involves some sunk costs, or any other element of irreversibility, it makes sense to wait until the uncertainty has been resolved. The convenience to postpone investment decisions is particularly strong when the uncertainty is likely to be resolved in the near future. There exists an extensive literature on the role, the conduct and the efficacy of monetary policy which we cannot completely review here. There are several papers which document possible scenarios of policy effectiveness.[51] But our attempt to link the theory of the "option value of waiting" to monetary policy is one of quite novel contributions according to our knowledge. However, this paper is not the first analysis of the link between option theory and the effectiveness of monetary policy. For instance, Rose (2000) examined the relationship between interest rates and aggregate investment by using a similar formal framework where a firm has a two-period window of opportunity to invest. Rose showed not only that the traditional investment function is shifted downward by the presence of uncertainty and irreversibility (as in our paper), but also that at the aggregate level it has a "hump". The policy implications of Rose's analysis "are perhaps reminiscent of the Keynesian liquidity trap, though rather more perverse. At the very least, . . . monetary policy is always less effective than Marshallian rules suggest" (Rose, 2000, p. 632). One main difference between Rose's analysis and our paper is the presence of a rather simple term structure of interest rates.

In contrast to other contributions in the field, our approach assumes that revenue uncertainty instead of interest rate uncertainty creates the "option value of waiting". In other words, we investigate which level of the risk-free policy rate triggers investment if investors have to take real option values into account. For reasons of simplicity, we model interest rate expectations in a deterministic fashion but let a stochastic process determine future revenues.

One can easily imagine investors assessing various investment projects. Some would be slightly profitable under the prevailing degree of uncertainty, but they would be even more profitable if uncertainty were favourably resolved, and would cause a loss if not. In such a situation, investors would lose little (in terms of forgone profits) if they postpone investment decisions: Once the uncertainty had been resolved, it would still have the option to proceed if that was to its advantage. An analogous argument applies to the consumers which might delay their decisions to buy a durable consumer good in times of uncertainty. According to the simple models, uncertainty which cannot be hedged raises the variability of revenues and induces the investors to apply a higher discount rate on (expected) future revenues. Dixit (1989) introduces an additional motive why uncertainty should hamper investment: if investments bear an irreversible sunk cost character, there is an incentive to wait until the uncertainty has resolved; this is the "option value of waiting".

A brief case study might be helpful to convey the spirit of the argument. For this purpose, we have a brief look at the ECB. Some time ago, it was widely believed that a war in Iraq would not have any appreciable direct consequences for the European economy due to its low degree of openness towards the Gulf region. However, the indirect effects could be substantial if the war lasted longer than expected, or if it led to a disruption of oil supplies and wider regional instability and geo-political frictions. Such an outcome could not be ruled out. This uncertainty was likely to be resolved soon, perhaps not in a matter of weeks, as the US administration maintained at that time, but certainly in a matter of months. However, while it

---

[51] See, for instance, Ammer and Brunner (1995), Goodfriend (1991), Guender (2003), Orphanides and Wieland (1998), and Taylor (1999).

remained, one expected demand – especially investment demand – to remain quite weak in the near future.

Shouldn't the ECB have tried to stimulate demand with an interest rate cut under this scenario? A first counter-argument would have been that the concept of the "option value of waiting" applied to the ECB just as much as it applies to everyone else. At that time, it was not clear whether a war might be averted, or it might be short and have little effect on oil prices. Hence, if the ECB would have cut policy rates, it would have risked having to reverse its decision almost immediately. The ECB should have cut its rates only if it was convinced that such a cut would make sense even if the uncertainty would be favorably resolved.

Let us add that we have no judgment to offer at all on whether the ECB had the right rate level or levels during 2001–2005. There is nothing in our paper that addresses this question. Since the same logic applies to (less benefits of) policy rate increases under an inflationary scenario, we are certainly not arguing in this paper for rate cuts or against them as a policy matter. However, in the context of the post-September 2001 depression which we use for illustration purposes, a cut as an insurance against a bad outcome does not make sense, since

(1) cutting interest rates is not effective if uncertainty is large,
(2) a central bank itself disposes of an option value of waiting with interest rate cuts. If, for instance the ECB cuts today, it kills this option to cut in the future (although this option might be very valuable in times of high uncertainty even if the interest rates are not zero).
(3) frequent interest rate changes by a central bank induce additional uncertainty which tends to aggravate the weakness of investment and consumer goods demand.

The models of decision-making under uncertainty also have further important implications for monetary policy. All economic decisions involve some transaction costs – whether they are about investment, or about hiring and firing. These last are especially important in Europe. This implies that businesses facing only a small change in prices may not respond (immediately). There is always a price range within which it does not pay to change course. The size of this range grows as uncertainty increases.

One might feel inclined to ascribe real impacts of revenue volatility solely to times of excessively high uncertainty, i.e. to crashing events like September 11th. However, since uncertainty ε was included additively in the revenue function it was straightforward to interpret ε as an all comprising expression of uncertain revenues like, e.g., disequilibria of the US economy since the turn-of-year 2000/01 (current account, consumer financial position, over-investment). Moreover, the relation (including the "weak reaction" characteristic) between investment/employment and all its determinants (not only interest rates but also e.g. the wages and the oil prices) was affected by uncertainty. Thus, the impacts implied by sunk costs and uncertainty are manifold. We only calculated interest rate triggers, holding other determinants of investment/employment constant. Summarising, compared to the prediction of the majority of models of monetary policy transmission, real world investment/employment may appear less sensitive to changes in the interest rate, due to uncertainty.

Of course it is true that when risk premiums are high, a given change in the riskless interest rate produces less of a proportional change in the user cost and required rate of return on capital than when the risk premium is low. If one assumes iso-elastic (log–log) investment response functions, one would deduce that changes in the riskless rate are less effective when uncertainty is high. However, with heterogeneous agents and projects, there are always some projects near the margin that respond to changes in the required rate of return at any level of uncertainty. Hence our "range of inaction" at first glance appears to be a discontinuity due to overly "representative" modeling, not to anything "real" that should concern monetary policy. However, in order to derive macroeconomic implications which are empirically testable, Belke and Goecke (2001a, 2001b) deal with the aggregation of the approach proposed in this paper. They assume that the firms have different exit ("disinvestment") and entry ("investment") triggers. Special attention is paid to the problem of aggregation under uncertainty. It is shown that under uncertainty "areas of weak reaction" have to be considered even at the macroeconomic level. Due to the similarities of the macro relations under uncertainty to the micro behaviour derived in this contribution our micro-approach can serve as a first base for empirical tests.

How do our formal considerations fit with the monetary policy strategy of the ECB in reality? According to its two-pillar strategy, the rationale for the ECB for taking investment/employment demand functions into account when deciding on interest rate cuts (or increases) is to support general economic policy in times of low (high) inflation. Moreover, empirical evidence as a stylised fact comes up with the result that Taylor-rule type monetary policy reaction functions describe the actual behaviour of the ECB quite well. The ECB will be confronted with an unusually highly uncertain environment still for some time for several reasons. First, many of the underlying causes of world wide uncertainty do not seem to be resolved, although the Iraq conflict itself was terminated unexpectedly early. Second, experience has shown that the effects of the quick termination of war actions in the Gulf region were more than compensated by an increase in uncertainty with respect to the shape of the post-war world order. As long as uncertainty stays relevant for consumers and investors, the approach of the option value of waiting should be relevant for the monetary policy of the world's leading central banks.

In the light of the results of the paper, the remarks on the ineffectiveness of monetary policy in the case of the ECB in the year 2003 made in the introduction are corroborated in a subtle sense. Under the presumption of a net reduction of revenue uncertainty, the investment/employment impacts of a lower interest rate level continue to be twofold. A reduction of uncertainty, e.g. after the potential end of the Iraq conflict, would have led to a contraction of the area of weak reaction. Hence, the interest rates triggering investments would not have needed to be as low as before. Hence, the effectiveness of expansionary monetary policy via cutting interest rates would have been increased (lowered) by a low (high) degree of uncertainty.

5.3.4 Monetary Policy and the Phillips Curve

The Phillips curve concept plays an important role for analysing the impact of monetary policy on output and employment. In the following, monetary policies according to the (i) Keynesian, (ii) monetarist, (iii) neo-classical, (iv) Neo-Keynesian and (v) hysteresis viewpoint will be outlined as far as the Phillips curve trade-off is concerned. Needless to say, assumptions about market *agents' inflation expectations* play the crucial role for the *diagnosed effectiveness* of monetary policy affecting real magnitudes.

5.3.4.1 Monetary Policy Under a Keynesian Phillips-Curve

Samuelson and Solow (1960) derived the modified Phillips curve under *static expectations*, which basically mean that market agents expect current inflation to equal future inflation:

$$\pi^e_{t+1} = \pi^e = \pi_t. \tag{5.81}$$

In such regime, how does an expansionary monetary policy affect employment? By increasing the money supply, the central bank reduces the interest rate. This, in turn, stimulates investment and overall demand as long as investment is a (negative) function of interest rates. A rising aggregate demand, in turn, meets a positively sloped labour supply curve. As a result, a rising output will be accompanied by an increase in the price level.

Under the assumption of *money illusion*, labour supply depends solely on nominal wages (W_t), which are assumed to be given. The demand for labour, however, is defined as a function of real wages (W_t/p). As a result, an increase in p lowers real wages, thereby increasing the demand for labour, and output and employment increase.

With output, Y, and unemployment, U, the Keynesian Phillips curve can be formulated as:

$$Y = f\left((\pi - \pi_t)\ldots\right), \text{ with } \partial Y/\partial(\pi - \pi_t) > 0 \text{ and}$$
$$U = f\left((\pi - \pi_t)\ldots\right), \text{ with } \partial U/\partial(\pi - \pi_t) < 0.$$

Figure 5.29 shows the Phillips curve in quadrant IV. Quadrant III depicts the relation between inflation and output (which is assumed to be positive), while quadrant II represents the 45° line, and quadrant I shows the economy's output-employment relation (which is assumed to be negative).

Let us assume the level of unemployment is A (A', A'', A'''), and that monetary policy wants to lower it to B. Under the assumption of static expectations, a lowering of interest rates (caused by an increase in the money supply) increases inflation, thereby lowering real wages. A rising demand for labour pushes down unemployment to B (B', B'', B''').

The benefit of inflation – that is the positive impact on output and employment – is a direct result of assumed behavioural differences between workers and

Fig. 5.29 Phillips curve
assuming static expectations

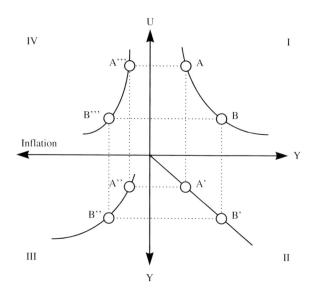

employers: whereas labour demand depends on real wages, labour supply is said to
depend on nominal wages. And so it is assumed that workers – but not employer
suffer from *money illusion* making inflation an effective instrument for increasing
employment.

5.3.4.2 Monetary Policy Under a Monetarist Phillips-Curve

Friedman (1968a, 1968b) and Phelps (1967) made *adaptive expectations* a key element of their analyses of the Phillips curve. They noted that market agents display
a kind of *learning behavior*, that is they tend to take into account estimation errors
made in the past when forming expectations about future developments. As a result,
the Phillips-curve effect is only temporary rather than persistent in nature: monetary
policy cannot "outsmart" market agents by *surprise inflation* on an ongoing basis.

To show this, assume that an expansionary monetary policy increases the stock
of money, thereby lowering the interest rate. Investment and as output rises above its
potential level the price level increases. Higher inflation reduces real wages, increasing the demand for labour. Sooner or later, however, employees will demand higher
nominal wages, which bring real wages back towards its original level. The demand
for labour declines as real wages rise, and output and employment fall back towards
their original levels.

That said, an expansionary monetary policy leaves the economy with higher
inflation, while output and unemployment remain unchanged. Monetary policy cannot make the economy deviating for long from its potential output, Y^*, and the natural rate of unemployment, U^*. The relation between production, Y, and unemployment, U, can be written as:

Fig. 5.30 Phillips curve
assuming adaptive
expectations

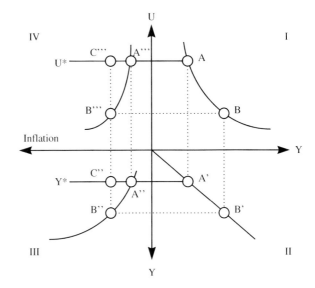

$$Y = Y^* + a(\pi - \pi^e), \text{ with } \delta Y/\delta(\pi - \pi^e) > 0 \text{ and}$$
$$U = U^* + b(\pi - \pi^e), \text{ with } \delta U/\delta(\pi - \pi^e) < 0,$$

whereas a and b are parameters showing the intensity with which expectations are corrected for by past estimation errors.

Starting from point A in Fig. 5.30, an expansionary monetary policy impulse pushes unemployment from point A (A', A'', A''') to point B (B', B'', B'''). However, as market agents sooner or later learn about the loss of purchasing power induced by higher inflation, nominal wages will be adjusted accordingly. A higher real wage brings output and employment back to the long-term equilibrium level, that is Y^* and U^*, respectively, in point $C'''(C'')$.

That said, under the regime of adaptive expectations a persistent increase in output and employment would be possible only if the central bank succeeds in keeping actual inflation above expected inflation (*surprise inflation*) – a requirement which would, under adaptive expectations, imply a monetary policy path towards hyperinflation. However, the Monetarist conclusion that monetary policy can, at least temporarily, affect output and employment via inducing surprise inflation was challenged by the economists analysing the Phillips curve theory under *rational expectations*.

5.3.4.3 Monetary Policy Under a Neo-Classical Phillips-Curve

The neo-classical Phillips-curve is based on the assumption that market agents form their expectations according to the theory of rational expectations: Market agents take into account all available information and have knowledge about the functioning of the economy. As a result, they do not commit systematic forecasting errors.

In a quantity theory framework, with given output and a constant velocity of money, the expected money supply growth (m^e) determines expected inflation (π^e). In this special case the relation $m^e = \pi^e$ holds. The production and unemployment function can be stated as:

$$Y = Y^* + a(m - m^e) + \varepsilon_Y, \text{ with } \delta Y/\delta(m - m^e) > 0 \text{ and}$$
$$U = U^* + b(m - m^e) + \varepsilon_U, \text{ with } \delta U/\delta(m - m^e) < 0,$$

whereas ε_Y and ε_U are i.i.d. error terms with expected means of zero, respectively.

Monetary policy affects output and unemployment only if an unexpected increase in money supply creates *surprise inflation* and/or if market agents commit expectation errors. However, both are assumed to be temporary rather than persistent in nature. As a result, output and employment are, in the long-term, independent from monetary variables not even hyperinflation would change that.

The Neo-Classical Model in More Formal Terms

Robert E. Lucas's aggregate supply function can be formulated as (Lucas, 1973, pp. 327ff.):

$$Y_t = Y^* + c(p_t - p_t^e) + v_t, \tag{5.82}$$

where Y_t is output, Y^* is potential output, p_t is the actual price level, p_t^e is the expected price level and v_t is the i.i.d. error term of the aggregate supply function; c is a behavioral parameter. If the actual price level equals the expected price level, and v_t is zero, actual output equals potential output $(Y_t = Y^*)$.

The aggregate demand function is:

$$Y_t = A_t + b(m_t - p_t) + u_t, \tag{5.83}$$

where A_t is autonomous demand, m_t is the stock of money, and u_t is the i.i.d. error term of aggregate demand; b is a behavioral parameter. Equation (5.83) says that actual demand is a function of *real balances*.

Now we assume that prices are fully flexible, and aggregate supply, Y_t^S, equals aggregate demand, Y_t^D:

$$Y_t^S = Y_t^D = Y_t. \tag{5.84}$$

If we impose rational expectations (RE) on the system, we can formulate the aggregate demand function as:

$$Y_t^e = A_t^e + b(m_t^e - p_t^e), \tag{5.85}$$

Accordingly, the aggregated supply function can be written as:

$$Y_t^e = Y^* + c(p_t - p_t^e).$$

(5.86)

To calculate Y_t and p_t, we simply subtract (5.85) from (5.83), and we yield:

$$Y_t - Y_t^e = (A_t - A_t^e) + b(m_t - m_t^e) - b(p_t - p_t^e) + u_t.$$

(5.87)

Likewise, we subtract (5.86) from (5.82), which yields:

$$Y_t - Y_t^e = c(p_t - p_t^e) + v_t;$$

(5.88)

note that we have $Y_t^e = Y^*$.

If we set (5.87) equal to (5.88), we can calculate the equilibrium price level, which is:

$$p_t = p_t^e + \frac{1}{b+c}\left[(A_t - A_t^e) + b(m_t - m_t^e) + u_t - v_t\right].$$

(5.89)

Inserting (5.89) in (5.88) gives us the equilibrium output:

$$Y_t = Y^* + \frac{c}{b+c}\left[(A_t - A_t^e) + b(m_t - m_t^e) + u_t + \frac{b}{c}v_t\right].$$

(5.90)

Equation (5.90) says that actual output will be at potential if there are no "surprises" and no demand and supply side shocks. Only *unexpected* increases in A_t, m_t and the emergence of supply and demand shocks can make Y_t deviating from Y^*.

What is more, in the neo-classical model, money supply growth does not affect output *as long as it is anticipated*. In that sense, it does not matter if money supply growth is 5 or 10% p.a. – provided it is correctly anticipated.[52] As a result, the *monetarist acceleration hypothesis* does not hold in the neo-classical model.

Finally, the neo-classical model says how an increase in the money supply affects real magnitudes and prices. If the rise in money supply is *expected*, prices will increase, while real magnitudes will remain unaffected. If the rise in money supply is *unexpected*, there will be effects on prices and real magnitudes as shown in Eqs. (5.89) and (5.90), respectively.

---

[52]Of course, the model does not take into account the costs of (high) inflation.

5.3.4.4 Re (iv): Neo-Keynesian Phillips-Curve

The assumption of rational expectations, e.g. the conclusions of the neo-classical theory, has been criticised by the Neo-Keynesian theorists for neglecting an important cost component governing market agents' behaviour, namely *transaction costs*. The concept of transaction costs has been introduced by Ronald Coase's (1937) article *The Nature of the Firm*. According to Coase, transaction costs subsume all costs for preparing, transacting and supervising contracts (wage agreements, rents and bond contracts, etc). Neo-Keynesians consider these costs to cause wage and *price rigidities*.

In view of the existence of such costs, it might be rational for market agents to agree to multi-period contracts. Such commitments would be changed only if certain *threshold* costs are reached. Three hypotheses emerge from such a view:

(1) The adjustment of real wages to changing inflation comes with a time lag (*wage-lag hypothesis*);
(2) price increases reduce the real value of outstanding debt instruments (*creditor-debtor hypothesis*); and
(3) nominal interest rates adjust to inflation with a time lag (*real rate hypothesis*), so inflation can – at least temporarily – reduce real interest rates.

In the Neo-Keynesian theory, the existence of nominal wage and price rigidities has an important impact on how monetary policy affects output and employment in the Phillips curve model. For instance, lower interest rates increase investment demand and therefore total output. A rising demand meets a positively sloped supply curve. As result, the price level increases as employment and output rise.

That said, Neo Keynesian theorists have de facto modified the Phillips curve in the formulation of Samuelson and Solow by simply replacing static expectations by rational expectations and, at the same time, introducing the assumption of rigid wages and prices, which are a result of transaction costs. Monetary policy might be in a position to affect output and employment as long as the changes in real wages and prices do not exceed critical values, inducing market agents to adjust their contracts. In the following, we will consider monetary policy under a hysteretic long-run Phillips curve. Due to the fact that we were able to derive macro hysteresis on the labor market without imposing any nominal rigidities, we do *not* classify the hysteresis approach as a *Neo-Keynesian* variant of the Phillips curve as it is, however sometimes done in the literature.

5.3.4.5 Re (v): Monetary Policy Under a Hysteretic Long-Run Phillips Curve

As argued above, the NAIRU essentially is a path-dependent variable if unemployment exhibits hysteresis. Hence, it is often argued that a *temporarily* expansionary monetary policy is able to lower unemployment *permanently*. Take, for instance, the Phillips curve under adaptive expectations (Fig. 5.30) or the Neo-Keynesian variant as an example. After an expansionary monetary policy impulse has lowered unemployment from point *A* to *B*, the insider-outsider and the human capital mechanisms come into play. According to the insider-outsider approach temporary lower unemployment is transformed to lower natural unemployment due to the power of labor unions that keep the equilibrium wage low in order to guarantee the continuation of the employment status of those bargaining for wages. By this, the natural rate of unemployment U^* is lowered and the natural rate of output Y^* is increased, as characterized by a downward shift of the horizontal lines denoting U^* respectively Y^* up to the point where they intersect with B''' respectively B. This exactly mirrors the fact that in a heavily unionized economy unions directly represent the interests only of those who are currently employed. In the case of a negative monetary shock, however, unionization would undermine the ability of those outside the union to compete for employment because in the wake of recovery unions would only negotiate (too) high wages to benefit the relatively small group consisting of those who are currently employed. After prolonged layoffs employed workers inside the union may seek the benefits of higher wages for themselves, rather than moderating wage demands to promote the rehiring of unemployed workers. In this case, a *temporarily* higher unemployment rate would typically result in a permanently higher natural rate of unemployment and hysteresis effects on the Phillips curve would be symmetric. Dual labour market consisting of employed insiders and unemployed outsiders would emerge.

These effects are reinforced by the *human capital effect*. In the wake of a temporarily expansionary monetary policy more people from the labour force enjoy training on the job which makes it easier for them to be effective competitors on the labor markets (which taken by itself should lower wages) and to cope with structural change. In the end, the equilibrium unemployment rate is lowered by a temporary positive macro shock. Also in this case, the hysteresis effect works the other way round in a *symmetric* fashion. If there is a negative monetary shock to the economy this would lead to human capital depreciation during spells of unemployment which lowers the (equilibrium) real wage necessary for re-entering the labor market. In other words, the ex ante equilibrium wage is neither the same as the ex post equilibrium wage nor it is the gravitation centre of the Phillips curve system any more. Instead, it has become path-dependent.

According to this view, the application of supply-side oriented measures (which directly lower U^*) lowers the magnitude of the demand shock necessary to reverse the effect of an adverse shock in the past ("coercive power" in the language of ferromagnetics). Demand-side measures lower the "remanence" of past shocks. Hence, some analysts feel legitimized to argue in favor of counter-cyclical policies especially in times of high macroeconomic uncertainty and, hence, excessive savings, pointing to hysteresis effects. For this purpose, they fade out the benefits of enacting supply-side reforms and, at the same time, over-emphasize the benefits of demand side policies. However, as our analysis in Sect. 5.3.3 has shown, an interest rate cut as an insurance against a bad outcome does not make sense, since cutting interest rates is not effective if uncertainty is large, a central bank itself disposes of an option value of waiting with interest rate cuts. If, for instance the central bank cuts today, it kills this option to cut in the future (although this option might be very valuable in times of high uncertainty even if the interest rates are not zero). Moreover, frequent interest rate changes by a central bank induce additional uncertainty which tends to aggravate the weakness of investment and consumer goods demand. Finally, they simply overlook the implications of macro hysteresis if the latter is carefully derived and aggregated from micro hysteresis. The latter implies that the effect of monetary policy on the labor market performance becomes weaker in case of hysteresis in (un-) employment since certain thresholds of the input variables have to be passed in order to have an impact at all. Hence, there are good reasons not to use the hysteresis argument to promote counter-cyclical monetary policies.

5.3.4.6 Summary

Table 5.7 summaries the effects of inflation on the real economy and the price level according to the alternative schools of thought.

5.3.4.7 Monetary Policy, the Phillips Curve and Partisan Political Business Cycles

The question of political impacts on labor markets and thus of the political dimension of unemployment has recently been asked repeatedly, since permanently high unemployment in Western Europe and the failure of implementing reforms cannot be explained anymore by purely economic approaches of Keynesian or neo-classical provenience. At the same time, first evidence from "cross-country-studies" of significant impacts of government ideology on unemployment in Western democracies is available (for an early survey see Belke, 1996, pp. 198ff.). Depending on the shape of the induced unemployment cycle, political business cycles of the Partisan type (PT), of the Rational Partisan type (RPT) and of the hysteresis-augmented RPT type (RPTHYS) are distinguished. The latter takes account of the path-dependence or at least persistence of unemployment (which in limited samples has nearly the same dynamic implications for political business cycles as hysteresis, see the passages

Table 5. 7   Effect of inflation on the real economy and the price level

School of thought	Output and employment	Price level
Keynesian theory	+ sustainable	+
Monetarism	+ short-term; 0 long-term	+ short-term; ++ long term
Neo-classical theory		
– under imperfect information	+ short-term; 0 long-term	+ short-term; ++ long-term
– with perfect information	0 short- and long-term	++ short- and long-term
Neo-Keynesianism	+ potentially sustainable	+ short-term; ++ potentially long term
Hysteresis	++ immediately and sustainable	++ short- and long-term

Legend: +/0 = positive/no effect.

above). Since this feature is a stylized fact at least for EU-countries like Germany it will be of special interest here as well.

Arguably, Germany had the world's most independent central bank. Surprisingly, however, some researchers have found political business cycles in German monetary aggregates (Berger and Woitek, 2001; Vaubel, 1997).[53] This feature is of course hard to explain this with standard models of opportunistic government behavior. Instead, these authors show that the cycles originated *from shifts in money demand tolerated by the Bundesbank*. Such shifts occur because, when inflation preferences differ between political parties and election results are uncertain, rational investors avoid entering into long-term financial contracts before elections. Contrary to the Bundesbank's stated commitment to a "monetarist" policy rule, it appears to have allowed these changes to have an impact on monetary aggregates. It remains to be seen whether this pattern is transferred to the regime of European Monetary Union and whether prove is evidence for a partisa cycle in monetary policy instrument (Belke and Potrafke, 2009). This will be one of the hot topics of research in the field of the *political economy of monetary policy* in the future.[54]

Since the "... Rational Partisan Theory has yet to be subjected to adequate empirical tests ... " (Hibbs, 1992, p. 361), Belke (2000) tries to develop appropriate testing procedures of the PT, RPT and the hysteresis-augmented RPT. The testing strategy proposed there goes on from the weaknesses of the economic procedures used. One striking weakness is recognized in the fact that the possibility of one or more unit roots in the time series of the individual variables and – even more important – in the relationship between the labor and goods market variables has not been considered.[55] Moreover, the literature on country-specific tests of the RPT is mainly limited to the U.S. case. This indicates the still considerable need of empirical research connected with the "... (as yet largely untested) partisan surprise hypothesis ..." (Hibbs, 1991, p. 24). A good description is Sheffrin (1989a): "The theory of rational partisan business cycles should apply to other democracies besides the United States. However, there have been few tests outside the United States ..." (Sheffrin, 1989a, p. 251; Sheffrin, 1989b, p. 166).

---

[53] Vaubel (1997) essentially argues that central bank staff depends positively on the country's population size, its per capita income and the central bank's independence with respect to salaries. In the developing countries, exchange rate pegging can reduce central bank staff. Among the industrial countries, France, Belgium/Luxembourg and Germany have the most overstaffed central banks. According to Vaubel, central bank revenue in Germany has a significantly positive effect on staff size. A non-parametric test for the German Bundesbank confirms the hypothesis that monetary expansion (M1) accelerates when the government has a political majority in the central bank council at the beginning of the pre-election period or when the political majority in the council changes in favor of the government during the pre-election period (and that monetary expansion decelerates if the reverse is true). For a survey of empirical tests of partisan monetary policy see Belke and Potrafke (2009)

[54] Sadeh (2006) argues that coordination of electoral cycles among European Union (EU) member states and greater similarity in the partisan bias of their governments would make their membership in the single currency easier and cheaper by harmonizing their fiscal policies and would thus contribute to the sustainability of the Economic and Monetary Union (EMU).

[55] One exception to this rule is Berger and Woitek (1997).

The politically founded Partisan Theory (PT) to explain ideology-specific business cycles has been propagated already in the seventies by Douglas A. Hibbs.[56] The PT has the assumption of non-rational expectations and an *exploitable Phillips-trade-off* in common with the also now-famous approach to an explanation of political business cycles, the model by Nordhaus (1975). However, it differs from the latter with respect to the specification of the utility functions of the parties. Political parties maximize, usually *arranged in a right-left-scheme*, party-specific utility functions. The latter express different preferences concerning the inflation-unemployment-trade-off by weighing the arguments in a different party-specific manner. The PT is generally regarded as empirically valid, if under left governments a significantly higher (trend in) inflation and a significantly lower (trend in) unemployment can be observed (Belke, 1996, pp. 36ff.; Gaertner, 1994).

Proponents of the Rational Partisan Theory (RPT) adopt from Hibbs the party-specific utility functions (Alesina, 1987; Chappell and Keech, 1986; Alesina and Rosenthal, 1995, pp. 161ff.). However, in contrast to Hibbs they assume rational expectations of all players in the polit-economic sphere. Moreover, they focus on uncertainty induced by elections. In the case of an election victory of the right-wing party positive deviations of the unemployment rate; in the case of a victory of the left-wing party negative deviations from the natural rate result. Inflation surprises occur, even if the current government party is reelected (Standard-RPT, "strict form"). However, inflation surprises result in any case, if there is a change in the governing party. If one acknowledges from a neo-Keynesian point of view that even anticipated monetary policies have a systematic impact in the short-term, the strongest real effects can be observed in the wake of a surprising substitution of a governing party (General RPT-version, "weaker form"). As a consequence, in the wake of elections transitory expansions (if left-wing governments) or contractions (if right-wing governments) appear alongside the short-term Phillips curve. According to the General RPT-version (Alesina, 1991, pp. 64f.; Alesina & Roubini, 1992, pp. 669f.; Annett, 1993, pp. 24) temporary real impacts – especially if electoral uncertainty is difficult to quantify – are only expected in the wake of actual changes in government.

As stressed by a large number of authors like Alesina (1991), Alesina and Roubini (1992), Annett (1993) – this General RPT-Version cannot at all be interpreted as a "corruption" of the RPT approach, but as a plausible modification of standard RPT that points the way ahead. One of the main reasons is that real impacts of nominal rigidities (which at least partially are compatible with rational expectations) are often emphasized by real rigidities (Jeanne, 1997). The latter have been relevant for the West German labor market since the midst of the seventies. Another important reason (at least with respect to right-wing post-election blips) is the "general downward nominal wage rigidity" as emphasized e.g. only recently by Akerlof et al. (1996). Note that all these approaches *assume* that partisan inflation cycles are induced by partisan cycles in monetary policy *instruments* (Belke and Potrafke, 2009).

---

[56]The most cited source is Hibbs (1977). Precursors are Lau and Frey (1971) and Frey and Lau (1968).

Numerous empirical tests of theories of political business cycles which abstract from rational expectations did not lead to unambiguously positive results, at least with respect to West European democracies. If at all the hypothesis of a political cycle could not be rejected, this should be more relevant with respect to policy instruments than with respect to macroeconomic variables. Moreover, the shape of the cycle in many cases proves to be unstable over time. However, the RPT proves to be successful more recently (Belke, 1996, pp. 56ff.). Problems with respect to tests of the RPT often emerge if one tries to specify the null and the alternative hypothesis correctly, i.e. in a compatible manner. Above all, proponents of the RPT face the question how to reconcile the RPT-inherent temporary "*post election blips*" with the persistence of unemployment in Western Europe resp. with the appearance of one or more unit roots in unemployment equations. Under these circumstances, they have to admit that these "post election blips" tend to perpetuate though RPT implies that real wage shocks will have reverted within one term of office.

This "*lag of the impact after its cause*" has often been termed hysteresis (see our discussion of hysteresis and the Phillips curve further above). Especially demand shocks, which in the RPT-framework boil down to real wage shocks, tend to have hysteretic impacts and have to be modelled correspondingly. However, in that case the *problem of an "observational equivalence"* of the time pattern of unemployment according to the PT and the RPT has to be solved: both theories imply permanent party differences in unemployment rates (Alogoskoufis, Lockwood, & Philippopoulos, 1992a, 1992b; Belke, 1996, pp. 158ff.; Hibbs, 1991, p. 5). The unemployment rate in the hysteresis-augmented RPT-case is not only dependent on current government policies and current expectations of the electorate (as in the Standard-RPTapproach) anymore. On the contrary, there exists a "carryover from past policies" (Alesina & Rosenthal, 1989, p. 375). The unemployment level stays the same over a whole office term; there is no "post election blip" as in the RPT. Under left-wing governments it is in any case lower and under rightwing governments in any case higher than the level of the preceding term of office. As a result, governments of different ideological couleur in the long term induce different unemployment rates similar to the PT. Future research in this area should, thus, not confine itself to an analysis of partisan-induced changes in the level of unemployment, but additionally focuses on the politically induced changes in the relationship between employment and its forcing variables. That is to say, one should not focus on a unit root in the (un-) employment time series itself but instead *on several unit roots in the system* (Belke, 2000, p. 229). Seen on the whole, creve is no consensus in the literature up to now how parties affect monetary policy, but monetary surprises appear as a unconvincing driving force of traditional partisan political cycles (Drazen 2000).

5.4 "Optimal" Inflation

Is there something like *optimal inflation*? In his article *The Optimum Quantity of Money*, Milton Friedman (1969) maintains that the optimal inflation is the negative of the real interest rate, implying a *zero nominal interest rate*. Friedman's reasoning make, a strong case against any inflationary policy.[57] To show this, consider an agent's asset portfolio consisting of both bonds and money. As bonds have a return (the nominal interest rate, i) and money (in the form of cash and sight deposits) has none, an agent who holds money must think that money is *useful* in some way. In other words, money must provide some utility which is peculiar to it and not provided by other assets. The marginal cost of holding an extra unit of money is the interest that is foregone by not holding bonds.

We can illustrate Friedman's argument by the *consumer surplus* underneath the money demand function M^d in Fig. 5.31 (Bailey, 1956). The money demand function is negatively related to the opportunity costs of money (the interest rate on bonds i). M/P represents real money holdings. Suppose there is a money holding of M_r/P, where inflation is zero, and the foregone interest rate is $i_0 = r$. In this case, the consumer surplus for money holders is the area CEF. Likewise, the producer surplus of money issuers is represented by the area $0(M_r/P)CE$.[58]

If inflation rises to π_1, the nominal interest rate becomes $i_1 = r + \pi_1$, and money demand declines to (M_i/P). The consumer surplus of the money holders is no longer represented by the area $ABCE$ but by FAB. The producer surplus also changes and becomes $0(M_i/P)BA$. The net social loss is the area $(M_i/P)(M_r/P)BC$, which has to be shouldered by money holders. In order to eliminate such a welfare loss, *inflation should be zero*, so that $i = r$, and the real money holdings would be (M_r/P). But is this really optimal?

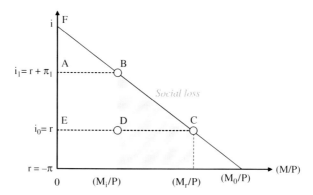

Fig. 5.31 Welfare costs of inflation and optimum quantity of money

---

[57] A more elaborate general equilibrium theoretic analysis of Friedman's optimum quantity of money proposition was pursued by Grandmont and Younes (1972) and Bewley (1980, 1983); for a critique see, for instance, Hahn (1971).

[58] Assuming that the marginal costs of money production are zero (which is not too far-fetched in a paper money standard), the producer surplus equals the seigniorage.

Economizing on money can be wasteful from society's point of view. Of course, money is costly to hold. At the same time, it is – under today's government controlled paper money system – costless for central banks to produce. By expanding the quantity of real money supply, the central bank could make everyone better off at no cost to itself. In that sense, Lucas (1987) writes that this is: "one of the few legitimate 'free lunches' economics has discovered in 200 years of trying."

Friedman argued that the optimal policy involves eliminating incentives to economize on the holdings of money. To do so, the central bank should seek to *eliminate the difference between interest rates on money and other securities*. This would make holding money costless. That said, the optimal amount of money is the one that has zero marginal opportunity cost, that is a zero nominal interest rate: here, money and bond holdings would yield the same return.

Hence, Friedman suggests that one could do even better than keeping inflation at zero – namely, by reducing the nominal rate of interest to zero (i.e. $r + \pi = 0$). As a result, the negative rate of inflation must equal the real rate of interest: $\pi = -r$. The optimal quantity of money holdings is determined by the maximum of the consumer surplus of money holders. This would be achieved if money demand reaches (M_0/P), which implies a nominal interest rate of zero. In an economy with a positive real interest rate inflation would therefore have to be the negative of the latter in order to keep the nominal interest at zero.

As a result, Friedman (1969) wrote that the optimal monetary policy is to steadily *contract* the supply of money (which determines inflation) at the real rate of interest: $\Delta m = -r$. In this case, the quantity theory (in which the income velocity of money is a stable function, so that $\Delta m = \pi$) says that the desired result is a zero nominal rate of interest: $i = r + -\pi = 0$.

In contrast, Phelps (1972, 1973) pointed out that, by weighing costs and benefits, optimum inflation should be positive. His line of argument takes recourse to the idea that *inflation is a tax*. In other words, any reduction of the consumer surplus – following economizing on money holdings because of inflation – is transferred to the government. What the government decides to do with this *extra revenue* must be included in any welfare analysis. Phelps argued that some inflation would be desirable if distortions associated with the inflation tax were less costly than distortions associated with other taxes to which the government might resort.

Fischer and Modigliani (1975) argue that the cost of (modest) inflation is largely the manner in which it distorts taxation. Consequently, as Phelps (1973) argued, optimal inflation ought to be treated as a public finance problem, effectively as an optimal taxation issue. However, note that optimal inflation arguments usually point to steady, modest inflation (2–3% per year or so); higher rates have a tendency to become highly variable and/or to spiral into hyperinflation, associated with negative consequences for economic activity.

Furthermore, even if the Friedman rule shouldn't be optimal in a strict sense, there are two reasons why it is likely to be nearly so. First, Lucas (1994) estimates that even low inflation involves substantial welfare costs. Second, seigniorage accounts for only a small fraction of tax revenue raised across developed countries, and the adjustments in other taxes needed to replace lost seigniorage revenue are likely to be minor.[59] These two facts might suggest that the optimal inflation tax is not likely to be far from Friedman's reasoning.

5.5 Deflation

In a dynamic economy, some prices tend to rise, and some prices tend to fall in relation to average prices. In an environment where average price increases are large, the relative prices of some items may decline even if money prices of individual goods or services do not actually fall. The lower the level of inflation is, the more likely it is that relative price changes will be associated with some rising prices and some falling prices.

However, if not only some but all prices of goods and services keep declining over time, the economy's price level would be trending downwards. Such an environment would be called *deflation*, defined as an ongoing decline in the economy's total price level.

Admittedly, deflation has a bad rap, largely based on the experience of the "Great Depression" period 1929–1933, when deflation was actually synonymous with *depression*: Falling output, employment and prices. However, *deflation is neither good nor bad*, and its consequences were not always a cause of concern. In fact, deflations were often benign, but sometimes they were not (Bordo & Filardo, 2004).

If prices decline as a consequence of increases in overall productivity, deflation would be associated with rising output and employment. If, in contrast, the money supply contracts – as a consequence of distress in the banking sector –, the ensuing deflation might very likely be associated with losses in output and employment.

In their analysis, Bordo, Lane, and Redish (2004), focusing on the US, the UK and Germany in the late 19th century, find that deflation at that time reflected both positive aggregate supply shocks and negative money supply shocks.[60] However, the negative money supply shocks had little effect on output. Thus, the authors conclude that deflation in the 19th century when money was backed by a commodity – was primarily good.

The burden that deflation might impose on the economy depends on whether it is *anticipated* or *unanticipated*. If, for instance, borrowers and lenders expect inflation to be 3% per year, then a decline in inflation to 1% per year will distribute wealth away from borrowers and *towards lenders*.

---

[59]Mulligan and Sala-i-Martin (1997) estimate that taking taxes into account raises optimal inflation by perhaps as much as 1%. Braun (1994) estimates that tax considerations raise optimal inflation by between 1 and 6%. Taking the average of Braun's estimates and subtracting a real interest rate of, say, 2.5% yields an optimal inflation of 1% p.a.

[60]See also the study of the International Monetary Fund (2003).

Moreover, the notion that nominal wages are downwardly rigid has a long history in macroeconomics, appearing most prominently in John Maynard Keynes' 1936 analysis of the business cycle (which was itself motivated by the experience of the Great Depression). Clearly, deflation might be problematic in such an environment. If employers cannot reduce nominal wages when prices are falling, the relative cost of labor increases and firms respond by using fewer workers. But the problems associated with downwardly rigid wages are not confined to deflation.

Keeping labor markets in equilibrium requires that individual wages continuously rise and fall in relation to one another, regardless of general price drift. Even if inflation is positive, changes in labor markets require wage reductions for some workers and wage rises for others. If employees are unwilling to accept nominal wage cuts in an environment of falling prices, their relative wages increase, resulting in employment losses.

Lower inflation obviously increases the number of workers affected by downwardly rigid nominal wages. Deflation does actually not change the nature of the problem, though. It is reasonable to assume that, should nominal wages be downwardly rigid, the economic disruptions are as large at low positive inflation as they would be at small deflation.

However, deflation can be expected to be blamed if (1) it coincides with events that have little or nothing to do with deflation (for instance, relative price movements); (2) complications arise from institutional features that are not unique to deflation (as in downward inflexibility of wages); or (3) output losses following from unanticipated disinflation (a type of price change in which deflation has no special status).

Against this backdrop it is of interest as to ask whether there could be a circumstance in which even perfectly anticipated and reasonably stable deflation could pose a problem. In fact, there might be one. The nominal market interest rate, in a simple world, has two components: the real interest rate and an inflation premium. If anticipated deflation is large enough relative to the real rate, the *nominal interest rate* might become *zero*.[61]

If nominal interest rates are zero, the symmetry between inflation and deflation may break down. In fact, there is no upper bound on nominal interest rates, but there should be a lower bound, as *interest rates cannot fall below zero*. If the nominal interest rate is negative, no one would bother to hold interest bearing assets because the return from holding money would be greater.

Once the nominal interest rate is zero, it is usually said, expectations of additional deflation mean that real interest rates move higher. Rising real interest rates, triggered by growing deflation expectations at the *zero nominal interest rate bound*, are the exact opposite of what the doctor would prescribe in times of economic stress. The central bank's inability to lower nominal rates that are zero, along with the implications for real rates if deflationary pressure continues, is perhaps the strongest case against policies that allow persistently negative inflation.

---

[61] While the Friedman rule suggests that nominal interest rates should be very low, this line of thinking suggests that reducing real rates to zero could be problematic.

Deflation in Japan – A Brief Review

During the late 1980s, Japan's economic system was widely seen as a model
to be emulated by other countries. Little more than a decade later, however, the
world again looked at Japan, but this time for a different reason: this time the
issue was not how to replicate Japan's success, but how to avoid an economic
slump and deflation.

The *collapse of the asset price boom* in the early 1990s marked the beginning of a long economic slump in Japan, with only moderate and rather short-
lived recoveries (Okina & Shiratsuka, 2004; Okina, Shirakawa, & Shiratsuka,
2001). From the early 1980s to the end of 1989 the Nikkei rose from less than
7,000 to around 39,000 points (Fig. 5.32(a)). Thereafter, it fell back to 7,800
points in April 2003. Japanese land prices, which had more than doubled in
the period from 1980 to early 1991, dropped in 2005-Q3 below the level seen
at the beginning of the 1980s (Fig. 5.32(b)).

What had caused the dismal development? There is a consensus among
policymakers and economists that one of the basic structural problems the
Japanese economy has faced is the *non-performing loan problem* of the banking sector. The impaired balance sheet situation of the banking sector, a direct
result of defaulting borrowers in the wake of the collapse of the asset price
boom, reduced the banking sector's willingness and/or ability to extend loans
to the private sector. Money and credit expansion fell sharply from the early
1990s (Fig. 5.33), accompanied by economic stagnation in terms of real GDP
and industrial production (Fig. 5.33(b)).

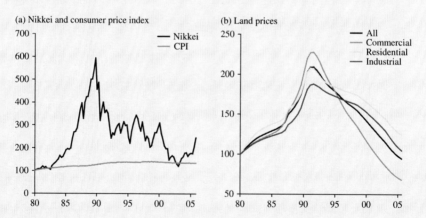

Fig. 5.32 Stock market and land prices in Japan
Source: Bloomberg, Thomson Financials; own calculations. All series take the value of 100
in 1980-Q1.

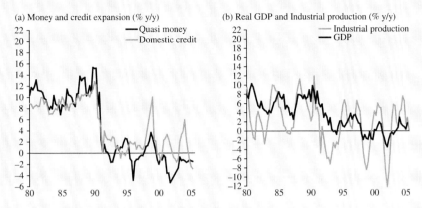

Fig. 5.33 Money and credit expansion and economic activity
Source: Bloomberg, IMF; own calculations.

The Bank of Japan (BoJ) started cutting interest rates in early 1991, thereby orchestrating a general downward trend in Japanese interest rates (Fig. 5.34). However, with consumer price inflation running at a relatively low level, real interest rates remained in positive territory (Mori, Shiratsuka, & Taguchi, 2000). In early 1995, the BoJ had little room for further interest rate reductions, with official short-term rates approaching zero. The BoJ maintained the uncollateralised overnight call rate as low as around 0.5% despite the fact that Japan's economy recovered at a more than 3% growth rate of GDP from 1995 to 1996. In autumn 1997, Japan's economy started to deteriorate, largely under the influence of financial system disturbance reflecting the failure of large financial institutions. The BoJ successively lowered the overnight call rate to 0.02% in February 1999.

The period between 1999 and 2000 is often termed the *zero interest rate period*. In August 2000, the BoJ lifted its zero interest rate policy and raised the overnight call rate to 0.25%, since the economy was showing signs of continued recovery. However, in late 2000, the economy started to deteriorate again, reflecting adjustments to global IT and related exports. Concerns over a potentially returning deflation intensified. The BoJ lowered the policy interest rate one last time to 0.15% and then adopted *quantitative monetary easing* in March 2001.

In terms of *fighting deflation*, the monetary policy of the BoJ has been controversially reviewed. A number of economists (such as, for instance, Blinder, 1999; Krugman, 1998; McCallum, 1999; Meltzer, 1999a, 1999b, 1999c, 1999d; Posen, 1998; Svensson, 1999) have suggested bold monetary policy actions. In contrast, responses from the BoJ, including Okina (1999) and Ueda (1999, 2000), have consistently defended a policy of not taking actions beyond lowering the policy rate to zero.

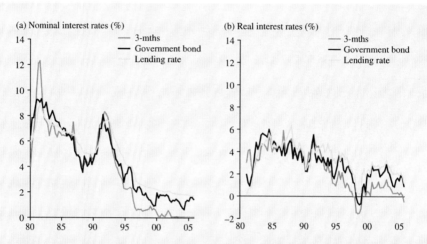

Fig. 5.34 Japanese yield environment
Source: Bloomberg, IMF, Thomson Financial; own calculations. Real rates are nominal rates minus annual consumer price inflation.

So has deflation been the actual cause of Japan's economic stagnation? Baba et al. (2005) argue that deflation has by no means been a major factor. The authors see the deflation of asset prices – land and stock prices – as being closely related to the economic difficulty of the Japanese economy at that time. The *negative shocks* generated by sharp declines in asset prices have been propagated and amplified by their interaction with the deterioration in the condition of the financial system.

Okina and Shiratsuka (2004) argue that asset price deflation in Japan in the 1990s is better understood as a *reflection of a significant downward shift in trend growth* rather than the bursting of a gigantic asset price bubble, which amplified the business cycle. A downward shift in the Japanese growth trend, resulting from incomplete economic adjustments to significant changes in relative prices, can be regarded as a large-scale and quite persistent adverse shock.

5.5.1 Demand and Supply Shocks and Deflation

There is a long tradition to analyse the wider consequences of demand and supply shocks in the traditional Keynesian *IS-LM* framework. In the following, (i) the Keynesian *investment trap*, (ii) the Keynesian *liquidity trap* and – to contrast the idea of a stable equilibrium below full employment – (iii) the *real balance effect* shall be briefly reviewed.

5.5.1.1 Keynesian Investment Trap

In Fig. 5.35, quadrant I shows the labour market, where labor demand (L^d) meets labor supply (L^s); both schedules are a function of the real wage (W/P), where W is the nominal wage and P is the price level. The production function is shown in quadrant II, where income (Y) is a function of labour (L). Aggregate demand (AD) and aggregate supply (AS), which are function of the price level, are shown in quadrant III. The IS- and LM-curves are shown in quadrant IV. The vertical IS-curve represents the investment trap: investment does not respond to the interest rate. Finally, quadrant V shows the (flexible) nominal wage for a given price level.

Let us assume the economy is running at full capacity. The intersection between the vertical IS(Y^*)-curve and the normally shaped LM(P^*)-curve in quadrant IV shows that effective demand determines actual output – independent from the LM-curve. In equilibrium, the interest rate is i^*, the real wage is W/P^* (where P^* is the equilibrium price level) and L^* is the equilibrium labor volume.

Now assume that a *negative shock* (for instance, a decline in consumption demand) pushes the IS-curve to the left. Aggregate demand (AD) shifts to the left. Income and the interest rate fall to Y_0 and i_1, respectively. An ensuing decline in the price level (from P^* to P_1) would shift the LM-curve (via a *real balance effect*) to LM(P_1). The interest rate would fall further to i_2. However, given an interest insensitive investment demand, any change in the interest rate would *leave actual output unchanged*.

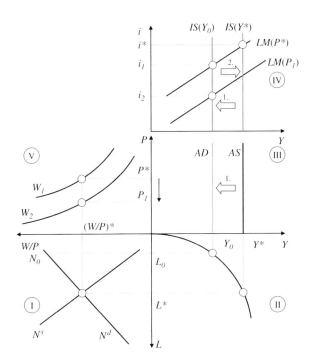

Fig. 5.35 *"Keynesian case I"*: the investment trap

With income at $Y_0 < Y^*$, labour demand would be just L_0 ($< L^*$) – as in the
Keynesian framework aggregate demand determines output. Unemployment would
be $\overline{L_0 L*}$. From a Keynesian point of view, the new constellation would be *stable*: In
a Keynesian investment trap, a decline in the price level, the interest or the nominal
wage would not bring output back to potential. In fact, the price level could keep
falling (leading to a protracted period of deflation) without restoring the economy
back to potential output.

5.5.1.2 Keynesian Liquidity Trap

The idea of the Keynesian liquidity trap is that the interest rate cannot fall below
a certain level, implying an infinite interest rate elasticity of money demand, as
graphically symbolised by a horizontal LM-curve.[62] If the interest rate level resulting from the liquidity trap is too high, aggregate demand will remain lower than
potential output. As was the case in the Keynesian investment trap, changes in inter-

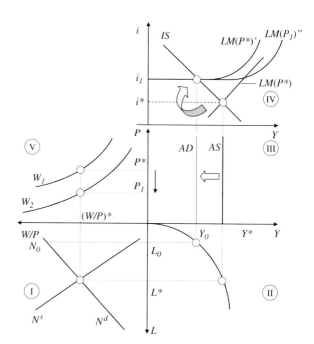

Fig. 5.36 *"Keynesian case
II"*: the liquidity trap

---

[62] Svensson (1999) reconsiders the idea of the liquidity trap using state-of-the-art monetary models
in which optimizing agents have rational expectations. In his money-in-the-utility-function model,
households become willing to hoard any additional money that the government chooses to supply
after the nominal interest rate reaches its lower bound of zero. The central bank then loses control
of the price level and perhaps other key variables as well.

est rates, prices and wages nominal cannot bring the economy back towards full employment.

Figure 5.36 shows a situation in which the economy is in equilibrium (with Y^*, i^*, P^* and W/P^*). Now, a shock makes the LM-curve completely interest rate insensitive in the area where it intersects with the IS-curve. As a result, equilibrium output falls to Y_0 ($< Y^*$), and the AD-curve moves to the left. The interest rate i_1 is clearly higher than i^* needed for bringing aggregate demand in line with potential output. A decline in the price level (from P^* to P_1) would move the LM-curve to the right via the *real balance effect*. However, given the infinite interest rate elasticity of the demand for money, the interest rate remains unchanged. Even ongoing deflation would not restore the economy back to full employment; again, unemployment would remain stable at $\overline{L_0 L*}$.

5.5.1.3 The Case Against (Persistent) Deflation

The Keynesian investment trap and the liquidity trap suggest that a situation of (persistent) unemployment might emerge even though wages and the price level are fully flexible. However, Gottfried von Haberler (1937), Tibor Scitovsky (1941) and Arthur C. Pigou (1941, 1943, 1947) put forward theoretical considerations which would argue against such a conclusion. According to these authors, consumption would be based not only on current income – as is the case in the traditional Keynesian model – but also on *real net wealth*.[63]

Accordingly, the IS-curve depends, in addition to current income, on real balances (M/P). A *negative supply shock*, for instance, shifts the IS-curve to the left, lowering income to Y_0 from Y^*. However, the ensuing decline in the price level (from P^* to P_1) would uno actu increase market agents' holdings of real balances. This, in turn, would induce additional spending (*wealth effect*), raising income. Also, a rise in real balances would move the LM-curve to the right (which, however, would have no effect in the case of an investment trap). In other words, the economy would restore itself back to equilibrium, and any deflation and loss in output and employment would be short-lived (Fig. 5.37).

Finally, the real balance effect gains further support from the notion that the (long-run) money demand would be rather interest rate insensitive, as maintained by Monetarists. In such a case, the LM-curve would tend to exhibit a vertical shape that is the *exact opposite* of a liquidity trap. In fact, the real balance effect could be quite powerful; the smaller the interest rate elasticity of money demand is, the bigger is the impact of changes in real money holdings on output and employment. (Note that the steeper the LM- and the AD-curves are, the lower is the price level in the AS-AD diagram following a negative supply shock).

Pigou (1943) proposed that even the Keynesian *special cases* – liquidity trap and investment trap – are not sufficient to maintain an unemployment equilibrium, as the rightward shifts of the IS curve via the Pigou effect will ensure that the economy

---

[63] *Real net wealth* refers to the real supply of money and the real supply of bonds.

Fig. 5.37 The case against
persistent deflation: the "*real
balance effect*"

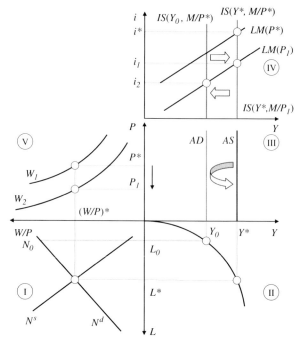

is taken back to full employment equilibrium.[64] Thus, the only theoretical way to
establish an unemployment equilibrium in the Keynesian model is assuming sticky
wages and prices.

5.5.2 Debt-Deflation Theories

It is fair to say that the role of financial crises for economic crises has received
relatively little attention in modern macroeconomics (Peter, 2005). Compared to
the earlier literature, financial distress became less prominent in the interwar period
(Tobin, 1975; Laidler, 2007), and even less prominent in the post World War II
period. Although there is now a growing interest in the topic (stimulated by the
series of financial crises since the second half of the 1990s and especially the recent
credit crises), research has not yet reached a stage in which the ideas of the "theory
of the crisies" literature have retained a prominent position.[65]

---

[64]Kalecki (1944) noted that the Pigou effect would in practice be confined to "*outside*" *money*,
as every other financial asset is a liability to some private debtor, who is correspondingly hurt by
deflation. In the classical model, the Pigou effect on outside money, relabelled "real balance effect"
by Patinkin, has a zero net effect when all money is "inside" and banks are perfectly competitive
(Patinkin, 1948, 1971).

[65]Few models allow for wide-spread default and losses to the banking system. This includes
Bernanke (1999), and Christiano, Motto, and Rostagno (2004). This issue is taken up in von Peter
(2004).

Financial distress seems to have been a characteristic feature of *bad deflation*. According to De Long (1999, p. 231), "almost every analyst placed general deflation, and the bankruptcies it caused, at or near the heart of the worst macroeconomic disaster the world has ever seen." In the case of Japan, Kiyotaki and Moore (1997) show that asset price declines had a severely negative impact on overall credit conditions, with negative effects on output and employment.

It was the Great Depression of 1929–1933 that inspired *debt deflation theories*, basically describing how debt and deflation might enforce each other. In the following, a brief look shall be taken at three (interrelated) debt deflation theories:

  (i) Irving Fisher (1933) argued that borrowers attempting to reduce their burden of debt (indebtedness) engage in distress selling to raise money for repaying their debt. But repayment in aggregate causes a contraction in the money supply and leads to deflation.
 (ii) Ludwig von Mises (1912) held excessive credit expansion, fostered by government controlled central banks, responsible for boom and bust periods, in which deflation would actually follow from inflation.
(iii) Hyman Minsky (1982) showed that, in a period of financial crisis, distress selling reduces asset prices, causing losses to agents with maturing debts. This reinforces distress selling and reduces consumption and investment spending, which deepens deflation.
(iv) Ben S. Bernanke (1983) observed that debt deflation involves wide-spread bankruptcy, impairing the process of credit intermediation. The resulting credit contraction of credit and money supply depresses aggregate demand.

5.5.2.1 Fisher's Debt-Deflation Theory

Irving Fisher's 1933 article *The Debt-Deflation Theory of Great Depressions* sets out a monetary theory of how financial distress relates, and exacerbates, deflation. Fisher's argument starts with a state of *over-indebtedness*. Agents seek to reduce their indebtedness by selling assets. The first and most important steps in Fisher's chain of consequences are (Fisher, 1933, p. 342):

  (i) the attempt to liquidate assets on the part of borrowers and liquidate debt holdings on the part of creditors leads to distress selling; this leads to
 (ii) a contraction of deposit currency, as bank loans are paid off. The contraction of deposits is accompanies lay a decline in the velocity of money. This causes
(iii) a fall in the level of prices, in other words, a swelling of the real value of money, worsening the real indebtedness of borrowers.

Fisher views price level deflation as "the root of almost all the evils" (and he elaborates on six further steps in this process (Fisher, 1932, p. 39)). He stressed the role of over-stretched borrowers for setting into motion deflation (1933, p. 344, his emphasis): "if the over-indebtedness with which we started was great enough, the liquidation of debts cannot keep up with the fall of prices which it causes. In that case, liquidation defeats itself. While it diminishes the number of dollars owed, it may not do so as fast as it increases the value of each dollar owed. Then, *the very effort of individuals to lessen their burden of debts increases it, because of the mass effect of the stampede to liquidate in swelling each dollar owed*. Then we have the great paradox which, I submit, is the chief secret of most, if not all, great depressions: *The more the debtors pay, the more they owe*. The more the economic boat tips, the more it tends to tip. It is not tending to right itself, but is capsizing. But if the over-indebtedness is not sufficiently great to make liquidation thus defeat itself, the situation is different and simpler. It is then more analogous to a stable equilibrium; the more the boat rocks the more it will tend to right itself."

Fisher's theory was innovative in at least three aspects. First, he introduced the idea that financial distress feeds back on deflation. Second, in contrast to the price specie flow mechanism, which saw deflation as an outcome of gold outflows, Fisher emphasised the role of liquidation of assets for causing deflation.[66] Third, in contrast to much of the subsequent literature, Fisher viewed deflation as destabilizing; as was shown earlier, to classical economists deflation would not necessarily be negative (von Haberler, 1937; Scitovsky, 1941; Pigou, 1941, 1943, 1947).

Finally, it should be noted that Fisher mentions a stability condition: if the initial over-indebtedness exceeds a *threshold*, the process becomes unstable. Debt deflation would only come to a halt in "almost universal bankruptcy". However, Fisher does not become more precise in the sense of putting a number to a *critical threshold* of over-indebtedness.

The US Great Depression and the Stock Market

Analysts generally agree that the economic collapse of the 1930s was extremely severe, actually the most severe in American history (Wheelock, 1992). Real (constant dollar) GNP fell 33% and the price level declined 25% from 1929 to 1933. The unemployment rate went from under 4% in 1929 to 25% in 1933. Real GNP did not recover to its 1929 level until 1937. The unemployment rate did not fall below 10% until World War II.

Personal and firm bankruptcies rose to unprecedented highs. In 1932 and 1933, aggregate corporate profits in the United States were negative. Some 9,000 banks failed between 1930 and 1933. Since some suspended banks eventually reopened and deposits were recovered, these numbers might overstate the extent of the banking distress. In any case, bank failures were numerous and their effects severe, even compared with the 1920s, when failures were high by any standards.

---

[66]Liquidation involves the selling of the borrower's possessions, "his stocks, his bonds, his farmland, or whatever his available assets may be" (Fisher, 1932, p. 13).

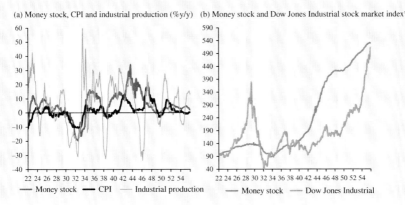

Fig. 5.38 Putting the Great Depression in the US into perspective
Source: Thomson Financial, Bloomberg, NBER, own calculations. – *Indexed, January
1922 = 100. – *Shaded areas* recession periods according to NBER.

Figure 5.38(a) shows the annual changes in the stock of money, industrial production and the CPI from 1922 to 1956. As can be seen, the stock
of money contracted sharply during the Great Depression, accompanied by a
strong decline in economic activity and the price level. Figure 5.38(b) plots the
US Dow Jones stock market index against the stock of money – highlighting
the decline in stock prices as the money stock contracted.

To put the Great Depression into perspective, Fig. 5.39 shows the US Dow
Jones Industrial index from 1910 to 1954 (in natural logarithms). The series
was indexed to 100 at its peak level in August 1929. Moreover, it shows the
developments of the stock markets in the US, Germany and Japan from the
early 1970s to January 2006. These indices were also set 100 in the respective
month when they reached their peak values in the period under review.

In the stock market crash of the late 1920s/early 1930s, the US Dow Jones
fell from it speak of around 380 points in August 1929 to less than 43 in June
1932. It took until November 1954 until the US Dow Jones Industrial had
returned back to its pre-crisis level – that is around 25 years. By contrast, the
decline in stock market prices worldwide, starting around autumn 2000, was
much less pronounced. In fact, most indices had returned close to, or even
exceeded their pre-crisis levels around autumn 2007.

Much of the debate about the causes of the Great Depression has focused
on bank failures. Were they merely a *result* of falling national income and
money demand? Or were they an important *cause* of the Great Depression?
Most contemporaries viewed bank failures as unfortunate for those who lost
deposits, but irrelevant for macroeconomic developments. Keynesian explanations of the Great Depression assigned little, if any, role to bank failures.

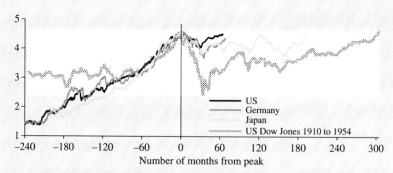

Fig. 5.39 Putting the "Black Friday 1929" into perspective
Source: Bloomberg, Thomson Financial; own calculations. – The US, German and Japanese stock markets are represented by broadly defined market capitalization indices. – The indices were set 100 (shown in natural logarithms) in the month when the respective index reached its maximum in the period under review (For the Dow Jones Industrial in 1910–1954: August 1929, for after WWII period in the US: September 2000, Germany: May 2000, Japan: January 1990).

In sharp contrast, Monetarists like Milton Friedman and Anna J. Schwartz (1963) and Alan Meltzer (1976) maintain that bank failures caused the money supply to fall which, in turn, caused much of the decline in economic activity. In these explanations, the US Federal Reserve bears much of the blame for the Great Depression because it failed to prevent the banking panics and the resulting contraction in the money stock. Bernanke (1983) notes that bank failures disrupted credit markets which, he argues, caused an increase in the cost of credit intermediation that significantly reduced output.

In a more recent work, Eichengreen and Mitchener (2003) analysed how well quantitative measures of the credit can explain the uneven expansion of the 1920s and the slump of the 1930s. The authors conclude that the *credit boom view* provides a useful perspective on both the boom of the 1920s and the subsequent slump. In particular, it would direct attention to the role played by the structure of the financial sector and the interaction of finance and innovation.

In addition, the management of the monetary regime at that time seems to have mattered greatly for explaining the Great Depression. The pro-cyclical character of the foreign exchange component of international reserves, and the failure of domestic monetary authorities that could have adopted stable policy rules following the emergence of the crisis, could also be important issues for explaining the developments in credit markets that helped to set the stage for the Great Depression.

5.5.2.2 Mises' Deflation Theory

The *Austrian Monetary Theory of the Trade Cycle,* put forward by Ludwig von Mises, maintains that depressions would be the inevitable consequence of an unhampered government sponsored *credit expansion.*[67] Mises' theory actually rests on two interrelated considerations. *First,* there is the notion that governments, the holders of the monetary monopoly, would pursue a policy against the free market (von Mises, 1996, p. 794): "Credit expansion is the governments' foremost tool in their struggle against the market economy". *Second,* Mises saw public pressure being brought to bear on the government and its central bank to keep interest rates as low as possible: "It is fact that today measures aimed at lowering the rate of interest are generally considered highly desirable and that credit expansion is viewed as the efficacious means for the attainment of this end."

Mises assumed that governments aim at pushing the market rate of interest to below Wicksell's *natural rate,* which requires a continuous expansion of bank credit.[68] As such, the boom is as a consequence of a policy of artificial and unsustainable credit expansion, in which capital and other resources are committed to excessive production at the expense of consumption. One may use the term *forced savings* to describe the policy induced reduction in consumption, and the term *malinvestment* to describe the increase in investment encouraged by a policy of artificially cheap credit.

To Mises, the economic crisis brought about by a cheap money policy would sooner or later unfold (von Mises, 1996, p. 565): "As soon as credit expansion comes to an end, these faults become manifest. Private households and firms would adjust their portfolios." Liquidating unprofitable activities plays an essential role in triggering the crisis: "It is this process of liquidation of the faults committed in the boom and readjustment to the wishes of the consumers which is called the depression".

Mises recognized, as did Wicksell, that *enlightened* central bank policy would avoid overly generous bank credit expansion, thus minimizing the divergence between the bank rate and the natural rate. Believing, however, that central bank policy as formulated by government officials would be ideologically biased towards cheap credit and artificially low interest rates, Mises favored institutional reform in the direction of a privatization of monetary affairs and free banking.[69]

---

[67]The idea that the market's responses to credit expansion contain the seeds of their own undoing is older than the Austrian or the Swedish (*Wicksell*) School. A self-reversing process triggered by bank credit expansion policy had been identified early in the nineteenth century by members of the *Currency School.* Actually, Mises considered his own theory as an extension of the circulation-credit theory rather than a uniquely Austrian theory.

[68]The divergence of the two rates of interest was of concern to Wicksell primarily because of its effect on the general level of prices. Wicksell acknowledged that bank policy might also affect the allocation of resources, but any such allocative effects were reduced to "tendencies only" by his simplifying assumptions and thus were no part of his formal theory.

[69]As a kind of "second best solution", Mises recommended (von Mises 1996, p. 795): "The inference to be drawn from the monetary cycle theory by those who want to prevent the recurrence of

To Mises, depression and deflation are the inevitable consequence of *government sponsored credit expansion policy* (Mises, 1996, p. 572): "The wavelike movement affecting the economic system, the recurrence of periods of boom which are followed by periods of depression, is the unavoidable outcome of the attempts, repeated again and again, to lower the gross market rate of interest by means of credit expansion. There is no means of avoiding the final collapse of a boom brought about by credit expansion. The alternative is only whether the crisis should come sooner as the result of a voluntary abandonment of further credit expansion, or later as a final and total catastrophe of the currency system involved."

5.5.2.3 Minsky's Debt Deflation Theory

Minsky's (1982) debt deflation theory emphasises the role of the asset market. Distress asset selling reduces asset prices, which reinforces distress selling and worsens deflation. Regarding Fisher's first channel, Minsky (1982, p. 383) wrote: "Fisher does not identify the ways a unit can get cash to repay loans that fall due. [...] Once a situation exists where debt payments cannot be made either by cash from operations or refinancing, so that assets have to be sold, then the requirements imposed by the debt structure can lead to a fall in the prices of assets. In a free market, the fall in asset prices can be so large that the sale of assets cannot realize the funds needed to fulfill commitments." As in Fisher's explanation, distress selling can be self-defeating, and the asset market and distress selling feedback on each other.[70]

Regarding Fisher' second channel, Minsky argues that the fall in asset prices reinforces deflation via a *negative wealth effect* (Minsky, 1963, p. 6): "If payment commitments cannot be met from the normal sources, then a unit is forced either to borrow or to sell assets. Both borrowing on unfavorable terms and the forced sale of assets usually result in a capital loss for the affected unit. However, for any unit, capital losses and gains are not symmetrical: there is a ceiling to the capital losses a unit can take and still fulfil its commitments. Any loss beyond this limit is passed on to its creditors by way of default or refinancing of the contracts. Such induced capital losses result in a further contraction of consumption and investment beyond that due to the initiating decline in income. This can result in a recursive debt-deflation process."

To Minsky, the debt structure determines stability and plays an important part in his financial instability hypothesis (1977, 1978, 1992). A robust debt structure makes the economy "an equilibrium seeking and containing system"; but under a fragile debt structure, it becomes "a deviation amplifying system" (Minsky, 1992, p. 7). Minsky's financial instability theory explains how a capitalist economy

---

booms and of the subsequent depressions is not that the banks should not lower the rate of interest, but that they should refrain from credit expansion."

[70] Kindleberger (1996), in his famous book *Manias, Panics, and Crashes*, takes Minsky's approach as the organising principle for casting the history of financial crises in terms of cycles of speculation on borrowed funds.

endogenously generates a financial structure susceptible to financial crises, and how the activity in financial markets gives rise to financial crises.

5.5.2.4 Bernanke's Debt Deflation Theory

Bernanke (1983) highlights the macroeconomic role of a credit contraction for aggregate spending. In the context of the Great Depression, he emphasized that widespread borrower default and bank runs reduced the effectiveness of financial intermediation (Bernanke, 1983, p. 264): "The banking problems of 1930–1933 disrupted the credit allocation process by creating large, unplanned changes in the channels of credit flow. [...] plus the actual failures, forced a contraction of the banking system's role in the intermediation of credit." "[...] experience does not seem to be inconsistent with the point that even good borrowers may find it more difficult or costly to obtain credit when there is extensive insolvency. The debt crisis should be added to the banking crisis as a potential source of disruption of the credit system. (p. 267)." "The effects of this credit squeeze on aggregate demand helped convert the severe but not unprecedented downturn of 1929–1930 into a protracted depression" (p. 257).

   Bernanke cautions that his theory does not offer a complete explanation of the Great Depression, however; it neither explains its beginning, nor excludes other theories (Bernanke, 1983, p. 258). His objective is to explain the depth and length of the Great Depression, but not what caused it.

5.6 Asset Price Inflation

5.6.1 From "Bubbles" to Asset Price Inflation

Prices, determined by demand and supply in free market, change over time and for various reasons. So do prices for assets such as stocks, bonds, real estate and housing. In an information efficient market, one would expect that an asset price corresponds with its fundamentally justified value (Shiller, 2000). The latter could be defined as the present value of the *true* earning capacity of an asset or the true value of the services that the holder of that asset will receive from using it.

   It is often said, however, that asset prices, stock prices in particular, do not always equal their fundamental value. Keynes (1936) observed that stock prices may not be governed by an objective view of fundamental factors but by *what average opinion expects average option to be*. Keynes' analogy for price actions in the stock market was that of trying to forecast a winner of a beauty contest. Here, subjective beauty is not necessarily the issue. What is important is how an individual thinks the other market agents' concepts of beauty will be reflected in their dispositions.

   The positive (negative) difference between an asset's market price and its fundamental value could therefore be termed *overvaluation* (*undervaluation*), represent-

ing a *positive (negative) bubble*.[71] To illustrate the bubble phenomenon, let us turn
to the stock market (Cuthbertson, 1996, p. 157). For simplicity it shall be assumed
that (i) agents are risk neutral and have RE and (ii) demand a constant real return on
the asset: $E_t R_t = k$. The Euler equation is:

$$P_t = \delta(E_t P_{t+1} + E_t D_{t+1}),\qquad(5.91)$$

where $\delta = 1/(1+k)$. Solving by repeated forward substitution yields the rational
formula of the stock price:

$$P_t = P_t^f = \sum_{i=1}^{\infty} \delta^i E_t D_{t+i},\qquad(5.92)$$

assuming that the transversality condition holds (meaning that $\lim(\delta^i E_t D_{t+n}) = 0$
as $n \to \infty$). The present value of the stock, P_t, as shown in (5.92), is the fundamental value of the stock, P_t^f.

However, the present value can also be shown including a rational bubble:

$$P_t = \sum_{i=1}^{\infty} \delta^i E_t D_{t+i} + B_t = P_t^f + B_t,\qquad(5.93)$$

where B_t represents the rational bubble term.

Bubbles and the RVF

Following Cuthbertson (1996), it can be shown that (5.93) can satisfy (5.92)
when some restrictions are placed on the properties of B_t. To start with, let
us lead Eq. (5.93) by one period and take expectations at time t. Such an
operation yields:

$$\begin{aligned} E_t P_{t+1} &= E_t \left[\delta E_{t+1} D_{t+2} + \delta^2 E_{t+1} D_{t+3} + \ldots + B_{t+1} \right] \\ &= \left[\delta E_t D_{t+2} + \delta^2 E_t D_{t+3} + \ldots + E_t B_{t+1} \right]. \end{aligned} \qquad(5.94)$$

Note that Eq. (5.94) is based on the law of iterated expectations:
$E_t(E_{t+1} D_{t+j}) = E_t D_{t+j}$.

The right hand side of the Euler equation (5.91) includes the term $P_t = \delta(E_t P_{t+1} + E_t D_{t+1})$. Using (5.94) we find the following result:

$$\delta(E_t P_{t+1} + E_t D_{t+1}) = \delta E_t D_{t+1} + \left[\delta^2 E_t D_{t+2} + \delta^3 E_t D_{t+3} + \ldots + \delta E_t B_{t+1} \right]. \qquad(5.95)$$

---

[71] Negative bubbles can occur when there is a banking crisis which forces banks to simultaneously
liquidate assets. Asset prices fall below their fundamental because of a lack of liquidity.

Substituting the fundamental value, P_t^f, in Eq. (5.93) yields:

$$\delta(E_t P_{t+1} + E_t D_{t+1}) = P_t^f + \delta E_t B_{t+1}. \tag{5.96}$$

When substituting (5.96) in (5.91), the result is:

$$P_t = P_t^f + \delta E_t B_{t+1}. \tag{5.97}$$

We can make solutions (5.93) and (5.97) equivalent, if the following relation holds:

$$E_t B_{t+m} = B_t/\delta = (1+k)B_t. \tag{5.98}$$

In this case, solutions (5.93) and (5.97) become the same expression and satisfy (5.91). More generally, (5.93) implies:

$$E_t B_{t+m} = B_t/\delta^m. \tag{5.99}$$

B_t (in addition to the known discount factor) is the best forecast of all future values of the bubble and it is determined by its current value. Note that whereas the bubble solution satisfies the Euler equation, it violates the transversality condition for $B_t \neq 0$.

A *bubble* might be characterised as the difference between an assets market value and its fundamentally justified value.[72] However, it might not always be easy to identify asset price bubbles. For example, price rise might simply reflect the adjustment to an increased fundamental value of the asset under review. In such a case, the price increase would represent a process leading towards a new equilibrium. Alternatively, a surge in an asset's market price could be driven by non-fundamental factors. Such a price rise would lead to a divergence between the asset's market price and its fundamentally justified valuation.

When dealing with *asset price inflation*, some initial remarks appear to be in order. The term *inflation* is usually defined as an ongoing rise in the economy's *total price level*. It refers to the *overall* upward drift of money prices, it does not refer to an increase in individual goods prices. In that sense, inflation denotes the loss of purchasing power of money: as the economy's total price level rises, the purchasing power of money declines. In a market economy, there are ever-changing *relative prices*. Prices of some goods may exhibit an ongoing rise over time. Such an observation, however, is not necessarily indicative of inflation, for price rises of

---

[72]On 5 December 1996, for instance, the former Chairman of the US Federal Reserve Board, Alan Greenspan, used the term "irrational exuberance" for describing the extraordinarily strong increases in stock prices. See Greenspan (1996).

one category of goods and services might be accompanied by price declines of other
categories, thereby keeping the economy's price level unchanged.

Assets such as stocks, bonds, housing etc., represent goods like any other goods
which are bought and sold in the market place. As a result, it would be actually
misleading to speak of *asset price inflation*. A better term would be "excessive
asset price rises". This is because the latter expression would denote a *relative* price
change. However, it has become common practise to use the term asset price inflation for denoting an *unusually strong* increase in asset prices.

Stock Prices and Consumer Goods Prices

Figure 5.40(a) plots the US S&P's 500 stock market index against the US consumer price index from 1870 to 2005. Up until the 1950s, both series appeared
to be drifting more or less closely together. Since then, however, the series
decoupled markedly: Stock prices have been trending upwards much stronger
than consumer goods prices.

Figure 5.40(b) shows the price earnings (PE) ratio of the S&P's 500 stock
market index. The latter has been oscillating around the long-term average of
15. However, the PE ratio has fluctuated widely in the period under review.
Perhaps most notably, it rose to unprecedented levels at the end of the 1990s,
that is towards the end of the *New Economy* era. It was actually then when, in
view of drastically rising stock prices and increasingly (over-)stretched stock
valuation measures, market observers started to increasingly talk about *asset
price inflation*.

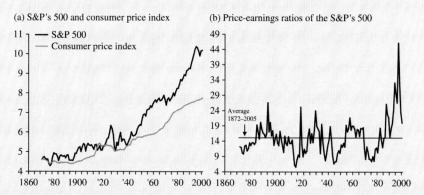

Fig. 5.40 US stock market, inflation, and stock market valuation
Source: Global Financial Data, Robert Shiller (update of data shown in Chap. 26 of market
volatility, R. Shiller, MIT Press, 1989, and Irrational Exuberance, Princeton 2005). One-
year PE-ratio starts in 1872. Price indices were set 100 in 1871 (natural logarithms).

5.6.2 Keeping Track of Asset Price Inflation

In recent years, the discussion about the role financial asset prices – and *asset price inflation* – should play in monetary policy has received growing attention (Gertler, 1998; Bank for International Settlement, 1998; Gertler & Bernanke, 1999; Filardo, 2000). The discussion has actually developed along four major lines:

(i)   the role financial asset prices play in the transmission mechanism;
(ii) the role of financial asset prices have for the stability of the financial system;
(iii) the use of financial assets prices as information and indicator variables for monetary policy; and
(iv) the role financial asset prices could play in formulating the central bank's policy objectives.

5.6.2.1 The Role Asset Prices Play in the Transmission Mechanism

Four major channels can be identified through which asset price developments may influence inflation or output. *First*, asset price developments have a direct impact on consumer prices to the extent that asset price changes affect the prices of services of capital goods (for instance, rents might rise when the underlying value of real estate increases). *Second*, changes in the value of assets may lead to adjustments in domestic expenditure. For instance, rising stock prices may increase the propensity to spend, affecting the prices of final demand. *Third*, asset price changes may spawn *confidence effects*, which will influence consumption and investment and thus prices (Gros, 2007). *Fourth*, asset price developments may generate a self-reinforcing effect through the *credit channel*, creating a pro-cyclical influence on economic activity. More specifically, rising asset prices could boost the value of available collateral, which, in turn, may fuel the growth of debt financed spending. Conversely, when asset prices decline and individuals experience difficulty in servicing their debt, banks will suffer losses and may react by reducing credit, magnifying a cyclical downturn.

Insights into the relationship between asset prices and consumer prices are essential in determining *whether monetary policy should react to asset price developments*. To the extent that consumer price inflation is directly influenced by asset price inflation, central bank would need to take into account asset prices for setting the money supply and interest rates. In particular, pronounced asset price developments may, in principle, thus influence the monetary policy stance, even when this policy is primarily focused on (developments of) consumer prices.

5.6.2.2 The Role of Financial Asset Prices for the Stability of the Financial System

In recent years, financial system stability has de facto become an additional objective of monetary policy. It requires that the principal components of the system –

banks and other financial institutions, markets and payment/settlement infrastructure – facilitate a smooth and efficient allocation of financial resources from savers to investors, that financial risk is assessed and priced reasonably, and that risks are efficiently managed. These requirements include that the financial system is capable of absorbing adverse disturbances.

As experience showed, a dysfunctional financial sector can severely hamper a smooth functioning of the creation of credit and money supply, thereby exerting a negative impact on output and employment. What is more, monetary policy is traditionally conducted via the (domestic) banking sector. If banks would suffer distress (from, say, loan write-offs that severely limit their equity capital base), the efficiency and effectiveness of monetary policy could be greatly diminished.

Boom and Bust Cycles in Asset Prices

Recently a number of studies has been analysing historical boom and bust cycles in asset prices in order to identify regularities in terms of their costs and to detect *dangerous booms* at an early stage (ECB, 2005, p. 55).[1] A recent IMF survey[2] reviewed periods of bust in housing and equity markets and reaches the following conclusions:

– Housing price busts appear to be less frequent than equity price busts. Peak-to-trough periods lasted, on average, longer in the housing than in the equity market (four years versus two and a half years). Price declines during housing (equity) price busts are in the order of around 30% (45%) on average. Forty percent (25%) of housing (equity) price booms were followed by busts.
– Output losses associated with asset price busts can be substantial. The loss incurred during a typical housing (equity) price bust amounts to 8% (4%) of GDP. One feature of housing price cycles that tends to be forgotten is their extraordinary length: many last for more than ten years (Gros, 2007).
– Bank based financial systems incur larger losses than market based financial systems during housing price busts, while the opposite is true for equity price busts. All major banking crises in industrial countries in the post-war period coincided with housing price busts.

An ECB Working Paper[3] focused on *aggregate asset price booms*. By distinguishing high and low cost booms[4], the analysis highlights the following findings:

- High cost booms typically last around a year longer than low cost booms (four versus three years), lead to a build-up of larger real and financial imbalances and are accompanied by stronger real estate price booms and higher inflation towards the end of the booms.
- During the early stages of booms, real money growth and real credit growth are larger for high cost booms.
- Towards the end of high cost booms the stance of monetary policy is typically looser than during low cost booms.[5]

---

[1] See ECB Workshop on Asset Prices and Monetary Policy in 2003.

[2] Helbling and Terrones (2003) base their results on a sample of 14 (for housing prices) or 19 (for equity prices) industrialised countries between 1959 and 2002. Busts are defined as bottom quartile peak to trough real price decreases.

[3] Detken and Smets (2004) use aggregate asset price indices, covering private residential and commercial housing prices as well as share prices for 18 industrialised countries for the period from 1970 to 2002. Booms are defined as periods in which real aggregate asset prices exceed a recursive, sluggishly adjusting (stochastic) trend by more than 10%.

[4] High cost booms are defined as a drop of more than 3% points in average three-year post-boom real GDP growth relative to average boom-year real GDP growth.

[5] This result is confirmed, in the case of the US Great Depression, by Christiano, Motto, and Rostagno (2003).

5.6.2.3 The Use of Assets Prices as Information and Indicator Variables

Asset price markets are forward-looking. Changes in asset prices can therefore be expected to reflect *news* about market agents' inflation and growth expectations. For example, in information efficient markets, investors implicitly reveal, by buying and selling bonds, their *expectations about future developments* in terms of real interest rates and inflation. That said, asset prices might be an important and timely source of information for market agents and central banks alike.

For instance, the spread between long- and short-term bonds might provide information about market agents' expectations as far as the business cycle is concerned. A steep (flat) yield curve might suggest expectations of ongoing strong (weak) economic expansion. The yield spread between comparable conventional bonds and inflation linked bonds – the so-called *break-even inflation* – might be seen as providing a timely indicator of market participants' inflation expectations. Furthermore, option prices can be used to obtain the distribution of market participants' expectations of bond yields over the very short term.

Break-Even Inflation

In recent years, many governments have issued bonds whose coupon and principal at redemption are indexed to a consumer price index. The yield spread between comparable conventional bonds and index linked bonds should therefore reflect market participants' inflation expectations over the remaining maturity of the bond. This yield spread is referred to as *break-even inflation* (BEI) because it provides an estimate of expected inflation at which, under certain assumptions, an investor would be indifferent as to which of the two types of bonds to hold.

Long-term inflation expectations are often used as a measure of the *credibility of monetary policy*: if the central bank's commitment to maintain price stability is credible, the private sector's long-term inflation expectations should correspond with the central bank's pre-announced inflation target (or definition of price stability).

In line with the *Fisher parity* (1907), the nominal yield of a bond, i_{nom}, can be stated as follows:

$$(1 + i_{nom}) = (1 + i_{real})(1 + \pi^e)(1 + \phi), \qquad (5.100)$$

with i_{real} = real rate component, π^e = inflation expectation and ϕ = risk premium. The BEI can be calculated as:

$$(1 + i_{nom})/(1 + i_{real}) = (1 + \pi^e)(1 + \phi). \qquad (5.101)$$

The BEI offers several important features as a source of information on the private sector's long-term inflation expectations. *First*, it is available at high frequency. *Second*, the BEI reflects free market trades, thereby giving insights into market agents' *true* inflation concerns. *Third*, as conventional and index linked bonds are issued over a variety of original maturities, they allow for the extraction of information about inflation expectations at a larger number of horizons than reported in surveys.

However, the BEI as indicator of market participants' long-term inflation expectations needs to be interpreted with caution (Sack, 2000):

– The BEI incorporates an *inflation risk premium* required by investors to be compensated for inflation uncertainty when holding long-term maturity nominal bonds. The rationale is as follows. Future inflation erodes the payments on a nominal security but not those on an index-linked bond. Investors are therefore likely to demand a premium as compensation for holding long-term nominal securities, and, as they are typically risk-averse, such a premium is likely to vary over time with the uncertainty about future

inflation. Moreover, it is natural for this inflation risk premium *to rise with the maturity of the bond*. This premium tends to *bias the BEI upwards*.
– The market liquidity of index linked bonds is typically lower than that of comparable nominal bonds. This may lead to the presence of a *higher liquidity premium* embedded in the yields on index linked bonds. The liquidity premium tends *to bias the BEI rate downwards*.
– The BEI may sometimes be biased as a result of technical and institutional market factors (tax distortions and regulation, thereby affecting the demand for index linked instruments), which may have little to do with changes in inflation expectations. Unfortunately, the *distortion effect* on the BEI is difficult to isolate and quantify.

Figure 5.41 shows the BEI and the real yield component for various bond maturities in percent for the euro area and the US for the period September 1998 to the beginning of August 2007. Throughout the period under review, the euro area BEIs have been oscillating around 2.0%, the level of inflation the ECB considers compatible with its price stability mandate. In the US, BEIs were around 2.5%, a level typically considered compatible with the US Fed's (implicit) definition of price stability.

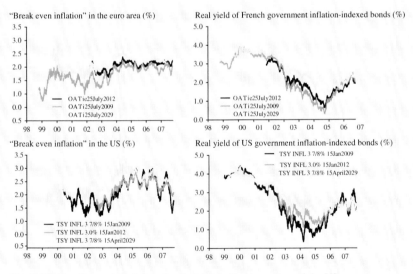

Fig. 5.41 Break-even-inflation and real yields in the euro area and the US
Source: Bloomberg; own calculations.

As far as the stock market is concerned, *expected aggregate dividends* might be closely linked to expected corporate profit growth, thereby providing useful additional information for assessing market participants' expectations for overall economic activity. Furthermore, *options on stock prices* can provide indications about the perceived volatility of overall stock market conditions.

While information derived from asset prices could in principle be useful for market agents and monetary policy purposes, it is important to bear in mind that their information content is generally based on theoretical assumptions concerning the link between asset prices and key economic variables and must therefore be interpreted with caution. Perhaps most important in this context, it is frequently argued that financial asset prices cannot, for logical reasons, serve as a reliable guide for monetary policy.

For instance, if market inflation expectations exceed (fall below) the central bank's envisaged inflation, monetary policy might be tempted to hike (cut) interest rates. However, by linking monetary policy decisions to market inflation expectations, the central bank could easily slide into a *vicious circle*: Policy instability and thus inflation instability can emerge if monetary policy relies not on external anchoring but on market expectations, which themselves are a function of the expected monetary policy decisions.

Is Stabilizing Consumer Price Enough?

In his 2006 article titled *Is price stability enough?*, the former BIS chief economist W. R. White maintains that the stability of consumer prices might not be sufficient to ensure macroeconomic stability, that is securing sustained output and employment gains. He shows that past experience is replete with examples of major economic and financial crises that were not preceded by consumer price inflation.

White notes (White, 2006, p. 1): "The core of the problem is that persistently easy monetary conditions can lead to the cumulative build-up over time of significant deviations from historical norms – whether in terms of debt levels, saving ratios, asset prices or other indicators of "imbalances". The historical record indicates that mean reversion is a common outcome, with associated and negative implications for future aggregate demand." A brief look at the development of consumer prices, today's widely accepted monetary policy target variable, and asset prices might be instructive in this context.

Figure 5.42(a) shows that in the US house and consumer prices moved fairly closely together from the early 1970s to around the middle of the 1990s. Thereafter, however, housing prices started rising much stronger than consumer prices; this is also shown by annual changes in the price indices under review (Fig. 5.42(b)). Figure 5.42(c) plots US stock prices against consumer prices. Whereas until the early half of the 1980s consumer prices went up (much) stronger than stock prices, the reverse held true for the period that followed; Fig. 5.42(d) shows annual changes in the indices under review.

The data point to two, actually interrelated, issues. *First*, asset prices can decouple from consumer prices over prolonged periods of time – thereby giving rise to the possibility of misalignments and misallocation of scarce resources which, when corrected at some point, might entail severe losses in output and employment. *Second*, if this is the case, the question is whether central banks, in an effort to support sustainable economic expansion, should take asset prices, in addition to consumer prices, explicitly into account when making monetary policy decisions.

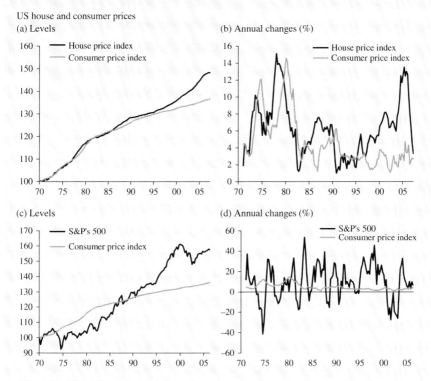

Fig. 5.42   US stock market and consumer prices
Source: Bloomberg; own calculations. Levels in natural logarithms, 1970-Q1 = 100.

5.6.2.4   The Discussion About Including Asset Prices in the Monetary Policy Objective

Back in the early 1970s, Alchian and Klein (1973) reasoned that from a welfare perspective the central bank should be concerned with price stability for both current and future consumer goods by focusing on a *cost-of-life index*.[73] Their proposal to include asset prices in the price index defining price stability is, by and large, considered to be the most radical proposal with regard to the importance of asset prices in the conduct of monetary policy.

According to Alchian and Klein's idea of stabilizing a cost-of-life index, changes in asset prices could reflect future inflation. The expenditure side of the consumer's life time budget constraint can be written as:

$$p_t c_t + \sum_{j=1}^{T} p_{t+j} c_{t+j}, \tag{5.102}$$

where p and c represent prices and consumption goods, respectively. Consumers allocate their wealth into current consumption and asset holdings ($p_A A_t$) in each time period. So the expenditure side of the budget constraint can be also formulated as:

$$p_t c_t + p_A A_t. \tag{5.103}$$

Subtracting the second equation from the first yields the link between asset prices and future prices:

$$p_A A_t + \sum_{j=1}^{T} p_{t+j} c_{t+j}. \tag{5.104}$$

If A_t and future consumption choices were known, then changes in p_A would reflect changing future prices. Shibuya (1992) exploits this link and further simplifies Alchian and Klein's theory for practical purposes.[74] He shows that their approach could define the economy's total price level as a weighted-sum of consumer and asset prices:

$$p_{total} = \alpha p_c + (1 - \alpha) p_A, \tag{5.105}$$

or, when expressed in inflation terms,

$$\pi_{total} = \alpha \pi_c + (1 - \alpha) \pi_A, \tag{5.106}$$

With $0 \leq \alpha \leq 1$. Here, α $(1 - \alpha)$ represents the weight of consumer goods (assets) in the total price index.

---

[73]See in this context also Pollak (1975). On the question about the information content of price indices see Carlson (1989).

[74]For Japan, see, for instance, Shibuya (1992) and Shiratsuka (1999).

A Simple Application of the Alchian and Klein Approach

Several analyses (Shiratsuka, 1999; Shibuya, 1992; Shiratsuka, 2001) have made attempts to calculate an intertemporal cost of life index in line with the work of Alchian and Klein (1973).[75] In what follows, a rather simple index shall be calculated based on the consumer price index and the stock market capitalisation (interpreted as a proxy for asset price developments in general) in the US and Japan.

Figure 5.43(a) shows measures of the US price level based on different weighting of the consumer price index versus the stock market index for the period 1973-Q2 to 2005-Q3. The higher the stock market weighting is, the higher is the rise in the measure of the economy's total price level. What is more, the higher (lower) the weighting for the stock market, the more volatile changes in the total index become (Fig. 5.42(b)). Similar results can be observed for Japan (Fig. 5.44(a) and (b)).

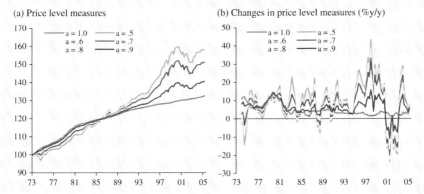

Fig. 5.43   Alternative measures of the price level in the US
Source: Bloomberg, Thomson Financial. – Period: 1973-Q2 to 2005-Q3. – In graph (**a**), the index series were set 100 in 1973-Q2 (shown as natural logarithms). – (**b**) The term $a(1-a)$ shows the weighting the consumer price index (stock market valuation) has in the total measure of the price level.

---

[75]For instance, Okina and Shiratsuka (2004) calculate an intertemporal cost of living index for Japan since the mid-1980s. In fact, they make use of dynamic equilibrium price index (DEPI) as proposed by Shibuya (1992). The DEPI rises sharply from 1986 to 1990 and then starts declining in 1991. During this period, although the GDP deflator remains relatively stable, inflation measured by the GDP deflator accelerates until 1991 and then remains subdued from 1992. The authors interpret the development of the DEPI as an understatement in conventional inflation measures regarding the inflationary pressure that occurred in the late 1980s and the deflationary pressure that has continued since the early 1990s (p. 11).

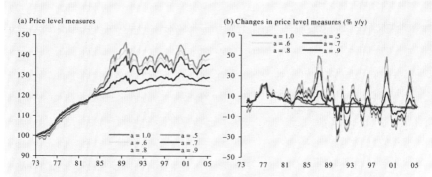

Fig. 5.44 Alternative measures of the price level in Japan
Source: Bloomberg, Thomson Financial. – Period: 1973-Q2 to 2005-Q2. – In graph (**a**), the index series were set 100 in 1973-Q2 (shown in natural logarithms). – (**b**) The term $a (1 - a)$ shows the weighting the consumer price index (stock market valuation) has in the total measure of the price level with $0 \leq \alpha \leq 1$.

Descriptive statistics the indices can be found in Table 5.8. From the point of view of a money holder, the total price level indices – as calculated above – suggest that in the period under review the *true* decline in the purchasing power of money has been considerably higher when compared to a consumer price index measure. In addition, the indices show that there were relatively long periods of time in which consumer and stock price indices did not move in tandem; consumer price changes seemed to *underestimate* changes in the loss of purchasing power of money.

Table 5.8 Descriptive statistics of total price level measures

	$\alpha = 0$	$\alpha = 1.0$	$\alpha = 0.5$	$\alpha = 0.6$	$\alpha = 0.7$	$\alpha = 0.8$	$\alpha = 0.9$
I. US							
Average	12.5	4.7	9.5	8.8	8.0	7.1	6.1
Maximum	61.6	14.6	43.2	38.7	33.0	25.7	15.8
Minimum	−42.5	1.0	−23.6	−22.1	−19.9	−16.6	−10.9
Standard deviation	18.8	3.2	11.4	10.0	8.4	6.6	4.5
II. Japan							
Average	10.3	3.7	7.4	6.8	6.1	5.3	4.5
Maximum	74.3	22.8	49.6	42.7	34.8	25.8	22.3
Minimum	−41.5	−1.6	−34.1	−31.3	−27.5	−22.1	−13.7
Standard deviation	23.5	4.8	16.4	14.5	12.2	9.7	6.7

Period: 1973-Q1 to 2005-Q3 for the US, 1973-Q2 to 2005-Q2 for Japan. – The term $a (1 - a)$ shows the weighting the consumer price index (stock market valuation) has in the total measure of the price level with $0 \leq \alpha \leq 1$. – The numbers are based on annual changes in the indices under review.

As noted earlier, Alchian and Klein assume that goods should be lumped into two categories: goods that are consumed today and goods that are consumed in the future. However, one may put forward a somewhat less sophisticated, but economically nevertheless viable, argument for seeing asset prices as an important component in the economy's total price level: namely that preserving the purchasing power of money would actually require that the economy's price level, including all kinds of goods and services bought and sold, remains unchanged over time. Viewed from this perspective, asset prices should be assigned the same role as consumer prices when it comes to stabilizing the economy's price level.

Goodhart (1995) took up on Alchian and Klein's recommendation and called upon monetary policy to give asset prices an explicit role in monetary policy. More recently, there has been an argument in favor of including housing prices, a particular type of asset price, in the index to be stabilized by monetary policy on account of their good forecasting properties for future consumer price inflation (Goodhart, 2001; Goodhart & Hofmann, 2000).[76]

5.6.2.5 Discussion

The point has been made that only a cost-of-life index would be unbiased in times of changing preferences between current and future consumption (Bryan, Cecchetti, & O'Sullivan, 2003). What is more, the mainstream economic viewpoint has identified *several additional conceptual problems* with regards to including asset prices in the objective function of monetary policy. Table 5.9 provides an overview of the major arguments against including asset price in the central bank's target inflation index and contrasts them with "non-mainstream" responses.

At this juncture it is fair to say that central banks consider asset price changes as *price changes sui generis*. Common wisdom is far from considering them in the same way as changes in consumer prices. This viewpoint is clearly expressed by US Fed Governor Donald L. Kohn (2006): "If we can identify bubbles quickly and accurately, are reasonably confident that tighter policy would materially check their expansion, and believe that severe market corrections have significant non-linear adverse effects on the economy, then extra action may well be merited. But if even one of these tough conditions is not met, then extra action would be more likely to lead to worse macroeconomic performance over time than that achievable with conventional policies that deal expeditiously with the effects of the unwinding of the bubbles when they occur. For my part, I am dubious that any central banker knows enough about the economy to overcome these hurdles. However, I would not want to rule out the possibility that in some circumstances, or perhaps at some point in the future when our understanding of asset markets and the economy has increased, such a course of action would be appropriate."

---

[76]See also Quan and Titman (1999) for an international analysis on the co-movement of estate and stock prices. Further on house price inflation see Breedon and Joyce (1992); also Capel and Houben (1998).

Table 5.9 Pros and cons including asset prices in the monetary policy objective

No.	Argument	Response
1.	Asset prices are likely to be a bad proxy for future goods prices and should therefore not be included in the index to be stabilized by monetary policy (ECB, 2005).	The rationale of including asset prices is to provide a *true picture of* the economy's total price level. For that reason, asset prices do not necessarily have to contain any indication properties as far as future consumer price inflation is concerned.
2.	The relevant asset price index should theoretically cover all assets, including human capital and the value of consumer durables (ECB, 2005).	Including all asset prices would indeed be highly desirable. Admittedly, at a technical level, the construction of a relevant (and timely) index might be problematic. However, technical arguments do not outweigh theoretical reasoning.
3.	Asset prices can move in directions unrelated to expectations about future inflation. In order to measure asset price inflation and react appropriately, the central bank would need to be able to determine the fundamental value of assets (Filardo, 2000; Diewert, 2002; Smets, 1997). Monetary policy cannot control the fundamental factors which affect asset prices in the long run, though. Attempts to steer asset prices on a mechanical basis could easily turn out to be futile.	The idea for including asset prices in a broadly defined price index shall allow the central bank to keep the economy's total price level stable over time. This is not to say that, with the relative price adjustment allowed to work, some prices (such as asset prices) could move up, while other prices could fall. From this view point, a central bank would not run into the *identification problem* of whether prices of specific items are appropriate from a fundamental point of view.
4.	Targeting asset prices by including them in a price index, and thus establishing a more or less mechanical policy response, creates *moral hazard problems* with regard to investor behavior towards risk. Risk taking would increase in anticipation of the asset price stabilizing attempts of monetary policy (Goodhart & Huang, 1999).	First, one could argue that the central bank should not respond to changes in the price level (the final objective of monetary policy) but to *forward-looking intermediate variables*, thereby preventing unwanted (future) movements in the price level. Second, as stated above, the central bank would not aim at stabilizing any asset prices in particular but the overall price level. Allowing the relative price adjustment to occur, the central bank might not run the risk of creating unwanted moral hazard which could artificially increase investor risk appetite.

Table 5.9 (continued)

No.	Argument	Response
5.	If the central bank is successful and credible in pursuing the objective of consumer price stability, this will also stabilize expectations of future inflation. It is then not clear what can be gained by explicitly targeting a (necessarily deficient) proxy for future consumer prices (Bernanke & Gertler, 2001; Cecchetti, Genberg, & Wadhwani, 2003). Indeed, this may be seen as a case whereby the central bank double-counts consumer price pressures in its information set.	This argument would be valid if consumer and asset price inflation were strongly moving in tandem (that is, statistically speaking, if they were cointegrated, even over short periods). However, this might not necessarily be the case. In fact, consumer and asset price inflation might decouple, potentially causing economic crisis when, later on, adjustment processes take place, leading to severe losses in output and employment.
6.	Inflation indeterminacy could arise as a result of circularity between asset price determination and a monetary policy stance with forward-looking behavior. If central banks conduct policy in response to asset price developments and asset prices themselves are at least partly the result of private agents' expectations of the future monetary policy stance, then – under certain conditions – inflation expectations can become self-fulfilling. Inflation will become *indeterminate* and could potentially be very volatile (Bernanke & Woodford, 1997).	As a rule, one may argue that a central bank should respond to information provided by *intermediate variables* (such as, for instance, money and credit expansion) rather than by actual deviations of the final policy objective from its target. That said, the inclusion of asset prices in the price index should not generate the problem outlined. In fact, under such a policy the purchasing power of money could be preserved – compared to a situation in which the money holder cannot be assured that asset and consumer prices exhibit a reliable and strong co-movement (in the long-run).
7.	The weight attached to current consumption goods prices and asset prices would have to be determined. Based on traditional expenditure shares, the weight of asset prices could easily exceed 90%, which would lead to an extremely volatile monetary policy. Other methods relate the shares to the forecasting ability of future consumption prices. Results for the weights differ substantially, depending on the method chosen (Bryan, Cecchetti, & O'Sullivan, 2003).	The finding that asset prices in the past did exhibit a much greater degree of volatility relative to consumer prices is, of course, a *regime dependent insight*. Stabilizing the economy's overall price level would presumably require all prices to become more flexible – to the upside as well as to the downside. This would presumably reduce the relative volatility of asset prices against consumer prices.

References

Akerlof, G. A., Dickens, W. T., & Perry, G. L. (1996). The macroeconomics of low inflation. *Brookings Papers on Economic Activity*, 1–59.

Albanesi, S., Chari, V. V., & Christiano, L. J. (2003). Expectation traps and monetary policy. *Review of Economic Studies*, *70*(4), 715–741.

Alchian, A. A., & Kessel, R. A. (1977/1959). Redistribution of wealth through inflation. Reprinted in Alchian, A. A., *Economic forces at work*. Indianapolis: Liberty Press.

Alchian, A., & Klein, B. (1973). On a correct measure of inflation. *Journal of Money, Credit and Banking*, *5*(1), 73–191.

Alesina, A. (1987). Macroeconomic policy in a two-party system as a repeated game. *Quarterly Journal of Economics*, *102*, 651–678.

Alesina, A. (1991). Evaluating rational partisan business cycle theory: A response. *Economics and Politics*, *3*, 63–72.

Alesina, A., & Rosenthal, H. (1989). Partisan cycles in congressional elections and the macro-economy. *American Political Science Review*, *83*, 373–398.

Alesina, A. & Rosenthal, H. (1995). Partisan Politics, Divided Government and the Economy, Cambridge University Press, Cambridge.

Alesina, A., & Roubini, N. (1992). Political cycles in OECD economies. *Review of Economic Studies*, *59*, 663–688.

Alogoskoufis, G. S., Lockwood, B., & Philippopoulos, A. (1992a). Wage inflation, electoral uncertainty and the exchange rate regime: Theory and UK evidence. *Economic Journal, 102*, 1370–1394.

Alogoskoufis, G. S., Lockwood, B., & Philippopoulos, A. (1992b). *Wage inflation, electoral uncertainty and the exchange rate regime: Theory and UK evidence* (CEPR Discussion Papers). London: Centre for Economic Policy Research, No. 657.

Amable, B., Henry, J., Lordon, F., & Topol, R. (1991). *Strong hysteresis: An application to foreign trade* (OFCE Working Paper/Document de travail 9103). Paris: Observatoire Français des Conjonctures Economiques.

Amable, B., Henry, J., Lordon, F., & Topol, R. (1994). Strong hysteresis versus zero-root dynamics. *Economic Letters*, *44*, 43–47.

Amable, B., Henry, J., Lordon, F., & Topol, R. (1995). Weak and strong hysteresis: An application to foreign trade. *Economic Notes*, *24*, 353–374.

Ammer, J., & Brunner, A. (1995, September). *When is monetary policy effective?* (Board of Governors of the Federal Reserve System International Finance Discussion Papers 520).

Angell, J. W. (1933). Money, prices and production: Some fundamental concepts. *Quarterly Journal of Economics*, *48*(1), 39–76.

Annett, A. M. (1993). Elections and macroeconomic outcomes in Ireland, 1948–91. *Economic and Social Review*, *25*, 21–47.

Arce, O. J. (2005). *The fiscal theory of the price level: A narrow theory for non-fiat money* (Documentos de Trabajo, 0501). Madrid: Banco d'España.

Baba, N., Nishioka, S., Oda, N., Shirakawa, M., Ueda, K., & Uga, H. (2005, November). *Japan's deflation, problems in the financial system and monetary policy* (BIS Working Papers, No. 188). Basle: Bank for International Settlements.

Bailey, M. J. (1956). The welfare cost of inflationary finance. *Journal of Political Economy*, *64*, 93–110.

Baldwin, R., & Krugman, P. (1989). Persistent trade effects of large exchange rate shocks. *Quarterly Journal of Economics*, *104*, 635–654.

Bank of England. Working Papers 141, London.

Barro, R. J. (1995). Inflation and economic growth. *Bank of England, Quarterly Bulletin*, *35*(2), 166–176.

Barro, R. J. (1997). *Macroeconomics* (5th ed.). Cambridge, MA: MIT Press.

Bassetto, M. (2002). A game-theoretic view of the fiscal theory of the price level. *Econometrica*, *70*, 2167–2195.

Belke, A. (1996). *Politische Konjunkturzyklen in Theorie und Empirie – Eine kritische Analyse der Zeitreihendynamik in Partisan-Ansätzen*. Tübingen: Mohr-Siebeck.

Belke, A. (2000). Political business cycles in the German labour market? Empirical tests in the light of the Lucas-Critique. *Public Choice, 104*, 225–283.

Belke, A. (2002). Towards a balanced policy mix under EMU: Co-ordination of macroeconomic policies and 'Economic Government'?, *Journal of Economic Integration, 17*, 21–53.

Belke, A. (2003). Hysteresis models and policy consulting. In B. Priddat & T. Theurl (Eds.). *Risiken der Politikberatung – Der Fall der Ökonomen* (pp. 209–221). Baden-Baden: Nomos.

Belke, A., & Goecke, M. (1999). A simple model of hysteresis in employment under exchange rate uncertainty. *Scottish Journal of Political Economy, 46*, 260–286.

Belke, A., & Goecke, M. (2001a). Exchange rate uncertainty and employment: An algorithm describing "play". *Applied Stochastic Models in Business and Industry, 17*(2), 181–204.

Belke, A., & Goecke, M. (2001b). Exchange rate uncertainty and 'play'-nonlinearity in aggregate employment. *International Advances in Economic Research, 7*, 38–50.

Belke, A., & Goecke, M. (2005). Real options effects on employment: Does exchange rate uncertainty matter for aggregation? *German Economic Review, 6*(2), 185–203.

Belke, A., & Goecke, M. (2008). European monetary policy in times of uncertainty. In A. Belke, S. Paul, & C. Schmidt (Eds.), *Fiskal- und Geldpolitik im Zeichen europäischer integration, RWI: Schriften*. Berlin: Duncker and Humblot.

Belke, A., & Gros, D. (2001). Evidence on the costs of intra-European exchange rate variability. *Open Economies Review, 12*, 231–264.

Belke, A., Koesters, W., Leschke, M., & Polleit, T. (2002, December). *International coordination of monetary policies – Challenges, concepts and consequences*. (ECB-Observer – Analyses of the monetary policy of the European System of Central Banks, No. 4). Frankfurt/Main.

Belke, A., & Patrafke, N. (2009). Does Government Ideology Matter in Monetary Policy & Public Economic Papers, 94, University of Duisburg-Essen.

Benhabib, J., Schmitt-Grohe, S., & Uribe, M. (2002). Avoiding liquidity traps. *Journal of Political Economy, 110*(3), 535–563.

Bentolila, S., & Bertola, G. (1990). Firing costs and labour demand: How bad is eurosclerosis? *Review of Economic Studies, 57*, 381–402.

Berger, H., & Woitek, U. (2001). The German political business cycle: Money demand rather than monetary policy. *European Journal of Political Economy, 17*(3), 609–631.

Berger, H., & Woitek, U. (1997). Searching for Political Business Cycles in Germany. *Public Choice, 91*(2), 179–197.

Bergin, P. R. (2000). Fiscal solvency and price level determination in a monetary union. *Journal of Monetary Economics, 45*, 37–53.

Bernanke, B. S. (1983, June). Nonmonetary effects of the financial crisis in propagation of the great depression. *American Economic Review, 73*(3), 257–276.

Bernanke, B. S. (1999). *Japanese monetary policy: A case of self-induced paralysis?* (Working Paper). Princeton, NJ: Princeton University.

Bernanke, B. S. (2006, February). *The benefits of price stability, remarks at the center for economic policy studies and on the occasion of the seventy-fifth anniversary of the Woodrow Wilson School of Public and International Affairs*. Princeton, NJ: Princeton University.

Bernanke, B. S., & Gertler, M. (1989, March). Agency costs, net worth, and business fluctuations. *American Economic Review, 79*(1), 14–31.

Bernanke, B. S., & Gertler, M. (2001). Should central banks respond to movements in asset prices? *American Economic Review, 91*, 253–257.

Bernanke, B. S., & Woodford, M. (1997). Inflation forecasts and monetary policy. *Journal of Money, Credit and Banking, 29*(4), 663–684.

Bewley, T. F. (1980). The optimum quantity of money. In J. H. Kareken & N. Wallace (Eds.), *Models of monetary economies* (pp. 169–210). Minneapolis, MN: Federal Reserve Bank of Minneapolis.

Bewley, T. F. (1983). A difficulty with the optimum quantity of money. *Econometrica, 51*, 1485–1504.

Blanchard, O. J., & Summers, L. H. (1986). *Hysteresis and the European unemployment problem, NBER Macroeconomics Annual* (Vol. 1, pp. 15–78). Cambridge, MA: MIT Press.

Blanchard, O. J., & Summers, L. H. (1988). Beyond the natural rate hypothesis. *American Economic Review, 78*(2), 182–187.

Blanchard, O. J., & Wolfers, J. (2000). The role of shocks and institutions in the rise of European unemployment: The aggregate evidence. *Economic Journal, 110*, C1–C33.

Blinder, A. S. (1982). The anatomy of double-digit inflation in the 1970s. In R. Hall (Ed.), *Inflation: Causes and effects* (pp. 261–282). Chicago: University of Chicago Press.

Blinder, A. S. (1997, May/June). Measuring short-run inflation for central bankers – Commentary. *Federal Reserve Bank of St. Louis, Review*, 157–160.

Blinder, A. S. (1999). *Monetary policy at the zero lower bound: Balancing the risks.* Presented at the Conference "Monetary Policy in a Low Inflation Environment," organized by the Federal Reserve Bank of Boston, October 18–20.

Bordo, M. D., & Filardo, A. (2004). *Deflation and monetary policy in a historical perspective: Remembering the past or being condemned to repeat it?* (NBER Working Paper No. 10833).

Bordo, M. D., Lane, J. L., & Redish, A. (2004, February). *Good versus bad deflation: Lessons from the gold standard era.* NBER Working Paper, 10329, National Bureau of Economic Research Cambridge, MA.

Braun, R. A. (1994). How large is the optimal inflation tax? *Journal of Monetary Economics, 34*, 201–214.

Breedon, F. J., & Joyce, M. A. (1992, May). House prices, arrears, and possessions. *Bank of England, Quarterly Bulletin*, 173–179.

Brokate, M., & Sprekels, J. (1996). Hysteresis and phase transitions. In J. E. Marsden, L. Sirovich, & F. John (Eds.), *Applied mathematical sciences* (Vol. 121). New York: Springer.

Bryan, M. F., & Cecchetti, S. G. (1993). *Measuring core inflation* (NBER Working Paper, No. 4303). National Bureau of Economic Research Cambridge, MA.

Bryan, M., & Cecchetti, S. G. (1994). Measuring Core Inflation, in: *Monetary Policy*, Greg Mankiw, N. G. (ed.), University of Chicago Press, Chicago, 195–215.

Bryan, M., Cecchetti, S., & O'Sullivan, R. (2003). A stochastic index of the cost of life. In W. Hunter, G. Kaufmann, & M. Pomerleano (Eds.), *Asset price bubbles*. Cambridge: MIT Press.

Bryan, M. F., Cecchetti, S. G., & Wiggins, R. L., II. (1997). *Efficient inflation estimation* (Working Paper 9707). Cleveland: Federal Reserve Bank of Cleveland.

Buiter, W. H. (1999). The fallacy of the fiscal theory of the price level NBER Working Paper, 7302, National Bureau of Economic Research Cambridge, MA. Buiter, W. (2002). The fiscal theory of the price level: A critique. *Economic Journal, 112*, 459–480.

Bullard, J. (1999, November/December). Testing long-run monetary neutrality propositions: Lessons from the recent research. *Federal Reserve Bank of St. Louis, 81*(6), 57–77.

Burda, M. (1988). Is there a capital shortage in Europe? *Weltwirtschaftliches Archiv – Review of World Economics, 124*, 38–57.

Caballero, R. J. (1991). On the sign of the investment–uncertainty relationship. *American Economic Review, 81*, 279–288.

Caballero, R. J., Engel, E. M. R. A., & Haltiwanger, J. (1997). Aggregate employment dynamics: Building from macro evidence. *American Economic Review, 87*, 115–137.

Cagan, P. C. (1956). The monetary dynamics of hyperinflation. In M. Friedman (Ed.), *Studies in the quantity theory of money*. Chicago: University of Chicago Press.

Capel, J., & Houben, A. (1998). Asset inflation in the Netherlands: Assessment, economic risks and monetary policy implications. In BIS, *The role of asset prices in the formulation of monetary policy*. Basle: Bank for International Settlements.

Caplin, A. S., & Spulber, D. (1987). Menu costs and the neutrality of money. *Quarterly Journal of Economics, 102*(4), 703–725.

Carlson, K. M. (1989, November/December). Do price indexes tell us about inflation? A review of the issues. *Federal Reserve Bank of St. Louis, Monthly Review*, 12–30.

Carlstrom, C. T., & Fuerst, T. S. (1999, December). The fiscal theory of the price level. *The Federal Reserve Bank of Cleveland*, Issue QI 22–32.

Carlstrom, C. T., & Fuerst, T. S. (2001). Monetary policy and self-fulfilling expectations: The danger of using forecasts. *Federal Reserve Bank of Cleveland, Economic Review*, *37*(1), 9–19.

Carlstrom, C. T., & Fuerst, T. S. (2002). Monetary policy rules and stability: Inflation targeting versus price-level targeting. *Federal Reserve Bank of Cleveland*, 15 February.

Castelnuovo, E., Nicoletti-Altimari, S., & Rodriguez-Palenzuela, D. (2003, November). Definition of price stability, range and point inflation targets: The anchoring of long-term inflation expectations. In O. Issing (Ed.), *Background studies for the ECB's evaluation of its monetary policy strategy* (pp. 43–90). Frankfurt, Main: European Central Bank Publisher.

Cecchetti, S. G. (1997, May/June). Measuring short-run inflation for central bankers. *Federal Reserve Bank of St. Louis, Review*, *79*(3), 143–155.

Cecchetti, S., Genberg, H., & Wadhwani, S. (2003). Asset prices in a flexible inflation targeting framework. In W. Hunter, G. Kaufmann, & M. Pomerleano (Eds.), *Asset price bubbles*. Cambridge: MIT Press.

Chadha, J. S., Haldane, A. G., & Janssen, N. G. J. (1998). Shoe-leather costs reconsidered. *The Economic Journal*, *108*, 363–382.

Chappell, H. W., & Keech, W. R. (1986). Party differences in macroeconomic policies and outcomes. *American Economic Review, Papers and Proceedings*, *76*, 71–74.

Chari, V. V., Christiano, L. J., & Kehoe, P. J. (1991). Optimal fiscal and monetary policy: Some recent results. *Journal of Money, Credit, and Banking*, *23*(3), 519–539.

Chari, V. V., & Kehoe, P. J. (2002). *Free riding problems in a monetary union, time consistency and free-riding in a monetary union* (NBER Working Paper, 9370). National Bureau of Economic Research Cambridge, MA.

Christiano, L. J., & Fitzgerald, T. J. (2000). Understanding the fiscal theory of the price level, economic review. *Federal Reserve Bank of Cleveland, Economic Review*, *36*(2), 2–38.

Christiano, L. J., & Gust, C. (1999). *The great inflation of the 1970s*, unpublished manuscript, Northwestern University and Board of Governors of the Federal Reserve System.

Christiano, L., Motto, R., & Rostagno, M. (2003). The great depression and the Friedman-Schwartz hypothesis. *Journal of Money, Credit and Banking*, *35*(6), 1119–1197.

Christiano, L., Motto, R., & Rostagno, M. (2004). *The great depression and the Friedman-Schwartz hypothesis*. (European Central Bank Working Paper 326). European Central Bank, Frankfurt/Main.

Clarida, R., Gali, J., & Gertler, M. (1999). The science of monetary policy: A new Keynesian perspective. *Journal of Economic Perspectives*, *37*(4), 1661–1707.

Clark, T. E. (2001). Comparing measures of core inflation. *Economic Review, Federal Reserve Bank of Kansas City, Q II*, 5–31.

Coase, R. H. (1937/1988). The nature of the firm. In R. H. Coase (Ed.), *The firm, the market, and the law* (pp. 33–55). Chicago-London: University of Chicago Press.

Cochrane, J. H. (1998a). A frictionless view of U.S. inflation. In B. S. Bernanke & J. Rotemberg (Eds.), *NBER Macroeconomics Annual* (pp. 323–384). Cambridge, Mass.: MIT Press.

Cochrane, J. H. (1998b, October). *Long-term debt and optimal policy in the fiscal theory of the price level* (NBER Working Paper, 6771). Cambridge, MA: National Bureau of Economic Research.

Cochrane, J. H. (2000, January). *Money as stock: Price level determination with no money demand* (NBER Working Paper 7498). Cambridge, MA: National Bureau of Economic Research.

Cochrane, J. (2003a). *Fiscal foundations of monetary regimes*. Mimeo, University of Chicago.

Cochrane, J. (2003b). *Money as stock*. University of Chicago Mimeo.

Côté, A. (1994). *Exchange rate volatility and trade – A survey, Bank of Canada* (Working Paper 94-5). Ottawa.

Cross, R. (1994). The macroeconomic consequences of discontinuous adjustment: Selective memory of non-dominated extrema. *Scottish Journal of Political Economy*, *41*, 212–221.

Cross, R. (Ed.) (1988, July 1986). *Unemployment, hysteresis, and the natural rate of unemployment*. Proceedings of a Conference held at the University of St. Andrews, Scotland, Blackwell Publishers.

Cushing, M. J. (1999). The indeterminacy of prices under interest rate pegging: The Non-Ricardian case. *Journal of Monetary Economics*, *44*, 131–148.

Cushman, D. (1985). Real exchange rate risk, expectations, and the level of direct investment. *Review of Economics and Statistics, 67*, 297–308.

Cuthbertson, K. (1996). *Quantitative financial economics: Stocks, bonds and foreign exchange.* New York: Wiley.

Cutler, J. (2001, March). *Core inflation in the UK, Bank of England* (Discussion Paper No. 3).

Daniel, B. C. (2003). *Fiscal policy, price surprises, and inflation.* New York: Mimeo, University at Albany (SUNY).

Daniel, B. C. (2004). *Monetary policy and inflation in a fiscal theory regime.* New York: Mimeo, University at Albany (SUNY).

Darby, J., Hughes Hallet, A., Ireland, J., & Piscitelli, L. (1998). *The impact of exchange rate uncertainty on the level of investment* (CEPR Discussion Paper 1896) London.

Davig, T., Leeper, E. M., & Chung, H. (2004). *Monetary and fiscal policy switching* (NBER Working Paper, 10362). Cambridge, MA: National Bureau of Economic Research.

de Grauwe, P., & Polan, M. (2005). Is inflation always and everywhere a monetary phenomenon? *Scandinavian Journal of Economics, 107*(2), 239–259.

de Grauwe, P., & Skudelny, F. (1997). *The impact of EMU on trade flows.* Katholieke Universiteit Leuven (Department of Economics Discussion Paper 133) Leuven.

De Long, J. B. (1995, December 19). *America's only peacetime inflation: The 1970s.* Cambridge, MA: National Bureau of Economic Research.

De Long, J. B. (1997). America's peacetime inflation: The 1970s. In C. Romer & D. H. Romer (Eds.), *Reducing inflation: Motivation and strategy* (pp. 247–276). Chicago: University of Chicago Press for NBER.

De Long, B. (1999). Should we fear deflation? *Brookings Papers on Economic Activity, 1999*(1), 225–252.

Detken, C., & Smets, F. (2004). *Asset price booms and monetary policy* (ECB Working Paper 364).

Deutsche Bundesbank (2000, April). Core inflation rates as a tool for price analysis. *Monthly Bulletin*, 45–58.

Dewald, W. G. (1998). Money still matters, review. *Federal Reserve Bank of St. Louis, 80*, 13–24.

Diewert, E. (2002). Harmonized indexes of consumer prices: Their conceptual foundations. *Swiss Journal of Economics and Statistics, 138*(4), 547–637.

Dittmar, R., Gavin, W. T., & Kydland, F. E. (1999, January/February). The inflation-output variability tradeoff and price-level targets. *Economic Review, Federal Reserve Bank of St. Louis, 81*(1), 23–32.

Dixit, A. (1989). Entry and exit decisions under uncertainty. *Journal of Political Economy, 97*, 620–638.

Dixit, A., & Pindyck, R. S. (1994). *Investment under uncertainty.* Princeton, NJ: Princeton Uninversity Press.

Dornbusch, R. (1987). *Open economy macroeconomics: New directions* (NBER Working Paper 2372).

Dowd, K. (1994). The costs of inflation and disinflation. *Cato Journal, 14*(2), 305–331.

Dowd, K. (1996). *Competition and finance: A new interpretation of financial and monetary economics.* London: Macmillan.

Drazen, A. (2000). The Political Business Cycle after 25 years, NBER Macro economics Annual 15, 75–117.

Dupor, B. (2000). Exchange rates and the fiscal theory of the price level. *Journal of Monetary Economics, 45*, 613–630.

Dwyer, G. P., & Hafner, R. W. (1998). Is Money Irrelevant?, in: Federal Reserve Bank of St. Louis Review, May/June, 3–17.

Dwyer, G. P., Jr., & Hafer, R. W. (1999). Are money growth and inflation still related? *Federal Reserve Bank of Atlanta, Economic Review, Second Quarter, 84*(2), 32–43.

Eichengreen, B., & Mitchener, K. (2003). *The great depression as a credit boom gone wrong* (BIS Working Paper, 137). Basle: Bank for International Settlements.

Emmons, W. R. (2000, November/December). The information content of treasury-index securities. *Federal Reserve Bank of St. Louis, 82*(4), 25–38.

Estrella, A., & Fuhrer, J. C. (2000). *Dynamic Inconsistencies: Counterfactual implications of a class of rational expectation models*, Working Paper, July.

European Central Bank. (2003). Workshop on asset prices and monetary policy (www.ecb.int/events/conferences/html/assetmp.en.html) Frankfurt/Main.

European Central Bank (2005, April). Asset price bubbles and monetary policy. *Monthly Bulletin*, 47–60.

Feldstein, M. (1997). The costs and benefits of going from low inflation to price stability. In C. Romer & D. H. Romer (Eds.), *Reducing inflation: Motivation and strategy, NBER Studies in Business Cycles* (Vol. 30). Chicago, IL: University of Chicago Press.

Feldstein, M. (1999). *The costs and benefits of price stability*. Chicago: University of Chicago Press.

Filardo, A. (2000). Monetary policy and asset prices. *Economic Review, Federal Reserve Bank of Kansas City*, third quarter, *85*(3).

Fischer, S., & Modigliani, F. (1975). Toward an understanding of the costs of inflation. *Carnegie-Rochester Conference Series on Public Policy*, *15*, 5–41.

Fisher, I. (1907). *The rate of interest*, New York: Macmillan.

Fisher, I. (1932). *Booms and depressions*. New York: Adelphi Company.

Fisher, I. (1933, October). The debt-deflation theory of great depressions, *Econometrica*, *1*(4), 337–357.

Fitzgerald, T. J. (1999, August 1). Money growth and inflation: How long is the long run? *Federal Reserve Bank of Cleveland*.

Formaini, R. L. (no date of release). Economic insight. *Federal Reserve Bank of Dallas*, *10*(1).

Frey, B. S., & Lau, L. J. (1968). Towards a mathematical model of government behavior. *Zeitschrift für Nationalökonomie*, *28*, 355–380.

Friedman, M. (1960). A Program for Monetary Stability, New York, Fordham, University Press.

Friedman, M. (1968a). The role of monetary policy. *American Economic Review*, *58*, 1–17 (Reprinted in Friedman, 1969).

Friedman, M. (1968b). Money: The quantity theory. *International Encyclopedia of the Social Sciences*, 432–437 (Reprinted in Friedman, 1969).

Friedman, M. (1969). *The optimum quantity of money and other essays*. London: Macmillan.

Friedman, M. (1994). *Money mischief, episodes in monetary history*. San Diego, New York, London: Hartcourt Brace & Company.

Friedman, M., & Schwartz, A. J. (1963). *A monetary history of the United States, 1867–1960*. Princeton, NJ: Princeton University Press.

Gaertner, M. (1994). Democracy, elections and macroeconomic policy: Two decades of progress. *Journal of Political Economy*, *10*, 85–100.

Gali, J., & Gertler, M. (1999, October). Inflation dynamics: A structural econometric analysis. *Journal of Monetary Economics*, *44*(2), 195–222.

Gavin, W. T., & Stockman, A. (1991). Why a rule for stable prices may dominate a rule for zero inflation. *Federal Reserve Bank of Cleveland, Economic Review*, *27*(1), 2–8.

Gertler, M. (1998). *Asset prices and monetary policy Four views*. Basle: Bank for International Settlements.

Gertler, M., & Bernanke, B. S. (1999, August 26–28). *Monetary policy and asset price volatility. New challenges for monetary policy, a Symposium* sponsored by the Federal Reserve Bank of Kansas City.

Goecke, M. (1994). Micro- and macro-hysteresis in foreign trade. *Aussenwirtschaft – Schweizerische Zeitschrift für internationale Wirtschaftsbeziehungen*, *49*, 555–578.

Goecke, M. (2002). Various concepts of hysteresis applied in economics. *Journal of Economic Surveys*, *16*(2), 167–188.

Goodfriend, M. (1991, Spring). Interest rate smoothing and the conduct of monetary policy. *Carnegie-Rochester Conference on Public Policy*, *34*, 7–30.

Goodhart, C. (1995). Price stability and financial fragility. In K. Sawamoto & Z. Nakajima (Eds.), *Financial stability in a changing environment*. New York: St. Martin's Press.

Goodhart, C. (2001). What weight should be given to asset prices in the measurement of inflation? *The Economic Journal, 111*, 335–356.

Goodhart, C., & Hofmann, B. (2000). Do asset prices help to predict consumer price inflation? *The Manchester School Supplement, 68*, 122–140.

Goodhart, C., & Huang, H. (1999). *A model of the lender of last resort* (IMF Working Paper, 99/39) Washington/DC.

Gordon, D. B., & Leeper, E. M. (2002). *The price level, the quantity theory of money, and the fiscal theory of the price level* (NBER Working Paper 9084). Cambridge, MA: National Bureau of Economic Research.

Grandmont, J., & Younes, Y. (1972). On the role of money and the existence of a monetary equilibrium. *Review of Economic Studies, 39*, 355–372.

Granger, C. W.J. (1969). Investigating causal relations by econometric and cross-sectional methods, in: *Econometrica*, 37, 424–438.

Greenspan, A. (1996, December). *The challenge of central banking in a democratic society.* Remarks at the annual dinner and Francis Boyer lecture of the American Enterprise Institute for Public Policy Research, Washington/DC.

Greenspan, A. (2001, October 11). "Transparency in Monetary Policy" Remarks by the Chairman at the Federal Reserve Bank of St. Louis, Economic Policy Conference.

Greenspan, A. (2004). Risk and uncertainty in monetary policy. *American Economic Review, Papers and Proceedings, 94*, 33–40.

Gros, D. (2007, October). *Bubbles in real estate? A longer-term comparative analysis of housing prices in Europe and the US* (CEPS Working Document No. 276). Brussels: Centre for European Policy Studies.

Guender, A. V. (2003). Optimal monetary policy under inflation targeting based on an instrument rule. *Economics Letters, 78*, 55–58.

Hahn, F. H. (1971). Equilibrium with transaction costs. *Econometrica, 39*(3), 417–439.

Hall, R. E. (1979). A theory of the natural unemployment rate and the duration of unemployment. *Journal of Monetary Economics, 5*, 153–170.

Hayek, A. F. v. (1960). *The constitution of liberty*. Chicago: The University of Chicago Press.

Hayek, A. F. v. (1976, October). *Denationalisation of money: An analysis of the theory and practice of concurrent currencies* (Hobart Paper Special 70). London: The Institute of Economic Affairs.

Hayek, F. A. (1945, September). The use of knowledge in society. *American Economic Review, XXXV*(4), 519–530.

Hayek, F. A. (1970, May 18). *Can we still avoid inflation?* Essay originally given as a lecture before the Trustees and guests of the Foundation for Economic Education at Tarrytown, New York.

Helbling, T., & Terrones, M. (2003, April). *When bubbles burst, world economic outlook*. (Chap. II).

Hess, G. D., & Morris, C. S. (1996). The long-run costs of moderate inflation. *Federal Reserve Bank of Kansas City Economic Review, 81*(2), 71–88.

Hetzel, R. L. (1998). Arthur burns and inflation. *Federal Reserve Bank of Richmond Economic Quarterly, 84*(1), 21–44.

Hibbs, D. (1977). Political Parties and Macroeconomic Policy. American Political Science Review, 71, 1467–1487.

Hibbs, D. A. (1991). *The partisan model of macroeconomic cycles: More theory and evidence for the United States* (Trade Union Institute for Economic Research Working Paper, 95, Stockholm, later appeared) in: *Economics and Politics, 6*, 1–23.

Hibbs, D. A. (1992). Partisan theory after fifteen years. *European Journal of Political Economy, 8*, 361–373.

Hogan, S., Johnson, M., & Lafleche, T. (2001, January). Evaluating Measures of Core inflation, in: Bank of Canada Review, Summer, 19–29.

Horwitz, S. (2003). The costs of inflation revisited. *The Review of Austrian Economics, 16*(1), 77–95.

International Monetary Fund (1999, October). *Safeguarding macroeconomic stability at low infla-tion*. World Economic Outlook Washington/DC.

International Monetary Fund (2003, April). *Deflation: Determinants, risk, and pol-icy options – Findings of an interdepartmental task force,* Washington/DC http://www.lavoce.info/news/images/deflation_imf_report18mag2003.pdf

Issing, O. (1999). Hayek – currency competition and European monetary union, Annual Hayek memorial lecture, hosted by the Institute of Economic Affairs in London on 27 May.

Jeanne, O. (1997, June 15–17). *Real and nominal rigidities over the cycle*. Paper presented at the International Seminar on Macroeconomics (NBER inc. EEA). Switzerland: Gerzensee.

Jenkins, P., & Longworth, D. (2002, Summer). Monetary policy and uncertainty. *Bank of Canada Review*, Ottawa 3–10.

Judd, K. (1989). *Optimal taxation in dynamic, stochastic economies: Theory and evidence*. Cali-fornia: Stanford University, Hoover Institution.

Kalecki, M. (1944). Professor Pigou on "The classical stationary state" – A comment. *The Eco-nomic Journal, 54*(213), 131–132.

Kerr, W., & King, R. G. (1996, Spring). Limits on interest rate rules in the IS model. *Federal Reserve Bank of Richmond Economic Quarterly, 82*, 47–76.

Keynes, J. M. (1936). *The general theory of employment, interest and money*. Cambridge: MacMil-lan, Cambridge University Press.

Kindleberger, C. (1996). *Manias, panics and crashes: A history of financial crises* (3rd ed.). New York: John Wiley & Sons, Inc.

King, M. (2002, March 13). Lecture at the First Economic Policy Forum held at the Banque de France, Paris.

King, R. G., & Watson, M. W. (1997, Summer). Testing long-run neutrality. *Federal Reserve Bank of Richmond: Economic Quarterly, 83*(3), 69–101.

Kiyotaki, N., & Moore, J. (1997). Credit cycles. *Journal of Political Economy, 105*(2), 211–248.

Kocherlakota, N. R., & Phelan, C. (1999). Explaining the fiscal theory of the price level. *Federal Reserve Bank of Minneapolis: Quarterly Review, 23*(4), 14–23.

Kohn, D. L. (2006, March 16). Monetary policy and asset prices, Speech given at "Monetary Policy: A Journey from Theory to Practice," European Central Bank Colloquium held in honor of Otmar Issing, Frankfurt, Germany.

Krasnosel'skii, M. A., & Pokrovskii, A. V. (1989). *Systems with hysteresis*. Berlin: Springer.

Krugman, P. (1989). *Exchange rate instability*. Cambridge, MA: MIT Press.

Krugman, P. (1998). *It's Baaack! Japan's slump and the return of the liquidity trap. Brookings Papers on Economic Activity*, 237–487.

Kydland, F. E., & Prescott, E. C. (1977, June). Rules rather than discretion: The inconsistency of optimal plans. *Journal of Political Economy, 85*(3), 473–491.

Laidler, D. (2007). *Financial stability, monetarism and the Wicksell connection* (Working Papers, 20073). University of Western Ontario: RBC Financial Group Economic Policy Research Insti-tute.

Lansing, K. J. (2000, July 7). Exploring the causes of the great inflation. *Federal Reserve Bank of San Francisco, 2000-21.*

Lansing, K. J. (2002, July 1). *Learning about a shift in trend output: Implications for monetary policy and inflation*. Unpublished paper, Federal Reserve Bank of San Francisco.

Lau, L. J., & Frey, B. S. (1971). Ideology, public approval and government behavior. *Public Choice, 10*, 21–40.

Layard, R., Nickell, S. J., & Jackman, R. (1991). *Unemployment, macroeconomic performance and the labor market*. Oxford: Oxford University Press.

Lee, J. K., & Wellington, D. C. (1984). Angell and the stable money rule. *Journal of Political Economy, 92*(5), 972–978.

Leeper, E. M. (1991). Equilibria under 'Active' and 'Passive' monetary and fiscal policies. *Journal of Monetary Economics, 27*(1), 129–147.

Lindbeck, A., & Snower, D. (1988). Cooperation, harassment and involuntary unemployment: An insider-outsider approach, *American Economic Review, 78*(1), 167–188.

Loyo, E. (1999). *Tight money paradox on the loose: A fiscalist hyperinflation*. Cambridge, MA: Harvard University, Kennedy School of Government.

Lucas, R. E., Jr. (1972). Econometric testing of the natural rate hypothesis. In O. Eckstein (Ed.), *Econometrics of price determination* (pp. 50–59). Board of Governors of the Federal Reserve System Washington/DC.

Lucas, R. E., Jr. (1973). Some international evidence on output-inflation tradeoffs. *American Economic Review*, *63*(3), 326–334.

Lucas, R. E. Jr. (1976). Econometric policy evaluation: A critique, in Brunner, K. Meltzer, A. H. (eds.), The Phillips curve and labour markets, Amsterdam, North Holland, 19–46.

Lucas, R. E., Jr. (1980). Two illustrations of the quantity theory of money. *American Economic Review*, *70*(5), 1005–1014.

Lucas, R. E., Jr. (1986, October). Adaptive behavior and economic theory. *Journal of Business*, *59*(4), 401–426.

Lucas, R. E., Jr. (1987). *Models of business cycles*, Oxford, Basil Blackwell.

Lucas, R. E., Jr. (1994). *On the welfare cost of inflation* (CEPR Working Paper No. 394). London: Center for Economic Policy Research.

Lucas, R. E., Jr. (1996, August). Nobel lecture: Monetary neutrality. *Journal of Political Economy*, *104*(4), 661–682.

Lutz, F. A., & Mints, L. W. (Eds.) (1951). *Readings in monetary theory*. New York: The Blakiston Company.

Marimón, R. (2001). The fiscal theory of money as an unorthodox financial theory of the firm. In A. Leijonhufvud (Ed.), *Monetary theory as a basis for monetary policy*. New York: Palgrave.

Mayer, T. (1999). *Monetary policy and the great inflation in the United States: The federal reserve and the failure of macroeconomic policy, 1965–79*. Cheltenham: Edward Elgar.

Mayergoyz, I. D. (1986). Mathematical models of hysteresis. *IEEE Transactions on Magnetics*, *22*, 603–608.

McCallum, B. T. (1998, March). *Indeterminacy, bubbles, and the fiscal theory of price level determination* (NBER Working Paper, 6456). Cambridge, MA: National Bureau of Economic Research.

McCallum, B. T. (1999a). *Theoretical analysis regarding a zero lower bound on nominal interest rates* (Working paper). Pittsburgh, PA: Carnegie Mellon University.

McCallum, B. T. (1999b). *Theoretical issues pertaining to monetary unions* (NBER Working Paper 7393). Cambridge, MA: National Bureau of Economic Research.

McCallum, B. T. (2001, July/August). Monetary policy analysis in models without money. *Federal Reserve Bank of St. Louis: Review*, *83*(4), 145–160.

McCallum, B. T., & Goodfriend, M. (1987). Demand for money: Theoretical analysis. *The New Palgrave Dictionary of Economics*, Newman, P., Milgate, M., Eatwell, J. (eds.), London, Mcmillan, 775–781.

McCallum, B. T., & Nelson, E. (1999, August). An optimizing IS-LM specification for monetary policy and business cycle analysis. *Journal of Money, Credit, and Banking*, *31*, 296–316.

McCandless, G. T., & Weber, W. E. (1995, Summer). Some monetary facts. *Federal Reserve Bank of Minneapolis: Quarterly Review*, *25*(4), 2–11.

Meltzer, A. H. (1976, November). Monetary and other explanations of the start of the great depression. *Journal of Monetary Economics*, *4*, 455–471.

Meltzer, A. H. (1999a). Commentary: How should monetary policy be conducted in an era of price stability? *New challenges for monetary policy*. Symposium organized by the Federal Reserve Bank of Kansas City.

Meltzer, A. H. (1999b). Commentary: What more can the Bank of Japan do? *Monetary and Economic Studies*, *17*(3), 189–191. Institute for Monetary and Economic Studies, Bank of Japan.

Meltzer, A. H. (1999c). *A policy for Japanese recovery* (Working Paper). Pittsburgh, PA: Carnegie Mellon University Mimeo.

Meltzer, A. H. (1999d, March). *The transmission process*. Presented at the Deutsche Bundesbank Conference on "The Monetary Transmission Process: Recent developments and lessons for Europe."

Minsky, H. (1963, 1977, 1978). Can 'it' happen again? chapter 1, The financial instability hypothesis, chapter 3, and The financial instability hypothesis: A restatement, chapter 5. In Minsky, H. (1982). *Can it happen again?* Essays on Instability and Finance. Armonk, New York: M. E. Sharpe, Inc.

Minsky, H. P. (1982). Can "it" happen again? Essays on Instability and Finance, Armonk, NY, M. E. Sharpe.

Minsky, H. (1992). *The financial instability hypothesis* (Working Paper 74). The Jerome Levy Economics Institute of Bard College.

Mishkin, F. S. (2007, October 20). *Headline versus core inflation in the conduct of monetary policy*. Speech given at the "Business cycles, International Transmission and Macroeconomic Policies" Conference. Montreal, Canada: HEC Montreal.

Mori, N., Shiratsuka, S., & Taguchi, H. (2000, May). *Policy responses to the post-bubble adjustments in Japan: A tentative review*. Bank of Japan, Institute for Monetary and Economic Studies Discussion Paper Tokyo.

Motely, B. (1997, April 18). Should monetary policy focus on "core" inflation? *Economic Letter*, Federal Reserve Bank of San Francisco.

Mulligan, C. B., & Sala-i-Martin, X. (1997). *The optimum quantity of money: Theory and evidence* (NBER Working Paper No. 5954). Cambridge, MA: National Bureau of Economic Research.

Mundschenk, S., & von Hagen, J. (2002). The political economy of policy coordination in Europe. *Swedish Review of Economic Policy, 8*, 11–41.

Muth, J. F. (1961). Rational expectations and the theory of price movements. *Econometrica, 29*, 315–335.

Neumann, M. J. M. (2003, March 03). *The European Central Bank's first pillar reassessed* (Working Paper). IIW Bonn University Bonn.

Neumann, M. J. M., & Greiber, C. (2004). *Inflation and core money growth in the euro area* (Deutsche Bundesbank Discussion Paper, No. 36) Frankfurt/Main.

Niepelt, D. (2004). The fiscal myth of the price level. *Quarterly Journal of Economics, 119*, 277–300.

Nordhaus, W. D. (1975). The political business cycle. *Review of Economic Studies, 42*, 169–190.

Obstfeld, M., & Rogoff, K. S. (1999). *Foundations of international macroeconomics*. Cambridge, MA: MIT Press.

Okina, K. (1999). Monetary policy under zero inflation – A response to criticism and questions regarding monetary policy. *Monetary and Economic Studies, 17*(3), 157–182. Institute for Monetary and Economic Studies, Bank of Japan Tokyo.

Okina, K., Shirakawa, M, & Shiratsuka, S. (2001). The asset price bubble and monetary policy: Experience of Japan's economy in the late 1980s and its lessons. *Monetary and Economic Studies, 19*(S-1), 395–450. Institute for Monetary and Economic Studies, Bank of Japan.

Okina, K., & Shiratsuka, S. (2004, September). *Asset price fluctuations, structural adjustments, and sustained economic growth: Lessons from Japan's experience since the late 1980s* (IMES Discussion Paper Series). Bank of Japan Tokyo.

Orphanides, A. (1999). *The quest for prosperity without inflation*. Unpublished manuscript, Federal Reserve Board, Division of Monetary Affairs, Washington/DC.

Orphanides, A., & Wieland, V. (1998, June). *Price stability and monetary policy effectiveness when nominal rates are bound to zero*. Board of Governors of the Federal Reserve System Finance and Economics Discussion Paper Series no. 98/35, Washington/DC.

Orphanides, A., & Williams, J. C. (2003, January 23–25). *Imperfect knowledge, inflation expectations and monetary policy*. Paper prepared for the NBER conference on Inflation Targeting, Mimeo.

Pakko, M. R. (1998). Shoe-leather costs of inflation and policy credibility. *Federal Reserve Bank of St. Louis Review, 80*(6), 37–50.

Parkin, M. (1993). Inflation in North America. In K. Shigehara (Ed.), *Price stabilization in the 1990s* (pp. 47–83). London: Macmillan.

Parsley, D. C., & Wei, S.-J. (1993). Insignificant and inconsequential hysteresis: the case of U.S. bilateral trade. *Review of Economics and Statistics, 75,* 606–613.

Patinkin, D. (1948). Price flexibility and full employment. *American Economic Review, 38,* 543–564 (Revised and reprinted as chap. 13 in Lutz and Mints (1951)).

Patinkin, D. (1971). Inside money, monopoly bank profits, and the real balance effect: Comment. *Journal of Money, Banking and Credit, 3*(2), 271–275.

Perron, P. (1989). The great crash, the oil price shock and the unit root hypothesis. *Econometrica, 57,* 1361–1401.

Pesaran, M. H., & Pesaran, B. (1997). *Working with Microfit 4.0 – Interactive econometric analysis.* Oxford: Oxford University Press.

Phelps, E. S. (1967). Phillips curves, expectations of inflation and optimal unemployment over time. *Economica, 34,* 254–281.

Phelps, E. S. (1968, August). Money-wage dynamics and labor market equilibrium. *Journal of Political Economy, 76*(4, Pt. 2), 678–711.

Phelps, E. S. (1973). Inflation in the theory of public finance. *Scandinavian Journal of Economics, 75,* 67–82.

Phelps, E. S. (1999). Behind the structural boom: The role of assets valuations. *American Economic Review, 89,* 63–68.

Phelps, E. S. (1972). *Inflation policy and unemployment theory. The cost-benefit approach to monetary planning.* London: Macmillan.

Phillips, A. W. (1958). The Relation between unemployment and the rate of change of money wage rates in the United Kingdom, 1861–1957, in: Economica, 25, 2, 283–99.

Pigou, A. C. (1941). *Employment and equilibrium.* London: Macmillan.

Pigou, A. C. (1943). The classical stationary state. *The Economic Journal, 53*(212), 343–351.

Pigou, A. C. (1947). *Economic progress in a stable environment.* Economica, *14*(55), 180–188.

Pill, H., & Rautanen, T. (2006, May 5). *Monetary analysis – The ECB experience.* Paper presented at the 8th "The ECB and Its Watchers Conference, session ECB watch – Review of the ECB's strategy and alternative approaches," Frankfurt, Main.

Pindyck, R. S. (1988). Irreversible investment, capacity choice and uncertainty. *American Economic Review, 78,* 969–985.

Pindyck, R. S. (1991). Irreversibility, uncertainty, and investment. *Journal of Economic Literature, 29,* 1110–1148.

Piscitelli, L., Cross, R., Grinfeld, M., & Lambda, H. (2000). A test for strong hysteresis. *Computational Economics, 15,* 59–78.

Pollak, R. A. (1975, Winter). The intertemporal cost-of-living index. *Annals of Economic and Social Measurement, 4*(1), 179–195.

Posen, A. S. (1998). *Restoring Japan's economic growth.* Washington, DC: Institute for International Economics.

Quan, D. C., & Titman, S. (1999, Summer). Do real estate prices and stock prices move together? *An Investment Analysis, Real Estate Economics, 27,* 183–207.

Roger, S. (1998). *Core inflation: Concepts, uses and measurement* (Reserve Bank of New Zealand Discussion Paper Series G, 8).

Rolnick, A. J., & Weber, W. E. (1995). *Inflation, money, and output under alternative monetary standards* (Federal Reserve Bank of Minneapolis Research Department, Staff Report 175).

Rolnick, A. J., & Weber, W. E. (1997). Money, inflation, and output under fiat and commodity standards. *Journal of Political Economy, 105*(6), 1308–1321.

Rose, C. (2000). The I-r hump: Irreversible investment under uncertainty. *Oxford Economic Papers, 52,* 626–636.

Sack, B. (2000, September). Deriving inflation expectations from nominal and inflation-indexed treasury yields. *Journal of Fixed Income, 10*(2), 1–12.

Sadeh, T. (2006). Adjusting to EMU. *European Union Politics, 7*(3), 347–372.

Saint-Paul, G. (1996). *Dual labor markets: A macroeconomic perspective*. Cambridge, MA: MIT Press.

Saint-Paul, G. (1996a). Exploring the political economy of labour market institutions. *Economic Policy, 23*, 265–315.

Samuelson, P. A., & Solow, R. M. (1960). Analytical aspects of anti-inflation policy. *American Economic Review, 50*(2), 177–194.

Sargent, T. J., & Wallace, N. (1981). Some unpleasant monetarist arithmetic. *Federal Reserve Bank of Minneapolis: Quarterly Review, 5*(3), 1–17.

Sargent, T. J. (1986). The ends of four big inflations. In *Rational expectations and inflation* (pp. 40–109). New York: Harper and Row.

Sargent, T. J. (1986). *Rational expectations and inflation*. New York: Harper and Row.

Sargent, T. J. (1987). *Macroeconomic theory* (2d ed.). Boston: Academic Press.

Sargent, T. J. (1999). *The conquest of American inflation*. Princeton, NJ: Princeton University Press.

Scitovsky, T. (1941). A note on welfare propositions in economics. *Review of Economic Studies, 9*, 77–88.

Sheffrin, S. M. (1989a). Evaluating rational partisan cycle theory. *Economics and Politics, 1*, 239–259.

Sheffrin, S. M. (1989b). *The making of economic policy: History, theory, politics*. Cambridge, Mass.: Oxford University Press.

Shibuya, H. (1992). Dynamic equilibrium price index: Asset price and inflation, monetary and economic studies. Institute for Monetary and Economic Studies. *Bank of Japan, 10*(1), 95–109.

Shiller, R. J. (2000). *Irrational exuberance*. Princeton, NJ: Princeton University Press.

Shiratsuka, S. (1999). Asset price fluctuation and price indices. *Monetary and Economic Studies, 17*(3), 103–128. Institute for Monetary and Economic Studies, Bank of Japan.

Shiratsuka, S. (2001). Asset prices, financial stability and monetary policy: Based on Japan's experience of the asset price bubble. In *Marrying the macro- and microprudential dimensions of financial stability* (BIS Papers, No. 1, pp. 261–284). Basle: Bank for International Settlements.

Sims, C. A. (1994). A simple model for the study of the determination of the price level and the interaction of monetary and fiscal policy. *Economic Theory, 4*(3), 381–399.

Sims, C. A. (1999). *Domestic currency denominated government debt as equity in the primary surplus*. Mimeo, Princeton University.

Sims, C. A. (2001). *Fiscal consequences for Mexico of adopting the dollar* (pp. 597–625). Proceedings, Federal Reserve Bank of Cleveland.

Smets, F. (1997). *Financial asset prices and monetary policy: Theory and evidence* (CEPR Discussion Paper, 1751).

Svensson, L. E. O. (1997a, August). *Price level targeting vs. inflation targeting: A free lunch?* Institute for International Economic Studies, Stockholm University Stockholm.

Svensson, L. E. O. (1997b, March). Optimal inflation targets, 'conservative' Central Banks, and linear inflation contracts. *American Economic Review, 87*, 98–114.

Svensson, L. E. O. (1999). How should monetary policy be conducted in an era of price stability? In *New challenges for monetary policy*. Symposium organized by the Federal Reserve Bank of Kansas City.

Svensson, L. E. O. (2002). Monetary policy and real stabilization. *Rethinking Stabilization Policy, Federal Reserve Bank of Kansas City*, Symposium, *29*(31), 261–312.

Taylor, J. B. (1993). Discretion versus policy rules in practice, Carnegie-Rochester Conference Series on Public Policy, 39, 195–214.

Taylor, J. B. (1999). The robustness and inefficiency of monetary policy rules as guidelines for interest rate setting by the European Central Bank. *Journal of Monetary Economics, 43*, 655–679.

Tobin, J. (1975). Keynesian models of recession and depression. *American Economic Review, 65*(2), 195–202.

Tullock, G. (1980/1967). The welfare costs of tariffs, monopolies, and theft. Reprinted in J. Buchanan, R. Tollison, & G. Tullock (Eds.), *Toward a theory of the rent-seeking society*, College Station, TX: Texas A & M University Press.

Ueda, K. (1999, October 18–20). *Japan's experience with zero interest rates*. Paper Presented at the conference Monetary Policy in a Low Inflation Environment, organized by the Federal Reserve Bank of Boston.

Ueda, K. (2000). Causes of Japan's banking problems in the 1990s. In T. Hoshi & H. Patrick (Eds.), *Crisis and change in the Japanese financial system*. Boston, MA: Kluwer Academic Publishers.

van Garderen, K. J., Lee, K., & Pesaran, M. H. (1997). *Cross-sectional aggregation of non-linear models* (DAE Working Paper 9803). Cambridge: University of Cambridge – Department of Applied Economics.

Vaubel, R. (1997). The bureaucratic and partisan behavior of independent central banks: German and international evidence. *European Journal of Political Economy, 13*, 201–224.

von Haberler, G. (1937). *Prosperity and depression – A theoretical analysis of cyclical movements*. Cambridge, MA: Harvard University Press.

von Hagen, J., & Hofmann, B. (2003). *Monetary policy in orientation in times of low inflation*. Paper presented at the conference on Monetary Policy Under Low Inflation, Federal Reserve Bank of Cleveland, 21–22 November 2003, forthcoming in the Conference Proceedings.

von Mises, L. (1966/1996). *Human action* (4th ed.). San Francisco: Fox & Wilkes.

von Peter, G. (2004). *Asset prices and banking distress: A macroeconomic approach*. (BIS Working Paper 167). Basle: Bank for International Settlements.

von Peter, G. (2005, April). *Debt-deflation: Concepts and a stylised model* (BIS Working Papers, No. 176). Basle: Bank for International Settlements.

Warburton, C. (1952). How much variation in the quantity of money is needed? *Southern Economic Journal, 18*(4), 495–509.

Weber, A. (1994). *Testing long-run neutrality: Empirical evidence for G7 countries with special emphasis on Germany* (pp. 67–117). Carnegie-Rochester Conference Series on Public Policy.

Wheelock, D. C. (1992). Monetary policy in the great depression: What the Fed did, and why. *Federal Reserve Bank of St. Louis, 74*(1), 3–28.

White, W. R. (2006, April). *Is price stability enough?* (BIS Working Paper No. 205). Basle: Bank for International Settlements, http://www.bis.org/publ/work205.pdf

Wicksell, K. (1898/1965). *Geldzins und Güterpreise* [Interest and Prices]. New York: Augustus M. Kelley. (Original edition 1898)

Woodford, M. (1994). Monetary policy and price level determinacy in a cash-in-advance economy. *Economic Theory, 4*(3), 345–380.

Woodford, M. (1995). Price level determinacy without control of a monetary aggregate. *Carnegie–Rochester Conference Series on Public Policy, 43*(3), 1–46.

Woodford, M. (1996, July). *Control of the public debt: A requirement for price stability?* (NBER Working Paper No. 5684). Cambridge, MA: National Bureau of Economic Research.

Woodford, M. (1998a, June 18–19). *Public debt and the price level*. Paper presented at the conference on Government Debt Structure and Monetary Conditions, Bank of England, available at http://www.princeton.edu/~woodford/BOE.pdf

Woodford, M. (1998b). Comment on Cochrane. In B. S. Bernanke & J. Rotemberg (Eds.), *NBER macroeconomics annual* (pp. 390–418). Cambridge, Mass.: MIT Press.

Woodford, M. (1998c). Doing without money: Controlling inflation in a post-monetary world. *Review of Economic Dynamics, 1*(1), 173–219.

Woodford, M. (2003). *Interest and Prices*. Foundations of a theory of Monetary Policy, Princeton University Press, Princeton.

Woodford, M. (1999). Optimal monetary policy inertia. *Manchester School, 67*(Suppl.), 1–35.

Woodford, M. (2001). Fiscal requirements for price stability. *Journal of Money, Credit, and Banking, 33*, 669–728.

Wynne, M. A. (1999, June). *Core inflation: A review of some conceptual issues* (ECB Working Paper, 5). Frankfurt, Main/Dallas: European Central Bank/Federal Reserve Bank of Dallas Research Department Working Paper 99-03.

Chapter 6
Theory of Monetary Policy

Semper aliquid haeret.
       – Francis Bacon to adapt Plutarch

6.1 Uncertainty in Monetary Policy Making

Central banks, which are committed to the primary objective of price stability, should be interested in counteracting medium- to long-term inflation risks at an early stage. This is because the central banks' changes in money supply affect real variables and prices by *time lags*. As a result, monetary policy must be implemented in a forward-looking manner. To make things worse, there is considerable uncertainty surrounding the exact impact of monetary policy instrument variables on the target variable. And there is uncertainty surrounding the state of the economy when the decision is being made (Issing, 2002; Deutsche Bundesbank, 2004).

On the Importance of *Time-Lags* for Monetary Policy

Assumptions about *time lags* between events guide our causal judgments. Suppose, for example, you are suffering from a cold, and you take a new medicine that promises relief. How long are you going to wait until you take more of this drug, because you think the first dose did not help? You will probably base our decision on assumptions about the *expected delay* between taking the drug (cause) and experiencing relief (effect). Assume you believe the delay is 30 min. If 45 min have passed by without yielding any effect, you will probably conclude that the drug was not effective – and perhaps decide to take more of the drug. However, if we assume that it will take more than 45 min then we may continue to wait before taking any further action.

That said, the same fact may lead to very different causal judgments and actions. And getting the timing wrong between *cause* (taking the drug) and *effect* (experiencing relief) might, in the example above, potentially lead to

A. Belke, T. Polleit, *Monetary Economics in Globalised Financial Markets*,
DOI 10.1007/978-3-540-71003-5_6, © Springer-Verlag Berlin Heidelberg 2009

(health) damage. Needless to say how important it is for central banks to know about the existence and workings of the time lags of monetary policy: that is the time a monetary impulse requires to affect real output and prices.

According to Milton Friedman (1961), changes in the stock of money affect nominal magnitudes with variable, and uncertain, *time lags* (Fig. 6.1). It will take time for the policy makers in the central bank to actually recognize that monetary policy action is required for preventing, say, inflation to unaccept-able highs. This is the *recognition lag*. Then, it will take time for the decision makers to actually make a decision about what needs to be done (*decision lag*), to be followed by the *administrative lag*, which represents the time span required for putting in place monetary policy measures. After a monetary pol-icy action has been taken (such as, for instance, an interest rate hike), it takes time for the banking sector – typically the counterpart for monetary policy – to adjust the terms of credit supplied to private agents (*intermediate lag*). Finally, it will take time – perhaps a great deal of time – for market agents to translate changes in the money supply into changes in nominal magnitudes (*outside lag*).

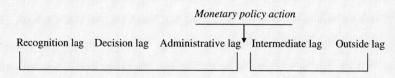

Fig. 6.1 Time lags in monetary policy

The debate about time lags has therefore very important implications for the institutional design of monetary policy. For instance, uncertainty about the time lags in monetary policy made Friedman a supporter of a *pre-announced fixed money supply growth rule*, preventing monetary policy from the possi-bility of taking ad hoc actions. Of course, Friedman was aware of the fact that such a strict monetary arrangement might not be best for every situation. However, he considered such a *rule based policy* as a *protection* against the costs from a *bad timing* (and the *misuse*) of monetary policy; weighing the pros and cons, Friedman came to favor a rule based policy over a *policy of discretion*.

While the academic profession has made tremendous progress in analysing risk in well-defined stochastic economies, the "Knightian uncertainty" that confronts monetary policy and sometimes markets is of an altogether different dimension. It was US economist Frank Knight (1885–1972) who, in his book *Risk, Uncertainty and Profit*, built his analysis on the distinction between risk and uncertainty (Knight,

1921, p. 205):[1] "Uncertainty must be taken in a sense radically distinct from the familiar notion of Risk, from which it has never been properly separated. (...) It will appear that a *measurable* uncertainty, or "risk" proper (...) is so far different from an *unmeasurable* one that it is not in effect an uncertainty at all."

Knight speaks of no less than the failure of the concept of probability calculus. In his seminal work "General Theory of Employment, Interest and Money", John Maynard Keynes (1883–1946) takes a very similar stance (Keynes, 1936, p. 161): "[Most of our decisions] to do something positive (...) can only be taken as a result of animal spirit (...) and not as the outcome of a weighted average of quantitative benefits multiplied by quantitative probabilities." In fact, Knight argues that the difficulty of the forecasting process extends far beyond the impossibility of applying mathematical propositions to forecasting the future. *A priori* reasoning, Knight insisted, cannot eliminate indeterminateness from the future. In the end, he considered reliance on the frequency of past occurrences extremely hazardous.

Issing (2002), distinguishing *three broad categories of uncertainty*, going from the more common to the more complex and "Knightian" ones, acknowledges that the uncertainty factors faced by central banks are myriad and interdependent. They are created by, for instance, competition between different theoretical models, constant structural change and the limited availability and reliability of key economic data. In this context, a distinction can be drawn between (1) *model uncertainty* and (2) *data uncertainty*.

6.1.1 Model Uncertainty

For analysing purposes, economists need to simplify complex realities. Such simplifications, which do not necessarily have to be formalistic, are generally referred to as theoretical models. Monetary policy makers need such models to form an idea about future inflation developments and gauge the impact of monetary policy actions in terms of direction, magnitude and timing. The models they use must adequately represent the relevant structural relationships between the price level, the monetary policy instruments and other factors affecting price movements; the latter include, inter alia, changes in oil prices or exchange rates as well as the introduction of new technologies or changes in the political and institutional framework. Since models simplify reality, they can only stress specific relationships while disregarding others.

The question of which relationships are *relevant* and which simplifications are *adequate* is a contentious one, though. Accordingly, there often exist *competing theoretical models* which explain the same phenomenon, differing in terms of the selection of explicitly included variables and the type of interrelatedness. This becomes a problem for the monetary policy maker if the relevant models characterise the

---

[1] Knight's emphasis on uncertainty decoupled him from the predominant economic theory of the time, which emphasized decision-making under conditions of perfect certainty or under the established laws of probability.

current situation differently and/or recommend differing monetary policy actions. It is possible, for example, that an assessment of the price outlook based on the *quantity theory of money model*, which emphasises the long-term relationship between money growth and inflation, may lead to a policy recommendation that is at odds with the results of a corresponding analysis based on a *Phillips curve model*, which stresses the link between inflation and the output gap.

Provided economists agree on the appropriate model, the next difficulty would be to *determine the values of the model's parameters* which provide information on the strength and dynamics of the relationship between the individual variables. Since parameter values are estimated based on an empirical analysis, the estimation results will be subject to statistical uncertainty. Moreover, the results will also depend on the choice of the estimation method. Policy makers are thus faced with an interlocking system of different forms of model uncertainty, with uncertainty about the adequate theoretical model being joined by uncertainty about which empirical model is suited to adequately quantify the relationships being studied.

In addition, theoretical models are often not very precise in *how they define the key variables*. It thus remains unclear for the most part how to operationalise the money stock or price level used in a theoretical model for the empirical analysis. This problem is also significant in light of the fact that different operationalisations (for instance, using M1 instead of M3 to measure money or using the GDP deflator instead of the CPI to measure the price level) can lead to different results regarding the strength and dynamics of the estimated relationships. The fact that empirical models can only capture basic features and behaviour patterns during a certain estimation period in the past remains a problem. The *choice of observation period* can, under some circumstances, have a considerable impact on the estimation result, especially if the relationships in question have changed fundamentally at some point in time.

This problem is *particularly severe* regarding the assessment of the economic situation *at the current end of the data*, since such "structural breaks" can often not be detected in a timely manner by econometric tests. And even if a regime shift has been detected, the parameters of the new structure cannot be captured with sufficient precision shortly after the break, owing to the small number of observations. It goes almost without saying that the extent of uncertainty about macroeconomic relationships in the euro area has been, and continues to be, especially large. After an event as pivotal as the establishment of a monetary union between formerly eleven (and by the time of writing this book already fifteen) nation-states, the likelihood of structural breaks will grow, and their impact on the monetary transmission process will initially be nearly impossible to gauge empirically because of the abovementioned problems.[2]

---

[2]Note, however, that those Central and Eastern European EU economies currently in the waiting room for entering the European Monetary Union (the so-called *members with a derogation*, a bulk off them being members of the ERM II) might strive to converge with the euro area economy before they will enter it as full members. For instance, they adapt their monetary policy strategies to that

6.1.2 Data Uncertainty

Data uncertainty arises because the relevant statistics (economic, financial and monetary statistics) provide often incomplete or even unreliable information about the *true* state of the economy. Data can be *incomplete* for a number of reasons. First, not all data which are relevant to analysing the economic situation are collected by the authorities from the statistics offices. Second, relevant data are available only with a time-lag. And third, key data (especially real economic data) tend to be subject to measurement problems, causing revisions of earlier estimates over time. In fact, gaps in collected data are a problem shared by virtually just about all central banks.

Besides the above cited problems of availability, timeliness and reliability of the underlying data, an additional type of data uncertainty exists and becomes relevant in practise. It occurs because many variables which play a decisive role in theoretical models *cannot be observed* directly in the real world and therefore *need to be estimated*. The estimation results, for their part, are strongly dependent on the underlying model. This shows how closely intertwined data uncertainty and model uncertainty are.

That applies to the calculation of equilibrium exchange rates as well as to determining the *natural level of interest rates* or the adequate valuation of assets. The most prominent examples of this, however, are undoubtedly *potential output* and the *output gap*, the latter defined as the deviation of real output from potential output. A number of recently published research papers has shown that estimates of potential output and therefore also of the output gap are fraught with considerable uncertainty, which is reflected also by the fact that the relevant time series are often revised years, if not even decades, later. This is due not so much to revisions in the data used for the estimations but to the fundamental *difficulty inherent in correctly estimating an economy's growth trend* – and especially changes in this trend.

Since such trend reversals are simply another example of the structural breaks described above, this is another region in which the boundary between data uncertainty and model uncertainty becomes blurry. As one case in point, until well into the 1980s it was not clear to what extent the oil price shocks of the 1970s had reduced potential output and the trend growth rate of developed industrial nations. This uncertainty apparently peaked in early 1975. Orphanides' research has shown that estimates of the US economy's output gap for early 1975, which were originally at –16%, were gradually revised upwards by over 10% points in the following years (Orphanides, 2003). Similar studies for the UK and German economies show that the output gap figures were revised to a similar extent in those countries. This can have severe implications for the quality of monetary policy making – especially if output gaps are largely exaggerated at real time.

To illustrate the issue of data uncertainty somewhat further, note that the US Bureau of Economic Analysis makes three successive "current quarterly" esti-

---

of the ECB and money demand might become more stable. Hence, the probability of structural breaks due to the entry of new members should be significantly lower than at the start of EMU.

mates of GDP, that is "advance," "preliminary," (following the advance release after around one month) and "final" (following the preliminary release by around one month). Annual revisions are released each July for the estimates of quarterly GDP for the three previous years; these annual-vintage estimates are labelled "first," "second," and "third" annual estimates. About every five years, comprehensive revisions are benchmarked to input-output tables.

But even then, data may still be expected to undergo a process of at times considerable revision which may last years (Bundesbank, 2004). For instance, Fig. 6.2(a) shows the relation between advance and final release of US real GDP quarter-on-quarter growth annualized (seasonally adjusted data). Figure 6.2(b) depicts the relation between preliminary and final releases. As can be seen, there were substantial differences between the final outcome and the indications given by advance and preliminary estimates. That said, making monetary policy decision on such data may well run the risk of making policy errors.

Another case in point in this context was the discussion about the "New Economy" phenomenon. In the second half of the 1990s there was growing uncertainty about whether, and by how much, the technology boom really pushed the US economy's trend growth rate upwards and whether such a shift would likely to persist for some time.

These examples again indicate how difficult it is to assess the economic situation at the point in time when monetary policy decisions need to be taken. Furthermore, they illustrate the connection between data uncertainty and model uncertainty. Consequently, the suitability of a theoretical model to monetary policy decision-making depends not only on how well it can explain past observations but also on the extent to which the data necessary for the model's empirical application are reliable and available in real time.

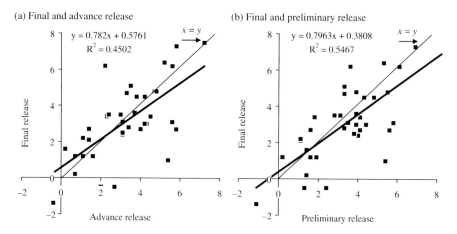

Fig. 6.2 Estimations and final outcomes for US real GDP
Source: Bloomberg; own calculations. – y = final release, x = advance/preliminary release. – Period: 1996-Q4 to 2007-Q2. – Quarter-on-quarter changes, annualised, in percent.

Data Uncertainty and Implications for Monetary Policy

Calls for downgrading the role of money in the ECB monetary policy strategy is a case in point for the implications data uncertainty has for monetary policy making. Advocates of inflation targeting dismiss the ECB's monetary pillar as superfluous and propose to rely on inflation forecasts as a guidepost for monetary policy. To produce these inflation forecasts, they generally recommend a *Phillips curve model*. However, this requires output gap estimates and forecasts, which are subject to considerable measurement error.[3]

An important factor in the evolution of fiscal policy in the early years of EMU was the *overestimation of potential output growth* in Europe. Under the influence of the *Lisbon euphoria*, it was generally assumed that potential growth in the euro area would increase because structural reforms were thought to raise *trend growth*. However, such an optimistic viewpoint was not matched by the data. This, in turn, had important implications for estimates of the euro area's output gap in 2000. Figure 6.3 shows for each year the output gap for the year 2000 as successively estimated by the OECD.

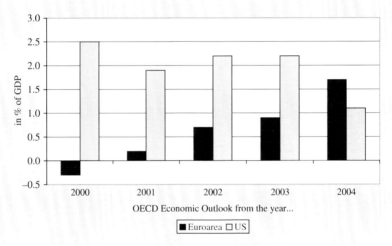

Fig. 6.3   Changing output gap estimates for the year 2000
Source: Gros et al. (2005, p. 10). OECD Economic Outlook, Autumn 2000, Autumn 2001, Autumn 2002, Autumn 2003, Autumn 2004.

At the end of 2000, the euro area output gap was estimated to be a negative 0.3%. However, this estimate was revised substantially in subsequent

---

[3] This leads to the real time data issue, an important aspect frequently stressed by the literature (Gros, Mayer, & Ubide, 2005, p. 40).

years. For instance, in 2004 the estimate for the output in 2000 was raised to a positive 1.7%. Turning to the US, the output gap was estimated to be a positive 2.5% in 2000. However, this estimate was subject to some changes in the following years, and in 2004 it was estimated to be only slight more than 1%.

Clearly, data uncertainty related to the output gap has important implications for monetary policy. Many economists fervently advocate a monetary policy of minimizing the output gap as a strategy for keeping inflation low. These economists have been criticising the ECB's decision to assign a prominent role to money unnecessary and confusing. From their viewpoint, only real economic data should guide ECB policy.[4] However, against the backdrop of the measurement and forecasting errors for the output gap, a monetary policy *focusing exclusively on the output gap* would surely have caused *severe errors* in policy as far as the objective of preserving price stability is concerned. *Monetary data are much less susceptible to revisions than real economic data.* Resting on a reliable data basis, the ECB's monetary analysis actually helps to avoid severe policy errors and support a medium-term orientation of monetary policy necessary to preserve price stability.

6.2 The Debate About "Rules Versus Discretion"

The debate about *rules versus discretion* for monetary policy has a long history in economic thinking.[5] Essentially, the discussion is about this: Shall monetary policy be allowed to take virtually any action deemed proper under prevailing conditions or shall it be forced to follow a (strict) rule? The latter could be operationalised by, for instance, Milton Friedman's k-percent rule, that is the central bank should expand the stock of money by a constant growth rate over time. Alternatively, monetary policy could be required to set interest rates in line with a flexible, or feedback (or open loop) rule.

The debate might be an old one, but it is all the more important in a fully-fledged government controlled paper money standard. As Milton Friedman put it (1994, p. 42): "(. . .) the world is now engaged in a great experiment to see whether it can fashion a different anchor, one that depends on government restraint rather than on the costs of acquiring a physical commodity." Irving Fisher (1929, p. 131), evaluating past experience, wrote on the same issue: "Irredeemable paper money has almost

---

[4] For a comprehensive reviewing of the critique being leveled against the ECB's monetary pillar see, for instance, Fischer, Lenza, Pill, and Reichlin (2006) and Woodford (2006). Belke and Gros (2007) take a critical look at the decision of the ECB to de facto downgrade the role of money and credit in policy making in recent years.

[5] For a classic statement see Simons (1948). See also Shaw (1958) and Fisher (1990).

invariably proved a curse to the country employing it." In the following, we will dig a little bit into the debate about rules versus discretion for monetary policy and, against this background, take a closer look at where international monetary policy stands and what challenges lie ahead when it comes to preserve sound money.

6.2.1 Arguments in Favour of Monetary Policy Discretion

The first argument in favour of relying upon discretion is that a room for manoeuvring on the part of the central bank may be used wisely to meet needs as they develop. No two sets of economic conditions are identical; the future is uncertain. So how can central bankers, with all their limitations as human beings, set a general rule for the future which will serve as well as the best that men can do as conditions do develop? Not enough is known about the ability of officials to implement a rule, almost any rule, to be confident of success. Can one not get the best total and combination of change if we deliberately make the monetary system adaptable?

Discretionary policy action tends to be held in high esteem because it is believed that monetary policy can contribute most when it is framed and administered in the light of conditions as the appear. To put it differently: monetary policy, or a change in money supply, is seen as the appropriate instrument to counteract recession, a view closely related to the viewpoint of Keynesian economics.

Second, a fixed rule would *fix into stone* the policy objective. However, society may find it desirable to change monetary policy goals over time. And a policy fixed to a rule may well be suited to achieving one goal (such as price stability), but it may be poorly adapted for another (economic growth), which may nevertheless increase in relative importance, or even reverse in priority. For instance, insulation from troubles coming from other countries may make necessary flexibility in monetary policy, it is said, for preventing foreign shocks (such as, for instance, financial crises, etc.) from spilling over into the domestic economy, causing output and employment losses.

Third, the great majority of those who have made policy, and in particular of those who are authorised to execute it, tend to prefer a considerable degree of discretion. Indeed, from an individual point of view, being responsible for taking decisions on a discretionary basis can be expected to be much more rewarding (in terms of prestige and job satisfaction) compared with implementing a policy slavishly following a strict rule (*auto pilot*).

6.2.2 Arguments in Favour of Rules

The first important reason for adhering to a (strict) rule is that, to start with, it assures protection against *human error*. Even if the rule may not be best for every situation, there is no danger of bad selection of alternative action or bad timing as authorities try to meet changing conditions. Thus, the public avoids not only the costs of uncertainty regarding policy action (in terms of timing and magnitude) but also some of the risks related to poor policy. At the worst, much may be sacrificed to obtain little because the potential superiority of flexible over fixed policy will not be large, whereas the losses from shifting to an inappropriate policy can be substantial.

Second, the selection of a fixed rule, once put in place, would require careful analysis and extensive public discussion. Though the final definition of policy would not be perfect, it would doubtless represent more carefully, and certainly more widely, considered thought than would be various decisions of an authority having extensive discretion to change policy at all times. The rule could represent the general public interest, whereas specific use of authority might be subject to pressure exerted by those concerned more with special than with general interest.

And third, experience may recommend that adhering to rules may simply be better than relying on discretion when it comes to preserving price stability. The record of discretionary management has by no means been brilliant. Perhaps it has not even been good. Judging the record is difficult, of course, if only because one cannot know what different actions would have produced. Nevertheless, the accomplishment certainly does not in itself provide convincing testimonial to the superiority of authority over rule.

6.3 The Time Inconsistency Problem

The debate about *rules versus discretion* was given a new impetus through the issue of *time inconsistency* as put forward by Kydland and Prescott (1977).[6] Later, Barro and Gordon (1983a, 1983b) showed that, even in view of *ideal* conditions for pursuing a discretionary monetary policy, a credible commitment on the part of the central bank to a (monetary) rule would be superior to pursuing a discretionary monetary policy. In what follows, we will take a brief look at the time inconsistency problem in (i) a one-period world and (ii) a multi-period world. Finally, we will (iii) summarise the discussion about time inconsistency.

What the Time Inconsistency Problem Is All About

To see how the time-inconsistency of optimal policies could lead to excessively high inflation, suppose that the central bank has the twin goals of keeping inflation close to some target level and unemployment close to the natural rate.[7] Suppose further that there are market imperfections (such as, for instance, monopolistic competition or strategic union behaviour) so that the

---

[6]See Kydland and Prescott (1977). The earlier literature focused on time inconsistency leading to the well-known inflation bias and on means of overcoming policy imperfections. More recently, time inconsistency issues have attracted renewed attention due to the large influence of the New Keynesian theoretical framework. See, for instance, Calvo (1978) and Clarida, Gali, and Gertler (1999).

[7]See in this context, for instance, Dennis (2003).

unemployment rate that clears the labour market is inefficiently high, lying above the natural rate. To keep unemployment close to the natural rate, the central bank must try to lower unemployment below the inefficiently high rate that would otherwise clear the labour market. In this model, workers negotiate their wage rate with firms based on what they expect inflation to be. To the extent that workers anticipate the inflation rate correctly, the prevailing unemployment rate is the (inefficiently high) market clearing rate.

Kydland and Prescott showed in their model that the central bank's desire to bring down unemployment to the natural rate leads to time-inconsistent behaviour of the monetary agent. Suppose that the inflation target is 2%; the optimal monetary policy recognizes that workers cannot be systematically fooled and, consequently, that the unemployment rate cannot systematically depart from the market-clearing rate. Despite its twin goals, therefore, the best the central bank can do is to announce that it will set monetary policy such that inflation equals 2%, and then follow through on that announcement and let the labour market clear at the market-clearing level.

But this optimal policy is *time inconsistent* and will not be realised – despite its pre-announcement. If workers believe the central bank's policy announcement and negotiate a contract with firms providing for a 2% nominal wage increase, then the central bank's range of options changes. Instead of following through and implementing the announced policy, the central bank can create a little more inflation (*surprise inflation*), which lowers workers' real wages, stimulating firms' demand for labour. With the nominal wage rate fixed, the labour market now clears at a lower unemployment rate. Thus, at the cost of slightly higher inflation, the economy reaps the benefit of lower unemployment. Kydland and Prescott showed that, in balancing these costs and benefits, the central bank would find it advantageous to create the inflation surprise and not implement the announced policy.

Of course, workers soon will realize that the central bank's announcements are not credible, and they will come to expect higher inflation. And when workers expect higher inflation, it becomes increasingly costly for the central bank to create any inflation surprise. The equilibrium outcome is for inflation to rise to the point where the central bank finds that the benefits of any additional inflation surprises are fully offset by their costs. At this inflation, the central bank has no incentive to create an inflation surprise. But because there are no inflation surprises, workers fully anticipate inflation, and the labour market does not clear at the natural rate of unemployment: instead the higher market-clearing rate prevails. Sadly, the fact that the central bank can revisit its announced policy after wages have been set leaves the economy with inefficiently high inflation, but no reduction in the unemployment rate. The discrepancy between the average inflation rate that occurs and the inflation target is known as the discretionary inflation bias.

6.3.1 Time Inconsistency in a Two-Period Model

The *cost function*, which the central bank wants to minimise, can be characterised as follows: Inflation, π, and deviations of actual real output, Y, from the production level envisaged by the central bank $(Y^* + \phi)$ lead to costs, where Y^* is potential real output, and ϕ represents the margin by which the central bank wishes to push actual real output beyond its potential level. In fact, Y^* is assumed to be the real output level which would be achieved if market agents do not make any inflation forecast errors. In simple linear terms, the cost function might look as follows:

$$L = \pi + \eta \left(Y - \left(Y^* + \phi \right) \right), \tag{6.1}$$

where $\eta > 0$ and $\phi > 0$.

If we assume further that total costs become increasingly painful with rising inflation and increasing deviations of actual output from the desired level, we can write:

$$L = \pi^2 + \eta \left(Y - \left(Y^* + \phi \right) \right)^2, \tag{6.2}$$

with $\eta > 0$ and $\phi > 1$.

Equation (6.2) represents an iso-cost line in the inflation-output space.

As noted above, the economy would be at Y^* if market agents do not make any inflation forecast errors. In that sense, Y^* corresponds to the *natural rate of unemployment*, as analysed in the Phillips curve theory. If it wants to bring actual real output beyond Y^*, the central bank obviously wants to fight the effects of *structural deficiencies* (regulation, etc.) on output through monetary policy.

To make this possible, the aggregate supply curve, *AS*, must, at least in the short-run, be positively related to inflation, at least:

$$\pi = \pi^e + \alpha \left(Y - Y^* \right), \tag{6.3}$$

while we assume, for the sake of simplicity, that $\alpha = 1$. Rearranging Eq. (6.3) yields:

$$Y = \pi - \pi^e + Y^*. \tag{6.4}$$

Equation (6.4) is actually a version of Robert Lucas's supply side function: actual real output will exceed potential real output if, and only if, actual inflation turns out to be higher than expected inflation. In such a (Keynesian-type) case, real wages decline, thereby lowering the cost of production and stimulating a rise in output; that is, output would rise through surprise inflation.

The economy's aggregate demand function can be written as:

$$Y_t = Y_{t-1} + \beta \left(\Delta m - \pi \right), \tag{6.5}$$

Fig. 6.4 Aggregate demand and supply and inflation expectations

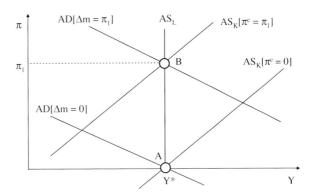

where $\beta > 0$, and we assume, again for the sake of simplicity, that $\beta = 1$. Equation (6.5) says that aggregate demand in period t will deviate from the level seen in period $t - 1$ only if money supply growth exceeds actual inflation; in that sense, aggregate demand is a function of real balances. Figure 6.4 shows the AS and AD curves in the (expected) inflation-output space; note that AS_L represents the long-run supply curve, while AS_K stands for the supply curves in the short-run.

It is assumed that the variable Y_{t-1} represents potential output in period $t - 1$. If actual inflation is determined by money growth, and the latter is zero ($AD[\Delta m = 0]$), actual output would equal potential output (any imply point A in Fig. 6.4). If, however, money growth is positive ($AD[\Delta m = \pi_1]$), and inflation is forecasted correctly ($\pi^e = \pi_1$), output remains at Y^*, while inflation runs at π_1 (point B).

Now assume market agents, in the current period, enter into multi-period contracts, which incorporate certain expectations as far as inflation in future periods is concerned. That said, the central bank has an incentive (according to Eqs. (6.2) and (6.3) to make actual inflation deviating from the level of expected inflation that is used in multi- (i.e two-) period contracts: The central bank can – via inducing *surprise inflation* – increase actual output beyond its potential (thereby minimising its cost function).

The crucial question in this context is: where do market agents' inflation expectations come from? Assume, for instance, that the central bank promises, before contracts are being made, to deliver zero inflation (that is promising to keep money growth at zero). Would such a promise be credible from the viewpoint of market agents? If the latter know about the central bank's cost function, it is fair to say that any such promise on the part of the central bank would not be credible from the viewpoint of market agents. This is because market agents can expect that the central bank would, as soon as contracts have been entered into, would pursue an inflation policy. This is actually where the *time inconsistency problem* strikes.

We would speak of *time inconsistency* if someone promises to take a certain measure at a future point in time, while we cannot expect the one to live up to that promise, as we would know that such an action is no longer optimal for the one who had made the promise. That said, in our example the central bank's announcement

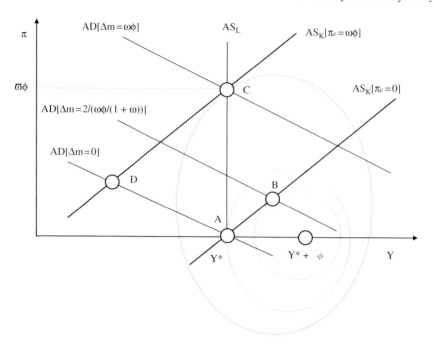

Fig. 6.5 Aggregated demand and supply and *time inconsistency*

to deliver zero inflation is time inconsistent. If market agents are rational, they won't put much trust in it. As a result, inflation expectations of zero, as promised by the central bank, are simply not rational.

Figure 6.5 inter alia shows the iso-cost lines for the central bank. The minimum costs imply an output $(Y^* + \phi)$ and zero inflation. The greater the distance of the iso-cost curve from this point is, the higher are the costs for the central bank. If, for instance, the central bank announces zero inflation – that is zero money growth –, point A would be realised. Here, actual inflation and realised output can be calculated by minimising Eq. (6.2), taking into account of Eq. (6.4):

$$L = \pi^2 + \varpi \left(\pi - \pi^e + Y - Y^* - \phi\right)^2 = \pi^2 + \varpi \left(\pi - \pi^e - \phi\right)^2. \qquad (6.6)$$

If $\pi^e = \pi = 0$, we have:

$$\frac{\partial L}{\partial \pi} = 2\pi = 0. \qquad (6.7)$$

In this case, we find that $Y = Y^*$.

However, point A is an unlikely outcome if market agents know about the central bank's cost function. This is because once market agents expect zero inflation, it is optimal for the central bank to make inflation higher than zero – that is pursuing a policy of surprise inflation –, thereby moving to point B in Fig. 6.5. The minimum cost solution for surprise inflation can be calculated as:

$$\frac{\partial L}{\partial \pi} = 2\pi + 2\varpi \left(\pi - \pi^e - \phi \right) = 0, \tag{6.8}$$

so that we yield

$$\pi = \frac{\varpi \left(\pi^e + \phi \right)}{1 + \pi}. \tag{6.9}$$

If we have zero inflation expectations, the level of inflation that minimises the central bank's cost function is:

$$\pi = \frac{\varpi \phi}{1 + \pi} > \pi^e = 0. \tag{6.10}$$

However, even if market agents have positive inflation expectations (that is expected inflation is higher than promised inflation), it remains optimal from the viewpoint of monetary policy to increase money growth. Such a policy would realise point C. Here, there are no output gains, but a (much) less favourable policy outcome as represented by point D can be prevented.

That said, if market agents realise the *logic of the incentive structure* on the par of the central bank, they would know that point A won't be realised, but that the *stable equilibrium* would be realised in point C. Here, inflation is higher than in point A, without output going beyond potential. In other words: without explicit measures for making the central bank's promise credible, *costs of higher inflation without will be the result, without yielding any benefits in terms of increasing actually output*.

How can the central bank's inflation announcement be made credible from the point of view of rational market agents? Quite simply: discretion on the part of monetary policy makers could be greatly reduced, or be eliminated altogether. For instance, the central bank authority could be reduced, via a country's constitution, to expanding the money supply at a constant and pre-determined rate over time (amounting to Friedman's *k-percent money supply growth rule*).

6.3.2 Time Inconsistency in a Multi-Period Model

So far, the analysis of the time inconsistency problem of monetary policy was made in a one-period world. If, however, the time inconsistency problem is analysed in a multi-period world, central banks have the chance to build up *reputation capital*, which makes a big difference to the model results in a one-period world (Backus & Driffill 1985). For instance, if point A in Fig. 6.4 appears to be favourable from the viewpoint of monetary policy makers, they might be (much) less inclined to pursue a policy that could put the outcome as shown in point A in danger.

That said, one solution to the time inconsistency problem of monetary policy (as formulated in Eq. (6.2)) is *lengthening the monetary policy makers' decision making period indefinitely*. For instance, let us assume that there is a constant probability $\theta \in [0, 1]$ that the current decision making period t is the last period. Ex ante, the probability that we will reach period t is $\text{Prob}[t] = (1 - \theta)^t$. With a rising t, the probability converges towards zero. What is important, however, is the fact that if we approach a remoter period (from today's viewpoint), the conditional probability that decision makers are still active in $t + 1$ is $\text{Prob}[t + 1 \mid t] = \theta$.

Against this backdrop, the costs of future periods can be discounted to the present period as follows:

$$\delta^t = \frac{1 - \theta}{1 + r}. \tag{6.11}$$

The nominator in Eq. (6.11) shows the probability that the decision making will reach period t, while the denominator represent the discount rate, r, plus 1. That said, if we assume an indefinite decision making horizon, the structure of decision making in future periods will actually be identical with decision making in the current period.

If, for instance, the central bank announces to pursue a monetary policy of zero inflation, and if such a policy announcement is seen credible from the point of view of market agents, the present value of discounted future costs is:

$$L_t^1 = L_A \cdot \left(1 + \delta + \delta^2 + \delta^3 + \ldots + \delta^t\right) = \frac{L_A}{1 - \delta}, \tag{6.12}$$

where L_A represents the cost in period t if point A in Fig. 6.4 is realised.

Alternatively, a monetary policy of *surprise inflation* would bring the economy immediately from point A to point B in Fig. 6.4. In this case, the AD-curve moves to the right, as the central bank increase money growth ($\Delta m > 0$), causing price rises ($\pi > 0$). However, inflation expectations rise further to $\pi = \varpi \phi$, moving the AD curve to the left. To avoid the unfavourable outcome in point D, the central bank increases money supply growth to $\Delta m = \varpi \phi$. The new equilibrium is reached in point C, where, while real output remains at Y^*. In this case, the present value (PV) of the costs is:

$$L_t^2 = L_B + L_C \left(\delta + \delta^2 + \delta^3 + \ldots + \delta^t\right) = L_B + \frac{\delta}{1 - \delta} L_C, \tag{6.13}$$

where L_B is the costs of pursuing a policy of surprise inflation (right from the start) and $\frac{\delta}{1-\delta} L_C$ is the PV of the costs of the long-term equilibrium solution if the central bank's announcement is not credible.

While the central bank can reduce the costs of delivering surprise inflation in the first period, it would cause higher costs in the future. As the latter enters the central bank's cost function in discounted terms, it is not clear whether or not it is optimal for the central bank to opt for surprise inflation. Generally speaking, it is optimal for the central bank to refrain from a policy of surprise inflation if:

$$L_t^1 \leq L_t^2, \text{ that is} \tag{6.14a}$$

$$\frac{L_A}{1 - \delta} \leq L_B + \frac{\delta}{1 - \delta} L_C. \tag{6.14b}$$

Solving Eq. (6.14b) for δ yields:

$$\delta \geq \frac{L_A - L_B}{L_C - L_B}. \tag{6.15}$$

That said, if it does not use too high a discount rate for valuing the future costs of its actions, the central bank's promise to pursue a zero inflation policy should be credible. If the discount factor on the left-hand side of (6.15) strictly exceeds the term on the right hand side of (6.15), a *finite horizon* in which market agents can sanction the central bank for any misconduct should be enough for keeping the policy promise credible (that is preventing the time inconsistency problem).

Predictability Versus Credibility

There is a distinction to be made between *predictability* and *credibility* of monetary policy. Predictability can be understood as the ability on the part of market agents to correctly forecast future monetary policy action. The term credibility refers to the believability of a promise. A policy promise (like, say, keeping future inflation low) may be credible from the viewpoint of market agents, while the policy action taken by the central bank to achieve its goal (that is to live up to its promise) might not (always) be predictable in terms of timing and magnitude.

For instance, market agents might well be confident that the central bank will keep future inflation low. However, their expectations about the timing of interest rate changes might not always be correct. Figure 6.6 shows changes in the ECB's main refinancing rate and the spreads of various money market rates over the ECB's main refinancing rate in basis points for the period January 1999–June 2008, a period in which the ECB monetary policy appeared to have been credible (as indicated by, for instance, relatively low market inflation expectations).

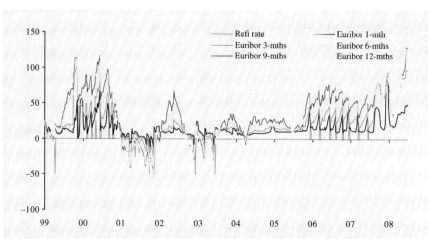

Fig. 6.6 Changes in ECB rates and spreads of money market rates over ECB main refinancing rates (in bp)
Source: Thomson Financial, own calculations.

In most cases market agents seemed to have predicted the timing and direction of forthcoming change in ECB interest rates, as evidenced by the widening spreads in the run-up to the day when interest rates were actually changed. However, there were also periods in which the market seemed to have got it wrong. For instance, in early 2002, when spread widening indicated the market expectation of rising short-term rates, the ECB did not raise rates – but lowered them in June 2002. In view of the example above, one may say that credibility and predictability of monetary policy actions went actually hand in hand.

In this context see, for instance, Blackburn and Christensen (1989), Blattner, Catenaro, Ehrmann, Strauch, and Turunen (2008), Ehrmann and Fratzscher (2005), Wilhelmsen and Zaghini (2005), Connolly and Kohler (2004).

6.3.3 Alternative Solutions to Inflation Bias

Following the work of Barro and Gordon, a large literature developed to examine alternative solutions to the inflation bias that arises under discretionary monetary policy (Persson & Tabellini, 1990, 1994). In the following, a brief overview will be given on (i) the concept of a conservative central banker, (ii) optimal contracts for central bankers and (iii) implementing economic reforms.

6.3.3.1 The Concept of a Conservative Central Banker

One might think of a solution to the inflation bias problem when the central bank can *earn its reputation* under a discretionary policy so that, over time, market agents expect inflation to be in line with the bank's promise to keep inflation low. Rogoff (1985) analysed the preferences of central bankers. He concluded that the government should appoint as central banker someone who places greater relative weight on the inflation objective than does the society as a whole. This concept has been labelled that of a *conservative central banker*; Svensson (1997) suggested the term *central banker conservatism for this*.

The intuition of the concept is easily understood by referring to the central banks' cost function. Assigning a lower weight to the output objective relative to the objective to keep inflation, the conservative central banker should give little rise to concern that he will be tempted to pursue a policy of surprise inflation. In an extreme case, η in Eq. (6.1) would become zero if the central banker just focuses on preventing inflation.

6.3.3.2 Optimal Contracts for Central Banker

Walsh (1995) suggests that a conservative central banker as required in the Rogoff solution may push the economy into recession too often for the general public's taste, in order to preserve low inflation. He proposes incentive-compatible contracts for central bankers that explicitly tie compensation to inflation performance.[8] Walsh shows that relative simple compensation arrangements – that is, for instance, tying pay to deviations of inflation from the envisaged target – are sufficient to make the central banker behave as to avoid an inflation bias.

However, McCallum (1995) points out that Walsh's contract solution to the inflation bias simply transfers the incentives that lead to the inflation bias one level up, namely from the monetary policy maker to the government that is charged with enforcement of the contract. All the logic that applied to the central bank applies to the government, so the incentive for the government to enforce the contract could lead to lax enforcement in the presence of employment-augmenting inflationary shocks, and once again end up with an inflation bias.

6.3.3.3 Implementing Economic Reforms

The pressing problem of unemployment and the choice of the appropriate monetary policy strategy are crucial challenges in current academic and political debates. Although both issues are usually connected in the public discussions the academic discourse had neglected, until the mid-nineties, to provide rational arguments for such an interrelation. Until then, the incentives and disincentives for labour, product and financial market reforms on the one side and the benefits and costs of monetary policy rules on the other side had typically been analyzed in isolation.

The pros and cons of different monetary policy strategies are usually investigated in the framework of Barro and Gordon (1983a, 1983b) and Kydland and Prescott (1977). Both contributions focus on the time inconsistency of discretionary

---

[8]The proper perspective for addressing such issues is found in the principal-agent literature. See, for instance, Persson and Tabellini (1993).

monetary policy (which presupposes monetary policy autonomy) and compare the efficiency of alternative monetary policy rules with the potential losses due to the inflexibility of rules under exogenous shocks. As possible solutions to the trade-off between the time-inconsistency problem of discretionary monetary policy and the inflexibility of rule-based monetary policy, various rules have been proposed. Prominent examples of such limitations of policy autonomy are feedback-rules in connection with distinct commitment technologies, e.g. the independence of central banks or incentive schemes for central bankers (Crowe & Meade, 2007; Persson & Tabellini, 1993; Svensson, 1997; Walsh, 1995).

However, the first-best solution to the time-inconsistency problem is to remove labour market rigidities, the fundamental cause of high structural unemployment (Berthold & Fehn (2006) Svensson, 1997, pp. 104 and 109; Duval & Elmeskov, 2005, p. 5).[9] Yet, such a proposal could be regarded as rather naive from a public choice perspective, which emphasizes that labour market institutions, as an outcome of rational political choice, have to be implemented in the loss function of politicians. In this paper, we argue that the design of labour market institutions can be interpreted as the result of utility maximizing political decisions. Therefore, it appears useful to augment the time-inconsistency models by an explicit consideration of labour market reforms (Herrendorf & Neumann, 2003).

Cross-country event studies are one way to empirically examine the impact of monetary policy strategies on the degree of economic reform in general. This approach has produced contradicting results, however. The U.S., e.g., are a monetary union with labour market institutions that encourage a low natural rate of unemployment. The EMS commitment was extremely helpful in fostering the reform process in the Netherlands and Denmark. The same holds for Austria under the DM peg (Hochreiter & Tavlas, 2005). In contrast, the UK and New Zealand experienced extensive labour market reforms without adhering to an international exchange rate arrangement. Hence, we choose an econometric analysis for a large sample of countries (and a large variety of reforms as well). Thereby, we go beyond the EMU case studies by van Poeck and Borghijs (2001), Bertola and Boeri (2001), and IMF (2004) which are rare examples of empirical investigations in this field.[10]

---

[9]OECD (2005) applies a consistent procedure to derive policy priorities to foster growth across OECD countries and identifies labour market reforms as being particularly important in, e.g., the Euro area. However, this does not at all imply that reforms in other areas are unimportant. Hence, we analyze a variety of different reform measures in the empirical part of this section.

[10]van Poeck and Borghijs (2001) argue that the prospect of qualifying for EMU should provide as big an incentive for labour-market reform as EMU membership itself. They conclude that EMU countries did not reform more than other countries and, unlike elsewhere, their progress on reform seemed unrelated to the initial level of unemployment. For a period from the early nineties up to 1999, Bertola and Boeri (2001) only focus on cash transfers to people of working age, e.g. unemployment benefits, and on job protection. They arrive at exactly opposite conclusions, i.e. reforms accelerated more in the euro area than outside. The IMF (2004) looks at the impact of a range of factors including macroeconomic conditions, political institutions, reform design and variables aimed to capture attitudes towards structural reform on different policy areas across OECD countries from the mid-1970s up to the late 1990s. It finds that EU membership leads to faster

6.3.4 Conflicting Views on the Relation Between the Degree of Monetary Policy Autonomy and Structural Reforms

The discussion of the relation between the degree of monetary policy autonomy and structural reforms is characterized by a wide spectrum of conflicting views. The identification of the impact of monetary regimes on structural reforms has motivated a couple of theoretical works that discuss whether monetary commitments tend to strengthen or reduce the degree of reforms. Importantly, most of these arguments are derived from reforms of the labour market.

We start with a sketch of the literature on monetary policy autonomy and reforms and refer to a prominent example of the loss of monetary autonomy, i.e. the irrevocable fixing of exchange rates under European Monetary Union (EMU). In the run-up to EMU a number of studies tried to assess the incentive effects of alternative monetary policy strategies on labour market reforms. According to the proponents of a liberal view, EMU, as a classical variant of a rule-based monetary policy, should have a disciplinary impact on national labour markets.[11] In the first place, EMU enhances the credibility of monetary policy and thereby lowers inflation expectations. Negative employment effects as a result of (too) high wage claims can no longer be accommodated by discretionary monetary policy. The responsibility of wage setters for unemployment increases significantly, because they no longer negotiate about nominal wage but real wage growth. The responsibility for existing unemployment is more transparently assigned to the parties which negotiate the relative price of labour. In contrast, autonomous discretionary monetary policy makes it more difficult to remove market rigidities because there is still the option to solve or at least to shift the unemployment problem onto third parties (Beetsma & Bovenberg 1998).

Insofar as the single currency increases transparency, the costs of structural rigidities become more obvious, as reflected in slowly changing relative prices. Lower trading costs and higher transparency jointly tend to foster competition in goods markets which, in turn, reduces the available product market rents. If these rents are smaller, the economic incentives to resist reforms that prevent such rents to be captured are smaller as well.

Overall, the incentives for extensive reforms of labour, goods, and capital markets increase under a regime of irrevocably fixed exchange rates.[12] If changes in monetary policy and the nominal exchange rate are not available, and if labour is immobile as is the case in most parts of the Euro area, there is no other option than to undertake reforms in order to facilitate the market-based adjustment to

---

moves towards liberalization of product markets. However, it does not clarify whether this represents an effect of EMU and/or policies to prepare for EMU. See also Duval and Elmeskov (2005, p. 10).

[11] For a recent survey of the arguments see Duval and Elmeskov (2005) and Hochreiter and Tavlas (2005).

[12] See Alogoskoufis (1994), Calmfors (1997), Duval and Elmeskov (2005, p. 6), Mélitz (1997), and Sibert and Sutherland (1997).

shocks. Hence, credible currency pegging has often been interpreted as a version of Mrs. Thatcher's There-Is-No-Alternative (TINA) strategy.[13] In this paper, we intend to generalize this striking TINA argument empirically and extend it to countries beyond the narrow focus of the Euro area, which is what e.g. Duval and Elmeskov (2005) concentrate on.

However, there are also important arguments against a positive impact of monetary rules on economic reform. First, based on OECD macro model simulations it was often argued with respect to EMU that the so-called up-front costs of structural of labour market reforms may be larger within a currency union. This holds especially in large, relatively closed countries for which changes in the real exchange rate by a period of low inflation are not so effective in alleviating the necessary "crowding-in" effect. Removing restrictions in financial markets tend to stimulate demand more than labour market reforms and hence allow an easier and quicker "crowding-in" of reforms (Bean, 1998; Blanchard 2006; Duval & Elmeskov, 2005, pp. 10–12; Saint-Paul & Bentolila, 2000). Hence, the prior in this case would be that rule-based monetary policy regimes like, e.g., EMU, lead to more reforms in the financial market than in the labour market.

Second, Calmfors (1997) and Sibert and Sutherland (1997) argue that one should not expect from monetary policy with its mainly short-run real economy effects to diminish structural unemployment significantly. Hence, rule-based monetary policy does not necessarily imply more labour market reform pressure. In the same line, empirical analysis indicates that the capability of exchange rates to absorb asymmetric shocks to labour and goods markets is rather low. Hence, flexibility of exchange rates does not seem to be a good substitute for reforms and, hence, the degree of reforms is not necessarily higher under fixed exchange rates (Belke & Gros, 1999).

Third, some analysts support the view that rule-based monetary policy, at least if it takes effect through entering a fixed exchange rate regime, has no disciplinary effects on the wage setting process, but leads to centralization processes and strengthens the incentives to claim high wages on the part of unions. Fourth, the limited evidence of price structure convergence for instance among core-EMS countries as compared with other countries speaks against any significant impact of credible exchange rate stabilization on product market competition. Hence, there are still product market rents to be captured and there will still be resistance to reforms (Haffner et al. 2000; Nicoletti et al. 2003).

From these introductory remarks it should be clear that the implementation of specific monetary policy rules significantly changes the conditions for and the efficiency of reforms (Calmfors, 1997, 1998; Grüner & Hefeker, 1996). Let us assume for the moment that we only focus on labour market reform and that the main aim of labour market reforms is to lower structural unemployment. At the same time, the term monetary policy rule is used in a more general fashion, i.e. that it comprises both monetary and exchange rate policy. The assessment of different monetary

---

[13]See, Bean (1998), Calmfors (1998, p. 28), Duval and Elmeskov (2005, p. 5), and Saint-Paul and Bentolila (2000).

policy rules from the employment perspective is then dependent on their specific impact on the implementation of labour market reforms: do they trigger or hinder market reforms? Moreover, it is decisive whether autonomous discretionary policy is able to settle the dispute between interest groups and to support the efficiency of reforms.

Monetary Policy as a Driver of Structural Reforms?

Recently, the economics of structural reforms have attracted increasing attention in the academic literature (Abiad & Mody, 2005; Helbling, Hakura, & Debrun, 2004; for a survey see Heinemann, 2004, 2005; Belke, Herz, & Vogel, 2005). This ongoing research is driven by the fact that, for a number of EU countries, the speed of structural changes lags behind what is necessary given high structural unemployment and imminent demographic change. Policy fields where a striking contrast between needs and deeds of institutional change has been identified are, for instance, labour markets, product markets, social security and tax systems.

Fruitful Interplay of Monetary Policy and Reforms

Although the existing empirical literature has started to identify important drivers and obstacles of reforms with regard to different policy field, the interplay of structural reforms and monetary policy has been neglected so far. While the theoretical literature has formulated some hypotheses how monetary policy may act as a catalyst for reform processes, thorough empirical studies based on the experience of a large number of industrial countries are only scarcely available.

Reforms aiming at an improvement of market efficiency can only be fruitful if there is monetary stability allowing price mechanisms to fulfil their allocative function. In this sense, theory suggests a clear basic link between monetary policy and reform policy: High inflation rates are not compatible with the successful implementation of structural reforms. This insight, however, does not exclude that – within a low inflation framework – there could be ways how monetary policy might encourage or smooth reform processes. A frequently cited argument relates to the so called "*two handed approach*" (for example: Bean, 1998): its basic logic is that monetary policy may be able to reduce upfront costs of certain kind of structural reforms, e.g. related to labour markets.

Hysteresis and Policy Complementarity

This is especially so if one accepts the main results of the now-famous *hysteresis* debate in the context of European unemployment, initiated by Olivier

Blanchard and others. According to this view, permanently high continental European unemployment can be best described as a hysteresis phenomenon. This implies that high structural unemployment (the "remanence") is the result of initially negative shocks impacting on the labour market which is prolonged by rigidities in labour and product markets. In order to get rid of the unemployment problem one has to use some "coercive" power, i.e. some counter-cyclical macro policies. However, the latter should be accompanied by significant supply side reforms which lead to more flexibility of the relevant markets in order to lower the costs of demand management. From this point of view, the "*two-handed approach*" to economic policy regains attention (for an overview of the hysteresis approach see Belke & Goecke, 1999, 2005). This approach is in accordance with the *policy complementarity* view proposed by Coe and Snower (1997) and Orszag and Snower (1998).

A different argument (frequently mentioned in various speeches and interviews of ECB officials) is closer to the primary objective of monetary policy itself and is unrelated to any demand management considerations: *Certain types of reforms of labour and product markets are able to reduce inflationary tendencies*, for example, if measures to strengthen competition on labour markets have a dampening effect on wage and price growth.

Still Some Lack of Empirical Backing

Obviously, these kinds of reflections rest on assumptions which do not all have a solid empirical backing. For example, the study of Helbling et al. (2004) indicates that *J-curve effects* where a (short-run) period of costs precedes the materialization of the long-run benefits are by no means typical for all reform fields. Furthermore, it is unclear, to which extent monetary policy can be effective to change the time profile of costs and benefits. Finally, difficult questions relate to monetary credibility which could be impaired if central banks accept a temporary divergence from stability oriented monetary policy for the sake of supporting governments in their policies.

In the monetary transmission literature much attention has been paid to the question how, e.g. labour market reforms, change the conditions for the conduct of monetary policy. The opposite question, *how relevant monetary policy is for structural reforms*, has not been covered in a systematic way although there have been some very rough first insights. The literature on the drivers of structural reforms sometimes includes the inflation rate (e.g. Pitlik & Wirth, 2003; Heinemann, 2005). Furthermore there are some works preoccupied with the question how relevant the exchange rate regime and EMU in particular is for reform processes (Belke, Herz, & Vogel, 2006a, b, c; Castrén, Takalo, & Wood, 2004; Duval & Elmeskov, 2005; Jimeno, 2005).

6.3.5 A Benchmark Model

In the following, we critically discuss the widely held view that the effects of changes in the monetary regime on the probability of labour market reforms are not predictable and speculative in the light of the Lucas critique. We endogenize labour market reforms in a Barro-Gordon-framework and focus on the long-run effects of reform.[14] The loss function of the policy maker includes as "bads" not only inflation and unemployment but also labour market reforms.

In political economy models it is generally assumed that politicians suffer welfare losses when implementing labour market reforms for two reasons. First, reforms tend to reduce at least in the short run the wages of employed insiders, who are frequently organized in powerful syndicates (trade unions) and who are the relevant political majority for re-electing the incumbent government. There is wide evidence that outsiders are generally compensated by active labour market policies and public transfers. Labour market reforms can be best interpreted as a downward shift of the seminal wage setting curve popularized by Layard, Jackman, and Nickell (1994) and Lindbeck (1992) towards the employment axis. This shift can be explained by the same factors that are emphasized by insider-outsider theories as arguments for the specific slope of the wage setting curve. A labour market reform could, e.g., reduce the period in which the unemployed receive unemployment benefits, which is a highly significant determinant of the diverging unemployment rates in OECD countries (Calmfors, 1998; Nickell, 1997). The real reservation wage of the unemployed would drop proportionally to the degree of reforms.[15]

Second, an intrinsic welfare-enhancing value is attached to existing labour market regulations. They diminish the susceptibility of the employed to shocks (protection against unlawful dismissal) and, as in the case of unemployment benefits, inherently bear an insurance character (Berthold & Fehn, 1996; Calmfors, 1998; Saint-Paul, 1993, 1996).

In order to account for these considerations, we augment the usual Lucas type unemployment equation and the hypothesis of rational expectations by an additional condition: the natural unemployment is linearly dependent on the chosen degree of labour market reforms. We distinguish between two scenarios, an autonomous and discretionary monetary policy and a non-autonomous, rule-based monetary policy.

---

[14] The analytical framework was initially developed by Barro and Gordon (1983a, 1983b), Kydland and Prescott (1977), Sibert and Sutherland (1997), and Svensson (1997).

[15] Alternatively, labour market reforms might contain the reduction of unemployment benefits, the rise of the efficiency of labour market policy, the substitution of collective by individual wage negotiations, lower minimum wages for young employees, the revision of the laws of wage negotiations (increasing the negotiation power of employees) and the reduction of both taxes and employment protection in general reform reduce equilibrium unemployment. See for instance, Buscher et al. (2005). Daveri & Tabellini (2000), Lindbeck and Snower, and Nicoletti and Scarpetta (2005). For the interrelation of product and labour market reforms see Ebell and Haefke (2003), Kugler and Pica (2004) and Nicoletti and Scarpetta (2005).

In order to interpret the degree of labour market reforms as a rational political choice of politicians, the common loss function L is augmented as follows:

$$V = 1/2 \left[(U - U^*)^2 + \lambda(\pi - \pi^*)^2 + \gamma r^2 \right],$$ (6.16)

where U is the actual unemployment, rate U^* is the unemployment target, π is the actual inflation rate, π^* is the inflation target, r corresponds to the actual degree of labour market reforms, λ is the weight of the deviation of inflation from its target and γ represents the weight of reforms in the loss function ($r \geq 0$). Assuming a constant relationship between output and unemployment and adding the variable measuring the degree of reforms, we are able to derive Eq. (6.17) straight from Eq. (6.2). To simplify the analysis, we assume separability of the loss function, although there are cases where the marginal utility of a reform depends on the level of unemployment (Saint-Paul, 1996).

Unemployment is determined by an expectation augmented Phillips-curve:

$$U = U^n - a(\pi - \pi^e) + \varepsilon, \text{ with}$$ (6.17)

$$\pi^e = E(\pi).$$ (6.18)

U^n is the natural rate of unemployment, π^e is the rationally expected inflation rate and ε is a stochastic i.i.d. shock. The parameter a characterizes the extent of nominal wage rigidities, i.e. the intensity with which real wages react to non-anticipated changes in the price level. If the government reduces the inflation rate by one percentage point per year it has to accept a additional percentage points of unemployment. Therefore, the parameter a can be considered as the sacrifice ratio (Layard et al., 1994).

An additional significant deviation from the standard Barro-Gordon-model is the assumption that the natural rate of unemployment depends on the chosen degree of labour market reform r in a linear fashion:

$$U^n = \tilde{u} - \delta r,$$ (6.19)

where $\tilde{u}$ is the natural unemployment in the absence of labour market reforms ($r = 0$) and δ represents the marginal effectiveness of reforms with respect to the reduction of structural unemployment (Blanchard and Giavazzi 2003) and for a non-lines relation Calmfors and Holmlund (2000).

In the following, we first analyze a *one-period game*, in which politicians determine labour market institutions and monetary policy. Decisions on the labour market institutions are made before stochastic exogenous shocks occur. They take the inflation-reaction function into consideration. Once the decision on the labour market arrangement is made, it is irreversible. Monetary policy is characterized by more flexibility. Under flexible exchange rates, the central bank is able to react to stochastic shocks within a period and can stabilize such shocks.

6.3.6 Results from the Benchmark Model I: Credible Commitment to a Strict Monetary Policy Rule

In order to develop a reference scenario, it is assumed that national politicians can be committed to a credible and optimal monetary policy rule. This could be attained either by membership in a currency union with an inflation-averse central bank, or by entering a credible exchange rate peg (Calmfors, 1998, p. 29).[16] The optimization problem consists of simultaneously identifying a monetary policy rule and the degree of labour market reforms that minimize the government's loss function.[17] Which values of π, π^e and r minimize Eq. (6.16) taking into account Eqs. (6.17) and (6.18) under the assumption of rational expectations?

If the natural and the targeted level of unemployment ($U^n = U^*$) are equal, the politicians choose the same inflation rate as in the case of the optimal monetary policy rule (Barro & Gordon, 1983b, p. 597; Svensson, 1997, pp. 101ff.). The optimization must therefore be carried out with respect to the condition $U^n = U^*$. Taking rational expectations into account and substituting π^* the optimal monetary policy rule yields:

$$\pi = \pi^* + (a/(\lambda + a^2))\varepsilon. \tag{6.20}$$

In the optimum, the inflation target π^* is pursued. To stabilize exogenous shocks, however, deviations from the inflation target are allowed for.

On average, neglecting the i.i.d. shocks,[18] the degree of labour market reforms amounts to:

$$-\delta(U^n - U^*) + \gamma r = 0 \tag{6.21}$$

or equivalently to:

$$r* = \delta(\tilde{u} - U^*)/(\gamma + \delta^2). \tag{6.22}$$

Equations (6.21) and (6.22) have a number of interesting implications. The degree of labour market reforms is chosen so that the marginal utility of a lower equilibrium unemployment (i.e. the deviation of structural from targeted unemployment weighted with the marginal efficiency of labour market reforms $-\delta(U^n - U^*)$) is equal to the marginal costs of reforms (γr). What is the economic intuition behind these results? The degree of labour market reforms is positively related to the level of structural unemployment without reforms and the deviation of the

---

[16]McCallum (1995) and Jensen (1997) both refer to the problem that the combination of "delegation and proper incentive schemes" is not able to eliminate the inflation bias completely as long as a discretionary national stabilization policy is maintained.

[17]Concerning the structure of the game, the expected loss function should be minimized. But for clarity of exposition, the expectations operator is left out.

[18]Strictly speaking, the monetary rule can in this case simply be expressed as a k-percent rule without feedback component.

structural from the politically targeted unemployment respectively ($\delta r * / \delta \tilde{u} > 0$). The degree of labour market reforms is nevertheless negatively related to the marginal costs of reforms ($\delta r * / \delta \gamma < 0$). Simultaneously, the degree of labour market reforms is independent of the nominal level of rigidities ($\delta r * / \delta a = 0$). Let us now turn to the analysis of discretionary policy, which is only possible if there is monetary policy autonomy.

6.3.7 Autonomy Results from the Benchmark Model II: Discretion and Time Inconsistency of Optimal Monetary Policy

The empirical literature on the time inconsistency problem of optimal monetary policy shows that it is realistic to model the economic decision process of discretionary monetary policy as a *two-stage game*. In the first stage, wage contracts are fixed on the basis of expected inflation. Moreover, the degree of labour market reforms is determined and exogenous stochastic shocks are realized. In the second stage, monetary policy sets its course in a discretionary way. One reason to suppose a discretionary character of the game is the low probability of successfully implementing credible commitments to an ex ante optimal monetary policy if the monetary policy institution is autonomous and has some leeway to act.

The optimization approach in our model essentially remains the same as in the commitment case analyzed in the previous section. The equation to determine the optimal inflation rate π^{opt} has remained unchanged (see Eq. (6.20)). However, the solution has become more complicated because in the discretionary case (remember the case of "surprise inflation" in the ordinary Barro Gordon framework) it cannot a priori taken for granted that $U^n = U^*$ is still valid. Taking rational expectations into account and substituting π^e yields the following monetary reaction function:

$$\pi = \pi^* + (a/\lambda)(U^n - U^*) + (a/(\lambda + a^2))\varepsilon. \tag{6.23}$$

In comparison to the commitment case, the additional term $(a/\lambda)(U^n - U^*)$ emerges on the RHS. It can directly be traced back to the time inconsistency problem. Several aspects of this result shed light on the relation between different monetary regimes and labour market reforms. It is significant that the degree of the inflation bias does not only dependent on λ, the relative weight of the inflation target in the loss function, but also on parameters which – directly or indirectly – are related to labour market reforms. First, there is the dependence on natural unemployment U^n which is according to Eq. (6.23) directly and negatively influenced by labour market reforms. Second, the sacrifice ratio a considerably affects the level of the inflation bias.[19]

---

[19] An increase of nominal rigidities intensifies the credibility problem of monetary policy. Hence, the incentive of politicians to reduce the increasing credibility problem by more labour market reforms expands. However, this effect should be – and actually is according to the extensive calibrations by Belke and Kamp (1999a, 1999b), Sect. 4.3 – less relevant in reality if the nominal rigidities are diminished by market-oriented reforms, resulting in higher wage flexibility.

In the first stage of the game, politicians decide on the degree of reforms, taken the inflation reaction function as given. They select r in such a way that the expected loss function (6.16) is minimized under the conditions of Eqs. (6.17), (6.19), and (6.23). In contrast to the previous section, the reaction function for the inflation rate is directly implemented in the loss function and not added as an additional condition. When fixing the degree of labour market reform denoted by r, the politicians have to consider that the equilibrium inflation rate depends on the level of natural unemployment. However, the realization of the stochastic shock is not recognized until the ex ante optimal degree of reforms is fixed. Therefore, not only the stochastic part of Eq. (6.23) – $(\pi^* + (a/\lambda)(U^n - U^*))$ – is used. After optimization, the degree of labour market reform is:

$$\gamma r - \delta(U^n - U^*) - \frac{a^2\delta}{\lambda}(U^n - U^*) = 0, \tag{6.24}$$

or, alternatively, after some rearrangement:

$$r* = \frac{\delta(a^2 + \lambda)}{\delta^2(a^2 + \lambda) + \gamma\lambda}(\tilde{u} - U^*). \tag{6.25}$$

In Eq. (6.24), the marginal utility of lower equilibrium unemployment equals the marginal cost of labour market reform. In comparison to the commitment case, an additional marginal utility component, $-a^2\delta(U^n - U^*)/\lambda$, is contained. It can be directly related to the increased utility of a smaller inflation bias $(a/\lambda)(U^n - U^*)$ which is induced by the implementation of reforms.

Most important in our context, it can be shown that the *degree of labour market reforms* is *less in the commitment case* than in the case of autonomous and, hence, discretionary monetary policy. For that purpose, the RHS of Eq. (6.25) – the degree of reforms under discretionary policy – and the RHS of Eq. (6.22) – the degree of reforms under commitment – are compared.

$$\frac{\delta(a^2 + \lambda)}{\delta^2(a^2 + \lambda) + \gamma\lambda}(\tilde{u} - U^*) - \frac{\delta}{(\gamma + \delta^2)}(\tilde{u} - U^*) =$$
$$\left[\frac{\delta(a^2 + \lambda)}{\delta^2(a^2 + \lambda) + \gamma\lambda} - \frac{\delta(a^2 + \lambda)}{\delta^2(a^2 + \lambda) + \gamma(a^2 + \lambda)}\right](\tilde{u} - U^*) > 0? \tag{6.26}$$

Obviously, this inequality is fulfilled because $\gamma(a^2 + \lambda)$ in the denominator of the second fraction is larger than $\gamma\lambda$ in the denominator of the first fraction. Both fractions only differ by these two parts. The degree of reforms is therefore higher in the case of autonomous policy (discretion) and lower in the case of commitment.

If monetary policy is autonomous, labour market reforms seem to achieve a "*double dividend*" since monetary policy is discretionary. First, the reforms directly reduce – like a rule-based monetary policy – the costs of structural unemployment. Secondly, they indirectly also lessen the level of equilibrium inflation since they diminish the credibility problem of discretionary monetary policy. The second effect is absent in the case of rule-based monetary policy. By definition, rule-based monetary policy does not suffer from a genuine credibility problem. Hence, one of the current central research questions relates to the correlation between reform intensity and the degree of autonomy of monetary policy, which might be determined to a large degree by the exchange rate regime, at least if the country is small and open (Duval & Elmeskov, 2005, pp. 9 and 23ff.). In the following, we focus on the notion of monetary policy *autonomy* instead of discretion since we consider autonomy as an important *prerequisite* of discretionary monetary policy. In this respect, our approach strictly follows Duval and Elmeskov (2005, p. 25) who measure the loss of autonomy of monetary policy by the degree of participation in any kind of fixed exchange rate agreement.

However, the observed reduction of inflation rates and perhaps also the increasing independence of national central banks in a currency union like, e.g., EMU may well be interpreted as mere temporary phenomena. Possibly, both phenomena are not sustainable but merely due to the intention to qualify for EMU at a certain point in time or at least to leave this opportunity open for the near future (Ozkan, Sibert, & Sutherland, 1997).

6.3.8 Welfare Comparisons of Different Monetary Policy Regimes

With an eye on the results derived in the preceding sections that discretionary policy with higher equilibrium inflation, one might be tempted to conclude that a higher degree of reforms and lower unemployment is generally superior to a rule-based monetary policy with a strong commitment. For instance, at the dawn of EMU some analysts argued exactly along these lines in the late nineties that it would be worthwhile for an EU country in terms of welfare to stay out of the euro area. However, in order to avoid premature conclusions on this politically important aspect, a formal welfare comparison of both alternatives is executed explicitly. Inserting the equilibrium values of employment, reform and inflation under both regimes which were calculated above into the loss function and comparing the results, leads to:

$$L(R) - L(D) = \frac{1}{2}(\tilde{u} - U^*)^2 \left[\frac{\delta^2(a^2 + \lambda)^2}{\delta^2(a^2 + \lambda)\lambda + \gamma\lambda^2} - \frac{\delta^2}{\gamma + \delta^2} - \frac{a^2}{\lambda} \right] \leq 0, \quad (6.27)$$

respectively.

$$L(R) - L(D) = \frac{1}{2}(\tilde{u} - U^*)^2 \left[-\frac{a^2\gamma^2}{(\delta^2(a^2 + \lambda) + \gamma\lambda)(\gamma + \delta^2)} \right] \leq 0. \quad (6.28)$$

The difference $L(R) - L(D)$ characterises the advantage of discretionary policy (stochastic shocks are neglected). It turns out that a monetary policy *rule* is generally *superior* to discretionary monetary policy. The difference between the welfare under a discretionary regime and a rule-based regime proves to be negative in general (see, for instance, Belke & Kamp, 1999a). This result might be surprising. However, it can be explained quite easily in economic terms.

Under discretionary monetary policy, labour-market reforms turn out to be more trenchant and come out to be more successful for the same reason (as measured by the degree of lowering the structural unemployment rate), simply because they are needed more pressingly. Insofar as a superior (and in the ideal case a perfect) instrument is available for the parallel reduction of the equilibrium inflation rate, namely a strict monetary policy rule, the higher degree of labour-market reforms under discretionary monetary policy only signals a kind of an overshooting.

6.3.9   Putting the Model into Perspective: Conditions for More Reforms Under a Discretionary Regime

According to the previous analysis, the incentives for market oriented reforms turn out to be higher under a discretionary monetary regime than under a rule-based regime: A lower equilibrium unemployment rate (as a result of structural reforms) reduces the *inflation bias*. Having said that, the problem of inflation bias can be reduced by market oriented reforms, which represent a second best substitute for a rule-based monetary policy.

If one considers that market-oriented reforms might reduce both the equilibrium unemployment and the nominal/real wage rigidities, the above mentioned effect is even reinforced. Both the degree of employment reaction to unanticipated monetary policy and the inflation bias itself are lowered by diminished rigidities. Taking the impacts of market-oriented reforms on the degree of nominal wage rigidities into account, the positive effect of discretionary policy on the implementation probability of market-oriented reforms is underlined. When the effect of unexpected inflation on employment is lowered, the incentive of politicians to deviate from a previously announced policy is reduced (Belke & Kamp, 1999a, 1999b).

With respect to the impact of nominal wage rigidities, there exists an additional argument which also favours more reform under monetary policy discretion. If downward nominal wage rigidities exist and at the same time the general level of inflation is low (as currently in most EU-countries and also observable worldwide), real wage reductions which are caused by market-oriented reforms and their effects on equilibrium unemployment are achieved only very slowly. In this case, a lot of time goes by until successful market-oriented reforms achieve positive employment gains (Akerlof, Dickens, & Perry, 1996; Carey, 1997; Gordon, 1996). With low inflation rates, a longer term negative relationship between inflation and equilibrium unemployment prevails. This leads to a non-linear long-run Phillips-curve. The lower the level of inflation is, the stronger are the incentives to inflate since the marginal gains of inflation, in the form of a lower natural rate of unemployment, rise with decreasing inflation (Calmfors, 1997, p. 24).

In the case of downward rigid real wages, real wage reductions which are necessary for the cutback of equilibrium unemployment and the enforcement of structural changes are not achieved by labour market reforms, at least in the short term. If the resistance of the affected interest groups against the implemented reforms simultaneously increases, the endurance of reforms without an accommodating monetary policy gets less and less credible. Uncertainties about the degree of real wage reductions caused by reforms and on the return on investment would lead to a lower present value of a *wait and see reform strategy* in the case of accommodating demand policy (Bean, 1998). Efficient market-oriented reforms are more likely hold out if they are accompanied by an expansive demand policy. A good timing with a fast and perceptible positive effect on employment reduces political resistance against reforms. This is the now famous *two-handed approach* originally proposed by Blanchard et al. (1986). However, monetary policy can only be varied in the absence of a fixed monetary policy rule. Additionally, one can argue that accommodating monetary policy is the suitable response on a negative supply shock in an inflation targeting regime. If reforms lead to a reduction in nominal wage growth, a negative deviation from the national consumer price index and the inflation target might be the result (Calmfors, 1998, pp. 32ff.).

In times of steadily increasing unemployment, e.g., in some continental European countries, it should also be taken into account that the degree of reforms should increase if unemployment is persistent and, hence, the inflation bias is larger (Alesina & Rosenthal, 1989; Jonsson, 1997; Svensson, 1997). Finally, the degree of reforms tend to be lower if credible entry conditions for a club of countries subordinated to a monetary rule are formulated (for instance, the Maastricht criteria for EMU) because lower inflation expectations lead to lower actual inflation rates without reform.

6.3.10 Conditions Favoring More Reforms Under a Rule-Based Regime

In our model some scenarios are possible where the incentives for structural reforms are higher in a rule-based regime. If employment fluctuations are assessed the more serious, the higher the average rate of unemployment is a precautionary motive for higher labour market reforms holds. The marginal utility of an unemployment decrease rises. Therefore, the marginal utility of reforms is sufficiently higher under a rule-based regime than under a discretionary regime only if the volatility of employment is higher under the rule-based regime than in the case of policy discretion (Calmfors, 1998, pp. 34ff.). Market-oriented reforms tend to achieve a stronger reaction of real wages to stochastic exogenous shocks. Since monetary policy is (because of the Lohmann trade-off) not unlimitedly at the disposal for stabilising asymmetric shocks,[20] this effect enhances the marginal utility and therefore creates a larger incentive to enact market-oriented reforms under a rule-based monetary policy than under a discretionary regime (see for example Layard, Jackman, & Nickell, 1991; Calmfors, 1997).

Additionally, the intensity of reforms in a rule-based regime is positively dependent on the degree of direct effects on structural unemployment resulting from the monetary policy rule. Employment effects of irrevocably fixed target inflation rates but also the corresponding effects of an accelerated structural change caused by a

---

[20]See Lohmann (1992). The Lohmann trade-off describes the trade-off between the utility of a monetary policy rule by commitment and the costs by the loss in flexibility.

monetary policy rule and the effects of a credible monetary policy on the wage-setting behaviour clearly belong to this aspect. If reforms have a positive impact on national structural unemployment the national degree of reforms increases and vice versa; the total effect remains therefore open to debate.

Moreover, one can imagine as a not remote possibility that the government might cancel an announced reform or does not realise it at all. If there are two time-inconsistency problems at the same time, first the traditional one concerning the inflation rate and second the incentive to deviate from a previously announced reform target, a rule-based monetary policy generally achieves a higher degree of reforms than discretionary monetary policy. In this setting, monetary policy rules are defined as regimes where the central bank can credibly commit itself to a target inflation rate and to a reform target. However, a discretionary regime cannot credibly commit itself to previously announce the inflation and the reform target. Therefore, the incentive to realise an announced reform target under a discretionary regime is rather low.

From the perspective of a national government, however, any reduction of reform, however, would lead to a subjective cost reduction and a rise in total economy welfare, without any pressure on wage contracts. The reason is that unions and management have already committed themselves to wage contracts. Private agents anticipate this mechanism and are not willing to negotiate low wages. Under a discretionary regime, an equilibrium with too high wages, too low employment and a too low degree of reforms is reached (Johansson, 1998).

Finally, if the inflation aversion λ is lowered by means of the appointment of a conservative government and/or conservative central bankers, would lower the tendency to more reforms under discretion.

6.3.11 Extension to the Open Economy Case

Economic openness is generally related to the share of exports and imports in GDP. A stronger exposure of firms to international competition is often assumed to increase the pressure and the incentives for market-oriented reforms. In open economies, output and employment tend to be highly responsive to price competitiveness so that there are stronger incentives to reform (Katzenstein, 1985; Nickell, 2005, pp. 2–3). However, empirical evidence is not especially supportive of the view that open economies are more likely to liberalize. Although Pitlik and Wirth (2003) report a positive impact of economic openness on market-oriented reforms, Herz and Vogel (2005) and Pitlik (2004) do not find robust significant coefficients of economic openness for their overall reform indicator. Only in the case of trade policy do they find a positive effect of economic openness on liberalization. Our above theoretical discussion seems to indicate a possible solution to this empirical puzzle. The key insight borrowed, for instance, from the political economy literature on openness, size of governments and reform efforts (Rodrik, 1996, and other papers by this author) is that more open economies are more

Table 6.1 Economic openness and exchange rate regimes 1970–2000

Degree of openness (Trade/ GDP)	Average	Median	Observations
< 0.25	2.65	2.93	60
0.25–0.75	2.27	2.00	471
0.75–1.25	1.98	2.00	200
> 1.25	1.51	1.00	59

Sources: The data on exchange rate flexibility are taken from Reinhart and Rogoff (2002). We measure economic openness as the sum of exports plus imports relative to GDP. The data are extracted from the World Development Indicators database (World Bank, 2002).

likely to implement rule-based exchange rate stabilization and, hence, generally implement less reforms. But is this really true?

Table 6.1 illustrates the empirical relation between economic openness and exchange rate policy in the overall sample of 123 countries. Exchange rate flexibility is measured on a scale from 1 (hard peg) to 4 (free float). The average and median statistics indicate that less open economies tend to have relatively flexible exchange rate regimes, whereas very open economies tend to favour currency pegs.

In the following we continue to assume that the main aim of reforms is to lower structural unemployment, and generalize the term monetary policy to include monetary and exchange rate policy. We equate the case of flexible exchange rates with an autonomous and discretionary monetary policy and use the notion of a fixed exchange rate system in cases which we originally addressed as rule-based monetary policy. But is this generalization legitimate? Can we interpret our model in terms of exchange rate regimes instead of monetary policy regimes?

As a stylized fact, money in an open economy is not controlled autonomously by the central bank but is determined endogenously by the exchange rate regime (Annett, 1993, p. 25; Krugman & Obstfeld, 2003, Chaps. 16 and 17). From early political business cycle research it is well-known that especially in the case of small open economies there is little evidence of high and increasing inflation rates under left-wing governments and low and diminishing inflation rates under right-wing regimes as a pattern of rational partisan cycles (e.g. Alesina & Roubini, 1992, p. 680; Annett, 1993, pp. 25 and 42). In the standard literature, the failure to establish partisan cycles is generally traced back to the fact that small open economies tend to have fixed exchange rates and, hence, the ability of these countries to exert an ide-ologically motivated impact on the inflation rate is limited.[21] If the limited degree of monetary policy autonomy under fixed exchange rates is raised by choosing a flexible exchange rate regime, there is more scope for partisan-oriented monetary policies. Wage negotiating parties tend to anticipate and account for different preferences of political parties only if exchange rates are flexible. Only in this case,

---

[21] See Alogoskoufis, Lockwood, and Philippopoulos (1992, p. 1384) and Ellis and Thoma (1990, pp. 17 and 24).

incumbent governments are able to manipulate the inflation rate by monetary and exchange rate policies. Hence, higher inflation rates under left-wing governments induced by a dynamic inconsistency problem can only arise, if exchange rates are flexible.[22]

A second argument underpins this view. Assume the existence of an international business cycle. In more open economies partisan considerations that arise at the domestic level are more likely to affect policymakers' incentives to engage in international cooperation. Left-wing governments cannot credibly commit themselves to international cooperation and prefer beggar-thy-neighbor policies so that the inflation bias of left-wing governments even increases in open economies. International cooperation by means of fixed exchange rate arrangements tends to eliminate the inflation bias via the same mechanism (Lohmann, 1993, p. 1374). The final argument in favor of our approach is that the hypothesis of a loss of monetary autonomy under fixed exchange rates rests on the assumption of capital which is perfectly mobile. International capital mobility has increased dramatically since the 1970s, the beginning of our estimation period.

Empirical studies of the rational partisan theory clearly show that – assuming a monetary model of the exchange rate – party-specific trajectories of money growth and inflation rates go along with proportional movements of the exchange rate. For instance, left-wing governments are more likely to experience inflation, capital flight, current account deficits and currency devaluation.[23] Hence, we feel justified to equate a flexible exchange rate system with a regime of autonomous and discretionary monetary policy and a system of fixed exchange rates with a rule-based monetary policy regime. Accordingly, the arguments that have been elaborated for the concepts "rule-based versus discretionary monetary policy" are transferred to the discussion of "fixed versus flexible exchange rate systems" and can be tested empirically in a straightforward fashion.

Reforms, Exchange Rates and Monetary Commitment – A Panel Analysis for OECD Countries

Belke et al. (2006), Belke, Herz, and Vogel (2007) were among the first to investigate the link between monetary policy and structural reforms in open economies. They test three hypotheses: (i) the Calmfors hypothesis according to which the degree of reforms is higher in the case of autonomous policy and lower in the case of commitment, (ii) the TINA hypothesis which implies a positive impact of a monetary policy rule on the extent of reforms, and (iii) a

---

[22]See Alesina and Roubini (1992, pp. 673–674), Alogoskoufis and Philippopoulos (1992, p. 397), Alogoskoufis et al. (1992, pp. 1370–1371), and Annett (1993, pp. 25 and 33).

[23]See Simmons (1994, p. 59), Ellis and Thoma (1990) estimate rational partisan theory approaches for open economies. In their study, party-specific inflation rates lead to party specific differences in exchange rate movements.

third factors hypothesis: if third factors dominate the relationship, monetary commitment should have little effect on reforms. Empirical estimations are performed with panel data on 23 OECD countries from 1980 to 2000 (three decennial periods). The structural reforms are proxied by the Economic Freedom of the World index whereas the monetary policy constraint is measured by a monetary commitment index and, alternatively, the exchange rate regime. The authors find little evidence of the Calmfors hypothesis, but evidence in favour of the TINA argument for labor-market and regulatory reform.

Hypotheses

The following section investigates the existence of a significant empirical correlation between monetary commitment and market liberalization conditional on the additional impact factors, such as the macroeconomic environment and political or institutional restrictions to economic reform. Hence, we test for a significant coefficient of monetary commitment in regressions using reform indices as the dependent variable. From Sects. 6.1, 6.2, and 6.3, we can derive the following hypotheses:

(1) If the view of an excessive intensity of reforms under monetary policy autonomy holds, labor market reforms will be stronger under higher monetary discretion, net of other factors.
(2) If the TINA-view of monetary commitment as a hard constraint is valid, one should expect the contrary, however. In this case monetary discretion negatively affects the degree of labor market reforms, net of other factors.

According to the sections above, this should be valid not only for labor market reforms but also for complementary reforms in the goods and the financial markets and, hence, in this sense also for a broader reform index. The latter typically comprises the major areas: (i) money and banking system, (ii) government size, (iii) freedom to trade, (iv) market regulation and (v) labor-market regulation.

(3) If third factors dominate the relationship, monetary commitment should have little effect on reforms, monetary commitment should have little effect on reforms.

Data and Definitions

We estimate and test the conjectured impact of monetary commitment on the degree of market-oriented reforms based on a panel of 23 OECD economies for the period 1970–2000.[24] Restricting our empirical analysis to this group of countries ensures a relatively homogeneous institutional setup. As dependent variable we use the extent of economic liberalization as measured by the Economic Freedom of the World (EFW) index and the sub-indices *money and banking system, freedom to trade, government size and labor market, credit and business regulation*, respectively (Gwartney & Lawson 2003; Gwartney, Lawson, Park, & Skipton, 2003). The empirical realizations of these indices range from one to ten, with a high value corresponding to a high level of economic freedom. The EFW index and the sub-indices are available in five-year intervals over the period 1970–2000.[25] An increase in the index value indicates a market-oriented reform. Hence, we use wider reform indicators and a wider time span than Duval and Elmeskov (2005), who investigate data from five policy areas: unemployment benefit systems, labor taxes, employment protection legislation, product market regulation and retirement schemes.

Among the explaining variables, our discussion focuses on the measure of monetary commitment (MC). We proxy the monetary commitment by the Freytag (2005) indicator. MC is a composed index, restricted to values between 0 and 1. Higher values indicate a stronger monetary commitment. MC consists of ten criteria such as the central bank's personal and political independence, the importance of price stability as an objective, and lending restrictions for the central bank (Freytag, 2005). The index is calculated as the non-weighted average of these criteria and comparable to Cukierman's (1992) index of central bank independence. In contrast to the latter, however, the variable MC includes information about external relations like the submission to an exchange-rate target, which appears quite appropriate in our open economy context (Freytag, 2005).

There are two theoretical reasons for these extensions: first, with a political decision about the exchange rate regime, especially in the case of a currency peg, governments are able to counter the central bank's monetary policy – thereby seriously questioning central bank independence. Second, if monetary reforms are backed by an exchange rate peg as a nominal anchor; external aspects become constitutive elements of the new monetary commitment.

---

[24]The 23 OECD economies correspond to the category high-income industrialized countries in the World Development Indicators database (World Bank, 2002) and cover Australia, Canada, the former EU-15, Iceland, Japan, New Zealand, Norway, Switzerland and the United States.

[25]We use the chain-weighted EFW index (Gwartney et al., 2003), which corrects for the limited availability of some components over time. Such chain-linked correction is only available for the summary indicator, however. For the sub-areas money and banking system, government size, freedom to trade, market regulation and labor-market regulation, we have to rely on uncorrected data instead. Missing data for indicator elements may distort the value of the sectoral indicators and distort the accuracy of these measures of economic reform.

The indicator is available for a set of high income countries only, which basically coincides with the 23 high-income OECD economies and also motivates
our restriction to this country sample. The data are available at decennial frequency only.

As an alternative proxy to account for monetary commitment we use
exchange rate flexibility (EXR) in our robustness checks. While the MC indicator includes legal aspects of the exchange rate regime and their impact on
monetary commitment, it does not account for the de facto implementation of
the exchange rate regime. As the de jure and de facto exchange rate regime of
a country may considerably differ, we employ the Reinhart and Rogoff (2002)
index of de facto exchange rate arrangements.[26] Reinhart and Rogoff (2002)
distinguish between exchange rate pegs (1), limited flexibility (2), managed
floating (3), and freely floating (4).[27] Thus, the index value increases in the de
facto exchange rate flexibility. For our purpose and due to the time structure of
the EFW data, we average the Reinhart and Rogoff (2002) index values over
ten-year intervals. Note that the monetary commitment indicator MC and our
measure of exchange rate flexibility both measure monetary policy autonomy,
but on an inverse scale.

The additional control variables that we consider include inflation, economic growth, real per capita GDP and openness as proxies of the pressure to
reform. Data are available from the World Development Indicators database
(World Bank, 2002). Economic openness is defined as exports plus imports
relative to GDP. To account for the potential endogeneity and in accordance
with other contributions (Herz & Vogel, 2005; Lora, 2000; Pitlik, 2004; Pitlik
& Wirth, 2003), we use these variables in first lags. A final set of controls
accounts for political and institutional barriers to policy reforms. Here we
include POLCON5 and the number of government changes. POLCON5
(Henisz, 2000, 2002) measures the effective political restrictions on executive
behavior. It accounts for the veto powers of the executive, two legislative
chambers, the sub-national entities and an independent judiciary. The index
ranges from zero to one, where a higher value indicates stronger political
constraints on the government. Given the time structure of our dependent
variable, we take average values of POLCON5 for the respective decade.
If political constraints and economic reforms were negatively correlated,

[26]The de facto measure improves on the de jure classification of IMF (2003) since it takes
into account that de jure exchange rate regimes are not necessarily applied in practice. This
has especially been the case in developing countries but also in industrialized countries.
Austria, e.g., had a de facto fixed exchange rate regime vis-à-vis Germany for a long time
without being a formal member of the exchange rate mechanism of the EMS. See Hochreiter
and Tavlas (2005).
[27]Reinhart and Rogoff (2002) include freely falling rates as an additional category. We add
the cases of freely falling rates to the free-float category, however.

we should obtain a significant negative coefficient on POLCON5.[28] GOVCHANGES counts the number of government changes in each period that entail a significant programmatic reorientation. The data are taken from Beck, Clarke, Groff, Keefer, and Walsh (2001). One could argue that frequent changes shorten the administration's time horizon and cause a stronger discounting of positive future payoffs. If frequent government changes decreased the credibility and reliability of economic policy and the government's decisiveness to reform, we should expect a significant negative coefficient for GOVCHANGES.

Empirical Model and Results

Empirical Model

To empirically analyze the role of monetary commitment, economic crisis, and political as well as institutional features for economic reform we estimate the equation:

$$\Delta EFW_{it} = \alpha_0 + \alpha_1 EFW_{i,t-1} + \alpha_2 MC_{it} + \alpha_3' X_{i,t-1} + \alpha_4' Y_{it} + \eta_i + \lambda_t + \varepsilon_{it},$$

where ΔEFW represents our index of reforms, i.e. the change in economic freedom, or the respective sub-indices. MC is our measure of monetary commitment, X is the vector of macroeconomic variables (growth, inflation, openness, per-capita GDP), Y captures the political and institutional impact on the capacity to reform, and i is a country index. Most importantly and according to the Calmfors perspective on labor market reform, we expect $\alpha_2 < 0$ for MC, and $\alpha_2 > 0$ under the EXR indicator, if monetary commitment and structural reforms were substitutes. The TINA-view should give the contrary, namely $\alpha_2 > 0$ for MC and $\alpha_2 > 0$ for EXR.

We add time-specific effects (λ_t) to account for unobserved heterogeneity across time. The short time dimension of our sample complicates the use of country fixed effects. As there are three observations per country at best, any estimate of individual effects would be very imprecise, and the insertion of country dummies would significantly reduce the degrees of freedom in the estimation. For this reason we do not include country dummies in our regression.

---

[28]Note that the political constraints may restrict changes in either direction, however. They may limit both liberalization and the restriction of economic freedom. Further evidence may be derived from an interaction between political constraints and the government's programmatic orientation. This extension is beyond the paper's focus, however. Herz and Vogel (2005) and Pitlik (2004) provide an in-depth discussion of the impact of political constraints.

The empirical model includes the lagged dependent variable among the regressors, which biases OLS estimates. In a first step we apply the GLS estimator that allows estimation in the presence of both heteroskedasticity and first-order residual autocorrelation (Baltagi, 1995; Hsiao, 2003). Secondly, we present GMM system estimates (Arellano & Bover, 1995; Blundell & Bond, 1998). We report the one-step estimates with robust standard error, which are to be preferred with potentially heteroskedastic error terms (Arellano & Bond, ;1991).[29]

Results

This section presents the regression results for our sample of OECD economies. We report the regression results for *overall liberalization, money and banking system, government size, freedom to trade, market regulation* and the sub-index *labor-market regulation* as dependent variables. Table 6.2 displays the GLS and Table 6.3 dynamic panel GMM estimates.

The two tables indicate a negative impact of initial levels of economic freedom on trade policy and labor market reform. The negative coefficients support the conjecture that higher initial levels of economic freedom reduce the scope and need for further liberalization. They also indicate a conditional convergence in economic policy (Duval & Elmeskov, 2005). Table 6.2 suggests similar results for the overall index of economic reforms, money and banking sector reform and government sector reform. Table 6.3 shows that the latter coefficient estimates are not robust against GMM however.

The paper focuses on the correlation between monetary commitment and market-oriented reforms. Tables 6.2 and 6.3 indicate a positive impact of monetary commitment on labor market reform. The GLS estimates in Table 6.2 furthermore suggest negative correlation between monetary commitment and money and banking sector, whereas GMM obtains a significantly positive commitment coefficient for overall regulatory reform. Neither of the coefficients is robust over both tables however. Trade policy, government size and the overall economic liberalization are uncorrelated with monetary commitment across the board.

With regard to the Calmfors hypothesis, the positive relation between monetary commitment and labor-market reform is the key finding. Notably, our estimates do not support the Calmfors hypothesis on labor-market reforms and its basic conclusion. We find no evidence for a negative impact of monetary commitment on labor-market reform. Both policies rather seem to

---

[29]The Sargan test for instrument validity is taken from the two-step estimates, however, because the one-step statistics tends to over-reject the test in the presence of heteroskedasticity (Arellano & Bond, 1991).

Table 6.2 Reforms and monetary commitment – GLS estimates with commitment indicator

	EFW	Money	Government size	Trade	Regulation	Labor market
Monetary	-0.24	**-0.90***	-0.04	-0.40	0.53	2.17**
commitment	(-0.77)	(-1.79)	(-0.05)	(-0.62)	(1.48)	**(2.41)**
EFW, M, G, T,	**-0.17***	**-0.48****	**-0.36****	**-0.56****	-0.03	**-0.23****
R, LM (t–1)	(-1.67)	(-5.54)	(-3.98)	(-5.19)	(-0.34)	**(-2.24)**
Inflation (t–1)	**2.41****	-3.20	**4.60***	**-3.29***	**1.70***	-0.30
	(2.79)	(-1.65)	(2.37)	(-1.80)	(2.23)	**(-0.08)**
Growth (t–1)	0.32	**11.0***	-9.09	-6.78	-3.00	-0.47
	(0.12)	(2.17)	(-1.33)	(-1.18)	(-0.94)	**(-0.06)**
Openness (t–1)	-0.16	0.28	-0.65	0.32	-0.08	-0.65
	(-1.02)	(1.25)	(-1.18)	(0.89)	(-0.43)	**(-0.97)**
LnRGDPpc (t–1)	0.28	**1.79****	-0.07	-0.48	-0.13	-0.18
	(1.12)	(4.37)	(-0.10)	(-0.92)	(-0.44)	(-0.18)
POLCON5	0.04	-1.42	**2.99***	2.19	0.77	1.00
	(0.06)	(-1.42)	(1.80)	(1.46)	(1.03)	**(0.53)**
GOVCHANGES	-0.02	-0.04	-0.06	-0.12	0.02	**0.09**
	(-0.29)	(-0.32)	(-0.39)	(-0.93)	(0.24)	**(0.54)**
Constant	-1.88	**-12.5****	-0.33	7.46	0.82	**1.60**
	(-0.90)	(-3.69)	(-0.05)	(1.63)	(0.33)	**(1.17)**
D1980s	0.63***	1.35***	0.91***	0.48	-0.24	**-0.10**
D1990s	1.04***	1.03***	1.16***	0.95**	0.91***	**-0.67**
AR (1) (p-value)	0.96	0.43	0.81	0.42	0.10*	**0.79**
R^2	0.77	0.72	0.77	0.45	0.73	**0.32**
Observations	**58**	**58**	**58**	**58**	57	51

Note: */**/*** indicates significance at the 10/5/1 percent level.

be complements, which supports the alternative TINA-view of monetary commitment as a hard constraint.

Most of the control variables are insignificant in most cases. If anything, political constraints have a positive rather than a negative impact on economic reform. We find a significant positive coefficient for government size across both tables. The result is compatible with the estimates of Pitlik (2004) for a larger and more diverse country sample and in line with his interpretation of political constraints as a commitment device. It may furthermore reflect the fact that constraints also tend to reduce the reversibility of reforms. The coefficient estimates for the number of government changes, which could be interpreted as an indicator for credibility and political commitment, are largely insignificant, a result which contrasts Herz and Vogel (2005) and Pitlik (2004) for larger country samples and shorter time intervals.

The macroeconomic control variables play a limited role in our regressions. High inflation which could indicate a greater need for reform has a robust

Table 6.3 Reforms and monetary commitment – 1-step GMM system estimates with commitment indicator

	EFW	Money	Government size	Trade	Regulation	Labor market
Monetary	−0.38	0.39	0.12	0.01	**0.77****	1.59**
commitment	(−0.73)	(0.25)	(0.13)	(0.02)	(2.29)	**(2.20)**
EFW, M, G, T,	0.34	0.21	−0.18	**−0.57*****	−0.23	−0.43**
R, LM (t–1)	(0.72)	(0.26)	(−0.94)	(−4.02)	(−1.54)	**(−2.38)**
Inflation (t–1)	**6.00*****	16.6	**4.62*****	**−1.80***	1.20	−1.17
	(3.17)	(1.31)	(3.56)	(−1.74)	(1.44)	**(−0.35)**
Growth (t–1)	5.15	**23.4****	**−13.7***	−3.85	−2.30	0.10
	(1.23)	(2.28)	(−1.77)	(−0.70)	(−0.82)	**(0.01)**
Openness (t–1)	−0.20	−0.12	−0.61	0.17	−0.13	−1.33
	(−1.02)	(−0.21)	(−1.09)	(0.52)	(−0.51)	**(−1.30)**
LnRGDPpc (t–1)	−0.04	0.53	0.13	−0.38	0.02	**0.37**
	(−0.09)	(0.25)	(0.20)	(−0.96)	(0.06)	**(0.51)**
POLCON5	−1.04	0.44	**2.93*****	**2.76****	0.68	1.89
	(−0.73)	(0.18)	(2.85)	(2.55)	(1.10)	**(1.13)**
GOVCHANGES	0.08	**0.41***	−0.05	−0.03	0.06	−0.02
	(0.86)	(1.73)	(−0.25)	(−0.25)	(0.87)	**(−0.19)**
Constant	−1.97	−9.67	−3.20	5.72	0.46	**−1.64**
	(−0.83)	(−0.72)	(−0.46)	(1.61)	(0.13)	**(−0.42)**
D1980s	0.68*	0.89**	1.06***	0.40	−0.18	**−0.07**
D1990s	1.09***	0.83	1.14**	0.80**	0.89***	**−0.67**
AR (1) (p-value)	0.01***	0.01***	0.05**	0.07*	0.02**	**0.49**
Sargan test (p-value)	0.90	0.15	0.35	0.24	0.30	**0.09***
Observations	**58**	**58**	**58**	**58**	**57**	**51**

Note: */**/*** indicates significance at the 10/5/1 percent level.

and positive impact on overall economic liberalization and the fiscal sector, but a negative impact on trade liberalization across both tables. The positive coefficient estimates are in line with Drazen and Easterly (2001) and Pitlik and Wirth (2003). Both studies consider more severe crises in their broader country sample, however. Our results indicate that in OECD countries smaller increases in inflation suffice to trigger structural reforms than in low and middle income countries.[30] Higher growth as an indicator of either the ability to

---

[30]The effect is limited, however. Given the estimates in Table 6.3, a one percentage-point inflation increase leads to 0.06 additional points on the reform index during the subsequent decade.

reform or the lack of pressure has a robust positive impact on money and banking system reform, whereas the negative impact on government sector reform only appears under GLS. The latter result coincides with the skeptic perspective that, if anything, governments react to fiscal pressure instead of pushing for consolidation in good times.

The estimates for economic openness are generally insignificant. The same holds for per-capita GDP, except in the GLS estimate for monetary and banking reform. The insignificance of economic openness does not support the hypothesis that the exposure to world markets increases the pressure for liberalization and that it leads to stronger market-oriented reforms. The time dummies are significant in most cases and indicate that, on average, monetary sector reform was especially pronounced during the 1980s and that overall, government size, trade-policy and regulatory reform were particularly prevalent during the 1990s.

Taken together, the estimates do not support the Calmfors hypothesis, which conjectures that monetary discretion promotes structural reforms and that monetary commitment and reforms are substitutes net of other factors. In contrast, we find evidence for the TINA hypothesis in market, especially labor-market regulation. Our result points to monetary commitment and labor market reforms being complements rather than substitutes.

Robustness Checks

To check our results with respect to the key hypothesis, we apply an alternative indicator for monetary commitment, namely *exchange rate flexibility*. In an open economy, flexible exchange rates closely correspond with monetary autonomy and the feasibility of monetary discretion, whereas an exchange rate peg indicates the adoption of a monetary rule. Monetary commitment does not necessarily imply a fixed exchange rate, however. Instead, a central bank may pursue inflation or monetary targeting. As discussed above, our exchange rate indicator accounts for the realization of the de facto exchange rate regime and might therefore provide additional information to the MC indicator, which focuses on de jure aspects of monetary commitment. Hence, we check the robustness of our results by using exchange rate flexibility to account for another important aspect of monetary autonomy.

Table 6.4 displays the results of this check. We focus on the estimates for exchange-rate commitment. The control estimates corroborate the results in Table 6.3 with regard to the insignificance of openness and initial per capita income, the mixed impact of inflation – positive on overall economic reform and public sector consolidation, negative on trade liberalization – and the rather positive effect of political constraints on liberalization.

Table 6.4   Reforms and monetary commitment – 1-step GMM system estimates with exchange-rate indicator

	EFW	Money	Government size	Trade	Regulation	Labor market
EXR flexibility	−0.09	**−0.36***	**0.24***	**−0.35****	0.00	−0.38
	(−1.03)	(1.79)	(1.80)	(−3.72)	(0.04)	**(−1.18)**
EFW, M, G, R,	−0.11	−0.23	−0.35	**−0.42****	**−0.36****	−0.23
T (t–1)	(−0.23)	(−0.48)	(−1.50)	(−2.74)	(−2.57)	**(−0.89)**
Inflation (t–1)	**3.76***	10.3	**3.97****	**−1.82****	1.38	−3.81
	(1.80)	(1.47)	(2.38)	(−2.09)	(1.39)	**(−1.12)**
Growth (t–1)	4.83	**23.0******	−6.42	−2.29	− 1.24	2.95
	(1.40)	(2.97)	(−1.16)	(−0.47)	(−0.47)	**(0.40)**
Openness (t–1)	−0.24	−0.30	0.03	−0.41	−0.08	−1.31
	(−0.69)	(−0.72)	(0.07)	(−1.46)	(−0.44)	**(−1.34)**
LnRGDPpc	0.27	1.87	−0.07	0.02	0.33	0.65
(t–1)	(0.50)	(1.61)	(−0.11)	(0.09)	(1.06)	**(0.87)**
POLCON5	0.33	1.32	**2.38***	**2.23***	0.35	1.47
	(0.25)	(0.85)	(1.83)	(1.91)	(0.75)	**(1.02)**
GOVCHANGES	−0.03	0.14	−0.03	−0.10	−0.03	−0.24*
	(−0.27)	(0.79)	(−0.14)	(−1.00)	(−0.33)	**(−2.00)**
Constant	−2.50	**−18.0****	−0.80	2.44	−1.19	**−4.24**
	(−0.89)	(−2.41)	(−0.12)	(1.09)	(−0.44)	**(−0.67)**
D1980s	0.83**	0.97**	0.73	0.42	−0.23	**0.27**
D1990s	1.32***	0.88***	1.13***	0.70***	0.99***	**−0.23**
AR (1) (p-value)	0.17	0.03**	0.05**	0.03**	0.01***	**0.12**
Sargan test (p-value)	0.34	0.11	0.88	0.58	0.65	**0.30**
Observations	**65**	**58**	**65**	**65**	**64**	52

Note: */**/*** indicates significance at the 10/5/1 percent level.

The estimates for exchange rate flexibility as a special form or aspect of monetary non-commitment point to the difference between exchange rate policy and general monetary commitment, however. As for monetary commitment in Tables 6.2 and 6.3, there is no evidence for a significant impact of exchange rate commitment on overall economic reform. However, we now find a negative impact of exchange-rate flexibility on monetary and banking sector reform and on trade liberalization as well as a positive estimate for our indicator of government size.

The positive correlation between exchange rate commitment and trade liberalization coincides with the view of the exchange rate peg as an instrument to facilitate international exchanges and to fully reap the benefits of economic integration. Indeed, the complementarity between trade and exchange rate commitment was a prominent argument in favor of EMU (Emerson, Gros, Italianer, Pisani-Ferry, & Reichenbach, 1992). The negative correlation between exchange rate flexibility and *money and banking sector* reform directly points to the commitment effect of an external anchor. Pegging the exchange rate increases the credibility of the monetary authority and allows importing stability. Lower inflation expectations and inflation rates translate in a positive indicator change. A credible exchange rate commitment might also reduced exchange rate risks leading to deeper domestic financial markets, increased competition and improved financing conditions. The positive correlation between exchange rate flexibility and government sector reform could finally result from governments being less reform-minded under flexible rates and an independent monetary policy, or from the lower costs of structural reforms under monetary accommodation that is not possible in monetary union.

Regarding the Calmfors hypothesis, the exchange rate indicator is insignificant for both overall regulation and labor-market reform. Again, there is no support for a complementarity between monetary discretion and structural reform. Neither does the insignificance of the exchange rate indicator support the TINA perspective from Tables 6.2 and 6.3. The exchange rate measure only captures part of the monetary commitment, and apparently not the decisive elements that shape the positive correlation between monetary commitment and structural reforms in our sample of OECD economies.

Both the sub-indicator for *money and banking sector reform* and, consequently, also the aggregate index of economic freedom contain information about lagged inflation rates. Therefore, the inclusion of lagged inflation as an explanatory variable is potentially problematic. In order to check the robustness of the estimates, we have rerun the regressions in Tables 6.2, 6.3, and 6.4 for overall and monetary and banking reform and excluded lagged inflation as a regressor. This modification has no qualitative impact on the estimates for monetary and exchange rate commitment. The lagged dependent variable becomes insignificant for monetary reform in Table 6.2, and the lagged levels of overall economic freedom and sound money are significantly negative in Tables 6.3 and 6.4. Political constraints are now significantly positive for overall economic freedom, and higher per-capita income seems to improve the prospect for reform. None of these changes does affect our conclusions on the complementarity or substitutability of monetary commitment and economic reforms and on the Calmfors hypothesis in particular, however.

Implications for Monetary Regime Choice

This paper investigates the link between monetary policy of open economies and structural reforms. We have confronted three hypotheses: (i) the (extended) Calmfors hypothesis, according to which the degree of reforms is higher in the case of autonomous policy and lower in the case of commitment, (ii) the TINA hypothesis which implies a positive impact of a monetary policy rule on the extent of reforms, and (iii) a third factors hypothesis: if third factors dominate the relationship, monetary commitment should turn out insignificant. Empirical estimations were performed with panel data on 23 OECD countries from 1970 to 2000 (3 decennial periods). The structural reforms are measured by the Economic Freedom of the World index, whereas the monetary policy constraint was measured by a monetary commitment index and the exchange rate regime. Our results provide little evidence to the hypothesis that monetary autonomy promotes structural reforms and economic freedom. Instead, our estimates for regulatory and labor-market reform are in favor of the TINA argument. Neither overall monetary nor exchange rate commitment affects the overall index of structural reforms. Exchange rate commitment and *money and banking sector reform* and exchange rate commitment and trade liberalization both appear to be complements.

Our empirical investigation leaves us with some open research questions. Addressing some of these issues raised in this paper on the adequacy of a composite reform indicator would require the estimation of a separate model of how labor market and complementary policies influence employment. In addition, a new composite reform indicator should be developed which does not aggregate reform steps in an additive manner but in a multiplicative fashion to pin down reform complementarities. We leave this task for future research.

6.4 Institutions for Safeguarding Price Stability

The past two decades have seen enormous changes in central banks and their practices. In some countries, older institutions have been fundamentally restructured. In other, such as the countries of the former Soviet Union, entirely new central banks have been established. The member countries of the European Union have created a supranational central bank that oversees a monetary union. In all of these situations, central bank law was either revised or written *de novo*, while institutional objectives, practices, and structures were amended or created from scratch.[31]

There are three major factors which, in modern day's monetary policy, shall safeguard the value of the currency: (1) central banks' independence, (2) their explicit

---

[31] Crowe and Meade (2007) survey and quantify the trends in two major areas of central bank governance: independence and transparency. We document the steady progress toward greater central bank independence and transparency in a large number of industrial and developing countries over the past 10–15 years and discuss the effects of these aspects of governance on inflation. See also Neumann (2002).

mandate to deliver low and stable inflation, and (3) institutional measures that shall prevent public finances from becoming insolvent – which, in turn, would most likely force the central bank to pursue an inflation policy. The first two institutional factors for stable money shall be reviewed in what follows, while the third factor will be outlined in some more detail in Sect. 6.5.

6.4.1 The Way Towards Central Bank Independence

During the 1970s and early 1980s, major industrialized economies experienced sustained periods of very high inflation. In virtually all countries, high inflation was associated with substantial societal costs in the form of output and employment losses. High inflation became not only intolerable in economics, but also in political terms. Perhaps most important, it was increasingly recognised that inflation was a direct result of central banks' monetary policy – as epitomised by Milton Friedman's famous dictum that *inflation is always and everywhere a monetary phenomenon.* Why did central banks allow high inflation to happen?

One line of argument pointed to the *inflation bias* inherent in discretionary monetary policy, which emerges if the central bank's objective for real output is above the economy's natural equilibrium level (Barro & Gordon, 1983a).[32] Under rational expectations, the public anticipates that the central bank will attempt to trade off low inflation against higher output. Due to the ensuing time inconsistency problem, real output would remain unchanged while inflation would be drifting higher.

Against the background of such an explanation, however, the question arises: why should central banks prefer economic expansion over stable money, or pursue unrealistic output goals? Economists have frequently pointed to *political pressure* as a potential answer. Elected politicians can be expected to be motivated by short-run considerations. As such, they may value short-run economic expansion more, while ignoring the long-run costs of inflation. In view of the political incentives to finance outlays via the printing press, countries whose central banks are (not) politically independent should experience lower (higher) inflation.

When is a central bank politically independent? Finding an answer to this question is critical for determining the optimal institutional design of monetary policy. Debelle and Fischer (1994) and Tootell (1996) maintain the view that a central bank cannot maintain its long-term independence from political pressure if it consistently acts contrary to the preferences of the constituency. However, how long the long-term is, and to what extent (if any) the central bank's short-term goals should deviate from the public's, are subject to considerable debate (Fuhrer, 1997).

With the issue of central bank independence appearing on the agenda, economists focused on the relationship between the central bank and the elected government as a key determinant of inflation (Bade & Parkin, 1984). Empirical research found that

---

[32]The notion that the central bank might be subject to an inflation bias has its roots in the literature on the *time inconsistency*, problem which is developed in Sect. 6.3 above.

inflation was negatively related to measures of central bank independence. Cukierman (1992) provides an excellent summary; references to the more recent literature can be found in Crowe and Meade (2007), Eijffinger and De Haan (1996), Hango and Hefeker (2002) and Walsh (2003); for a most recent survey see De Haan, Masciandaro and Quintyn (2008). Meanwhile, many countries have implemented reforms designed to grant their central banks greater independence from day-to-day government politics.

Disinflation and the Sacrifice Ratio

As a monetary policy of driving up inflation is costly, it will sooner or later be followed by a policy of *disinflation*, with the latter denoting a development that brings a currently high level of inflation down to a lower level. Periods of disinflation tend to be costly in terms of output and employment losses. The *sacrifice ratio* is typically defined as the cumulative output loss resulting from a permanent reduction in inflation (Barro, 1996; Feldstein, 1999).

The concept of the sacrifice ratio has attracted considerable attention among economists and policy makers. However, estimating its size is a difficult exercise (Cecchetti & Rich, 1999). In fact, it requires the identification of changes in the stance of monetary policy and an evaluation of their impact on the path of output and inflation. Neither one of these determinations is straightforward.

A great deal of discretion is actually needed on the part of the researcher to gauge the timing and extent of shifts in policy as well as to separate changes in output and inflation into those that were caused by policy and those that were not. For instance, Cecchetti and Rich (1999) estimate sacrifice ratios, ranging from just over 1 to nearly 10, for the US in the period 1959–1996. In other words, they estimate that for inflation to fall one percentage point, between 1 and 10% of one year's GDP must be sacrificed, a rather wide range.

The concept of the sacrifice ratio needs to be interpreted with caution for another reason: In a normative sense it could actually evoke the impression that it is the monetary policy of disinflation – rather than the monetary policy of inflation – that causes of losses in employment and output. In the US, for instance, rising inflation from the late 1960 to the early 1980s was followed by *rising* unemployment, while the period of disinflation was accompanied with *declining* unemployment (Fig. 6.7(a)).

What is more, the strong rise in inflation in the early 1970s and 1980s was accompanied by strongly declining real output, while subsiding inflation was accompanied by a rise in real GDP growth rates (Fig. 6.7(b)). When viewed from this perspective, it appears that in the US it was inflation – not disinflation – that appeared costly in terms of losses in employment and output.

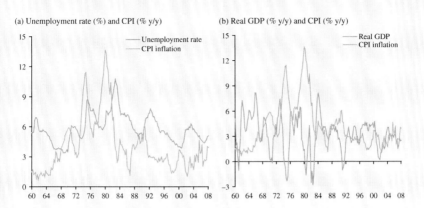

Fig. 6.7   Unemployment, real GDP and CPI inflation in the US
Source: Thomson Financial, own calculations.

Finally, Fig. 6.8(a) points out that, on average, there was indeed a negative relation between real GDP growth and CPI inflation for the period 1950-Q1 to 2008-Q1 and – for a period of inflation and disinflation – 1960-Q1 to 1986-Q4. Figure 6.8(b) shows that, on average, changes in unemployment and CPI were positively related to changes in the unemployment rate. Against this backdrop, reducing inflation seems to have been *beneficial* in terms of output and employment gains.

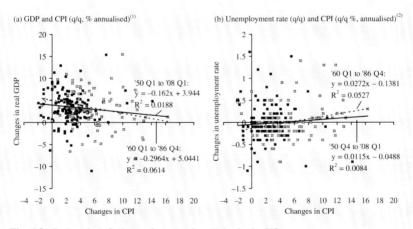

Fig. 6.8   Swings in inflation and economic activity in the US
Source: Thomson Financial, own calculations. (1) Real GDP and CPI in first differences of log levels, annualized. – (2) Changes in the unemployment rate in percentage points; CPI in first differences of log levels, annualized.

6.4.2 Dimensions of Central Bank Independence

Central bank independence can be characterised as a multifaceted institutional design. It basically refers to the freedom of monetary policy makers from direct political or governmental influence in the conduct of policy. As such, the concept of central bank independence includes, inter alia, the role of the government in appointing, and dismissing, members of the central bank decision making body; the voting power of the government on the board; the degree to which the central bank is subject to the government's budgetary control; the extent to which the central bank is required to lend to the government; and whether there are clearly defined policy goals established in the central bank's charter (Crowe & Meade, 2007).

Discussions about central bank independence tend to focus on two key aspects: *First*, there are the dimensions that encompass institutional characteristics which insulate the central bank from political influence in setting the goal of monetary policy. *Second*, there are the dimensions that include those aspects that allow the central bank to freely implement policy in pursuit of monetary policy goals. With Debelle and Fischer (1994), these two aspects are called *goal independence* and *instrument independence*.

– *Goal independence* refers to the central bank's ability to determine the goals of policy without the influence of the government. In the US, for instance, the Federal Reserve's goals are set in its legal charter. According to the Federal Reserve Act, Section 2A: "The Board of Governors of the Federal Reserve System and the Federal Open Market Committee shall maintain long run growth of the monetary and credit aggregates commensurate with the economy's long run potential to increase production, so as to promote effectively the goals of maximum employment, stable prices, and moderate long-term interest rates." These goals are described in vague terms, though, leaving it to the Fed to translate them into operational goals. That said, the Fed has a high level of goal independence. The same holds true for the ECB, which can interpret this goal in terms of a specific price index and definition of price stability. In the UK, in contrast, the Bank of England lacks goal independence since the inflation target is set by the government.
– *Instrument independence* refers to the central bank's ability to freely adjust its policy tools in pursuit of the goals of monetary policy. The Bank of England, while lacking goal independence, has instrument independence. Similarly, the inflation target range for the Reserve Bank of New Zealand is set in its Policy Targets Agreement (PTA) with the government, but given the PTA, the Reserve Bank has the authority to sets its instruments without political interference. In contrast, the US Fed and the ECB have complete instrument independence.

Goal and instrument independence needs to be backed by *organisational independence* and *financial independence*. The former allows the central bank to hire staff without having to seek the government's approval, while the latter makes sure that the central bank has available the means to finance its outlays without having to turn to the government budget; the central bank should be able to finance its expenditures out of current profits.

Finally, the relation between central banks' monetary policy making and their role for financial supervision deserves attention in this context. If central banks are involved in supervising the financial sector, a *conflict of interest* might arise which could undermine central bank independence. Such an argument is based on the possibility that (liquidity and/or solvency) crises in the financial system might de facto force the central bank to pursue an inflation policy in an attempt to *bail-out* financial institutions. Such a conflict of interest could actually be exacerbated if the emergence of financial crises would be related to central banks' role in safeguarding financial stability: *Moral hazard* could provoke excessive risk taking by financial market agents, as the central bank would be believed to come to the rescue of the banks via emergency liquidity assistance, adopting a policy stance that is not compatible with keeping inflation low.

6.4.3 Measuring Independence

Cukierman, Webb, and Neyapti (1992) have established the most widely employed index of central bank independence; alternative measures were developed by Alesina and Summers (1993), Bade and Parkin (1982), Crowe and Meade (2007), and Grilli, Masciandaro, and Tabellini (1991), among others. The Cukierman, Webb, and Neyapti index is based on four legal characteristics as described in a central bank's charter (Table 6.5):

- *First*, a bank has a high degree of independence if its chief executive is appointed by the central bank board rather than by the government, is not subject to dismissal, and has a long-term of office. These features, it is said, help insulate the central bank from political pressures.
- *Second*, the greater the extent to which policy decisions are made independently of government involvement is, the higher it the central bank's degree of independence.
- *Third*, a central bank is more independent if its charter states that price stability is the sole, or primary, goal of monetary policy; in that sense, political conflicts are thought to be reduced greatly.
- *Fourth*, the central bank's independence is greater if there are (strict) limitations on the government's ability to (directly) borrow from the central bank.

Cukierman et al. (1992) combine these four aspects into a single measure of legal independence. They find that Switzerland had the highest degree of central bank independence, closely followed by Germany. At the other end of the scale, the central banks of Poland and the former Yugoslavia were found to have the least independence. However, legal measures of central bank independence may not reflect the relationship between the central bank and the government that actually exists in practice.

Table 6.5 Cukierman index of central bank independence

Major components	Specific variables
Chief Exective Officer (CEO)	– Term of office of CEO – Who appoints the CEO? – Provisions for dismissal of CEO – Is CEO allowed to hold another office?
Policy formulation	– Who formulates policy (central bank alone, central bank with government)? – Who has final authority for policy? – Central bank active in formulating government budget?
Central bank objectives	– Price stability alone, or other?
Limitations on lending	– Limitations on advances to government – Limitations on securitised lending – Who controls terms of lending? – How wide is the circle of borrowers from the bank? – Type of lending limit, if it exists (absolute, relative to government revenue) – Maturity of loans – Restrictions on interest rates – Prohibition on lending in primary market

Cukierman (1992) measures aspects of legal central bank independence by examining the charters and associated legislation governing central banks in 70 countries. He categorises the differences between central banks using 16 variables, grouped into four major areas as shown in the table above. Cukierman ranks each variable on a scale from zero to one according to the author's subjective judgement about the degree of independence represented. The combined indices are weighted averages of the components. In practise, the combined indices range from 0.1 to 0.7, with no country being either completely independent or completely subservient, according to Cukierman's categorisation.
Source: Fuhrer (1997, p. 27).

In countries where the rule of law is less strongly embedded in the political culture, there can be wide gaps between the formal, legal institutional arrangements and their role in practice. This is particularly likely in many developing economies. That said, for developing economies, one should supplement, or even replace, measures of central bank independence based on legal definitions with measures that reflect the degree to which legally established independence is honored in practice. Based on Cukierman work, measures of central bank governor turnover, or turnover relative to the formally specified term length, may also be used to measure independence. High actual turnover is interpreted as indicating political interference in the conduct of monetary policy.

6.4.4 Empirical Evidence

Among the developed economies, most research results indicate that central bank independence is negatively correlated with inflation: The higher (lower) the central banks' degree of independence is, the lower (higher) is inflation, on average

(Eijffinger & de Haan, 1996). Clearly, the specific form of independence may matter for inflation. Debelle and Fischer (1994) maintain it is goal *dependence* and instrument *independence* that would produce low inflation. In fact, such an arrangement may prevent policy makers from changing the objective of policy on a frequent basis, thereby provoking the time inconsistency problem.

What is more, even if central bank independence leads to low inflation, the case for independence might be greatly weakened if it is accompanied by a growing real economic instability. However, little relationship was found between measures of real economic activity and central bank independence (Alesina & Summers, 1993). In other words, countries with more independence central banks enjoyed lower inflation yet suffered no cost in terms of more volatile real economic activity. Viewed from this point, one may be inclined to see central bank independence as a kind of *free lunch* (Fuhrer, 1997, p. 28).

While standard indices of central bank independence were negatively associated with inflation among developed economies, this was not the case among developing economies. Here, turnover rates of central bank governors were positively correlated with inflation. This is a case, however, in which causality is difficult to evaluate: Was inflation high *because* of political interference that leads to rapid turnover of central bank officials? Or did central bank officials get fired because they couldn't keep inflation low?

The empirical work attributing low inflation to central bank independence has been criticized along two dimensions. *First*, studies of central bank independence and inflation often failed to control adequately for other factors that may play a role for keeping inflation low. For instance, even an independent central bank is no guarantee for keeping inflation low if policy makers make *policy mistakes* that cause inflation. Also, political independence may not prevent that monetary policy makers become susceptible to *special interest groups* such as the commercial and investment banking sector. Finally, authors like Campillo and Miron (1997) find that central bank independence had no effect on inflation when controlling for other variables like openness.

Second, simply characterising central bank independence as an exogenous variable for explaining inflation may be problematic. Posen (1993) has argued that central bank independence and low inflation would reflect the constituency's preference for low inflation. In that sense, inflation and the degree of central bank independence are jointly determined by peoples' determinedness to keep inflation low. If the constituency's preference for low inflation would be absent, making, or increasing, the central bank's independence might not yield low inflation.

6.5 The Relation Between Fiscal and Monetary Policy

If the government spends more (less) than it pays out, it runs up a deficit (surplus). Government debt is simply the accumulation of deficits (surpluses) run up in the past. For the government, there is actually just one source of income: and that is raising taxes. It can raise taxes today, or it can do it at later point in time: that is issuing debt. In the first case, current tax payers have to shoulder the fiscal burden (and enjoy the benefits, if there are any, from government handouts), while in the second case, current income earners exchange money balances against financial claims against future taxpayers.

In fact, there is no other source of revenue for the government than raising taxes. If the government sells state assets, for instance, it merely returns assets back into the hands of the private sector which had been bought previously by raising taxes (or issuing debt). Also, auctioning off newly created assets (such as, for instance, licences) to the private sector amounts to just another form of taxation. What is more, there is a rather specific source of taxation, namely *inflation tax*.

6.5.1 The Government's Single-Period Budget Constraint

The government budget constraint (all variables in nominal terms) can be written as (Walsh, 2003):

$$G_t + i_{t-1} B_{t-1}^T = T_t + (B_t^T - B_{t-1}^T). \qquad (6.29)$$

The left hand side represents government expenditures, G_t, plus interest payments on outstanding debt, $i_{t-1} B_{t-1}^T$ (the superscript T denotes total debt). Debt issued in period $t-1$ pays the interest rate i_{t-1}. The right hand side of the equation shows tax revenues, T_t, and the deficit, that is the change in outstanding debt from $t-1$ to t, $B_t^T - B_{t-1}^T$.

The central bank's budget constraint links changes in assets and liabilities and takes the form:

$$(B_t^M - B_{t-1}^M) = i_{t-1} B_{t-1}^M + (H_t - H_{t-1}). \qquad (6.30)$$

The left hand side of the equation shows the change in the central bank's purchase of government debt from $t-1$ to t, which is $B_t^M - B_{t-1}^M$. The term $i_{t-1} B_{t-1}^M$ on the right hand side represents the interest payment from holding government debt; and $H_t - H_{t-1}$ is the change in high powered money in the portfolio of the private sector.

Combining the budget constraints of the government (6.29) and the central bank (6.30) by letting $B = B^T - B^M$, where B then represents the stock of interest bearing government debt by the public, one yields the government sector budget constraint:

$$G_t + i_{t-1} B_{t-1} = T_t + (B_t - B_{t-1}) + (H_t - H_{t-1}). \qquad (6.31)$$

From the viewpoint of the government sector, only debt held by the public represents an interest bearing liability. What is more, total government outlays can be financed by raising taxes (other than inflation), issuing additional debt and/or printing (non-interest bearing) additional money.

Dividing (6.31) by $P_t Y_t$, where P is the price level and Y is real output, one obtains:

$$\frac{G_t}{P_t Y_t} + i_{t-1}\left(\frac{B_{t-1}}{P_t Y_t}\right) = \frac{T_t}{P_t Y_t} + \frac{B_t - B_{t-1}}{P_t Y_t} + \frac{H_t - H_{t-1}}{P_t Y_t}. \tag{6.32}$$

The term $B_{t-1}/(P_t Y_t)$ can be multiplied and divided by $P_{t-1}Y_{t-1}$ (that is nominal output in $t-1$), which yields:

$$\frac{B_{t-1}}{P_t Y_t} = \left(\frac{B_{t-1}}{P_{t-1}Y_{t-1}}\right)\left(\frac{P_{t-1}Y_{t-1}}{P_t Y_t}\right), \text{ or} \tag{6.33}$$

$$b_{t-1} = \left[\frac{1}{(1 + \pi_t)(1 + \gamma_t)}\right], \tag{6.34}$$

where $b_{t-1} = B_{t-1}/(P_{t-1}Y_{t-1})$ is the stock of real government debt relative to income held by the public, π is inflation and γ is the growth rate of output. Using lower case letter for variables deflated by nominal output, the government's budget identity is therefore:

$$g_t + \bar{r}_{t-1}b_{t-1} = t_t + (b_t - b_{t-1}) + \left(h_t - \frac{h_{t-1}}{(1 + \pi)(1 + \gamma)}\right), \tag{6.35}$$

where $\bar{r}_{t-1} = (1 + i_{t-1})/[(1 + \pi_t)(1 + \gamma_t)] - 1$ is the *ex post* real return from $t-1$ to t.

6.5.2 Seigniorage and the Budget Constraint

The equations above allow analysing the respective roles of anticipated and unanticipated inflation on the government budget constraint. We define as r_t the *ex ante* real interest rate and π_t^e as expected inflation in t, formed in $t-1$. The nominal return on government debt is: $1 + i_{t-1} = (1 + r_{t-1})(1 + \pi_t^e)$. The difference between the ex ante and ex post real interest payments on real debt is:

$$(r_{t-1} - \bar{r}_{t-1})b_{t-1} = (\pi_t - \pi_t^e)(1 + r_{t-1})b_{t-1}/(1 + \pi_t). \tag{6.36}$$

When this term is added to both sides of (6.35), the budget constraint becomes:

$$g_t + \bar{r}_{t-1}b_{t-1} = t_t + (b_t - b_{t-1}) + \left(\frac{\pi_t - \pi_t^e}{1 + \pi_t}\right)(1 + r_{t-1})b_{t-1} + \left[h_t - \left(\frac{1}{1 + \pi_t}\right)h_{t-1}\right]. \tag{6.37}$$

The expression $(\pi_t - \pi_t^e)b_{t-1}$ on the right hand side of (6.37) shows government revenue generated when actual inflation in t exceeds anticipated inflation (expected in $t-1$, when the contract was made). To the extent that inflation is anticipated, it will be reflected in a higher nominal yield that the government must pay. That said, inflation by itself does not reduce the government's interest bearing nominal debt; only *surprise inflation* has such an effect.

Seigniorage, – the profit from issuing base money – can be formulated as:

$$s_t \equiv \frac{H_t - H_{t-1}}{P_t Y_t} = (h_t - h_{t-1}) + \left(\frac{\pi_t}{1+\pi_t}\right) h_{t-1}. \tag{6.38}$$

It can arise from two sources. The *first source* of seigniorage is $h_t - h_{t-1}$, which represents the change in the real holdings of central bank money relative to output. With the government holding the monopoly for issuing money, an increase in the amount of central bank money in the hands of the public increases resources in the hands of the government. In a steady state equilibrium, h will be constant and seigniorage will be zero. The *second source* of seigniorage is represented by the second term in (6.38). To maintain a constant level of real money holdings relative to income, the private sector needs to increase its nominal holdings of money (approximately) at the rate of inflation to offset the effect of inflation on real money holdings. By increasing central bank money to meet this *compensating* demand for money, the government is able to obtain goods and services and/or reduce other taxes.

6.5.3 Inflation and the Single-Period Budget Constraint

In a more simple representation assume real seignorage, φ, in t is given by:

$$\varphi_t = \frac{\Delta M_t}{P_t} = \frac{\Delta M_t}{M_t} \frac{M_t}{P_t} = \mu_t \frac{M_t}{P_t}. \tag{6.39}$$

According to Eq. (6.39), seigniorage increases with the rate of money creation, μ, and with the amount of real balances, M_t/P_t, that people are willing to hold. An increase in real seigniorage necessary to ensure government solvency requires an increase in the rate of money growth for a given demand of real balances.

Does real seigniorage relate to money growth and inflation? To answer that question, let us take a simple money demand function based on the quantity theory of money:

$$\frac{M}{P} = \frac{Y}{V(\pi^e)}, \tag{6.40}$$

where the velocity of money is a function of expected inflation. Equilibrium requires the two sides of the equation to grow at the same rate, or, more specifically:

$$\mu - \frac{\Delta P}{P} = \frac{\Delta Y}{Y} - \frac{\Delta V}{V}. \tag{6.41}$$

If μ was constant in the past and is expected to remain so for the foreseeable future, actual and expected inflation coincide. With a constant velocity of money, we can write:

$$\mu - \pi = \gamma. \tag{6.42}$$

Only the increase in money supply in excess of the increase in real output is thus inflationary. For the same reasoning, seignorage is related to, but does not coincide with, the inflation tax. The latter is the loss in real money holdings associated with inflation: $\pi M/P$. Seignorage is positive even if inflation is zero as long as people are willing to increase their real money holdings. Seignorage and the inflation tax are equal if money growth is positive ($\mu > 0$) and the economy doesn't grow ($\gamma = 0$).

6.5.4 The Limits to Seignorage Deficit Financing

However, can any deficit in present value terms be financed by seignorage as suggested by the intertemporal budget constraint? To put it differently: will countries always remain solvent, because they can always finance their deficits by printing money? In the following it will be shown that this is not the case: excessive money growth may actually result in lower rather than higher seignorage revenue.

To start with, the demand for real money holdings is:

$$L = Y[a - b(r + \pi^e)]. \tag{6.43}$$

The velocity of money is simply the reciprocal of the demand for real balances (that is $1/L$):

$$V = \frac{1}{Y[a - b(r + \pi^e)]} \tag{6.44}$$

In equilibrium, where real money supply (M/P) equals real money demand (L), and actual inflation equals expected inflation, we have: $\pi = \pi^e = \mu - \gamma$. As a result, the function of real seignorage can be written as:

$$\varphi = \mu \frac{M}{P} = \mu Y[a - b(r + \mu - \gamma)]. \tag{6.45}$$

Money growth has an ambiguous effect on φ. The latter increases when μ rises. At the same time, however, high money growth reduces real money holdings (hence equilibrium real balances) for a given γ, as it increases inflation expectations which, in turn, makes people reducing their real money holdings. That said, higher money growth increases seignorage only to the extent that it does not reduce real money holdings more than proportionally; in fact, this mechanism is reminiscent of the *Laffer curve*.

To show that increasing money growth above a certain *threshold* level reduces rather increases real seignorage, we can maximise Eq. (6.44) with respect to μ:

$$\frac{\partial \varphi}{\partial \mu} = a - b(r + \mu - \gamma) - b\mu = 0, \qquad (6.46)$$

which corresponds to:

$$\mu^* = \frac{a - b(r - \gamma)}{2b}. \qquad (6.47)$$

Substituting the latter in Eq. (6.46), we find that the maximum amount of real seignorage is:

$$\varphi^* = \frac{[a - b(r - \gamma)]^2}{2b}. \qquad (6.48)$$

That said, a country cannot finance any deficit by money printing and is bankrupt if the government budget constraint is satisfied only with a level of real seignorage in excess of φ^*. A country which is increasing money supply at a rate of $\mu < \mu^*$ can (always) resort to deficit financing by printing money.

6.5.5 The Intertemporal Budget Constraint

Ignoring the effects of surprise inflation, the single-period budget identity of the government can be written as:

$$g_t + r_{t-1}b_{t-1} = t_t + (b_t - b_{t-1}) + s_t, \qquad (6.49)$$

where s_t is seigniorage. If we assume that r is constant, (6.49) can be solved forward, yielding:

$$\sum_{i=0}^{\infty} \frac{g_{t+i}}{(1+r)^i} + (1+r)b_{t-1} = \sum_{i=0}^{\infty} \frac{t_{t+i}}{(1+r)^i} + \sum_{i=0}^{\infty} \frac{s_{t+i}}{(1+r)^i} + \lim_{i \to \infty} \frac{b_{t+i}}{(1+r)^i}. \qquad (6.50)$$

The government's expenditure and tax plans satisfy the requirements of the intertemporal budget balance ("no Ponzi condition") if the last term in (6.50) is zero:

$$\lim_{i \to \infty} \frac{b_{t+i}}{(1+r)^i} = 0.$$

If the latter holds, the right hand side of (6.50) becomes the present value of all current and future tax and seignior age revenues, and this is equal to the left hand side of the equation, that is the present value of all current and future outlays plus repayments for debt outstanding (principal plus interest). To put it differently, the government must raise sufficient revenue, in present value terms, to repay existing debt and finance its planned outlays. The primary deficit is: $f = g - t - s$, so the intertemporal budget constraint (6.49) requires:

$$(1 + r)b_{t-1} = - \sum_{i=0}^{\infty} \frac{f_{t+i}}{(1 + r)^i}.$$ (6.51)

In the case that government debt outstanding is positive ($b_{t-1} > 0$), the present value of future primary deficits must be negative (the government must run a primary surplus in present value terms). The surplus can be generated through adjustments in expenditures, taxes or seigniorage.

Putting a Limit to Government Debt – *The EMU Case*

Attaining and preserving a macroeconomic balance as a prerequisite for economic and social progress has been the foremost objective guiding European economic and monetary integration in the 1990s. The aim both to buttress the mandate of the European System of Central Banks (ESCB) to safeguard price stability and to apply the principle of subsidiarity to non-monetary policies of participating governments figured high on the agenda of the founders of Economic and Monetary Union (EMU).

At the same time they held the belief that sound government finances are an indispensable requisite for macroeconomic stability, and that financial stability is also rooted in disciplined fiscal policies. Hence an EU-wide commitment to sound public finances, such as that laid down in the Treaty and further developed in the Stability and Growth Pact, commands respect and constitutes a permanent guarantee that a responsible course of fiscal policy will be pursued.

The experience accumulated in past decades has shown that increased debt ratios – as well as the implicit debt associated with social security systems in ageing societies – cast a permanent shadow over economic prospects and, together with large deficits, constantly limit the scope for fiscal policy to act as a stabilising instrument. Long-term real interest rates are higher, private investment is lower and physical capital formation is at least partially crowded out. This reduces production, output suffers a permanent loss and consumption possibilities are diminished in the long run. Indeed, empirical evidence points to a significant negative relationship between fiscal imbalances and total gross domestic investment, and between deficits and income per capita over the medium term.

Moreover, fiscal laxity also appears to reduce the flexibility with which fiscal structures respond to economic fluctuations and help to dampen their effects on aggregate income. Fiscal structures have become more rigid over the past few decades. This has been partly due to discretionary policies to increase government employment or implement high replacement ratios and early retirement dates for pensioners, and has been partly a budgetary by-product of adverse demographic trends which have increased the proportion of retirees in populations. Far from facilitating the smoothing of income through the different phases of the cycle, growing structural deficits have systematically impeded the policy-makers' response to severe recession, even when endogenous spending and tax adjustments were most needed.

Inflation is a monetary phenomenon in the medium to long term. Since the long-run association between the monetary financing of fiscal deficits and inflation is well established, a credible and definitive prohibition of this, along with an institutional framework that assigns the monetary authority a credible and lasting mandate to pursue an objective of price stability, are essential preconditions for the maintenance of price stability over the medium term.

However, the task of a stability-oriented monetary policy can also be affected by the stance of fiscal policies. In the short run regulated prices and indirect taxes have a direct impact on HICP inflation. Over an extended period of time, unbalanced public finances have a negative impact on economic efficiency and hence on the process of price formation. High structural deficits tend to divert resources from private capital formation and to increase the gap between aggregate demand and supply. This tends to alter the composition of aggregate supply and creates rigidities and bottlenecks that contribute to heightened pressures on prices. In this way, persistent deficits might force monetary authorities to keep short-term rates higher than would otherwise be necessary. By contrast, an institutional framework that guarantees sound government finances fosters macroeconomic stability conducive to sustained growth in output and employment, and supports the maintenance of price stability as well as a steady improvement in living standards.

In certain circumstances, fiscal policies might also affect expectations and exacerbate the effects of economic and financial shocks. If market participants perceive fiscal structures to be overly exposed to economic fluctuations or changes in interest rates (e.g. because of insufficient safety margins built into primary balances to withstand adverse contingencies) such shocks might lead to increases in risk premia and long-term interest rates.

In a monetary union among sovereign states the case is strengthened for a responsible policy course with regard to fiscal choices. A newly established monetary union eliminates long-standing interest rate differentials which used to compensate investors for differences in inflation and depreciation prospects across the range of previously existing currencies. In this way, borrowers lose an element – a depreciating national currency – which used to signal market distress over misguided policies, not least on the fiscal front. At the same time, as national financial markets become more integrated, sovereign issuers can draw on a larger and more liquid capital market than was possible under monetary autonomy. For those member countries that had been penalised in relative terms in the market for government loans, vanishing risk and liquidity premia may consequently make borrowing a more attractive policy option than non-deficit spending as a means of financing public expenditure. This feature, in turn, tends to lend a deficit bias to the area as a whole, which, again, provides a major incentive for an economic constitution which discourages unsound fiscal practices.

When the fiscal authority is dispersed, errant fiscal choices pursued by individual members of a monetary union can have negative repercussions on their neighbouring economies. These negative external effects are generally transmitted via long-term interest rates, as fiscal laxity in one country and the drain that this exerts on union-wide private savings both put pressure on the cost of long-term finance for the area as a whole.

In principle, market forces could act as an effective deterrent against deviant policies. Indeed, even in the absence of explicit institutional constraints on fiscal deficits, the possibility of country-specific default premia penalising excessive borrowing could discourage deviation from fiscal discipline by individual governments. However, in practice there seems to be no firm evidence that the discipline exerted by financial markets has been sufficient to induce governments always to take heed of long-term budget constraints. Under such circumstances, unfettered fiscal regimes at the national level are inevitably conducive to tensions, and there is an obvious argument for supplementing market forces with commonly shared rules of fiscal restraint. These induce national policy-makers to internalise the area-wide impact of their decisions. In so doing, supranational rules improve co-ordination and inspire mutual trust among members.

The worst scenario we can think of, however, loomed at the horizon in spring 2009. At that time markets anticipated that the ECB would feel forced very soon to engage in quantitative easing and would be buying government bonds – maybe even euro bonds. Even if the spread between European government bonds was at that time likely to be exaggerated due to financial panic, the ECB should not have privileged the buying of Irish, Greek, Spanish and Italian government bonds. In doing so, it would have eliminated the incentives for further structural reform that these spreads (credit default swaps, CDS) create. The reason is that the denationalization of debt would lead to moral hazard and calls for a supranational fiscal bailout by governments and enterprises which have postponed reforms in the past (Belke, Schnabl, & Zemanek, 2009).

Source: Belke (2002), Belke, Schnabl, & Zemanek (2009), ECB (1999, pp. 45–46), Eichengreen and von Hagen (1996), Gros and Thygesen (1998, pp. 317ff.), and Mundschenk and von Hagen (2002).

6.5.6 The Government Debt Dynamics

The relation between government's deficits and debts can be explained as follows. The government's deficit is simply the difference between the stock of debt between period t and $t + 1$:

$$D_t = B_{t+1} - B_t, \tag{6.52}$$

where B represents the government's stock of debt (that is accumulation of the deficits of the past). In percent of nominal GDP, represented by Y, Eq. (6.52) can be written as:

$$\frac{D_t}{Y_t} = \frac{B_{t+1}}{Y_t} - \frac{B_t}{Y_t} \quad \text{or} \tag{6.53a}$$

$$= \frac{B_{t+1}}{Y_{t+1}} \frac{Y_{t+1}}{Y_t} - \frac{B_t}{Y_t} \tag{6.53b}$$

$$d_t = (1 + g)b_{t+1} - b_t. \tag{6.53c}$$

Here, the variable g represents a constant growth rate of nominal GDP: $Y_{t+1} = (1 + g)Y_t$. Assuming a time-invariant deficit-to-GDP ratio ($d_t := d$), the increase of the stock of debt in percent of GDP over time can be explained as follows. Starting in $t = 0$, the debt-to-GDP ratio in $t + 1$ is:

$$b_1 = \frac{b_0 + d}{1 + g}. \tag{6.54}$$

For the following periods ($t + 2, t + 3, \dots t + T$), one yields:

$$b_2 = \frac{b_1 + d}{1 + g} = \frac{\frac{b_0 + d}{1+g} + d}{1 + g} = \frac{b_0 + d}{(1 + g)^2} + \frac{d}{1 + g}$$

$$b_3 = \frac{b_0 + d}{(1 + g)^3} + \frac{d}{(1 + g)^3} + \frac{d}{(1 + g)^2} + \frac{d}{1 + g} \tag{6.55}$$

$$\vdots$$

$$b_T = \frac{b_0}{(1 + g)^T} + d\left(\sum_{t=1}^{T} \left(\frac{1}{1 + g}\right)^t\right).$$

Using the geometric series $\sum_{t=0}^{T-1} q^t = \frac{q^T - 1}{q - 1}$ and defining $q = 1/(1+g)$, one yields:

$$b_T = \frac{b_0}{(1 + g)^T} + d\left(\frac{\left(\frac{1}{1 + g}\right)^{T+1} - \left(\frac{1}{1 + g}\right)^1}{\frac{1}{1 + g} - 1}\right) \tag{6.56}$$

$$b_T = \frac{b_0}{(1+g)^T} + d\left(\frac{\dfrac{1}{(1+g)^{T+1}} - \dfrac{1}{1+g}}{\dfrac{-g}{1+g}}\right)$$

$$b_T = \frac{b_0}{(1+g)^T} + d\left(\frac{\dfrac{1}{(1+g)^T} - 1}{-g}\right) \tag{6.57}$$

$$b_T = \frac{b_0}{(1+g)^T} + \frac{d}{g}\left(1 - \frac{1}{(1+g)^T}\right).$$

The long-run relation between the ratios and the growth rate of output is can be obtained by letting T runs against infinity:

$$\lim_{T \to \infty} b_T = \frac{d}{g}. \tag{6.58}$$

Equation (6.58) shows that the debt-to-GDP ratio converges, given a time-invariant deficit-ratio, to d/g. For instance, a country's deficit-to-GDP ratio is 3% and its nominal output growth 5%, the debt-to-GDP ratio would converge towards 60%.

6.5.7 Extension of the Analysis

A country's *primary deficit*, F_t, is the gap between tax revenues, T_t, and expenditures, G_t: $F_t = G_t - T_t$. (So a primary surplus would be: $-F_t = T_t - G_t$.) The government's total budget deficit is:

$$D_t = F_t + r B_t, \tag{6.59a}$$

where $D_t = B_{t+1} - B_t$. Equation (6.59a) can be rearranged to yield:

$$B_{t+1} = (1+r)B_t + F_t. \tag{6.59b}$$

In percent of nominal output, Eq. (6.59b) is:

$$b_{t+1} = \left(\frac{1+r}{1+g}\right)b_t + \frac{1}{1+g}f_t. \tag{6.59c}$$

The change in the debt-to-GDP ratio is

$$b_{t+1} - b_t = \left(\frac{1+r}{1+g}\right) b_t + \frac{1}{1+g} f_t - b_t$$

$$= \left(\frac{1+r}{1+g} - \frac{1+g}{1+g}\right) b_t + \frac{1}{1+g} f_t \qquad (6.60)$$

$$= \left(\frac{r-g}{1+g}\right) b_t + \frac{1}{1+g} f_t$$

As can be seen, if $r > g$, a primary surplus would be needed, that is $f < 0$, for keeping the debt-to-GDP ratio from rising.

Figure 6.9 shows the evolution of debt- and deficit-to-GDP levels over time, starting with a level of 67%, under various assumptions regarding the deficit-to-GDP ratio, interest rates and output growth. In the first case ($d = 4\%$, $r = 4.5\%$, $g = 3\%$),

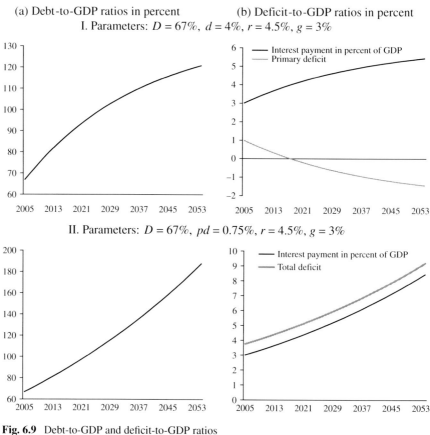

Fig. 6.9 Debt-to-GDP and deficit-to-GDP ratios
Source: own calculations. – The ratios were calculated using the formulas outlined in the Appendix.
– D = debt-to-GDP ratio, d = deficit-to-GDP ratio, pd = primary deficit, r = interest rate to be paid on government debt, g = economic growth rate.

the debt-to-GDP level would rise to 120% in the coming 50 years, with the interest rate payments rising to more than 5% of GDP. In the second case ($pd = 0.75\%$, $r = 4.5\%$, $g = 3\%$), the debt-to-GDP ratio would actually spin out of control, reaching 200% after 50 years with interest payments in percent of GDP climbing to 6.6%.

6.5.8 Consolidation Efforts

If the government debt-to-GDP shall be reduced under the assumption of a constant primary deficit ratio (that is $f > 0$), starting in period $t = 0$,

$$b_1 = \left(\frac{1+r}{1+g}\right) b_0 + \frac{1}{1+g} f_t$$

$$b_2 = \left(\frac{1+r}{1+g}\right) b_1 + \frac{1}{1+g} f_t$$

$$\vdots$$

$$b_T = \left(\frac{1+r}{1+g}\right) b_{T-1} + \frac{1}{1+g} f_t. \tag{6.61}$$

Substituting the debt-to-GDP ratios from one period to the next yields:

$$
\begin{aligned}
b_2 &= \left(\frac{1+r}{1+g}\right) \left[\left(\frac{1+r}{1+g}\right) b_0 + \frac{1}{1+g} f \right] + \frac{1}{1+g} f \\
&= \left(\frac{1+r}{1+g}\right)^2 b_0 + \left(\frac{1+r}{1+g} + 1\right) \frac{1}{1+g} f
\end{aligned}
\tag{6.62}
$$

$$\vdots$$

$$b_T = \left(\frac{1+r}{1+g}\right)^T b_0 + \left[\sum_{t=0}^{T-1} \left(\frac{1+r}{1+g}\right) \right] \frac{1}{1+g} f.$$

Using the geometric series, we can write:

$$
\begin{aligned}
b_T &= \left(\frac{1+r}{1+g}\right)^T b_0 + \left[\frac{\left(\frac{1+r}{1+g}\right)^T - 1}{\frac{1+r}{1+g} - 1} \right] \frac{1}{1+g} f \\
&= \left(\frac{1+r}{1+g}\right)^T b_0 + \frac{1+g}{r-n} \left[\left(\frac{1+r}{1+g}\right)^T - 1 \right] \frac{1}{1+g} f \\
&= \left(\frac{1+r}{1+g}\right)^T b_0 + \left[\left(\frac{1+r}{1+g}\right)^T - 1 \right] \frac{1}{r-g} f
\end{aligned}
\tag{6.63}
$$

To calculate the primary deficit, which reduces the debt-to-GDP ratio towards an envisaged level in the future, the equation must be solved for f:

$$b_T - b_0 \left(\frac{1+r}{1+g}\right)^T = \left[\left(\frac{1+r}{1+g}\right)^T - 1\right]\frac{1}{r-g}f, \text{ or} \qquad (6.64)$$

$$f = \left[b_T - b_0\left(\frac{1+r}{1+g}\right)^T\right]\left[\left(\frac{1+r}{1+n}\right)^T - 1\right]^{-1}(r-g). \qquad (6.65)$$

The equation above can be used to calculate the primary deficit ratio which is needed to stabilize the debt-to-GDP ratio at a desired level? Figure 6.10 shows in the first column the difference between the interest rate, r, and economy's output growth rate, g. The first row shows the prevailing debt-to-GDP ratio in percent of GDP.

The fields show the required primary deficits (> 0) or surpluses (< 0) to achieve a debt-to-GDP ratio of 60% in five years ($T = 5$). For example, a country having a debt-to-GDP ratio of 70% would need primary surpluses of more than 3% to bring the debt-to-GDP ratio to 60% in the coming five years under the assumption that $r - n = 0.01$. The second part of the table shows the primary surpluses required to bring about the desired 60% deficit-to-GDP ratio after twenty years ($T = 20$). Here, a country with a deficit-to-GDP of 70% would need a primary surplus ratio of nearly 1.2%. Taken a closer look at the data history provides a notion about the challenge which is ahead of many countries.

Difference between interest rate and growth $(r-g)$	Debt-to-GDP ratio in $t = 0$				
	1.4	1.2	1.0	0.8	0.7
		$T = 5$			
0.01	−0.179	−0.136	−0.092	−0.049	−0.028
0.02	−0.190	−0.145	−0.101	−0.056	−0.034
0.03	−0.201	−0.155	−0.109	−0.064	−0.041
0.04	−0.212	−0.165	−0.118	−0.071	−0.047
0.05	−0.223	−0.175	−0.126	−0.078	−0.054
		$T = 20$			
0.01	−0.052	−0.041	−0.029	−0.018	−0.012
0.02	−0.063	−0.050	−0.037	−0.025	−0.018
0.03	−0.074	−0.060	−0.046	−0.032	−0.025
0.04	−0.085	−0.070	−0.054	−0.039	−0.032
0.05	−0.096	−0.080	−0.063	−0.047	−0.038

Fig. 6.10 Primary deficit-to-GDP ratios under various parameter constellations
Note: When calculating $r - g$, we started with $r = 0.06$ and $g = 0.05$ and increased r thereafter.
– A negative (positive) sign indicates a primary surplus (deficit).

6.5.9 When Does It Become a "Ponzi Game"?

The development of the debt-to-GDP ratio is captured by the following equation:

$$b_T = \left(\frac{1+r}{1+g}\right)^T b_0 + \left[\left(\frac{1+r}{1+g}\right)^T - 1\right]\frac{1}{r-g}f. \tag{6.66}$$

In the first case that $r > g$ and $T \to \infty$, we would yield:

$$\lim_{T\to\infty} b_t = \infty.$$

Here, the government would become (sooner or later) insolvent – as the debt-to-GDP ratio would keep rising over time and the government would be unable to service its obligations. If, however, the following condition holds:

$$b_T = -\frac{1}{r-g}f, \tag{6.67}$$

the government debt-to-GDP ratio would not explode; this result can be easily calculated by assuming $b_T = b_0$. However, this would imply that the government must produce primary surpluses (as $f < 0$).

In the second case, $r < g$ holds and with $T \to \infty$ the result would be:

$$\lim_{T\to\infty} b_t = \frac{1}{g-r}f.$$

Here, when the growth rate exceeds interest rate, a Ponzi game would be possible. The government debt would rise over time. But as output rises even stronger, the debt-to-GDP ratio would converge. In the long-run, primary surpluses can be generated because $g - r$ is positive.

As a kind of case study of institutional arrangement destined to safeguard price stability in spite of and with an eye on governments keen on creation of seigniorage by the central bank, the following section analyzes the reform of the European Central Bank (ECB) Governing Council's voting procedures following enlargement of the euro area. Using the "one-member, one-vote" rule as a benchmark, it calculates voting shares and two well-known power indexes that have their origin in solutions of cooperative games to examine the reform effects (Belke & Styczynska, 2006).

Digression: The Allocation of Power in the Enlarged ECB Governing Council

Introduction

At the end of quite secretive discussions, the Governing Council of the European Central Bank (ECB) finally published its proposal for the reform of its decision-making process in early 2003. Meeting in Brussels on 21 March 2003, the heads of state of EU member countries approved the ECB's proposal on the rotation model. This unanimous decision came somewhat as a surprise to analysts, in view of the heavy resistance to the proposal as late as the middle of March in countries such as Finland and the Netherlands, whose parliaments felt that it placed them at a disadvantage. Nevertheless, it has been ratified by all Member States and finally entered into force on 1 June 2004 (European Central Bank, 2004, p. 164).

It is well known that the now bind ECB's reform proposal consists of a "minimum representation model", which combines elements of rotation as applied by the Federal Open Market Committee (FOMC) and elements of representation, i.e. the formation of country groups with group representatives following the examples set by the International Monetary Fund (IMF), the World Bank or the Bundesbank Council after German unification (see for example ECB, 2003). In this context, it is important to emphasis that enhancing efficiency was not the main motivation for the introduction of the rotation principle in the FOMC. Instead, the voting power of regional presidents was restricted in order to be able to run a common monetary policy for a common region instead of a monetary policy driven by regional interests. Most remarkably, the delegation of decision-making competences in the ECB to a small committee with only a few national representatives (delegation or centralisation) was not regarded as an option at all. It was consistently argued by the former President of the ECB, Wim Duisenberg (although questioned by European jurisprudence), that the wording of Art. 5 of the Treaty of Nice, along with Art. 10.2 and Art. 10.6 (the so-called "enabling clause") of the statute of the European System of Central Banks prohibited a delegation or centralisation solution and limited the scope of Council reform to a mere change in the voting procedures. However, supporting this view would imply accepting that the blueprint of the Treaty of Nice was flawed and that the present lopsided construction was owing to the lack of political power to correct the mistake.

By speeding up the process of passing the reform, the ECB Governing Council met two strategic targets at once. First, its own proposal could be completely discussed before the new members participated in the decision. Second, the ECB itself took the initiative to put forward a proposal and did not leave it, for instance, to the EU Commission. But how do we finally assess the ECB's proposal?

Without any doubt, the expansion of the euro area from 2004 on required a reform of the highest decision-making body of the European Central Bank, because otherwise the ECB Governing Council was going to comprise more than 30 members. The increase in the size of the Council gave and will give rise to efficiency problems[33] in the body that is responsible for the stability of one of the most important world currencies (i.e. a "numbers problem" – see for example Amend, 2003, & Berger, 2002).

Unfortunately, according to a plethora of authors (e.g. Bofinger, 2003; Gros, 2003; Meade, 2003b), the "new" rotation model seems to have significant drawbacks. For instance, it violates the fundamental principle of "one member, one vote",

---

[33] An efficient decision making is given in this context, if no unnecessary delays occur in monetary policy making and the decisions are made at minimal costs.

which is intended to ensure that ECB Governing Council members participate in the Council's meetings personally and independently, and not as national stakeholders. The rotation model cultivates thinking in national terms, reduces the responsibility of the rotating members for monetary decisions and diminishes transparency. As suggested above, it can be supposed that it was also constructed to disadvantage of the future EMU members. Furthermore, the cap on the total Council number of rights to vote at 21 is far too generous by international standards and will lead to more inefficiency in the decision-making process. In addition, the rotation model is inconsistent and contains arbitrary elements. For instance, the frequency of the voting rights' rotation is not explained and a very small country such as Luxembourg is endowed with a similar number of voting rights as Poland. Nevertheless, the reform brings about also some improvements. The position of the Executive Board seems to be stabilized because its voting share is retained at 6 while the number of overall votes is capped at 21. Under the status quo rule it would have decreased with each accession. At the same time an improvement in terms of representativeness, i.e. a reduction of the discrepancy between the political and economic weight has to be expected after the rotation model has been established.

The arguments above result from a narrative discussion of the ECB rotation model. In this digression we want to show that it is possible to support some of these arguments (e.g. the improvement of representativeness) and reveal new aspects by means of an analysis of the distribution of power in a voting system, with power being understood as the potential influence of a voter on the voting outcome. We apply the game theoretical concept of power indices in order to reveal features of this voting mechanism that are not visible when considering only the distribution of voting weights. Without consideration of information about the likelihood of coalition formation between National Bank Governors which can be due to common interest rates preferences, we calculate power indices of members of the Governing Council (Shapley-Shubik-Index, Banzhaf-Index) and hence concentrate on theoretical characteristics of the rotation model. We take an inter-temporal point of view because in a voting system with rotation, the consideration of several meetings is more significant than the analysis of a particular situation. The results reveal details of the mechanisms imposed by the rotation model. An advantage of this approach is that this analysis is independent of the actual interest rates preferences of Governing Council members which can change over time.[34]

In this digression, the first main section presents the ECB's reform proposal for the decision-making process in an enlarged euro area, i.e. the minimum representation model. The remaining parts offer an empirical assessment of the resulting shifts in power among the euro-area member states. For this purpose, the second main section introduces the power index concept and explains how to apply it to the new rotation model. The final and central section presents some algorithm-based results and compares them to the respective power indices prevailing in the status quo. Moreover, it investigate whether the new rotation model serves the important principle

---

[34]This advantage can also be understood as a handicap of our approach because voting situation in the ECB Governing Council is not displayed with all its particularities. This argument will be considered shortly in the conclusions, where we show up possibilities for further research.

of representativeness. Finally, conclusions and potentials for further research and applications to monetary policy analysis are presented.

Minimum Representation: The ECB's Reform Proposal

A (price) stability-oriented European monetary policy represents a collective good for the euro countries because a low and stable rate of inflation is the best precondition for investment, growth and employment. By contrast, a monetary policy prone to inflation may bring unemployment down in the short term but reduces medium- and long-term growth and employment (see Chapter 5). It is the central task of any monetary policy constitution to assure that a central bank like the ECB is not tempted to jeopardise a reasonable stabilisation policy because of the short-term demands of governments or well-organised lobbyists. In Europe, this constitution comprises: (1) the anchoring of the goal of price stability in the EU Treaty; (2) a concept of monetary policy that allows a viable policy of price stability as well as the documentation and verification of the ECB's willingness to maintain stability; and (3) the organisation of the monetary policy decision-making. Particularly the latter item is of central importance, because this is where the framework for daily decisions is laid down. This is valid not only in "normal" times but especially in times of crisis.

The necessity of reforming the decision-making process in the ECB Governing Council was beyond question in the wake of the enlargement of the EU (Berger, 2002 and Berger, de Haan and Inklaar, 2002). Under an unchanged body of rules, an expanded euro area would have led to a large ECB Governing Council that is hardly capable of acting. Including the six members of the Executive Board, the Governing Council would in the end consist of more than 30 members. Guided by national interests, the latter would as a rule tenaciously struggle to arrive at day-to-day decisions. Hence, this absolute increase in the number of members of the ECB Council would have caused efficiency problems. Another dimension of the problem is that the formation of coalitions among smaller euro-area member countries could lead to interest rate decisions that are not optimal for the euro area as a whole. The period of natural coalition among the governors of the larger member countries and the Executive Board, resulting from the dominating influence of the economic development of these countries on the European aggregates (which form the basis of consideration for members of the Executive Board), would end. This coalition so far enabled consensus decisions within the Council.

Finally, the discrepancy between the economic and the political weights of the euro member countries in the Council would have even increased without reform because of the fact that the new members tend to be (in economic terms) smaller in size. An overly strong representation of the acceding countries which are characterised by higher inflation owing to the Samuelson-Balassa effect could have led to additional economic costs for the eurozone. According to some critics, these costs would consist of either higher inflation in the euro area (although the latter should not be estimated as very high, i.e. above 0.2% points of total euro-area inflation) or higher nominal and real interest rates in the euro area than otherwise (if the ECB reacts to this inflationary bias). Of course this argument heavily depends on whether there really are differences in "inflation incentives" between the old member countries of the euro area and the newcomers. Nevertheless, one should not be so confident that the core countries of the economic and monetary union (EMU) will not endanger the stability mandate of the ECB to a lesser extent than the new member states will do (consider, for example, the erosion of the Stability and Growth Pact initiated not least by its early proponent Germany or the largely enhanced sovereign debt default risk of Ireland, Greece and some other euro area members in the wake of the financial and economics crises in 2009). The central question raised in this contribution is whether the ECB's reform proposal is able to handle and solve these future problems.

Based on the assumption of a future euro area with 27 member countries (the 12 members as of before 2004, plus the United Kingdom, Sweden and Denmark, plus the 10 Central and Eastern European countries (CEECs) that joined the EU in 2004 and Bulgaria and Romania) the ECB's Governing Council would consist of 27 national central bank (NCB) governors and six directors. According to the ECB's rotation model, voting rights would in the end be divided as follows (see Table 6.6).

- The six directors would possess a permanent right to vote.
- The five biggest countries (Germany, France, Italy, the UK and Spain) would represent the first group according to the criteria of a five-sixth share of euro GDP at market prices and a one-sixth share in the aggregated balance sheet of the euro area monetary financial institutions (MFIs). Together these countries would be allocated a total of four votes – i.e. these national central bank governors would have to suspend their voting right in one-fifth of the meetings.
- A total of eight votes would be assigned to the NCB governors of 14 middle-sized member countries. Thus, the participants of this group would be entitled to vote in only 57% of all decisions.

Table 6.6 ECB rotation model – Voting shares and frequencies of voting (three groups)[35]

		Number of governors in the Governing Council					
		22	23	24	25	26	27
Group 1	Frequency of voting	4/5	4/5	4/5	4/5	4/5	4/5
	Relative frequency of voting	0.0381	0.0381	0.0381	0.0381	0.0381	0.0381
Group 2	Frequency of voting	8/11	8/12	8/12	8/13	8/13	8/14
	Relative frequency of voting	0.035	0.032	0.032	0.030	0.030	0.027
Group 3	Frequency of voting	3/6	3/6	3/7	3/7	3/8	3/8
	Relative frequency of voting	0.024	0.024	0.020	0.020	0.018	0.018
Sum		15	15	15	15	15	15

Source: European Central Bank (2003, p. 79).

---

[35] Additionally to the frequencies of voting which result after the introduction of the rotation model, Tables 6.6 and 6.7 also show the relative frequencies of voting which will be useful later in our sections on how to apply the power index concept and the section containing our results.

Table 6.7   ECB rotation model – Voting shares and frequencies of voting (two groups)

		Number of governors in the Governing Council					
		16	17	18	19	20	21
Group 1	Frequency of voting	5/5	5/5	5/5	4/5	4/5	4/5
	Relative frequency of voting	0.0476	0.0476	0.0476	0.0381	0.0381	0.0381
Group 2	Frequency of voting	10/11	10/12	10/13	11/14	11/15	11/16
	Relative frequency of voting	0.043	0.040	0.037	0.037	0.035	0.033
Sum		15	15	15	15	15	15

Note: The relative frequency of voting is defined as the frequency of voting divided by number of members in the Executive Board (21) (the Executive Board) (see second section of this digression). Source: European Central Bank (2003, p. 78) and own calculations.

- The remaining eight NCB governors would only be allocated three rights to vote, which implies that these representatives would be suspended from 62.5% of the voting dates.
- Irrespective of their specific voting rights, all NCB governors would be able to participate in the discussions on the monetary policy of the ECB Governing Council.
- The problem of countries not joining the euro area at the same time was solved by forming two groups until the accession of the 22nd member (Table 6.7).

The implication of the ECB proposal in terms of the distribution of the voting rights between the Executive Board on the one hand and the NCB Governors from small, medium-sized and large euro-member countries on the other hand can be best analysed (though rarely performed up to now) using the game-theoretical concept of power indices which is presented from a theoretical perspective in the second section and applied empirically to the ECB decision-making process in the third section of this digression. In this sense, this study reaches beyond the early, more narrative discussions of the adjustment of voting modalities in the ECB Governing Council (see for example Belke, 2003; Gros, 2003; Lommatzsch and Tober 2003).

How to Apply the Power Index Concept

The classical power indices which have their origin in solutions for cooperative games are often used to observe and quantify the allocation of power in a voting system. In this approach, the voting power is roughly defined as the influence of players on a voting outcome. Its distribution usually differs from the purely formal distribution of voting rights as has been shown in different studies (Owen, 1995, p. 460; Holler & Kellermann, 1978; Leech, 2001a, 2001b).

Two power indices, the Shapley-Shubik index (Shapley, 1997) and the Banzhaf index (Banzhaf, 1965) have received the most attention in the theoretical literature and their application to political structures. We will use both of them in our analysis. For this purpose, will briefly introduce, formally define and compare them. In order to calculate the power indices a voting situation has to be defined as a game and the voting members of the considered committee as players. This game is then represented by the (relative) voting weights of the players, w_i for player i, as well as by the given majority rule, the quota q. By considering only these two aspects, the approach obviously abstracts from the particular preferences of agents when forming winning coalitions. However these two characteristics are sufficient to identify all winning and losing coalitions, which differ in the value attributed to them by the characteristic function v,[36] $v(C)=1$ for winning, $v(C)=0$ for losing coalitions. Winning coalitions are characterised by a sum of their members voting weights that exceeds the quota ($\sum_{i \in C} w_i \geq q$) whereas the contrary is the case for losing coalitions: their voting share is lower than the required majority ($\sum_{i \in C} w_i < q$). A game, where a winning coalition receives the maximum possible gain of 1 is called a simple game.[37] In this setup power indices identify the voting power of every player as his influence on the voting outcome. These measure take into account that the voting weight is not a good measure of power, and that a suitable power index can only result by considering the interaction of the players. Most of them work with the idea of a swing: a player i has a swing when his exit out of a winning coalition C turns it to a losing one. Player i is then "decisive" for the coalition C. When the number of swings of a player i is set in relation to the total number of swings in this game, the resulting number will be an indication of the power i.

This is exactly the way voting power is calculated by the Banzhaf index. Its formula counts the swings of the player i in all possible coalitions (Ω is the set of all coalitions). The numerator is equal to 1 if the player i has a swing in the coalition C and a value of 0 if it does not. This sum is then divided by the number of all coalitions including player i (2^{n-1}).

$$\beta_i^* = \sum_{C \subseteq \Omega} \frac{[v(C) - v(C - \{i\})]}{2^{n-1}}. \tag{6.68}$$

In order to make it comparable to the Shapley-Shubik power index (which will be explained later), we use the normalised Banzhaf index in our analysis. The normalised index has the property that the indices of all players always sum up to 1, which makes an interpretation as a share of power possible. For normalizing purposes the Banzhaf index of player i is divided by the sum of all indices. The formula for the normalised Banzhaf index is finally given by:

$$\beta_i = \frac{\beta_i^*}{\sum_{i=1}^{n} \beta_i^*}. \tag{6.69}$$

---

[36] The characteristic function is a function, denoted v, that associates a number, denoted $v(C)$ with every subset C (coalition) of N (player set). The number $v(C)$ is interpreted as the value created when the members of C cooperate.

[37] Additionally, the following conditions should hold: The set of all players forms a winning coalition, the set of zero players represents a losing coalition and the addition of players to a coalition cannot turn it from winning to losing.

The idea behind the Shapley-Shubik power index is slightly different. The number of swings is equally important, but in this index each permutation (ordering) of the set of players is taken into account. Since all orderings are considered, the idea of the swing is refined and described by the term pivotal position. A player is "pivotal", if his entry to a coalition turns it from losing into winning. Expressed differently, a pivotal player must be the last to enter a minimum winning coalition. The Shapley-Shubik index of player i then results in the division of the number of orderings of N for which i is pivotal by the total number of possible orderings of the set N.

Formally, this index can be expressed as:

$$\phi_i (N, v) = \sum_{i \in C; C \subseteq N} \frac{(|C| - 1)! \, (n - |C|)!}{n!} \, [v(C) - v(C - \{i\})] .^{38}$$

The line of reasoning in this section will be mainly based on the Shapley-Shubik index. The preference is given to the Shapley-Shubik index for two reasons. Firstly, this index is more appropriate for the analysis of voting bodies in which there is considerable communication among the voters and coalition formation is active (Straffin, 1988). This condition is surely met by the ECB Governing Council, owing to, for example, the informal meetings on the eve of the official sessions and the collegial definition of the voting body. The same can also be assumed to hold for the enlarged Governing Council which applies the Rotation model, because all NCB presidents are present in discussions independently of their voting rights. Secondly, it should be emphasised that the main difference between the two power indices lies in the specific probability model used by them. The fact that the Shapley-Shubik index takes into account all possible permutations does not only guarantee its neutrality towards ad hoc beliefs concerning coalition building. It also allows us to interpret the Shapley-Shubik index as the expected value of player i. In our study, this interpretation makes it possible to apply an inter-temporal approach and, furthermore, to interpret the inter-temporal power as the expected value of a player across several meetings.

Nevertheless, it could still be argued that the application of the Banzhaf index is more appropriate. This argument might derive from the distinction of power indices based on their interpretation as I-power or P-Power (see Felsenthal & Machover, 1998, p. 84). The power measured by the Banzhaf index is understood as I-Power, and is in this context interpreted in terms of "influence". An I-power index implies that voting behaviour is motivated by "policy-seeking" over a public good. On the contrary P-power (e.g., the Shapley-Shubik index) presupposes "office-seeking

---

[38] Here $|C|$ is the number of the members of the coalition C, n the general number of players, $v(C)$ the return of coalition C and $v(C - \{i\})$ the payoff of the coalition C after the exit of player i. In simple games, the expression $[v(C) - v(C - \{i\})]$ defines the appreciation of the value of coalition C by the player i, it shows whether in the considered permutation player i has a pivotal position. To obtain the Shapley-Shubik value of player i formally, the marginal contributions of player i to all possible coalitions are summed up and weighted with the probability that the player i is the last player who enters the coalition of the strength $|C|$.

behaviour" and a voting over a prize that will be accredited only to the winning party. Of course, we are aware of the fact that the ECB Governing Council is voting on a public good (monetary policy) and, hence, that also the aspect of power as "influence" should be captured by the research. However, we mainly refer to the Shapley-Shubik index in our analysis because we attach a higher importance to the arguments in favour of the applicability of this power index.[39] But at the same time we also compute and display the Banzhaf index as well in order to give additional support to our results. It turns out that in almost all cases the Banzhaf index is in line with the results gained with the Shapley index.

Up to now, concept of power indices has been frequently used to study the distribution of voting power in different national and international voting systems. For instance, Dreyer and Schotter (1980) and Leech (2001a) published studies of power distribution in the IMF, while Owen (1995, p. 460) analysed the United Nations Security Council. The voting power of European institutions has also been the subject of many studies. Bilbao, Fernandez, Jimenez, and Lopez (2002), Sutter (2001), and Widgrén (1994) estimated the power of member states in the EU Council, while the European Parliament was subject to a power index application in Lane and Maeland (2000). Yet the distribution of power in the ECB Council has been the subject of only a few studies, probably because of the triviality of the analysis of the status quo, the one member-one vote rule. Actually, the reform of this decision-making body resulted in a change of the equal distribution of the votes. Hence, the consideration of power distribution has become an important source of further insights into the impact of the reform of voting rights in the ECB Council. We are especially aware of one other study in the field, namely the study by Fahrholz and Mohl (2004). This study comes up with different, sometimes opposite results. These differences in results might be traced back to different assumptions made in order to model the specific voting scenario as a simple game. We will investigate this topic more deeply at the end of the current section, after the discussion of the assumptions made in our own research.

In the following calculations, the decision-making process in the ECB Governing Council is assumed to be a weighted voting game. Each of the NCB governors as well as the Executive Board is considered to be one separate player. Furthermore, the following three assumptions are crucial to hold. First, it is assumed that all the present members of the Governing Council cooperate over several meetings. After the introduction of the rotation model, the members of the Council will not be allowed to vote at every session. Nevertheless, all of them will still attend each session. Hence, it seems plausible in fact that the members will form coalitions that persist during several meetings.

In decision-making, it is not decisive if a vote is formally taken. Of much greater importance is the possibility of using a vote on an average of several meetings. This strategy leads to an active formation of inter-temporal coalitions during the

---

[39]Widgrén (1994) also calculates both indices for the Council of Ministers of the European Community. Nevertheless he interprets the Shapley-Shubik index despite the fact that the analyzed council decides over public goods. His main argument is the high level of communication within the committee.

preparations for decision-making. For this reason, we consider the decision-making process within the ECB Governing Council as an *inter-temporally cooperative game*.

Our second assumption refers to the preferences and the voting behaviour of the players. The NCB governors are regarded as representatives of their countries, who are thus voting with a *national bias*. This assumption stems from the classical analyses by Meade (2003a, 2003b, p. 131, 2003c, p. 2) and by Meade and Sheets (2002, 2005), which have shown that a national bias in the decision-making of the ECB Council cannot be excluded.[40] As long as the members of the Council are regarded as representatives of their countries because of their heritage, an incentive strengthened by the new rotation model also for the euro area, the suspicion persists that national aspects still play an important role.

Finally, our third assumption defines the role of the Executive Board. In the following calculations *the Executive Board is considered as one player* with six votes. The reason for this assumption is that we focus on the allocation of power among the national representatives. As the Executive Board is frequently assumed to represent the interests of the whole euro area, this unanimity assumption appears to be highly plausible.[41] Yet there is no *a priori* restriction in coalition-forming among the national central bank presidents.

Technically speaking, the relative frequency of voting (see Tables 6.3 and 6.4) is interpreted as the relative inter-temporal voting weight. It is defined as the frequency of voting resulting from the rotation, divided by the number of voters, which is 21 under the rotation model. For the Executive Board, for instance, this means dividing 6 (the voting frequency) by 21 which gives 0.27 for all accession phases.[42] The inter-temporal voting weight enters the calculations as the voting weight of a player in the classical applications. Furthermore, a simple majority rule has been assumed for the calculations of the inter-temporal voting power, closely following the approach by Gruener (1998, p. 4). The numerous calculations have been conducted based on an algorithm originally developed by Bräuninger and König (2001), namely the Indices of Power IOP 2.0 programme.

There are many important differences between our assumptions and the ones made in the study by Fahrholz and Mohl (2004). First, it is important to note that the authors of this study are not interested in an inter-temporal approach, while this aspect is central for our study. Second, they model the voting situation differently, i.e. they interpret each group of national bank presidents as one player and compute the power index of a single NCB president by dividing the power of the group

---

[40]The assumption of nationally biased voting behaviour of national central bank presidents has also been applied in Bindseil (2001) and de Grauwe (2003, p. 21).

[41]The consideration of the Executive Board as one player also significantly simplifies the calculations. Power Indices can be calculated exactly for games with approximately not more than 27 players. This restriction results of the time of calculation which doubles when adding one new player.

[42]Tables 6.6 and 6.7 reveal the relative voting frequencies that have been used in the calculation of power indices.

by the number of members. The modelling of a voting block is possible if we feel legitimized to assume that the members of the group form an a priori coalition with common interests. But the power of the block is in this case larger than the sum of the individual power indices (Straffin, 1980). In our study each NCB president is seen as a single player, because we are interested in a power index which considers the strategic interaction between all players. We believe that it would be useful to consider some a priori information on block building, but we do not agree that the assumption of common interests in the groups holds in general. In our view, there are some significant counter-arguments against the view that the NCB presidents will vote in a common fashion simply because they are part of a group. For instance, for two large countries that clearly belong to group 1 under the scenario of a euro area-27, namely Germany and the UK (with its cycle connected more closely to the US cycle than to that of the euro area), the business cycle pattern may not be synchronous. Moreover, it has been frequently argued by academics that the rotation model leads to a "re-nationalisation" of monetary policy, i.e. that in this bloated reformed Council, each governor will experience that it is mainly his national provenience what will play a role in the monetary decision making (Belke, 2003; Meade, 2003a, 2003b, 2003c). These points were two of the reasons, for instance, for Belke and Styczynska (2006) to choose and stick to the inter-temporal approach.

The third difference lies in the assumption concerning the behaviour of the Executive Board. In our study, the Executive Board is interpreted as a voting block, i.e. one player. Fahrholz and Mohl study two scenarios, the first one (non-partisan) similar to our approach and a partisan scenario where the members of the Executive Board build voting blocks with the representative of the NCB of his country. Our arguments for choosing only the non-partisan scenario have already been listed above. Fourth, the study by Fahrholz and Mohl compares three alternatives, namely "no reform", "reform to the rotation model" and a second reform option called according to its proponent, the German research institute DIW "à la DIW". This third alternative is not considered in our study, because (only) the rotation model has already been ratified and will come into force with EU Enlargement.

Finally, the main difference in results should be mentioned as well. Fahrholz and Mohl find that the power of the Executive Board diminishes as a result of the introduction of the rotation model, whereas in our study the opposite occurs. The specific set of assumptions underlying each of the two approaches accounts for this difference. In our approach, the Executive Board is the largest player in both cases: with and without reform. After the reform the Executive Board is one player who faces players with shrinking voting weights, which leads to a stabilisation of its power. Whereas in the study of Fahrholz and Mohl (in a non-partisan scenario with rotation model) the Executive Board faces blocks of players with voting shares nearly as high as its own as opposed to the status quo where the Executive Board builds a voting block but not the NCB presidents. Here the question may be raised why several countries vote in a block after, but not before the introduction of the rotation model and how the results of such different approaches can be compared. After having anticipated some of our results we now come to a detailed presentation and interpretation of them.

Results

Relative Voting Share and Power in the Reformed ECB Council

The relative voting weights usually allow a first view of the allocation of power in the ECB Council. But these numbers also form the basis for the calculation of the more elaborated power indices. We see the numerical derivation of the voting shares and the resulting power indices as the main ingredient of a detailed description of the characteristics of each of the voting rules compared in this study, i.e. the one person-one vote rule and the new rotation model. As a first step, the shifts of voting shares during an accession in a reformed ECB Council are investigated. As a second step, the results of the calculation of voting power for this case are discussed. Later, the results are compared with those derived for the status quo, the one person-one vote rule. Finally this comparison allows a comparative judgment about the usefulness and applicability of the new rotation model.

Under the rotation model, the relative voting weights do not change proportionally with each enlargement of the euro area. The relative voting weight of the Executive Board is stabilised at 6/21 and the voting weights of the national central bank presidents depend on the group to which the considered member of the European Central Bank Council can be counted, as can be seen in Fig. 6.11. While the relative voting weight of a national central bank governor who is a member of the first group falls only once as the Union is enlarged to 19 members, the relative weight of the members of the other groups changes almost with every accession.

As a result of the enlargement of the euro area, the relative voting weights of all groups fall as a trend, but for the members of group 2 a sudden rise in voting weight can be observed, i.e. when the 19th and the 22nd members accede. Figure 6.11 also clearly reveals the discrepancy between the relative voting weights of the members of different groups. The graph of group 1 is always located above the graphs for the

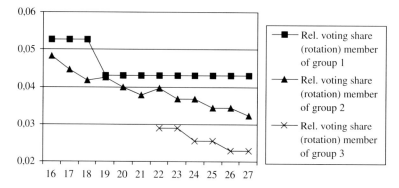

Fig. 6.11 Voting shares of national central bank presidents under the rotation model
Source: Own calculations. Refers to Belke & Styczynska (2006) in all figures and tables in this digression.

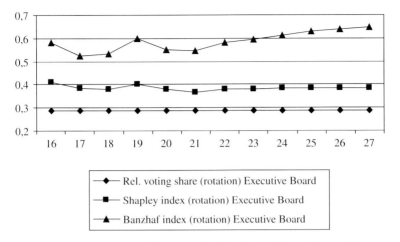

Fig. 6.12 Power and voting shares of the Executive Board under the rotation model
Source: Own calculations.

other groups. Only once do the curves of groups 1 and 2 move closer to each other, whereas the relative voting share of group 3 is always visibly smaller.

What are the consequences of this allocation of voting rights on the distribution of power among the different members of the Governing Council? After the discussion of the relative voting weights, we anticipate a stabilisation of Executive Board's power and rising differences between the power indices of members of different groups. As revealed in Fig. 6.12, the power index of the Executive Board is much less stable over time as could have been expected after examination of the relative voting shares. After the accession of the 17th member country, a sudden reduction of both power indices can be observed. The accession of the 17th country leads to an opposite reaction of power associated with the Executive Board, i.e. it rises. During the following accession both indices decrease. This trend is reversed after the accession of the 22nd member state to the euro area. In the midst of subsequent euro-area enlargement rounds, the Banzhaf index rises whereas the Shapley index remains relatively stable throughout the enlargement process, which prompts the question of why such changes occur.

In the first case, the power of the Executive Board decreases because the size of the Council rises without a reduction of the voting shares of group 1 members. But the accession of the 19th member country (in the second case) leads to a cut in the voting share in group 1 from one to four-fifths. The influence of the Executive Board thus rises because the members of group 1 are less frequently "decisive" for the coalitions than before.[43] Yet the voting share of group 1 never shrinks below

---

[43] Remember that in our setup power indices identify the voting power of every player according to his influence on the voting outcome. Most of these indices start from the idea of a swing: a player i has a swing when his exit out of a winning coalition C turns it to a losing one. Player i is then decisive for the coalition C. See extensively our above section on how to apply the power index concept.

Table 6.8 The relative power of the Executive Board under the rotation model

Member countries of the euro area	16	17	18	19	20	21	22	23	24	25	26	27
Shapley index Executive Bd. Shapley index group 1	11.2	6.9	9.6	12.7	9.0	11.7	11.2	11.1	11.9	12.2	11.6	12.0
Shapley index Executive Bd. Shapley index group 2	11.2	12.5	11.6	12.7	13.9	12.2	12.7	13.8	13.9	15.2	15.6	16.1
Shapley index Executive Bd. Shapley index group 3	–	–	–	–	–	–	19.2	19.5	21.4	19.9	23.6	24.3

Source: Own calculations.

this mark of four-fifths. Hence, the power of the Executive Board drops until it is stabilised (in terms of the Shapley index) by the introduction of group 3 (after the accession of the 22nd member state), as a result of a reduction of the voting shares of group 2.

Before we discuss the results of the calculation for each group, Table 6.8 shows the relation between the power indices of the Executive Board and each of the NCB governor groups 1–3. It becomes obvious that the power of the Executive Board exceeds the power of the national central bank presidents by a factor between 8 (in relation to group 1) and 24 (in relation to group 3).[44]

The development of the Shapley index of group 1, which is dependent on enlargement of the euro area, seems to be nearly opposite to that of the Executive Board, as can be seen in Fig. 6.13. The Shapley index rises suddenly as the 17th member state accedes to the euro area. Hence, it can be assumed that the members of the first group win the power initially lost by the Executive Board at this stage of enlargement. As could have been expected, the power of the representative members of group 1 decreases sharply after the accession of the 19th member state to the euro area, because at this point the voting rights are cut for the first time during the enlargement process.

It proves to be more difficult, however, to explain the surprising rise of the Shapley index after the accession of the 20th euro-area member state. At this step of enlargement, power even exceeds the relative voting weight. As the votes of the Executive Board and the considered group do not change at this point, the shift in the distribution of power can only be explained through the decrease of the voting weights of the members of group 2. This shift in the allocation of voting rights

---

[44]If the Banzhaf index is considered instead, the differences are even larger. In this case, the Executive Board has 14 to 70 times more power at its disposal.

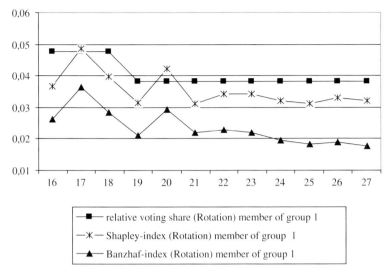

Fig. 6.13 Power and voting shares of a member of group 1 under the rotation model
Source: Own calculations.

changes the number of possibilities that are decisive in voting situations for group 1 members and raises their power in this specific scenario. After the next accession, the power of group 1 returns to the initial level again. The division of the NCB governors into three different groups does not affect the power of group 1 to a greater extent – it stays at a relatively stable level.[45]

When discussing the allocation of power to group 2 (Fig. 6.14), changes observed up to the accession of the 22nd member can be explained in a similar way. The only surprising change is the sudden rise in power after the accession of the 18th country. Despite the decreasing voting share, the power as indicated by both indices rises. Hence, this stage of enlargement can be interpreted as a favourable constellation of voting shares that aids group 2. This reminds us of paradoxes such as "the paradox of redistribution" or "the paradox of size" typically discussed in the literature on power indices because the power rises in spite of falling voting shares.[46] After the accession of the 22nd country, the members of group 2 lose power continuously – their Shapley index decreases from 0.042 for a euro area comprising 20 member states to a realisation of 0.032 in the case of 27 members.

For group 3, a negatively shaped curve can also be observed (Fig. 6.15). It is noteworthy that this group 3 emerges from the accession of the 22nd country. The members of this group have a lower share of the voting rights at their disposal than members of other groups and the power assigned to them is even lower than the

---

[45]The development of the Banzhaf index reveals significant breaks at similar stages of the euro-area enlargement process as the Shapley index does (Fig. 7.13).

[46]For a review of such paradoxes see Holler and Kellermann (1978, p. 107).

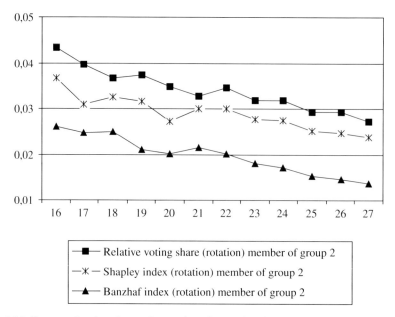

Fig. 6.14 Power and voting shares of a member of group 2 under the rotation model
Source: Own calculations.

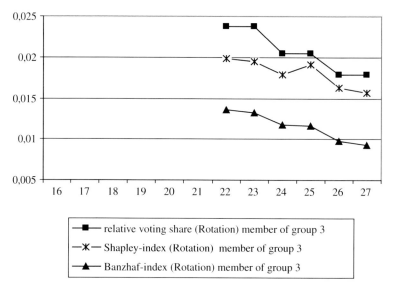

Fig. 6.15 Power and voting shares of a member of group 3 under the rotation model
Source: Own calculations.

voting share. During the enlargement process, their Shapley index decreases from 0.02 to 0.015 in the final scenario of the accession process. The power index of a representative member of group 2 exceeds the power of his or her counterpart in group 3 by two times in the final stage of a euro area consisting of 27 members.

Have the observed voting shares thus been good indicators of the distribution of power within the reformed ECB Governing Council? The first hypothesis was that the power of the Executive Board would be stabilised by the reform. Our numerical application of the power index concept has shown that the position of this "sub-Council" would not only be stabilised but also possibly strengthened. (This result is also confirmed by comparison to the power indices under the status quo rule.) The Shapley index of the Executive Board amounts to approximately 0.4 under all scenarios. This means that after the reform of the ECB decision-making process, 40% of the voting power devolves to the Executive Board.[47]

Our second hypothesis concerning the discrepancy between the power values of members of the different groups can be confirmed clearly. The five largest member states in the euro area in economic terms have between 19 and 24% of the voting power at their disposal, the sum of the calculated power indices for the five members of the first group. The medium-sized group, which has 11–14 member states, can exercise between 30 and 40% of the voting power, while group 3 with six to eight members has about 11–13% of the available voting power. But the consideration of the allocation of power has also revealed a new and unexpected feature of the rotation model. Surprising shifts of power between the groups have been observed, especially in the sequential enlargement scenarios prior to the construction of the three groups.

Comparison with the Status Quo: One Person, One Vote

In the previous subsection, the voting shares and power indices for all members of the Governing Council were presented under the assumption of the rotation model already being in place. The following comparison to the status quo (one person, one vote), however, is helpful in order to assess the changes that are generated by the projected reform. For this purpose, the voting shares and power indices in the unreformed European Central Bank Governing Council are first briefly reported. To check the robustness of our results, both the Shapley and the Banzhaf indices are indicated in some figures.[48] Nevertheless, our discussion predominately refers to the Shapley index.[49]

For the unreformed Governing Council, under the one member-one vote rule each of the national central bank governors has one vote. Hence, their relative voting weight amounts to $1/N$, with N as the number of all members of the Governing Council. As previously discussed, the Executive Board is regarded as one

---

[47]The numbers refer to the calculated Shapley values.

[48]The exact results are summarised in Belke and Styczynska (2006), Annex, Table A.3.

[49]See the discussion of the assumptions in our above section on how to apply the power index concept.

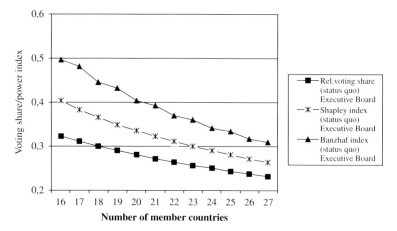

Fig. 6.16 Power of the Executive Board under the one member-one vote rule
Source: Own calculations.

player; consequently the voting weight of this specific player is 6/*N*. If a continuous enlargement of the Government Council is assumed, *N* increases and the relative voting shares of every player fall. Figure 6.16 shows the power indices for the Executive Board and additionally its relative voting weight. It becomes obvious that all the displayed curves reveal negative slopes. But both indices show a higher power index of the Executive Board than could have been expected after the examination of the allocation of relative voting weights.[50] The voting power that is attributed to the Executive Board by the Shapley index exceeds the relative voting rights to a smaller degree than the respective power expressed by the Banzhaf index. The voting power shown by the first index is between 20 and 30% higher than the voting share, while the Banzhaf index reveals it to be between 45 and 60% higher. In both cases, the distance to the relative voting weights is reduced by each successive accession.

But what impact does this allocation of voting rights have on the distribution of power among the NCB governors? The presentation of the voting power and voting weights of the national central bank presidents in Fig. 6.17 is very similar to Fig. 6.16 at first glance, but a closer inspection immediately reveals that the curves have a different order. The NCB governors have less influence on the voting result than expected if relative voting weights are examined. Contrary to the results for the Executive Board, the Shapley indices now exceed the Banzhaf values.[51]

This result, however, does not come as a surprise because a number of empirical applications confirm that the voting power of the "largest" player often tends to be higher than his or her voting share. The opposite is true for the "smallest" player,

---

[50]The Shapley index is normally closer to the voting rights than the Banzhaf index, as discussed in Sutter (2001, p. 341).

[51]The explanation is that the indices can always be summed up to one and the Banzhaf indices were higher for the Executive Board.

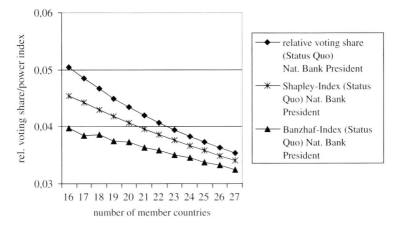

Fig. 6.17 Power of national central bank presidents under the one member-one vote rule
Source: Own calculations.

as discussed in Widgrén (1994, p. 1154). Here the Executive Board with six votes is the "largest player" and its power is several times higher than the corresponding power values of an individual NCB governor. Under the status quo rule, the voting weights of the Executive Board are always six times higher than the voting share of a single NCB governor, while the difference between the respective power indices is even more considerable.

Figures 6.18 to 6.21 present a comparison of power indices resulting for each considered group of the ECB Council. In Fig. 6.18, the realisations of the power indices of the Executive Board under the rotation model are compared with those under the status quo ante. It is clearly visible that the rotation model not only stabilises the power of the Executive Board, it even gains power after the reform proposed by the ECB: its Shapley index nearly doubles in the long term.

But not only the Executive Board benefits from the adaptation of the rotation model – the members of group 1 are vested with more voting power in the reformed Council in nearly all the accession phases as compared with their power in an unreformed Council (Fig. 6.19). Hence, there are also groups who lose their ability to influence the voting outcome. In this case, the losers under the reform are groups 2 and 3, as demonstrated in Figures 6.20 and 6.21. Thus, the NCB governors of group 2 have to give up less power than the members of group 3. While group 2 members lose 10–20% of their initial power, the power indices of the NCB governors from the economically less important member states are between 38 and 45% lower than under the one member-one vote rule.

Figures 6.18 to 6.21 also show very clearly that in the reformed Council the enlargement of the monetary union leads to unexpected shifts in the power of groups, as already discussed in the previous subsection. Here it is apparent that this development cannot be observed in the case of an unreformed Council. According

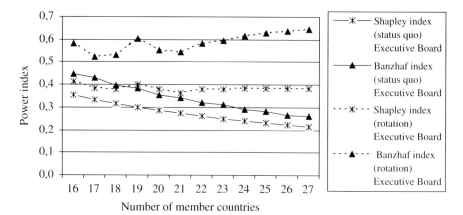

Fig. 6.18 Power of the Executive Board (status quo and rotation)
Source: Own calculations.

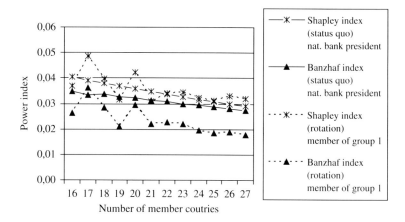

Fig. 6.19 Power of a representative member of group 1 (status quo and rotation)
Source: Own calculations.

to the preceding analysis, the rotation model cannot be considered as a robust voting rule, as the accession of new euro-area member states can lead to unexpected and probably unintended shifts in the allocation of power. The prediction of the actual possibilities for forming a majority in a Council vote changes in a way that cannot be extrapolated from a mere visual inspection of the voting shares. However, these unexpected changes taken in isolation probably do not make it significantly more difficult for the public to form accurate inflation expectations as long as the accession process is incomplete. This would likely only be the case with a much greater instability in the shares. But if the median of the member countries' inflation

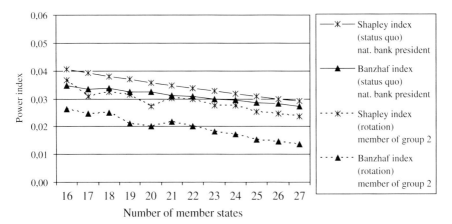

Fig. 6.20   Power of a representative member of group 2 (status quo and rotation)
Source: Own calculations.

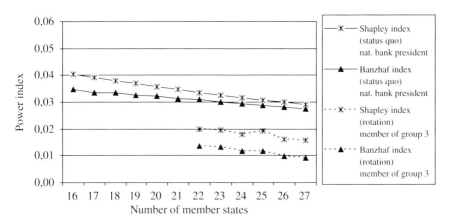

Fig. 6.21   Power of a representative member of group 3 (status quo and rotation)
Source: Own calculations.

preferences becomes more volatile in the wake of the rotation model (an issue not tackled in this paper), this would still become a matter of concern (Schulze, 2005).

Thus seen on the whole, both positive and negative characteristics of the rotation model have been identified in the wake of our systematic comparison with the status quo. The strengthening of the Executive Board can be considered as a benefit. Its influence on the voting outcome is much more important within the reformed Governing Council. Hence, the representatives of the European perspective versus those with a national bias have a stronger standing in the reformed Council when compared with the status quo.

Nevertheless, the lack of robustness must be seen as a disadvantage of the rotation model. Given the new voting shares, it is impossible to predict how the relations of power will really change. This voting system cannot be judged as transparent, because intuition does not enable one to come to similar conclusions as those arrived at through the relatively complex calculation of power indices. Moreover, the fact that after reform of the Council the members of group 3 are the only members that lose considerable voting power confirms the suspicion that the present Governing Council wanted to protect its voting influence at the expense of the accession countries.

An Assessment of Principle of Representativeness

In designing the precise features of the rotation system, the Governing Council was guided by some fundamental principles such as one member-one vote, ad personam participation, representativeness, automaticity and transparency.[52] In the following discussion, we only focus on the important principle of representativeness. Its justification by the ECB runs as follows. The introduction of a rotation of voting rights could lead to situations in which the group of governors with a voting right are from member states that, taken together, may be perceived as not being sufficiently representative of the euro area economy as a whole. The new voting system, therefore, should be designed in a manner that would safeguard against such outcomes.

In this subsection, one important aspect of this guiding principle of representativeness is examined. According to this definition, any ECB Council voting system which minimises the discrepancy between the voting share and the respective economic weight of each of the member countries meets this criterion. As a modification of this definition, the discrepancy between the voting power and the economic weight, represented either by the share on the common GDP or, alternatively, by a GDP plus population weight (GDP weight 50% and population weight 50%) and their development in the wake of the euro area enlargement process is examined. More concretely, we analyse whether this difference is diminished through the implicit abandonment of the one member-one vote principle and its substitution by the rotation model. For this purpose, four numbers are compared and presented in Fig. 6.22.

The first two numbers express the relative voting power of a single NCB governor. The relative power is calculated as the voting power of an NCB governor divided by the power of all NCB governors, both expressed through the Shapley value.[53] The white bars in Fig. 6.22 result under the rotation model, the striped ones without reform. As the third number, the GDP ratio of the respective country in the euro area GDP has been chosen as an approximation of the relative economic weight (black bar). Table 6.9 summarises the GDP data for EU member states and candidate countries.

---

[52] See ECB (2003, p. 75). See also Bofinger (2003, p. 3) and Gros (2003).

[53] See also Belke and Styczynska (2006), Table A.2; using this definition, we closely follow Berger (2002, p. 12) and Gros (2003, p. 125).

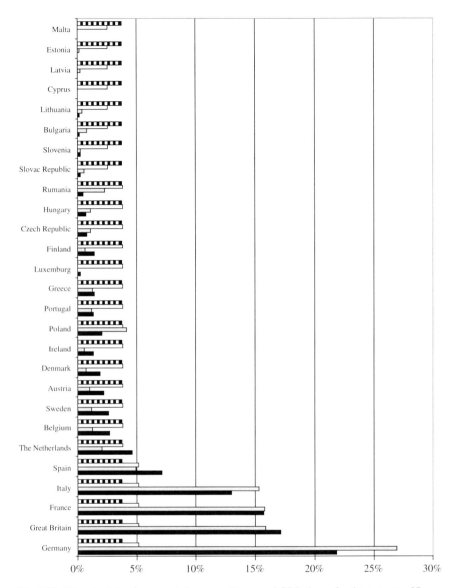

Fig. 6.22   The principle of representativeness – Power and GDP shares for the euro area-27
Notes: The *black bars* denote the respective GDP share, *grey bars* the GDP plus population weight
(GDP weight 50% and population weight 50%). *White bars* indicate the shares in the sum of
Shapley values under the rotation model and the striped ones the share of the sum of Shapley
values under the status quo rule
Source: Own calculations.

Table 6.9 Gross domestic product (in € millions) and population (in thousands) of EU member and candidate countries 2003

Country	Population	GDP
Germany	82,536.7	2,108,200.00
Great Britain	59,437.7	1,659,111.90
France	59,855.8	1,520,804.00
Italy	57,321.1	1,258,349.00
Spain	41,663.7	693,925.00
The Netherlands	16,192.6	444,033.00
Belgium	10,355.8	260,744.00
Sweden	8,940.8	255,423.10
Austria	8,102.2	216,830.50
Denmark	5,383.5	182,799.80
Ireland	3,963.7	128,187.40
Poland	38,218.5	200,198.00
Portugal	10,407.5	129,187.60
Greece	11,006.4	141,132.00
Luxembourg	448.3	22,340.50
Finland	5,206.3	139,734.00
Czech Republic	10,203.3	73,874.80
Hungary	10,142.4	69,888.90
Romania	21,772.8	48,361.80
Slovakia	5,379.2	25,147.00
Slovenia	1,995.0	23,385.10
Bulgaria	7,845.8	16,583.00
Lithuania	3,462.6	14,649.40
Cyprus	715.1	10,762.20
Latvia	2,331.5	8,940.20
Estonia	1,356.0	6,904.00
Malta	397.3	4,096.60

Source: Eurostat (2003a, 2003b).

While the fourth number is a country's GDP plus population weight (GDP weight 50% and population weight 50%). All figures are compared in Fig. 6.22 for each country in the case of a hypothetical euro area consisting of 27 member countries. The order of the countries is chosen to correspond with the ranking that results from the indicators proposed by the ECB.

A first inspection of Fig. 6.22 allows the non-rejection of the hypothesis that the introduction of the rotation model (white bars) leads to an improvement of representativeness because under the status quo rule (striped bars) the difference between the economic weights and the political weights of member states is larger. Nevertheless, the differences between political power and GDP respectively GDP plus population ratios of member countries are still large after the reform, especially so for the members of group 1. It is worth noting, that the consideration of population changes the degree of representativeness slightly. Some new EU-Members have large differences between the share in GDP and population (e.g. Poland).

Considering the sum of squared deviations enables us to enact a more exact comparison of the degrees of representativeness under the status quo rule and under the rotation model (Gros, 2003, p. 125). The sum results from the differences between

Table 6.10 Differences between the GDP-weight and the relative voting power – squared deviations

	Squared deviation status quo	Squared deviation rotation
Euro area-17	0.12	0.09
Euro area-22	0.12	0.10
Euro area-24	0.12	0.10
Euro area-27	0.09	0.07

Source: Own calculations.

the GDP weight and the relative power as measured for each member country. Table 6.10 shows the sums of squared deviations in four different scenarios of possible accession phases.

In each scenario, this sum proves to be smaller under the rotation model than under the status quo rule. The sum of the squares under the status quo in the case of a euro area consisting of 27 countries is 0.09. As already supposed after the examination of Fig. 6.22, this sum is smaller under the rotation model at 0.07. Consequently, we feel justified to conclude that the rotation model leads to an improvement compared with the status quo concerning the criterion of representativeness. Nevertheless, even after the reform large differences between the shares in voting power and in GDP can be found. This result is comparable to the results discussed in the literature (e.g. Bofinger, 2003; Gros, 2003) where only a slight improvement concerning this criterion is ascertained.

Conclusions and Potential for Further Research

Our analysis of the inter-temporal power indices in the context of the ECB Governing Council has revealed and highlighted some interesting aspects of both the reformed and unreformed voting system. One negative feature of the proposed voting reform is the sharp shift of the allocation of power during the early euro-area accession phases. This shift could have negative effects on the transparency of ECB decision-making and may result in a bias of inflation expectations. The second aspect of the rotation model that comes at a cost is the fact that the reform leads to a voting system where especially the acceding countries lose influence on the voting result compared with their voting power under the status quo. This could lead to a re-nationalisation of monetary policy in the euro area.

One benefit associated with the reform, however, is the higher degree of representativeness it would entail. But this effect is numerically very small and thus should not be overvalued. A further more important result is that the voting power of the Executive Board would be considerably strengthened through the reform. Under the quite realistic presumption that the Executive Board represents the interests of the euro area, this result tends to come as a benefit. In this case, the rotation model could have a stabilising effect on inflation expectations, which would alleviate the negative impact of the sudden shifts of power allocation. Moreover, European versus national aggregates could be more easily accepted by the public as an anchor for setting inflation expectations.

It is also conceivable to extend the approach taken in this study to the analysis of certain aspects of decision-making in the Governing Council, such as the modalities of decision-making. For instance, it is well known that both the tradition of deciding in a consensual fashion and the agenda-setting power of the Executive Board are some of the main features of the meetings of the ECB Council. Von Hagen (2003, p. 108) has taken these aspects into account in his analysis of the Governing Council prior to the reform. He essentially applies the median voter model to investigate what impact the traditional terms of decision-making have on the results of monetary policy. New insights could be gained if the rotation model is analyzed along these lines.

As a further possibility of extending our analysis, the monetary policy preferences of national central bank presidents could be explicitly included. The inclusion of such preferences in the analysis would make it possible to identify likely coalitions among Governing Council members who represent similar interests. The probability models used in the studies which model the Governing Council could be modified in accordance with information about the probabilities of certain coalitions forming. This could be achieved by defining the subsystems within which coalitions are joined with a higher probability. This approach was first used in Owen (1977) and has been applied to the EU Council in Widgrén (1994, p. 1154). In a similar fashion, this approach could be used to register the subsystems inside the Governing Council, wherein the Executive Board could be defined as one subsystem. Analogously, those groups of national central bank presidents whose home countries traditionally have a similar business cycle pattern could also be modelled as subsystems.

Why is such kind of rather complex voting power analysis as conducted by us above so relevant for the more recent analysis of European monetary policy? Cyprus and Malta embrace the euro since January 1st 2008, boosting Europe's monetary union to 15 states and adding another two Club Med votes to the policy board of the European Central Bank. The two islands – one near the coast of Africa and the other kissing the Levant – make up just 0.3pc of euro area GDP and barely flicker on the radar screen of the 320 m-strong currency bloc. Yet their arrival marks a crucial stage in the declining dominance of the German Bundesbank. The Latin and Hellenic cluster of states now has a majority of the votes on the Governing Council for the first time, with 11 of the 21 members.

While they hold a variety of views – and are in principle obliged to disregard their own national interest when they set foot inside the Eurotower – they share an economic culture that is often far removed from the German way of life. As the economic rift between the eurozone's North and South grows ever wider, the thorny question of which camp holds the majority of votes is likely to come into starker focus. Both the French and Italian leaders have already called for a shift in policy to curb the rise of the euro and shield struggling industries. "The lira-ization of the euro can no longer be excluded" (Belke & Gros, 2007, also cited by the Daily Telegraph (2007) on December 31st 2007).

Cyprus has carved out a niche as a tourist hub and off-shore banking centre, the money mecca of Russia's oligarchs and the new capitalists of the Balkans.

The current Cypriot leader, Tassos Papadopoulos, used to be legal adviser to the Yugoslav state bank used by Slobodan Milosevic to evade UN sanctions. With a per capita income of 94pc of the EU average, it is well able to cope with the rigours of the euro. It enters the euro area divided, leaving the North with the Turkish lira. Malta is too small to count on the monetary radar screen, though its plucky lira has been one of the strongest currencies in the world since breaking the link to sterling in the 1970s.

What worried officials in Frankfurt already at the start of 2008 was that the new-comers will tend to side with Greece, Spain, Portugal, Italy, France and Ireland should deflating property booms across the region prompt demands for a looser monetary policy. Germany has not had a property bubble. Instead it has used the time since the launch of the euro to screw down wages and claw back competitive-ness. Lean and fit again, it is gaining export share across southern Europe. While Germany at the start of 2008 had a current account surplus of 5.6pc of GDP, Spain had a deficit of 9.3pc, Portugal of 10pc, and Greece of 13pc. The deficits will have to be corrected, perhaps harshly as foreseen, for instance, by Belke & Gros, 2007.

Tensions are likely to grow not least because in the meantime also Slovakia entered the euro area. If you get sharp slowdowns in the peripheral economies, they are going to want rate cuts. It could lead to much more heated discussions although this might not necessarily transmit to the public since the ECB maintains total secrecy over meetings, refusing to release minutes or reveal how members voted. Ambrose Evans-Pritchard from the Daily Telegraph commented on this scenario as follows (Daily Telegraph, 2007):

The new Cypriot bank governor, Athanasios Orphanides, was a top official at US Federal Reserve until mid-2007 and made his name as an economic theorist arguing that central banks should let inflation spikes subside naturally – if possible – rather than slamming on the brakes in a rigid or mechanical fashion. The doctrine is known as "the Opportunistic Approach to Disinflation". It has had a major influence over US monetary strategy. Mr Orphanides played to his reputation as an inflation dove in an interview with Dow Jones in October, insisting that Europe enjoyed "an environment of very-well-anchored inflation expectations". This puts him in direct conflict with the two German board members, Axel Weber and Jürgen Stark, who have both warned repeatedly that eurozone inflation of 3.1pc is reaching levels that could set off the beginnings of a wage-price spiral. "Orphanides is going to bring a Fed-style framework to the ECB; the old Bundesbank perspective is progressively losing influence," said Julian Callow, eurozone economist at Barclays Capital.

A clutch of American-educated ECB board members from Italy, Spain and Greece is now taking over the key levers of power in Europe's monetary system. The Bundesbank lockhold was broken two years ago with the retirement of Otmar Issing, the doyen of German monetarism who held unchallenged mastery of the ECB as both chief economist and head of the research apparatus. A chunk of his empire went to Greek member Lucas Papademos, a former MIT professor and an intellectual force in his own right.

The ECB still cleaves to monetarist orthodoxy in a sort of ancestral deference to the Bundesbank – dutifully combing the M3 money supply data each month – but the bank is in reality shifting into a different orbit. The German-led group now seems determined to prevent a fresh wave of newcomers from Eastern Europe making the system even more inflation-prone and unmanageable. Mr Stark said these countries faced "substantial chal-lenges" and needed to achieve durable convergence before thinking of joining. Lorenzo Bini-Smaghi, head of the ECB's international division, said a number of Eastern European states should ditch their pegs to the euro, which was forcing them to hold interest rates too low for the needs of their fast-growing catch-up economies. "This might lead to boom-and-bust cycles, with potentially very severe adjustment costs," he said.

We would like to leave these strong statements largely uncommented here. But we would like to argue that it may be many years before the euro zone really welcomes its seventeenth member.

References

Abiad, A., & Mody, A. (2005). Financial reform: What shakes it? What shapes it? *American Economic Review, 95*(1), 66–88.

Akerlof, G., Dickens, W., & Perry, G. (1996). The macroeconomics of low inflation. *Brookings Papers on Economic Activity, 27*, 1–59.

Alesina, A., & Rosenthal, H. (1989). Partisan cycles in congressional elections and the macroeconomy. *American Political Science Review, 83*, 373–398.

Alesina, A., & Roubini, N. (1992). Political cycles in OECD economies. *Review of Economic Studies, 59*, 663–688.

Alesina, A., & Summers, L. (1993). Central bank independence and macroeconomic performance. *Journal of Money, Credit, and Banking, 25*(2), 157–162.

Alogoskoufis, G. S. (1994). On inflation, unemployment and the optimal exchange rate regime. In F. van der Ploeg (Ed.), *The handbook of international macroeconomics* (pp. 192–223). Cambridge, Oxford: Blackwell.

Alogoskoufis, G. S., Lockwood, B., & Philippopoulos, A. (1992). Wage inflation, electoral uncertainty and the exchange rate regime – theory and UK evidence. *Economic Journal, 102*, 1370–1394.

Alogoskoufis, G. S., & Philippopoulos, A. (1992). Inflationary expectations, electoral uncertainty and the exchange rate regime – Greece 1958–1989. *European Journal of Political Economy, 8*(3), 375–399.

Amend, T. (2003). Mittel- und Osteuropa: Auf dem Weg zum Euro. In *HBSC Trinkhaus und Burkhardt* (Hrsg.) (pp. 20–23). Währungen 2003/2004.

Annett, A. M. (1993). Elections and macroeconomic outcomes in Ireland – 1948–1991. *The Economic and Social Review, 25*, 21–47.

Arellano, M., & Bond, S. (1991). Some tests of specification for panel data: Monte Carlo evidence and an application to employment equations. *Review of Economic Studies, 58*, 277–297.

Arellano, M., & Bover, O. (1995). Another look at the instrumental variables estimation of error-component models. *Journal of Econometrics, 68*, 29–51.

Backus, D., & Driffill, J. (1985). Inflation and reputation. *American Economic Review, 75*(3), 530–538.

Bade, R., & Parkin, M. (1982). *Central bank laws and monetary policy*. Unpublished manuscript, Department of Economics, University of Western Ontario, Canada.

Bade, R. and M. Parkin. (1984). Central Bank Laws and Monetary Policy. Department of Economics, University of Western Ontario, Canada.

Baltagi, B. (1995). *Econometric analysis of panel data*. Chichester: John Wiley & Sons.

Banzhaf, J. F. (1965). Weighted voting doesn't work: A mathematical analysis. *Rutgers Law Review, 19*, 317–343.

Barro, R. J. (1996, May/June). Inflation and growth. *Federal Reserve Bank of St. Louis, Economic Review, 28*(3), 153–169.

Barro, R. J., & Gordon, D. B. (1983a). Rules, discretion and reputation in a model of monetary policy. *Journal of Monetary Economics, 12*(1), 101–121.

Barro, R. J., & Gordon, D. B. (1983b). A positive theory of monetary policy in a natural rate model. *Journal of Political Economy, 91*(4), 589–610.

Bean, C. (1998). The interaction of aggregate-demand policies and labor-market reform. *Swedish Economic Policy Review, 5*, 353–382.

Beck, T., Clarke, G., Groff, A., Keefer, P., & Walsh, P. (2001). New tools in comparative political economy: The database of political institutions. *World Bank Economic Review, 15*(1), 165–176.

Beetsma, R., & Bovenberg, L. (1998, September). *The optimality of a monetary union without a fiscal union* (CEPR Discussion Paper 1975) London.

Belke, A. (2002). Towards a Balanced Policy Mix under EMU: Co-ordination of Macroeconomic Policies and 'Economic Government'?. in: Journal of Economic Integration, Vol. 17(1), pp. 21–53.

Belke, A. (2003). The rotation model is not sustainable. *Intereconomics: Review of European Economic Policy, 38*, 119–124.

Belke, A., & Goecke, M. (1999). A simple model of hysteresis in employment under exchange rate uncertainty. *Scottish Journal of Political Economy, 46*(3), 260–286.

Belke, A., & Goecke, M. (2005). Real options effects on employment: Does exchange rate uncertainty matter for aggregation? *German Economic Review, 6*(2), 185–203.

Belke, A., & Gros, D. (1999). Estimating the costs and benefits of EMU: The impact of external shocks on labor markets. *Weltwirtschaftliches Archiv, 135*, 1–48.

Belke, A., & Gros, D. (2007). Instability of the Eurozone? In M. Heise, R. Tilly, P. J. J. Welfens (Eds.), *50 Years of EU dynamics – Integration, financial markets and innovations* (pp. 75–108). Berlin: Springer

Belke, A., Herz, B., & Vogel, L. (2006a). Reforms, exchange rates and monetary commitment: A panel analysis for OECD countries. *Open Economies Review, 18*, 369–388.

Belke, A., Herz, B., & Vogel, L. (2006b). Beyond trade – is reform effort affected by the exchange rate regime? A panel analysis for the world versus OECD countries. *Économie Internationale, 107*, 29–58.

Belke, A., Herz, B., & Vogel, L. (2006c). Exchange rate regimes and reforms – a panel analysis for the world versus OECD countries. *International Finance, 9*(3), 317–342.

Belke, A., Herz, B., & Vogel, L. (2007). Structural reforms and European monetary union: What can a panel analysis for the world versus OECD countries tell us? In D. Cobham (Ed.), *The travails of the eurozone: Economic policies and economic developments* (pp. 179–204). Houndmills, Basingstoke, UK: Palgrave Macmillan.

Belke, A., & Kamp, A. (1999a). When do labor market reforms achieve a double dividend under EMU? Discretionary versus rule based monetary policy revisited. *Journal of Economic Integration, 14*(4), 572–605.

Belke, A., & Kamp, M. (1999b). Doppelte 'Dividende' oder nur doppelte 'Funktion' von Arbeitsmarktreformen bei diskretionärer Geldpolitik? Anmerkungen zum Calmfors-Modell. *Jahrbücher für Nationalökonomie und Statistik, 218*(5+6), 543–555.

Belke, A., Schnable, G., & Zemanek, H. (2009). Current Account Imbalances and Structural Adjustment in the Euro Area: How to Rebalance Competitiveness, forthcoming IZA Discussion Paper, Bonn.

Belke, A., & Styczynska, B. (2006). The allocation of power in the enlarged ECB Governing Council – an assessment of the ECB rotation model. *Journal of Common Market Studies, 44*(5), 865–895.

Berger, H. (2002). *The ECB and euro area enlargement* (IMF Working Paper, No. 02/175) Washington/DC.

Berger, H., de Haan, J., & Inklaar, R. (2002, September 13–14). *Should the ECB be restructured, and if so, how?* Paper presented at the CESifo Delphi conference on Managing EU Enlargement, Munich.

Berthold, N., & Fehn, R. (1996). The positive economics of unemployment and labor market inflexibility. *Kyklos, 49*, 583–613.

Berthold, N., & Fehn, R. (2006). Unemployment in Germany – reasons and remedies, In M. Werding (Ed.), *Unemployment in Europe*, CESifo seminar series. Cambridge: MIT Press.

Bertola, G., & Boeri, T. (2001, March 21–22, April 27). *EMU labor markets two years on: Microeconomic tensions and institutional evolution.* Paper presented at the Workshop on "The Functioning of EMU: Challenges of the Early Years". Brussels: Directorate General for Economic and Financial Affairs, European Commission, p. 498.

Bilbao, J. M., Fernandez, J. R., Jimenez, N., & Lopez, J. J. (2002). Voting power in the European union enlargement. *European Journal of Operational Research, 143*, 181–96.

Bindseil, U. (2001). A coalition-form analysis of the one country-one vote rule in the Governing Council of the European central bank. *International Economic Journal, 15*, 141–64.

Blackburn, K., & Christensen, M. (1989). Monetary policy and policy credibility: Theory and evidence. *Journal of Economic Literature, 27*, 1–45.

Blanchard, O. (2006). European unemployment – the evolution of facts and ideas. *Economic Policy, 45*, 5–47.

Blanchard, O., Dornbusch, R., Dreze, J., Giersch, H., Layard, R., & Monti, M. (1986). Employment and growth in Europe – a two-handed approach. In O. Blanchard, R. Dornbusch, & R. Layard (Eds.), *Restoring Europe's prosperity* (pp. 95–124). Cambridge, Mass.: MIT Press.

Blanchard, O., & Giavazzi, F. (2003). Macroeconomic effects of regulations and deregulation in goods and labour markets. *Quarterly Journal of Economics, 118*(3), 879–907.

Blattner, T., Catenaro, M., Ehrmann, M., Strauch, R., & Turunen, J. (2008, March). The predictability of Monetary Policy ECB Occasional Paper Series, No. 83 Frankfurt/Main.

Blundell, R., & Bond, S. (1998). Initial conditions and moment restrictions in dynamic panel data models. *Journal of Econometrics, 87*, 115–143.

Bofinger, P. (2003). *Consequences of the modification of the Governing Council rules.* Briefing Paper for the committee for monetary and economic affairs (ECON) of the European Parliament, Brussels.

Bräuninger, T., & König, T. (2001). *Indices of power IOP 2.0* [Computer Programme]. University of Konstanz. Retrieved from http://www.uni-konstanz.de/FuF/Verwiss/koenig/IOP.html, 12 June 2004.

Buscher, H., Dreger, C., Ramos, R., & Surinach, J. (2005). *The impact of institutions on the employment performance in European labour markets* (IZA Discussion Paper 1732). Bonn: Institute for the Study of Labor.

Calmfors, L. (1997). *Unemployment, labor-market reform and EMU* (IIES Seminar Paper 639). Stockholm: Institute for International Economic Studies.

Calmfors, L. (1998). Macroeconomic policy, wage setting and employment – what difference does the EMU make? *Oxford Economic Policy Review, 14*, 125–151.

Calmfors, L. (2001). Unemployment, labor-market reform and monetary union. *Journal of Labor Economics, 19*(2), 265–289.

Calmfors, L., & Holmlund, B. (2000). Unemployment and economic growth: A partial survey. *Swedish Economic Review, 7*, 107–153 (Update of Calmfors, 1997).

Calvo, G. A. (1978). On the time consistency of optimal policy in a monetary economy. *Econometrica, 46*(6), 1411–1428.

Campillo, M., & Miron, J. (1997). Why does inflation differ across countries? In C. D. Romer & D. H. Romer (Eds.), *Reducing inflation: Motivation and strategy* (pp. 335–357). Chicago: University of Chicago Press.

Carey, K. (1997). "High Unemployment in the OECD. Does the Diagnosis of the 1980s Apply to the 1990s?," American University, Washington, mimeo.

Castrén, O., Takalo, T., & Wood, G. (2004, November). *Labor market reform and the sustainability of exchange rate pegs* (ECB Working Paper Series No. 406). Frankfurt, Main: European Central Bank.

Cecchetti, S. G., & Rich, R. W. (1999, March 15). *Structural estimates of the U.S. sacrifice ratio.* New York: Federal Reserve Bank of New York, Research and Market Analysis Group.

Clarida, R. Gali, J., & Gertler, M. (1999). The science of monetary policy: A new Keynesian perspective. *Journal of Economic Literature, 37*(4), 1661–1707.

Coe, D. T., & Snower, D. (1997). Policy complementarities: The case for fundamental labor market reform. *IMF Staff Papers, 44*(1), 1–35.

Connolly, E., & Kohler, M. (2004). *News and interest rate expectations: A study of six central banks* (Reserve Bank of Australia Research Discussion Paper, 10).

Crowe, C., & Meade, E. E. (2007). The evolution of central bank governance around the world. *Journal of Economic Perspectives, 21*(4), 69–90.

Cukierman, A. (1992). *Central bank strategy, credibility, and independence: Theory and evidence.* Cambridge, MA: The MIT Press.

Cukierman, A., Webb, S. B., & Neyapti, B. (1992). Measuring the independence of central banks and its effects on policy outcomes, *The World Bank Economic Review, 6*, 353–398.

Daily Telegraph. (2007, December 31). Cyprus and Malta Tip Euro balance, by Ambrose Evans-Pritchard, http://www.telegraph.co.uk/money/main.jhtml?xml=/money/2007/12/31/cceuro131.xml

Daveri, F., & Tabellini, G. (2000). Unemployment, growth and taxation in industrial countries. *Economic Policy, 15*, 47–104.

De Grauwe, P. (2003, 4 April). *The challenge of enlargement of Euroland.* Paper presented at the Spring Meeting of Young Economists, Leuven.

Debelle, G., & Fischer, S. (1994). How independent should a central bank be? In J. C. Fuhrer (Ed.), *Goals, guidelines and constraints facing monetary policymakers* (pp. 195–221). Boston: Federal Reserve Bank of Boston.

De Haan, J., Masciandaro, D., & Quintyn, M. (2008). Does central bank independence still matter? European Journal of Political Economy, 24, 717–721.

Dennis, R. (2003, April 11). Time-inconsistent monetary policies: Recent research. *FRBSF Economic Letter, 2003–10.*

Deutsche Bundesbank. (2004, June). Monetary policy under uncertainty. *Monthly Bulletin,* 15–28.

Drazen, A., & Easterly, W. (2001). Do crises induce reform? Simple empirical tests of conventional wisdom. *Economics and Politics, 13*, 139–157.

Dreyer, J., & Schotter, A. (1980). Power relationship in the International Monetary Fund: The consequences of quota changes. *Review of Economics and Statistics, 62*, 97–106.

Duval, R., & Elmeskov, J. (2005). *The effects of EMU on structural reforms in labor and product markets* (OECD Economics Department Working Papers 438). Paris: Organization for Economic Co-operation and Development.

Ebell, M., & Haefke, C. (2003). *Product market deregulation and labour market outcomes* (Swiss National Bank Working Papers 02, 08).

Ehrmann, M., & Fratzscher, M. (2005). *Communication and decision-making by central bank committees: Different strategies, same effectiveness?* (ECB Working Paper, 488). Frankfurt, Main: European Central Bank.

Eichengreen, B., & von Hagen, J. (1996). Federalism, fiscal restraints and European monetary union. *American Economic Review, 86*, 134–138.

Eijffinger, S., & de Haan, J. (1996). *The political economy of central-bank independence* (Special Papers in International Economics, No. 19). Princeton, NJ: Princeton University Press.

Ellis, C. J., & Thoma, M. A. (1990). *The implications for an open economy of partisan political business cycles: Theory and evidence* (Department of Economics Working Paper 90/2), University of Oregon.

Emerson, M., Gros, D., Italianer, A., Pisani-Ferry, J., & Reichenbach, H. (1992). *One market, one money. An evaluation of the potential benefits and costs of forming an economic and monetary union.* Oxford: Oxford University Press.

European Central Bank. (1999, May). *The implementation of the stability and growth pact.* Monthly Bulletin, Frankfurt/Main: European Central Bank.

European Central Bank. (2003, May). The adjustment of voting modalities in the Governing Council. In *Monthly bulletin* (pp. 73–83). Frankfurt, Main: European Central Bank.

European Central Bank. (2004). ECB annual report. Frankfurt, Main: European Central Bank.

European Central Bank. (2006, January). The predictability of the ECB's monetary policy. In *ECB monthly bulletin* (pp. 51–61). Frankfurt, Main: European Central Bank.

Eurostat. (2003a, September 23) *The GDP of the acceding countries.* Retrieved from http://europa.eu.int/comm/eurostat/, catalogue number: KS-NJ-03-047-DE-N.

Eurostat. (2003b, September 23) *The GDP*. Retrieved from http://europa.eu.int/comm/eurostat/, catalogue number: KS-NJ-03-035-DE-N.

Fahrholz, C., & Mohl, P. (2004, June 1). *EMU-enlargement and the reshaping of decision-making within the ECB Governing Council: A voting-power analysis* (Ezoneplus Working Paper, No. 23). Berlin (draft version).

Feldstein, M. (1999). *The costs and benefits of price stability*. National Bureau of Economic Research, Conference Report.

Felsenthal, D. S., & Machover, M. (1998). *The measurement of voting power: Theory and practice, problems and paradoxes*. Cheltenham: Edward Elgar.

Fischer, B., Lenza, M., Pill, H., & Reichlin, L. (2006, November 9–10). *Money and monetary policy: ECB 1999–2006*. Paper prepared for the Fourth ECB Central Banking Conference on "The Role of Money: Money and Monetary Policy in the Twenty-First Century". Frankfurt, Main: European Central Bank.

Fisher, I. (1929). *The purchasing power of money* (2nd ed.). New York: Macmillan, 1911, New York: Macmillan, 1913, New ed., New York: Macmillan, p. 486.

Fisher, S. (1990). Rules versus discretion in monetary policy. In B. Friedman & F. H. Hahn (Eds.), *Handbook of monetary economics, II* (pp. 1155–1184). Amsterdam, North Holland: Elsevier Science Publishers.

Freytag, A. (2005). The credibility of monetary reform: New evidence. *Public Choice, 124*(3), 391–409.

Friedman, M. (1961). The lag in effect of monetary policy. *Journal of Political Economy, 69*, 447–466.

Friedman, M. (1994). *Money mischief*. San Diego, CA: Harcourt Brace & Company.

Fuhrer, J. (1997, January). Central bank independence and inflation targeting: Monetary policy paradigms for the next millenium? *New England Economic Review*, Federal Reserve Bank of Boston, January 19–36.

Gordon, R. (1996). "Macroeconomic Policy in the Presence of Structural Maladjustments," Paper presented at the OECD Proceedings on Interactions between Structural Reform, Macroeconomic Policies and Economic Performance, Paris.

Grilli, V., Masciandaro, D., & Tabellini, G. (1991). Political and monetary institutions and public financial policies in the industrial countries. *Economic Policy, 6*, 341–392.

Gros, D. (2003). Reforming the composition of the ECB Governing Council in view of enlargement: An opportunity missed!, Intereconomics. *Review of European Economic Policy, 38*, 124–29.

Gros, D., & Thygesen, N. (1998). *European monetary integration – From the European monetary system to economic and monetary union* (2nd ed.). Longman, Harlow: Addison Wesley.

Gros, D., Mayer, T., & Ubide, A. (2005, June). *EMU at risk, 7th annual report of the CEPS macroeconomic policy group*. Brussels: Centre for European Policy Studies (CEPS).

Gruener, H. P. (1998). *On the role of conflicting national interests in the ECB-Council* (CEPR Discussion Paper No. 2216) London: Centre for Economic Policy Research.

Grüner, H. S., & Hefeker, C. (1996). *Militant labor and inflation aversion – The impact of EMU on labor union interaction* (SFB 303 Discussion Paper A-539), University of Bonn.

Gwartney, J., & Lawson, R. (2003). The concept and measurement of economic freedom. *European Journal of Political Economy, 19*, 405–430.

Gwartney, J., Lawson, R., Park, W., & Skipton, C. (2003). *Economic freedom of the world: 2003 annual report*. Vancouver: Fraser Institute.

Haffner, R. C. G., Nickell, S., Nicoletti, G., Scarpetta, S., & Zoega, G. (2000). European integration, liberalisation and labor market performance: Report for the Fondazione Rodolfo De Benedetti.

Hango, B., & Hefeker, C. (2002). Reconsidering Central Bank Independence, European Journal of Political Economy, *78*, 653–674.

Heinemann, F. (2004). Explaining reform deadlocks. *Applied Economics Quarterly Supplement, 55*, 9–26.

Heinemann, F. (2005). How distant is Lisbon from Maastricht? The Short-run Link Between Structural Reforms and Budgetary Performance, mimeo, prepared for the DG ECFIN workshop 'Budgetary implications of structural reforms', Brussels, 2 December 2005.

Helbling, T., Hakura, D., & Debrun, X. (2004). Fostering structural reforms in industrial countries. In *World economic outlook 2004* (chap. III, pp. 103–146). Washington, DC: International Monetary Fund.

Henisz, W. (2000). The institutional environment for economic growth. *Economics and Politics, 12*(1), 1–31.

Henisz, W. (2002). The institutional environment for infrastructure investment. *Industrial and Corporate Change, 11*(2), 355–389.

Herrendorf, B., & Neumann, M. J. M. (2003). The political economy of inflation, labour market distortions, and central bank independence. *The Economic Journal, 113*, 43–64.

Herz, B., & Vogel, L. (2005). *Determinants of market-oriented policy reforms: An empirical analysis*. Mimeo.

Hochreiter, E., & Tavlas, G. S. (2005). The two roads to the euro: The monetary experiences of Austria and Greece. In S. Schadler (Ed.), *Euro Adoption in Central and Eastern Europe – Opportunities and Challenges* (pp. 187–201). Washington, DC: International Monetary Fund.

Holler, M. J., & Kellermann, J. (1978). Die a-priori-Abstimmungsstärke im europäischen Parlament. *Kyklos, 31*, 107–111.

Hsiao, C. (2003). *Analysis of panel data*. Cambridge: Cambridge University Press.

IMF (2003). *International financial statistics. CD-ROM*. Washington, DC: International Monetary Fund.

IMF (2004). *Fostering structural reforms in industrial countries*. Chapter III in World Economic Outlook, Advancing Structural Reforms, International Monetary Fund, Washington, DC.

Issing, O. (2002, December 9). *Monetary policy in a world of uncertainty*. Fondation Banque de France Centre d'Etudes Prospectives et d.Informations Internationales CEPII Université Aix-Marseille IDE, Paris, http://www.banque-france.fr/gb/fondatio/telechar/issing.pdf

Jensen, H. (1997). Credibility of optimal monetary delegation. *American Economic Review, 87*, 911–920.

Jimeno, J. (2005, June). Comments on Duval, R., & Elmeskov, J. *The effects of EMU on structural reforms in labor and product markets*. Paper prepared for the Conference on "What Effects is EMU Having on the Euro Area and its Member Countries?", Frankfurt, Main: European Central Bank.

Johansson, A. (1998, April). *The interaction between labor market policy and monetary policy: An analysis of time inconsistency, Mimeo*. Paper presented at the Institute for International Economic Studies Seminar, Stockholm.

Jonsson, G. (1997). Monetary politics and unemployment persistence. *Journal of Monetary Economics, 39*(2), 303–325.

Katzenstein, P. (1985). *Small states in world markets*. Ithaca: Cornell University Press.

Keynes, J. M. (1936). The General Theory of Employment, Interest and Money, New York: Harcourt, Brace.

Knight, F. (1964, 1921), Risk, Uncertainty and Profit, New York: Century Press.

Krugman, P., & Obstfeld, M. (2003). *International economics – Theory and policy*. Boston, Mass.: Addison Wesley.

Kugler, A., & Pica, G. (2004, June). *Effects of employment protection and product market regulation on the Italian labor market*. Paper presented at the CEPR/ECB Workshop.

Kydland, F., & Prescott, E. (1977). Rules rather than discretion: The inconsistency of optimal plans. *Journal of Political Economy, 87*, 473–492.

Lane, J.-E., & Maeland, R. (2000). Constitutional analysis: The power index approach. *European Journal of Political Research, 37*, 31–56.

Layard, R., Jackman, R., & Nickell, S. (1991). *Unemployment*. Oxford: Oxford University Press.

Layard, R, Jackman, R., & Nickell, S. (1994). *The unemployment crisis*. Oxford: Oxford University Press.

Leech, D. (2001a). *Members voting power in the governance of the international monetary fund* (CSGR Working Paper No. 68/01), University of Warwick.

Leech, D. (2001b). *Fair re-weighting of the votes in the EU Council of Ministers and the choice of majority requirement for qualified majority voting during successive enlargements* (Warwick Economic Research Paper No. 587), University of Warwick.

Lindbeck, A. (1992). Macroeconomic theory and the labor market. *European Economic Review, 36*(2–3), 209–235.

Lindbeck, A., & Snower, D. (1997). *Centralized bargaining, multi-tasking and work incentives* (CEPR Discussion Paper 1563). London: Center for Economic Policy Research.

Lohmann, S. (1992). "The Optimal Degree of Commitment: Credibility and Flexibility," *American Economic Review* 82; pp. 273–286.

Lohmann, S. (1993). Electoral cycles and international policy coordination. *European Economic Review, 37*(7), 1373–1391.

Lommatzsch, K., & Tober, S. (2003). Voting rules in the ECB Governing Council following enlargement of the euro area. *Economic Bulletin, 40*, 91–94.

Lora, E. (2000). *What makes reforms likely? Timing and sequencing of structural reforms in latin America* (Inter-American Development Bank Working Papers, 424), Washington, DC.

McCallum, B. (1995, May). Two fallacies concerning central bank independence. *American Economic Review, Papers and Proceedings, 85*(2), 207–211.

Meade, E. E. (2003a, July 28). *EU enlargement and ECB decision making.* Online Article, Project syndicate. Retrieved from http://www.project-syndicate.org

Meade, E. E. (2003b). A (critical) appraisal of the ECB's voting reform, intereconomics. *Review of European Economic Policy, 38*, 129–131.

Meade, E. E. (2003c, July 28). *How independent is the ECB?* Online Article, Project syndicate. Retrieved from http://www.project-sydicate.org

Meade E. E., & Sheets, D. N. (2002). Regional Influences on U.S. Monetary Policy: Some Implications for Europe, CEP Discussion Paper, No. 523 London.

Meade, E. E., & Sheets, D. N. (2005). Regional influences on FOMC voting patterns. *Journal of Money Credit and Banking, 33*, 661–678.

Mélitz, J. (1997). The evidence about the costs and benefits of EMU. *Swedish Economic Policy Review, 4*(2), 191–234.

Mundschenk, S., & von Hagen, J. (2002). The political economy of policy coordination in Europe. *Swedish Review of Economic Policy, 8*, 11–41.

Neumann, M. J. M. (2002). Transparency in monetary policy. *Atlantic Economic Journal, 30*(4), 353–364.

Nickell, S. (1997). Unemployment and European labor market rigidities – Europe versus North America. *Journal of Economic Perspectives, 11*, 55–74.

Nickell, S. (2005, June). Comments on Duval, R., & Elmeskov, J. *The effects of EMU on structural reforms in labor and product markets, Mimeo.* Paper prepared for the Conference on "What Effects is EMU Having on the Euro Area and its Member Countries?" Frankfurt, Main: European Central Bank.

Nicoletti G., Golub, S., Hajkova, D., Mirza, D., & Yoo, K.-Y. (2003). *Policies and international integration: Influences on trade and foreign direct investment* (OECD Economics Department Working Papers 359).

Nicoletti, G., & Scarpetta, S. (2005). *Product market reforms and employment in OECD countries* (OECD Economics Department Working Paper 472), Paris: OECD = Organisation for Economic Cooperation and Development.

OECD. (2005). *Economic policy reforms, going for growth.* Paris: OECD = Organisation for Economic Cooperation and Development.

Orphanides, A. (2003). The quest for prosperity without inflation. *Journal of Monetary Economics, 50*(3), 633–663.

Orszag, M., & Snower, D. (1998). Anatomy of policy complementarities. *Swedish Economic Policy Review, 5*(2), 303–345.

Owen, G. (1977). Values of games with a priori unions. In R. Hein & O. Moeschlin (Eds.), *Essays in mathematical economics and game theory.* Berlin: Springer.

Owen, G. (1995). *Game theory* (3rd ed.). Orlando: Academic Press.

Ozkan, F. G., Sibert, A. C., & Sutherland, A. (1997, November). *Monetary union, entry conditions and economic reform* (CEPR Discussion Paper 1720), Center for Economic Policy Research, London.

Persson, T., & Tabellini, G. (1990). *Macroeconomic policy, credibility and politics, fundamentals of pure and applied economics.* Chur: Harwood Academic Publishers.

Persson, T., & Tabellini, G. (1993). Designing institutions for monetary stability. *Carnegie-Rochester Conference Series on Public Policy, 39,* 53–84.

Persson, T., & Tabellini, G. (1994). *Monetary and fiscal policy, Volume 2: Politics.* Cambridge, MA: MIT Press.

Pitlik, H. (2004). Are Less Constrained Governments Really More Successful in Executing Market-Oriented Policy Changes?, Diskussionsbeiträge aus dem Institut für Volkswirtschaftslehre der Universität Hohenheim 255/2005, University Hohenheim, Stuttgart.

Pitlik, H., & Wirth, S. (2003). Do crises promote the extent of economic liberalization? *European Journal of Political Economy, 19*(3), 565–581.

Posen, A. (1993). Why central bank independence does not cause low inflation: There is no institutional fix for politics. In R. O'Brien (Ed.), *Finance and the international economy 7* (pp. 40–65). Oxford: Oxford University Press.

Reinhart, C. M., & Rogoff, K S. (2002). *The modern history of exchange rate regime arrangements: A reinterpretation* (NBER Working Paper 8963). Cambridge, Mass.: National Bureau of Economic Research.

Rodrik, D. (1996). Understanding economic policy reform. *Journal of Economic Literature, 34*(1), 9–41.

Rogoff, K. S. (1985). The optimal commitment to an intermediate monetary target. *Quarterly Journal of Economics, 100,* 1169–1189.

Saint-Paul, G. (1993). On the political economy of labor market flexibility. *NBER Macroeconomics Annual, 78,* 151–187.

Saint-Paul, G. (1996). Exploring the political economy of labor market institutions. *Economic Policy, 23,* 265–315.

Saint-Paul, G., & Bentolila, S. (2000, April). Will EMU increase eurosclerosis? *International macroeconomics and labor economics* (CEPR Discussion Paper 2423), Center of Economic Policy Research, London.

Schulze, L. (2005). Reform der Abstimmungsregeln und Inflationspräferenz im EZB-Rat. *Wirtschaftsdienst, 85,* 724–730.

Shapley, L. S. (1997). A value on n-person games. In H. W. Kuhn (Ed.), *Classics in game theory.* Princeton, NJ: Princeton University Press.

Shaw, E. S. (1958). Money supply and stable economic growth. In *United States monetary policy* (pp. 49–71). New York: American Assembly.

Sibert, A. C., & Sutherland, A. (1997, November). *Monetary regimes and labor market reform* (CEPR Discussion Paper 1731), London.

Simmons, B. A. (1994). *Who adjusts? – Domestic sources of foreign economic policy during the interwar years.* Princeton, NJ: Princeton University Press.

Simons, H. C. (1948). Rules versus authorities in monetary policy. In *Economic policy for a free society* (pp. 40–77). Chicago: University of Chicago Press.

Straffin, P. (1980). *Topics in the theory of voting.* Boston: Birkhauser.

Straffin, P. (1988). The Shapley-Shubik and Banzhaf power indices as probabilities, In A. E. Roth (Ed.), *The shapley value: Essays in honor of Lloyd S. Shapley.* Cambridge: Cambridge University Press.

Sutter, M. (2001). Messung der Abstimmungsmacht und Anwendung auf den EU-Ministerrat. *Wirtschaftliches Studium, 6,* 339–341.

Svensson, L. (1997). Optimal inflation targets, "conservative" central banks, and linear inflation contracts. *American Economic Review, 87,* 98–114.

6 Theory of Monetary Policy

Tootell, G. M. B. (1996, November). *Whose monetary policy is it, anyway?* Boston: Mimeo, Federal Reserve Bank of Boston.

van Poeck, A., & Borghijs, A. (2001). *EMU and labor market reform: Needs, incentives and realisations.* Oxford: Blackwell Publishers.

Von Hagen, J. (2003). EMU: Monetary policy issues and challenges, In M. Baimbridge (Ed.), *Economic and monetary union in europe.* Cheltenham: Edward Elgar.

Walsh, C. E. (1995). Optimal contracts for central bankers. *American Economic Review, 85,* 150–167.

Walsh, C. E. (2003). *Monetary theory and policy* (2nd ed.). Cambridge, Mass.: MIT Press.

Widgrén, M. (1994). Voting power in the EC decision-making and the consequences of two different enlargements. *European Economic Review, 38,* 1153–1170.

Wilhelmsen, B.-R., & Zaghini, A. (2005, July). *Monetary policy predictability in the euro area: An international comparison* (ECB Working Paper No 504). Frankfurt, Main: European Central Bank.

Woodford, M. (2006, November 9–10). *How important is money in the conduct of monetary policy, Columbia University.* Paper prepared for the Fourth ECB Central Banking conference on The Role of Money: Money and Monetary Policy in the Twenty-First Century. Frankfurt, Main: European Central Bank.

World Bank. (2002). *World development indicators.* Washington, DC: World Bank Publications.

Chapter 7
Transmission Mechanisms

(. . .) the task of economics is to foretell the remoter effects, and so to allow us to avoid such acts as attempt to remedy a present ill by sowing the seeds of a much greater ill for the future.
    —*Ludwig von Mises (1981, 1934), The Theory of Money and Credit, Preface to the English Edition, p. 23.*

7.1 The Effects of Changes in Money Supply

When central banks under take monetary policy actions, they set into motion a series of consequences. However, little is known about when and how changes in the stock of money and short-term interest rates affect real and nominal magnitudes. It is generally assumed that monetary policy effects start with changes in financial market conditions, work through changes in firms' and private household spending, and eventually exert – via demand and supply – effects on the economy's price level. The path of consequences a change in the economy's stock of money triggers in terms of inflation and real magnitudes is known as *transmission mechanism*.

The instrument that central banks have at their disposal in monetary policy making is the control over the price and the quantity of base money. Base money – consisting of coins and notes in circulation and commercial banks' deposits held with central bank – represents the ultimate form of money in today's monetary systems. As explained earlier, central banks hold the monopoly over the money supply. Commercial bank money can only be produced on the back of base money. Therefore, the interest rate the central bank charges on base money credits typically exerts a strong impact on banks' willingness and capacity to extend credit and money to the private sector – and eventually output and prices.

A. Belke, T. Polleit, *Monetary Economics in Globalised Financial Markets*,
DOI 10.1007/978-3-540-71003-5_7, © Springer-Verlag Berlin Heidelberg 2009

The Central Bank's Grip on the Money Supply

Today's monetary systems around the world over represent government controlled money supply monopolies. Central banks, as agents of governments, determine the price and the quality of the money that people keep in their wallets and their bank accounts. It is fair to say that the power of central banks over the money supply is absolute: Central banks are the sole providers of *base money*, the necessary ingredient for commercial banks to extend credit to non-banks and thereby creating commercial bank money; this was actually shown in chapter 1 of this book.

Figure 7.1(a) shows US dollar in circulation in percent of the US monetary base (cash in circulation and banks' deposits with the central bank) from 1919 to May 2008. Ever since, currency in circulation has represented the bulk of US base money. Changes in the stock of the monetary base (including currency in circulation) varied greatly over time, though. They were most pronounced in the early 1930 s and during the World War II period (Fig. 7.1(b)). Since around the beginning of the 21st century, however, annual growth of US base money has slowed down substantially. Actually, the growth in outstanding US dollar cash (presumably in and outside the United States) has declined markedly.

For making the government controlled money supply monopoly effective, banks *must* demand base money; note that the absolute level of the stock of base money demanded by banks, or the degree of volatility in base money demand, do not change such a conclusion. Generally speaking, central banks can affect the demand for banks' base money easily by requiring banks to hold minimum reserves. For instance, changes in reserve ratios and/or changes in the reserve base would, other things being equal, affect the banking sector's demand for base money.

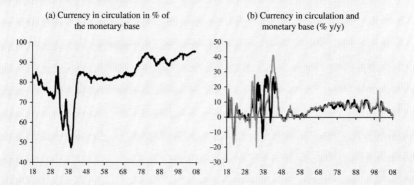

Fig. 7.1 Monetary base and currency in circulation in the US
Source: Federal Reserve Bank of St. Louis, own calculations. – St. Louis adjusted monetary base (AMBNS)

In that sense, there should be no doubt that *government sponsored central banks hold absolute power in terms of setting the price and quantity of the outstanding money supply*. What people do with the money stock supplied by central banks, however, is a rather different story. The latter issue is actually at the heart of the theories of the transmission of monetary policy, which will be reviewed in this part of the book.

The transmission mechanism of monetary policy can be expected to work through *various channels*, affecting variables and several market segments, at various speeds and intensities. Identifying these transmission channels is important and attracts a lot of attention from economists, policy makers and investors alike. Understanding the transmission mechanism of monetary policy should allow us, for instance, to better determine the most effective set of policy instrument, the timing of policy changes, and hence the main restrictions that central banks face in making their decisions.

Figure 7.2 provides a very simple overview of potential relationships between monetary policy actions – that are changes in the central bank short-term interest rate and the quantity of base money supplied – and of various stages of the transmission mechanism. For instance, it seem reasonable to stipulate that a rise in the supply of base money might cause market interest rates to fall in the market for base money, asset prices to rise and business confidence to improve, thereby stimulating domestic demand, output and eventually prices to increase.

In general, it seems fair to say that there is great uncertainty about how and when monetary policy measures affect real and nominal magnitudes. Looking at the economic literature, however, four major channels can be identified through which monetary policy might affect macroeconomic outcomes. Following Taylor (1995), these channels can be grouped as follows: (1.1) the interest rate channel, (1.2) the asset price channel, (1.3) the credit channel (including the theory of credit rationing) and (1.4) the exchange rate channel. In what follows we will take a closer look at these theoretical concepts.

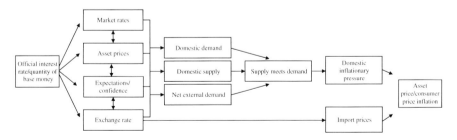

Fig. 7.2 Monetary policy transmission mechanisms
Source: BoE. – For simplicity, this figure does not show all interactions between variables, but these can be important.

7.1.1 Interest Rate Channel

The *conventional interest rate channel* of monetary policy transmission operates within the Keynesian *IS-LM* framework. A restrictive monetary policy, for instance, reduces the stock of money (M). Given an unchanged demand for money, the interest rate rises (i). This is actually the well-known *liquidity effect*. If investment spending (I) depends negatively on the interest rate, a rising interest rate reduces investment, thereby lowering aggregate demand and output (Y); this is the *income effect*. The interest rate transmission mechanism can therefore be described as follows:

$$M_{\downarrow} \Rightarrow i_{\uparrow} \Rightarrow I_{\downarrow} \Rightarrow Y_{\downarrow}. \tag{7.1}$$

There are two important assumptions related to the interest channel, though. *First*, it is assumed that money is used as a means of exchange, and that there is no (perfect) substitute for the stock of money supplied by banks. *Second*, it is assumed that commercial banks cannot perfectly shield themselves from changes in central bank official interest rates; so that a rise (lower) of official interest rates inevitably leads to a rise (decline) in the economy's market interest rates.

According to Bernanke and Gertler (1995), however, the conventional interest rate channel was not successful in explaining US data, and the authors provide two explanations why the conventional story is actually incomplete. *First*, empirical studies find that aggregate spending is fairly insensitive to interest rates. *Second*, monetary policy should have its strongest influence on short-term interest rates and its weakest effect on long-term rates. It is therefore puzzling that monetary policy has large effects on purchases of long-lived assets which respond to\break long-term rates.

However, economists tend to recognize the importance of the monetary transmission mechanism through interest rates. Taylor (1995) argues that financial market prices are key components of how monetary policy affects real activities. For instance, a restrictive monetary policy raises short-term interest rates. Since prices and wages are assumed to be rigid, real long-term interest rates increase as well. These higher real long-term rates lead to a decline in real investment, real consumption and real output.

The Reaction of M1, M3 and Loans to Changes in Interest Rates – An Example for the Euro Area

How do monetary and credit aggregates react to a change in the short-term interest rate? Do higher short-term rates really reduce bank lending and thereby money creation? And if this is the case, how long does it take for a restrictive monetary policy to affect overall credit and money supply?

All these questions can actually be addressed by using Vector Autoregressive models (VAR); actually, there models will be reviewed in some more details later in this chapter. VAR models impose very little theoretical structure on the data and can be used to establish the *stylised facts* about the cause-and-response relations among the variables under review.

In a VAR model, one can introduce a transitory increase in the level of one variable and to investigate the dynamic effects of this so-called "shock" on all variables in the system. The dynamic relations between a shock to one variable and the others in the system can be illustrated with so-called "impulse response functions". While all variables are exogenous in the VAR, a shock on, say, the short-term interest rate offers an empirical assessment of the implications of a change in the stance of monetary policy on other macroeconomic variables.

The following charts are based on the estimation of two VAR systems, both of which include a linear trend, a commodity price index[2] and an oil price index as (pre-determined) explanatory variables (ECB, 2007). The first system is intended to capture the behaviour of the components of M3 and consequently includes: a consumer price index, real GDP, M3, M1, and a long-term and a short-term (that is 3-month) nominal interest rate. The second system models the counterpart side of M3 and (in contrast to the first model) includes bank loans to the private sector (rather than M1) and MFI longer-term financial liabilities.

Since the focus is on the long-run relationships between the variables under review, the VAR is estimated in the level of the variables.[3] Figure 7.3 illustrates the reactions of the short-term interest rate, M1, M3 and loans to the private sector to a transitory (that is one-off) shock in the "policy rate" of one standard deviation (and the respective 65% confidence intervals).[4] The estimation is based on the period 1980-Q1 to 2004-Q4.

The *response pattern* of the short-term interest rate (upper left-hand side graph) shows a peak after two quarters, followed by a steady decline reaching a trough between eight and ten quarters before returning to the zero line. This could be interpreted such that following an initial restrictive interest rate policy, the central bank subsequently lowers interest rates in response to a decline in real activity and lower prices.

The increase in the short-term interest rate is followed by a rather immediate decline in euro area M1, a result that confirms the rather high interest rate sensitivity of this aggregate (upper right-hand side graph). It is also apparent that, after the interest rate effect has faded out over time, the effect of a decrease and subsequent recovery in GDP comes to the fore. A similar pattern can be observed for the dynamic response of nominal loans (lower left-hand side graph). At the same time, the reaction of loans as compared to that of M1 is somewhat delayed.

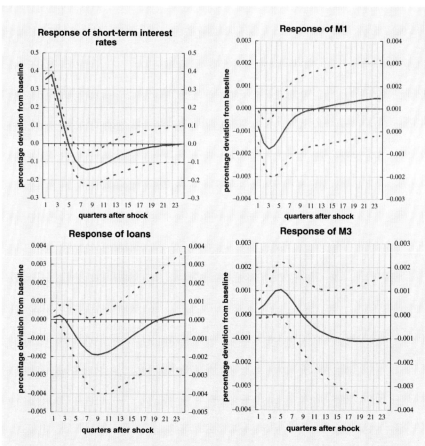

Fig. 7.3 Impulse response functions following a transitory increase in the short-term interest rate by one standard deviation. *Note*: Sample period 1981-Q1 to 2004-Q4, *solid lines* show percentage deviations from baseline and *dashed lines* the respective 65% confidence band, all variables but interest rates are in logarithms.
Source: ECB (2007)

In contrast to these findings, a rise in the short-term interest rate is followed by a significant and permanent decline in the stock of euro area M3, which starts to materialise after around ten quarters. The permanent decrease, however, is preceded by a positive reaction of M3 to a rise in interest rates, which may be linked to the speculative demand for money as materialising in the M3 components outside M1 (M3–M1). This positive initial response of M3 to the unanticipated increase in short-term interest rates can be relatively persistent, and is consistent in direction with what has been observed in the euro area over the past year as key ECB rates have risen.

[1]The use of a commodity price index as a leading indicator for domestic inflation in the policy reaction function could eliminate the positive response of
prices to a contractionary monetary policy shock. See Sims (1992).

[2]The impulse response analysis is carried out using generalised impulse
response functions. The purpose of generalised impulse response functions
to circumvent the problem of the dependence of the orthogonalised impulse
responses on the ordering of the variables in the VAR. See Pesaran and Shin
(1998).

[3]Sims, Stock, Watson (1990).

[4]It is common in the VAR literature to use a 65% confidence interval (although
this is narrower than for other statistical exercises). See Bagliano and Favero
(1999)

7.1.2 Asset Price Channel

Changes in official interest rates affect the market value of financial assets – such as
bonds and stocks. For instance, the price of bonds is inversely related to the interest
rate, so that a rise in interest rates lowers bond prices and *vice versa*. Declining
bond prices dampen the net equity capital in the balance sheet of lenders (banks and
other financial intermediaries), thereby reducing their willingness and/or ability to
layout credit. As a result, the decline in debt prices might exert a restrictive impact
on credit financed investment and consumption spending.

What is more, higher interest rates might also imply lower stock prices: as interest
rates rise, firms' expected future cash flows are discounted by a larger factor, so
the present value of any given future income stream declines. In addition, rising
borrowing costs raise leveraged firms' interest rate burden, thereby reducing their
profits. This, in turn, might also lower their stock prices in terms of lowering the
present value of firms' discounted future cash flows. Like in the case of falling bond
prices, dropping stock valuations might exert – via reducing lenders' equity capital –
a restrictive impact on the real economy congdon, 2005.

7.1.2.1   The Role of the Stock in the Transmission Process

In an information efficient stock market, stock prices would reflect market agents'
expectations regarding the firms' future profitability. For instance, rising stock prices
might indicate market expectation of an improving profitability of firms' investments, thereby pushing up firms' stock prices. Likewise, declining stock valuation
might indicate the expectation of unfavourable corporate profits in the future. That
said, fluctuations of stock market prices can be expected to convey important information about the future state of the economy.

Likewise, one could argue that changes in stock prices affect investment and
consumption; in this sense, a change in stock prices is a *forcing variable* for real
economic activity. For instance, declining stock prices would increase the cost of

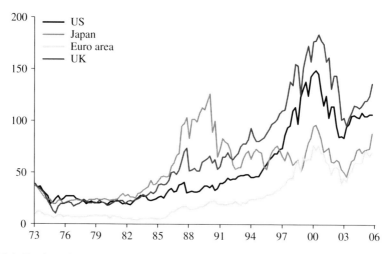

Fig. 7.4 Stock market capitalisation in percent of GDP
Source: IMF, Bloomberg, Thomson Financial. – Market capitalisation divided by nominal GDP.
– 1973-Q2 to 2006-Q1

equity capital, thereby increasing firms' total cost of capital. The latter, in turn, leads to less investment, dampening output and employment gains. Likewise, strongly rising stock prices could actually encourage additional investment and economic growth.

Clearly, one would expect that the higher an economy's stock market capitalisation is, the more likely it is that changes in stock valuations would be associated with (expected) the direction and intensity of (future) economic activity. One measure of the importance of the stock market for the economy is the stock market capitalization in percent of GDP.[1] Figure 7.4 shows the capitalisation ratios in the US, the euro area the UK and Japan in the period from the early 1970 s to the beginning of 2006. Capitalisation ratios have trending upwards in the US, euro area and the UK since the early 1970 s. In Japan, however, the ratio peaked at the beginning of the 1990 s and has (so far) not returned to its former highs.

How Do Stocks and Monetary Policy Interact?

How important are changes in stock market prices for economic growth? Can, and do, central banks affect stock prices via changing interest rates (or other monetary policy instruments), thereby exerting an impact on the real economy and consumer price inflation? Or is it the other way round: do central banks react to price action in stock markets?

---

[1] Other indications are, for instance, are the number of listed companies or the percentage of quoted shares in non-financial corporations' main liabilities.

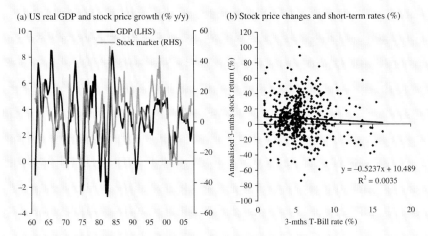

Fig. 7.5 US growth and stock prices (% y/y) and the short-term interest rate (%)
Source: Bloomberg; own calculations. S&P 500 stock market index

In the US, annual changes in real GDP and stock prices show a relatively close and positive correlation for the period 1961–2007 (Fig. 7.5 (a)). This could either suggest that stock price changes *induce* changes in economic activity (and therefore ultimately corporate profitability); or that changes in stock market prices merely reflect forthcoming changes in economic activity. The fact is: simple correlation coefficients do not tell us anything about *causality*.

What about the relation between stock price changes and the stance of monetary policy? The relation between US 3-months interest rates (which are actually determined by monetary policy) and changes in US stock market prices, when measured on the basis of the coefficient of determination, was, on average, very small in the period under review (Fig. 7.5(b)). However, based on the scatter plotter we would not reject the hypothesis that, at least in the short-term, stock prices did react to the short-term interest rate.

In fact, all the questions raise above are still pretty much open to debate. For instance, Rigobon and Sack (2002, 2003) note that movements in the US stock market can exert a significant impact on the US economy. At the same time, however, the authors note that there is little knowledge about the magnitude of the US Fed monetary policy reaction (which, in turn, can be expected to affect the real economy at least in the short-run) to the stock market. One reason is that it is difficult to estimate the policy reaction because of the simultaneous response of equity prices to interest rate changes.

No doubt, the questions regarding potential consequences of stock market developments on macroeconomic developments enjoy great attention among economists, monetary policy makers and the public at large. This is all too plausible, given that stock prices can be expected, as a rule, to be closely related to productive economic activity. In what follows, a closer look shall therefore be taken at three transmission channels involving price action in the stock market: (i) the stock market effect on investment, (ii) the household wealth effects, and (iii) the household liquidity effects.

Stock Market Effects on Investment

James Tobin's q-theory (Tobin, 1969) gives an explanation for how changes in stock prices might affect real output. To start with, Tobin's q is defined as the market value of firms divided by the replacement cost of capital:

$$Tobin's q = \frac{market\ value\ of\ the\ firm}{replacement\ costs}, \tag{7.2}$$

whereas Tobin's q can be greater 1, smaller than 1 or equal to 1.

If, for instance, Tobin's q exceeds 1, the market price of firms is high relative to the replacement cost of capital. Companies can issue stocks and get a high price for it relative to the cost of the facilities and equipment they are buying. In other words, new plant and equipment investment is cheap relative to the market value of firms, and the economy expands.

Likewise, if Tobin's q is smaller than 1, firms will demand existing investment projects. New investment declines, and so does the economy. If, however, Tobin's q is 1, the economy is in equilibrium: with the market value of the firm being equal to its replacement costs, there is no economic incentive to expand or contract investments.

Alternatively, Tobin's q can be stated *in terms of return rates*. To show this, let R be the discount rate (interest rate) which makes the expected future earnings of a new investment project, E, equal to the purchase price of the existing investment projects, I, so that:

$$I = \frac{E}{R}. \tag{7.3}$$

Equation (7.3) corresponds to the replacement investment costs as shown in Eq. (7.2).

What is more, we can write the internal interest rate on existing investment, C, as:

$$C = \frac{E}{r_C}, \tag{7.4}$$

where C is the market value of existing investment projects and r_C is the discount rate (interest rate) that brings E into line with C. Equation (7.4) gives us the value of the *existing firm*. As a result, Tobin's q can be restated as (7.4) divided by (7.3), which yields:

$$Tobin'sq = \frac{C}{I} = \frac{E}{r_C} \cdot \frac{R}{E} = \frac{R}{r_C}. \qquad (7.5)$$

Equation (7.2) and its equivalent, Eq. (7.5) both suggest that changes in R to r_C would an effect on real economic activity (via affecting investment spending). Take, for instance, the equilibrium case in which Tobin's q equals 1. If the central bank, via an expansionary monetary policy, increases the money supply and lowers the market interest rates, firms' earnings expectation, E, might increase, thereby raising R. According to Tobin's q, which now exceeds 1, the economy would expand (other things being equal).

"Tobin's q" in a Neo-Classical Perspective

Assume that economic production, Y, is a function of the stock of capital, K, and labour, L:

$$Y = f(K, L), \qquad (7.6)$$

while assuming constant returns to scale (*linear homogenous*). What is more, output equals the sum of factor marginal products multiplied by factor inputs:

$$Y = f(K, L) = f_K(K, L)K + f_L(K, L)L, \qquad (7.7)$$

where f_K and f_L are the marginal products of capital and labour, respectively. In the following, we assume that L is constant.[2]
    The firm's profit is given by the following function:

$$A_S f(K_S, L_S) - w_S L_S - (K_{S+1} - K_S). \qquad (7.8)$$

Here, A is a scale variable, w is wage, while the subscript s represents the period under review.

---

[2]In general it is assumed that (for linearly homogenous production functions) the marginal products of capital and labour depend only on the capital-labor ratio, that is $k \equiv K/L$. Given $f(K, L) = Lf(K, 1)$, the marginal product of capital is: $f_K(K, L) = f'(k)$, where $f(k) \equiv f(K/L, 1)$ is the per worker production function. Finally, the marginal products of capital and labor can be expressed as functions of k; for the marginal product of labor we can have: $f_L(K, L) = f(k) - f'(k)k$.

An additional assumption we make is that for making an investment, I (a change in the stock of capital ($I_S = K_{S+1} - K_S$) between s and $s + 1$), the firm must pay a deadweight installation cost of $\chi I_S^2/2K_S$ over and above the actual investment cost I_S (Obstfeld & Rogoff, 1996, p. 106).

The firm's present and discounted future profits in period t is:

$$d_t + V_t = \sum_{S=t}^{\infty} \left(\frac{1}{1+r}\right)^{S-t} \left[A_S f(K_S, L_S) - \chi I_S^2/2K_S - w_S L_S - I_S\right].$$

The left hand side of the equation above simple says that the firm's value equals current dividend payments, received in period t, plus the present value of future discounted dividends, V_t (the latter is therefore the market value *ex dividends* in t).

Using the Lagrange technique, maximising the above equation for a given K_t, subject to $I_S = K_{S+1} - K_S$, is based on the following expression:

$$L_t = \sum_{S=t}^{\infty} \left(\frac{1}{1+r}\right)^{S-t} \left[A_S f(K_S, L_S) - \chi I_S^2/2K_S \right. \tag{7.10}$$
$$\left. -w_S L_S - I_S - q_S(K_{S+1} - K_S - I_S)\right].$$

The first-order condition for investment is $\partial L_t/\partial I_S = 0$, which implies:

$$-\frac{\chi I_S}{K_S} - 1 + q_S = 0. \tag{7.11}$$

Here, q_S is the *shadow price* of capital already installed at the end of period s. That said, the condition above implies that the shadow price of capital equals the marginal cost of investment (including installation costs), that is $1 + \chi I_S/K_S$. The condition can be rewritten as a version of Tobin's q:

$$I_S = \frac{q_S - 1}{\chi} K_S. \tag{7.12}$$

According to Eq. (7.12), investment is positive only if the shadow price of installed capital q_S exceeds 1, the price of new, uninstalled capital.

The first-order condition for capital in $s+1$ is $\partial L_t/\partial K_{S+1} = 0$, which can be written as:

$$\frac{A_{S+1} f_K(K_{S+1}, L_{S+1}) + 0.5\chi(I_{S+1}/K_{S+1})^2 + q_{S+1}}{1+r} - q_S = 0. \tag{7.13}$$

The equation above is the investment *Euler equation*. At the optimum, the period t shadow price of an extra unit of capital is a function of:

- the capital's marginal product in the coming period, that is in $s + 1$;
- the marginal contribution of capital to lower installation costs in the next period [that is the term $0.5\chi(I_{S+1}/I_{S+1})^2$]; and
- the shadow price of capital in the next period, $s+1$.

Finally, if a firm is in equilibrium, it does not benefit from increasing capital by an additional unit in s [which entails the marginal costs of $q_s = 1 + \chi(I_S/K_S)$], reaping a higher marginal product and lower investment costs in $s+1$ [that is $A_{S+1} f(K_{S+1}, L_{S+1})$ and $0.5\chi(I_{S+1}/I_{S+1})^2$, respectively], then disinvesting the additional capital unit in $s+1$ [which would yield a net marginal benefit of $q_{s+1} = 1 + \chi(I_{S+1}/K_{S+1})$].

Finally, we can write:

$$q_t = \sum_{S=t+1}^{\infty} \left(\frac{1}{1+r} \right)^{S-t} \left[A_{S+1} f_K(K_{S+1}, L_{S+1}) + 0.5\chi(I_{S+1}/K_{S+1})^2 \right].$$

(7.14)

Tobin's q, or the shadow price of already installed capital, is a function of the discounted stream of future marginal products of capital (given the stock of labor) and the discounted stream of marginal contributions to the reduction in future capital installation costs.

As was outlined above, Tobin's q assumes that there exists a (reliable) link between stock prices (reflecting the value of firms) and new investment. *But how might monetary policy affect stock prices?* One could think of the following process. An increase in money supply ($M_\uparrow$), which lowers interest rates, makes bonds less attractive relative to stocks, thereby raising the demand for stocks. The rise in stock prices ($P_{s\uparrow}$) increases Tobin's q ($q_\uparrow$). Combining the latter with the fact that higher stock prices will result in higher investment ($I_\uparrow$) and output ($Y_\uparrow$) yields:

$$M_\uparrow \Rightarrow P_{s\uparrow} \Rightarrow q_\uparrow \Rightarrow I_\uparrow \Rightarrow Y_\uparrow.$$

(7.15)

Alternatively, one could think of firms financing their new investment projects by issuing new equities (*commonly stock*). When stock prices rise (as a result of lower market interest rates), it becomes cheaper for firms to finance their investment via equity because each share that is issued produces more funds. Thus, a rise in stock prices encourages new investment. That said, an alternative description of the mechanism is that a rise in the stock of money ($M_\uparrow$) raises stock prices ($P_{s\uparrow}$), thereby lowering the cost of capital ($c_\downarrow$), and real investment and output rise ($I_\uparrow$ and $Y_\uparrow$):[3]

$$M_\uparrow \Rightarrow P_{s\uparrow} \Rightarrow c_\downarrow \Rightarrow I_\uparrow \Rightarrow Y_\uparrow.$$

(7.16)

---

[3]For a comparison to Tobin's q approach, see Bosworth (1975) and Hayashi (1982).

Household Wealth Effects

Another channel through which asset prices may affect the real economy is the so-called *wealth effect* for households. The life cycle model of Franco Modigliani (1966) holds that individual consumption is determined by the lifetime resources of consumers. An important component of consumers' lifetime resources is – at least in developed countries – their stock of financial wealth. If stocks are a major component of peoples' total wealth, an increase in money supply, which raises stock prices, would increase the value of individuals' wealth, thereby increasing the lifetime resources of consumers. This, in turn, might cause consumption to rise. The ensuing transmission process would be:

$$M_\uparrow \Rightarrow P_{s\uparrow} \Rightarrow W_\uparrow \Rightarrow C_\uparrow \Rightarrow Y_\uparrow, \tag{7.17}$$

where $W_\uparrow$ and $C_\uparrow$ indicate increases in household wealth and consumption, respectively. Research has found this transmission mechanism to be quite strong in the United States, but the size of the wealth effect is still controversial (Modigliani, 1971; Ludvigson & Steindel, 1999).

Illing and Klueh (2005), for instance, illustrate how the integration of modern theory of finance and stochastic dynamic macroeconomic analysis may provide a deeper understanding of the link between asset prices and consumption. They show convincingly that this approach gives only a partial explanation for recent trends in US consumption. Comparing wealth effects in Anglo-Saxon countries with continental Europe, the article provides a perspective of the challenges for European monetary policy arising from wealth effects on consumption.

Household Liquidity Effects

Monetary policy can exert *liquidity effects* on household balance sheets, which can impact consumer durables and housing expenditures (Mishkin, 1976, 1977); in that sense, the liquidity effect impacts consumers' desire to spend. To start with, consumer durables (and, in some economies also) housing are relatively illiquid assets. If, as a result of a negative income shock (that is, for instance, an unexpected economic downturn, accompanied by lower-than-expected pay rises), consumers need to sell their assets to raise money, they would expect a big loss because they could not get the full value of their assets in a distress sale. In contrast, if consumers hold *financial* assets (such as, for instance, money, stocks and bonds), they could sell them *quickly* against cash, with relatively little loss in value.

That said, the structure the consumer's balance sheet should be an important factor determining the *likelihood of suffering financial distress*. If consumers have a large amount of financial assets relative to debt, their estimate of the probability of financial distress is low, and they will be more willing to keep spending. When stock prices rise, the value of financial assets rises ($FA_\uparrow$); and consumer expenditures might also rise because consumers have a more secure financial position and a lower estimate of the likelihood of suffering financial distress ($FD_\uparrow$). The transmission mechanism can therefore be formulated as:

$$M_\uparrow \Rightarrow P_{s\uparrow} \Rightarrow FA_\uparrow \Rightarrow FD_\downarrow \Rightarrow C_{d\uparrow}, H_\uparrow \Rightarrow Y_\uparrow, \qquad (7.18)$$

where $C_{d\uparrow}$ indicates a rise in expenditure on consumer durables and $H_\uparrow$ rise in residential housing spending.

7.1.2.2 Real Estate Prices

In the more recent past, house prices in many western industrial have shown more or less pronounced, and often volatile, swings, mostly to the upside, though and quite often outpacing the increase in consumer prices (Fig. 7.6). From a theoretical point of view, real estate prices might affect aggregate demand via *two channels*: (i) direct effects on housing expenditure and (ii) affecting household wealth.

Direct Effects on Housing Expenditure

A rise in the stock of money ($M_\uparrow$), the result of an expansionary monetary policy, lowers the cost of financing housing. An ensuing rising demand for housing assets pushes house prices up ($P_{h\uparrow}$), provided housing supply doesn't grow accordingly. With higher housing prices relative to construction costs, construction firms find it more profitable to build houses, and thus houses expenditure will rise ($H_\uparrow$). With H being a component of overall production, total output will rise. In this case, the transmission process would be characterized as (Belke & Wiedmann, 2005, 2006):

$$M_\uparrow \Rightarrow P_{h\uparrow} \Rightarrow H_\uparrow \Rightarrow Y_\uparrow. \qquad (7.19)$$

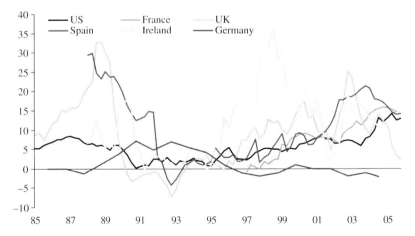

Fig. 7.6 Selected measures of house price changes (% y/y)
Source: Various central banks and national statistics offices; own calculations. – Germany: annual numbers, interpolated (last data point: 2004)

Household Wealth Effects

In many countries, housing prices represent an important component of household wealth, which can be expected to affect consumption spending. Hence, an expansionary monetary policy ($M_\uparrow$), which raises housing prices ($P_{h\uparrow}$) via lowering interest rates, also raises household wealth ($W_\uparrow$), which, in turn, increases consumption spending ($C_\uparrow$) and aggregate demand ($Y_\uparrow$):

$$M_\uparrow \Rightarrow P_{h\uparrow} \Rightarrow W_\uparrow \Rightarrow C_\uparrow \Rightarrow Y_\uparrow. \tag{7.20}$$

What is the empirical evidence? By now, there are some papers around which examine the literature on the relationship between stock and house prices and consumer spending. For instance, there is a study by Campbell and Cocco (2005) who start from the insight that housing is a major component of wealth. Since house prices fluctuate considerably over time, it is important to understand how these fluctuations affect households' consumption decisions. Rising house prices may stimulate consumption by increasing households' perceived wealth, or by relaxing borrowing constraints. Campbell and Cocco (2005) investigate the response of household consumption to house prices using UK micro data. They estimate the largest effect of house prices on consumption for older homeowners, and the smallest effect, insignificantly different from zero, for younger renters. This finding is consistent with heterogeneity in the wealth effect across these groups. In addition, they corroborate that regional house prices affect regional consumption growth. Predictable changes in house prices are correlated with predictable changes in consumption, particularly for households that are more likely to be borrowing constrained. However, this effect is driven by national rather than regional house prices and is important for renters as well as homeowners, suggesting that UK house prices are correlated with aggregate financial market conditions.

Paiella (2008) reviews both the time-series studies and the microeconomic evidence. The time-series approach allows her to distinguish between short-run and long-run links between consumption, income and wealth. Moreover, it enables her to identify which variables adjust to restore the long-run equilibrium in the case of a shock, and to determine the time taken by the adjustment process. The microeconomic literature improves our understanding of the link between wealth and expenditure and distinguishes among the alternative hypotheses – of direct wealth effect, common causality, and collateral channel – that have been proposed to explain this relationship. Based on the evidence, *the relationship between wealth and consumer spending appears to be strong*, although there is some disagreement as to the size and nature of the link. Furthermore, there also appear to be *some important differences across countries*, which should be allowed for by policymakers when appraising the policy implications of a change in asset prices.

Moreover, Bassanetti and Zollino (2008) focus on Italian aggregate quarterly time series covering the sample period 1980–2006 and test the presence and size of wealth effects on consumption, taking separately account of financial assets and residential property on the basis of new stock measures. They find sound evidence in favour of a cointegrating relation, in which both wealth components display the expected, positive effect on households' consumption. In particular, their results point to a *lower marginal propensity to consume out of housing than out of non housing net worth*, with a respective size of two and four cents. Following the estimate of a vector error correction model, they discuss the role played by transitory and permanent shocks in driving changes in the variables they consider. They find that *both consumption and wealth respond almost exclusively to permanent shocks*, which are the sole determinants of the common stochastic trend in their theoretical set-up. As a result, they are quite confident that their estimates of wealth coefficients in the cointegrating vector match very closely the true long run marginal propensity to consume for Italian households.

A further example is Hamilton (2008) who offers an explication of the hump-shaped response of real economic activity to changes in monetary policy, focusing on the particular channel operating through new home sales. He suggests *that the conventional notion of a monetary policy shock as a surprise change in the fed funds rate is misspecified.* The primary news for market participants is not what the Fed just did, but is instead *new information* about what the Fed is going to do in the near future. *Revisions in these anticipations show up instantaneously in long-term mortgage rates.* Although mortgage rates respond well before the Fed actually changes its target rate, home sales do not respond until much later. Hamilton (2008) attributes this delay to cross-sectional heterogeneity in search times. This framework offers a description of the lags in the effects of monetary policy that is both more detailed, allowing one in principle to measure the consequences at the daily frequency, and more believable than traditional measures.

7.1.3 Credit Channel

The *credit channel* literature discusses two distinct (but complementary) ways how financial market imperfections might affect real economic activity and inflation (Hall, 2001). First, the *bank lending channel* focuses on the (cost) consequences which shocks to banks' balance sheets have on borrowers who depend on bank credit. Second, under the *firm balance sheet channel* it is the balance sheet of borrowers, rather than lenders, which matters for financing costs and, as a result, investment and consumption spending.

7.1.3.1 Bank Lending Channel

The *credit view* of the monetary transmission process maintains that banks play a special role in the financial system because they solve asymmetric information problems in credit markets. Most borrowers do not have direct access to the credit availed in capital markets, but need to borrow from banks (Kashyap & Stein, 1994; Gertler & Gilchrist, 1994). Banks lend against collateral (such as, for instance, real estate or financial asset portfolios). If the price of collateral ($P_{h\uparrow}$) rises as a result of monetary expansion ($M_\uparrow$), banks enjoy capital gains, thereby increasing their equity capital (net worth $NW_{b\uparrow}$). A rise in equity capital, in turn, allows banks to engage in more lending ($L_\uparrow$), raising debt financed investment ($I_\uparrow$) and thus output ($Y_\uparrow$):

$$M_\uparrow \Rightarrow P_{h\uparrow} \Rightarrow NW_{b\uparrow} \Rightarrow L_\uparrow \Rightarrow I_\uparrow \Rightarrow Y_\uparrow. \tag{7.21a}$$

If prices of collateral against which banks have extended credit fall, however, a restrictive impact on output could be expected, as banks would have to reign in loans extended relative to a diminished capital base. Such a transmission mechanism can be described as a *capital crunch*. It was actually operational in the US in the early 1990 s, during the *savings and loans crisis* (Bernanke, Lown, & Friedman, 1991), and it is also said to have been an important source of stagnation in Japan in the 1990s.

Moreover, recent research emphasizes a strong link between banking globalization, monetary transmission and the lending channel (Cetorelli & Goldberg, 2008). The globalization of banking in the United States is influencing the monetary transmission mechanism both domestically and in foreign markets. Using quarterly information from all U.S. banks comprising call reports between 1980 and 2005, Cetorelli and Goldberg find evidence *supporting the lending channel for monetary policy* in large banks. However, this is valid *only* for those banks which are *domestically-oriented* and without international operations. The authors demonstrate that the large globally-oriented banks *rely on internal capital markets* with their foreign affiliates to help smooth domestic liquidity shocks. They are also able to show that the existence of such internal capital markets contributes to an *international propagation of domestic liquidity shocks* to lending by affiliated banks abroad (see digression I on the financial crisis of 2007/2008 in this chapter). While these results imply a substantially more active lending channel than documented in the seminal work of Kashyap and Stein (2000), the lending channel within the United States is declining in strength as banking becomes more globalized.

7.1.3.2 Firm Balance Sheet Channel

The presence of *asymmetric information* in credit markets provides another transmission process for monetary policy. The so-called *balance sheet channel* (Bernanke & Gertler, 1989, 1995; Cecchetti, 1995; Hubbard, 1995; Bernanke, Gertler, & Gilchrist, 1999) works via changes in borrowers' asset values and cash flows as a result of, for instance, monetary policy. This, in turn, can affect borrowers' creditworthiness and hence the credit risk/finance premium they are charged. Changes in firms' net value also influence *adverse selection* and *moral hazard* in lending to these firms. In other words, the balance sheet channel explains how the financial health of borrowers might affect their access to credit and cause and/or amplify shocks to economy-wide spending

Take, for instance, a restrictive monetary policy, which lowers firms' net value. It means that there is now less collateral for the loans made to a firm. This, in turn, increases adverse selection, reducing credit supply made available to firms for financing investment. Also, the lower firms' net worth is, *the higher becomes the moral hazard:* owners of firms have a lower equity stake in the firm, giving them greater incentives to engage in risky investment projects. Since taking on riskier investment projects makes it more likely that loans might not be paid back, a decrease in net worth leads to a decrease in lending and hence in investment.

Following this line of thinking, an expansionary monetary policy ($M_\uparrow$) would cause a rise in stock prices ($P_{s\uparrow}$) and raises the net worth of firms ($NW_\uparrow$). A rise in firms' net worth, in turn, reduces adverse selection and moral hazard, encouraging higher (bank) lending to firms ($L_\uparrow$). Investment ($I_\uparrow$) and aggregate spending ($Y_\uparrow$) rise:

$$M_\uparrow \Rightarrow P_{s\uparrow} \Rightarrow NW_\uparrow \Rightarrow L_\uparrow \Rightarrow I_\uparrow \Rightarrow Y_\uparrow. \tag{7.21b}$$

In the context of analysing the interactions between borrowers' financial positions and their external financing costs, the *financial accelerator model* of Bernanke, Gertler, and Gilchrist (1999) deserves special attention. It assumes that lending is costly for creditors, in terms of monitoring the outcome of borrowers' investment projects. These costs (*external finance premium*), which are part to the credit costs and to be borne by borrowers, are actually determined by lenders' financial positions (*net worth*). The higher (lower) borrowing firms' net worth is, the lower (higher) is the finance premium. The underlying idea is that corporate net worth represents borrowers' own stake in an investment project and serves as a signal to lenders of borrowers' likely incentive to default on loans.

The financial accelerator model offers two explanations of the monetary transmission process. *First*, the transmission can run via changes in corporate cash flow. For instance, a rise in policy interest rates reduces firms' cash flows and raises the proportion of a given investment project that must now be financed with credit. A decline in firms' net worth increases the external finance premium. Higher funding costs reduce investment and thereby output. *Second*, an (unanticipated) monetary tightening reduces the demand for physical capital and lowers the net present value of asset prices. This, in turn, reduces the value of collateral available to back loans, raises the external finance premium and reduces current investment and output. Clearly, the higher (lower) firms' leverage is, the stronger (smaller) will be the impact changes in monetary policy (or a kind of *adverse shock*) exert on real magnitudes (and prices).

7.1.4 Credit Rationing

Modern credit market analysis is based on the imperfect information theory (Jaffee & Russell, 1976; Keeton, 1979; Stiglitz & Weiss, 1981). *Credit rationing models* rely on the assumption of asymmetrically distributed information between lenders and borrowers. Most important, the models *assume that at some point lenders' expected profit will decline with an increase in the interest rate charged to the borrower.* As a result, rational lenders won't increase the interest on loans past the rate at which expected profits start to decline, even if there are borrowers who would be willing to pay an even higher interest rate. As a result, credit market equilibrium may be characterised by a situation in which there is an excess demand for loans over supply.

"Credit Rationing" Versus "Credit Crunch"

A *credit rationing* occurs when banks' loan supply at a given interest rate falls short of borrowers' loan demand at that specific rate. How can that happen? As banks' are unwilling to extend loan supply even though borrowers would be prepared to pay a higher interest rate, the market would find an equilibrium in which the demand for loans exceeds credit supply (Fig. 7.7 (a)). A *credit crunch* represents a situation in which, starting from a given equilibrium, the supply of credit declines (sharply) relative to demand, leading to a new equilibrium – characterised by a higher interest rate and a lower equilibrium amount of credit (Fig. 7.7(b)). Whereas under a credit crunch the market mechanism works in the sense that interest rate adjustments bring supply of and demand for loans in equilibrium, credit rationing implies an equilibrium in which there is an excess demand for loans over credit supply (Green & Oh, 1991).

It seems fair to say that, from an analytical perspective, it might be difficult to distinguish between evidence of credit rationing and significance of a credit crunch, even if data about ongoing developments are available. For instance, Fig. 7.8 shows annual growth rates of various bank lending aggregates from January 1989 to April 2008. For instance, bank lending to firms contracted in the late 1980 s/early 1990 s (*savings and loans crisis*), and also at the start of the 21st century (bursting of the *New Economy boom*).

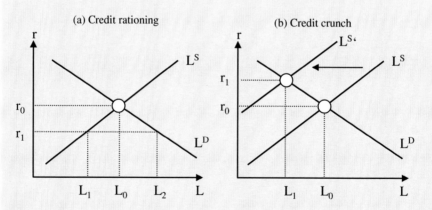

Fig. 7.7 Credit rationing versus credit crunch

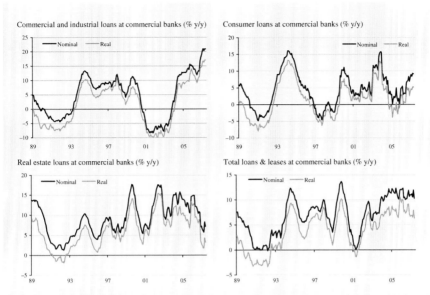

Fig. 7.8 US bank lending in the more recent past
Source: Federal Reserve Bank of St. Louis, Thomson Financial. Real rates were calculated
by subtracting the annual change from the US CPI from nominal growth rates

In general, changes in bank lending to the private sector might be indicative of *supply-side as well as demand-side* factors. For instance, a decline in
bank lending to firms might reflect banks' declining willingness and/or ability
to extend credit to firms and private households. At the same time, it could
reflect a decline in corporates' investment activities (or corporates' deliberate
de-leveraging efforts), translating into a lower demand for credit.
Figure 7.8(a-d) show the growth rates of various US bank loan aggregates.
For instance, starting with the collapse of the stock market boom around
2000/2001, US bank lending started contracting, presumably because firms
refrained from taking on more debt, while banks became increasingly unwilling to extend credit.

Stiglitz and Weiss (1981, p. 394) define equilibrium *credit rationing* as a situation
in which "either (a) among loan applicants who appear to be identical some receive
a loan and others do not, and the rejected applicants would not receive a loan even
if they offered to pay a higher interest rate; or (b) there are identifiable groups of
individuals in the population who, with a given supply of credit, are unable to obtain
loans at any interest rate, even though with a larger supply of credit, they would."
The critical aspect of this definition is that the equilibrium in the credit market might
represent a situation in which there is an unsatisfied loan demand that cannot be
eliminated through an increase in the interest rate the borrower is willing to pay.

To start with the Stiglitz and Weiss model, the borrower would default on his loan, B, if the return on the credit financed investment, R, plus the collateral, C, is insufficient to pay back the loan plus the interest rate payment, based on the cost of credit, r':

$$C + R \leq (1 + r')B. \tag{7.22}$$

That said, the net return to the borrower $\pi(R, r')$ can be written as:

$$\pi(R, r') = \max[R - (1 + r')B; -C]. \tag{7.23}$$

The return to the bank is:

$$p(R, r') = \min[R + C; (1 + r')B], \tag{7.24}$$

that is the borrower must either pay back the loan (plus interest payments) or the maximum amount he can pay $(R + C)$.

Now assume the bank has identified a group of funding projects. For each project θ there is a probability distribution of (gross) returns R; a greater (smaller) θ corresponds to higher (lower) risk. Furthermore, let us assume that the bank is able to distinguish projects with different mean returns, but that it is in a position to ascertain the riskiness of the projects.

The distribution of returns is $F(R, \theta)$ and the density function $f(R, \theta)$. If a greater θ corresponds to greater risk in the sense of mean preserving spreads (Rothschild & Stiglitz, 1970), i.e., for $\theta_1 > \theta_2$, if:

$$\int_0^\infty R f(R, \theta_1) dR = \int_0^\infty R f(R, \theta_2) dR, \tag{7.25}$$

then for $y \geq 0$, we have

$$\int_0^y F(R, \theta_1) dR \geq \int_0^y F(R, \theta_2) dR. \tag{7.26}$$

Theorem 1. *For a given interest rate r', there is a critical θ' such that a firm borrows from the bank if and only if $\theta' > \theta$.*

This follows directly from the finding that the firm's profit area is a convex function of R (Fig. 7.9 (a)), whereas the bank's profit is a concave function of R (Fig. 7.9(b)).

It is assumed that the returns to the bank decrease with a rise in the interest rate, which leads to Theorem 2.

Theorem 2. *As the interest rate rises, the critical value of θ, below which individuals do not apply for loans, increases.*

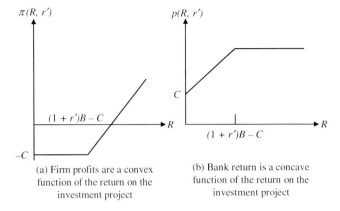

(a) Firm profits are a convex
function of the return on the
investment project

(b) Bank return is a concave
function of the return on the
investment project

Fig. 7.9 Firms' and bank profit functions

To show this, note that the value of θ' for which expected profits are zero satisfies:

$$\Pi(r', \theta') \equiv \int_0^{\infty} \max[R - (1 + r')B; -C]\, dF(R, \theta') = 0. \tag{7.27}$$

Differentiating yields:

$$\frac{d\theta'}{dr'} = \frac{B \int_{(1+r')B-C}^{\infty} dF(R, \theta')}{\partial \Pi / \partial \theta'} > 0. \tag{7.28}$$

Now let us turn to Theorem 3.

Theorem 3. *The expected return on a bank loan extended to a firm is a decreasing function of the riskiness of the credit financed investment project.*

The graphs earlier have made clear that the bank's (firm's) profit is a concave (convex) function of R. Theorem 2 and 3 imply that a rise in the interest rate increases the bank's return. In addition to this direct effect, however, there is an indirect, or: *adverse selection*, effect acting in the opposite direction. The intuition is quite similar to the work of Akerlof's market for lemons (Akerlof, 1970).

To see this, assume there are two groups of borrowers. The "safe" group borrows only at an interest rate below r_1, the risky group below r_2, with $r_1 < r_2$. A rise of the interest rate above r_1 changes the portfolio mix of applicants dramatically: the low risk group withdraws, the high risk borrowers keep demanding loans (Fig. 7.10). This leads to Theorem 4.

Theorem 4. *If there are a discrete number of potential borrowers each with a different θ, then $\bar{p}(r')$ will not be a monotonic function of r', since each successive group drops out of the market, there is a discrete fall in $\bar{p}$.*

Fig. 7.10 The optimal
interest rate from banks'
point of view

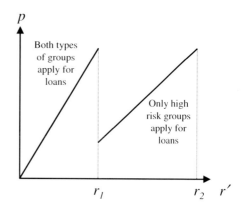

That said,

Theorem 5. *Whenever $\bar{p}(r')$ has an interior mode, there are supply functions such that market equilibrium entails credit rationing.*

Figure 7.11 illustrates such a situation. The demand for loans, L^D, is a decreasing function of the interest rate. This relation is shown in the upper right quadrant. The non-monotonic relation between the interest rate to be paid by borrowers and the expected return to the bank per dollar loaned, $\bar{p}$, is depicted in the lower right quadrant. The relation between $\bar{p}$ and loan supply, L^S, is shown in the lower left quadrant.[4]

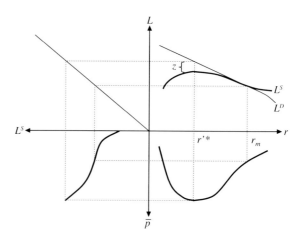

Fig. 7.11 Determining the
market equilibrium

---

[4]It should be noted that it is not necessary for the analysis that the supply of loans is positively related to the bank's profit as shown here.

At interest rate r'^*, the demand for loans exceeds the supply of loans. A bank that would increase the interest rate beyond r'^* would lower its return per money unit loaned. The excess of loan demand is measured by z. Of course, there is an interest rate r_m at which demand for loans equates supply. However, r_m does not represent a market equilibrium. The bank could increase profits by charging r'^* rather than r_m and would make a larger profit from each money unit loaned.

Finally, Fig. 7.12 shows a $\bar{p}(r')$ function with multiple modes. The equilibrium for such a function is described by Theorem 6.

Theorem 6. *If $\bar{p}(r')$ has several modes, market equilibrium could be either a situation in which there is a single interest rate at or below the market clearing level or by two interest rates, with an excess demand for credit at the lower one.*

Let r_m be the lowest Walrasian equilibrium interest rate and r'' the interest rate which maximises $\bar{p}(r)$. If $r'' < r_m$, the analysis for Theorem 5 is unaffected by the multiplicity of modes. With the interest rate at r'', credit will be rationed.

If, however, $r'' > r_m$, loans made be provided at two different interest rates, say r_1 and r_2. r_1 is the interest rate which maximises $p(r)$ conditional on $r \leq r_m$; r_2 is the lowest rate greater than r_m such that $p(r_1) = p(r_2)$. From $r_1 < r_m < r_2$, there will be an excess demand for loans at r_1, that is credit rationing. Rejected borrowers will apply for loans at the higher rate. Since there would be an excess supply of loans at r_2 if there would be no loans at r_1, and an aggregate excess of demand for loans if no loans were made at r_2, a distribution of available loans exists at r_1 and r_2 such that all applicants who are rejected at r_1 and who apply for loans at r_2 will get credit at the higher interest rate.

Credit supply available at $p(r_1)$ will either be loaned at r_1 and r_2. Clearly, there would be no incentive for small deviations from r_1, which represents a local maximum of $p(r)$. That said, a bank would not make available loans at an interest rate r_3 such that $p(r_3) < p(r_1)$. As a result, no bank would offer loans between r_1 and r_2. If a bank would offer loans at an interest rate of r_4 such that $p(r_4) > p(r_1)$ would not attract any borrowers since by definition $r_4 > r_2$; there would be no excess demand at interest rate r_2.

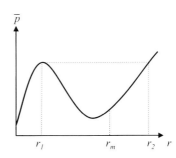

Fig. 7.12 A two-interest rate
equilibrium

Digression: The Financial Crisis of 2007/2008 – Overview and Policy Lessons

The financial crisis and (late on also economic) that started in the summer of 2007 is *one of the most dramatic and important crises* of recent decades. Its causes and unfolding impacts have highlighted a number of *new concerns and issues* for policy makers, practitioners as well as academics interested in financial and monetary issues (Allen & Carletti, 2008a, for a more commonplace representation of the initial phases of the downturn in facts and figures see BBC, 2007). When the fog of the crisis will have lifted, this may necessitate a revision of some of our textbook knowledge.

The crisis came as a surprise to many people. However, for others it was not a surprise. John Paulson, the hedge fund manager, correctly predicted the subprime debacle and earned \$3.7 billion in 2007 as a result.[5] The vulnerabilities that the global financial system has displayed were hinted at beforehand in the Bank of England and other Financial Stability Reports.[6] The Economist magazine had been predicting for some time that property prices in the US and a number of other countries were a bubble and were set to fall.[7]

How did problems with subprime mortgages result in a systemic crisis, a panic? The ongoing Panic of 2007 is due to a *loss of information* about the location and size of risks of loss due to default on a number of interlinked securities, special purpose vehicles, and derivatives, all related to subprime mortgages (see, among others, the very readable paper by Gorton, 2008).[8]

Subprime mortgages are a financial innovation designed to provide home ownership opportunities to riskier borrowers. Addressing their risk required a particular design feature, linked to house price appreciation. Subprime mortgages were then financed via securitization, which in turn has a unique design reflecting the subprime mortgage design. Subprime securitization tranches were often sold to (collateral debt obligations CDOs), which were, in turn, often purchased by market value off-balance sheet vehicles. Additional subprime risk was created (though not on net) with derivatives. When the housing price bubble burst, this chain of securities, derivatives, and off-balance sheet vehicles could not be penetrated by most investors to determine the location and size of the risks. The introduction of the ABX indices, synthetics related to portfolios of subprime bonds, in 2006 created common knowledge about the effects of these risks by providing centralized prices and

---

[5]Financial Times, January 15, 2008, and June 18, 2008.

[6]See, for example, Bank of England (2006, 2007).

[7]See, for example, Economist (2005, 2006).

[8]Mulligan and Threinen (2008) model the panic of 2008 as part of the wealth and substitution effects stemming from a housing price crash that began in 2006. The dissipation of the wealth effect stimulates a re-organization of the banking sector and is fostered by employment, GDP, and unemployment. The release of resources from the real estate sector lets investment goods prices shrink and thus devalues existing non-residential capital while it is stimulating non-residential investment. These predictions are compared with measured U.S. economic performance from 2006 to 2008 Q2.

a mechanism for shorting. Gorton (2008) describes the relevant securities, derivatives, and vehicles and provides some very simple, stylized, examples to show: (1) how asymmetric information between the sell-side and the buy-side was created via complexity; (2) how the chain of interlinked securities was sensitive to house prices; (3) how the risk was spread in an opaque way; and (4) how the ABX indices allowed information to be aggregated and revealed. We would like to argue that these details are at the heart of the answer to the question of the origin of the Panic of 2007 (Gorton, 2008).

Let us now consider the sequence of events in more detail. This provides a starting point for our discussion in subsequent sections. This description is mostly drawn from Federal Reserve Bank (2008a, 2008b; Bank of England, 2008; Bernanke, 2008; European Central Bank, 2008; International Monetary Fund, 2007a, 2007b, 2008; Kohn, 2008).

Symptoms and Chronicle of the Credit Crisis

The crisis started in the first half of 2007 when the credit quality of subprime residential mortgages, in particular adjustable-rate ones, started to deteriorate. Mortgage companies specializing in subprime products experienced funding pressures and many failed.

Although problems were initially confined to the subprime mortgage markets, further deterioration of credit quality and increases in the delinquency rates led to a spread of the crisis to other markets and products. By mid-2007 investors started to retreat from structured credit products and risky assets more generally, as rating agencies started downgrading many mortgage-backed securities. The prices of AAA-rated tranches of subprime securitizations fell dramatically in a short period of time. When markets are efficient this indicates that information about the underlying quality of the assets deteriorated. This led to the conventional wisdom that bad incentives in the mortgage industry were to blame.

The securitization market for subprime mortgages finally simply broke down. Figure 7.13 shows that in July 2007 there was a tremendous jump in the co-movement of AAA-rated tranches of subprime mortgage backed securities, commercial mortgage backed securities, and securities linked to corporate credit quality.

The prices of AAA tranches of securitizations went to levels that were very difficult to explain on the basis of fundamentals. The April 2008 Bank of England Financial Stability Report deduced that prices of these securities at that time implied a 38% loss rate – consistent with a 76% default rate and an eventual 50% loss given default – that seemed much too high. How can prices be so low if it is not fundamentals? We will turn to this important issue in the "lessons from the crisis" section.

As from late summer 2007, defaults in the *US subprime mortgage market* triggered the severest global financial market turmoil in the more recent financial market history. Bank stock market valuations across the globe started declining strongly with investors fearing growing losses, and perhaps even defaults, among major financial institutions (Fig. 7.14). Most notable, the losses in bank stock valuations were much higher than those for non-financial stocks.

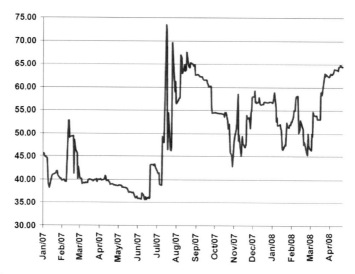

Fig. 7.13 Co-movement between AAA-rated US structured financial instruments (in percent)
Source: Bank of England calculations using data from JP Morgan Chase and Co. – Bank of England
Financial Stability Report (2008, p. 24, Chart 1.19)

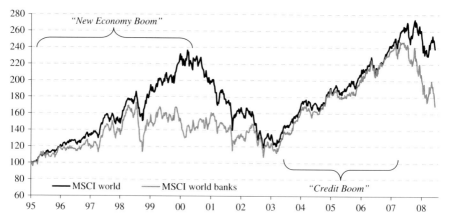

Fig. 7.14 Global stock markets (MSCI indices)
Source: Bloomberg, own calculations. Indexed: January 1995 = 100, weekly data

   Growing investor concern about the financial solidity of individual banks – and
presumably the banking sector as a whole – led to strongly rising spreads between
interbank money market rates and official central bank rates (Fig. 7.15), accompanied by a drastic drop in *market liquidity*. As a response to the financial market
turbulence, the US Federal Reserve slashed interest rates as from September 2007,
lowering the Federal Funds Target Rate to 2.0% until April 2008.
   Investment and commercial banks cut their exposures across business lines. The
tightening of repo haircuts caused a number of hedge funds and other leveraged

(a) US money market rates (%)   (b) Euro area money market rates (%)

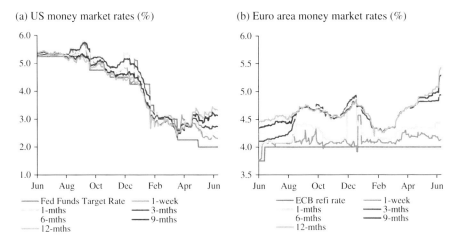

Fig. 7.15 Money market rates in the US and the euro area (%)
Source: Thomson Financial; own calculations. – The US Fed lowered the Federal Funds Target Rate from 5.25% on 18 September 2007 to 2.0% on 30 April 2008

investors to unwind existing positions (*distress selling*).[9] Spreads on even the most highly rated assets reached unusually wide levels, and market liquidity virtually disappeared across many fixed income markets.

For instance, new issuance activities in the US asset backed commercial paper (ABCP) market fell sharply (Fig. 7.16, ABCP is short-term (mostly due within a year) and is backed by (longer-term assets) assets such as, for instance, real estate, autos and other commercial debt; it is just another example of a Collater-ized Debt Obligation (CDO). ABCP issuers (mostly conduits, special investment vehicles (SIVs)) felt it increasingly difficult, if not impossible, to "roll over" their outstanding liabilities.

As commercial banks had committed liquidity lines to SIVs, banks found them-selves in need of funding. The effective closure of asset backed security (ABS) and leveraged loan markets – another consequence of an unfolding credit crisis – left major financial institutions in need of funds to finance warehouses of assets that they had not expected to retain on their balances.

As investor concern about a looming worldwide economic and financial crisis rose – including bankruptcies in the financial and non-financial sector –, the market prices for *credit insurance* – as expressed by the European iTraxx indices (which represent a sample of credit default swaps (CDS)) – rose dramatically (Fig. 7.17).

Write-offs against bank equity capital and rising funding costs as a result of heightened investor risk aversion could make banks reducing their loan supply vis-à-vis non-banks. That said, the credit market turmoil episode would have the

---

[9] A valuation haircut is a risk control measure applied to underlying assets used in reverse transac-tions, implying that the central bank calculates the value of underlying assets as the market value of the assets reduced by a certain percentage (haircut). The Eurosystem applies valuation haircuts reflecting features of the specific assets, such as the residual maturity.

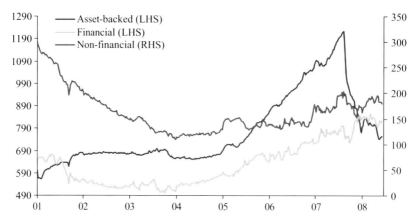

Fig. 7.16 Outstanding US commercial paper, US$bn
Source: US Federal Reserve

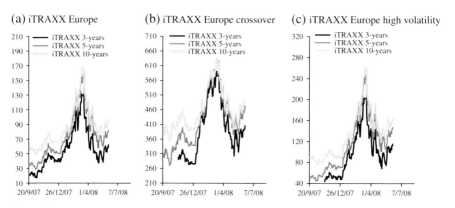

Fig. 7.17 iTraxx indices
Source: Bloomberg

potential to spill-over from the financial sector into credit supply conditions for firms and private households. Figure 7.17 chronicles the initial parts of the credit market turmoil which started in early August 2007.

In summary, a *general loss of confidence* started to become pervasive. Signs of strain appeared in the leveraged syndicated loan market and in other leveraged lending markets in late June 2007, in the asset-backed commercial paper (ABCP) and in the term bank funding markets in August 2007. Spreads of collateralized loan obligations (CLOs) increased while the issuance of such debt reduced significantly, thus also reducing leveraged lending. Spreads on US ABCP widened significantly in mid August, while the volume of ABCP outstanding dropped significantly. This put substantial pressure on the structured investment vehicles (SIVs) that had heavily invested in structured financial products. Many had to activate the contingent liquidity support from their sponsor banks.

At the same time, problems arose in the term interbank funding markets in the US, Europe and the UK. Banks suddenly became much more unwilling to provide liquidity to other banks, especially for maturities longer than a few days. Reflecting that, Libor spreads rose significantly. The apparent reason for this liquidity hoarding was twofold. On the one hand, banks wanted to protect themselves against potential larger-than-anticipated liquidity needs deriving from the disruptions in the mortgage, syndicated loans and commercial paper markets. On the other hand, uncertainty about the counterparty risk increased as banks could not precisely assess their counterparties' exposure to the subprime related securities and also to the other disrupted markets (Allen & Carletti, 2008). A chronicle of the initial phases of the credit market turmoil is conveyed by us in Fig. 7.18 below.

After a relief of the tensions in September and October following a 50 basis point reduction in the Federal Funds rate, tensions mounted again in November and December when end-of-the-year considerations became an additional element fueling the uncertainty deriving from the subprime market crisis. Spreads widened significantly again in all affected markets and a flight to quality led to a strong demand for safe assets and a sharp drop in Treasury bill yields (Allen & Carletti, 2008).

Problems mounted again in March 2008 when the release of news of further losses and write-downs due to the use of mark-to-market accounting increased con-

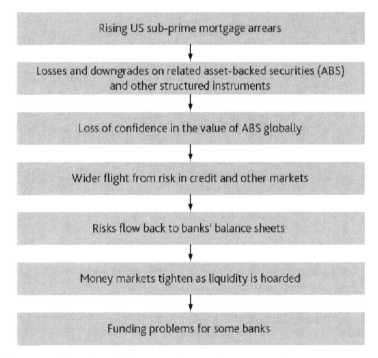

Fig. 7.18 A chronicle of the initial phases of the credit market turmoil
Source: Bank of England (2007 October)

cerns about the creditworthiness and the capital position of several institutions. Financial markets continued to be under great stress, particularly the markets for short-term uncollateralized and collateralized funding. Tensions culminated in mid-March 2008 when a sudden wholesale run on Bear Stearns impeded the investment bank obtaining funding on both unsecured and collateralized short term financing markets. Indicators of counterparty risk started being more significantly affected. For example, the cost of insurance against the default of large complex financial institutions (LCFIs), as measured by the credit default swap spreads, rose steadily in 2008 and reached an unprecedented peak around the time of the collapse of Bear Stearns.

Central banks around the world accompanied the unfolding of the crisis with *numerous interventions*. Some of these interventions concerned *reductions in policy rates* (but the Fed also reduced the discount window rate in September 2007) as well as *liquidity injections* into the system. Other interventions concerned *changes in the standard operational frameworks* or the creation of more unusual, innovative forms of special liquidity schemes. Changes involved extensions in the maturity of central bank lending (in the US both with respect to the discount window loans in September 2007 and the open market operations in March 2008), and widening of the collateral accepted.

Special liquidity schemes introduced in the US during the crisis include the Term Auction Facility in December 2007 through which credit is auctioned to depository institutions against Discount Window collateral, the Term Securities Lending Facility in March 2008 which allows primary dealers to swap less-liquid mortgage and other asset backed securities for Treasury securities, and, after the collapse of Bear Stearns, the Primary Dealer Credit Facility through which the discount window was extended to primary dealers. Similarly, a special liquidity scheme was introduced in the UK in April 2008 according to which institutions eligible for the standing facilities can swap collateral with Treasury Bills. Furthermore, both the Bank of England and the Federal Reserve were *directly involved in managing and orchestrating the rescue,* respectively, *of Northern Rock and Bear Stearns*; and the Federal Reserve recently established a temporary arrangement to provide emergency liquidity to Fannie Mae and Freddie Mac, should it become necessary. More recently, the US Treasury has been given the power, though on a temporary basis, to extend unlimited credit to (and invest in the equity of) the two Government Sponsored Enterprises (Allen & Carletti, 2008).

Although the *real effects of the crisis* have so far been contained to some extent, initial signs of propagation seem to be emerging at the time of writing this book. Credit standards and terms on both commercial and industrial (C&I) loans and commercial real estate loans tightened and the yields on corporate bonds increased significantly over the first half of 2008 (see Federal Reserve Bank, 2008a, 2008b), indicating increasing pressures and risks for the nonfinancial corporate sector. Credit has remained available to the business sector so far, but household borrowing has slowed. Similar changes are occurring in the UK and Europe. The exchange rate of the dollar fluctuated during the crisis with a general trend towards depreciation against most currencies. Private payroll employment started falling substantially in

February 2008, and inflation started also to be a source of concern. Economic growth remained slow in the first half of 2008, and the persistent weaknesses in the housing markets together with the tightened conditions for credit to businesses and households also weakened the projections for the second half of the year.

Real Effects of the Subprime Mortgage Crisis: Is It a Demand or a Finance Shock?

Tong and Wei (2008) develop a methodology to investigate whether and how a financial-sector crisis can spill over to the real economy. They apply the latter to the case of financial crisis of 2007/2008 and ask: if there is a spillover, does it express itself primarily in a lower degree of consumer confidence and consumer demand? Does there also exist a supply-side channel through a tightened liquidity constraint faced by non-financial firms? As the majority of firms seems to have much larger cash holdings than in earlier times, some observers claim that a liquidity constraint is not likely to be a significant factor for non-financial firms.

Tong and Wei (2008) propose a methodology to assess the importance of the former two channels for spillovers. They first propose an index of a firm's sensitivity to a shock to consumer confidence, based on the firms' response to the September 11th shock in 2001. They then construct a separate firm-level index of the degree of financial constraints starting from Whited and Wu (2006). To check for robustness, they additionally construct an alternative sector-level index of a firm's intrinsic demand for external finance (Rajan & Zingales, 1998). They find robust evidence in favour of *both channels* being at work, but that a tightened liquidity squeeze is economically more important than a reduction of consumer confidence or spending in determining cross-firm differences in stock price declines.

Monetary Policy Before and During the Subprime Crisis

Realizing that their *traditional instruments were inadequate* for responding to the crisis that began on 9 August 2007, Federal Reserve officials improvised. Beginning in mid-December 2007, they implemented a series of changes directed at ensuring that liquidity would be distributed to those institutions that needed it most. Conceptually, this meant America's central bankers shifted from focusing solely on the size of their balance sheet, which they use to keep the overnight interbank lending rate close to their chosen target, to manipulating the composition of their assets as well. We described the necessary details further above under the headline "Symptoms and chronicle of the credit crisis".

Among others, Cecchetti (2008) investigates the Federal Reserve's conventional and unconventional responses to the financial crisis of 2007–2008. Finally, Borio and Nelson (2008) put the monetary operations of the world's most important central banks in the wake of the financial turmoil under scrutiny and in perspective. They correctly argue that a proper understanding of central bank operations in response to the recent financial turmoil and of their implications for the monetary policy stance and for market functioning calls for a deeper understanding of operating frameworks. Not only are these the least familiar aspect of monetary policy, they also differ considerably across countries. It is important to note that the frameworks can have a first-order influence on the size and type of liquidity injections employed and on the need for exceptional measures.

Does Liquidity Provision Help at All?

Models of interaction between risk taking in the financial sector and central bank policy show that in the absence of central bank intervention, the incentive of financial intermediaries to free ride on liquidity in good states may result in excessively low liquidity in bad states (Illing, 2007a). In the prevailing mixed-strategy equilibrium, depositors are worse off than if banks would coordinate on more liquid investment. It is shown that public provision of liquidity improves the allocation, even though it encourages more risk taking (less liquid investment) by private banks.

Illing (2007b) presents a stylized framework to analyze conditions under which monetary policy contributes to amplified movements in the housing market. Building on work by Hyun Shin (2005), he analyses self enforcing feedback mechanisms resulting in amplifier effects in a credit constrained economy. Illing (2007b) characterizes conditions for asymmetric effects, causing systemic crises. By injecting liquidity, monetary policy can prevent a meltdown. Anticipating such a response, private agents are encouraged to take higher risks. Provision of liquidity works as a public good, but it may create potential conflicts with other policy objectives and may give incentives to build up leverage with a high systemic exposure to small probability events. The decisive keywords in such kind of models is: confidence, confidence and confidence!

Did Monetary Policy Trigger the Credit Crisis?

However, some critiques argue that there never would have been a sub-prime mortgage crisis if the Fed had been alert (Belke and Wiedmann 2005, 2006). They are scornful of Bernanke's campaign to clear his name by blaming the bubble on an Asian saving glut, which purportedly created stimulus beyond the control of the Fed by driving down global bond rates. Bernanke's attempt to exculpate himself does not appear to them too convincing (Belke & Gros, 2007).

According to the critiques, the basic issue is that regulators, the private sector and monetary policy have combined to lead to an outcome with unintended consequences: the potential for a serious recession and spill-over to countries and markets where excesses were less marked. While short-run policies are needed to avoid this, the long-run cost may be severe if the system is not fundamentally reformed. Liquidity doesn't do anything in this situation. It cannot deal with the underlying fear that lots of firms are going bankrupt (see, for instance, Buiter, 2008, and Anna Schwartz in different contexts and at numerous occasions).

Responding to the credit and liquidity crunch that has spooked global financial markets, the Federal Reserve, for instance, reduced, on Friday 17 August 2007, its primary discount rate from 6.25 to 5.75%. The discount rate is the rate that the Fed charges eligible financial institutions for borrowing from the Fed against what the Fed deems to be eligible collateral. It is normally 100 bps above the target Federal Funds rate, which is the Fed's primary monetary policy instrument and which is currently 5.25%. The critiques believe that this cut in the discount rate was an inappropriate response to the financial turmoil.

The market failure that prompted this response was not that financial institutions are unable to pay 6.25% at the discount window and survive (given that they have eligible collateral). The problem is that banks and other financial institutions are holding a lot of assets which are suddenly illiquid and cannot be sold at any price. In other words, there is no longer a market that matches willing buyers and sellers at a price reflecting economic fundamentals. Lowering the discount rate does not solve this problem; it just provides a 50 bps subsidy to any institution able and willing to borrow at the discount window.

Addressing the problem of illiquid financial markets using the blunt instrument of monetary policy, a cut in the monetary policy rate, would be clear confirmation that the Fed is concerned about financial markets over and above what these markets imply for the real economy. Such regulatory capture would effectively redirect the "Greenspan put" from the equity markets in general to the profits and viability of a small number of financial institutions. It would not be a proper use of public money Belke and Wiedmann 2005 and 2006.

Note that much of the academic literature on the role of liquidity in financial crises has focused *on the effects on the real economy*, mainly through the provision of liquidity to non-financial firms. However, Allen and Carletti (2008) argue this has not been a significant factor in the financial crisis of 2007/2008 at the time of writing this book. However, one should note that this may change going forward according to our above section on "Symptoms and chronicle of the credit crisis". A first indication was the alleged impact on the financial situation of the automobile industry in the US and in Europe.

There is by now a growing literature on understanding the current crisis. Brunnermeier 2009 provides an excellent account of the sequence of events in the crisis focusing on a wide range of factors. Adrian and Shin (2008) argue that the dynamics of the crisis are driven by deleveraging. However, Allen and Carletti (2008), for instance, set their very readable study apart from these papers in its primary focus on liquidity.

How to Avoid Planting the Seeds of the Next Crisis?

It is of course essential that *"moral hazard" has to be minimised*. This "bail out" of the illiquid institution by the Fed should be *sufficiently costly* that those paying the price would still remember it during the next credit boom, and act more prudently. Second, where no market price is available, the Fed should base its valuation on *conservative assumptions about the creditworthiness* of the counterparty and the collateral offered by the counterparty. They counterparty should not expect to get 90 cents on the dollar for securities that it could not find a willing private taker for at any price. Third, the highest "liquidity haircut" in the central bank's (here: the Fed's) arsenal should be applied to this conservative valuation.

To summarize, some of the usual causes of the crisis of 2007/2008 that are given in the press and are considered as conventional wisdom are ratings agencies, lack of transparency, poor incentives in the origination of mortgages, the securitization of them, the provision of ratings for securitizations and risk management systems which proved to be inadequate.

However, the main cause was *that the Federal Reserve provided too much liquidity and held interest rates too low* for too long and this caused a bubble in property prices. Without the significant drop in property prices there would not have been a problem. Further questions come immediate to our minds. Why was there a proliferation in subprime mortgages? What was the reason subprime mortgages became so important? Why were they introduced and why have they caused such a problem? If we regulate them will we prevent the problem going forward?

Another important and complementary driver of the US financial crisis was the fact that *subprime mortgages were used for tax arbitrage* by US-homeowners. What is tax arbitrage? In the US interest is tax deductible but rent is not. This creates a significant incentive to turn rent payments into tax deductible interest payments. This is what 100% mortgages do. The buyer doesn't own the house, the bank does. The user of the house makes a fixed payment each month to cover the interest. This is just like paying rent except it is tax deductible. This worked pretty well as long as property prices keep rising. If they fall, the arbitrage no longer works. But property prices in the US had not fallen on average since the Great Depression (isn't there a special relevance of Asia?). In recent years property has outperformed other assets so it seemed like a good bet.

What Kind of Research Program Should Be Drawn from the Financial Crisis?

The financial crisis of 2007/2008 has for sure paved the way for a gigantic *new research program* for next five to ten years in the fields of finance and macroeconomics and hybrids consisting of both areas. According to the preceding passages, we feel legitimized to claim that the most important component of a research program emerging from the financial crisis is the following one.

Claim 1: *Central banks need to think carefully about the effects of monetary policy on asset prices, particularly property prices and about global imbalances.* In the past, very few central banks have done this. For example, the Federal Reserve argued this was not possible and focused solely on consumer price indices of inflation.

Let us now derive further important lessons from the financial crisis (Allen, 2008; Allen & Carletti, 2008). For this purpose, let us start from the observation that the most important elements of the crisis were the role of liquidity or the late there of in this crisis and its effects on interbank markets and collateralized markets. For this purpose, we now first address the role of liquidity. Our background is the theoretical framework of liquidity provision derived earlier in Sect. 4.7 of this textbook.

Role of Liquidity in the Credit Crisis– Cash-in-the Market Pricing

One of the most puzzling features of the crisis has been the pricing of AAA tranches of a wide range of securitized products. It appears that the market prices of many of these instruments are *significantly below what plausible fundamentals would suggest* they should be. This *pricing risk* has come as a great surprise to many. Allen and Carletti (2008) propose an alternative to the view of bad incentives in the mortgage industry and call it the "*mispricing view*". According to this view, new information about subprime defaults led to a realization they were more risky than previously thought. This led to sales of the AAA tranches as portfolios were readjusted. The volume of sales overwhelmed the absorption capacity of the secondary markets for securitized assets and prices fell below fundamentals.

Furthermore, they argue that the sharp change in pricing regimes that started in August 2007 is consistent with what is known in the academic literature as "cash-in-the-market" pricing. Holding liquidity is costly because less liquid assets usually have higher returns. In order for providers of liquidity to markets to be compensated for this opportunity cost, they must on occasion be able to make a profit by buying up assets at prices below fundamentals. Once the link between prices and fundamentals is broken, arbitrage becomes risky and the usual forces that drive prices and fundamentals together no longer work (Shleifer & Vishny, 1997). This *limit to arbitrage* means that prices can deviate from fundamentals for protracted periods (see in detail Sect. 4.7 of this textbook).[10]

There is also a direct link to mispricing from the *Paulson Plan*.[11] The mispricing view of the crisis underlay the Treasury and Fed view that subprime mortgage assets could be bought at "hold-to-maturity" prices well above market prices and taxpayers could also make money. This was not well explained when the plan was presented to the public and Congress.

---

[10] It is like during the dot.com bubble in that trying to arbitrage internet stocks led to bankruptcy. The LTCM crisis arguably also exhibited mispricing.

[11] U.S. Treasury Secretary Henry Paulson proposed a plan under which the U.S. Treasury would acquire up to $700 billion worth of mortgage-backed securities. The plan was introduced on September 20 by U.S. Treasury Secretary Henry Paulson. Named the Troubled Asset Relief Program, but also known as the Paulson Proposal or Paulson Plan, it should not be confused with Paulson's earlier 212-page plan, the blueprint for a modernized financial regulatory reform, which was released on March 31, 2008. A key part of the proposal is the federal government's plan to buy up to US$700 billion of illiquid mortgage backed securities (MBS) with the intent to increase the liquidity of the secondary mortgage markets and reduce potential losses encountered by financial institutions owning the securities.

The Effects on Interbank Markets and Collateralized Markets

The second surprise has been the way in which the money markets have operated. The interbank markets for terms longer than a few days have experienced considerable pressures. In addition, the way that the collateralized markets operate has changed significantly. Haircuts have increased and low quality collateral has become more difficult to borrow against. The Federal Reserve and other central banks have introduced *a wide range of measures* to try to improve the smooth functioning of the money markets. The extent to which these events affect the functioning of the financial system and justifies central bank intervention depends on the possible explanations as to why the markets stopped operating smoothly.

One of the main roles of interbank markets is to reallocate liquidity among banks that are subject to idiosyncratic shocks. If banks hoard liquidity and as a result they are able to cover idiosyncratic shocks from their own liquidity holdings, then their unwillingness to lend to other banks is *not a problem*. If, on the contrary, the liquidity hoarding prevents the reshuffling of liquidity to deficient, but solvent banks, then the badly functioning interbank market is a problem warranting central bank liquidity provision. Allowing banks to exchange mortgage backed securities for Treasuries *is desirable if* it improves collateralized lending in the repo market *but is not if* it simply leads to more window dressing by financial institutions. In this case the actions of the Federal Reserve *are simply removing market discipline*.

Hence, the most important market failures identified above are: mispricing due to limits to arbitrage, inefficient liquidity provision and finally also contagion. Let us address the third issue once again because it might – contrary to the first two – not have been explained by us in the necessary detail.

Fear of Contagion

The controversial use of public funds in the arranged merger of Bear Stearns with J. P. Morgan was justified by the possibility of contagion. If Bear Stearns had been allowed to fail, its extensive involvement as counterparty in many derivatives markets may have caused a string of defaults. There is a large literature on the likelihood of contagion between banks based on simulations. The conclusion of this literature is that contagion in banking is unlikely. However, some have argued that these simulations do not capture important elements of the process. Whatever one's view of the likelihood of contagion in banking, it is important to conduct similar studies in the context of counterparty risk in derivatives and other markets (Allen & Carletti, 2008).

The above considerations lead us to formulate our second policy lesson from the subprime crisis.

Claim 2: *Careful research is needed to distinguish the relative importance of the bad (mortgage markets) incentives view and the mispricing vie* (because the two views have distinctly different implications for regulation and risk management going forward, e.g. mark-to-market accounting).

A further pressing question is why regulation didn't prevent the financial crisis? First, banking regulation is different from other kinds of regulation in that there is no wide agreement on the market failures it is designed to correct. Second, it is backward looking in the sense that it was put in place to prevent the recurrence of past types of crises. Current regulation did not prevent the crisis.

The question then is how banking regulation should be designed in the aftermath of the crisis? What are the benefits and costs of regulation? What exactly are the market failures? The Basel agreements illustrate the lack of a widely agreed theoretical framework by now. Hence, our third claim connected with the financial crisis of 2007/2008 which should be put under scientific scrutiny amounts to the following.

Claim 3: *Banking regulation needs to be designed to solve market failures rather than being imposed piecemeal as a reaction to crises* (because many banks focus on satisfying current regulations rather than thinking ahead and arguably current regulation hurts rather than helps).

Let us now readdress the quite popular bad incentives argument in order to arrive at our next claim. The former is also well-known as the *moral hazard* problem of bank bailouts. It can best be illustrated by referring to the Fed and Bear Sterns example. It is very important the Fed does not bail out shareholders as they did with Bear Sterns. The Fed should *have charged* for the guarantee. By this, they could have avoided systemic risk while taking out the shareholders and ensuring senior management was replaced.

Why has Goldman Sachs been able to avoid the worst effects of the crisis while other financial institutions such as Merrill Lynch did not? The answer is that Goldman has had a long run incentive system while firms such as Merrill Lynch do not. This leads us to conclude that it is very important to conduct further research on the question whether and how financial institutions need to fundamentally reform the way they reward executives and base compensation on long run performance not annual performance (policy lesson 4).

Claim 4: *Incentives of bankers need to be reformed but this should be a matter for the private sector and not regulated. However, the Fed – just like other central banks – must not undermine private sector moves in this regard.*

Another very topical research issue is the sense or non-sense of *cross-border cooperation of policy reactions to the financial crisis* because one of the most worrying aspects of the current crisis is the possibility for contagion across borders. In the US case this was demonstrated rather clearly by the UBS and the "too big to save" problem and is currently so in Europe where banks have a significantly higher leverage than their US counterparts. To save the European banking system, Daniel Gros and others have suggested a coordinated approach by all EU member countries under which the large banks are re-capitalised and each government guarantees the lending of its own banks to other EU banks (see http.www.voxeu.com and Gros & Micossi, 2008). Their claim is the international community needs to do much more to coordinate crisis management. The recent financial crisis has provided many examples of lack of cooperation. For instance, the Société Générale problem provides an example of how not to do it (Allen & Carletti, 2008).

The Federal Reserve, for instance, could easily prevent the threat of contagion posed by Bear Stearns. Even the threat of contagion posed by the failure of the largest banks in the US such as Citigroup and Bank of America could be avoided by central bank and government intervention even though this may require the outlay of very large amounts of government funds. However, some banks are so large relative to the countries in which they are based that this is not the case.

One example at hand was Fortis in Belgium. This bank had assets that are greater in size than the GDP of Belgium. If it were to fail it would be quite likely that a Belgian government (if one existed at the time) would be unwilling to intervene and assume fiscal responsibility because of the large size of the burden. In this case the key issue would be how the burden would be shared between countries of the European Union. The Ecofin (2008, p. 5) specifies that "If public resources are involved, direct budgetary net costs are shared among affected Member States on the basis of equitable and balanced criteria, . . . ".

Unfortunately, this lack of specificity is likely to lead to substantial delays in dealing with the situation as each country vies to improve its fiscal position. During this time the prospect of contagion could effectively freeze many European and some global capital markets with enormous effects on the real economy. It is an urgent matter for the European Union to agree on specific ex ante burden sharing criteria for the costs of preventing large banking crises. The work along these lines that is currently under way needs to proceed rapidly.

Even more worrying is the fact that there exist banks that may fail in small countries that are not part of a larger grouping. The classic example here is UBS (as stated above) and Credit Suisse in Switzerland. These two banks both have assets significantly in excess of Swiss GDP. It may literally be infeasible for the Swiss government to raise the funds to prevent their failure. In such cases the potential damage caused by the prospect of contagion if one of them were to fail is very large. It is again an urgent task to devise a system to prevent this kind of problem from occurring. The International Monetary Fund and the Bank for International Settlements are obvious institutions to be assigned to deal with such problems. The alternative is to wait for the catastrophe to occur. In that case consumers will subsequently be unwilling to invest in large banks in small countries. In the meantime, however, very large costs will have been imposed on the global economy. Hence, the fifth hypothesis to be investigated more deeply in further research from the financial crisis is the following one.

Claim 5: *Put in place a system of burden sharing so that crisis management can be effective in case a large multinational bank is faced with bankruptcy* (which might be particularly important for the EU with its goal of a single market in financial services).

Some observers argue that the financial crisis also stresses the importance of an even narrower *focus on financial stability*. For this purpose, they refer to the observation that, after the crises in Norway and Sweden, the Norges Bank and Riksbank started publishing Financial Stability Reviews and now many central banks do it. It would be helpful if the Federal Reserve did this. Moreover, the governance of the US regional banks, and in particular the New York Fed, needs to be reformed to avoid conflicts of interest in crisis situations, like, for instance, in case of Lehman Brothers. Based on these arguments, the sixth potential research topic might be as follows.

Claim 6: *The Federal Reserve System needs to place more emphasis on financial stability.* This may not have helped them to avoid the current crisis but on the other hand it may have led them to think through many of the issues that they are now faced with more carefully.

To conclude, there are still many issues remaining to be investigated more deeply by means of scientific methods, among them the *provision of liquidity at quarter-end and year-end and window dressing and that the mark-to-market accounting in financial institutions has severe drawbacks in times of crisis and needs to be reformed.* We suggested further above that one of the exacerbating factors in the recent crisis was that markets have not been pricing the AAA tranches of securitized products in a way that reflects fundamentals. If that occurs, mark-to-market accounting for financial institutions has the disadvantage that it can understate the value of banks and other intermediaries and makes them appear insolvent when in fact they are not. Historic cost accounting has the advantage that it does not do this. On the other hand, it leads to bankrupt institutions that deserve to be closed being able to continue and possibly gamble for resurrection. Allen and Carletti (2008b) suggest that in financial crisis situations where liquidity is scarce and prices are low as a result, market prices should be supplemented with both model-based and historic cost valuations. The rest of the time and in particular when asset prices are low because expectations of future cash flows have fallen, mark-to-market accounting should instead be used.

A further issue not to be solved here certainly is the Fed view versus the ECB view on the financial crisis and problems caused by exchange rate movements. Moreover, a question not only interesting for analysts, of course, is what's going to happen next? What precedents provide the best guide? The US has not had situations like this on a nationwide basis since the Great Depression but in other parts of the world there have been many financial crises. What is the most similar? While scholars like Franklin D. Allen from Wharton argue that it is important to understand the experience of Japan in the 1990's and the determinants of feedback effects such as corporate governance (and that this is a key area for research going forward), Barry Eichengreen, for instance, compares the crisis of 2007/2008 with the Asian crisis in the 90 s.

Finally, at the time of writing this book, commentators are busy with analyzing the *UK action plan to fight the financial* crisis and its European successors. Nationalizing the banking system is of course a bold step removing bankruptcy risk and contagion risk. But why should one bail out equity holders? In case of a debt overhang – why should the government bail out bondholders if this transfers risk to governments (see, for instance, the Irish debt). Above, we already argued that the credit market and interbank markets freeze might be due either to fear of default or to liquidity hoarding – with specific policy conclusions in either case.

7.1.5 Exchange Rate Channel

In an increasingly globalised world, national economies are no longer unaffected by real and monetary developments outside their own borders. In this sense, Taylor (1995) and Obstfeld and Rogoff (1996) stress the importance of international developments in the transmission process of monetary policy. In this context, the exchange rate can be expected to play an important role. One could think of two major transmission processes that operate through exchange rates: (i) exchange rate effects on net exports and (ii) exchange rate effects on market agents' balance sheets.

7.1.5.1 Exchange Rate Effects on Net Exports

In a world of free capital flows and flexible exchange rate, attention needs to be paid to how monetary policies affect exchange rates, which, in turn, affect net exports and aggregate output and prices. Clearly, this channel does not operate if a country has a fixed exchange rate, and the more open an economy is, the stronger this channel might become.

A change in monetary policy affects exchange rates when and if it affects the (perceived) attractiveness of investing in the domestic economy relative to investing abroad. For instance, an easier domestic monetary policy makes holding assets denominated in domestic currency less attractive relative to assets denominated in foreign currencies. As investors offer domestic currency against foreign currency in the FX market, the exchange rate of the domestic currency depreciates $(E_\downarrow)$. A lower value of the domestic currency makes domestic goods cheaper relative to foreign goods, thereby causing a rise in net exports $(NX_\uparrow)$ and hence in aggregate spending $(Y_\uparrow)$:

$$M_\uparrow \Rightarrow E_\downarrow \Rightarrow NX_\uparrow \Rightarrow Y_\uparrow. \tag{7.29}$$

7.1.5.2 Exchange Rate Effects on Balance Sheets

Monetary policy induced changes in exchange rates can have an effects on aggregate demand by affecting the balance sheets of both financial and non-financial firms if, for instance, a substantial amount of their debt is denominated in foreign currency. With debt contracts denominated in foreign currency, an expansionary monetary policy $(M_\uparrow)$, if it leads to a depreciation of the domestic currency, increases the debt burden of domestic borrowers. If assets are predominantly denominated in domestic currency (and therefore do not change in value in response to exchange rate changes), there would be a decline in firms' net worth $(NW_\downarrow)$. This deterioration in balance sheet positions can induce adverse selection and moral hazard, which, as discussed above, can lead to a decline in lending $(L_\downarrow)$, investment $(I_\downarrow)$ and overall economic activity $(Y_\downarrow)$:[12]

$$M_\uparrow \Rightarrow E_\downarrow \Rightarrow NW_\downarrow \Rightarrow L_\downarrow \Rightarrow I_\downarrow \Rightarrow Y_\downarrow. \tag{7.30}$$

---

[12]Mishkin (1996, 1999) considers this mechanism to be very important explaining the financial crises in Mexico and East Asia.

7.2 Theory of Crisis: The Austrian Theory of the Business Cycle

The *Austrian Monetary Theory of the Trade Cycle* (MTTC) remains a distinct, and actually non-mainstream, explanation of how monetary policy impacts the economy. In sharp contrast to the transmission processes outlined above, the Austrian MTTC considers monetary policy induced changes in the money stock as pushing the economy into disequilibrium, thereby sowing the seeds of economic crises.

The Austrian MTTC has its origin in Carl Menger's *Principles of Economics* (1871), and it builds on the notion of a capital-using production process as outlined in Eugen von Böhm-Bawerk's *Capital and Interest* (1890). Ludwig von Mises actually developed the Austrian MTTC in his *Theory of Money and Credit* (1912), and it was further enriched by Friedrich August von Hayek's *Prices and Production* (1935).

The Austrian MTTC incorporates important elements of Knut Wicksell's *Interest and Prices* (1898). Wicksell based his theory on the temporary divergence between the *market interest* and the *natural interest rate*. The former denotes the interest rate as determined by free market forces. The latter represents the interest rate that keeps the economy in equilibrium – that is the rate of interest that allows the economy to grow at full employment without causing inflation.

Let us start with an economic equilibrium situation, in which the market interest rate equals the natural rate. If the central bank makes base money cheaper (thereby increasing commercial banks' loan supply), the market rate of interest falls below the economy's natural interest rate. It becomes economically attractive to increase debt financed investments. With total demand outstripping supply, prices rise. Sooner or later the central bank adopts a restrictive policy to combat inflation. A tightening of monetary policy brings market interest rate back to the economy's natural rate, and the boom turns into bust.

The Austrian MTTC makes a distinction between a *savings-induced boom*, which is sustainable, and a *credit-induced boom*, which is not. Figure 7.19 (a) shows an increased thriftiness by households, as represented by a shift of the supply curve from S to S'. Households' time preference declines: They prefer to shift consumption from the present to the future. As a result, the rate of interest falls from i_0 to i_1, enticing businesses to undertake investment projects previously considered unprofitable. At a lower market clearing interest rate, saving and investment increase by the amount AB. This increase in the economy's productive capacity constitutes *genuine growth*.

Figure 7.19(b) shows the effect of an artificial increase in credit and money supply, brought about by the central bank. The savings curve moves from S to $S+\Delta M$. However, households have *not* become more thrifty, or future-oriented; in other words: peoples' time preference has not changed. As the market clearing interest rate falls from i_0 to i_1, businesses are encouraged to increase investment by the amount AB, while genuine savings actually fall by the amount AC.

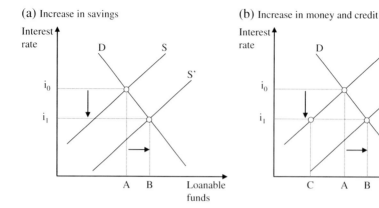

Fig. 7.19 The Austrian MTTC

The increase in the money stock *artificially* lowers the market interest rate, and actual investment now exceeds genuine savings by *CB*. That is to say, the economy's resources have not increased; and this is why Austrians term *CB* as *forced savings*. What is more, a rise in investment reduces consumption, causing a distortion in peoples' initial savings-consumption equilibrium. Sooner or later, people can be expected to reduce their savings and increase their consumption for bringing their savings-consumption profile back to the preferred initial relation. As a result, the savings curve would move back to the left, raising the interest rate back to i_0 and reducing investment. That said, a lowering of the market interest rate below the neutral rate provokes a temporary boom, to be followed by bust.

Ludwig von Mises out the Austrian MTTC succinctly (von Mises, 1996, p. 572): "The wavelike movement affecting the economic system, the recurrence of periods of boom which are followed by periods of depression, is the unavoidable outcome of the attempts, repeated again and again, to lower the gross market rate of interest by means of credit expansion. There is no means of avoiding the final collapse of a boom brought about by credit expansion. The alternative is only whether the crisis should come sooner as the result of a voluntary abandonment of further credit expansion, or later as a final and total catastrophe of the currency system involved."

7.3 The Vector-Autoregressive (VAR) Model – A Benchmark for Analysing Transmission Mechanisms

Vector autoregressive (VAR) models have become a standard empirical procedure for analysing the impact monetary policy exerts on variables such as, for instance, output, market interest rates and inflation. In what follows we will take a closer look at the structure and application of VAR models in the context of the transmission process of monetary policy.

7.3.1 Overview on VAR Models

Since the basic principles were put forward by Sims (1980), VAR models have been used extensively for analysing the monetary transmission process. [13] These models try to answer questions such as, for instance: What, precisely, is the effect of a 1% increase in the money supply growth rate on CPI inflation in the future? How does CPI inflation react to a given change in the central bank rate? Or: How big an interest rate cut is needed to offset an expected half percentage point rise in the unemployment rate? What fraction of the variation in inflation in the past forty years is due to monetary policy as opposed to external shocks?

Simple VAR models provide a systematic way to capture rich dynamics in multiple time series, and the statistical toolkit that came with VARs was easy to use and interpret. As Sims and others argued, VAR models provide a coherent and structural approach to data description, forecasting, structural inference, and policy analysis. Generally speaking, VAR models come in three forms:

– A *reduced form VAR* expresses each variable as a linear function of its own past values, the past values of all other variables being considered, and a serially uncorrelated error term. Consider a three variable reduced VAR, ordered as (1) x, (2) y and (3) z. In the first equation, x would be represented by past values of x, y and z. In the second equation, y would be represented by past realisations of y, x ands z; and similarly for z in the third equation.
– A *recursive VAR* constructs the error terms in the each regression equation to be uncorrelated with the error in the preceding equations. This is done by inserting contemporaneous values as regressors. In the first equation of the corresponding recursive three variable VAR, x is then the dependent variable, and the regressors are lagged values of all three variables. In the second equation, y is the dependent variable and the regressors are lags of all three variables *plus* the current value of x. z is the dependent variable in the third equation, and the regressors are lags of all three variables, the current value of x *plus* the current value of y. Estimations of each equation by OLS produce residuals that are uncorrelated across equations. Of course, the results depend on the order of the variables: changing the order changes the VAR equations, coefficients, and residuals, and there are $n!$ recursive VARs, representing all possible orderings.

---

[13]Open economy studies include Sims (1992), Eichenbaum and Evans (1995), Cushman and Zha (1997), and Kim and Roubini (1999). Closed economy studies include Sims (1986), Gali (1992), Gordon and Leeper (1994), Christiano, Eichenbaum, and Evans (1996), Bernanke and Mihov (1998), and Sims and Zha (1998).

– A *structural VAR* uses economic theory to sort out the contemporaneous links between the variables (Bernanke, 1986; Blanchard & Watson, 1986; Sims, 1986). Structural VARs require *identifying assumptions* that allow correlations to be interpreted causally. These identifying assumptions can involve the entire VAR, so that all of the causal links in the model need to be spelled out (or just a single equation, so that only a specific causal link is identified). This produces instrumental variables which permit the contemporaneous links to be estimated using instrumental variables regression.

7.3.2 Technicalities of the VAR Model

In a two variable case (Enders, 2004, p. 264), the time path of $\{y_t\}$ shall be affected by past realisations of $\{y_t\}$ and current and past realisations of $\{z_t\}$; the time path of $\{z_t\}$ is affected by past realisations of $\{z_t\}$ and current and past realisations of $\{y_t\}$. A simple bivariate system is:

$$y_t = b_{10} - b_{12}z_t + \gamma_{11}y_{t-1} + \gamma_{12}z_{t-1} + \varepsilon_{yt} \tag{7.31}$$

$$z_t = b_{20} - b_{21}y_t + \gamma_{21}y_{t-1} + \gamma_{22}z_{t-1} + \varepsilon_{zt}, \tag{7.32}$$

where ε_{yt} and ε_{zt} are white noise disturbances with standard deviations of σ_y and σ_z, respectively, that $\{\varepsilon_{yt}\}$ and $\{\varepsilon_{zt}\}$ are uncorrelated, and that y and z are $I(0)$ variables. The two equations above form a first-order VAR model, as the longest time lag length it unity.

The structure of the system allows feedback: y and z are allowed to affect each other. For instance, b_{12} is the contemporaneous effect of a change in z_t on y_t and γ_{12} shows the affect of a change in z_{t-1} on y_t. What is more, if b_{21} is not zero, the disturbance term ε_{yt} has an indirect contemporaneous effect on z_t (namely via y_t); and if b_{12} is not zero, ε_{zt} will have an effect on y_t (namely via z_t). Equations (7.31) and (7.32) are *not* reduced equations: y_t has a contemporaneous effect on z_t, and z_t has a contemporaneous effect on y_t.

The equations cannot be estimated directly by OLS, though, because the regressors are correlated with the error term: z_t is correlated with the error term ε_{yt} and y_t is correlated with ε_{zt}. It is possible, however, to transform the system into a form, which can be estimated with OLS. In compact form, the system can be expressed as follows:

$$\begin{bmatrix} 1 & b_{12} \\ b_{212} & 1 \end{bmatrix} \begin{bmatrix} y_t \\ z_t \end{bmatrix} = \begin{bmatrix} b_{10} \\ b_{20} \end{bmatrix} + \begin{bmatrix} \gamma_{11} & \gamma_{12} \\ \gamma_{21} & \gamma_{22} \end{bmatrix} \begin{bmatrix} y_{t-1} \\ z_{t-1} \end{bmatrix} + \begin{bmatrix} \varepsilon_{yt} \\ \varepsilon_{zt} \end{bmatrix}, \tag{7.33}$$

Alternatively, we can write:

$$Bx_t = \Gamma_0 + \Gamma_1 x_{t-1} + \varepsilon_t, \tag{7.34}$$

where

$$B = \begin{bmatrix} 1 & b_{12} \\ b_{21} & 1 \end{bmatrix}, x = \begin{bmatrix} y_t \\ z_t \end{bmatrix}, \Gamma_0 = \begin{bmatrix} b_{10} \\ b_{20} \end{bmatrix}, \Gamma_0 = \begin{bmatrix} b_{10} \\ b_{20} \end{bmatrix}, \varepsilon_t = \begin{bmatrix} \varepsilon_{yt} \\ \varepsilon_{zt} \end{bmatrix}. \quad (7.35)$$

A *VAR model in standard form* can be obtained by pre-multiplication by B^{-1}:

$$x_t = A_0 + A_1 x_{t-1} + e_t, \quad (7.36)$$

where $A_0 = B^{-1}\Gamma_0$, $A_1 = B^{-1}\Gamma_1$ and $e_t = B^{-1}\varepsilon_t$.

Using a new notation, a_{i0} is defined at the i element of vector A_0, a_{ij} the element in row i of column j of the matrix A_1, and e_{it} as the element i of the vector e_t. That said, (7.36) can be rewritten as:

$$y_t = a_{10} + a_{11} y_{t-1} + a_{12} z_{t-1} + e_{1t} \quad (7.37)$$

$$z_t = a_{10} + a_{11} y_{t-1} + a_{12} z_{t-1} + e_{1t} \quad (7.38)$$

It is important to note that the error terms e_{1t} and e_{2t} are composites of the two shocks ε_{yt} and ε_{zt}. Since we defined $e_t = B^{-1}\varepsilon_t$, the error terms e_{1t} and e_{2t} are:

$$e_{1t} = (\varepsilon_{yt} - b_{12}\varepsilon_{zt})/(1 - b_{12}b_{21}) \quad (7.39)$$

$$e_{2t} = (\varepsilon_{zt} - b_{21}\varepsilon_{yt})/(1 - b_{12}b_{21}). \quad (7.40)$$

The error terms ε_{yt} and ε_{zt} represent white-noise processes. What follows is that e_{1t} and e_{2t} have zero means, constant variances and are individually uncorrelated.

7.3.3 Imposing Restrictions

The system represented by (7.31) and (7.32) is under-identified, and we need to restrict one of the parameters to identify the primitive system. One way to do this is to use the type of recursive system as suggested by Sims (1980). Let's assume the coefficient $b_{21} = 0$, so that:

$$B^{-1} = \begin{bmatrix} 1 & -b_{12} \\ 0 & 1 \end{bmatrix}. \quad (7.41)$$

Multiplying the primitive system (7.31) and (7.32) by B^{-1} yields:

$$\begin{bmatrix} y_t \\ z_t \end{bmatrix} = \begin{bmatrix} 1 & -b_{12} \\ 0 & 1 \end{bmatrix} \begin{bmatrix} b_{10} \\ b_{20} \end{bmatrix} + \begin{bmatrix} 1 & -b_{12} \\ 0 & 1 \end{bmatrix} \begin{bmatrix} \gamma_{11} & \gamma_{12} \\ \gamma_{21} & \gamma_{22} \end{bmatrix} \begin{bmatrix} y_{t-1} \\ z_{t-1} \end{bmatrix} + \begin{bmatrix} 1 & -b_{12} \\ 0 & 1 \end{bmatrix} \begin{bmatrix} \varepsilon_{yt} \\ \varepsilon_{zt} \end{bmatrix}.$$

$$(7.42)$$

The above can be rewritten as:

$$y_t = a_{10} + a_{11}y_{t-1} + a_{12}z_{t-1} + e_{1t} \tag{7.43}$$

$$z_t = a_{20} + a_{21}y_{t-1} + a_{22}z_{t-1} + e_{2t}, \tag{7.44}$$

where

$$a_{10} = b_{10} - b_{12}b_{20}$$
$$a_{11} = \gamma_{11} - b_{12}\gamma_{21}$$
$$a_{12} = \gamma_{12} - b_{12}\gamma_{22}$$
$$a_{20} = b_{20}$$
$$a_{21} = \gamma_{21}$$
$$a_{22} = \gamma_{22}$$

Given that $b_{21} = 0$, $e_{1t} = \varepsilon_{yt} - b_{12}\varepsilon_{zt}$ and $e_{2t} = \varepsilon_{zt}$. The variances of e_1 and e_2 are:

$$\text{Var}(e_1) = \sigma_y^2 + b_{12}^2\sigma_z^2$$
$$\text{Var}(e_2) = \sigma_z^2.$$

The covariance is: $\text{Cov}(e_1, e_2) = -b_{12}\sigma_z^2$.

The restriction $b_{21} = 0$ imposed upon the system makes ε_{yt} and ε_{zt} shocks to affect contemporaneous value of y_t, but only ε_{zt} affects the cotemporaneous value of z_t. That said, the values of e_{2t} are solely attributed to the shocks in the $\{z_t\}$ sequence. Decomposing the residuals in this triangular fashion is called Choleski decomposition.

7.3.4 Impulse Response Functions

The VAR model can be presented as a vector moving average (VMA). Indeed, the variables in Eq. (7.36), that is y_t and z_t, are functions of the current and past shocks of e_{1t} and e_{2t}. The VMA representation allows tracing out the time path of shocks on the variables included in the VAR system. To see this, the first-order VAR model in standard form is:

$$x_t = A_o + A_1 x_{t-1} + e_t. \tag{7.45}$$

Solving the equation by backward iteration, one obtains:

$$\begin{aligned} x_t &= A_0 + A_1(A_0 + A_1 x_{t-2} + e_{t-1}) + e_t \\ &= (I + A_1)A_0 + A_1^2 x_{t-2} + A_1 e_{t-1} + e_t, \end{aligned} \tag{7.46}$$

where $I = 2 \cdot 2$ matrix. After n iterations, one yields:

$$x_t = (I + A_1 + \ldots + A_1^n)A_0 + \sum_{i=0}^{n} A_1^i e_{t-i} + A_1^{n+1} x_{t-n-1} + e_t. \qquad (7.47)$$

The stability condition requires that the expression A_1^n vanishes as n approaches infinity. If this particular condition is met, the particular solution for x_t is:

$$x_t = \mu + \sum_{i=0}^{n} A_1^i e_{t-1}, \qquad (7.48)$$

where $\mu = [\bar{y}, \bar{z}]'$.

With this in mind, let's turn back to the two variable first-order VAR model, which can be written in matrix form:

$$\begin{bmatrix} y_t \\ z_t \end{bmatrix} = \begin{bmatrix} a_{10} \\ a_{20} \end{bmatrix} + \begin{bmatrix} a_{11} & a_{12} \\ a_{21} & a_{22} \end{bmatrix} \begin{bmatrix} y_{t-1} \\ z_{t-1} \end{bmatrix} + \begin{bmatrix} e_{1t-1} \\ e_{2t-2} \end{bmatrix}. \qquad (7.49)$$

Using Eq. (7.48), one can write:

$$\begin{bmatrix} y_t \\ z_t \end{bmatrix} = \begin{bmatrix} \bar{y} \\ \bar{z} \end{bmatrix} + \sum_{i=0}^{\infty} \begin{bmatrix} a_{11} & a_{12} \\ a_{21} & a_{22} \end{bmatrix}^i + \begin{bmatrix} e_{1t-1} \\ e_{2t-2} \end{bmatrix}. \qquad (7.50)$$

Equation (7.50) can be expressed in terms of the $\{\varepsilon_{yt}\}$ and $\{\varepsilon_{zt}\}$. From (7.39) and (7.40), the vector errors are:

$$\begin{bmatrix} e_{1t} \\ e_{2t} \end{bmatrix} = \frac{1}{1 - b_{12}b_{21}} \begin{bmatrix} 1 & -b_{12} \\ -b_{21} & 1 \end{bmatrix} \begin{bmatrix} \varepsilon_{yt} \\ \varepsilon_{zt} \end{bmatrix}. \qquad (7.51)$$

Combining (7.50) with (7.51) yields:

$$\begin{bmatrix} y_t \\ z_t \end{bmatrix} = \begin{bmatrix} \bar{y} \\ \bar{z} \end{bmatrix} + \frac{1}{1 - b_{12}b_{21}} \sum_{i=0}^{\infty} \begin{bmatrix} a_{11} & a_{12} \\ a_{21} & a_{22} \end{bmatrix}^i \begin{bmatrix} 1 & -b_{12} \\ -b_{21} & 1 \end{bmatrix} + \begin{bmatrix} \varepsilon_{yt-i} \\ \varepsilon_{zt-i} \end{bmatrix}. \qquad (7.52)$$

Equation (7.52) can be simplified by defining the $2 \cdot 2$ matrix as ϕ_i with elements $\phi_{ik}(i)$:

$$\phi_i = \frac{A_1^i}{1 - b_{12}b_{21}} \begin{bmatrix} 1 & -b_{12} \\ -b_{21} & 1 \end{bmatrix}. \qquad (7.53)$$

That said, the moving average representations (7.51) and (7.52) can be expressed in terms of the $\{\varepsilon_{yt}\}$ and $\{\varepsilon_{zt}\}$ sequences:

$$\begin{bmatrix} y_t \\ z_t \end{bmatrix} = \begin{bmatrix} \bar{y} \\ \bar{z} \end{bmatrix} + \sum_{i=0}^{\infty} \begin{bmatrix} \phi_{11}(i) & \phi_{12}(i) \\ \phi_{21}(i) & \phi_{22}(i) \end{bmatrix}^i \begin{bmatrix} \varepsilon_{yt-i} \\ e_{zt-i} \end{bmatrix}, \qquad (7.54)$$

or, more compactly:

$$x_t = \mu + \sum_{i=0}^{n} \phi_i \varepsilon_{t-1}. \qquad (7.55)$$

The coefficients ϕ_i quantify the effects of ε_{yt} and ε_{zt} shocks on the time path of $\{\varepsilon_{yt}\}$ and $\{\varepsilon_{zt}\}$. The four elements represented by $\phi_{ik}(i)$ are *impact multipliers*. For example, $\phi_{11}(1)$ and $\phi_{12}(1)$ are the one-period responses of a shock to $\{\varepsilon_{yt-1}\}$ and $\{\varepsilon_{zt-1}\}$, respectively, on y_t.

Summing up the coefficients of the impulse response functions stemming from shocks to ε_{yt} and ε_{zt} yield the cumulative effect. For instance, after n periods, the effect of ε_{zt} on the variable y_{t+n} is $\phi_{12}(n)$, or:

$$\sum_{i=0}^{n} \phi_{12}(i). \qquad (7.56)$$

In the two variable case, $\phi_{11}(i)$, $\phi_{12}(i)$, $\phi_{21}(i)$ and $\phi_{22}(i)$ represent the coefficients of the so-called *impulse response functions*. By plotting these coefficients against i (the time), the behaviour of $\{y_t\}$ and $\{z_t\}$ in response to the various shocks can be graphically illustrated; these are the so-called *impulse-response functions*.

7.3.5 A Simple VAR Model for the US

In the following, the results of a simple VAR model for the US economy are presented. The time period under review is 1972-Q1 to 2005-Q4. The following endogeneous variables enter the VAR system (in that order): real GDP, GDP deflator, the stock of M1 and real stock prices (that is stock prices deflated with the GDP deflator). All variables are expressed in levels of logarithms. Furthermore, the Federal Funds Target Rate and the 10-year US Treasury yield are included, expressed in logarithms (that is $r_t = \ln(1 + i_t/100)$). Regarding the lag length, the Akaike information criterion (AIC) suggests 6 lags, and the Schwarz (SC) and Hannan-Quinn criterion 1 lag. The number of lags for the VAR was chosen to be 6 quarters (for which the LM-test does no longer indicate serial correlations in the residuals, Table 7.1).

Figure 7.20 (a) shows the impulse-response function of the 10-year Treasury yield following a one-off shock (innovation) of the monetary policy rate. The horizontal axis shows the number of quarters following the innovation, while the vertical axis shows the quarterly change in the responding variable. The dotted lines show the statistical significance of the quarterly parameter at the 95% confidence band.

Table 7.1 Results of the LM-test for the null hypothesis that there is no serial correlation at lag order h

Lags	LM-Stat	p-values
1	35.11	0.510
2	40.91	0.263
3	32.79	0.621
4	41.33	0.248
5	49.24	0.069
6	30.32	0.735
7	39.39	0.320
8	48.45	0.080

Probabilities from chi-square with 36 df. Source: Thomson Financial; Bloomberg, Federal Reserve Bank of St. Louis; own calculations. – Sample period: 1972-Q1 to 2005-Q4.

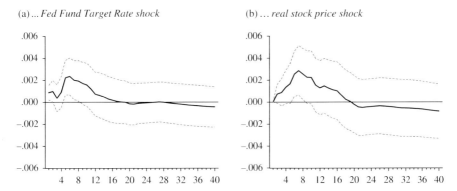

(a) ... *Fed Fund Target Rate shock*

(b) ... *real stock price shock*

Fig. 7.20 Impulse-response function of the 10-year bond yield to . . .

A one-off increase in the Federal Funds Target Rate (in the amount of one standard deviation of the sample mean) leads to an increase in the 10-year US Treasury yield. That said, monetary policy rates seem to exert an economically plausible reaction of long-term yields. Statistical significance can be detected for quarters 1–2 and 5–9 following the shock.

The 10-year Treasury yield rises following a one-off increase in real stock prices (Fig. 7.20(b)). Such a finding might be explained by rising stock prices being accompanied by rising growth and/or rising inflation (concerns), thereby dragging long-term bonds with it. Here, statistical significance can be assigned to quarters 5–8 following the innovation.

The response of the Federal Funds Target Rate to a one-off real GDP innovation is shown in Fig. 7.21 (a). An increase in real GDP is followed by a rise the Fed's official rate. A similar reaction can be observed following a one-off shock in the GDP deflator (Fig. 7.21(b)). Presumably, these two impulse response functions capture the Fed's monetary policy reaction function: raising rates with rising real growth and inflation.

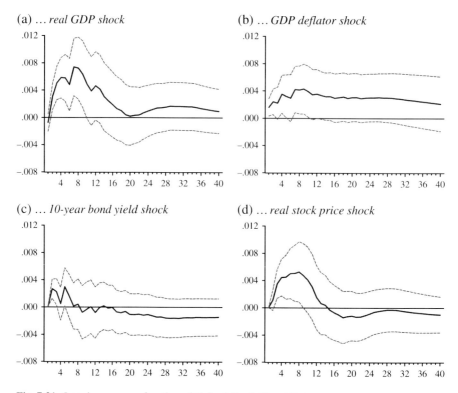

(a) ... *real GDP shock*

(b) ... *GDP deflator shock*

(c) ... *10-year bond yield shock*

(d) ... *real stock price shock*

Fig. 7.21 Impulse response function of Federal Funds Target Rate to a ...

Figure 7.21(c) suggests that short-term money policy rates react (somewhat) to higher long-term yields (significance can be assigned to the parameters in quarter 1–3 and quarter 5 following the shock). This relation might reflect the Fed's reaction to rising inflation which, in turn, translates in higher inflation expectations and thus

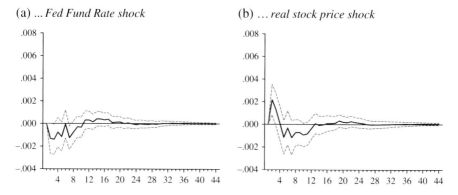

(a) ... *Fed Fund Rate shock*

(b) ... *real stock price shock*

Fig. 7.22 Impulse response function of real GDP to a ...

higher long bond yields. A rise in real stock prices is accompanied by a rise in the official policy rate 7.21. (d).

A rise in the Federal Funds Target Rate leads to a reduction in real GDP growth (Fig. 7.22 (a)), while an increase in the real stock price is accompanied by a rise in real output (Fig. 7.22(b)). The latter might be explained by the "leading property" of stock prices: an improvement in economic perspectives might be reflected in rising stock prices at an early stage when compared to real economic data.

We continue with a second practical example of a VAR analysis, but this time on the global level.

Digression: Global Liquidity and the Dynamic Pattern of Price Adjustment: A VAR Analysis for OECD Countries

Motivation

Global liquidity has been expanding steadily since 2001. In most industrial countries and more recently also in some emerging market economies with a dollar peg, especially China, broad money growth has been running well ahead of nominal GDP.[14] Surprisingly enough, for a long time goods price inflation had been widely unaffected by the strong monetary dynamics in many regions in the world. Only recently surplus liquidity poured into raw material, food and goods markets. Over the same time horizon, however, many countries have experienced sharp but sequential booms in asset prices, such as real estate or share prices (Schnabl and Hoffmann, 2007). Between 2001 and 2006, for instance, house prices strongly increased in the US (55%), the euro area (41%), Australia (59%), Canada (61%) and a number of further OECD countries; the HWWI commodity price index surged by 110% in the same period and stock prices more than doubled in nearly all major markets from 2003 to 2006. Many observers interpret the sequence of increases of asset prices as the result of liquidity spill-overs to certain asset markets (Adalid & Detken, 2007; Greiber & Setzer, 2007).

From a monetary policy perspective, the different price dynamics of assets and goods prices in recent years raises the question as to whether the money-inflation nexus has been changed (thereby calling into question the close long-term relationship between monetary and goods price developments that was observed in the past) or whether effects from previous policy actions are still in the pipeline. To investigate the relative importance of these developments, this study tries to establish an empirical link between money, asset prices and goods prices. For this purpose, we estimate a variety of VAR models including a measure of global liquidity, proxied by a broad monetary aggregate in the OECD countries under consideration (United States, Euro area, Japan, United Kingdom, Canada, South Korea, Australia, Switzerland, Sweden, Norway and Denmark) and analyse the impact of a shock

---

[14]This section heavily relies on Belke, Orth, and Setzer (2008a).

to global liquidity on global asset and goods price inflation. The basic idea is that different price elasticities of supply lead to differences in the dynamic pattern of price adjustment to a global liquidity shock. While goods prices adjust only very slowly to changing global monetary conditions due to plentiful supply of consumer goods from emerging markets, asset prices such as housing and commodity prices react much faster since the supply of real estate and commodities cannot be easily expanded. Thus disequilibria on these markets are generally balanced out by price adjustments (Roffia & Zaghini, 2007).

The main emphasis is on globally aggregated variables, which implies that we do not explicitly deal with spill-overs of global liquidity to national variables. The main motivation for this specific way of proceeding is heavily related to recent research according to which inflation appears to be a global phenomenon. So far, the relationship between money growth, different categories of asset prices and goods prices has been little studied in an international context. Only recently, a number of authors suggested specific interactions of global liquidity with global consumer price and asset price inflation (Baks & Kramer, 1999; Sousa & Zaghini, 2006; Rueffer & Stracca, 2006). However, so far no study has tried to systematically analyze differences between asset classes and goods in the dynamic pattern of price adjustment to a global liquidity shock.

The remainder of this section is organised as follows: first, we convey an impression of the global perspective of the monetary transmission process. Second, we develop some simple theoretical considerations to illustrate the potential role of different supply elasticities as potential drivers of asset- and goods-specific price adjustments to global liquidity shocks. Third, we turn to an econometric analysis using the VAR technique on a global scale. Moreover, we conduct a wide array of robustness checks. We finish with some policy conclusions.

The Global Perspective of Monetary Transmission

Both with respect to global inflation and to global liquidity performance, available evidence becomes stronger that the global instead of the national perspective is more important when the monetary transmission mechanism has to be identified and interpreted. For instance, Ciccarelli and Mojon (2005) find empirical evidence in favour of a robust error-correction mechanism, meaning that deviations of national inflation from global inflation are corrected over time. Similarly, Borio and Filardo (2007) argue that the traditional way of modelling inflation is too country-centred and a global approach is more adequate. Considering the development of global liquidity over time, the question is often raised whether and to what extent global factors are responsible for it. Rueffer and Stracca (2006) investigate this aspect for the G7 countries in the framework of a factor analysis and conclude that around 50% of the variance of a narrow monetary aggregate can be traced back to one common global factor. One prominent example of such a global factor is, for instance, the expansionary monetary policy stance of the Bank of Japan (BoJ) during the last years. It has been characterised by a significant accumulation of foreign reserves and by extremely low interest rates – at some time even approaching zero. By means of carry trades, financial investors took up loans in Japan and invested the proceeds in currencies with higher interest rates. Such kind of capital transactions has impacts on the development of monetary aggregates far beyond the special case of Japan and national borders in general (see, e.g., Schnabl & Hoffmann, 2007).

An additional argument in favour of focusing on global instead of national liquidity is that national monetary aggregates have become more difficult to interpret due to the huge increase of international capital flows. Simply accounting for the external sources of money growth and then mechanically correcting for cross-border portfolio flows or M&A activity, on the presumption of their likely less relevant direct effects on consumer prices, is not a sufficient reaction. Instead, these transactions have to be investigated with respect to their information content and potential wealth effects on residents' income and on asset prices which might backfire to goods prices as well (Papademos, 2007, p. 4; Pepper & Olivier, 2006). In the same vein, Sousa and Zaghini (2006) argue that global aggregates are likely to internalize cross-country movements in monetary aggregates – due to capital flows between different regions – that may make the link between money, inflation and output more difficult to disentangle at the country level. Giese and Tuxen (2007) stress the fact that in today's linked financial markets shifts in the money supply in one country may be absorbed by demand elsewhere, but simultaneous shifts in major economies may have significant effects on worldwide asset and goods price inflation.

Some critics might argue that global liquidity, as measured in one currency, can only change in quantitative terms if one assumes a fixed exchange rate system worldwide. Note, however, that international liquidity spill-over effects may occur regardless of the exchange rate system. Under pegged exchange rate regimes official foreign exchange interventions result in a transmission of monetary policy shocks from one country to another. In a system of flexible exchange rates, the validity of the "uncovered interest rate parity" relationship should in theory prevent cross-border monetary spill-overs. According to this theory, the expected appreciation of the low-yielding currency in terms of the high-yielding currency should be equal to the difference between interest rates in the two economies. However, the enduring existence of carry trades can be taken as evidence that exchange rates diverge from fundamentals for lengthy periods, as the exposure of a carry trade position involves a bet that uncovered interest rate parity does not hold over the investment period. Note as well that exchange rates might quite rarely be considered as truly flexible across our estimation period anyway, as, for instance, Reinhart and Rogoff (2004) classify only 4.5% of the exchange rate regimes under their investigation as currently "freely floating".

The concept of "global liquidity" has attracted growing attention in the empirical literature in recent years. One of the first studies in this field is Baks and Kramer (1999) who use different indices of liquidity in seven industrial countries to explore the dimension of the relationship between liquidity and asset returns. The authors find evidence that there are important common components in G7 money growth and that an increase in G7 money growth is consistent with higher G7 real stock returns and lower G7 real interest rates.

Recently, a number of studies have applied VAR or VECM models to data aggregated on a global level. Important contributions include Rueffer and Stracca (2006), Sousa and Zaghini (2006), and Giese and Tuxen (2007). These studies find significant and distinctive reaction of consumer prices to a global liquidity shock. In contrast, the relationship between global liquidity and asset prices is mixed. In the study by Rueffer and Stracca (2006), e.g., a composite real asset price index that incorporates property and equity prices does not show any significant reaction to a global liquidity shock. Giese and Tuxen (2007) find no evidence that share prices increase as liquidity expands, however, they cannot empirically reject cointegration relationships which imply a positive impact of global liquidity on house prices.

The Price Adjustment Process

As far as the impact of monetary policy on asset prices is concerned, the most recent and innovative studies are – with an eye on the subprime crisis not surprisingly – concerned with the relationship between monetary policy and house prices. However, we will show below that large parts of the arguments can be transferred without major modifications to other asset classes as well. Some authors have recently emphasized the role of housing for the transmission of monetary policy, although drawing on interest rate changes as policy instruments rather than on changes in money aggregates (see e.g. Del Negro & Otrok, 2007; Giuliodori, 2005; Goodhart & Hofmann, 2001; Mishkin, 2007; Iacoviello, 2005).

Recently, the global aspects of house price developments have gained importance. A study by the IMF deals with this issue and analyses the recent house price boom from a global point of view. [15] Similar to some of the studies mentioned above a factor analysis is performed and a global factor is extracted. It is estimated that 40% of national house price developments can be explained by global factors. The study concludes that there are strong international linkages of the factors that determine house prices and that the recent house price bubble is indeed a highly global phenomenon. There are at least two possible explanations of these findings. First, there is empirical evidence for the existence of a global business cycle (Canova, Ciccarelli, & Ortega, 2007) and since house prices are meant to move largely procyclically, this can be seen as one major common force that drives house prices all over the world. Second, if there are arbitrage relationships between house prices and globally traded securities like shares, the global factors that affect these securities influence house prices as well (think, for instance, of a global stock market crash).[16]

---

[15] See the essay "The Global House Price Boom" in International Monetary Fund (2004), Chap. 2.
[16] See IMF (2004) for this argument.

One aspect which has been largely neglected by the previous literature is why house prices (and other asset prices) have risen so sharply in recent years while consumer price development has been subdued. Some insights into the relationship between money, asset prices and consumer prices can be derived from the dynamic price adjustment to a liquidity shock across different sectors of the economy. In the short term, an expansionary monetary policy providing the markets with more liquidity should trigger an immediate price reaction in sectors with low price elasticity of supply, but a more subdued price reaction in sectors with high elasticity of supply. Over time, however, elastic good prices also adjust to the new equilibrium by proportional changes of the price level, i.e. it is plausible to argue that in the long term changes in money supply do not lead to any effects on real money or real output.

Like many other assets, housing prices are quite volatile relative to observable changes in fundamentals. If we are going to understand boom-bust housing cycles, we must incorporate housing supply. Glaeser, Gyourko, and Saiz (2008) present a simple model of housing bubbles which predicts that places with more elastic housing supply have fewer and shorter bubbles, with smaller price increases. However, the welfare consequences of bubbles may actually be higher in more elastic places because those places will overbuild more in response to a bubble. The data show that the price run-ups of the 1980 s were almost exclusively experienced in cities where housing supply is more inelastic. More elastic places had slightly larger increases in building during that period. Over the past five years, a modest number of more elastic places also experienced large price booms, but as the model suggests, these booms seem to have been quite short. Prices are already moving back towards construction costs in those areas.

Figure 7.23 illustrates (admittedly, in a rather extreme representation) the price-quantity changes as a result of a monetary expansion in markets with high (left graph) and low (right graph) price elasticity of supply. The aggregated supply of price elastic goods Se in the short-term (SR) is characterized by infinite price

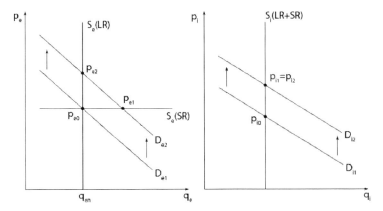

Fig. 7.23 Short- and long-run impact of a liquidity shock to price elastic (*left-hand side*) and price inelastic good (*right-hand side*)

elasticity so that additional demand triggered by a liquidity shock (from D_{e1} to D_{e2}) can be satisfied without any price increase. Consequently, the liquidity shock translates into an increase in output achieving a new short-term equilibrium at p_{e1}. In contrast, goods characterized by restrictions in supply cannot be expanded easily and are thus quantity insensitive to a monetary expansion. Additional demand (shift from D_{i1} to D_{i2}) is then fully reflected in a rise of house prices to p_{i1}.

In the long-term, prices will also react on the price elastic good market as the well-documented neutrality of money holds; any change in money supply is met with a proportional change in the price level that keeps real money and real output in both sectors unchanged (at p_{e2} and p_{i2}).

The possibility of different dynamic adjustments of price elastic and inelastic goods to a monetary shock may provide an explanation for the recent upward shift in relative prices between assets and consumer goods.

This assumption can be well motivated with developments in international trade. Due to high degree of competition in international goods markets and vast supply of cheap labour in many emerging markets around the world, which weighs heavily on the prices of manufactured goods, in the short-term goods prices remain unaffected by the increase in aggregate demand. Only in the long-term, increasing capacity utilization will translate into higher wages, putting upward pressure on prices.

In contrast, asset prices such as housing, but also commodity prices are generally assumed to be restricted in supply. Land cannot be expanded easily (Japan) and/or all real estate transactions involve high costs (continental Europe). The latter implies that housing supply is inelastic at least within a certain price interval. [17] Thus, additional demand for housing is immediately reflected in a rise of house prices.

Similarly, a number of constraints in the commodity market such as finite supply prevent producers in the commodity market from adjusting quantities to short-term price incentives. Moreover, as argued by Browne and Cronin (2007), the price adjustment process in commodity markets is relatively fast because participants are more equally empowered with more balanced information and resources than their consumer goods counterparts. This enables them to react quickly to changes in monetary conditions.

Empirical Analysis

Data Description and Aggregation Issues

In the following empirical analysis, we analyze whether monetary transmission corresponds with our prior that different price elasticities of supply determine the ordering of the different asset/goods classes in the transmission process of global liquidity. For this purpose we use quarterly time series from 1984-Q1 to 2006-Q4 for the United States, the euro area, Japan, United Kingdom, Canada, South Korea,

---

[17]For a detailed discussion of the relevance of these arguments see Gros (2007), OECD (2005), and Shiller (2005).

Australia, Switzerland, Sweden, Norway and Denmark, so that in our analysis 72.2% of the world GDP in 2006 and presumably a considerably larger share of global financial markets are represented.[18]

For the aforementioned 11 countries, we gather real GDP (GDP), the GDP defla- tor (PGDP), the short term money market rate (IS), and a broad monetary aggregate (M). Further, to capture developments in asset and commodity markets, we include a nominal house price index (HPI) and the HWWI commodity price index (COM).[19] The latter is already a global variable (measured in US dollars) so that no aggrega- tion is needed. The monetary aggregate we use is M2 for the US, M3 for the Euro Area, M2 plus cash deposits for Japan, M4 for the UK and mostly M3 for the other countries. The data stem from the IMF, the OECD, the BIS and the ECB and are seasonally adjusted if available or treated with the X12-ARIMA procedure. [20]

In the next step, we aggregate the country-specific series to obtain global series considering the principles mentioned by Beyer, Doornik, and Hendry (2000) and employing the method as used by Giese and Tuxen (2007) in the same context. First, we calculate variable GDP weights for each country by using market exchange rates to convert nominal GDP into a single currency. This is in contrast to previous literature which has mostly relied on aggregation by purchasing power exchange rates. However, precise purchasing power rates are difficult to measure and not uncontroversial. Moreover, as a stylized fact, deviations from actual and purchasing power rates have proven to be quite persistent and should therefore not be neglected (Taylor, 2000). Nevertheless, we check for the sensitivity of our results to the choice of exchange rates in our robustness section. The weight of a country i in period t therefore is:

$$w_{i,t} = \frac{GDP_{i,t}e_{i,t}}{GDP_{agg,t}} \tag{7.57}$$

Second, we compute for each variable (measured in domestic currency) the growth rate, denoted by $g_{i,t}$ and aggregate them by using the weights calculated in (1):

$$g_{agg,t} = \sum_{i=1}^{11} w_{i,t} g_{i,t} \tag{7.58}$$

Finally, aggregate levels are then obtained by choosing an initial value of 100 and multiplying with the computed global growth rates. This gives the level of each variable as an index:

---

[18]Own calculations based on IMF data.

[19]The HWWI commodity price index provides an encompassing gauge of price trends in com- modity markets. It consists of crude oil (63%), industrial raw materials (23%), coal (4%), and foodstuffs (10%).

[20]House price are based on OECD data (see Schich & Weth, 2008).

$$index_T = \prod_{t=2}^{T}(1 + g_{agg,t})$$ (7.59)

This method is applied to all variables except the interest rate, for which aggregation is performed without calculating growth rates.

The main advantage of the chosen aggregation scheme is that it avoids a potential bias resulting from different national definitions of broad money. Given the different definitions of monetary aggregates across countries, the building of a simple sum of national monetary aggregates – a method frequently applied in the related literature – would under-represent countries with narrower definitions of the monetary aggregate and vice versa.

To illustrate the development of global liquidity since 1984, Fig. 7.24 shows global monetary aggregates in absolute and relative terms as well as the inverse of income velocity of money. All three series find themselves above their time trend since about 2001 when monetary policymakers turned to a more expansionary policy in the course of the rapid downturn in stock markets and a number of further shocks such as September 11th. Money growth remained strong throughout the last years, as indicated by the persistent growth of the ratio of nominal money to nominal GDP – a measure frequently applied as an indicator of excess liquidity.[21] Overall, the graphical inspection provides some first glance for the view that global liquidity is indeed at a high level and that the term excess liquidity can be justified rather easily when analyzing the most recent period.

Figure 7.25 displays the remaining aggregated economic variables of interest. The GDP deflator series clearly elucidates the moderate inflation which started to emerge around the mid-90 s and has persisted until 2006 although monetary aggregates expanded heavily in recent years. Global short-term interest rates were at a historically low level from 2002 to 2005, since the monetary policy stance was extremely loose during this period. [22] Interestingly, the global time series show that the recent years of global excess liquidity are accompanied by strong price increases in both housing and commodity markets. The ongoing discussion about the linkage of global excess liquidity and asset price inflation is not least based on this phenomenon. In the following econometric analysis we will investigate the causal connection of global liquidity and asset and commodity price inflation in a more formal framework.

The VAR Methodology Again

The econometric framework employed is a vectorautoregressive model (VAR) which allows us to model the impact of monetary shocks on the economy while

---

[21] See, for instance, Rueffer and Stracca (2006).

[22] One might regard the deviation from an estimated Taylor rate as a more accurate measure in this respect. However, these numbers create a rather similar picture. See International Monetary Fund (2007), Chap. 1, Box 1.4.

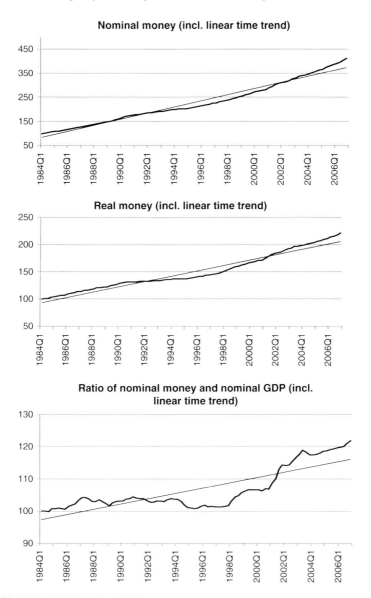

Fig. 7.24 Global liquidity since 1984

taking care of the feedback between the variables since all of them are treated as endogenous.[23] Consider first the traditional reduced-form VAR model:

---

[23]Of course, one could model exogenous variables as well, but this option is not used here. One reason is that Belke et al. (2008) consider a world model, where there are no exogenous variables by definition. Moreover, from an econometric point of view, we refer to our point estimates.

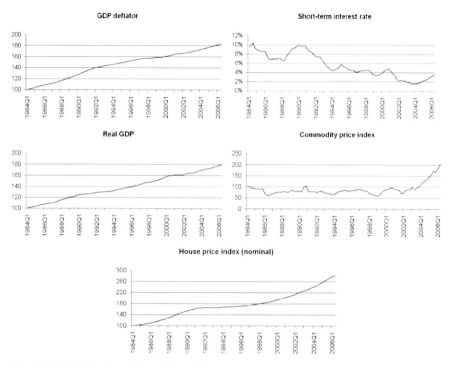

Fig. 7.25 Global series of GDP deflator, short-term interest rate, real GDP, commodity prices and house prices

$$\Gamma(L)Y_t = CZ_t + u_t \tag{7.60}$$

where Y_t is the vector of the endogenous variables and $\Gamma(L)$ is a matrix polynomial in the lag operator L for which $\Gamma(L) = I + \sum_{i=1}^{p} A_i L^i$, so that we have p lags. Z_t is a matrix with deterministic terms, C is the corresponding matrix of coefficients, and u_t is the vector of the white noise residuals where serial correlation is excluded, so that:

$$E(u_t) = 0$$

$$E(u_t u_s^{|}) = \begin{cases} \Sigma : t = s \\ 0 : t \neq s \end{cases}$$

Since Σ is not a diagonal matrix, contemporaneous correlation is allowed. In order to model uncorrelated shocks, a transformation of the system is needed. Using the Cholesky decomposition $\Sigma = PP'$, taking the main diagonal of P to define the

---

They reveal that no variable is weakly exogenous. Instead, all variables cannot be rejected to be endogenous.

diagonal matrix D and pre-multiplying (7.60) with $\Psi := DP^{-1}$ yields the structural VAR (SVAR) representation:

$$K(L)Y_t = C^* Z_t + e_t \tag{7.61}$$

$$K(L) = \Psi + \sum_{i=1}^{p} A_i^* L^i \tag{7.62}$$

The contemporaneous relations between the variables are now directly explained in Ψ, which is a lower triangular matrix with all elements of the main diagonal being one. The innovations e_t are by construction uncorrelated: $E(e_t e_t') = \Psi \Sigma \Psi' = \Psi PP' \Psi' = DP^{-1} PP' P^{-1'} D' = DD'$. Similarly, the Cholesky decomposition is used to construct orthogonal innovations out of the moving average representation of the system which is the cornerstone of the impulse response analysis.

Furthermore, the use of the Cholesky decomposition implies a recursive identification scheme which involves restrictions about the contemporaneous relations between the variables. The latter are given by the (Cholesky) ordering of the variables and might considerably influence the results of the analysis. Therefore, different orderings are used to prove the robustness of our results.

Unit root tests indicate that all our series are integrated of order one. Thus the question arises whether one should take differences of the variables in order to eliminate the stochastic trend. However, Sims, Stock, and Watson (1990) show that Ordinary Least Squares estimates of VAR coefficients are consistent under a broad range of circumstances even if the variables are nonstationary. [24] Therefore, we strictly follow this approach and estimate the VAR model in levels.

Empirical Findings

The Baseline Model

We are starting our VAR analysis by estimating a benchmark model which includes the traditional macroeconomic variables output (GDP), GDP deflator (PGDP), short-term interest rate (IS), and broad money (M). Further, we include the house (HPI) and the commodity price index (COM) in our model in order to test for dif-

---

[24] Estimating the VAR in levels does not pose any problems, if all variables are stationary (I(0)). If some variables have a unit root (I(1)) and the series are not cointegrated, a VAR in levels or 1st differences makes no difference asymptotically. Taking first differences only tends to be better in samples smaller than ours (Hamilton, 1994, pp. 553 and 652). However, if two or more variables are I(1) and cointegrated, the first difference estimates are biased if there is cointegration because the error-correction term is omitted. An alternative in the latter case would be to estimate a VECM. However, since it is hard to identify with any degree of accuracy the underlying structural parameters of a VECM which includes a large number of variables, for practical reasons we derive impulse responses from a VAR in levels, which due to its simplicity seems to be a more appropriate technique.

ferent price reaction of assets and goods to a liquidity shock. In addition, a constant and a linear time trend are added. All variables are taken in log-levels except the interest rate. Our benchmark specification is thus given by the following vector of endogenous variables (along with the corresponding Cholesky ordering):

$$x_t = (GDP, GDP, COM, HPI, M, IS)_t \tag{7.63}$$

The Cholesky ordering of the basic specification follows the principle that monetary variables should be ordered last, since they are expected to react faster to the real economy than vice versa (Favero, 2001). The price variables PGDP, COM and HPI are ordered in the middle given that they are supposed to react to the monetary variables only with a lag. In general, the results are very robust to changes in the ordering within the three blocks. To determine lag length, we apply the usual criteria. [25] Most of the criteria point at a lag length of 2, which is also sufficient to avoid serial correlation among the residuals and seems to be appropriate in order to estimate a model which is parsimonious where possible. [26] While this is true not only for the benchmark specification but also for the following models we will continue with two lags for the whole analysis.

Figure 7.26 displays the impulse responses with respect to an unexpected increase in global liquidity. (See the appendix of Belke, Orth, & Setzer, 2008a, for the whole array of impulse responses) It has all features expected from our theoretical considerations: The GDP deflator reacts slowly but moves upwards significantly after about eleven quarters. Thus, in our model money matters for and causes goods price inflation although substantial time lags have to be taken into account. Quicker positive responses to a global liquidity shock are given by the house price and the commodity price index (after three and nine quarters respectively). From a theoretical point of view, the lower price elasticity of supply in the housing and in the commodity market compared to the goods market should contribute to this finding. Based on these findings we interpret the current situation that abundant global liquidity contributed to the bull market in the real estate sector and that – following the downturn in the housing market triggered by the subprime crisis – money balances are now flowing largely into commodity markets putting upward pressure on commodity prices.

It is also of interest that commodity prices react later than house prices to a shock of global liquidity. This is consistent with anecdotic evidence during the recent food price hike when global demand, driven by "hunger for return", turned to commodities after house prices had collapsed. On a more theoretical level, one could argue that house prices react faster than commodity prices to an unexpected increase in liquidity since expectations of future economic growth might be even more important for commodities than for real estate and, thus, shocks to global liquidity only pour

---

[25]To be explicit, Belke et al. (2008) use the Likelihood Ratio test, the Final Prediction Error, the Akaike information criterion, the Schwarz criterion and the Hannan-Quinn criterion.

[26]To test for autocorrelation of the residuals, Belke et al. (2008) perform the Lagrange Multiplier test.

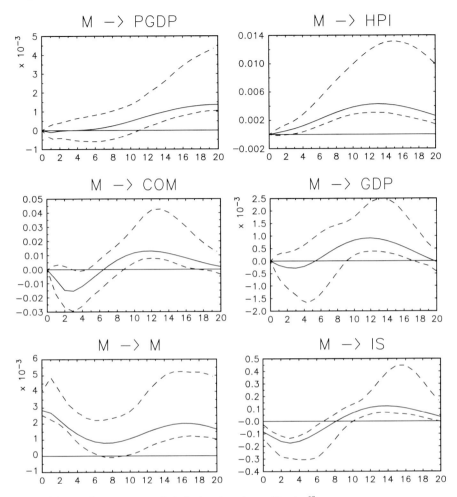

Fig. 7.26 Impulse response analysis for benchmark specification[27]

into commodity markets when economic growth accelerates.[28] Moreover, speculation may play a more important role in housing markets. If assets can be stored,
people expecting a price rise can take some amount off today's market, driving up
the price now, in the expectation that they can sell it at a higher price later. Commodities which are characterized by a lower degree of storability than housing, then
display less distinguished and slower price increases than housing (Krugman, 2008).

---

[27]The confidence intervals of our impulse responses display two standard deviations and are calculated via the studentized Hall bootstrap method.

[28]Note the striking similarity in the impulse responses of a liquidity shock to output and to commodity prices.

The remaining impulse responses of our benchmark model are also in line with economic theory. GDP moves up temporarily but not permanently as a result of a liquidity shock, which is in line with the theoretical assumption that money is neutral for the real economy in the long run. Interestingly, the price puzzle (the absence of a decline of the price level due to a positive interest rate shock), which is often found in similar VAR models, does not appear in our model (see Fig. A1 in the appendix to Belke, Orth, & Setzer, 2008a). Note also that the response of our variables to an interest rate shock is very consistent with the dynamic adjustment to a global liquidity shock. Further, it is of interest to see that house price shocks have predictive content for future goods price inflation suggesting that house prices should be taken into account by monetary authorities as they signal changes in expected goods price inflation (see Goodhart and Hofmann, 2007, for similar results).

Augmenting the VAR with Gold and Stocks

Given that the dynamics of the benchmark model is found to be plausible, the next step in our VAR analysis is to augment our baseline model with further asset variables. Specifically, we include the gold price (in US dollars) and, alternatively, a globally aggregated stock price index in our model. [29] Similar to house and commodity prices these time series are characterized by significant upwards movements in recent years (Fig. 7.27).

Gold prices are of particular interest given that the actual amount of gold which can be produced in any year is only a minor share of the stock of gold. Thus the increase in the quantity of gold supplied in response to an aggregate demand shock is only a small fraction of the stock of gold, resulting a in a very steep supply curve.

In the Cholesky ordering, we put gold just behind the house price index, given its assumed sensitiveness to monetary policy shocks; however, results are again very robust to changes in the ordering within the "price block":

$$x_t = (\text{GDP, PGDP, COM, HPI, GOLD, M, IS})_t \tag{7.64}$$

Figure 7.28 displays the impulse responses of our extended model that are of main interest. Global liquidity shocks again positively and significantly influence the price level for goods and services (GDP deflator), housing and commodities. Interestingly, the response of the gold price is even faster. Gold prices react significantly after three quarters to an unexpected increase in global liquidity. This confirms our theoretical assumption that the price elasticity of supply is decisive to what degree global liquidity shocks are reflected in the price level. The quantity of gold cannot be easily extended so that the supply of gold is relatively price-inelastic and the reaction speed of the gold price is therefore quicker compared to other asset prices.

---

[29] Note that the HWWI commodity price index does not include gold and thus there arise no problems of multicollinearity. Data for stock prices are from Datastream. For each country in our sample we use the key national stock market index and aggregate the series to a global index as described above.

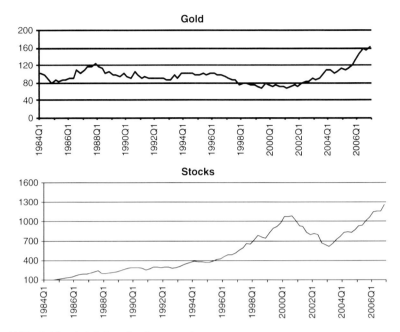

Fig. 7.27   Gold and global stock prices over time

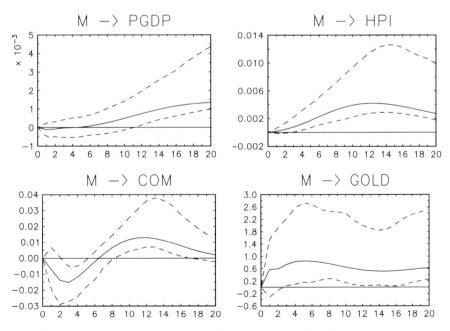

Fig. 7.28   Impulse response analysis for the VAR model augmented with gold price

As a further alternative we substitute gold prices with the global stock price index. As a financial market variable, stocks are last in our Cholesky ordering so that we now have the following vector of endogenous variables: [30]

$$x_t = (\text{GDP, PGDP, COM, HPI, M, IS, STOCKS})_t \qquad (7.65)$$

As can be seen in Fig. 7.29, the positive and significant reactions of the GDP deflator, the house price index and the commodity price index to a global liquidity shock prove to be stable. However, stock prices do not show a positive response to a monetary impulse. This might serve as an indication that the relationship between monetary developments and shares is less pronounced. One of the reasons is that the relationship between the developments in the stock market and money holdings is not clear cut. On the one hand, higher liquidity tends to increase household's assets, and a part of the associated asset growth may be held in the form of shares. On the other hand, high (expected) securities returns make the holding of shares more attractive than holding money. This may trigger important substitution effects, i.e. shifts between money and shares.

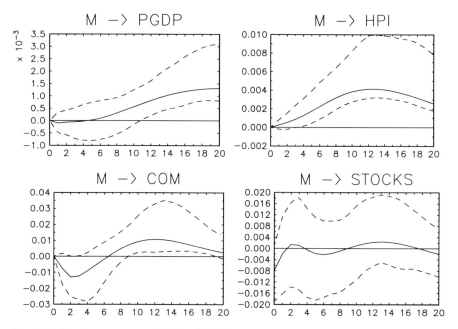

Fig. 7.29 Impulse response analysis for the VAR model augmented with stock prices

---

[30]Stock prices are often ordered last in similar VAR models. See, for instance, Millard and Wells (2003) and Thorbecke (1997).

Robustness Checks

To check for the robustness of our results, we additionally estimated several alternative versions of our model. First, we changed the lag lengths (especially 4 lags) with nearly no consequences for our results. Second, we used different Cholesky orderings in order to avoid that our results rely on any particular assumption regarding the structural equations of our VAR model. No major changes in the results occurred. Third, we used an alternative aggregation scheme for our global aggregates in order to find out if the results are sensible in this respect. As we used market exchange rates so far for the calculation of the individual country weights we also checked for the alternative of using PPP exchange rates in the aggregation procedure. (This results in a substitution in Eq. (7.57) of $e_{i,t}$): by $e_{i,t}^{PPP}$.[31] Figure 7.30 displays selected impulse responses of our benchmark model when using PPP aggregation. (See Belke, Orth, and Setzer, 2008 Appendix A2 for the full set of impulse responses.) The main empirical findings are not affected. Global liquidity shocks again lead to a temporary increase of the output variable and to a permanent and significant increase of the GDP deflator, the house price index and the commodity price index. The high robustness of our results to the aggregation

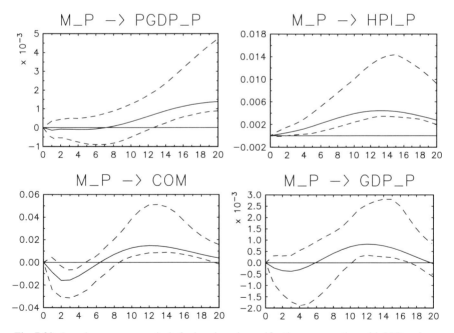

Fig. 7.30 Impulse response analysis for benchmark specification; aggregation with PPP exchange rates

---

[31] The base year for our PPP exchange rates is 1999.

scheme should not come as a surprise given that many variables in our sample are highly correlated at an international level – a phenomenon which renders the form of aggregation less important.

Conclusions

In this section, we have analyzed the effects of global liquidity shocks on goods prices and a variety of asset prices. We come up with the following empirical results: First, we find support of the conjecture that monetary aggregates may convey useful leading indicator information on variables such as house prices, gold prices, commodity prices and the GDP deflator at the global level. In contrast, stock prices do not show any positive response to a liquidity shock – a result which might be related to the relatively higher importance of substitution effects for this asset class. Second, our VAR results support the view that different price elasticities on asset and goods markets explain the recently observed relative price change between asset classes and consumer goods. In line with theoretical reasoning, the price reaction of asset prices takes place faster than that of goods prices. Third, we find significant spill-over effects from housing markets to goods price inflation suggesting that a forward-looking monetary policy has to take asset price developments into account. In sum, we would therefore like to argue that global liquidity deserves at least the same attention as the worldwide level of interest rates has received in the recent intensive debate on the world savings versus liquidity glut hypothesis, if not possibly more.

Against the background of our results the still high level of global liquidity has to be interpreted as a threat for future stable and low inflation and financial stability. Since global excess liquidity is found to be an important determinant of asset and goods prices, there might be at least two implications for the adequate conduct of monetary policy. First, monetary policy has to be aware of different time lags in the transmission from liquidity to different categories of prices. In particular, strong money growth might be a good indicator of emerging future bubbles in the real estate sector and later on also of bubbles in gold and commodity markets. However, it does not seem to be a good leading indicator for stock prices. Second, this pattern should, on the contrary, also be taken into account when assessing the consequences of a slowing down or smooth reversal in global excess liquidity – for instance, the risks and options in the light of Bretton Woods II.

How Has the Euro Changed the Monetary Transmission?

Boivin, Mojon, AND Giannoni (2008) characterize the transmission mechanism of monetary shocks across countries of the euro area, documents how this mechanism has changed with the introduction of the euro, and explores some potential explanations. The factor-augmented VAR (FAVAR) framework used is sufficiently rich to jointly model the euro area dynamics while permitting the transmission of shocks to be different across countries. They find important heterogeneity across countries in the effect of monetary shocks before the launch of the euro. In particular, we find that German interest-rate shocks triggered stronger responses of interest rates and consumption in some countries such as Italy and Spain than in Germany itself. According to their estimates, the creation of the euro has contributed (1) to a greater homogeneity of the transmission mechanism across countries, and (2) to an overall reduction in the effects of monetary shocks. Using a structural open-economy model, they argue that the combination of a change in the policy reaction function – mainly toward a more aggressive response to inflation and output – and the elimination of an exchange-rate risk can explain the evolution of the monetary transmission mechanism observed empirically.

7.4 Monetary Policy and the "Zero Bound" to Nominal Interest Rates

Nominal interest rates should not fall below zero.[32] If, for instance, the nominal yield of an asset would be negative – that is its nominal value declines over time –, no rational investor would willingly hold it. He would do better holding money (which typically does not yield interest payments). Theoretically speaking, if the nominal yield of an asset would be negative, market agents would increasingly exchange it against money, thereby lowering its money price and thereby, *uno actu*, raising its nominal yield, bringing it back at least to a zero return – that is the (opportunity) return on money balances.

In the economic literature, however, the *zero bound on nominal interest rates* (or: *zero bound*) is seen as a major constraint for monetary policy that wants to keep the economy – via changing the short-term interest rate – at full employment. This view rests on the very notion that *the short-term interest rate is the key variable for monetary policy*. As a result, the zero bound is seen as a problem when nominal interest rates are low (which is typically the case when long-term inflation is low (Johnson, Small, & Tyron, 1999). This is because a decline in inflation could then push the real short-term interest rate above the level compatible with keeping the economy at full employment.

For instance, if economic activity is weak, and short-term interest rates hit the zero bound, a dangerous dynamic might be set in motion. With actual output falling below potential, inflation might slow down further, increasing the real rate of interest. If the resulting real interest rate is higher than the real interest rate needed for keeping the economy at full employment, a downward deflationary spiral might be set into motion: declining output, falling prices and real interest rate.

The issue of the zero bound is in great part related to the experience made in the Great Depression period in the US and came up to the surface again with

---

[32]However, Johnson (1998) notes that nominal yields dropped very slightly below zero in the US during the Great Depression and in Japan recently.

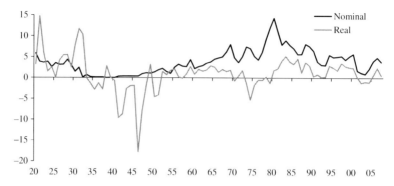

Fig. 7.31 US 3-months T-Bill rates, nominal and real (%)
Source: Global Financial Data; own calculations. – The real interest rate is the nominal rate minus annual CPI inflation. – The *shaded area* reflects the Great Depression 1929–1933. – Last data point: October 2007

unanticipated force at the start of 2009 in the ware of the financial crisis.[33] While nominal short-term interest rates actually declined from 1928, and became virtually zero by 1932, real interest rates – calculated as nominal interest rates minus the annual change in the CPI – actually rose from 1929 to 1931 and remained high thereafter, as the decline in annual CPI inflation was higher than the nominal interest rate (Fig. 7.31).

The risk associated with hitting the zero bound – and the severity of the consequences – is usually assessed on the basis of empirical analyses. Detailed studies of the US economy by Fuhrer and Madigan (1997), Orphanides and Wieland (1998), Tetlow and Williams (1998) and Reifschneider and Williams (1999) suggest that the risk associated with zero inflation may be significant, but that inflation of 1–3% p.a. should be sufficient to alleviate most of that risk (Fuhrer & Sniderman 2000). Orphanides and Wieland (1998) find that the zero bound has a significant detrimental impact on economic performance if policymakers strive to target inflation below 1% p.a., and recessions would be more frequent and last longer.

That said, monetary policy might choose a sufficiently high level of target inflation so that, on average, nominal interest rates can remain sufficiently high at all times, thereby providing more room to lower (real) interest rates should it become necessary (Phelps, 1972; Summers, 1991; Fischer, 1996). Summers and Fischer conclude, based on the zero bound, that inflation should be maintained in a range of 1–3%, Svensson (1999) suggests a 2% p.a. target for inflation.

In their model for the US economy Reifschneider and Williams (1999) find that the zero bound becomes important for inflation targets below 1% p.a. At an inflation target of zero, the authors find the policy rate is essentially at the zero bound nearly one-fourth of the time (compared to about 2% p.a. of the time when inflation

---

[33]The debate gained momentum in the late 1990 s, when economic growth in many countries was weak and, at the same time, CPI inflation had reached rather low levels by historical standards.

averages 3% p.a.) and the percentage of the time the economy is in a state of low economic activity is 10% p.a. (versus 2% p.a. at average inflation of 3% p.a.).

Many of the studies on the zero bound use stochastic simulations of empirical macro models, resting on certain assumptions (Johnson, 1998). Most important, in most models the transmission mechanism of monetary policy is solely from official short-term to longer-term government bond yields, and then to other asset prices. That said, alternative channels through which monetary policy can exert an impact on prices and real magnitudes tend to be mostly ignored.

7.4.1 Alternative Channels for Monetary Policy

When nominal rates are zero, there is still be a great number of instruments through which monetary policy can exert an impact on prices and (at least in the short-term) output (Johnson, 1998; Yates, 2002). That said, the debate about the zero bound at first glance appeared to be of rather little importance in the discussion about *optimal inflation*. However in the wake of the credit crisis it has become the heart of the controversies about the options of monetary policy. In what follows, a brief look shall be taken at how a central bank can (1) increase the quantity of money and (2) affect market agents' inflation expectations – two potential strategies for coping with the zero bound. Finally, (3) we will draw some policy lessons from the discussion about the zero bound.

7.4.1.1 Increasing the Quantity of Money

Even if nominal short-term interest rates are at zero, the central bank can increase the stock of money in the portfolio market agents – be it banks or non-banks – by simply buying assets from them (such as, for instance, short- and long-term government securities and corporate bonds). By doing so, the central bank can increase the amount of base money in peoples' portfolios. This is actually what is meant by "quantitative easing." Quantitative refers to the fact that a specfic quantity of money is being created. "Easing" refers to reducing the preserves on banks (Buiter, 2008).

Growing concern about forthcoming inflation as a result of a growing money supply would induce money holders to exchange money against (inflation protected) *real assets*, thereby pushing up *expected inflation* and thereby nominal market interest rates (across the maturity spectrum). For outstanding debt contract, a rise in actual inflation would lower borrowers' real debt levels (at the expense of creditors). That said, the central bank – the monopoly supplier of money – seems to be in a position to increase the stock of money at actually any point in time in any quantity desired. It can keep inflation positive through its *traditional open market operations*.

Fed Funds Rates and the Long-Term Interest Rate

Over sufficiently long periods of time long-term and short-term rates move together quite closely in the US. Figure 7.32 shows this by plotting the Federal Funds Target Rate, the 10-year Treasury yield, and the ratio of the 10-year yield to the Federal Funds Target Rate from January 1971 to March 2008. Until the early 1990 s, the deviation of the ratio from 1 remained within a relatively limited range.

As rates continued to fall in the early 1990 s (the funds rate declined more than the 10-year yield), the ratio increased to a peak of nearly 2.32 in December 1992. Moreover, the deviation of the ratio from 1.0 was very persistent, with the ratio remaining above the previous peak from the May 1991 to January 1995 sample period. The ratio began increasing dramatically in early 2001, reaching a peak of 4.59 by June 2004 before falling back to 1.0; during this time, the FOMC was increasing its target federal funds rate relative to an essentially unchanged 10-year yield.

The findings above suggest that the impact of short-term rate interest rates, as set by the US Fed, on long-term yields has declined dramatically since the early 1990 s. That said, the US central bank's ability to influence the market yield environment appears to have become much less obvious compared with the preceding decades.

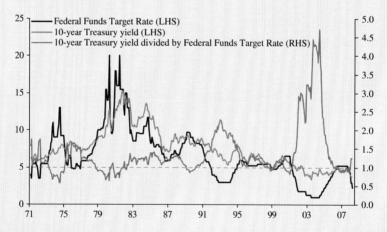

Fig. 7.32   Fed funds rates and the long-term interest rate (%)
Source: Federal Reserve Bank of St. Louis, Thomson Financial, own calculations

Buying Credit Bonds

If short-term interest rates are at zero, and the economy is in recession, *credit risk premiums* can be expected to be high. If this prevents the economy from recovering, the central bank could potentially exert a positive impact on the *easiness* of credit supply by taking (part of) the private sector's credit risk onto its balance sheet, for example, through purchases of risky private sector securities from financial institutions. By doing so, the central bank would reduce the corporate risk exposure of financial firms, thereby increasing their ability and/or willingness to extend credit to the non-bank sector – supported by a rise in base money supply in the hands of the financial sector. [34]

Writing Options

For giving a *signal about keeping inflation alive in the future*, a central bank could also enter into options contracts (Johnston, 1999, p. 84). For instance, if future short-term interest rates rise above a specified level, the central bank would commit itself to extent base money to its counterparty. By doing so, the central bank could actually *express its determination* that it will inject additional money into the economy if interest rates decline to an unwanted level – and that future inflation will therefore be kept in positive territory.

Purchasing Foreign Exchange

Purchasing foreign exchange would be another strategy for increasing the supply of base money. Irrespective of whether the central bank purchases foreign currency holdings from residents or non-resident, by doing so it would increase the supply of base money. Buying foreign currency against issuing domestic base money can be expected to have a depreciating impact on the exchange rate – as it would either spark inflation fears (if the intervention is not sterilised[35]), or because it entails an increase in domestic base money relative to money supply in foreign countries.

---

[34] Such action might require some changes in central bank statues, though. For instance, in the US the Fed can only purchase private sector debt which is eligible for discount operations, generally excluding corporate debt and mortgages. Johnston (1999, p. 94) notes, however, that the range of eligible instruments could be expanded: "Under 13 (3), if the Board of Governors found there to be "unusual and exigent circumstances" and voted by a majority of at least five governors to authorize lending under 13 (3), the Federal Reserve could discount to individuals, partnerships, and corporations "notes, drafts and bills of exchange . . . indorsed or otherwise secured to the satisfaction of the Federal Reserve Banks . . ." This broadening of the class of instruments eligible for discount would correspondingly broaden the class eligible for purchase."

[35] In unsterilized intervention, the authorities exchange cash or reserves for securities denominated in foreign currency, with the result that the domestic monetary base changes and, normally, domestic interest rates change. In sterilized intervention, the change in the domestic base is offset by a purchase or sale of domestic currency securities and domestic interest rates are normally left unchanged.

Quantitative and Qualitative Easing – A Primer

Concepts and Definitions

Willem Buiter (2008) has come up with a terminology to distinguish *quantitative easing*, i.e. an expansion of a central bank's balance sheet, from something which he labels *qualitative easing*, i.e. a central bank tasking riskier assets onto its balance sheet.

Quantitative easing denotes an increase in the size of the balance sheet of the central bank through a boost it is monetary liabilities, i.e. base money, holding the composition of its assets constant. The notion of asset composition refers to the proportional shares of the different financial instruments held by the central bank in the total value of its assets. In other words, quantitative easing can be defined as an increase in the size of the central bank balance sheet through a rise in its monetary liabilities which holds the (average) liquidity and riskiness of its asset portfolio constant.

Qualitative easing means a shift in the composition of the central bank assets towards less liquid and riskier assets, holding the size of the balance sheet and the official interest rate constant. Private securities as well as sovereign or sovereign-guaranteed instruments can make up for the less liquid and more risky assets. All kinds of risk, among them also credit risks and default risks are included.

Motivation

The aim of quantitative easing and the follow on process of deposit multiplication is to raise the amount of money in circulation by means of an increase of credit. Hence, the flow of money around the economy is intended to be stimulated by increased spending. Whereas setting official policy rates represents the usual method of regulating the money supply, quantitative easing is regarded to be a solution when the normal process of raising the money supply by cutting interest rates does not work. This is most obviously the case when interest rates are located at a zero level and it is impossible to cut them even further (Bernanke, 2002).

Historical Experiences

One of the prominent examples where quantitative easing was used is Japan in the early 2000s when the Bank of Japan (BOJ) fiercely fought domestic deflation (Spiegel, 2001). The BOJ had been maintaining short-term interest rates at close to their minimum attainable zero values since 1999. When it started its policy of quantitative easing, the BOJ flooded commercial banks with excess liquidity to foster private lending. Commercial banks were left with large stocks of excess reserves and, hence, rather little risk of a liquidity shortage emanating. The BOJ accomplished this by buying more government bonds than would be required to settle the interest rate at a zero level. Moreover, it bought asset-backed securities and equities and extended the terms of its commercial paper purchasing operation.

More recently during the credit crisis, policies announced and finally implemented by the US Federal Reserve under its chairman Ben Bernanke to neutralize the impacts of the crisis also represent a variant of quantitative easing. The Fed's balance sheet has expanded dramatically by adding new assets and new liabilities without sterilizing them by corresponding subtractions. The Bank of England (BOE) has also been using quantitative easing as an additional instrument of its monetary policy in order to counter the credit crisis.

The ECB has been employing quantitative easing–although it is not too explicit about this - through a process of expanding the assets which banks can offer as collateral to be posted to the ECB' in return for euros. this process has finally produced bonds being "structured for the ECB". In contrast, other central banks were comparatively restrictive in terms of the collateral accepted. The Fed usually accepted primarily treasuries. More recently, it has moved to buying almost any relatively safe dollar-denominated securities. The Bank of England applies a large haircut.

Limits and Risks

Quantitative easing is seen as a risky strategy that could trigger higher inflation than desired or even hyperinflation if it is used improperly, too much money is created and this money is not collected again when fears of deflations are gone. The latter might not take place if one considers re-election oriented governments which will heavily oppose against the necessary interest increases in times of post-credit crisis lower growth. Moreover, any creation of money out of "thin air" will ultimately have the same effect since the respective currency will inevitably devalue proportionally to the amount of new currency created, regardless of the final use of the new money.

However, it is argued by some that the risk of such outcomes becomes smaller when a central bank employs quantitative easing strictly to ease credit markets (e.g. by buying commercial paper). Hyperinflation is yet more likely to be triggered when money is created for the purpose of buying up government debts (as, for instance, treasury securities) which in turn can create a political temptation and moral hazard for governments and legislatures to spend more than their revenues, without either raising taxes or risking default on financial obligations.

7.4.1.2 Increasing Inflation (Expectations)

As outlined earlier, the nominal interest rate on bonds as determined by supply and demand in the free market can be stated as:

$$Nominal\ interest\ rate = real\ interest\ rate + inflation\ (expectation).$$

Let us consider a scenario in which nominal yields would become (close to) zero and the economy is in recession. Paul Krugman (1998), for instance, suggests that the central banks should lower real interest rates by pushing up *inflation expectations*, for this could bring the economy back into growth territory: "The way to make monetary policy effective, then, is for the central bank to credibly promise to be irresponsible – to make a persuasive case that it will permit inflation to occur, thereby producing the negative real interest rates the countries need."

However, what matters for real funding costs is *actual inflation*, not *expected inflation*. To show this, assume that a US$100 bond is paying a fixed coupon of 5% p.a., and that the market yield at the time of issue was 5% (that is a real rate of 3% p.a. and an inflation expectation of 2% p.a.). Now, the central bank increases the money supply (via buying bonds from bonds). Inflation expectations rise to, say, 4%, and the current market yield rises to 7% p.a. Accordingly, the market price of the bond declines to below US$100. However, as long as *actual inflation* remains at 2% p.a., real borrowing costs for existing debtors remain unchanged, whatever the bond market yield may be; the investor suffers a capital loss. Only if *actual inflation* rises to 4% p.a. does the loss of purchasing power of money reduce the borrower's real debt burden (at the expense of the creditor).

Clearly, if the central bank delivers *surprise inflation*, it would lower the real interest rate on outstanding nominal coupon bearing bonds. But monetary policy may succeed in producing surprise inflation only once. *Smart market agents* will find out that there is a discrepancy between monetary policy promises made and subsequent actions – and this very insight would most likely provoke the *time-inconsistency problem*. People would start expecting inflation to be higher than what monetary policy makers claim they are trying to achieve. Nominal yields on newly issued debt will go up, without lowering the real interest rate. The economy would end up in a rather unfavourable position: there would be additional costs due to higher inflation without any benefits from higher employment.

At this juncture it should be noted that is hard to imagine that an economy's *real interest rate* should ever reach zero. As long as human desires are not fully satisfied, there is always something to gain from investing part of current income, thereby increasing future income. As a consequence, there should always be a positive real interest rate.

If the central bank promises to keep inflation at, say, 2% p.a., zero nominal market interest rates would suggest that the *central banks' inflation promise is not credible*. Creating positive inflation expectations, however, should be an easy undertaking under a government controlled paper money regime: there should be hardly any doubt that the central bank can increase, if it wants to, the stock of money at any time in any quantity desired. The zero bound is therefore is a rather unlikely even in today's monetary environment.

7.4.1.3 Lessons to Be Learned from the Zero Bound Nominal Interest Rate Discussion

One should highlight that the discussion about potential problems related to the zero bound rests on *Keynesian economics*: the *short-term interest rate* is typically seen as the only available instrument through which the central bank affects prices and output. The discussion basically ignores alternative chancels through which monetary policy can affect prices and, at least in the short-run, real magnitudes, most notably through (direct) changes in the base money supply.

While nominal short-term interest rates may indeed approach zero – simply because under a money supply monopoly the central bank has the power to do so – there is no evidence so far that longer-term market interest rate have ever reached zero under a government paper money regime. The *normative recommendations* based on the zero bound nominal interest rates debate – namely better choosing higher than a lower inflation as a kind of *insurance* against zero nominal interest rates – are therefore to be taken with a great deal of caution.

In fact, Wolman (1998) shows that *optimal inflation* is very low, even if one takes into account the zero bound issue. He points out that when a policy of targeting the price level is followed, and market agents' inflation expectations are forward looking, the constraint on nominal interest rates imposes essentially no constraint on real interest rates. Similarly, Wolman (2005) shows that price level targeting combined with forward-looking price-setting behaviour implies that the real implications of the zero bound for monetary policy are very small.

After all, it appears that the alleged zero bound nominal interest rate problem is perhaps no problem at all, as Ben S. Bernanke noted in 2002: "Indeed, under a fiat (that is, paper) money system, a government (in practice, the central bank in cooperation with other agencies) should always be able to generate increased nominal spending and inflation, even when the short-term nominal interest rate is at zero."

What remains is indeed a word of caution. The danger in today's government controlled paper money regimes is too high a level of inflation – and not too low a level of inflation – because the government has control over the money supply. As Ben S. Bernanke (2002) also said: "(. . .) the U.S. government has a technology, called a printing press (or, today, its electronic equivalent), that allows it to produce as many U.S. dollars as it wishes at essentially no cost. By increasing the number of U.S. dollars in circulation, or even by credibly threatening to do so, the U.S. government can also reduce the value of a dollar in terms of goods and services, which is equivalent to raising the prices in dollars of those goods and services. We conclude that, under a paper-money system, a determined government can always generate higher spending and hence positive inflation."

References

Adalid, R., & Detken, C. (2007). *Liquidity shocks and asset price boom/bust cycles* (ECB Working Paper Series 732). Frankfurt, Main: European Central Bank.

Adrian, T., & Shin, H. (2008). *Liquidity and leverage* (Working Paper 328). New York: Federal Reserve Bank of New York.

Akerlof, G. A. (1970). The market for "lemons"; quality uncertainty and the market mechanism. *Quarterly Journal of Economics, 84*, 503–515.

Allen, F. D. (2008, October 11). *Lessons from the subprime crisis.* Presidential address. Montreal: International Atlantic Economic Society.

Allen, F. D., & Carletti, E. (2008a). *The role of liquidity in financial crises* (Working Paper 08–33). Philadelphia, PA: Wharton Financial Institutions Center, University of Pennsylvania.

Allen, F. D., & Carletti, E. (2008b, October). Should financial institutions mark to market?. *Banque de France Financial Stability Review*, 12, 1–6.

Bagliano, F. C., & Favero, C. A. (1999). Information from financial markets and VAR measures of monetary policy. *European Economic Review, 43*, 825–837.

Baks, K., & Kramer, C. F. (1999). *Global liquidity and asset prices: Measurement, implications, and spillovers* (IMF Working Papers 99/168). Washington, DC: International Monetary Fund.

Bank of England. (no date available). *The transmission of monetary policy*, http://www.bankofengland.co.uk/publications/other/monetary/montrans.pdf

Bank of England (2006, October). *Financial stability report.*

Bank of England (2007, April). *Financial stability report.*

Bank of England (2007, October). *Financial Stability report.*

Bank of England (2008, April). *Financial stability report.*

Bassanetti, A., & Zollino, F. (2008). *The effects of housing and financial wealth on personal consumption: Aggregate evidence for Italian households* (Bank of Italy Research Paper No. A12). Rome: Bank of Italy.

BBC (2007). *The downturn in facts and figures*, web (as of September 5, 2008), http://news.bbc.co.uk/2/hi/business/7073131.stm

Belke, A., & Gros, D., (2007). Instability of the eurozone? *On monetary policy, house prices and labor market reforms* (IZA Discussion Papers 2547), Bonn: Institute for the Study of Labor.

Belke, A., Orth, W., & Setzer, R. (2008a). Sowing the seeds of the subprime crisis – Does global liquidity matter for housing and other asset prices?. International Economics and Economic Policy, 5, 403–424.

Belke, A., & Wiedmann M. (2005). Boom or bubble in the US real estate market? *Intereconomics – Review of International Trade and Development, 40*(5), 273–284.

Belke, A., & Wiedmann M. (2006). Real estate bubbles and monetary policy – the US case. *Journal of Economics, 9*(54), 898–917.

Bernanke, B. S. (1986). *Alternative explorations of the money-income correlation* (pp. 49–99). Carnegie-Rochester Conference Series on Public Policy, 25.

Bernanke, B. S. (2002, November 21). *Deflation: Making sure "It" doesn't happen here.* Remarks by Governor before the national economists club, Washington, DC, http://www.federalreserve.gov/boardDocs/speeches/2002/20021121/default.htm

Bernanke, B. (2008). *Liquidity provision by the Federal Reserve.* Speech, May 13, Board of Governors of the Federal Reserve System, www.federalreserve.gov/newsevents/speech/bernanke20080513.htm

Bernanke, B. S., & Gertler, M. (1989, March). Agency costs, net worth, and business fluctuations. *American Economic Review, 79*(1), 14–31.

Bernanke, B. S., & Gertler, M. (1995). Inside the black box: The credit channel of monetary policy transmission. *Journal of Economic Perspectives, Fall 9*, 27–48.

Bernanke, B. S., Gertler, M., & Gilchrist, S. (1999). The financial accelerator in a quantitative business cycle framework, In J. Taylor & M. Woodford (Eds.), *Handbook of Macroeconomics* (Vol. 10, pp. 1341–1393). Amsterdam: Elsevier.

Bernanke, B. S., Lown, C. S., & Friedman, B. M. (1991). The credit crunch. *Brookings Papers on Economic Activity, 2*, 205–239.

Bernanke, B. S., & Mihov, I. (1998). *The liquidity effect and long-run neutrality* (pp. 149–194). Carnegie-Rochester Conference on Public Policy Series, 49.

Beyer, A., Doornik, J. A., & Hendry, D. F. (2000). Constructing historical euro-zone data. *The Economic Journal, 111,* 308–327.

Blanchard, O. J., & Watson, M. W. (1986). Are business cycles all alike?. In R. J. Gordon (Ed.), *The American business cycle*. Chicago: University of Chicago Press.

Boivin, J., Mojon, B., & Giannoni, M. P. (2008). *How has the euro changed the monetary trans-mission?* (NBER Working Paper No. 14190). Cambridge, MA: National Bureau of Economic Research.

Borio, C. E. V., & Filardo, A. (2007). *Globalisation and inflation: New cross-country evidence on the global determinants of domestic inflation* (BIS Working Papers 227). Basle: Bank for International Settlements.

Borio, C. E. V., & Nelson, W. (2008, March). *Monetary operations and the financial turmoil, BIS Quarterly Review*. Basle: Bank for International Settlements.

Bosworth, B. (1975). The stock market and the economy. *Brookings Papers on Economic Activity 2,* 257–290.

Browne, F., & Cronin, D. (2007). *Commodity prices, money and inflation* (ECB Working Paper 738). Frankfurt, Main: European Central Bank.

Brunnermeier M. (2009). Deciphering the 2007–08 liquidity and credit crunch. *Journal of Economic Perspectives*, 23 (1), 77–100.

Buiter, W. (2008, August 21–23). *Central banks and financial crises*. Paper presented at the Federal Reserve Bank of Kansas City's Symposium on "Maintaining Stability in a Changing Financial System", Jackson Hole, Wyoming.

Buiter, W. (2008a). Quantitative Easing and Qualitative Easing: A terminological and taxonomic proposal, December 9, ft.com/maverecon.

Campbell, J. Y., & Cocco, J. F. (2005, August). *How do house prices affect consumption? Evidence from micro data* (NBER Working Paper, 11534). Cambridge, MA: National Bureau of Economic Research.

Canova, F., Ciccarelli, M., & Ortega, E. (2007). Similarities and convergence in G-7 cycles. *Journal of Monetary Economics, 54*(3), 850–878.

Cecchetti, S. G. (1995, May/June). Distinguishing theories of the monetary transmission mechanism. *Federal Reserve Bank of St. Louis Review, 77,* 83–97.

Cecchetti, S. G. (2008). *Crisis and responses: The federal reserve and the financial crisis of 2007–2008* (NBER Working Paper, 14134). Cambridge, MA: National Bureau of Economic Research.

Cetorelli, N., & Goldberg, L. S. (2008, November). *Banking globalization, monetary transmission and the lending channel* (Bundesbank Research Centre Discussion Paper, 21/2008, Series 1 – Economic Studies). Frankfurt, Main: Bundesbank Research Centre.

Christiano, L. J., Eichenbaum, M., & Evans, C. (1996). The effects of monetary policy shocks: Evidence from the flow of funds. *Review of Economics and Statistics, 78*(1), 16–34.

Ciccarelli, M., & Mojon, B. (2005). *Global inflation* (ECB Working Paper Series 537). Frankfurt, Main: European Central Bank.

Congdon, T. (2005). *Money and asset prices in boom and bust*. London: The Institute of Economic Affairs.

Cushman, D. O., & Zha, T. A. (1997). Identifying monetary policy in a small open economy under flexible exchange rates. *Journal of Monetary Economics, 39*(3), 433–448.

Del Negro, M., & Otrok, C. (2007). 99 Luftballons: Monetary policy and the house price boom across US States. *Journal of Monetary Economics, 54*(7), 1962–1985.

Ecofin. (2008, June 1). *Memorandum of understanding on cooperation between the financial supervisory authorities*. Central Banks and Finance Ministries of the European Union on Cross-Border Financial Stability.

Economist. (2005, December 8). Hear that hissing sound. *The Economist*.

Economist. (2006, August 24). What's that hissing sound? *The Economist.*

Eichenbaum, M., & Evans, C. (1995). Some empirical evidence on the effects of shocks to monetary policy on exchange rates. *Quarterly Journal of Economics, 110*(4), 975–1009.

Enders, W. (2004). *Applied econometric time series* (2nd ed.). New York: Wiley & Sons, Inc.

European Central Bank (2007, July). *Monthly bulletin.* Frankfurt, Main: European Central Bank.

European Central Bank (2008, June). *Financial stability review.* Frankfurt, Main: European Central Bank.

Favero, C. A. (2001). *Applied macroeconometrics* New York: Oxford University Press.

Federal Reserve Bank (2008a, February). *Monetary policy report to the congress* Washington/DC.

Federal Reserve Bank (2008b, July). *Monetary policy report to the congress* Washington/DC.

Fischer, S. (1996, August 29–31). Why are central banks pursuing long-run price stability? In *Achieving price stability.* A symposium sponsored by the Federal Reserve Bank of Kansas City, Jackson Hole, Wyoming.

Fuhrer, J., & Madigan B. F. (1997). Monetary policy when interest rates are bounded at zero. *The Review of Economics and Statistics, 74*(4), 573–585, MIT Press.

Fuhrer, J., & Sniderman, M. (2000, November). In J. Fuhrer & M. Schneiderman (Eds.), *Monetary policy in a low-inflation environment. Journal of Money, Credit and Banking. 32*(4), 845–869.

Gali, J. (1992). How well does the IS-LM model fit postwar US data. *Quarterly Journal of Economics, 107*(2), 709–738.

Gertler, M., & Gilchrist, S. (1994). Monetary policy, business cycles and the behavior of small manufacturing firms. *Quarterly Journal of Economics, 109,* 309–340.

Giese, J. V., & Tuxen, C. K. (2007). *Global liquidity, asset prices and monetary policy: Evidence from cointegrated VAR models.* Unpublished Working Paper, University of Oxford, Nuffield College and University of Copenhagen, Department of Economics.

Giuliodori, M. (2005). The role of house prices in the monetary transmission mechanism across European countries. *Scottish Journal of Political Economy, 52*(4), 519–543.

Glaeser, E. L., Gyourko, J., & Saiz, A. (2008). *Housing supply and housing bubbles* (Harvard Institute of Economic Research Discussion Paper, 2158). Cambridge, MA: Harvard Institute of Economic Research.

Goodhart, C. A. E., & Hofmann, B. (2001, March). *Asset prices, financial conditions, and the transmission of monetary policy.* Federal Reserve Bank of Kansas City Proceedings.

Goodhart, C. A. E., & Hofmann, B. (2007). *House prices and the macroeconomy: Implications for banking and price stability.* Oxford: Oxford University Press.

Gordon, D. B., & Leeper, E. M. (1994). The dynamic impacts of monetary policy: An exercise in tentative identification. *Journal of Political Economy, 102*(6), 1228–1247.

Gorton, G. B. (2008). *The Panic of 2007* (NBER Working Paper, 14358). Cambridge, MA: National Bureau of Economic Research.

Green, E. J., & Oh, S. N. (1991). Can a "credit crunch" be efficient? *Federal Reserve Bank of Minneapolis, Quarterly Review, Fall, 15*(4), 3–17.

Greiber, C., & Setzer, R. (2007). *Money and housing: Evidence for the euro area and the US* (Deutsche Bundesbank Discussion Paper Series 1: Economic Studies 07/12). Frankfurt, Main: European Central Bank.

Gros, D. (2007, October). *Bubbles in real estate? A longer-term comparative analysis of housing prices in Europe and the US* (CEPS Working Document No. 276). Brussels: Centre for European Policy Studies.

Gros, D, & Micossi, S. (2008, October 10). *A concerted approach to re-start the interbank market, CEPS commentary.* Brussels: Centre for European Policy Studies.

Hall, S. (2001, Winter). Credit channel effects in the monetary transmission mechanism. *Bank of England Quarterly Bulletin,* 442–448.

Hamilton, J. D. (1994). *Time series analysis.* Princeton, NJ: Princeton University Press.

Hamilton, J. D. (2008). *Daily monetary policy shocks and the delayed response of new home sales* (NBER Working Paper, 14223). Cambridge, MA: National Bureau of Economic Research.

Hayashi, F. (1982). Tobin's marginal q and average q: A neoclassical interpretation. *Econometrica, 50*(1), 213–224.

Hubbard, R. G. (1995, May/June). Is there a "credit channel" for monetary policy?. *Federal Reserve Bank of St. Louis Review, 77,* 63–74.

Iacoviello, M. (2005). House prices, borrowing constraints, and monetary policy in the business cycle. *American Economic Review, 95*(3), 739–764.

Illing, G. (2007a). *Liquidity shortages and monetary policy* (Discussion Papers in Economics, 2008). Munich: University of Munich, Department of Economics.

Illing, G. (2007b). *Financial stability and monetary policy, a framework* (CESifo Working Paper Series, 1971). Munich.

Illing, G., & Klueh, U. (2005). Vermögenspreise und Konsum: Neue Erkenntnisse, amerikanische Erfahrungen und europäische Herausforderungen. *Perspektiven der Wirtschaftspolitik, 6*(1), 1–22.

International Monetary Fund (2004, September). The global house price boom. In *World economic outlook – The global demographic transition* (chap. II, pp. 71–89). Washington, DC: International Monetary Fund.

International Monetary Fund (2007a, October). *Global financial stability report.* Washington, DC: International Monetary Fund.

International Monetary Fund (2007b, October). What is global liquidity? In *World economic outlook – Globalization and inequality* (chap. I, pp. 34–37). Washington, DC: International Monetary Fund.

International Monetary Fund (2008, April). *Global financial stability report.* Washington, DC: International Monetary Fund.

Jaffee, D. M., & Russell, T. (1976). Imperfect information, uncertainty and credit rationing. *Quarterly Journal of Economics, 90*(4), 651–666.

Johnson, H.C. (1998), Gold, France, and the Great Depression, 1919–1932, New Haven, Yale University Press.

Johnson, K., Small, D., & Tyron, R. (1999). *Monetary policy and price stability* (International Economics and Finance Discussion Paper, 641). Washington, DC: Board of Governors of the Federal Reserve System.

Kashyap, A. K., & Stein, J. C. (1994). Monetary policy and bank lending. In N. G. Mankiw (Ed.), *Monetary policy.* Chicago: University of Chicago Press.

Kashyap, A. K., & Stein, J. C. (2000). What do a million observations on banks say about the transmission of monetary policy?. *American Economic Review, 90*(3), 407–428.

Keeton, W. R. (1979). *Equilibrium credit rationing.* New York: London.

Kim, S., N. & Roubini, N. (1999). *Exchange rate anomalies in the industrial countries: A solution with a structural VAR approach*, Urbana-Champaign: University of Illinois, Mimeo.

Kohn, D. (2008). *Money markets and financial stability.* Speech May 29, Board of Governors of the Federal Reserve System, www.federalreserve.gov/newsevents/speech/kohn20080529a.htm

Krugman, P. (1998). *Japan's trap.* Available at http://web.mit.edu/krugman/www.

Krugman, P. (2008, March 19). *Commodity prices (Wonkish).* New York: New York Times.

Ludvigson, S., Steindel, C. (1999). How important is the stock market effect on consumption?," Economic Policy Review, Federal Reserve Bank of New York, issue Jul, pages 29–51.

Menger, C. (1871). *Principles of economics.* Alabama: Ludwig von Mises Institute.

Millard, S. P., & Wells, S. J. (2003). *The role of asset prices in transmitting monetary and other shocks* (BoE Working Papers 188). London: Bank of England.

Mishkin, F. S. (1976). Illiquidity, consumer durable expenditure, and monetary policy. *American Economic Review, 66*(4), 642–654.

Mishkin, F. S. (1977). What depressed the consumer? The household balance-sheet and the 1973–75 recession. *Brookings Paper on Economic Activity, 1,* 123–164.

Mishkin, F. S. (1996). Understanding financial crises: A developing country perspective. In M. Bruno & B. Pleskovic (Eds.), *Annual world bank conference on Development Economics* (pp. 29–62). Washington, DC: World Bank.

Mishkin, F. S. (1999). Lessons from the Asian crisis. *Journal of International Money and Finance, 18*(4), 709–723.

Mishkin, F. S. (2007). *Housing and the monetary transmission mechanism* (NBER Working Paper 13518). Cambridge, MA: National Bureau of Economic Research.

Modigliani, F. (1966). The life cycle hypothesis of saving, the demand for wealth and the supply of capital. *Social Research, 33,* 160–217.

Modigliani, F. (1971). Monetary policy and consumption. *Consumer spending and monetary policy: The linkages* (pp. 9–84). Boston: Federal Reserve Bank of Boston.

Mulligan, C. B., & Threinen, L. (2008). *Market responses to the panic of 2008* (NBER Working Paper, 14446). Cambridge, MA: National Bureau of Economic Research.

Obstfeld, M., & Rogoff, K. (1996). *Foundations of international macroeconomics.* Cambridge, MA: MIT Press.

OECD (2005). *Recent house price developments: The role of fundamentals.* OECD Economic Outlook 78 (chap. III, pp. 193–234).

Orphanides, A., & Wieland, V. (1998, August). *Price stability and monetary policy effectiveness when nominal interest rates are bounded at zero* (Finance and Economics Discussion Series, 1998–35). Washington, DC: Board of Governors of the Federal Reserve System.

Paiella, M. (2008). *The stock market, housing and consumer spending: A survey of the evidence on wealth effects* (Bank of Italy Research Paper, A8), Rome.

Papademos, L. (2007, June 11). *The effects of globalisation on inflation, liquidity and monetary policy*. Speech at the conference on the "International Dimensions of Monetary Policy" organised by the National Bureau of Economic Research, S'Agar`o, Girona.

Pepper, G. & Olivier, M. (2006). *The liquidity theory of asset prices*. New York: Wiley Finance.

Pesaran, M. H., & Shin, Y. (1998). Generalized impulse response functions in linear multivariate models. *Economic Letters, 58,* 17–29.

Phelps, E. S. (1972). *Inflation policy and unemployment theory*. London: The McMillan Press Ltd.

Rajan, R. G., & Zingales, L. (1998). Financial dependence and growth. *American Economic Review, 88*(3), 559–586.

Reifschneider, D., & Williams, J. C. (1999, September). Three *lessons for monetary policy in a low inflation era* (Board of Governors of the Federal Reserve System, Working Paper). Washington, DC: Board of Governors of the Federal Reserve System.

Reinhart, C. M., & Rogoff, K. S. (2004). The modern history of exchange rate arrangements: A reinterpretation. *Quarterly Journal of Economics, 119*(1), 1–48.

Rigobon, R., & Sack, B. (2002). *The impact of monetary policy on asset prices* (NBER Working Paper 8794). Cambridge, Massachusetts: National Bureau of Economic Research.

Rigobon, R., & Sack, B. (2003, May). Measuring the reaction of monetary policy to the stock market. *Quarterly Journal of Economics, 2,* 639–669.

Roffia, B., & Zaghini, A. (2007). *Excess money growth and inflation dynamics* (ECB Working Paper Series 749). Frankfurt, Main: European Central Bank.

Rothschild, M., Stiglitz, J.E. (1970). Increasing Risk: I. A Definition, in: *Journal of Economic Theory, 2,* 225–243.

Rueffer, R., & Stracca, L. (2006). *What is global excess liquidity, and does it matter?* (ECB Working Paper Series 696). Frankfurt, Main: European Central Bank.

Schich, S., & Weth, M. (2008). *Demographic changes and real house prices*. Deutsche Bundesbank, Frankfurt, Main: European Central Bank, (forthcoming).

Schnabl, G., & Hoffmann, A. (2007). *Monetary policy, vagabonding liquidity and bursting bubbles in new and emerging markets – An overinvestment view* (CESifo Working Paper 2100). Munich: CESifo.

Shiller, R. (2005). *Irrational exuberance* (2nd ed.). Princeton, NJ: Princeton University Press.

Shin, H. S. (2005, December). *Risk and liquidity in a system context* (LSE Working Paper). Paper presented at the BIS conference on Accounting, Risk Management and Prudential Regulation, London School of Economics, London.

Shleifer, A., & Vishny, R. (1997). The limits to arbitrage. *Journal of Finance, 52,* 35– 55.

Sims, C. A. (1980). Macroeconomics and reality. *Econometrica, 48*(1), 1–48.

Sims, C. A. (1986). Are forecasting models usable for policy analysis. *Federal Reserve Bank of Minneapolis Quarterly Review, 10*(1), 2–15.

Sims, C. A. (1992). Interpreting the time series facts: The effects of monetary policy. *European Economic Review, 36*(5), 975–1000.

Sims, C.A., Stock, J.H., Watson, M. W., (1990). Inference in Linear Time Series Models with Some Unit Roots. Econometrica *58* (1), 113–144.

Sims, C. A., & Zha, T. A. (1998). *Does monetary policy generate recessions?* (Federal Reserve Bank of Atlanta Working Paper No. 98–12). Atlanta: Federal Reserve Bank of Atlanta.

Sousa, J. M., & Zaghini, A. (2006). *Global monetary policy shocks in the G5: A SVAR approach* (CFS Working Paper Series 2006/30). Frankfurt, Main: Center for Financial Studies.

Spigel, M. (2001). FRBSF: Economic Letter – Quantitative Easing by the Bank of Japan (11/02/2001), Federal Reserve Bank of San Francisco.

Stiglitz, J. E., & Weiss, A. (1981). Credit rationing in markets with imperfect information. *American Economic Review, 71*, 393–410.

Summers, L. (1991). How should long-term monetary policy be determined?. *Journal of Money, Credit and Banking, 23*(3), 625–631.

Svensson, L. E. O. (1999, August). *How should monetary policy be conducted in an Era of price stability?* Stockholm University: Institute for International Economic Studies.

Taylor, J. B. (1995). The monetary transmission mechanism: An empirical framework. *Journal of Economic Perspectives, 9*(4), 11–26.

Taylor, M. (2000). Purchasing power parity over two centuries: Strengthening the case for real exchange rate stability. *Journal of International Money and Finance, 19*, 759–764.

Tetlow, R., & Williams, J. C. (1998, March). *Implementing price stability: Bands, boundaries and inflation targeting* (Federal Reserve Board Staff Working Paper).

Thorbecke, W. (1997). On stock market returns and monetary policy. *Journal of Finance, 52*(2), 635–654.

Thornton, D. L. (2007, May). The federal funds and long-term rates. *Monetary Trends*, Federal Reserve Bank of St. Louis p.1.

Tobin, J. (1969, February). A general equilibrium approach to monetary theory. *Journal of Money, Credit, and Banking, 1*, 15–29.

Tong, H., & Wei, S.-J. (2008). *Real effects of the subprime mortgage crisis: Is it a demand or a finance shock?* (NBER Working Paper, 14205). Cambridge, MA: National Bureau of Economic Research.

Von Hayek, F. A. (1935). *Prices and production.* US Alabama: Ludwig von Mises Institute.

von Mises, L. (1912). *Theory of money and credit.* US Alabama: Ludwig von Mises Institute.

von Mises, L. (1981/1934). *The theory of money and credit.* (Preface to the English Editon, p. 23).

von Mises, L. (1996). *Human action.* (4th revised ed,). San Francisco: Fox & Wilkes.

Wicksell, K. (1898). *Interest and prices.* New York: Augustus M. Kelley.

Whited, T. M, & Wu, G. (2006). Financial constraints risk. *Review of Financial Studies, 19*(2), 531–559.

Wolman, A. (1998). Staggered price setting and the zero bound on nominal interest rates. *Federal Reserve Bank of Richmond Economic Quarterly, 84*, 1–22.

Wolman, A. (2005). Real implications of the zero bound on nominal interest rates. *Journal of Money, Credit and Banking, 37*(2), 273–296.

Yates, T. (2002). *Monetary policy and the zero bound to nominal interest rates: A review* (ECB Working Paper No. 190). Frankfurt, Main: European Central Bank.

Chapter 8
Monetary Policy Strategies

There Is No Such Thing As A Free Lunch

In 1950, a New York Times columnist ascribed this phrase to economist (and Army General) Leonard P. Ayres of the Cleveland Trust Company (and not to Milton Friedman). "It seems that shortly before the General's death [in 1946]. . . a group of reporters approached the general with the request that perhaps he might give them one of several immutable economic truisms which he had gathered from his long years of economic study. . . 'It is an immutable economic fact,' said the general, 'that there is no such thing as a free lunch.'"

Fetridge, Robert H., "Along the Highways and Byways of Finance," The New York Times, Nov 12, 1950, p. 135.

8.1 Strategy Requirements

8.1.1 On the Monetary Policy Strategy

In most western industrialised countries, the primary objective of monetary policy is the maintenance of price stability. However, central banks cannot control the prices directly by using the monetary policy instruments at its disposal. Instead, they face a complex *transmission process,* which describes the stages with which a change in money supply/short-term interest rates leads to changes in the economy's price level Friedman 1975. The transmission process is typically subject to variable and not fully predictable time lags. In fact, it can be expected to be continuously changing in response to changes in economic behaviour and institutional structures.

Under a monetary policy regime with discretionary elements, there is a need for an *organizing analytical framework* for monetary policy decision makers. Such framework would help to order, analyse and interpret monetary policy relevant data and present and announce policy decisions made to the outside world. This is actually the role of a central bank's *monetary policy strategy* (European Central Bank, 1999a, p. 43): "A monetary policy strategy is a coherent and structured description of how monetary policy decisions will be made in the light of the behaviour of economic indicators, in order to achieve the overriding objective of price stability." A monetary policy strategy should fulfil *two crucial tasks:*

– *First*, the strategy puts an ordering and coherent structure on policy makers' internal decision process. It should make sure that central bank decision makers take into account the information and analyses required to take policy decisions compatible with preserving low inflation.
– *Second*, a monetary policy strategy is a vehicle for communicating with the outside world. Monetary policy is most effective when it is credible – that is, when the public is completely confident that monetary policy is fully committed to keeping inflation low. The monetary policy strategy must not only signal the overriding objective of monetary policy, but must also convince the public that this objective will be achieved by adhering to it.

In that sense, the monetary policy addresses basically *three issues* (Blinder, 1995): (i) the goal of monetary policy, (ii) the instruments at the disposal of the central bank for achieving the policy goals and (iii) when and how the central bank uses its instruments.

For designing a monetary policy strategy which can fulfil these requirements, a great deal of knowledge about the functioning of the economy is essential. Perhaps most important, what is the needed is *knowledge* about the actual causes of inflation. What is more, as monetary policy works with time lags, future threats to price stability must be extracted from currently available variables; in other words, the *indicator properties* of monetary, financial and other economic variables for price developments must be analysed and understood. It is important for designing an effective policy strategy to understand how monetary policy, through changes in base money supply/short-term interest rates, affects the economy in general and, ultimately, inflation. Understanding the *transmission process* will help to from a view about what kind of the policy action is appropriate to prevent inflation in the future as revealed by the indicator variables.

To fulfil the tasks as outlined above, a central bank's monetary policy strategy must satisfy certain general criteria (European Central Bank, 1999a, p. 44). Foremost among them is the principle of *effectiveness*. It means that strategy must make policy makers to response to changes in variables which influence the final objective, i.e. keeping inflation low. It must also represent a *credible and realistic commitment* to achieving the monetary policy objective. The strategy must convince the public that the central bank's monetary policy actions will, and can be made, in line with the strategy requirements.

In order to build up *reputation capital* and *credibility* – which are necessary requirements for implementing monetary policy effectively and successfully –, a monetary policy strategy has to satisfy a number of additional criteria (European Central Bank, 1999a, p. 44):

– The strategy must be *understandable* from the viewpoint of the public at large and financial market participants in particular. Ambiguity about how the monetary policy objective will be achieved can cause a great deal of (costly) uncertainty.

- The strategy must be *transparent*. The public must be presented ex ante with information about how monetary policy decisions are being made by the central bank and the economic rationale on which they are based.
- A strategy is typically formulated with the view of providing the central bank with some *discretion* (*escape clause*). The reason being that delivering low inflation shall be achieved over the *medium-term*.
- The strategy must be *consistent* with the independent status granted to monetary policy and should support it as far as possible.
- The strategy must ensure that the central bank *decision makers are accountable* both for policy actions and the performance in achieving the policy goal.

A central bank's strategy may change over time, as former Fed Vice Chairman Alan Blinder (1995) noted: "People often misunderstand and think that we can't have a long-run strategy because of all these uncertainties and because the world is constantly changing. That is quite wrong. You must have a long-run strategy, but you must be willing to modify it as new information becomes available. Can this stitch-in-time strategy lead you into error anyway? You bet it can! But the other strategy – the Bunker Hill strategy – is sure to lead you into error. And that makes it, to me, a very easy choice."

8.1.2 Intermediate Variable

In view of the *time lags* of monetary policy, the need for pursuing a *pre-emptive* and *forward-looking* monetary policy has become common wisdom.[1] Consider, for instance, the remarks made by former US Federal Reserve Chairman Alan Greenspan (1999): "For monetary policy to foster maximum sustainable economic growth, it is useful to preempt forces of imbalance before they threaten economic stability. But this may not always be possible – the future at times can be too opaque to penetrate. When we can be preemptive, we should be, because modest preemptive actions can obviate more drastic actions at a later date that would destabilize the economy."

In the same vein, former US Federal Reserve Chairman W. M. Martin said (1965): "To me, the effective time to act against inflationary pressures is when they are in the development stage – before they have become full-blown and the damage has been done. Precautionary measures are more likely to be effective than remedial action: the old proverb that an ounce of prevention is worth a pound of cure applies to monetary policy as well as to anything else."

In general, a pre-emptive, forward-looking monetary policy takes action if and when there is a divergence between expected, or projected, inflation (π_t^e) and envisaged inflation ($\hat{\pi}_t$). The policy recommendation could be described as follows:

---

[1] Note that the case for having intermediate variables in monetary policy rests on the argument of the existence of time lags per se, not because there is uncertainty about the actually length and variability of time lags.

Table 8.1 Indicator versus intermediate variable

	Intermediate variable/target	Indicator variable
• Central bank must be able to control the variable (perfectly)	X	
• Monetary policy must exert a predominant influence on the variable.	X	X
• Changes in the variable must be followed by predictable changes in prices.	X	X
• Variable must be (exactly) measurable by the central bank.	X	X
• Timely access to the information provided by the variable.	X	X

$$\Delta i = \lambda^{\pi} f(\pi_t^e - \hat{\pi}_t). \tag{8.1}$$

The bank would have to increase (decrease) the interest rate, i, that is $\Delta i > 0$ ($\Delta i < 0$), if expected future inflation exceeds target inflation; $\lambda^{\pi} > 0$ shows the intensity with which rates are changed in response to the expected deviation from target inflation. In Eq. (8.1), the inflation forecast actually de facto represents an *intermediate variable*, or *intermediate target*, for monetary policy.

To qualify as an intermediate target, a variable must meet a number of requirements (Table 8.1). *First*, the central bank must be able to control it via changes in base money supply and/short-term interest rates, implying, *second*, that monetary policy exerts the predominant influence on the variable. *Third*, changes in the intermediate variable must be followed by predictable changes in future prices. *Four*, the intermediate variable must be (exactly) measurable by the central bank with, *five*, a sufficient degree of timeliness and accuracy. In contrast to the intermediate variable, an *indicator variable* cannot be (fully, or perfectly) controlled by monetary policy (Belongia & Batten, 1992).

8.1.3 A Model for Intermediate Targeting

The need for an intermediate variable for monetary policy rests on the notion that (i) the central bank cannot control inflation directly and that (ii) that policy measures affect inflation with time lags. Under such conditions, monetary policy would have to rely on an intermediate variable (Neumann, 2000). In what follows, we will take a closer look at optimal monetary policy which makes use of an intermediate target for achieving its policy objective.

To start with, aggregate supply, aggregate demand and money demand system are as follows (Walsh, 2003, p. 440):

$$y_t = a(\pi_t - E_{t-1}\pi_t) + z_t \tag{8.2a}$$

$$y_t = -\alpha(i_t - E_t\pi_{t+1}) + u_t \tag{8.2b}$$

$$m_t - p_t = m_t - \pi_t - p_{t-1} = y_t - ci_t + v_t, \tag{8.2c}$$

where (8.2a) is the Lucas supply curve, (8.2b) is the aggregate demand function (negatively related to the real interest rate) and (8.2c) is the money demand function. The error terms z, u and v follow an autoregressive process:

$$z_t = \rho_z z_{t-1} + e_t,$$
$$u_t = \rho_u u_{t-1} + \varphi_t \text{ and}$$
$$v_t = \rho_v v_{t-1} + \psi_t,$$

where $0 < \rho_i < 1$ for $i = z$, u and v. The shocks e, φ and ψ have a zero mean, are i.i.d. and are mutually uncorrelated processes.

8.1.3.1 Optimal Interest Rate Policy

Assume that monetary policy's objective is to minimise the expected squared deviation of inflation around its target level π^*. If i_t is the policy's instrument, the objective function is:

$$V = E(\pi_t - \pi^*)^2 \rightarrow \min. \tag{8.3}$$

Furthermore, assume that the interest rate i_t is set before e_t, φ_t and ψ_t are known but that y_{t-1}, π_{t-1} and m_{t-1} (and, as a result, p_{t-1}, z_{t-1}, u_{t-1} and v_{t-1}) are known when i_t is set.

Monetary policy will set i_t to ensure that expected inflation will equal the desired, or target, rate π^*. Actual inflation will differ from π^*, if there are shocks to aggregate supply, demand and/or money demand. This is because monetary policy offset these effects, but it will offset any expected effect from lagged disturbances so that $E_{t-1}\pi_t = E_t\pi_{t+1} = \pi^*$. Inserting the latter in (8.2a) and setting (8.2a) equal to (8.2b) yields:

$$\pi_t = \frac{(a + \alpha)\pi^* - \alpha i_t + u_t - z_t}{a}. \tag{8.4}$$

If full information about z_t and u_t is available, monetary policy would set the interest equal to $i_t^* = \pi^* + (1/\alpha)(u_t - z_t)$, as this would make actual inflation equal to target inflation.

If, however, i_t must be set prior to observing the realisation of the innovations in period t, the optimal policy can be obtained by taking expectations of (8.4), conditional on information available in period $t - 1$:

$$\hat{i} = \pi^* + (1/\alpha)(\rho_u u_{t-1} - \rho_z z_t).\tag{8.5}$$

Substituting the latter in (8.4) yields:

$$\pi_t(\hat{i}) = \pi^* + \frac{\varphi_t - e_t}{a}.\tag{8.6}$$

The loss of the objective function is:

$$V(\hat{i}) = (1/a)^2(\sigma_\varphi^2 + \sigma_e^2),\tag{8.7}$$

where σ_φ^2 and σ_e^2 are the variances of φ and e.

8.1.3.2 Optimal Money Supply

Of course, monetary policy could identify the stock of money consistent with π^* and then choosing i_t to achieve the required m_t. Using (8.2c) to eliminate i_t from the aggregate demand function (8.2b) yields:

$$y_t = \left(\frac{\alpha}{\alpha + c}\right)(m_t - \pi_t - p_{t-1} - v_t) + \left(\frac{c}{\alpha + c}\right)(u_t + \alpha\pi^*).\tag{8.8}$$

Using the aggregate supply curve (8.2a), the equilibrium inflation is:

$$\pi_t = \pi^* + (1/a)\left[\left(\frac{\alpha}{\alpha + c}\right)(m_t - \pi_t - p_{t-1} - v_t) + \left(\frac{c}{\alpha + c}\right)(u_t + \alpha\pi^*) - z_t\right]$$

$$= \frac{[a(\alpha + c) + \alpha c]\pi^* + \alpha(m_t - p_{t-1} - v_t) + cu_t - (\alpha + c)z_t}{a(\alpha + c) + \alpha}.\tag{8.9}$$

The stock of m_t, which would yield $\pi_t = \pi^*$, is:

$$\hat{m}_t = (1 - c)\pi^* + p_{t-1} - (c/\alpha)u_t + \left(1 + \frac{c}{\alpha}\right)z_t + v_t\tag{8.10}$$

If, however, the money stock is set before the occurrence of the shocks, the optimal money supply is:

$$\hat{m}_t = (1 - c)\pi^* + p_{t-1} - (c/\alpha)\rho_u u_{t-1} + \left(1 + \frac{c}{\alpha}\right)\rho_z z_{t-1} + p_v v_{t-1}.\tag{8.11}$$

The interest rate which is consistent with the objective of bringing about $\hat{m}_t$ is $\hat{i}_t$. That said, a monetary policy for minimising the loss function can either set the optimal interest rate or calculating the optimal money supply first and then setting the interest rate; both procedures yield the same result as far as the levels of $\hat{m}_t$ and $\hat{i}_t$ are concerned.

8.1.3.3 Responding to the Actual Stock of Money

A monetary policy that sets the actual interest rate equal to $\hat{i}$, Eq. (8.2c) actual money supply will be:

$$\hat{m}_t(\hat{i}) = \pi_t(\hat{i}) + p_{t-1} + y(\hat{i}) - c\hat{i}_t + v_t. \tag{8.12}$$

Equation (8.12) can be stated as:

$$\hat{m}_t(\hat{i}) = \hat{m}_t - \left(\frac{1}{a}\right) e_t + \left(1 + \frac{1}{a}\right) \varphi_t + \psi_t. \tag{8.13}$$

A divergence of m_t from $\hat{m}_t$ gives information about shocks, and this can be used to adjust the interest rate to keep inflation close to the target. Let us assume, for instance, that there is a *positive demand side shock* ($\varphi > 0$), all other things being equal. It will, for a given nominal interest rate, increase output and inflation, both of which contribute to an increase in nominal money demand. Under a policy of keeping i fixed, the policy maker would let m rise in response to the increased demand for money. However, if the central bank focuses on money supply, the increase in m_t above $\hat{m}_t$ would signal that the nominal interest rate should be increased. If the central bank keeps m_t at its target level $\hat{m}_t$, the objective of keeping the inflation at π^* would be achieved. That said, if money serves as an intermediate target, monetary policy is better able to achieve the target for the goal variable π_t.

A *positive shock to money demand*, ψ_t, however, does not require a change in i_t to maintain inflation on target. Equation (8.20) indicates that a positive money demand shock causes m_t to rise above its target level $m_t(\hat{i})$. Under a policy of adjusting i to keep m close to its target, the nominal interest rate would be raised, which would make π deviating from π^*. That said, if there is a money demand shock, raising rates to keep m at the target level would not produce the appropriate policy for keeping π on target.

8.1.3.4 The Emergence of Several Shocks Under Intermediate Targeting

Now assume that several shocks (to demand- and supply-side and to money demand) emerge at the same time. Under a policy that keeps m_t always equals to its target level $\hat{m}_t$, the interest rate is:[2]

$$i_t^T = \hat{i}_t + \frac{(1+a)\varphi_t - e_t + a\psi_t}{ac + \alpha(1+a)}. \tag{8.14}$$

---

[2]Note that individual disturbances cannot be observed by the policy maker. If m_t can be observed, i_t can be adjusted.

If the interest rate is at i_t^T, inflation would be:

$$\pi_t(i_t^T) = \pi^* + \left(\frac{1}{a}\right)[-\alpha(i_t^T - \hat{\imath}) + \varphi_t - e_t]$$

$$= \pi^* + \frac{c\varphi_t - (\alpha + c)e_t - \alpha\psi_t}{ac + \alpha(1 + a)}. \tag{8.15}$$

If we comparing Eq. (8.15) with the level of inflation according to $\pi_t(\hat{\imath}_t)$ as shown in Eq. (8.6) – the latter showing the money supply if the information about money supply is not used –, we can draw two conclusions. *First*, the impact of an aggregate demand shock, φ, on inflation is reduced by $c/[ac + \alpha(1 + a)] < 1/a$. This is because a positive φ tends to raise money demand, which requires an interest rate hike to keep m on target. This interest rate increase partially offsets the effect of a demand shock on inflation.

Second, the impact of an aggregate supply shock (e) under a money targeting is also reduced. *Third*, money demand shocks, ψ_t, affect inflation. For instance, a positive ψ_t pushes m above target. If i is raised to offset this shock, inflation will fall below target.

For an intermediate targeting, we have the following loss function:

$$V(i_t^T) = \left(\frac{1}{ac + \alpha(1 + a)}\right)^2 [c^2\sigma_\varphi^2 + (\alpha + c)^2\sigma_e^2 + \alpha^2\sigma_\psi^2]. \tag{8.16}$$

If we compare Eq. (8.16) with (8.7), the loss of pursuing an intermediate targeting should be increased by the variance of money demand shocks, σ_ψ^2. However, it the latter is not too large, an intermediate targeting should do better than simply keeping the nominal interest rate at $\hat{\imath}$.

8.1.3.5 Interest Rate Rule Under Intermediate Targeting

Under an intermediate targeting, the rule is to adjust the interest rate (that is the operating target of monetary policy) to information provided by the intermediate target. Using (8.13) and (8.14), the monetary policy rule is:

$$i_t^T - \hat{\imath} = \left[\frac{a}{ac + \alpha(1 + a)}\right](m_t(\hat{\imath}) - \hat{m})$$

$$= \mu^T [m_t(\hat{\imath}) - \hat{m}]. \tag{8.17}$$

If, according to Eq. (8.17), actual money supply ($m_t(\hat{\imath})$) deviates from the target level ($\hat{m}$), the central bank changes its interest rate. Of course, the optimal policy would depend on the kind of shock hitting the system. Changing interest rates in response to deviations of money from its target without taking into account the kind of shocks (φ, e or ψ) exerting an effect on money, however, would be an inefficient use of the information in m.

The Lucas Critique

In 1976 Robert E. Lucas published his article *Econometric Policy Evaluation: A Critique*, in which he argued against the widespread use of econometric models to evaluate policies. His argument is that policy *regime shifts* change the structure of the economic system under investigation, changing hitherto observable relations between different variables. As a result, policy induced regime shifts render hitherto existing relations ineffective (*Lucas Critique*).

According to the Lucas Critique, regime shifts, that are quantitative changes of policy instruments (such as changes in tax rates, government spending or interest rate policies), will influence peoples' behaviour. As a result of policy changes, hitherto observed parameters linking, say, interest rates to overall spending, might change as a consequence. It is against this backdrop that, according to the Lucas Critique, econometric analysis (based as it is on past experience) cannot be used to analyse and or predict the economic impact of changes in economic policies on an *ex ante* basis. The Lucas critique would be even more true if policies are qualitative in the sense of Tinbergen (1952), that is if policy makers change the institutions (and thus directly the structure of the economy).

The Lucas Critique has made an important impact in the field of economics; Lucas's article is probably one of most influential macroeconomic articles of the 1970s (LeRoy, 1992, p. 235). It should have helped to change the economic profession's view about the usefulness of macro econometric modelling for implementing macro-economic policies: The rather optimistic view prevailing in the 1960s and early 1970s as far as *de facto state planning exercises* were concerned was turned into a somewhat less euphoric stance.

However, the empirical relevance of the Lucas Critique has actually not been established beyond doubt. In analysing the multitude of articles that quoted Lucas's original contribution, Ericsson and Irons (1992), for instance, found that only 43 articles investigated the validity of the Lucas Critique on an empirical basis, whereas the majority of quotations (more than 90%) were actually taken the Lucas Critique and its implications for granted.

8.2 Monetary Targeting (MT)

The Chicago economist Milton Friedman has become the epitome of *monetarism*. In his famous *Program for Monetary Stability* (1959), he dropped the proposal of a countercyclical monetary policy rule as put forward by the earlier *Chicago Plan* and opted in favor of a *constant money growth rule* (or *k-percent rule*) Specifically, Friedman (1959, 1962) proposed that instead of trying to smooth out the cycle, the central bank should just follow *a strict rule of expanding the money supply at a constant rate*. Such a rule had actually been earlier favoured by James W. Angell (1933, 1935) and Clark Warburton (1952).[3]

Friedman's policy proposal was derived from experience that discretionary countercyclical monetary policy would do more damage than good. He was inspired by his analysis of the *time lag* it takes for monetary policy to affect the economy. He found time lags to be quite *long* and *highly variable*. Especially in the field of monetary policy, time lags would create *serious policy problems*, according to Friedman. For instance, an expansionary monetary policy seeking to prevent a current recession would presumably impact the real economy at a later stage, perhaps when it is already on the way back to normal – when a monetary stimulus is no longer needed. In view of time lags, Friedman concluded that it would be less damaging to just stick to a constant money growth rule rather than take recourse to ad hoc changes in the money supply.

According to Friedman and Schwartz (1963) the US Fed had often been the source of economic instability. A central bank, they argued, is run by humans and humans are, unlike rules, subject to ineptitude and error. What is more, they are vulnerable to political influence – an argument echoing Simons (1936). Friedman (1959, 1962, 1984, 1985) argued that far too often central banks' discretionary power over the money supply can be swayed by politicians or public opinion, without regard for preserving sound money. For instance, central banks will often undertake expansionary monetary policy in order to provide a boost for the election efforts of their political masters – the inflation consequences of which will only be felt after they are safely in office.

8.2.1 Money Growth Targets

Friedman's concept for the constant money growth rule can be expressed in terms of the quantity theory. The equation of exchange is:

$$M \cdot V = Y \cdot P, \tag{8.18}$$

where M denotes the stock of money, V represents the income velocity of money, whereas Y and P stand for real output and the price level, respectively. Equation (8.18) simply states that the stock of money, multiplied by the number of times a

---

[3]The monetarism paradigm has later on also spread to Germany. Founded by the late Karl Brunner in 1970, the Konstanz Seminar celebrated its thirtieth anniversary in 1999. Brunner started the Seminar with two objectives, to close the gap in the quality of research and teaching of economics between the United States and Europe, Germany and Switzerland in particular, and to provide an alternative to the dominant Keynesian paradigm to European monetary policy makers. At its beginnings, the Konstanz Seminar was at the fringe of the economics profession; today it is part of the mainstream. Fratianni and von Hagen (2001) review the academic and policy accomplishments of the Konstanz Seminar.

money unit is used for financing purposes, equals real output multiplied with the price level.

To calculate a money supply which is consistent with the economy's inflation and output objectives, Eq. (8.18) can be transformed as follows:

$$\Delta m + \Delta v = \Delta y + \Delta p \qquad (8.19)$$

where small case letters represent logarithms and Δ represent first differences.[4] Solving equation (8.19) for Δm yields:

$$\Delta m = \Delta y + \Delta p - \Delta v. \qquad (8.20)$$

According to Eq. (8.20), money supply growth is driven by real income growth plus the envisaged rise in the price level, i.e. inflation, minus the trend change in the income velocity of the stock of money.

The ECB, for instance, used the formula presented above to derive its *reference value* for the growth of the stock of M3.[5] By assuming an average annual growth rate of output (or potential) of between 2.0 to 2.5%, an envisaged inflation rate of around 1.5% per year and an annual trend decline in the velocity of money of between 0.5 and 1.0%, the ECB's reference value of to $4\frac{1}{2}\%$ could be derived as:

$$\Delta m^{reference} = \Delta y^{potential} + \Delta p^{target} - \Delta v^{trend}$$
$$\approx 2.25\% + 1.5\% - (-0.75\%) \approx 4.5\%.^{6}$$

In view of the considerations outlined above it becomes clear that the demand for money – which is simply the reciprocal of the income velocity of money – plays a crucial role for money to have a reliable impact on (future) inflation. If, and only if, the demand for money proves to be (trend) stable, changes in the stock of money can be expected to have a predictable bearing on inflation.[7]

---

[4] The calculus-minded reader knows that $d (\ln X) d X = 1/X$ or $d (\ln X) = dX / X$, that is for infinitesimal small changes a change in $\ln X$ is equal to the relative or proportional change in X.

[5] For a detailed survey of German policy of monetary targeting at the times of the Bundesbank see, for instance, Neumann and von Hagen (1993). See also von Hagen (1999).

[6] To eliminate *noise*, the ECB compares actual M3 growth rates with the reference value on a 3-month moving average basis. Persistent deviations in M3 growth from the reference value shall, under normal circumstances, signal to the ECB risks to future price stability and, consequently, a need for policy action.

[7] "Extracting the stable long-run relationship (...) from shorter term developments in M3 is, in essence, the filtering of signals from noise. This analysis is demanding, since it requires both a strong command of economic theory and a detailed knowledge of the institutional environment", Issing (2001, p. 6).

Alternative Views on Money Supply Growth

In the literature, there are numerous proposal concepts determining optimal money supply, each of them deriving their support almost solely from the expositors of the theories on which they are based (Carilli, Dempster, & Rohan, 2004, p. 36).

To start with, Milton Friedman proposed a money supply rule based on the equation of exchange. In that sense, money supply growth should be determined by potential income growth, Δy^*, and an acceptable rise in the price level, Δp, whereas a long-term stability of the demand for money would suggest a trend change the velocity of money of zero ($\Delta v = 0$):

$$\Delta m = \Delta y^* + \Delta p. \tag{8.21}$$

Irving Fisher (1935) proposed a money supply rule that would change the money stock if and when the actual price level, p, would deviate from the target price level, p^T, so that:

$$\Delta m = p^T - p. \tag{8.22}$$

According to Eq. (8.22), the change in the money supply should be positive (negative) if $p^T > p$ ($p^T < p$). In that sense, Fisher's money growth rule actually represented a price level stabilisation rule.

Representatives of the Austrian School of Economics like, for instance, Friedrich August von Hayek (1975, p. 199) and Murray N. Rothbard (2000, pp. 59 and pp. 169–181) have proposed *alternative optimal money supply growth rules*. These proposals can be seen against the backdrop of concerns that a price level stabilization policy would hinder the adjustment of relative prices and would therefore do more harm than good.

Austrian economists would point out that some price level deflation should be expected if, for instance, real output growth is fuelled by rising productivity (Horwitz, 1996, p. 317). In one his contributions, Hayek (1935, p. 27) expressed the optimal monetary policy as one which would keep unchanged the *effective amount of money in circulation*. In other words, the appropriate monetary policy would be:

$$\Delta m = \Delta v, \tag{8.23}$$

which means that changes in the average price level resulting from changes in the demand for money should be stabilized. Hayek thus effectively combines policy elements of the Austrian School and variants of the quantity theory; one could term Hayek's proposal as a *combined view* (Selgin, 1990, 1997).[8]

Murray N. Rothbard (2000) argued that the optimal money supply growth rule would actually be zero money growth (in the shortrun). His money growth rule would be:

$$\Delta m = 0. \tag{8.24}$$

The quantity theory view takes a portfolio approach to explaining the demand for money, treating money as an alternative to the holding of wealth in other (financial or real) assets. However, according to Rothbard (2000), which is espoused by Salerno (1983) and Reisman (2000), money is not primarily a store of wealth, it is the means of exchange.

Money supply is just the flipside of the demand for goods, while the supply of goods equals the demand for money. For keeping the exchange between goods and money efficient, nothing would be won if the money stock increases. A rise in the money stock would, other things being equal, just reduce the exchange value of the money unit. "We come to the startling truth that it doesn't matter what the supply of money is. Any supply will do as well as any other supply" (Rothbard, 2000).

In fact, Rothbard, in line with most libertarian economists, argued fervently in favour of money being returned to the free market (Hoppe, 1994). Such a proposal rests on the idea that monopolising the money supply by the government would do more harm than good to economic welfare and societal freedom: "[D]etermining the supply of money, like all other goods, is best left to the free Typeet. Aside from the general moral and economic advantages of freedom over coercion, no dictated quantity of money will do the work better, and the free Typeet will set the production of gold in accordance with its relative ability to satisfy the needs of consumers, as compared with all other productive goods."

8.2.2 The Income Velocity of Money

The (trend) change in velocity can be derived from approximating the behaviour of the ratio between nominal output and the stock of money by various trend measures. Alternatively, the trend in the velocity of money can be estimated by using long-run money demand functions, which usually represent the demand for real money

---

[8]Support for the Hayek's position can, by the way, be found even among traditional monetarists – for example, Warburton (1951) submits that an exception to the price level stabilization rule might be made in the context of secular output growth (Horwitz, 1996, p. 297).

holdings as depending on variables such as, for instance, a transaction variable and various interest rates (Brand, Gerdesmeier & Roffia, 2002).

In this context, attention usually focuses on the long-run money demand relationship, which – together with the assumption of real trend growth – can be viewed as capturing the *long-run income velocity of money* which is actually relevant for determining money growth compatible with price stability. A simple money demand relationship (which shall be homogenous in terms of prices) can be represented by:

$$m - p = \beta_0 + \beta_y y + \gamma i + \varepsilon, \tag{8.25}$$

where m represents the logarithm of money, p is the logarithm of the price level, y is the logarithm of real GDP, i is the interest rate and ε is the (i.i.d) error term (*white noise*).

The change in the income velocity of money is:

$$\Delta v = \Delta y + \Delta p - \Delta m \text{ or,} \tag{8.26a}$$

equivalently, if we assume an environment of price stability (Δp dropping out of Eq. (8.26a)) and stationarity of real interest rates (i excluded from Eq.(8.25)) and $\varepsilon = 0$:

$$\Delta v = (1 - \beta_y)\Delta y, \tag{8.26b}$$

Equation (8.26b) shows that in this case the change in velocity would be solely driven by real output; neither interest rates nor inflation would have an impact on trend income velocity. Moreover, with $\beta_y > 1$, income velocity of money would show a *declining trend* over time.[9]

Assuming a stable money demand equation, monetary policy actors are able to calculate a steady-state money growth rate (or, to use the ECB's term: reference value) that is consistent with price stability and the assumed trend behaviour of real output. Using Eq. (8.26b) eq. in (8.26a), taking first differences and substituting inflation consistent with price stability and trend real output growth gives:

$$\Delta m_t^{t\,\arg et} = \pi^{envisaged} + \beta_y \Delta y_t^{potential}. \tag{8.27}$$

8.2.3 Inflation Indicators – Measures of Excess Liquidity

The aim of this section is to provide an overview of *various measures of excess liquidity*, which can be defined as the deviation of the actual stock of money from an

---

[9]The declining trend of income velocity can be explained by the *omitted wealth effect*. As market agents do not only demand real balances for financing actual output but also already existing wealth, nominal money growth might exceed nominal output growth. See Gerdesmeier (1996) for more details.

estimated equilibrium level. Given their dynamic nature, the excess liquidity measures under review are – in the light of long and variable lags of monetary policy – very *useful tools to quantify future price pressures*. In addition, excess liquidity measures consider inflation as a purely monetary phenomenon: neither the *output gap* nor the *liquidity gap* – although both form an integral part of the concepts – can be held responsible for inducing a persistent rise in the price level. Despite strong theoretical support, the usefulness of excess liquidity measures *depends on the stability of money demand*, a question which has of course to be answered in the realm of empirical research.

Among the very few central banks, the European Central Bank has explicitly assigned a prominent role to money in its two pillar strategy. The bank has set a reference value against which actual money expansion shall be measured. Continuing deviations of money growth from the reference value should raise questions and should, at the least, require a careful reassessment of whether the prevailing monetary policy is consistent with the ECB's definition of price stability. Against this background, the ECB has advocated some *excess liquidity measures*, which can be defined as the deviation of the actual stock of money from an estimated equilibrium level. Most prominent among them ranks the so-called *real money gap* (European Central Bank, 1999a, b, 2000). Meanwhile, various measures of excess liquidity have been put forward in the literature in recent years.[10] In the following, we highlight *four* of these concepts, namely (i) the price gap, or *P*-star concept, (ii) the real money gap, (iii) the nominal money gap and (iv) the money overhang. Finally, we provide a comparison between the various measures.

8.2.4 The Price Gap

Presumably the most prominent measure of excess liquidity stems from the work of Hallman, Porter and Small (1991).[11] To start with, the authors define a short- and a long-run price level as follows:

$$p_t = m_t + v_t - y_t \text{ and} \tag{8.28}$$

$$p_t^* = m_t + v_t^{trend} - y_t^{potential}, \tag{8.29}$$

where p_t^* represents the long-run or equilibrium price level. The difference between Eq. (8.29) and (8.28) is the so-called *price gap*:

$$p_t^* - p_t = (v_t^{trend} - v_t) + (y_t - y_t^{potential}). \tag{8.30}$$

---

[10]See, European Central Bank (2004), p. 45. To our knowledge, the ECB introduced the real money gap in its June 2001 Bulletin, p. 8. For the results of the latest strategy revision see ECB (2003).

[11]See Hallman, Porter, and Small (1991) for more details. At roughly the same time, for price level stability purposes, Irving Fisher (1935) proposed an automatic variation in the stock of money to correct deviations from target.

If the actual price level is below (above) the long-term level, upwards (down-ward) pressure on the (future) price level can be expected, as p_t would be expected to converge towards p_t^*.

According to Eq. (8.30), the price gap is a function of the *liquidity gap* ($v_t^{trend} - v_t$) and the *output gap* ($y_t - y_t^{potential}$).[12] However, when analysing the forces driving inflation in this concept it is important to note that an increase in real output above potential will *not* cause a change of the price gap as Eq. (8.30) would suggest at first glance. This is because v (remember that $v = y + p - m$) will rise as y increases and vice versa. A positive (negative) output gap is compensated by a negative (positive) liquidity gap.

Reformulating Eq. (8.28) as $-v_t = m_t - p_t - y_t$ and inserting this expression into Eq. (8.30) shows that the *price gap* is the difference between real money adjusted for the trend velocity and real potential output:

$$(p_t^* - p_t) = (m_t + v_t^{trend} - p_t) - y_t^{potential}. \tag{8.31}$$

That said, inflation – defined as a persistent rise in the price level over time – can only occur when *too much money is chasing too few goods* or, to put it differently, money is always and everywhere a monetary phenomenon in this concept.

An empirically testable *inflation forecasting* model using the price gap as infla-tion indicator could then look as follows (Belke & Polleit, 2006):

$$\pi_{t+1} = \beta_0 + \beta_1(p_t^* - p_t) + \sum_{i=1}^{n} \beta_i \pi_{t-i} + N_t + \varepsilon_t \tag{8.32}$$

where π_{t+1} is future inflation.[13] If the actual price level is *lower* (higher) than the equilibrium price level, future inflation will *increase* (fall) to close the *gap*. As a result, one would expect the parameter β_1 to be positive. Given the *stickiness* of inflation, one may also take into account past inflation as shown by $\sum_{i=1}^{n} \beta_i \pi_{t-i}$. N_t represents a vector of non-monetary *cost push* variables (oil, wages, exchange rate, unemployment etc.). In econometric studies using German data, the *P*-star model has proven to be quite successful (Tödter & Reimers, 1994; Clostermann & Seitz, 1999) – but only if M3 instead of, say, M1 was used as the monetary aggregate under review. Moreover, this has also been the case for studies with a focus on the euro area (Nicoletti-Altimari, 2001).

---

[12]For an extension of the model for small and open economies (especially in view of fixed exchange rates) see Clemens and Tatom (1994).

[13]For calculating the price gap, one may approximate v^{**} and y^* applying the Hodrick-Prescott-Filter (HP-Filter), which has become a standard procedure in many applied econometric work (Orr, Edey & Kennedy, 1995; Martins & Scarpetta, 1999), to v and y.

8.2.4.1 A Constant Money Growth Rate and the Role of Money Growth Seen in the Past

It can again be shown that a comparison between the *actual* stock of money growth rate and a *constant* money growth, or reference, rate might give *misleading policy signals* since monetary expansion, which occurred in the past, will have a bearing on future prices might be systematically neglected. To show this, let us assume the stock of money at the end of period t, is m_t. The constant, or reference, growth rate r (which is the rate compatible with price stability) gives a *reference stock of money* at the end of period $t + 1$:[14]

$$m_t + r = m_{t+1}^{reference}. \tag{8.33}$$

The actual growth rate of money is a_1, so that the actual stock of money at the end of period $t + 1$ is:

$$m_t + a_1 = m_{t+1}^A. \tag{8.34}$$

The difference between m_{t+1}^A and $m_{t+1}^{reference}$ is:

$$m_{t+1}^A - m_{t+1}^{reference} = a_1 - r. \tag{8.35}$$

In period $t + 1$, a simple comparison between the actual and reference growth rate says that if $a_1 > r$ ($a_1 < r$), upward (downward) pressure on the future price level can be expected; in the case of $a_1 = r$, inflation pressure would be zero.

Now, let us look what happens in the *next period*. If the growth rate r is now applied to the *actual* stock of money *at the end of $t + 1$* rather than to the equilibrium stock of money – which is implied under a constant reference growth rate concept –, the reference stock of money at the end of period $t + 2$ would be:

$$m_{t+1}^A + r = m_{t+2}^{reference}, \tag{8.36}$$

whereas the *actual* stock of money at the end of period $t + 2$ is determined by the actual growth rate in that period, a_2:

$$m_{t+1}^A + a_2 = m_{t+2}^A. \tag{8.37}$$

The difference between m_{t+2}^A and $m_{t+2}^{reference}$ is:

$$(m_{t+1}^A + a_2) - (m_{t+1}^{reference} + r) \text{ or} \tag{8.38a}$$

$$(a_1 - r) + (a_2 - r). \tag{8.38b}$$

---

[14]Here $a = \ln(1 + A)$ and $r = \ln(1 + R)$, where A and R represent the growth rates in percentage points divided by 100.

In period $t + 2$, a simple comparison between the actual growth rate (a_2) and the target growth rate (r) of the stock of money does not necessarily provide a proper yardstick as far as detecting inflation pressure is concerned. The finding of, say $a_2 = r$, in period $t + 2$ cannot say that excess liquidity is *absent*. For instance, if actual money growth in $t + 1$ was $a_1 > r$, upward pressure on the (future) price level can be expected, even if $a_2 = r$. In fact, only *under the condition that the price gap is zero* can a comparison between the actual and a constant money growth rate provide adequate insights into future inflation.

This can be shown by taking a look at the equilibrium price level, which is:

$$p_t^{target} = m_t^{target} + v_t^{trend} - y_t^{potential}, \tag{8.39}$$

where m_t^{target} is the envisaged money supply as determined by the constant money supply growth concept. The deviation between the target price level and the actual price level is:

$$\begin{aligned} p_t^{target} - p_t &= m_t^{target} + v_t^{trend} - y_t^{potential} - (m_t + v_t - y_t) \\ &= (m_t^{target} - m_t) + (p_t^* - p_t) \end{aligned} \tag{8.40}$$

Inflation pressure is determined by (i) the deviation of the target money stock from the actual stock of money in period t plus (ii) the price gap. So only if the price gap is zero, it makes sense to base monetary policy decisions on signals provided by deviations of actual money growth from a constant reference value.

8.2.4.2 The Price Gap and Money Demand

Alternatively, the equilibrium price level can also be defined as the price level that would emerge (given the current holdings of money) if both the goods and money Typeet were in equilibrium:

$$p_t^* = m_t - \beta_y y_t^{potential} + \gamma i_t^*, \tag{8.41}$$

where i_t^* is the equilibrium interest rate. Accordingly, the short-term price level would be:

$$p_t = m_t - \beta_y y_t + \gamma i_t. \tag{8.42}$$

Subtracting (8.42) from (8.41) yields the price gap:

$$p_t^* - p_t = \beta_y \left(y_t - y_t^{potential} \right) + \gamma (i_t^* - i_t). \tag{8.43}$$

In this representation, the price gap is a function of the output gap ($y_t - y_t^{potential}$) and the interest rate gap ($i_t^* - i_t$).

Like in Eq. (8.30), a positive price gap can only arise through an increase in the money stock. For instance, a rise in m_t, which is not accompanied by a rise in y_t, would lower the interest rate i_t to below i_t^*, so that $p_t^* - p_t > 0$. If a rise in m_t raises y_t above $y_t^{potential}$, while i_t remains unchanged, the price gap would become positive, indicating inflation pressure.

8.2.5 The Real Money Gap

More recently, an alternative version of the price gap concept, namely the *real money gap* has been proposed (Gerlach & Svensson, 2003). In this context, actual real money is defined as the actual nominal money supply less the actual price level:

$$m_{real,t} = m_t - p_t, \tag{8.44}$$

whereas the equilibrium real money holding can be modelled as follows:

$$m_{real,t}^* = m_t - p_t^*. \tag{8.45}$$

The difference between Eq. (8.45) and (8.44) can be referred to as the *real money gap*. It thus follows:

$$m_{real,t}^* - m_{real,t} = (m_t - p_t^*) - (m_t - p_t) = -p_t^* + p_t. \tag{8.46}$$

Against this background, it is easy to see that the real money gap and the price gap represent the same concept, but simply express it using different variables and with the *sign reversed*:

$$p_t^* - p_t = -(p_t - p_t^*). \tag{8.47}$$

8.2.6 The Nominal Money Gap

The nominal money gap is defined as the difference between the actual stock of money, m_t, from the level implied by the normative money stock, that is the stock of money that would have built up had money expanded in line with an envisaged growth path (Masuch, Pill, & Willeke, 2001). Using a (somewhat arbitrary) base period ($t = 0$), the money gap is:

$$m_t - m_t^{target} = m_t - \left(m_0 + t\left(\pi^* + \beta_y \Delta y_t^{potential} \right) \right), \tag{8.48}$$

with $m_t^{target} = m_0 + t \cdot \Delta m_t^{target}$ with $m_0 = y_0 + p_0 - v_0$. The equation can thus be re-written as:

$$m_t - m_t^{target} = y_t + p_t - v_t - \left(y_0 + p_0 - v_t^* + t\left(\pi^* + \beta_y \Delta y_t^{potential} \right) \right) \text{ or,} \tag{8.49}$$

equivalently,

$$m_t - m_t^{target} = (p_t + \hat{p}_t) + (p_t^* - p_t),\qquad(8.50)$$

where $\hat{p}_t = p_0 + \sum_{t=1}^{n} \pi_t^*$. The nominal money gap is thus made up of the *price target gap* $(p_t + \hat{p}_t)$ and the price gap $(p_t^* - p_t)$. That said, the nominal money gap contains price rises which have already been realised in the past. It thus reflects the cumulative deviations of actual inflation and output in the past from their envisaged (trend/equilibrium) values.

8.2.7 The Monetary Overhang

The *monetary overhang* (or, if negative, the *monetary shortfall*) is defined as the difference between the actual nominal stock of money and the equilibrium stock of money calculated on the basis of actual values of y and i (Tödter, 2002). Using the parameters of the long-run money demand equation, the monetary overhang is:

$$m_t - m_t^{equilibrium} = m_t - (\beta_0 + p_t + \beta_y y_t + \gamma i_t + \varepsilon_t).\qquad(8.51)$$

Under certain assumptions, the monetary overhang is de facto an indicator of disequilibria in the money Typeet rather than an inflation indicator:[15] If the money demand function implies a stable cointegration relationship, the monetary overhang is a stationary variable (i.e. an error correction term) which should contain information on the future development of the money stock. Dynamic processes of adjustment would ensure that, following a shock, the money holdings adjust to the path defined by the long-run money demand.

8.2.8 Comparisons of the Measures of Excess Liquidity

Figure 8.1(a) shows annual M3 growth for the period January 1999 to May 2008. In addition the graph also shows the growth rates of *M3 corrected for portfolio shifts*.[16] As a result of money expansion rates above the ECB's $4\frac{1}{2}\%$ reference value, excess liquidity, as measured by the real money gap, has increased over time (Fig. 8.1(b)). The real money gap stood at around 16% in May 2008, with the real money gap calculated on the basis of M3 corrected for portfolio shifts was close to 12.5%. In what follows, a closer look shall be taken at the information content of the alternative measures of excess liquidity.

---

[15]This result, however, crucially hinges on the question whether the long-run relationship is found to be weakly exogenous with respect to real income and interest rates.

[16]In view of extraordinary portfolio shifts, the ECB constructed a monetary aggregate called "M3 corrected" (ECB, 2004, p. 43.). It basically represents the monthly M3 series excluding the net purchases of non-monetary securities by the money-holding sector from MFIs and nonresidents.

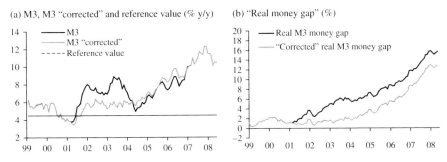

Fig. 8.1 Money and excess liquidity in the euro area
Source: Thomson Financial, ECB, own calculations. – The *real money gap* is defined as the difference between the actual level of M3 deflated by the HICP and the deflated level of M3 that would have resulted from constant nominal M3 growth at its reference value of $4\frac{1}{2}\%$ and HICP inflation in line with the ECB's definition of price stability, taking December 1998 as the base period.

8.2.9 The Difference Between the Nominal Money Gap and the Monetary Overhang

In line with the considerations outlined above, the difference between the money gap and the monetary overhang (or monetary shortfall) can be modelled as follows:[17]

$$\left(m_t - m_t^{target}\right) - \left(m_t - m_t^{equilibrium}\right) = m_t^{equilibrium} - m_t^{target}$$

$$= \left(k\prime + p_t + \beta_y y_t + \gamma i_t\right) - \left(m_0 + t\left(\pi^* + \beta_y \Delta y_t^{potential}\right)\right) \text{ or, equivalently,}$$

$$= (k\prime - m_0) + (p_t - (p_0 + t\pi^*)) + \beta_y \left(y_t - \left(y_0 + t\Delta y_t^{potential}\right)\right) + \gamma(i_t - i_0) \tag{8.15}$$

Following this expression, the difference between the money gap $(m_t - m_t^{target})$ and the monetary overhang is related to four determinants: (i) the extent to which the money stock in the chosen base period (k') differs from a level consistent with long-run money demand at the macroeconomic variables obtained in the base period $(k' - m_0)$; (ii) the difference between the actual price level and its equivalent extrapolated from the base period on the basis of the inflation objective $(p_t - (p_0 + t\pi^*))$; (iii) a term related to the cumulated output gap since the base period $\beta_y(y_t - (y_0 + t\Delta y_t^{potential}))$; and (iv) a term related to the difference in the level of nominal interest rates prevailing in the current and the base period $\gamma(i_t - i_0)$.

If the base period is chosen appropriately, the first component of this difference will be zero. If nominal interest rates are broadly speaking unchanged (as one might expect over a period of several years in an environment of price stability), then the last component will also be zero. Therefore, there are two main substantive differences between the money gap and the monetary overhang as defined above:

---

[17] For the following, see Masuch, Pill, and Willeke (2001).

First, the nominal money gap implicitly includes the cumulated impact on the money stock of deviations of the actual price level from a price level path which is determined ex ante (e.g. a price level objective determined by the base period and the desired inflation rate). In contrast, the monetary overhang automatically accepts "base drift" in the price level. In other words, at a conceptual level the money gap is an indicator more consistent with price level objectives, whereas the monetary overhang as defined above is more consistent with an inflation objective (and allows the price level to behave as a random walk, accepting one-off shifts in the price level on the principle that *bygones are bygones*).

Second, the money gap increases relative to the monetary overhang in proportion to the output gap. In other words, the money gap incorporates the impact on the money stock of cumulated deviations of actual output from potential. Thus, if real growth since the base period is higher than potential growth, the money gap is larger than the overhang. In this sense, the money gap is a form of summary statistic, whereas the overhang merely reflects the additional information in money which is not included in its determinants (GDP and interest rates). A similar comparison can be made between the money gap and the real money gap.

8.2.10 The Difference Between the Nominal Money Gap and the Real Money Gap

Following again the basic considerations outlined in the last sections, the difference between the money gap and the real money gap as outlined above is:

$$
\begin{aligned}
&(m_t - m_t^{target}) - (m_t - m_t^*) \\
&= (k' + p_t + \beta_y y_t^{potential} + \gamma i_t) - \left(m_0 + t \left(\pi^* + \beta_y \Delta y_t^{potential} \right) \right) \\
&= (k' - m_0) + (p_t - (p_0 + t\pi^*)) + \gamma (i_t - i_0).
\end{aligned} \tag{8.53}
$$

The real money gap (as can be derived out of the P-star approach) represents an intermediate approach, where the impact of the output gap – that is the cumulated deviations of actual output growth from potential – on the money stock is included in the measure of excess liquidity (in this respect the real money gap is similar to the nominal money gap). At the same time, however, the impact of cumulated deviations of the actual price level from an implicit price level objective on the money stock is excluded (in this respect the real money gap is similar to the overhang concept). In assessing which of the measures of excess liquidity is most useful for monetary policy purposes, a number of considerations have to be borne in mind.

First, at a conceptual level, the importance of price level objectives, as opposed to inflation objectives, needs to be considered. If price level objectives are deemed important, a money gap measure may be more appropriate since this measure incorporates the impact on the money stock of deviations of such an objective. *Second*, consideration should be given to whether money should be used, at least in part, as a summary statistic of developments in the determinants of money or whether the focus of attention should be on the information in monetary developments which is not provided by alternative indicators which are included in the money demand framework.

In the former case, focusing on estimates of the money gap or real money gap (the *P*-star approach) may be more useful, since, for example, these measures encompass developments in the output gap. Alternatively, if analysing the additional information in monetary developments is deemed more useful, a focus on the monetary overhang/shortfall may be more appropriate since this does not incorporate the effects of the output gap or deviations of the price level from a desired level on the stock of money and measure of excess liquidity. Obviously, the weight assigned to the gap measure relative to the overhang measure may thus also depend on the uncertainty regarding the estimates of the output gap in real time.

Effectiveness and Costs of the Inflation Indicator Under Alternative Policy Rules

If we measure forthcoming inflation pressure on the basis of the price gap, monetary policy can take recourse to a *constant, proportional, derivative* or *integral* monetary policy rule when it comes to responding to deviations of actual from target inflation (Humphrey, 1992).

Under a *constant money supply growth rule*, the central bank would simple set the money stock and leave it there. A *proportional policy rule* would change the money stock in proportion to current price deviations from the target. In Fig. 8.2, such a policy would correspond to reducing the price level in the amount of $a - t_1$.

A *derivative policy* would decrease the money stock in proportion to the change in the price gap, which is indicated by the slope of the tangent to the curve at point a. An *integral policy* would decrease the money stock in proportion to the cumulative value of the price gap over time, which would be indicated by the area under the curve.

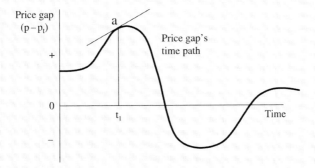

Fig. 8.2 Price gap and the proportional, derivative, and integral policy rule
Source: Humphrey (1992).

The analyses of the effectiveness and costs of the three policy rules under review will be based on Fisher's transaction equation. It can be formulated as: $\dot{p} = \alpha(m - kqp)$, where $\dot{p}$ represents changes in prices to excess money supply, where the latter is the product of k, the Cambridge cash holding coefficient, q, which is output, and p, which is the price level. The parameter α shows the responsiveness of prices adjusting to excess money.[18]

Policy Rules

Under a *constant money rule*, the central bank sets the money stock at the level: $m_T = kqp_T$, which makes the money supply equal money demand at the target price level p_T. Accordingly, the money stock rule is: $m_c = m_T$, where m_c is the constant money supply policy.

Under a *proportional feedback rule*, the central bank increases (decreases) the envisaged stock of money m_T as the price level is below (above) its target. The policy rule is: $m_p = m_T - \beta(p - p_T)$, where m_p is the proportional policy rule. The coefficient β is the proportional correction coefficient.

Under the *derivative feedback rule*, the central bank would adjust the money supply in response to the speed with which the price gap, $p - p_T$, changes. In other words: The central bank changes the money stock to prevent increases or decreases in the price level $\dot{p}$ (note that p_T is fixed). The policy response function is therefore: $m_d = m_T - \gamma\dot{p}$, where m_d is the derivative policy and γ is the derivate correction coefficient.

Under the *integral feedback rule,* the central bank changes the money stock to correct cumulative price gaps, that is the sum of all past policy target deviations made in the past. In other words: The monetary policy uses the information given by their integral to determine the current setting of the money stock. Accordingly, the policy equation is: $m_i = m_T - \delta \int_0^\infty (p - p_T)dt$. Here, m_i is the integral policy rule, $\int_0^\infty (\quad)dt$ is the integral operator, and δ denotes the integral correction operator. If we differentiate the integral policy rule, it can be written as: $\dot{m} = -\delta(p - p_T)$, which says that monetary policy sets the money stock change opposite to changes in prices currently deviating from target.

---

[18] Let the model's time unit be a calendar quarter. Define $T = 1/\alpha$ as the number of quarters required for prices to adjust to clear the Typeet for money balances. Then Fisher's 1920 finding that prices follow money with a lag of close to three months implies that both α and T are approximately equal to unity in magnitude.

Central Bank Loss Function

In what follows, it is assumed that monetary policy tries to keep prices as close to target as possible. Any failure to do so causes societal losses. These societal losses shall be measured by a quadratic cost function, showing the loss L as the cumulative squared deviation of prices from their desired target level:

$$L = \int_0^\infty (p - p_T)^2 dt.$$

Effectiveness of Activist Policy Rules and Its Costs

In a first step, we will substitute the *constant money supply rule* in the price equation $\dot{p} = \alpha(m - kqp)$, so that we yield: $\dot{p} = \alpha kq(p_T - p)$. Solving this first order equation for the time path of prices gives: $p = p_T + (p_0 - p_T)e^{-at}$, where p_0 is the price level in $t = 0$, e is the base of the natural logarithm and $\alpha = aky$ is the speed of convergence to target. As t grows large the system converges to p_T, and the system would end when p has reached p_T. If we insert the price path of the constant money supply in the loss function and integrating yields: $L_c = (p_0 - p_T)^2/2a$. For evaluating purposes assume that $p_T = 1$, $p_0 = 2$, $\alpha = 1$, $k = \frac{1}{2}$, $y = 100$ and $a = 50$. The loss of the constant money supply rule would then amount to $L_c = 1/100$.

The *proportional money supply rule* yields the price path $p = p_T + (p_0 - p_T)e^{-bt}$, and the loss is $L_c = (p_0 - p_T)^2/2b$, where $b = \alpha(kq + \beta)$ represents the speed of convergence parameter. Since $b > a$, prices under the proportional rule converge faster – and therefore deviate for shorter period of time from the target – than under a constant money supply rule. Numerically, the loss of the proportional money supply rule would be $L_p = 1/102$, comparing favourably with the constant money supply rule.

The *derivative money supply rule* would require changes in the money stock opposite to the direction prices are moving. In that sense, it would exert a stabilizing effect when prices are moving away from target. However, a problem would occur when prices move toward target: When prices fall toward target, the derivative rule interferes perversely by expanding the money stock. In so doing, it hampers convergence and becomes an unattractive policy rule. The derivative rule yields the price path: $p = p_T + (p_0 - p_T)e^{-ct}$. The loss function is: $L_d = (p_0 - p_T)^2/2c$, whereas the speed parameter is $c = \alpha ky/(1 + \alpha y)$. With c being smaller than a and b, convergence is slower, target deviations longer and higher losses, which amount to $L_d = 1/50$ under the assumption that γ takes on the value of 1.

Now let us turn to the *integral money supply rule*. It follows the time path: $p = p_T + A_1 e^{r_1 t} + A_2 e^{r_2 t}$, whereas A_1 and A_2 are the constants of integration determined by initial conditions; and $r_1, r_2 = (-\alpha k y/2) \pm \sqrt{(\alpha k y)^2 - 4\alpha\delta}/2$ are the characteristic roots of the left-hand side (or homogenous part) of the second order expression $\ddot{p} + (\alpha k y)\dot{p} + \alpha\delta p = \alpha\delta p_T$, which was derived from differentiating the policy reaction function to eliminate the integral and substituting the result into price change equation. Dampened oscillations about target result if $(\alpha k y)^2 < 4\alpha\delta$ or if $\delta > \alpha k^2 y^2/4$. Monotonic convergence results for small values of the integral correction factor δ. In any case, convergence is slower under the integral rule than under the proportional and constant money supply rules, as the above mentioned characteristic roots would reveal. The loss function shows a large reputation loss associated with the integral rule:

$$L_i = -\left[A_1^2/2r_1\right] - [2A_1 A_2/(r_1 + r_2)] - \left[A_2^2/2r_2\right]$$

where $A_1 = [\dot{p}_0 - r_2(p_0 - p_T)]/(r_1 - r_2)$ and $A_2 = [r_1(p_0 - p_T) - \dot{p}_0]/(r_1 - r_2)$. Of course, this result is difficult to evaluate analytically. However, using numerical calculations, and assuming $\dot{p}_0 = -1$, the loss is 26, much higher than the losses under the alternative rules.

Summary

Of the constant money growth rule and the three activist feedback rules analysed, only the proportional rule – which actually represents a policy based on the price gap or, equivalently, a deviation of projected from actual inflation – outperforms Friedman's non-activist *constant money growth rule*; in fact, proportional policy's loss is the smallest. The proportional feedback rule also dominates the derivative and integral rules. That said, a policy based on a price gap measure seems – under the given assumptions of the model used – indeed appropriate for pursuing price stability with as little costs as possible.

Source: Humphrey (1992).

Monetary Policy of the People's Bank of China

In December 1993, the State Council of the People's Republic of China established that the goals of monetary policy were to maintain the stability of the value of the currency, promoting economic growth (Geiger, 2008, p. 3). In that sense, the monetary policy of People's Bank of China (PBC) considers low inflation as being conducive to growth and employment.

In 1994, the PBC announced three monetary aggregates, M0, M1 and M2, which were in 1996 given an intermediate target status, and under the Ninth Five-Year Plan, control target ranges were announced (Laurens & Maino, 2007) (Table 8.2). The money growth targets are published in the annual monetary policy report for the subsequent year. In that sense, the PBC appears to formally pursue a money-oriented intermediate targeting. Figure 8.3(a) shows the annual growth rates of the Chinese monetary aggregates, while Fig. 8.3(b) depicts various bank lending aggregates.

Table 8.2 PBC monetary aggregates, targets and actual outcomes

	M1, % y/y		M2, % y/y	
	Target	Actual outcome	Target	Actual outcome
1994	21	26.2	24	34.5
1995	21–23	16.8	23–25	29.5
1996	18	18.9	25	25.3
1997	18	16.5	23	17.3
1998	17	11.9	16–18	15.3
1999	14	17.7	14–15	14.7
2000	15–17	16	14–15	12.3
2001	13–14	12.7	15–16	14.4
2002	13	16.8	13	16.8
2003	16	18.7	15	19.6
2004	17	13.6	17	14.6
2005	15	11.8	15	17.6
2006	14	17.5	14	16.9

Source: Geiger (2008, p. 21).

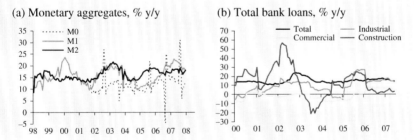

(a) Monetary aggregates, % y/y   (b) Total bank loans, % y/y

Fig. 8.3 Bank loans and money supply
Source: Bloomberg, own calculations. – M0: currency in circulation. – M1: currency outside the banks and demand deposits other than those of the central government. – M2: M1 plus time, savings, and foreign currency deposits of resident sectors other than central government

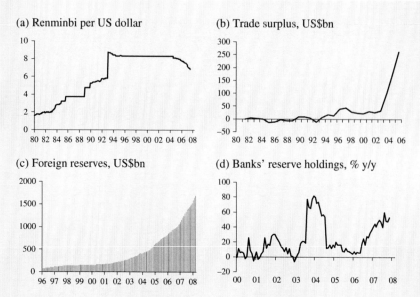

Fig. 8.4 Exchange rate and stock markets
Source: Bloomberg, own calculations.

Between 1997 and 2005, China had a de facto *exchange rate peg* vis-a-vis
the US dollar, while the exchange rate was allowed to fluctuate within a certain
bandwidth. On 21 July 2005, the peg against the US dollar was replaced by a
managed floating exchange rate system based on Typeet supply and demand
with a reference to a basket of currencies (the four main currencies in the
basket are the US dollar, the euro, the Japanese yen and the Korean won).
Since then, the Renminbi (RMB) appreciated from RMB8.11 per US dollar to
RMB6.85 per US dollar in June 2008 (Fig. 8.4).

In recent years, China's exchange system has become more open. An
important step in China's path of liberalization was the ac ceptance of Article
VIII of the IMF's Articles of Agreement in 1996 (*current account convertibility*). Nonetheless, China retains an extensive system of controls, involving
discretionary control of capital flows and approval and verification of both current and capital account transactions. That said, substantial controls remain in
place; so far, renminbi is not yet a fully convertible currency.

China's *trade surplus* rose strongly in recent years, standing at US$262.1bn
at the end of 2007 (Fig. 8.4(b)). Reflecting ongoing capital account surpluses,
China's foreign reserves stood at US$1.68trn in March 2008 (Fig. 8.4(c)): The
PBC had to buy foreign currencies against issuing domestic base money for
keeping the exchange rate at the desired level. To prevent an overly expansionary domestic monetary policy as a result of FX market interventionism,

the PBC runs *sterilizing operations* in the inter-bank money markets. Increasing minimum reserve requirements is one of the instruments used for reducing inter-bank liquidity (Fig. 8.4(d)).

The PBC applies a number of monetary policy instruments: (i) minimum reserve requirements for (actively) influencing the banking sector's liquidity situation; (ii) central bank lending rates, for determining banks' refinancing costs, and (iii) open market operations (for various maturities) for steering money market conditions. In addition, the PBC has at its disposal the (non-market based) instruments of *window guidance* (since 1998) and direct lending for influencing the allocation of credit supply.

On 4 January 2007, the Shanghai Inter-bank Offered Rate (Shibor) formally launched, in an attempt to build a money market interest rate system (PBC, 2008, p. 22) (Fig. 8.5(a)). Via influencing inter-bank refinancing conditions, the PBC can influence the borrowing rates banks charge to their customers (Fig. 8.5(b)). In that sense, the PBC has implemented a monetary policy concept which bears quite some similarities to those in operation in many Western industrialised countries.

(a) Shibor interest rates (%)   (b) Lending interest rates (%)

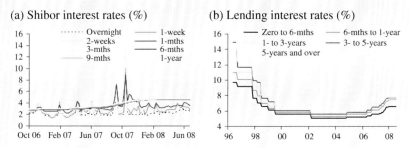

Fig. 8.5 Exchange rate and stock markets
Source: Bloomberg, Thomson Financial, own calculations.

(a) CPI, % y/y   (b) Chinese and world stock markets

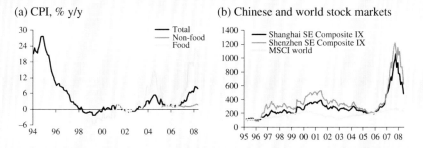

Fig. 8.6 Exchange rate and stock markets
Source: Bloomberg, Thomson Financial, own calculations.

While annual consumer price inflation declined substantially from the first half of the 1990s, it started rising from around 2003 (Fig. 8.6(a)), at the time when China's trade surpluses built up strongly, and stood at 7.7% in May 2008. What is more, Chinese stock markets rose rather strongly from the middle of the 1990s to late 2007 when compared to world stock markets (Fig. 8.6(b)), presumably strongly driven by capital inflows and euphoria about China's economic perspectives in an increasingly globalised world economy.

8.3 Inflation Targeting (IT)

(...) most advocates of inflation targeting – at least those referring to simple rules for monetary policy decisions – ultimately rely on a view of the economy whose essence can be captured by no more than three equations. The defining characteristics of these equations are: (i) staggered pricing, (ii) the centrality of the output gap (or Phillips curve), and (iii) the notion that monetary impulses propagate primarily via a price (interest rate) channel, with monetary quantities playing no role.

Issing, O. (2004, p. 173).

Many central banks, for instance, the Reserve Bank of New Zealand, Bank of England, the Swedish Riksbank, the Bank of Norway and the Reserve Bank of Australia, pursue an *inflation targeting* (IT). New Zealand first instituted this monetary policy framework in early 1990. Since that time, 22 countries have formally adopted inflation targeting. After being forced to withdraw from the European Exchange Rate Mechanism (ERM) in November 1992, for instance, the Swedish Riksbank's Governing Board decided in January 1993 to adopt the strategy of IT as from 1995 on.[19]

Meanwhile, there is a vast amount of literature on IT. Different authors have proposed different, and in some cases conflicting, definitions. Although the practice of IT is anything but uniform across countries, a number of elements are common to central banks' IT policies (Bernanke et al., 1999; Dotsey, 2006; Neumann & von Hagen, 2002). These include:

– An emphasis on *long-run price stability* as the principal goal of monetary policy. Under IT, policy objectives (such as, for instance, high growth and full employment) can be pursued only to the extent that they are compatible with the inflation target.

---

[19]See Heikensten and Vredin (2002, p. 8). For a detailed discussion of how IT was put into practise in Sweden, see Svensson (1999, 2003). More generally on IT, see also Baltensperger (2000), Bernanke (2003), Bernanke, Laubach, Mishkin, & Posen (1999), Neumann and von Hagen (2002, p. 127ff) and Kuttner (2004).

– An explicit *numerical target* for inflation and a *timetable* for reaching that target. Most inflation targets are in the neighborhood of 2 percent p.a., and most of them shall achieve the inflation target at a horizon of no more than two years.
– A high degree of *transparency* with regard to monetary policy formulation. Many central banks that pursue IT publish a detailed report on general economic conditions and the outlook for inflation to inform the public at large about the central bank's thinking.
– In terms of *accountability*, central banks' published inflation reports under IT provide a means for ex post evaluation of inflation performance. Failure to fulfil the inflation target may require the central bank to take specific steps. For example, should inflation deviate by more than 1 percentage point from its 2.5% target, the Governor of the Bank of England is obliged to submit an open letter to the Chancellor of the Exchequer explaining the reason for the deviation and presenting a timetable for a return to the target.

Against this backdrop, one could argue that all central banks that wish to keep inflation low would follow IT. In fact, IT can be understood as a *broadly* defined monetary policy strategy, *subsuming* inflation fighting monetary policy concepts. In that sense, MT could be interpreted as a specific form of IT. Here, monetary policy would take action according to the signal provided by money expansion to achieve its objective of keeping inflation low. In other words: IT and MT are not mutually exclusive strategies.

Proponents of a forward-looking IT would argue that inflation forecasts should serve as the *intermediate variable* of monetary policy. By doing so, IT would actually become an *inflation forecast targeting* (Svensson, 1997; Woodford, 2007). That said, whenever the (conditional) inflation forecast would exceed (fall below) target inflation, the central bank would switch to a more restrictive (expansionary) monetary policy to avoid deviations of future inflation from the central bank's pre-announced target inflation. Whereas under MT *money expansion* (or the concept of the *price gap*) would be the intermediate target of monetary policy, the intermediate target of IT would be the central bank's *self-made inflation forecast*.

While most central banks that pursue an IT publish inflation forecasts on a regular basis, *little is known about the structure of the inflation forecast models* used. Typically, central banks under IT remain actually silent about the specific structure of the forecasting model. They don't tell which variables enter the forecasting system, what weight is assigned to the variables under review, whether (and if so, how) these variables are interrelated, whether or not the structure of the model is changed over time, etc. Given that the inflation forecast plays such an important role, IT – in more or less sharp contrast to MT – can be characterised as a monetary policy with a strong discretionary bias – which creeps into monetary policy through the inflation forecasts.

Inflation Targeting in Practise

At the level of implementation of IT, central banks differ with respect to choice of the price index. Some would focus on *headline CPI inflation*, while other would focus on measures of *core CPI inflation*. There might also be differences as far as pre-announcing a *point inflation target* (of, say, 2% p.a.) or a range *inflation target* (of, say, between 0 and 3% p.a.).

Under IT, most central banks publish an *inflation report* on a regular (quarterly or semi-annual) basis. Such a report tends to outline central banks' views on developments which are expected to influence the currency area's inflation outlook. It typically also includes various assumptions about economic developments in other major economies. In that sense, the inflation report is typically an *important communication tool* of monetary policy under IT (Fracasso, Genberg, & Wyplosz, 2003).

To most proponents of IT, *communication* is an important means to create transparency and accountability of monetary policy, thereby establishing its *credibility*. One hypothesis is that transparency allows the central bank to overcome the time consistency problem. King (1997) has argued that transparency, accountability, and a clearly defined objective all would enhance central bank credibility, defined as the ability to convince the private sector that it will carry out policies that may be time inconsistent, and thus implement the optimal state-contingent rule.

One may also distinguish between *full-fledged IT* and *near-IT*. For example, some central banks – particularly those of emerging market or post-communist countries – have set up most of the mechanics of IT, but may lack the institutional means to make a long-run commitment to price stability (such as, for instance, *full* political independence). According to Carare and Stone (2003) and Stone (2003), these policies can be characterised as *IT light*.

There are central banks which seem to have implicitly adopted some aspects of IT, without officially pursuing such a strategy. For instance, the US Fed, traditionally operating under a dual mandate, has made inflation fighting an increasingly important objective of its policy. At the same time, however, the Fed still lacks an explicit numerical definition of price stability (or an inflation target), and its monetary policy formulation can be said to have remained more opaque compared with central banks pursuing IT (Kuttner & Posen, 2001).

For instance, the Swiss National Bank (SNB) publishes an inflation forecast on a quarterly basis, which serves as an important guidepost of monetary policy making. In that sense, the SNB concept has moved closer to an IT. The ECB, in contrast, publishes its staff inflation projections – which are not classified as *inflation forecasts*. In fact, the ECB has taken great efforts in distinguishing itself from the impression it has adopted IT – for instance, by stressing that it has a *price stability definition*, but would not follow an *inflation target*.

8.3.1 The Role of the Inflation Forecast Under IT

A crucial ingredient any inflation forecasts is the assumption about the course of monetary policy in the forecasting period. In what follows, we will take a brief look at the *information content* of inflation forecasts based the assumption that the central bank: (i) keeps rates constant; and (ii) bases its inflation forecast on the market's expected future short-term interest rates (or *forward interest rates*). Thereafter, we will (iii) critically review IT inflation forecasting exercises.

8.3.1.1 Inflation Forecast Assuming Unchanged Official Interest Rates

When producing an inflation forecast, the researcher may assume that the central bank keeps interest rates constant over the forecast period. For instance, the BoE in its inflation reports prior to August 2004, the ECB (for its *inflation projection*) and the Swiss National Bank (SNB) followed such a practise, publishing *conditional* inflation forecasts (Jansson & Vredin, 2003; Vickers, 1998; Woodford, 2007, p. 13). The message of the conditional inflation forecast is simple: there would be no need to take action if the central bank's inflation forecast coincides with target inflation. If, however, forecast inflation diverges from target inflation, the bank would have to take action to bring about the desired result.

That said, conditional inflation forecasts based on unchanged interest rates do not inform neither policy makers nor the public at large about actual inflation in the future, as the monetary policy stance may well change over time. In that sense, inflation forecasts which were made on the assumption that official interest rates are held constant in the forecast period are merely an instrument to show what level of inflation would emerge if, and only if, the central bank does *not* take policy action.

Inflation Projections of the ECB and the SNB

On 13 October 1998, the ECB presented its stability oriented monetary policy strategy for the single currency area, consisting of three main elements: (i) a quantitative definition of price stability and, as far as analysing the risks to price stability are concerned, (ii) a prominent role for money, and (iii) a broadly based assessment of real economic developments.

On 23 November 2000, the first President of the ECB, Wim F. Duisenberg, announced that the bank would, following an ECB Governing Council decision from 16 November 2000, be responding to one of the EU Parliament's demands for more transparency by starting the publication of the *staff macro-economic projections* for growth and inflation as from December 2000 on a semi-annual basis (Duisenberg, 2000). Since 3 June 2004, staff projections are published on a quarterly rather than semi-annual basis(Table 8.3).

Table 8.3 Euro area HICP inflation and ECB inflation projections

	2000	2001	2002	2003	2004	2005	2006	2007	2008	2009
Actual HICP inflation	2.1	2.3	2.3	2.1	2.1	2.2	2.2	2.1	...	...
Forecasts in:										
December 2000	2.4	2.3	1.9	...	...	...	...	...	...	...
June 2001		2.5	1.8	...	...	...	...	...	...	...
December 2001		2.7	1.6	1.5	...	...	...	...	...	...
June 2002			2.3	1.9	...	...	...	...	...	...
December 2002			2.2	1.8	1.6	...	...	...	...	...
June 2003				2.0	1.3	...	...	...	...	...
December 2003				2.1	1.8	1.6	...	...	...	...
June 2004					2.1	1.7	...	...	...	...
September 2004					2.2	1.8	...	...	...	...
December 2004					2.2	2.0	1.6	...	...	...
March 2005					2.1	1.9	1.6	...	...	...
June 2005					2.1	2.0	1.5	...	...	...
September 2005					2.1	2.2	1.9	...	...	...
December 2005						2.2	2.1	2.0	...	...
March 2006						2.2	2.2	2.2	...	...
June 2006							2.3	2.2	...	...
September 2006							2.4	2.4	...	...
December 2006							2.2	2.0	1.9	...
March 2007								1.8	2.0	...
June 2007								2.0	2.0	...
September 2007								2.0	2.0	...
December 2007								2.1	2.5	1.8

Source: Thomson Financial, ECB, Monthly Bulletin. In percent, annual averages.

At the beginning, the *Eurosystem staff inflation projections* for the coming two years were calculated on the assumption that, inter alia, the central bank's *short-term interest rate would remain unchanged in the forecast period* (European Central Bank, 2001). That said, staff inflation projections were not, in principle, a reliable predictor for future inflation. Rather, they outlined a scenario which was likely to be falsified in practice, since monetary policy would act to address threats to future price stability.

What is more, it should be noted that ECB inflation projections are based on real economic variables, while the information content of monetary variables (money, price gaps, bank credit to the non-bank sector) does not enter the forecasting exercise. In that sense, ECB staff inflation projections would paint an incomplete picture of actual inflation to be expected in the future.

In November 2000, ECB President Duisenberg took extensive effort to outline the role of staff inflation projections in the ECB' monetary policy (Duisenberg, 2000): "I should emphasize that we use the word 'projection' in order to signal that the published projections are the results of a scenario based on a set of underlying technical assumptions, including the *assumption of unchanged monetary policy*. This is the way forecasts are produced in many central banks in order to best inform monetary policy decision-makers. As the Eurosystem's staff economic projections are the products of a technical exercise, which assumes, inter alia, that short-term interest rates and the exchange rate will not change over the forecast horizon, it should be clear that the staff projection will not, in general, be the best predictor of future outcomes, in particular for somewhat longer horizons. Rather, it represents a scenario which is likely to be falsified in practice, since monetary policy will always act to address any threats to price stability."

Since June 2006, the Eurosystem inflation projections have been based on the technical assumption that short-term market interest rates (that is the 3-months Euribor rate) *move in line with market expectations* (reflected by *forward rates*) over the projection horizon: As far the assumed policy rate is concerned, the projections make use of the market expectation, prevailing at the point in time when the forecasts are made. The consequences of such a procedure will be discussed below.

The Swiss National Bank (SNB) monetary policy concept, which is in place since the beginning of 2000, consists of three elements (Olivei, 2002; Jordan & Kugler, 2004; Jordan, Peytrignet & Rich, 2001; Swiss National Bank, 2005): the quantitative definition of price stability, a medium-term inflation forecast and an operational target range for the three-month London interbank offered rate (Libor) for Swiss francs, the bank's chosen reference interest rate. The SNB publishes, on a quarterly basis, forecasts for CPI inflation over the three subsequent years. A period of three years is seen as corresponding more or less to the time required for running through the complete transmission of monetary stimuli. By publishing a medium to long-term forecast, the SNB emphasises the need to adopt a forward-looking stance and react at an early stage to any inflation or deflation threat. Figure 8.7 shows Swiss annul CPI inflation and three Swiss National Bank CPI inflation forecasts.

The SNB's inflation forecasts are based on the assumption that the three-month Libor will remain constant over the forecasting period. If the inflation forecast indicates future inflation to rise above (fall below) 2% – the bank's upper ceiling for acceptable inflation –, it would signal a need for tighter (easier) monetary policy. In practise, however, the SNB would not react mechanically to inflation forecasts. To determine the scale and timing of its response, it also takes account of the general economic situation.

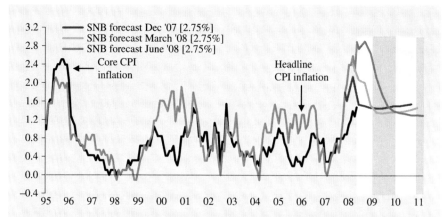

Fig. 8.7 Swiss CPI inflation, actual and SNB forecast (%)
Source: Thomson Financial; SNB. 3-months Libor target rate for the forecast in brackets.

While the SNB states that it would combat inflation that persistently exceeds the 2% level, there are situations in which it would allow this threshold to be temporarily exceeded. In a small open economy, exceptional situations with sharp exchange rate fluctuations could arise, causing CPI inflation to overstep the price stability threshold in the short-term. Marked price rises for imported goods, such as oil, can also result in a temporary breach of price stability (*cost push effects*). The SNB has so far explicitly stated that it is not possible – or necessary – for the central bank to prevent this.

8.3.1.2 Inflation Forecasts Using Market Expectations of Interest Rates

A central bank may decide to produce inflation forecasts based the market's expectations of the future path of policy rates. If confident that the central bank is committed to achieving its inflation target, financial markets would expect the central bank's inflation forecast to converge, sooner or later, towards the central bank's pre-announced inflation target.[20] This is because if monetary policy is credible, the central bank would take action to prevent deviations of future inflation from target inflation.

So why would IT pursuing central banks decide to (also) publish forecasts based on forward rates instead of just assuming a constant official interest

---

[20]For instance, the Riksbank's inflation forecasts for inflation two-years ahead come reasonably close to their stated targets, at least since 1997. This observation, along with the well-known instability problems associated with constant-interest-rate rules, led Vredin (2003) to question whether these central banks' forecasts represent true constant-interest-rate forecasts.

rate in the forecasting period? In general, such a decision is based on various deficiencies of forecasts based on constant rates (Bank of England, 2004; Heikensten, 2005):

– One may argue that the impact of monetary policy depends on people's expectations as far as the level of future is concerned. If the monetary policy objective is to convey more *reliable* information about future inflation, it could be helpful to base inflation forecasts on market interest rate; expectations.
– An interest rate assumption that is in line with the market's view of how official interest rates will develop could make central bank communication easier. Using constant rates, a central bank's forecasts would be difficult to compare with others, since other forecasters do not normally base their forecasts on an unchanged policy rate. *Ex post* assessments of forecasts of economic and inflation developments become generally easier if they are based on assumptions that better reflect the interest rate expectations of market agents.
– One may argue that using market forward rates should make it easier to produce consistent projection scenarios, which is particularly important when preparing estimates for a long-term perspective (longer than the quite common two years). The assumption of a constant rate horizion should become more unrealistic the longer it extends. When the difference between the market's view of the future short-term interest rates and the assumption of an unchanged repo rate has been large, it might be difficult to link assumptions about short-term interest rates to a reasonable picture of, for instance, future long-term rates, since long-term rates depend on expectations of how short-term rates; will evolve.

Inflation Forecasts of the BoE and the Riksbank

Since it was established in 1997, the Monetary Policy Committee (MPC) of the Bank of England (BoE) has been publishing an inflation projection in the *Inflation Report* based on unchanged official interest rates. Given that the future is uncertainty, the BoE presents its inflation forecasts in probability terms. The *fan charts*, which the BoE has been publishing since 1996, are graphical illustration of those probabilities. For instance, Fig. 8.8(a) shows the BoE's May 2008 inflation forecast based on an unchanged interest rate of 5% throughout the forecast horizon. The width of the coloured bands is an indication of how uncertain policy makers are about the outlook for inflation Britton, Fishes & Whitley (1998).

Starting in 1998, the MPC has also been producing an inflation projection using an assumed path for official interest rates estimated from market yields

(a) Annual CPI inflation projection based on constant   (b) CPI inflation projection based on market
      nominal interest rates at 5%, May 2008   interest rate expectations, May 2008

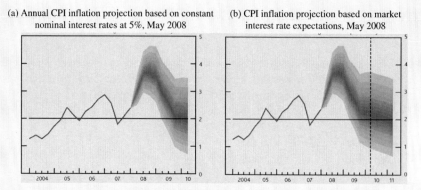

Fig. 8.8   Bank of England inflation projections
Source: Bank of England, May 2008. – The fan charts depict the probability of various outcomes of CPI inflation in the future. If economic circumstances identical to today's were to
prevail on 100 occasions, the MPC's best collective judgement is that inflation over the subsequent three years would lie within the darkest central band on only 10 of those occasions.
The fan charts are constructed so that outturns of inflation are also expected to lie within
each pair of the lighter red areas on 10 occasions. Consequently, inflation is expected to
lie somewhere within the entire fan charts on 90 out of 100 occasions. The bands widen as
the time horizon is extended, indicating the increasing uncertainty about outcomes (Bank
of England, 2002, p. 48)

on government liabilities (Bank of England, 1998, 2001, 2004). Figure 8.8(b)
shows the BoE's inflation forecast May 2008 based on the market's implied
forward interest rates. Table 8.4 shows the central bank's short-term interest
rate path as implied by the forward market as of May 2008 and February 2008,
respectively. As can be seen, there wasn't much of a change between these two
months in terms of expected rate changes on the part of the BoE.

Table 8.4   Bank Rate implied by forward market interest rates[a]

	2008			2009				2010				2011	
	Q2[b]	Q3	Q4	Q1	Q2	Q3	Q4	Q1	Q2	Q3	Q4	Q1	Q2
May	4.9	4.7	4.6	4.6	4.5	4.6	4.6	4.6	4.6	4.7	4.7	4.7	4.7
February	4.8	4.6	4.5	4.4	4.4	4.4	4.4	4.5	4.5	4.6	4.6	4.7	

[a]The data are fifteen working day averages of one-day forward rates to 7 May and 6 February 2008, respectively. They have been derived from general collateral (GC) gilt repo rates
at maturities up to a year and instruments that settle on Libor (including futures, swaps,
interbank loans and forward rate agreements) further out, adjusted for credit risk.
[b]The May figure for 2008 Q2 is an average of realised spot rates to 7 May, and forward
rates thereafter
Source: Bank of England, May 2008.

It should be noted that monetary policy makers must make a (*subjective*) decision about the balance of risks when making inflation forecasts. If policy makers think that risks are evenly spread around the *mode*, then the distribution curve would be symmetrical. If policy makers believe that there is a higher probability that inflation would be above (below) the mode, the area under the probability function would be skewed to the right (left). The risks around the BoE's central projection for inflation in May 2008 and February 2008 was skewed to the upside, as illustrated by Fig. 8.9(a) and (b), respectively.

On 19 November 1992, the Swedish krona was forced out of the ERM and, in January 1993, the Swedish Riksbank announced the monetary policy objective of ensuring that consumer price inflation remained at 2% p.a., with a toleration band of ±1 percentage point (over the coming two years). The inflation target formally applied as from 1995.

Up until October 2005, the Riksbank published its inflation forecasts under the assumption that the policy rate would not change during the forecast period (Riksbank, 2005a, b; Ingves, 2007). From October 2005, the Riksbank published its inflation forecasts based on market expectations of the future development of the policy rate. As from February 2007, the Riksbank publishes inflation forecasts based on its own forecast of short-term interest rates (Table 8.5).

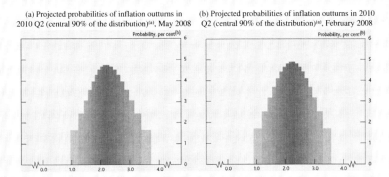

(a) Projected probabilities of inflation outturns in 2010 Q2 (central 90% of the distribution)[a], May 2008

(b) Projected probabilities of inflation outturns in 2010 Q2 (central 90% of the distribution)[a], February 2008

Fig. 8.9 Bank of England inflation projections
Source: Bank of England, May 2008. – [a]Chart (**a**) represents a cross-section of the CPI inflation fan chart in 2010 Q2 for the market interest rate projection. The coloured bands have a similar interpretation to those on the fan charts. Like the fan charts, they portray the central 90% of the probability distribution. If economic circumstances identical to today's were to prevail on 100 occasions, the MPC's best collective judgement is that inflation in 2010 Q2 would lie somewhere within the range covered by the histogram on 90 occasions. Inflation would lie outside the range covered by the histogram on 10 out of 100 occasions. Chart (**b**) shows the corresponding cross-section of the February 2008 Inflation Report fan chart. – [b]Average probability within each band. The figures on the y-axis indicate the probability of inflation being within ±0.05 percentage points of any given inflation, specified to one decimal place.

Table 8.5   Riksbank's own repo rate forecasts (%)

	Q2 2008	Q3 2008	Q4 2008	Q3 2009	Q3 2010	Q3 2011
Repo rate	4.25	4.5(4.3)	4.8(4.3)	4.9(4.3)	4.6(4.3)	4.4

Source: Riksbank Policy Report, 2008/2. – Note that the assessment in
the Monetary Policy Update in April 2008 is stated in parentheses.

Figure 8.10(a) shows the Riksbank's forecast assumptions (according to
its half year 2008 policy assessment) as far as the future path of its official
short-term interest rate are concerned, including the uncertainty band. Figure
8.10(b) displays annual CPI inflation forecasts, based on its half year policy
report in 2008. Again the bands around the forecasts represent the uncertainty
bands.

Most interesting in this context, inflation forecasts based on the market's
expected future short-term interest rates (as in the case of the BoE) and the
central bank's own forecasts of the future path of short-term interest rates (as
is the case of the Riksbank) yield inflation projections that, sooner or later,
converge back towards the central banks' inflation target. What is the *hidden
message* of these findings?

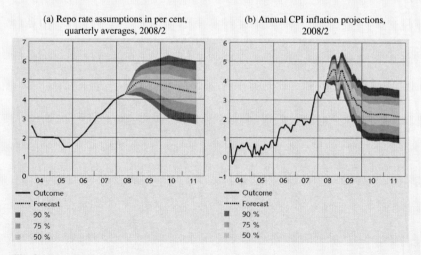

(a) Repo rate assumptions in per cent,   (b) Annual CPI inflation projections,
quarterly averages, 2008/2   2008/2

Fig. 8.10   Swedish Riksbank inflation and CPI projections
Source: Riksbank Monetary Policy Report, 2008/2. – The uncertainty bands in the figures
are based on historical forecast errors.

The finding that inflation projections, which were made on the basis of the market's implied forward short-term rates, converge back to the central bank's inflation target is that market agents considers the central bank's inflation promise *credible*; otherwise, future inflation would deviate from the central bank's announced inflation target.

If inflation forecasts, which were calculated on the central bank's own views about how it will set short-term rates in the future, converge to the central bank's pre-announced inflation target, it merely says that monetary policy makers are confident that they are going to meet their inflation target in the future. Only in the case that the central bank's own short-term rate forecasts are in line with the market's expected future short-term rates can one say that the market considers monetary policy to be credible as far as achieving the inflation target is concerned.

8.3.2 A Critical Review of the Inflation Forecasting Exercises

While IT has actually become a rather prominent concept in monetary policy theory and monetary policy practice, we will now take a critical review of the inflation forecasting exercise (see, Neumann & von Hagen, 2002, p. 128ff.), who give a generally positive assessment of IT but cannot confirm the superiority of IT over other monetary policy strategies geared at price stability, and Woodford (2007, p. 13), who investigates whether forecast targeting is inter-temporally inconsistent).

8.3.2.1 Do Inflation Projections Qualify as an Intermediate Target of Monetary Policy?

It is widely agreed that monetary policy affects inflation with time lags.[21] This is the reason why monetary policy is well advised to base its actions on forward-looking inflation indicators, or intermediate targets. According to Saving (1967) and Brunner and Meltzer (1967), an intermediate variable must (a) have a stable relation to the final monetary policy goal, (b) be controllable through monetary policy instruments, (c) have a causal relationship to the final policy goal (d) be timely in terms of data availability.

Indisputably, *inflation forecasts* would meet the requirements (b) and (d). When it comes to requirements (a) and (c), however, a favourable assessment is far from

---

[21] Of course, if there was no uncertainty about the transmission mechanism and parameter constancy, there would be no need for an intermediate variable approach. For a discussion of intermediate targets see Neumann (1974). The debate about the best choice of an intermediate target has been revived in the 1990s following the adoption of IT in a number of countries; see Leidermann and Svensson (1995).

ensured.[22] To start with, it is not (yet) clear how inflation projections and actual future inflation interact. It might be intellectually appealing to assume that if a central bank reacts to deviations of projected from target inflation it could keep future inflation in line with the central bank's objective. However, most central banks using inflation forecasts have so far not brought forward convincing empirical evidence indicating such a causal and stable relation exists between inflation projections and future inflation. That is to say, IT frameworks *do not specify a transmission mechanism.* (Issing, 2004, p. 173). However, such insights are essential for monetary policy being able to identify *shocks* to the economy appropriately and, in turn, deliver action in a pre-emptive manner. Without such knowledge, (costly) policy mistakes must be expected to occur.

One could argue, though, that the publication of inflation forecasts would keep market agents' inflation expectations in line with the central bank's inflation promise, thereby keeping future inflation at the target level. Such an interpretation of the transmission mechanism would de facto classify the *market agents' inflation expectations* as the central bank's *true* intermediate target: changes in market agents' inflation expectations – which are interpreted as a function of inflation projections – would determine future actual inflation.

However, for inducing a desired change in market agents' inflation expectations the central bank would have to deliver a change in the intermediate target. As monetary policy would then act to bring about the desired change in the inflation projection, the latter could actually no longer serve as an intermediate variable to monetary policy: the reverse would actually hold true. In fact, under such a policy approach the central bank would slide directly into an *infinite regress*, translating into the risk that inflation expectations loose its mooring to monetary policy altogether (this issue which will be discussed below in more detail).

8.3.2.2 Inflation Expectations and Central Bank Credibility

So even if inflation forecasts (based on constant interest rates) do provide relatively little information about actual inflation in the future, one may argue that inflation forecasts would help to keep inflation expectations in line with the central bank's inflation objective, that is supporting *monetary policy credibility*. However, the latter can be expected to be influenced to a great deal by the *time inconsistency problem* as outlined by Kydland and Prescott (1977), with their message being clarified and extended by Barro and Gordon (1983a, b) and Barro (1996). According to these seminal works, institutional arrangements – such as imposing a (flexible) policy rule or designing a proper central bank constitution – are to be seen as eliminating the *inflation bias* of monetary policy when markets are populated by rational agents. It is, at theoretically, highly questionable whether a central bank's inflation forecasts help eliminating the inflation bias.

---

[22]It should be noted at this juncture that, for instance, Haldane (1995) notes that the Bank of England's inflation forecast satisfies criteria (a–c).

   Such scepticism may be justified by, for instance, the fact that to the outside world, inflation projections are rather opaque: it is not known which variables are included in the forecasting model; nor is it known how much weight is assigned to each of the variables.[23] The public's confidence in the accuracy of the inflation projections – and the appropriateness of its policy recommendations – can therefore be assumed to hinge on the central bank's already established credibility.[24] That said, it is questionable whether inflation forecasts further monetary policy credibility. It seems to work the other way round: inflation forecasts are credible if central bank credibility is already in place.

8.3.2.3 Optimism Bias

There is also the issue of a potential *optimism bias* inherent in central banks' inflation forecasts, which could potentially undermine central bank credibility. Inflation forecasts are subject to a (non-negligible) degree of discretion and vulnerable to *theory fads*. In particular, forecasters might have a preference for projecting future inflation that does not deviate too much from the bank's inflation promise. This, in turn, might lead to target deviations if the need for policy action is not properly indicated. An optimism bias might occur especially in a period when future inflation is at risk of deviating strongly from the target (due to, for instance, unfavourable price shocks). Under such circumstances, the central bank could opt for publishing a *more optimistic projection* in order to prevent market agents from becoming too concerned about the inflation outlook, thereby producing an inappropriate policy recommendation and damaging credibility.

8.3.2.4 The Circularity Problem

At first glance, the case for using *market* interest rates in calculating the inflation forecast might appear theoretically convincing and intellectually challenging. However, a second glance would reveal that such a procedure could actually run the risk of falling victim to the well-known *circularity problem* of monetary policy.[25] To see this, one has to take into account that market interest rate expectations are *conditional*: They reflect, at any given point in time, the expectation about a certain monetary policy stance in the future.

   If monetary policy uses market interest rates in assessing the policy outlook, *policy instability* could emerge: an *infinite regress* could unfold, in which the public's

---

[23]Svensson (2003, p. 450) argues that forecast targeting "does not imply that forecasts must be exclusively model-based", which, of course, suggests a rather pronounced degree of discretion in formulating the inflation forecast. The same view is expressed by, for instance, the Sachverständigenrat (2003), p. 26.

[24]On the determinants of central bank credibility see ECB Observer (2001).

[25]For an exposition of the circularity problem induced by monetary policy which mechanically responds to private inflation forecasts see Woodford (1994) and Bernanke and Woodford (1997). See also Carlstrom and Fuerst (2001).

behaviour and monetary policy affect each other, and there is nothing objective on which to pin down either; outcomes are determined by each side's beliefs about what the other side will do. A situation arises in which monetary policy does not rely on external anchoring but on market expectations, which themselves are a function of the expected monetary policy decisions. This problem would presumably become particularly virulent if monetary policy enters a period of inflation exceeding the pre-announced target.

8.3.2.5 The Potential for Confusion

If the central bank publishes its inflation forecasts based on constant central bank rates, and if these forecasts indicate deviations from target inflation, there might be the situation in which there is no reason for market agents to change their hitherto held interest rate expectations. This would actually be the case in which market agents have already *priced in* changes in future short-term interest rates relative to the rates used by the central bank in its inflation forecast.

It could be a rather different story, however, if the central bank calculates its inflation forecasts on the basis of implied forward short-term rates. If, for instance, the inflation forecast is higher than target inflation, the central bank's message to the market would be that short-term interest rates have to be increased – because the prevailing interest rate expectations would not be sufficient to keep future inflation in line with target inflation. However, will that allow the market to form a precise view about forthcoming changes in official rates?

This would be the case *if the central bank publishes its rate profile used in forecasting*: market agents can then compare the bank's rate assumption with currently prevailing interest; any gap between the two would signal forthcoming central bank action. If the central does not inform about the exact structure of the implied forward rates used in calculating the inflation forecast, (a great deal of) uncertainty would remain as to what level the central bank wants to bring its future short-term rates. In that sense, inflation forecasts based on implied forward yields require somewhat higher attention on the part of market agents when compared to inflation forecasts based on constant rates.

8.4 Nominal Income Targeting (NIT)

Meltzer (1987), Gordon (1985), Hall and Mankiw (1994) and Feldstein and Stock (1994), inter alia, recommended a nominal GDP targeting rule for monetary policy (for simulations see Judd & Motley, 1993). Nominal GDP, $Y_{n,t}^*$, is defined as the target price level, P_t^*, multiplied with real income, $Y_{r,t}^*$, in period t. Under a *nominal income targeting* (NIT), the target of nominal income in period t is:

$$Y_{n,t}^* = P_t^* \cdot Y_{r,t}^P. \tag{8.54}$$

The target path of NIT, assuming the desired price level, P_0, and full employment output, Y_0^P, can written as:

$$Y_n(t) = P_0 \cdot Y_0^P \cdot e^{\Delta y^T \cdot t}, \tag{8.55}$$

whereas y represents the NIT growth target.

The NIT can be formulated in growth terms, which would be:

$$\Delta y^T = \pi^* + y^*, \tag{8.56}$$

where Δy^T is target nominal income growth, y^* is potential real growth and π^* is annual target inflation.

In what follows, we want to analyse the monetary policy reactions under NIT if there is (i) a positive demand side shock, (ii) a negative demand side shock, (iii) a positive supply side shock, and (iv) a negative supply side shock. The ensuing potential stabilisation problems shall be discussed in a simple *IS-LM-* and *AD-AS-* framework. Thereafter, we will (v) take a look at the implied assumptions under NIT and, in a final step, compare NIT with MT.

8.4.1 Positive Demand Side Shock

Figure 8.11(a) shows equilibrium in the goods and money market in point A. The NIT (level) is represented by the hyperbola Y_n^* (Bradley & Jansen, 1989, p. 33). It represents all price and output combinations compatible with a given NIT. A positive supply side shock shifts (in the form of, say, productivity gains) pushes the *IS*-curve from IS_0 to IS_1, moving AD_0 to AD_1. The new equilibrium is B, where output has increased from Y_0 to Y_1 and the interest rate from i_0 to i_1. As B is incompatible with Y_n^*, the central bank has to follow a restrictive policy. The reduction of money supply shifts the *LM*-curve from LM_0 to LM_1. The reduction of interest-sensitive spending lowers output to the original output level A. Here, the price level is P_0, output Y_0, while the interest rate is now i_2.

8.4.2 Negative Demand Side Shock

Starting in equilibrium A in Fig. 8.11(b), a negative demand side shock (in the form of, say, a sharp oil price rise) shifts IS_0 to IS_1, and AD_0 to AD_1. Output declines from Y_0 to Y_1. The declining demand for transaction balances reduces the interest rate to i_1. However, the new equilibrium is incompatible with NIT. An expansionary monetary policy is required, moving LM_0 to LM_1. The additional money supply lowers the interest rate, increases aggregate demand. In the final equilibrium (points C and A), output and prices are at their original level while the interest rate has declined to i_1.

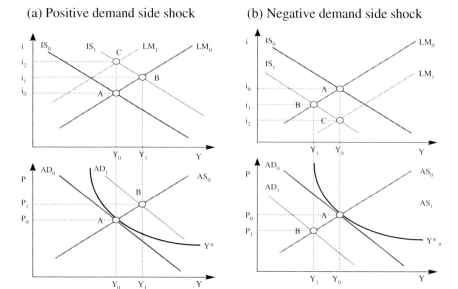

Fig. 8.11 Demand side shocks and monetary policy under NIT

8.4.3 Positive Supply Side Shock

In Fig. 8.12(a) a positive supply side shock (say, a sharp drop in energy prices) shifts AS_0 to AS_1, and LM_0 to LM_1 as the price level has declined from P_0 to P_1. The declining interest rate stimulates demand, increasing output to Y_1. In point B both nominal income deviate from NIT. The central bank would have to pursue an expansionary policy. An increase in money supply moves LM_1 to LM_2, and AD_0 to AD_1. In point C, actual output is above the envisaged level, while prices are below the target level.

That said, in the case of a positive supply side shock, the central bank can keep a given NIT only at the expense of violating the output target or the price level target. If, for instance, the central bank would decide to restore P_0, it has to pursue an even more expansionary course. However, the new equilibrium output level would imply an even higher output target deviation. If, however, the central bank would attempt to restore Y_0, it would have to accept a price level below the target level.

8.4.4 Negative Supply Side Shock

In Fig. 8.12(b), a negative supply side shock increases the price level to P_1. As the real money supply contracts, LM_0 shifts to LM_1. If the central bank sticks to its NIT, it has to respond with an expansionary policy. Realising point C, however,

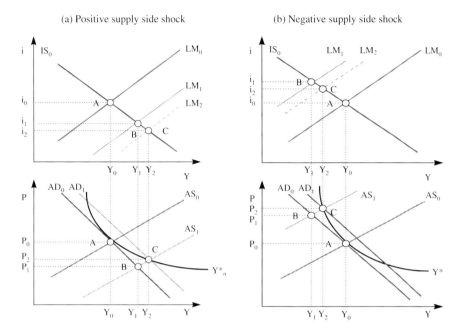

Fig. 8.12 Supply side shocks and monetary policy under NIT

output and prices deviate from their targets. If the central bank pursues an even more expansionary policy it could restore the original output level but only at the expense of an even higher price level deviation. A restrictive monetary policy would shift the *AD*-curve to the left, and P_0 could be restored with output falling below the target level.

The results of our analyses are shown in Table 8.6. Under NIT, (positive as well as negative) demand side shocks can, in principle, be successfully counteracted by monetary policy in terms of achieving the target output and the target price level. Supply side shocks (positive as well as negative), however, force the central bank to trade off the output target against the price level target.

8.4.5 A Critical Review of NIT

If the central bank has to comply with a pre-determined nominal income target, based on specified price level and output targets, the central bank's discretion to trade-off the price level objective against the output objective is not completely eliminated, but may be greatly reduced. This is that least the case when there is a negative relation between inflation and growth.

Table 8.6 NIT and monetary policy responses to shocks

	Demand side shock		Supply side shock	
	Positive	Negative	Positive	Negative
Monetary policy reaction	restrictive *(anti-cyclical)*	expansionary *(anti-cyclical)*	expansionary *(pro-cyclical)*	*(slightly)* expansionary
Nominal GDP target compliance	*yes*	*yes*	*For achieving the NIT, the price (output) target has to be traded-off against an output (price) deviation.*	
Price target compliance	*yes*	*yes*		
Output target compliance	*yes*	*yes*		

At this juncture, a number of additional problems of using NIT as a monetary policy strategy shall be highlighted:

- As the central bank has to take action under NIT as demand and supply side shocks materialise, *knowledge* about the transmission mechanism is required. The existence of time lags gives rise to the concern that monetary policy impulses may affect the economy at a point in time when policy action is no longer needed. In fact, an anti-cyclical monetary policy may actually turn out to be a pro-cyclical policy; a shock-absorbing policy action may translate into a shock-increasing impulse.

- In general, a NIT monetary policy requires the central bank to have *reliable forecasts* for the forthcoming business cycle in order to be able to implement monetary policy in a pre-emptive way – given that policy works with time lags. However, it is questionable as to whether this kind of information would available (at all times).

- In contrast to MT, economists in favour of NIT assume that monetary policy can, at least in the short-term, affect real output in a *systematic fashion*. Such a view must assume that people do not form expectations according to the rational expectations model.

- NIT raises the question as to whether the central bank's *political independence* could be put at risk (Sachverständigenrat, 1974, p. 146). Assume, for instance, that poor tax policies dampen real output. In this case, a NIT might have to pursue an expansionary monetary policy, running the risk of violating the price level target.

- Finally, one has to take into account that if NIT is classified as a monetary policy strategy, such a concept does not give the central bank any idea *how to achieve this goal*. In f the price level and output targets are basically final, but in no way, intermediate targets.

– NIT may force the central bank to pursue an *activist monetary policy*, especially
  when there are demand and supply-side shocks. This, in turn, may increase the
  risk of monetary policy actually becoming a destabilising force for the economy's
  expansion path.

It is against the backdrop of these critical remarks that we will now compare NIT
with an alternative strategy candidate, namely MT.

8.4.6 Comparing NIT with MT

In a final step, we want to highlight the major difference between NIT and MT.
Using the familiar transaction equation, the stock of money is:

$$M_t = P_t + Y_r - V_t, \tag{8.57}$$

where M is the stock of money and V is the income velocity of the money stock.
   Under NIT, Eq. (8.57) can be formulated as:

$$M^{NIT} = P_t^* + Y_{r,t}^P - V^{Actual}, \tag{8.58}$$

where V^{Actual} is the actual (or cyclical) income velocity of money.
   In contrast, under MT Eq. (8.57) would be:

$$M_t^{MT} = P_t^* + Y_{r,t}^P - V_t^{Trend}, \tag{8.59}$$

where V^{Trend} is the (long-term) trend income velocity of money. That said, the
difference between M^{MT} and M^{NIT} is:

$$M_t^{MT} - M_t^{NIT} = V_t^{Actual} - V_t^{Trend}. \tag{8.60}$$

That said, the differences between MT and NIT can be explained by different
monetary policy responses to changes in the income velocity of money. Whereas
under MT the central bank would not change the money supply to deviations of
actual velocity from its trend value, a monetary policy of NIT would make the actual
velocity a determining factor of the money supply.
   If we assume that the prices, output and the velocity of money might temporarily
deviate from their long-term values, while the central bank keeps the money stock
according to the long-term formulation of the equation of exchange, we can write:

$$M^{MT} = P_t^{Actual} + Y_{r,t}^{Actual} - V_t^{Actual}. \tag{8.61}$$

If we subtract Eq. (8.58) from (8.61), we yield:

$$M^{MT} - M^{NIT} = (P_t^{Actual} - P_t^*) + (Y_{r,t}^{Actual} - Y_{r,t}^*). \tag{8.62}$$

Table 8.7 Money supply growth under MT and NIT

Strategy	Δp_t^*	$\Delta y_{r,t}^*$	Assumed Δv_t	Δm_t
MT	2.5%	2.5%	Trend: −1.0%	6.0%
			Bust: −1.0%	6.0%
			Boom: −1.0%	6.0%
NIT	2.5%	2.5%	Trend: −1.0%	6.0%
			Bust: −2.0%	7.0%
			Boom: 0.0%	5.0%

Legend: The change in the stock of money, Δm_t, is calculated as Δp_t^* plus $\Delta y_{r,t}^*$ minus the assumed (trend) of Δv_t.

Of course, Eq. (8.62) is merely another representation of the divergence of the actual income velocity from its trend. However, it points out that under a monetary policy of MT, the nominal income target will be met in the long-run, but not necessarily in the short-run.

In view of the above, it should be clear that the central bank would smooth the money supply growth under MT, whereas under NIT the central bank would be required change the money stock on the basis of cyclical developments. In that sense, NIT would result in a (much) more activist policy compared to MT.

This is all the more obvious in view of the finding that in times of booms (busts) the income velocity of money tends to rise above (fall below) its trend value. Whereas this would have implications for NIT, it would have not impact for MT. Table 8.7 provides a simple example for money supply growth under MT and NIT due to changes in the income velocity of money.

In sum, NIT is a concept based on the generally accepted monetary policy objectives of keeping inflation low and supporting positive real output growth. However, NIT does actually not meet the requirements of a monetary policy strategy. It does not provide the policy makers with insights about how to achieve a given nominal income target. What is more, a policy following NIT would most likely run into situations in which it cannot achieve both, low inflation and high growth; in other words, it would have to favour one objective at the expense of the other.

8.5 The Taylor Rule

It is well over a decade since John B. Taylor set out what has become part of the current orthodoxy of monetary economics by now.

In his seminal paper, John B. Taylor (1993) shows that the monetary policy decisions of the US Fed between 1982 and 1992 can be described reasonably well by a simple *reaction equation*. For the period from 1965 to 1980, however, his equation could not explain the Fed's decisions; the rule recommends a much higher interest rate than that actually set by the Fed. From this observation, Taylor (1999b) reaches the normative conclusion that high inflation, which the US experienced in the 1970s, had likely been avoided, had the Fed followed his rule. Since then, Taylor's approach has become quite popular in describing and forecasting the rate setting behaviour of central banks (Orphanides, 2003a).

More specifically, according to the Taylor rule, the *Taylor rate* is calculated as follows (Taylor, 1993, p. 195):

$$i_t = r^* + \Delta p^e_{t+1} + a_y \cdot (\Delta y_t - \Delta y^*) + a_p \cdot (\Delta p_t - \Delta p^*), \qquad (8.63)$$

where:

i_t = nominal Taylor-rate in period t,
r^* = real equilibrium rate,
Δp^e_{t+1} = expected inflation (prevailing in period $t+1$),
Δy_t = change in actual real output,
Δy^* = change in trend output,
Δp_t = actual inflation,
Δp^* = target inflation;

here, a_y, a_p = weightings for the output gap $(\Delta y_t - \Delta y^*)$ and the inflation gap $(\Delta p_t - \Delta p^*)$, respectively, and have positive weights $(a_y, a_p > 0)$. With the exception of the interest rate, lower case letters stand for logarithms, Δ for fourth differences (that is annual changes).

The output gap is the deviation of the actual from the potential growth, and the inflation gap is the deviation of the actual inflation from the target inflation. The Taylor rate is calculated by adjusting the real short-term equilibrium rate with the (expected) inflation and the weighted output gap and inflation gap.[26] So if the economy runs above trend growth and/or actual inflation exceeds target inflation, the central bank should raise the short-term interest rate (other things being equal). If, however, the economy grows below potential, or actual inflation falls short of target inflation, the central bank must lower the interest rate (other things being equal). If the output gap and inflation gap are zero and the Taylor-rate is thus in equilibrium, monetary policy is *neutral* in terms of influencing real output and inflation.

This is, at its roots, a Wicksellian view of the world (see in detail Sect. 2.4 of this book). By fixing the short-run nominal rate, the central bank can, given stickiness in prices over the short run, shift the short *real* interest rate – both in absolute terms and, more particularly, relative to the short-run real rate that would equilibriate demand and supply (Tucker, 2008).

Typically, policymakers think about that in terms of the "output gap", reflecting firms' capacity utilization and slack/pressure in the labor market. By contrast, in the academic literature – notably Michael Woodford's Interest and Prices – the benchmark is to set monetary policy in order to offset the frictions in the economy, so as to obtain the conditions that would prevail if prices, wages etc were fully flexible

---

[26] See Gerlach and Schnabel (1999, p. 1).

(Woodford, 2003). According to our view, policymakers and academics still need to resolve how big the gap is between those two approaches.

Hence, that gap between the short real rate and its "equilibrium" can be thought of as representing the stance of monetary policy, which should be chosen by the central bank in the light of the extent to which inflation deviates from target, and to which aggregate demand deviates from the supply capacity of the economy. Implicit in this rule is that the textbook policymaker knows how the degree of slack in the real economy acts on future inflation or the slope of the Phillips curve (see Sect. 5.3 of this book).

However, the two forces sweeping through the world economy in the wake of the recent credit crisis – rises in commodity prices combined with a credit crunch – test the way policymakers typically apply various elements of this set up in more routine circumstances.

In his original paper, Taylor (1993) made a deliberately simple approach for selecting the non-observable variables. He substituted *realised* inflation of the preceding four quarters for *expected* inflation over the same period. What is more, Taylor assumed a 2.2% annual rate of growth for the US production potential (which corresponded to the trend growth of real income in the United States between 1984 and 1992). The equilibrium real short-term interest rate was set at 2% p.a. The inflation gap was calculated as the difference between actual inflation and an inflation target of 2%. Finally, Taylor assigned a weighting of 0.5 to the output and inflation gap, respectively. Against the backdrop of these assumptions, the Taylor interest rate captured the behaviour of the US Fed in terms of setting interest rates quite well (Orphanides, 2003).

Gerlach and Schnabel (1999) were among the first authors applying the Taylor rule approach to the euro area. For the period 1982 to 1997, the authors calculated a *credibility-adjusted* real short-term equilibrium rate of 3.55%, based on weighted 3-month rates, deflated by consumer prices. The national output gaps were taken from the OECD and were then aggregated. Target inflation was set at 2.0%. The authors' empirical results – excluding EMS turbulence in 1992 and 1993 – were consistent and statistically significant. The weight of the output gap and inflation gap were 0.5 and 1.5, respectively. Gerlach and Schnabel (1999, p. 4) conclude that the results "suggest that if the ECB were to conduct monetary policy using the [Taylor rule], it would in fact not deviate much from past (weighted) interest rate setting behaviour in the countries forming the EMU area."

A Normative Taylor Rate for the US

In its monthly publication *Monetary Trends*, the Federal Reserve Bank of St. Louis contrasts the actual US Federal Funds Rate with various *Taylor interest rate* levels, calculated on the basis of alternative inflation targets. By comparing the actual interest rate with *normative Taylor rates* one can actually make an assessment as far as the monetary policy stance is concerned: if the actual

Federal Funds Rate is higher (lower) than the normative Taylor rate, monetary policy is restrictive (expansionary).

Using Taylor's (1993) equation, the nominal Taylor rate as calculated by the Federal Reserve Bank of St. Louis is:

$$f_t^* = r + \pi_{t-1} + (\pi_{t-1} - \pi^*)/2 + 100 \cdot (y_{t-1} - y_{t-1}^p)/2,$$

where f_t^* is the normative Taylor rate, r is the long-run real short-term interest rate, π_{t-1} is the previous period's annual inflation in percent (measured on the basis of the consumer price index), π^* is the inflation target, y_{t-1} is the log of the previous period's level of real gross domestic product (GDP) and y_{t-1}^p is the log of an estimate of the previous period's level of potential output (which can be approximated by, for instance, applying the HP-Filter to real GDP); the Federal Reserve Bank of St. Louis uses five alternative target inflation rates (π^*), namely 0, 1, 2, 3, 4 percent p.a.

Figure 8.13 provides an illustration for US monetary policy in the period 1972-Q1 to 2008-Q1. Until the early 1980s, the actual Federal Funds Rate tended to be (well) below the level suggested by the Taylor rule compatible with inflation of between zero and 4 percent p.a. In the period thereafter, however, the actual Fed rate was set more in line with the Taylor rate. Most notably, in the periods of economic downturns, that is in the early 1990s and 2001–2002, the Fed had lowered its official rate well below the levels recommended by a Taylor rate compatible with inflation of 4%.

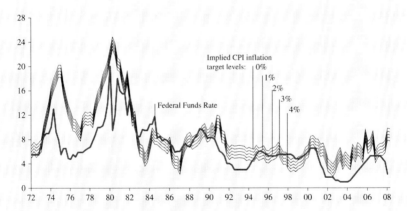

Fig. 8.13 Normative Taylor rates for the US Fed
Source: Bloomberg; Thomson Financial; own calculations.

8.5.1 *A Taylor Rule for the Swedish Riksbank*

In the following, we present estimations of Taylor rates for the Swedish economy from the early 1990s to 2004. In the specifications of the Taylor rule we used the central bank's interest rate which is explained as a function of the inflation gap and the output gap:

$$\tilde{i}_t = (1 - \rho)i^* + \beta_1 \bar{\pi}_t + \beta_2 \bar{y}_t + \rho i_{t-1} + \varepsilon_t, \qquad (8.64)$$

where:

$\tilde{i}_t$ = Taylor interest rate,
i^* = steady state nominal rate of interest, which, in turn, is defined as the equilibrium real rate of interest plus inflation target; the former was approximated by the average real GDP growth rate for the period under review, which amounted to 2.5%;
$\bar{\pi}_t$ = deviation of actual from target inflation (*inflation gap*);
$\bar{y}_t$ = actual output growth minus potential growth (*output gap*);
i = short-term interest rate, here the 3-month money market rate; and
ε_t = error term (i.i.d.).

The parameters β_1 and β_2 denote how the central bank responds to deviations in the inflation gap and the output gap, respectively. The only addition to the *classical* Taylor rule specification is the lagged interest rate term, taking into account the central bank's *interest rate smoothing* or *policy inertia*. In this parameterization, the long-run response of the nominal interest rate to inflation is $\beta_1/(1 - \rho)$. The latter assumes that the lagged interest rate corresponds with the real equilibrium interest rate plus expected inflation. Figures 8.14(a-d) show the macro-economic variables under review in Sweden for the period 1980-Q1 to 2004-Q3.

The trend values for GDP growth and CPI inflation were calculated by using the Hodrick-Prescott (HP) filter. As the Riksbank switched to an inflation targeting regime in 1993, we took this year as a starting point fore calculating Taylor rates. Table 8.8 shows the OLS regression results of various Taylor rules, based on *headline inflation* and *underlying inflation* for two periods, namely 1993-Q1 to 2004-Q3 and – to exclude the effect of the aftermath of the bursting of the "New Economy" stock market bubble on monetary policy behaviour – a shorter period from 1993-Q1 to 2001-Q3.

The estimates of the Taylor rates give a relatively good fit. However, this is largely due to the estimated coefficient ρ on the lagged interest rate, which is large and highly significant in all cases, indicating that the Riksbank has pursued a rather pronounced interest rate smoothing. All coefficients – with the exception of the inflation gap when using underlying inflation for the period 1993-Q1 to 2001-Q3 – are statistically significant at standard levels. Moreover, all coefficients have the correct sign, that is, for instance, a shrinking (rising) of the output gap was accompanied by rising (declining) short-term interest rates. The coefficients suggest that

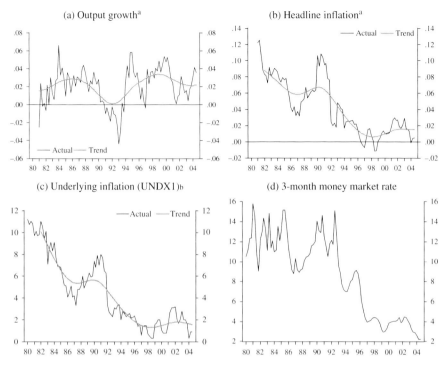

Fig. 8.14 Macroeconomic variables in Sweden
Legend: [a]Fourth differences of log values, trend is represented by the Hodrick-Prescott filter. –
[b]Annual change in percent. –
Source: Thomson Financial, Riksbank; own calculations.

the Riksbank has assigned a slightly higher weight to inflation target deviations compared to deviations of actual output from potential when settings policy rates.

Figures 8.15 (a) and (b) show the actual 3-month money market rate in Sweden and the estimated Taylor rates using headline inflation for the period 1993-Q1 to 2003-Q3 and 1993-Q1 to 2001-Q3, respectively. The Taylor rates were estimated using (i) *dynamic estimates*, that is calculating multi-steps estimates of the Taylor rate by starting from the first period in the forecast sample; and (ii) *static estimates*, that is calculating the Taylor rate as a sequence of one-step ahead estimates using actual rather than estimated values for the lagged interest rate (dependent variable).

The static estimates fit the actual 3-month money market rate quite well. If we want to form a view about the policy stance, however, the dynamic estimates are of greater interest. For the estimate in the period 1993-Q1 to 2004-Q3, the Taylor rate had recommended a somewhat easier monetary policy from the middle of 1996 to the beginning of 1999, whereas the opposite held true for the period thereafter, especially since end-2002. The Taylor rule estimate on the basis of period 1993-Q1 to 2001-Q3, in turn, would have recommended an even easier policy from the

Table 8.8 Estimates of the Taylor rule specification of the instrument rule using "headline" and "underlying" inflation

Dependent variable = policy interest rate i

Period	N	Coefficient on				Ad-justed R2	LM test for 2nd and 4th order AC
		Intercept	Output gap	Inflation gap	Lagged i		
I. Headline inflation							
Q193–Q304	47	.15**	19.7***	24.0***	.89***	0.97	.21 [.80]
		(.06)	(3.2)	(6.8)	(.03)		.57 [.68]
Q193–Q301	35	.21***	19.2***	24.5***	.86***	0.97	.28 [.76]
		(.08)	(3.6)	(8.6)	(.03)		.54 [.71]
II. Underlying inflation (UND1X)							
Q193–Q304	47	.09*	19.2***	19.3*	.88***	0.96	1.42 [.25]
		(.05)	(3.5)	(9.6)	(.04)		1.43 [.24]
Q193–Q301	35	.16**	19.1***	17.4	.84***	0.96	1.49 [.24]
		(.06)	(3.8)	(13.1)	(.05)		1.49 [.23]

Legend: ***/**/* indicate significance at the 1/5/10 percent levels, respectively. Estimation is by ordinary least squares. Numbers in parentheses are standard errors. The *LM*-test statistic for second-order autocorrelation is N times the R^2 from a regression of the residual onto all the regressors from the original regression and two and 4 lags of the residual. The p value from the $\chi 2$ distribution is reported underneath the test statistic. Sample period reflects the Riksbank's switch to inflation targeting around 1993.

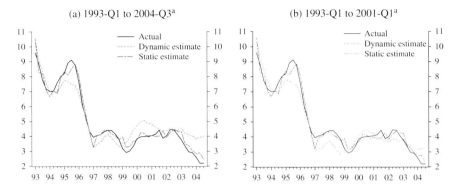

Fig. 8.15 3-month money market rates for Sweden, actual and Taylor rates

middle of 1996 to the beginning of 1999 and, a considerably tighter policy since the beginning of 2003 when compared with the actual rate set by the Riksbank.

8.5.2 The Measurement Problems of the Taylor Rule

There are at least four major measurement problems with the Taylor rate. *First*, the weightings of the output and inflation gaps have to be determined. The weighting scheme used by Taylor is not necessarily appropriate (Ball, 1997). The central bank's orientation and the structure of the economy have to be taken into consideration when determining the coefficients. The *weights* have to be *estimated* and are therefore *method dependent*. Depending on the relative weights, there may be considerable differences in the Taylor interest rate at different periods resulting in a correspondingly varied assessment and recommendations of current monetary policy.

Second, the real interest rate is calculated as the nominal interest rates minus a *measure of inflation*. As a result, the choice of the inflation measure influences the real interest rate estimate. In general, broadly based indices such as the consumer price index or the GDP deflator might be considered to be appropriate measures of inflation. If, however, inflation measures on the basis of the CPI and GDP differ, so will the resulting measures of the real interest rate.

Third, there are also *different options available for estimating the output gap*. Depending on the method used for determining the potential – for example, a log-linear trend, a Hodrick-Prescott trend or the estimation of a production function –, there might be different measures of the output gap, which would have a direct impact on the level and the behaviour of the Taylor rate – notwithstanding the significant data uncertainty about output gap data at the time of policy decision making in real time (see also chapter 6.1). One Solution might be to use growth rates of the output gap (Gorter, Jacobs, & De Haan, 2008).

Fourth, there is also considerable uncertainty about how to calculate the non-observable *equilibrium real interest rate* (Ferguson, 2004, and Giammarioli & Valla, 2003). It may be approximated by a multi-year average of the difference between the actual nominal interest rate and inflation. However, such a measure would depend on the period used for forming the average. Alternatively, assuming a constant equilibrium real interest rate over long periods may not appropriate either. Besides the expected rate of return on tangible fixed assets and the general propensity to save, the equilibrium real interest rate may also depend on the general assessment of the uncertainty in the economy and the degree of credibility of the central bank. If these aspects are not taken into account, the resulting Taylor rate may be of questionable informative value (Amato, 2005; Mésonnier & Renne, 2004).

The Taylor-Rule Framework and the Credit Crisis – the UK Case

How may the credit market turmoil affect the equilibrium short-term real interest rate? Would it be reasonable to assume that the (hitherto observable) relationship between economic slack and future inflation remains intact? For addressing these questions, a closer look will be taken at the developments in the UK.

To start with, it would be *overly simplistic* to assume that the equilibrium real short-term interest rate would be *stable* over time. In fact, that rate can be expected to change over time (Neiss & Nelson, 2001). If the equilibrium real interest rate and inflation expectations rise (fall), the central bank needs, under a Taylor-rule regime, to increase (lower) its nominal policy rate to keep its monetary stance unchanged. That said, a *financial market crisis* may affect both, the equilibrium real interest rate and market inflation expectations.

In efficient financial markets, the risk-free rate should be a satisfactory *summary statistic*. Under *normal* market conditions, it can be assumed that interest rates for private sector loans show a *fairly stable spread* relative to the risk-free yield. It can also be assumed that the *degree of credit rationing* in the economy should be fairly *constant* over time. However, these assumptions might be put into questions in a period of severe market strain.

For instance, premia on unsecured interbank lending rose sharply, reflecting heightened investor risk aversion (Fig. 8.16). Faced with deteriorating refinancing conditions and mounting shareholder concern about rising losses, banks were required to start *de-leveraging* their balance sheets. This was basically done via raising fresh equity capital, demanding repayment of outstanding loans and selling of assets (Tucker, 2008a, and Sect. 7.1.4). Of course, any shrinking of banks' balance sheets would imply a decline in the economy's overall credit and money supply.

Fig. 8.16 Premia on
unsecured interbank lending
in the UK Libor-OIS
Source: Tucker (2008, p. 18).

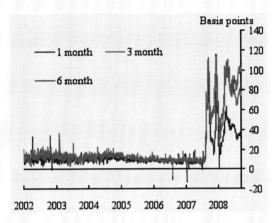

Lending rates for corporates and households edged higher as interbank interest rates went up. In an attempt to lower the private sector's funding costs, the BoE started cutting interest rates in December 2007, bringing the Bank Rate down from 5.75% to 5.50%, and lowering borrowing costs further to 4.50% until October 2008. However, market borrowing rates for the private sector declined much less, as spreads between loan yields and the short-term risk-free rate rose (Fig. 8.17). The *Credit Conditions Survey* of the BoE signalled tightening (Fig. 8.18).

Fig. 8.17 Selective effective
rates and the Bank rate in the
UK
Source: Tucker (2008, p. 18).

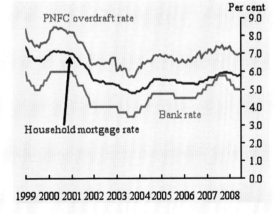

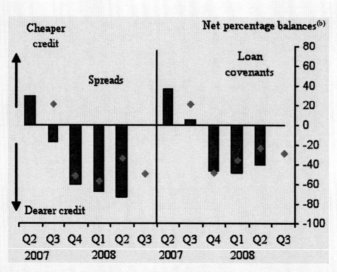

Fig. 8.18 BoE Credit condition survey – large corporates
Source: Tucker (2008, p. 18). The blue bars show responses over the past three months. The red diamonds show expectations over the next three months. Expectations balances have been moved forward one quarter so that they can be compared with the actual outturns in the following quarter. A positive balance indicates that spreads have become narrower, such that it is cheaper to borrow, or that the terms and conditions on which credit is provided have become looser.

John B. Taylor (2008) suggested that in such a market environment *the policy rate should be reduced by the extent of the widening in spreads* to maintain an unchanged policy stance (McCulley & Touli, 2008, see also section 8.5). Such a view was challenged by Tucker (2008), though. To him, the challenging aspect of a period of credit market turmoil is *quantity rationing*, which cannot be solved by lowering central bank borrowing costs. Curdia and Woodford (2008) added that borrowers and savers have a different propensity to consume. Consequently, a change in credit spreads will affect the average rate faced by borrowers and savers in a different way from a change in the policy rate – so that Taylor's proposal might not yield the desired effect.

From theoretical viewpoint it seems that the financial market turmoil should have reduced the *equilibrium real interest rate*, which, in turn, would argue for a lowering of the central bank nominal interest rate to keep the monetary stance unchanged; declining inflation expectations would work in the same direction. In this context it should also be noted that for calculating the equilibrium nominal central bank rate, the consumer price index (CPI) may not necessarily be the appropriate price index.

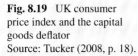

Fig. 8.19 UK consumer price index and the capital goods deflator
Source: Tucker (2008, p. 18).

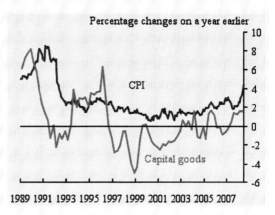

For instance, firms' investment decisions might depend on the price development of capital goods rather than our consumer price inflation. The latest pickup in consumer price inflation (in great part driven by higher energy prices) was much higher than increases in capital goods prices (Fig. 8.19). This could suggest a higher real interest rate for businesses than is suggested by subtracting CPI inflation from nominal interest rates CPI. That said, *it is not at all straightforward to calibrate monetary conditions* in a period of financial market turmoil.

Curdia and Woodford (2008) conclude that the information content of money and credit quantities would not add anything to analysing credit market yield spreads. However, such a conclusion ignores the issue of *quantity rationing*. When such rationing occurs, data on the quantity of lending and money may be more useful than the shadow prices (Brigden & Mizen, 1999). Tucker (2008) and others do not recommend using on Monetary Conditions Indices, as such measures – due to their theoretical deficiencies – run the risk of becoming a source of policy instability. However, the authors correctly stress the need for a better quantitative understanding *of how the equilibrium real rate (r*) shifts with shocks to the financial parts of the economy.*

8.5.3 Does the Taylor Rule Qualify as a Policy Strategy?

Notably, John B. Taylor (1998) recommended his concept for the euro area monetary policy, arguing that his rule had proved itself in simulation studies (ranging over a large number of model economies) to be a reasonably good monetary policy guideline when it comes to stabilising inflation and output. What is more, Taylor holds the view that the risk of following an incorrect monetary policy rule, which is the risk associated with the uncertainty about the *true structure of the economy* (McCallum, 1988), is smaller using a Taylor rule when compared with alternative rules.

However, there are a number of theoretical and practical aspects which should make a central bank hesitant to accept the Taylor rule as a monetary policy strategy candidate (Svensson, 2003). *First*, the Taylor rule is not a policy strategy as such: it does not show *how* to achieve a certain policy goal. It simply adds the objective of keeping the output gap zero to the objective of keeping inflation in line with the target rate.

Second, a Taylor rule based policy ignores the need for identifying *intermediate variables* which have a reliable relation to future developments in terms of inflation (and output). While it is known that monetary policy affects the economy with time lags, under the Taylor rule the central bank would therefore not pursue a forward-looking policy and would presumably (always) act too late to prevent target deviations.

Third, under the Taylor rule the *feedback effects* of the inflation gap and output gap can compensate each other which, in turn, can lead to questionable monetary policy recommendations. For instance, an inflation gap of zero, accompanied by a negative output gap (which is basically the scenario in the case of a forthcoming stagnation), requires the central bank to pursue an expansionary monetary policy. However, the central bank cannot be sure whether an increase of the money supply will affect growth or merely inflate prices.

To give another example, the Taylor rule would indicate a need for monetary policy action if there is merely a *one-off increase in the price level*, caused, for instance, by an increase in the oil price. One could argue, however, that monetary policy should tolerate such a first-round effect on the price level. This shows that the Taylor rule calls for a more detailed analysis of the individual determinants of price level changes.

Fourth, if the central bank is required to respond to output gaps as is the case under the Taylor rule, its independence might be severely undermined. Take, for instance, the case in which the economy experiences declining growth because of bad macro-economic policies. In this case, the central bank would be required to *bail out* government's poor policies. Basically, the central bank would be held responsible for macroeconomic mismanagement, which, in turn, could conflict with the objective of price stability.

Finally, one may quote former FOMC member L. H. Meyer (2002), who noted: "Although the Taylor rule has been a useful benchmark for policymakers, my experience during the last 5-1/2 years on the FOMC has been that considerations that are not explicit in the Taylor rule have played an important role in policy deliberations. In particular, forecasts clearly have played a powerful role in shaping the response of monetary policy in a way not reflected in the simple Taylor rule."

Note, however, that several papers have documented a regime switch in US monetary policy from"passive" and destabilizing in the pre-1979 period to"active" and stabilizing afterwards. These studies typically work with *dynamic stochastic general equilibrium (DSGE) models* with rational expectations. Milani (2008) relaxes the assumption of rational expectations and allows for *learning* instead. Economic agents form expectations from simple models and update the parameters through constant-gain learning. In this setting, he aims to test whether monetary policy may have been a source of macroeconomic instability in the 1970s by inducing unstable learning dynamics. The model is estimated by Bayesian methods. The constant-gain coefficient is jointly estimated with the structural and policy parameters in the system. The results show that monetary policy was *respecting the Taylor principle also in the pre-1979 period* and, therefore, did not trigger macroeconomic instability.

Eusepi and Preston (2008) analyze how the formation of expectations constrains monetary and fiscal policy design. Economic agents have imperfect knowledge about the economic environment and the policy regime in place. Households and firms learn about the policy regime using historical data. Regime uncertainty substantially narrows, relative to a rational expectations analysis of the model, the menu of policies consistent with expectations stabilization. When agents are learning about the policy regime, there is greater need for policy coordination: the specific choice of monetary policy limits the set of fiscal policies consistent with macroeconomic stability and *simple Taylor-type rules* frequently lead to *expectations-driven instability*. In contrast, non-Ricardian fiscal policies combined with an interest rate peg promote stability (see Sect. 5.2.3 of this book). Resolving uncertainty about the prevailing monetary policy regime improves stabilization policy, enlarging the menu of policy options consistent with stability. However, there are limits to the benefits of communicating the monetary policy regime: the more heavily indebted the economy, the greater is the likelihood of expectations-driven instability. More generally, regardless of agents' knowledge of the policy regime, when expectations are anchored in the long term, short-term dynamics display greater volatility than under rational expectations.

Note also that central bank communication plays an important role in shaping market participants' expectations. Eusepi (2008), for instance, studies a simple nonlinear model of monetary policy in which agents have incomplete information about the economic environment. He shows *that agents' learning and the dynamics of the economy are heavily affected by central bank transparency about its policy rule*. A central bank that does not communicate its rule can induce "learning equilibria" in which the economy alternates between periods of deflation coupled with low output and periods of high economic activity with excessive inflation. More generally, initial beliefs that are arbitrarily close to the inflation target equilibrium can result in complex economic dynamics, resulting in welfare-reducing fluctuations. On the contrary, central bank communication of policy rules helps stabilize expectations around the inflation target equilibrium (see also Sect. 6.4 of our book).

8.5.4 Comparing the Taylor Rule with MT

Now, does the Taylor rule qualify as an appropriate monetary policy strategy candidate? This question should be answered by comparing its merits with those of the alternative strategy. In the following, we will compare the Taylor rule with MT (Deutsche Bundesbank, 1999, p. 53). Under MT, the central bank's reaction function is:

$$\Delta i = \lambda^m f(\Delta m_t - \Delta m^T), \tag{8.65}$$

that is the bank raises (lowers) its interest rate i, that is $\Delta i > 0$ ($\Delta i < 0$), if actual money supply growth, m_t, exceeds (falls below) desired money growth, m^T; $\lambda^m > 0$ shows the intensity with which rates are changed in response to the expected deviation of actual money growth from target growth. Note that:

$$\Delta m^T = \Delta y^* + \Delta p^T - \Delta v^* \text{ and} \tag{8.66a}$$

$$\Delta m = \Delta y + \Delta p - \Delta v. \tag{8.66b}$$

Inserting Eqs. (8.66a) and (8.66b) into Eq. (8.65), the following MT interest rate rule emerges:

$$i = i_{t-1} + \lambda^m \left[(\Delta p - \Delta p^T) + (\Delta y - \Delta y^*) - (\Delta v - \Delta v^*) \right]. \tag{8.67}$$

At this juncture it should be noted that the (trend) income velocity of money, V, is simply the reciprocal of the (trend) cash holding coefficient, K: $V = 1 / K$ and $V^* = 1 / K^*$. In logs, we have:

$$v = -k \text{ and } v^* = -k^*.$$

We can therefore substitute $(\Delta v^* - \Delta v)$ by $(-\Delta k^* - (-\Delta k))$. Inserting the latter into Eq. (8.67) yields:

$$i = i_{t-1} + \lambda \cdot [(\Delta p - \Delta p^*) + (\Delta y - \Delta y^*) + (\Delta k - \Delta k^*)]. \tag{8.68}$$

Equation (8.68) shows that the reaction function under MT is determined by the one-period lagged interest rate i_{t-1}, the inflation gap $(\Delta p - \Delta p^*)$, the change in the output gap $(\Delta y - \Delta y^*)$, and the change in the liquidity gap $(\Delta k - \Delta k^*)$. Like the Taylor rule, a MT based monetary policy contains the inflation gap and output gap as policy determining variables. However, there are *important conceptual differences* between the two concepts:

- In addition to the output and inflation gap, MT takes into account the liquidity gap (that is actual money holdings relative to long-term equilibrium money holdings). As a result, MT rests on a *richer* set of information.
- In contrast to the Taylor-rule, MT does not require the central bank to know the economy's equilibrium real interest rate level. Under MT the central bank merely changes the interest rate from the *previous* period to keep actual money supply on target.

- In contrast to the Taylor rule, MT makes explicit use of an intermediate variable, namely money supply growth relative to its target. In view of the well know time-lag problem, MT might therefore be less prone to policy mistakes compared with the Taylor rule.
- In contrast to a Taylor rule, MT does not take action related to the cyclical behaviour of the economy (as represented by the output gap); in that sense, it is non-interventionist. In fact, MT is just about stabilizing money supply growth.

To show in some more detail why a monetary policy under MT reacts in a rather different fashion that under the Taylor rule, let us consider some examples.

Equation (8.68) could suggest that if actual inflation exceeds target inflation, the central bank would raise the interest rate; at least, this is what the Taylor rule would say. Under MT, however, there would be no such action on the part of the central bank. This is because an increase in the inflation gap *would be compensated for by a decline in the liquidity gap* in the same amount. Likewise, under MT a change of the output gap would not make the central bank change its interest rate: A change in the output gap would be compensated for by a change in the liquidity gap in the same amount. This is because v (remember that $v = y + p - m$) will rise as y and p increase and vice versa.

The only development that can make a central bank pursuing MT to change interest rates is a rise of money supply over its target rate. In such a case actual money holdings (k) would rise above their long-term equilibrium level (k^*), thereby signalling to the central bank the need to switch to a restrictive policy course, that is raising its interest rate; the change in the liquidity gap could not be compensated for by either changes in the inflation gap or changes in the output gap.

8.6 The McCallum Rule

The *McCallum rule* (McCallum, 1987, 1988, 1993) calculates a growth rate of base money that is compatible with a pre-determined nominal output growth target.[27] The comparison between actual base money growth with McCallum's rate gives an indication as to whether monetary policy is restrictive or expansionary: If McCallum's rate is higher (lower) than actual base money, monetary policy is restrictive (expansionary).

The McCallum rule rests on the *equation of exchange* in the sense that McCallum's base money growth is determined on the basis of the economy's growth potential, the income velocity of money and the desired increase in the price level. As such, the McCallum rule might be characterised as an *alternative to Milton Friedman's constant money supply growth rule*, with the major difference being the handling of the velocity of money for calculating target money supply growth.

---

[27] The monetary base is the sum of currency held by the non-bank public and bank reserves. As the latter is recorded on the liability side of its balance sheet, the central bank can monitor it on a daily basis and make adjustments as needed to keep it at any desired level on average over (say) a week.

Whereas Friedman's constant money supply growth assumes a constant (change in the) income velocity of money, the McCallum rule takes into account the development of the income velocity of base money seen in the past. In that sense the McCallum equation allows for (gradual) changes in the income velocity of base money over time. McCallum (1994) argues that such an *averaging* is actually a correction for long lasting changes in velocity stemming from, for instance, regulatory and technological changes. In that sense, the McCallum rule qualifies as a *nominal feedback rule*, as it reacts to *past* economic developments.

In this context it should be noted that even though most central banks of industrial nations implement monetary policy by controlling short-term interest rates – the operating target in the Taylor rule concept. However, the McCallum rule would by no means be *less realistic*. In fact, we should have no doubt that central banks, which hold the base money supply monopoly, can actually control (at least a narrow definition of) the stock of base money if they wish to do so.

8.6.1 Calculating the McCallum Rule

In a formal way, the McCallum rule can be formulated as follows:

$$\Delta b_t = \Delta y^{nom} - \Delta v_t^b + \lambda(\Delta y^{nom*} - \Delta y_{t-1}^{nom}). \tag{8.69}$$

Here, the symbols are:

Δb_t annual rate of growth of base money in percent;
Δv_t^b annual change in the income velocity of base money, as an average over the previous four years, in percent;
λ intensity with which the central bank responds to deviations of target nominal output from actual nominal output in period $t - 1$;
Δy^{nom*} annual change in target nominal output in percent; and
Δy_{t-1}^{nom} annual change in actual nominal output in period $t - 1$ in percent.

In Eq. (8.69) the target value of nominal output growth can be defined as the sum of target inflation and the long-run average rate of growth of real GDP (which is not affected by monetary policy). McCallum takes the latter to be 3% p.a. for the US. With an inflation target of 2% p.a., target nominal output growth would amount to 5% p.a.

The term Δv_t^b reflects the notion that the income velocity of base money could – due to technological and regulatory changes – change over time. Relating it to the past four years is intended to model a forecast of the average growth rate of velocity over the foreseeable future; it is not intended to reflect current cyclical conditions. The latter are represented by the final term, $\Delta y^{nom*} - \Delta y_{t-1}^{nom}$, which is positive (negative) if the recent increase in nominal output turns out to be smaller (larger) than target nominal output growth. For instance, a positive $\Delta y^{nom*} - \Delta y_{t-1}^{nom}$ would, other things being equal, argue in favor of conducting an easier monetary policy.

8.6.2 Illustrations of the Basic McCallum Equation

In its monthly publication *MonetaryTrends*, the Federal Reserve Bank of St. Louis publishes a (modified) McCallum equation for the US, taking into account alternative inflation targets. It uses the following formula:[28]

$$\Delta b_t = \pi^* + (10 - year\ moving\ average\ growth\ of\ real\ GDP) - \\ (4 - year\ moving\ average\ of\ base\ velocity\ growth) \tag{8.70}$$

The 10-year moving average growth rate of real GDP for a quarter t is the average quarterly growth during the previous 40 quarters. At an annual rate, the formula is: $((y_t - y_{t-40})/40) \times 400$, where y_t is the log of quarterly real GDP. The 4-year moving average of base velocity growth is calculated similarly. The alternative inflation targets are $\pi^* = 0, 1, 2, 3, 4$ percent per annum respectively. Figure 8.20(a) shows the results of the McCallum equation for base money growth for alternative inflation targets over the period 1970-Q1 to 2008-Q1. Figure 8.20(b) and (c) show the components of the McCallum equation, that is actual and long-term average output growth and actual and long-term income velocity growth of base money, respectively.

From the early 1970s to around the middle of the 1980s, US base money growth exceeded the McCallum rates, suggesting that the Fed's monetary policy stance was too expansionary. Since then, however, base money growth has basically remained within the band, suggesting that base money growth supported inflation to be between 1 and 4% p.a. Since around 2001, however, base money growth has declined to a level compatible with inflation of around zero percent.

Of course, one may apply the McCallum equation to *alternative monetary aggregates*.[29] For instance, Fig. 8.21(a) shows the McCallum rule on the basis of the stock of US M2 for the period 1970-Q1 to 2007-Q2 (and Fig. 8.21(b) and (c) its components). As can be seen, M2 growth was well above the McCallum growth rates compatible with inflation of less than 4% p.a. until the middle of the 1980s. Since then, however, M2 has expended at rates which suggested that inflation would remain in a band of between zero and 4%. Lately, however, M2 growth would suggest that monetary policy has become *too easy*, financing an inflation of more than 4% p.a.

---

[28] In contrast to our illustration, the Federal Reserve Bank of St. Louis uses a modified money base, including an estimate of the effect of sweep programs: To adjust the monetary base for the effect of retail-deposit sweep programs, the bank adds to the monetary base an amount equal to 10 percent of the total amount swept, as estimated by the Federal Reserve Board staff. These estimates are imprecise, at best. Sweep program data are found at research.stlouisfed.org/aggreg/swdata.html.

[29] In this case, however, we have to take into account that a change in base money supply might not be accompanied by a predictable change in a more broadly defined monetary aggregate – as the money multiplier might not be stable.

(a) Monetary base growth and inflation target levels, % y/y

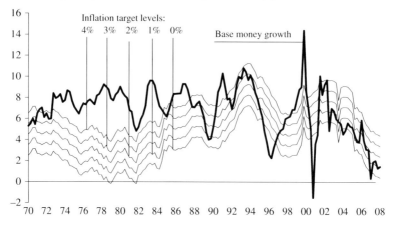

Components of McCallum's rule

(b) Real output growth, % y/y

(c) Monetary base velocity growth, % y/y

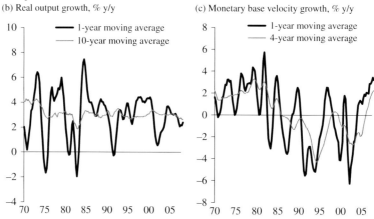

Fig. 8.20 McCallum's rule for US base money
Source: Bloomberg; Federal Reserve Bank of St. Louis, Monetary Trends; own calculations. –
Monetary base growth and inflation targets show the quarterly growth of the monetary base implied
by applying McCallum's (1988, 1993) equation: $\Delta MB_t = \pi^* + $ *(10-year moving average growth
of real GDP) – (4-year moving average of base velocity growth)* to five alternative target inflation
rates, $\pi^* = 0, 1, 2, 3, 4$ percent, where ΔMB_t is the implied growth rate of the adjusted monetary
base. – The 10-year moving average growth of real GDP for a quarter t is calculated as the average
quarterly growth during the previous 40 quarters, at an annual rate, by the formula $((y_t - y_{t-40})/40)$
$\times$ 400, where y_t is the log of real GDP. – The 4-year moving average of base velocity growth is
calculated similarly. – The spike in base money growth at the end of 1999 reflects actions taken to
accommodate expected change-of-millennium demand.

(a) M2 growth and inflation target levels, % y/y

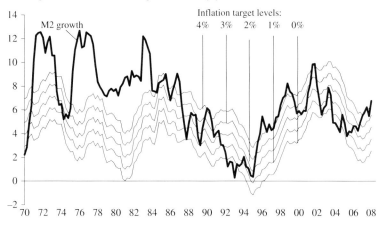

Components of McCallum's rule
(b) Real output growth, % y/y   (c) M2 veocity growth, % y/y

Fig. 8.21   McCallum's rule for US M2
Source: Bloomberg; Federal Reserve Bank of St. Louis, Monetary Trends; own calculations. – For
further explanations, see comment below the previous graph.

8.6.3 Extensions of the McCallum Rule

The McCallum rule ranks among the most widely analyzed nominal feedback
rules for policy *simulation* (Dueker & Fischer 1998). Of course, these analyses
should be interpreted with quite some caution: Modelling how an economy would
have developed *if* a certain set of policy measures had been taken is of course
a highly controversial approach – especially so if such analyses are based on
historical data.

One objective of simulations is to analyse how well the McCallum rule has tracked actual monetary policy. McCallum conducts simulations for the US that include shocks in a system consisting of the rule in the following representation (using quarterly data):

$$\Delta b_t = 0.00739 - \frac{1}{16}(y_{t-1}^{nom} - b_{t-1} - y_{t-17}^{nom} + b_{t-17}) + 0.25(y^{nom*} - y)_{t-1}. \quad (8.70a)$$

The first term on the right hand side of the equation is the constant 0.00739, which implies a 3% annual nominal growth rate translated into quarterly logarithmic units; it corresponds to the rate of long-term annual growth in nominal US GDP (McCallum, 1989, p. 341). The second term subtracts the average growth rate of the income velocity of base money, approximated by the average quarterly difference in the logarithm of velocity over the previous four years; this term is the estimate of trend income velocity. The third term specifies how policy is to respond to deviations of nominal income from its target; McCallum recommends to set the feedback value $\lambda = 0.25$.

The equation above says that if nominal output was below target in the preceding period (other things being equal), monetary policy should increase base money supply growth, for making the economy to actually *catch up*. In fact, this term adds a cyclical element to the McCallum rule – thereby actually running counter to the very idea of the McCallum equation, namely ironing out the effects of short-term swings in income velocity of base money on base money supply growth. Like any anti-cyclical monetary policy, the McCallum rule could become destabilising, if we take into account that money works with a long time lag on output and prices.

As noted earlier, McCallum uses a four year average of income velocity growth base money because trends in velocity growth can (gradually) shift over time, but not every change in base velocity represents a long-lasting shift in trend. Clearly, the possibility of changes in the income velocity of base money represents the critical issue in the McCallum rule. According to Dueker (1993), the McCallum concept for nominal GDP targeting proves to be simple yet robust to potential changes in income velocity of money. Dueker (1993, p. 27), who developed an alternative forecast-based model for calculating changes in income velocity of money, gives a *political-economic argument* in favour of pursuing McCallum's simple approach: "Given that it would be easier for the public to verify that the Fed is following McCallum's rule, relative to the forecast-based rule, the former may garner the Fed more credibility, even though it is technically less able to stabilize nominal GDP growth."

International evidence gained from simulation analyses of the McCallum's rule is somewhat mixed. Hall (1990) applied McCallum's rule with a feedback value of 0.25 to the US, Canada, Japan and Germany. He found that if the US and Canada had followed the McCallum rule, inflation would have been much lower. In contrast, simulations for West Germany and Japan indicated that the rule would have increased nominal GNP variability around its trend. Hall's results show that modifications of the rule's specification are often needed. One reason for Hall's disappointing results rests on the choice of the feedback value.

Describing past monetary policy with a feedback rule allows ascertaining the implicit or explicit policy goals pursued in the past and identifying the point in time when these goals changed. Dueker and Fischer (1996) extend the McCallum rule to Swiss monetary policy, allowing for feedback from the exchange rate to the policy rule. The results show that Swiss monetary policy would have been tighter during relatively high inflation at the beginning of the 1990s compared with the recommendation given by the amended McCallum rule. The gap between the actual and the model implied base money growth rate was closed gradually by mid 1993 – after higher than normal inflation had been observed for more than three years.

8.6.4 Final Remarks

A major concern about the outlook for low inflation is that the monetary policy strategy may *lack sufficient institutional discipline* to assure that short-term objectives – such as, for instance, smoothing business cycle swings and the wish to avoid interest rate volatility – do not interfere with the long-term objective of safeguarding sound money. It has led to renewed interest in nominal feedback strategies – such as the McCallum rule –, as they are *closer to a pure rule* on the continuum between a fixed rule and pure discretion.

More specifically, the McCallum rule belongs to a class of nominal feedback rules which were developed in response to politically unpopular constant money supply growth rules and the inflation bias inherent in discretionary monetary policy. McCallum argues that a monetary policy following his rule is (more likely than a constant money supply growth rule) to achieve price stability and muster support from the public at large: The feedback mechanism would smooth out swings in the business cycle and safeguard a money-orientated monetary policy against the consequences of financial and regulatory changes.

At the current juncture, however, it appears that central banks are unlikely to give up their discretionary powers to a nominal feedback rule. In that sense, a more promising avenue for the McCallum rule is its use as *indicators for monetary policy*. Rather than stating that monetary policy should follow a specific fixed rule, the McCallum rule could be used as a *reference guide*. A repeated argument against the simulations performed with nominal feedback rules, however, is that they suffer from the *Lucas critique*. The latter basically says that the parameters used to simulate the data generating process for economic variables are calibrated in a world devoid of a nominal feedback rules, and they would presumably change if a nominal feedback rule were put into place. That said, the class of *normative studies* that attempt to make policy recommendations based on *counterfactual simulations* have to be interpreted with great caution. In fact, the relative merits of pursuing a nominal feedback rule such as the McCallum rule simply cannot be assessed on the basis simulation analyses.

8.7 Interest Rate Targeting

8.7.1 Monetary Policy and the Neutral Real Interest Rate

Under an *interest rate targeting*, the central bank would set the real (short-term) interest rate at the neutral level, at which inflation is low and stable, and output is equal to potential (Judd & Motley, 1992). Over the *medium- to long term*, it can be assumed that a successful monetary policy sets the real interest rate close to the natural rate. In the *short-term*, however, a *lack of knowledge* on the part of policy makers about the exact level of the neutral interest rate may cause unfavourable policy results in terms of deviations of actual inflation and output from their desired levels (Cuaresma, Gnan, & Ritzberger-Gruenwald, 2003).

On a theoretical level, one could argue that it is the emergence of *shocks* that would require monetary policy action to prevent unfavourable policy results. Because it is here where we can assume that the central bank's actual real interest rate will differ (considerably) from the long-term natural interest rate (Amato, 2005). A central bank following a stability-oriented monetary policy would want to offset any such effects on the final objectives (inflation and output) by adjusting its policy instruments.

Deviations between the actual real interest rate and its neutral level can be regarded as a *measure of the monetary policy stance*. If, for instance, the actual real interest rate exceeds (falls below) the neutral level, monetary policy can be expected to exert a *contractionary* (expansionary) impact on economic activity and downward (upward) pressure on inflation. Clearly, the extent and duration of the deviation of the actual real short-term rate from its natural level can be expected to determine the impact on real economic activity and prices. Having said that, the *level of the natural real interest rate* is an important *benchmark variable for monetary policy*. If it is possible to estimate the level of the natural real interest rate with precision in real time, it would allow central banks to gain a better understanding of the impact of monetary policy on economic activity and prices.

While the natural real interest rate is, in principle, a useful concept, tit cannot be observed directly. While it is difficult to assess the level of the natural rate *ex-post*, the difficulties are exacerbated even further in *real time*. Therefore, central banks would have to take recourse to estimates which are subject to a high degree of uncertainty. Indeed, research results suggest more generally that monetary policy recommendations based on real-time estimates of the neutral interest rate level can differ significantly from those based on ex-post (revised) data (Orphanides, 2003b). As a result, the natural real interest rate is, in practice, often a concept which *does not add much value to monetary policy-making* from an operational perspective (European Central Bank, 2004a).

For example, how do the commodity price rises and, separately, the credit crunch in 2007/2008 affect the "equilibrium" short-term real rate? Many analysts doubt that the actual short real rate is still an adequate proxy measure of monetary conditions (Tucker, 2008, p. 6 ff.).

8.7.2 Poole's Analysis of Interest Rate Targeting Versus Monetary Targeting

Poole (1970) studies the optimal choice of the monetary policy instrument in an *IS-LM*-framework with a fixed price level. Under the objective of keeping the economy's price level stable, monetary targeting is an effective strategy if there are (positive and negative) demand and supply side shocks (Table 8.9). If, however, there are shocks to money demand, interest rate targeting proves to be the effective strategy. Given that many economists and monetary policy makers assume instability of money demand, Poole's analytical result is frequently used to support arguments for casting monetary policy in terms of *pure interest rate rules*.

However, the effectiveness of the policy strategies under review rests on (i) the assumed objective of monetary policy and (ii) the nature of the shocks. In what follows, we will highlight the implications of (i) a (positive) demand shock under interest rate targeting and (ii) a (positive) shock to money demand under monetary targeting. In both cases the objective of monetary policy is keeping the price level stable. It will be shown that in the first case, the economy's price level would actually spiral out of control, whereas in the second case the price level would be subject to a one-off level shift.

8.7.2.1 Positive Demand Shock Under Interest Rate Targeting

To start with, we assume that the economy's equilibrium output is Y_0, the equilibrium interest rate is i_0 – that is the *target interest rate* –, the money supply M_0 and the price level P_0 (Fig. 8.22). We assume a (neo-classical) aggregated supply curve, which implies that AS is a vertical line. A *positive demand shock* moves IS to IS' and, accordingly, AD to AD'. The interest rate rises to i_1 ($> i_0$) and the price level to P_1 ($>P_0$). With an unchanged money supply, the increase in the price level pushes the LM curve to the left (*negative real balance effect*), increasing the interest rate further to i_2 ($> i_1 > i_0$).

Under an interest rate targeting, the central bank would have to expand the money supply for bringing the interest rate back to i_0. A rise in money supply from M_0 to

Table 8.9 Effectiveness of monetary targeting versus interest rate targeting under a policy of price level stabilization

Kind of shock Strategy	Demand side shocks	Supply side shocks	Money demand shocks
Monetary targeting	*yes*	*yes*	*No (one –off target deviation)*
Interest rate targeting	*no (growing target deviations)*	*no (growing target deviations)*	*yes*

Note: The shocks can be *positive* or *negative*. Assuming that, at the start of the analysis, actual output is at potential.

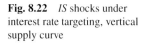

Fig. 8.22 *IS* shocks under interest rate targeting, vertical supply curve

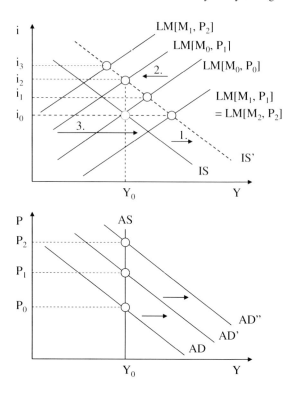

M_1 moves the *LM* curve to the right. However, this would move *AD'* to *AD''*, which pushes up the price level to P_2. As the *LM* curve moves to the left, the interest rate rises to i_3. As a result, monetary policy has to increase the stock of money further to push down the interest rate – a policy that leads to a further increase in the price level.

That said, under interest rate targeting a *demand shock* would actually lead to a monetary policy that makes the price level spinning out of control (*dynamic instability*). Keeping the interest rate at its (pre-shock) target level leads the price level further and further away from its target value. An interest rate targeting strategy would therefore be incompatible with the monetary policy objective of keeping the price level firmly anchored.

8.7.2.2 Money Demand Shock Under Monetary Targeting

Under a monetary targeting, the target money supply is M_0. A *positive shock* to the demand for money moves the *LM* curve to the left: at a given income peoples' demand for money has been increased (Fig. 8.23). As a result, the interest rate rises from i_0 to i_1. A rise in money demand moves *AD* to *AD'*, so that the price level drops to P_1. This, in turn, moves the *LM* curve back to the right. As a result, in the new

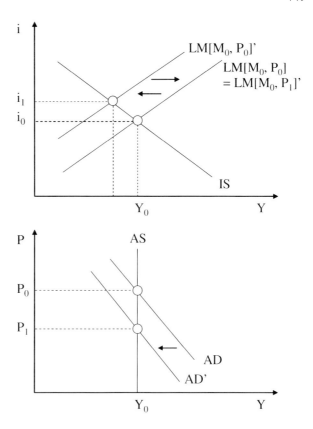

Fig. 8.23 *LM* shock under monetary targeting, vertical supply curve

equilibrium the price level is below P_0. In other words, monetary targeting cannot achieve the objective of keeping the price level constant if three is a (positive) shock to money demand.

In view of this result one should note, however, that the *money demand shock* would actually lead to a *one-off shift* in the price level – in contrast to a demand shock under interest rate targeting, which would actually make monetary policy raising the price level further and further away from its target level. In that sense, monetary targeting would not prove any dynamic instability as an interest rate targeting does.

8.7.3 Poole's Analysis in the Context of Stochastic Shocks

Following Walsh (2003, p. 432), we will now outline alternative forms of the Poole model, focusing on (ii) control errors for broad money, (iii) the policy of base money adjustments and (iv) the role of variances for optimal policy. It should be noted that in all cases, the objective of monetary policy is minimizing output fluctuations (rather than stabilizing the price level), and there are no time lags of monetary policy. We start with outlining the basic model.

8.7.3.1 Basic Model

We start with a version of Poole's model, based on the IS-LM-framework, where the price level is fixed:

$$y_t = -\alpha i_t + u_t \text{ and} \tag{8.71}$$

$$m_t = y_t - c i_t + v_t, \tag{8.72}$$

whereas small letters denoted logs. Equation (8.71) is output, y, which is negatively related to the interest rate, i. Output also depends on a disturbance term u, which has the variance σ_u^2. Equation (8.72) shows the real demand for money. (Note that the price level P has been normalised to 1, so that its log value is $p = 0$). It depends positively on output and negatively on the interest rate and a disturbance term v, which has the variance σ_v^2. The disturbance terms u and v are assumed to have a zero mean and represent serially and mutually uncorrelated processes.

The central bank's objective function is assumed to be the minimization of output fluctuations:

$$E[y_t]^2. \tag{8.73}$$

Note that the output level was normalized to 1, so that in logarithms we have: $y = 0$ (absence of shocks).

In terms of monetary policy action, the central bank sets either i or m at the start of period t. The random shocks u and v occur in the course of the period. They determine the endogenous variables, that is either y and m if i is the policy instrument or y and i if m is the policy instrument.

Let us start with considering i as the policy instrument. In this case, Eq. (8.71) can be solved directly for output. The stock of money, m, would simply be adjusted to y and i to ensure equilibrium in the money market. Setting i_t that leads to $E[y_t]^2 = 0$, output is u_t. Output variation is thus:

$$E_i[y_t]^2 = \sigma_u^2. \tag{8.74}$$

If, however, m is the policy instrument, the joint equilibrium of Eqs. (8.71) and (8.72) is:

$$y_t = \frac{\alpha m_t + c u_t - \alpha v_t}{\alpha + c}. \tag{8.75}$$

When determining the amount of m_t that implies $E[y_t]^2 = 0$, we get $y_t = (c u_t - \alpha v_t)/(\alpha + c)$. For the objective function under setting the money supply we yield:

$$E_m[y]^2 = \frac{c^2\sigma_u^2 + \alpha^2\sigma_v^2}{(\alpha + c)^2}. \tag{8.76}$$

The two alternative policy strategies – interest rate steering or money supply setting – can be evaluated in terms of output volatility: the lower output volatility, the better. For instance, interest rate targeting would be the preferred to the money supply setting policy if $E_i[y_t]^2 < E_m[y_t]^2$. In view of Eqs. (8.75) and (8.76), this condition is satisfied if and only if:

$$\sigma_v^2 > \left(1 + \frac{2c}{\alpha}\right)\sigma_u^2. \tag{8.77}$$

Equation (8.77) shows that the interest rate strategy is the preferred strategy if (i) the variance of money demand shocks (σ_u^2) is larger, (ii) the *LM* curve is steep (which is represented by its slope $1/c$) and/or (iii) the *IS* curve is flat (the slope is $-1/\alpha$). In contrast, the money supply setting is preferred if the variance of output shocks (σ_v^2) is high, the *LM* curve is flat and/or the *IS* curve is steep.

If there are only *demand shocks*, a money supply setting leads to a smaller output variance than interest rate setting. This is because under a constant money supply a positive *IS* shock leads to a higher output and a rise in the interest rate. The latter, however, dampens output brings production back to its original level. A fixing of i would lead to higher output variation.

If, however, the system is hit by *shocks to money demand*, while aggregate demand shocks are absent, output could be stabilized perfectly under an interest rate steering. This is because a money demand shock would affect the interest rate which, in turn, leads to output fluctuations. By steering the interest rate, however, such an outcome could be prevented; output variance could be prevented.

If both types of shocks are present, however, the optimal choice depends on the relative variances u and v as well as on the slopes of the *IS* and *LM* curves.

8.7.3.2 Control Errors for Broad Money

Under a system of fractional reserve banking, how do the results above change if allowance is made for potential control errors in setting the money supply? The broadly defined money supply m can be formulated (in log terms) as follows (Walsh, 2003, p. 435):

$$m_t = b_t + hi_t + \omega_t, \tag{8.78}$$

where b is base money, i is the interest rate, and ω is a random disturbance term. The money multiplier $m_t - b_t$ depends positively on the interest rate ($h > 0$); it also depends on ω. If the central bank pursues an interest rate steering, Eq. (8.78) would be irrelevant for output variations ($E_i[y_t]^2 = \sigma_u^2$).

Under a monetary base rule, however, output can be written as:

$$y_t = \frac{(c+h)u_t - \alpha v_t + \alpha \omega_t}{\alpha + c + h}. \tag{8.79}$$

That said, output variation under a monetary base steering is:

$$E_b[y_t]^2 = \left(\frac{1}{\alpha + c + h}\right)^2 \left[(c+h)^2 \sigma_u^2 + \alpha^2(\sigma_v^2 + \sigma_\omega^2)\right]. \tag{8.80}$$

If the central bank's objective is to minimize output fluctuations, we find that interest rate steering is the preferred strategy over monetary base steering if and only if:

$$\sigma_v^2 + \sigma_\omega^2 > \left(1 + \frac{2(c+h)}{\alpha}\right)\sigma_u^2. \tag{8.81}$$

The disturbance ω does not affect output variance under an interest rate steering, but it would do so under a monetary base steering. So the presence of money multiplier disturbances suggests that, other things being equal, a base steering might be less attractive and makes it more likely that an interest rate steering procedure proves to be the favorable alternative when it comes to minimizing output fluctuations.

8.7.3.3 Base Money Adjustments

Let us assume that base money supply, b, is the central bank's instrument, and it will change b in response to the interest rate, i. The policy rule would be:

$$b_t = \mu i_t. \tag{8.82}$$

The parameter μ, both its sign and magnitude, show how the central bank varies the monetary base as the interest rate vary. If base money is kept constant (that is $b = 0$ according to the normalization), μ would be 0. If $\mu = -h$, base money would be adjusted to keep m equal to zero on average. (Note that actual m might still vary due to the control error ω.) If we combining Eqs. (8.82), (8.71) and (8.72) yields:

$$i_t = \frac{v_t - \omega_t + u_t}{\alpha + c + \mu + h}. \tag{8.83}$$

As can be seen, large (small) values of μ reduce (increase) the variance of the interest rate. In the case that $\mu \to \infty$, Eq. (8.83) would converge to a policy of keeping the interest rate at a fixed level.

If we insert Eq. (8.83) in (8.71), we have the output as:

$$y_t = \frac{(c + \mu + h)u_t - \alpha(v_t - \omega_t)}{\alpha + c + \mu + h}. \tag{8.84}$$

Accordingly, the variance of output is:

$$\sigma_y^2 = \frac{(c + \mu + h)^2 \sigma_u^2 + \alpha^2 (\sigma_v^2 + \sigma_\omega^2)}{(\alpha + c + \mu + h)^2}. \tag{8.85}$$

Minimizing the equation with respect to μ, the optimal policy rule – that is the one that minimizes output variance – is given by:

$$\mu^* = -(c + h) + \frac{\alpha(\sigma_v^2 + \sigma_\omega^2)}{\sigma_u^2}. \tag{8.86}$$

In fact, neither an interest rate steering ($\mu \rightarrow \infty$), nor a base money steering ($\mu = 0$) nor a money supply steering policy would be optimal. In fact, the optimal policy strategy depends on the relative variances of the shocks.

8.7.3.4 The Role of Variances for Optimal Policy

How do the variances of affect the choice of the optimal policy rule (which aims at minimizing output variance)? To start with, let us assume under given monetary base, there are no disturbances in money supply and demand ($v = \omega = 0$), that is $\sigma_v^2 = \sigma_\omega^2 = 0$. In the traditional Poole analysis, base money steering would dominate an interest rate steering.

According to Eq. (8.86), however, the result could be improved if the stock of base money is not held constant but is reduced when the interest rate rises: $b_t = -(c+h)i_t$. Given a positive demand shock ($u_t > 0$), a rise in the interest rate reflects a rise in output. A monetary policy designed to stabilize output should reduce m_t, which, in turn, would require a reduction of base money. That said, the optimal policy would be a deliberately restrictive policy, pushing the interest rate up even further.

If, however, σ_v^2 and σ_ω^2 are positive, an interest rate increase could be a result of either an increase in money demand or a reduction of money supply. An increase in base money would be optimal when there is a positive money demand and or a negative money supply shock, as by doing so the interest rate effect on output fluctuations could be offset. The optimal policy would be $\mu^* > -(c + h)$ when $\sigma_v^2 + \sigma_\omega^2$ becomes large.

No let us assume that the central bank needs to find out what kind of shock is at work. For the sake of simplicity, suppose the central bank can only respond to *observed shocks* v, u and ω. The policy rule would then be:

$$b_t = \mu_u u_t + \mu_v v_t + \mu_\omega \omega_t, \tag{8.87}$$

where μ_u, μ_v and μ_ω are the reaction parameters for the respective disturbances. Inserting the new policy rule in Eqs. (8.71) and (8.72) yields:

$$y_t = \frac{(c + h + \alpha\mu_u)u_t - \alpha(1 - \mu_v)v_t + \alpha(1 + \mu_\omega)\omega_t}{\alpha + c + h}. \tag{8.88}$$

In the case where there is perfect information about the nature and magnitude of the shocks, the central bank could minimize output variance if: $\mu_u = -(c+h)/\alpha$, $\mu_v = 1$ and $\mu_\omega = -1$.

If, however, monetary policy cannot observe the underlying shocks, it might decide to react on the basis of forecasts of these disturbances. As we have a model that has a linear structure, the optimal policy can be written as:

$$b_t = \mu_u \hat{u}_t + \mu_v \hat{v}_t + \mu_\omega \hat{\omega}_t = -[(c+h)/\alpha]\hat{u}_t + \hat{v}_t - \hat{\omega}_t, \qquad (8.89)$$

where $\hat{u}_t$, $\hat{v}_t$ and $\hat{\omega}_t$ are forecast values of the shocks. In the Poole model, the central bank observes the interest rate, i_t, that is it sets policy actions conditional on i_t. That said, the forecast shocks depends on i_t, and we can say that $\hat{u}_t = \delta_u i_t$, $\hat{v}_t = \delta_v i_t$ and $\hat{\omega}_t = \delta_\omega i_t$. The policy rule under forecasting the disturbances would be:

$$b_t = -\left(\frac{c+h}{\alpha}\right)\hat{u}_t + \hat{v}_t - \hat{\omega}_t = \left(-\frac{c+h}{\alpha}\delta_u + \delta_v - \delta_\omega\right)i_t. \qquad (8.90)$$

If we use this policy rule to solve for the equilibrium interest rate, determining the δ_i from the assumption that forecasts are equal to the projection of the shocks on i_t, the coefficient on i_t in the equation above is equal to the value μ^* in Eq. (8.86). That said, the optimal policy response to an interest rate change is actually an optimal response to the central bank's forecasts of the underlying disturbances, where the forecasts depend on the observed interest rate.

8.8 The Monetary Conditions Index (MCI)

The idea of the monetary conditions index (MCI) is to combine interest rate and exchange rate movements in a consistent manner, thereby expressing the change in *underlying monetary conditions* in a single variable. Using its original form as developed by the Bank of Canada, the MCI is, at a given time t, the weighted sum of the (relative) change in the effective real exchange rate and the (absolute) change in the short-term real rate of interest compared with a base period (Freedman, 1994):

$$MCI_t = w_e \cdot \left[\frac{weighted\ real\ external\ value\ t}{weighted\ real\ value\ in\ base\ period} - 1\right]$$
$$+ w_r \cdot \left[\begin{array}{l}(short\text{-}term\ real\ interest\ rate\ in\ t)\ -\\ (short\text{-}term\ real\ interest\ rate\ in\ base\ period)\end{array}\right]$$

Exchange rate movements are included in the MCI with a weight of *we*, while interest rate movements carry a weight of *wr*. As the MCI relates to an arbitrarily chosen base period, no significance is to be ascribed to its absolute level. The development of the MCI over time indicates whether the underlying monetary conditions have eased (decline in the MCI) or tightened (increase in the MCI).[30]

The indicator properties of MCI for monetary policy are controversial for a number of reasons (Deutsche Bundesbank, 1999). *First*, the MCI actually relates, first and foremost, to the real economy rather than the objective of low inflation. It assumes that a higher interest rate and appreciating real effective exchange rate dampen economic growth and vice versa. That said, it is far from clear as to whether the MCI has – as a theoretical concept – any relation to (future) inflation. Most important in this context, the MCI does not incorporate any monetary variables (like credit and money supply) which could explain systematic changes in the economy's price level.

Second, the definition of the real exchange rate and the choice of the real interest rate included in the MCI influence greatly the computation of the indicator. In fact, the MCI concept does not suggest which interest rate (short- or long-term, money market rates or corporate funding rates) would be appropriate. For instance, countries in which long-term (real) financing relationships play a major role, it would be economically plausible to base the MCI on a long-term (real) interest rate rather than a short-term money market interest rate.

Third, the relative weights with which the individual components are included in the MCI are not directly observable and must therefore be guessed or estimated econometrically. The MCI therefore depends markedly on the specification and the assumptions of these estimations. *Fourth*, it might not be easy and straightforward to interpret changes in the MCI in terms of their significance for monetary policy. If, for instance, the appreciation of the real exchange rate is due to, say, a rise in foreign demand for domestic goods, it would not be at all appropriate for monetary policy to reduce the MCI to its original level: The positive demand shock might be accompanied by an increased inflationary pressure (as, for instance, stronger domestic growth could translate into stronger demand for credit and money). Mechanistically adjusting policy rates in response to exchange rate movements – as suggested by a simple interpretation of the MCI – might not be appropriate.

Figure 8.24(a) shows the German short-term interest rates in nominal and real terms for the period 1972-Q1 to 2007-Q3, while Fig. 8.24(b) depicts a measure of the country's real effective exchange rate. Figure 8.24(c) shows the real short-term interest rate and the real effective exchange rate starting from the base period 1972-Q1, while Fig. 8.24(d) presents various measures of the MCI. The MCI has eased substantially since the early 1990s. In particular the Deutsche Bundesbank

---

[30]For instance, the Bank of Canada used the MCI as a short-term operational reference variable; however, the bank has discontinued the calculation of the MCI as from 31 December 2006 and has not used it as an input into its monetary policy decisions for some time. See in this context Freedman (1994, 1995, 1996). For the use of the MCI in New Zealand see Reserve Bank of New Zealand (1996).

(a) German 3–mths money market rate (%)[1]

(b) Real effective exchange rate of Germany[2]

(c) Changes against the base period

(c) Measures of the MCI

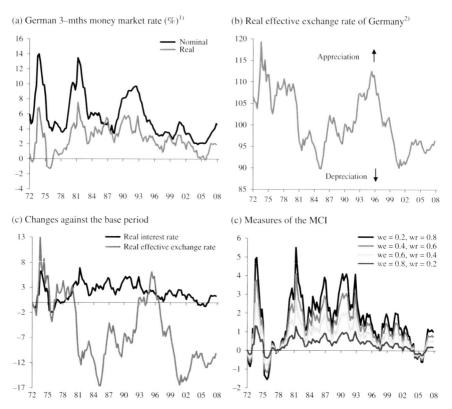

Fig. 8.24   A monetary conditions index (MCI) for Germany
Source: Thomson Financial, Deutsche Bundesbank, own calculations. [1]Real interest rates were calculated by subtracting annual CPI inflation from nominal rates. – [2]Indicator of the German economy's price competitiveness against 20 trading partner countries, based on the deflators of total sales. – Period: 1972-Q1 to 2007-Q3; first quarter 1972 = 0.

monetary policy of lowering the interest rate in the wake of the German reunification recession, accompanied by the depreciation of the real effective exchange rate of the D-mark, which set in in the second half of the 1990s, contributed to a marked lowering of the MCI.

If anything, the MCI appears to be positively related to German real GDP growth – and would (in an ex-post analysis) have given pro-cyclical policy recommendations (Fig. 8.25(a)). As maintaining price stability has become the overriding goal of monetary policy, however, it should be of particular interest to take a look at the relation between the MCI and CPI inflation (Fig. 8.25(b)). For instance, in Germany there was, in anything, a *positive correlation* between the two series: higher (lower) inflation was accompanied by a tighter (easier) MCI. Of course, the MCI would have given rather controversial monetary policy recommendations.

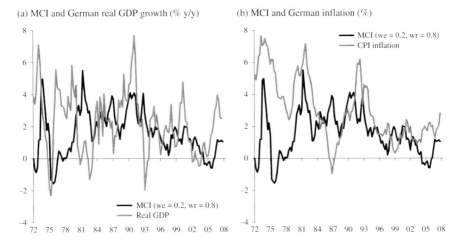

(a) MCI and German real GDP growth (% y/y)   (b) MCI and German inflation (%)

Fig. 8.25   MCI for Germany, GDP growth (% y/y) and CPI inflation (%)
Source: Thomson Financial, Deutsche Bundesbank, own calculations. For the explanation of the
MCI, see previous graph

Digression: **How the ECB and the US Fed Set Interest Rates**

Monetary policies of the ECB and US Fed can be characterised by Taylor rules. In
what follows, we test *classical Taylor rules* as well as *extended Taylor rules*, with
the latter incorporating money growth and the euro-dollar exchange rate (Belke &
Polleit, 2007). For the period under review is 1999–2005. The result might help
shedding light on two aspects: (i) whether the ECB has consistently followed a
(stabilising) rule, and (ii) whether and how the ECB behaved differently than the
US Fed.

Central Bank Reaction Function: The "Taylor Rule"

The monetary policy strategy of the ECB is of particular interest for the analysis
of business cycles but even more so for the ongoing debate on rules versus discretion in monetary policy.[31] In order to explain the interest rate decisions of the
ECB, one may estimate Taylor rule (1993) type reaction functions, according to
which an interest rate under the control of the ECB is made dependent on variables like the domestic inflation rate and the output gap. Due to the short history
of EMU data, most papers on ECB monetary policy have up to now estimated a
Bundesbank or a hypothetical ECB reaction function prior to 1999 and then, e.g.

---

[31] See Carstensen and Colavecchio (2004). For the estimation of monetary policy reaction functions
in general see, e.g., Huang and Lin (2006), Florio (2005) and Altavilla and Landolfo (2005). For
an application to regime shifts in reaction functions see, for instance, Valente (2003).

by testing its out-of-sample forecast properties, compared the implied interest rates with actual ECB rates.[32] There are only a few studies such as, for instance, Fourçans and Vranceanu (2004), Gerdesmeier and Roffia (2003), Ullrich (2003) and Surico (2003) which have actually estimated an ECB reaction function.

Most authors have so far chained up pre-EMU and post-EMU data to obtain long series. However, the implicit assumption of structural stability at the time of the EMU start inherent in these studies is hardly tenable according to our view. Moreover, it is questionable whether one can assume that the national central banks in the pre-EMU period followed on average a consistent strategy which can be compared without frictions with the strategy of the ECB (Belke & Gros, 2005; Gali, 2002). Hence, we base our analysis in this contribution purely on the euro area regime which started in January 1999.

Theory of the Taylor Rule

We start from the usual baseline specification of the Taylor rule concept which looks as follows:

$$i_t = \rho \cdot i_{t-1} + (1 - \rho) \cdot (\beta_0 + \beta_1 \cdot y_t + \beta_2 \cdot \pi_t + \varepsilon_t). \qquad (8.91)$$

The variables included in this specification are the short-term interest rate i_t, the output gap y_t, and the domestic inflation rate π_t. The parameters β_1 and β_2 reflect the long-run weight of the variables output gap (y) and the inflation rate (π), respectively, while the parameter ρ describes the extent of interest rate smoothing chosen by monetary policy. Exactly following other studies in this field, the money market rate is used to approximate the relevant policy rate. As usual, we base our output gap and inflation rate variables on time series which are measured ex post for period t.

An important empirical question relates to the estimated weight on inflation, i.e. to the parameter β_2. Since it is the real interest rate which actually drives private decisions, the size of β_2 needs to assure that – as a response to a rise in inflation – the nominal interest rate is raised sufficiently to actually increase the real interest rate. This so-called *Taylor principle* implies that the coefficient β_2 has to be larger than 1 (Taylor, 1999b; Clarida, Galí, & Gertler, 1998). If not, self-fulfilling bursts of inflation may be possible (see e.g., Bernanke & Woodford, 1997; Clarida et al., 1998; Clarida, Galí, & Gertler, 1999, 2000; Woodford, 2001). For monetary policy to have a stabilising impact on output, a less restrictive condition has to be fulfilled, i.e. β_1 should be positive.

In practice, it is usually observed that, especially since the early 1990s, central banks worldwide tend to move policy interest rates in small steps without reversing

---

[32]See, e.g. Clausen and Hayo (2005), Faust et al. (2001), and Smant (2002) for the first approach and e.g. Clausen and Hayo (2005) and Gerlach-Kristen (2003) for the latter. For a good survey see Sauer and Sturm (2003).

their direction quickly (Amato & Laubach, 1999; Castelnuovo, 2003; Rudebusch, 2002). To incorporate this pattern of interest rate smoothing, our Eq. (8.91) is viewed as the mechanism by which the target interest rate i* is determined. The actual interest rate partially adjusts to this target according to $i_t = (1 - \rho) \cdot i* + \rho \cdot i_{t-1}$, where ρ is the smoothing parameter. This results finally in estimating equation.

In addition to this baseline model, we consider either money growth or the nominal dollar-euro exchange rate as an additional argument contained in the ECB reaction function. The influence of the monetary pillar of the ECB monetary policy strategy is examined by the specification:

$$i_t = \rho \cdot i_{t-1} + (1 - \rho) \cdot (\beta_0 + \beta_1 \cdot y_t + \beta_2 \cdot \pi_t + \beta_3 \cdot \Delta m_t + \varepsilon_t), \qquad (8.92)$$

which additionally includes the annual growth rate of money balances M3, m_t. We include money growth to model the monetary pillar of the ECB strategy which emphasizes the prominent role of M3 growth for interest rate decisions. This may reflect the leading indicator properties of money growth both for inflation (Altimari, 2001) and for the output gap (Coenen, Levin, & Wieland, 2001).

We also analyse whether ECB interest rate decisions are affected by changes in the nominal exchange rate of the dollar against the euro, exr_t:

$$i_t = \rho \cdot i_{t-1} + (1 - \rho) \cdot (\beta_0 + \beta_1 \cdot y_t + \beta_2 \cdot \pi_t + \beta_3 \cdot \Delta exr_t + \varepsilon_t). \qquad (8.93)$$

According to its monetary policy strategy, the ECB claims to pay attention to a broad set of economic variables that may help to assess the presence of threats to price stability. We see two arguments which speak in favour of an inclusion of the exchange rate in the reaction function. *First*, while it is not clear whether central banks directly react to exchange rate changes (Taylor, 2001), the ECB might have been particularly tempted to counteract devaluations in the first years of EMU in an attempt to establishing the reputation of the single currency as a successful successor of the D-mark. *Second*, a direct influence of exchange rate changes in the instrument rule can pay off in terms of reduced inflation variance (Ball, 1999; Taylor, 1999b).

Empirical Evidence of the Taylor Rule

Preliminaries. – Many studies show that monetary policy in Germany[33] and the hypothetical euro area prior to 1999 followed the Taylor principle with β_2 exceeding 1.[34] With respect to ECB policy, however, the preliminary consensus reached looks rather different. The results gained by Gerdesmeier and Roffia (2003) and Ullrich (2003) who use standard output gap measures based on

---

[33]See, for instance, Clarida et al. (1998), Clausen and Hayo (2005), Faust et al. (2001), Peersman and Smets (1998) and Smant (2002).

[34]See, e.g., Clausen and Hayo (2005), Gerlach-Kristen (2003), Gerlach and Schnabel (2000), Peersman and Smets (1998) and Ullrich (2003).

Hodrick-Prescott-filtered industrial production contradict those brought forward both by Fourçans and Vranceanu (2004) who take the annual growth rate of industrial production as a measure of the business cycle and by the literature on Taylor rules for both Germany and the hypothetical euro area. While Fourçans and Vranceanu (2004) find the ECB to react strongly to variations in the inflation rate and much less to output variations, both Gerdesmeier and Roffia (2003) and Ullrich (2003) somewhat surprisingly identify small reactions to inflation and – both in relative and in absolute terms – strong responses to output deviations. Fourçans and Vranceanu (2004) arrive at coefficient estimates of $\beta_1 = 0.18$ and $\beta_2 = 1.16$ for the sample 1999:4-2002:2. Gerdesmeier and Roffia (2003) estimate $\beta_1 = 0.30$ and $\beta_2 = 0.45$ based on a sample 1999:1-2002:1. For a sample of 1999:1-2002:8, Ullrich (2003) comes up with $\beta_1 = 0.63$ and $\beta_2 = 0.25$.[35] Furthermore, Ullrich (2003) observes a structural break between pre-1999 and post-1999 monetary policy in the euro area.

Data and methods. – Following most of the literature, we use ex-post realized data and apply the generalized method of moments (GMM) to estimate the ECB and the Fed reaction function. In order to compare a Taylor Rule with actual monetary policy, we need to find proxies for the stance of monetary policy, inflation and the output gap. We conduct the GMM estimations both for quarterly and monthly data. The sample period for our estimations of the ECB and Fed interest setting behaviour is 1999Q1 to 2005Q02. We measure actual monetary policy by the three-month money market rates (ISR_EU and ISR_US). Euro area inflation is measured by the year-on-year percentage change in the harmonised index of consumer prices for the euro area (D4LNCPI_EU). US inflation is calculated on the basis of the consumer price index (D4LNCPI_US). Money growth is measured by the year-on-year percentage change in M3 for the euro area (D4LNM3_EU), and by the year-on-year percentage change in M2 for the US (D4LNM2_US). The output gap (OUTPUTGAP_EU and OUTPUTGAP_US) is calculated by the first difference between real GDP in logs and the Hodrick-Prescott filtered log real GDP with the smoothing parameter set at $\lambda = 1600$).[36] As exchange rate variable we used the annual growth rate of the nominal dollar exchange rate vis-à-vis the euro (GROWTH_EUROUSD), i.e. the first difference of order 4 of the log exchange rate (Taylor, 2001, p. 6). Since the null hypothesis of non-stationarity cannot be rejected for the levels of our exchange rate variable but can be rejected for the first differences at the usual 5 percent level, we used first differences of the exchange rate variable in our regressions.[37] As usual, we applied the first difference of order 4 in

---

[35] A further example is Surico (2003a) who comes up with the following estimates: $\beta_1 = 0.77$ and $\beta_2 = 0.47$ for the sample 1997:07-2002:10.

[36] However, in the simulations part of this paper, we complementarily use monthly data (Belke & Gros, 2005). Since our measure of the output gap based on industrial production is much more volatile than Taylor's (1993) original GDP-based output gap, the results might be biased and we mainly focus on the results based on GDP series and quarterly data, as is also sometimes preferred in the literature (see, e.g. the survey by Ullrich, 2003).

[37] We used a wide spectrum of unit root tests, among others, e.g., the ADF-test, the Elliott-Rothenberg-Stock DF-GLS test and the Kwiatkowski-Phillips-Schmidt-Shin test. The results are available on request.

strict analogy with our measure of the inflation rate. An increase of the exchange rate variable indicates an appreciation of the euro.

As far as the output gap specification is concerned, we strictly follow Clarida et al. (1998) and Faust, Rogers, and Wright (2001) and finalize our analysis with the complementary use of monthly data. In this case of monthly data, we use the industrial production index for the euro area and apply a standard Hodrick-Prescott filter (with the smoothing parameter set at $\lambda = 14,400$) to calculate the output gap as the deviation of the logarithm of actual industrial production from its trend.[38]

In the case of monthly data, we base our analysis of the ECB behaviour on the period from January 1999 to August 2005. The analysed time period for the US comprises the *Greenspan era*, starting in August 1987. As exchange rate variable we used the annual growth rate of the nominal dollar exchange rate vis-à-vis the euro (GROWTH_USEUR), i.e. the first difference of order 12 of the log exchange rate. An increase of the exchange rate variable indicates an appreciation of the euro.

The GMM approach essentially consists of an instrumental variables estimation of Eq. (1) and becomes necessary because at the time of an interest rate decision, the ECB cannot observe the ex post realized contemporaneous right-hand side variables in Eqs. (8.91), (8.92) and (8.93). Hence, it bases its decisions on information which comprises lagged variables only. The weighting matrix in the objective function is chosen in order to allow the GMM estimates to be robust to possible heteroskedasticity and serial correlation of unknown form in the error terms (for a recent application see Carstensen & Colavecchio, 2004).

The chosen instruments need to be predetermined at the time of an interest rate decision. Hence, they have to be dated on period t-1 or earlier. They should help to predict the contemporaneous variables which are still unobserved at time t. For exactly this purpose, we include the first four lags of the nominal interest rate, inflation, the output gap, money growth, and the euro-dollar exchange rate. The former three variables are typically used as instruments in related work (Sauer & Sturm, 2003; Gerdesmeier & Roffia, 2003; Ullrich, 2003). We also include money growth and the nominal euro-dollar exchange rate. The choice of a relatively small number of lags for the instruments is intended to minimize the potential small sample bias that may arise when too many over-identifying restrictions are imposed. To confirm that we have chosen an appropriate instrument set, we run a first stage regression of inflation and other variables of Eqs. (1), (2) and (3) on the instrumental variables and perform an F-test for their joint significance (Kamps & Pierdzioch, 2002).

A second important property of the instrumental variables is their exogeneity with respect to the central bank decisions and, hence, their uncorrelatedness with the disturbances which reflect deviations from the policy rule that are unpredictable ex ante. To test this property, we perform a standard J-test for the validity of the over-identifying restrictions (Hansen, 1982, and Tables 8.13 and 8.14 below). We dispense with the robustness checks by means of the ordinary OLS procedure which

---

[38]Despite the increasing share of services in the overall economy, it is still commonly assumed that the industrial sector is the 'cycle maker' and that it leads significant parts of the economy. See Sauer and Sturm (2003).

are widely used in the literature because otherwise the regressors would unlikely be weakly exogenous.

Empirical results for ECB monetary policy. –Table 8.10 presents a review of three different Taylor rule estimations based on our Eqs. (8.91), (8.92) and (8.93), using quarterly data. Column 3, shows the results for our baseline specification of the Taylor rule according to Eq. (8.91). The degree of interest rate smoothing and the ECB's response to inflation is rather small, whereas the weight of the output gap is large (and significantly larger than for inflation).

Compared to the original Taylor rule which postulates weights of 0.5 both for the output gap and inflation, respectively, the influence of the business cycle situation on the decisions of the ECB seems to be strong. However, the inflation weight proves to be smaller than according to the original Taylor rule and falls considerably below 1. Hence, the so-called Taylor principle $\beta_2 > 1$ which would guarantee that an increase in the nominal interest rate causes an increase in the real interest rate with the desired dampening impact on inflation is clearly not fulfilled. However, note that our findings are in line with the few other available studies.

Adding money growth and the exchange rate change to the Taylor rule specification (column 4 which corresponds with our Eq. (8.92)), leads to a slightly different picture. Independent from the significance of the output gap and the inflation rate, we are able to establish a significant impact of money on the interest rate decisions. Moreover, the coefficient of money growth is positive as expected from theory. Presumably, this result is caused by the fact that the ECB considered the high money growth rates in the aftermath of the stock market downswing as portfolio adjustments that did make interest rate responses necessary.[39] At the same time and most remarkably, the coefficient of inflation changes becomes negative. One explanation for this quite striking result might be that the ECB pursued its anti-inflationary course by means of reacting to higher money growth rather than to actual inflation.

Another explanation might be that the ECB might not have responded strongly to actual inflation due to uncertainty and data release lags. Since inflation expectations on the part of the ECB (operationalised by the bank's near-term inflation outlook as published in the Bulletins) tended to fall short of actual future inflation in our sample, it should make a difference for the estimates which variables are used – actual or expected ones.[40] Finally, the time profile of the lag structure in the relation

---

[39]For a detailed analysis of the effects of the stock market downswing and the accompanying financial uncertainty on EMU money demand and on measures of excess liquidity derived from money demand, see Carstensen (2004) and Greiber and Lemke (2005).

[40]Giannone, Reichlin, and Sala (2002, p. 11), deliver a third competing argument. They argue that the reaction function used here is not conditioned on shocks like demand or technology shocks but on the variables themselves. The use of a reaction function not conditioned on shocks might result in a coefficient smaller than unity depending on the ratio of inflation variance caused by demand to inflation variance caused by technology. A low value of this ratio causes a small coefficient. For a similar argument see also Ullrich (2003, p. 10).

Table 8.10 Empirical Taylor reaction functions of the ECB GMM estimations, Quarterly data, 1999Q1–2005Q2

Explanatory variable	Parameter	Specification Eq. (1)	Specification Eq. (2)	Specification Eq. (3)
Lagged interest rate	ρ	0.75***	0.70***	0.65***
		(0.02)	(0.01)	(0.02)
Constant	β_0	0.02***	0.02***	0.03***
		(0.004)	(0.001)	(0.002)
Output gap	β_1	1.94***	2.41***	1.12***
		(0.08)	(0.06)	(0.14)
Inflation rate	β_2	0.49***,**	−0.16***	0.01
		(0.19)	(0.03)	(0.09)
Money	β_3		0.19***	
			(0.03)	
Exchange rate	β_4			−0.04*** (0.009)
Statistics				
J-statistic		0.15 (p>0.75, df=8)	0.18 (p>0.90, df=11)	0.14 (p>0.75, df=7)
R-squared		0.95	0.95	0.95

Notes: Standard errors are given in parentheses below the estimated values (*/**/*** indicating significance on the 10/5/1 percent level). p-values are given in parentheses below the J-test statistics (df = degrees of freedom). For the GMM estimation the first four lags of the short-term interest rate, the inflation rate, the output gap, the money growth rate (if implemented), and the rate of change of the dollar-euro exchange rate (if implemented) are used as instruments (see, e.g., Kamps & Pierdzioch, 2002; Carstensen & Colavecchio, 2004).

between money growth and consumer price inflation works reasonably well as an explanation – as shown by an additional investigation of the correlations between the respective time series. Although both parameters for inflation and for money growth appear to be very close, a simple Wald test of coefficient restrictions (whose results are available on request) reveals that the sum between both coefficient estimates is significant, i.e. we have to reject the null hypothesis that the estimates are numerically the same in absolute values. Hence, there is no need to look for a special explanation of numerically equal parameter estimates.

In our final specification (column (5) which corresponds with our Eq. (8.93)), the inflation variable even becomes insignificant. However, the coefficient of the output gap, albeit smaller, stays highly significant. Again, also in specification 3 the high significance and the high value of the estimated coefficient of the output gap in the ECB reaction function deserves special attention, even though it possesses a coefficient lower than the other tabulated specifications. Thus, there is again clear evidence of a business cycle orientation of the ECB.

Even though the coefficient of the exchange rate is relatively small compared to the ones of the other explanatory variables, it is highly significant and displays the expected negative sign. As discussed in Taylor (2001), an appreciation of the euro leads to a relaxation of monetary policy. Moreover, our point estimates are in the range analysed by Taylor (1999b). According to our estimates, a one percent devaluation of the euro leads to a long-run interest increase of four basis points. The significance of the coefficient of the exchange rate – although it is quite small – suggests that including the exchange rate leads to a stable specification (8.93) which describes the monetary policy rule of the ECB pretty well. By this, we empirically corroborate the rule of thumb that – as a monetary policy rule – a substantial appreciation of the exchange rate furnishes a prima facie case for relaxing monetary policy (Obstfeld & Rogoff, 1995, p. 93, and Sect. II).

One interpretation of this rule of thumb would be that the coefficient of the exchange rate change is less than zero. Then a higher than normal exchange rate would call on the central bank to lower the short-term interest rate, which presumably would represent a relaxing of monetary policy. Or, the appreciation of the exchange rate today (period t, say) will increase the probability that the central bank will lower the interest rate in the future (period t+1, say). With a rational expectations model of the term structure of interest rates, these expectations of lower future short term interest rates will tend to lower long-term interest rates today. Thus the appreciation of the exchange rate, through the effects of exchange rate transmission and the existence of a policy rule, will result in a decline in interest rates today. However, our results do not support the competing view that policy makers should heed the Obstfeld-Rogoff warning that substantial departures from PPP, in the short run and even over decades make such a policy reaction to the exchange rate undesirable.

Let us finally turn to the issue of interest rate smoothing. Note that our estimates of ρ, which range from 0.65 to 0.75, are quite high. However, coefficients are not so close to 1 so that the estimation uncertainty of the long-run weights would become really large. In fact, our results are in line with Gerdesmeier and Roffia (2003) who estimate ρ to be 0.72 and Fourçans and Vranceanu (2004) who arrive at an estimate of $\rho = 0.73$.

The findings above appear to be robust in the sense that the J-statistic testing the over-identifying restrictions is insignificant across all specifications tested. In Table 8.10, we use the J-statistic to test the validity of over-identifying restrictions when we have (as in our case) more instruments than parameters to estimate. Under the null-hypothesis, that is the over-identifying restrictions are satisfied, the J-statistic multiplied by the number of regression observations is asymptotically distributed with degrees of freedom equal to the number of over-identifying restrictions (Favero, 2001). According to the results tabulated in the second last row of Table 8.10, all our models are correctly specified because all p-values are higher than their critical counterparts.

Overall, the results displayed in Table 8.10 are conclusive. All regressions show that interest rate policy from 1999 on did not follow the Taylor principle as β_2 does not exceed 1 consistently. The inflation parameter for the ECB period (β_2) is usually lower than the output parameter (β_1) and does not exceed one. Hence, from this pattern one might even conclude that the ECB tended to accommodate changes in inflation. This is also suggested by the standard specification in column 3 of Table 8.10 which reports a positive and significant coefficient for inflation.

The results presented above accentuate those of Gerdesmeier and Roffia (2003) and Ullrich (2003), who suggest that the ECB reacts to a rise in expected inflation by raising nominal short-term interest rates by a relatively small amount and thus letting real short-term interest rates decline. Hence, instead of continuing the Bundesbank's inflation stabilising policy, the ECB appears to have followed a policy rather comparable to the pre-Volcker era of the Fed, for which e.g. Taylor (1999a) and Clarida et al. (2000) have found values for β_2 well below one.[41]

Estimation results for Fed policy. – Table 8.11 presents a review of three different Taylor rule estimations based on Eqs. (8.91), (8.92) and (8.93) for the US, again using quarterly data. The results for the basic specification are displayed in Table 8.11 (column (3), Eq. (8.91)). Using ex post measured variables in the baseline specification (1) leads to a rather strong interest rate smoothing, a large weight of the output gap and an even larger one of inflation. Compared to the original Taylor rule with weights of 0.5 both for the output gap and inflation, respectively, the impact of inflation on Fed decisions is relatively strong. However, the weights of inflation and of the output gap are not too different. The inflation weight is larger than in the original Taylor rule and considerably above 1. Hence, the so-called Taylor principle

---

[41] Taylor (1999a) arrives at values of $\beta_1 = 0.25$ and $\beta_2 = 0.81$ with ex-post data for the US for that period, while Orphanides (2001) estimates a forward-looking rule with real-time data and reports $\beta_1 = 0.57$ and $\beta_2 = 1.64$.

$\beta_2 > 1$ is clearly fulfilled. Hence, an increase in the nominal interest rate tends to cause an increase in the real interest rate and a dampening of inflation.

Adding money growth to the baseline variables yields (column (4), Eq. (8.92)), which has a stronger degree of interest rate smoothing than before. This does not change the pattern of the results for inflation and the output gap at all. However, in contrast to our estimates for the ECB, the sign of the coefficient of M2 growth is negative. Hence, higher M2 growth tends to lead to lower realisations of the policy variable.

If we finally include dollar-euro exchange rate changes in our Taylor rule specification (column (5) of Table 8.11), the coefficient of inflation remains highly significant. The coefficient of the output gap is even larger and again highly significant. Even though the coefficient of the exchange rate is relatively small compared to the ones of the other explanatory variables, it is clearly significant and has the expected positive sign. An appreciation of the euro (a rising exchange rate) leads to a more restrictive monetary policy of the Fed. According to our estimates, a one percent devaluation of the dollar leads to a long-run interest increase of twelve basis points. This interest rate reaction is three times as high as in the ECB case.

At last, we should make some comments on the estimated extent of the Fed's interest rate smoothing behaviour (row 2 of Table 8.11). The parameter ρ is estimated to be significantly larger than in the euro area and falls into a range between 0.84 and 0.91. From an economic point of view, our evidence on interest rate smoothing can be interpreted as follows. Since it captures the impact of the lagged interest rate on the current interest rate decision i becomes more and more important as ρ tends to one. Consequently, the relative importance of other explanatory variables should diminish. It may even be the case that they are not suitable anymore to explain the long run patterns of the policy variable (see, e.g., Carstensen and Colavecchio, 2004, p. 11). However, we observe exactly the opposite in the case of the Fed. The additional variables are highly significant and have coefficients which are large in absolute and relative terms. Overall, the smoothing parameter estimates a bit more away from 1 are obtained in the specifications (8.91) and (8.93) in which our money growth indicator is not included.

Simulations

To shed light on the question as to whether the central bank complied with the Taylor rule in the more recent past, we make use of one-period-ahead forecasts. By doing so, we should be able to quantify the difference between the actual and the fitted, or Taylor, interest rate. We make use of static one-step-ahead forecasts based on our specifications of the Taylor reaction functions including interest smoothing behaviour. In this context, (a) in-sample and (b) out-of-sample forecasts will be produced. Case (a) allows to investigate whether the central bank sets interests rates according to a Taylor rule which is estimated based on data for the whole available

Table 8.11 Empirical Taylor reaction functions of the Fed GMM estimations, quarterly data, 1999Q1-2005Q2

Explanatory variable	Parameter	Specification Eq. (1)	Specification Eq. (2)	Specification Eq. (3)
Lagged interest rate	ρ	0.87***	0.91***	0.84***
		(0.02)	(0.03)	(0.02)
Constant	β_0	−0.03***	0.02	−0.03**
		(0.01)	(0.04)	(0.01)
Output gap	β_1	1.98***	1.77***	2.97***
		(0.22)	(0.35)	(0.31)
Inflation rate	β_2	2.57***	2.51***	2.27***
		(0.52)	(0.98)	(0.48)
Money	β_3		−0.85*	
			(0.59)	
Exchange rate	β_4			0.12***
				(0.03)
Statistics				
J-statistic		0.26 (p>0.50, df=8)	0.20 (p>0.50, df=7)	0.21 (p>0.90, df=11)
R-squared		0.97	0.97	0.96

For notes see Table 8.10.

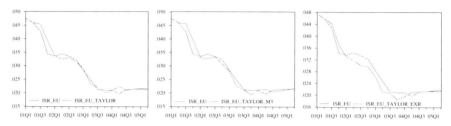

Fig. 8.26 Short-term interest rate and Taylor rate in the euro area 2001Q3-2005Q, full-sample estimates and in-sample forecasts
Note: One-Period-ahead in-sample forecasts based on GMM estimates. For details see footnotes to Table 8.10.

sample period. Case (b) shall provide insights as to whether the central banks stuck to their rule, which was estimated for a sub-period, throughout the total period under review.

While our in-sample forecasts (case (a)) are based on exactly the same estimations and especially the same estimation period which were presented in Tables 8.10 and 8.11, our out-of-sample forecasts (case (b)) necessitate the re-estimation of the same specifications for a shorter time-horizon. This ex-ante forecasting or post-sample prediction exercise helps forecasting observations that do not appear in the data set used to estimate the forecasting equation. Since case (b) would have resulted in a serious lack of degrees of freedom due to insufficient data points, we decided to make use of monthly data if we enact out-of-sample forecasts.[42]

Figures 8.26 and 8.27 illustrate the results of the in-sample forecasts of monetary policy according to a Taylor rule which is estimated over the whole available sample independent on the start of the forecast period (case (a)). Figures 8.28 and 8.29 exhibit the prediction of a Taylor rule over the whole sample when this Taylor rule is estimated only up to the start of the out-of-sample forecast period (case (b)).

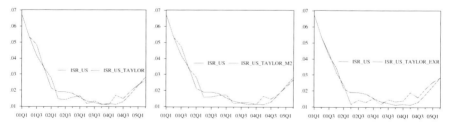

Fig. 8.27 Short-term interest rate and Taylor rate in the US 2001Q3-2005Q2, full-sample estimates and in-sample forecasts
Note: One-Period-ahead in-sample forecasts based on GMM estimates. For details see footnotes to Table 8.11.

---

[42]Inoue and Kilian (2002) show that in-sample tests of predictability are at least as credible as the results of out-of-sample tests. Hence, there is no reason to emphasize only one type of forecasts a priori.

Fig. 8.28 Short-term interest rate and Taylor rate in the euro area 2001M05-2005M08, Out-of-sample forecasts based on GMM estimates
Note: Out-of-sample forecasts based on GMM estimates. Estimation period is 1999M01 2001M04 for the first two figures and 1999M01 2001M05 for the last figure. For the first two figures, the forecast period amounts to 2001M05-2005M08, and for the last figure it is 2001M06-2005M08. For further details see footnotes to Table 8.10.

Each Figure contains three graphs which depict the course of actual monetary policy together with the Taylor rule estimated by Eqs. (8.91), (8.92) and (8.93).

Our first choice for setting the start date of the forecast period is (the 11th) September 2001, because this started a period of unprecedented political and financial market instability. The second choice would be the turn-of-year 2000/2001, with which came the meltdown of stock market valuations (Belke & Gros, 2005). The exact dates of the chosen sample splits are recorded in the tables.

As far as the in-sample forecasts for the euro area are concerned, the estimated realisations of the central bank rate follow closely the actual interest rate. This should be of little surprise, given the rather high R-squared of the estimations in Tables 8.10 and 8.11. In the most recent quarters in 2005, however, the Taylor rate slightly exceeded the actual ECB rate (the opposite is the case for the first two quarters of 2005 with regard to the Fed). This would imply that euro interest rates are currently slightly too low as compared with the implicit Taylor rule.

Next, according to the Taylor specifications including money growth, both monetary policies have been too expansionary during the third and the fourth quarter

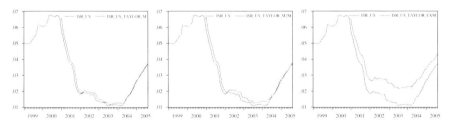

Fig. 8.29 -Short-term interest rate and Taylor rate in the US 2001M01-2005M08, out-of-sample forecasts based on GMM estimates
Note: Out-of-sample forecasts based on GMM estimates. Estimation period lasts from the start of the Greenspan area August 1987 until the start of the crisis of 2000/2001 in December 2000. For details see footnotes to Table 8.11.

of 2001 and the first and the second quarter of 2004. A similar pattern emerges for specifications (8.92) and (8.93). In contrast, if one considers the specification including the exchange rate, euro area monetary policy appeared to have slightly too strict from the first quarter of 2002 until the first quarter of 2004. Let us now turn to our out-of-sample forecasts of the policy variable for the ECB and the Fed.

Note again that out-of-sample forecasting represents a particularly interesting exercise, as it allows detecting deviations of actual monetary policy rates from normative Taylor rate levels. Since it is generally agreed that evaluating forecasts must be done exclusively on their ex ante performance, we mainly comment on Figs. 8.24 and 8.29.

As far as the euro area is concerned, one finds a significant negative deviation of the actual interest rate from the estimated interest rate which corresponds to the (Taylor) rule from the midst-of-2003 on up to August 2005. This is striking especially because we also included the estimated extent of interest rate smoothing in the normative Taylor interest rate and, by this, corrected for stickiness in interest rate setting in times of uncertainty. Overall, we conclude that ECB monetary policy has been to be too expansionary already since two years. The negative deviations of actual rates from the rule might be interpreted as a clear sign that the bank has significantly downgraded the role of money in its policy strategy and actual policy making since May 2003.

Fed actions appear to have been significantly different from that of the ECB. In fact, the Fed seems to have strictly followed its Taylor rule since 2000/2001. Such a conclusion alters only if the change of the euro-dollar exchange rate is included in the Taylor rule specification. Here, the Fed did not react to the depreciation of the dollar as sharply as it did prior to 2000/2001. One explanation for this pattern might be that, given its multi-indicator approach, the Fed might have tried to help reducing the current account deficit by short-term rate changes. This could also explain why the fit between the actual and Taylor rate as shown in Fig. 8.29, third graph, is not as perfect as depicted in Taylor (1993).

In general, the standard Taylor rule, with the Taylor's normative weights, appears to be a much better way to characterise the rate setting behaviour of the Fed than that of the ECB. Moreover, the Fed has shown a stronger (preference for) interest rate smoothing under the Taylor rule compared with the ECB. That might explain why, following the crisis of 2000/2001, the Fed's rates have remained in line with the Taylor rate whereas the ECB has deviated from its pre-crisis Taylor rule policy behaviour.

Concluding Remarks

According to the findings presented in this section, the interest rate setting behaviour of the ECB and the Fed in the period 1999–2005 and 1987–2005, respectively, can be pretty well characterised by some form of Taylor rule. However, the standard

Taylor rule appears to be a much better tool for modelling the behaviour of the Fed than that of the ECB.[43]

The empirical estimates for the euro area suggest that the ECB puts a larger weight on the output gap relative to inflation. Such a conclusion is shared by other authors. Faust et al. (2001) argue that the ECB puts too high a weight on the output gap relative to inflation, especially in comparison to the Bundesbank. However, the low weight which the ECB has assigned to inflation might be due to the fact that inflation was fairly low in the sample period. Moreover, the estimates also show that money growth appear to have played an important role in the ECB' rate setting. Moreover, the exchange rate has a small, albeit significant effect as well.

The test results indicate that the Fed has been following the estimated Taylor rule in a rather stable manner during the Greenspan era. This does not change if money growth is included as an additional variable in the Taylor rule, but it becomes somewhat less obvious when the change of the euro-dollar exchange rate is taken into account. As a particularly interesting side-aspect, money growth seems to have played an important role in Fed rate decisions as well.

Comparing the Taylor rule estimations of the two central banks, the Fed displayed a much greater tendency for interest rate smoothing compared with its counterpart in the euro area. This might explain why, following the crisis of 2000/2001, the Fed's rates have remained fairly in line with the Taylor rate (even in view of a series of unprecedented interest rate cuts), whereas the ECB has deviated from its pre-crisis Taylor rule policy behaviour.

In fact, the findings do not suggest that the ECB has followed a stable rate setting pattern stabilizing throughout the sample period, whereas the Fed appears to have adhered to its rate setting behaviour. In fact, the ECB seems to have pursued too expansionary a policy after 2000/01.

Looking at contemporaneous Taylor rules, our results suggests that the ECB has de facto even accommodated changes in inflation and, hence, might have even followed a pro-cyclical, e.g. destabilising, policy. In contrast to the Fed, the ECB's nominal policy rate changes were not large enough to actually influence real short term interest rates. Such an interpretation gives rise to the conjecture that the ECB follows a policy quite similar to the pre-Volcker era of US monetary policy, a time also known as the "Great Inflation" (Taylor, 1999a).

However, some words of caution might be in order. In general and in relation to data used in the applications, the number of the observations is rather small (only 26 – 1999Q1 to 2005Q2). Therefore, the estimations risk not to be robust. It is important to recognize this drawback in the analysis. We addressed this caveat in this section for instance when we enhanced the frequency of the data set, i.e. applied monthly instead of quarterly data.

Moreover, one should always be aware of the fact that time series properties are more a question of the time span (sample issue) than of the numbers of observations investigated. Hence, we will be able to come up with more satisfactory results in

---

[43] See, however, Österholm (2005) who conjectures that the Taylor rule appears to be a questionable tool for evaluation of the Federal Reserve during the investigated samples.

terms of degrees of freedom only when some further time will have elapsed. Never-theless, it is time now to follow pioneers in the field (see Sect. 3.1) and to actually estimate an ECB reaction function. We feel all the more legitimised to do so because (a) our time span clearly goes beyond those samples used in the above mentioned studies by nearly 100 percent and (b) we follow those studies by complementarily using monthly data in order to escape the problem of limited degrees of freedom (although one should be aware that this is only a limited device to assess time series properties more accurately).

More specifically, Clarida et al. (2000, p. 154) argue that a short sample with little variability in inflation, especially with only small deviations from the target rate, might lead to too low an estimate of the inflation parameter. So far, data are only available for less than two completed business cycles and the actual inflation rate is close to the target the ECB has set itself. In that sense, recent inflation rates are not at all comparable to those during the 1970s. It might also be the case that the ECB would act much more aggressively against larger deviations of inflation from its own goal than can be seen in the data so far. As suggested by e.g. Clarida and Gertler (1996), central banks react differently to expected inflation above trend as compared to expected inflation below trend. They show that the Bundesbank clearly reacted in the former case, whereas in the latter case they hardly responded. Given data limitations, it is too early for us to tell whether or not the same holds for the ECB.

A final but important caveat relates to Svensson's (2003) observation that interest rate changes affect inflation and output with a sizeable lag. Hence, monetary policy should be modeled in a forward-looking fashion. Any Taylor rule estimation should be based on expected inflation and output. The results gained by Gorter, Jacobs, & De Haan (2008) suggest that the use of expectations leads to different estimates of a Taylor rule model.

In the final section (Digression II) we would like to ask whether there are asym-metries in trans-Atlantic monetary policy making in the sense that the ECB follows the Fed in its decisions. This question is more topical than ever in the wake of the recent and at the time of writing this textbook still ongoing subprime credit crisis and the fundamentally different reactions of the Fed and the ECB to the latter (see Chap. 8). Since the central banks' interest rate cycle connected with the crisis does not appear to be run through completely up to now, we would like to argue that it makes much sense to investigate, instead, the most recent completed episode of an inactive ECB and a pro-active Fed as a case study – namely the period up around the years 2000, 2001 and afterwards. This is done in the following.

Digression II: Does the ECB Follow the Fed?

The belief that the ECB follows the US Federal reserve in setting its policy is so entrenched with market participants and commentators that the search for empirical support would seem to be a trivial task. However, this is not the case. We find that the ECB is indeed often influenced by the Fed, but the reverse is true at least as often if one considers longer sample periods. There is empirically little support for the proposition that there has been for a long time a systematic asymmetric leader-follower relationship between the ECB and the Fed. Only after September 2001 is there more evidence of such an asymmetry. We also find a clear cut structural break between the pre-EMU and the EMU period in terms of the relationship between short term interest rates on both sides of the Atlantic (Belke & Gros, 2005).

Motivation

In this digression we will address the question of whether the ECB has systematically followed the US Federal Reserve in setting interest rates. It is difficult to document "conventional wisdom" because it seems so obvious to everybody that few bother to actually provide evidence for it. One of the few instances in which it is possible to document the widespread expectation that the ECB follows the Fed is related in Garcia-Cervero (2002). In a Reuters poll of economists taken in November, 2002, the proportion of those expecting a cut by the ECB almost doubled (from 21–43%) the day after the Fed did cut rates on November 5th. Later on, these analysts were proved to be wrong, but were they wrong at changing their mind in the first place?

While many seem to be convinced that the ECB does follow the Fed, few seem to ask the obvious question: What could be the rationale for the ECB to follow the Fed? The simplest explanation would be that moves by the Fed provide the ECB with an important signal about the state of the US economy and financial markets. One implication of this explanation would be that the ECB should follow the Fed almost immediately because it would not have any reason to delay its move once the signal has been given. One could thus account for the episode related above (Begg, Canova, de Grauwe, Fatás, & Lane, 2002, p. 42). The problem with this argument is that it implies that then the Fed should also follow the ECB because the euro area is of a similar size as the US economy. However, nobody seems to suggest that the Fed might also follow the ECB.

Another explanation might be that the US cycle precedes that of the euro area so that the ECB might appear to follow the Fed, but in reality it just reacts to the evolution of the euro area's cycle, which happens to lag that of the US. The problem with this explanation is that leads and lags in macroeconomic variables like output and employment are usually measured in months or quarters (Begg et al., 2002, p. 41 ff., estimate the lag at 3–5 months), whereas the ECB is usually assumed to follow the Fed within a much shorter time frame. (See the example reported above.) Moreover, the business cycle effect should be accounted for by the autoregressive element that is present in standard causality tests. Finally, recent research clearly demonstrated that the impact of the US business cycle has become significantly weaker throughout the nineties as compared to the seventies and eighties. This is mainly due to the emergence of multinational firms which can afford to stick to longer-term strategies independent of business cycle troughs (Schroeder et al., 2002). Hence, this approach is not well-suited as an explanation for the "leader-follower" pattern.

Perhaps the most popular explanation why the ECB might follow the Fed is that the ECB is simply slow and inefficient. This explanation would roughly run as follows: The world's financial markets were buffeted over the last years by the emergence and then the bursting of an asset price bubble. The leadership of the Fed (Alan Greenspan in particular) is simply smarter and was quicker to spot the problems. By contrast, so the story seems to go, the ECB is a new institution that still has to find its ways, and its decision making body is too large to come to quick decisions, especially given that it usually tries to forge a consensus before moving (Belke, Koesters, Leschke, & Polleit, 2002; Wyplosz, 2001).

Another explanation could be grounded in a fundamental difference between the US and the euro zone economies: namely that the US economy is more flexible. This has important implications especially in times of heightened uncertainty (Belke & Goecke, 2008). This can be seen most easily through the concept of the "option value of waiting" already explained in depth in Sect. 5.3.3 of this book where we discussed the path-dependent natural rate of (un)employment as a target of monetary policy and the impact of uncertainty on it. Remember that this concept formalises a common sense decision rule: if a decision involves some sunk costs, or any other element of irreversibility, it makes sense to postpone the decision until the uncertainty has been resolved. The temptation to postpone investment decisions is particularly strong when sunk costs are high and when the uncertainty is likely to be resolved in the near future. One can imagine in particular enterprises that have to consider normal investment projects, i.e. projects that would be slightly profitable under current circumstances and even more profitable in case the uncertainty is resolved in a positive sense, but would lead to losses if the uncertainty is resolved in a negative sense. In this case the enterprise would lose little (in terms of foregone profits) if it waited with the decision. Once the uncertainty has been resolved it would still have the option to proceed if the outcome is positive.[44]

The concept of the "option value of waiting" applies also to the ECB. If, during times of unusual uncertainty, it cuts rates today it risks having to reverse its decision soon. The ECB should thus cut today only if it is convinced that such a cut would make sense even if the uncertainty is resolved in a positive way. In this sense, monetary policy is not a game of "follow the leader", but of setting the right policy in the light of domestic inflation and growth prospects.

The models of decision-making under uncertainty also have a second implication. All decisions involve some transaction costs – whether they are about investment, or about hiring and firing. These last are especially important in Europe. This implies that businesses facing only a small change in prices may not respond immediately. There is always a band of inaction – a price range within which it does not pay to change course. The size of this band of inaction increases as uncertainty increases. And, given the structural rigidities in the euro zone economy, uncertainties probably affect decision-making in Europe more than they do in the US. As transactions costs (which are effectively sunk costs) are more important in the euro area than in the US it follows that for the ECB the option value of waiting for more

---

[44]See Belke and Gros (2003). For a more formalized treatment of monetary policy effectiveness under uncertainty based on the real option approach see Belke and Goecke (2003).

information should be higher and might thus explain why the ECB is slower to react to signals than the Fed.

The problem with this explanation, however, is that it should hold only for periods when volatility is temporarily higher than usual because the option value argument is valid only if the uncertainty is resolved (diminished) after a certain period. The option value of waiting argument should thus apply only when financial markets are "excessively" turbulent. We find some evidence for this hypothesis in the sense that we find that it is mainly after September 2001 that the Fed seems to influence the ECB (and not vice versa).

The remainder of this part of the book applies a battery of quantitative and qualitative techniques to validate the hypothesis that *the ECB systematically follows the US Federal Reserve* with its decisions. This hypothesis can also be put as a question: Does the probability of an interest rate move by the ECB increase after the Fed has moved (but not the other way round)? In other words, we check whether the behaviour of the analysts in the poll mentioned at the beginning can be backed up by a careful statistical analysis of the data. We proceed as follows: we first examine some prima facie evidence and then proceed to a more detailed econometric analysis using Granger causality methods. To ensure robustness we use several different indicators and time periods and a variety of lag structures. Finally, we then look closer at the EMU period and find that there is a clear structural break around September 2001.

ECB and Fed Interest Rate Setting – First Prima Facie Evidence

A simple way to answer the question whether the ECB follows the Fed might be to look at the behaviour of the official rates set by the ECB and the Fed. However, these rates do not move frequently enough to allow the use of standard statistical methods without great caution. Hence one has to find indicators from financial markets, for example short term interest rates, which complement the analysis and make it more robust. Although central banks do not directly set the most widely watched indicator of short-term monetary conditions, namely the 1-month interest rate, they can nevertheless determine pretty much its evolution. If the ECB had systematically followed the evolution in the US (moves by the Fed as well as changes in US financial markets), one would expect to find that changes in US interest rates tend to lead changes in euro area short-term rates. At first sight this seems to have been the case if one looks at the short life span of the euro. Figure 8.30 plots the central bank (ECB_REFIN and FED_FUNDS) and the 1-month money market interest rate series (EURO_1 M and USD_1 M) for the euro zone and for the US since the start of EMU. We plot both levels and first differences. As expected, the 1-month rates closely move around to the central bank rates. Hence, we feel free to use money market rates to test whether the ECB follows the Fed.

This figure suggests at first sight that the US was leading the euro area by around one quarter both when interest rates were going up, from the trough in early 1999

Fig. 8.30 Central bank rates and one-month interest rates in the euro zone and the US (January 1st 1999 to April 25th 2003)

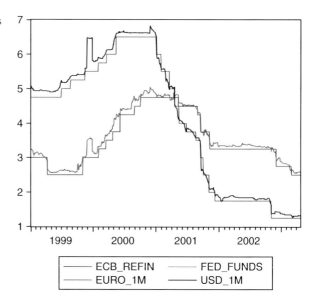

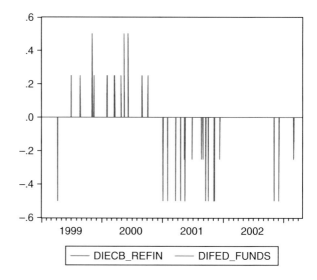

and when they started falling in early 2001. Many observers concluded from this apparent relationship that the ECB mimicked the Fed in its monetary decisions. However, this popular belief was not corroborated by simple statistical analyses with data for monthly realisations of 3-month interest rates up to 2001 (Belke et al., 2002; Belke & Gros 2002a; Gros et al., 2002, p. 45 ff. and 62 ff.). This early period was followed by a phase in which the Fed lowered its interest rate with an unprecedented speed while the ECB was more hesitant in this respect. The surprise cut by the Federal Reserve of 50 bp on 3 January, 2001 is often cited as a telling example of the leader-follower relationship because after this move by the Federal Reserve the ECB found itself under increasing and incredibly strong pressure to cut its own rates as well.[45] The last period which can be identified by visual inspection is characterized by the fact that the ECB follows the direction of the Fed steps but not by the same magnitude leading by mid-2001 to a positive gap in the interest rate levels between the euro zone and the US (in reversal of the development at the start of EMU). The sample period thus contains two periods with different interest rate differentials.

Interestingly enough these two periods of different interest differentials also broadly cover two different periods on the foreign exchange markets in the sense that until 2001 the euro declined from a temporary peak reached when EMU started, but this was then followed by a period of dollar weakness. The period of dollar strength was associated with higher US interest rates and the period of dollar weakness was associated with lower US interest rates. This is what one would expect in general. But, as usual, it is difficult to disentangle cause and effect. Did changes in (policy) interest rates drive the exchange rate, or did exogenous shocks to the foreign exchange market affect the business cycle on both sides of the Atlantic and hence caused changes in interest rates? We do not want to be drawn in a discussion of this general issue and note just that if exchange rates movement were the exogenous factor one would expect a negative relationship between euro area and US interest rates: a weaker dollar should, ceteris paribus, make it more likely that the Federal Reserve will raise rates, whereas the ECB should become more inclined to cut rates. We did not observe any negative correlation of this kind in the data (whether on a contemporaneous or lagged basis).

We complement the description of stylized facts by a more institutional view of the monetary policy decision making process. In Table 8.12 we display a chronology of FED and ECB interest rates movements since 1999 by only referring to meeting dates where at least one of the central banks changed its rate. We assign a change of the interest rate to the day when it is agreed upon since we assume that it is priced into expectations from this day on. Note that the FED has always led the turning points in the interest rate cycle both in June 1999 and in January 2001. In order to address the relationship between interest rate movements among the two central banks we first need to consider how often they take interest rate decisions. Then we comment upon such decisions.

The ECB used to discuss monetary policy at each of its fortnightly meeting. Then on 8 November 2001, this was changed and the ECB decided to discuss monetary

---

[45]Wyplosz (2001, p. 1), reports clear anecdotic evidence of the demand by the markets, the media and even by Finance Ministers to cut rates during this period.

Table 8.12 Chronology of central bank rate changes by the Eurosystem and the Fed

Date	Level		Change	
	FED	ECB	FED	ECB
1-Jan-99		3		0
8-Apr-99		2.5		-50
30-Jun-99	5.00		25	
24-Aug-99	5.25		25	
4-Nov-99		3		50
16-Nov-99	5.50		25	
2-Feb-00	5.75		25	
3-Feb-00		3.25		25
16-Mar-00		3.5		25
21-Mar-00	6.00		25	
27-Apr-00		3.75		25
16-May-00	6.50		50	
8-Jun-00		4.25		50
31-Aug-00		4.5		25
5-Oct-00		4.75		25
3-Jan-01	6.00		-50	
31-Jan-01	5.50		-50	
20-Mar-01	5.00		-50	
18-Apr-01	4.50		-50	
10-May-01		4.5		-25
14-May-01	4.00		-50	
27-Jun-01	3.75		-25	
21-Aug-01	3.50		-25	
30-Aug-01		4.25		-25
17-Sep-01	3.00	3.75	-50	-50
2-Oct-01	2.50		-50	
6-Nov-01	2.00		-50	
8-Nov-01		3.25		-50
11-Dec-01	1.75		-25	
6-Nov-02	1.25		-50	
5-Dec-02		2.75		-50
6-Mar-03		2.5		-25

Note: For the US, the Fed funds rate http://www.federalreserve.gov/fomc/fundsrate.htm2), and for the euro zone the ECB refi rate (http://www.ecb.int/index.html) is tabulated.

policy only once every four weeks (Perez-Quiros & Sicilia, 2002, p. 8). This brought the ECB's rhythm closer to that of the FED, which meets every six weeks. If it were not for the possibility of inter-meeting moves the one month rate should thus open a window of 2 weeks after a Fed meeting during which no change should be expected. But the FED has made three inter-meetings cuts while the ECB made only one in the aftermath of the terrorist attacks in the US. Indeed this constituted an extraordinary situation resulting in the only co-ordinated inter-meeting when the three central banks ECB, Fed and the Bank of England, cut by 50 bp within 3 days.[46] There are two further instances (in January 2001, the first easing of the cycle and in November 2001) when the FED made inter-meetings cuts not triggered by extraordinary events. The ECB does not seem to have this "urgency" to react to economic information. However, the Fed and the ECB have moved within a week on four occasions (apart from the inter-meeting cuts in September 2001) in February 2000, in May 2001 and finally in November 2001. Hence, we could tentatively conclude that the FED leads the ECB.[47]

Note however, that the FED could be leading the ECB due to pure "cyclical" considerations (international transmission of the cycle). It is a well-known fact that the business cycle in the US has led Euroland's in the period under consideration by about 1–2 quarters and thus it makes perfect sense that the FED is the first one to change direction on interest rates movements.[48] A statement of an influential member of the ECB Board, Issing, on BBC News one day after the Fed's quarter-point cut of interest rates on June 27th, 2001, is illuminating in this respect. Asked whether the ECB would follow the Fed's lead, he said: "The Fed did what was necessary for the US and we will do what is necessary for Europe"[49]. This statement would suggest that any leader-follower relationship would purely accidental. It has to seen, however, in the context of the "objective functions" or mandates of the two institutions. It is widely perceived that the Federal Reserve pays relatively more attention to growth than the ECB. This is another piece of perceived wisdom that is hard to document since estimates of standard Taylor rule functions fit both the US and the euro area data and the estimates do not yield significant differences in the relative weights attached to inflation and the output gap. We not want to take a stance on this issue, but it is clear that if the hypothesis that the ECB pays more attention to inflation were true one would expect the ECB to be more cautious in following the Fed during an easing cycle.

---

[46] The ECB has been criticised for making reactive, rather than proactive monetary policy decisions in the wake of September 11th. Perhaps, the ECB and other central banks would have waited longer before assessing the outcome of the terrorist strikes, and formulating and timing policy responses without the lead of the Fed. However, the decision by the ECB to follow the Fed's lead represents a shift to a more pre-emptive policy stance. In cutting interest rates without a clear indication of the likely economic impact of events in the US and the impact on oil prices, the ECB took a risk that cheaper money in Euroland may induce greater price pressures over the medium term that could threaten its 2% inflation target. However, according to our option value-argument (Gros & Belke, 2003), the ECB was correct in its assessment of the risks to EU growth, and the decision to cut its interest rate has contributed to enhancing the ECB's credibility as a global monetary authority.

[47] In the spring of 1999, the ECB somewhat belatedly reacted to fears of deflation triggered by the LTCM crisis as another exceptional event in our sample.

[48] Begg et al. (2002, p. 42) and Breuss (2002, p. 13) see a time lag between Fed and ECB interest rate decisions. They attribute the reason for the Fed's moving first to the US cycle leading the euro zone's.

[49] See BBC-News (2001).

But the key question we want to address is rather whether, even without any news on the evolution of the euro area economy, a FED decision to cut rates increases the probability of a cut by the ECB (see for instance the Reuters poll mentioned in the introduction). With our high frequency data (daily and weekly) we can differentiate between time lags caused by different positions along the economic cycle from those which are related to other issues (e.g. the alleged inability of the ECB to react quickly to financial market developments because of the need to reach a consensus in the Governing Council).

If the leader-follower relationship were purely a function of the business cycle lag one would expect that ECB to follow the Fed with a corresponding lag, i.e. 3–6 months later. If the ECB were just slower to react to financial market shocks one would expect it to be able reach a new consensus in its Governing Council about 1 or two meetings after the Fed (where there is only one decision maker who counts: Chairman Greenspan), implying a lag of about 1-2 months. Finally, in the crude perception of financial markets that the ECB just does not know what to do and just follows immediately the Fed on would expect a lag of less than a month in terms of policy rates, which should translate in a (partial) immediate reaction in the one month rates used by us.

The procedure used in this part of the book to ascertain the existence of a leader-follower relationship essentially is a Granger-causality (GC) test procedure. These tests can show whether past values of a certain variable (e.g. US interest rates) influence another variable (e.g. euro interest rates) after one has taken into account the patterns that might link the second variable (euro rates) to its own past. If this is not the case, we speak of Granger non-causality (Greene, 2003, p. 590 ff.). However, Granger causality measures precedence and information content but does not by itself indicate causality in the more common use of the term.

A battery of statistical tests is run covering the entire sample period (1989–2003) to test the leader-follower hypothesis also for the Bundesbank and the Fed as well as only the euro period. The latter period is even split further into sub-samples to test for robustness of our results.[50] Overall, this gave the result that US interest rates do not influence euro interest rates in the sense of a one-way causation. The US interest rate of the previous time periods did not have a statistically significant one-way influence on the current euro interest rate when all other factors were taken into account. This suggests that the visual impression of a US leadership over the entire period might be misleading for most of the periods analysed by us.

Empirical Analysis

The first section of this chapter will outline our statistical approach in more detail. As explained in the first chapter, the administratively set central bank interest rates

---

[50]We used first differences, i.e. changes in interest rates, when the level series seemed to contain a unit root.

as well as the 1-month money market rates of the US and the euro area were used as both rates are widely watched indicators of the monetary policy stance. In order to cope with the relatively short sample available for the EMU period we also include up to 9 years before the start of EMU in our analysis, implicitly testing the validity of the leader-follower hypothesis for the ECB's predecessor, the German Bundesbank, as well. We clearly separate between the Deutsche Mark era and the euro era in our empirical analysis. Our prior was that the results should not be very different between these two sub-periods, the reason being that the goal in monetary policy was almost the same for the Bundesbank than it is for the ECB. However, as will become clear below our prior was not at all confirmed.

The data for the central bank rates, the targeted federal funds rate (funds rate) and the ECB interest rate for main refinancing operations (refi rate), comprise the sample 1999–2003, and are taken from the homepages of the European Central Bank and the Federal Reserve (http://www.ecb.int/index.html, http://www.federalreserve.gov/fomc/fundsrate.htm). The data for the weekly and daily realisations of the 1-month LIBOR euro and dollar interest rates are taken from Datastream Primark. Our pre-EMU rates are synthetic euro rates. We have used the following samples: for central bank rates: January 1st 1999 to April 25th 2003, for weekly realisations of 1-month rates: from January 6th, 1989, to April 25th 2003, for daily realisations of 1-month rates: May 8th 1989 to May 8th 2003.[51]

Preliminaries

The first step in the empirical work concerned the choice of the statistical procedure. The simplest available procedure was chosen to ascertain the existence of a leader-follower relationship, i.e., the so-called Granger-causality tests (and related approaches). In order to make sure that our results do not depend on the particular test period chosen, we ran a battery of statistical tests for a number of periods, e.g. covering the entire euro period (1999 until 2003) and different periods from the end of 1989 onwards. What are the appropriate interest rates in our context? Optimally, we should investigate the instrument of the central bank for monetary policy. Both the ECB and the Fed operate in the money market, but at slightly different maturities. They cannot influence longer term interest rates directly (Borio, 2001), their direct influence is limited to the overnight money market rate in the case of the US and the rate for fortnightly operations in the case of the ECB.[52] The monthly rates we use are of course, influenced by the expectations about the future path of the shorter rates controlled by the central banks.[53]

---

[51] Daily data refer to working days only. Weekends and holidays were eliminated.

[52] The ECB also provides some funds at longer maturities (three months).

[53] See Ulrich 2003, p. 7, and Wyplosz 2001, p. 6 f. Perez-Quiros and Sicilia (2002), p. 7 ff., argue that policy announcements made on Council meetings should not trigger any reaction of asset prices in case of full predictability, since market participants have already correctly anticipated these policy decisions on the day when the central bank rate is changed. However, in a world of uncertainty, collective decisions on monetary policy and lack of transparency, effective communi-

A priori, if one uses market interest rate data, it becomes inherently difficult to distinguish policy maker's intentions from demand disturbances in financial markets (Bergin & Jordá, 2004). However, Fig. 8.30. has clearly shown that central bank rates and market rates move closely together. Moreover, using market rates has the advantage that one captures, although maybe imperfectly, probabilities of future moves of the central bank rates. If one uses only the latter one has only the realisations, not the expectations, which determine market rates which are in turn the rates that influence the economy. Hence, we decided to operationalise the interest rates as follows:

1. daily realisations of Central bank rates (targeted Fed funds rate and ECB refi rate),
2. weekly realisations of 1-month money market rates, and
3. daily realisations of 1-month money market rates.

Ad 1: The Federal Reserve announces an objective for the federal funds rate, the federal funds target. Hence, it makes sense to use the latter variable as the operating target in our estimations. Hamilton and Jordá (2000) argue that the target data for the federal funds rate accurately reflect the monetary policy stance since they reflect policy considerations instead of demand innovations. ECB decisions concern the setting of the main refinancing operations. So the operating target is the refi rate. With an eye on their impact on the markets, we feel legitimized to include changes in the central bank rates starting with the day of the meeting they were decided upon, i.e. in some cases earlier than their date of de-facto effectiveness.[54]

Ad 2: We preferred 1-month rates to 3-month rates (as used in Belke & Gros, 2002a; Gros et al., 2002) because it is rather difficult to measure reaction lags of less than 3 months based on 3-month rates. With daily rates we have the maximum of information, but most news on a daily basis come presumably from financial markets. We used LIBOR rates because they are highly comparable since they refer to the same market and to the same time zone, etc.

Ad 3: Here we also used LIBOR rates, but weekly realisations to eliminate (at the price of a smaller sample) some of the noise that might come from short term disturbances in money markets. With weekly realisations the average number of observations available to detect a leader-follower pattern would be 1–2 if the ECB had followed the Fed tightly.

---

cation and active guidance to the markets, predictability and the anticipation of the exact timing of interest rate changes might not be fully attainable. This justifies the use of the refi and the targeted funds rate in our case.

[54]For instance, the Governing council of the ECB decided to lower the minimum bid rate on the main refinancing operations by 0.25 percentage points to 2.50%, starting from the operation to be settled on March 12th, 2003. In this case, we assigned the change already to March 6th, 2003.

Before the regressions were run, however, an important empirical caveat had to be taken into account. Since the level series seem to contain a unit root[55] and Granger causality tests tend to give misleading results if the variables considered contain unit roots, it was first tested whether the interest rates were actually stationary during the time period considered. The results of the unit root tests are available on request and suggest that the series have to be differenced once (to get the change in interest rates between two periods) in order to make them stationary.

Granger Causality?

The next step was to use Granger-causality (GC) analysis to establish whether there is a follower-leader relationship between the changes in the relevant Euro and US interest rates. We conduct separate GC analyses for all of the relevant variables.

First, we used central bank rates. In order to test for the existence of some policy link between the FED decisions on the one hand and the ECB on the other, we perform Granger causality tests among the two intervention rates. This means that we are dealing with daily observations of series that move with discrete jumps (the refi rate for the ECB and the fund rate for the FED). This is somewhat of an extreme exercise because this sort of test is designed for smooth variables instead of variables that jump from one value to another. Note, however, that targets are typically modified in discrete increments rather than continuously. Hence, the very nature of what we want to capture is discrete and represents a structural break in the series. Moreover, the changes in targets are spaced irregularly in time (Hamilton and Jordá 2000). We could argue that by using this dataset we are forcing the series to maximise its co-movements. If we do not find empirical evidence with this data set, it is doubtful that we would find it either with a more "conventional" dataset. The smoother the series (take for instance the monthly 3-month LIBOR money market rates we used in Belke & Gros, 2002a; Gros et al., 2002) the more difficult to capture any reaction to abrupt rates changes and the more contaminated this series would be with irrelevant information (Garcia-Cervero, 2002).

Second, we compromised on 1-month market rates with an eye on Fig. 8.30 which clearly demonstrates that the time pattern of the latter is not too different from that of the central bank rates. Hence, we conducted Granger causality tests for weekly realisations of 1-month money market rates and daily realisations of 1-month money market rates.

The main results of the Granger-causality tests are tabulated below in Figs. 8.31, 8.32 and 8.33 and Tables 8.13 and 8.14. We have used the same samples like in our unit root tests to run GC tests. However, we decided to use different numbers of lags. Note that the daily data refer to weekdays and thus a month is about 21 observations

---

[55]The level series does not fluctuate around a constant mean and its variance is not constant and finite.

a) For central bank rates (daily realisations, in levels)

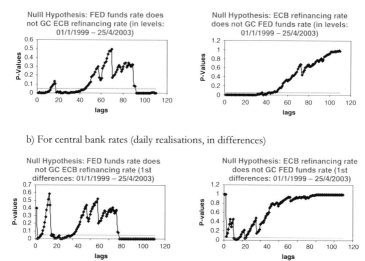

b) For central bank rates (daily realisations, in differences)

Fig. 8.31 Results of Granger causality tests (P-values dependent on lag-length)

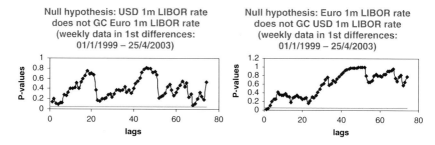

Fig. 8.32 P-values for Granger Causality tests of weekly realisations of the 1-month LIBOR rates

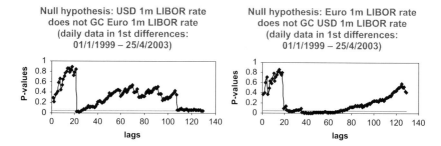

Fig. 8.33 P-values for Granger Causality tests of daily realisations of the 1-month LIBOR rates

Table 8.13 Results of Granger causality tests by sample period and lag length (first differences of weekly realisations of the 1-month LIBOR rates)

Lag length in weeks	Full sample: 1989–2003		Pre-EMU: 1989–1998		EMU: 1999–2003	
	US does not GC EU	EU does not GC US	US does not GC EU	EU does not GC US	US does not GC EU	EU does not GC US
1	–	–	–	–	–	0.011
2	–	–	–	–	–	0.045
3	–	–	–	–	–	–
4	–	–	–	–	–	–
9	–	0.008	–	0.000	–	–
13	–	0.022	–	0.002	–	–

Note: Full sample: 06/01/89 – 25/4/2003, pre-EMU period: 06/01/89 – 25/12/1998, EMU period: 01/1/1999 – 25/4/2003.

Table 8.14 Results of Granger causality tests by sample period and lag length (first differences of daily realisations of the 1-month LIBOR rates)

Lag length in working days	Full sample: 1989–2003		Pre-EMU: 1989–1998		EMU: 1999–2003	
	US does not GC EU	EU does not GC US	US does not GC EU	EU does not GC US	US does not GC EU	EU does not GC US
1	–	0.021	–	0.015	–	–
5	–	0.004	–	0.008	–	–
10	0.008	0.001	0.005	0.001	–	–
21	0.001	0.000	0.002	0.001	–	–
42	0.000	0.000	0.000	0.000	–	0.004

Note: Full sample: 08/05/89 – 08/05/2003, pre-EMU period: 08/05/89 – 31/12/1998, EMU period: 01/1/1999 – 08/05/2003.

rather than 30. In order to limit the loss of degrees of freedom (and limit the analysis to a time span that does not exceed the reaction lag of even the slowest central bank), we do not test for more than 5 months of history (about 110 working days), and, for simplicity, report results only at the standard 5% significance level.

One should also be well aware that the results often depend greatly on the lag structure. For central bank rates we used lags from 1 to 110, for weekly realisations of the 1-month rates we applied 1, 2, 3, 4, 9 and 13 (since interest rate decisions are often met closely to each other a lower lag is more probable) and for daily realisations of these rates 1, 5 (one week), 10, 21, 42 (2 months). This procedure enabled us to take into account that the periodicity of the lag is not a priori fixed by theory. For robustness reasons and with an eye on our hypothesis of a possible break in the relation around the start of EMU (and the turn of the year 2000–2001), different sample periods were used in a fashion coherent with our unit root tests. By investigating (a) the whole sample of available data from the end of the eighties on until "today", (b) the limited sample from the end of the eighties on until the end of 1998 and (c) the sample consisting of the EMU period, we clearly separate between the deutsche mark era and the euro era in our empirical analysis. Our prior is that the results should not be so much affected – the reason being that the goal in monetary policy was almost the same for the Deutsche Bundesbank than it is for the ECB. However, the behaviour of the Bundesbank might have also been influenced by the anticipation of EMU. We will discuss this issue later on by asking whether the ECB systematically follows the US Federal Reserve to a larger or smaller extent than the Bundesbank.

The whole range of GC results for levels and first differences of the central bank rates and first differences of the market rates is summarized below. In some cases, we plot the sequence of probability values dependent on the lag structure jointly with the 5 percent significance level as illustrative examples. We regard the hypothesis that the ECB followed the Fed as a one-way causality which is corroborated exactly if the p-values are below 5 percent for the GC test with the null hypothesis "The US rate does not GC the euro rate", but at the same time the p-values are above 5% for the GC test with the null hypothesis "The euro rate does not GC the US rate".

Ad 1) *Results for (administratively set) central bank rates*: In a first step, we summarise the results of the GC analysis for the levels of the central bank rates. There is strong and consistent evidence that the *FED GC (Granger-causes) the ECB*, when we limit the analysis to lags up to around 40 days. The relationship holds at virtually all-relevant lags within this sample (left graph of Fig. 8.31(a)). Interestingly there is also evidence that at the same time the ECB Granger causes the Fed (right graph of Fig. 8.31(a)); but this unwinds as soon as we extend the study to more than 40 working days lags (possibly due to the few breaks). When we extend the number of lags to lags of at least around 90 working days (about 4.5 months) we find again evidence that the FED GC the ECB; this time the relation again holds for all relevant lags. At the same time the hypothesis that the Fed does not follow the ECB cannot be rejected at the usual significance level of 5 percent. Hence, we find evidence that the *ECB follows the Fed in a one-way direction*. However, this holds only with long lags. We interpret this as evidence in favour of relevance of cyclical considerations instead of policy interaction. However, given the special time series behaviour of the official central bank rates we do not put a lot of weight on these results.

As a second step and as a complementary check, we performed an additional exercise to see whether the main results still hold, this time with the *first differences* of the central bank interest rates rather than interest rates levels. Note that now we test whether daily changes in the fund rate GC daily changes in the ECB refinancing rate. The risk is that, due to the high proportion of zeros (since rates do not often change on a daily basis) results get distorted, especially if we include few lags. In order to minimize this risk we include as many lags as needed so as to guarantee at least one observation different from zero in the history of each variable. Here, we need about 20 working days of history in order to find evidence that *the FED GC the ECB*, which holds from 20 to 40 and from 90 to more than 120 daily lags and disappears in between. We cannot find any GC running between the Fed and the ECB for short lags (10–15 day lags), but for these lags there is evidence that the *FED GC the ECB*. For extremely short lags, the Fed seems to impact the ECB in a one-way direction. Hence, it is seems to be possible to find some causality, but we again would warn against putting too much emphasis on these results.

Ad 2) *Results for weekly realisations of the 1-month rates*: In Table 8.13, a surprising pattern emerges. At the usual 0.05 significance level there is no case in which we have to reject the null hypothesis that the US does not influence the euro area. But we also find that in six out of the 18 cases considered we have to reject the hypothesis that the euro area interest rates do not influence US rates. This is the case for short lags (1–2 weeks) during the EMU period and for longer lags (9 or 13 weeks) for both the full sample and the Pre-EMU period.

Ad 3) *Results for daily realisations of the 1-month rates*: The evidence in Table 8.14 is less one sided against the hypothesis that the ECB follows the Fed. In six cases we find evidence that the Fed Granger causes the ECB. However, in all of these cases it is also found at the same time that the US rate is simultaneously determined by the euro interest rate. Hence this cannot be interpreted as evidence for a leader-follower relationship either.[56] As for the weekly data, however, we find several (in this case 5) cases in which one has to reject decisively the hypothesis that the ECB does not influence the Fed (or more precisely that euro area (pre-EMU: DM or synthetic euro) interest rates do not influence dollar rates).

Do the results deliver an answer to the question whether the Euro area systematically followed the US Federal Reserve? When we look at Tables 8.13 and 8.14 we

---

[56]Overall, our new results confirm those contained in the studies by Belke and Gros (2002a) and Gros et al. (2000) which were based on an investigation of monthly realisations of the 3-month LIBOR interest rates and a smaller sample: In no case does one have to reject the null hypothesis that the US interest rate does not 'Granger cause' the euro interest rate and at the same time not reject the null hypothesis that the euro interest rate does not Granger cause the US rate.

would be tempted to turn the question around: has the Fed systematically followed Euro area developments? And has the euro area influence on the Fed been stronger or weaker before EMU? While great caution must exercised in interpreting these results with fixed lag lengths it is clear that they do not give any support to the null hypothesis that the ECB follows in an asymmetric way the Fed (nor seems the Bundesbank have done this during the pre-EMU period). If we limit our analysis to the euro period, the hypothesis of the Fed being a follower dominates clearly that of the US being the leader and the euro zone being the follower.

We regard these results with some caution because we are – at least with respect to the correct treatment of the central bank interest rate series – on the "frontier" of standard time series analysis. We are not surprised that we find a strong structural break between the pre- and post-EMU period. While the ECB has taken over most of the trappings of the Bundesbank (emphasis on price stability, use of monetary indicator, etc.) its behaviour should be different because it is responsible for a much larger and somewhat less open economy (Belke & Gros, 2002). Moreover, our pre-EMU rates are synthetic euro rates. Hence they contain over 40% DEM rates (plus satellites like NL and AUS), but also LIT and FF rates, which at times diverged from DEM rates. While it is generally assumed that the DEM dominated the other currencies, there has been some discussion to what extent the Deutsche Bundesbank did really dominate the EMS. For instance, Fratianni and von Hagen (1990) found that Germany had a limited leadership role among European countries before the start of EMU. Hence it is not surprising that we find a clear cut structural break between the pre-EMU and the EMU period in terms of the relationship between short-term interest rates.[57]

Does the Relationship Change Over Time?

Our main finding so far has been that for the EMU period one does not find an asymmetric and one way influence of the Fed on the ECB. However, just as there was a clear structural break around the start of EMU there might have been another break within the EMU period. Our main candidate for a structural break is September (to be more precise 11th of September) 2001, because this started a period of unprecedented political and financial market instability. Our second candidate is in

---

[57]Belke and Gros (2006) address two additional questions within the Johansen-framework of a cointegrating VAR analysis (Johansen 1991, 1995). Is there a stochastic co-movement between the US and the euro interest rate? And: If there is a co-movement, is it driven by the US interest rate? Hence, we checked for cointegration between the US and the euro interest rates and for weak exogeneity of the US interest rate in the cointegrating VAR. In the preceding chapter, we argued that due to the non-stationary character of the time series, we had to conduct our GC analysis in first differences for the 1-month LIBOR rates. This clearly needs not be the case if the US and the euro zone time series are cointegrated. In this case, we can additionally use level information in order to identify the nature of the relationship of the two series in the data-generating process. The results are available on request.

the run-up to the first one, namely the turn-of-year 2000/2001 with the uncertainty about an unravelling of the financial equilibrium in the US economy. As explained in the introduction we consider that this (combined) increase in uncertainty should lead to an asymmetry in monetary policy because the increase in uncertainty increases the "option value of waiting" for policy makers much more in the Euro area, whose economic system is much less flexible than that of the US.

The Role of the 11th of September 2001: Evidence Based on GC Tests

In order to test this kind of reasoning, we expend some efforts *to search for breaks in the relation between US and euro interest rates around September 11th*, 2003 via the Granger causality test procedure. For this purpose, we again split up the EMU sample in two sub-periods. This time, the first sub-sample ranges from 1999 until the 11th of September 2001 and the second comprises the dates from 12th of September 2001 until "today". We conducted the tests for Granger-causality for the same three variables than before: the central bank rates (levels and differences), the weekly (only differences) and the daily realisations (only differences) of the 1-month money market rate. The results are displayed graphically in Figs. 8.34, 8.35 and 8.36. Like before, we plot the sequence of probability values dependent on the lag structure jointly with the 5% significance level. We again feel legitimized to accept the hypothesis of the ECB following the Fed as a one-way causality exactly if the p-values are below 5% for the null hypothesis "The US rate does not GC the euro rate", but at the same time the p-values are above 5 percent for the null hypothesis "The euro rate does not GC the US rate". In other words, we expect the Fed to GC the ECB, but at the same time the ECB not to GC the Fed. This time we focus on the difference in results across the sub-samples before and after the 11th of September.

The results of our sample-split tests are striking. While there is no evidence that the ECB followed the Fed before the 11th of September, it seems as if the ECB has done so afterwards. After September 11th, the Fed Granger causes the ECB, but at the same time the ECB does not Granger cause the Fed. Hence, changes in the euro interest rate appear to follow changes in the US rate by one-way causation. A leader-follower pattern according to the option value of waiting emerges. Moreover, the difference between the levels of the interest rates still remains high (see Fig. 8.30). Hence, the option value of waiting with interest decisions also manifests itself in this level difference. All in all, our findings are consistent with the pattern that September 11th, 2001, raised the uncertainty for monetary policy making in addition to the generally observed rising uncertainty near turning points of the cycle.[58]

---

[58]For a general discussion of interest rate decisions in an uncertain environment see Begg et al. (2002, p. 31ff).

a) For levels

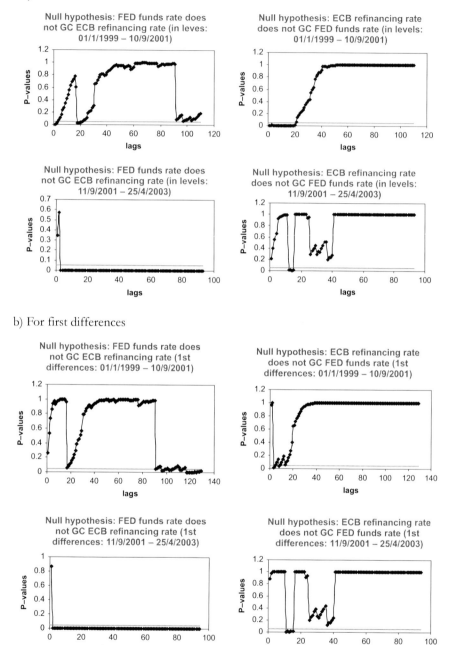

b) For first differences

Fig. 8.34   P-values for Granger Causality tests of central bank rates (sample split at September 11th 2001)

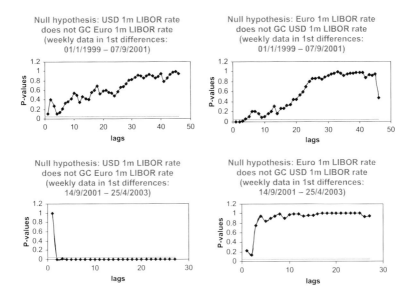

Fig. 8.35 P-values for Granger Causality tests of weekly realisations of the 1-month LIBOR rates for first differences (sample split at September 11th 2001)

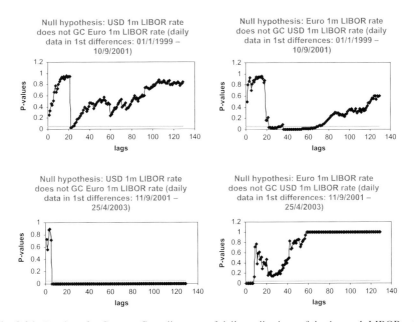

Fig. 8.36 P-values for Granger Causality tests of daily realisations of the 1-month LIBOR rates for first differences (sample split at September 11th 2001)

Breaks Around the Turn-of-Year 2000/01? Evidence Based on GC Tests

One might still argue that interest rates in Europe tended to be influenced by what had happened on the other side of the Atlantic but that this had changed during 2001. In that year the Fed cut interest rates at an unprecedented speed (and by an unprecedented magnitude) because it feared an unravelling of the financial equilibrium in the US. The ECB took a more relaxed stance on this point as the euro area economy did not show any of the (potential) disequilibria of the US economy (current account, consumer financial position, over-investment). For the ECB interest rate setting, this might have induced uncertainty and an option value of waiting. Hence, one might be tempted to conclude that over the whole sample the relationship between the US and the euro interest rate was contemporaneous, while a leader-follower relationship with the Fed as the leader becomes significant if only two sub-samples of the EMU period (namely until December 2000) are considered. In order to test whether this kind of reasoning is correct, we take some efforts to search for breaks in the relation between US and euro interest rates around the turn of year 2000–2001.

For this purpose, we again split up the EMU sample in two sub-periods. This time, the first sub-sample ranges from 1999 until the end-of-year 2000 and the second comprises the dates from 2001 until "today". We conducted the tests for Granger-causality for the same three variables than before: the central bank rates (levels and differences), the weekly (only differences) and the daily realisations (only differences) of the 1-month rate. A representative selection of the results is displayed graphically in Figs. 8.37 and 8.38. Like before, we plot the sequence of probability values dependent on the lag structure jointly with the 5% significance level. We again regard the hypothesis of the ECB following the Fed as a one-way causality as corroborated if the p-values are below 5% for the null hypothesis "The US rate does not GC the euro rate", but at the same time the p-values are above 5 percent for the null hypothesis "The euro rate does not GC the US rate". However, this time we focus on the difference in results across the sub-samples before and after the turn-of-year 2000/2001. We only display the results for the first differences of the central bank rates and of the weekly realisations of the 1-month LIBOR rates (Figs. 8.37 and 8.38).[59]

With respect to the results for weekly data the main impression is that before the suspected break there is a two-way causation between the US interest rate and the euro interest rate for short lags (from 4 to 10 weeks). After this potential break, this mutual impact of US and euro interest rates can be established only for longer lags (from 23 weeks on). Moreover, for very short lags there is even evidence for the ECB leading the Fed. However, for the central bank rates, the evidence for the leader-follower hypothesis after the break is much stronger. All in all and although evidence appears to a certain extent weaker, already the turn-of-year 2000/2001 (combined with September 2001) represents the starting point for higher general

---

[59]The tests for the remaining variables display a similar pattern and are available on request.

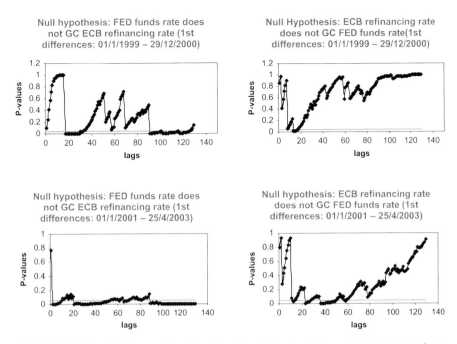

Fig. 8.37   P-values for Granger Causality tests of central bank rates (sample split at turn-of-year 2000/2001)

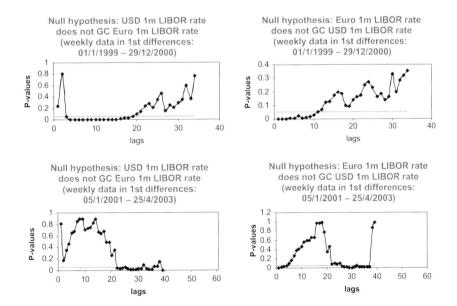

Fig. 8.38   P-values for Granger Causality tests of weekly realisations of 1-month LIBOR rates for first differences (sample split at turn-of-year 2000/2001)

uncertainty which is strong enough to induce for the ECB an option value of waiting with interest rate decisions.[60]

Policy Conclusions

So does the ECB follow the Fed?[61] Our answer would be: no, except for the period after the turn-of-year 2000/2001 and, more significantly, September 2001. To be more precise, we find that the relationship between the interest rate decisions of the Fed and the ECB changes over time. Most of the time, it is symmetric. Only after September 2001 do we find a preponderance of the evidence hinting at a significant influence of the US on the euro area, but little in the other direction. However, a note of caution applies here. Since the merger of European national central banks almost certainly resulted in a change of the parameters of the central bank reaction function, the length of the time period which has elapsed since the start of EMU respectively since September 11th is only beginning to be sufficient for our empirical tests. Hence, one should find even more investigations of this highly relevant topic in the future.

What could account for this finding? One hypothesis mentioned in the introduction is that the cyclical position of Euroland lags that of the US, implying that the leader-follower relationship might be spurious. However, the US business cycle has led the euro area one for quite some time now, but we find that the Fed leads the ECB only during the most recent period. The emergence of an asymmetric leader-follower relationship renders less likely the popular explanation that the ECB is just slow because it is a new institution that has to find its way in unfamiliar territory. If this had been the case, one would have expected to find evidence for the hypothesis that the Fed leads the ECB mainly during the early EMU period, not more recently.

It is always difficult to determine the deeper reasons for correlations over time. But the fact that the asymmetric leader-follower relationship appears only after a major shock which increases global uncertainty suggests to us that the deeper reason why the ECB appears to follow the Fed is simply that the Euro area economy is less flexible. This makes it optimal also for the ECB to take into account the "option value of waiting" and react later to shocks. This implies that even if both economies are hit mainly by common shocks (Peiró, 2002) one would find econometrically

---

[60]Begg et al. (2002) report in their MECB 4 update that since September 2001, the economic environment has become dramatically more uncertain. In this respect, they refer to, e.g. the sharp drop in stock markets, the large swings in HICP inflation largely unconnected with food or energy prices. See also Belke and Goecke (2008).

[61]The ECB has, understandably, not taken any position on this issue. But a recent ECB Working Document (Ehrmann & Fratzscher, 2002) analyses one part of this issue, namely the extent to which the US influences the euro area. The conclusions are interesting: "There are in particular some US macroeconomic announcements to which European markets react significantly, especially in times of increased uncertainty, like the initial period of EMU or the 2001 recession" and, "throughout a learning process, the importance given to US news has declined". As will become clearer below our own results are consistent with the first quote, but go in the opposite direction of the second quote.

that the Fed seems to be leading the ECB. From this perspective, common shocks imply that the US interest cycle leads the EU if the US is more flexible and also contracts more quickly in response to negative shocks. In contrast to Begg et al. (2002), we do not argue that such rigidities may require monetary policy to play a bigger role. Instead, waiting with interest rate changes becomes valuable if there is a large degree of uncertainty.

We are nearly sure that we will see more kind of this research in the future – most probably based on Taylor rules – when the fogs of the current still ongoing credit crisis will have thinned out.

References

Altavilla, C., & Landolfo, L. (2005). Do Central Banks Act asymmetrically? Empirical Evidence from the ECB and the Bank of England. *Applied Economics, 37*, 507–519.

Altimari, S. N. (2001) *Does money lead inflation in the euro area?* ECB Working Paper, 63, European Central Bank, Frankfurt/Main.

Amato, J. D. (2005). *The role of the natural rate of interest in monetary policy*. BIS Working Paper No. 171, March.

Amato, J. D., & Laubach, T. (1999). The value of interest-rate smoothing: How the private sector helps the Federal Reserve. *Federal Reserve Bank of Kansas City Economic Review, 84*(3), 47–64.

Angell, J. W. (1933). Money, Prices and production: Some fundamental concepts. *Quarterly Journal of Economics, 48* (1), 39–76.

Angell, J. W. (1935, November). The 100 per cent reserve plan. *Quarterly Journal of Economics, 750*, 1–35.

Ball, L. (1997). *Efficient rules for monetary policy*. NBER Working Paper No. 5952, Cambridge, MA.

Ball, L. (1999). Policy rules for open economies. In J. B. Taylor (Ed.), *Monetary policy rules* (pp. 127–144). Chicago: University Press.

Baltensperger, E. (2000). Die Europäische Zentralbank und ihre Geldpolitik, Swiss National Central Bank. *Quarterly Bulletin, 1*, 49–73.

Bank of England. (1998, February). The Inflation Report Projections: Understanding the Fan Chart. *Quarterly Bulletin, 38*(4), 30–37.

Bank of England. (2001). The Formulation of Monetary Policy at the Bank of England. *Quarterly Bulletin, 41*(4), 434–441.

Bank of England. (2002). Inflation Report.

Bank of England. (2003). Modelling and forecasting at the Bank of England – The Pagan Report and the Bank's Response, 30 January.

Bank of England. (2004). Inflation Report.

Bank of England. (2008, May). Inflation Report.

Barro and Gordon (1983b). Rules, discretion, and reputation in a model of monetary policy. *Journal of Monetary Economics, 12*(1), 101–121.

Barro, R. J. (1996, May/June). Inflation and growth. *Federal Reserve Bank of St. Louis, 78*(3), 153–169.

Barro, R. J., & Gordon, D. B. (1983a). A positive theory of monetary policy in a natural-rate model. *Journal of Political Economy, 91*(4), 589–610.

BBC-News. (2001). *Europe defies calls for rate cut, BBC News Business*. Web: http://news.bbc.co.uk/1/hi/business/1412137.stm, access May 2nd, 2003.

Begg, D., Canova, F., de Grauwe, P., Fatás, A., & Lane, P. (2002). *Surviving the slowdown: Monitoring the European Central Bank 4*. London: Centre for Economic Policy Research (CEPR).

Belke, A., & Goecke, M. (2008). European monetary policy in times of uncertainty. In A. Belke, S. Paul, & C. Schmidt (Eds.), *Fiskal- und Geldpolitik im Zeichen europäischer Integration* RWI: Schriften, Duncker und Humblot, Berlin (forthcoming).

Belke, A., & Gros, D. (2002). Designing EU-US monetary relations: The impact of exchange rate variability on labor markets on both sides of the Atlantic. *World Economy, 25*, 789–813.

Belke, A., & Gros, D. (2002a). *Does the ECB follow the Fed?* Department of Economics Discussion Paper 211/2002, University of Hohenheim, Stuttgart.

Belke, A., & Gros, D. (2003). If the ECB cuts rates it should do so boldly, Financial Times International, Comment & Analysis, March 2nd, p. 13.

Belke, A., & Gros, D. (2005). Asymmetries in transatlantic monetary policy-making: Does the ECB follow the Fed? *Journal of Common Market Studies, 43*(5), 921–946.

Belke, A., & Gros, D. (2006). Asymmetries in monetary policy making – ECB versus Fed. In V. Alexander, & H.-H. Kotz (Eds.), Global *divergence in trade* (pp. 141–171). Edward Elgar: Money and Policy.

Belke, A., Koesters, W., Leschke, M., & Polleit, T. (2002). International coordination of monetary policies – challenges, concepts and consequences, ECB-Observer – Analyses of the Monetary Policy of the European System of Central Banks 4, December, Frankfurt, Part 1: Impact of exchange rate volatility on labour markets – a case for transatlantic monetary policy coordination?.

Belke, A., & Polleit, T. (2006). Money and Swedish inflation. *Journal of Policy Modeling, 28*(8), 931–942.

Belke, A., & Polleit, T. (2007). How the ECB and the US Fed set interest rates. *Applied Economics, 39*(17), 2197–2209.

Belongia, M. T., & Batten, D. S. (1992). *Selecting an intermediate target variable for monetary policy when the goal is price stability.* Federal Reserve Bank of St. Louis, Working Paper, 008A.

Bergin, P. R., & Jordá, O. (2004). Measuring monetary policy interdependence. *Journal of International Money and Finance, 23* (5), 761–783.

Bernanke, B. S. (2003, March 25). A Perspective on inflation targeting. Remarks At the Annual Washington Policy Conference of the National Association of Business Economists, Washington, DC.

Bernanke, B. S., Laubach, T., Mishkin, F., & Posen, A. (1999). *Inflation targeting: Lessons from the international experience.* Princeton: Princeton University Press.

Bernanke, B. S., & Woodford, M. (1997). Inflation forecasts and monetary policy, *Journal of Money, Credit, and Banking, 24*, 653–684.

Blinder, A. (1995, June). The strategy of monetary policy, Remarks Delivered Before the Minnesota Meeting, a Business Forum, Minneapolis.

Borio, C. (2001). *Comparing monetary policy operating procedures across the United States, Japan, and the euro area,* BIS Paper, 9, Bank for International Settlements, Basle, pp. 1–22.

Bradley M. D., & Jansen D. W. (1989). Understanding Nominal GDP Targeting. *Federal Reserve Bank of St. Louis Review, 71*(6), 31–40.

Brand, C., Gerdesmeier, D., & Roffia, B. (2002). *Estimating the trend of M3 income velocity underlying the reference value for monetary growth.* ECB Occasional Paper, No. 3, May.

Breuss, F. (2002). *Is ECB's monetary policy optimal already?* Paper presented at the International Conference on Policy Modeling, EcoMod, July 4–6, Brussels.

Brigden, A., & Mizen, P. (1999). *Money, credit and investment in the UK corporate sector.* Bank of England Working Paper, 100, BOE London.

Britton, E., Fisher, P., & Whitley, J. (1998, February). The inflation report projections: Understanding the fan chart. *Bank of England Quarterly Bulletin, 30*–37.

Brunner, K., & Meltzer, A. H. (1967). The meaning of monetary indicators. In Horwich, G. (Ed.), *Monetary process and policy: A symposium. Homewood,* Illinois: Richard D. Irwin, Inc.

Carare, A., & Stone, M. R. (2003). *Inflation targeting regimes.* International Monetary Fund Working Paper No 03/9, January Washington/DC.

Carilli, A. M., Dempster, G. M., & Rohan, J. R. (2004). Monetary reform from a comparative-theoretical perspective. *The Quarterly Journal of Austrian Economics, 7*(3), 29–44.

Carlstrom C. T., & Fuerst, T. S. (2001, April). Timing and real indeterminacy in monetary models. *Journal of Monetary Economics, 47*(2), 285–298.

Carstensen, K. (2004). Estimating the ECB policy reaction function. *German Economic Review 7*(1), 1–34.

Carstensen, K., & Colavecchio, R. (2004). *Did the revision of the ECB monetary policy strategy affect the reaction function?* Kiel Working Papers, 1221, Kiel Institute for World Economics, Kiel.

Castelnuovo, E. (2003). *Describing the Fed's conduct with Taylor rules: Is interest rate smoothing important?* ECB Working Paper, 232, European Central Bank, Frankfurt/Main.

Clarida, R., & Gertler, M. (1996). *How the Bundesbank conducts monetary policy.* NBER Working Paper, 5581, NBER, Cambridge, MA.

Clarida, R., Galí, J., & Gertler, M. (1998). Monetary policy rules in practise: Some international evidence. *European Economic Review, 42*, 1033–1067.

Clarida, R., Galí, J., & Gertler, M. (1999). The science of monetary policy: A New Keynesian perspective. *Journal of Economic Literature, 37*(4), 1661–1707.

Clarida, R., Galí, J., & Gertler, M. (2000). Monetary policy rules and macroeconomic stability: Evidence and some theory. *Quarterly Journal of Economics, 115*, 147–180.

Clausen, V., & Hayo, B. (2005). Monetary policy in the euro area – Lessons from the first years. *International Economics and Economic Policy, 1*(4), 349–364.

Clemens, J. M. K., & Tatom, J. A. (1994, May/June). The P-Star model in five small economies. *Federal Reserve Bank of St. Louis Monthly Review, 76*(3), 11–29.

Clostermann, J., & Seitz, F. (1999). Der Zusammenhang zwischen Geldmenge, Output und Preisen in Deutschland – Ein modifizierter P-Star-Ansatz, ifo Diskussionsbeiträge No. 60, Munich.

Coenen, G., Levin, A., & Wieland, V. (2001). *Data uncertainty and the role of money as an information variable for monetary policy.* ECB Working Paper, 84, European Central Bank, Frankfurt/Main.

Cuaresma, J. C., Gnan, E., & Ritzberger-Gruenwald, D. (2003). *Searching for the Natural Rate of Interest*: A Euro Area Perspective OeNB Working Paper No. 84, Vienna Oesterreichische Nationalbank July.

Curdia, V., & Woodford, M. (2008). *Credit frictions and optimal monetary policy.* Paper discussed at the BIS Annual Conference, Bank for International Settlements Basle, June.

Deutsche Bundesbank (1999). *Taylor interest rate and monetary conditions index.* Monthly Report, April, pp. 47–63.

Dotsey, M. (2006). A review of inflation targeting in developed countries. *Federal Reserve Bank of Philadelphia Business Review*, 3rd quarter, 10–20.

Dueker, M. (1993, May/June). Can nominal GDP targeting rules stabilize the economy? *Federal Reserve Bank of St. Louis, Review,* 15–29.

Dueker, M. J., & Fischer, A. M. (1998, July/August). A guide to nominal feedback rules and their use for monetary policy, *Federal Reserve Bank of St. Louis, Review*, 55–63.

Dueker, M., & Fischer, A. M. (1996, February). Inflation targeting in a small open economy: Empirical results for Switzerland. *Journal of Monetary Economics*, 89–103.

Duisenberg, W. F. (2000, November 23). Hearing before the Committee on Economic and Monetary Affairs of the European Parliament with the President of the European Central Bank, in accordance with Article 113(3) of the Treaty on European Union, Brussels.

ECB Observer (2001, April 19). Inflationsperspektiven im Euroraum, www.ecb-observer.com.

Ehrmann, M., & Fratzscher, M. (2002). *Interdependence between the euro area and the US: What Role for EMU?*, European Central Bank Working Paper 200, December, Frankfurt/Main.

Ericsson N. R., & Irons J. S. (1992). The Lucas critique in practice: Theory without measurement. In K. D. Hoover (Ed.), *Macroeconometrics: Developments, tensions and prospects* (pp. 263–312). Boston: Kluwer.

European Central Bank (1999a). The stability-oriented monetary policy strategy of the eurosystem. ECB Monthly Bulletin, European Central Bank, Frankfurt/Main, January, pp. 39–50.

European Central Bank (1999b). euro area monetary aggregates and their role in the eurosystem's monetary policy strategy. ECB Monthly Bulletin, European Central Bank, Frankfurt/Main, February, pp. 29–46.

European Central Bank (2000). The two pillars of the ECB's monetary policy strategy. ECB Monthly Bulletin, November, pp. 37–48.

European Central Bank (2001, June). A guide to Eurosystem staff macroeconomic projection exercise. (www.ecb.int), Frankfurt/Main.

European Central Bank (2003, June). The outcome of the ECB's evaluation of its monetary policy strategy. ECB Monthly Bulletin, European Central Bank, Frankfurt/Main, pp. 79–92.

European Central Bank (2004). Monetary analysis in real time. Monthly Bulletin October, European Central Bank, Frankfurt/Main, pp. 43–66.

European Central Bank (2004a). The neutral real interest rate in the Euro area. ECB Monthly Bulletin, European Central Bank, Frankfurt/Main, May, pp. 57–69.

Eusepi, S. (2008, September). Central Bank transparency and nonlinear learning dynamics. Federal Reserve Bank of New York Staff Report, 342, New York.

Eusepi, S., & Preston, B. (2008, September). Stabilizing expectations under monetary and fiscal policy coordination. Federal Reserve Bank of New York Staff Report, 343, New York.

Faust, J., Rogers, J. H., & Wright J. H. (2001). *An empirical comparison of Bundesbank and ECB monetary policy rules.* International Finance Discussion Papers, 705, Board of Governors of the Federal Reserve System.

Favero, C. (2001). *Applied macroeconometrics.* Oxford: Oxford University Press.

Feldstein, M., & Stock, J. (1994). The use of a monetary aggregate to target nominal GDP. In G. Mankiw (Ed.), *Monetary policy* (pp. 7–62) University of Chicago Press, Chicago.

Ferguson, R. W. (2004, October 29). Equilibrium real interest rates: Theory and application. Speech at the University of Connecticut.

Fisher, I. (1920). *Stabilizing the dollar.* New York: Macmillan.

Fisher, I. (1935). *100% Money.* New York: Adelphi.

Florio, A. (2005). Asymmetric monetary policy – empirical evidence for Italy. *Applied Economics, 37,* 751–764.

Fourçans, A., & Vranceanu, R. (2004). The ECB interest rule under the Duisenberg Press, European Journal of Political Economy, *29,* 81–194.

Fracasso, A., Genberg, H., & Wyplosz, C. (2003). How do Central Banks write an evaluation of inflation targeting. CEPR, Geneva Reports on the World Economy, Special Report 2.

Fratianni, M., & von Hagen, J. (1990). German dominance in the EMS: Evidence from interest rates. *Journal of International Money and Finance, 9,* 358–375.

Fratianni, M., & von Hagen, J. (2001). The konstanz seminar on monetary theory and policy at 30. *European Journal of Political Economy, 17,* 641–664.

Freedman, C. (1994). The use of indicators and the monetary conditions index in Canada. In T. J. T. Baliæo, & C. Cottarelli (Eds.), *Frameworks for monetary stability – policy issues and country experiences* (pp. 458–476). Washington: IMF, IDE.

Freedman, C. (1995, Autumn). The role of monetary conditions and the monetary conditions index in the conduct of policy. *Bank of Canada Review,* 53–59.

Freedman, C. (1996). The use of indicators and of the monetary conditions index in Canada. The Transmission of Monetary Policy in Canada, Bank of Canada, Ottawa, pp. 67–80.

Friedman, B. M. (1975, October). Targets, instruments and indicators of monetary policy. *Journal of Monetary Economics, 1*(4), 443–473.

Friedman, M. (1959). *A program for monetary stability.* New York: Fordham University Press.

Friedman, M. (1962*). Capitalism and freedom.* Fortieth Anniversary Edition, Chicago: University of Chicago Press.

Friedman, M. (1984). Lessons from the 1979-82 monetary policy experiment. *The American Economic Review,*74(2), Papers and Proceedings of the Ninety-Sixth Annual Meeting of the American Economic Association, pp. 397–400.

Friedman, M. (1985). The case for overhauling the Federal Reserve. *Challenge, 28*(3), 4–12.

Friedman, M., & Schwartz, A. (1963). *A monetary history of the United States, 1867–1960*. Princeton, NJ: Princeton University Press.

Gali, J. (2002). Monetary policy in the early years of EMU. In M. Buti & A. Sapir (Eds.), *EMU and Economic policy in Europe: The challenges of the early years*. Cheltenham: Edward Elgar.

Garcia-Cervero, S. (2002). Is the Fed really leading the way?, Deutsche Bank Europe Weekly 22 November 2002, Global Markets Research, London, pp. 8–10.

Geiger, M. (2008, February). *Instruments of monetary policy in China and their effectiveness: 1994–1996*. United Nations Conference On Trade and Development, Discussion Papers, No. 187 New York.

Gerdesmeier, D. (1996). *The role of wealth in money demand*. Discussion Paper 5/96, Deutsche Bundesbank, Fankfurt/Main.

Gerdesmeier, D., & Roffia, B. (2003). *Empirical estimates of reaction functions for the euro area*. ECB Working Paper, 206, European Central Bank, Frankfurt Main.

Gerlach, S., & Schnabel, G. (1999, August). *The Taylor rule and interest rates in the EMU Area: A note*. BIS Working Paper, No. 73, www.bis.org/publ/work73.pdf.

Gerlach, S., & Schnabel, G. (2000). The Taylor rule and interest rates in the EMU area. *Economics Letters, 67*, 165–171.

Gerlach, S., & Svensson, L. E. O. (2003). Money and inflation in the euro area: A case for monetary indicators? *Journal of Monetary Economics, 50*, 1649–1672.

Gerlach-Kristen, P. (2003). *Interest rate reaction function and the Taylor rule in the Euro area*. ECB Working Paper, 258, European Central Bank, Frankfurt am Main.

Giannone, D., Reichlin, L., & Sala, L. (2002). *Tracking Greenspan: Systematic and unsystematic monetary policy revisited*. CEPR Discussion Paper, 3550, London.

Gordon, R. (1985). The conduct of domestic monetary policy. In A. Ando, et al. (Eds.), *Monetary policy in our times* (pp. 45–81). Proceedings of the First International Conference Held by the Institute for Monetary and Economic Studies of the Bank of Japan, Cambridge/MA and London: The MIT Press.

Gortes, J., Jacobs, J., & De Haan, J. (2008). Taylor Rules for the ECB Using Expectations Data. Scandinavian Journal of Economics, *110*, 473–488.

Greene, W. H. (2003). *Econometric analysis* (5th ed.) Prentice Hall, New Jersey.

Greenspan, A. (1988, July 28). Statement before the Subcommittee on Domestic Monetary Policy Committee on Banking Finance and Urban Affairs, U.S. House of Representatives.

Greenspan, A. (1999, July 22). The Federal Reserve's semiannual report on monetary policy. Testimony before the Committee on Banking and Financial Services, U.S. House of Representatives.

Greenspan, A. (2003, August 29). Monetary policy under uncertainty. Remarks by Chairman Alan Greenspan At a Symposium sponsored by the Federal Reserve Bank of Kansas City, Jackson Hole, Wyoming.

Greiber, C., & Lemke W. (2005). *Money demand and macroeconomic uncertainty*. Bundesbank Discussion Paper, Economic Studies, 26/2005, Frankfurt am Main.

Gros, D., Durrer, K., Jimeno, J., Monticelli, C., Perotti, P., & Daveri, F. (2002). Fiscal and monetary policy for a low-speed Europe. 4th Annual Report of the CEPS Macroeconomic Policy Group, Centre for European Policy Studies, Brussels.

Haldane, A. G. (ed.) (1995, March). Targeting Inflation: A Conference of Central Banks on the Use of Inflation Targets, Bank of England, London.

Hall, R., & Mankiw, G. (1994). Nominal income targeting. In G. Mankiw, (Ed.), *Monetary policy* (pp. 1–93), Chicago: Chicago University Press.

Hall, T. E. (1990). McCallum's base growth rule: Results for the United States, West Germany, Japan and Canada. *Weltwirtschaftliches Archiv* (pp. 630–642).

Hallman, J. J., Porter, R. D., & Small, D. H. (1991). Is the price level tied to the M2 monetary aggregate in the long run?. *American Economic Review, 81*(4), 841–858.

Hamilton, J. D., & Jordá, O. (2000). *A Model for the Federal Funds rate target*. NBER Working Paper 7847, National Bureau of Economic Research, Cambridge/MA.

Hansen, L. P. (1982). Large sample properties of generalized method of moments estimators. *Econometrica, 50*, 1029–1054.

Heikensten, L., & Vredin, A. (2002). The art of targeting inflation. *Riksbank Economic Review, 4*, 5–34.

Heikensten, L. (2005, February 22). Thoughts on How to Develop the Riksbank's Monetary Policy Work, Speech at the Swedish Economics Association.

Hoppe, H.-H. (1994). How is fiat money possible? or, the devolution of money and credit. *Review of Austrian Economics, 7*(2), 49–74.

Horwitz, S. (1996). Capital theory, inflation and deflation: the austrians and monetary disequilibrium theory compared. *Journal of the History of Economic Thought, 18*, 287–308.

Huang, H.-C., & Lin, S.-C. (2006). Time-varying discrete monetary policy reaction functions. *Applied Economics, Journal, 38*, 449–464.

Humphrey, T. M. (1992, November/December). A simple model of Irving Fisher's price-level stabilization rule. *Economic Review, Federal Reserve Bank of Richmond*, 12–18.

Ingves, S. (2007, January 19). *Swedish experiences of monetary policy with an inflation target.* Speech given at the Conference on Inflation Targeting, Budapest, Hungary.

Inoue, A., & Kilian, L. (2002). *In-sample or out-of-sample tests of predictability: which one should we use?.* ECB Working Paper, 195, European Central Bank, Frankfurt/Main.

Issing, O. (2001). Monetary Analysis, Tools and Applications, ECB Conference. In: J.-W. Klöckers, & C. Willeke (Eds.), *Foreword*, Frankfurt.

Issing, O. (2004, July/August). Inflation targeting: A view from the ECB. *Federal Reserve Bank of St. Louis Review, 86*(4), 169–179.

Jansson, P., & Vredin, A. (2003). Forecast-based monetary policy: The case of Sweden. *International Finance, 6*(3), 349–380.

Johansen, S. (1991). Estimation and hypothesis testing of cointegration vectors in gaussian vectorautoregressive models. *Econometrica, 59*, 1551–1580.

Johansen, S. (1995). *Likelihood-based inference in cointegrated vector autoregressive models.* Oxford: Oxford University Press.

Jordan, T. J., & Kugler, P. (2004). Implementing Swiss Monetary Policy: Steering the M3-Libor with Repo Transactions, in: Swiss Journal of Economics and Statistics, 140, pp. 381–393.

Judd, J. P., & Motley, B. (1992). Controlling inflation with an interest rate instrument. *Federal Reserve Bank of San Francisco Economic Review, 3*, 3–22.

Judd, J. P., & Motley, B. (1993). Using a nominal GDP rule to guide discretionary monetary policy. *Federal Reserve Bank of San Francisco Economic Review, 3*, 3–11.

Kamps, C., & Pierdzioch C. (2002). Geldpolitik und vorausschauende Taylor-Regeln – Theorie und Empirie am Beispiel der Deutschen Bundesbank, Kieler Arbeitspapiere, 1089, Institut für Weltwirtschaft, Kiel.

King, M. (1997). The Inflation Targeting Five Years On, Lecture delivered at the London School of Economics, 29 October.

Kuttner, K. N., & Posen, A. S. (2001). Inflation, monetary transparency, and G3 exchange rate volatility. In M. Balling, E. H. Hochreiter, & E. Hennessy, (Eds.), *Adapting to financial globalisation: international studies in monetary banking* (Vol. 14, pp. 229–258). London: Routledge.

Kuttner, N. K. (2004, July/August). The role of policy rules in inflation targeting. *Economic Review, Federal Reserve Bank of St. Louis*, 89–112.

Kydland, F. E., & Prescott, E. C. (1977, June). Rules rather than discretion: The inconsistency of optimal plans. *Journal of Political Economy, 85*(3), 473–491.

Laubach, T., & Posen, A. S. (1997, January). *Disciplined discretion: The German and Swiss monetary targeting frameworks in operation.* Federal Reserve Bank of New York Working Paper No. 9707.

Laubach, T., & Williams, J. (2001). Measuring the natural rate of interest. Finance and Economics Discussion Series 2001–56, Board of Governors of the Federal Reserve System (U.S.) Washington.

Laubach, T., & Williams, J. C. (2003, November). Measuring the natural rate of interest. *The Review of Economics and Statistics, 85*(4), 1063–1070.

Laurens, B. J., & Maino, R. (2007). *China: Strenghtening monetary policy implementation*. IMF Working Paper, 07/14, International Monetary Fund Washington/DC.

Leidermann, L., & Svensson, L. E. O. (Eds.) (1995). Inflation targets. London: Centre for Economic Policy Research (CEPR).

LeRoy, S.F. (1992). On policy regimes. In K. D. Hoover (Ed.), *Macroeconometrics: Developments, tensions and prospects* (pp. 235–251). Boston: Kluwer.

Leschke, M., & Polleit T. (2000, May). Die Taylor-Regel: ein Konzept für die Europäische Zentralbank?, in: *Bankarchiv, Zeitschrift für das gesamte Bank- und Börsenwesen*, *48*, 355–359.

Lucas, R. E. (1972, April). Expectations and the neutrality of money. *Journal of Economic Theory, 4*(2), 103–124.

Lucas, R. E. (1976). Econometric policy evaluation: A critique. In R.E. Lucas (Ed.), *Studies in business-cycle theory* (pp. 104–130). Cambridge, MA: MIT Press.

Manrique, M., & Marques, J. M. (2004). An empirical approximation of the natural rate of interest and potential growth. Banco de Espana Documentos de Trabajo No. 0416 Madrid.

Martin, W. M. (1965, December 8). Remarks Before the 59th Annual Meeting of the Life Insurance Association of America, New York City.

Martins, J. O., & Scarpetta, S. (1999). *The levels and cyclical behaviour of mark-ups across countries and market structures*. OECD Economics Department, Working Paper No. 213 Organisation for Economic Cooperation and Development Paris.

Masuch, K., Pill, H., & Willeke, C. (2001, August). Framework and tools of monetary analysis. Monetary Analysis: Tools and Applications, European Central Bank, Frankfurt, 117–144.

McCallum, B. T. (1987, September/October). The case for rules in the conduct of monetary policy: A concrete example. *Federal Reserve Bank of Richmond Economic Review, 73*, 10–18.

McCallum, B. T. (1988). Robustness properties of a rule for monetary policy. *Carnegie-Rochester Conference Series on Public Policy, 29*, 173–203.

McCallum, B. T. (1989). Monetary Economics: Theory and Policy, New York, Macmillan.

McCallum, B. T. (1990a). Targets, Indicators, and instruments of monetary policy. In W. Haraf, Cagan, W. (Eds.), *Monetary policy for a changing financial environment*. Washington, DC: AEI Press.

McCallum, B. T. (1990b, August). Could a monetary base rule have prevented the great depression? *Journal of Monetary Economics, 26*, 3–26.

McCallum, B. T. (1993, November). Specification and analysis of a monetary policy rule for Japan. *Monetary and Economic Studies*, Bank of Japan, *11*, 1–45.

McCallum, B. T. (1994). *Monetary policy rules and financial stability*. NBER Working Paper No. 4692, National Bureau of Economic Research, Cambridge/MA.

McCallum, B. T. (2002, November 18). The use of policy rules in monetary policy analysis Shadow Open Market Committee.

McCulley, P., & Touli, R. (2008). Chasing the neutral rate down: financial conditions, monetary policy, and the Taylor rule, Global Central Bank Focus, PIMCO.

Meltzer A, (1987). Limits of short-run stabilisation policy. *Economic Inquiry, 25*, 1–13.

Mésonnier, J. S., & Renne, J. P. (2004, September). Une estimation du taux d'intérêt naturel pour la zone euro, Banque de France, Note d'études et de recherché, No. 115.

Meyer, L. H. (2002, January 16). Rules and Discretion, Remarks At the Owen Graduate School of Management, Vanderbilt University, Nashville, Tennessee.

Milani, F. (2008). Learning, monetary policy rules, and macroeconomic stability. *Journal of Economic Dynamics and Control, 32*(10), 3148–3165.

Neiss, K., & Nelson, E. (2001). *The real interest rate as an inflation indicator*. Bank of England Working Paper No 130, London.

Neumann, M. J. M. (1974). Zwischenziele und Indikatoren als Grundlagen geldpolitischer Entscheidungen, Wirtschaftswissenschaftliches Studium, pp. 421–427.

Neumann, M. J. M. (2000). Strategien der Geldpolitik, in: G. Obst, O. Hintner, *Geld-, Bank- und Börsenwesen*, 40. Aufl., v. J. Hagen, v. J. H. Stein, Stuttgart, Schäffer-Pöschel, 1594–1604.

Neumann, M. J. M., & von Hagen, J. (2002). Does inflation targeting matter? *Federal Reserve Bank of St. Louis Review, 84*(4), 127–148.

Neumann, M. J. M., & von Hagen, J. (1993). Monetary policy in Germany. In M. Fratianni & D. Salvatore (Eds.), *Handbook on Monetary Policy* (pp. 299–334). New York: Greenwood Press.

Nicoletti-Altimari, S. (2001, May). *Does money lead inflation in the euro area?*. ECB Working Paper No. 63, European Central Bank Frankfurt/Main.

Obstfeld, M., & Rogoff, R. (1995). The mirage of fixed exchange rates. *Journal of Economic Perspectives, 9*, 73–96.

Olivei, G. P. (2002). Switzerland's approach to monetary policy. *New England Economic Review, Federal Reserve Bank of Boston*, Second Quarter, 57–60.

Orphanides, A. (2001). *Monetary policy rules, macroeconomic stability and inflation: A view from the trenches*, Federal Reserve Board, Finance and Economics Discussion Series, 2001–62.

Orphanides, A. (2003a, June). *Historical monetary policy analysis and the Taylor Rule*. Board of Governors of the Federal Reserve System.

Orphanides, A. (2003b). Monetary policy rules based on real-time data. *American Economic Review, 91*(4), 964–985.

Orr, A., Edey, M., & Kennedy, M. (1995). *The determination of real long term interest rates: 17 Country pooled-time-series evidence*, OECD Working Paper No. 155 Organization for Economic Co-operation and Development Paris.

Österholm, P. (2005). The Taylor Rule and real-time data – a critical appraisal. *Applied Economics Letters, 12*, 679–685.

Peersman G., & Smets, F. (1998). *Uncertainty and the Taylor rule in a simple model of the euro-area economy*. Ghent University Working Paper Ghent.

Peiró, A. (2002). Macroeconomic synchronization between G3 countries. *German Economic Review, 3*(2), 137–153.

Perez-Quiros, G., & Sicilia, J. (2002, November). *Is the European Central Bank (and the United States Federal Reserve) predictable?* European Central Bank Working Paper 192, Frankfurt/Main.

Perron, P. (1989). The great crash, the oil price shock, and the unit root hypothesis. *Econometrica, 57*, 1361–1401.

Poole, W. (1970, May). Optimal choice of monetary policy instruments in a simple stochastic macro model. *Quarterly Journal of Economics, 84*, 197–216.

Reifschneider, D., & Williams, J. (2000). Three lessons for monetary policy in a low-inflation era. *Journal of Money, Credit and Banking, 32*(4), 936–966.

Reisman, G. (2000). The goal of monetary reform. *Quarterly Journal of Austrian Economics, 3*(3), 3–18.

Reserve Bank of New Zealand (1996). Summary indicators of monetary conditions. *Reserve Bank Bulletin, 59*(3), 223–228.

Riksbank (2005a). *Changes in the Riksbank's forecasting methods*. Inflation Report 2005:1, Stockholm.

Riksbank (2005b). *Longer-term forecasts under the assumption that the Repo rate evolves in line with implied forward rates*. Inflation Report, 2, 56–59, Stockholm.

Riksbank (2008). Monetary Policy Report, 2, Stockholm.

Rothbard, M. N. (2000, 1963). *America's great depression* (5th ed.), Auburn, Alabama: Ludwig von Mises Institute.

Rudebusch, G. D. (2002). Term structure evidence on interest-rate smoothing and monetary policy inertia. *Journal of Monetary Economics, 49*, 1161–1187.

Sachverständigenrat zur Begutachtung der gesamtwirtschaftlichen Entwicklung (1974). Jahresgutachten 1974/75, Statistisches Bundesamt, Wiesbaden.

Sachverständigenrat zur Begutachtung der gesamtwirtschaftlichen Entwicklung (2003). Jahresgutachten 2003/04, Statistisches Bundesamt, Wiesbaden.

Sack, B. (2000, September). Deriving inflation expectations from nominal and inflation-indexed treasury yields. *Journal of Fixed Income, 10*(2), 1–12.

Sack, B., & Elsasser, R. (2004, May). Treasury inflation-indexed debt: A review of the US experience. *Economic Policy Review*, Federal Reserve Bank of New York, 47–63.

Salerno, J. T. (1983). Gold standards: True and false. *Cato Journal, 3*(1), 239–267.

Sauer, S., & Sturm, J.-E. (2003). *Using Taylor rules to understand ECB monetary policy*. CESifo
Working Paper, 1110, Centre for Economic Studies, University of Munich appeared in 2007 in:
German Economic Review, *8*, 375–398.

Saving, T. R. (1967, August). Monetary-policy targets and indicators. *Journal of Political Economy*, 446–456.

Schaechter, A., Stone, M. R., & Zelmer, M. (2000). *Adopting inflation targeting: practical issues
for emerging market countries*. Occasional Paper 202, International Monetary Fund, Washing-
ton/DC.

Schroeder, M. et al. (2002). Neue Übertragungsmechanismen in einer globalisierten
Weltwirtschaft – Deutschland und Europa im internationalen Verbund, Gutachten für das
Bundesministerium für Wirtschaft und Technologie, Centre for European Economic Research
(ZEW) Mannheim, documented in Frankfurter Allgemeine Zeitung, June 7th, (2002). Der Ein-
fluss der amerikanischen Konjunktur wird schwächer.

Selgin, G. A. (1990). Monetary equilibrium and the productivity norm of price-level policy. *Cato
Journal, 10*(1), 265–87.

Selgin, G. A. (1997). *Less than zero: The case for a falling price level in a growing economy*.
Hobart Paper 132, London, Institute for Economic Affairs.

Simons, H. C. (1936). Rules versus authorities in monetary policy. In F. A. Lutz & L. W. Mints
(Eds.), 1951, Readings in Monetary Theory, The American Economic Association, , Homewood, IL: Richard D. Irwin.

Smant, D. J. C. (2002). Has the European Central Bank followed a Bundesbank policy? Evidence
from the early years. *Kredit und Kapital, 35*(3), 327–443.

Smets, F., & Wouters, R. (2002). *An estimated stochastic dynamic general equilibrium model of
the Euro area*. ECB Working Paper, No. 171.

Stone, M. R. (2003). *Inflation targeting lite*. IMF Working Paper 03/12, International Monetary
Fund, Washington D.C.

Surico, P. (2003). *How does the ECB target inflation?* ECB Working Paper, 229, European Central
Bank, Frankfurt/Main.

Surico, P. (2003a). Asymmetric reaction functions for the Euro area. *Oxford Review of Economic
Policy, 19*(1), pp. 44–57.

Svensson, L. E. O. (1997). Inflation forecast targeting: Implementing and monitoring inflation
targets. *European Economic Review, 41*, 1111–1146.

Svensson, L. E. O. (1999). Inflation targeting as a monetary policy rule. *Journal of Monetary
Economics, 43*, 607–654.

Svensson, L. E. O. (2003). What is wrong with Taylor rules? Using judgment in monetary policy
through targeting rules. *Journal of Economic Literature, 41*(2), 426–477.

Swiss National Bank (1999). Monetary policy decisions of the Swiss National Bank. *Quarterly
Report, 4*, 19–23.

Swiss National Bank (2005). *The monetary policy concept as of January 2005*,
http://www.snb.ch/e/geldpolitik/geldpol.html.

Taylor, J. B. (1993). Discretion versus policy rules in practice. *Carnegie-Rochester Conference
Series on Public Policy, 39*, 195–214.

Taylor, J. B. (1998). *The robustness and efficiency of monetary policy rules as guidelines for interest rate setting by the European Central Bank*, Conference on Monetary Policy Rules organized
by the Sveriges Riksbank and the Institute for International Economics (Stockholm University),
Stockholm, June 12–13, 1998.

Taylor, J. B. (1999a). A historical analysis of monetary policy rules. In J. B. Taylor (Ed.), *Monetary
policy rules*. Chicago: University of Chicago.

Taylor, J. B. (1999b). The robustness and efficiency of monetary policy rules as guidelines for interest rate setting by the European Central Bank. *Journal of Monetary Economics, 43*, 655–679.

Taylor, J. B. (2001). The role of the exchange rate in monetary policy rules. *American Economic Review, 91*, 263–267.

Taylor, J. B. (2008, February). *Monetary policy and the state of the economy*. Testimony before the Committee on Financial Services, US House of Representatives, Washington, DC.

Tinbergen, J. (1952). *On the theory of economic policy*. North-Holland: Amsterdam.

Tödter, K.-H. (2002, June). *Monetary indicators and policy rules in the p-star model*. Deutsche Bundesbank, Discussion Paper 18/02, Frankfurt/Main.

Tödter, K.-H., & Reimers, H.-E. (1994). P-Star as a link between money and prices in Germany. *Weltwirtschaftliches Archiv, 130*, 273–289.

Tucker, P. (2008, September 12). *Money and Credit, Twelve Months On*, Speech delivered at the Money, Macro and Finance Research Group 40th Annual Conference, Birkbeck College, London.

Tucker, P. (2008a). *The credit crisis: Lessons from a protracted peacetime*. Remarks given at the Chatham House conference on "The New Financial Frontiers". Forthcoming in the 2008 Q3 edition of the Bank of England Quarterly Bulletin.

Ullrich, K. (2003). *A comparison between the Fed and the ECB: Taylor rules*. ZEW Discussion Paper, 03-19, Centre for European Economic Research, Mannheim.

Valente, G. (2003). Monetary policy rules and regime shifts. *Applied Financial Economics, 13*, 525–535.

Vickers, J. (1998, November). *Inflation targeting in practice – the U.K. experience*. Bank of England Quarterly Bulletin November 368–3.

von Hagen, J. (1999). Monetary targeting in Germany. *Journal of Monetary Economics, 43*, 681–701.

von Hayek, F. A. (1978). *The denationalisation of money*. London: Institute for Economic Affairs.

Walsh, C. (2003). *Monetary theory and practise* (2nd ed.), Cambridge, Massachusetts: MIT Press.

Warburton, C. (1951, 1946). The misplaced emphasis in contemporary business fluctuation theory. reprinted in AEA Readings in Monetary Theory, New York, Blakiston.

Warburton, C. (1952). How Much Variation in the Quality of Money Is Needed?, in: South Economic Journal, *18*(4), 495–509.

Woodford, M. (1994). Monetary policy and price level determinacy in a cash-in-advance economy. *Economic Theory, 4*(3), 345–380.

Woodford, M. (2001). The Taylor rule and optimal monetary policy. *American Economic Review, 91*, 232–237.

Woodford, M. (2003). *Interest and prices – foundations of a theory of monetary policy*. Princeton: Princeton University Press.

Woodford, M. (2007). The case for forecast targeting as a monetary strategy. *Journal of Economic Perspectives, 21*(4), 3–24.

Wyplosz, C. (2001, September 12). *The Fed and the ECB*, Briefing Note to the Committee for Economic and Monetary Affairs of the European Parliament. Brussels.

Index